Anthropology
NINTH EDITION

WILLIAM A. HAVILAND
University of Vermont

Harcourt College Publishers
Fort Worth Philadelphia San Diego New York Orlando Austin San Antonio
Toronto Montreal London Sydney Tokyo

To My Anthropological Kin:

Frank Hamilton Cushing
Frederica de Laguna

PUBLISHER	EARL MCPEEK
ACQUISITIONS EDITOR	LIN MARSHALL
MARKET STRATEGIST	KATHLEEN SHARP
DEVELOPMENTAL EDITOR	MARGARET MCANDREW BEASLEY
PROJECT EDITOR	ELAINE RICHARDS
ART DIRECTOR	BURL SLOAN
PRODUCTION MANAGER	ANDREA ARCHER

Cover images: (tl) Tim Hursley/SuperStock; (tr) Patrick N. Lucero/SuperStock; (br) ®Rommel/Masterfile; (bc) SuperStock; (bl) ©Telegraph Colour Library/FPG International; (cl) ©Freeman Patterson/Masterfile.

ISBN: 0-15-506755-9
Library of Congress Catalog Card Number: 99-64170

Copyright © 2000, 1997, 1994, 1991, 1989, 1985, 1982, 1978, 1974 by Harcourt, Inc.

Address for Domestic Orders
Harcourt College Publishers, 6277 Sea Harbor Drive, Orlando, FL 32887-6777
800-782-4479

Address for International Orders
International Customer Service
Harcourt, Inc., 6277 Sea Harbor Drive, Orlando, FL 32887-6777
407-345-3800
(fax) 407-345-4060
(e-mail) hbintl@harcourtbrace.com

Address for Editorial Correspondence
Harcourt College Publishers, 301 Commerce Street, Suite 3700, Fort Worth, TX 76102

Web Site Address
http://www.harcourtcollege.com

Printed in the United States of America

0 1 2 3 4 5 6 7 8 048 9 8 7 6 5 4 3

Harcourt College Publishers

Using
Anthropology
A Guide to Learning From Your Textbook

Anthropology, **Ninth Edition** is designed to give students a thorough, college-level introduction to the principles and processes of anthropology. It covers the basic divisions of anthropology—physical and cultural anthropology, including ethnology, linguistics, and prehistoric archaeology—and presents the key concepts and terminology relevant to each.

Anthropology, **Ninth Edition,**

- incorporates a **unifying theme.** Although each chapter has been developed as a self-contained unit of study, a common theme runs through all of the chapters: Cultures must produce behavior which is generally adaptive.

- provides a **readable and engaging** introduction to the discipline of anthropology. Using numerous and colorful examples, Dr. Haviland presents even the most complex concepts in prose that is clear, straightforward, and easy for today's first- and second-year students to understand.

- utilizes print and non-print **media** to explore the different "literacies" which anthropologists draw upon. The Ninth Edition offers many new student resources online at www.harbrace.com/anthro/.

- maintains **moderate length.** The textbook is of sufficient length to avoid superficiality, yet it does not present more material than can reasonably be absorbed in the space of a single semester.

The following pages will introduce you to the many features of *Anthropology,* **Ninth Edition,** and show you how to make the best use of the learning aids provided to enhance your study of anthropology.

 Web Links Web Link icons, appearing in the margin of each chapter, refer to additional related material located on the text's web site: the Anthropology Internet Connection (www.harbrace.com/anthro/). Content ranges from Internet research activities to annotated links to quizzing materials for each chapter.

Original Studies

These unique selections are from case studies and other original works of men and women who have been or are currently actively involved in important anthropological fieldwork. Each study sheds additional light on some important anthropological concept or subject area found within the chapter.

Anthropology Applied Boxes

These boxed features demonstrate the many practical applications of anthropological knowledge, the important work conducted by anthropologists outside of academic settings, and the variety of careers pursued by trained anthropologists.

Bio Boxes

Throughout the textbook, profile boxes provide biographical information about important people in the field of anthropology.

Illustrations

Dr. Haviland has chosen numerous four-color photos to catch your eye and mind and make important anthropological points. The line drawings, maps, charts, and tables were selected specifically for their usefulness in illustrating, emphasizing, or clarifying certain anthropological concepts.

Chapter 2
METHODS OF STUDYING THE HUMAN PAST

THIS EXCAVATION IS OF A HALF-MILLION-YEAR-OLD SITE IN ISRAEL. BECAUSE EXCAVATION OF SITES DESTROYS THEM, METICULOUS RECORDS MUST BE KEPT. WITHOUT SUCH RECORDS, THE FINDS TELL US NOTHING ABOUT THE HUMAN PAST.

Previews and Summaries

Each chapter begins with a set of **preview** questions providing a framework for studying the contents of the chapter. At the end of each chapter is a summary containing kernels of the most significant ideas presented in that chapter.

148 PART II Primate Evolution and the Emergence of the Hominines

be considered hominines. No matter how much some of them may have resorted to bipedalism, they had not yet developed the anatomical specializations for this mode of locomotion that are seen in the earliest known hominines. They were optional rather than obligatory bipeds. Nevertheless, existing evidence allows the hypothesis that apes and humans separated from a common evolutionary line sometime during the late Miocene, and some fossils, particularly the smaller African ramamorphs, do possess traits associated with humans. Moreover, the Miocene apes possessed a

limb structure less specialized for brachiation than modern apes; this structure could well have provided the basis for the development of human as well as ape limb types.

Clearly not all ramamorphs evolved into the forests and woodlands continued to develop as arboreal apes, although ultimately some of them took up a more terrestrial life. These are the bonobos, chimpanzees, and gorillas, who have changed far more from the ancestral condition than have the still arboreal orangutans.

Chapter Preview

What Forces Are Responsible for the Diversity of Primates in the World Today?

Although all primates—lemurs, lorises, tarsiers, monkeys, apes, and humans—share a common ancestry, they have come to differ through the operation of evolutionary forces which have permitted them to adapt to a variety of environments in a variety of ways. Although biologists agree upon the fact of evolution, they are still unraveling the details of how it has proceeded.

What Are the Processes of Evolution?

Evolution works through mutation, producing genetic variation, which is then acted upon by drift (accidental changes in gene frequencies in a population), gene flow (the introduction of new genes from other populations), and natural selection. Natural selection is the adaptive mechanism of evolution that works through differential reproduction as individuals with genes for adaptive traits produce more offspring than those without.

How Do These Processes Produce New Forms of Organisms?

Populations may evolve in a linear manner, as small changes from one generation to another improve that population's adaptation. Through the accumulation of such changes over many generations, an older species may evolve into a new one. Or evolution may proceed in a branching manner, in response to isolating mechanisms. These serve to separate populations, preventing gene flow between them so that drift and selection may proceed in different ways. This may lead to the appearance first of divergent races and then of divergent species.

63

Points for Consideration

New to this edition, these questions appear at the end of each chapter and are intended to provoke thought and stretch the individual's concepts of culture and human behavior.

Suggested Readings and Bibliography

At the conclusion of each chapter is an annotated list of suggested readings which will supply the inquisitive student with further information about specific anthropological points. A complete bibliography can be found at the end of the book.

---

be considered hominines. No matter how much some of them may have resorted to bipedalism, they had not yet developed the anatomical specializations for this mode of locomotion that are seen in the earliest known hominines. They were optional rather than obligatory bipeds. Nevertheless, existing evidence allows the hypothesis that apes and humans separated from a common evolutionary line sometime during the late Miocene, and some fossils, particularly the smaller African ramamorphs, do possess traits associated with humans. Moreover, the Miocene apes possessed a

limb structure less specialized for brachiation than modern apes; this structure could have provided the basis for the development of human as well as ape limb types.

Clearly not all ramamorphs evolved into hominines. Those that remained in the forests and woodlands continued to develop as arboreal apes, although ultimately some of them took up a more terrestrial life. These are the bonobos, chimpanzees, and gorillas, who have changed far more from the ancestral condition than have the still arboreal orangutans.

CHAPTER SUMMARY

Although the study of comparative anatomy and biochemistry of living animals indicates much about their evolution, the most direct evidence comes from fossils. For animals that have often lived where conditions for fossilization are generally poor, we do have a surprisingly large number of primate fossils. Some are relatively complete skeletons, while most are teeth and jaw fragments.

The primates arose as part of a great adaptive radiation that began more than 100 million years after the appearance of the first mammals. The reason for this late diversification of mammals was that most ecological niches that they have since occupied were either preempted by the reptiles or were nonexistent until the flowering plants became widespread beginning about 65 million years ago.

The first primates were arboreal insect eaters, and the characteristics of the initial tree-dwelling environment. While some primates no longer inhabit the trees, it is certain that those adaptations which evolved to a life in the trees were preadaptive to the adaptive zone now occupied by the hominines.

The earliest primates had developed by 60 million years ago in the Paleocene epoch and were small arboreal creatures. Lemurlike adapids were common in the Eocene, as were species of tarsierlike omomyids. By the late Eocene, perhaps 45 million years ago, small primates combining features of both monkeys and apes were on the scene. In the Miocene epoch, apes proliferated and spread over many parts of the Old World. Among them were the ramamorphs, which appeared by 16 million years ago and were widespread even as recently as 8 million years ago. Although remarkably similar to orangutans in some respects, details of dentition suggest that hominines, as well as the African apes, arose from the ramamorphs. At least some populations of these primates lived in parts of Africa where the right kind of selective pressures existed to transform a creature just like it into a primitive hominine. Other populations remained in the forests, developing into today's bonobo, chimpanzee, gorilla, and orangutan. Of these, the orangutan has changed less from the ancestral condition than have the bonobo, chimp, and gorilla.

POINTS FOR CONSIDERATION

1. How do physical anthropology and paleontology advance our understanding of the origins and functions of modern human culture?

2. What do we mean by culture? Is it exclusive to humans?

3. Given the limited amount of evidence often available, what can be deduced from examining the elements of a complete skull (a rather rich find), i.e., cranium, eye sockets, jaw, etc.? What would you expect to find among modern primates? How and why does this differ from other mammals?

BIBLIOGRAPHY

Aberle, D. F., Bronfenbrenner, U., Hess, E. H., Miller, D. R., Schneider, D. H., & Spuhler, J. N. (1963). The incest taboo and the mating patterns of animals. *American Anthropologist*, 65, 253–265.

Abu-Lughod, L. (1986). *Veiled sentiments: Honor and poetry in a Bedouin society.* Berkeley, CA: University of California Press.

Adams, R. E. W. (1977). *Prehistoric Mesoamerica.* Boston: Little, Brown.

Adams, R. M. (1966). *The evolution of urban society.* Chicago: Aldine.

AIDS Monthly Surveillance Summary (through July 1997). (1997). San Francisco.

Aébua, L. & Denais, W. (Eds.), *cultural studies of behavior.* Holt, Rinehart & Winston.

Alland, A., Jr. (1970). *Adaptation in cultural evolution: An approach to medical anthropology.* New York: Columbia Press.

Alland, A., Jr. (1971). *Human nature.* New York: Columbia University Press.

Allen, S. L. (1994). Media as public. Building a public perspective. *Newsletter*, 21, 6.

Allen, J. S., & Chrrr, S. M. A density genotype. *Current* 831–842.

Amábile-Cuevas, C. F., & C. (1993). Horizontal gene *Scientist*, 81, 332–341.

American Anthropological Statement on "race." An www.ameranthassn.org.

Amiran, R. (1965). The begi pottery-making in the N Mattson (Ed.), *Ceramics a* ogist, 91, 127–340.

Anderson, J. R., & Nelkin, I curve: A statement. *Scien*

Ankel-Simons, E., Fleagle, J. S. (1998). Femoral anato pithecine zoesis; an early pology, 106, 413–424.

Appenzeller, T. (1998). Are *lution? Science*, 282, 1451

Accensborg, G. M. (1961). Th object and sample *Americ* 63, 241–264.

Armstrong, D. F., Stokoe, W. S. E. (1995). Signs of the *Current Anthropology*, 34

Armstrong, K. (1991). *Muhai cism: cism: Fighting a cr *Scientist*, 42–47.

Ashmore, W. (Ed.). (1981). *Settlement patterns.* Albuqu New Mexico Press.

Avoiding the next crisis. (199 *Washington Post National* p. 26.

Balandier, G. (1971). *Politica* New York: Pantheon.

Baltes, M. (1998). Why settle ory of communities. *Scien* 1444.

Bastom, M. (1968). Voluntary association: anthropological aspects. In *International encyclopedia of the social sciences* (Vol. 16, pp. 357–362). New York: Macmillan.

Bar-Yosef, O. (1986). The Walls of Jericho: An Alternative Interpretation. *Current Anthropology*, 27, 157–162.

Bar-Yosef, O., Vandermeersch, A, Arensburg, B., Belfer-Cohen, A., Goldberg, P., Laville, H., Meignen, L., Rak, Y., Speth, J. D., Tchernov, E., Tillier, A-M., & Weiner, S. (1992). The Excavations in Kebara Cave. *Mt. Carmel. Current Anthropology*, 11,

Berdan, F. F. (1982). *The Aztecs of Central Mexico.* New York: Holt, Rinehart & Winston.

Bermúdez de Castro, J. M., Arsuaga, J. L., Caboné, E., Rosas, A., Martínez, I., & Mosquera, M. (1997). A Hominid from the lower Pleistocene of Atapuerca, Spain: Possible ancestor to Neandertals and modern humans. *Science*, 276, 1392–1393.

Bernal, I. (1969). *The Olmec world.* Berkeley: University of California Press.

Bernard, H. R., & Sibley, W. E. (1975). *Anthropology and jobs.* Washington, DC:

SUGGESTED READINGS

Birdwhistell, R. L. (1970). *Kinesics and context: Essays in body motion communication.* Philadelphia: University of Pennsylvania Press.

Kinesics was first delineated as an area for anthropological research by Birdwhistell, so this book is particularly appropriate for those who wish to know more about the phenomenon.

Crane, L. B., Yeager, E. & Whitman, R. L. (1981). *An introduction to linguistics.* Boston: Little, Brown.

This book gives balanced coverage to all subfields of linguistics, including topics traditionally ignored in textbooks.

Eastman, C. M. (1990). *Aspects of language and culture* (2nd ed.). Novato, CA: Chandler and Sharp.

The bulk of this book is devoted to the subjects of worldview, ethnography of communication, nonverbal behavior, animal communication, discourse pragmatics, conversational analysis, semiotics, and ethnicity. A single chapter deals with linguistics as a field tool.

Gardner, R. A., Gardner, B. T., & Van Cantfort, T. E. (Eds.). (1989). *Teaching sign language to chimpanzees.* Albany, NY: State University of New York Press.

In 10 jargon-free chapters, easily accessible to the interested layperson as well as professionals, the methods and results of the Gardners

and their students are laid out in great detail. Psychologists and anthropologists who reviewed the book agree it represents a milestone in ape language research and, as one put it, should be read by all interested in the evolution of human behavior.

Hickerson, N. P. (1980). *Linguistic anthropology.* New York: Holt, Rinehart and Winston.

A description and explanation of what anthropological linguistics is all about, written so beginning students understand it.

Ruhlen, M. (1994). *The origin of language: Tracing the evolution of the mother tongue.* New York: John Wiley and Sons.

Scholarly in substance but written for a popular audience, this book argues for a good introduction to comparative linguistics for beginning anthropology students. With an evolutionary theme, it cuts through the difficult problems of our linguistic ancestors with plausible though still controversial results.

Trager, G. L. (1964). Paralanguage: A first approximation. In D. Hymes (Ed.), *Language in culture and society* (pp. 274–279). New York: Harper & Row.

The author was the pioneer in paralinguistic research, and in this article he discusses what paralanguage is, why it should be studied, and how.

Running Glossary

This textbook includes a running glossary which offers on-page definitions of terms relevant to the study of anthropology.

Pronunciation Guide

A pronunciation guide is printed inside the front and back covers of the book to aid you in learning and pronouncing unfamiliar words that appear in the text.

Putting the World in Perspective

This section, found in the introduction to the book, illustrates the many ways in which the world can be viewed. A discussion of **cartography** and **projections** shows their benefits to anthropology.

PREFACE

PURPOSE

Anthropology is designed for introductory anthropology courses at the college level. The text deals primarily with the basic divisions of anthropology—physical and cultural anthropology, including ethnology, linguistics, and prehistoric archaeology—and presents the key concepts and terminology germane to each.

Most anthropology instructors have two goals for their introductory classes: to provide an overview of principles and processes of anthropology, and to plant a seed of cultural awareness in their students that will continue to grow and challenge ethnocentrism long past the end of the semester.

All nine editions of *Anthropology* have tried to support and further these goals. The majority of our students come to class intrigued with anthropology but with little more than a vague sense of the discipline. The first and most obvious aim of the text, therefore, is to give students a comprehensive introduction to anthropology. Because it draws from the research and ideas of a number of schools of anthropological thought, the text exposes students to a mix of such approaches as evolutionism, historical particularism, diffusionism, functionalism, French structuralism, structural functionalism, and others. This inclusiveness reflects my conviction that different approaches all have important things to say about human behavior. To restrict oneself to one approach, at the expense of the others, is to cut oneself off from significant insights.

If most students have little substantive concept of anthropology, they often have less clear—and potentially more destructive—views of the primacy of their own culture and its place in the world. A secondary goal of the text, then, is to persuade our students to understand the true complexity and breadth of human behavior and the human condition. Debates in North America and Europe regarding the "naturalness" of the nuclear family, the place of nonstandard English dialects in public education, and the supposed fixedness of racial differences or gender roles all greatly benefit from the perspectives gained through cultural anthropology. This questioning aspect of anthropology is perhaps the most relevant gift we can pass on to our students. Indeed, "debunking" is close to the spirit of anthropology, and questioning the superiority of European (and European-American) peoples and cultures is something anthropologists have always been good at. Anthropology is, in this sense, a tool to enable students to think both in and out of context.

A UNIFYING THEME

I have often found in my own teaching that introductory students lack a sense of the bigger picture in their studies of human behavior. The best solution seems to be the use of a theme that allows students to contextualize each chapter and part introduction, regardless of the order in which they are read. Accordingly, each chapter has been developed as a self-contained unit of study that may be used in any sequence by the instructor.

In earlier editions of this book, I referred to this common theme as one of environmental adaptation, although I was never very happy with that phrase. Its principal defect is its implication of fairly straightforward behavioral responses to environmental stimuli. Of course, people do not react to an environment as a given; rather, they react to an environment as they perceive it, and different groups of people may perceive the same environment in radically different ways. People also react to things other than the environment: their own biological natures, for one, and their beliefs, attitudes, and the consequences of their behavior, for others. All of these factors present them with problems, and people maintain cultures to deal with problems or matters that concern them. To be sure, their cultures must produce behavior that is generally adaptive, or at least not maladaptive, but this is far from saying that cultural practices necessarily arise because they are adaptive in a particular environment.

MANY MESSAGES, MANY MEDIA

For most of the discipline's history, anthropologists have relied upon print resources to share information, especially the very linear genre of ethnography, occasionally supplemented with photographs and, in fewer cases, film and analog recordings. The ethnography in particular reflects our discipline's roots in the Western approach to scholarly work.

However, many of the people anthropologists have studied and worked with have different "literacies" that they draw upon. Indeed, cultural anthropologists work with numerous guises of human behavior, ranging from music to oral narrative, ritual dance, weaving, and spray-paint graffiti. Anthropology is arguably among the most naturally "multimedia" of all studies.

The ninth edition of Anthropology recognizes students' level of comfort with nonprint media as well as the many potential paths to exploring the techniques, processes, and findings of anthropology. The art program, discussed in more detail below, is an important part of the text's narrative. The accompanying videos (discussed with the rest of the supplements) show culture in motion and bring action and life into the circle of ideas. The Web Links, signified by a marginal icon (also discussed in more detail below) build skills for analysis and research, and move the content of the text from standard linear textbook format to a multimedia package. PowerPoint slides and Overhead Transparencies bring the ideas and art of the text to life in the classroom. And, of course, the suggested readings and bibliography continue to show the rich library of anthropological texts students can draw upon.

The ninth edition thus allows instructors to utilize a broad set of instructional tools to expand their classrooms. Anthropology has been an archive of human behavior, and it is important that the discipline show the richness and diversity of humanity through the appropriate media.

▲▼▲▼▲▼▲▼▲▼▲▼▲▼▲▼▲▼▲▼▲▼▲▼▲▼▲▼▲▼▲▼

SPECIAL FEATURES OF THE BOOK

READABILITY

The purpose of a textbook is to transmit and register ideas and information, to induce the readers to see old things in new ways, and then to ask readers to think about what they see. A book may be the most elegantly written, most handsomely designed, most lavishly illustrated text available on the subject, but if it is not interesting, clear, and comprehensible to the student, it is valueless as a teaching tool. The trick is not just to present facts and concepts; the trick is to make them *memorable*.

The readability of the text is enhanced by the writing style. The book is designed to present even the most difficult concepts in prose that is clear, straightforward, and easy for today's first- and second-year students to understand, without feeling that they are being "spoken down to." Where technical terms are necessary, they appear in bold-faced type, are carefully defined in the text, and defined again in the running glossary in simple, clear language.

THE SELECTION OF CROSS-CULTURAL EXAMPLES

Because much learning is based on analogy, numerous and engaging examples have been utilized to illustrate, emphasize, and clarify anthropological concepts. Cross-cultural perspectives infuse the text, comparing cultural practices in a great variety of societies, often including the student's own. But these examples have been chosen with the knowledge that while students should be aware that anthropology has important statements to make about the student's own culture and society, the emphasis in introductory anthropology should be on non-Western societies and cultures for illustrative purposes. Why?

It is a fact of life that North Americans share the same planet with great numbers of people who are not only not North American but are non-Western as well. Moreover, North Americans constitute a minority, for they account for far less than one-quarter of the world's population. Yet traditional school curricula in North America emphasize their own surroundings and backgrounds, saying little about the rest of the world. In its March 8, 1976, issue (p. 32), the Chronicle of Higher Education documented an increasing tendency toward cultural insularity and ethnocentrism in North American higher education. That the problem persists is clear from a report made public in 1989 by the National Governors' Association, which warned that the economic well-being of the United States is in jeopardy because so many of its citizens are ignorant of the languages and cultures of other nations. The situation has not changed much since then. More than ever, college students need to acquire knowledge about the rest of the world and its peoples. Such a background gives them the global perspective they need to better understand their own culture and society and their place in today's world. Anthropology, of all disciplines, has a long-standing commitment to combating ethnocentrism, which gives instructors a unique obligation to provide this perspective.

MAPS, PHOTOGRAPHS, AND OTHER ILLUSTRATIONS

In this text, numerous four-color photos have been used to make important anthropological points by catching the students' eyes and minds. Many are unusual in the sense that they are not "standard" anthropological textbook photographs; each has been chosen because it complements the text in some distinctive way. And many photographs are shown in groups to contrast and compare their messages. In the ninth edition, for instance, Chapter 27 has two photos that compare colonial and modern violence against indigenous people in Guatemala. The success of these photographs can be measured in the number of comments I have received from students and other instructors over the years about the vividness of particular selections.

In addition, the line drawings, maps, charts, and tables were selected especially for their usefulness in illustrating, emphasizing, or clarifying particular anthropological concepts and have also proven to be valuable and memorable teaching aids.

Maps in particular have proven to be a popular aid through each edition of *Anthropology*, and the ninth edition builds on this success. Approximately 70 percent of the marginal locator maps are new or have been revised. And we have returned to one feature initially utilized in the first edition: placing a world map (a Robinson projection) in the front matter which shows where all of the cultures mentioned in the text are located.

ORIGINAL STUDIES

A special feature of this text is the Original Study that appears in each chapter. These studies consist of selections from case studies and other original works by women and men who have done, or are doing, important anthropological work. Each study, integrated within the flow of the text, sheds additional light on an important anthropological concept or subject area found in the chapter. Their content is not "extraneous" or supplemental. The Original Studies bring specific concepts to life through specific examples. And a number of Original Studies also demonstrate the anthropological tradition of the case study, albeit in abbreviated form.

The idea behind the Original Studies is to coordinate the two halves of the human brain, which have different functions. While the left (dominant) hemisphere is "logical" and processes verbal inputs in a linear manner, the right hemisphere is "creative" and less impressed with linear logic. Psychologist James V. McConnell described it as "an analog computer of sorts—a kind of intellectual monitor that not only handles abstractions, but also organizes and stores material in terms of Gestalts [that] include the emotional relevance of the experience." Logical thinking, as well as creative problem-solving, occurs when the two sides of the brain cooperate. The implication for textbook writers is obvious: To be truly effective, they must reach both sides of the brain. The Original Studies help to do this by conveying some "feel" for humans and their behavior and how anthropologists actually study them. For example, in the Chapter 16 Original Study, adapted from The Blessed Curse by R. K. Williamson, students hear the author describe growing up as an "intersexed" person and the clash of her parents' fundamentalist Christian worldview with that of her Cherokee grandmother regarding her identity. Her state of existence "between" genders is considered alternately as a blessing and a curse. As with other Original Studies, the striking nature of her experiences drives the discussion of a host of issues deeply relevant to students and anthropology.

INTEGRATED GENDER COVERAGE

Unlike many introductory texts, the ninth edition of Anthropology integrates rather than separates gender coverage. This approach gives the ninth edition a very large amount of gender-related material: the equivalent of three full chapters for the ninth edition. This much content far exceeds the single chapter most introductory textbooks contain.

Why is the gender-related material integrated? Anthropology is itself an integrative discipline; concepts and issues surrounding gender are almost always too complicated to remove from their context. Moreover, spreading this material through all of the chapters emphasizes how considerations of gender enter into virtually everything people do.

Much of the new content for the ninth edition (listed below) relates to gender in some way. These changes generally fall into at least one of three categories: changes in thinking about gender within the discipline, examples that have important ramifications on gender in a particular society or culture, and cross-cultural implications about gender and gender relations. Examples of new material range from an expanded definition of marriage and additional material on homo-

sexual identity to current thinking on the role of Hadza women in food provisioning and recent news in regard to female genital mutilation. Through a steady drumbeat of such coverage, the ninth edition avoids a thunderous crash of relegating "gender" to a single chapter that is preceded and followed by silence.

PREVIEWS AND SUMMARIES

An old and effective pedagogical technique is repetition: "Tell 'em what you're going to tell 'em, tell 'em, and then tell 'em what you've told 'em." To do this, each chapter begins with preview questions that set up a framework for studying the contents of the chapter. At the end of the chapter is a summary containing the kernels of the more important ideas just presented. The summaries provide handy reviews for students without being so long and detailed as to seduce students into thinking they can get by without reading the chapter itself.

WEB LINKS

The Internet has proven to be an increasingly important means of communication and will no doubt continue to grow in relevance and complexity. The ninth edition draws upon the World Wide Web both as an instructional tool and as a new set of examples of culture and cultural change. Every chapter contains several marginal icons called Web Links, which refer the student and instructor to additional content on the marked subject located on the text's associated web site, called the Harcourt Anthropology Internet Connection (http://www.harbrace.com/anthro/). This content ranges from Internet research activities to updated annotated links to quizzing materials for each chapter. A special emphasis has been placed on applied anthropology links. Students visiting the site will be able to see anthropology in action. Extensive resources for students and instructors are located at the site (see Supplements below for more information).

POINTS FOR CONSIDERATION

Much of the instruction in introductory anthropology classes is geared to stimulate and provoke how students think about human behavior. And traditionally instructors try to challenge students to discuss and consider the issues and implications of each chapter. Points for Consideration, which are new to the ninth edition, are discussion questions that have been added to the end of each chapter. These questions have been designed to further this technique by igniting discussion and stretching students inside and outside of the classroom.

SUGGESTED READINGS AND BIBLIOGRAPHY

Each chapter also includes a list of suggested readings that will supply the inquisitive student with further information about specific anthropological points that may be of interest. The books suggested are oriented toward the general reader and toward the interested student who wishes to explore further the more technical aspects of the subject. In addition, the bibliography at the end of the book contains a listing of more than 500 books, monographs, and articles from scholarly journals and popular magazines on virtually every topic covered in the text that a student might wish to investigate further.

RUNNING GLOSSARY

The running glossary is designed to catch the students' eyes as they read, reinforcing the meaning of each newly introduced term. It is also useful for chapter review, as the student may readily isolate those terms introduced from those in other chapters. The glossary defines each term in clear, understandable language. As a result, less class time is required going over terms, leaving instructors free to pursue matters of greater interest.

LENGTH

Careful consideration has been given to the length of this book. On the one hand, it had to be of sufficient length to avoid superficiality or misrepresentation of the discipline by ignoring or otherwise slighting some important aspect of anthropology. On the other hand, it could not be so long as to present more material than can be reasonably dealt with in the space of a single semester, or to be prohibitively expensive. The resultant text is comparable in length to introductory texts in the sister disciplines of economics, psychology, and sociology, even though there is more ground to be covered in an introduction to general anthropology.

▲▽▲▽▲▽▲▽▲▽▲▽▲▽▲▽▲▽▲▽▲▽▲▽▲▽▲▽▲▽▲

THE NINTH EDITION

Every chapter in the ninth edition has been thoroughly updated, considered, and fine-tuned. Major changes for the ninth edition include:

CHAPTER 1 Expanded material on objectivity and falsification in science, the replication of results in anthropology, discussion of the Piltdown hoax to illustrate scientific methodology in physical anthropology, the methodology of cross-cultural comparison and use of tools such as the Human Relations Area File (HRAF), a new discussion of informants, and cross-cultural differences in infant sleeping arrangements and the implication of these differences for child development.

CHAPTER 2 New description of the excavation of an archaeological site in Alaska.

CHAPTER 3 Expanded discussion of linear evolution.

CHAPTER 4 A revised section on primate behavior to bring in material on bonobos.

CHAPTER 5 New material on *Eosimias* and *Morotopithecus*.

CHAPTER 6 Revised discussion of *Ardipithecus*.

CHAPTER 7 Revised discussion of evolution from *H. habilis* to *H. erectus*.

CHAPTER 8 New material on *Homo erectus* fossils in Spain and Italy, evidence for *H. erectus'* ability to cross open water and make and use spears, and possible emergence of speech.

CHAPTER 9 New material on archaic *H. sapiens* in Spain (Sima de los Huesos), new material on language capabilities of Neandertals, expanded discussion of DNA analysis and the relationship between archaic and modern *H. sapiens*.

CHAPTER 10 Revised discussion of Cro-Magnon-Neandertal relationship, expanded discussion of *H. sapiens* spread into the Americas.

CHAPTER 11 New material on early farming in China, Southwest Asia and the Americas.

CHAPTER 12 New discussion of Atalhyk and Teotihuacan, and the "action theory" of civilization's origins.

CHAPTER 13 New reference to AAA statement on race, new discussion of time depth of differential skin pigmentation, new discussion of thrifty and nonthrifty genotypes, new discussion of hormone disrupting chemicals.

CHAPTER 14 New material on culture and race.

CHAPTER 15 New information on multilingualism in general and the Ebonics controversy in particular.

CHAPTER 16 Expanded material on homosexual identity.

CHAPTER 17 A revised section on horticulture and a new discussion of the anthropological "myth" of patrilocality among food foragers (also in Chapter 1).

CHAPTER 18 New material on the role of Hadza women in child provisioning and an expanded discussion of child labor in the modern global economy.

CHAPTER 19 A revised definition of marriage, especially same-sex marriage, and new material on polyandry.

CHAPTER 20 A revised discussion of residence patterns, with new material on structural problems of polyandrous families.

CHAPTER 21 An expanded discussion of phratries and moieties.

CHAPTER 22 A revised section on common-interest associations and new material on linguistic markers of class, as well as information on issues surrounding slavery, race, and class in the United States.

CHAPTER 23 New material on the distinction between social and cultural control, as well as an expanded discussion on the recent trends in the United States toward negotiation and mediation versus legal action and the implications of these trends for the distribution of justice.

CHAPTER 24 A revised discussion of science and religion, additional information on female genital mutilation, and new material on revitalization movements and the millennium.

CHAPTER 25 A completely revised section on ethnomusicology.

CHAPTER 26 New material on resistance to change, the buying and selling of brides in modern China, and indigenous rights in Brazil.

CHAPTER 27 Expanded material on global corporations, revised discussions of population and consequences of reduced growth, and new material on global warming and the Asian financial crisis.

NEW ORIGINAL STUDIES

In addition, nine of the twenty-seven Original Studies are new to the ninth edition:

Chapter 2 Whispers from the Ice, by Sherry Simpson (1995).

Chapter 3 The Drunkard's Walk, by Stephen Jay Gould (1996).

Chapter 9 African Origin or Ancient Population Size Differences? By Milford Wolpoff and Rachel Caspari (1998).

Chapter 15 The Great Ebonics Controversy, by Monoghan, Hinton and Kephart (1997).

Chapter 16 The Blessed Curse, by R. K. Williamson (1995)

Chapter 19 Arranging Marriage in India, by Serena Nanda (1992)

Chapter 26 Violence on Indian Day in Brazil, by Robin M. Wright (1997)

Chapter 27 Standardizing the Body: The Question of Choice, by Laura Nader (1997)

NEW ANTHROPOLOGY APPLIED BOXES

Moreover, there are seven new Anthropology Applied boxes. These include The Practical Importance of Evolution (Chapter 3), Forensic Archaeology (Chapter 9), Archaeology By and For American Indians (Chapter 11), Anthropology and the World of Business, with a section by Susan Squires (Chapter 18), Anthropology and AIDS, written specifically for this edition by

anthropologist A. M. Williams (Chapter 19), Federal Recognition for Native Americans, written specifically for this edition by anthropologist Harald E. L. Prins (Chapter 21), and Dispute Resolution and the Anthropologist (Chapter 23).

NEW BIO BOXES

Four Bio Boxes are new to the ninth edition as well. Chapter 1 now contains brief biographies of Frank Hamilton Cushing and Matilda Coxe Stevenson; Franz Boas, Frederick Ward Putnam, and John Wesley Powell; and George Peter Murdock. And Chapter 25 includes a Bio Box on Frederica de Laguna.

SUPPLEMENTS TO THE TEXT

In keeping with the ninth edition's recognition that the use of many messages requires many media, the selection of ancillaries accompanying *Anthropology* should meet most instructors' and students' needs.

PRINT SUPPLEMENTS

A separate Study Guide is provided to aid comprehension of the textbook material. Each chapter begins with concise learning objectives, then offers chapter exercises, review questions, and a glossary review to help students achieve these objectives. This supplement also includes hints on reading anthropology texts and studying for tests.

An Instructor's Manual offers teaching objectives and lecture and class activity suggestions that correspond to each chapter of the textbook. An extensive Test Bank, available in both printed and computerized forms, offers nearly 2000 items, including multiple choice, true/false, matching, short answer, and essay questions.

MEDIA SUPPLEMENTS

PowerPoint slides and a four-color overhead transparency set bring the ideas and art of anthropology to life in the classroom.

There are several videos available to accompany the text. *Millennium: Tribal Wisdom and the Modern World*, hosted by anthropologist David Maybury-Lewis, presents a thoughtful exploration of cultures across the world. Many issues are covered, including indigenous rights, definitions of gender and gender roles, and the construction of the self. Instructors can choose from ten 60-minute programs.

In addition, *Faces of Culture*, prepared by Coast Telecourses in Fountain Valley, California, through the Coast Community College District, has been an important part of *Anthropology* since 1983. Most of the twenty-six half-hour programs focus on key anthropological concepts, while several episodes are devoted to presenting rich ethnographic detail on specific cultures. These videos are available for standalone use or in the context of a telecourse. A Telecourse Study Guide is also available.

ONLINE SUPPLEMENTS

Perhaps the most striking addition to the many supplements options for the ninth edition is the Harcourt Anthropology Internet Connection, the web site for Anthropology located at http://www.harbrace.com/anthro/. Features of the Anthropology Exchange include:

Anthropology in the News. A section providing current news articles related to all fields of anthropology, updated monthly by David Carlson of Texas A&M University.

Quizzing and Testing. Student self-assessment supplies reinforcement on important concepts. Testing tools allow the results to be forwarded to instructors.

Online Case Study Resources. Located in the Anthropology Exchange section of the site, this material supports Harcourt's well-known Spindler case studies series and provides additional information on concepts and research covered in the text.

Anthropology in Action. Focused on indigenous rights, applied anthropology, and human rights issues, these links provide a forum for current news and events.

Media Guide. The media guide contains a substantial body of references—documentaries, ethnographic films, URLs, Listserv addresses, CD-ROMs, and books and journals—that provide additional resources for the student and instructor, arranged by topic.

Downloadable Supplements. Instructors can download many of the printed ancillaries and some media items as well.

Professional Contacts Area. In this career center, students can read about and find professional opportunities in anthropology and related fields.

CD-ROM SUPPLEMENT

The *Yąnomamö Interactive: The Ax Fight* CD-ROM has set an award-winning standard in the use of nonprint media in the anthropology classroom. The CD-ROM begins with complete digital QuickTime footage of Chagnon and Asch's classic ethnographic film *The Ax Fight* used by numerous instructors. And since this is a digital film, the viewer can fast forward, reverse, and skip around at will. Moreover, the film itself is extensively supplemented with transcripts, supporting maps, genealogical tables, photos, up-to-date biographies of individuals shown in the film, post-film still photos, and important historical and contemporary analyses of the film and its events. Even individuals important to the events in the film but not included in the actual footage are included in the resource material.

How would the *Yąnomamö Interactive* CD-ROM assist in the introductory classroom? Like many of the best case studies, *Yąnomamö Interactive* contains layers of meaning, interrelating such factors as kinship and kinship charts, the role of the ethnographer, and violence and conflict. But the digital nature of the medium provides a new way of exploring these relationships. All of the data on *Yąnomamö Interactive* is cross-referenced and hyperlinked, allowing the student or instructor to create wholly original texts and analyses of the film and its corollary parts. For instance, an explanation of the kinship dynamics underlying the conflict between two men can move from the genealogical chart to the biography of each individual and then to a listing of each of the men's "scenes" in the film. The viewer could then go directly to all of these scenes to watch these men in action. And unlike a traditional case study, such nonlinear paths through the CD-ROM mean that the events in the film—and the film itself—are open to interpretations that would be difficult or impossible to achieve in a nondigital medium.

ACKNOWLEDGMENTS

Many people assisted in the preparation of this book, some of them directly, some of them indirectly. In the latter category are all of the anthropologists under whom I was privileged to study at the University of Pennsylvania: Robbins Burling, William R. Coe, Carleton S. Coon, Robert Ehrich, Loren Eisley, J. Louis Giddings, Ward H. Goodenough, A. Irving Hallowell, Alfred V. Kidder II, Wilton M. Krogman, Froelich Rainey, Ruben Reina, and Linton Satterthwaite all contributed to it in important ways.

A similar debt is owed to all those anthropologists with whom I have worked or discussed research interests

and the field in general. There are too many of them to list here, but surely they have had an important impact on my own thinking and so on this book. Finally, the influence of all those who assisted in the preparation of the first eight editions must linger on in this new one. They are all listed in the prefaces to the earlier editions, and the ninth edition benefits from their past influence.

The ninth edition owes a special debt to several contributing writers. Anthropologist Harald E. L. Prins wrote an Anthropology Applied feature on Federal Recognition for Native Americans specifically for this edition about his work for the Aroostook Band of the

Mi'kmaqs. And anthropologist A. M. Williams also wrote an original Anthropology Applied feature on Anthropology and AIDS based on her work in San Francisco. I am grateful for their expertise, skill, and willingness to share their work. Wallace Haviland, my son and a Ph.D. candidate at the University of Pennsylvania, deserves much thanks for his expertise and depth in his rewrite of Chapter 25, as well as his assistance with the Points for Consideration. Anthropologist David Carlson of Texas A&M University and David Houston, who was a student of mine at the University of Vermont, have supplied a great deal of time, originality, and effort for the Web Links and the book's other World Wide Web resources.

This revision also benefits from my continued association with valued colleagues at the University of Vermont: Deborah Blom, Robert Gordon, Carroll M. P. Lewin, Stephen L. Pastner, James Petersen, Jeanne Shea, Peter A. Thomas, Luis Vivanco, and A. Peter Woolfson. All have responded graciously at one time or another to my requests for sources and advice in their various fields of expertise. We all share freely our successes and failures in trying to teach anthropology to introductory students.

In 1984, I was given the opportunity to participate in an open discussion between textbook authors and users at the American Anthropological Association's Annual Meeting (a session organized and chaired by Walter Packard and the Council on Anthropology and Education). From this I got a good grounding in what instructors at institutions ranging from community colleges to major universities were looking for in anthropology texts; subsequent insights have come from a special symposium on the teaching of anthropology at the University of Vermont in 1986 (organized by A. Peter Woolfson), a meeting of textbook authors with members of the Gender and the Anthropology Curriculum Project at the American Anthropological Association's Annual Meeting in 1988, and a special session on Central Themes in the Teaching of Anthropology at the American Anthropological Association's Annual Meeting in 1990 (organized by Richard Furlow). To the organizers and sponsors of all these events, my sincere thanks.

Most recently, I was asked to prepare a paper entitled, "Cleansing Young Minds, or What Should We Be Doing in Introductory Anthropology?" for *The Teaching of Anthropology: Problems, Issues, and Decisions*. This essay is a good summary of why I teach introductory anthropology classes and how I approach my students. And these ideas are also very important to understanding how this textbook is put together. I appreciate the editors of this volume inviting me to participate on this project.

Thanks are also due the anthropologists who made suggestions for this edition. They include: Henry H. Bagish, Santa Barbara City College; Janet E. Benson, Kansas State University; Janis Binam, Riverside Community College; James Bindon, University of Alabama; James G. Chadney, University of Northern Iowa; Rebecca Cramer, Johnson County Community College; Rene Descartes, SUNY at Cobleskill; Anne L. Grauer, Loyola University of Chicago; Glenice Guthrie, Buffalo State College; James Hamill, Miami University; Timothy J. Kloberdanz, North Dakota State University; Susan Lees, Hunter College, CUNY; Anthony J. Mendonca, Community College of Alleheny County; James L. Merryman, Wilkes University; Malvin Miranda, University of Nevada, Las Vegas; C. Roger Nance, University of Alabama, Birmingham; Thomas P. Ostrom, Rochester Community & Technical College; Steven Reif, Kilgore College; Bruce D. Roberts, University of Southern Mississippi; Larry Ross, University of Missouri; Anne C. Woodrick, University of Northern Iowa.

All of their comments were carefully considered; how I have responded to them has been determined by my own perspective of anthropology, as well as my thirty-seven years of experience with undergraduate students. Therefore, neither they nor any of the other anthropologists mentioned here should be held responsible for any shortcomings in this book.

I also wish to acknowledge my debt to a number of nonanthropologists who helped me with this book. The influence of David Boynton, winner of the 1985 Distinguished Service Award of the American Anthropological Association and my editor at Holt, Rinehart and Winston until his retirement in 1983, I am sure lingers on. Helpful in seeing this edition through to publication have been Lin Marshall, acquisitions editor, and Margaret McAndrew Beasley, developmental editor, as well as Shannon Oram, editorial assistant, Sandra Lord, freelance photo researcher, and Sarah Davis Packard, Web developmental editor. I also wish to thank the skilled editorial, design, and production team: Elaine Richards, project editor; Burl Sloan, designer; and Andrea Archer, production manager.

The greatest debt of all is owed my wife, Anita de Laguna Haviland, who has not only had to put up with my preoccupation with this revision, but has fed revised text into the word processor. Finally, she has been a source of endless good ideas to include and ways to express concepts. The book has benefited enormously from her involvement.

William A. Haviland
June 1999

CONTENTS

Preface   viii

Putting the World in Perspective   xxiv

PART I
THE STUDY OF HUMANKIND   2

Introduction   3

CHAPTER 1
THE NATURE OF ANTHROPOLOGY   4

Chapter Preview   5
The Development of Anthropology   7

Bio Box: **Frank Hamilton Cushing, Matilda Coxe Stevenson**   8

Anthropology and the Other Sciences   8
The Discipline of Anthropology   9
   Physical Anthropology   9
   Cultural Anthropology   9

Anthropology Applied: **Forensic Anthropology**   10

   Archaeology   12
   Linguistic Anthropology   14
   Ethnology   15

Original Study: **Two Tales From the Trukese Taproom**   16

Anthropology and Science   22

Bio Box: **George Peter Murdock**   23
   Difficulties of the Scientific Approach   25

Bio Box: **Franz Boas, Fredric Ward Putnam, John Wesley Powell**   26

Anthropology and the Humanities   29
Questions of Ethics   30
Anthropology and Contemporary Life   31

Chapter Summary   32
Points for Consideration   33
Suggested Readings   33

CHAPTER 2
METHODS OF STUDYING THE HUMAN PAST   34

Chapter Preview   35
Methods of Data Recovery   36
   The Nature of Fossils   37

Original Study: **Whispers From the Ice**   38

Sites and Fossil Localities   43
   Site and Locality Identification   44

Anthropology Applied: **Cultural Resource Management**   46

   Site and Locality Excavation   47
     Archaeological Excavation   47

     Excavation of Fossils   50
   State of Preservation of Archaeological and Fossil Evidence   51
Sorting Out The Evidence   52
   Dating the Past   55
   Methods of Relative Dating   55
   Methods of Chronometric Dating   56
   Chance and Study of the Past   59

Chapter Summary   59
Points for Consideration   60
Suggested Readings   60

CHAPTER 3
BIOLOGY AND EVOLUTION   62

Chapter Preview   63
Heredity   64
   The Transmission of Genes   64
     DNA   64
     Genes   65
     Chromosomes   66
     Cell Division   66
     Polygenetic Inheritance   69
Population Genetics   69
   The Stability of the Population   70
   Factors for Change   70
     Mutation   70
   Genetic Drift   72
   Gene Flow   73
   Natural Selection   74

Bio Box: **Charles R. Darwin**   76

Adaptation   77
   The Case of Sickle-Cell Anemia   78
   Evolution of Populations   80

Original Study: **The Drunkard's Walk**   81

   Speciation   83
   Isolating Mechanisms   83
   The Nondirectness of Evolution   84

Anthropology Applied: **The Practical Importance of Evolution**   85

Chapter Summary   87
Points for Consideration   88
Suggested Readings   89

PART II
PRIMATE EVOLUTION AND THE EMERGENCE OF THE HOMININES   90

Introduction   91

CHAPTER 4
MONKEYS, APES, AND HUMANS: THE MODERN PRIMATES   92

Chapter Preview   93
The Classification System   94
The Primate Order   95
Primate Characteristics   98
  Primate Sense Organs   98
  The Primate Brain   99
  Primate Dentition   100
  The Primate Skeleton   101
  Reproduction and Care of Young   102
  Establishing Evolutionary Relationships   104
Modern Primates   105
  Strepsirhines   105
  Haplorhines   106
    Tarsiers   106
    New World Monkeys   107
    Old World Monkeys   107
    Small and Great Apes   107
The Social Behavior of Primates   110

Anthropology Applied: **Primate Conservation**   110
  The Group   111

Bio Box: **Jane Goodall**   112

  Individual Interaction   112
  Sexual Behavior   113
  Play   115
  Communication   115
  Home Ranges   117
  Learning   117

Original Study: **The Intellectual Abilities of Orangutans**   118

  Use of Objects as Tools   123
  Hunting   124
  Primate Behavior and Human Evolution   125

Chapter Summary   125
Points for Consideration   126
Suggested Readings   126

CHAPTER 5
FOSSIL PRIMATES   128

Chapter Preview   129
Primate Fossils   130
Mammalian Evolution and Primate Origins   130
Rise of the Primates   132
  Paleocene Primates   134
  Eocene Primates   134

Original Study: **Catopithecus and Anthropoid (Catarrhine and Platyrrhine) Origins**   135

  Oligocene Monkeys and Apes   138
  Miocene Apes   139
  Ramamorphs   141
  Ramamorphs and Human Origins   143

Ramamorph Adaptations   144
Early Apes and Human Evolution   147

Chapter Summary   148
Points for Consideration   148
Suggested Readings   149

CHAPTER 6
THE EARLIEST HOMININES   150

Chapter Preview   151
Australopithecus   152
  A. afarensis and A. africanus   154
  A. robustus and A. boisei   159

Bio Box: **Louis S. B. Leakey and Mary Leakey**   162

  Australopithecus anamensis and Ardipithecus ramidus   164
  Environment, Diet and Australopithecine Origins   165
  Humans Stand on Their Own Two Feet   166

Original Study: **The Naked and the Bipedal**   168

Chapter Summary   172
Points for Consideration   173
Suggested Readings   173

PART III
EVOLUTION OF THE GENUS HOMO AND THE DEVELOPMENT OF EARLY HUMAN CULTURE   174

Introduction   175

CHAPTER 7
HOMO HABILIS AND CULTURAL ORIGINS   176

Chapter Preview   177
Early Representatives of the Genus *Homo*   178
  Relations Between Homo habilis *and Australopithecus*   181
Lower Paleolithic Tools   183
  Olduvai Gorge   183
  Oldowan Tools   184
  Tools, Meat and Brains   185

Original Study: **Cat in the Human Cradle**   188

Bio Box: **Adrienne Zihlman**   193

  The Earliest Signs of Culture: Tools   194
  Cooperation and Sharing   195
  Language Origins   197

Chapter Summary   197
Points for Consideration   198
Suggested Readings   198

CHAPTER 8

HOMO ERECTUS AND THE EMERGENCE OF HUNTING AND GATHERING — 200

Chapter Preview — 201
Homo erectus Fossils — 202
  Homo erectus *From Java* — 202
  Homo erectus *From China* — 202
  Homo erectus *From Africa* — 204
  Homo erectus *From Europe* — 206
  Physical Characteristics of Homo erectus — 207
  Relationship Between Homo erectus
    and Homo habilis — 208
The Culture of *Homo erectus* — 209
  The Acheulean Tool Tradition — 209

Original Study: **Homo erectus and the use of Bamboo** — 211
  Use of Fire — 215
Other Aspects of *Homo erectus'* Culture — 217

Chapter Summary — 221
Points for Consideration — 222
Suggested Readings — 222

CHAPTER 9

ARCHAIC HOMO SAPIENS AND THE MIDDLE PALEOLITHIC — 224

Chapter Preview — 225
The Appearance of *Homo sapiens* — 226
  Levalloisian Technique — 227
  Archaic Homo sapiens — 228
    African, Chinese, and Javanese
      Populations — 232
The Culture of Archaic *Homo sapiens* — 232
  Middle Paleolithic — 232
  The Mousterian Tradition — 232

Anthropology Applied: **Forensic Archaeology** — 234
  The Symbolic Life of Neandertals — 235
  Neandertals and Spoken Language — 236
  Archaic Homo sapiens *and Modern
    Human Origins* — 237

Bio Box: **Franz Weidenreich** — 238
  The "Eve" of "Out of Africa" Hypothesis — 240

Original Study: **African Origin or Ancient Population Size Differences?** — 243

Chapter Summary — 245
Points for Consideration — 246
Suggested Readings — 246

CHAPTER 10

HOMO SAPIENS AND THE UPPER PALEOLITHIC — 248

Chapter Preview — 249
Upper Paleolithic Peoples: **The First Modern Humans** — 250

Anthropology Applied: **Stone Tools for Modern Surgeons** — 251
  Upper Paleolithic Tools — 253
  Upper Paleolithic Art — 258

Original Study: **Paleolithic Paint Job** — 261
  *Other Aspects of Upper Paleolithic
    Culture* — 265
  The Spread of Upper Paleolithic Peoples — 266
  *Where Did Upper Paleolithic People
    Come From?* — 268
The Mesolithic Era — 271
  Mesolithic Tools and Weapons — 271
  Cultural Diversity in the Mesolithic — 273
Major Paleolithic and Mesolithic Trends — 274

Chapter Summary — 275
Points for Consideration — 276
Suggested Readings — 276

PART IV

HUMAN BIOLOGICAL AND CULTURAL EVOLUTION SINCE THE OLD STONE AGE — 278

Introduction — 279

CHAPTER 11

CULTIVATION AND DOMESTICATION — 280

Chapter Preview — 281
The Mesolithic Roots of Farming and
  Pastoralism — 283
The Neolithic Revolution — 283
  Domestication: What Is It? — 283
  Evidence of Early Plant Domestication — 284
  Evidence of Early Animal Domestication — 285
  Beginnings of Domestication — 286
  Why Humans Became Food Producers — 287

Bio Box: **V. Gordon Childe** — 288
  Other Centers of Domestication — 294

Anthropology Applied: **Archaeology For and By Native Americans** — 296
  The Spread of Food Production — 297
Culture of Neolithic Settlements — 299
  Earliest Full-Fledged Farming Settlements — 299
  Jericho: An Early Farming Community — 300
  Neolithic Technology — 301
    Pottery — 301
    Housing — 303
    Clothing — 303
  Social Structure — 303

Neolithic Culture in the New World   304
The Neolithic and Human Biology   305

Original Study: **History of Mortality and
Physiological Stress**   305
The Neolithic and the Idea of Progress   308

Chapter Summary   309
Points for Consideration   310
Suggested Readings   310

CHAPTER 12
THE RISE OF CITIES AND CIVILIZATION   312

Chapter Preview   313
What Civilization Means   314
Tikal: A Case Study   317
   Surveying the Site   318
   Evidence From the Excavation   319
Cities and Cultural Change   321
   Agricultural Innovation   321
   Diversification of Labor   322

Anthropology Applied: **Economic
Development and Tropical Forests**   323
   Central Government   326
      Evidence of Centralized Authority   326
      The Earliest Governments   328
   Social Stratification   329
      Evidence of Social Stratification   329

Original Study: **Finding the Tomb of a
Moche Priestess**   330
The Making of Civilization   336
   Theories of Civilization's Emergence   336
      Irrigation Systems   336
      Trade Networks   337
      Environmental and Social
         Circumscription   337
      Religion   337
Civilization and Stress   339

Chapter Summary   340
Points for Consideration   342
Suggested Readings   342

CHAPTER 13
MODERN HUMAN DIVERSITY   344

Chapter Preview   345
Variation and Evolution   346
   Physical Variability   346
The Meaning of Race   348
   Race as a Biological Concept   349

Original Study: **Race Without Color**   350
   The Concept of Human Races   355

Some Physical Variables   357
   Skin Color: A Case Study in Adaptation   359
The Social Significance of Race: Racism   363
   Race and Behavior   363
   Race and Intelligence   364
   Intelligence: What Is It?   366
Continuing Human Biological Evolution   368

Anthropology Applied: **Studying the
Emergence of New Diseases**   373
Chapter Summary   374
Points for Consideration   376
Suggested Readings   376

PART V
CULTURE AND SURVIVAL: COMMUNICATING, RAISING CHILDREN, AND STAYING ALIVE   378

Introduction   379

CHAPTER 14
THE NATURE OF CULTURE   380

Chapter Preview   381
The Concept of Culture   382
Characteristics of Culture   382
   Culture Is Shared   382

Anthropology Applied: **New Houses for
Apache Indians**   384
   Culture Is Learned   388
   Culture Is Based on Symbols   389
Bio Box: **Leslie A. White**   390
   Culture Is Integrated   390
Bio Box: **A. R. Radcliffe-Brown**   391
Studying Culture in the Field   392
Bio Box: **Bronislaw Malinowski**   393

Original Study: **The Importance of
Trobriand Women**   394
Culture and Adaptation   396
   Functions of Culture   397
   Culture and Change   398
Culture, Society, and the Individual   399
Evaluation of Culture   399

Chapter Summary   402
Points for Consideration   403
Suggested Readings   403

CHAPTER 15
LANGUAGE AND COMMUNICATION   404

Chapter Preview 405
The Nature of Language 407
The Sound and Shape of Language 408
Phonology 409
Morphology 410
Grammar and Syntax 410
The Gesture-Call System 411
Kinesics 412
Paralanguage 412
Voice Qualities 412
Vocalizations 416
Linguistic Change 416

Anthropology Applied: **Language Renewal
Among the Northern Ute** 419

Language In Its Cultural Setting 420
Language and Thought 421
Kinship Terms 423
Language and Gender 424
Social Dialects 424

Original Study: **The Great Ebonics
Controversy** 425
The Origins of Language 428

Chapter Summary 431
Points for Consideration 432
Suggested Readings 433

CHAPTER 16
GROWING UP HUMAN 434

Chapter Preview 435
The Self and the Behavioral Environment 436
The Self 436
The Behavioral Environment 439
The Penobscot 440

Original Study: **The Blessed Curse** 442

Personality 446
The Development of Personality 446
Dependence Training 448

Bio Box: **Margaret Mead** 449

Independence Training 451
Combined Dependence/Independence
Training 452
Group Personality 452
Modal Personality 453

Bio Box: **Ruth Fulton Benedict** 455

National Character 455
The Japanese 456
Objections to National Character
Studies 456
Normal and Abnormal Personality 458

Anthropology Applied: **Anthropologists
and Mental Health** 460
Chapter Summary 464
Points for Consideration 465
Suggested Readings 465

CHAPTER 17
PATTERNS OF SUBSISTENCE 466

Chapter Preview 467
Adaptation 468
The Unit of Adaptation 470
Evolutionary Adaptation 471
Culture Areas 473

Bio Box: **Julian H. Steward** 475

Culture Core 475
The Food-Foraging Way of Life 476
Characteristics of the Food-Foraging Life 479
*The Impact of Food Foraging on Human
Society* 480
Subsistence and Gender 480
Food Sharing 482
Cultural Adaptations and Material
Technology 482
Egalitarian Society 483
Food-Producing Society 484
The Settled Life of Farmers 484

Original Study: **Gardens of the
Mekranoti Kayapo** 486
Pastoralism: The Bakhtiari 490
*Intensive Agriculture and Nonindustrial
Cities* 493

Anthropology Applied: **Agricultural
Development and the Anthropologist** 494
Aztec City Life 495
Nonindustrial Cities in the Modern World 498

Chapter Summary 499
Points for Consideration 500
Suggested Readings 500

CHAPTER 18
ECONOMIC SYSTEMS 502

Chapter Preview 503
Economic Anthropology 504
Resources 506
Patterns of Labor 506
Sexual Division of Labor 506
Age Division of Labor 509
Cooperation 510
Craft Specialization 511
Control of Land 511

Technology 512
Leveling Mechanisms 513
Distribution and Exchange 514
Reciprocity 514
Barter and Trade 517
The Kula Ring 518
Redistribution 519
Distribution of Wealth 521

Original Study: **Prestige Economics in Papua New Guinea** 522

Market Exchange 525
Economics, Culture, and the World of Business 529

Anthropology Applied: **Anthropology and the World of Business** 530

Chapter Summary 532
Points for Consideration 533
Suggested Readings 533

PART VI
THE FORMATION OF GROUPS: SOLVING THE PROBLEM OF COOPERATION **534**

Introduction 535

CHAPTER 19
SEX AND MARRIAGE 536

Chapter Preview 537
Control of Sexual Relations 539

Anthropology Applied: **Anthropology and AIDS** 540

Rules of Sexual Access 542
The Incest Taboo 545
Endogamy and Exogamy 547

Bio Box: **Claude Lévi-Strauss** 548

The Distinction Between Marriage and Mating 548
Marriage and the Family 549
Forms of Marriage 550
The Levirate and the Sororate 552
Serial Monogamy 552
Choice of Spouse 553

Original Study: **Arranging Marriage in India** 554

Cousin Marriage 559
Marriage Exchanges 560
Same-Sex Marriage 562
Divorce 563

Chapter Summary 565
Points for Consideration 566
Suggested Readings 566

CHAPTER 20
FAMILY AND HOUSEHOLD 568

Chapter Preview 569
Family and Society 572

Original Study: **The Ephemeral Modern Family** 572

Functions of the Family 575
Nurturance of Children 576
Economic Cooperation 576
Family and Household 578
Form of the Family 579
The Nuclear Family 579
The Extended Family 581
Residence Patterns 582
Problems of Family and Household Organization 586
Polygamous Families 586
Extended Families 587
Nuclear Families 588

Anthropology Applied: **Dealing With Infant Mortality** 589

Female-Headed Households 591

Chapter Summary 594
Points for Consideration 595
Suggested Readings 595

CHAPTER 21
KINSHIP AND DESCENT 596

Chapter Preview 597
Descent Groups 598
Unilineal Descent 599
Patrilineal Descent and Organization 600
Traditional China: A Patrilineal Society 600

Original Study: **Coping as a Woman in a Man's World** 602

Matrilineal Descent and Organization 604
The Hopi: A Matrilineal Society 605
Double Descent 607
Ambilineal Descent 607
Ambilineal Descent Among New York City Jews 607
Forms and Functions of Descent Groups 609
Lineage 610
Clan 610

Anthropology Applied: **Federal Recognition for Native Americans** 611

Phratries and Moieties 612
Bilateral Descent and the Kindred 613
Evolution of the Descent Group 615

Kinship Terminology and Kinship Groups   616
   Eskimo System   617
   Hawaiian System   618
   Iroquois System   618
   Crow System   619

Bio Box: Lewis Henry Morgan   619

   Omaha System   620
   Sudanese or Descriptive System   620

Chapter Summary   622
Points for Consideration   623
Suggested Readings   623

CHAPTER 22
GROUPING BY SEX, AGE, COMMON INTEREST, AND CLASS   624

Chapter Preview   625
Grouping by Gender   626
Age Grouping   628
   Institutions of Age Grouping   629
   Age Grouping in African Societies   630
Common-Interest Associations   631
   Kinds of Common-Interest Associations   632
      Men's and Women's Associations   632
Social Stratification   634

Anthropology Applied: Anthropologists and Social Impact Assessment   635

   Class and Caste   636
   Mobility   640
   Gender Stratification   641
   Development of Stratification   642

Original Study: Genocide in Rwanda   644

Chapter Summary   647
Points for Consideration   648
Suggested Readings   649

PART VII
THE SEARCH FOR ORDER: SOLVING THE PROBLEM OF DISORDER   650

Introduction   651

CHAPTER 23
POLITICAL ORGANIZATION AND THE MAINTENANCE OF ORDER   652

Chapter Preview   653
Kinds of Political Systems   654
   Uncentralized Political Systems   654
      Band Organization   654
      Tribal Organization   656

Kinship Organization   659
Age-Grade Organization   660
Association Organization   661
   Centralized Political Systems   661
      Chiefdoms   662
      State Systems   663
   Political Leadership and Gender   666
Political Organization and the Maintenance
   of Order   668
   Internalized Controls   668
   Externalized Controls   669

Original Study: Limits on Power in Bedouin Society   671

Social Control Through Law   674
   Definition of Law   674
   Functions of Law   674
   Crime   677

Anthropology Applied: Dispute Resolution and the Anthropologist   678

Political Organization and External Affairs   680
   War   680
Political Systems and the Question of
   Legitimacy   683
Religion and Politics   685

Chapter Summary   685
Points for Consideration   687
Suggested Readings   688

CHAPTER 24
RELIGION AND THE SUPERNATURAL   690

Chapter Preview   691
The Anthropological Approach to Religion   694
The Practice of Religion   694
   Supernatural Beings and Powers   696
      Gods and Goddesses   696
      Ancestral Spirits   697
      Animism   698

Bio Box: Sir Edward B. Tylor   699

   Animitism   700
   Religious Specialists   701
      Priests and Priestesses   701
      Shamans   701

Original Study: Healing Among the Ju/'hoansi of the Kalahari   703

   Rituals and Ceremonies   705
      Rites of Passage   705
      Rites of Intensification   707
Religion, Magic, and Witchcraft   708
   Witchcraft   710
      Ibibio Witchcraft   711

The Functions of Witchcraft   712
  Psychological Functions of Witchcraft
    Among the Navajo   712

***Anthropology Applied:* Reconciling
Modern Medicine With Traditional
Beliefs in Swaziland**   713

The Functions of Religion   714
Religion and Cultural Change   716
  Revitalization Movements   717

Chapter Summary   719
Points for Consideration   721
Suggested Readings   721

CHAPTER 25
THE ARTS   722

Chapter Preview   723
The Anthropological Study of Art   726

***Anthropology Applied:* Protecting
Cultural Heritages**   727

Verbal Arts   728
  Myth   729
  Legend   731
  Tale   733
  Other Verbal Arts   734
The Art of Music   736

***Bio Box:* Frederica de Laguna**   736

  Functions of Music   739
Pictorial Art   741
  Southern African Rock Art   742

***Original Study:* Bushman Rock Art and
Political Power**   747

Chapter Summary   750
Points for Consideration   750
Suggested Readings   751

PART VIII
**CHANGE AND THE FUTURE: SOLVING
THE PROBLEM OF ADJUSTING TO
CHANGED CONDITIONS**   **752**

Introduction   753

CHAPTER 26
CULTURAL CHANGE   754

Chapter Preview   755
Mechanisms of Change   757
  Innovation   757
  Diffusion   761
  Cultural Loss   763
Forcible Change   764

Acculturation   764
Genocide   766
Directed Change   768

***Anthropology Applied:* Growing Trees
in Haiti**   769

***Bio Box:* Franz Boas**   770

Reactions to Forcible Change   771
  Revitalization Movements   772
Rebellion and Revolution   774
Modernization   777
  *Skolt Lapps and the Snowmobile
    Revolution*   778
  The Shuar Solution   780

***Original Study:* Violence on Indian Day
in Brazil 1997**   781

  *Modernization and the "Underdeveloped"
    World*   785
  Modernization: Must It Always Be Painful?   786

Chapter Summary   787
Points for Consideration   788
Suggested Readings   788

CHAPTER 27
ANTHROPOLOGY AND THE FUTURE   790

Chapter Preview   791
The Cultural Future of Humanity   792
  One-World Culture   793
  The Rise of the Multinational Corporations   795

***Original Study:* Standardizing the Body:
The Question of Choice**   798

  One-World Culture: A Good Idea or Not?   802
  Ethnic Resurgence   803
  Cultural Pluralism   804
    Guatemalan Cultural Pluralism   804
  Ethnocentrism   808

***Anthropology Applied:* Advocacy for the
Rights of Indigenous Peoples**   809

  Global Arpartheid   810
Problems of Structural Violence   812
  World Hunger   812
  Pollution   814
  Population Control   818
  The Culture of Discontent   820

Chapter Summary   821
Points for Consideration   822
Suggested Readings   822

Bibliography   B-1
Index   I-1
Photo Permissions   P-1
Literary Permissions   L-1

ABOUT THE AUTHOR

Dr. William A. Haviland is professor of anthropology at the University of Vermont, where he has taught since 1965. He holds a doctorate degree in anthropology from the University of Pennsylvania and has published widely on archaeological, ethnological, and physical anthropological research carried out in Guatemala, Maine, and Vermont. Dr. Haviland is a member of many professional societies, including the American Anthropological Association and the American Association for the Advancement of Science. In 1988, he participated in the project on "Gender and the Anthropology Curriculum," sponsored by the American Anthropological Association.

One of Dr. Haviland's greatest loves is teaching, which originally prompted him to write *Cultural Anthropology*. He says he learns something new every year from his students about what they need out of their first college course in anthropology. In addition to writing *Cultural Anthropology*, Dr. Haviland has authored several other popular Harcourt Brace works for anthropology students.

PUTTING THE WORLD IN PERSPECTIVE

Although all humans that we know about are capable of producing accurate sketches of localities and regions with which they are familiar, CARTOGRAPHY (the craft of mapmaking as we know it today) had its beginnings in 13th century Europe, and its subsequent development is related to the expansion of Europeans to all parts of the globe. From the beginning, there have been two problems with maps: the technical one of how to depict on a two-dimensional, flat surface a three-dimensional spherical object, and the cultural one of whose worldview they reflect. In fact, the two issues are inseparable, for the particular projection one uses inevitably makes a statement about how one views one's own people and their place in the world. Indeed, maps often shape our perception of reality as much as they reflect it.

In cartography, a PROJECTION refers to the system of intersecting lines (of longitude and latitude) by which part or all of the globe is represented on a flat surface. There are more than 100 different projections in use today, ranging from polar perspectives to interrupted "butterflies" to rectangles to heart shapes. Each projection causes distortion in size, shape, or distance in some way or another. A map that shows the shape of land masses correctly will of necessity misrepresent the size. A map that is accurate along the equator will be deceptive at the poles.

Perhaps no projection has had more influence on the way we see the world than that of Gerhardus Mercator, who devised his map in 1569 as a navigational aid for mariners. So well suited was Mercator's map for this purpose that it continues to be used for navigational charts today. At the same time, the Mercator projection became a standard for depicting land masses, something for which it was never intended. Although an accurate navigational tool, the Mercator projection greatly exaggerates the size of land masses in higher latitudes, giving about two-thirds of the map's surface to the northern hemisphere. Thus,

the lands occupied by Europeans and European descendants appear far larger than those of other people. For example, North America (19 million square kilometers) appears almost twice the size of Africa (30 million square kilometers), while Europe is shown as equal in size to South America, which actually has nearly twice the land mass of Europe.

A map developed in 1805 by Karl B. Mollweide was one of the earlier equal-area projections of the world. Equal-area projections portray land masses in correct relative size, but, as a result, distort the shape of continents more than other projections. They most often compress and warp lands in the higher latitudes and vertically stretch land masses close to the equator. Other equal-area projections include the Lambert Cylindrical Equal-Area Projection (1772), the Hammer Equal-Area Projection (1892), and the Eckert Equal-Area Projection (1906).

The Van der Grinten Projection (1904) was a compromise aimed at minimizing both the distortions of size in the Mercator and the distortion of shape in equal-area maps such as the Mollweide. Allthough an improvement, the lands of the northern hemisphere are still emphasized at the expense of the southern. For example, in the Van der Grinten, the Commonwealth of Independent States (the former Soviet Union) and Canada are shown at more than twice their relative size.

The Robinson Projection, which was adopted by the National Geographic Society in 1988 to replace the Van der Grinten, is one of the best compromises to date between the distortion of size and shape. Although an improvement over the Van der Grinten, the Robinson projection still depicts lands in the northern latitudes as proportionally larger at the same time that it depicts lands in the lower latitudes (representing most third-world nations) as proportionally smaller. Like European maps before it, the Robinson projection places Europe at the center of the map with the Atlantic Ocean and the Americas to the left, emphasizing the cultural connection between Europe and North America, while neglecting the geographical closeness of northwestern North America to northeast Asia.

The following pages show four maps that each convey quite different "cultural messages." Included among them is the Peters Projection, an equal-area map that has been adopted as the official map of UNESCO (the United Nations Educational, Scientific, and Cultural Organization), and a map made in Japan, showing us how the world looks from the other side.

INUIT

INUIT

INUIT

INUIT

TORY
ISLANDE

TLINGIT

•BELLA COOLA
•KWAKIUTL

WESTERN
ABENAKI

NASKAPI

OJIBWA

IROQUOIS

MONTAGNAIS

•CROW

MALISEET
MI'KMAQ

•N. PAIUTE
•SHOSHONE

•SIOUX

PENOBSCOT

•POMO

•UTE

•OMAHA

AMISH

PEQUOT

S. PAIUTE

•CHEYENNE

NEW YORK CITY JEWS

NAVAJO

•CHEROKEE

CANARY
ISLANDERS

PUEBLO (HOPI,
TEWA, ZUNI)

•COMANCHE

APACHE

AZTEC

MAYA

PUERTO RICANS

HAWAIIAN

ZAPOTEC

HAITIANS
CARIBBEAN

MENDE

SHUAR

YANOMAMI

KPEL

INCA

MUNDURUCU

SHERENTE

INCA

CINTA-LARGA

SAMOAN

AYMARA

KAYAPO

INCA

YAGHAN

THE ROBINSON PROJECTION   The map above is based on the Robinson Projection, which is used
today by the National Geographic Society and Rand McNally. Although the Robinson Projection distorts
the relative size of land masses, it does so to a much lesser degree than most other projections. Still, it

places Europe at the center of the map. This particular view of the world has been used to identify the location of many of the cultures discussed in this text.

THE PETERS PROJECTION   The map above is based on the Peters Projection, which has been adopted as the official map of UNESCO. While it distorts the shape of continents (countries near the equator are vertically elongated by a ratio of two to one), the Peters Projection does show all continents according to their correct relative size. Though Europe is still at the center, it is not shown as larger and more extensive than the third world.

JAPANESE MAP   Not all maps place Europe at the center of the world, as this Japanese map illustrates.
Besides reflecting the importance the Japanese attach to themselves in the world, this map has the virtue

of showing the geographic proximity of North America to Asia, a fact easily overlooked when maps place Europe at their center.

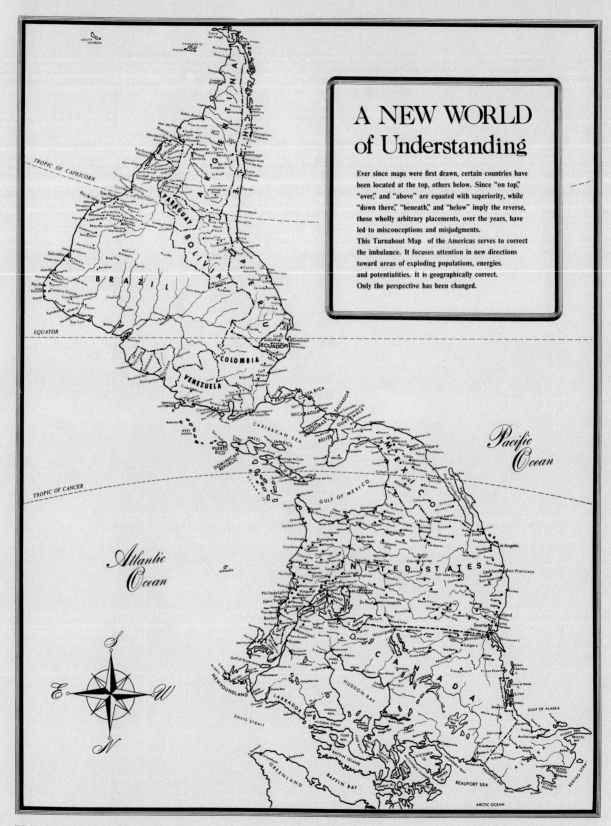

A NEW WORLD
of Understanding

Ever since maps were first drawn, certain countries have been located at the top, others below. Since "on top," "over," and "above" are equated with superiority, while "down there," "beneath," and "below" imply the reverse, these wholly arbitrary placements, over the years, have led to misconceptions and misjudgments.

This Turnabout Map of the Americas serves to correct the imbalance. It focuses attention in new directions toward areas of exploding populations, energies, and potentialities. It is geographically correct. Only the perspective has been changed.

THE TURNABOUT MAP   The way maps may reflect (and influence) our thinking is exemplified by the "Turnabout Map," which places the South Pole at the top and the North Pole at the bottom. Words and phrases such as "on top," "over," and "above" tend to be equated by some people with superiority. Turning things upside down may cause us to rethink the way North Americans regard themselves in relation to the people of Central America. © 1982 by Jesse Levine Turnabout Map™ —Dist. by Laguna Sales, Inc., 7040 Via Valverde, San Jose, CA 95135

NINTH EDITION

Anthropology

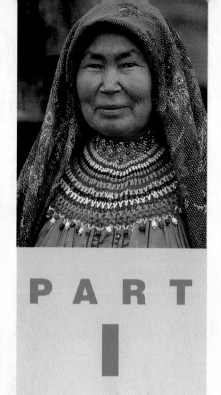

PART

I

THE STUDY OF HUMANKIND

Chapter 1
THE NATURE OF ANTHROPOLOGY

Chapter 2
METHODS OF STUDYING THE HUMAN PAST

Chapter 3
BIOLOGY AND EVOLUTION

Introduction

Anthropology is the most liberating of all the sciences. Not only has it exposed the fallacies of racial and cultural superiority, but also its devotion to the study of all peoples, regardless of where and when they lived, has cast more light on human nature than all the reflections of sages or the studies of laboratory scientists. If this sounds like the assertion of an overly enthusiastic anthropologist, it is not; it was all said long ago in 1941 by the philosopher Grace de Laguna in her presidential address to the Eastern Division of the American Philosophical Association.

The subject matter of anthropology is vast, as we shall see in this book: It includes everything that has to do with human beings, past and present. Of course, many other disciplines are concerned in one way or another with human beings. Some, such as anatomy and physiology, study humans as biological organisms. The social sciences are concerned with the distinctive forms of human relationships, while the humanities examine the great achievements of human culture. Anthropologists are interested in all of these things, too, but they try to deal with them all together, in all places and times. It is this unique, broad perspective that equips anthropologists so well to deal with that elusive thing called human nature.

Needless to say, no single anthropologist is able to investigate personally everything that has to do with people. For practical purposes, the discipline is divided into various subfields, and individual anthropologists specialize in one or more of these. Whatever their specialization, though, they retain a commitment to a broader, overall perspective on humankind. For example, cultural anthropologists specialize in the study of human behavior, while physical anthropologists specialize in the study of humans as biological organisms. Yet neither can afford to ignore the work of the other, for human behavior and biology are inextricably intertwined, with each affecting the other in important ways. We can see, for example, how biology affects a cultural practice such as color-naming behavior. Human populations differ in the density of pigmentation within the eye itself, which in turn affects people's ability to distinguish the color blue from green, black, or both. Consequently, a number of cultures identify blue with green, black, or both. We can see also how a cultural practice may affect human biology, as exemplified by abnormal forms of hemoglobin, the substance that transports oxy-gen in the blood. In certain parts of Asia and Africa, when humans took up the practice of farming, they altered the ecology in a way that, by chance, created ideal conditions for the breeding of mosquitoes. As a result, malaria became a serious problem (mosquitoes carry the malarial parasite), and a biological response to this was the spread of certain genes that, in those people who inherit the gene from only one parent, produced a built-in resistance to the disease. Although those who inherit the gene from both parents contract a potentially lethal anemia, such as sickle-cell anemia, those without the gene are apt to succumb to malaria. (We will take up this topic in Chapter 3.)

To begin our introduction to the study of anthropology, we will look closely at the nature of the discipline. In Chapter 1 we will see how the field of anthropology is subdivided, how the subdivisions relate to one another, and how they relate to the other sciences and humanities. Chapter 1 introduces us as well to the methods anthropologists use to study human cultures, especially those of today, or the very recent past. However, since the next two parts of the book take us far back into the human past, to see where we came from and how we got to be the way we are today, further discussion of methods used to study contemporary cultures is deferred to Parts V and VIII (especially Chapter 14). The very different methods used to find out about the ancient past are the subject of Chapter 2, which discusses the nature of fossils and archaeological materials, where they are found, how they are (quite literally) unearthed, and how they are dealt with once unearthed. From this, one can begin to appreciate what the evidence can tell us if handled properly, as well as its limitations. In order to understand what fossils have to tell us about our past, some knowledge of how biological evolution works is necessary. But fossils, unlike flesh and blood people, do not speak for themselves, and so they must be interpreted. If we are to have confidence in an interpretation of a particular fossil, we must be sure the interpretation is consistent with what we know about the workings of evolution; therefore, Chapter 3 is devoted to a discussion of evolution. With this done, we will have set the stage for our detailed look at human biological and cultural evolution in Parts II, III, and IV.

Chapter 1
THE NATURE OF ANTHROPOLOGY

A DEPICTION OF FIRST CONTACT BETWEEN
HERNANDO CORTÉS AND THE AZTEC RULER
MOCTEZUMA. SUCH CONTACTS SPARKED THE
INTEREST IN OTHER PEOPLES THAT LED TO THE
DEVELOPMENT OF ANTHROPOLOGY.

Chapter Preview

What Is Anthropology?

Anthropology, the study of humankind everywhere, throughout time, seeks to produce reliable knowledge about people and their behavior, both about what makes them different and what they all share in common.

What Do Anthropologists Do?

Physical anthropologists study humans as biological organisms, tracing the evolutionary development of the human animal and looking at biological variations within the species, past and present. Cultural anthropologists are concerned with human cultures, or the ways of life in societies. Within the field of cultural anthropology are archaeologists, who seek to explain human behavior by studying material objects, usually from past cultures; linguists, who study languages, by which cultures are maintained and passed on to succeeding generations; and ethnologists, who study cultures as they have been observed, experienced, and discussed with persons whose culture they seek to understand.

How Do Anthropologists Do What They Do?

Anthropologists, in common with other scientists, are concerned with the formulation and testing of hypotheses, or tentative explanations of observed phenomena. In so doing, they hope to develop reliable theories—explanations supported by bodies of data—although they recognize that no theory is ever completely beyond challenge. In order to frame hypotheses that are as objective and free of cultural bias as possible, anthropologists typically develop them through a kind of total immersion in the field, becoming so familiar with the minute details of the situation that they can begin to recognize patterns inherent in the data. It is also through fieldwork that anthropologists test existing hypotheses.

5

A common part of the mythology of all peoples is a legend that explains the appearance of humans on earth. Such a myth, for example, is the account of creation recorded in the Bible's Book of Genesis. Another vastly different example, which nonetheless serves the same function, is the belief of the Nez Perce (a people native to the American Northwest) that humanity is the creation of Coyote, one of the animal people that inhabited the earth before humans. Coyote chased the giant beaver monster, Wishpoosh, in an epic chase whose trail formed the Columbia River. When Coyote caught Wishpoosh, he killed him and dragged his body to the riverbank. Ella Clark retells the story:

> With his sharp knife Coyote cut up the big body of the monster.
>
> "From your body, mighty Wishpoosh," he said, "I will make a new race of people. They will live near the shores of Big River and along the streams which flow into it."
>
> From the lower part of the animal's body, Coyote made people who were to live along the coast. "You shall live near the mouth of Big River and shall be traders."
>
> "You shall live along the coast," he said to others. "You shall live in villages facing the ocean and shall get your food by spearing salmon and digging clams. You shall always be short and fat and have weak legs."
>
> From the legs of the beaver monster he made the Klickitat Indians. "You shall live along the rivers that flow down from the big white mountain north of Big River. You shall be swift of foot and keen of wit. You shall be famous runners and great horsemen."
>
> From the arms of the monster he made the Cayuse Indians. "You shall be powerful with bow and arrows and with war clubs."
>
> From the ribs he made the Yakima Indians. "You shall live near the new Yakima River, east of the mountains. You shall be the helpers and the protectors of all the poor people."
>
> From the head he created the Nez Perce Indians. "You shall live in the valleys of the Kookooskia and Wallowa rivers. You shall be men of brains, great in council and in speech making. You shall also be skillful horsemen and brave warriors."

> Then Coyote gathered up the hair and blood and waste. He hurled them far eastward, over the big mountains. "You shall be the Snake River Indians," said Coyote. "You shall be people of blood and violence. You shall be buffalo hunters and shall wander far and wide."[1]

For as long as they have been on earth, people have needed answers to questions about who they are, where they came from, why they act the way they do, and why other people look and act differently. Throughout most of their history, though, people relied on myth and folklore for their answers to these questions, rather than the systematic testing of data obtained through careful observation. Anthropology, over the last 200 years, has emerged as a scientific approach to answering these questions. Simply stated, **anthropology** is the study of humankind in all places and throughout time. The anthropologist is concerned primarily with a single species—*Homo sapiens*—the human species, its ancestors, and its near relatives. Because anthropologists are members of the species they study, it is difficult for them to maintain a scientific detachment toward those whom they study. This, of course, is part of a larger problem in science. As one leading U.S. scientist puts it:

> Nature is objective, and nature is knowable, but we can only view her through a glass darkly—and many clouds upon our vision are of our own making: social and cultural biases, psychological preferences, and mental limitations (in universal modes of thought, not just human stupidity).
>
> The human contribution to this equation of difficulty becomes ever greater as the subject under investigation comes closer to the heart of our practical and philosophical concerns.[2]

Since nothing comes closer to the heart of our practical and philosophical concerns than ourselves and others of our kind, can we ever hope to gain truly

---

[1]Clark, E. E. (1966). *Indian legends of the Pacific Northwest* (p. 174). Berkeley: University of California Press.
[2]Gould, S. J. (1996). *Full house* (p. 8). New York: Harmony Books.

Anthropology. The study of humankind in all times and places.

objective knowledge about peoples' behavior? Anthropologists worry about this a great deal, but have found that by maintaining a critical awareness of their assumptions, and constantly testing their conclusions against new sources of data, they can achieve a useful understanding of human behavior. By scientifically approaching how people live, anthropologists have learned a great deal both about human differences, and about the many things all humans have in common beneath all these differences.

THE DEVELOPMENT OF ANTHROPOLOGY

Although works of anthropological significance have a considerable antiquity—two examples are the accounts of other peoples written by Herodotus the Greek in the 5th century B.C., and by the Arab Ibn Khaldun in the 14th century A.D.—anthropology as a distinct field of inquiry is a relatively recent product of Western civilization. In the United States, for example, the first course in general anthropology to carry credit in a college or university (the University of Rochester) was not offered until 1879. If people have always been concerned about themselves, other people, and their origins, why then did it take such a long time for a systematic discipline of anthropology to appear? The answer to this is as complex as human history. In part, it relates to the limits of human technology. Throughout most of their time on earth, people have been restricted in their geographical horizons. Without the means of traveling to distant places, observation of cultures and peoples far from one's own was a difficult—if not impossible—venture. Extensive travel was usually the exclusive prerogative of a few; the study of foreign peoples and cultures was not likely to flourish until adequate modes of transportation and communication could be developed.

This is not to say that people have always been unaware of the existence of others in the world who look and act differently from themselves. The Old and New Testaments of the Bible, for example, are full of references to such diverse peoples as Jews, Egyptians, Hittites, Babylonians, Ethiopians, Romans, and so forth. Still, the differences between these people pale by comparison to those between

any of them on the one hand and (for example) indigenous people of Australia, the Amazon forest, or arctic North America. With the means to travel to truly faraway places, it became possible to meet for the first time such radically different people. It was the massive encounter with hitherto unknown peoples, which came as Europeans sought to extend their trade and political domination to all parts of the world, that focused attention on human differences in all their glory.

Another significant element that contributed to the slow growth of anthropology was the failure of Europeans to recognize that beneath all the differences, they might share a basic "humanity" with people everywhere. Societies that did not share the fundamental cultural values of Europeans were labeled as "savage" or "barbarian." Not until the late 18th century did a significant number of Europeans

Not only are all anthropologists *not* all male, neither are they all European or European American. Mamphela Ramphele, who is vice chancellor of the University of Cape Town, is a native South African anthropologist who has studied the migrant labor hostels of Cape Town.

Frank Hamilton Cushing *(1857–1900)*
Matilda Coxe Stevenson *(1849–1915)*

In the United States, anthropology began in the 19th century when a number of dedicated amateurs went into the field to gain a better understanding of what many European Americans still regarded as "primitive people." Exemplifying their emphasis on firsthand observation is Frank Hamilton Cushing, who lived among the Zuni Indians for $4\frac{1}{2}$ years (he is shown here in full dress as a war chief).

Among these founders of North American anthropology were a number of women whose work was highly influential among those who spoke out in the 19th century on behalf of women's rights. One of these pioneering anthropologists was Matilda Coxe Stevenson, who also did fieldwork among the Zuni. In 1885, she founded the Women's Anthropological Society, the first professional association for women scientists. Three years later, she was hired by the Bureau of American Ethnology, making her one of the first women in the United States to receive a full-time position in science. The tradition of women being active in anthropology continues, and since World War II more than half the presidents of the American Anthropological Association have been women.

consider the behavior of such people to be at all relevant to an understanding of themselves. This growing interest in human diversity, coming at a time when efforts to explain things in terms of natural laws were increasing, cast doubts on the traditional biblical mythology, which no longer adequately "explained" human diversity.

Although anthropology originated within the context of Western civilization, it has long since gone global. Today, it is an exciting, international discipline whose practitioners are drawn from diverse societies in all parts of the world. Even societies that have long been studied by European and North American anthropologists—several African and Native American societies, for example—have produced anthropologists who continue to make their mark on the discipline. Their distinctive perspectives help shed new light not only on their own societies, but on those of others (including Western societies) as well.

ANTHROPOLOGY AND THE OTHER SCIENCES

It would be incorrect to infer from the foregoing that serious attempts were never made to analyze human diversity before the 18th century. Anthropologists are not the only scholars who study people. In this respect they share their objectives with the other social and natural scientists. Anthropologists do not think of their findings as something quite apart from those of psychologists, economists, sociologists, or biologists; rather, they welcome the contributions these other disciplines have to make to the common goal of understanding humanity, and they gladly offer their own findings for the benefit of these other disciplines. Anthropologists do not expect, for example, to know as much about the structure of the human eye as anatomists, or as much about the perception of color as psychologists. As synthesizers, however, they are better prepared to understand how these relate to color-naming behavior in different human societies than any of their fellow scientists. Because they look for the broad basis of human behavior without limiting themselves to any single social or biological aspect of that behavior, anthropologists can acquire an especially extensive overview of the complex biological and cultural organism that is the human being.

THE DISCIPLINE OF ANTHROPOLOGY

Anthropology is traditionally divided into four fields: physical anthropology and the three branches of cultural anthropology, which are archaeology, linguistic anthropology, and ethnology. **Physical anthropology** is concerned primarily with humans as biological organisms, while **cultural anthropology** deals with humans as cultural animals. Both, of course, are closely related; we cannot understand what people do unless we know what people are. And we want to know how biology does and does not influence culture, as well as how culture affects biology.

PHYSICAL ANTHROPOLOGY

Physical anthropology (or, alternatively, biological anthropology) is the branch of anthropology that focuses on humans as biological organisms, and one of its many interests is human evolution. Whatever distinctions people may claim for themselves, they are mammals—specifically, primates—and, as such, they share a common ancestry with other primates, most specifically apes and monkeys. Through the analysis of fossils and observation of living primates, physical anthropologists try to trace the ancestry of the human species in order to understand how, when, and why we became the kind of animal we are today.

Another major concern of physical anthropology is the study of present-day human variation.

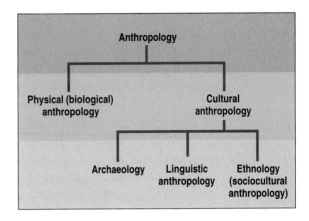

FIGURE 1.1
The subfields of anthropology.

Although we are all members of a single species, we differ from each other in many obvious and not so obvious ways. We differ not only in such visible traits as the color of our skins or the shape of our noses, but also in such biochemical factors as our blood types and our susceptibility to certain diseases. The physical anthropologist applies all the techniques of modern molecular biology to achieve fuller understanding of human variation and the ways in which it relates to the different environments people have lived in. We shall come back to physical anthropology later in this chapter, after looking at the fields of cultural anthropology.

CULTURAL ANTHROPOLOGY

Because the capacity for culture is rooted in our biological natures, the work of the physical anthropologist provides a necessary background for the cultural anthropologist. In order to understand the work of the cultural anthropologist, we must clarify what we mean when we refer to culture. For our purposes here, we may think of culture as the often unconscious standards by which societies—groups of people—operate. These standards are learned rather than acquired through biological inheritance. Since they determine, or at least guide, the day-to-day behavior of the members of a society, human behavior is above all cultural behavior. The manifestations of culture may vary considerably from

---

Physical anthropology. The systematic study of humans as biological organisms. **>** **Cultural anthropology.** The branch of anthropology that focuses on human behavior.

anthropology *applied* Forensic Anthropology

In the public mind, anthropology is often identified with the recovery of the bones of remote human ancestors, the unearthing of ancient campsites and "lost cities," or the study of present-day tribal peoples whose way of life is erroneously seen as being something "out of the past." What people are often unaware of are the many practical applications of anthropological knowledge. One field of applied anthropology—known as **forensic anthropology**—specializes in the identification of human skeletal remains for legal purposes. Forensic anthropologists are routinely called upon by police and other authorities to identify the remains of murder victims, missing persons, or people who have died in disasters such as plane crashes. From skeletal remains, the forensic anthropologist can establish the age, sex, population affilia-

tion, and stature of the deceased, and often whether he/she were right or left handed, exhibited any physical abnormalities, or evidence of trauma (broken bones and the like). In addition, some details of an individual's health and nutritional history can be read from the bones.

One well-known forensic anthropologist is Clyde C. Snow, who has been practicing in this field for over 35 years, first for the Federal Aviation Administration and more recently as a freelance consultant. In addition to the usual police work, Snow has studied the remains of General George Armstrong Custer and his men from the 1876 battlefield at Little Big Horn, and in 1985, he went to Brazil where he identified the remains of the notorious Nazi war criminal Josef Mengele. He was also instrumental in establishing the first forensic team devoted

Physical anthropologists do not just study fossil skulls. Shown here is Clyde Snow, whose specialty is forensic anthropology and who is widely known for his work identifying victims of state-sponsored terrorism. In this photo he holds the skull of a Kurdish youth who was executed by Iraqi security forces.

Forensic anthropology.   Field of applied physical anthropology that specializes in the identification of human skeletal remains for legal purposes.

to documenting cases of human rights abuses around the world. This mission began in 1984, when he went to Argentina at the request of a newly elected civilian government as part of a team to help with the identification of remains of the *desaparecidos,* or "disappeared ones," the 9,000 or more people who were eliminated by government death squads during 7 years of military rule. A year later, he returned to give expert testimony at the trial of nine junta members, and to teach Argentineans how to recover, clean, repair, preserve, photograph, x-ray, and analyze bones. Besides providing factual accounts of the fate of victims to their surviving kin, and refuting the assertions of "revisionists" that the massacres never happened, the work of Snow and his Argentinean associates was crucial in convicting several military officers of kidnapping, torture, and murder. Since Snow's pioneering work, forensic anthropologists have become increasingly involved in the investigation of human rights abuses in all parts of the world, from Chile to Guatemala, Haiti, the Philippines, Iraqi Kurdistan, Rwanda, and (most recently) Bosnia. Meanwhile, they continue to do important work for regular clients in the United States. Snow, for example, is regularly consulted by the medical examiners' offices of Oklahoma; Cook County, Illinois; and the Federal Bureau of Investigation. Although not all cases he investigates involve abuse of police powers, when this is an issue, evidence provided by forensic anthropologists is often crucial for bringing the culprits to justice. To quote Snow: "Of all the forms of murder, none is more monstrous than that committed by a state against its own citizens. And of all murder victims, those of the state are the most helpless and vulnerable since the very entity to which they have entrusted their lives and safety becomes their killer."* Thus, it is especially important that states be called to account for their deeds.

---

*Joyce, C. (1991). *Witnesses from the grave: The stories bones tell.* Boston: Little, Brown.

---

place to place, but no person is "more cultured" in the anthropological sense than any other.

Just as physical anthropology is closely related to the other biological sciences, cultural anthropology is closely related to the other social sciences. The one it has most often been compared to is sociology, since the business of both is the description and explanation of behavior of people within a social context. Sociologists, however, have concentrated heavily on studies of people living in modern—or at least recent—North American and European societies, thereby increasing the probability that their theories of human behavior will be culture-bound: that is, based on assumptions about the world and reality that are part of the sociologists' Western culture, usually the middle-class version most typical of professional people. Since cultural anthropologists, too, are products of the culture they grew up with, they too are capable of culture-bound theorizing. However, they constantly seek to minimize the problem by studying the whole of humanity in all times and places, and do not limit themselves to the study of recent Western peoples; anthropologists have found that to fully understand human behavior, all humans, past and present, must be studied. More than any other feature, this unique cross-cultural and evolutionary perspective distinguishes cultural anthropology from the other social sciences. It provides anthropology with a far richer body of data than that of any other social science, and it can also be applied to any current issue. As a case in point, consider the way infants in the United States are routinely made to sleep apart from their parents, their mothers in particular. To North Americans, this seems normal, but cross-cultural studies show that "cosleeping" is the rule. Only in the past 200 years, generally in Western industrialized societies, has it been considered proper for mother and infant to sleep apart. In fact, it amounts to a cultural experiment in child rearing.

Recent studies have shown that this unusual degree of separation of mother and infant in Western societies has important consequences. For one thing, it increases the length of the infant's crying bouts, which may last in excess of 3 hours a day in the child's 2nd and 3rd months. Some mothers incorrectly interpret the cause as a deficiency in breast milk and switch to less healthy bottle-fed formulas, but in

---

Culture-bound. Theories about the world and reality based on the assumptions and values of one's own culture.

Sociologists conduct structured interviews and administer questionnaires to respondents, while psychologists experiment with participants. Anthropologists, by contrast, learn from informants.

extreme cases, the crying may provoke physical abuse, sometimes with lethal effects. But the benefits of cosleeping go beyond significant reductions in crying: Infants also nurse more often and three times as long per feeding; they receive more stimuli (important for neurological development); and they are apparently less susceptible to sudden infant death syndrome ("crib death"). Moreover, there are benefits to the mother as well: Frequent nursing prevents early ovulation after childbirth, and she gets at least as much sleep as mothers who sleep without their infants.[3]

The emphasis cultural anthropology places on studies of prehistoric or more recent non-Western cultures has often led to findings that dispute existing beliefs derived from Western studies. Thus, cultural anthropologists were the first to demonstrate "that the world does not divide into the pious and the superstitious; that there are sculptures in jungles and paintings in deserts; that political order is possible without centralized power and principled justice without codified rules; that the norms of reason were not fixed in Greece, the evolution of morality not consummated in England. . . . We have, with no little success, sought to keep the world off balance; pulling out rugs, upsetting tea tables, setting off firecrackers. It has been the office of oth-

ers to reassure; ours to unsettle."[4] Although the findings of cultural anthropologists have often challenged the conclusions of sociologists, psychologists, and economists, anthropology is absolutely indispensable to them, as it is the only consistent check against culture-bound assertions. Anthropology is to these disciplines what the laboratory is to physics and chemistry: the essential testing ground for their theories.

Cultural anthropology may be divided into the areas of archaeology, linguistic anthropology, and ethnology (often called sociocultural anthropology; see Figure 1.1). Although each has its own special interests and methods, all deal with cultural data. The archaeologist, the linguist, and the ethnologist take different approaches to the subject, but each gathers and analyzes data that are useful in explaining similarities and differences between human cultures, as well as the ways that cultures everywhere develop, adapt, and continue to change.

Archaeology

Archaeology is the branch of cultural anthropology that studies material remains in order to describe and explain human behavior. Traditionally, it has

---

[3]Barr, R. G. (1997, October). The crying game. *Natural History*, 47. Also McKenna, J. J. (1997, October). Bedtime story, *Natural History*, 50.

[4]Geertz, C. (1984). Distinguished lecture: Anti anti-relativism, *American Anthropologist*, 86, 275.

Archaeology.   The study of material remains, usually from the past, to describe and explain human behavior.

focused on the human past, for material products of behavior, rather than behavior itself, are all that survive of that past. The archaeologist studies the tools, pottery, and other enduring relics that remain as the legacy of extinct cultures, some of them as many as 2.5 million years old. Such objects, and the way they were left in the ground, reflect past human behavior. For example, shallow, restricted concentrations of charcoal that include oxidized earth, bone fragments, and charred plant remains, and near which are pieces of fire-cracked rock, pottery, and tools suitable for food preparation, are indicative of cooking and associated food processing. From such remains much can be learned about a people's diet and subsistence activities. Thus the archaeologist is able to find out about human behavior in the past, far beyond the mere 5,000 years to which historians are limited by their dependence upon written records. But archaeologists are not limited to the study of prehistoric societies; they also may study those for which historic documents are available to supplement the other material remains that people left behind them. In most literate societies, written records are associated with governing elites rather than with people at the "grass roots." Thus, while they can tell archaeologists much that they might not know from archaeological evidence alone, it is equally true that archaeological remains can tell historians much about a society that is not apparent from its written documents.

Although archaeologists have concentrated on the human past, significant numbers of them are concerned with the study of material objects in contemporary settings. One example is the University of Arizona's Garbage Project, which, through a carefully controlled study of household waste, continues to produce information about contemporary social issues. One aim of this project has been to test the validity of interview-survey techniques, upon which sociologists, economists, other social scientists, and policymakers rely heavily for their data. The tests clearly show a significant difference between what people say they do and what garbage analysis shows they actually do. For example, in 1973, conventional techniques were used to construct and administer a questionnaire to find out

While history tells us something of the horrors of slavery in North America, the full horror is revealed only by archeological investigation of such sites as the African burial ground in New York. Even young children were worked so far beyond their ability to endure that their spines actually fractured.

about the rate of alcohol consumption in Tucson. In one part of town, 15% of respondent households affirmed consumption of beer, but no household reported consumption of more than eight cans a week. Analysis of garbage from the same area, however, demonstrated that some beer was consumed in over 80% of households, and 50% discarded more than eight empty cans a week. Another interesting finding of the Garbage Project is that when beef prices reached an all-time high in 1973, so did the amount of beef wasted by households (not just in Tucson, but in other parts of the country as well). Although common sense would lead us to suppose just the opposite, high prices and scarcity correlate with more, rather than less, waste. Obviously, such findings are important, for they show that ideas about human behavior based on conventional interview-survey techniques alone can be seriously in error.

In 1987, the Garbage Project began a program of test excavations in landfills in various parts of the country. From this work has come the first reliable data on what materials actually go into landfills and what happens to them once there. And once again, we are finding that our existing beliefs are at odds with the actual situation. For example, biodegradable materials, like newspapers, take a

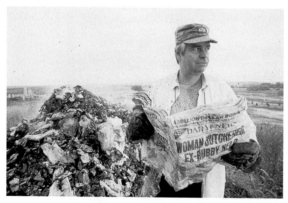

William Rathje, director of the University of Arizona's Garbage Project, holds a newspaper retrieved from deep in a landfill, a vivid demonstration that biodegradables in compacted landfills do not biodegrade as expected.

much longer time to decay when buried in deep, compacted landfills than anyone previously expected. Needless to say, this kind of information is vital if the United States is ever to solve its waste disposal problems.

Linguistic Anthropology

Perhaps the most distinctive feature of humanity is its ability to speak. Humans are not alone in the use of symbolic communication. Studies have shown that the sounds and gestures made by some other animals—especially by apes—may serve functions comparable to those of human speech; yet no other animal has developed a system of symbolic communication as complex as that of humans. Ultimately, language is what allows people to preserve and transmit their culture from generation to generation. The branch of cultural anthropology that studies human languages is called **linguistic anthropology.** Linguists may deal with the description of a language (the way a sentence is formed or a verb conjugated) or with the history of languages (the way languages develop and influence each other over time). Both approaches yield valuable information, not only about the ways people communicate but also about the ways they understand the world around them. The everyday language of North Americans, for example, includes a number of slang words, such as *dough, greenback, dust, loot, cash, bucks, change,* and *bread,* to identify what an indigenous native of Papua-New Guinea would recognize only as *money.* Such phenomena help identify things that are considered of special importance to a culture. Through the study of language in its social setting, anthropologists can understand how people perceive themselves and the world around them.

Anthropological linguists may also make a significant contribution to our understanding of the human past. By working out the genealogical relationships among languages, and examining the distributions of those languages, they may estimate how long the speakers of those languages have lived where they do. By identifying those words in related languages that have survived from an ancient

---

Linguistic anthropology. The branch of cultural anthropology that studies human language.

ancestral tongue, they can also suggest both where, and how, the speakers of the ancestral language lived.

Ethnology

As the archaeologist has traditionally concentrated on cultures of the past, so the **ethnologist,** or socio-cultural anthropologist, concentrates on cultures of the present. And unlike the archaeologist, who focuses on the study of material objects to learn about human behavior, the ethnologist concentrates on the study of human behavior as it can be seen, experienced, and even discussed with those whose culture is to be understood.

Fundamental to the ethnologist's approach is descriptive **ethnography.** Whenever possible, the ethnologist becomes ethnographer by going to live among the people under study. Through **participant observation**—eating a people's food, speaking their language, and personally experiencing their habits and customs—the ethnographer is able to understand their way of life to a far greater extent than any nonparticipant anthropologist or other social scientist ever could; one learns a culture best by learning how to behave acceptably in the society in which one is doing fieldwork. To become a participant observer in the culture under study does not mean that the ethnographer must join in a people's battles in order to study a culture in which warfare is prominent; but by living among a warlike people, the ethnographer should be able to understand the role of warfare in the overall cultural scheme. He or she must be a meticulous observer in order to be able to get a broad overview of a culture without placing undue emphasis on one of its parts at the expense of another. Only by discovering how all cultural institutions—social, political, economic, religious—relate to one another can

the ethnographer begin to understand the cultural system. Anthropologists refer to this as the **holistic perspective,** and it is one of the fundamental principles of anthropology. Robert Gordon, an anthropologist from Namibia, speaks of it in this way: "Whereas the sociologist or the political scientist might examine the beauty of a flower petal by petal, the anthropologist is the person that stands on the top of the mountain and looks at the beauty of the field. In other words, we try and go for the wider perspective."[5]

In participating in an unfamiliar culture, ethnographers do not just blunder about blindly, but enlist the assistance of individual **informants.** These are members of the society the anthropologist as ethnographer is working in, who she or he develops close relationships with, and who help interpret whatever activities are occurring. As a child learns proper behavior from its parents, so do informants help the anthropologist in the field unravel the "mysteries" of what is, at first, a strange culture.

So basic is ethnographic fieldwork to ethnology that the British anthropologist C. G. Seligman once asserted, "Field research in anthropology is what the blood of the martyrs is to the church."[6] Something of its flavor is conveyed by the experience of one young anthropologist, in this case working in relatively comfortable conditions on an island in the western Pacific. In particular, the following Original Study illustrates the impossibility of going into the field free of all naïveté, the importance of "the unexpected" in the field, the problems of freeing oneself from the assumptions and biases of one's own culture, and the necessity of establishing rapport with those whom one wishes to study.

---

[5]Gordon, R. (1981, December). [Interview for Coast Telecourses, Inc.]. Los Angeles.
[6]Lewis, I. M. (1976). *Social anthropology in perspective* (p. 27). Harmondsworth, England: Penguin.

Ethnologist. An anthropologist who studies cultures from a comparative or historical point of view, using ethnographic accounts. **> Ethnography.** The systematic description of a particular culture based on firsthand observation. **> Participant observation.** In ethnography, the technique of learning a people's culture through direct participation in their everyday life for an extended period of time. **> Holistic perspective.** A fundamental principle of anthropology, that the various parts of culture must be viewed in the broadest possible context to understand their interconnections and interdependence. **> Informants.** Members of a society the ethnographer works in who help interpret what she or he sees taking place.

In Cartagena, Colombia, an ethnographer interviews local fishermen.

Two Tales From the Trukese Taproom[7]

▲▽

It was nearing sundown in Mwáán Village on Moen Island, Truk, as we bounced slowly along in the Datsun pickup. The landscape glowed, and the Pacific island blues and greens heightened in intensity as the shadows lengthened. The village's daily rhythm slowed, and the moist air was heavy with incompatible aromas: acrid smoke from cooking fires, sweet fragrance of plumeria blossoms, foul stench of the mangrove swamp, and the pleasant warm earth smells of a tropical island at dusk. All was peaceful, somnolent, even stuporous. And then the quiet was shattered by an ear-splitting shout out of nowhere: "Waaaaa Ho!" The horrible roar was repeated, and its source—a muscular young man clad only in blue jeans and zoris [a kind of sandal]—materialized directly in the path of our truck, brandishing a two-foot-long machete.

The three of us in the pickup were all new to Truk. Bill, the driver, was an American anthropologist in his sixties traveling with his wife through Micronesia en route home from Asia, and he'd only been in Truk for a couple of days. Leslie and I, the passengers, had been there for approximately a month awaiting a field-trip ship to take us to our outer island research site on Namoluk Atoll. In the interim she and I were staying in a small guest facility on the grounds of a Protestant church-sponsored high school a couple miles from the town center. We had met Bill and his wife by chance the day before at a local restaurant. The four of us had spent this day voyaging by motorboat to another island in Truk Lagoon to explore the ruins of the former Japanese headquarters that had been destroyed in World War II. On our return we agreed to meet for dinner, and Bill had just come for us in his

[7]Marshall, M. (1990). Two tales from the Trukese taproom. In P. R. DeVita (Ed.), *The humbled anthropologist* (pp. 12–17). Belmont, CA: Wadsworth.

rented truck to drive back to town for supper. None of us had ever before heard the frightening yell, "Waaaaa Ho!" Nor had any of us been confronted by a young Trukese man built like a fullback and waving a machete over his head.

"What in the hell?" Bill asked, but before I could respond we were nearly upon the young man. Fortunately, the bumpiness of the dirt road limited our speed to perhaps five miles per hour, and Bill avoided hitting our challenger by swerving to the left just in time. As he did so, the young man brought the machete down with all the force he could muster on top of the cab, once again announcing his presence with a loud "Waaaaa Ho!" The machete cut into the edge of the cab approximately half an inch deep right where I had been holding on to the door frame a split second before. As steel hit steel, Bill panicked and floored the truck, but our attacker managed to strike another powerful blow with the knife on the edge of the truck bed before we escaped. We jolted along at 15 miles per hour the rest of the way to town, the maximum we and the pickup could sustain given road conditions. We were completely shaken by what had just befallen us.

"Why in the hell did he do that?" Bill wanted to know. I was new to Truk, there to study and learn about Trukese society and culture. I had no answer to Bill's question. We literally did not know what had hit us, or more accurately, why we had been attacked. Over dinner we speculated on the possibilities. The young man might have been angry with foreigners and decided to take out his bad feelings on us. No, we rejected that hypothesis because it was clear that the young man would not have been able to tell who was in the truck when he burst out of the bushes and lunged at us. It all happened too fast. A second thought we had was that the young man had it in for someone who owned a blue Datsun pickup, saw our truck approaching, and mistook us for someone else. But this hypothesis failed for the same reason: Because of the dwindling light and the thick brush along the roadside it seemed unlikely our attacker could see the color and make of the truck before he leapt into its path. Finally, based on our collective experience as persons reared in American [U.S.] culture, the four of us concluded either that the young man was emotionally distraught over a recent major trauma in his life or that he was mentally ill and a clear danger to the general public.

We were puzzled and truly frightened. What made the incident all the more bizarre was that Leslie and I had been treated with unfailing kindness by all the Trukese we had met from the moment of our arrival. We had walked through Mwáán Village several times daily for four weeks, many times after dark, and always we had been greeted by warm smiles and a cheery "*Ran Annim!*" What could have provoked this attack? Why in the hell did he do that? Although I could not know it at the time, this incident presaged much of my later research involvement with the people of Truk and directed my attention to a series of questions and puzzles that I continue to pursue. I can now, with some degree of confidence, provide an answer to why the young man did what he did: He was drunk. The fearsome yell announced that fact immediately to anyone who knew the code surrounding drunken behavior in Truk, but we were ignorant of this as outsiders and novices in the subtleties of Trukese life. When young Trukese men drink, they are perceived to become dangerous, explosive, unpredictably aggressive. Given the option, the received wisdom is to avoid Trukese drunks if at all possible. We, of course, did not have that option, and we became yet one more target of the violence associated with alcohol consumption in contemporary Truk. In fact, we were lucky that no one was hurt. Quite often the aggression of Trukese drinkers results in injuries and, occasionally, deaths.

How long has alcohol been available in the islands? Why do young men drink in Truk and why do women almost uniformly abstain? Why do drinkers so often become violent after consuming alcohol? What happens to the perpetrators of such violence? Questions such as these surrounding the Trukese encounter with alcoholic beverages are legion, and when pursued they open myriad windows into Trukese personality, culture, history, and social organization. Before I came to understand this, however, I had another traumatic experience involving Trukese and alcohol.

By the time this second incident occurred, Leslie and I had been in Truk for 4 months. We had left the headquarters island of Moen and sailed 130 miles to the southeast to a tiny and remote coral atoll which was to be the focus of my dissertation research. Namoluk was idyllic, an emerald necklace of land surrounding a turquoise lagoon bounded by the deep sapphire blue of the open ocean. Namoluk was a close-knit kin community of 350 persons where people knew one another in terms of "total biography": All the details of one's life and the lives of one's relatives and ancestors were part of local lore and general public knowledge. Everyone had a particular role to play that in some senses seemed almost predestined from childhood onward. Namoluk was fascinating, an integrated yet intricate community with a long history of its own which had been studied only briefly half a century before by a German scholar. I became totally engrossed in my research and in trying to master the local language.

We had taken up residence in a comfortable new cement house with a corrugated iron roof located more or less in the center of the village area. Our house sat at the intersection of two main paths and in between the locations of two of the island's three licensed bingo games. Since bingo was played daily by a large part of the population, a steady stream of islanders strolled past our front door. The family on whose homestead we lived slept in a wooden house next door, but members of the family were in and out of our house continually.

Soon after our arrival in Namoluk I learned that alcohol use was the subject of considerable controversy. Technically the island was dry by local consensus, but the legality of the local prohibition ordinance was questionable because proper procedures for enacting such a law had not been followed. At the time we came on the scene an intergenerational struggle was under way between men over roughly the age of 40 or 45 and younger men for control of the elective municipal government. Alcohol became a central issue in this struggle, with older men supporting prohibition and younger men enthusiastically drinking booze when ever possible. Even so, drinking was certainly not a regular event on Namoluk, and when it did take place, it often led to nothing more than boisterous singing and loud laughter late at night in the canoe houses. I began to get the impression that drunkenness on Namoluk was categorically different from what we had experienced on Truk a few months before. And then it happened. Late on a Sunday afternoon we were lolling about our house, just being lazy and chatting with our landlord when suddenly a huge commotion arose in the distance. Sounds of anguish, anger, and anxiety swirled toward us and then, out of the milling mob of men, women, and noise, came that unforgettable yell: "Waaaaa Ho!"

I sprang to my feet, jumped into my zoris, and dashed out the door to find a crowd of 20 to 30 agitated people at the intersection of the two paths, yelling, shouting at one another, and keeping two persons separated. As I took in the pattern of what was happening, I realized that a fight was threatening between two men who had been drinking. Each was being upbraided by female relatives to refrain from fighting, while at the same time men were standing by to make sure that their own male kinsman was not injured. Before I could stop to coolly assess the situation and record it objectively in my data notebook I found myself next to the antagonists. The larger man suddenly jumped on his opponent, wrestling him to the ground. Instantly he began pummeling and pounding the smaller man with his fists. I acted almost instinctively. Before I fully realized what I was doing I had a full nelson on the larger man, had pulled him off of his victim, and was trying to convince him to desist from such behavior.

Though strong enough to protect myself from harm, it occurred to me as I stood there that I had made a terrible mistake. All through graduate school my professors had emphasized the importance of not taking sides or getting involved in local political or interpersonal squabbles in the research community, lest one make enemies, close off potential sources of information, or even get thrown out of the research site. All of those warnings flashed through my mind as I pressed the full nelson on the struggling man. I was convinced that I had blown it and that this whole sorry episode would have nothing but negative repercussions for my work—and just at a time when Leslie and I were beginning to feel like we really fit into the community.

But, oh, how wrong I was.

In learning why I was wrong, I also learned an important lesson about masculinity and how masculinity relates to fighting and to alcohol use in Trukese culture. And I had taken a major step toward what has become the central focus of my research over the past fifteen years: the study of alcohol and culture.

Once tempers calmed and it was clear that the fighting was over, I released my hold and returned to my house, shaken and chagrined. How could I have been so stupid as to get involved in a silly drunken brawl? As I sat there feeling sorry for myself, a knock on the door roused me from dejection. It was two of the teenagers on the island, boys of about 14 years of age, who were among our most loyal and patient language teachers. They asked if they could come in and, though I didn't really feel like company, I said, "Sure." The three of us sat on the woven pandanus mat on the floor, and one of them immediately commented, "Wow, you were really strong out there a few minutes ago!" I wasn't sure whether I was being flattered or mocked, but before I gave a snide response I glanced at the boys and recognized the earnestness in their faces. I made some uncommittal answer, and they elaborated. My behavior had been thought impressive and salutory by everyone present: They said it demonstrated strength and bravery or fearlessness. If they only knew, I thought, that it actually demonstrated nothing more than the ignorance of an interloper endeavoring to keep the peace according to the inappropriate canons of his own culture!

Later that evening the man I had restrained, who was among the most influential and important younger men in the community, and on whose bad side I could ill afford to be, knocked on my door, accompanied by an older male relative. My landlord was with me and, while he knew what was about to take place, I was completely in the dark. The older man spoke long and rapidly in the Namoluk language and I understood only a little of what he said. Then the younger man spoke directly to me in English, asking my forgiveness for any problems he may have caused and noting that he would not have acted the way he had if he hadn't been drinking. "It was the alcohol that made me do it," he said. "We Trukese just don't know how to drink like you Americans. We drink and drink until our supply is gone and then we often get into fights." I was enormously relieved that *he* wasn't angry with *me*, and we begged one another's pardon through a mixture of Trukese apology ritual and American-style making up after an unpleasantness.

What I didn't recognize at the time, and only later came to fully understand, was that the incident that upset me so for fear I had botched my community rapport not only improved my rapport (including with the man I had restrained!) but also contributed to the development of my personal reputation on Namoluk. I noted earlier that Namoluk persons know one another in terms of total biography. As a foreigner from outside the system, I was an unknown quantity. Initially, people didn't know whether I was a good or a bad person, whether I would prove disruptive or cooperative, whether I would flaunt local custom or abide by it. Like every Trukese young adult— but especially like young men—I had to prove myself by my actions and deeds. I had to create and sustain an impression, to develop a reputation. At the time I didn't know this. Luckily for me, and purely by accident, my actions that afternoon accorded closely with core Trukese values that contribute to the image of a good person: respectfulness, bravery, and the humble demonstration of nonbullying strength in thought and deed. What I first believed to have been a colossal blunder turned out to be a fortunate coincidence of impulsive action with deep-seated cultural beliefs about desirable masculine behavior. Now I, the unknown outsider, had begun to develop a local biography. But this was something I came to understand only after several more years of fieldwork in Trukese society.

The popular image of ethnographic fieldwork is that it takes place among far-off, exotic peoples. To be sure, much of ethnographic work has been done in places like Africa, the islands of the Pacific Ocean, the deserts of Australia, and so on. One very good reason for this is that non-Western peoples have been too often ignored by other social scientists. Still, anthropologists have recognized from the start that an understanding of human behavior depends upon knowledge of all cultures and peoples, including their own. During the years of the Great Depression and World War II, for example, many anthropologists in the United States worked in settings ranging from factories to whole communities. One of the landmark studies of this period was W. Lloyd Warner's study of "Yankee City" (Newburyport, Massachusetts). Less well known is that it was an anthropologist, Philleo Nash, working on the White House staffs of Presidents Roosevelt and Truman, who was instrumental in desegregating the armed forces and moving the federal government into the field of civil rights. What Nash did was to put his anthropological expertise to work in order to accomplish a particular goal; an example of applied anthropology. Later on, he served as lieutenant governor of Wisconsin, and as Indian Commissioner in President Kennedy's administration. Today, numerous anthropologists work outside of academic settings as applied anthropologists, and we shall see examples of their work in succeeding chapters of this book.

In the 1950s, the availability of large amounts of money for research in foreign lands diverted attention from work at home. Later on, as political unrest made fieldwork increasingly difficult to carry out, there was renewed awareness of important anthropological problems that needed to be dealt with in North American society. Many of these problems involve people that anthropologists knew from other settings. Thus, as people from South and Central America have moved into the cities and suburbs of the United States, or as refugees have arrived from Haiti, Southeast Asia, and other places, anthropologists have been there not just to study them, but to help them adjust to their new circumstances. Simultaneously, anthropologists are applying the same research techniques that served them so well in the study of non-Western peoples to the study of such diverse things as street gangs, corporate bureaucracies, religious cults, healthcare delivery systems, schools, and how people deal with consumer complaints.

An important discovery from such research is that it produces knowledge that usually does not emerge from the kinds of research done by other social scientists. For example, the theory of cultural deprivation arose during the 1960s as a way of explaining the educational failure of many children of minorities. In order to account for their lack of achievement, some social scientists proposed that such children were "culturally deprived." They then proceeded to "confirm" this idea by studying children, mostly from Native American, African American, and Hispanic populations, interpreting the results through the protective screen of their theory. By contrast, ethnographic research on the cultures of "culturally deprived" children reveals a different story. Far from being culturally deprived, they have elaborate, sophisticated, and adaptive

Anthropologists carry out fieldwork at home as well as abroad. One who has done this is Dr. Miriam Lee Kaprow of John Jay College, whose work was with New York firefighters.

cultures that are simply different from the ones espoused by the educational system. Although some still cling to it, the cultural-deprivation theory is culture-bound, and is merely a way of saying that people are "deprived" of "my culture." One cannot argue that such children do not speak adequate Spanish, Ebonics (sometimes called "Black English"), or whatever; clearly they do well the things that are considered important in *their* cultures.

Though it has much to offer, the anthropological study of one's own culture is not without its own special problems. Sir Edmund Leach, a major figure in British anthropology, put it this way:

> Surprising though it may seem, fieldwork in a cultural context of which you already have intimate first-hand experience seems to be much more difficult than fieldwork which is approached from the naive viewpoint of a total stranger. When anthropologists study facets of their own society their vision seems to become distorted by prejudices which derive from private rather than public experience.[8]

Although ethnographers strive to get inside views of other cultures, they do so very self-consciously

---

[8]Leach, E. (1982). *Social anthropology* (p. 124). Glasgow, Scotland: Fontana Paperbacks.

as outsiders. And the most successful anthropological studies of their own culture by North Americans have been done by those who first worked in some other culture. Lloyd Warner, for example, had studied the Murngin of Australia before he tackled Newburyport. The more one learns of "other" cultures, the more one gains a different perspective on one's own. Put another way, as other cultures come to be seen as less exotic, the more exotic one's own seems to become. In addition to North American ethnographers going outside their own culture before trying to study it (so that they may see themselves as *others* see them), much is to be gained by encouraging anthropologists from Africa, Asia, and South America to do fieldwork in North America. From their outsiders' perspective come insights all too easily overlooked by an insider. This is not to say that the special difficulties of studying one's own culture can not be overcome; what is required is an acute awareness of those difficulties.

Although ethnographic fieldwork is basic to ethnology, it is not the sole occupation of the ethnologist. Largely descriptive in nature, ethnography provides the basic data the ethnologist (who is more theoretically oriented) may then use to study one particular aspect of a culture by comparing it with that same aspect in others. Anthropologists constantly make such cross-cultural comparisons, and this is another hallmark of the discipline. Interesting insights into our own practices may come from cross-cultural comparisons, as when one compares the time that people devote to what we consider to be "housework." In North American society, there is a widespread belief that the ever-increasing output of household appliance consumer goods has resulted in a steady reduction in housework, with a consequent increase in leisure time. Thus, consumer appliances have become principal indicators of a high standard of living. Anthropological research among food foragers (people who rely on wild plant and animal resources for subsistence), however, has shown that they work far less at household tasks, and indeed less at all subsistence pursuits, than do people in industrialized societies. Aboriginal Australian women, for example, devote an average of approximately 20 hours per week to collecting and preparing food, as well as other domestic chores. By contrast, women in the rural United States in the 1920s, without the benefit of labor-saving appliances, devoted approximately 52 hours a week to their housework. One might suppose that this has changed in the decades since, yet some 50 years later, urban U.S. women who were not working for wages outside their homes were putting 55 hours a week into their housework; this in spite of all their "labor-saving" dishwashers, washing machines, clothes dryers, vacuum cleaners, food processors, and microwave ovens.[9]

Cross-cultural comparisons highlight alternative ways of doing things, and so have much to offer North Americans, large numbers of whom, opinion polls show, continue to doubt the effectiveness of their own ways of doing things. In this sense, one may think of ethnology as the study of alternative ways of doing things. At the same time, by making systematic cross-cultural comparisons of cultures, ethnologists seek to arrive at valid conclusions concerning the nature of culture in all times and places.

ANTHROPOLOGY AND SCIENCE

The primary concern of all anthropologists is the careful and systematic study of humankind. Anthropology has been called a social or a behavioral science by some, a natural science by others, and one of the humanities by still others. Can the work of the anthropologist properly be labeled scientific? What exactly do we mean by the term "science"?

Science is a powerful and elegant way people have hit upon to understand the workings of the visible world and universe. Science seeks testable explanations for observed phenomena, ideally in terms of the workings of hidden but universal and immutable principles, or laws. Two basic ingredients are essential for this: imagination and skepticism. *Imagination,* though capable of leading us astray, is required in order that we may envision the ways in which phenomena might be ordered, and think of old things in new ways. Without it, science cannot exist. *Skepticism* is what allows us

---

[9]Bodley, J. H. (1985). *Anthropology and contemporary human problems* (2nd ed., p. 69). Palo Alto, CA: Mayfield.

George Peter Murdock *(1897–1985)*

Modern cross-cultural studies in anthropology derive from George Peter Murdock's efforts to develop a rigorous methodology. Educated at Yale University, he was strongly influenced by the firm belief of his mentor, Albert Keller, in history's "lawfulness" (in the sense of scientific laws). Influenced as well by an early attempt at statistical comparison by the 19th century British anthropologist Sir Edward B. Tylor, in 1937 Murdock instituted the Cross Cultural Survey in Yale's Institute of Human Relations. This later became the Human Relations Area File (HRAF), a catalogue of cross-indexed ethnographic data filed under uniform headings. In a landmark book, *Social Structure* (published in 1949) he demonstrated the utility of this tool for researching the ways in which human societies were structured and changed. Later in life, Murdock used HRAF as the model for his *World Ethnographic Sample* (1957) and (after he moved to the University of Pittsburgh) *An Ethnographic Atlas*. The latter is a database of over 100 coded cultural characteristics in almost 1,200 societies.

The value of HRAF (now available at many colleges and universities) and other such research tools is that they permit a search for causal relationships, utilizing statistical techniques to provide testable generalizations. To cite one example, anthropologist Peggy Reeves Sanday examined a sample of 156 societies drawn from HRAF in an attempt to answer such questions as these: Why do women play a more dominant role in some societies than others? Why, and under what circumstances, do men dominate women? Her study, published in 1981 *(Female Power and Male Dominance)*, besides disproving the common myth that women are universally subordinate to men, shed important light on the way men and women relate to one another in human societies, and ranks as a major landmark in the study of gender. (So important is this topic, since gender considerations enter into just about everything people do, that it is included in every single chapter of this textbook.)

Valuable though HRAF is, the files are not without their problems. Although they permit blind searches for correlations between customs, such correlations say nothing about cause and effect. All too easily they are rationalized by construction of elaborate causal chains that may amount to little more than "just so" stories. Further historical analysis of particular practices is required. The strength of Sanday's study is that she did not ignore the particular historical contexts of the societies in her sample.

Other problems consist of errors in the files from inadequate ethnographies or unsystematic sources; the nonrandom nature of the sample (cultures are included or rejected in accordance with the quality of available literature); and the fact that items are wrenched out of context. In short, HRAF and similar databases are useful tools, but they are not foolproof; they can lead to false conclusions unless carefully (and critically) used.

to distinguish **fact** from fancy, to test our speculations, and to prevent our imaginations from running away with us.

In their search for explanations, scientists do not assume reality is always as it appears on the surface. After all, what could be more obvious than that the earth is a stable entity, around which the sun travels every day? And yet, it isn't so. Supernatural explanations are rejected, as are all explanations and appeals to authority not supported by

---

Fact. An observation verified by several observers skilled in the necessary techniques of observation.

To many people, a scientist is someone (usually a white male) who works in a laboratory, carrying out experiments with the aid of specialized equipment. Contrary to the stereotypical image, not all scientists work in laboratories, nor is experimentation the only technique they use (nor are scientists invariably white males in lab coats).

strong empirical (observational) evidence. Because explanations are constantly challenged by new observations and novel ideas, science is self-correcting; that is, inadequate explanations are sooner or later shown as such, to be replaced by more reliable explanations.

The scientist begins with a **hypothesis,** or tentative explanation of the relationship between certain phenomena. By gathering various data that seem to support such generalizations, and, equally important, by showing why alternative hypotheses may be falsified, or eliminated from consideration, the scientist arrives at a system of validated hypotheses, or **theory.** Thus a theory, contrary to everyday use of the term, is more than mere speculation; it is a well-supported explanation of natural phenomena. Even so, no theory is ever considered to be beyond challenge. Truth, in science, is not considered to be absolute but rather a matter of varying degrees of probability; what is considered to be true is what is most probable. This is just as true in anthropology as it is in biology or physics. But while nothing can be proven to be absolutely true, incorrect assumptions can be proven false. So it is that, as our knowledge expands, the odds in favor of some theories over others are generally in-

creased, even though old "truths" sometimes must be discarded as alternative theories are shown to be more probable.

To illustrate how scientific methodology works, we will look at a famous case from physical anthropology. In 1910, parts of a human skull and an almost intact lower jaw were found in the Piltdown gravels, in Sussex, England. Although the gravels were thought to be quite ancient, the skull was remarkably modern in appearance. The jaw, however, was exceedingly apelike. The find, Piltdown I, was named *Eoanthropus dawsoni,* Dawson's "dawn man," after its discoverer, an amateur archeologist, paleontologist, and practicing lawyer, Charles Dawson. In 1913 an apelike canine tooth was found to go with the jaw, and in 1915 Piltdown II, fragments of skull plus a molar tooth, was found two miles from Piltdown I. So much for the facts, but what to make of them? Two hypotheses come to mind. The first is that the remains are just what they seem: an ape jaw found in proximity to human skull remains. The other is that skulls and jaw belong to some kind of "missing link" with a modern-sized human brain, but primitive, apelike jaws. It was the second hypothesis, even though it aroused occasional dissension, that was generally accepted until the early 1950s.

The reasons for widespread acceptance of hypothesis 2 are as follow. With the publication in 1859 of Darwin's theory of evolution by natural selection, intense interest developed in finding traces of prehistoric human ancestors. Accordingly, predictions were made as to what those ancestors looked like. Darwin himself, on the basis of his knowledge of embryology and the comparative anatomy of living apes and humans, suggested in his later book *The Descent of Man* that early humans had, among other things, a large brain and an apelike face and jaw.

Although the tools made by prehistoric peoples were forthcoming, their bones were not. To be sure, a few Neandertal and Cro-Magnon skeletons came to light in Europe, but they weren't at all like the predicted "missing link." Moreover, more ancient and primitive *Homo erectus* fossils found in Java were the subject of a heated debate. Their discoverer reacted to this controversy by burying the fos-

---

Hypothesis. A tentative explanation of the relations among certain phenomena. > **Theory.** In science, an explanation of natural phenomena supported by reliable data.

sils beneath his dining room floor, where no one could get at them to examine them. Given this state of affairs, the Piltdown finds could not have come at a better time. Here at last was the long-awaited "missing link," and it was almost exactly as predicted. Even better, so far as English-speaking scientists were concerned, it was found in English soil!

In the context of the evidence available in the early 1900s, the idea of an ancient human with a large brain and an apelike face could become widely accepted as valid. A reexamination of this theory, however, was forced by the discovery of more and more fossils, primarily in Africa, China, and Java. These seemed to show that modern-looking human jaws preceded the development of large-sized brains, rather than the other way around. Thus, the Piltdown remains became more and more of a problem. This led one physical anthropologist, J. S. Weiner, to reconsider the Piltdown fossils, and this is what he found:[10]

1. The only actual human characteristic of the jaw was the apparent tooth wear; otherwise, it was just like the jaw of an ape.
2. The muscle attachments indicate an apelike arrangement of jaw muscles, which would not produce a human wear pattern.
3. The heavy wear of the canine tooth is inconsistent with other features of the tooth that clearly indicate it came from an immature individual.
4. The parts of the jaw that would give it away as surely that of an ape were missing.
5. When drilling for a dentine sample from a tooth, it was found that this was pure white beneath a thin surface stain—not what one would expect in a very ancient fossil.

On the basis of these findings, Weiner returned to the first of our two original plausible hypotheses—that the remains were human skulls and an ape jaw. But now there was a corollary hypothesis that someone had faked the evidence, causing widespread acceptance of the "big-brained human with apelike jaws" hypothesis. Specifically, Weiner proposed that someone had stained the jaw of an ape, destroyed the parts that would give it away for what it was, filed the teeth, and then planted them to-

gether with the human skull parts in the Piltdown gravels. He and two of his colleagues then devised a series of appropriate procedures to test the logical consequences of his hypothesis. For example, microscopic examination revealed the presence of abrasion on the teeth, as would be produced by filing. Chemical tests revealed significant differences in chemical content between jaw and skull; these would be expected if they were from different sources, but not if they belonged together. In short, they were able conclusively to falsify the "big-brained human with apelike jaws" hypothesis and confirm Weiner's version of the "ape jaw with human skull" hypothesis.

DIFFICULTIES OF THE SCIENTIFIC APPROACH

Straightforward though the scientific approach may appear to be, there are serious difficulties in its application in anthropology. One of them is that once researchers have stated a hypothesis, they are strongly motivated to verify it, and this can cause them unwittingly to overlook negative evidence, not to mention all sorts of other unexpected things. This is a familiar problem in science; as paleontologist Stephen Jay Gould puts it: "The greatest impediment to scientific innovation is usually a conceptual lock, not a factual lock."[11] In the fields of cultural anthropology there is a further difficulty: In order to arrive at useful theories concerning human behavior, one must begin with hypotheses that are as objective and as little culture-bound as possible. And here lies a major—some people would say insurmountable—problem: It is difficult for someone who has grown up in one culture to frame hypotheses about others that are not culture-bound.

As one example of this sort of problem, we may look at attempts by archaeologists to understand the nature of settlement in the Classic period of Maya civilization. This civilization flourished between A.D. 250 and 900 in what is now northern Guatemala, Belize, and adjacent portions of Mexico and Honduras. Today much of this region is covered by a dense tropical forest of the sort that people of European background find difficult to deal with. In recent times this forest has been

[10]Weiner, J. S. (1955). *The Piltdown forgery.* New York: Oxford University Press.

[11]Gould, S. J. (1989). *Wonderful life* (p. 226). New York: Norton.

Franz Boas   *(1858–1942)*
Fredric Ward Putnam   *(1839–1915)*
John Wesley Powell   *(1834–1902)*

In North America, anthropology among the social sciences has a unique character, owing in large part to the natural science (rather than social science) background of the three men pictured above. Franz Boas (left), educated in physics, was not the first to teach anthropology in the United States, but it was he and his students, with their insistence on scientific rigor, who made such courses a common part of college and university curricula. Putnam (center), a zoologist specializing in the study of birds and fishes, and permanent secretary of the American Association for the Advancement of Science, made a decision in 1875 to devote himself to the promotion of anthropology. Through his efforts many of the great anthropology museums were established: at the University of California (now the Phoebe Hearst Museum), Harvard University (the Peabody Museum), the Field Museum in Chicago; and in New York he founded the anthropology department of the American Museum of Natural History. Powell (right) was a geologist and founder of the United States Geological Survey, but he also carried out ethnographic and linguistic research (his classification of Indian languages north of Mexico is still consulted by scholars today). In 1879, he founded the Bureau of American Ethnology (ultimately absorbed by the Smithsonian Institution), thereby establishing anthropology within the United States government.

inhabited by few people, who sustain themselves through slash-and-burn farming. (After cutting and burning the natural vegetation, crops are grown for two years or so before fertility is exhausted and a new field must be cleared.) Yet numerous archaeological sites featuring temples sometimes as tall as modern 20-story buildings, other sorts of monumental architecture, and carved stone monuments are found there. Because of their cultural bias against tropical forests as places to live, and against slash-and-burn farming as a means of raising food, North American and European archaeologists asked the question: How could the Maya have maintained large, permanent settlements on the basis of slash-and-burn farming? The answer seemed self-evident: They could not; therefore, the great archaeological sites must have been ceremonial centers inhabited by few, if any, people. Periodically a rural peasantry, living scattered in small hamlets over the countryside, must have gathered in these centers for rituals, or to provide labor for their construction and maintenance.

This view dominated for several decades, and not until 1960 did archaeologists working at Tikal, one of the largest of all Maya sites, decide to ask the simplest and least biased questions they could think of: Did anyone live at this particular site on a permanent basis? If so, how many, and how were they supported? Working intensively over the next decade, with as few preconceived notions as possible, the archaeologists were able to establish that Tikal was a large settlement inhabited on a permanent basis by tens of thousands of people who were supported by forms of agriculture more productive than slash-and-burn alone. This work at Tikal falsified the older culture-bound ideas and paved the way for a new understanding of Classic Maya civilization.

By recognizing the potential problems of framing hypotheses that are not culture-bound, anthropologists have relied heavily on a technique that has proved successful in other fields of the natural sciences. As did the archaeologists working at Tikal, they immerse themselves in the data to the fullest extent possible. By doing so, they become so thoroughly familiar with the minute details that they can begin to see patterns inherent in the data, many of which might otherwise have been overlooked. These patterns are what allow the anthropologist to frame hypotheses, which then may be subjected to further testing.

This approach is most easily seen in ethnographic fieldwork, but it is just as important in archaeology. Unlike many social scientists, the ethnographer usually does not go into the field armed with prefigured questionnaires; rather, the ethnographer recognizes that there are probably all sorts of unguessed things, to be found out only by maintaining as open a mind as possible. This does not mean that anthropologists never use questionnaires, for sometimes they do. Generally, though, they use them as a means of supplementing or clarifying information gained through other methods. As the fieldwork proceeds, ethnographers sort their complex observations into a meaningful whole, sometimes by formulating and testing limited or low-level hypotheses, but as often as not by making use of intuition and playing hunches. What is important is that the results are constantly scrutinized for consistency, for if the parts fail to fit together in an internally consistent manner, then the ethnographer knows that a mistake has been made and that further work is necessary.

The contrast between the anthropological and other social-science approaches is dramatically illustrated by the following example—one of several—presented by Robert Chambers in his book *Rural Development*. Since Chambers is a highly respected professional in the field of international development, he speaks with a greater degree of detachment than could an anthropologist (or sociologist).

> Sean Conlin lived as a social anthropologist in a village in Peru. While he was there a sociologist came and carried out a survey. According to the sociologist's results, people in the village invariably worked together on each others' individually owned plots of land. That was what they told him. But in the period of over a year during which Conlin lived in the village, he observed the practice only once. The belief in exchange relations was, he concludes, important for the people's understanding of themselves, but it was not an economic fact.[12]

This does not mean all sociological research is bad and all anthropological research is good; merely, reliance on questionnaire surveys is a risky business, no matter who does it. Robert Chambers sums up the difficulties:

> Unless careful appraisal precedes drawing up a questionnaire, the survey will embody the concepts and categories of outsiders rather than those of rural people, and thus impose meanings on the social reality. The misfit between the concepts of urban professionals and those of poor rural people is likely to be substantial, and the questions asked may construct artificial chunks of "knowledge" which distort or mutilate the reality which poor people experience. Nor are questionnaire surveys on their own good ways of identifying causal relationships—a correlation alone tells us nothing definite about cause—or of exploring social relationships such as reciprocity, dependence, exploitation, and so on. Their penetration is usually shallow, concentrating on what is measurable, answerable, and acceptable as a question, rather than probing less tangible and more qualitative aspects of society. For many

---

[12]Chambers, R. (1983). *Rural development: Putting the last first* (p. 51). New York: Longman.

reasons—fear, prudence, ignorance, exhaustion, hostility, hope of benefit—poor people give information which is slanted or false.[13]

Chambers then points out that for these and numerous other reasons, conventional questionnaire surveys have many drawbacks if the aim is to gain insight into the lives and conditions of poor rural people. Other methods are required, either alone, or together with surveys. To the degree that extensive questionnaire surveys preempt resources, tying up staff as well as money, they prevent other approaches. Yet another problem in scientific anthropology is the matter of replication. In the other physical and natural sciences, replication of observations and/or experiments is a major means of establishing the reliability of a researcher's conclusions. The problem in ethnology is that observational access is far more limited. As anthropologist Paul Roscoe notes:

> In the natural sciences, the ubiquity of the physical world, coupled with liberal funding, traditionally has furnished a comparatively democratic access to observation and representation: The solar spectrum, for example, is accessible to, and describable by, almost any astronomer with access to the requisite equipment.[14]

Thus, researchers can see for themselves if a colleague has "gotten it right." Access to a non-Western culture, by contrast, is constrained by the difficulty of getting there and being accepted; by the limited number of ethnographers; by often inadequate funding; by the fact that cultures change, so what is observable at one time may not be at another; and so on. Thus, one cannot easily see for oneself whether the ethnographer "got it right." For this reason, an ethnographer bears a special responsibility for accurate reporting.

The result of archaeological or ethnographic fieldwork, if properly carried out, is a coherent account of a culture, which provides an explanatory framework for understanding the behavior of the people who have been studied. And this, in turn, is what permits the anthropologist to frame broader hypotheses about human behavior. Plausible though

such hypotheses may be, however, the consideration of a single society is generally insufficient for their testing. Without some basis for comparison, the hypothesis grounded in a single case may be no more than an historical coincidence. On the other hand, a single case may be enough to cast doubt on, if not refute, a theory that had previously been held valid. The discovery in 1948 that aborigines living in Australia's Arnhem Land put in an average work day of less than 6 hours, while living well above a level of bare sufficiency, was enough to call into question the widely accepted notion that food foraging peoples are so preoccupied with finding food that they lack time for any of life's more pleasurable activities. Even today, economists are prone to label such peoples as "backward," even though the observations made in the Arnhem Land study have since been confirmed many times over in various parts of the world.

Hypothetical explanations of cultural phenomena may be tested by the comparison of archaeological and/or ethnographic data for several societies found in a particular region. Carefully controlled comparison provides a broader context for understanding cultural phenomena than does the study of a single culture. The anthropologist who undertakes such a comparison may be more confident that the conditions believed to be related really are related, at least within the region that is under investigation; however, an explanation that is valid in one region is not necessarily so in another.

Ideally, theories in cultural anthropology are generated from worldwide comparisons. The cross-cultural researcher examines a worldwide sample of societies in order to discover whether or not hypotheses proposed to explain cultural phenomena seem to be universally applicable. Ideally the sample should be selected at random, thereby enhancing the probability that the conclusions of the cross-cultural researcher will be valid; however, the greater the number of societies being compared, the less likely it is that the investigator will have a detailed understanding of all the societies encompassed by the study. The cross-cultural researcher depends upon other ethnographers for data. It is impossible for any single individual personally to perform in-depth analyses of a broad sample of human cultures throughout the world.

In anthropology, cultural comparisons need not be restricted to ethnographic data. Anthropologists can, for example, turn to archaeological data

[13]Ibid., p. 51.
[14]Roscoe, P. B. (1995). The perils of "positivism" in cultural anthropology. *American Anthropologist, 97*, 497.

Development schemes in nonindustrial countries have traditionally favored projects like dam building that more often than not fail to deliver the expected benefits, owing to the developers' lack of understanding of local peoples' practices and needs.

to test hypotheses about cultural change. Cultural characteristics thought to be caused by certain specified conditions can be tested archaeologically by investigating situations where such conditions actually occurred. Also useful are data provided by the ethnohistorian.

Ethnohistory is a kind of historical ethnography that studies cultures of the recent past through oral histories; through the accounts of explorers, missionaries, and traders; and through analysis of such data as land titles, birth and death records, and other archival materials. The ethnohistorical analysis of cultures, like archaeology, is a valuable approach to understanding change. By examining the conditions believed to have caused certain phenomena, we can discover whether or not those conditions truly precede those phenomena.

Ethnohistoric research is also valuable for assessing the reliability of data used for making cross-cultural comparisons. For example, anthropologists working with data from such resources as the Human Relations Area Files (see the biography on George Peter Murdock in this chapter) have sometimes concluded that among food foragers it is (and was) the practice for married couples to live in or near the household of the husband's parents (known as patrilocal residence). To be sure, this is what many ethnographers reported. But what this

fails to take into account is that most such ethnographies were done among food foragers whose traditional practices had been severely altered by pressures emanating (usually) from the expansion of Europeans to all parts of the globe. For example, the Western Abenaki people of northwestern New England are asserted to have practiced patrilocal residence prior to the actual invasion of their homeland by English colonists. Ethnohistoric research shows, however, that their participation in the fur trade with Europeans, coupled with increasing involvement in warfare to stave off incursions of outsiders, led to increased importance of men's activities and a change from more flexible to patrilocal residence patterns.[15] Upon close examination, other cases of patrilocal residence among food foragers turn out to be similar responses to circumstances associated with the rise of colonialism. Far from wives regularly going to live with their husbands in proximity to the latter's male relations, food foraging peoples originally seem to have been far more flexible in their postmarital residence arrangements.

Ethnohistorical research, like the field studies of archaeologists, is valuable for testing and confirming hypotheses about culture. And like much of anthropology, it has practical utility as well. In the United States, ethnohistorical research has flourished, for it often provides the key evidence necessary for deciding legal cases involving Native American land claims. And here again is an example of a practical application of anthropological knowledge.

▲▼▲▼▲▼▲▼▲▼▲▼▲▼▲▼▲▼▲▼▲▼▲▼▲▼▲▼
ANTHROPOLOGY AND THE HUMANITIES

Although the sciences and humanities are often thought of as mutually exclusive approaches to learning, they both come together in anthropology. That is why, for example, anthropological research is funded not only by "hard science" agencies like

[15]Haviland, W. A., & Power, M. W. (1994). *The original Vermonters* (Rev. and exp. ed., pp. 174–175, 215–216, 297–299). Hanover, NH: University Press of New England.

Ethnohistory. The study of cultures of the recent past through oral histories; through accounts left by explorers, missionaries, and traders; and through the analysis of such records as land titles, birth and death records, and other archival materials.

the National Science Foundation, but also by organizations such as the National Endowment for the Humanities. As noted by Roy Rappaport, a past president of the American Anthropological Association, the amalgamation of scientific and humanistic approaches

> is and always has been a source of tension. It has been crucial to anthropology because it truly reflects the condition of a species that lives and can only live in terms of meanings that it must construct in a world devoid of intrinsic meaning, yet subject to natural law. . . . Without the continued grounding in the empirical that scientific aspects of our tradition provide, our interpretive efforts may float off into literary criticism and into particularistic forms of history. Without the interpretive tradition, the scientific tradition that grounds us will never get off the ground.[16]

The humanistic side of anthropology is perhaps most immediately evident in its concern with other cultures' languages, values, and achievements in the arts and literature (including oral literature among peoples who lack writing). Beyond this, anthropologists remain committed to the proposition that one cannot fully understand another culture by simply observing it; as the term "participant observation" implies, one must *experience* it as well. Thus, ethnographers spend prolonged periods of time living with the people whom they study, sharing their joys and suffering their deprivations, including sickness and, sometimes, premature death. They are not so naive as to believe that they can be, or even should be, dispassionate about the people whose trials and tribulations they share. As Robin Fox puts it, "Our hearts, as well as our brains, should be with our men and women."[17] Nor are anthropologists so self-deceived as to believe that they can avoid dealing with the moral and political consequences of their findings. Indeed, anthropology has a long tradition of advocacy for the rights of indigenous peoples, a topic to which we shall return in later chapters of this book.

The humanistic side of anthropology is evident as well in its emphasis on qualitative, as opposed to quantitative, research. This is not to say that anthro-

---

[16]Rappaport, R. A. (1994). Commentary. *Anthropology Newsletter, 35,* 76.

[17]Fox, R. (1968). *Encounter with anthropology* (p. 290). New York: Dell.

pologists are not aware of the value of quantification and statistical procedures; they do make use of them for various purposes. However, reducing people and what they do to numbers has a definite "dehumanizing" effect (it is easier to ignore the concerns of "impersonal" numbers than it is those of flesh-and-blood human beings) and ignores important issues not susceptible to numeration. For all these reasons, anthropologists tend to place less emphasis on numerical data than do other social scientists.

Given their intense encounters with other peoples, it should come as no surprise that anthropologists have amassed as much information about human frailty and nobility—the stuff of the humanities—as any other discipline. Small wonder, too, that above all they intend to avoid allowing a "coldly" scientific approach to blind them to the fact that human societies are made up of individuals with rich assortments of emotions and aspirations who demand respect. Anthropology has sometimes been called the most human of the sciences, a designation in which anthropologists take considerable pride.

QUESTIONS OF ETHICS

The kinds of research carried out by anthropologists, and the settings within which they work, raise a number of important questions concerning ethics. Who will make use of the findings of anthropologists, and for what purposes? In the case of a militant minority, for example, will others use anthropological data to suppress that minority? And what of traditional communities around the world? Who is to decide what changes should or should not be introduced for community "betterment"? By whose definition is it betterment—the community's, some remote government's, or an international agency's such as the World Bank? Then consider the problem of privacy.

Anthropologists deal with people's private and sensitive matters, including things that people would not care to have generally known about themselves. How does one write about such matters and at the same time protect the privacy of informants? Not surprisingly, because of these and other questions, there has been much discussion among anthropologists over the past two decades on the subject of ethics.

Anthropologists recognize that they have obligations to three sets of people: those they study, those who fund the research, and those in the profession who expect them to publish their findings so that they may be used to further knowledge.[18] Because fieldwork requires a relationship of trust between fieldworker and informants, the anthropologist's first responsibility clearly is to his or her informants and their people. Everything possible must be done to protect their physical, social, and psychological welfare and to honor their dignity and privacy. In other words, *do no harm*. Although early ethnographers often provided the kind of information colonial administrators needed to control the "natives," they have long since ceased to be comfortable with such work, and regard as basic a people's right to their own culture.

As an example of how the sometimes conflicting interests of the people studied, of the profession, and of funding agencies may be dealt with, we may turn to a 1981 interview given by Laura Nader:

> In the case of the Zapotec, I was dealing with very sensitive materials about law and disputes and conflicts and so forth. And I was very sensitive about how much of that to report while people were still alive and while things might still be warm, so I waited on that. . . . I feel comfortable now releasing that information. With regard to a funder in that case, it was the Mexican government, and I feel that I have written enough to have paid off the [money] which they gave me to support that work for a year. So, I've not felt particularly strained for my Zapotec work in those three areas. On energy research that I've done, it's been another story. Much of what people wanted me to do energy research for was . . . to tell people in decision-making positions about [North] American consumers in such a way that they could be manipulated better, and I didn't want to do that. So what I said was I would be willing to study a vertical slice. That is, I would never study the consumer without studying the producer. And once you take a vertical slice like that, then it's fair because you're telling the consumer about the producer and the producer about the consumer. But just to do a study of consumers for producers, I think I would feel uncomfortable.[19]

[18]American Anthropological Association (1998). Code of ethics of the American Anthropological Association. *Anthropology Newsletter, 39*(6), 19–20.
[19]Nader, L. (1981, December). [Interview for Coast Telecourses, Inc.]. Los Angeles.

ANTHROPOLOGY AND CONTEMPORARY LIFE

Anthropology, with its long-standing commitment to understanding people in all parts of the world, coupled with its holistic perspective, is better equipped than any other discipline to grapple with a problem of overriding importance for all of humanity at the beginning of the 21st century. An inescapable fact of life is that North Americans—a small minority of the world's people—live in a global community in which all people are interdependent. Widespread awareness of this exists in the business community, which relies on foreign sources for raw materials, sees the non-Western world as its major area for market expansion, and is increasingly manufacturing its products abroad. Nevertheless, citizens of the United States are on the whole as ignorant about the cultures of the rest of the world as they have ever been. This is true not just of "average citizens" but of highly educated people, too. In Guatemala, for example, where over half the population is made up of Maya Indians, U.S. Foreign Service personnel are largely ignorant of the literature—most of it by anthropologists—pertaining to these people.[20] As a result, too many of us are poorly equipped to handle the demands of living in the modern world.

Anthropologist Dennis Shaw sums up the implications of this state of affairs:

> Such provinciality raises questions about the welfare of our nation and the global context in which it is a major force. We have, as a nation, continued to interpret the political actions of other nations in terms of the cultural and political norms of our own culture and have thus made major misinterpretations of global political affairs. Our economic interests have been pursued from the perspective of our own cultural norms, and thus, we have failed to keep up with other nations that have shown a sensitivity to cultural differences. Domestically, a serious question can be raised about the viability of a democracy in which a major portion of the electorate is basically ignorant of the issues which our political leaders must confront. Internationally, one can speculate

[20]Nance, C. R. (1997). Review of Haviland's *Cultural Anthropology* (p. 2). [Manuscript in author's possession.]

Ignorance of other cultures can have serious consequences, as the failed United Nations intervention in Somalia shows. Blinded by their own cultures' assumption of the universality of centralized political structure, the powers intervening in Somalia misunderstood the nature of that country's uncentralized, segmentary system.

about the well-being of a world in which the citizens of one of the most powerful nations are seriously deficient in their ability to evaluate global issues."[21]

Former ambassador Edwin Reischauer once put it more tersely: "Education is not moving rapidly enough in the right directions to produce the knowledge about the outside world and attitudes toward other peoples that may be essential for human survival.[22] What anthropology has to contribute to contemporary life, then, is an understanding of and a way of looking at the world's peoples, or nothing less than basic skills for survival in the modern world.

[21]Quoted in Haviland, W. A. (1997). Cleansing young minds, or what should we be doing in introductory anthropology? In C. P. Kottak, J. J. White, R. H. Furlow, & P. C. Rice (Eds.), *The teaching of anthropology: Problems, issues, and decisions* (p. 35). Mountain View, CA: Mayfield.

[22]Ibid., p. 35.

CHAPTER SUMMARY

Throughout human history, people have needed to know who they are, where they came from, and why they behave as they do. Traditionally, myths and legends provided the answers to these questions. Anthropology, as it has emerged over the last 200 years, offers another approach to answering the questions people ask about themselves.

Anthropology is the study of humankind. In employing a scientific approach, anthropologists seek to produce a reasonably objective understanding of human diversity as well as those things all humans have in common. The two major branches of anthropology are physical and cultural anthropology.

Physical anthropology focuses on humans as biological organisms. Particular emphasis is given by physical anthropologists to tracing the evolutionary development of the human animal and studying biological variation within the species today. Cultural anthropologists study humans in terms of their cultures, the often unconscious standards by which societies operate. Three areas of cultural anthropology are archaeology, anthropological linguistics, and ethnology. Archaeologists study material objects usually from past cultures in order to explain human behavior. Linguists, who study human languages, may deal with the description of a language, with the history of languages, or how they are used in particular social settings. Ethnologists concentrate on cultures of the present or recent past; in doing comparative studies of culture, they focus on a particular aspect of culture, such as religious or economic practices, or as ethnographers they may go into the field to observe and describe human behavior as it can be seen, experienced, and discussed with persons whose culture is to be understood.

Anthropology is unique among the social and natural sciences in that it is concerned with formulating explanations of human diversity based on a study of all aspects of human biology and behavior in all known societies, rather than in European and North American societies alone. Thus anthropologists have devoted much attention to the study of non-Western peoples.

Anthropologists are concerned with the objective and systematic study of humankind. The anthropologist employs the methods of other scientists by developing a hypothesis, or assumed explanation, using other data to test the hypothesis, and ultimately arriving at a theory—an explanation supported by reliable data. The data used by the cultural anthropologist may be from a single society or from numerous societies, which are then compared.

In anthropology, the humanities and sciences come together into a genuinely human science. Anthropology's link with the humanities can be seen in its concern with people's values, languages, arts, and literature—oral as well as written—but above all in its attempt to convey the experience of living as other people do. As both a science and one of the humanities, anthropology has essential skills to offer the modern world, where understanding the other people with whom we share the globe has become a matter of survival.

POINTS FOR CONSIDERATION

1. Think about movies you have seen and novels you have read that have anthropologists as characters. How are they portrayed? How do these characterizations contrast with the discipline as presented in this chapter?

2. How could the kind of information anthropologists gather be useful in resolving contemporary national political debates? What about international political issues? How might this information change these debates?

SUGGESTED READINGS

Lett, J. (1987). *The human enterprise: A critical introduction to anthropological theory*. Boulder, CO: Westview.

Part 1 examines the philosophical foundations of anthropological theory, paying special attention to the nature of scientific inquiry and the mechanisms of scientific progress. Part 2 deals with the nature of social science as well as the particular features of anthropology.

Peacock, J. L. (1986). *The anthropological lens: Harsh light, soft focus*. New York: Cambridge University Press.

This lively and innovative book manages to give the reader a good understanding of the diversity of activities undertaken by anthropologists, while at the same time identifying the unifying themes that hold the discipline together.

Spradley, J. P. (1979). *The ethnographic interview*. New York: Holt, Rinehart & Winston.

This book contains one of the best discussions of the nature and value of ethnographic research to be found. The bulk of the book is devoted to a step-by-step, easy-to-understand account of how one carries out ethnographic research with the assistance of informants. Numerous examples drawn from the author's own research in such diverse settings as skid row, courtrooms, and bars make for interesting reading. A companion volume, *Participant Observation*, also is highly recommended.

Vogt, F. W. (1975). *A history of ethnology*. New York: Holt, Rinehart & Winston.

This history of cultural anthropology attempts to describe and interpret the major intellectual strands, in their cultural and historical contexts, that influenced the development of the field. The author tries for a balanced view of this subject rather than one that would support a particular theoretical position.

Chapter 2
METHODS OF STUDYING THE HUMAN PAST

THIS EXCAVATION IS OF A HALF-MILLION-YEAR-OLD
SITE IN ISRAEL. BECAUSE EXCAVATION OF SITES
DESTROYS THEM, METICULOUS RECORDS MUST
BE KEPT. WITHOUT SUCH RECORDS,
THE FINDS TELL US NOTHING ABOUT
THE HUMAN PAST.

Chapter Preview

What Are Archaeological Sites and Fossil Localities, and How Are They Found?

Archaeological sites are places containing the remains of past human activity. They are revealed by the presence of artifacts—objects fashioned or altered by humans—as well as certain kinds of soil marks, changes in vegetation, irregularities of the surface, and the like. Fossil localities are places containing the actual remains of organisms that lived in the past. They are revealed by the presence of fossils—any trace or impression of an organism of past geological time that has been preserved in the earth. Although fossils are sometimes found in archaeological sites, not all archaeological sites contain fossils, and localities are often found apart from archaeological sites. Though often discovered by accident, sites and localities are generally located by systematically surveying a region.

How Are Sites and Localities Investigated?

Archaeologists and paleoanthropologists face something of a dilemma. The only way to thoroughly investigate a site or locality is by excavation, which results in its destruction. Thus, every attempt is made to excavate in such a way that the location of everything found, no matter how small, is precisely recorded. Without such records little sense can be made of the data, and the potential of the site or locality to contribute to our knowledge of the past would be lost forever.

How Are Archaeological or Fossil Remains Dated?

Remains can be dated in relative terms by noting their stratigraphic position, by measuring the amount of fluorine contained in fossil bones, or by associating them with different floral or faunal remains. More precise dating is achieved by counting the tree rings in wood from archaeological contexts, by measuring the amount of carbon 14 remaining in organic materials, or by measuring the percentage of potassium that has decayed to argon in volcanic materials. Some other techniques are less commonly used, but they are often expensive, are not always as widely available, or else they have not yet been proved as reliable.

A popular stereotype of anthropologists is that they are concerned exclusively with the human past. This is not the case, as should now be evident; not even archaeologists and physical anthropologists, those most likely to be engaged in the study of the past, devote all of their time to such pursuits. As we have seen, some archaeologists study the refuse of modern peoples, and many physical anthropologists engage in research on such issues as present-day human variation and adaptation. Nevertheless, the study of the human past is an important *part* of anthropology, given its concern with peoples in all places and times. Moreover, knowledge of the human past is essential if we are to understand what it was that made us distinctively human, as well as how the processes of change—both biological and cultural—affect the human species. Indeed, given the radical changes taking place in the world today, one may say that an understanding of the nature of change has never been more important. Although it is not their sole concern, archaeology and physical anthropology are the two branches of anthropology most involved in the study of the human past.

Archaeologists (apart from those engaged in the analysis of modern garbage) study things left behind by people who lived in historic or prehistoric times—tools, trash, traces of shelters, and the like. As the British archaeologist Stuart Piggot put it, "Archaeology is the science of rubbish."[1] Most of us are familiar with some kind of archaeological material: the coin dug out of the earth, the fragment of an ancient jar, the spear point used by some ancient hunter. The finding and cataloging of such objects is often thought by nonprofessionals to be the chief goal of archaeology. While this was true in the last century, the situation changed several decades ago. Today, the aim is to use archaeological remains to reconstruct human societies that can no longer be observed firsthand, in order to understand and explain human behavior. Although it may look as if the archaeologist is digging up things, he or she is really digging up human behavior.

The actual remains of our ancestors, as opposed to the things they lost or discarded, are the concern of physical anthropologists. Those physical anthropologists engaged in the recovery and study of the fossil evidence for human evolution, as opposed to those who study present-day peoples, are generally known as **paleoanthropologists.** Unlike paleontologists, who study all forms of past life, paleoanthropologists confine their attention to humans, near humans, and other ancient primates, the group to which humans belong. Just as the finding and cataloging of objects was once the chief concern of the archaeologist, so the finding and cataloging of human and other primate fossils was once the chief concern of the paleoanthropologist. But, again, there has been a major change in the field; while recovery, description, and organization of fossil materials are still important, the emphasis since the 1950s has been on what those fossils can tell us about the processes at work in human biological evolution. It is not so much a case of what you find, but what you find out.

In Chapter 1, we surveyed at some length just what it is that anthropologists do, and why they do it. We also looked briefly at the ethnographic methods used by anthropologists to study the cultures of living peoples. Other methods are required, however, when studying peoples of the past—especially those of the prehistoric past, before the existence of written records. Since the next two parts of this book are about the prehistoric past, in this chapter we shall look at how archaeologists and paleoanthropologists go about their study of the human past.

▲▽▲▽▲▽▲▽▲▽▲▽▲▽▲▽▲▽▲▽▲▽▲▽▲▽▲▽▲▽▲▽▲▽

METHODS OF DATA RECOVERY

Archaeologists, one way or another, work with **artifacts,** any object fashioned or altered by

---

[1]Quoted in Fagan, B. M. (1995). The quest for the past. In L. L. Hasten (Ed.), *Annual Editions 95/96, Archaeology* (p. 10). Guilford, CT: Dushkin.

Paleoanthropologist.   An anthropologist who studies human evolution from fossil remains. > **Artifact.**   Any object fashioned or altered by humans.

humans—a flint chip, a basket, an axe, a pipe, or such nonportable things as house ruins or walls. An artifact expresses a facet of human culture. Because it is something that someone made, archaeologists like to say that an artifact is a product of human behavior or, in more technical words, that it is a material representation of an abstract ideal.

Just as important as the artifacts themselves is the way they were left in the ground. What people do with the things they have made, how they dispose of them, and how they lose them also reflect important aspects of human behavior. Furthermore, the context in which the artifacts were found tells us which objects were contemporary with which other objects, which are older, and which are younger. Without this information, the archaeologist is in no position at all even to identify, let alone understand, specific cultures of the past. This importance of context cannot be overstated; without context, the archaeologist in effect knows nothing! Unfortunately, such information is easily lost if the materials have been disturbed, whether by bulldozers or by the activities of relic collectors.

While archaeologists work with artifacts, paleoanthropologists work with human or other primate fossils—the remains of past forms of life. And just as the context of a find is as important to the archaeologist as the find itself, so is the context of a fossil absolutely critical to the paleoanthropologist. Not only does it tell which fossils are earlier or later in time than other fossils, but also by noting the association of human fossils with other nonhuman remains, the paleoanthropologist may also go a long way toward reconstructing the environmental setting in which the human lived.

THE NATURE OF FOSSILS

Broadly defined, a **fossil** is any trace or impression of an organism of past geologic time that has been preserved in the earth's crust. Fossilization typically involves the hard parts of an organism: Bones, teeth, shells, horns, and the woody tissues of plants are the most successfully fossilized materials. Although the soft parts of an organism are

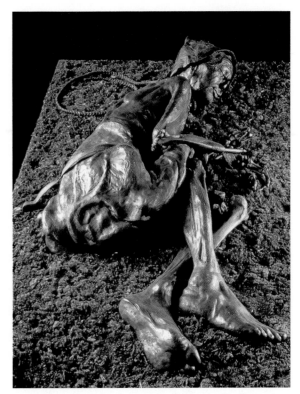

In northern Europe, human bodies periodically recovered from bogs were so well preserved that they were commonly mistaken for recent corpses. Shown here is "Tolland Man," mistaken in 1950 for a lost Danish schoolboy. In fact, he died by hanging more than 2,000 years ago.

rarely fossilized, the casts or impressions of footprints, and even whole bodies, have sometimes been found.

An organism or part of an organism may be preserved in a number of ways. The whole animal may be frozen in ice, like the famous mammoths found in Siberia, safe from the actions of predators, weathering, and bacteria. Or it may be enclosed in a fossil resin such as amber. Specimens of spiders and insects dating back millions of years have been preserved in the Baltic Sea area, which is rich in resin-producing conifers. It may be preserved in the bottoms of lakes and sea basins,

---

Fossil.   The preserved remains of plants and animals that lived in the past.

where the accumulation of chemicals renders the environment antiseptic. The entire organism may also be mummified or preserved in tar pits, peat, oil, or asphalt bogs, in which the chemical environment prevents the growth of decay-producing bacteria. Such **unaltered fossils,** although not common, are often quite spectacular and may be particularly informative. As an example, consider the recovery in 1994 of the remains of a young girl in Barrow, Alaska.

Unaltered fossil.   Remains of plants and animals which lived in the past that have not been altered in any significant way.

Whispers From the Ice[2]

People grew excited when a summer rainstorm softened the bluff known as Ukkuqsi, sloughing off huge chunks of earth containing remains of historic and prehistoric houses, part of the old village that predates the modern community of Barrow. Left protruding from the slope was a human head. Archaeologist Anne Jensen happened to be in Barrow buying strapping tape when the body appeared. Her firm, SJS Archaeological Services, Inc., was closing a field season at nearby Point Franklin, and Jensen offered the team's help in a kind of archaeological triage to remove the body before it eroded completely from the earth. The North Slope Borough hired her and Glenn Sheehan, both associated with Pennsylvania's Bryn Mawr College, to conduct the work. The National Science Foundation, which supported the three-year Point Franklin project, agreed to fund the autopsy and subsequent analysis of the body and artifacts. The Ukkuqsi excavation quickly became a community event. In remarkably sunny and calm weather, volunteers troweled and picked through the thawing soil, finding trade beads, animal bones, and other items. Teen-age boys worked alongside grandmothers. The smell of sea mammal oil, sweet at first then corrupt, mingled with ancient organic odors of decomposed vegetation. One man searched the beach for artifacts that had eroded from the bluff, discovering such treasures as two feather parkas. Elder Silas Negovanna, originally of Wainwright, visited several times, "more or less out of curiosity to see what they have in mind," he says. George Leavitt, who lives in a house on the bluff, stopped by one day while carrying home groceries and suggested a way to spray water to thaw the soil without washing away valuable artifacts. Tour groups added the excavation to their rounds.

"This community has a great interest in archaeology up here just because it's so recent to their experience," says oral historian Karen Brewster, a tall, young woman who interviews elders as part of her work with the North Slope Borough's division of Inupiat History, Language, and Culture. "The site's right in town, and everybody was really fascinated by it."

Slowly, as the workers scraped and shoveled, the earth surrendered its historical hoard: carved wooden bowls, ladles, and such clothing as a mitten made from polar bear hide, birdskin parkas, and mukluks. The items spanned prehistoric times, dated in Barrow to before explorers first arrived in 1826.

---

[2]Adapted from Simpson, S. (1995, April). Whispers from the ice. *Alaska,* 23–28.

Among the objects found at Ukkuqsi are these wooden devices for throwing spears.

The work prompted visiting elders to recall when they or their parents lived in traditional sod houses, and relied wholly on the land and sea for sustenance. Some remembered sliding down the hill as children, before the sea gnawed away the slope. Others described the site's use as a lookout for whales or ships. For the archaeologists, having elders stand beside them and identify items and historical context is like hearing the past whispering in their ears. Elders often know from experience, or from stories, the answers to the scientists' questions about how items were used or made. "In this instance, usually the only puzzled people are the archaeologists," jokes archaeologist Sheehan.

A modern town of 4,000, Barrow exists in a cultural continuum, where history is not detached or remote, but still pulses through contemporary life. People live, hunt, and fish where their ancestors did, but they can also buy fresh vegetables at the store and jet to other places. Elementary school classes include computer and Inupiaq language studies. Caribou skins, still ruddy with blood, and black brant carcasses hang near late-model cars outside homes equipped with television antennas. A man uses power tools to work on his whaling boat. And those who appear from the earth are not just bodies, but relatives. "We're not a people frozen in time," says Jana Harcharek, an Inupiat Eskimo who teaches Inupiaq and nurtures her culture among young people. "There will always be that connection between us [and our ancestors]. They're not a separate entity."

The past drew still closer as the archaeologists neared the body. After several days of digging through thawed soil, they used water supplied by the local fire station's tanker truck to melt through permafrost until they reached the remains, about 3 feet below the surface. A shell of clear ice encased the body, which rested in what appeared to be a former meat cellar. With the low-pressure play of water from the tanker, the archaeologists teased the icy casket from the frozen earth, exposing a tiny foot. Only then did they realize they had uncovered a child. "That was kind of sad, because she was about my daughter's size," says archaeologist Jensen.

The girl was curled up beneath a baleen toboggan and part of a covering that Inupiat elder Bertha Leavitt identified as a kayak skin by its stitching. The child, who appeared to be 5 or 6, remained remarkably intact after her dark passage through time. Her face was cloaked by a covering that puzzled some onlookers. It didn't look like human hair, or even fur, but something with a feathery residue. Finally they concluded it was a hood from a feather parka made of bird skins. The rest of her body was delineated muscle that had freeze-dried into a dark brick-red color. Her hands rested on her knees, which were drawn up to her chin. Frost particles coated the bends of her arms and legs.

"We decided we needed to go talk to the elders and see what they wanted, to get some kind of feeling as to whether they wanted to bury her right away, or whether they were willing to allow some studies in a respectful manner—studies that would be of some use to residents of the North Slope," Jensen says. Working with community elders is not a radical idea to Jensen or Sheehan, whose previous work in the Arctic has earned them high regard from local officials who appreciate their sensitivity. The researchers feel obligated not only to follow community wishes, but to invite villagers to sites and to share all information through public presentations. In fact, Jensen is reluctant to discuss findings with the press before the townspeople themselves hear it.

"It seems like it's a matter of simple common courtesy," she says. Such consideration can only help researchers, she points out. "If people don't get along with you, they're not going to talk to you, and they're liable to throw you out on your ear." In the past, scientists were not terribly sensitive about such matters, generally regarding human remains—and sometimes living Natives—as artifacts themselves. Once, the girl's body would have been hauled off to the catacombs of some university or museum, and relics would have disappeared into exhibit drawers in what Sheehan describes as "hit-and-run archaeology."

"Grave robbers" is how Inupiat Jana Harcharek refers to early Arctic researchers. "They took human remains and their burial goods. It's pretty gruesome. But, of course, at the time they thought they were doing science a big favor. Thank goodness attitudes have changed."

Today, not only scientists but municipal officials confer with the Barrow Elders Council when local people find skeletons from traditional platform burials out on the tundra, or when bodies appear in the house mounds. The elders appreciate such consultations, says Samuel Simmonds, a tall, dignified man known for his carving. A retired Presbyterian minister, he presided at burial ceremonies of the famous "frozen family" that ancient Inupiats discovered in Barrow 13 years ago. "They were part of us, we know that," he says simply, as if the connection between old bones and bodies, and living relatives, is self-evident. In the case of the newly discovered body, he says, "We were concerned that it was reburied in a respectful manner. They were nice enough to come over and ask us."

The elders also wanted to restrict media attention and prevent photographs of the body except for a few showing her position at the site. They approved a limited autopsy to help answer questions about the body's sex, age, and state of health. She was placed in an orange plastic body bag in a stainless steel morgue with the temperature turned down to below freezing.

With the help of staff at the Indian Health Service Hospital, Jensen sent the girl's still-frozen body to Anchorage's Providence Hospital. There she assisted with an autopsy performed by Dr. Michael Zimmerman of New York City's Mount Sinai Hospital. Zimmerman, an expert on prehistoric frozen bodies, had autopsied Barrow's frozen family in 1982, and was on his way to work on the prehistoric man recently discovered in the Alps.

The findings suggest the girl's life was very hard. She ultimately died of starvation, but also had emphysema caused by a rare congenital disease—the lack of an enzyme that protects the lungs. She probably was sickly and needed extra care all her brief life. The autopsy also found soot in her lungs from the family's sea mammal oil lamps, and she had osteoporosis, which was caused by a diet exclusively of meat from marine mammals.

The girl's stomach was empty, but her intestinal tract contained dirt and animal fur. That remains a mystery, and raises questions about the condition of the rest of the family. "It's not likely that she would be hungry and everyone else well fed," Jensen says.

That the girl appears to have been placed deliberately in the cellar provokes further questions about precontact burial practices, which the researchers hope Barrow elders can help answer. Historic accounts indicate the dead often were wrapped in skins and laid out on the tundra on wooden platforms, rather than buried in the frozen earth. But perhaps the entire family was starving and too weak to remove the dead girl from the house, Jensen speculates. "We probably won't ever be able to say, 'This is the way it was,'" she adds. "For that you need a time machine."

The scientific team reported to the elders that radiocarbon dating places the girl's death in about 1200 A.D. If correct—for dating is technically tricky in the Arctic—the date would set the girl's life about 100 years before her people formed settled whaling villages, Sheehan says.

Following the autopsy and the body's return to Barrow in August, one last request by the elders was honored. The little girl, wrapped in her feather parka, was placed in a casket and buried in a small Christian ceremony next to the grave of the other prehistoric bodies. Hundreds of years after her death, an Inupiat daughter was welcomed back into the midst of her community.

The "rescue" of the little girl's body from the raw forces of time and nature means researchers and the Inupiat people will continue to learn still more about the region's culture. Sheehan and Jensen returned to Barrow in winter 1994 to explain their findings to townspeople. "We expect to learn just as much from them," Sheehan said before the trip. A North Slope Cultural Center scheduled for completion in 1996 will store and display artifacts from the dig sites.

Laboratory tests and analysis also will contribute information. The archaeologists hope measurements of heavy metals in the girl's body will allow comparisons with modern-day pollution contaminating the sea mammals that

Inupiats eat today. The soot damage in her lungs might offer health implications for Third World people who rely on oil lamps, dung fires, and charcoal for heat and light. Genetic tests could illuminate early population movements of Inupiats. The project also serves as a model for good relations between archaeologists and Native people. "The larger overall message from this work is that scientists and communities don't have to be at odds," Sheehan says. "In fact, there are mutual interests that we all have. Scientists have obligations to communities. And when more scientists realize that, and when more communities hold scientists to those standards, then everybody will be happier."

Cases in which an entire organism of any sort, let alone a human, is preserved in a relatively unaltered state are rare and comprise possibly less than 1 percent of all fossil finds. The majority of **fossils** have been **altered** in some way. They generally consist of such things as scattered teeth and fragments of bones found embedded in the earth's crust as part of rock deposits. Thousands, and even millions, of years ago, the organisms died and were deposited in the earth; they may then have been covered by sediments and silt, or sand. These materials gradually hardened, forming a protective shell around the skeleton of the organism. The internal cavities of bones or teeth and other parts of the skeleton are generally filled in with mineral deposits from the sediment immediately surrounding the specimen. Then the external walls of the bone decay and are replaced by calcium carbonate or silica.

Fossilization is most apt to occur among marine animals and other creatures that live near water, because their remains accumulate on shallow sea or river bottoms, away from waves and tidal action. These concentrations of shells and other parts of organisms are covered and completely enclosed by the soft marine sediments that eventually harden into shale and limestone.

Terrestrial animals, however, are not so successfully fossilized unless they happened to die in a cave, or their remains were dragged there by some other meat-eating animal. In caves, condi-

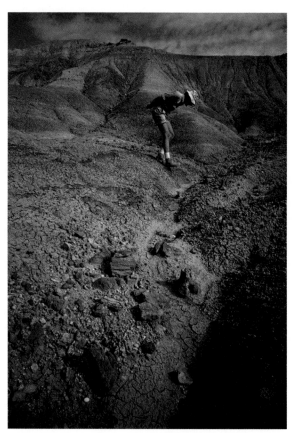

Fossils are not always found in the ground. In this picture, paleoanthropologist Donald Johanson searches for fossils in a gully in Ethiopia. The fossils in the foreground were once buried beneath sediments on an ancient lake bottom, but rains in more recent times have eroded the sediments from around them so that they lie exposed on the surface.

Altered fossils.   Remains of plants and animals that lived in the past that have been altered, as by the replacement of organic material by calcium carbonate or silica.

tions are often excellent for fossilization, as minerals contained in water dripping from the ceiling may harden over bones left on the cave floor. In northern China, for example, many fossils of *Homo erectus* (discussed in Chapter 8) and other animals were found in a cave at a place called Zhoukoudian, in deposits consisting of consolidated clays and rock that had fallen from the cave's limestone ceiling. The cave had been frequented by both humans and predatory animals, who left remains of many a meal there.

Outside of caves, the bones of a land dweller, having been picked clean and often broken by predators and scavengers, are then scattered and exposed to the deteriorating influence of the elements. The fossil record for many primates, for example, is poor, because organic materials decay rapidly in the tropical forests in which they lived. The records are much more complete in the case of primates that lived on the grassy plains, or savannas, where conditions are far more favorable to the formation of fossils. This is particularly true in places where ash deposited from volcanic eruptions or waterborne sediments along lakes and streams could quickly cover over the skeletons of primates that lived there. At several localities in Ethiopia, Kenya, and Tanzania in East Africa, numerous fossils important for our understanding of human evolution have been found near ancient lakes and streams, often "sandwiched" between layers of volcanic ash.

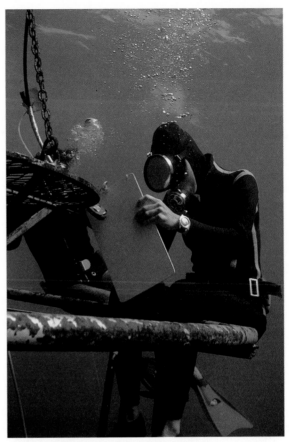

Archaeological remains may be found underwater as well as in the soil, giving rise to the specialized field of underwater archaeology.

SITES AND FOSSIL LOCALITIES

Places containing archaeological remains of previous human activity are known as **sites**. There are many kinds of sites, and sometimes it is difficult to define their boundaries, for remains may be strewn over large areas. Some examples are hunting campsites, in which hunters waited for game to pass; kill sites, in which game was killed and butchered; village sites, in which domestic activities took place; and cemeteries, in which the dead, and sometimes their belongings, were buried.

Sometimes human fossil remains are present at archaeological sites. This is the case, for example, at certain early sites in East Africa. Sometimes, though, human remains are found at other localities. For example, in South Africa the fossil remains of early human ancestors have been found in rock fissures, where their remains were dropped by predators. Such places are usually referred to as **fossil localities**.

Site. In archaeology, a place containing remains of previous human activity. **> Fossil locality.** In paleoanthropology, a place where fossils are found.

SITE AND LOCALITY IDENTIFICATION

Archaeological sites, particularly very old ones, frequently lie buried underground, and therefore the first task for the archaeologist is actually finding sites to investigate. Most sites are revealed by the presence of artifacts. Chance may play a beneficial role in the discovery, as in the previously discussed case of the site at Barrow, Alaska. Usually, however, the archaeologist will have to survey a region in order to plot the sites available for excavation. A survey can be made from the ground, but nowadays more and more use is made of remote sensing techniques, many of them byproducts of space-age technology. Aerial photographs have been used off and on by archaeologists since the 1920s and are widely used today. Among other things, they were used for the discovery and interpretation of the huge geometric and zoomorphic markings on the coastal desert of Peru. More recently, use of high-resolution aerial photographs, including satellite imagery, resulted in the astonishing discovery of over 500 miles of prehistoric roadways connecting sites in the four-corners region (where Arizona, New Mexico, Colorado, and Utah meet) with other sites in ways that archaeologists had never suspected. This led to a whole new understanding of prehistoric Pueblo Indian economic, social, and political organization. Evidently, large centers like Pueblo Bonito were able to exercise political control over a number of satellite communities, mobilize labor for large public works, and see to the regular redistribution of goods over substantial distances.

On the ground, sites can be spotted by **soil marks,** or stains, that often show up on the surface of recently plowed fields. From soil marks, many Bronze Age burial mounds were discovered in northern Hertfordshire and southwestern Cambridgeshire, England. The mounds hardly rose out of the ground, yet each was circled at its core by chalky soil marks. Sometimes the very presence of certain chalky rock is significant. A search for

Some archaeological features are best seen from the air, such as this figure of a hummingbird made in prehistoric times on the Nazca Desert of Peru.

Soil marks. Stains which show up on the surface of recently plowed fields that reveal an archaeological site.

Stone Age cave sites in Europe would be simplified with the aid of a geological map showing where limestone—a mineral necessary in the formation of caves—is to be found.

Some sites may be spotted by the kind of vegetation they grow. For example, the topsoil of ancient storage and refuse pits is often richer in organic matter than that of the surrounding areas, and so it grows a distinct vegetation. At Tikal, an ancient Maya site in Guatemala (Chapter 12), breadnut trees usually grow near the remains of ancient houses, so that an archaeologist looking for the remains of houses at Tikal would do well to search where these trees grow. In England, a wooden monument of the Stonehenge type at Darrington, Wiltshire, was discovered from an aerial photograph showing a distinct pattern of vegetation growing where the ancient structure once stood.

Documents, maps, folklore—ethnohistorical data—are also useful to the archaeologist. Heinrich Schliemann, the famous (and controversial) 19th-century German archaeologist, was led to the discovery of Troy after a reading of Homer's *Iliad.* He assumed that the city described by Homer as Ilium was really Troy. Place-names and local lore often are an indication that an archaeological site is to be found in the area. Archaeological surveys in North America depend a great deal upon amateur collectors who are usually familiar with local history.

Sometimes sites in eastern North America are exposed by natural agents, such as soil erosion or droughts. Many prehistoric Indian shell refuse mounds have been exposed by the erosion of river banks. A whole village of stone huts was exposed at Skara Brae in the Orkney Islands by the action of wind as it blew away sand. And during the long drought of 1853–1854, a well-preserved prehistoric village was exposed when the water level of Lake Zurich, Switzerland, fell dramatically. In 1991, the mummified body of a late Neolithic man was found in the Tyrolean Alps, where it had been released by glacial melting.

Often, archaeological remains are accidentally discovered in the course of some other human

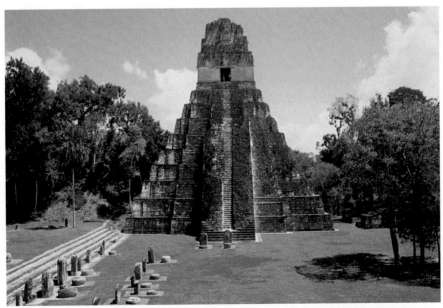

Sometimes archaeological sites are marked by dramatic ruins, as shown here. This temple stands at the heart of the ancient Maya city of Tikal. Built by piling up rubble and facing it with limestone blocks held together with mortar, it served as the funerary monument of a king, whose body was placed in a tomb beneath the pyramidal base.

anthropology applied   Cultural Resource Management

In June 1979, on a knoll next to a river not far from Lake Champlain, a survey crew working for Peter A. Thomas of the University of Vermont's Consulting Archaeology Program discovered archaeological materials unlike any found before in the region. The following June, Thomas returned to the site with a crew of five in order to excavate a portion of it. What they found were the remains of an 8,000-year-old hunting and fishing camp that had been occupied for up to a few months in the spring or fall by perhaps one or two families. From the site they recovered a distinctive tool inventory never recognized before, as well as data related to hunting and fishing subsistence practices, butchery or hide processing, cooking, tool manufacture, and a possible shelter. Since many archaeologists had previously believed the region to be devoid of human occupation 8,000 years ago, recovery of these data was especially important.

What sets this work apart from conventional archaeological research is that it was conducted as part of cultural resource management activities required by state and federal laws to preserve important aspects of the country's prehistoric and historic heritage. In this case, the Vermont Agency of Transportation planned to replace an inadequate highway bridge with a new one. Since the project was partially funded by the U.S. government, steps had to be taken to identify and protect any significant prehistoric or historic resources that might be adversely affected. To do so, the Vermont Agency of Transportation hired Thomas, first to see if such resources existed in the project area, and then to retrieve data from the endangered portions of the one site that was found. As a result, an important contribution was made to our knowledge of the prehistory of northeastern North America.

Since passage of the Historic Preservation Act of 1966, the National Environmental Policy Act of 1969, and the Archaeological and Historical Preservation Act of 1974, the field of cultural resource management has flourished. Consequently, many archaeologists are employed by such agencies as the Army Corps of Engineers, the National Park Service, the U.S. Forest Service, and the U.S. Soil and Conservation Service to assist in the preservation, restoration, and salvage of archaeological resources. Archaeologists are also employed by state historic preservation agencies. Finally, they do a considerable amount of consulting work for engineering firms to help them prepare environmental impact statements. Some of these archaeologists, like Thomas, operate out of universities and colleges, while others are on the staffs of independent consulting firms.

---

activity. Plowing sometimes turns up bones, fragments of pots, and other archaeological objects. Stone quarrying at Swanscombe, Kent, in England revealed one of the most important sites of the Old Stone Age, with human remains thought to be about 250,000 years old. In 1995, strip mining near the town of Schoningen in Germany led to the discovery of 400,000-year-old spears of *Homo erectus* (see Chapter 8). So frequently do construction projects uncover archaeological remains that in many countries, including the United States, projects that require government approval will not be authorized unless measures are first taken to identify and protect archaeological remains on the construction sites. Archaeological surveys in the United States are now routinely carried out as part of the environmental review process for federally funded or licensed construction projects.

Conspicuous sites such as the great mounds or "tells" of the Middle East are easy to spot, for the country is open. But it is difficult to locate ruins, even those that are well above ground, where there is a dense forest cover. Thus, the discovery of archaeological sites is strongly affected by local geography.

While archaeological sites may be found just about anywhere, the same is not true for fossil localities. One will find fossils only in geological contexts where conditions are known to have been right for fossilization. Once the paleoanthropologist has identified such regions, specific localities are identified in much the same ways as archaeological sites. Indeed, the discovery of ancient stone tools may lead to the discovery of human fossil remains. For example, it was the presence of very crude stone tools in Olduvai Gorge, East Africa, which prompted Mary and Louis Leakey to search there for the human fossils (discussed in Chapters 6 and 7) they eventually found.

SITE AND LOCALITY EXCAVATION

Before the archaeologist or paleoanthropologist plans an excavation, he or she must ask the question, "Why am I digging?" Then he or she must consider the amount of time, money, and labor that can be committed to the enterprise. The recovery of archaeological and fossil material long ago ceased to be the province of the enlightened amateur, as it once was when any enterprising collector went out to dig for the sake of digging. A modern excavation is carefully planned and rigorously conducted; it should not only shed light on the human past but should also help us to understand cultural and evolutionary processes in general.

Archaeological Excavation

After a site is chosen for excavation, on the basis of its potential contribution to the solution of some important research problem, the land is cleared and the places to be excavated are plotted. This is usually done by means of a **grid system.** The surface of the site is divided into squares, each square being numbered and marked with stakes. Each object found may then be located precisely in the square from which it came. (Remember, in archaeology, context is everything!) The starting point of a grid system may be a large rock, the

edge of a stone wall, or an iron rod sunk into the ground. The starting point is also known as the reference or **datum point.** At a large site covering several square miles, this kind of grid system is not feasible because of the large size of the ruins. In such cases, the plotting may be done in terms of individual structures, numbered according to the square of a "giant grid" in which they are found (Figure 2.1).

In a gridded site, each square is dug separately with great care. Trowels are used to scrape the soil, and screens are used to sift all the loose soils so that even the smallest artifacts, such as flint chips or beads, are recovered.

A technique employed when looking for very fine objects, such as fish scales or very small bones, is called **flotation.** Flotation consists of immersing soil in water, causing the particles to separate. Some will float, others will sink to the bottom, and the remains can be easily retrieved. If the site is **stratified**—that is, if the remains lie in layers one upon the other—each layer, or stratum, will be dug separately (see Figure 2.2 for an example of stratigraphy). Each layer, having been laid down during a particular span of time, will contain artifacts deposited at the same time and belonging to the same culture. Culture change can be traced through the order in which artifacts were deposited. But, say archaeologists Frank Hole and Robert F. Heizer, "because of difficulties in analyzing stratigraphy, archaeologists must use the greatest caution in drawing conclusions. Almost all interpretations of time, space, and culture contexts depend on stratigraphy. The refinements of laboratory techniques for analysis are wasted if archaeologists cannot specify the stratigraphic position of their artifacts."[3] If no stratification is present, then the archaeologist digs by arbitrary levels.

---

[3]Hole, F., & Heizer, R. F. (1969). *An introduction to prehistoric archeology* (p. 113). New York: Holt, Rinehart & Winston.

Grid system. A system for recording data from an archaeological excavation. > **Datum point.** The starting, or reference, point for a grid system. > **Flotation.** An archaeological technique employed to recover very tiny objects by immersion of soil samples in water to separate heavy from light particles. > **Stratified.** Layered; said of archaeological sites where the remains lie in layers, one upon another.

FIGURE 2.1

At large sites covering several square miles, a giant grid is constructed, as shown in this map of the center of the ancient Maya city of Tikal. Each square of the grid is one quarter of a square kilometer; individual structures are numbered according to the square in which they are found. The temple shown on page 45 can be located near the center of the map, on the east edge of the Great Plaza.

To recover very small objects easily missed in excavation, archaeologists routinely screen the earth they remove.

FIGURE 2.2
This drawing shows the strata (layers) uncovered on the North Acropolis of Tikal. The remains of at least 22 structures were found at this one location. The North Acropolis is shown near the center of the map in Figure 2.1, just north of the Great Plaza.

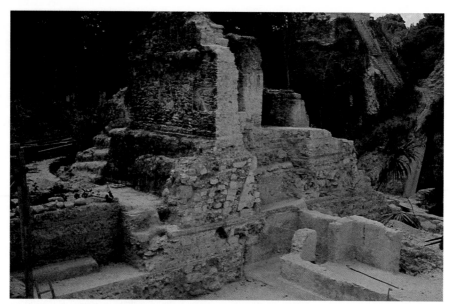

This photo shows the stratigraphy associated with one of the structures (5D-26) shown schematically in Figure 2.2.

Each square must be dug so that its edges and profiles are straight; walls between squares are often left standing to serve as visual correlates of the grid system.

Excavation of Fossils

Excavating for fossils is in many ways like archaeological excavation, although there are some differences. The paleoanthropologist must be particularly skilled in the techniques of geology, or else have ready access to geological expertise, because a fossil is of little value unless its temporal place in the sequence of rocks that contain it can be determined. In addition, the paleoanthropologist must be able to identify the fossil-laden rocks, their deposition, and other geological details. In order to provide all the necessary expertise, paleoanthropological expeditions these days generally are made up of teams of experts in various fields in addition to physical anthropology. A great deal of skill and caution is required to remove a fossil from its burial place without damage. An unusual combination of tools and materials is usually contained in the kit of the paleoanthropologist—pickaxes, enamel coating, burlap for bandages, and plaster of paris.

To remove newly discovered bones, the paleoanthropologist begins uncovering the specimen, using pick and shovel for initial excavation, then small camel hair brushes and dental picks to remove loose and easily detachable debris surrounding the bones. Once the entire specimen has been uncovered (a process that may take days of back-breaking, patient labor), the bones are covered with shellac and tissue paper to prevent cracking and damage during further excavation and handling.

Both the fossil and the earth immediately surrounding it, or the matrix, are prepared for removal as a single block. The bones and matrix are cut out of the earth (but not removed), and more shellac is applied to the entire block to harden it. The bones are covered with burlap bandages dipped in plaster of paris. Then the entire block is enclosed in plaster and burlap bandages, perhaps splinted with tree branches, and allowed to dry overnight. After it has hardened, the entire block is carefully removed from the earth, ready for packing and transport to a laboratory. Before leaving the discovery area, the investigator makes a thorough sketch map of the terrain and pinpoints the find on geological maps to aid future investigators.

FIGURE 2.3

Although the wooden posts of a house may have long since decayed, their positions may still be marked by discoloration of the soil. The plan shown on the left, of an ancient posthole pattern and depression at Snaketown, Arizona, permits the hypothetical house reconstruction on the right.

STATE OF PRESERVATION OF ARCHAEOLOGICAL AND FOSSIL EVIDENCE

What is recovered in the course of excavation depends upon the nature of the remains as much as upon the excavator's digging skills. Inorganic materials such as stone and metal are more resistant to decay than organic ones such as wood and bone. Often an archaeologist comes upon an assemblage—a collection of artifacts—made of durable inorganic materials, such as stone tools, and traces of organic ones long since decomposed, such as woodwork (Figure 2.3), textiles, or food.

State of preservation is affected by climate; under favorable climatic conditions, even the most perishable objects may survive over vast periods of time. For example, predynastic Egyptian burials consisting of shallow pits in the sand often yield well-preserved corpses. Since these bodies were buried long before mummification was ever practiced, their preservation can only be the result of rapid desiccation in the very warm, dry climate. The tombs of dynastic Egypt often contain wooden furniture, textiles, flowers, and papyri barely touched by time, seemingly as fresh looking as they were when deposited in the tomb 3,000 years ago—a consequence of the dryness of the atmosphere.

The dryness of certain caves is also a factor in the preservation of fossilized human or animal feces. Human feces are a source of information on prehistoric foods and can be analyzed for dietary remains. From such analysis archaeologists

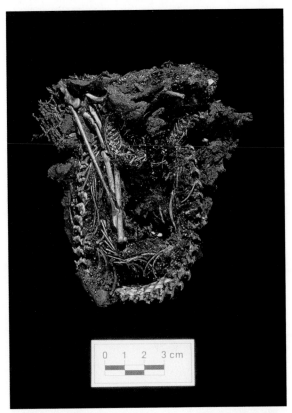

This 2,500-year-old sacred "medicine bag" made of animal hide contained a fishhook and a variety of animal remains, including a timber rattlesnake, black rat snake, and pine marten foreleg. In the acidic soils of New England, these materials would have long since decayed had it not been for the copper salts from beads buried with the bag.

can determine not only what the inhabitants ate but also how the food was prepared. Because many sources of food are available only in certain seasons, it is even possible to tell the time of year in which the food was eaten and the excrement deposited.

Certain climates can soon obliterate all evidence of organic remains. Maya ruins found in the very warm and moist tropical rain forests of Mesoamerica are often in a state of collapse—notwithstanding the fact that many are massive structures of stone—as a result of the pressure exerted upon them by the heavy forest vegetation. The rain and humidity soon destroy almost all traces of woodwork, textiles, or basketry. Fortunately, impressions of these artifacts can sometimes be preserved in plaster, and some objects made of wood or plant fibers are depicted in stone carvings and pottery figurines. Thus, even in the face of complete decay of organic substances, something may still be learned about them.

The cultural practices of ancient humans may also account for the preservation of archaeological remains. The ancient Egyptians believed that eternal life could be achieved only if the dead person were buried with his or her worldly posses-

At the Maya site of Tikal, these manikin sceptre figures originally made of wood were recovered from a king's tomb by pouring plaster into a cavity in the soil, left when the original organic material decayed.

sions. Hence, their tombs are usually filled with a wealth of artifacts. Many skeletal remains of Neandertals (Chapter 9) are known because they practiced burial, probably because they too believed in some sort of afterlife. By contrast, skeletal remains of pre-Neandertal peoples are rare and when found usually consist of mere fragments rather than complete skeletons.

SORTING OUT THE EVIDENCE

It cannot be stressed too strongly that the value of archaeological materials is virtually destroyed if an accurate and detailed record of the excavations has not been kept. As one eminent anthropologist has put it:

> The fundamental premise of excavation is that all digging is destructive, even that done by experts. The archaeologist's primary responsibility, therefore, is to record a site for posterity as it is dug because there are no second chances.[4]

Excavation records include a scale map of all the features, the stratification of each excavated square, a description of the exact location and depth of every artifact or bone unearthed, and photographs and scale drawings of the objects. This is the only way archaeological evidence can later be pieced together so as to arrive at a plausible reconstruction of a culture. Although the archaeologist may be interested only in certain kinds of remains, every aspect of the site must be recorded, whether it is relevant to the particular investigation or not, because such evidence may be useful to others and would otherwise be permanently lost. One must remember that archaeological sites are nonrenewable resources, and that their destruction, whether by proper excavation or by looting, is permanent.

After photographs and scale drawings are made, the materials recovered are processed in the laboratory. In the case of fossils, the block in which they have been removed from the field is cut open,

[4]Fagan, B. M. (1995). *People of the earth* (8th ed., p. 19). New York: HarperCollins.

and the fossil is separated from the matrix. Like the initial removal from the earth, this is a long, painstaking job involving a great deal of skill and special tools. This task may be done with hammer and chisel, dental drills, rotary grinders, or pneumatic chisels, and, in the case of very small pieces, with awls and tiny needles under a microscope.

Chemical means, such as hydrochloric and hydrofluoric acids, are also used in the separation process. Some fossils require processing by other methods. For example, precise identification can be obtained by examining thin, almost transparent strips of some fossils under a microscope. Casts of the insides of skulls are made by filling the skull wall with an acid-resistant material, then removing the wall with acid. A skull may be cleaned out and the inside painted with latex. After the latex hardens, it is removed in a single piece, revealing indirect evidence of brain shape and outer appearance. Such a cast of the skull's interior is helpful in determining the size and complexity of the specimen's brain.

Archaeologists, as a rule of thumb, plan on at least three hours of laboratory work for each hour of fieldwork. In the lab, artifacts which have been recovered must first be cleaned and cataloged—often a tedious and time-consuming job—before they are ready for analysis. From the shapes of the artifacts and from the traces of manufacture and wear, archaeologists can usually determine their function. For example, the Russian archaeologist S. A. Semenov devoted many years to the study of prehistoric technology. In the case of a flint tool used as a scraper, he was able to determine, by examining the wear patterns of the tool under a microscope, that the prehistoric individuals who used it began to scrape from right to left and then scraped from left to right, and in so doing avoided straining the muscles of the hand.[5] (See also Figure 2.4).

Analysis of vegetable and animal remains provides clues about the environment and the eco-

FIGURE 2.4

In northern New England, prehistoric pottery was often decorated by impressing the damp clay with a cord-wrapped stick. Examination of cord impressions reveals that coastal people twisted fibers used to make cordage to the left (Z twist), while those living inland did the opposite (S twist). The nonfunctional differences reflect motor habits so deeply ingrained as to seem completely natural to the cordage makers. From this, we may infer two distinctively different populations.

nomic activities of the occupants of a site (see Figure 2.5). Such analysis may help clarify peoples' relationship to their environment and its influence upon the development of their **technology**—the knowledge they employ to make and use objects. For example, we know that the people responsible for Serpent Mound in Ontario, Canada, (a mound having the form of a serpent, consisting of burials and a shell midden) were there only in the spring and early summer, when they came to collect shellfish and perform their annual burial rites; apparently they moved elsewhere at the beginning of summer to pursue other seasonal subsistence activities. Archaeologists have inferred that the mound was unoccupied in winter, because this is the season when deer shed their antlers, yet no deer antlers were found on the site. Nor were duck bones found, and so archaeologists conclude that the mound was also unoccupied in the fall, when ducks stopped on their migratory route southward to feed on the wild rice that grew in the region.

Analysis of human skeletal material also provides important insights into ancient peoples' diets. Microscopic wear patterns on teeth, for

[5]Semenov, S. A. (1964). *Prehistoric technology.* New York: Barnes & Noble.

Technology. The knowledge people employ to make and use objects.

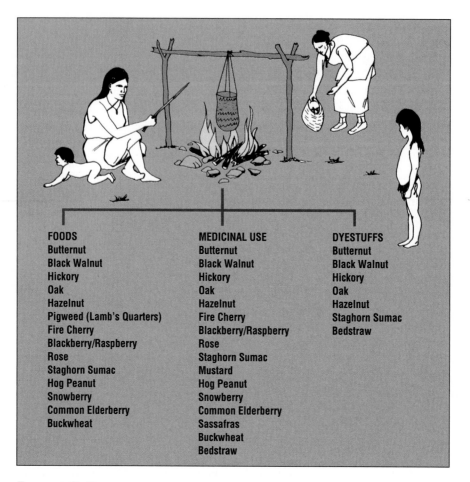

FOODS	MEDICINAL USE	DYESTUFFS
Butternut	Butternut	Butternut
Black Walnut	Black Walnut	Black Walnut
Hickory	Hickory	Hickory
Oak	Oak	Oak
Hazelnut	Hazelnut	Hazelnut
Pigweed (Lamb's Quarters)	Fire Cherry	Staghorn Sumac
Fire Cherry	Blackberry/Raspberry	Bedstraw
Blackberry/Raspberry	Rose	
Rose	Staghorn Sumac	
Staghorn Sumac	Mustard	
Hog Peanut	Hog Peanut	
Snowberry	Snowberry	
Common Elderberry	Common Elderberry	
Buckwheat	Sassafras	
	Buckwheat	
	Bedstraw	

FIGURE 2.5

Plant remains recovered from hearths used by people between one and two thousand years ago at an archaeological site in Vermont may have been utilized as shown here, based on our knowledge of how the same plants were used by Indians in the region when first encountered by Europeans. Occupation of the site must have been in the summer and fall, the seasons when these plants are available.

example, may reveal whether abrasive plants were important foods. Similarly, people who eat more plants than meat will have a higher ratio of strontium to calcium in their bones. At the ancient Maya city of Tikal, analysis of human skeletons showed that elite members of society had access to better diets than lower ranking members of society, allowing them to reach their full growth potential with greater regularity. Important insights into life expectancy, mortality, and health status also emerge from the study of human skeletal remains. Unfortunately, such studies have become more difficult to carry out, especially in the United States, as Native American communities demand (and federal law requires) the return of skeletons from archaeological excavations for reburial. Archaeologists find themselves in something of a quandary over this requirement; as scientists, they know the importance of the information that can be gleaned from studies of human skeletons, but as anthropologists, they are bound to respect the feelings of those whose ancestors those skeletons represent. Currently (as illustrated in the Original Study in this chapter), archaeologists are consulting with representatives of Native American communities to work out procedures with which both parties can live.

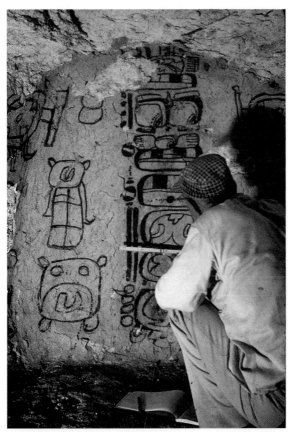

Some ancient societies devised precise ways of recording dates that archaeologists have been able to correlate with our own calendar. Here is the tomb of an important ruler, Stormy Sky, at the ancient Maya city of Tikal. The glyphs painted on the wall give the date of the burial in the Maya calendar, which is the same as March 18, A.D. 457, in our calendar. The tomb, Burial 48, is shown in Figure 2.2 above the 30-meter mark.

DATING THE PAST

Reliable methods of dating objects and events are necessary if archaeologists and paleoanthropologists are to know the sequence of events in the situation under study. But since archaeologists and paleoanthropologists deal mostly with peoples and events in times far removed from our own, the calendar of historic times is of little use to them. So they must rely on two kinds of dating: relative and "absolute." **Relative dating** consists simply of finding out if an event or object is younger or older than another. **"Absolute"** or (more properly) **chronometric dates** are dates based upon solar years and are reckoned in "years before the present" (B.P., with "present" defined as A.D. 1950). Many relative and chronometric techniques are available; here, there is space to discuss only the ones most often relied upon. Ideally, archaeologists try to utilize as many methods as are appropriate, given the materials available to work with and the funds at their disposal. By doing so, they significantly reduce the risk of arriving at erroneous dates.

METHODS OF RELATIVE DATING

Of the many relative dating techniques available, **stratigraphy** is probably the most reliable. Stratigraphy is based on the simple principle that the oldest layer, or stratum, was deposited first (it is the deepest) while the newest layer was deposited last (in undisturbed situations, it lies at the top). Therefore, in an archaeological site the evidence is usually deposited in chronological order. The lowest stratum contains the oldest artifacts and/or fossils, whereas the uppermost stratum contains the most recent ones. Thus, even in the absence of precise dates, one knows the *relative* age of objects in one stratum compared with the ages of those in other strata.

Another method of relative dating is the **fluorine test.** It is based on the fact that the amount of fluorine deposited in bones is proportional to their age. The oldest bones contain the greatest amount of fluorine, and vice versa. The fluorine test is useful in dating bones that cannot be ascribed with certainty to any particular stratum and

Relative dating. In archaeology and paleoanthropology, designating an event, object, or fossil as being older or younger than another. **>** **"Absolute" or chronometric dates.** In archaeology and paleoanthropology, dates for archaeological materials based on solar years, centuries, or other units of absolute time. **>** **Stratigraphy.** In archaeology and paleoanthropology, the most reliable method of relative dating by means of strata. **>** **Fluorine test.** In archaeology or paleoanthropology, a technique for relative dating based on the fact that the amount of fluorine in bones is proportional to their age.

cannot be dated according to the stratigraphic method. A shortcoming of this method is that the rate of fluorine formation is not constant, but varies from region to region.

Relative dating can also be done on the evidence of botanical and animal remains. A common method, known as **palynology**, involves the study of pollen grains. The kind of pollen found in any geologic stratum depends on the kind of vegetation that existed at the time that stratum was deposited. A site or locality can therefore be dated by determining what kind of pollen was found associated with it. In addition, palynology is also an important technique for reconstructing past environments in which people lived.

Another method relies on our knowledge of paleontology. Sites containing the bones of extinct animal species are usually older than sites in which the remains of these animals are absent. Very early North American Indian sites have yielded the remains of mastodons and mammoths—animals now extinct—and on this basis the sites can be dated to a time before these animals died out, roughly 10,000 years ago.

Methods of Chronometric Dating

One of the most widely used methods of "absolute" or chronometric dating is **radiocarbon analysis.** It is based on the fact that all living organisms absorb radioactive carbon (known as carbon 14), maintaining equilibrium with the level of this isotope in the atmosphere, and that this absorption ceases at the time of death. It is possible to measure in the laboratory the amount of radioactive carbon left in a given organic substance, because radioactive substances break down or decay slowly and at a constant rate over a fixed period of time. Carbon 14 begins to disintegrate, returning to nitrogen 14, emitting radioactive (beta) particles in the process. At death, about 15 beta

radiations per minute per gram of material are emitted. The rate of decay is known as "half-life," and the half-life of carbon 14 is 5,730 years. This means that it takes 5,730 years for one-half of the original amount of carbon 14 to decay into nitrogen 14. Beta radiation will be about 7.5 counts per minute per gram. In another 5,730 years, one-half of this amount of carbon 14 will also have decayed. In other words, after 11,460 years, only one-fourth of the original amount of carbon 14 will be present. Thus the age of an organic substance such as charcoal, wood, shell, or bone can be measured by counting the beta rays emitted by the remaining carbon 14. The radiocarbon method can adequately date organic materials up to 70,000 years old. Of course, one has to be sure that the association between organic remains and archaeological materials is valid. For example, charcoal found on a site may have gotten there from a recent forest fire, rather than more ancient activity; or wood used to make something by the people who lived at a site may have been retrieved from some older context.

Because there is always a certain amount of error involved, radiocarbon dates are not as "absolute" as is sometimes thought. This is why any stated date always has a plus-or-minus ($\pm$) factor attached to it. For example, a date of 5,200 $\pm$ 120 years ago means that there is a two out of three chance that the true date falls somewhere within the 240 years between 5,080 and 5,320 radiocarbon years ago. The qualification "radiocarbon years" is necessary, because we have discovered that radiocarbon years are not precisely equivalent to calendar years.

The discovery that radiocarbon years are not precisely equivalent to calendar years was made possible by another method of "absolute" dating, **dendrochronology.** Originally devised for dating Pueblo Indian sites in the North American Southwest, this method is based on the fact that in the right kind of climate, trees add one (and only one)

Palynology. In archaeology and paleoanthropology, a method of relative dating based on changes in fossil pollen over time. **> Radiocarbon analysis.** In archaeology and paleoanthropology, a technique for chronometric dating based on measuring the amount of radioactive carbon (C-14) left in organic materials found in archaeological sites. **> Dendrochronology.** In archaeology, a method of chronometric dating based on the number of rings of growth found in a tree trunk.

new growth ring to their trunks every year (see Figure 2.6). The rings vary in thickness, depending upon the amount of rainfall received in a year, so that climatic fluctuation is registered in the growth ring. By taking a sample of wood, such as a beam from a Pueblo Indian house, and by comparing its pattern of rings with those in the trunk of a tree known to be as old as the artifact, archaeologists can date the archaeological material. Dendrochronology is applicable only to wooden objects. Furthermore, it can be used only in regions in which trees of great age, such as the giant sequoias and the bristlecone pine, are known to grow. On the other hand, radiocarbon dating of wood from bristlecone pines that have been dated by dendrochronology allows us to "correct" carbon 14 dates so as to bring them into agreement with calendar dates.

Potassium-argon analysis, another commonly used method of "absolute" dating, is based on a technique similar to that of radiocarbon analysis. Following intense heating, as from a volcanic erup-

tion, radioactive potassium decays at a known rate to form argon, any previously existing argon having been released by the heating. The half-life of radioactive potassium is 1.3 billion years. Deposits that are millions of years old can now be dated by measuring the ratio of potassium to argon in a given rock. Volcanic debris, such as at Olduvai Gorge and other localities in East Africa, can be dated by potassium-argon analysis; thus we know when the volcanic eruption occurred. If fossils or artifacts are found sandwiched between layers of volcanic ash, as they are at Olduvai and other sites in East Africa, they can therefore be dated with some precision. But as with radiocarbon dates, there are limits to that precision, and potassium-argon dates are always stated with a ± margin of error attached.

Amino acid racemization dating, yet another chronometric technique, is of potential importance because it bridges a time gap between the effective ranges of the radiocarbon and potassium-argon methods. It is based on the fact that amino

Living tree, cutting date known

Beams from archaeological sites

Tree stumps

FIGURE 2.6

Chronometric dating based on tree rings is called *dendrochronology*. Starting with a sample of known age, ring patterns toward the inner part are matched with those from the outer part of the older sample, and so on, back in time.

Potassium-argon analysis. In archaeology and paleoanthropology, a technique for chronometric dating that measures the ratio of radioactive potassium to argon in volcanic debris associated with human remains. **>** **Amino acid racemization dating.** In archaeology and paleoanthropology, a technique for chronometric dating that measures the ratio of right-to-left-handed amino acids.

acids trapped in organic materials gradually change, or "racemize" after death, from left-handed forms to right-handed forms. Thus, the ratio of left- to right-handed forms should indicate the specimen's age. Unfortunately, in substances like bone, moisture and acids in the soil can leach out the amino acids, thereby introducing a serious source of error. However, ostrich eggshells have proven immune to this problem, the amino acids being so effectively locked up in a tight mineral matrix that they are preserved for thousands of years. Because ostrich eggs were widely used as food, and the shells as containers in Africa and the Middle East, they provide a powerful means of dating sites of the middle part of the Old Stone Age (Paleolithic), between 40,000 and 180,000 years ago.

Radiocarbon, potassium-argon, and amino acid racemization dating are only three of several "high-tech" dating methods that have been developed in the past few decades. Radiocarbon and potassium-argon, in particular, are the chronometric methods most heavily relied upon by archaeologists and paleoanthropologists; nevertheless, other methods are increasingly used as a check on accuracy and to supplement dates determined by other means. To cite one example, a technique called **electron spin resonance** measures the trapped electron population in bone or shell (the number of trapped electrons indicates the specimen's age). Because electron spin resonance dates derived from an important Middle Paleolithic skull from Qafzeh, Israel, (discussed in Chapter 9) agree with those based on amino acid racemization, we

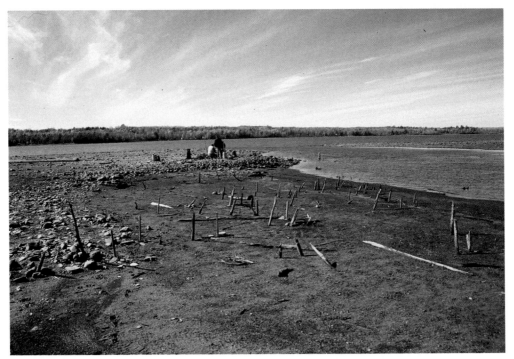

Shown here is what remains of a 1,700-year-old fish weir, for trapping fish, in Maine. Submersion beneath the water preserved the lower portions of wooden stakes, which were revealed by unusually low water levels.

Electron spin resonance. In archaeology and paleoanthropology, a technique for chronometric dating that measures the number of trapped electrons in bone or shell.

can have confidence that the dating is correct. Because other methods of chronometric dating are often quite complicated to carry out, they tend to be expensive; many can be carried out only on specific kinds of materials, and in the case of some, are so new that their reliability is not yet unequivocally established. It is for these reasons that they have not been as widely used as radiocarbon and potassium-argon.

CHANCE AND THE STUDY OF THE PAST

It is important to understand the imperfect nature of the archaeological and fossil records. They are imperfect, first of all, because the chance circumstances of preservation have determined what has and what has not survived the ravages of time. Thus, cultures must be reconstructed on the basis of incomplete and, possibly, unrepresentative samples of artifacts. The problems are further compounded by the large role chance continues to play in the discovery of prehistoric remains. Therefore, one must always be cautious when trying to interpret the human past. No matter how elegant a particular theory may be about what happened in the past, new evidence may at any time force its reexamination and modification, or even rejection, in favor of some better theory.

CHAPTER SUMMARY

Archaeology and physical anthropology, though they do not neglect the present, are the two branches of anthropology most involved in the study of the human past. Archaeologists study material remains to describe and explain human behavior; physical anthropologists called paleoanthropologists study fossil remains to understand and explain the processes at work in human biological evolution.

Artifacts are objects fashioned or altered by humans, such as a flint chip, a pottery vessel, or even a house. A fossil is any trace of an organism of past geological time that has been preserved in the earth's crust. Fossilization typically involves the hard parts of an organism and may take place through freezing in ice, preservation in bogs or tar pits, immersion in water, or inclusion in rock deposits. Fossilization is most apt to occur among marine animals and other organisms that live near water because of the likelihood that their corpses will be buried and preserved on sea and river bottoms. On land, conditions in caves or near active volcanic activity may be conducive to fossilization.

Places containing archaeological remains of previous human occupation are known as sites. Sometimes human fossils are present at archaeological sites, but they may occur by themselves at fossil localities. Sites and localities are generally located by a survey of a region. While fossil localities are revealed by the presence of fossils, archaeological sites are revealed by the presence of artifacts. Irregularities of the ground surface, unusual soil discoloration, and unexpected variations in vegetation type and coloring may also indicate the location of a site. Ethnohistorical data—maps, documents, and folklore—may provide further clues to the location of archaeological sites. Sometimes both fossils and archaeological remains are discovered accidentally, for example, in plowing, quarrying, or in building construction.

Once a site or locality has been selected for excavation, the area is divided and carefully marked with a grid system; the starting point of the dig is called the datum point. Each square within the grid is carefully excavated, and any archaeological or fossil remains are recovered through employment of various tools and screens; for very fine objects, the method of flotation is employed. The location of each artifact when found must be carefully noted. Once excavated, artifacts and fossils undergo further cleaning and preservation in the laboratory with the use of specialized tools and chemicals.

The durability of archaeological evidence depends upon climate and the nature of the artifacts. Inorganic materials are more resistant to decay than organic ones. However, given a very dry climate, even organic materials may be well preserved. Warm, moist climates as well as thick vegetation act to decompose organic material quickly, and even inorganic material may suffer from the effects of humidity and vegetation growth. The durability of archaeological evidence is also dependent upon the social customs of ancient people.

Because excavation in fact destroys a site, the archaeologist must maintain a thorough record in the form of maps, descriptions, scale drawings, and photographs of every aspect of the excavation. All artifacts must be cleaned and classified before being sent to the laboratory for analysis. Often the shape and markings of artifacts can determine their function, and the analysis of vegetable and animal remains may provide information.

There are two kinds of methods for dating archaeological and fossil remains. Relative dating is a method of determining the age of objects relative to each other and includes the method of stratigraphy, based on the position of the artifact or fossil in relation to different layers of soil deposits. The fluorine test is based on the determination of the amount of fluorine deposited in the bones. The analysis of floral remains (including palynology) and faunal deposits is also widely employed. Methods of "absolute," or chronometric, dating include radiocarbon analysis, which measures the amount of carbon 14 that remains in organic objects; potassium-argon analysis, which measures the percentage of radioactive potassium which has decayed to argon in volcanic material; dendrochronology, dating based upon tree rings; and amino acid racemization, based on changes from left- to right-handed amino acids in organic materials, especially eggshells. Other chronometric methods exist, such as electron spin resonance, but are not as widely used, because of limited applicability, difficulty of application, expense, or (as yet) unproven reliability.

POINTS FOR CONSIDERATION

1. Why would archaeologists be so concerned about having recourse to so many different methods of dating materials? How does this relate to site location?

2. Why is it vital for anthropologists to develop good relations with both the "official" powers and the individual members of the community within which they are working? How can these relationships, good or bad, impact fieldwork and methodology?

3. How can material objects give insight into cultural beliefs, patterns of behavior, and values? What items might archaeologists find particularly revealing when unearthing our own remains in the far future?

SUGGESTED READINGS

Fagan, B. M. (1998). *People of the earth: An introduction to world prehistory* (9th ed.). New York: Longman.

There are a number of good texts that, like this one, try to summarize the findings of archaeologists on a worldwide scale. This book, being one of the more recent ones, is reasonably up to date.

Feder, K. L. (1999). *Frauds, myths, and mysteries* (3rd ed.). Mountain View, CA: Mayfield.

This very readable book is written to enlighten readers about the many pseudo-scientific and even crackpot theories about past cultures that all too often have been presented to the public as "solid" archaeology.

Joukowsky, M. (1980). *A complete field manual of archaeology: Tools and techniques of fieldwork for archaeologists.* Englewood Cliffs, NJ: Prentice-Hall.

This book, encyclopedic in its coverage, explains for the novice and professional alike all of the methods and techniques used by archaeologists in the field. Two concluding chapters discuss fieldwork opportunities and financial aid for archaeological research.

Sharer, R. J., & Ashmore, W. (1993). *Archaeology: discovering our past* (2nd ed.). Palo Alto, CA: Mayfield.

One of the best presentations of the body of method, technique, and theory that most archaeologists accept as fundamental to their discipline. The authors confine themselves to the operational modes, guiding strategies, and theoretical orientations of anthropological archaeology in a manner well designed to lead the beginner into the discipline.

Shipman, P. (1981). *Life history of a fossil: An introduction to taphonomy and paleoecology.* Cambridge, MA: Harvard University Press.

In order to understand what a fossil has to tell us, one must know how it came to be where the paleoanthropologist found it. In this book, anthropologist-turned-science-writer Pat Shipman explains how animal remains are acted upon and altered from death to fossilization.

Thomas, D. H. (1998). *Archaeology* (3rd ed.). Fort Worth, TX: Harcourt Brace.

Some books tell us how to do archaeology, some tell us what archaeologists have found out, but this one tells us why we do archaeology. It does so in a coherent and thorough way, and Thomas's blend of ideas, quotations, biographies, and case studies makes for really interesting reading.

Chapter 3
BIOLOGY AND EVOLUTION

EVOLUTION HAS PRODUCED A VARIETY OF
PRIMATES, RANGING ALL THE WAY FROM LEMURS
TO HUMANS. SUCH VARIETY IS NOT THE RESULT
OF PROGRESSIVE CHANGE BUT RATHER THE
ADAPTATION OF ORGANISMS TO CONDITIONS AS
THEY ARE. ONCE THOSE CONDITIONS CHANGE,
NEW ADAPTATIONS ARE REQUIRED.

Chapter Preview

What Forces Are Responsible for the Diversity of Primates in the World Today?

Although all primates—lemurs, lorises, tarsiers, monkeys, apes, and humans—share a common ancestry, they have come to differ through the operation of evolutionary forces which have permitted them to adapt to a variety of environments in a variety of ways. Although biologists agree upon the fact of evolution, they are still unraveling the details of how it has proceeded.

What Are the Processes of Evolution?

Evolution works through mutation, producing genetic variation, which is then acted upon by drift (accidental changes in gene frequencies in a population), gene flow (the introduction of new genes from other populations), and natural selection. Natural selection is the adaptive mechanism of evolution that works through differential reproduction as individuals with genes for adaptive traits produce more offspring than those without.

How Do These Processes Produce New Forms of Organisms?

Populations may evolve in a linear manner, as small changes from one generation to another improve that population's adaptation. Through the accumulation of such changes over many generations, an older species may evolve into a new one. Or evolution may proceed in a branching manner, in response to isolating mechanisms. These serve to separate populations, preventing gene flow between them so that drift and selection may proceed in different ways. This may lead to the appearance first of divergent races and then of divergent species.

Humans have long had close contact with other animals. Some, such as dogs, horses, and cows, have lived close to people for so long that little attention is paid to their behavior. We are interested only in how well they do what they were bred for—companionship, racing, milk-giving, or whatever. Domestic animals are so dependent on humans that they have lost many of the behavioral traits of their wild ancestors. Except to a small child, perhaps, and a dairy farmer, a cow is not a very interesting animal to watch.

By contrast, wild animals, especially exotic ones, have always fascinated people, as the popularity of circuses and zoos attests. In cultures very different from those of the industrialized countries of the world, like those of some American Indians, people can have a special relationship with particular animals, believing their fates to be intertwined. Such companion animals may be called upon for assistance to serve as messengers, or the person may be able to transfer his or her state of being into the animal's body.

A curious feature of this interest is the desire of humans to see animals as mirror images of themselves, a phenomenon known as **anthropomorphism**. Stories in which animals talk, wear clothes, and exhibit human virtues and vices go back to antiquity. Many children today learn of Mickey Mouse, Garfield the cat, or Kermit the Frog and Miss Piggy; the animals created by Walt Disney, Jim Henson, and others have become an integral part of contemporary North American culture. Occasionally one sees on television trained apes dressed like humans eating at a table, pushing a stroller, or riding a tricycle. They are amusing because they look so "human."

Over the ages, people have trained animals to perform tricks, making them mimic human behavior. But never did people suspect the full extent of the relationship they have with animals. The close biological tie between humans and the other **primate order**—the group of animals which, besides humans, includes lemurs, lorises, tarsiers, monkeys, and apes—is now better understood. The diversity of primates existing today is the result of the operation of evolutionary forces which have permitted them to adapt to environments in a variety of ways. These evolutionary processes are the subject of this chapter.

HEREDITY

In order to understand how evolution works, one must first have some understanding of the mechanisms of heredity, because heritable variation constitutes the raw material for evolution. Our knowledge of the mechanisms of heredity is fairly recent; most of the fruitful research into the molecular level of inheritance has taken place in the past four decades. Although certain aspects remain puzzling, the outlines by now are reasonably clear.

THE TRANSMISSION OF GENES

Biologists call the actual units of heredity **genes**, a term that comes from the Greek word for "birth." The presence and activity of genes were originally deduced rather than observed by an Austrian monk, Gregor Mendel, in the 19th century. Working shortly after publication of Darwin's theory of evolution, Mendel sought to answer some of the riddles posed by that theory by experimenting with garden peas to determine how various traits are inherited. Specifically, he discovered what Darwin never knew: how variation, so important to his theory, was passed from one generation to the next. Interestingly, Mendel's work was generally ignored until it was rediscovered at the turn of the 20th century. Since then, the function of genes has been pretty well known, even though no one really knew what genes were until quite recently.

DNA

In 1953, James Watson and Francis Crick discovered that genes are actually portions of molecules

---

Anthropomorphism. The ascription of human attributes to nonhuman beings. **> Primate order.** The group of mammals that include lemurs, lorises, tarsiers, monkeys, apes, and humans. **> Genes.** Portions of DNA molecules that direct the development of observable or identifiable traits.

Gregor Mendel performed carefully controlled breeding experiments with garden peas that led to the discovery, in 1865, of the basic laws of heredity.

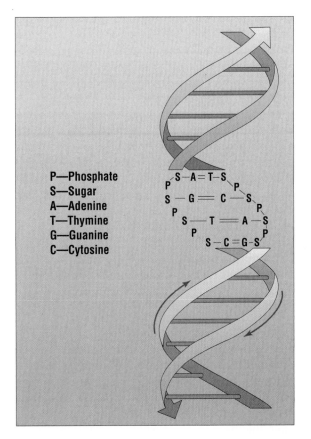

P—Phosphate
S—Sugar
A—Adenine
T—Thymine
G—Guanine
C—Cytosine

FIGURE 3.1
This diagrammatic representation of a portion of a deoxyribonucleic acid (DNA) molecule represents the double helix strands and the connecting nitrogenous base pairs. The helix strands are formed by alternating sugar and phosphate groups. The connection is produced by complementary bases—adenine with thymine, cytosine with guanine—as shown for a section of the molecule.

of deoxyribonucleic acid, or **DNA.** DNA is a complex molecule with an unusual shape, rather like two strands of a rope twisted around one another. The chemical bases that connect the two strands (Figure 3.1) constitute a code that contains information to direct the production of proteins. It is at this level that the development of certain traits occurs. The code directs the formation of such things as the protein that colors the iris of the eye (thereby determining eye color) or the hemoglobin molecule in red blood cells. Recently there has been great progress in cracking the genetic code, in a series of events as fascinating as any spy story.

DNA molecules have the unique property of being able to produce exact copies of themselves. Thus a copy can be made and passed to another organism; as long as no errors are made in the replication process, new organisms will contain genetic material exactly like that in ancestral organisms.

Genes

A gene is a segment of the DNA molecule containing several base pairs that directs the development of particular observable or identifiable traits. Thus, when we speak of the gene for a human

DNA. The genetic material, deoxyribonucleic acid; a complex molecule with information to direct the synthesis of proteins. DNA molecules have the unique property of being able to produce exact copies of themselves.

blood type in the A-B-O system, we are referring to the portion of a DNA molecule that contains the genetic code for the proteins that result in the attachment of different sugar molecules to certain other molecules carried on the surface of red blood cells, and which determine one's blood type. A gene, then, is not really a separate structure, as had once been imagined, but a location, like a dot on a map. These genes provide the blueprint for about 60,000 proteins that keep us alive and healthy. Interestingly, only about 10% of human DNA encodes proteins. As Jerold Lowenstein puts it, our DNA, "like daytime television, is nine-tenths junk."[1] The genes themselves are split by long stretches of this "junk" DNA which, in the course of producing proteins, is metaphorically "snipped out" and left on the "cutting room floor."

Chromosomes

DNA molecules do not float freely about in our bodies; they are located on structures called **chromosomes** found in the nucleus of each cell. Chromosomes are nothing more than long strands of DNA combined with protein to produce structures that can actually be seen under a conventional light microscope. Each kind of organism has a characteristic number of chromosomes, which are usually found in pairs. For example, the body cells of the fruit fly each contain four pairs of chromosomes; those of humans contain 23 pairs; those of some brine shrimp have as many as 160 pairs. The two chromosomes in each pair contain genes for the same traits. The gene for eye color, for instance, will be found on each chromosome of a particular pair, but there may be variant forms of these genes. One might be for brown and the other for blue eyes. Forms of genes that are located on paired chromosomes and that code for different versions of the same trait are called **alleles.**

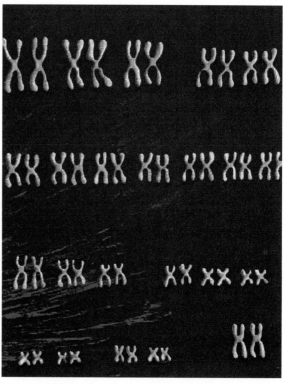

This is a photomicrograph of human chromosomes.

Cell Division

In order to grow and maintain good health, the body cells of an organism must divide and produce new cells. Cell division is initiated when the chromosomes, and hence the genes, replicate, forming a second pair that duplicates the original pair of chromosomes in the nucleus. To do this, the DNA metaphorically "unzips" between the base pairs—adenine from thymine and guanine from cytosine—following which each base on each now-single strand attracts its complementary base, reconstituting the second half of the double helix. Each new pair is surrounded by a membrane, and becomes the nucleus that directs the activities of a new cell. This kind of cell division is called **mitosis,** and it produces new cells that have exactly the same number of chromosome pairs, and hence genes, as did the parent cell.

---

[1]Lowenstein, J. M. (1992). Genetic surprises. *Discover,* *13*(12), 86.

Chromosome. In the cell nucleus, long strands of DNA combined with a protein that can be seen under the microscope. **> Alleles.** Alternate forms of a single gene **> Mitosis.** A kind of cell division that produces new cells having exactly the same number of chromosome pairs, and hence genes, as the parent cell.

When new individuals are produced through sexual reproduction, the process involves the merging of two cells, one from each parent. If two regular body cells, each containing 23 pairs of chromosomes, were to merge, the result would be a new individual with 46 pairs of chromosomes; such an individual, if it lived at all, would surely be a monster. But this increase in chromosome number does not occur, because the sex cells that join to form a new individual are the product of a different kind of cell division, called **meiosis.**

Although meiosis begins like mitosis, with the replication and doubling of the original genes and chromosomes, it proceeds to divide that number into four new cells rather than two (Figure 3.2). Thus each new cell has only half the number

FIGURE 3.2
In cell division both mitosis (a) and meiosis (b) create new cells. However, in mitosis the new cell has the same number of chromosomes as the parent cell, while in meiosis there are half of the chromosomes. Chromosomes in blue originally came from one parent, those in pink from the other.

Meiosis. A kind of cell division that produces the sex cells, each of which has half the number of chromosomes, and hence genes, as the parent cell.

of chromosomes with their genes found in the parent cell. Human eggs and sperm, for example, have only 23 single chromosomes (half of a pair), whereas body cells have 23 pairs, or 46 chromosomes.

The process of meiotic division has important implications for genetics. Since paired chromosomes are separated, two different types of new cells will be formed; two of the four new cells will have one half of a pair of chromosomes, and the other two will have the second half of the original chromosome pair. At the same time, corresponding portions of one chromosome may "cross over" to the other one, somewhat scrambling the genetic material compared to the original chromosomes. Of course, none of this will make any difference if the original pair was **homozygous,** or identical in genetic material. For example, if in both chromosomes of the original pair the gene for blood type in the A-B-O system was represented by the allele for Type A blood, then all new cells will have the "A" allele. But if the original pair was **heterozygous,** with the "A" allele on one chromosome and the allele for Type O blood on the other, then half of the new cells will contain only the "O" allele; the offspring have a 50-50 chance of getting either one. It is impossible to predict any single individual's **genotype,** or genetic composition, but statistical probabilities can be established.

What happens when a child inherits the allele for Type O blood from one parent and that for Type A from the other? Will the child have blood of Type A, O, or some mixture of the two? Many of these questions were answered by Mendel's original experiments.

Mendel discovered that certain alleles are able to mask the presence of others; one allele is dominant, whereas the other is recessive. Actually, it is the traits that are dominant or recessive, rather than the alleles themselves; geneticists merely speak of dominant and recessive alleles for the sake of convenience. Thus, one might speak of the allele

for Type A blood as being dominant to the one for Type O. An individual whose blood type genes are heterozygous, with one "A" and one "O" allele, will have Type A blood. In other words the heterozygous condition (AO) will show exactly the same physical characteristic, or **phenotype,** as the homozygous (AA), even though the two have a somewhat different genetic composition, or genotype. Only the homozygous recessive genotype (OO) will show the phenotype of Type O blood.

The dominance of one allele does not mean that the recessive one is lost or in some way blended. A Type A heterozygous parent (AO) will produce sex cells containing both "A" and "O" alleles. Recessive alleles, such as that for albinism in humans, can be handed down for generations before they are matched with another recessive in the process of sexual reproduction and show up in the phenotype. The presence of the dominant allele simply renders the recessive allele inactive.

All of the traits Mendel studied in garden peas showed this dominant-recessive relationship, and so for some years it was believed that this was the only relationship possible. Later studies, however, have indicated that patterns of inheritance are not always so simple. In some cases, neither allele is dominant; they are both codominant. An example of codominance in human heredity can be seen also in the inheritance of blood types. Type A is produced by one allele; Type B by another. A heterozygous individual will have a phenotype of AB, since neither allele can dominate the other.

The inheritance of blood types points out another complexity of heredity. The number of alleles is by no means limited to two; certain traits have three or more allelic genes. Of course, only one allele can appear on each of the pairs of chromosomes, so each individual is limited to two alleles.

Another discovery is the fact that dominance need not always be complete. This is the case with the alleles for normal **hemoglobin** (the protein that

---

Homozygous. Refers to a chromosome pair that bears identical alleles for a single gene. **>** **Heterozygous.** Refers to a chromosome pair that bears different alleles for a single gene. **>** **Genotype.** The actual genetic makeup of an organism. **>** **Phenotype.** The physical appearance of an organism that may or may not reflect a particular genotype because the latter may or may not include recessive alleles. **>** **Hemoglobin.** The protein that carries oxygen in the red blood cells.

Sickle-cell anemia is caused by an abnormal hemoglobin, called hemoglobin S. Those afflicted by the disease are homozygous for the allele S; heterozygotes are not afflicted. Shown here is a sickle cell among normal red blood cells.

carries oxygen in the red blood cells) and the abnormal hemoglobin that is responsible for **sickle-cell anemia** in humans. Sickle-cell anemia occurs in individuals who are homozygous for a particular allele. In those with two such alleles, the red blood cells take on a characteristic sickle shape which, because they are more rapidly removed from circulation than normal cells, leads to anemia. To compound the problem, the sickle cells tend to clump together, blocking the capillaries and so causing tissue damage. Such individuals normally die before reaching adulthood. The homozygous dominant condition ($Hb^A Hb^S$; normal hemoglobin is

known as hemoglobin A, not to be confused with blood type A) produces only normal molecules of hemoglobin while the heterozygous condition ($Hb^A Hb^S$) produces some normal and some abnormal molecules; except under low-oxygen conditions, such individuals suffer no ill effects. Although the normal seems dominant to the abnormal, the dominance is incomplete, and therefore the other allele is not completely inactive. It is now believed that many instances in which phenotypes appear to indicate complete dominance may show incomplete dominance on the molecular level. We shall return to the sickle-cell condition later, for we now know that under certain conditions the heterozygous condition is actually more advantageous than is the "normal," homozygous condition.

Polygenetic Inheritance

So far, we have spoken as if the traits of organisms are single-gene traits, that is, the alleles of one particular gene determine one particular trait. Certainly this is the case with the A-B-O blood groups and some other things, but in humans, the most obvious traits are usually not single gene. Skin color, for example, is programmed by the action of many genes, each of which produces a small effect. In such cases, we speak of **polygenetic inheritance,** where two or more genes (as opposed to just two or more alleles) work together to effect one particular phenotypic character. Because so many genes are involved, each of which may have alternative alleles, it is difficult to unravel the genetic underpinnings of a trait like skin color. Theoretically, the observed range of variation in human skin color seems to require the presence of at least three, if not as many as six, separate genes, each of which produces a small additive effect.

POPULATION GENETICS

At the level of the individual, the study of genetics shows how traits are transmitted from one

---

Sickle-cell anemia.   An inherited form of anemia caused by the red blood cells assuming a sickled shape. **>** **Polygenetic inheritance.**   When two or more genes work together to effect a single phenotypic character.

generation to the next and enables a prediction about the chances that any given individual will display some phenotypic characteristic. At the level of the group, the study of genetics takes on additional significance, revealing mechanisms that support evolutionary interpretations of the diversity of life.

A key concept in genetics is that of the **population,** or a group of individuals within which breeding takes place. It is on the population level that natural selection takes place, as some members of the population produce more than their share of the next generation, while others produce less than their share. Thus, over a period of generations, the population shows a measure of adaptation to its environment due to this evolutionary mechanism.

THE STABILITY OF THE POPULATION

In theory, the characteristics of any given population should remain remarkably stable. And indeed, generation after generation, the bullfrogs in my farm pond, for example, look much alike, have the same calls, exhibit the same behavior when breeding. Another way to look at this remarkable consistency is to say that the **gene pool** of the population—the total number of different genes and alleles—seems to remain the same.

The theoretical stability of the gene pool of a population is not only easy to observe; it is also easy to understand. Mendel's experiments with garden peas, and all subsequent genetic experiments as well, have shown that, although some alleles may be dominant to others, the recessive alleles are not just lost or destroyed. Statistically, a heterozygous individual has a 50% chance of passing on to the next generation the dominant allele; he or she also has a 50% chance of passing on the recessive allele. The recessive allele may again be masked by the presence of a dominant allele in the

next generation, but it is there nonetheless and will be passed on again.

Since alleles are not "lost" in the process of reproduction, the frequency with which certain ones occur in the population should remain exactly the same from one generation to the next. The **Hardy-Weinberg Principle,** named for the English mathematician and the German physician who worked it out in 1908, demonstrates algebraically that the percentage of individuals that are homozygous for the dominant allele, homozygous for the recessive allele, and heterozygous will remain the same from one generation to the next provided that certain specified conditions are met: that mating is entirely random; that the population is sufficiently large for statistical averages to express themselves; that no new variants will be introduced into the population's gene pool; and that all individuals are equally successful at surviving and reproducing. In real life, however, these conditions are rarely met, as geographical, physiological, or behavioral factors may favor matings between certain individuals over others; as populations—on islands, for example—may be quite small; as new genetic variants may be introduced through mutation or gene flow; and as natural selection may favor the carriers of some alleles over others. Thus, changes in the gene pools of populations, without which there could be no evolution, can and do take place. Formally defined, **evolution** is a heritable change in genotype which becomes effective in the gene pool of a population.

FACTORS FOR CHANGE

Mutation

The ultimate source of change is **mutation** of genes. This amounts to an alteration of a gene that produces a new allele—one not inherited from an ancestor, but heritable by descendants. The fact is, every second that you read this page, the DNA in

---

> **Population.** In biology, a group of similar individuals that can and do interbreed. > **Gene pool.** The total genes of a population. > **Hardy-Weinberg Principle.** Demonstrates algebraically that the percentage of individuals that are homozygous for the dominant allele, homozygous for the recessive allele, and heterozygous should remain constant from one generation to the next, provided that certain specified conditions are met. > **Evolution.** A heritable change in genotype that becomes effective in the gene pool of a population. > **Mutation.** Chemical alteration of a gene that produces a new allele.

each cell of your body is being damaged.[2] Fortunately, DNA repair enzymes exist that constantly scan DNA for mistakes, slicing out damaged segments and patching up gaps. Were it not for this repair mechanism, we would have diseases like cancer at a much higher frequency than we do, and we would not get a faithful copy of our parental inheritance. Not only would we not live long, but our species would not exist for long. But because the repair mechanism itself is not perfect, not all mistakes are corrected; otherwise, there would be no possibility for evolution to occur.

Geneticists have calculated the rate at which various types of mutant genes appear. In human populations, they run from a low of about five mutations per million sex cells formed, in the case of a gene abnormality that leads to the absence of an iris in the eye, to a high of about 100 per million, in the case of a gene involved in a form of muscular dystrophy. (Note that the human male ejaculates hundreds of millions of sperm cells at a single time.) The average is about 30 mutants per million. Although mutations sometimes produce

---

[2]Culotta, E., & Koshland, D. E. Jr. (1994). DNA repair works its way to the top. *Science, 266*, 1926.

marked abnormalities, the great majority of them produce more subtle effects.

Research with a variety of organisms indicates that certain factors increase the rate at which mutations occur. These include a number of chemicals, such as some dyes, certain antibiotics, and some chemicals used in the preservation of food. Another important cause of increased mutation rates is irradiation. The ultraviolet rays of sunshine are capable of producing mutations, as are X rays. Radioactive rays have the same mutation-causing effect, as was so sadly demonstrated by the high rates of mutation found in the children of survivors of the Hiroshima and Nagasaki bombings.

In humans, as in all multicelled animals, the very nature of the genetic material itself ensures that mutations will occur. For instance, the fact that genes are split by stretches of "junk" DNA increases the chances that a simple editing mistake in the process of copying DNA will cause significant gene mutations. To cite one example, the gene for collagen (the main structural protein of the skin, bones, and teeth) is fragmented by no less than 50 segments of "junk" DNA. As a consequence, there are 50 chances for error each time the gene is copied. One result of this seemingly inefficient, if not dangerous situation is that it

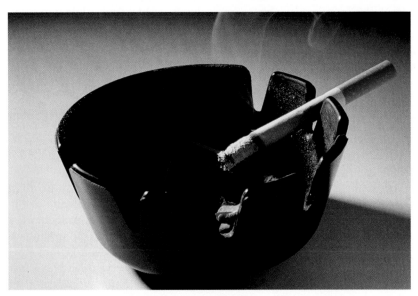

One of the most potent mutagenic agents known is tobacco smoke.

becomes possible to shuffle the gene segments themselves like a deck of cards, putting together new proteins with new functions. Although individuals may suffer as a result (the French artist Henri Toulouse-Lautrec's growth abnormality resulted from a mutation of the collagen gene), it does make it possible for an evolving species to adapt more quickly to a new environment. Another source of genetic remodeling from within is the movement of whole DNA sequences from one locality or chromosome to another. This may disrupt the function of other genes or, in the case of so-called "jumping genes," carry important functional messages of their own.

One recent finding is that humans have longer strings of repetitious DNA within and between genes than do other primates, so it is not surprising that we have a higher mutation rate. And a consequence of this is an increased incidence of such genetic diseases as Huntington's Disease and Fragile X Syndrome (a form of mental retardation).[3]

It is important to realize that mutations do not arise out of need for some new adaptation. Indeed, there is no tendency for the frequency of a particular mutation to correlate with the direction in which a population is evolving. They are purely chance events; what happens once they appear depends on whether or not they happen (by chance) to enhance the survival and reproductive success of the individuals who carry them.

GENETIC DRIFT

Each individual is subject to a number of chance events that determine life or death. For example, an individual squirrel in good health and possessed of a number of advantageous traits may be killed in a forest fire; a genetically well-adapted baby cougar may not live longer than a day if its mother gets caught in an avalanche, whereas the weaker offspring of a mother that does not die may survive. In a large population, such accidents of nature are unimportant; the accidents that preserve

French artist Henri Toulouse-Lautrec, whose growth abnormality resulted from a mutation of the collagen gene.

individuals with certain genes will be balanced out by the accidents that destroy them. However, in small populations, such averaging out may not be possible. Since human populations are so large, we might suppose that human beings are unaffected by chance events. While it is true that a rock slide which kills five campers whose home community has a total population of 100,000 is not statistically significant, a rock slide which killed five hunters from a small group of food foragers could significantly alter frequencies of alleles in the local gene pool. The average size of local groups of historically known food foragers (people who hunt, fish, and gather other wild foods for subsistence) varies between about 25 and 50.

Another sort of chance event may occur when an existing population splits up into two or more new ones, especially if one of these new populations is founded by a particularly small number of individuals. What this amounts to is a sampling error; in such cases, it is unlikely that the gene frequencies of the smaller population will duplicate those of the larger population. Even if a popula-

[3]Glausiusz, J. (1995). Micro gets macro. *Discover, 16*(11), 40.

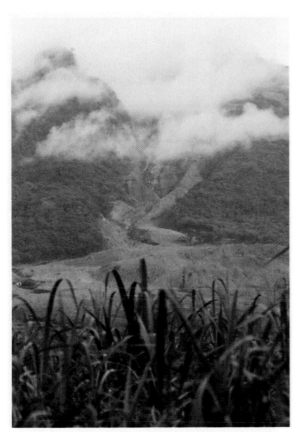

The 1998 Casitas Volcano mudslide in Nicaragua, triggered by the rains of Hurricane Mitch, buried a village, killing over 1,200 people. This is one kind of accident that can produce chance alterations of allele frequency in human gene pools.

tion does not split in this way, in a small population, the same sort of sampling error may occur as, by chance, parental alleles may not be passed on to the next generation in the same frequencies. If, for example, a person's genotype for blood type is AO, but he has only one offspring, only one of those alleles will be passed on.

The effect of chance events on the gene pool of small populations is called **genetic drift.** Genetic drift plays an important role in causing the sometimes bizarre characteristics found in animals in isolated island populations. It is also likely to have

been an important factor in human evolution, because until 10,000 years ago all humans were food foragers who probably lived in relatively small, self-contained populations.

GENE FLOW

Another factor that brings change to the gene pool of a population is **gene flow,** or the introduction of new alleles from nearby populations. Gene flow occurs when previously separated groups are once again able to interbreed, as, for example, when a river that once separated two populations of small mammals changes course. Migration of individuals or groups into the territory occupied by others may also lead to gene flow. This genetic change has been observed in several North American rodents that have been forced to leave their territory due to changes in environmental conditions. Gene flow has been an important factor in human evolution, both in terms of early human or near-human groups and in terms of current so-called racial variation. For example, the last 400 years have seen the establishment of a new phenotype throughout much of Central and South America as a result of the introduction into the native Indian gene pool of alleles from both the Spanish colonists and the Africans whom Europeans imported as slaves.

Although we think of gene flow as occurring between populations of related organisms, it has recently become apparent that it can, in fact, occur between unrelated organisms as well. In this case, though, it does not take place by interbreeding, but through other means. Such gene transfer is well known between different kinds of bacteria, but seems to take place even among vertebrate animals. In some cases, the agent of transfer can be a retrovirus, one of the most diverse and widespread infectious entities of vertebrates.[4]

---

[4]Amábile-Cuevas, C. F., & Chicurel, M. E. (1993). Horizontal gene transfer. *American Scientist, 81,* 338.

Genetic drift. Chance fluctuations of allele frequencies in the gene pool of a population. **> Gene flow.** The introduction of alleles from the gene pool of one population into that of another.

In Central America, gene flow between Native Americans (upper left), Spaniards (upper right), and Africans (lower left) has led to the emergence of a new phenotype (lower right).

How this takes place is depicted in Figure 3.3. Retroviruses are responsible for many diseases that affect humans, such as immunodeficiencies (including AIDS), hepatitis, anemias, and some neurological disorders.

NATURAL SELECTION

Although the factors discussed above may produce change in a population, that change would not necessarily make the population better adapted to its biological and social environment. By **adaptation** is meant both a process, by which organisms achieve a beneficial adjustment to an available environment, and the results of that process, the characteristics of organisms that fit them to the particular set of conditions of the environment in which they are generally found. Genetic drift, for example, often produces strange characteristics that have no survival value; mutant genes may be either helpful or harmful to survival, or simply neutral. It is the action of natural selection that makes evolutionary change adaptive.

Natural selection refers to the evolutionary process through which the environment exerts pressure that selects some individuals and not others to reproduce the next generation of the group. In other words, instead of a completely random selection of

---

Adaptation.   A process by which organisms achieve a beneficial adjustment to an available environment; and also the results of that process, the characteristics of organisms that fit them to the particular set of conditions of the environment in which they are generally found. > **Natural selection.**   The evolutionary process through which factors in the environment exert pressure that favors some individuals over others to produce the next generation.

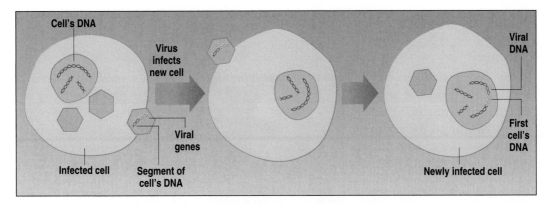

FIGURE 3.3
How viruses can transfer genetic material from one species to another.

individuals whose traits will be passed on to the next generation, there is selection by the forces of nature. In the process, the frequency of genetic variants for harmful or maladaptive traits within the population is reduced while the frequency of genetic variants for adaptive traits is increased.

In popular writing, natural selection is often thought of as "survival of the fittest," (a phrase Darwin never used), the idea being that the physically weak, being unfit, are eliminated from the population by disease, predation, or starvation. Obviously, the survival of the fittest has some bearing on natural selection; one need hardly point out that the dead do not reproduce. But there are many cases in which individuals survive, and even do quite well, but do not reproduce. They may be incapable of attracting mates, or they may be sterile, or they may produce offspring that do not survive after birth. For example, among the Uganda Kob, a kind of antelope native to eastern Africa, males that are unable to attract females form all-male herds in which they live out their lives. As members of a herd, they are reasonably well protected against predators, and so they may survive to relatively ripe old ages. They do not, however, pass their genes on to succeeding generations. This is an instance of natural selection at work, leading to different rates of reproduction for different types of individuals within a population. Change

brought about by natural selection in the frequency with which certain genetic variants appear in a population is actually a very slow process. For example, the present frequency of the sickle-cell allele is 0.05 in the entire U.S. population. A 5% reduction per generation (about 25 years) would take about 2,000 years to reach a frequency of 0.01, assuming complete selection against those homozygous for the allele. Yet given the great time span involved—life on earth has existed for 3 to 4 billion years—even such small and slow changes will have a significant cumulative impact on both the genotypes and phenotypes of any population.

Natural selection, as it acts to promote change in gene frequencies, is referred to as **directional selection.** Another form it may take is **stabilizing selection,** in which it acts to promote stability, rather than change. This occurs in populations which are already well adapted or where change would be disadvantageous. In humans, for instance, there has been no significant increase in brain size for the last 200,000 years or so. Stabilizing selection seems to be operating here, as the human birth canal is not adequate for the birth of larger-brained offspring. In cases where change is disadvantageous, natural selection will favor the retention of gene frequencies as they are. For this reason, the evolutionary history of most forms of

Directional selection.   Natural selection as it acts to promote change in a population's gene pool. **> Stabilizing selection.**   Natural selection as it acts to promote stability, rather than change, in a population's gene pool.

Charles R. Darwin (1809–1882)

Grandson of Erasmus Darwin (a physician, scientist, poet, and originator of a theory of evolution himself), Charles Darwin began the study of medicine at the University of Edinburgh. Finding himself unfitted for this profession, he then went to Christ's College, Cambridge, to study theology. Upon completion of his studies there, he took the position of naturalist and companion to Captain Fitzroy on the *HMS Beagle*, which was about to embark on an expedition to various poorly mapped parts of the world. The voyage lasted for close to 5 years, taking Darwin along the coasts of South America, over to the Galapagos Islands, across the Pacific to Australia, and then across the Indian and Atlantic oceans back to South America before returning to England. The observations he made on this voyage, and the arguments he had with the orthodox and dogmatic Fitzroy, had a powerful influence on the development of the ideas culminating in Darwin's most famous book, *On the Origin of Species*, which was published in 1859.

Contrary to what many people seem to think, Darwin did not "discover" or "invent" evolution. The general idea of evolution had been put forward by a number of writers, including his grandfather, long before Darwin's time. Nor is evolution a theory, as some people seem to believe, any more than gravity is a theory. To be sure, there are competing theories of gravity—the Newtonian and Einsteinian—that seek to explain its workings, but the evidence in favor of gravity is overwhelming. Similarly, the evidence in favor of evolution is overwhelming, even though there have been competing theories that seek to explain how it works.

Darwin's contribution was one such theory—that of evolution through natural selection. His was the theory that was best able to account both for change within species and for the emergence of new species in purely naturalistic terms. As is usually the case with pioneering ventures, there were flaws in Darwin's original theory. Today, we can say that Darwin's basic idea has stood the test of scientific scrutiny remarkably well, and the evidence in its favor is about as good as we had for the theory that the earth is spherical, until we were able to put up an astronaut who could see with his own eyes that this indeed is the case.

---

life is not one of constant change, proceeding as a steady, stately progression over vast periods of time; rather, it is one of prolonged periods of stability punctuated by shorter periods of change (or extinction) when altered conditions require new adaptations. According to the fossil record, most species survive somewhere between 3 and 5 million years.[5]

Discussions of the action of natural selection typically focus on anatomical or structural changes, such as the evolutionary change in the types of teeth found in primates; ample evidence (fossilized teeth, for example) exists to interpret such changes. By extrapolation, biologists assume that the same mechanisms work on behavioral traits as well. It seems reasonable that a hive of bees capable of communicating the location of nectar-bearing flowers would have a significant survival advantage over those that must search for food by trial and error. One biologist's simple example, in which money substitutes for fitness,

---

[5]Thomson, K. S. (1997). Natural selection and evolution's smoking gun. *American Scientist, 85,* 516.

An example of stabilizing selection: The brain of the modern skull on the left is no bigger than that in the c. 50,000-year-old skull on the right, even though the outer appearance of the skulls has changed.

illustrates how such cooperative behavior may come about:

> You are given a choice. Either you can receive $10 and keep it all or you can receive $10 million if you give $6 million to your next door neighbor. Which would you do? Guessing that most selfish people would be happy with a net gain of $4 million, I consider the second option to be a form of selfish behavior in which a neighbor gains an incidental benefit. I have termed such selfish behavior benevolent.[6]

Natural selection of beneficial social traits was probably a particularly important influence on human evolution, since in the primates, some degree of cooperative social behavior became important for food-getting, defense, and mate attraction.

ADAPTATION

As a consequence of the process of natural selection, those populations that do not become extinct generally become well adapted to their environments. Anyone who has ever looked carefully at the plants and animals that survive in the deserts

of the western United States can cite many instances of adaptation. For example, members of the cactus family have extensive root networks close to the surface of the soil, enabling them to soak up the slightest drop of moisture; they are able to store large quantities of water whenever it is available; they are shaped so as to expose the smallest possible surface to the dry air and are generally leafless as adults, thereby preventing water loss through evaporation; and a covering of spines discourages animals from chewing into the juicy flesh of the plant.

Desert animals are also adapted to their environment. The kangaroo rat can survive without drinking water; many reptiles live in burrows where the temperature is lower; most animals are nocturnal, or active only in the cool of the night. Many of the stories traditionally offered to explain observable cases of adaptation rely heavily on the purposeful acts of a world creator. The legend of Coyote and Wishpoosh (Chapter 1) is one such example; the belief popular among Europeans early in the 19th century that God created each animal separately to occupy a specific place in a hierarchical ladder of being is another.

The adaptability of organic structures and functions, no matter how much a source of wonder and fascination, nevertheless falls short of perfection. This is so because natural selection can only work with what the existing store of genetic variation provides; it cannot create something

---

[6]Nunney, L. (1998). Are we selfish, are we nice, or are we nice because we are selfish? *Science, 281,* 1619.

The moths shown in these two pictures are varieties of a single species. While the mottled brown variant is well-camouflaged on relatively clean tree trunks, it is readily visible on sooty tree trunks. The reverse is true for the black variant, which became especially common when coal fueled British industry.

entirely new. That exquisite design is not the rule is illustrated by the pains of aching backs, the annoyances of hernias, and problems with hemorrhoids that we humans must endure because the body of a four-footed vertebrate, designed for horizontal posture, has been "jury-rigged" to be held vertically above the two hind limbs. Furthermore, the structural alterations that enable us to walk erect have made it more difficult than it is for any other species of mammal to bear offspring. Yet, these defects have been perpetuated by natural selection, because they are outweighed by other aspects of human adaptation that enhance the reproductive success of the species as a whole.

THE CASE OF SICKLE-CELL ANEMIA

Among human beings, a particularly well-studied case of an adaptation paid for by the misery of many individuals brings us back to the case of sickle-cell anemia. Sickle-cell anemia first came to the attention of geneticists when it was observed that most North Americans who suffer from it are of African ancestry. Investigation traced the abnormality to populations that live in a clearly defined belt throughout central Africa (although brought to North America from central Africa, the abnormality also exists in some non-African populations, as will be noted below).

Geneticists were curious to know why such a deleterious hereditary disability persisted in these populations. According to the theory of natural selection, any alleles that are harmful will tend to disappear from the group, since the individuals who are homozygous for the abnormality generally die—are "selected out"—before they are able to reproduce. Why, then, had this seemingly harmful condition remained in populations from central Africa?

The answer to this mystery began to emerge when it was noticed that the areas in which sickle-cell anemia is prevalent are also areas in which falciparum malaria is common (Figure 3.4). This severe form of malaria causes high fevers that significantly interfere with the reproductive abilities of those who do not actually die from the disease. Moreover, it was discovered that the same hemoglobin abnormalities are found in residents of parts of the Arabian Peninsula, Greece, Algeria, and Syria as well as in certain East Indians, all of whom also live in regions where falciparum malaria is common. Further research established that the abnormal hemoglobin was associated with an increased ability to survive the effects of the malarial parasite; it seems that the effects of the abnormal hemoglobin in limited amounts were less injurious than the effects of the malarial parasite.

Thus, selection favored heterozygous individuals ($Hb^A Hb^S$). The loss of alleles for abnormal hemoglobin caused by the death of those ho-

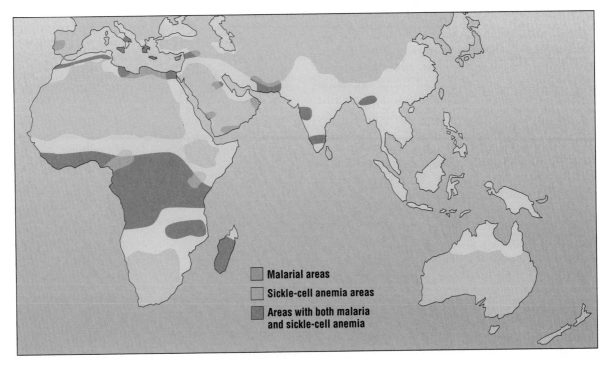

FIGURE 3.4

The allele that, in homozygotes, causes sickle-cell anemia makes heterozygotes resistant to falciparum malaria. Thus, the allele is most common in populations native to regions where this strain of malaria is common.

mozygous for it (from sickle-cell anemia) was balanced out by the loss of alleles for normal hemoglobin, as those homozygous for it experienced reproductive failure.

This example also points out how adaptations tend to be specific; the abnormal hemoglobin was an adaptation to the particular parts of the world in which the malarial parasite flourished. When Africans adapted to that region came to North America, where falciparum malaria is unknown, what had been an adaptive characteristic became an injurious one. Where there is no malaria to attack those with normal hemoglobin, the abnormal hemoglobin becomes comparatively disadvantageous. Although the rates of sickle-cell trait are still relatively high among African Americans— about 9% show the sickling trait—this represents a significant decline from the approximately 22% who are estimated to have shown the trait when the first slaves were brought from Africa. A further decline over the next several generations is to

be expected, as selection pressure continues to work against it.

This example also illustrates the important role culture may play even with respect to biological adaptation. In West Africa, falciparum malaria was not a significant problem until humans abandoned food foraging for farming a few thousand years ago. In order to farm, they had to clear areas of the natural forest cover. In the forest, decaying vegetation on the forest floor had imparted an absorbent quality to the ground so that the heavy rainfall of the region rapidly soaked into the soil. But once stripped of its natural vegetation, the soil lost this quality. Furthermore, the forest canopy was no longer there to break the force of the rainfall, and so the impact of the heavy rains tended to compact the soil further. The result was that stagnant puddles commonly formed after rains, and these were perfect for the breeding purposes of mosquitoes. Mosquitoes then began to flourish, and it is mosquitoes that carry the malarial parasite and inflict it on humans. Thus, humans unwittingly created the kind of environment that made a hitherto disadvantageous trait, the abnormal hemoglobin associated with sickle-cell anemia, advantageous.

Although it is true that all living organisms have many adaptive characteristics, it is not true that all characteristics are adaptive. All male mammals, for example, possess nipples, even though they serve no useful purpose. To female mammals, however, nipples are essential to reproductive success, which is why males have them. The two sexes are not separate entities, shaped independently by natural selection, but are variants upon a single ground plan, elaborated in later embryology. Precursors of mammary glands are built in all mammalian fetuses, enlarging later in the development of females, but remaining small and without function in males.

Nor is it true that current utility is a reliable guide to historical origin. For one thing, non-adaptive characters may be co-opted for later utility following origins as developmental consequences of changing patterns in embryonic and postnatal growth. The unusually large size of a kiwi's egg, for example, enhances the survivability of kiwi chicks, in that they are particularly large and capable when hatched. Nevertheless, kiwi eggs probably did not evolve such large size because it is adaptive. Kiwis evolved from large, Moa-sized ancestors, and in birds, egg size reduces at a slower rate than does body size. Therefore, the out-sized eggs of kiwi birds seem to be no more than a developmental byproduct of a reduction in body size.[7] Similarly, an existing adaptation may come under strong selective pressure for some new purpose, as did insect wings. These did not arise so that insects might fly, but rather as gills that were used to "row," and later skim, across the surface of the water.[8] Later, the larger ones by chance proved useful for purposes of flight. In both these cases, what we see is natural selection operating as "a creative scavenger,

This X-ray illustrates the unusually large size of a kiwi's egg.

taking what is available and putting it to new use."[9]

EVOLUTION OF POPULATIONS

One consequence of the process of natural selection is that a population may become increasingly well adapted to its environment. This kind of evolutionary change can be thought of as a refinement of the organism. As it moves from the rather generalized prototype to more and more specialized versions, the organism becomes better and better adapted; each new "model" replaces the old, in a process somewhat analogous to the changes that have been made to automobiles since their first appearance. Still, a car remains a car, no matter how "improved" the latest model may be; it has not been transformed into something radically different. The same principle holds for linear evolution (Figure 3.5, see p. 82). Ultimately, stabilizing selection is likely to take over, as available alleles reach their most adaptive frequencies in a species' gene pool. There will be little change thereafter, so long as the adaptation remains viable.

One important difference from the automobile analysis is that linear evolution does not represent a directed thrust of causality, but rather arises as a consequence of entirely random movement. Paleontologist Stephen Jay Gould explains:

[7]Gould, S. J. (1991). *Bully for brontosaurus* (pp. 109–123). New York: W. W. Norton.

[8]Kaiser, J. (1994). A new theory of insect wing origins takes off. *Science, 266,* 363.

[9]Doist, R. (1997). Molecular evolution and scientific inquiry, misperceived. *American Scientist, 85,* 475.

The Drunkard's Walk[10]

▲▼

The overall directionality in certain kinds of random motion—an apparent paradox to many—can best be illustrated by a paradigm known as the "drunkard's walk." A man staggers out of a bar dead drunk. He stands on the sidewalk in front of the bar, with the wall of the bar on one side and the gutter on the other. If he reaches the gutter, he falls down into a stupor and the sequence ends. Let's say that the sidewalk is 30 feet wide, and that our drunkard is staggering at random with an average of 5 feet in either direction for each stagger. (See Figure 3.6 for an illustration of this paradigm.) For simplicity's sake—since this is an abstract model and not the real world—we will say that the drunkard staggers in a single line only, either toward the wall or toward the gutter. He does not move at right angles along the sidewalk parallel to the wall and gutter.

Where will the drunkard end up if we let him stagger long enough and entirely at random? He will finish in the gutter—absolutely every time, and for the following reason: Each stagger goes in either direction with 50% probability. The bar wall at one side is a "reflecting boundary." If the drunkard hits the wall, he just stays there until a subsequent stagger propels him in the other direction. In other words, only one direction of movement remains open for continuous advance—toward the gutter. We can even calculate the average amount of time required to reach the gutter. (Many readers will have recognized this paradigm as just another way of illustrating a preferred result in coin tossing. Falling into the gutter on one unreversed trajectory, after beginning at the wall, has the same probability as flipping six heads in a row [one chance in sixty-four]—5 feet with each stagger, to reach the gutter in 30 feet. Start in any other position, and probabilities change accordingly. For example, once the drunkard stands in the middle, 15 feet from the wall, then three staggers in the same direction [one chance in eight for a single trajectory] put him into the gutter. Each stagger is independent of all others, so previous histories don't count, and you need to know only the initial position to make the calculation.)

FIGURE 3.6
The drunkard's walk.

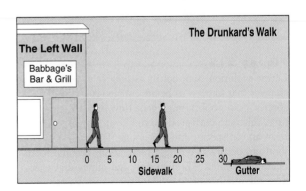

[10]Gould, S. J. (1996). *Full house: The spread of excellence from Plato to Darwin* (pp. 149–151). New York: Harmony Books.

I bring up this old example to illustrate but one salient point: In a system of linear motion structurally constrained by a wall at one end, random movement, with no preferred directionality whatever, will inevitably propel the average position away from a starting point at the wall. The drunkard falls into the gutter every time, but his motion includes no trend whatever toward this form of perdition. Similarly, some average or extreme measure of life might move in a particular direction even if no evolutionary advantage, and no inherent trend, favor that pathway.

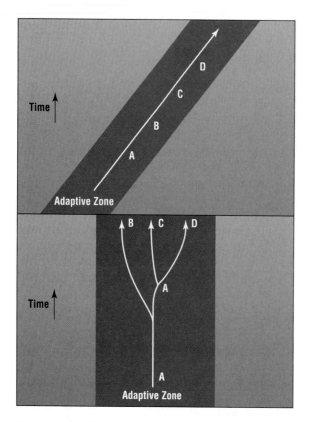

FIGURE 3.5

Linear evolution (top) occurs as relatively small scale changes that happen to be advantageous accumulate in a species' gene pool through gene flow and selection. Over time, this map may produce sufficient change to transform an old species into a new one. Divergent evolution (bottom) occurs as different populations become reproductively isolated. Through drift and differential selection, the number of descendant species increases.

Ironically, a species may become extinct if it becomes too well adapted. If the environment changes for some reason, those organisms most highly adapted to the old environment will have the greatest difficulty surviving in a new one. Such changes took place a number of times during the course of vertebrate evolution; one of the most dramatic examples was the sudden extinction of the dinosaurs. In such cases, it is usually the more generalized organisms that survive; later they may give rise to new lines of specialists.

But not all evolution is a linear progression from one form to more specialized forms of the same type. Evolution is also **divergent,** or branching (Figure 3.5 bottom). This happens when a single ancestral species gives rise to two or more descendant species. Divergent evolution is probably responsible for much of the diversity of life to be observed today. Evolution may also be **convergent,** when two dissimilar forms develop greater similarities; birds and bats, for example. Convergent evolution takes place in circumstances where an environment exerts similar pressures on different organisms, so that unrelated species become more like one another. Because evolution can take so many different courses, it is often difficult to reconstruct the sequence of events that led to the emergence of any given group or species, especially when that evidence, such as fossil remains, is often fragmentary and incomplete. We are fortunate, though, in that the fossil record for human evolution is particularly rich.

Divergent evolution.   An evolutionary process in which an ancestral population gives rise to two or more descendant populations that differ from one another. **>** **Convergent evolution.**   A process in which two phylogenetically unrelated organisms develop greater similarities.

SPECIATION

Both linear and divergent evolution can result in the establishment of a new **species**. The term *species* is usually defined as a population or group of populations that is mechanically capable of interbreeding and reproductively isolated from other such populations. Thus the bullfrogs in my farm pond are the same species as those in my neighbor's pond, even though the two populations may never actually interbreed; in theory, they are capable of it if they are brought together. This definition is not altogether satisfactory, because isolated populations may be in the process of evolving into different species, and it is hard to tell exactly when they become separate. For example, all dogs belong to the same species, but a male Saint Bernard and a female Chihuahua are not capable of producing offspring; even if they could somehow manage the feat of copulation, the Chihuahua would die trying to give birth to such large pups. On the other hand, Alaskan sled dogs are able to breed with wolves, even though they are of different species. In nature, however, wolves most often mate with their own kind. Although all species definitions are relative rather than absolute, the modern concept of species puts more stress on the question of whether breeding actually takes place in the wild than on the more academic question of whether breeding is technically feasible.

Populations within species that are quite capable of interbreeding but may not regularly do so are called **races**, or subspecies. Evolutionary theory suggests that species evolve from races through the accumulation of differences in the gene pools of the separated groups. This can happen, however, only in situations where one race is isolated from others of its species for prolonged periods of time. There is nothing inevitable about races evolving into new species. Because they are by definition genetically open—that is, members of different races are capable of interbreeding—races are impermanent and subject to reamalga-

mation. This is precisely what happens as long as gene flow remains open.

In the case of humans, as we shall see in Chapter 13, the race concept is difficult to apply. For one thing, the human propensity for gene flow makes the definition of biological races particularly arbitrary; for another, there has been a deplorable tendency to confuse cultural with biological phenomena under the heading of "race."

ISOLATING MECHANISMS

Certain factors, known as **isolating mechanisms**, separate breeding populations, leading to the appearance first of divergent races and then divergent species. This happens as mutations may appear in one of the isolated populations but not in the other, as genetic drift affects the two populations in different ways, and as selective pressures may come to differ slightly in the two places. Because isolation prevents gene flow, changes that affect the gene pool of one population cannot be introduced into the gene pool of the other.

Some isolating mechanisms are geographical, preventing travel, hence gene flow, between members of separated populations. Anatomical structure can also serve as an isolating mechanism, as we saw in the case of the Saint Bernard and the Chihuahua. Other physical isolating factors include early miscarriage of the offspring; weakness or presence of maladaptive traits that cause early death in the offspring; or, as in the case of horses and asses, sterility of the hybrid offspring (mules).

Although physical barriers to reproduction may develop in geographical isolation, as genetic differences accumulate in the gene pools of separate populations, they may also result from accidents as cells undergo meiosis. In the course of such accidents genetic material may be broken off, transposed, or transferred from one chromosome to another. Even a relatively minor mutation, if it involves a gene that regulates the growth and

---

Species.   In biology, a population or group of populations that is capable of interbreeding, but that is reproductively isolated from other such populations. > **Race.**   In biology, a population of a species that differs in the frequency of some allele or alleles from other populations of the same species. > **Isolating mechanisms.**   Factors that separate breeding populations, creating divergent races and ultimately (if maintained) divergent species.

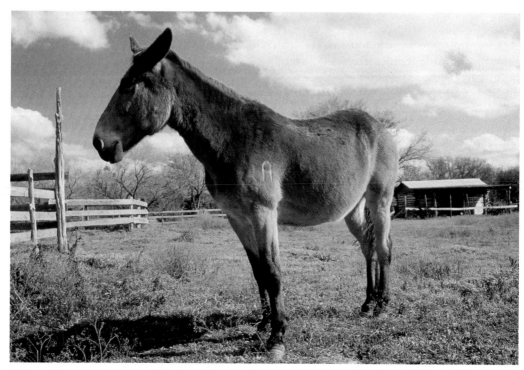

Although horses and asses (two separate species) can mate and produce live offspring (mules, pictured here), sterility of mules maintains the reproductive isolation of the parental species.

development of an organism, may have a major effect on its adult form.

Isolating mechanisms may also be social rather than physical. Speciation due to this mechanism is particularly common among birds. For example, cuckoos (birds that do not build nests of their own but lay their eggs in other birds' nests) attract mates by mimicking the song of the bird species whose nests they usurp; thus cuckoos that are physically capable of mating may have different courtship behavior, which effectively isolates them from others of their kind.

Social isolating mechanisms are thought to have been important factors in human evolution. They continue to play a part in the maintenance of so-called racial barriers. Although mating is physically possible between any two mature humans of the opposite sex, awareness of social and cultural differences often makes the idea distasteful, perhaps even unthinkable; in India, for example, someone of an upper caste would not think of marrying an "untouchable." This isolation results from the culturally implanted concept of a significant difference between "us" and "them." Yet, as evidenced by the blending of human populations that has so often taken place in the world, people are also capable of suspending or even reasoning away social isolating mechanisms that would, in the case of other animals, lead separate races to evolve into separate species. Such speciation is extremely unlikely in *Homo sapiens*.

THE NONDIRECTEDNESS OF EVOLUTION

In the popular mind, evolution is often seen as leading in a predictable and determined way from one-celled organisms, through various multicelled forms, to humans, who occupy the top rung of a "ladder of progress." To be sure, one-celled organisms appeared long before multicellular forms, but the latter could hardly develop before the basic structure of the cell existed. Furthermore, single-celled organisms were not replaced by multicellular descendants, but remain today as in the past the dominant forms of life. They exist in greater numbers and diversity than all forms of multicellular life, and live in all habitats accessible to *any* form of life.[11]

[11]Ibid., pp. 176–195.

 The Practical Importance of Evolution

So fundamental to the organization of life is evolution that its applications go far beyond anthropology to all biological science. To illustrate, consider the following, extracted from an editorial in *Science*, the premier scientific journal of North America:*

Evolution is now widely perceived and appreciated as the organizing principle at all levels of life. This principle so pervades research that the evolutionary underpinning of many experimental approaches is unstated. For example, studies in the developmental genetics of fruit flies led to the discovery of genes that control development in all segmented organisms. Protein alignments are used to identify conserved amino acid residues that are potentially important to function. Even the hierarchical use of model organisms, from bacteria to humans, in biomedical testing and research is implicitly based on a recognition that the same building blocks underlie all life and that levels of increasing similarity are nested.

Today, the study of evolution is motivated by the human drive to understand the world and our place in it. But the field has now become socially and economically relevant. Heavy use of pesticides and antibiotics has fostered the evolution of resistant pathogens and pests. Phylogenies (the underpinnings of evolutionary theory) are used to track infectious diseases, and they have just been admitted into Louisiana criminal courts to infer sources of HIV transmission. [Phylogenies are evolutionary genealogies.] Drug development makes use of "directed" evolution, using in vitro selection, mutation, and recombination— some of nature's evolutionary mechanisms—to find molecules for specific tasks. Bioremediation exploits the evolution of novel functions in microbes to clean up toxic waste. Do we face future challenges from evolution in genetically engineered organisms or from bioterrorists producing new capabilities in pathogenic microbes?

Evolutionary biology continues to face the social and legal opposition it has experienced since before the Scopes trial. It is viewed by some as a threat to cultural values and has been misused by others to condone bad behavior. Nonetheless, the science continues to advance profoundly, solving public health and environmental problems far beyond anything imaginable even a generation ago. However, at a time when evolution is the unifying fabric of biology, it is barely mentioned in some high school textbooks and classrooms. Will the next generation of scientists be prepared to exploit these advances?

*Bull, J. J., & Wichman, H. A. (1998). A revolution in evolution. *Science*, 281, 1959.

As for humans, we are indeed recent arrivals in the world (though not as recent as some new strains of bacteria), but our appearance—like that of any kind of organism—was made possible only as a consequence of a whole string of historical accidents. To cite but one example: About 65 million years ago, some sort of extraterrestrial body slammed into earth where the Yucatan Peninsula now exists, so disrupting the world's climate as to cause the extinction of the dinosaurs (not to mention numerous other species as well). For 100 million years, dinosaurs had ruled most terrestrial environments available for vertebrate animals, and would probably have continued to do so were it not for this event. Although mammals appeared at about the same time as reptiles, they existed as small, inconspicuous creatures that an observer from outer space would probably have dismissed as insignificant. But with the demise of the dinosaurs, all sorts of opportunities became available, and mammals began their great expansion into new niches, including the one in which our own ancestors evolved. So it is that an essentially random event—the collision with a comet or asteroid—made possible our own existence. Had it not happened, or had it happened at some other time (before the existence of mammals), we would not be here, and there would probably be no consciously intelligent life on earth.[12]

The history of any species is an outcome of many such contingencies. At any point in the chain of events, had any one element been different, the final result would be markedly different. As Stephen Jay Gould puts it: "All evolutionary sequences include . . . a fortuitous series of accidents with respect to future evolutionary success. Human brains and bodies did not evolve along a direct and inevitable ladder, but by a circuitous and tortuous route carved by adaptations evolved for different reasons, and fortunately suited to later needs."[13]

The history of life is not one of progressive advancement in complexity; if anything, it is one of proliferation of enormously varied designs which subsequently have been restricted to a few

---

[12]Gould, S. J. (1985). *The flamingo's smile: Reflections in natural history* (p. 409). New York: W. W. Norton.
[13]Ibid., p. 410.

For more than 260 million years, dinosaurs were the dominant land vertebrates. The later success of mammals was made possible by a chance event: the collision with earth of an asteroid or comet, the effects of which brought about the dinosaurs' extinction.

highly successful forms. Even at that, imperfections remain. As Gould so aptly puts it:

> Our world is not an optimal place, fine tuned by omnipotent forces of selection. It is a quirky mass of imperfections, working well enough (often admirably); a jury-rigged set of adaptations built of

curious parts made available by past histories in different contexts.[14]

_____

[14]Ibid., p. 54.

CHAPTER SUMMARY

Evolution may be defined as a heritable change in genotype which becomes effective in the gene pool of a population. Genes, the actual units of heredity, are portions of molecules of DNA (deoxyribonucleic acid), a complex molecule resembling two strands of rope twisted around one another. The way smaller molecules are arranged in this giant molecule is actually a code that contains information to direct the synthesis of proteins. DNA molecules have the unique property of being able to produce exact copies of themselves. As long as no errors are made in the process of replication, new organisms will contain genetic material exactly like that in ancestral organisms. A gene is a unit of the DNA molecule that directs the development of identifiable traits, for example, blood type. Human DNA provides the blueprint for about 60,000 proteins that keep us alive and healthy.

DNA molecules are located on chromosomes, structures found in the nucleus of each cell. Each kind of organism has a characteristic number of chromosomes, which are usually found in pairs. Humans have 23 pairs. Genes that are located on paired chromosomes and coded for different versions of the same trait are called alleles.

Mitosis, one kind of cell division, begins when the chromosomes (hence the genes) replicate, forming a second pair that duplicates the original pair of chromosomes in the nucleus. It results in new cells with exactly the same number of chromosome pairs as the parent cell. Meiosis, a different kind of cell division, results from sexual reproduction. It begins with the replication of original chromosomes, but these are divided into four cells, each containing 23 single chromosomes.

The Austrian monk Gregor Mendel studied the mechanism of inheritance with garden peas. He discovered that some alleles are able to mask the presence of others. They are called dominant. The allele not expressed is recessive. The allele for Type A blood in humans, for example, is dominant to the allele for Type O blood.

Phenotype refers to the physical characteristics of an organism, whereas genotype refers to its genetic composition. Two organisms may have the same phenotype, but different genotypes.

A key concept is that of population, or a group of similar individuals within which most breeding takes place. It is populations, rather than individuals, that evolve. The total number of different genes and alleles available to a population is called its gene pool. The frequency with which certain genes occur in the same gene pool theoretically remains the same from one generation to another; this is known as the Hardy-Weinberg Principle. Nonetheless, change does take place in gene pools as a result of several factors.

The ultimate source of genetic change is mutation. These are accidents that cause changes in sequences of DNA. Although mutations are inevitable given the nature of cellular chemistry, extrinsic factors, such as heat, certain chemicals, or various kinds of radiation can increase the mutation rate.

The effects of chance events (other than mutations) on the gene pool of a small population is called genetic drift. Genetic drift may have been an important factor in human evolution because until 10,000 years ago all humans probably lived in relatively small populations. Another factor that brings change to the gene pool of a population is gene flow, or the introduction of new variants of genes from nearby populations. Gene flow occurs when previously separated groups are able to breed again. It may also occur as retroviruses transfer DNA from members of one species to those of another.

Natural selection is the force that makes evolutionary change adaptive. It reduces the frequency of alleles for harmful or maladaptive traits within a population and increases the frequency of alleles for adaptive traits. By adaptation is meant both the process by which organisms achieve a beneficial adjustment to an available environment, and the results of the process, the characteristics of organisms that fit them to the particular set of conditions of the environment in which they are generally found. A well-studied example of adaptation through natural selection in humans is inheritance of the trait for sickling red blood cells. The sickle-cell trait, caused by the inheritance of an abnormal form of hemoglobin, is an adaptation to life in regions in which falciparum malaria is common. In these regions, the sickle-cell trait plays a beneficial role, but in other parts of the world, the sickling trait is no longer advantageous, while the associated sickle-cell anemia remains injurious. Geneticists predict that as malaria is brought under control, within several generations, there will be a decline in the number of individuals who carry the allele responsible for the sickle-cell anemia.

Evolution is the process whereby organisms change into a new form from a previous form. Evolution is not a linear progression but rather the outcome of random changes that, in hindsight, may appear linear. It may be divergent, or branching; or convergent, where two dissimilar forms develop similarities.

A species is a population or a group of populations that is mechanically capable of interbreeding. The concept of species is relative rather than absolute; whether breeding actually takes place in the wild or not is more important than the academic question of whether it is technically feasible. Populations within species that are capable of interbreeding but do so to a limited extent are called races. While species are reasonably discreet and stable units in nature, races are impermanent and subject to reamalgamation.

Isolating mechanisms serve to separate breeding populations, creating first divergent races and then (if isolation continues) divergent species. Isolating mechanisms can be geographical; physical, as in the differing anatomical structures of the Saint Bernard and Chihuahua; or social, such as in the caste system of India.

Evolution is not a "ladder of progress" leading in a predictable and determined way to ever more complex forms. Rather, it has produced, through a series of accidents, a diversity of enormously varied designs which subsequently have been restricted to a lesser number of still-less-than-perfect forms.

POINTS FOR CONSIDERATION

1. Commonly held are the ideas that individual creatures were created/designed by some divine power to fit their specific niches in the world, or that all living things undergo a process of continual refinement and improvement called "evolution." How do these two views resemble each other, and how do they differ from the anthropologist's view of the process of evolution?

2. Members of the Hapsburgian royal family shared certain genetic characteristics which resulted in the trait of hemophilia (a condition in which the blood does not clot properly around a wound). What factors allowed this disadvantageous trait to continue to manifest itself in the family, rather than being bred out, and what does it say about the power of culture to interfere with or enhance the underlying "engines" of evolution?

3. Consider the concepts *evolution, survival of the fittest, natural selection, adaptation,* and *mutation.* They are used interchangeably by many people; however, they have very specific meanings within anthropology. How do they differ from each other, and why are they all useful terms, as defined within anthropology?

4. What is the significance of the heterozygous genotype in terms of adaptation and the success of a species? Is it a benefit or a liability? Are such terms even valid?

SUGGESTED READINGS

Berra, T. M. (1990). *Evolution and the myth of creationism.* Stanford, CA.: Stanford University Press.

Written by a zoologist, this book is a basic guide to the facts in the debate over evolution. It is not an attack on religion, but a successful effort to assist in understanding the scientific basis for evolution.

Cavalli-Sforza, L. L. (1977). *Elements of human genetics.* Menlo Park, CA: Benjamin.

A short book for those who want to know something about genetics, and who would like basic genetic principles discussed from a "human" angle.

Edey, M. A., & Johanson, D. (1989). *Blueprints: Solving the mystery of evolution.* Boston: Little, Brown.

This book is about the evolution of the idea of evolution, told as a scientific detective story. As much about the discoverers of evolution as it is about their discoveries, the book provides insights into the workings of science and gives readers the information they need to ponder the significance of our newfound ability, through genetic engineering, to actually direct the evolution of living things, including ourselves.

Gould, S. J. (1991). *Bully for Brontosaurus: Reflections in Natural History.* New York: Norton.

A collection of Gould's essays from *Natural History* magazine, in which he ranges over various issues in evolutionary biology. No one is better at explaining how evolution works, or exposing common fallacies, than Gould. Collections of his earlier essays, also highly recommended, are *Ever Since Darwin, The Panda's Thumb, Hens' Teeth and Horses' Toes,* and *The Flamingo's Smile.*

Gould, S. J. (1996). *Full house: The spread of excellence from Plato to Darwin.* New York: Harmony.

In this highly readable book, Gould explodes the misconception that evolution is inherently progressive. In the process, he shows how trends should be read as changes in variation within systems.

Woodward, V. (1992). *Human heredity and society.* St. Paul, MN: West.

Written for college students, this book discusses the implications of our knowledge of modern genetics for public policy. Concerned with the rise of interest in genetic engineering for the fixing of social ills, Woodward's premise is that it is as important to know what genes *aren't,* as what they are.

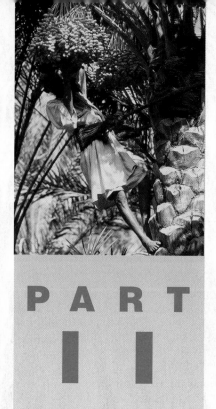

PART II

PRIMATE EVOLUTION AND THE EMERGENCE OF THE HOMININES

Chapter 4
MONKEYS, APES, AND HUMANS: THE MODERN PRIMATES

Chapter 5
FOSSIL PRIMATES

Chapter 6
THE EARLIEST HOMININES

Introduction

In Chapter 1, we saw how the Nez Perce Indians of North America explained their existence in the world. Indeed, all human cultures of which we have record have grappled with such age-old questions as: Where do we come from? What is our place in the overall scheme of things? Each culture has answered these questions in its own way, through bodies of myth and folklore, as did the Nez Perce. It was not until the twentieth century that hard scientific evidence was available to apply to these questions. In particular, as physical anthropologists and archaeologists have unearthed the bones and tools of our earliest ancestors, we have begun to glimpse the outline of a fantastic saga in which a tropics-dwelling apelike creature is transformed into a creative being capable of inventing solutions to problems of existence, rather than passively accepting what the environment and its own biology dictate.

This section of the book discusses developments that set the stage for this transformation. We begin, in Chapter 4, with a review of the modern primates (the zoological order to which humans belong), in order to understand how we humans are like the other primates. In particular, we can begin to appreciate that many of the physical characteristics we think of as distinctively human are simply exaggerated versions of characteristics common to other primates. For example, primate brains tend to be large and heavy relative to body size and weight; in humans, this trait is realized to a greater degree than it is in other primates. We can begin to appreciate as well the kind of behavioral versatility of which present-day members of this order are capable. In the range of modern primate behavior patterns, we find clues to patterns that were characteristic of primates that lived in the past, from which humans descended.

Knowledge of the modern primates sets the stage for a review of the fossil evidence for primate evolution. In Chapter 5, the important fossils are interpreted in light of evolutionary theory, our understanding of the biological variation of modern primates, and the behavioral correlates of that variation. This brings us to the apelike creatures of 8 to 16 million years ago, from some of which human ancestors evolved. Our early apelike ancestors seem to have spent more and more time on the ground, and probably possessed mental abilities more or less equivalent to those of modern great apes. Because they were small and vulnerable, we think that the greatest measure of reproductive success came to those that were able to rear up on their hind limbs and scan the savanna, threaten predators with their forelimbs, transport food to a tree or other place where it could be eaten in relative safety, and transport offspring instead of relying on them to hang on by themselves, all the while managing to keep cool in the heat of the day.

With the appearance by 4 million years ago of *Australopithecus,* one of the earliest true hominines, the stage was set for the human transformation. *Australopithecus* may best be thought of as an apelike human; it walked bipedally in a fully human manner, but its mental abilities do not seem to have differed greatly from those of its ancestors of a few million years earlier. This implies essentially apelike behavior patterns, and it is appropriate to complete this section of the book with a chapter on *Australopithecus.*

Chapter 4
MONKEYS, APES, AND HUMANS: THE MODERN PRIMATES

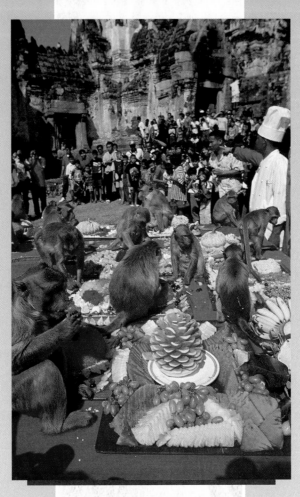

MONKEYS AND APES HAVE LONG FASCINATED HUMANS,
OWING TO THEIR MANY ANATOMICAL AND BEHAVIORAL
RESEMBLANCES TO US. THIS IS EXEMPLIFIED HERE BY
TEMPLE MONKEYS IN THAILAND PARTAKING OF AN
ANNUAL MONKEY FEAST. THE STUDY OF OTHER PRIMATES
PROVIDES US WITH IMPORTANT CLUES AS TO WHAT LIFE
MAY HAVE BEEN LIKE FOR OUR OWN ANCESTORS.

Chapter Preview

What Is the Place of Humanity Among the Other Animals?

Humans are classified by biologists as belonging to the primate order, a group that also includes lemurs, lorises, tarsiers, monkeys, and apes. They are so classified on the basis of shared characteristics of anatomy, physiology, protein structure, and even the genetic material itself. Among the primates, humans resemble monkeys, but most closely resemble apes.

What Are the Implications of the Shared Characteristics Between Humans and the Other Primates?

The similarities on which the modern classification of animals is based are indicative of evolutionary relationships. Therefore, by studying the anatomy, physiology, and molecular structure of the other primates, we can gain a better understanding of what human characteristics we owe to our general primate ancestry, and what traits are uniquely ours as humans. Such studies indicate that many of the differences between apes and humans are differences of degree rather than kind.

Why Do Anthropologists Study the Social Behavior of Monkeys and Apes?

By studying the behavior of apes and monkeys living today—especially those most closely related to us—we may find essential clues from which to reconstruct the adaptations and behavior patterns involved in the emergence of our earliest ancestors.

All living creatures, be they great or small, fierce or timid, active or inactive, face a fundamental problem in common—that of survival. Simply put, unless they are able to adapt themselves to some available environment, they cannot survive. Adaptation requires the development of behavior patterns that will help an organism utilize the environment to its advantage—to find food and sustenance, avoid hazards, and, if the species is to survive, reproduce its own kind. In turn, organisms need to have the biological equipment that makes possible the development of appropriate patterns of behavior. For the hundreds of millions of years that life has existed on earth, biological adaptation has been the primary means by which the problem of survival has been solved. This is accomplished as those organisms of a particular kind whose biological equipment is best suited to a particular way of life produce more offspring than those whose equipment is not so adapted. In this way, advantageous characteristics become more common in succeeding generations, while less advantageous ones become less common.

In this chapter, we will look at the biological equipment possessed by the primates, the group of animals to which humans belong. By doing so, we will gain a firmer understanding of those characteristics we share with other primates, as well as those that distinguish us from them, and make us distinctively human. We shall also sample the behavior made possible by the biological equipment of primates. The study of that behavior is important to help us understand something of the origins of human culture and the origin of humanity itself.

▲▽▲▽▲▽▲▽▲▽▲▽▲▽▲▽▲▽▲▽▲▽▲▽▲▽▲▽▲▽▲

THE CLASSIFICATION SYSTEM

In order to understand the exact place of humanity among the animals, it is helpful to describe briefly the system used by biologists to classify living things. The basic system was devised by the 18th-century Swedish naturalist Carl von Linné. The purpose of the Linnaean system was simply to create order in the great mass of confusing biological data that had accumulated by that time. Von Linné—or Linnaeus, as he is generally called—classified living things on the basis of overall similarities into small groups, or species. Modern classification has gone a step further by distinguishing superficial similarities between organisms—called **analogies**—from basic ones—called **homologies**. The latter are possessed by organisms that share a common ancestry; even though homologous structures may serve different functions (the arm of a human and the forefoot of a dog, for instance), they arise in similar fashion and pass through similar stages in embryonic development prior to their ultimate differentiation. By contrast, analogous structures look similar and may serve the same purpose (the wings of birds and bats, for example), but they are built from different parts, do not pass through similar stages in embryonic development, nor do the organisms share a common ancestry.

On the basis of homologies, groups of like species are organized into larger, more inclusive groups, called **genera** (the singular term is genus). The characteristics on which Linnaeus based his system were the following:

1. *Body structure:* A Guernsey cow and a Holstein cow are of the same species because they have identical body structure. A cow and a horse do not.
2. *Body function:* Cows and horses bear their young in the same way. Although they are of different species, they are closer than either cows or horses are to chickens, which lay eggs and have no mammary glands.
3. *Sequence of bodily growth:* Both cows and chickens give birth to—or hatch out of the egg—fully formed young. They are therefore more closely related to each other than either one is to the frog, whose tadpoles undergo a series of changes before attaining adult form.

Analogies. In biology, structures that are superficially similar; the result of convergent evolution. > **Homologies.** In biology, structures possessed by two different organisms that arise in similar fashion and pass through similar stages during embryonic development. The two structures may or may not be similar in adults, but have evolved from a common ancestral stock. > **Genera; genus.** In the system of plant and animal classification, a group of like species.

Birds and bats exemplify analogy: Both have wings that are used for flight, but the wings are built differently.

Modern taxonomy (scientific classification) is based on more than body structure, function, and growth. One must also compare chemical reactions of blood, protein structure, and even the genetic material itself. Even comparison of parasites is useful, for they tend to show the same degree of relationship as the forms they infest.

Through careful comparison and analysis, Linnaeus and those who have come after him have been able to classify specific animals into a series of larger and more inclusive groups up to the largest and most inclusive of all, the animal kingdom. In Table 4.1 are the main categories of the Linnaean system applied to the classification of the human species, with some of the more important distinguishing features noted for each category.

(Other categories of primates will be dealt with later in this chapter.)

THE PRIMATE ORDER

The primate order is only one of several mammalian orders, such as rodents, carnivores, ungulates (hoofed mammals), and so on. As such, primates share a number of features with other mammals. Generally speaking, mammals are intelligent animals, having more in the way of brains than reptiles or other kinds of vertebrates. In most species, the young are born live, the egg being retained within the womb of the female until it

An example of homology: Fish have gills but humans do not. Gill structures do develop in the human embryo but are modified to serve other purposes. From the rudimentary, gill-like structures are built such things as the jaw, bones of the inner ear, thymus, and parathyroid glands.

TABLE 4.1	Classification of Humans	
Kingdom	Animals	Do not make their own food, but depend on intake of living food.
Phylum	Chordata	Have at some stage gill slits as well as **notochord** (a rodlike structure of cartilage) and a nerve chord running along the back of the body.
Subphylum*	Vertebrata	Notochord replaced by vertebral column ("backbone") to form internal skeleton along with skull, ribs, and limb bones.
Class	Mammalia	Maintain constant body temperature; young nourished after birth by milk from mother's mammary glands.
Order	Primates	Hands and feet capable of grasping; tendency to erect posture with head balanced on spinal column; acute development of vision rather than sense of smell; tendency to larger brains.
Family	Hominidae	More rigid bodies, longer arms than other primates, ability to hang vertically from arms; 98% identical at the genetic level.
Subfamily	Homininae	Ground-dwelling with bipedal locomotion; more reliance on learned, as opposed to biologically determined, behavior.
Genus	*Homo*	Larger brains; reliance on cultural, as opposed to biological adaptation.
Species	*sapiens*	Brains of modern size; relatively small faces.

*Most categories can be expanded or narrowed by adding the prefix "sub" or "super." A family could thus be part of a superfamily, and in turn contain two or more subfamilies.

achieves an advanced state of growth. Once born, the young are nourished by their mothers with milk provided from the mammary glands, from which the class Mammalia gets its name. During this period of infant dependency, young mammals are able to learn some of the things that they will need for survival as adults.

Mammals are also active animals. This is made possible by their relatively constant body temperature, an efficient respiratory system featuring a separation between the nasal and mouth cavities, a diaphragm to assist in drawing in and letting out breath, and an efficient four-chambered heart that prevents mixing of oxygenated and deoxygenated blood. It is facilitated as well by a skeleton in which the limbs are positioned beneath the body, rather than out at the sides, for ease and economy of movement. The bones of the limbs have joints constructed so as to permit growth in the young while simultaneously providing strong, hard joint surfaces that will stand up to the stresses of sustained activity.

The skeleton of most mammals is simplified, compared to that of most reptiles, in that it has fewer bones. For example, the lower jaw consists of a single bone, rather than several. The teeth, however, are another matter. Instead of the relatively simple, pointed, peglike teeth of reptiles, mammals have special teeth for special purposes: incisors for nipping, gnawing, and cutting; canines for ripping, tearing, killing, and fighting; premolars that may either slice and tear or crush and grind (depending on the kind of animal); and molars for crushing and grinding. This enables mammals to eat a wide variety of food—an advantage to them, since they require more food than do reptiles to sustain their high activity. But they pay a

Notochord.   A rodlike structure of cartilage that, in vertebrates, is replaced by the vertebral column.

Order	Suborder	Infraorder	Superfamily	Family
Primates	Strepsirhini	Lemuriformes	Lemuroidea	Five families of lemurs and lemurlike animals
			Lorisoidea	One family of lorises
	Haplorhini	Tarsii	Tarsioidea	One family, represented solely by tarsiers
		Platyrrhini	Ceboidea	Two families of New World monkeys
		Catarrhini	Cercopithecoidea	Two families of Old World monkeys
			Hominoidea	Hylobatidae (small apes)
				Pongidae (Asian great apes)
				Hominidae (African apes, humans, and near humans)

TABLE 4.2   The Primate Order

price: reptiles have unlimited tooth replacement, whereas mammals are limited to two sets. The first set serves the immature animal, and is replaced by the "permanent" or adult dentition.

The primate order is divided into two suborders (Table 4.2), of which one is the **Strepsirhini** (from the Greek for "turned nose"), which includes lemurs and lorises (all members of the infraorder **Lemuriformes**). On the whole, strepsirhines are cat-sized or smaller, although there have been some larger forms in the past. Generally, they do not exhibit the characteristics of their order as much as do the members of the other suborder, the **Haplorhini** (from the Greek for "simple nose"). The strepsirhines also retain certain features common among nonprimate mammals, such as claws and moist, naked skin on their noses, that have not been retained by the haplorhines.

The haplorhine suborder is divided into three infraorders: the **Tarsii**, or tarsiers; the **Platyrrhini**, or New World monkeys; and the **Catarrhini**, consisting of the superfamilies Cercopithecoidea (Old World monkeys) and Hominoidea. Within the Hominoidea are the families Hylobatidae (small apes, like the gibbon), Pongidae, and Hominidae. Although the traditional classification of primates placed all great apes (bonobo, chimpanzee, gorilla, and orangutan) together in the pongid family, and humans alone as hominids, it is now recognized that this way of grouping apes and humans violates evolutionary relationships. Since the way we classify is supposed to reflect evolutionary genealogies, recent classifications restrict the Pongidae to orangutans, while bonobos, chimps and gorillas are included with humans in the Hominidae, as a reflection of their closer relation to each other than to orangs. Unfortunately, old habits die hard, and it is still common to find scientists using the family names in the old way. But because it misleads, this obsolete practice should be dropped; therefore, in this

---

Strepsirhini. A primate suborder that includes the single infraorder Lemuriformes. ▷ **Lemuriformes.** A strepsirhine infraorder that includes lemurs and lorises. ▷ **Haplorhini.** A primate suborder that includes tarsiers, monkeys, apes, and humans. ▷ **Tarsii.** A haplorhine infraorder that includes tarsiers. ▷ **Platyrrhini.** A haplorhine infraorder that includes the New World monkeys. ▷ **Catarrhini.** A haplorhine infraorder that includes Old World monkeys, apes, and humans.

book we shall use classificatory terminology more reflective of evolutionary genealogy. Only at the level of the subfamily will humans (homininae) be separated from bonobos, chimps and gorillas, although a case can be made that the separation should be made below even the level of the subfamily.[1]

PRIMATE CHARACTERISTICS

Although the living primates are a varied group of animals, they do share a number of features in common. These features are, however, displayed in varying degree by the different kinds of primate; in some they are barely detectable, while in others they are greatly elaborated. All are useful in one way or another to **arboreal,** or tree-dwelling, animals, although (as any squirrel knows) they are not essential to life in the trees. For animals preying upon the many insects living on the fruit and flowers of trees and shrubs, however, such primate characteristics as manipulative hands and keen vision would have been enormously adaptive. Probably, it was as arboreal animals relying on visual predation of insects that primates got their start in life.

PRIMATE SENSE ORGANS

The primates' adaptation to their way of life in the trees coincided with changes in the form and function of their sensory apparatus: The senses of sight and touch became highly developed, and the sense of smell declined. When primates took to the trees in search of insects, they no longer needed to live a "nose-to-the-ground" existence, sniffing

close to the ground in search of food. The haplorhines especially have the least-developed sense of smell of all land animals.

Catching insects in the trees, as the early primates did and many still do, demands quickness of movement and the ability to land in the right place without falling. Thus, they had to be adept at judging depth, direction, distance, and the relationships of objects in space, abilities that remain useful to animals that travel through the trees (as most primates still do today), even though they may have given up most insect eating in favor of fruits and leaves. In the haplorhines, these abilities are provided by their **stereoscopic vision,** the ability to see the world in three dimensions—height, width, and depth. It requires two eyes set apart from one another on the same plane. Each eye thus views an object from a slightly different angle, and the object assumes a three-dimensional appearance, indicating spatial relationships. Stereoscopic vision is one of the most important factors in primate evolution, for it evidently led to increased brain size in the visual area and a great complexity at nerve connections.

Visual acuity, however, varies throughout the primate order. Lemuriformes, for example, are the most visually primitive of the primates. Lacking stereoscopic vision, their eyes look out from either side of their muzzle or snout, much like those of a cow or a rabbit. Nor do they possess color vision. All other primates possess both color and stereoscopic vision, as well as a unique structure called the **fovea centralis,** or central pit in the retina of each eye. Like a camera lens, this feature enables the animal to focus on a particular object for acutely clear perception, without sacrificing visual contact with the object's surroundings.

Primate sense of touch also became highly developed as a result of arboreal living. Primates found useful an effective feeling and grasping mechanism to grab their insect prey, and to prevent them from falling and tumbling while moving through the trees. The primitive mammals from which primates descended possessed tiny

[1]Goodman, M., Bailey, W. J., Hayasaka, K., Stanhope, M. J., Slighton J., & Czelusniak, J. (1994). Molecular evidence on primate phylogeny from DNA sequences. *American Journal of Physical Anthropology, 94,* 7.

Arboreal. Tree-dwelling. > **Stereoscopic vision.** Three-dimensional vision. > **Fovea centralis.** A shallow pit in the retina of the eye that enables an animal to focus on an object while maintaining visual contact with its surroundings.

Hands that grasp and eyes that see in three dimensions enable primates, like these South American monkeys, to live effectively in the trees.

tactile hairs that gave them extremely sensitive tactile capacities. In primates, these hairs were replaced by informative pads on the tips of the animals' fingers and toes.

THE PRIMATE BRAIN

By far the most outstanding characteristic of primate evolution has been the enlargement of the brain among members of the order. Primate brains tend to be large, heavy in proportion to body weight, and very complex. The cerebral hemispheres (the areas of conscious thought) have enlarged dramatically and, in catarrhines, completely cover the cerebellum, which is the part of the brain that coordinates the muscles and maintains body equilibrium.

The reasons for this important change in brain size are many, but it likely began as the earliest primates, along with many other mammals, began to carry out their activities in the daylight hours. Prior to 65 million years ago, mammals seem to have been nocturnal in their habits, but with the extinction of the dinosaurs, inconspicuous, night-time activity was no longer the key to survival. With the change to diurnal, or daytime, activity the sense of vision took on greater importance, and so visual acuity was favored by natural selec-

tion. Unlike reptile vision, where the information-processing neurons are in the retina, mammalian vision is processed in the brain, permitting integration with information received by hearing and smelling.

If the evolution of visual acuity led to larger brains, it is likely that the primates' arboreal existence played a major role in furthering enlargement of the brain. Paleontologist Alfred S. Romer states:

> Locomotion in the trees requires great agility and muscular coordination, which in itself demands development of the brain centers; and it is of interest that much of the higher mental faculties are apparently developed in an area alongside the motor centers of the brain.[2]

Another interesting hypothesis that may help account for primate brain enlargement involves the use of the hand as a tactile organ to replace the teeth and jaws or snout. The hands assumed some of the grasping, tearing, and dividing functions of the snout, again requiring development of the

---

[2]Romer, A. S. (1945). *Vertebrate paleontology* (p. 103). Chicago: University of Chicago Press.

brain centers for more complete coordination. Thus, while the skull and brain expanded, the teeth and jaws grew smaller. Certain areas of the brain became more elaborate and intricate. One of these areas is the cortex, considered to be the center of an animal's intelligence; it receives impressions from the animal's various sensory receptors, analyzes them, and sends responses back down the motor nerves to the proper receptor.

An animal living in the trees is constantly acting on and reacting to the environment. Messages from the hands, feet, eyes, and ears, as well as from the sensors of balance, movement, heat, touch, and pain, are relayed to the cortex, individually and simultaneously. The cortex, then, must be developed to a considerable degree of complexity to receive and coordinate these impressions and to transmit back the appropriate responses. It is assumed that such development must have occurred early in the history of the primates.

The enlarged cortex not only provided the primates with a greater degree of efficiency in the daily struggle for survival but also gave them the basis for more sophisticated cerebration, or thought. The ability to think probably played a decisive role in the evolution of the primates from which human beings emerged.

PRIMATE DENTITION

Although they have added other things than insects to their diets, primates have retained less specialized teeth than other mammals. According to primatologist W. E. LeGros Clark:

> An arboreal life obviates the necessity for developing highly specialized grinding teeth, since the diet available to most tree-living mammals in the tropics, consisting of leaves, shoots, soft fruits, and insects, can be adequately masticated by molar teeth of relatively simple structure.[3]

In most primates, on each side of each jaw, in front, are two straight-edged, chisel-like broad teeth called incisors (Figure 4.1). Behind the inci-

[3]LeGros Clark, W. E. (1966). *History of the primates* (5th ed., p. 271). Chicago: University of Chicago Press.

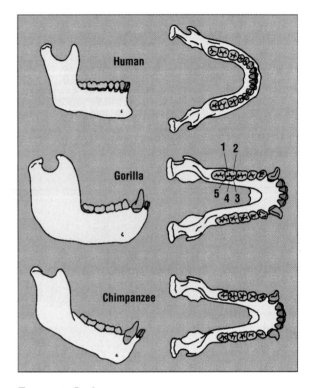

FIGURE 4.1

In this depiction of the lower jaws of a human, a gorilla, and a chimpanzee, incisors are shown in blue, canines in red, and premolars and molars in yellow. On one of the gorilla molars, the cusps are numbered to facilitate their identification.

sors is a canine, which in many mammals is large, flaring, and fanglike and is used for defense as well as for tearing and shredding food. Among some catarrhines the canine is somewhat reduced in size, especially in females, though it is still large in males. In humans, though, incisors and canines are practically indistinguishable, although the canine has an oversized root, suggestive of larger canines some time back in our ancestry. Behind the canines are the premolars. Last come the molars, usually with four or five cusps, used mostly for crushing or grinding food. This basic dentition contrasts sharply with that of nonprimate mammals.

On the evidence of comparative anatomy and the fossil record, LeGros Clark postulated the existence of an early primate ancestor that possessed three incisors, one canine, four premolars, and three molars on each side of the jaw, top and bottom, for a total of 44 teeth. In the early stages of primate evolution, four incisors (one on each side of each jaw) were lost. This change differentiated the primates, with their two incisors on each side of each jaw, from other mammals. The canines of most primates develop into long, daggerlike teeth that enable them to rip open tough husks of fruit and other foods. In a combat situation, male baboons, apes, and other primates flash these formidable teeth at their enemies, intending to scare them off. Only infrequently, when this bluffing action fails, are teeth used to inflict bodily harm.

Other evolutionary changes in primate dentition involve the premolar and molar teeth. Over the millennia, the first and second premolars became smaller and eventually disappeared altogether, while the third and fourth premolars grew larger with the addition of a second pointed projection, or cusp, thus becoming "bicuspid." The molars, meanwhile, evolved from a three-cusp pattern to one with four and even five cusps. This kind of molar economically combined the functions of grasping, cutting, and grinding in one tooth.

The evolutionary trend for primate dentition has generally been toward economy, with fewer, smaller, more efficient teeth doing more work. Thus our own 32 teeth are fewer in number than those of some, and more generalized than those of most, primates. Indeed, the absence of third molars in many individuals indicates that the human dentition is undergoing further reduction.

THE PRIMATE SKELETON

The skeleton gives an animal its basic shape or silhouette, supports the soft tissues, and helps protect the vital internal organs. In primates (Figure 4.2), for example, the skull protects the brain and the eyes. A number of factors are responsible for the shape of the primate skull as compared with those of most other mammals: changes in dentition, changes in the sensory organs of sight and smell, and increased brain size. The primate

FIGURE 4.2
Note where the skulls and vertebral columns are joined in these skeletons of a bison (left) and a gorilla (right). In the bison (as in most mammals) the skull projects forward from the vertebral column, but in the semierect gorilla, the vertebral column is well beneath the skull.

brain case, or **cranium,** tends to be high and vaulted. A solid partition exists in most primate species between the eye and the temple, affording maximum protection to the eyes from the contraction of the chewing muscles positioned directly next to the eyes.

The **foramen magnum** (the large opening in the skull through which the spinal cord passes and connects to the brain) is an important clue to evolutionary relationships. In primates, the evolutionary trend has been for this to shift forward, toward the center of the skull's base, so that it faces downward, as in humans, rather than directly backward, as in dogs, horses, and other mammals. Thus, the skull does not project forward from the vertebral column. Instead, the vertebral column joins the skull toward the center of its base, thereby placing the skull in a balanced position in animals that frequently assume upright posture.

In most primates, the snout or muzzle portion of the skull has grown smaller as the acuity of the sense of smell declined. The smaller snout offers less interference with stereoscopic vision; it also enables the eyes to be placed in the frontal position. As a result, primates have more of a humanlike face than other mammals. Below the primate skull and the neck is the **clavicle,** or collarbone, a holdover from primitive mammal ancestors. This serves as a strut that prevents the arm from collapsing inward when brought across the front of the body. It allows greater maneuverability of the arms, permitting them to swing sideways and outward from the trunk of the body. The clavicle also supports the **scapula** and allows for the muscle development that is required for flexible, yet powerful, arm movement. This shoulder and limb structure is associated with considerable acrobatic agility and, in the case of all apes and some New World monkeys, the ability to **brachiate**— use their arms to swing and hang beneath the branches of trees with the body in a vertical (upright) position.

Primates have retained also the characteristic, found in early mammals, of **pentadactyly.** Pentadactyly, which means possessing five digits, is a primitive characteristic found in many nonarboreal animals, but it proved to be of special advantage to tree-dwelling primates. Their grasping feet and hands (Figure 4.3) have sensitive pads at the tips of their digits, backed up (except in some strepsirhines) by flattened nails. This unique combination of pad and nail provides the animal with an excellent **prehensile** (grasping) device for use when moving from tree to tree. The structural characteristics of the primate foot and hand make grasping possible; the digits are extremely flexible, the big toe is fully opposable to the other digits in most species, and the thumb is opposable to the other digits to varying degrees.

Hindsight indicates that the flexible, unspecialized primate hand was to prove a valuable asset for future evolution of this group. Had they not had generalized grasping hands, early hominines (members of the human subfamily) would not have been able to manufacture and utilize tools and thus embark on the new and unique evolutionary pathway that led to the revolutionary ability to adapt through culture.

REPRODUCTION AND CARE OF YOUNG

The breeding of most mammals occurs once or twice a year, but most primate species are able to breed at any time during the course of the year. Generally, the male is ready to engage in sexual activity whenever females are in **estrus,** around the time of ovulation. The female's receptivity is cyclical, corresponding to her period of estrus, which occurs once each month.

This is not to say that females are receptive regularly each month. Rather, the average adult female monkey or ape spends most of her time

---

Cranium. The brain case of the skull. **> Foramen magnum.** A large opening in the skull through which the spinal cord passes and connects to the brain. **> Clavicle.** The collarbone. **> Scapula.** The shoulder blade. **> Brachiate.** To use the arms to move from branch to branch, with the body hanging suspended from the arms. **> Pentadactyly.** Possessing five digits (fingers and toes). **> Prehensile.** Having the ability to grasp. **> Estrus.** In primate females, the time of sexual receptivity during which ovulation takes place.

Tarsier **Gibbon** **Chimpanzee** **Human**

FIGURE 4.3
The hands of primates are similar. However, human hands are distinguished by well-developed thumbs that can be used in opposition to the fingers. The highly specialized hands of the brachiators (gibbons and chimpanzees) are characterized by long fingers and weakly developed thumbs.

either pregnant or nursing, at which times she is not sexually receptive. But after her infant is weaned, she will come into estrus for a few days each month, until she becomes pregnant again. Since this can happen at any time, it is advantageous to have males present throughout the year. Thus, sex plays a role in keeping both sexes constantly together, except among some orangutans, among whom adults only come together when females are in estrus. In most species, however, sex is not the only, or even the most important, cause of males and females remaining together.

One of the most noticeable adaptations to arboreal life among primates is a trend toward reduction in the number of offspring born at one time to a female. The most primitive primates,

Swelling of her sexual skin indicates that this baboon is in estrus. Females of most primates come into estrus once a month until pregnant; thereafter, they will not come into estrus until their infant is weaned.

A young baboon clings to its mother. Because the mother's hands are used in locomotion, she cannot carry her infant. Consequently, it must be able to hold on for itself.

lemurs and marmosets, produce two or three young at each birth. Catarrhines, however, usually produce only a single offspring at a time. Natural selection may have favored single births among primate tree dwellers because the primate infant, which has a highly developed grasping ability (the grasping reflex can also be seen in human infants), must be transported about by its mother, and more than one clinging infant would seriously encumber her as she moved about the trees. Moreover, a female pregnant with a large litter would be unable to lead a very active life as a tree dweller.

Primates bear fewer young at a time, and so they must devote more time and effort to their care if the species is to survive. This usually means a longer period during which the infant is dependent upon its mother. As a general rule, the more closely related to humans the species is, the smaller, more helpless, and more immature the newborn offspring tend to be. For example, a lemur is dependent upon the mother for only a few months after birth; an ape, for four or five years; and a human for more than a decade. Longer infancy is typically associated with an increase in longevity (see Figure 4.4). If the breeding life of primates had not extended, the lengthened infancy could have led to a decrease in numbers of individuals. Something approaching this can be seen in the great apes: A female chimpanzee, for example, does not reach sexual maturity until about the age of 10, and once she produces her first live offspring, there is a period of about 5.6 years before she will bear another. Furthermore, a chimpanzee infant cannot survive if its mother dies before it reaches the age of 4 at the very least. Thus, assuming that none of her offspring die before adulthood, a female chimpanzee must survive for at least 20 or 21 years just to maintain the size of chimpanzee populations at their current levels. In fact, chimpanzee infants and juveniles do die from time to time, and not all females live full reproductive lives. This is one reason why apes are not as abundant in the world today as are monkeys.

The young of catarrhine, and especially hominoid, species are born with relatively underdeveloped nervous systems; moreover, they lack the social knowledge that guides behavior. Thus they depend upon adults not only for protection but also

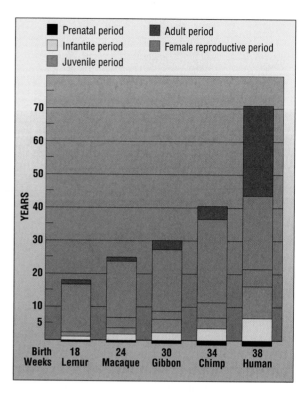

FIGURE 4.4
Primates are born at earlier stages of development than other animals. Humans are born at a particularly early stage because of their larger brain; if born later, the baby's head would be too large for the mother's pelvis.

for instruction, as they must learn how to survive. The longer period of dependence in these primates makes possible a longer period of learning, which appears to be a distinct evolutionary advantage.

ESTABLISHING EVOLUTIONARY RELATIONSHIPS

Most of the primate characteristics so far discussed are present at least in a rudimentary sort of way in the strepsirhines, but all are seen to a much greater degree in the haplorhines. The differences between humans and the other haplorhines, especially catarrhines, are rather like those between strepsirhines and haplorhines. In humans most of the characteristic primate traits are developed to a degree not realized by any other species. Among some strepsirhines, some of the distinctive primate traits are missing, while others are clearly present, so that the borderline between primate and non-primate becomes blurred, and the difference is one of degree rather than kind. All of this is fully expectable, given an evolutionary history in which primitive primates having a rough resemblance to today's strepsirhines developed out of some other mammalian order and eventually gave rise to primitive haplorhines; from these emerged the catarrhines and, ultimately, hominids.

Just how close our evolutionary relationship is to other primates is indicated by molecular evidence. There is a striking similarity in blood and protein chemistry among the hominoids especially, indicating close evolutionary relationships. On the basis of tests with blood proteins, it has been shown that the bonobo, chimpanzee, and gorilla are closest to humans; next comes the orangutan; then the smaller apes (gibbons and siamangs); Old World monkeys; New World monkeys; and finally the strepsirhines. Measurements of genetic affinity confirm these findings, providing further evidence of humanity's close kinship to the great apes, especially those of Africa (Figure 4.5). The classification of humans, two species of genus *Pan* (bonobos and chimpanzees), and gorillas together in the family hominidae, distinct from the pongidae, reflects the fact that the three genera are more closely related to one another than any is to the orangutan.

At the genetic level, humans and chimpanzees are at least 98.5% identical. The differences are that chimps have an extra pair of chromosomes; of the other pairs, 18 are virtually identical whereas the remaining ones have been reshuffled. Overall, the differences are fewer than those between gibbons (with 44 chromosomes) and siamangs (50 chromosomes) which, in captivity, have produced live hybrid offspring. Although some studies of molecular similarities have suggested a closer relationship between the genus *Pan* and humans than either has to gorillas, others disagree, and the safest course at the moment is to regard all three hominid genera as having an equal degree of relationship (the two species of genus *Pan* are, of course, more closely related to each other than either is to gorillas or humans).[4]

▲▽▲▽▲▽▲▽▲▽▲▽▲▽▲▽▲▽▲▽▲▽▲▽▲▽▲▽▲▽

MODERN PRIMATES

The modern primates are mostly restricted to warm areas of the world. As already noted, they are divided into two suborders, Strepsirhini and Haplorhini. Strepsirhines are small, mostly quadrupedal, Old World animals; haplorhines include tarsiers, monkeys, apes, and humans.

STREPSIRHINES

The strepsirhines, the most primitive primates, are represented by the single infraorder Lemuriformes, within which are the lemurs and lorises. Although lemurs are restricted to the island of Madagascar, off the east coast of Africa, lorises range from Africa to southern and eastern Asia. All are small, with none larger than a good-sized dog. In general body outline, they resemble rodents and insectivores, with short pointed snouts, large pointed ears, and big eyes. In the anatomy of the upper lip and snout, lemuriformes resemble nonprimate mammals, in that the upper lip is bound down to the gum and the naked skin on the nose around

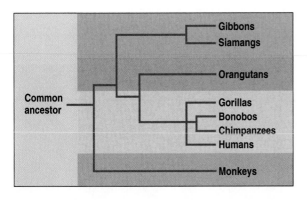

FIGURE 4.5

Based on molecular similarities and differences, a relationship can be established among various catarrhine primates. Present thinking is that the split between the human and African ape lineages took place no more than 8 million years ago.

[4]Rogers, J. (1994). Levels of the genealogical hierarchy and the problem of hominid phylogeny. *American Journal of Physical Anthropology, 94,* 81.

the nostrils is moist. They also have long tails, with that of a ring-tail lemur somewhat like the tail of a raccoon.

In brain structure, lemuriformes are clearly primates, and they have characteristically primate "hands," although they use them in pairs, rather than one at a time. They move on all fours, with the forelimbs in a "palms down" position, and also cling in near vertical positions to branches. Although they retain a claw on their second toe, which they use for scratching and grooming, all other digits are equipped with flattened nails. With their distinctive mix of characteristics, strepsirhine primates appear to occupy a place between the haplorhines and insectivores.

HAPLORHINES

The suborder Haplorhini is divided into three infraorders: the Tarsii (tarsiers), Platyrrhini (New World monkeys), and Catarrhini (Old World monkeys, apes, and humans). Most haplorhines are bigger than the strepsirhines and are strikingly humanlike in appearance. Actually, it is more accurate to say that humans are remarkably like monkeys, but even more like apes, in appearance. The defining traits of the strepsirhines—large cranium, well-developed brain, acute vision, chisel-like incisors, prehensile digits—are even more marked in the haplorhines. Most haplorhines generally move on all four limbs, but many stand erect to reach fruit hanging in trees: Some apes occa-

sionally walk on two feet. Monkeys are often highly arboreal, and New World species have prehensile tails that wrap around a tree branch, freeing the forelimbs to grasp food. Some New World monkeys brachiate; Old World monkeys almost never do.

All apes may once have been fully arboreal brachiators, but among modern apes, only the gibbon and siamang still are. The bonobo, chimpanzee, and gorilla spend most of their time on the ground, but sleep in the trees and may also find food there. Orangutans, too, spend time down on the ground, but are more arboreal than the African apes. When on the ground, they move mostly on all fours.

Tarsiers

Tarsiers are the haplorhine primates most like the lemuriformes, and in the past they were usually classified in the same suborder with them. The head, eyes, and ears of these kitten-sized arboreal creatures are huge in proportion to the body. They have the remarkable ability to turn their heads 180 degrees, so they can see where they have been as well as where they are going. The digits end in platelike, adhesive discs. Tarsiers are named for the elongated tarsal, or foot bone, that provides leverage for jumps of 6 feet or more. Tarsiers are mainly nocturnal insect eaters. In the structure of the nose and lips, and the part of the brain governing vision, tarsiers resemble monkeys.

Modern strepsirhines represent highly evolved variants of an early primate model. In them, primate characteristics are not as prominent as they are in monkeys, apes, and humans.

In tarsiers, primary characteristics are somewhat more prominent than among strepsirhines.

New World Monkeys

New World monkeys live in forests and swamps of South and Central America. They are characterized by flat noses with widely separated, outward flaring nostrils, from which comes their name of platyrrhine monkeys. All are arboreal and some have long, prehensile tails by which they hang from trees. These features and the presence of three, rather than two, premolars on each side of each jaw distinguish them from the Old World monkeys, apes, and humans. Platyrrhines walk on all fours with their palms down and scamper along tree branches in search of fruit, which they eat sitting upright. Spider monkeys are accomplished brachiators as well. Although other New World monkeys spend much of their time in the trees, they do not often hang or swing from limb to limb by their arms and have not developed the extremely long forelimbs characteristic of brachiators.

Old World Monkeys

Old World, or catarrhine, monkeys are characterized by noses with closely spaced, downward-pointing nostrils, the presence of two, rather than three, premolars on each side of each jaw, and their lack of prehensile tails. They may be either arboreal or terrestrial. The arboreal species include the guereza monkey, the Asiatic langur, and the strange-looking proboscis monkey. Some are equally at home on the ground and in the trees, such as the macaques, of which some 19 species range from Gibraltar (the misnamed "Barbary ape") to Japan.

Several species of baboons are largely terrestrial, living in the savannas, deserts, and highlands of Africa. They have long, fierce faces and move quadrupedally, with all fours in the palms-down position. Their diet consists of leaves, seeds, insects, and lizards, and they live in large, well-organized troops consisting of related females and adult males that have transferred out of other troops. Because baboons have abandoned trees (except for sleeping and refuge) and live in environments like that in which humans may have originated, they are of great interest to primatologists.

Small and Great Apes

The apes are the closest living relatives we humans have in the animal world. Their general appearance and way of life are related to their semierect posture. In their body chemistry, the position of their internal organs, and even their diseases, they are remarkably close to humans. They are arboreal to varying degrees, but their generally greater size and weight are obstacles to swinging and jumping as freely as monkeys. The small, lithe gibbon can both climb and swing freely through the trees and so spends virtually all of its time in them. At the opposite extreme are gorillas, who climb trees, using their prehensile hands and feet to grip the trunk and branches. Their swinging is limited to leaning outward as they reach for fruit, clasping a limb for support. Most of their time is spent on the ground.

The apes, like humans, have no external tail. But, unlike humans, their arms are longer than their legs, indicating that their ancestors specialized for arboreal brachiation in a way that our own did not. In moving on the ground, the African apes "knuckle-walk" on the backs of their hands, resting their weight on the middle joints of the fingers. They stand erect when reaching for fruit, looking over tall grass, or in any activity where they find the erect position advantageous.

The semierect position is natural in apes when on the ground because the curvature of their vertebral column places their center of gravity, which is high in their bodies, in front of their hip joint. Thus, they are both "top heavy" and "front heavy." Furthermore, the structure of the ape pelvis is not well suited to support the weight of the torso and limbs easily. Nor do apes have the arrangement of leg muscles that enables humans to stand erect and swing their legs freely before and behind.

Gibbons and siamangs, which are found in Southeast Asia and Malaya, have compact, slim bodies with extraordinarily long arms compared to their short legs, and stand about three feet high. Although their usual form of locomotion is brachiation, they can run erect, holding their arms out for balance. Gibbons and siamangs resemble monkeys in size and general appearance more than the other apes.

Orangutans are found in Borneo and Sumatra. They are somewhat taller than gibbons and siamangs and are much heavier, with the bulk characteristic of apes. In the closeness of the eyes and facial prominence, an orangutan looks a little like a chimpanzee, except that its hair is reddish. Orangs walk with their forelimbs in a fists-sideways or a palms-down position. They are, however, somewhat more arboreal than the

Gibbons and orangutans are Southeast Asian apes. Gibbons are brachiators that use their long arms and hands to swing through the trees. Although orangutans sometimes brachiate, their legs move like arms and their feet are like hands; thus, much of their movement is by four-handed climbing.

African apes. Although sociable by nature, the orangs of upland Borneo spend most of their time alone, as they have to forage over a wide area to obtain sufficient food. By contrast, fruits and insects are sufficiently abundant in the swamps of Sumatra to sustain groups and permit coordinated group travel. Thus, gregariousness is a function of habitat productivity.[5]

Gorillas, found in equatorial Africa, are the largest of the apes; an adult male can weigh over 400 pounds. The body is covered with a thick coat of glossy black hair, and mature males have a silvery gray upper back. There is a strikingly human look about the face, and like humans, gorillas focus on things in their field of vision by directing the eyes rather than moving the head. Gorillas are mostly ground dwellers, but may sleep in trees in carefully constructed nests. Because of their weight, brachiation is limited to raising and lowering themselves among the tree branches when searching for fruit. They

"knuckle-walk," using all four limbs with the fingers of the hand flexed, placing the knuckles instead of the palm of the hand on the ground. They will stand erect to reach for fruit, to see something more easily, or to threaten perceived sources of danger with their famous "chest beating" displays. Although gorillas are gentle and tolerant, bluffing is an important part of their behavioral repertoire.

Chimpanzees and bonobos are two species of the same genus (*Pan*), bonobos being the least well-known and restricted in their distribution to the rain forests of the Democratic Republic of Congo. The common chimpanzee, by contrast, is widely distributed throughout sub-Saharan Africa. They are probably the best known of the apes, and have long been favorites in zoos and circuses. Although thought of as particularly quick and clever, all four great apes are of equal intelligence, despite some differences in cognitive styles. More arboreal than gorillas, but less so than orangs, chimpanzees and bonobos forage on the ground much of the day, "knuckle-walking" like gorillas. At sunset, they return to the trees, where they build their nests.

---

[5]Normile, D. (1998). Habitat seen as playing larger role in shaping behavior. *Science, 279*, 1454.

Chimpanzees and gorillas are African apes.

▲▽▲▽▲▽▲▽▲▽▲▽▲▽▲▽▲▽▲▽▲▽▲▽▲▽▲▽▲▽▲

THE SOCIAL BEHAVIOR OF PRIMATES

The physical resemblance of human beings to the other catarrhines is striking, but the most startling resemblance of all is in their social behavior. Because of their highly developed brains, monkeys and apes behave in a manner far more complex than most other animals except humans. Only over the past four decades have primatologists made prolonged close-range observations of catarrhines in their natural habitats, and we are discovering much about social organization, learning ability, and communication among our closest relatives in the animal kingdom. In particular, we are finding that a number of behavioral traits that we used to think of as distinctively human are found to one degree or another among other primates, reminding us once again that many of the differences between us and them are differences of degree, rather than kind.

The range of behavior shown by living primates is great—too great to be adequately surveyed in this book. Instead, we shall look primarily at the behavior of those species most closely related to humans, bonobos, chimpanzees, and gorillas.

anthropology applied   Primate Conservation

At present, no fewer than 76 species of primates are recognized as being in danger of extinction. Included among them are all of the great apes, as well as such formerly widespread and adaptable species as rhesus macaques. In the wild, they are threatened by destruction of their habitat in the name of "development," by hunting for food and trophies, and by trapping for pets and research. Because monkeys and apes are so closely related to humans, they are regarded as essential for biomedical research in which humans cannot be used. It is ironic that trade in live primates to supply laboratories can be a major factor in their local extinction.

Because of their vulnerability, the conservation of primates has become a matter of urgency. Two approaches to the problem may be taken, both of which require application of knowledge gained from studies of free-ranging animals. One is to maintain some populations in the wild, either by establishing preserves where animals are already living, or by moving populations to localities where suitable habitat exists. In either case, constant monitoring and management are necessary to assure that sufficient space and resources remain available. The other approach is to maintain breeding colonies in captivity, in which case care must be taken to provide the kind of physical and social environment that will encourage psychological as well as physical well-being, and also reproductive success. Without such amenities as things to climb, materials to use for nest building, others to socialize with, and places to withdraw not only from humans but from each other, primates in zoos and laboratories do not successfully reproduce.

The value of field studies for effective wild animal management is illustrated by Shirley Strum's relocation in 1984 of three troops of free-ranging baboons in Kenya. The troop she had been studying for 15 years had become a problem, raiding peoples' crops and garbage. Accordingly, it was decided to move this and two other local troops—130 animals in all—to more sparsely inhabited country 150 miles away. Knowing their habits, Strum was able to trap, tranquilize, and transport the animals to their new home in such a way as not to disrupt their social relationships, cause them to abandon their new home, or block the transfer into their troops of new males, with their all-important knowledge of local resources. The success of her effort, which had never been tried with baboons before, proves that relocation is a realistic technique for saving endangered primate populations.

The Group

Primates are social animals, living and traveling in groups that vary in size from species to species. In most species, females and their offspring constitute the core of the social system. This is true of chimpanzees to a degree. In two Tanzanian communities studied, females often leave their natal group for another, although up to 50% do not.[6] In both cases, however, females in ovulation may temporarily leave their group to mate with males of another. But whatever the case, their sons, and often their daughters, remain in their mother's group for life. That there is variation among chimpanzees is illustrated by a community in Guinea, where both females and especially males leave the group as adolescents.[7] Among bonobos, it is females that transfer to another group, in which they establish bonds of friendship with females already there. Female bonobos are especially skilled at establishing bonds of friendship with one another, so that they are far more sociable than are chimpanzee females. Among the latter, the stronger bonds are between males, as young ones reaching maturity join groups of adult males. In the case of gorillas, either sex may or may not leave its natal group for another.

Among chimps, the largest organizational unit is the community, composed of 50 or more individuals. Rarely, however, are all these animals together at a single time. Instead, they are usually found ranging singly or in small subgroups consisting of adult males together, females with their young, or males and females together with their young. In the course of their travels, subgroups may join forces and forage together, but sooner or later these will break up again into smaller units. When they do, members are often exchanged, so that new subunits are different in their composition from the ones that initially came together.

Although relationships between individuals within the community are relatively harmonious, dominance hierarchies exist. Generally, males outrank females, although high-ranking females may dominate low-ranking males. Physical strength and size help determine an animal's rank, as do the rank of its mother, its skill at enlisting the aid of other individuals, and, in the case of the male, its motivation to achieve high status. Highly motivated males, even though they may not be the biggest in their group, may bring considerable intelligence and ingenuity to bear in their quest for high rank. For example, in the community studied by Jane Goodall, a pioneer in the study of primate behavior, one chimp hit upon the idea of incorporating noisy kerosene cans into his charging displays, thereby intimidating all the other males.[8] As a result, he rose from relatively low status to the number one (alpha) position.

On the whole, bonobo females form stronger bonds with one another than do their chimpanzee counterparts. Moreover, the strength of the bond between mother and son is such as to interfere with that between males. Thus, instead of the male dominance among chimps, one sees female dominance. Not only do bonobo males defer to females in feeding, but alpha females have been observed chasing high-ranking males. Alpha males even yield to low-ranking females, and groups of females form alliances in which they may cooperatively attack males, to the point of inflicting blood-drawing injuries.[9]

The gorilla group is a "family" of 5 to 20 individuals led by a mature, silverbacked male and including younger, black-backed males, females, the young, and sometimes other silverbacks. Subordinate males, however, are usually prevented by the dominant male from mating with the group's females, although he may occasionally allow access to lower ranking ones. Thus, young silverbacks often leave their natal family to start their own families by winning outside females. If the dominant male is weakening with age, however, one of his sons may remain with the group to succeed to his father's position. Unlike chimpanzees, gorillas rarely fight over food, territory, or sex, but will fight fiercely to maintain the integrity of the group.

[6]Moore, J. (1998). Comment. *Current Anthropology, 39,* 412.
[7]Normile, p. 1454.
[8]Goodall, J. (1986). *The chimpanzees of Gombe: Patterns of behavior* (p. 424). Cambridge, MA: Belknap Press.
[9]de Waal, F., Kano, T., & Parish, A. R. (1998). Comments. *Current Anthropology, 39,* 408, 410, 413.

Jane Goodall   *(b. 1934)*

In July 1960 Jane Goodall arrived with her mother at the Gombe Chimpanzee Reserve on the shores of Lake Tanganyika in Tanzania. The first of three women Kenyan anthropologist Lewis Leaky sent out to study great apes in the wild (the others were Dian Fossey and Birute Galdikas, who were to study gorillas and orangutans, respectively), her task was to begin a long-term study of chimpanzees. Little did she realize that more than 35 years later she would still be at it.

Though born in London, Jane grew up and was schooled in Bournemouth, England. Upon her graduation at 18, she enrolled in secretarial school, followed by taking jobs in England before the opportunity came to go to Africa. As a child, she had always dreamed of going there to live among animals, so when an invitation arrived to visit a friend in Kenya, she jumped at the opportunity. Quitting her regular job, Goodall worked as a waitress to raise the money for travel and was then on her way. Once in Kenya, she met Louis Leaky, who gave her a job as an assistant secretary. Before long, she was on her way to Gombe. Within a year, the outside world began to hear the most extraordinary things about this pioneering woman and her work: tales of tool-making apes, cooperative hunts by chimpanzees, and what seemed like exotic chimpanzee rain dances. By the mid-1960s, her work had earned her a Ph.D. from Cambridge University, and Gombe was on its way to becoming one of the most dynamic field stations for the study of animal behavior anywhere in the world.

Although field studies of primates in their natural habitats had been undertaken prior to 1960, they were few in number, and most had produced extremely limited information. It was Goodall's particular blend of patience and determination that showed what could be achieved, and before long her field station became something of a Mecca for aspiring young students interested in primate behavior. The list of those who have worked with her at Gombe, many of them women, reads like a *Who's Who* of eminent scholars in primate behavior.

Although Goodall is still very much involved with her chimpanzees, she spends a good deal of time these days lecturing, writing, and overseeing the work of others. She also is heavily committed to primate conservation, and no one is more dedicated to efforts to halt the illegal trafficking in captive chimps nor a more eloquent champion for humane treatment of captive chimpanzees.

INDIVIDUAL INTERACTION

One of the most notable primate activities is grooming, the ritual cleaning of another animal's coat to remove parasites, shreds of grass, or other matter. The grooming animal deftly parts the hair of the one being groomed with two fingers, and with the thumb and forefinger of the other hand removes any foreign object, often eating it. Among gorillas, grooming is mainly hygienic; but among bonobos and chimpanzees it is a gesture of friendliness, submission, appeasement, or closeness. Embracing, touching, and jumping up and down are forms of greeting behavior among chimpanzees. Touching is also a form of reassurance.

Among gorillas, as among most primates, the mother-infant bond is strong.

Gorillas, though gentle and tolerant, are also aloof and independent, and individual interaction among adults tends to be quite restrained. Friendship or closeness between adults and infants is more evident. Among bonobos, chimpanzees, and gorillas, as among most other primates, the mother-infant bond is the strongest and most long-lasting in the group. It may last for many years; commonly for the lifetime of the mother. Gorilla infants share their mothers' nests and have been seen sharing nests with mature, childless females. Bonobo, chimpanzee, and gorilla males are attentive to juveniles, and may share in parental responsibilities. Bonobo males seem most involved with their young and even carry infants on occasion, including those from different groups. Moreover, a male's interest in a youngster does not elicit the nervous reaction from the mother as it does among chimps. This latter relates to the regular, if infrequent, practice of infanticide on the part of chimpanzee males, a practice never observed among bonobos.

SEXUAL BEHAVIOR

Among the three foregoing species, as with humans, there is no fixed breeding season. Sexual activity between the sexes, however—initiated by either the male or the female—occurs only during the period each month when the female is receptive to impregnation. This is signaled, in the case of chimps and bonobos, by vivid swelling of the skin around their genitals. Because this swelling continues even after conception until youngsters are weaned (at about age 4), females continue to attract attention of males. Gorillas, by contrast, show little interest in sex after conception. To a degree, chimps are promiscuous in their sexual behavior, and 12 to 14 males have been observed to have as many as 50 copulations in one day with a single female. Nor do females appear to show preference for known over strange males, sometimes wandering off to mate with males of another group. Generally,

Grooming is an important activity among all catarrhine primates, as shown here. Such activity is important for strengthening bonds between individual members of the group.

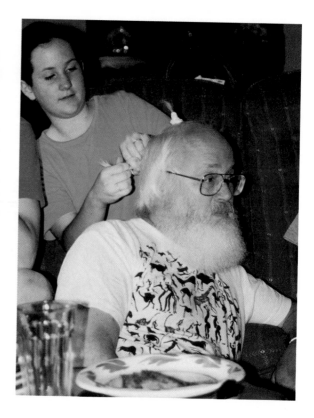

dominant males try to monopolize females in full estrus, although cooperation from the female is usually required for this to succeed. By making herself scarce, she may be able to exercise some choice, showing preference for a male who has previously shared food and groomed her. An alpha male, however, is able to monopolize the females to some extent, and some alphas have been seen to monopolize several estrus females at the same time.

Although mating behavior among bonobos resembles that of chimps, there are differences. For example forced copulation has never been observed among bonobos.[10] But their sexuality goes far beyond male-female mating, as they have been observed having sex in virtually all combinations of ages and sex. Between adult males and females, it occurs primarily when the female is swollen; other forms of sex may occur at other times. Particularly common is genital rubbing among females, which functions to reduce tensions. Whereas chimps often settle disputes by aggressive behavior, bonobos often do so through sex.

In gorilla families, the dominant silverback has exclusive breeding rights with the females, although he may allow a young silverback occasional access to a low-ranking female. Otherwise, the young silverback must leave "home" in order to find sex partners, usually by luring them away from other established groups.

Although the vast majority of primate species are not "monogamous" in their mating habits, many smaller species of New World monkeys, a few island-dwelling populations of leaf-eating Old World monkeys, and all of the smaller apes (gibbons and siamangs) do mate for life with a single individual of the opposite sex. None of these species is closely related to human beings, nor do "monogamous" species ever display the degree of

---

[10]de Waal, F. (1998). Comment. *Current Anthropology, 39,* 407.

Female bonobos frequently engage in genital rubbing, as here. Such sexual activity is an important means of reducing tension.

sexual dimorphism—anatomical differences between males and females—that is characteristic of our closest primate relatives, or that was characteristic of our own ancient ancestors.

PLAY

Frequent play activity among primate infants and juveniles is a means of learning about the environment, testing strength (rank in dominance hierarchies is based partially—but only partially—on size and strength), and generally learning how to behave as adults. Chimpanzee infants mimic the food-getting activities of their mothers, "attack" dozing adults, and "harass" adolescents.

Observers have watched young gorillas do somersaults, wrestle, and play tug-of-war, follow the leader, and king of the mountain. One juvenile, becoming annoyed at repeated harassment by an infant, picked it up, climbed a tree, and deposited it on a branch from which it was unable to get down on its own, and its mother had to retrieve it.

COMMUNICATION

Primates, like many animals, vocalize. They have a great range of calls that are often used together with movements of the face or body to convey a message. Observers have not yet established the meaning of all the sounds, but a good number have been distinguished, such as warning calls, threat calls, defense calls, and gathering calls; the behavioral reactions of other animals hearing the call have also been studied. Among bonobos, chimpanzees, and gorillas, vocalizations are mainly emotional rather than propositional. Much of these species' communication takes place by the use of specific gestures and postures. Indeed, a number of these, such as kissing and embracing, are in virtually universal use today among humans, as well as apes.

Primatologists have classified numerous kinds of chimpanzee vocalization and visual communication (see Figure 4.6). Together, these facilitate group protection, coordination of group efforts,

---

Sexual dimorphism. Within a single species, the presence of marked anatomical differences between males and females.

and social interaction in general. One form of communication appears to be unique to bonobos: the use of trail markers. When foraging, the community breaks up into smaller groups, rejoining again in the evening to nest together. To keep track of each party's whereabouts, those in the lead will, at the intersections of trails or where downed trees obscure trails, deliberately stomp down the vegetation so as to indicate their direction, or rip off large leaves and place them

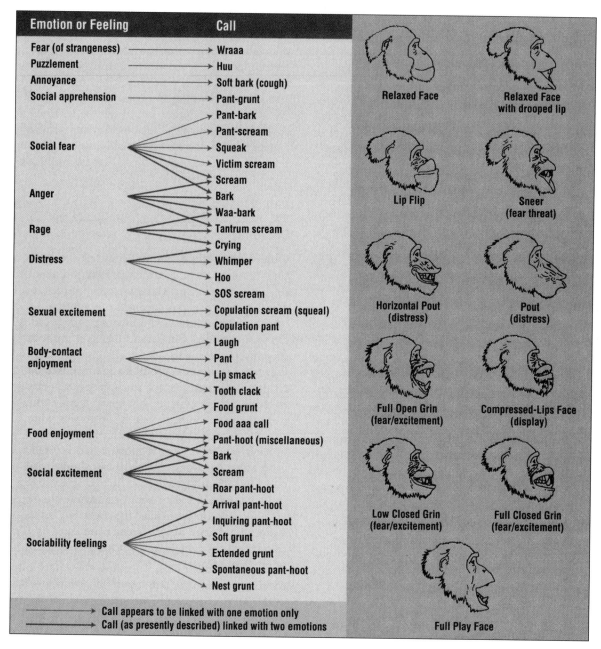

FIGURE 4.6

Chimpanzee communication combines a number of distinctive calls with different facial expressions.

carefully for the same purpose. Thus, they all know where to come together at the end of the day.[11]

Experiments with captive apes, discussed later in this chapter, reveal that their communicative abilities exceed what they make use of in the wild. From such experiments, we may learn something about the origin of human language.

HOME RANGES

Primates usually move about within circumscribed areas, or **home ranges,** which are of varying sizes, depending on the size of the group and on ecological factors such as availability of food. Ranges are often moved seasonally. The distance traveled by a group in a day varies, but may include many miles. Some areas of a range, known as "core areas," are used more often than others; they may contain water, food sources, resting places, and sleeping trees. The ranges of different groups may overlap, as among bonobos, where 65% of one "territory" may overlap with another.[12] By contrast, chimpanzee territories, at least in some regions, are exclusively occupied.

Gorillas do not defend their home ranges against incursions of others of their kind, although they certainly will defend their group if it is in any way threatened. Thus, they may be said to be nonterritorial. In encounters with other communities, bonobos will defend their immediate space through vocalizations and displays, but rarely through fighting. Usually, they settle down and feed side by side, not infrequently grooming, playing, and engaging in sexual activity between groups as well. Chimpanzees, by contrast, have been observed patrolling their territories to ward off potential trespassers. Moreover, Goodall has recorded the destruction of one chimpanzee community by another

that invaded the first one's turf. This sort of lethal intercommunity interaction has never been observed among bonobos. Although it has been interpreted as territorial behavior, another interpretation is possible.[13] In Africa today, human encroachment is squeezing chimpanzees into ever smaller pockets of forest. This places considerable stress on animals whose levels of violence tend to increase in the absence of sufficient space. Perhaps the violence that Goodall witnessed was a response to crowding as a consequence of human encroachment. Another factor may be frustration engendered by artificial feeding. Among primates in general, the clearest territoriality appears in forest species, rather than in those that are more terrestrial in their habits.

LEARNING

Observation of monkeys and apes has shown that their learning abilities are remarkably humanlike. In an experiment carried out by some Japanese primatologists, a group of Japanese macaques was fed wheat; within four hours, wheat eating had spread to the entire group of macaques living in the valley. Inventive behavior has also been observed among Japanese macaques. A group living on an island off the Japanese coast learned to clean sweet potatoes by dipping them in water after observing the young macaque who had first done it. From this youngster, the behavior spread to its playmates and some of their mothers. Once a mother had learned to wash sweet potatoes, this skill was always passed on to her offspring.

The more we learn about catarrhines in general, and apes in particular, the more we become aware of a degree of intelligence and capacity for conceptual thought hitherto unsuspected for any nonhuman primate.

---

[11]Recer, P. (1998, February 16). Apes shown to communicate in the wild. *Burlington Free Press,* p. 12A.

[12]Parish, A. R. (1998). Comment. *Current Anthropology, 39,* 414.

---

[13]Power, M. G. (1995). Gombe revisited: Are chimpanzees violent and hierarchical in the "free" state? *General Anthropology, 2*(1), 5–9.

Home range.   The area within which a group of primates usually moves.

The Intellectual Abilities of Orangutans[14]

Both the fossil data and comparisons of DNA and other biochemical measures suggest that the orangutan is the most conservative, or primitive, of the great apes. They are most like the ancestral hominoid (ape-like primate) living about 12 million years ago that later gave rise to apes and humans. Orangutans have retained more of the characteristics of this hominoid than have the African apes. As a result, orangutans have been labeled a "living fossil," and thus are a kind of time traveler.

Orangutans have amazing abilities that need wider recognition within both the general population and the scientific community. Cognitive studies with orangutans have shown that they are at least as intelligent as the African apes, and have revealed a humanlike insightful thinking style characterized by longer attention spans and quiet deliberate action. Susan Essock and Duane Rumbaugh commented: "Chimpanzees are often reputed to be the 'smartest' of the apes, and orangutans have the reputation of being dull and sluggish. Such tags are unfortunate and contrary to the results of studies."

Orangutans make shelters and other tools in their natural setting. In captivity, they learn to tie knots, recognize themselves in mirrors, use one tool to make another, and are the most skilled of the apes in manipulating objects. They are the escape artists of zoos because of their ability to cleverly manipulate bolts and wires to get out of their enclosures, a trait with which I have become very familiar. In discussing these tendencies, Benjamin Beck has compared the probable use of a screwdriver by chimpanzees, gorillas, and orangutans. The gorilla would largely ignore it, the chimpanzee would try to use it in a number of ways other than as a screwdriver, and:

> The orangutan would notice the tool at once but ignore it lest a keeper discover the oversight. If a keeper did notice, the ape would rush to the tool and surrender it only in trade for a quantity of preferred food. If the keeper did not notice, the ape would wait until night and then proceed to use the screwdriver to pick the locks or dismantle the cage and escape.

Wright showed an orangutan named Abang how to strike flakes from a piece of flint to make a knife, as our hominid ancestors did 2 million years ago. After Abang learned to make flakes, he opened a box containing food by cutting a string that held it closed.

Finding that orangutan and human brains are similar in areas specialized for language prompted scientists to speculate that orangutans could possibly be taught to use gestural signs. Since 1973, I have been doing just that, first with chimpanzees, and, more recently, with an orangutan named Chantek. Now we do not have to wonder about what might be in the

Chantek: An Orangutan Who Uses Sign Language

[14]Miles, H. L. W. (1993). Language and the orangutan: The old "person" of the forest. In P. Cavalieri & P. Singer (Eds.), *The great ape project* (pp. 45–50). New York: St. Martin's Press.

mind of apes, or what emotions they might feel. If we keep our expectations realistic and use human children as our model, we can just ask them. I have learned much about these creatures, and like my colleagues doing similar research, I have found myself unconsciously experiencing them as persons.

The similarities between apes and humans seemed in conflict with our behavioral differences, until ape language experiments shifted scientific opinion and began to fill in the gap. Attempts to teach speech to orangutans have not been very successful because apes lack the flexible right angle bend to their vocal tract that is necessary to make the range of human vocal sounds. After researchers began to use American Sign Language for the deaf to communicate with chimpanzees and gorillas, I began the first longitudinal study of the language ability of an orangutan named Chantek, who was born at the Yerkes Primate Center in Atlanta, Georgia, USA. There was criticism that symbol-using apes might just be imitating their human caregivers, but there is now growing agreement that orangutans, gorillas, and both chimpanzee species can develop language skills at the level of a 2- to 3-year-old human child.

The goal of Project Chantek was to investigate the mind of an orangutan through a developmental study of his cognitive and linguistic skills. It was a great ethical and emotional responsibility to engage an orangutan in what anthropologists call "enculturation," since I would not only be teaching a form of communication, I would be teaching aspects of the culture upon which that language was based. If my developmental project was successful, I would create a symbol-using creature which would be somewhere between an ape living under natural conditions and an adult human, which threatened to raise as many questions as I sought to answer.

Beginning at 9 months of age, Chantek was raised at the University of Tennessee at Chattanooga by a small group of caregivers who communicated with him by using gestural signs based on American Sign Language for the deaf. Chantek produced his first signs after 1 month and eventually learned to use approximately 150 different signs, forming a vocabulary similar to that of a very young child. Chantek learned names for people (LYN, JOHN), places (YARD, BROCK-HALL), things to eat (YOGURT, CHOCOLATE), actions (WORK, HUG), objects (SCREWDRIVER, MONEY), animals (DOG, APE), colors (RED, BLACK), pronouns (YOU, ME), location (UP, POINT), attributes (GOOD, HURT), and emphasis (MORE, TIME-TO-DO). We found that Chantek's signing was spontaneous and nonrepetitious. He did not merely imitate his caregivers as had been claimed for the sign language-trained chimpanzee Nim; rather, Chantek actively used his signs to initiate communications and meet his needs.

Almost immediately, Chantek began to use his signs in combinations and modulated their meanings with slight changes in how he articulated and arranged his signs. He commented "COKE DRINK" after drinking his coke, "PULL BEARD" while pulling a caregiver's hair through a fence, "TIME HUG" while locked in his cage as his caregiver looked at her watch, and "RED BLACK PAINT" for a group of colored paint jars. At first he used signs to manipulate people and objects to meet his needs, rather than to refer to them. He knew the meaning of his signs the way a pet might associate a can of food or a word with feeding time. But, could he use these signs as symbols, that is, more abstractly to represent a person, thing, action, or idea, even apart from its context or when it was not present?

One indication of the capacity to use symbolic language in both deaf and hearing human children is the ability to point, which some researchers argued that apes could not do spontaneously. Chantek began to point to objects when he was 2 years old, somewhat later than human children, as we might expect. First, he showed and gave us objects, and then he began pointing to where he wanted to be tickled and to where he wanted to be carried. Finally, he could answer questions like WHERE HAT?, WHICH DIFFERENT?, and WHAT WANT? by pointing to the correct object.

As Chantek's vocabulary increased, the ideas that he was expressing became more complex, such as when he signed "BAD BIRD" at noisy birds giving alarm calls, and "WHITE CHEESE FOOD-EAT" for cottage cheese. He understood that things had characteristics or attributes that could be described. He also created combinations of signs that we had never used before. In the way that a child learns language, Chantek began to over- or under-extend the meaning of his signs, which gave us insight into his emotions and how he was beginning to classify his world. For example, he used the sign "DOG" for dogs, a picture of a dog in his viewmaster, orangutans on television, barking noises on the radio, birds, horses, a tiger at the circus, a herd of cows, a picture of a cheetah, and a noisy helicopter that presumably sounded like it was barking. For Chantek, the sign BUG included crickets, cockroaches, a picture of a cockroach, beetles, slugs, small moths, spiders, worms, flies, a picture of a graph shaped like a butterfly, tiny brown pieces of cat food, and small bits of feces. He signed "BREAK" before he broke and shared pieces of crackers, and after he broke his toilet. He signed "BAD" to himself before he grabbed a cat, when he bit into a radish, and for a dead bird.

We also discovered that Chantek could comprehend our spoken English (after the first couple of years we used speech as well as signing). One day when the radio was on, a children's story about a cat was being broadcast. When the narrator said "cat" or made meow sounds, Chantek signed "CAT." We then verbally asked Chantek to sign a number of the words in his vocabulary, which he promptly did, showing that he had developed sign-speech correspondences without intentional training.

Another component of the capacity to use symbols is displacement: the ability to refer to things or events not present. It is an important indicator that symbols are also mental representations that can be held in the mind when the objects to which they refer are not present. This was an extremely important development in the evolution of human language because it freed individuals from the immediate environment and allowed our ancestors to talk about distant times and places. When he was 2 years old, Chantek began to sign for things that were not present. He frequently asked to go to places in his yard to look for animals, such as his pet squirrel and cat who served as playmates. He also made requests for "ICE CREAM," signing "CAR RIDE" and pulling us toward the parking lot for a trip to a local ice-cream shop.

We learned that an orangutan can tell lies. Deception is an important indicator of language abilities since it requires a deliberate and intentional misrepresentation of reality. In order to deceive, you must be able to see events from the other person's perspective and negate his or her perception. Chantek began to deceive from a relatively early age, and we caught him in lies about three times a week. He learned that he could sign DIRTY to get into the bathroom to play with the washing machine, dryer, soap, etc., instead of using the toilet. He also used his signs deceptively to gain social advantage in games, to divert attention in social interactions, and to avoid testing situations and coming home after walks on campus. On one occasion, Chantek stole food from my pocket while he simultaneously pulled my hand away in the opposite direction. On another occasion, he stole a pencil eraser, pretended to swallow it, and "supported" his case by opening his mouth and signing "FOOD-EAT," as if to say that he had swallowed it. However, he really held the eraser in his cheek, and later it was found in his bedroom where he commonly hid objects.

We carried out tests of Chantek's mental ability using measures developed for human children. Chantek reached a mental age equivalent to that of a 2- to 3-year-old child, with some skills of even older children. On some tasks done readily by children, such as using one object to represent another and pretend play, Chantek performed as well as children, but less frequently. He engaged in chase games in which he would look over his shoulder as he darted about, although no one was chasing him. He also signed to his toys and offered them food and drink. Like children, Chantek showed evidence of animism, a tendency to endow objects and events with the attributes of living things. Although none of these symbolic play behaviors were as extensive as they would have been in a human child, the difference appears to be one of degree, not kind.

Chantek also experimented in play and problem solving; for example, he tried vacuuming himself and investigated a number of clever ways to short out the electric fence that surrounded his yard. He learned how to use several tools, such as hammers, nails, and screwdrivers, and he was able to complete tasks using tools with up to 22 problem-solving steps. By the time he was 2 years old, he was imitating signs and actions. We would perform an action and ask him to copy it by signing "DO SAME." He would immediately imitate the behavior, sometimes with novel twists, as when he winked by moving his eyelid up and down with his finger. Chantek also liked to use paints, and his own free-style drawings resembled those of 3-year-old human children. He learned to copy horizontal lines, vertical lines, and circles. By $4\frac{1}{2}$ years of age, Chantek could identify himself in the mirror and use it to groom himself. He showed evidence of planning, creative simulation, and the use of objects in novel relations to one another to invent new meanings. For example, he simulated the context for food preparation by giving his caregiver two objects needed to prepare his milk formula and staring at the location of the remaining ingredient.

The above examples show evidence of intentionality, premeditation, taking the perspective of the other, displacement, and symbolic use of language. These cognitive processes require that some form of mental image about the outcome of events be created. A further indication that Chantek had mental images is found in his ability to respond to his caregiver's request that he improve the articulation of a sign. When his articulation became careless, we would ask him to "SIGN BETTER." Looking closely at us, he would sign slowly and emphatically, taking one hand to put the other into the proper shape. Evidence for mental images also comes from Chantek's spontaneous execution of signs with his feet, which we did not teach him to do. Chantek even began to use objects in relation to each other to form signs. For example, he used the blades of scissors instead of his hands to make the sign for biting.

Chantek was extremely curious and inventive. When he wanted to know the name of something, he offered his hands to be molded into the shape of the proper sign. But language is a creative process, so we were pleased to see that Chantek began to invent his own signs. He invented: NO-TEETH (to show us that he would not use his teeth during rough play); EYE-DRINK (for contact lens solution used by his caregivers); DAVE-MISSING-FINGER (a name for a favorite university employee who had a hand injury); VIEWMASTER (a toy that displays small pictures); and BALLOON. Like our ancestors, Chantek had become a creator of language, the criterion that 200 years earlier Lord Monboddo had said would define orangutans as persons.

We had a close relationship with Chantek. He became extremely attached to his caregivers, and began to show empathy and jealousy toward us. He would quickly "protect" us from an "attacking" toy animal or other pretence. He clearly missed favorite caregivers and occasionally asked to see us. When he was 8 years old, he became too large to live on campus, and he returned to the Yerkes Center in Atlanta, Georgia, to live. It was a difficult transition, and he missed his familiar companions and activities. One day he sat sadly, and signed "POINT GIVE ANN" while gesturing toward the front door. He watched the door and the different cars and individuals that passed by—waiting for Ann. His loneliness was somewhat relieved when he was introduced to two female orangutans at the Yerkes Center. Although he impregnated one of them, the offspring died shortly after birth. In the future, not only is it important that Chantek have an opportunity to continue to interact with other orangutans, but it is also important that his enculturation not be forgotten. My goal is for our interaction to continue, and for Chantek to have an opportunity to use his signs not only with other humans, but with other orangutans as well.

We have lived day to day with Chantek and have shared common experiences, as if he were a child. We have healed his hurts, comforted his fears of stray cats, played keep-away games, cracked nuts in the woods with stones, watched him sign to himself, felt fooled by his deceptions and frustrated when he became bored with his tasks. We have dreamed about him, had conversations in our imagination with him, and loved him. Through these rare events shared with another species, I have no doubt I was experiencing Chantek as a person.

USE OF OBJECTS AS TOOLS

In the wild, gorillas do not make or use tools in any significant way, but chimpanzees (like orangutans) do. For our purposes, a **tool** may be defined simply as an object used to facilitate some task or activity. Here, a distinction must be made between simple tool *use,* as when one pounds something with a convenient stone when a hammer is not available, and tool *making,* which involves deliberate modification of some material for its intended use. Thus, otters that use unmodified stones to crack open clams may be tool users, but they are not toolmakers. Not only do chimpanzees modify objects to make them suitable for particular purposes, but chimps can to some extent modify them to regular and set patterns. They can also pick up, and even prepare, objects for future use at some other location, and they can use objects as tools to solve new and novel problems. For example, chimps have been observed using stalks of grass, twigs that they have stripped of leaves, and even sticks up to 3 feet long that they have smoothed down to "fish" for termites. They insert the modified stick into a termite nest, wait a few minutes, pull the stick out, and eat the insects clinging to it, all of which requires considerable dexterity. Chimpanzees are equally deliberate in their nest building. They test the vines and branches to make sure they are usable. If they are not, the animal moves to another site.

Other examples of chimpanzee use of objects as tools involve leaves, used as wipes or as sponges, to get water out of a hollow to drink. Large sticks may serve as clubs or as missiles (as may stones) in aggressive or defensive displays. Stones or rocks are also used as hammers and anvils to open palm nuts and hard fruits. Interestingly, tool use to fish for termites or to crack open nuts is most often exhibited by females, whereas aimed throwing of rocks and sticks is most often exhibited by males. Such tool-using behavior, which young animals learn from their mothers and other adults in their group, may reflect one of the preliminary adaptations that, in the past, led to human cultural behavior.

In the wild, bonobos have not been observed making and using tools to the extent that chimpanzees do. However, the use of large leaves as trail markers may be considered a form of tool use. That these animals do have further capabilities is exemplified by a captive bonobo who has figured out how to make tools of stone that are remarkably like the earliest such tools made by our own ancestors.

Although (like bonobos and chimps) gorillas build nests, they are the only one of the four great apes that have not been observed to make and use other tools in the wild. The reason for this is probably not that gorillas lack the intelligence or skill to do so; rather, their easy diet of leaves and nettles makes tools pointless.

The chimpanzee is using a tool to fish for termites.

Tool. An object used to facilitate some task or activity. While toolmaking involves intentional modification of the material of which it is made, tool use may involve objects either modified for some particular purpose or completely unmodified.

Among chimpanzees, meat is commonly shared with other adults. Here, a group of related males shares the prey.

HUNTING

The hunting, killing, and eating of small to medium-sized mammals, something that is unusual among primates, has been observed among bonobos and chimps, but not among gorillas. Although chimpanzee females sometimes hunt, males do so far more frequently. When on the hunt, they may spend up to 2 hours watching, following, and chasing intended prey. Moreover, in contrast to the usual primate practice of each animal finding its own food for itself, hunting frequently involves teamwork to trap and kill prey. The most sophisticated examples of this occur when hunting baboons; once a potential victim has been partially isolated from its troop, three or more adults will carefully position themselves so as to block off escape routes while another climbs toward the prey for the kill. Once a kill has been made, it is common for most of those present to get a share of the meat, either by grabbing a piece as the chance affords, or by sitting and begging for a piece. Whatever the nutritional value of meat, hunting is not done purely for dietary purposes, but for political and sociosexual reasons as well. The giving of meat helps cement alliances between males, and its sharing may be used also to entice a swollen female to have sex. In fact, males are more apt to hunt if a swollen female is present, and females in estrus are more successful at begging for meat.

Bonobos, too, hunt, but in their case it is usually the females who do so, duikers (a kind of antelope) being the most frequent prey. The huntresses regularly share the carcasses with other females, but less often with males. Even when the most dominant male throws a tantrum nearby, he may still be denied a share.[15] Not only do females control the spoils of the hunt, they are unusual also in the degree to which they will share fruit. Otherwise, it is interesting to note that, in primates, as among many carnivores, increased cooperation seems to go hand in hand with predation and meat eating.

---

[15]Ingmanson, E. J. (1998). Comment. *Current Anthropology, 39*, 409.

Primate Behavior and Human Evolution

Studies of monkeys and apes living today—especially those most closely related to us, gorillas, bonobos, and chimpanzees—afford essential clues in the reconstruction of adaptations and behavior patterns involved in the emergence of our earliest ancestors. At the same time, we must be careful about how we reconstruct this development. Primates have changed in various ways from earlier times, and undoubtedly certain forms of behavior that they now exhibit were not found among their ancestors. Furthermore, it is important to remember that present-day primate behavior shows considerable variation, not just from one species to another but also from one population to another within a single species. To ignore such variation is to run the risk of faulty generalization—something often seen in the popular literature.

CHAPTER SUMMARY

The Linnaean system classifies living things on the basis of overall similarities into small groups, or species. The characteristics on which Carl von Linné based his system were body structure, body function, and sequence of bodily growth. Modern taxonomy also utilizes such characteristics as chemical reactions of blood, protein structure, and the makeup of the genetic material itself.

The modern primates, like most mammals, are intelligent animals that bear their young live and then nourish them with milk from their mothers. Like other mammals, they maintain constant body temperature and have respiratory and circulatory systems that will sustain high activity. Their skeleton and teeth also resemble those of other mammals, although there are differences of detail.

Modern primates are divided into two suborders. The strepsirhines include lemurs and lorises, which resemble small rodents in body outline. The haplorhines include tarsiers, New and Old World monkeys, apes, and humans. To a greater degree among the haplorhines, and a lesser degree among the strepsirhines, primates show a number of characteristics that developed as adaptations to insect predation in the trees. These adaptive characteristics include a generalized set of teeth, suited to insect eating but also a variety of fruits and leaves as well. These teeth are fewer in number and set in a smaller jaw than in most mammals. Other evolutionary adaptations in the primate line include stereoscopic vision, or depth perception, and an intensified sense of touch. Each of these developments had an effect upon the primate brain, resulting in a general trend toward larger size and greater complexity. There were also changes in the primate skeleton; in particular, a reduction of the snout, an enlargement of the brain case, and numerous adaptations for upright posture and flexibility of limb movement. In addition, changes in the reproductive pattern resulted in fewer offspring born to each female and a longer period of infant dependency.

The apes are humans' closest relatives. Apes include gibbons, siamangs, orangutans, gorillas, bonobos, and chimpanzees. In genetic structure, biochemistry, and anatomy, bonobos, chimpanzees, and gorillas are closest to humans, and thus must share a common ancestry.

The social life of primates is very complex. Primates are social animals, and most species live and travel in groups. Among bonobos and chimpanzees, it is females that may transfer, though not all do so; their sons and often their daughters remain with their mothers for life. In some chimpanzee communities, there is male as well as female transfer. Among gorillas, either males or females may transfer. In all three species, both males and females are organized into dominance hierarchies. In the case of females, the better food and reduced harassment that are a consequence of high rank enhance reproductive success.

A characteristic primate activity is grooming, which is a sign of closeness between individuals. Among bonobos, gorillas, and chimpanzees, sexual interaction between adults of opposite sex generally takes place only when a female is in estrus. Although dominant males try to monopolize females while they are in estrus, the cooperation of the females is usually required for this to succeed. Among bonobos, sex serves as a means of reducing tensions, as in the genital rubbing that frequently takes place between females. Primates have elaborate systems of communication based on vocalizations and gestures. In addition, bonobos employ trail signs to communicate their whereabouts to others. Usually primates move about within home ranges, rather than defended territories.

The diet of most primates is made up of a variety of fruits, leaves, and insects, but bonobos and chimpanzees sometimes hunt, kill, and eat animals as well. Among chimps, most hunting is done by males, and may require considerable teamwork. By contrast, it is usually bonobo females that hunt. Once a kill is made, the meat is generally shared with other animals.

POINTS FOR CONSIDERATION

1. How does physical development relate to the development of "culture" among primates?

2. In what ways can habitat affect the level of cognition, and how has this been important in human evolution?

3. How do humans display similar tendencies of territoriality to other primates? Is it individual, or does this occur at a broader level, as well? What stress-reducing activities or rituals do humans engage in?

4. In the section on Chantek, the orangutan, the author of the study voices a concern over "enculturating" Chantek. What does this say about the author's perceptions of orangutan cognitive abilities? How is this supported within the text, and what are some of the implications about the value and validity of primate studies as a means of recreating possible early human behavior?

SUGGESTED READINGS

de Waal, F. (1996). *Good natured: The origins of right and wrong in humans and other animals.* Cambridge, MA: Harvard University Press.

Primatologist Frans de Waal, though fully up on field studies of wild primates, has spent much of his career studying bonobos and chimpanzees in captivity. In this book he argues that moral behavior can be found in nonhuman animals, most clearly in apes but also in other primates and even nonprimate species. Written for a general audience, but with a strong scientific foundation, the book communicates its message in a clear and responsible way.

Fossey, D. (1983). *Gorillas in the mist.* Burlington, MA: Houghton Mifflin.

Dian Fossey is to gorillas what Jane Goodall is to chimpanzees. Up until the time of her death, Fossey had devoted years to the study of gorilla behavior in the field. This book is about the first 13 years of her study; as well as being readable and informative, it is well illustrated.

Goodall, J. (1990). *Through a window.* Boston: Houghton Mifflin.

This fascinating book is a personal account of Goodall's experiences over 35 years of studying wild chimpanzees in Tanzania. A pleasure to read and a fount of information on the behavior of these apes, the book is profusely illustrated as well.

LeGros Clark, W. E. (1966). *History of the primates* (5th ed.). Chicago: University of Chicago Press.

An old classic, this remains a fine introduction to the comparative anatomy of the primates.

Patterson, F., & Linden, E. (1981). *The education of Koko*. New York: Holt, Rinehart and Winston.

Several experiments with captive apes have sought to investigate the full potential of their communicative abilities, and one of the most interesting is that involving Koko the gorilla. This is a particularly readable account of those experiments and their results.

Chapter 5
FOSSIL PRIMATES

OUR KNOWLEDGE OF THE EARLIEST CATARRHINE
PRIMATES IS BASED PRIMARILY ON FOSSILS FROM
EGYPT'S FAYUM DEPRESSION IN THE DESERT WEST
OF CAIRO. HERE, WINDS AND FLASH FLOODS
HAVE UNCOVERED SEDIMENTS MORE THAN 22
MILLION YEARS OLD, EXPOSING THE REMAINS OF
A TROPICAL RAIN FOREST THAT WAS HOME TO A
VARIETY OF MONKEY-LIKE ANIMALS.

Chapter Preview

When Did the First Primates Appear, and What Were They Like?

The earliest primates had developed by 60 million years ago and were small, arboreal insect eaters. Their initial adaptation to life in the trees set the stage for the subsequent appearance of other primate models.

When Did the First Monkeys and Apes Appear, and What Were They Like?

By the late Eocene epoch, about 37 million years ago, monkeys and apes about the size of modern house cats were living in Africa. By about 20 million years ago, they had proliferated and soon spread over many parts of the Old World. Some forms remained relatively small, while others became quite large, some even larger than present-day gorillas.

What Group of Primates Gave Rise to the Human Line of Evolution?

Present evidence suggests that our own ancestors are to be found among the "ramamorphs," which were widespread between approximately 17 and 8 million years ago. Small versions of these apelike primates seem to have had the right kind of anatomy, and at least some of them lived in situations in which the right kind of selective pressures existed to transform them into primitive hominines.

Almost a century and a half ago, Charles Darwin shattered the surface calm of the Victorian world with his startling theory that humans are cousins of the living apes and monkeys and are descended from the same prehistoric ancestors. What would have been the public reaction, one wonders, if they had known, as we do, that even earlier ancestors were small, mouse-sized creatures that subsisted chiefly on insects and worms? Such primitive creatures date back about 60 million years. These ancient forebears of ours evolved over time into different species as mutations produced variation, which was acted upon by natural selection and genetic drift.

Although many of the primates discussed in this chapter no longer exist, their descendants, which were reviewed in Chapter 4, are to be found living throughout the world. The successful adaptation of the primates is believed to be due largely to their intelligence, a characteristic that reaches its culmination in human beings and which provides for adaptive flexibility. Other physical traits, such as stereoscopic vision and a grasping hand, have also been instrumental in the success of the primates.

What is the justification for studying a form of life whose history is, at best, fragmentary and which existed millions of years ago? The study of these prehistoric primates tells us something we can use to interpret the evolution of the entire primate line, including ourselves. It gives us a better understanding of the physical forces that caused these primitive creatures to evolve into today's primates. Ultimately, the study of these ancient ancestors gives us a fuller knowledge of the processes through which insect-eating, small-brained animals evolved into a toolmaker and thinker that is recognizably human.

▲▽▲▽▲▽▲▽▲▽▲▽▲▽▲▽▲▽▲▽▲▽▲▽▲▽▲

PRIMATE FOSSILS

Considering that primates have tended through the ages to live in environments where the conditions for fossilization are generally poor, we have a surprising number of fossils to work with. While some nearly complete skeletons of ancient primates do exist, more often what we have are specimens of teeth and jawbones, because these structures are durable and are often the only remains of an animal to be found. Thus a whole branch of fossil study based on tooth structures, or dentition, has arisen. Dentition is extremely important in helping to identify and classify different fossil forms; often investigators are able to infer a good deal about the total animal on the basis of only a few teeth found lying in the earth. For example, knowledge of the way the teeth fit together indicates much about the operation of the jaws, suggesting the types of muscles needed. This in turn indicates how the skull must have been shaped to provide accommodation for the musculature. The shape of the jaws and details of the teeth also suggest the type of food that they were suited to deal with, indicating the probable diet of the specimen. Thus a mere jawbone can tell paleoanthropologists a great deal about the animal from which it came.

▲▽▲▽▲▽▲▽▲▽▲▽▲▽▲▽▲▽▲▽▲▽▲▽▲▽▲

MAMMALIAN EVOLUTION AND PRIMATE ORIGINS

An interesting fact about the evolution of the mammals is that the diverse forms with which we are familiar today, including the primates, are the products of an **adaptive radiation** that did not begin until after mammals had been present on the earth for over 100 million years. Actually, the story of mammalian evolution starts as long ago as 280 to 230 million years ago (Figure 5.1). From deposits of this period, which geologists call the Permian, we have the remains of reptiles with features pointing in a distinctly mammalian direction. These mammal-like reptiles were slimmer than most other reptiles, and were flesh eaters. In a series of graded fossils, we can see in them a reduction of bones to a more mammalian number, the shifting of limbs underneath the body, development of a separation between the mouth and nasal cavity, differentiation of the teeth, and so forth.

Adaptive radiation. Rapid diversification of an evolving population as it adapts to a variety of available niches.

MILLIONS OF YEARS AGO	PERIODS	EPOCHS	LIFE FORMS
2		Pleistocene	
5		Pliocene	First undoubted hominines
23		Miocene	
34		Oligocene	
55		Eocene	First undoubted monkey-ape ancestors
65		Paleocene	First undoubted primates
135	Cretaceous		
180	Jurassic		First undoubted mammals
230	Triassic		
280	Permian		Mammal-like reptiles
345	Carboniferous		First reptiles

FIGURE 5.1

This timeline highlights some major milestones in the evolution of mammals.

By 180 million years ago—the end of what geologists call the Triassic period—true mammals were on the scene. We know these and the mammals from the succeeding Jurassic and Cretaceous periods (180 to 65 million years ago) from hundreds of finds of mostly teeth and jaw parts. All of these creatures were small eaters of flesh—such things as insects, worms, and eggs. They seem to have been nocturnal in their habits, which is probably why the senses of smell and hearing became

so developed in mammals. Although things cannot be seen as well in the dark as they can in the light, they can be heard and smelled just as well. Both sound and smell are more complex than sight. If something can be seen it is right there in the animal's line of vision. By contrast, it is possible to smell and hear things around corners and in other hidden places, and in addition to figuring out what it is that is smelled or heard and how far away it is, the animal must also figure out where it is. A further complication is the fact that smells linger, and so the animal must figure out if the cause of an odor is still there or, if not, how old the odor is.

As mammals' senses of hearing and smell became keener, they lost the ability (possessed by reptiles) to see in color. But the new, keener senses and the importance of outwitting both prey and predators served to improve their information-processing capacities and enlarge the part of the brain that handles these—the cerebral cortex—beyond that of reptiles.

Since mammals were developing as such bright, active creatures, it may seem puzzling at first why reptiles continued to be the dominant land animals for more than 100 million years.

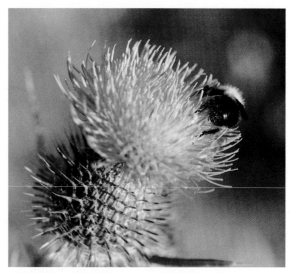

The appearance of angiosperm plants provided not only highly nutritious fruits, seeds, and flowers, but also a host of habitats for numerous edible insects and worms—just the sorts of foods required by mammals with their high metabolism.

After all, mammals, with their constant body temperature, can be active at any time, whereas reptiles become more sluggish as the surrounding temperature drops. Furthermore, mammals provide care for their young, whereas most reptiles leave theirs to fend for themselves. But the mammals faced two limitations. For one, their high activity demanded more nutrition than did the less constant activity of reptiles. Such high-quality nutrition is provided by the fruits, nuts, and seeds of flowering plants, but these plants did not become common until late in the Cretaceous period. It is also provided by the flesh of other animals, but the mammals were small and therefore dependent particularly on small prey such as insects and worms. These were limited in numbers until flowers and fruits provided them with a host of new **ecological niches,** or functional positions in their habitats, to exploit.

The second limitation that affected mammals was the slight head start enjoyed by reptiles; this allowed them to preempt most available niches, which therefore were not available to mammals. With the mass extinction of many reptiles at the end of the Cretaceous, however, a number of existing niches became available to mammals; at the same time, whole new niches were opened up as the new grasses provided abundant food in arid places, and other flowering plants provided abundant, high-quality food elsewhere. By chance, the mammals had what it took in the way of biological equipment to take advantage of the new opportunities available to them.

RISE OF THE PRIMATES

The early primates emerged during a time of great change all over the world. The separation of continents was under way as the result of movement of the great platelike segments of the earth's crust on which they rest. Although Europe was still joined to North America, South America and India were isolated, while a narrow body of water separated Africa from Eurasia (Figure 5.2). On the land itself the great dinosaurs had but recently become extinct, and the

The abilities to judge depth correctly and grasp branches strongly are of obvious importance to animals as active in the trees as most primates.

Ecological niche.   A species' way of life considered in the context of its environment, including other species found in that environment.

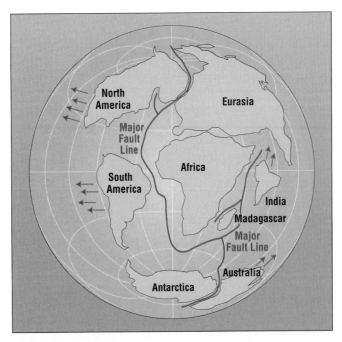

FIGURE 5.2
The separation of the continents resulted from massive shifting in the platelike segments of the earth's crust as illustrated by the position of continents at the end of the Cretaceous period some 65 million years ago.

mammals were undergoing the great adaptive radiation which ultimately led to the development of the diverse forms with which we are familiar today. At the same time, the newly evolved grasses, ivies, shrubs, and other flowering plants were undergoing an enormous proliferation. This diversification, along with a milder climate, favored the spread of dense, lush tropical and subtropical forests over much of the earth, including North and South America and much of Eurasia and Africa. With the spread of these huge belts of forest, the stage was set for the evolution of some mammals from a rodentlike ground existence to the arboreal primate condition. Forests would provide our early ancestors with the ecological niches in which they would flourish.

The move to an arboreal existence brought for early primates a combination of the problems of earthbound existence with those of flight. In their move into the air, birds developed highly stereotyped behavior; tree-dwelling primates, on the other hand, exhibit flexible decision-making behavior. The initial forays into the trees must have produced many misjudgments and errors of coordination, leading to falls that injured or killed the individuals badly adapted to arboreal life. Natural selection favored those that judged depth correctly and gripped the branches strongly. It is quite likely that the early primates that took to the trees were in some measure preadapted, with better vision and more dexterous fingers than their contemporaries.

The relatively small size of the early primates allowed them to make use of the smaller branches of trees; larger, heavier competitors, and most predators, could not follow. The move to the smaller branches also opened up a more abundant food supply; the primates were able to gather insects, leaves, flowers, and fruits directly rather than waiting for them to fall to the ground.

The utilization of a new environment led to an acceleration in the rate of change of primate characteristics. Paradoxically, these changes eventually made possible a return to the ground on the part of some primates, including the ancestors of the genus *Homo*.

Paleocene Primates

Far back in the reaches of geologic time, small, squirrel-like animals resembling today's tree shrews scampered along the branches of trees in tropical forests. Members of the now extinct suborder **Plesiadapiformes,** these creatures appeared during the Paleocene Epoch, about 65 million years ago. They lived mostly on seeds and insects; their muzzles were long and pointed, their ears were small, their wrists and ankles were capable of turning toward each other, enabling them to climb trees, and their digits were flexible and suitable for grasping in spite of the presence of claws.

Since their survival depended on catching live food, these animals had to be quick and intelligent; the latter characteristic was reflected in their brains, which were larger than those of the tree shrews they otherwise resembled. Plesiadapiformes, of which there were a number of species, are known from a series of fossils from North America and Europe. Clearly, they were successful animals in their day, for in North America they account for a bit over a third of late Paleocene mammalian fossils.

Until 1990, plesiadapiformes were generally considered very primitive primates. The subsequent discovery of a particularly well preserved fossil from Wyoming, however, revealed that they were not; rather, they are related to the colugos— gliding mammals that are represented today by two species of "flying lemurs" (which aren't lemurs, nor do they fly; like flying squirrels, they glide). Flying lemurs are found today only in Borneo and the Philippines. Since colugos and primates show a close genetic relationship, both likely shared a common ancestry among the insectivores, probably going their separate evolutionary ways by 60 million years ago. Thus, primates would have arisen as part of the great Paleocene adaptive radiation of mammals.

In fact, the earliest surely known primate fossils, ten teeth from a site in Morocco, are about 60 million years old. These cheek teeth (molars and premolars) are very similar to the correspon-

ding teeth of the modern mouse lemur, a tiny strepsirhine primate weighing a mere two ounces.

Eocene Primates

The Eocene epoch, which lasted from about 55 to 34 million years ago, began with an abrupt warming trend, at which time many older forms of mammals became extinct, to be replaced by recognizable progenitors of many of today's forms. Among the latter were numerous forms of lemurlike and tarsierlike primates, of which over 50 genera are known. Fossils of these creatures have been found in Africa, North America, Europe, and Asia, where the warm, wet conditions of the Eocene sustained extensive rain forests.

Most Eocene primates are classified into two families, the **Adapidae** and the **Omomyidae.** The former were mostly diurnal (active during daylight) and generally ate fruit and leaves. Generally small, some were a bit larger than the smallest of today's monkeys. In many ways they were remarkably similar to modern lemurs and lorises, which likely are their descendants. Smaller than adapids are the omomyids, which were nocturnal eaters of fruits and insects. Tarsierlike in their anatomy, they are closely related to today's tarsier.

What these early primates have in common are somewhat enlarged brain cases, slightly reduced snouts, and a somewhat forward position of the eye orbits, which are surrounded by a complete bony ring (Figure 5.3). Their dentition, however, was primitive and unlike that of modern forms. In their limb skeleton, they were well adapted to grasping, leaping, and perching. Moreover, nails, rather than claws, may be seen on some digits.

A third group of Eocene primates is represented by fossils from late Eocene deposits in Egypt's Fayum depression.[1] Known as *Cato-*

---

[1]Culatta, E. (1992). A new take on anthropoid origins. *Science, 256,* 1516–1517.

Plesiadapiformes. Now-extinct mammals once considered to be primates, now known to be related to colugos (gliding mammals), which share a common ancestry with primates. > **Adapidae.** Extinct family of lemurlike primates. > **Omomyidae.** Extinct family of tarsierlike primates.

pithecus, these 37-million-year-old fossils include several skulls, jaws, and teeth, clearly revealing them to be catarrhine primates. Whether they are the earliest fossils to represent this group is a matter of debate. In 1992, some teeth were discovered in Algeria that could be as many as 46 to 50 million years old, but this is not certain. At least some of the teeth do resemble those of Oligocene hominoids. As for *Catopithecus,* this small creature displays the catarrhine dental formula (two incisors, a canine, two premolars, and three molars on each side of each jaw), a foramen magnum in a somewhat forward position beneath the skull, a com-

pletely walled eye orbit, and a brain about 3.1 cubic centimeters in size.[2]

Whether the group of primates that gave rise to *Catopithecus* arose at the same time as the adapids and omomyids, or from some early form of one or the other of these two families, has been a matter of lively debate, as illustrated by the following Original Study.

---

[2]Simons, E. (1995). Skulls and anterior teeth of *Catopithecus* (Primates: Anthropoidea) from the Eocene and anthropoid origins. *Science, 268,* 1885–1888.

Catopithecus and Anthropoid (Catarrhine and Platyrrhine) Origins[3]

▲▽

When paleontologists disagree, they rarely have the luxury of doing another experiment to see who's right. Instead, they must resort to a more chancy and time-consuming enterprise: returning to the field and unearthing more fossils that prove their point. Paleoanthropologist Elwyn Simons of Duke University claims to have done just that. He presents new fossils from the Fayum Desert in Egypt to help resolve one of the most contentious issues in paleoprimatology: What was the common ancestor of apes, monkeys, and humans?

The new fossils, estimated to be 37 million years old, include rarely preserved front teeth of the oldest undisputed higher primate, a small leaf- or insect-eating creature called *Catopithecus.* But given the difficulty of proving kinship among ancient primates, the finds are unlikely to forge consensus about this divisive issue. "These are neat specimens, but they don't address all the competing hypotheses. Until we have more complete material from Asia and Egypt, questions will remain," says early-primate expert Herbert Covert of the University of Colorado, Boulder.

The problem of the origin of higher primates, also known as anthropoids, has sparked scientific fireworks for decades. Currently, there are at least four competing theories about how, when, and where anthropoids split from lower primates such as the primitive living lemurs. One theory favors an extinct group of primates, the diminutive omomyids, as anthropoid ancestors. Another camp, relying on fragmentary fossils from Africa and Asia, suggests that anthropoids themselves are an ancient group, extending back nearly to the dawn of all primates. And Simons says his new specimens support yet a third idea: Another extinct group, the lemurlike adapids, eventually led to all higher primates, including humans. "The oldest documented anthropoids don't look like omomyids. They look like adapids," he says.

Simons bases this conclusion on newly discovered fossils from an extraordinarily productive area of the Fayum Desert in Egypt where he and

---

[3]Culatta, E. (1995). New finds rekindle debate over anthropoid origins. *Science, 268,* 1851.

his crew have already unearthed 21 different primate species. The new fossils are skulls and jaws of *Catopithecus*, which has held the status of oldest undisputed anthropoid since Simons published the first skull 5 years ago. The new skulls—five or six in all—confirm that this small primate had the accepted anthropoid traits, such as a complete bony cone around the eye socket and forehead bones that are fused together rather than separate.

The new material also preserves incisors and canine teeth in the jaws, a rare find, as front teeth are often broken or lost. These teeth have adapoid traits such as shovel-shaped incisors, says Simons. In contrast, omomyid incisors are pointed, "like carrots," he says.

What's more, *Catopithecus'* upper jaw reveals two big front teeth flanked by smaller ones (just as in humans), while in the lower jaw the lateral incisors are bigger than the central ones. Adapids have exactly the same pattern, but omomyids do not. All in all, according to Simons, *Catopithecus'* teeth look very similar to adapids' and nothing like omomyids', suggesting that anthropoids evolved from a branch of the adapid family tree. "The dental resemblances, taken together, show ties between the early anthropoid of the Fayum and one group of adapids, the cercamoniines," he says. He believes early cercamoniines led to higher primates.

Simons gets support from Philip Gingerich of the University of Michigan, who came to similar conclusions in the 1970s. At the time, Gingerich was comparing adapids to later anthropoids because the front teeth of early anthropoids were unknown. "It was a case of waiting for more evidence to catch up with the idea," he says.

But those who favor competing theories question whether the similarities between adapids and *Catopithecus* in fact prove they have a common ancestor. "The front teeth are not necessarily compelling characters," says Covert. "They look the same, but do they indicate shared ancestry?" Covert and others think the answer is probably not. Rather than indicating a common ancestry, some of the similarities may have evolved independently in adapids and anthropoids, says anthropologist Robert D. Martin of the University of Zurich in Switzerland: "I think that there is convergence between late adapids and simians (or anthropoids)." Martin praises the Fayum fossils, but says, "I don't find this adapid argument any more convincing than when it was suggested in the 1920s."

Also, although the Fayum deposits hold the first known anthropoids, the group likely evolved much earlier, so *Catopithecus* may look very different from the first higher primates, says Martin. "The Fayum is simply too late," agrees K. Christopher Beard of the Carnegie Museum of Natural History in Pittsburgh, who has his own candidate for the earliest anthropoid. This is a controversial Chinese primate, about 45 million years old and known from two jaws as well as from unpublished material.

Beard named the fossil *Eosimias*, or "dawn ape," but Simons counters that so far, there's no proof that *Eosimias* or any other older specimens are higher primates. "The trouble with all the other early 'anthropoids' is that they are just known from jaw fragments or even teeth. So for them, none of the confirming features of anthropoids can be discerned," he says. "Only the Fayum has certifiable early anthropoids." Simons is not alone in his skepticism about Beard's finds. Says Martin: "About *Eosimias*, I'm on the fence for now."

Artist's reconstruction of *Eosimias*, an early catarrhine primate.

Still, Beard continues to unearth fragmentary fossils to support his case, most recently a fossil ear bone that he says conflicts with the notion of an adapid ancestor for anthropoids. In an article in press in the *Journal of Human Evolution,* Beard and Ross MacPhee of the American Museum of Natural History show that this ear bone looks much more like an omomyid than an adapid. Thus, although they believe that the anthropoid lineage extends back at least 45 million years, MacPhee and Beard also conclude that anthropoids are more closely related to omomyids than to adapids.

But that argument hasn't won over the skeptics either. The bone was found isolated, so MacPhee and Beard can't prove that it truly belongs to *Eosimias.* And the ear bone looks so much like that of an omomyid that it doesn't boost *Eosimias'* uncertain status as an anthropoid, says paleoanthropologist Richard Kay of Duke. Agrees Gingerich: "That ear bone looks most like an omomyid, which I take to mean that it probably is an omomyid."

These recent volleys of evidence, some promoting an adapid ancestor for anthropoids, others suggesting an ancient link to omomyids, seem unlikely to end the debate. So how to solve the mystery of which early primate group led to our own lineage? On this, even Beard and Simons agree: more field seasons, and more fossils.

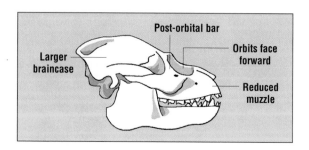

Figure 5.3

The Eocene genus Adapis represents the Adapidae.

Since the above study was written, additional fragments of *Eosimias* have come to light, including fragments of cranium and other parts of the skeleton. These have strengthened the case that it was a small, probably insect-eating relative of platyrrhine and catarrhine primates. Furthermore, it now appears that adapid primates really can be ruled out as ancestral to haplorhines; the shared dental resemblances seem to be retained from more ancient primate ancestors. Omomyids probably resemble the ancestral stock that gave rise to the haplorhines, but the latter (like the adapids) were probably diurnal rather than nocturnal. Omomyids and tarsiers, with their large eyes, seem to have reverted to nocturnal habits, whereas the ancestors of platyrrhines and catarrhines did not. They shifted to a more herbivorous diet, with greater emphasis on arboreal quadrupedalism, in contrast to the emphasis on leaping seen in omomyids and tarsiers.[4]

With the end of the Eocene, substantial changes took place among the primates, as among other mammals. In North America, primates became extinct and elsewhere their range seems to have been reduced considerably. A driving force in all this was probably climatic change. Already,

through the late Eocene, climates were becoming somewhat cooler and drier, but at the end temperatures took a sudden dive, sufficient to trigger formation of a substantial ice cap over Antarctica. The result was a marked reduction of the environments to which early primates were adapted. At the same time, some early primate niches may have been more effectively utilized by newly evolved rodent forms. Finally, the precursors of monkeys and apes, up to then overshadowed by adapids and omomyids, may have been able to take over some other niches formerly occupied by the early adapids and omomyids.

Oligocene Monkeys and Apes

The Oligocene epoch began about 34 million and ended about 23 million years ago. Primate fossils that have thus far been discovered and definitely placed in the Oligocene are not common, but enough exist to prove that haplorhines were becoming quite prominent and diverse by this time. The scarcity of Oligocene primate fossils stems from the reduced habitat available to them and from the arboreal nature of primates then living, which restricted them to damp forest environments where conditions are exceedingly poor for fossil formation.

Fortunately, Egypt's Fayum depression has yielded sufficient fossils (more than 1,000) to reveal that by 33 million years ago, haplorhine primates existed in considerable diversity. Moreover, the "cast of characters" is growing, as new fossils continue to be found in the Fayum, as well as in newly discovered localities in Algeria and Oman. At present, we have evidence of at least 60 genera included in two families, **Parapithecidae** and **Propliopithecidae**. Included in the latter is *Catopithecus*. Both families show a combination of monkeylike and apelike features, but the parapithecids are generally smaller than the propliopithecids. The origins of both families probably lie in the third, less numerous group of Eocene primates just discussed, but in the Oligocene the tables have been turned;

---

[4]Kay, R. F., Ross, C., & Williams, B. A. (1997). Anthropoid origins. *Science, 275,* 803–804.

Parapithecidae. Extinct family of small haplorhine primates. ▶ **Propliopithecidae.** Extinct family of haplorhine primates, probably ancestral to hominoids.

This *Aegyptopithecus* skull dates to the Oligocene epoch. The enclosed eye sockets and dentition mark it as a catarrhine primate, probably ancestral to *Proconsul.*

now lemurlike and tarsierlike forms have become far less prominent than forms that combine monkeylike and apelike features.

Included among the parapithecids may be the ancestors of monkeys. In their dental formula and limb bones, these small primates (about the size of a modern squirrel monkey) resemble platyrrhine monkeys. Some of them could easily have gotten to South America via exposed oceanic ridges and islands between the two continents which, in the Oligocene, were far closer to each other than they are today. The earliest surely known catarrhine monkey fossil comes from the Miocene epoch, but its molars look as if they evolved from an earlier pattern much like one seen in parapithecids.

More apelike in their dentition are a number of other genera, of which the best known is *Aegyptopithecus* (the "Egyptian ape"). Its lower molars have the five cusps of an ape, and the upper canine and lower first premolar provide the sort of shearing mechanism found in apes. Its skull possesses eye sockets that are in a forward position and completely protected by a bony wall, as is typical of modern monkeys and apes. Evidently *Aegyptopithecus*, and probably the other propliopithecids and parapithecids as well, possessed vision superior to that of the Eocene adapids and omomyids, not to mention their modern relatives, the lemurs and tarsiers. In fact, the inside of the skull of *Aegyptopithecus* reveals that its brain had

a larger visual cortex and smaller olfactory lobes than do lemurs or tarsiers. Although the brain of *Aegyptopithecus* was smaller relative to body size than that of more recent catarrhines, this primate seems to have had a larger brain than any lemur or tarsier, past or present.

Aegyptopithecus, besides being the best-known Oligocene primate, is also of interest to us for its teeth, which suggest that it belongs in the ancestry of those Miocene forms that gave rise to both humans and today's African apes. Although no bigger than a modern house cat, *Aegyptopithecus* was nonetheless one of the larger Oligocene primates. Possessed of a monkeylike skull and body, with limb proportions not unlike those seen in some modern platyrrhine monkeys, and fingers and toes capable of powerful grasping, it evidently moved about in a quadrupedal monkeylike manner.[5] Differences between males and females include more formidable canine teeth and deeper mandibles (lower jaws) in the males. In modern catarrhines, species with these traits generally live in groups that include several adult females with one or more adult males.

MIOCENE APES

The beginning of the Miocene epoch, which succeeded the Oligocene about 23 million years ago, saw the catarrhine primates still restricted to Africa, where they had originated. Around 17 million years ago, however, Africa came into contact with the Eurasian landmass, permitting the spread and proliferation of apes in the forests that covered many parts of the Old World.

East Africa is an area particularly rich in the fossils of apes from the early through the middle part of the Miocene. The earliest of these apes, *Proconsul,* is one of the best known, owing to the preservation of almost all elements of its skeleton. Four recognized species of *Proconsul* varied considerably in size, the smallest being no larger than

---

[5]Ankel-Simons, F., Fleagle, J. G., & Chatrath, P. S. (1998). Femoral anatomy of *Aegyptopithecus zeuxis,* an early Oligocene anthropoid. *American Journal of Physical Anthropology, 106,* 421–422.

Paleoanthropologist Alan Walker displays bones of *Proconsul,* an unspecialized tree-dwelling, fruit-eating hominoid of the early Miocene.

knee, and foot anatomy of *Proconsul* is similar to what one sees in living hominoids, and like them, it had no tail (Figure 5.4). The wrist and pelvis, however, are monkeylike and the lumbar vertebrae and leg bones show features that are intermediate between those of a gibbon and a monkey. Over-all, the vertebral column was longer and more flex-ible, and the torso narrower than in apes, but the hind limb was less monkeylike, being more mobile as are ape hind limbs. The consensus is that *Proconsul* represents an unspecialized tree-dwelling, fruit-eating **hominoid** (the catarrhine superfamily to which modern apes and humans belong). Easily derivable from an animal like *Aegyptopithecus,* it was almost certainly ancestral to hominoids of the middle Miocene. Like its prob-able ancestor as well as its descendants, all species of *Proconsul* were sexually dimorphic, the males being the larger sex with more formidable canine teeth.

Contemporary with *Proconsul* is *Moroto-pithecus,* whose limb bones have recently been found at Moroto, in Uganda. What they indicate is a shoulder joint more like that of an ape than *Proconsul's,* permitting suspension of the body when hanging by the arms. Leg bones suggest strong climbing ability, and previously found ver-tebrae are indicative of a stiffer, apelike body. Otherwise details of teeth, face, and body are comparable to *Proconsul.*[6]

Most hominoids of the middle and late Miocene (from roughly 16 million to 5 million years ago) can be divided into two broad groups, informally labeled dryomorphs and ramamorphs (a third group, pliomorphs, retain more primitive characteristics and need not concern us here).[7] In the former group are several species of forest-dwelling primates having teeth and jaws very much like those of the earlier *Proconsul.* They

a modern female baboon, while the largest was the size of a female gorilla. That they were apes is clearly shown by their dentition, particularly the five-cusped lower molars. Moreover, their skull, compared to that of the Oligocene proto-apes, shows a reduced snout and a fuller, more rounded brain case. Cranial capacity for one species is es-timated at about 167 cubic centimeters, about 1.5 times larger than that typical of a mammal of com-parable body size, and relatively larger than in modern monkeys. Still, some features are reminis-cent of monkeys, particularly the forward thrust and narrowness of the face.

Although its overall configuration is not quite like any living monkey or ape, the elbow, hip,

[6]Gebo, D. L., MacLatchy, L., Kityo, R., Deino, A., Kingston, J., & Pilbeam, D. (1997). A hominoid genus from the early Miocene of Uganda. *Science, 276,* 401–404.

[7]Conroy, G. C. (1997). *Reconstructing human origins: A modern synthesis* (p. 94). New York: W. W. Norton.

Hominoid. A catarrhine primate superfamily that includes apes and humans.

FIGURE 5.4

Reconstructed skeleton of *Proconsul*. Note apelike absence of tail, but monkeylike limb proportions. *Proconsul*, however, was capable of greater rotation of forelimbs than monkeys.

seem to have been somewhat more apelike, rather than monkeylike in their overall appearance, however; like earlier *Morotopithecus,* they had relatively rigid bodies as well as limb bones well adapted for suspension and climbing. Dry-omorphs ranged over a remarkably wide geographical area: Their fossils have been found in Europe, Asia, and Africa. Such abundance and wide distribution indicates that these primates were very successful animals.

RAMAMORPHS

Also living in parts of Africa, Asia, and Europe were various genera of hominoids lumped together as **ramamorphs** (sometimes called "sivapithecines" and sometimes "ramapithecines") (Figure 5.5). Closely related to the dryomorphs, they too may be descendants of the earlier *Proconsul* or *Moro-topithecus.* According to David Pilbeam, who has made the study of Miocene hominoids his life-

Ramamorphs. A group of hominoids that includes the ancestor of orangutans, and probably of bonobos, chimpanzees, gorillas, and humans as well.

FIGURE 5.5
Ramamorph fossils have been found in East Africa, Europe and Asia.

work: "Any of [the ramamorphs] would make excellent ancestors for the living hominoids: human bipeds, chimpanzee and gorilla knucklewalkers, Orangutan contortionists."[8] For many years, ra-

---

[8]Pilbeam, D. (1986). *Human origins* (p. 6). David Skamp Distinguished Lecture in Anthropology, Indiana University.

mamorphs were known exclusively from the remains of teeth and jaws. Relative to the size of the cheek teeth (premolars and molars), their incisor teeth are comparable in size to those of the dryomorphs, although they are placed a bit more vertically in the mouth. The canines are substantially larger in males than in females, but even in males they are significantly smaller relative to the cheek teeth than the canines of any dryomorph. Still, they do project beyond adjacent teeth so that, when closed, the jaws of ramamorphs interlock. Furthermore, the shearing function of the upper canine with the first lower premolar is retained. The molars, which show the same five-cusp pattern as the dryomorphs, have noticeably thicker enamel and low, rounded cusps. The shape of the tooth row tends to be slightly V-shaped, while that of the dryomorphs is more like a U, with the rows of cheek teeth parallel to one another (Figure 5.6). The palate, or roof of the mouth, is high and arched. Finally, the lower facial region of the ramamorphs is narrow, short, and deep. Overall, the dental apparatus was built for powerful chewing, especially on the back teeth.

In the past three decades, our dependence on teeth and jaws for our knowledge of the ramamorphs has lessened as a number of their skull

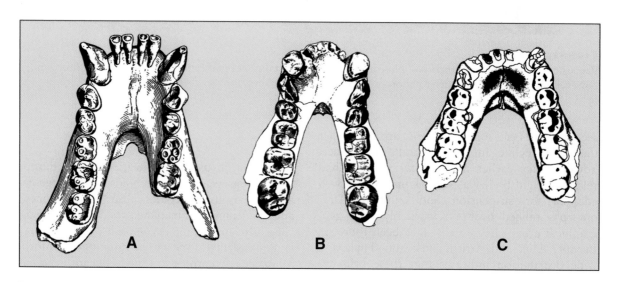

FIGURE 5.6
The lower jaws of a dryomorph (A), ramamorph (B), and early *Australopithecus* (C), a hominine who lived 4 million years ago, demonstrate some important similarities and differences between the three hominoids. Relative to the cheek teeth, all have comparatively small teeth at the front of the jaw. There is general similarity between A and B, as well as B and C. The major difference between the latter is that the rows of cheek teeth are farther apart in the hominine.

This *Sivapithecus* skull is remarkably similar to skulls of modern orangutans, so much so that an ancestor-descendant relationship is probable. The last common ancestor of chimpanzees, gorillas, and humans may not have differed greatly from *Sivapithecus*.

and limb bone fragments have been found in China, Greece, Hungary, Pakistan, and Turkey. In the best-known genus *(Sivapithecus)*, the face is remarkably orangutanlike in its profile and a number of other details. The mandible, however, is only broadly rather than specifically similar to that of an orang, nor are the upper arm bones quite the same.

RAMAMORPHS AND HUMAN ORIGINS

As long as ramamorphs were known only from fossils of teeth and jaws, it was easy to postulate some sort of relationship between them and our-

selves. This was because a number of features—the position of the incisors, the reduced canines, the thick enamel of the molars, and the shape of the tooth row—seemed to point in a somewhat human direction. Some fossils (notably *Kenyapithecus* from East Africa) even show a shallow concavity above the position of the canine tooth, a feature not found in any ape, but often found in humans. Indeed, some even went so far as to see ramamorphs as the earliest representatives of a human, as opposed to any ape lineage. With the discovery of the orangutan-like skulls and apelike limb bones of *Sivapithecus*, however, it became clear that this could not be so, and many anthropologists concluded that ramamorphs could have nothing to do with human origins. Rather, orangutans were seen as the sole modern survivors of an ancient group from which the line leading to the African apes and humans had branched off some 18 to 12 million years ago.

Recently, opinion has shifted back to a middle position. While the link between Miocene *Sivapithecus* and modern orangutans seems undeniable this does not rule out the possibility of a link between other ramamorphs on the one hand and African apes and humans on the other.[9] For example, both orangutans and humans have a thick coat of enamel on their molars, whereas the African apes do not. It now appears that humans, like orangs, retain the thick enamel seen in ramamorphs, whereas chimps and gorillas lost it sometime after the separation of **hominids** from pongids.[10] Then, too, some ramamorphs, such as *Ouranopithecus* from northern Greece, seem closer in dental proportions and other features of their teeth to early hominines than do Asian fossils ascribed to this group.[11]

[9]Ciochon, R. L., & Fleagle, J. G. (1987). *Ramapithecus and human origins*. In R. L. Ciochon & J. G. Fleagle (Eds.), *Primate evolution and human origins* (p. 208). Hawthorne, NY: Aldine de Gruyter.

[10]Lewin, R. (1983). Tooth enamel tells a complex story. *Science, 228*, 707.

[11]Koufos, G. (1993). Mandible of *Ouranopithecus macedoniensis* (Hominidae, Primates) from a new late Miocene locality in Macedonia (Greece). *American Journal of Physical Anthropology, 91*, 232–234.

Hominid. Hominoid family to which humans alone used to be assigned; now includes African apes and humans, with the latter assigned to the subfamily *Homininae*.

Although not identical, the modern ape most like *Sivapithecus* is the orangutan. Chimpanzees and gorillas, like humans, have come to differ more from the ancestral condition than have these Asian apes.

That the ancestry of humans may ultimately be among the apelike ramamorphs, then, is consistent with dental evidence. It is consistent as well with resemblances between the shoulder girdle of the earliest well-known **hominine**, *Australopithecus* (discussed in the next chapter), and that of orangutans (it is elevated in both). This suggests that humans evolved from a primate capable of arm movements like those of orangutans; the ramamorphs were capable of just such arm movements. Finally, the opinion that ramamorphs are ancestral to humans as well as all of today's great apes (Figure 5.7) is in accord with estimates, based on molecular similarities and differences between

humans, bonobos, chimpanzees, and gorillas, that they could not have separated from a common ancestral stock more than 10 million years ago. We know from the fossils that the ramamorphs were still on the scene 8 million years ago (indeed, a form larger than a modern gorilla survived in Asia until about 300,000 years ago) and also that our own human ancestors were going their separate evolutionary way by at least 4.4 million, if not 6 million, years ago.

RAMAMORPH ADAPTATIONS

Molar teeth like those of the ramamorphs, having low crown relief, thick enamel, and surfaces poorly developed for cutting, are found in a number of modern primates.[12] Some of these species are terrestrial and some are arboreal, but all have one thing in common: They eat very hard nuts, fruits with very tough rinds, and some seeds. This provides them with a rich source of easily digested nutrients that are not accessible to species with thin molar enamel incapable of standing up to the stresses of tough rind removal or nut cracking. Thus the ramamorphs probably ate food similar to that eaten by these latter-day nut crackers.

Analysis of other materials from deposits in which ramamorph fossils have been found suggests utilization of a broad range of habitats, including tropical rain forests as well as drier bush country. Of particular interest to us, from the standpoint of human origins, are those populations that lived on the edge of open country, where food could be obtained through foraging on the ground out in the open, as well as in the trees of the forests. As it happened, there was a climatic shift under way, causing a gradual but persistent breaking up of forested areas, with a consequent expansion of open grassland.[13] Under such circumstances, it seems likely that those populations

[12]Kay, R. F. (1981). The nut-crackers—A new theory of the adaptations of the Ramapithecinae. *American Journal of Physical Anthropology, 55,* 141–151.
[13]Conroy, G. C. (1997). *Reconstructing human origins: A modern synthesis* (pp. 84–86). New York: W. W. Norton.

Hominine. Member of the *Homininae,* the subfamily of hominids to which humans belong.

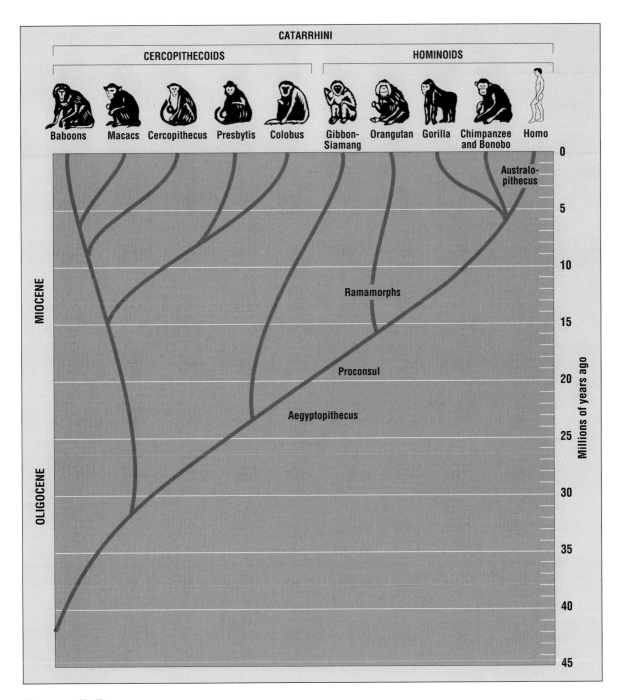

FIGURE 5.7
Although debate continues over details, this chart represents a reasonable reconstruction of evolutionary relationships among the catarrhine primates.

Kenyapithecus, a ramamorph fossil from east East Africa, has relatively small canine teeth and a facial profile suitable for an ancestor of African apes and humans.

Ground-dwelling primates, like this male baboon, depend heavily on their massive canine teeth for protection from other animals. Ramamorphs, by contrast, lacked such massive weapons of defense.

of ramamorphs living at the edge of the forests were obliged to supplement food from the forest more and more with other foods readily available on the ground in more open country. Consistent with this theory, late ramamorph fossils are typically found in association with greater numbers of the remains of animals adapted to grasslands than are earlier ones.

Because ramamorphs already had large, thickly enameled molars, those that had to were capable of dealing with the tough and abrasive foods available on the savanna. What they lacked, however, were canine teeth of sufficient size to have served as effective "weapons" of defense. By contrast, most modern monkeys and apes that spend much time down on the ground rely heavily for defense on the massive, fanglike canines possessed by the males. Since catlike predators were even more nu-

merous on the ground than now, ramamorphs, especially the smaller ones (which probably weighed no more than about 40 pounds[14]), would seem to have been especially vulnerable primates. Probably the forest fringe was more than just a source of foods different from those of the grasslands; its trees would have provided refuge when danger threatened. Yet, with continued expansion of open country, trees for refuge would have become fewer and farther between.

Slowly, however, physical and behavioral changes must have improved these primates' chances for survival out in the open on the ground. For one thing, those that were able to gather food and then carry it to the safety of a tree probably had a better rate of survival than those that did not. Although many species of monkeys have cheek pouches in which to carry food, apes do not. Occasionally, modern apes will assume a bipedal stance in order to transport food in their arms, but they are quite awkward about it. The center of gravity, however, is higher in the body of modern apes than it seems to have been in their earlier ancestors, so that bipedal food transport may not have been quite so awkward for the ramamorphs, especially the smaller ones.

[14]Pilbeam, D. R. (1987). Rethinking human origins. In Ciochon & Fleagle, p. 217.

A young baboon clings to its mother's back. The ability of apes as well as monkeys to carry their infants is limited by their need to use their arms in locomotion.

Food may not have been the only thing transported. Among modern primates, infants must be able to cling to their mothers in order to be transported; since the mother is using her forelimbs in locomotion, either to walk or swing by, she can't very well carry her infant. Chimpanzee infants, for example, must cling for themselves to their mothers, and even at the age of 4 years, they make long journeys on her back. Injuries caused by falling from the mother are a significant cause of infant mortality. Thus, females able to carry their infants would have made a significant contribution to the survivorship of their offspring.

Another advantage of at least the occasional assumption of a bipedal stance would have been the ability to scan the grasslands, so that predators could be spotted before they got too close. Such scanning can be seen from time to time among baboons and chimps today when out on the savanna, even though their anatomy is less suited for this than the ramamorph's was. Bipedalism, too, would have enhanced the ability to use the hands to wield and throw things at predators. Among primates, "threat gestures" typically involve shaking branches and large sticks. On the ground, chimpanzees have been observed on numerous occasions throwing rocks at leopards.

Lacking the large body size and formidable canines of chimps, there is every reason to suppose that the ramamorphs, when away from the trees and faced by a predator, resorted to the same kind of intimidating displays.

Yet another incentive to stand bipedally would be to make use of one of the more abundant food sources available in open country[15]— the thornbushes that are too spiny and unsturdy to be climbed and whose edible seeds, leaves, and pods would have been too high to pick for a primate standing on four (or three) feet. Moreover, by using two hands (rather than one) to feed on seeds, the time necessary for such feeding would be cut in half, thereby reducing the period of vulnerability.

Another crucial consideration is the matter of avoiding overheating when out in the open, exposed to the direct rays of the sun. Since all hominoids lack the special physiological mechanisms possessed by most savanna mammals that protect their brains from damaging elevations of temperature, those that ventured out in the open would have been at risk without some other way of dealing with this problem. Bipedalism would have made a significant contribution, for when the sun is directly overhead, the heat load on an upright hominine is only about 40 percent of that received by a same-sized quadruped.[16] Moreover, bipedalism raises the body well above the ground, where heat is most intense; this also increases exposure to faster-moving air currents for effective heat loss though convection.

EARLY APES AND HUMAN EVOLUTION

Although the ramamorphs display a number of features from which hominine characteristics may be derived, and some may occasionally have walked bipedally, they were much too apelike to

---

[15]Jolly, C. J., & Plog, F. (1986). *Physical Anthropology and Archaeology* (4th ed., p. 216). New York: Knopf.
[16]Wheeler, P. (1993). Human ancestors walked tall, stayed cool. *Natural History, 102*(8), 66.

be considered hominines. No matter how much some of them may have resorted to bipedalism, they had not yet developed the anatomical specializations for this mode of locomotion that are seen in the earliest known hominines. They were optional rather than obligatory bipeds. Nevertheless, existing evidence allows the hypothesis that apes and humans separated from a common evolutionary line sometime during the late Miocene, and some fossils, particularly the smaller African ramamorphs, do possess traits associated with humans. Moreover, the Miocene apes possessed a limb structure less specialized for brachiation than modern apes; this structure could well have provided the basis for the development of human as well as ape limb types.

Clearly not all ramamorphs evolved into hominines. Those that remained in the forests and woodlands continued to develop as arboreal apes, although ultimately some of them took up a more terrestrial life. These are the bonobos, chimpanzees, and gorillas, who have changed far more from the ancestral condition than have the still arboreal orangutans.

CHAPTER SUMMARY

Although the study of comparative anatomy and biochemistry of living animals indicates much about their evolution, the most direct evidence comes from fossils. For animals that have often lived where conditions for fossilization are generally poor, we do have a surprisingly large number of primate fossils. Some are relatively complete skeletons, while most are teeth and jaw fragments.

The primates arose as part of a great adaptive radiation that began more than 100 million years after the appearance of the first mammals. The reason for this late diversification of mammals was that most ecological niches that they have since occupied were either preempted by the reptiles or were nonexistent until the flowering plants became widespread beginning about 65 million years ago.

The first primates were arboreal insect eaters, and the characteristics of all primates developed as an adaptation to the initial tree-dwelling environment. While some primates no longer inhabit the trees, it is certain that those adaptations which evolved to a life in the trees were preadaptive to the adaptive zone now occupied by the hominines.

The earliest primates had developed by 60 million years ago in the Paleocene epoch and were small arboreal creatures. Lemurlike adapids were common in the Eocene, as were species of tarsierlike omomyids. By the late Eocene, perhaps 45 million years ago, small primates combining features of both monkeys and apes were on the scene. In the Miocene epoch, apes proliferated and spread over many parts of the Old World. Among them were the ramamorphs, which appeared by 16 million years ago and were widespread even as recently as 8 million years ago. Although remarkably similar to orangutans in some respects, details of dentition suggest that hominines, as well as the African apes, arose from the ramamorphs. At least some populations of these primates lived in parts of Africa where the right kind of selective pressures existed to transform a creature just like it into a primitive hominine. Other populations remained in the forests, developing into today's bonobo, chimpanzee, gorilla, and orangutan. Of these, the orangutan has changed less from the ancestral condition than have the bonobo, chimp, and gorilla.

POINTS FOR CONSIDERATION

1. How do physical anthropology and paleontology advance our understanding of the origins and functions of modern human culture?

2. What do we mean by culture? Is it exclusive to humans?

3. Given the limited amount of evidence often available, what can be deduced from examining the elements of a complete skull (a rather rich find), i.e., cranium, eye sockets, jaw, etc.? What would you expect to find among modern primates? How and why does this differ from other mammals?

4. Do humans represent the "ultimate" in evolution, as is often thought? Are we the result of continual evolutionary "progress," or are we merely an accident, another branch in the trail? How does this relate to the concept of niches?

SUGGESTED READINGS

Ciochon, R. L., & Fleagle, J. (Eds.). (1987). *Primate evolution and human origins.* Hawthorne, NY: Aldine de Gruyter.

Articles in Part IV of this book summarize recent knowledge of early catarrhine evolution, while those in Part V examine the ramamorphs and their possible significance respecting human origins. Editors' introductions to each section provide the necessary overall perspective on the issues discussed in the articles.

Conroy, G. C. (1997). *Reconstructing human origins: A modern synthesis.* New York: W. W. Norton.

Though it says little about earlier primates, this book has an excellent, up-to-date chapter (3) on the Miocene hominoids. *Proconsul,* the dryomorphs, and ramamorphs are discussed in the context of climate changes in Africa and elsewhere in the Old World.

France, D. L., and Horn, A. D. (1992). *Lab manual and workbook for physical anthropology* (2nd ed.). New York: West.

Two chapters of this useful manual are devoted to a review of early primate fossils through the Miocene. Included are excellent drawings and photos.

Chapter 6
THE EARLIEST HOMININES

DISCOVERED IN 1998 AT A SITE IN SOUTH AFRICA,
THIS SKULL, SHOWN HERE EMBEDDED IN A STONE MATRIX,
IS PART OF THE MOST COMPLETE *AUSTRALOPITHECUS*
SKELETON EVER FOUND (ITS FOOT SKELETON, FOUND
EARLIER, IS SHOWN IN FIGURE 6.6). THOUGH THEIR
BEHAVIOR PATTERNS WERE MORE APELIKE THAN HUMAN,
AUSTRALOPITHECUS MOVED AROUND ON THE GROUND
ON TWO LEGS, JUST AS HUMANS DO TODAY.

Chapter Preview

When and Where Did the First Hominines Appear, and What Were They Like?

The earliest undoubted hominine, *Ardipithecus*, evolved in Africa by 4.4 million years ago. By 4 million years ago, this gave rise to *Australopithecus,* an African hominine remarkably human from the waist down that had become fully adapted for moving about on the ground on its hind legs in the distinctive human manner. But from the waist up, *Australopithecus* was still essentially apelike, with a brain suggesting intellectual abilities roughly comparable to those of a modern-day African ape.

What Is the Relation Between the Various Forms of *Australopithecus?*

The earliest forms of *Australopithecus* preserve a number of features indicative of a more apelike ancestor. By 2.5 millions years ago, this form gave rise to one whose chewing apparatus had become larger and more massive, at the same time that its brain size remained relatively stable. For a while, this late form coexisted with a less radically altered version of the earlier form.

Why Had *Australopithecus* Become a Bipedal Walker?

Early hominines venturing out in the open on the ground would have been vulnerable in two ways: to damaging buildup of heat in the brain from direct exposure to the sun, and to the many predators that prowled on the ground. Bipedal locomotion solves the heat problem by reducing the exposure of the body to direct solar radiation and positioning the body for most effective heat loss through convection. It also enabled *Australopithecus* to scan the savanna for danger, carry food to places where it could be consumed in safety, transport offspring, and grab hold of objects with which to threaten predators.

The period between about 7.5 and 4.5 million years ago was one of change; climates became dramatically drier than before, and in Africa, as many species of forest- or bush-dwelling mammals became extinct, several new groups made their appearance. Among the latter was the first undoubted hominine, known as *Ardipithecus ramidus*. Discovered in 1994, this species is known so far from several fragments of teeth, skull, and other parts of the skeleton. Much better known is its apparent descendant, *Australopithecus,* the oldest fossils of which date back to between 4.2 and 3.9 million years ago at two sites not far from Lake Turkana in northern Kenya. The earlier fossils of *Ardipithecus* are from deposits 4.4 million years old in Ethiopia. We know far less about *Ardipithecus* than about *Australopithecus*, which walked about on the ground on two (rather than four) feet and possessed manipulative and dexterous hands capable of using objects as tools. In spite of its ability to walk in a human manner, its behavior patterns otherwise were probably more apelike than human. Among other things, it spent more time in trees than later hominines, probably even sleeping in them.

For a long time, the fossil evidence of the early stages of human evolution was both sparse and tenuous. In the 1960s, however, there began a rush of paleoanthropologists into the field. Numerous international expeditions, including over 100 researchers from Belgium, Great Britain, Canada, France, Israel, Kenya, the Netherlands, and the United States, swarmed over parts of East Africa, where they have since unearthed unprecedented amounts of fossil material. So many fossils, coming fast and furiously, have been difficult to digest, and our ideas of early human evolution have had to be constantly revised. Now, there is widespread agreement over the broad outline, even though debate continues over details. What is clear is that the course of human evolution has not been a simple, steady "advance" in the direction of modern humanity. Rather, it appears that at least three divergent hominine lines evolved in the past. In this chapter we will discuss two of them, beginning with the best-known fossils of *Australopithecus*. We will then see how they relate to earlier forms.

AUSTRALOPITHECUS

In 1924, an unusual fossil was brought to the attention of Professor Raymond Dart of the University of Witwatersrand in Johannesburg; it was the partial cranium and natural brain cast of an animal unlike any he had ever seen before in South Africa. Recognizing in this unusual fossil an intriguing mixture of simian and human characteristics, anatomist Dart named his discovery *Australopithecus africanus*, or southern ape of

Raymond Dart, who described the first fossil of *Australopithecus* and correctly diagnosed its bipedal mode of locomotion.

Ardipithecus ramidus.   The oldest known hominine; lived about 4.4 million years ago. **> *Australopithecus.***   The first well-known hominine; lived between 4.2 and 1 million years ago. Characterized by bipedal locomotion when on the ground, but with an apelike brain; includes at least five species: *afarensis, africanus, anamensis, boisei,* and *robustus.*

Africa. Based on the position of the foramen magnum, the large hole in the skull where the spinal cord enters, Dart claimed that *Australopithecus* was probably a biped.

Since Dart's original find, hundreds of other fossils of *Australopithecus* have been found, first in South Africa and later in Tanzania, Kenya, Ethiopia, and Chad (Figure 6.1). As they were discovered, many were given a number of different specific and generic names, but usually all are now considered to belong to the single genus

Australopithecus. Most anthropologists recognize at least four species of the genus: *A. afarensis, A. africanus, A. boisei,* and *A. robustus.* (A fifth species, *A. anamensis,* will be discussed later in the chapter.). The latter two, from eastern and southern Africa respectively, are notable for having jaws that are massive relative to the size of the brain case. *A. afarensis* and *A. africanus,* also from eastern and southern Africa respectively, are slightly smaller on average and lack such massive jaws.

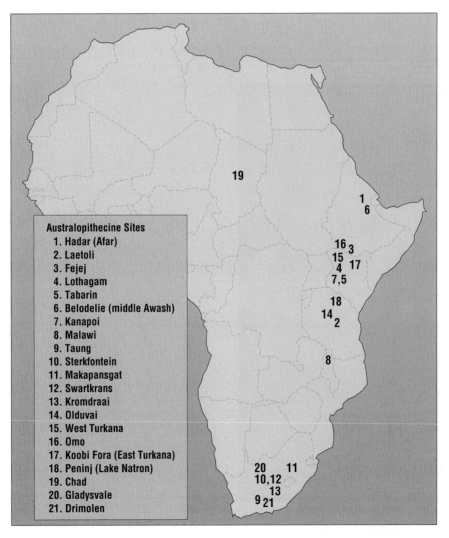

FIGURE 6.1

Australopithecus fossils have been found in South Africa, Malawi, Tanzania, Kenya, Ethiopia, and Chad.

A. afarensis and A. africanus

Included in the species *A. africanus* are numerous fossils found beginning in the 1930s at Sterkfontein and Makapansgat in South Africa, in addition to Dart's original find from Taung. All date between 3 and 2.3 million years ago (though a partial foot skeleton may be as old as 3.5 million years). Included in *A. afarensis* are parts of a large number of individuals who lived between 3.9 and 2.9 million years ago; the first of these were found in the 1970s in northern Ethiopia's Afar region. Discovered by Donald Jo-

hanson of the United States, they include the famous "Lucy," represented by bones from almost all parts of a single skeleton, and "the First Family," a collection of bones from at least 13 individuals of both sexes, ranging in age from infancy to adulthood, who died together as a result of some single calamity.

Similar material, close to 4 million years old, found by a team led by Mary Leakey at Laetoli, in Tanzania, is usually assigned to the same species as the Afar fossils. Although some have interpreted the wide variation exhibited by the *afarensis* specimens as indicative of the presence of two separate

Sufficient parts of the skeleton of "Lucy," a hominine that lived between 3.3 and 2.6 million years ago, survived to permit this reconstruction. Her hip and leg bones reveal that she walked about in a distinctively human manner.

Body weight	28 kg	27 kg
Stature	123 cm	105 cm
Cranial capacity	1,072 cc	410 cc
Tooth area (cheek)	255 mm^2	384 mm^2
Upper arm length	244	235
Thigh length	333	280

Figure 6.2

Reconstructed body proportions of a female *A. afarensis* compared to a modern pygmy.

This comparison of two skulls illustrates the degree of sexual dimorphism exhibited by Australopithecines about 2 million years ago. The skull on the left is a female and the skull on the right is a male. Earlier Australopithecines were equally dimorphic.

species, recent studies tend to support the single-species hypothesis,[1] indicating that *afarensis* was sexually dimorphic, with the males about one and a half times the size of females. In this respect, they were somewhat like the Miocene apes, with size differences greater than one sees in a modern chimpanzee, but less than one sees in gorillas or orangs.

Other pieces of Australopithecines similar to *A. afarensis* or *africanus* have been found at other East African sites that generally are 2 million or more years old. Both species were erect, bipedal hominines about the size of modern pygmies (Figure 6.2), though far more powerfully built. Their stature ranged between 3.5 and 5 feet, and they are estimated to have weighed between 29 and 45 kilograms.[2] Their physical appearance was un-usual by our standards: They may be described as looking like an ape from the waist up (see Figure 6.3) and like a human from the waist down. Their cranium was relatively low, the forehead sloped backward, and the brow ridge that helps give apes such massive-looking foreheads was also present. The lower half of the face was chinless and accented by jaws that were quite large, relative to the size of the skull.

Much has been written about *Australopithecus* teeth. Speaking generally, both *A. afarensis* and *africanus* possessed small incisors, short canines in line with adjacent teeth, and a rounded dental arch. The molars and premolars are larger in size but similar in form to modern human teeth (Figure 6.4). The molars are unevenly worn; the upper cheek teeth are worn from the inside, and the lower cheek teeth are worn from the outside. This indicates that both species chewed food in a hominine fashion, even though they were probably capable of two to four times the crushing force of modern human beings. Heavy wear indicates that the food chewed was high in tough plant fibers. There is usually no gap between the canines

[1]Leonard, W. R., & Hegman, M. (1987). Evolution of P3 morphology in *Australopithecus afarensis*. *American Journal of Physical Anthropology, 73,* 60.

[2]McHenry, H. M. (1992). Body size and proportions in early hominids. *American Journal of Physical Anthropology, 87,* 407.

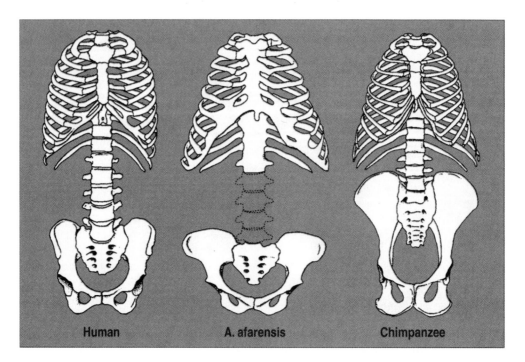

FIGURE 6.3

Trunk skeletons of modern human, *A. afarensis*, and chimpanzee, compared. In its pelvis, *afarensis* resembles the modern human, but its ribcage shows the pyramidal configuration of the ape.

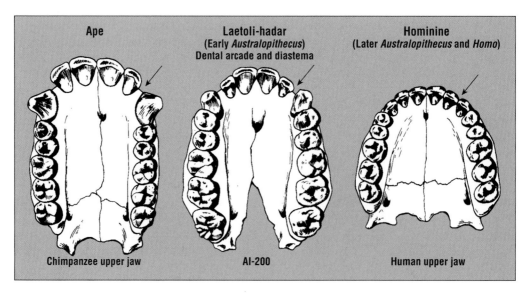

FIGURE 6.4

The upper jaws of an ape, *Australopithecus*, and modern human show important differences in the dental arch and the spacing between the canines and adjoining teeth. Only in the earliest australopithecines can a diastema (a large gap between the teeth) be seen.

FIGURE 6.5
Sexual dimorphism in canine teeth.

and the teeth next to them on the upper jaw, as there would be in apes. Further, the large mandible is very similar to that of the later hominine, *Homo erectus.*

As one might expect, these features are most evident in the fossils of *A. africanus,* the more recent of the two species; the teeth of the earlier *afarensis,* from Ethiopia but especially from Laetoli, show numerous features reminiscent of the late Miocene ramamorphs which the later ones (of *africanus*) do not (see Figure 5.6). Generally, the incisors and canines are a bit larger in *afarensis,* there is sometimes a gap between upper lateral incisors and canines, the canines tend to project noticeably, the first lower premolars are less like molars and show more shearing wear, and the dental arch is less rounded. One jaw from Laetoli even shows a partial interlock of upper canines with lower canines and premolars. All of this strongly suggests a ramamorphlike ancestor for *Australopithecus* back in Miocene times.

In addition to differences in the teeth between earlier *afarensis* and later *africanus,* there were also differences between the sexes. For example, male canines are significantly larger than those of females (Figure 6.5). There is as well a clear evolutionary trend for the first lower premolar of males to become more molarlike, through development of a second cusp. Those of females, by contrast, do not. Such differences are to be expected if male and female foraging patterns were not quite the same—for example, if females got more of their food from the trees, while males consumed large amounts of lower-quality food to be found on or near the ground. Consistent with this pattern, some features of the skeleton are somewhat better suited to climbing in females than in males.[3]

Although the brain is small and apelike and the general conformation of the skull seems nonhuman (even the semicircular canal, a part of the ear crucial to maintenance of balance, is apelike), the foramen magnum of these Australopithecines is placed forward and is downward-looking, as it is in later bipedal hominines of the **genus** *Homo.* Cranial capacity, commonly used as an index of brain size, varied from 310 to 485 cubic centimeters in *A. afarensis* and 428 to 510 cubic centimeters in *A. africanus,*[4] roughly the size of a large

[3]Simons, E. L. (1989). Human origins. *Science, 245,* 1346.

[4]Grine, F. E. (1993). Australopithecine taxonomy and phylogeny: Historical background and recent interpretation. In R. L. Ciochon & J. G. Fleagle (Eds.), *The human evolution source book,* (pp. 201–202). Englewood Cliffs, NJ: Prentice Hall.

Homo erectus. Members of the genus *Homo* that immediately precede *Homo sapiens.* ▸ **Genus Homo.** Hominine genus characterized by expansion of brain and reduction of jaws; includes at least three species: *habilis, erectus,* and *sapiens.*

chimpanzee brain. While 3 times larger than the brain of any Miocene ape, it was only about a third the size of a modern human brain. Intelligence, however, is not indicated by absolute brain size alone, but is roughly indicated by the ratio of brain to body size. Unfortunately, with such a wide range of adult weights it is not clear whether brain size was larger than a modern ape's relative to body size. Although some researchers think they see evidence for some expansion of the brain, others vigorously disagree. Moreover, the outside appearance of the brain, as revealed by casts of the insides of skulls, is more apelike than human, suggesting that cerebral reorganization toward a human condition had not yet occurred.[5] Consistent is the fact that the system for drainage of the blood from the cranium of *A. afarensis* is significantly different from that of the genus *Homo*. At the moment, the weight of the evidence favors mental capabilities for both *afarensis* and *africanus* as being comparable to those of modern great apes.

The fossil remains of *Australopithecus afarensis* and *africanus* have provided anthropology with two striking facts. First, as early as 4 million years ago, this hominine was bipedal, walking erect. This is indicated first of all by the curvature of the spine, which is like that of humans rather than of apes. This served to place the center of gravity over, rather than in front of, the hip joint. In addition, a forearm bone from "Lucy," which is shorter than that of an ape, suggests that the upper limb was lighter and the center of gravity lower in the body than in apes. Still, the arms of *A. afarensis* are long compared to its relatively short legs. While these make for a shorter stride length than in *Homo*, they were well suited to vertical climbing. Moreover, the somewhat elevated position of the shoulder joint was more adapted to arboreal performance; fingers and toes show more curvature; and a partial foot skeleton between 3.5 and 3 million years old from Sterkfontein, South Africa, (Figure 6.6) shows a long, flexible toe still useful for grabbing onto tree limbs.[6] The

[5]Falk, D. (1989). Apelike endocast of "ape-man" Taung. *American Journal of Physical Anthropology, 80,* 339.

[6]Oliwenstein, L. (1995). New footsteps into walking debate. *Science, 269,* 476.

Shown here is an *A. afarensis* skull from Ethiopia.

FIGURE 6.6
Drawing of the foot bones of a 3- to 3.5-million-year-old *Australopithecus* from Sterkfontein, as they would have been in the complete foot. Note how long and flexible the first toe (at right) is.

combination of traits indicate that the tree-climbing abilities of *A. afarensis* exceeded those of more recent hominines, and that they spent time in trees as well as on the ground.

Bipedal locomotion is also indicated by a number of leg and hip remains (Figure 6.7). There is general agreement that even the relatively short legs are much more human than apelike. In fact, a trait-by-trait comparison of individual bones shows that *Australopithecus* frequently falls within the range of modern *Homo,* even though the overall configuration is not exactly the same. But the most dramatic confirmation of *Australopithecus'* walking ability comes from Laetoli, where, nearly 4 million years ago, three individuals walked across newly fallen volcanic ash. Because it was damp, the ash took the impressions of their feet and these were sealed beneath subsequent ash falls until discovered by Dr. Paul Abell in 1978. The shape of the footprints, the linear

distance between the heels where they struck, and the amount of "toe out" are all quite human.

The second striking fact provided by *Australopithecus afarensis* and *africanus* is that hominines acquired their erect bipedal position long before they acquired their highly developed and enlarged brain. Not only is the latter more apelike than human in its size and structure, but also it is evident that *Australopithecus* did not have prolonged maturation as do modern humans; instead they grew up rapidly as do apes.[7] Thus, no matter how important bipedal locomotion may have been in setting the stage for the later expansion and elaboration of the human brain, it cannot by itself account for those developments.

A. robustus and *A. boisei*

The remains of what is now known as *Australopithecus robustus* were first found at Kromdraai and Swartkrans in South Africa by Robert Broom and John Robinson in 1948 in deposits that, unfortunately, cannot be securely dated. Current thinking puts them anywhere from 1.8 to 1.0 million years ago.

A. robustus shared practically all of the traits listed for the two species of *Australopithecus* just discussed, especially *A. africanus* from South Africa. Although similar in size to *A. africanus,* the bones of *robustus'* body were thick for their size, with prominent markings where their muscles attached. The skull of *A. robustus* was thicker and larger than that of *africanus,* with a slightly larger cranial capacity (around 530 cubic centimeters). Its skull also possessed a simianlike sagittal crest running from front to back along the top. This feature provides sufficient area on a relatively small braincase for attachment of the huge temporal muscles required to operate powerful jaws, such as *A. robustus* possessed and gorillas have today; hence what we have here is an example of convergent evolution in gorillas and hominines.

---

[7]Tardieu, C. (1998). Short adolescence in early hominids: Infantile and adolescent growth of the human femur. *American Journal of Physical Anthropology, 107,* 173–174.

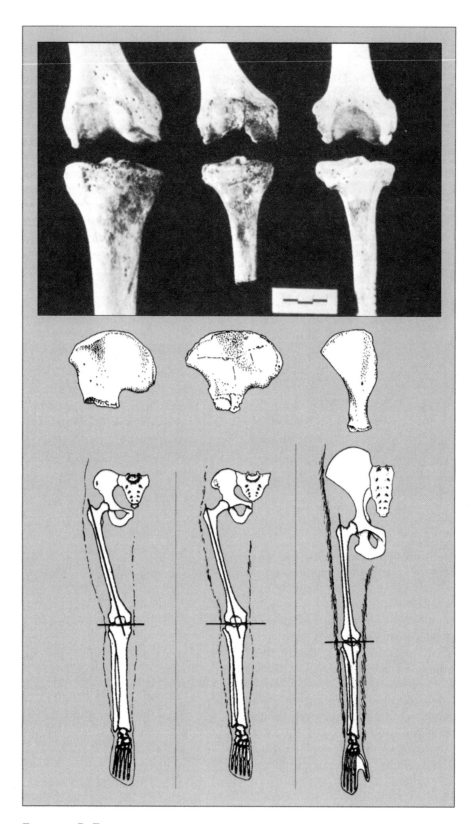

FIGURE 6.7

Examination of the upper hip bones and lower limbs of (from left) *Homo sapiens*, *Australopithecus*, and an ape can be used to determine means of locomotion. The similarities of the human and australopithecine bones are striking and are indicative of bipedal locomotion. (The reconstruction of the australopithecine limb is based on the knee joint shown in the photograph.)

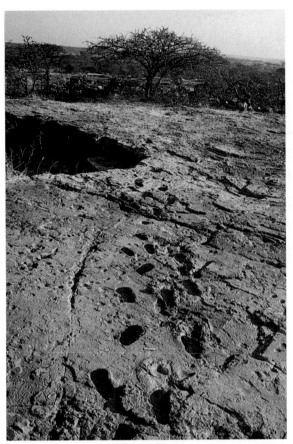

These footprints from Laetoli, Tanzania, confirm that *Australopithecus* walked bipedally. They were made by three individuals, one of whom was careful to walk directly in the footsteps of one in front.

The first specimen of *Australopithecus boisei* to be found in East Africa was discovered by Mary Leakey in the summer of 1959, the centennial year of the publication of Darwin's *On the Origin of Species.* She found it in Olduvai Gorge, a fossil-rich area near Ngorongoro Crater, on the Serengeti Plain of Tanzania, East Africa. Olduvai is a huge gash in the earth, about 25 miles long and 300 feet deep, which cuts through Pleistocene and recent geological strata revealing close to 2 million years of the earth's history.

Mary Leakey's discovery was reconstructed by her husband, Louis, who gave it the name *"Zinjanthropus boisei."* At first, he thought this hominine seemed more humanlike than *Australopithecus* and extremely close to modern humans

in evolutionary development. Further study, however, revealed that *"Zinjanthropus,"* the remains of which consisted of a skull and a few limb bones, was an East African representative of *Australopithecus.* Although similar in many ways to *A. robustus,* most commonly it is referred to as *Australopithecus boisei.* Potassium argon dating places this early hominine at about 1.75 million years old. Since the time of Mary Leakey's original find, numerous other fossils of *A. boisei* have been found at Olduvai, as well as north and east of Lake Turkana in Ethiopia and Kenya. While one (often referred to as the "Black Skull," sometimes as *A. aethiopicus*) is known to be as many as 2.5 million years old, some date to as recently as 1.3 million years ago.

The size of the teeth and certain cranial features of *A. boisei* are reminiscent of *A. robustus.* Molars and premolars are enormous, as are the mandible and palate. Even so, the anterior teeth (canines and incisors) are often crowded, owing to the room needed for the cheek teeth. The heavy skull, more massive even than its robust South African relative's, has a sagittal crest and prominent brow ridges; cranial capacity ranges from about 500 to 530 cubic centimeters. Body size, too, is somewhat larger; whereas *robustus* is estimated to have weighed between 32 and 40 kilograms, *boisei* probably weighed from 34 to 49 kilograms.

Because the earliest skull (2.5 million years) in the *boisei* lineage, the so-called "Black Skull" from Kenya, retains a number of primitive features shared with *A. afarensis,* it is probable that *A. boisei* evolved from *afarensis* ancestors. Whether *A. robustus* represents a southern offshoot of the *boisei* lineage or convergent evolution from an *africanus* ancestor is so far not settled; arguments can be presented in favor of both interpretations. In either case, what happened was that the later Australopithecines developed molars and premolars that are both absolutely and relatively larger than those of earlier *afarensis* and *africanus* (though some tendency in this direction can be seen in *africanus*). Larger teeth require more bone to support them, hence the prominent jaws of *boisei* and *robustus.* Finally, the larger jaws and the chewing of more food require more jaw musculature that attaches to the skull. The marked crests seen on the skulls

Louis S. B. Leakey   (1903–1972)
Mary Leakey   (1913–1996)

Few figures in the history of paleoanthropology have discovered so many key fossils, received so much public acclaim, or stirred up as much controversy as Louis Leakey and his second wife, Mary Leakey. Born in Kenya of missionary parents, Louis received his early education from an English governess, and subsequently was sent to England for a university education. He returned to Kenya in the 1920s to begin his career there.

It was in 1931 that Louis and his research assistant from England, Mary Nicol (whom he married in 1936), began working in their spare time at Olduvai Gorge in Tanzania, searching patiently and persistently for remains of early hominines. It seemed a good place to look, for there were numerous animal fossils, as well as crude stone tools lying scattered on the ground and eroding out of the walls of the gorge. Their patience and persistence were not rewarded until 1959, when Mary found the first hominine fossil. A year later, another skull was found, and Olduvai was on its way to being recognized as one of the most important sources of hominine fossils in all of Africa. While Louis reconstructed, described, and interpreted the fossil material, Mary made the definitive study of the Oldowan tools.

The Leakeys' important discoveries were not limited to those at Olduvai. In the early 1930s, they found the first dryomorph fossils in Africa at Rusinga Island in Lake Victoria. Also in the 1930s, Louis found a number of skulls at Kanjera, Kenya, which show a mixture of modern and more primitive features. In 1961, at Fort Ternan, Kenya, the Leakeys found the first remains of a ramamorph in Africa. After Louis's death, a member of an expedition led by Mary Leakey found the first footprints of *Australopithecus,* at Laetoli, Tanzania. In addition to their own work, Louis Leakey promoted a good deal of important work on the part of others. He made it possible for Jane Goodall to begin her landmark field studies of chimpanzees; later on, he was instrumental in setting up similar studies among gorillas (by Dian Fossey) and orangutans (by Birute Galdikas).

Louis Leakey had a flamboyant personality and a way of making interpretations of fossil materials that frequently did not stand up very well to careful scrutiny, but this did not stop him from publicly presenting his views as if they were the "gospel truth." It was this aspect of the Leakeys' work that generated controversy. Nonetheless the Leakeys accomplished and promoted more work that resulted in the accumulation of knowledge about human origins than anyone before them. Anthropology clearly owes them a great deal.

of the late Australopithecines provide for the attachment of such a musculature on a skull that has increased very little in size. In effect, *boisei* and *robustus* had evolved into highly efficient "chewing machines." Clearly, their immense cheek teeth and powerful chewing muscles bespeak the kind of heavy chewing a diet restricted to uncooked plant foods requires. Many anthropologists believe that, by becoming a specialized consumer of plant foods, the late Australopithecines avoided competing for the same niche with early *Homo,* with which they were contemporaries (see Chapter 7).

The so-called "Black Skull," found at West Turkana, Kenya, is the earliest known "robust" *Australopithecus*. At 2.5 million years old, it appears ancestral to later *A. boisei*.

Skulls of *A. africanus* (left) and *A. boisei* (right) show significant differences. Both specimens are male.

In the course of evolution, the **law of competitive exclusion** dictates that when two closely related species compete for the same niche, one will outcompete the other, bringing about the "loser's" extinction. That early *Homo* and late *Australopithecus* did not compete for the same niche is suggested by their coexistence for something like 1.5 million years.

Australopithecus anamensis and *Ardipithecus ramidus*

As already noted, *A. afarensis* fossils displayed a number of traits suggestive of a ramamorphlike ancestry. In addition to the features of the teeth, hands, and feet already noted, the skull of *afarensis* is thick boned and has a forward thrust to the face, large flaring cheek bones, and heavy cresting. Older than *afarensis* is *A. anamensis*, which dates to between 4.2 and 3.9 million years ago. Represented by an arm bone found in 1965 and two jaws and a shin bone found in 1995, this species had an even more apelike jaw with a shallow palate, large canines, and nearly parallel rows of cheek teeth. The shinbone, however, is like that of *afarensis*, and is the oldest direct evidence so far for bipedalism.

Ardipithecus ramidus, found in Ethiopia in 1994 and represented by pieces of several individuals was, as one might expect at 4.4 million years old, even more apelike than *A. anamensis*. Like chimpanzees, *Ardipithecus* had relatively small molars, large canines, and the same sort of first lower premolar. The shapes of the canine and vertebral elements, however, are like those of hominines. Unfortunately, no foot, leg, or pelvic remains have yet been described, but since this hominine lived in a more forested environment than its successors, it undoubtedly spent significant time in the trees. On the other hand, because the fossils of *A. anamensis* fit so neatly in between those of *A. afarensis* on the one hand, and *Ardipithecus* on the other, the latter must have had a preference for bipedal locomotion when on the ground. Consistent with this is the forward position of the foramen magnum.

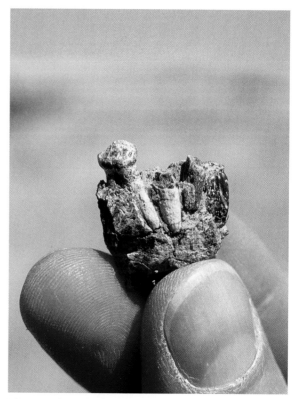

These teeth and jaw fragment are from *Ardipithecus*, the earliest known hominine, which lived 4.4 million years ago.

The picture that emerges, then, is of the emergence of *Australopithecus*, via *Ardipithecus*, from a ramamorphlike ancestor around the end of the Miocene epoch. This is not to say that this evolution took place at a steady pace, for it probably did not. For example, fragments of an *afarensis* skull 3.9 million years old are virtually identical to the corresponding parts of one 3 million years old. Evidently, once the bipedal adaptation was achieved, stabilizing selection took over and there was little change for at least a million years. By 2.5 million years ago, change was again in the works, resulting in the appearance of new forms including *A. boisei* and *A. robustus* (see Figure 7.5). But again, from about 2.3 million years until the species became extinct around 1 million

---

Law of competitive exclusion. When two closely related species compete for the same niche, one will outcompete the other, bringing about the latter's extinction.

years ago, *A. boisei*, at least, shows relatively little change.[8] Evidently, the pattern in early hominine evolution has been relatively short periods of marked change separated by prolonged periods of relative stasis.

ENVIRONMENT, DIET, AND AUSTRALOPITHECINE ORIGINS

Having described the fossil material, we may now consider the evolutionary forces responsible for the appearance of *Australopithecus*. Since a major driving force in evolution is climatic change, we must take into account the effects of such changes in the late Miocene epoch profound enough to cause the temporary drying up of the Mediterranean Sea. On the land, tropical forests underwent reduction or, more commonly, broke up into mosaics where patches of forest were interspersed with savanna or other types of open country. The forebears of the hominine line, probably to be found among African ramamorphs, lived in places where there was access to both trees and open country. With the breaking up of forests, these early ancestors of ours found themselves spending more and more time on the ground and had to adapt to this new, more open environment.

The most obvious problem facing these hominine ancestors in their new situation, other than getting from one patch of trees to another, was food getting. As the forest shrank, the traditional ape-type foods found in trees became less available to them. Therefore, it became more and more necessary to forage on the ground for foods such as seeds, grasses, and roots. Associated with this change in diet is a change in their dentition; male canines (used by other primates as defensive weapons), not large to begin with, became as small as those of females (Figure 6.8), leaving both sexes relatively defenseless when down on the ground and easy targets for numerous carnivorous predators. Many investigators have concluded that the hands of early hominines took over the weapon functions of the reduced canines, enabling them to

FIGURE 6.8
This lower jaw from Laetoli, Tanzania, is between 3.6 and 3.8 million years old and belonged to a hominine known as *Australopithecus*. Although its canine tooth projects a bit beyond the other teeth, it is a far cry from the projection seen in most other primates.

threaten predators by using wooden objects as clubs and throwing stones. This set the stage for the much later manufacture of more efficient weapons from bone, wood, and stone. Although the hands of the later Australopithecines were suitable for toolmaking, there is no evidence that any of them ever made stone tools. To illustrate the problem: Experiments with captive bonobos have shown that they are capable of making crude chipped stone tools, but they have never been known to do so under natural conditions. Thus, to have a potential is one thing, but whether it is realized is quite another. In fact, the earliest known

[8]Wood, B., Wood, C., & Konigsberg, L. (1994). *Paranthropus boisei*: An example of evolutionary stasis? *American Journal of Physical Anthropology, 95,* 134.

stone tools are at least 1.5 million years younger than the oldest undoubted fossils of *Australopithecus*, nor has anyone been able to establish a clear association between stone tools and later *Australopithecus* (as opposed to *Homo*) fossils. Considering the number of sites and fossils known (several hundred), this appears to be significant. However, *Australopithecus* certainly had no less intelligence and dexterity than do modern great apes, all of whom are capable of using tools when it is to their advantage to do so. Both orangutans and chimpanzees have been observed in the wild making and using simple tools such as wooden probes to get termites and ants. Gorillas seem not to do so in the wild only because they developed a diet of leaves and nettles that made tools pointless. Most likely, the ability to make and use simple tools is something that goes back to the last common ancestor of the Asian and African apes, before the appearance of hominines.

It is reasonable to suppose, then, that Australopithecines were tool users, though not toolmakers. Unfortunately, few tools that they used are likely to have survived for a million and more years, and any that did would be hard to recognize as such. Although we cannot be certain about this, in addition to clubs and missiles for defense, stout sticks may have been used to dig up edible roots, and convenient stones may have been used (as some chimpanzees do) to crack open nuts. In fact, some animal bones from Australopithecine sites in South Africa show microscopic wear patterns suggesting their use to dig up edible roots from the ground. We may also allow the possibility that, like chimpanzees, females may more often have used tools to get and process food than males, but the latter may more often have used tools as "weapons."[9]

HUMANS STAND ON THEIR OWN TWO FEET

From an apelike carriage, the early hominines developed a fully erect posture; they became bipedal. Ramamorphs seem to have been primates that combined quadrupedal climbing with at least some brachiation and that, on the ground, were capable of assuming an upright stance, at least on occasion (optional, versus obligatory, bipedalism). Since no hominine fossils have been found dating from the period of 2 or more million years between the last known African ramamorphs and the first known *Australopithecus*, we may assume that those hominine ancestors that did exist during the period were evolving into fully erect bipeds. *Australopithecus* is the first fully bipedal hominine of which we have a record.

Bipedalism, as a means of locomotion, has its drawbacks. For example, it makes an animal more visible to predators, exposes its "soft underbelly," or gut, and interferes with the ability to change direction instantly while running. Nor does it make for particularly fast running; quadrupedal chimpanzees and baboons, for example, are 30 to 34% faster than we bipeds. For 100 meter distances, our

This bonobo (pygmy chimpanzee) figured out by himself how to make stone tools like those made by our own ancestors 2.5 million years ago.

---

[9]Goodall, J. (1986). *The chimpanzees of Gombe: Patterns of behavior* (pp. 552, 564). Cambridge, MA: Belknap Press.

Just as chimpanzees use wooden probes to fish for termites, so do orangutans use probes to extract termites, ants, or honey. Such tool use likely goes back to a time preceding the split between Asian and African hominoids, long before the appearance of hominines.

best athletes today may attain speeds of 34–37 kilometers per hour, but the larger African carnivores can attain speeds up to 60–70 kilometers per hour. Other drawbacks include the frequent lower back problems, hernias, hemorrhoids, and other circulatory problems to which humans are prone by virtue of their bipedal specialization. Nor can we overlook the consequences of a serious leg or foot injury; a quadruped can do amazingly well on three legs, but a biped with only one functional leg is seriously hindered. Each of these drawbacks would have placed our early hominine ancestors at risk from predators, and so, we must ask, what made bipedal locomotion worth paying such a high price?

One once-popular suggestion is that it allowed males to gather food on the savanna and transport it back to females, who were restricted from doing so by the dependence of their offspring.[10] This explanation is unlikely, however, since female apes, not to mention women among food-foraging peoples, routinely combine infant care with foraging for food. Indeed, among food foragers, it is the women who normally supply the bulk of the food eaten by both sexes. Moreover, the pair-bonding (one male attached to one female) required by this model is not characteristic of terrestrial primates, nor of those displaying the degree of sexual dimorphism that was characteristic of *Australopithecus*. Nor is it really characteristic of *Homo sapiens*; in a substantial majority of recent human societies, including those in which people forage for their food, some form of polygamy—marriage to two or more people at the same time—is not only permitted, but preferred. And even in the supposedly monogamous society of the United States, it is relatively common for an individual to marry two or more others (the only requirement is that he or she not be married to them at one and the same time).

Another suggestion, that bipedal locomotion arose as an adaptation for nonterritorial scavenging of meat,[11] is also unlikely. While it is true that

[10]Lovejoy, C. O. (1981). The origin of man. *Science, 211,* 341–350.

[11]Lewin, R. (1987). Four legs good, two legs bad. *Science, 235,* 969–971.

a biped is able to travel long distances without tiring, and that a daily supply of dead animal carcasses would have been available to hominines only if they were capable of ranging over vast areas, there is no evidence that hominines did much in the way of scavenging prior to about 2.5 million years ago. Furthermore, the heavy wear seen on Australopithecine teeth is indicative of a diet high in tough, fibrous plant foods. Thus, scavenging was likely an unforeseen byproduct of bipedal locomotion, rather than a cause of it.

Yet more recent is the suggestion that our ancestors stood up as a way to cope with heat stress out in the open.

The Naked and the Bipedal[12]

▲▼

Human beings are a peculiar species. Among other things, we're the only mostly hairless, consistently bipedal primate. Ever since Darwin, evolutionary biologists have wondered how we acquired these unique traits. Not long ago most would have argued that our upright stance evolved as part of a feedback loop that helped free our hands to use tools. But by the early 1980s a series of discoveries in Africa—including fossilized footprints and early hominine bones—made it clear that bipedalism preceded tool use by at least 2 million years. Lately a new theory has been gaining ground: It holds that our forebears reared up on two legs to escape the heat of the African savanna.

"The African savanna is one of the most thermally stressing habitats on the planet as far as large mammals are concerned," says Pete Wheeler, a physiologist at Liverpool John Moores University in England. For several years now Wheeler has been studying just how stressful such an environment would have been for the first primates to venture out of the shade of the forest. Among the apes, our ancestors are the only ones that managed the switch; no other ape today lives on the savanna full-time.

Most savanna animals, says Wheeler, cope with the heat by simply letting their body temperature rise during the day, rather than waste scarce water by sweating. (Some antelope allow their body temperature to climb above 110 degrees.) These animals have evolved elaborate ways of protecting the brain's delicate neural circuitry from overheating. Antelope, for instance, allow venous blood to cool in their large muzzles (the cooling results from water evaporation in the mucous lining), then run that cool blood by the arteries that supply the brain, thereby cooling it, too.

"But the interesting thing about humans and other primates," says Wheeler, "is that we lack the mechanisms other savanna animals have. The only way an ape wanting to colonize the savanna could protect its brain is by actually keeping the whole body cool. We can't uncouple brain temperature from the rest of the body, the way an antelope does, so we've got to prevent *any* damaging elevations in body temperature. And of course the problem is even more acute for an ape, because in general, the larger and more complex the brain, the more easily it is damaged. So there were incredible selective pressures on early hominines favoring adaptations that would reduce thermal stress—pressures that may have favored bipedalism."

---

[12]Adapted from Folger, T. (1993). The naked and the bipedal. *Discover, 14*(11), 34–35.

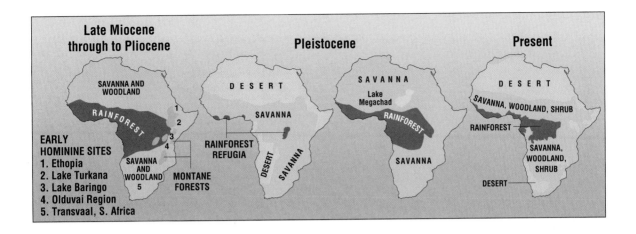

Late Miocene through to Pliocene — Pleistocene — Present

SAVANNA AND WOODLAND
RAINFOREST
EARLY HOMININE SITES
1. Ethopia
2. Lake Turkana
3. Lake Baringo
4. Olduvai Region
5. Transvaal, S. Africa
SAVANNA AND WOODLAND
MONTANE FORESTS

DESERT
SAVANNA
RAINFOREST REFUGIA
DESERT
SAVANNA

SAVANNA
Lake Megachad
RAINFOREST
SAVANNA

DESERT
SAVANNA, WOODLAND, SHRUB
RAINFOREST
SAVANNA, WOODLAND, SHRUB
DESERT

Just how would bipedalism have protected the brain from heat? And why did our ancestors become bipedal rather than evolve some other way to keep cool? Before moving out onto the savanna, says Wheeler, our forebears were preadapted to evolve into bipeds. Swinging from branch to branch in the trees, they had already evolved a body plan that could, under the right environmental pressures, be altered to accommodate an upright stance. Such a posture, says Wheeler, greatly reduces the amount of the body's surface area that is directly exposed to the intense midday sun. It thereby reduces the amount of heat the body absorbs.

Although this observation is not new, Wheeler has done the first careful measurements and calculations of the advantages such a stance would have offered the early hominines. His measurements were rather simple. He took a 1-foot-tall scale model of a hominine similar to Lucy—the 3-million-year-old, chimp-size Australopithecine that is known from the structure of her pelvis and legs to have been at least a part-time biped. Wheeler mounted a camera on an overhead track and moved it in a semicircular arc above the model, mimicking the daily path of the sun. Every five degrees along that path—the equivalent of 20 minutes on a summer day—Wheeler stopped the camera and snapped a photograph of the model. He repeated this process with the model in a variety of postures, both quadrupedal and bipedal. To determine how much of the hominine's surface area would have been exposed to the sun's rays, Wheeler simply measured how much of the model's surface area was visible in the sun's-eye-view photos. He found that a quadrupedal stance would have exposed the hominine to about 60% more solar radiation than a bipedal one.

Not only does a biped expose less of its body to the sun, it also exposes more of its body to the cooler breezes a few feet above ground. The bottom line, says Wheeler, is that "on a typical savanna day, a knuckle-walking chimp-size hominine would require something in the region of five pints of water a day. Whereas simply by standing upright you cut that to something like three pints. In addition to that, you can also remain out in the open away from shade for longer, and at higher temperatures. So for an animal that was foraging for scattered resources in these habitats, bipedalism is really an excellent mode of locomotion."

FIGURE 6.9

How the human brain is cooled: Blood from the face and scalp, instead of returning directly to the heart, may be shunted instead into the braincase, and then to the heart. Already cooled at the surface of the skin, it is able to carry away heat from the brain.

Wheeler suspects that bipedalism also made possible two other uniquely human traits: our naked skin and large brains. "Our work suggests that you can't get a naked skin until you've become bipedal," he says.

"The problem has always been explaining why we don't see naked antelope or cheetahs. The answer appears to be that in those conditions in which animals are exposed to high radiation loads, the body hair acts as a shield. We always think of body hair as keeping heat in, but it also keeps heat out. If you take the fleece off a sheep and stand the animal out in the desert in the outback of Australia, the sheep will end up gaining more heat than you're helping it to dissipate. However, if you do that to a bipedal ape, because the exposure to solar radiation is so much less, it helps the ape lose more heat. Bipedalism, by reducing exposure to the sun, is tipping the balance and turning hair loss, which in quadrupeds would be a disadvantage, into an asset."

We bipeds maximize our heat loss, says Wheeler, by retaining a heat shield only on our most exposed surface—the top of our skull—and by exposing the rest of our body to cooling breezes. And bipedalism and naked skin together, he says, probably allowed us to evolve our oversize brains.

"The brain is one of the most metabolically active tissues in the body," he explains. "In the case of humans it accounts for something like 20 percent of total energy consumption. So you've got an organ producing a lot of heat that you've got to dump. Once we'd become bipedal and naked and achieved this ability to dump heat, that may have allowed the expansion of the brain that took place later in human evolution. It didn't cause it, but you can't have a large brain unless you can cool it."

An objection to the above scenario might be that when bipedalism developed, savanna was not as extensive in Africa as it is today. In both East and South Africa, environments included both closed and open bush and woodlands. In fact, fossil flora and fauna found with *Ardipithecus* are typical of a closed, wooded habitat. Yet even today, similar floral and faunal elements can be found in the otherwise rather desolate region where *Ardipithecus* once lived,[13] and between 5

---

[13]Conroy, G. C. (1997). *Reconstructing human origins: A modern synthesis* (p.152). New York: W. W. Norton.

and 4 million years ago, the environments of eastern and southern Africa can best be described as a mosaic of both open and closed country. Although climbing ability would still have been useful to hominine ancestors, inevitably they would have had to spend significant amounts of time out in the open, away from trees.

Persuasive though the "stand up to keep cool" hypothesis may be, we should not overlook other life-or-death considerations. The fact is that the causes of bipedalism are likely to have been multiple. While we may reject the idea of male "breadwinners" provisioning "stay-at-home" females as culture bound, it is true that

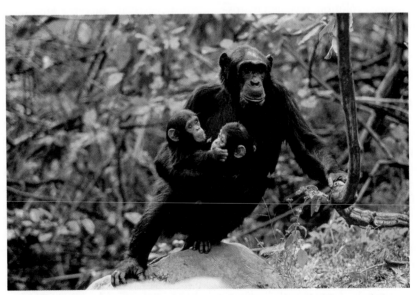

Because apes do not normally walk bipedally, they cannot hold on to their infants when moving about. By holding on to their infants while walking bipedally, our own ancestors probably reduced the risk of fatal falls for their infants.

bipedal locomotion does make food transport possible. A fully erect biped on the ground—whether male or female—has the ability to gather substantial quantities of food for transport back to a tree or other place of safety for consumption; the animal does not have to remain out in the open, exposed and vulnerable, to do all of its eating. But food may not have been the only thing transported. As we saw in Chapter 4, primate infants must be able to cling to their mothers in order to be transported; since the mother is using her forelimbs in locomotion, to either walk or swing by, she can't very well carry her infant. Chimpanzee infants, for example, must cling for themselves to their mother, and even at the age of 4, they make long journeys on their mothers' backs. Injuries caused by falling from the mother are a significant cause of infant mortality. Thus, mothers able to carry their infants would have made a significant contribution to the survivorship of their offspring, and the ancestors of *Australopithecus* would have been capable of doing just this.

Besides making food transport possible, bipedalism could have facilitated the food quest in other ways. With their hands free and body upright, the animals could reach otherwise unobtainable food on thorn trees too flimsy to climb. Furthermore, with both hands free, they could gather food twice as fast. And in times of scarcity, their ability to travel far without tiring would help get them between widely distributed sources of food. Since the head is positioned higher than in a quadrupedal stance, sources of food and water may be spotted from afar, thereby facilitating their location.

Still other advantages of bipedalism would have enhanced survivability. With their heads well up above the ground, bipeds are able to spot predators before they get too close for safety. Finally, if hominines did get caught away from a safe place of refuge by a predator, manipulative and dexterous hands freed from locomotion provided them with a means of protecting themselves by brandishing and throwing objects at their attackers.

CHAPTER SUMMARY

The course of hominine evolution, revealed by fossil finds, has not been a simple, steady "advance" in the direction of modern humans. One early hominine which appeared by at least 4 million years ago was *Australopithecus*, a genus that anthropologists divide into five species. *Australopithecus afarensis* and *africanus* walked erect; they were about the size of a modern human pygmy; they chewed food like humans; and their general appearance was that of an apelike human. The size and outward appearance of their brain suggest a degree of intelligence probably not greatly different from that of a modern chimpanzee or gorilla. Like chimpanzees, *afarensis* and *africanus* may have made some use of objects as tools.

Australopithecus boisei and *robustus* shared practically all of the traits listed for *afarensis* and *africanus*, but were more highly specialized for the consumption of plant foods. *Australopithecus anamensis*, the earliest documented biped, fits neatly between the later *A. afarensis* and the earlier (at 4.4 million years) *Ardipithecus ramidus*. The lat-

ter suggests an ancestry among the Miocene ramamorphs of Africa.

During the late Miocene and Pliocene, the climate became markedly cooler and drier; many areas that had once been heavily forested became a mosaic of woodland and more open country. The ancestors of hominines found themselves spending more and more time on the ground; they had to adapt to this altered, more open environment, and food getting became a problem. As their diet changed, so did their dentition. On the whole, teeth became smaller, and many of the defensive functions once performed by the teeth seem to have been taken over by the hands.

Ramamorphs are believed to have been part-time brachiators who may at times have walked erect. *Australopithecus* is the first fully bipedal hominine with erect posture that we know about. Some disadvantages of bipedalism as a means of locomotion, besides anatomical and circulatory weaknesses, are that it makes an animal more visible to predators, exposes its "soft underbelly," slows the animal down, interferes with its ability to change direction instantly while running, and leaves nothing to fall back on when one leg is injured. Its advantages are that it provides hominines with a means of keeping their brains from overheating, of protecting themselves and holding objects while running, of traveling long distances without tiring, and of seeing farther.

POINTS FOR CONSIDERATION

1. What can the comparison of dental remains tell us about significant similarities or differences in terms of "lifestyle" and behavior between species, or within a species between sexes? What are the possible pitfalls of relying too heavily upon any one piece of evidence?

2. How have scientists used *Australopithecus* remains to deduce early hominine habitat? What have been their conclusions?

3. Why would so many people assume that hominine bipedalism is directly related to tool use? What view of human development does this seem to imply? How does evidence of a variety of species of *Australopithecus* call these views into question?

SUGGESTED READINGS

Ciochon, R. L., & Fleagle, J. G. (Eds.). (1993). *The human evolution source book*. Englewood Cliffs, NJ: Prentice Hall.

In the first four parts of this book, the editors have assembled articles to present data and survey different theories on the evolution and diversification of the earliest hominines. A short editors' introduction to each section places the various articles in context.

Conroy, G. C. (1997). *Reconstructing human origins: A modern synthesis*. New York: W. W. Norton.

This text devotes two chapters to *Australopithecus* that are reasonably up-to-date and are comprehensive in their description of the various fossils, discussion of environmental considerations, and coverage of competing interpretations of the material.

Johanson, D., & Edey, M. (1981). *Lucy: The beginnings of humankind*. New York: Simon and Schuster.

This book tells the story of the discovery of "Lucy" and the other fossils of *Australopithecus afarensis,* and how they have enhanced our understanding of the early stages of human evolution. It reads like a first-rate detective story, while giving one of the best descriptions of Australopithecines and one of the best accounts of how paleoanthropologists analyze their fossils to be found in literature.

PART III

EVOLUTION OF THE GENUS *HOMO* AND THE DEVELOPMENT OF EARLY HUMAN CULTURE

Chapter 7
HOMO HABILIS AND CULTURAL ORIGINS

Chapter 8
HOMO ERECTUS AND THE EMERGENCE OF HUNTING AND GATHERING

Chapter 9
ARCHAIC HOMO SAPIENS AND THE MIDDLE PALEOLITHIC

Chapter 10
HOMO SAPIENS AND THE UPPER PALEOLITHIC

Introduction

By 2.5 million years ago, long after the line of human evolution had branched off from that of apes, a new kind of evolutionary process was set in motion. Early hominines began to manipulate the physical world, inventing solutions to the problems of human existence. With the passage of time, they came to rely more on cultural, rather than biological, adaptation as a more rapid and effective way of adjusting to environmental pressures. No longer did they have to depend predominately on physical attributes to survive. Moreover, as culture became more efficient at solving the problems of existence, human populations began to spread geographically, inhabiting new and even harsh environments, all of which is illustrated by human habitations of the cold regions of the world. Instead of being dependent on the evolution of humans capable of growing heavy coats of fur, as do other mammals that live in such regions, humans devised forms of clothing and shelter that, coupled with the use of fire, enabled them to overcome the cold. Moreover, once this kind of "cold adaptation" was accomplished, it could readily be changed when circumstances required it. The fact is that cultural equipment and techniques can change rapidly, whereas biological change can be accomplished only over many generations.

The next four chapters discuss how evolving hominines acquired the ability to invent their own solutions to the problems of existence and how this ingenuity gained primacy over biological change as the human mechanism for adapting to the environment. We begin, in Chapter 7, with the appearance of the genus *Homo*. Although the earliest members of this genus had far smaller brains than ours, they were significantly larger than those of *Australopithecus*. Their appearance is associated with a new way of surviving: Instead of foraging, as do most primates, on a more or less individualistic basis for vegetables and fruits, supplemented by eggs, grubs, lizards, and similar sources of animal protein, early *Homo* invented stone tools with which they could butcher the carcasses of even larger animals. Thus, they were able to increase significantly the amount of meat in their diet. This made possible a degree of economic specialization; males scavenged for meat, and females gathered a wide variety of other wild foods. It also made possible new patterns of social interaction: Females and males began sharing the results of their food-getting activities on a regular basis.

Over the next nearly 2.5 million years—a period known as the Paleolithic, or Old Stone Age—the evolving genus *Homo* relied increasingly on improved mental abilities for survival, as we shall see in Chapters 8, 9, and 10. In the process, hunting came to replace scavenging as the main means by which meat was procured, and other improvements of this food-foraging way of life took place. As a consequence, the human species, essentially a tropical one, was able to free itself from its tropical habitat and, through invention, adapt itself to colder climates. By 200,000 years ago, humans had acquired essentially modern brains. Shortly thereafter, they achieved the ability to survive under true Arctic conditions. To invent ways of surviving under such forbidding and difficult conditions ranks as no less an achievement than sending the first man to the moon.

Chapter 7
HOMO HABILIS AND CULTURAL ORIGINS

THOUGH FIRST FOUND AT OLDUVAI GORGE
IN TANZANIA, SOME OF THE BEST FINDS OF
HOMO HABILIS HAVE COME FROM KOOBI FORA
IN KENYA (ABOVE). *HOMO HABILIS*, THE
EARLIEST MAKER OF STONE TOOLS, WAS A
SCAVENGER OF DEAD CARCASSES FOR MEAT AND
THE FIRST HOMININE TO SHOW EVIDENCE OF
SIGNIFICANT INCREASE IN BRAIN SIZE BEYOND
WHAT IS SEEN IN APES.

Chapter Preview

When, Where, and How Did Human Culture Develop?

Human culture appears to have developed in Africa as some populations of early hominines began making stone tools with which they could butcher animals for their meat. Actually, the earliest stone tools and evidence of significant meat eating date to about 2.5 million years ago, just prior to the appearance of the genus *Homo*.

When Did Reorganization and Expansion of the Human Brain Begin?

Reorganization and expansion of the human brain did not begin until at least 1.5 million years after the development of bipedal locomotion. It began in conjunction with scavenging and the making of stone tools. This marks the appearance of the genus *Homo*, an evolutionary offshoot of *Australopithecus*. The two forms appear to have coexisted for a million years or so, during the course of which *Australopithecus* relied on a vegetarian diet while developing a massive chewing apparatus. In contrast, *Homo* ate more meat and became brainier.

Why Did the Eating of More Meat Lead to Improved Brains?

The making of stone tools—needed to skin, butcher, and crack open the bones of animals for marrow—put a premium on improved eye-hand coordination and precision grip, both of which selected for more complex brains. Increased meat eating, too, led to changes in the subsistence activities of both females and males. These changes required both sexes to do more in the way of thinking and planning, which again selected for larger, more complex brains.

In 1931 when Louis and Mary Leakey began work at Olduvai Gorge, they did so because of the presence of crude stone tools in deposits dating back to very early in the Pleistocene epoch, which began almost 2 million years ago. When they found the bones of *Australopithecus boisei* in 1959, in association with some of these tools, they thought they had found the remains of one of the toolmakers. They later changed their minds, however, and suggested that these tools were not produced by *A. boisei*, nor were the bones of the birds, reptiles, antelopes, and an extinct kind of pig found with the remains of *A. boisei* the remains of the latter's dinner. Instead, *A. boisei* may have been a victim of a rather different contemporary who created the tools, ate the animals, and possibly had the unfortunate *A. boisei* for dessert. That contemporary was called by the Leakeys *Homo habilis* ("handy man").

EARLY REPRESENTATIVES OF THE GENUS *HOMO*

The Leakeys discovered the remains of this second hominine in 1960, only a few months after their earlier discovery, just a few feet below it. The

remains, which were those of more than one individual, consisted of a few cranial bones, a lower jaw, a clavicle, some finger bones (Figure 7.1), and the nearly complete left foot of an adult (Figure 7.2). These fossils date from about 1.8 million years ago and represent a hominine with a cranial capacity in the 650 to 690 cubic centimeter range, a skull that lacks noticeable bony crests, and almost modern-looking hands and feet. Subsequent work at Olduvai has unearthed not only more skull fragments, but other parts of the skeleton of *Homo habilis* as well. These indicated that, aside from their more modern-looking heads, hands, and feet, the skeleton of this hominine from the neck down does not differ greatly from that of *Australopithecus afarensis* or *africanus*. Overall size was about the same, as was the degree of sexual dimorphism (Figure 7.3), and they still climbed trees, although perhaps not quite so much as *Australopithecus*.[1] Moreover, dental evidence suggests that, as with *A. afarensis* and *africanus*, the period of infancy and childhood in *H. habilis* was not prolonged, as it is in modern humans, but was more in line with apes.[2]

Since the late 1960s, fossils of the genus *Homo* that are essentially contemporaneous with those from Olduvai have been recognized elsewhere in Africa—in South Africa, in Kenya near Lake Baringo as well as east of Lake Turkana at Koobi Fora, and in Ethiopia just north of Lake Turkana. One of the best of these, known as KNM ER 1470, was discovered by the Leakeys' son Richard. (The letters *KNM* stand for Kenya National Museum; the *ER*, for East Rudolf, the former name for Lake Turkana.) The deposits in which it was found are about 1.9 million years old; these deposits, like those at Olduvai, also contain crude stone tools. The KNM ER 1470 skull is more modern in appearance than any *Australopithecus* skull and has a cranial capacity of 752 cubic centimeters. Furthermore, the inside of the skull shows a pattern in the left cerebral hemisphere that, in living people, is associated with a speech area.[3] This shape is in keeping with indications of brain asymmetry more like that of humans than apes, as is evidence from wear patterns on tools evidently used by early *Homo* that reveal that these hominines were predominately right-handed. In humans, the speech organs and the right hand are controlled

---

[1]Lewin, R. (1987). The earliest "humans" were more like apes. *Science, 236,* 106–163.

[2]Lewin, R. (1987). Debate over emergence of human tooth pattern. *Science, 235,* 749.

[3]Falk, D. (1993). Hominid paleoneurology. In R. L. Ciochon & J. G. Fleagle (Eds.), *The human evolution source book* (p. 62). Englewood Cliffs, NJ: Prentice Hall.

FIGURE 7.1

A comparison of hand bones of a juvenile gorilla, *Homo habilis* from Olduvai, and a modern human highlights important differences in the structure of fingers and thumbs. In the top row are fingers and in the second row are terminal thumb bones. While terminal finger bones are more human, lower finger bones are more curved and powerful. The bottom row compares thumb length and angle relative to the index finger.

FIGURE 7.2

A partial foot skeleton of *Homo habilis* (center) is compared with the same bones of a chimpanzee (left) and modern human (right). Note how *habilis'* bone at the base of the great toe is in line with the others, as in modern humans, making for effective walking but poor grasping.

by adjacent areas in the left cerebral hemisphere. While this doesn't prove that early *Homo* had a spoken language, it does indicate that its brain was not only larger than that of *Australopithecus,* but was reorganized along more human lines.

Although the 1470 skull and other early *Homo* fossils from localities other than Olduvai are frequently assigned to the same species, *H. habilis,* there are those who argue that two distinct species may be present. In favor of this interpretation is what appears to be an unusually wide range of variation; however, those who suspect that two species are present cannot agree on how to apportion the fossils between them.[4] Nor have they so far been able to demonstrate that the two proposed species occupied different parts of the paleolandscape. Unless and until these difficulties are overcome, it seems best to regard all of this material as representative of a single species, ***Homo habilis.***

---

[4]Conroy, G. C. (1997). *Reconstructing human origins: A modern synthesis* (pp. 264–265 & 269–270). New York: W. W. Norton.

Homo habilis.   Earliest representative of the genus *Homo;* lived between 2.4 and 1.6 million years ago. Characterized by expansion and reorganization of the brain, compared to *Australopithecus.*

FIGURE 7.3
As these two skulls from Koobi Fora demonstrate, that of female *H. habilis* (right) was markedly smaller than that of the male (left).

RELATIONS BETWEEN *HOMO HABILIS* AND *AUSTRALOPITHECUS*

A consideration of brain size relative to body size clearly indicates that *Homo habilis* had undergone enlargement of the brain far in excess of values predicted on the basis of body size alone. This means that there was a marked advance in information-processing capacity over that of the Australopithecines. Because larger brains generate more heat, it is not surprising to find that *habilis'*

brain was provided with a heat exchanger of a sort not seen in *Australopithecus*, save to a very rudimentary degree in *africanus*.[5] This heat-exchange system consists of small openings in the braincase through which veins pass allowing cooled blood from the face and scalp to be shunted to the brain, from which the blood can then carry off excess

---

[5]Falk, D. (1993). A good brain is hard to cool. *Natural History, 102*(8), 65.

ER 1470: One of the most complete skulls of *Homo habilis* is close to 2 million years old.

heat (see Figure 6.9). In this way, damage to the brain from excessive heat is prevented.

Although these hominines had teeth that are large by modern standards—or even by those of

a half-million years ago—they are smaller in relation to the size of the skull than those of Australopithecines. Since major brain-size increase and tooth-size reduction are important trends in the evolution of the genus *Homo*, but not of *Australopithecus*, it looks as if ER 1470 and similar hominines were becoming somewhat more human. Consistent with this are the indications that the brain of KNM ER 1470 was less apelike and more human in structure. It is probably no accident that the earliest fossils to exhibit these features appear by 2.4 million years ago (the age of the Baringo fossil), soon after the earliest evidence (to be discussed shortly) for stone toolmaking and increased consumption of meat.

As noted earlier, the Australopithecine diet seems to have consisted for the most part of plant foods, although *A. afarensis* and *africanus* may have consumed limited amounts of animal protein as well. Later Australopithecines *boisei* and *robustus* evolved into more specialized "grinding machines" as their jaws became markedly larger (Figure 7.4), while their brain size did not. Nor is there firm evidence that they made stone tools. Thus, in the period between 2.5 and 1 million years ago, two kinds of hominines were headed in very different evolutionary directions.

FIGURE 7.4

Premolars (left) and molars (right) of *Australopithecus* and *Homo habilis* show significant differences in size. The teeth of *Australopithecus* show a clear tendency to enlarge with time over those of *A. afarensis,* while the teeth of *H. habilis* differ little from those of *A. afarensis.*

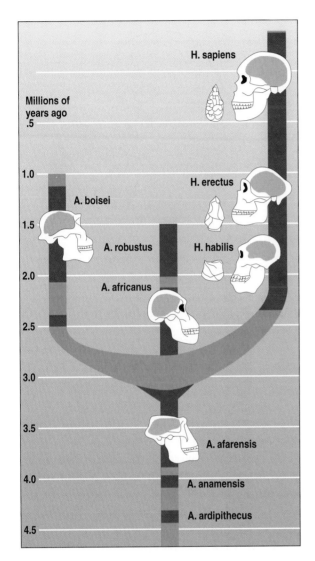

either species. Precisely which of the two gave rise to *H. habilis* is vigorously debated. Most see *A. afarensis* as sufficiently generalized to have given rise to both the *Homo* and *boisei-robustus* patterns, noting that the earliest skull to show the latter, the so-called "Black Skull," nonetheless shows some holdovers from *A. afarensis*. This skull's age, 2.5 million years, is too old for any but the very earliest *africanus* to have figured in its ancestry. Since the earliest *Homo habilis* skull is nearly as old, the same must be true for it. Evidently, a three-way split was under way by 2.5 million years ago, with the third line represented by *A. africanus* (Figure 7.5). This persisted until about 2 million years ago (or later, if *A. robustus* is a descendent of *africanus,* rather than an offshoot of *boisei*) by which time the other two lineages had become widespread in nonforested parts of Africa.

FIGURE 7.5
This diagram presents one plausible view of early human evolution.

If neither *Australopithecus boisei* nor *robustus* belong in the direct line of human ancestry, what of earlier species of *Australopithecus*? From the standpoint of anatomy alone, it has long been recognized that either *Australopithecus afarensis* or *africanus* constitutes a good ancestor for the genus *Homo,* and it now seems clear that the body of *Homo habilis* had changed little from that of

LOWER PALEOLITHIC TOOLS

The earliest tools known to have been made by hominines have been found in the vicinity of Lake Turkana in Kenya and southern Ethiopia, Olduvai Gorge in Tanzania, and Hadar in Ethiopia. Their appearance marks the beginning of the **Lower Paleolithic,** the first part of the Old Stone Age.

These early tools show striking similarities, indicating that they were the results of a cultural tradition of manufacturing tools according to a particular preconceived model or pattern. At Olduvai and Lake Turkana, these tools are close to 2 million years old. The Hadar tools have been found below a deposit dated by potassium argon to about 1.8 million years ago, but above another dated to about 2.8 million years; thus they are estimated to be about 2.5 million years old.

OLDUVAI GORGE

What is now Olduvai Gorge was once a lake. Almost 2 million years ago, its shores were inhabited not only by numerous wild animals but also by groups of hominines, including *Australopithecus boisei* and *Homo habilis* as well as the later

Lower Paleolithic.   The first part of the "Old Stone Age"; its beginning is marked by the appearance of Oldowan tools.

Homo erectus (Chapter 8). The gorge, therefore, is a rich source of Paleolithic remains as well as a key site providing evidence of human evolutionary development. Among the finds are assemblages of stone tools that are about 2 million years old. These were found little disturbed from when they were left, together with the bones of now-extinct animals that provided food. At one spot, in the lowest level of the gorge, the bones of an elephant lay in close association with more than 200 stone tools. Apparently, the animal was butchered here; there are no indications of any other activity. At another spot, on an occupation surface 1.8 million years old, basalt stones were found grouped in small heaps forming a circle. The interior of the circle was practically empty, while numerous tools and food debris littered the ground outside, right up to the edge of the circle. Some have interpreted this as evidence for some sort of shelter, seeing the stone piles as supports for the framework of a protective fence of thorn branches, or perhaps a hut with a covering of animal skins or grass. Another possibility is that the stones were "stockpiled" ahead of time, to be made into tools as needed, or to be hurled as missiles to hold off carnivorous animals while the hominines extracted meat, marrow, hide, and sinew from pieces of animal carcass.

OLDOWAN TOOLS

The oldest tools found at Olduvai Gorge belong to the **Oldowan tool tradition,** which is characterized by an all-purpose generalized chopping tool, produced by removing a few flakes from a stone (often a large, water-worn pebble) either by using another stone as a hammer (a hammerstone) or by striking the pebble against a large rock (anvil) to remove the flakes. This system of manufacture is called the **percussion method** (Figure 7.6). The finished product had a jagged, sharp edge, effective for cutting and chopping. The generalized form of the chopping tool suggests that it served many purposes, such as butchering meat, splitting bones for marrow, and perhaps also defending the user. Also used were the flakes, which

FIGURE 7.6

By 2.5 million years ago, hominines in Africa had invented the percussion method of stone tool manufacture. This technological breakthrough, which is associated with a significant increase in brain size, made possible the butchering of meat from scavenged carcasses.

had sharp, useful edges (in fact, many so-called choppers may be no more than by-products of flake manufacture). Some flakes were used "as is" for cutting tools, while others were retouched for use as scrapers.

Crude as they were, Oldowan choppers and flakes mark an important technological advance for early hominines; previously, they depended on found objects requiring little or no modification, such as bones, sticks, or conveniently shaped stones. Oldowan tools made possible new additions to the diet, because, without such tools, hominines could eat few animals (only those that could be skinned by tooth or nail); therefore, their diet was limited in terms of animal proteins. The advent of Oldowan choppers and flakes meant more than merely saving labor and time—they made possible the addition of meat to the diet on a frequent, rather than occasional, basis. Much popular literature has been written about this penchant for meat, often with numerous colorful references to "killer apes." Such references are quite misleading, not only

---

Oldowan tool tradition. The earliest identifiable stone tools. > **Percussion method.** A technique of stone tool manufacture performed by striking the raw material with a hammerstone or by striking raw material against a stone anvil to remove flakes.

because hominines are not apes but also because killing has been greatly overemphasized. Meat can be obtained, after all, by scavenging or by stealing it from other predators. What is significant is that a dentition such as that possessed by *Australopithecus* and *Homo habilis* is poorly suited for meat eating. What is needed if substantial amounts of meat are to be eaten, without teeth like those possessed by carnivorous animals, are sharp tools for butchering.

The initial use of tools was probably the result of adaptation to an environment that we know was changing between 3 and 2 million years ago from forests to grasslands. The physical changes that adapted hominines for spending increasing amounts of time on the new grassy terrain encouraged toolmaking. It has been observed that monkeys and apes, for example, often use objects, such as sticks and stones, in their threat displays. The change to a nearly upright bipedal posture, coupled with existing flexibility at the shoulder, arms, and hands, allowed hominines to do so as well, helping them to compete successfully with the large predatory carnivores that shared their environment.

What else do these assemblages of Oldowan tools and broken animal bones have to tell us about the life way of early *Homo*? First, they tell us that both *Homo habilis* and large carnivorous animals were active at these locations, for in addition to marks on the bones made by slicing, scraping, and chopping with stone tools, there are tooth marks from gnawing. Some of the gnawing marks overlie the butcher marks, indicating that enough flesh was left on the bones after the hominines were done with them to attract the other carnivores. In other cases, though, the butcher marks overlie the tooth marks of carnivores, indicating that the animals got there first. This is what we would expect if *H. habilis* were scavenging the kills of other animals, rather than doing its own killing. Consistent with this picture is that whole carcasses are not represented; evidently, only parts were transported away from the original location where they were obtained, again what we would expect if they were "stolen" from the kill of some other animal. The stone tools, too, were made of raw material procured at some distance from where they were used to process the parts of carcasses. Finally, the incredible density of bones at

some of the sites and patterns of weathering indicate that, although *H. habilis* didn't linger longer than necessary at any one time (and for good reason—the carnivores attracted by the meat could have made short work of *habilis* as well), the sites were repeatedly used over periods guessed to be on the order of 5 to 15 years.

All of this is quite unlike the behavior of historically known food-foraging peoples, who bring whole carcasses back to camp, where they are completely processed; neither meat nor marrow is left (as they were at Oldowan sites), and the bones themselves are broken up (as they were not at Oldowan sites) both to get at the marrow and to fabricate tools and other objects of bone. Nor do historically known food foragers normally camp in the midst of so much garbage. The picture that emerges of our Oldowan forbears, then, is of scavengers, getting their meat from the lower Paleolithic equivalent of modern-day road kills, taking the spoils of their scavenging to particular places where tools, and the raw materials for making them, had been stockpiled in advance for the purpose of butchering. At these sites, the remains were quickly processed, so that those doing the butchering could clear out before their lives were endangered by carnivores attracted by the meat. Thus, the Oldowan sites were not campsites or "home bases" at all. Quite likely, *H. habilis* continued to sleep in trees or rocky cliffs, as do other small-bodied terrestrial or semiterrestrial primates, in order to be safe from predators. However, the advanced preparation for meat processing implied by the caching of stone tools, and the raw materials for making tools, attests to considerable foresight and ability to plan ahead.

TOOLS, MEAT, AND BRAINS

As we have seen, by 1.5 million years or so after early hominines became fully bipedal, the size and structure of the brain were beginning to change. Until about 2.5 million years ago, early hominines lived on foods that could be picked or gathered: plants, fruits, invertebrate animals such as ants and termites, and perhaps even an occasional piece of meat scavenged from kills made by other animals. After 2.5 million years ago, meat became more important in their diet, and they began to scavenge for it on a more regular basis.

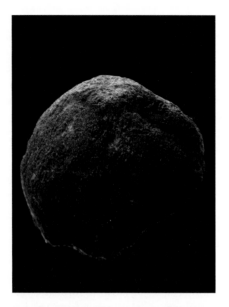

The stone tools used by *Homo habilis* included lava cobbles, choppers, and flakes like those shown here. Most choppers were probably the result of being struck from one cobble by another. These flakes were used to remove meat from bones, leaving cut marks (lower left). The cobbles and choppers were used to break open bones (middle left) to get at the marrow.

Homo habilis filled the same niche on the ground that these vultures fill in the air: a nonterritorial scavenger.

Since early hominines lacked size and strength to drive off predators, or to compete directly with other scavengers attracted to kills, they must have had to rely on their wit and cunning for success. One may imagine them lurking in the vicinity of a kill, sizing up the situation as the predator ate its fill while hyenas and other scavengers gathered, and devising strategies to outwit them all so as to seize a piece of the carcass. A hominine depending on stereotyped instinctual behavior in such a

Becoming scavengers put *Homo habilis* in competition with formidable adversaries like hyenas.

situation would have been at a competitive disadvantage. One that could anticipate problems, devise distractions, bluff competitors into temporary retreat, and recognize, the instant it came, its opportunity to rush in and grab what it could of the carcass stood a much better chance of surviving, reproducing, and proliferating.

One means by which early hominines gained access to a reasonably steady supply of carcasses while at the same time minimizing the risks involved is suggested by recent field studies of leopards. How this could have worked and the arguments in favor of it are the subject of the following Original Study.

Cat in the Human Cradle[6]

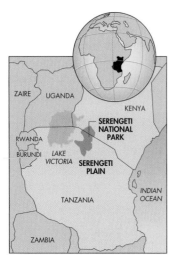

▲▽.

Recent evidence, such as marks on some of the Olduvai bones, indicates that animals the size of wildebeests or larger were killed, eaten, and abandoned by large predators such as lions, hyenas, and saber-toothed cats; hominines may have merely scavenged the leftovers. Several specialists now agree that early hominines obtained at least marrow mainly in this way. The picture with regard to the remains of smaller animals, such as gazelle-sized antelopes, is less certain. Paleoanthropologists Henry Bunn and Ellen Kroll believe that the cut-marked upper limb bones of small, medium-sized, and large animals found at Olduvai Gorge demonstrate that hominines were butchering the meaty limbs with cutting tools. Since modern-day lions and hyenas rapidly and completely consume small prey, leaving little or nothing for potential scavengers, Bunn and Kroll conclude that hominines must have acquired the smaller animals by hunting. But another scholar, Kay Behrensmeyer, suggests that a small group of hominines could have obtained these bones, not by hunting, but by driving off timid predators, such as cheetahs or jackals, from their kills.

Since carnivores play a key role in all these scenarios, three years ago I began thinking about studying their behavior and ecology. About the same time, a colleague directed me to a paper on the tree-climbing abilities of early hominines. The authors (anatomists Randall L. Susman, Jack T. Stern, and William L. Jungers) analyzed the limb bones of *Homo habilis* specimens from Olduvai Gorge, as well as those of the early hominine *Australopithecus afarensis* (better known as Lucy). They concluded that early hominines were probably not as efficient as we are at walking on two feet, but they were better than we are at climbing trees and suspending themselves from branches. At the very least, given their apparent lack of fire, early hominines must have used trees as refuges from large predators and as sleeping sites.

One evening, as I watched a documentary film by Hugh Miles about a female leopard and her cubs in Kenya's Masai Mara Reserve, carnivore behavior and early hominine tree climbing suddenly connected for me. In the film, a pack of hyenas attempt to scavenge an antelope that the mother leopard has killed. At the sight of the hyenas, the leopard grabs the prey in her jaws and carries it up a small tree. This striking behavior sparked my curiosity and sent me to the library the next morning to find out more about leopards.

---

[6]Adapted from Cavallo, J. A. (1990). Cat in the human cradle. *Natural History*, 54–56 & 58–60.

This leopard has carried part of a Thomson's gazelle up into a tree to prevent other scavengers from consuming what is left. Such tree-stored carcasses may have been the principal source of meat for *Homo habilis*.

I learned that the leopard differs from other large African carnivores in a variety of ways. Although it occasionally kills large animals, such as adult wildebeests and topi or young giraffes, the leopard preys primarily on smaller antelopes, such as Thomson's gazelles, impala, and Grant's gazelles, and on the young of both large and small species. Unable to defend its kills on the ground from scavenging by lions and spotted hyenas, both of which often forage in groups, the usually solitary leopard stores each kill in a tree, returning to feed but otherwise frequently abandoning it for varying lengths of time.

Although the leopard may not consume its entire prey immediately, the tree-stored kills are relatively safe from theft. (Even lions, which can climb trees, usually take little notice of this resource.) As a result, a kill can persist in a tree for several days. Also, leopard kills appear to be more predictably located than those of lions and hyenas because leopards tend to maintain a small territorial range for several years and occasionally reuse feeding trees. Finally, leopard kills are usually found in the woodlands near lakes and rivers, the habitat apparently preferred by early hominines. Such circumstances, I reasoned, might have once provided an ideal feeding opportunity for tree-climbing hominines, particularly *Homo habilis*. By scavenging from the leopard's temporarily abandoned larder, early hominines could have obtained the fleshy and marrow-rich bones of small- to medium-sized prey animals in relative safety.

Fossil evidence shows that ancestors of present-day leopards were contemporaneous with early hominines and shared the same habitats. The antiquity of tree-caching behavior is harder to prove, but it is supported by paleoanthropologist C. K. Brain's excavations of ancient caves in southern Africa's Sterkfontein Valley. In the vertical, shaftlike caves, Brain found the fossil remains of hominines, baboons, and antelopes, and of leopards and other large carnivores. The size of the prey animals and the selection of body parts, as well as puncture marks on some of the cranial bones of hominines and baboons, suggested that many of these fossils were the remains of leopard meals. Brain guessed that they had fallen into the caves from leopard feeding trees growing out of the mouths of the caves.

Given its similarities to the ancient environments represented at the early archeological sites—extensive grasslands with wooded lakes, rivers, and streams—the Serengeti National Park in northern Tanzania seemed an ideal living laboratory in which to test my hypothesis. I traveled there in July 1987, accompanied by Robert J. Blumenschine, who had conducted an earlier study there on scavenging opportunities provided by lions and hyenas. Along the Wandamu River, a tributary of the Seronera, we were fortunate to find an adult female leopard and her 13-month-old (nearly full-grown) male cub that tolerated our Land-Rover. We spent a total of about 50 hours, during the day and at night, observing these leopards at three fresh, tree-stored kills of Thomson's gazelles. The leopards frequently left the carcasses unguarded between feedings. On one occasion, a complete young Thomson's gazelle, killed the previous evening, was abandoned for 9 daylight hours (we found the leopards resting approximately 2 miles away). Without directly confronting these predators, therefore, a creature able to climb trees could have easily carried off the same amount of flesh and marrow as it could obtain from hunting.

While Brain's work in South Africa implicates leopards as predators of early hominines, including the genus *Homo,* some hominines may have also benefited from living near these carnivores. Tree-stored leopard kills could have provided an important resource to early scavenging hominines and the sharp, broken limb bones from the partly eaten prey could have been used to peel back the hide, expose the flesh of the carcasses, and remove large muscle bundles. This activity may even have given early hominines the initial impetus to make and use tools in the extraction of animal nutrients.

Some paleoanthropologists have argued that scavenging was an unlikely subsistence strategy for early hominines, since large predators require expansive home ranges and kills by these carnivores are rare in any particular area. They also contend that very little is left over from such kills after the predator is finished and that hominine competition with large carnivores for these leftovers would be a dangerous activity. My 1988 observations suggest something quite different. During approximately 2 months in the dry season, I documented 16 kills of small and medium antelopes made by my adult male and female leopards within an approximately 4-by-8-mile area. The majority of these kills, still retaining abundant flesh and marrow, were temporarily abandoned by the leopard for 3 to $8\frac{1}{2}$ hours during a single day.

The tree-stored leopard kills consisted mainly of adult and juvenile Thomson's gazelles. Compared with kills of similar-sized prey made on the ground by Serengeti lions and hyenas, as recorded by Blumenschine, the tree-stored leopard kills lasted longer, offering large quantities of flesh and marrow for 2 or more days. In part this was because they were not subject to many scavengers. The leopard kills were also more predictably located on the landscape than those of lions in the same area. In modern leopard populations, a male maintains a relatively large territory that overlaps with the usually smaller territories of several females. This pattern often means that several tree-stored kills are available simultaneously during a given period of time within a relatively small area.

An obvious question is how leopards would have responded to repeated theft of their tree-stored kills by early hominines. Would they, perhaps, have abandoned portions of their ranges if such thefts occurred with sufficient regularity? Although I haven't yet tested this, I don't think they would have. According to my observations and those of other researchers, leopards are usually more successful at hunting larger prey, such as gazelles and impala, at night. This gives them the opportunity to consume part of such kills before the arrival of any daytime scavengers. They thus should be able to obtain enough nourishment to warrant remaining in a territory, despite some such losses.

Like modern baboons and chimpanzees, early hominines may have killed some small animals, such as newborn antelopes. But they could have acquired all sizes of animal carcasses without hunting if the prey killed by leopards is taken into account. The wide assortment of animal bones at sites like Olduvai Gorge, which have been attributed to ground-based hunting and scavenging, could instead be attributed to scavenging only, both in trees and on the ground. Leopard kills would then have provided much of the flesh consumed by early hominines, while carcasses abandoned on the ground by other large predators would have yielded primarily bone marrow. Additional flesh may have come from the remains of large kills made by saber-toothed cats or from the carcasses of animals that drowned when herds migrated across ancient lakes.

While we can't observe the behavior of our early ancestors, the present-day interactions between leopards and some other primate species can be instructive. Baboons, for example, often fall victim to leopards while they sleep at night in trees or caves. During the day, however, baboons regularly attack, displace, and according to one account, even kill leopards. In western Tanzania, a park ranger reported that during the day, a group of baboons saw a leopard in a tree with the carcass of an impala. Barking out alarm calls, the adult and adolescent male baboons chased the leopard for about $\frac{3}{10}$ of a mile. The females and young baboons stayed with the carcass and began to eat, until the males returned and took possession of the kill.

Similarly, although chimpanzees in western Tanzania are the occasional prey of leopards, there is a report that one day some chimpanzees scavenged what was apparently a tree-stored leopard kill. On a more dramatic occasion, also during the day, a group of chimpanzees was observed noisily surrounding a leopard lair from which an adult leopard was heard growling. A male chimpanzee entered the lair and emerged with a leopard cub, which it and the others killed without reprisal from the adult leopard. This type of shifting day-night, predatory-parasitic relationship may once have existed between leopards and our early hominine ancestors.

Several lines of evidence suggest it was probably the early hominine males, rather than females, who did most of the scavenging. What predisposed them for this division of labor may have been the foraging habits of the earlier Australopithecines. As already noted (in Chapter 6), dental and skeletal differences between males and females suggest that males may have fed on the ground and lower levels of trees more heavily than females, who had a higher proportion of fruit in their diet.[7] Something like this pattern is seen today among orangutans, where it is a response to highly dispersed resources. As a consequence, males consume larger amounts of low-quality food such as bark than do females. A major difference, of course, is that orangutan males still forage in the forest, whereas male *Australopithecus* did not. In such a situation, the latter may have been forced to try out supplementary sources of food on the ground, especially if existing sources became scarcer, as they likely did; in the crucial period between 3 and 2 million years ago climates became markedly cold and dry.[8] Already bipedal, Australopithecines were capable of covering, in an energetically efficient way, the considerable distances (on the order of 32 square miles, based on the Original Study) necessary to ensure a steady supply of meat.

Another consideration is that, without contraceptive devices and formulas that could be bottle-fed to infants, females in their prime, when not pregnant, must have had infants to nurse. While this would not have restricted their local mobility, any more than it does a female ape or monkey or a woman among historically known food-foraging peoples, it would have been less easy for them than for males to range over the substantial distances required to search out carcasses. Also essential for the successful scavenger would have been the capacity for the massive bursts of energy needed to elude the many carnivores active on the savanna. Although anatomical and physiological

differences between the sexes in humans today are relatively insignificant compared to *H. habilis*, as a general rule, men can still run faster than women (even though some women can certainly run faster than some men). Finally, even for the smartest and swiftest individuals, scavenging would still have been a risky business. To place early *Homo* females at risk would have been to place their offspring, actual and potential, at risk as well. Males, on the other hand, would have been relatively expendable, for, to put the matter bluntly, a very few males are capable of impregnating a large number of females. In evolutionary terms, the population that places its males at risk is less likely to jeopardize its chances for reproductive success than is the one that places its females at risk.

Early hominine females, as well as males, had to "sharpen their wits" in order to gain access to some of the meat scavenged. For the most part, females continued to gather the same kinds of foods that their ancestors had been eating all along. But instead of consuming all this food themselves as they gathered it (as other primates do), they provided some to the males who, in turn, provided the females with meat. To do this, they had to plan ahead so as to know where food would be found in sufficient quantities, devise means by which it could be transported to some agreed-upon location for division at the proper time, while at the same time preventing its loss through spoilage or to such animals as rats and mice. At the least, this may have required fabrication of carrying devices such as net bags, and use of trail signs of the sort (described in Chapter 4) used by modern bonobos. Thus, female gathering played just as important a role in the development of larger, more complex brains as did male scavenging.

Evolving hominines' new interest in meat is a point of major importance. Out on the savanna, it is hard for a primate with a digestive system like that of humans to satisfy its amino-acid requirements from available plant resources. Moreover, failure to do so has serious consequences: growth depression, malnutrition, and ultimately death. The most readily accessible plant sources would have been the proteins available in leaves and legumes (nitrogen-fixing plants, familiar modern examples being beans and peas), but these are hard for primates like us to digest unless they are

[7]Leonard, W. R., & Hegman, M. (1987). Evolution of P3 morphology in *Australopithecus afarensis*. *American Journal of Physical Anthropology, 73*, 60.

[8]Behrensmeyer, A. K., Todd, N. E., Potts, R., & McBrinn, G. E. (1997). Late Pliocene faunal turnover in the Turkana basin, Kenya and Ethiopia. *Science, 278,* 1589–1594.

Adrienne Zihlman *(b. 1940)*

Up until the 1970s, the study of human evolution, from its very beginnings, was permeated by a deep-seated bias reflecting the privileged status enjoyed by men in Western society. Beyond the obvious labeling of fossils as particular types of "men," irrespective of the sex of the individual represented, it took the form of portraying males as the active sex in human evolution. Thus, it was males who were seen as providers and innovators, using their wits to become ever more effective providers of food and protection for passive females. The latter were seen as spending their time getting pregnant and caring for offspring, while the men were "getting ahead" by becoming ever smarter. Central to such thinking was the idea of "man the hunter," constantly honing his wits through the pursuit and killing of animals. Thus, hunting by men was seen as the pivotal humanizing activity in evolution.

We now know, of course, that such ideas are culture bound, reflecting the hopes and expectations of late-19th- and early-20th-century European and European-American culture. This recognition came in the 1970s and was a direct consequence of the entry of a number of highly capable women into the profession of paleoanthropology. Up until the 1960s, there were few women in any field of physical anthropology, but with the expansion of graduate programs and

changing attitudes towards the role of women in society, increasing numbers of them went on to earn a PhD. One of these was Adrienne Zihlman, who earned her doctorate at the University of California at Berkeley in 1967. Subsequently, she authored a number of important papers critical of "man the hunter" scenarios. She was not the first to do so; as early as 1971, Sally Linton had published a preliminary paper on "Woman the Gatherer," but it was Zihlman from 1976 on who especially elaborated on the importance of woman's activities for human evolution. Others have joined in the effort, including Zihlman's companion in graduate school and later colleague, Nancy Tanner, who collaborated with Zihlman on some of her papers and has produced important works of her own.

The work of Zihlman and her coworkers was crucial in forcing a reexamination of existing "man the hunter" scenarios, out of which came recognition of the importance of scavenging in early human evolution as well as the importance of female gathering and other activities. While there is still plenty to learn about human evolution, thanks to these women we now know that it wasn't a case of women being "uplifted" as a consequence of their association with progressively evolving men. Rather, the two sexes evolved together with each making its own important contribution to the process.

cooked. The problem is that leaves and legumes contain substances that cause the proteins to pass right through the gut without being absorbed.[9]

---

[9]Stahl, A. B. (1984) Hominid dietary selection before fire. *Current Anthropology*, 25, 151–168.

Chimpanzees have a similar problem when out on the savanna. In such a setting, they spend about 37 percent of their time on a yearly basis going after insects like ants and termites, while at the same time increasing their predation of eggs and vertebrate animals. Such animal foods not only are easily digestible, but they provide high-

One means by which bonobos indicate to others where they are headed is to deliberately trample down the vegetation. *H. habilis* may have made use of similar trail signs.

quality proteins that contain all the essential amino acids in just the right percentages. No one plant food does this by itself; only if the right combination is consumed can plants provide what meat does by itself in the way of amino acids. Moreover, there is abundant meat to be had on the savanna. All things considered, then, we should not be surprised if our own ancestors solved their "protein problem" in somewhat the same way that chimps on the savanna do today.

Increased meat consumption on the part of early hominines did more than merely ensure an adequate intake of essential amino acids, important though this was. Animals that live on plant foods must eat large quantities of vegetation, and obtaining such foods consumes much of their time. Meat eaters, by contrast, have no need to eat so much, or so often. Consequently, meat-eating hominines may have had more leisure time available to explore and manipulate their environment; like lions and leopards, they would have time to spend lying around and playing. Such activity, coupled with the other factors already mentioned, probably was a stimulus to hominine brain development.

The importance of meat eating for early hominine brain development is suggested by the size of their brains: The cranial capacity of the largely plant-eating *Australopithecus* ranged from 310 to 530 cubic centimeters; that of the most primitive known meat eater, *Homo habilis* from East Africa, ranged from 580 to 752 cc; whereas *Homo erectus*, who eventually hunted as well as scavenged for meat, possessed a cranial capacity of 775 to 1,225 cc.

THE EARLIEST SIGNS OF CULTURE: TOOLS

The use of specially made tools of stone appears to have arisen as a result of the need for implements to butcher and prepare meat, because hominine teeth were inadequate for the task. Even chimpanzees, whose canine teeth are far larger and sharper, frequently have trouble tearing through the skin of other animals.[10] Besides overcoming this problem, the manufacture of stone tools must have played a role in the evolution of the human brain, first by putting a premium on manual dexterity and fine manipulation over mere power in the use of the hands. This in turn put a premium on improved organization of the nervous system. Second, the transformation of a lump of stone into a "chopper," "knife," or "scraper" is a far cry from what a chimpanzee does when it transforms a stick into a termite probe. While the probe is not unlike the stick, the stone tool is (with the exception of hammerstones) quite unlike the lump of stone. Thus, the toolmaker must have in mind an

---

[10]Goodall, J. (1986) *The chimpanzees of Gombe: Patterns of behavior* (p. 372). Cambridge, MA: Belknap Press.

Meat-eating animals, like these lions, do not have to spend as much time eating as do those that rely on plant foods alone. Consequently, they have more time available for play and exploration.

abstract idea of the tool to be made, as well as a specific set of steps that will accomplish the transformation from raw material to finished product. Furthermore, only certain kinds of stone have the flaking properties that will allow the transformation to take place, and the toolmaker must know about these.

COOPERATION AND SHARING

With an apelike brain and a diet like that of monkeys and apes when out in open country, *Australopithecus* probably behaved much like other hominoids. Like apes, adults probably foraged for their own food, which was rarely shared with other adults. Among modern apes, however, there are two notable exceptions to this behavior. Among bonobos, females sometimes share meat and even fruits with each other and (sometimes) males. Adult chimpanzees, by contrast, rarely share plant food with one another, but males almost always share meat, frequently with females. Increased consumption of meat on the part of *Homo habilis* may have promoted even more sharing among adults. Moreover, a regular supply of meat would have required that substantial amounts of time and energy be devoted to the search for carcasses, and food gathered by females and shared with males could have provided the latter with both.

Sharing and cooperation between the sexes need not necessarily have been between mated males and females, but may just as well have been between brothers and sisters and mothers and sons. On the other hand, the capacity to engage in sexual activity at any time the female deemed appropriate may have promoted sharing and cooperation between a male and one or more sex partners. Among most catarrhine primates, males attempt to monopolize females

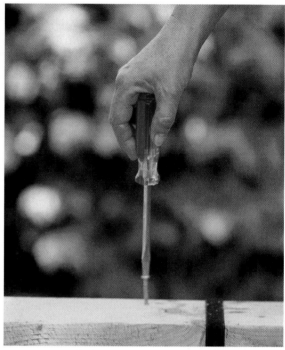

A power grip (left) utilizes more of the hand, while the precision grip (right) relies on the fingers for control.

when the latter are at the height of sexual receptivity. Moreover, male chimpanzees frequently use the sharing of meat to entice females to have sex, and females in estrus are more successful at begging for meat from males. Males, too, are more apt to hunt if a sexually receptive female is present.[11] The ability of the human female, alone among primates, to engage in sex at any time seems to be a consequence of bipedal locomotion. The reason for this is that this mode of locomotion requires a higher hormonal output than in other primates, to catalyze the steady release of energy to muscles needed for endurance.[12]

Hence, constant sexual activity should go back to the earliest hominines. Sharing of sex partners (who may have been multiple) seems likely.

Although chimpanzees can and do hunt singly, they frequently cooperate in the task. In the case of *Homo habilis*, cooperation would seem to have been even more crucial to success in scavenging. It is hard to imagine a creature lacking the formidable canines of a chimpanzee competing on an individual basis with carnivores far more powerful than itself.

In summary, then, it seems reasonable to assume that *Homo habilis* engaged in more sharing and cooperative behavior than one sees among present-day chimpanzees. How much more is certainly not known, and probably fell far short of what has been observed among any historically known food-foraging peoples. After all, *Homo habilis* was not just a different sort of hominine from *Australopithecus*; it was different from *Homo sapiens* as well.

---

[11]Moore, J. (1998). Comment. *Current anthropology, 39,* 413.

[12]Spuhler, J. N. (1979). Continuities and discontinuities in anthropoid-hominid behavioral evolution: Bipedal locomotion and sexual reception. In N. A. Chagnon & W. Irons (Eds.), *Evolutionary biology and human social behavior* (pp. 454–461). North Scituate, MA: Duxbury Press.

LANGUAGE ORIGINS

The evident importance of cooperation, planning, and foresight in the life of *H. habilis* raises the issue of this species' ability to communicate. Modern apes communicate through a combination of calls and gestures, and humans, though we rely on spoken language, also use this gesture-call system. Like the apes, we have inherited this from ancient ancestors that predate the evolutionary split between hominids and pongids. After three decades of experiments by several different researchers with captive apes, there is a growing consensus that all great apes share an ability to develop language skills at least to the level of a 2- to 3-year-old.[13]

---

[13]Miles, H. L. W. (1993). Language and the orangutan: The old person of the forest. In P. Singer (Ed.), *The great ape project* (p. 46). New York: St. Martin's.

(See the Original Study in Chapter 4.) Of course, they do not do so in the wild, even though the potential is there (just as bonobos do not make chipped stone tools in the wild, even though experiments show they are capable of it). Nor do they develop these language skills through speech, but rather through use of gestures. Again, because this linguistic potential is shared, it must be one which the earliest hominines possessed as well. In view of these considerations, the previously noted features of the brain of *H. habilis* that in modern humans are associated with language take on added interest.

Moreover, the speech area is adjacent to that which controls the right hand. Putting this all together, we must at least allow the possibility that *H. habilis* had developed a perhaps quite rudimentary gestural language. With the hands freed from locomotion to do other things, they were certainly more available for communication than are the hands of apes.

CHAPTER SUMMARY

Since 1960 a number of fossils have been found in East Africa at Olduvai Gorge, Lake Baringo, and east of Lake Turkana, and in South Africa at Sterkfontein and Swartkrans, which have been attributed to *Homo habilis*, the earliest representative of this genus. Among them is the well-known KNM ER 1470 skull, which is more modern in appearance than any *Australopithecus* skull. From the neck down, however, the skeleton of *Homo habilis* differs little from that of *Australopithecus*. Because it does show a significant increase in brain size, and some reorganization of its structure, *Homo habilis*' mental abilities must have exceeded those of *Australopithecus*. By 2.4 million years ago, the evolution of *Homo* was proceeding in a direction different from that of *Australopithecus*.

The same geological strata that have produced *Homo habilis* have also produced the earliest known stone tools. These lower Paleolithic artifacts from Olduvai Gorge, Lake Turkana, and Hadar in Ethiopia, are remarkably similar, suggesting that they were the products of a cultural

tradition in which tools were manufactured according to a model.

Finds made at Olduvai Gorge have provided important evidence of human evolutionary development. The oldest Lower Paleolithic tools found at Olduvai are in the Oldowan tool tradition, which is characterized by all-purpose generalized chopping tools and flakes. Used to make them was the percussion method of manufacture. The simple but effective Oldowan choppers and flakes made possible the addition of meat to the diet on a regular basis because people could now butcher meat, skin any animal, and split bones for marrow. Many Oldowan archaeological sites appear to be temporary places where meat was processed, rather than campsites.

Some changes in the brain structure of *Homo habilis* seem to have been the result of the changed diet. Increased consumption of meat, beginning about 2.5 million years ago, made new demands on their coordination and behavior. Successful procurement of meat through scavenging depended on *H. habilis*' ability to outthink far more powerful predators and scavengers. Obtaining animal food presented problems that very often had to be solved on the spot; a small scavenger depending on stereotyped instinctual behavior alone would have been at a competitive disadvantage in such a situation. Moreover, eaters of high-protein foods, such as meats, do not have to eat as often as vegetarians do. Consequently, meat-eating hominines may have had more leisure time available to explore and experiment with their environment.

Toolmaking and use also favored the development of a more complex brain. To make stone tools, one must have in mind at the beginning a clear vision of the tool to be made, one must know the precise set of steps necessary to transform the raw material into the tool, and one must be able to recognize the kind of stone that can be successfully worked. Advanced eye-hand coordination is also required.

A prime factor in the success of early hominines was the development of some cooperation in the procurement of foods. While the males probably supplied much of the meat, the females continued to gather the sorts of food eaten by other primates; however, instead of consuming what they gathered as they gathered it, they shared a portion with the males in exchange for meat. This required foresight and planning on the part of females, which played as important a role as male scavenging in favoring the development of larger, more complex brains. Food sharing with a sexual division of labor is characteristic of modern food foragers, and some hint of it can be seen among chimpanzees, among whom meat is frequently shared.

The cooperation, planning, and foresight exhibited by *Homo habilis* suggest the existence of some sort of rudimentary language, as do some features of this species' brain. Experiments with captive apes favor some sort of gestural language.

POINTS FOR CONSIDERATION

1. How does meat consumption relate to brain size? How does this recall earlier discussions regarding early primate development and arboreality?

2. What is the significance of the asymmetrical brain development demonstrated in early *Homo habilis*? How does it imply the presence of abstract thought and symbolism? What are the ramifications in terms of the creation and propagation of "culture?"

3. How have hominines managed, apparently, to augment or interfere with the natural processes of evolution? Have they really done this, or are they still subject to those same forces? Explain your answer.

4. Think about the old punch line stated by the sculptor: "I just chip away everything that doesn't look like a person." What is the importance of this statement? How does it relate to *Homo habilis* and the beginning of the paleolithic? What important evidence does it reveal about *H. habilis*?

SUGGESTED READINGS

Campbell, B. G., & Loy, J. D. (1995). *Humankind emerging* (7th ed.). New York: HarperCollins.

This well-written and lavishly illustrated text has excellent coverage of the earliest hominines.

Ciochon, R. L., & Fleagle, J. G. (Eds.). (1993). *The human evolution source book*. Englewood Cliffs, NJ: Prentice Hall.

This collection of articles by specialists provides a more detailed look at the different theories on early hominine evolution.

Johanson, D., and Shreeve, J. (1989). *Lucy's child: The discovery of a human ancestor*. New York: Avon.

This sequel to *Lucy* is written in the same engaging style. Although it covers some of the same ground with respect to *Australopithecus*, its focus is on *Homo habilis*. Besides giving a good description of this earliest member of the genus *Homo*, it presents one of the best discussions of the issues concerning when (and why) *Homo* appeared.

Chapter 8
HOMO ERECTUS AND THE EMERGENCE OF HUNTING AND GATHERING

MORE "HUMAN" THAN *HOMO HABILIS*, THOUGH LESS SO THAN *HOMO SAPIENS*, *HOMO ERECTUS* EMERGED ABOUT 1.8 MILLION YEARS AGO, BY WHICH TIME THE GENUS *HOMO* WAS SPREADING TO PARTS OF ASIA. SHOWN HERE IS EXCAVATION OF A *HOMO ERECTUS* SITE IN NORTHERN SPAIN, WHICH *H. ERECTUS* OCCUPIED BY 800,000 YEARS AGO.

Chapter Preview

Who Was *Homo erectus?*

Homo erectus was the direct descendant of early members of the genus *Homo,* as evidenced by findings in various parts of Africa. Populations of *Homo erectus* were widespread between about 1.8 million and 400,000 years ago, from Africa and Europe in the West, to Southeast Asia and China in the East.

What Were the Cultural Capabilities of *Homo erectus?*

Having a larger brain than its ancestors, *Homo erectus* became increasingly able to adapt to different situations through the medium of culture. This is reflected by better-made tools, a greater variety of tool types, regional diversification of tool kits, use of fire, and improved organizational skills.

What Were the Consequences of *Homo erectus'* Improved Abilities to Adapt Through Culture?

As culture became more important as the vehicle through which this species secured its survival, life became somewhat easier than it had been. As a result, selective pressures other than those favoring increased capacity for culture were reduced, reproduction became easier, and more offspring survived than before. This allowed populations to grow, causing "spillover" into previously uninhabited regions. This expansion in turn contributed to the further evolution of culture, as populations of *Homo erectus* had to find solutions to new problems of existence in newly inhabited regions.

In 1891, the Dutch army surgeon Eugene Dubois, intent upon finding the fossils of a "missing link" between humans and apes, set out for Indonesia (then the Dutch East Indies), which he considered to have provided a suitable environment for such a creature. At Trinil, on the island of Java, Dubois found what he was searching for: the fossil remains of a primitive kind of hominine, consisting of a skull cap, a few teeth, and a thighbone. Its features seemed to Dubois part ape, part human. Indeed Dubois at first thought the remains did not even belong to the same individual. The flat skull, for example, with its low forehead and enormous brow ridges, appeared to be like that of an ape; but it possessed a cranial capacity much larger than an ape's, even though small by modern human standards. The femur, or thighbone, was clearly human in shape and proportions and indicated the creature was a biped. Although Dubois called his find *Pithecanthropus erectus*, or "erect ape man," it has since been assigned to the species *Homo erectus*.

These casts of the skull cap and thigh bone of *Homo erectus* were made from the original bones found by Eugene Dubois at Trinil, Java.

HOMO ERECTUS FOSSILS

Until 1.8 million years ago, hominines were not to be found outside of Africa. It was on this continent that hominines, and later the genus *Homo*, originated. It was also in Africa that the first stone tools were invented. But by the time of *Homo erectus*, hominines had spread far beyond the confines of their original homeland. Fossils of this species are now known from a number of localities not just in Africa, but in China, Europe, Georgia, and India, as well as Java (Figure 8.1). Despite the fact that remains of this species have been found in so many different places in three continents, the remains show very little significant physical variation. Evidence suggests, however, that populations of *H. erectus* in different parts of the world do show some differences from one another on a subspecific level.

HOMO ERECTUS FROM JAVA

For a long time, the scientific community was reluctant to accept Dubois's claim that his Javanese fossils were of human lineage. It was not until the 1930s, particularly when other fossils of *H. erec-*

tus were discovered by G. H. R. von Königswald at Sangiran, Java, in the Early Pleistocene Djetis beds, that scientists almost without exception agreed that both discoveries were the remains of an entirely new kind of early hominine. Von Königswald found a small skull that fluorine analysis and (later) potassium-argon dating indicated to be older than Dubois's approximately 500,000- to 700,000-year-old Trinil specimen. Since 1960, additional fossils have been found in Java, and we now have remains of something like 40 individuals. A long continuity of *H. erectus* populations in Southeast Asia is indicated, from perhaps as many as 1.8 million to about 500,000 years ago. Interestingly, the teeth and jaws of some of the earliest Javanese fossils are in many ways quite similar to those of *Homo habilis*.[1]

HOMO ERECTUS FROM CHINA

A second population of *H. erectus* was found in the mid-1920s by Davidson Black, a Canadian anatomist then teaching at Peking Union Medical College. After purchasing in a Peking drugstore a few teeth for sale to local inhabitants for their supposed medicinal properties, Black set out for the nearby countryside to discover the owner of the

---

[1]Tobias, P. V., & von Königswald, G. H. R. (1964). A comparison between the Olduvi hominines and those of Java and some implications for hominid phylogeny. *Nature, 204*, 515–518.

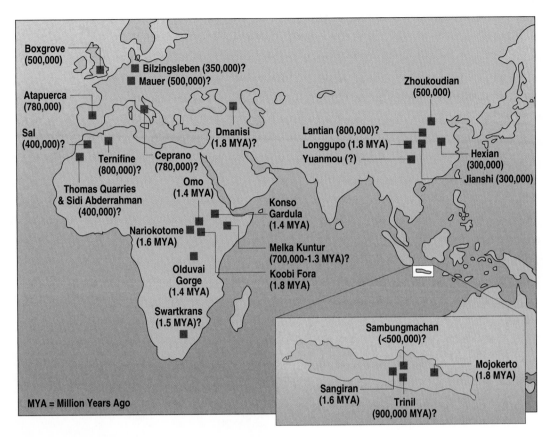

FIGURE 8.1
Sites, with dates, at which *Homo erectus* remains have been found.

The fragment of the early *Homo erectus* jaw from Java on the left is nearly identical to the jaw of *Homo habilis* from Olduvai Gorge on the right.

teeth and perhaps a species of early hominine. At a place called Dragon Bone Hill in Zhoukoudian, 30 miles from Beijing, on the day before closing camp at the end of his first year of excavation, he found one molar tooth. Subsequently, a skull encased in limestone was found by W. C. Pei, Black's associate; and between 1929 and 1934, the year of his death, Black labored along with Pei in the fossil-rich deposits of Zhoukoudian, uncovering fragment after fragment of the hominine Black had named, on the basis of that first molar tooth, *Sinanthropus pekinensis,* or "Chinese man of Peking"—now recognized as an East Asian representative of *H. erectus.*

After his death, Black's work was continued by Franz Weidenreich, a Jewish refugee from Nazi Germany. By 1938, the remains of more than 40 individuals, consisting of teeth, jawbones, and incomplete skulls, had been dug out of the limestone. World War II brought a halt to the digging, and

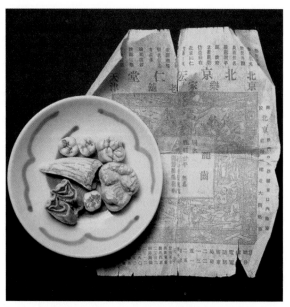

In Asia, Chinese drug stores are good places to look for fossils—including those of *Homo erectus*—among "dragon" bones and teeth. Actually fossils from many species of animals, these are ground up to make various medicines. This typical assortment of dragon teeth, including some from hominines (top row), is accompanied by the formula for converting them into medicine.

the original Zhoukoudian specimens were lost during the Japanese invasion of China. Fortunately, Weidenreich had made superb casts of most of the fossils and sent them to the United States. After the war, other specimens of *H. erectus* were discovered in China, at Zhoukoudian and at a number of other localities (Figure 8.1). The oldest skull is about 700,000 to 800,000 years old and comes from Lantian in Shensi Province. Even older is a fragment of a lower jaw from a cave in south-central China (Lunggupo) that is as old as the oldest Javanese fossils. Like some of their Javanese contemporaries, this Chinese fossil is reminiscent of African *H. habilis*. By contrast with these ancient remains, the original Zhoukoudian fossils appear to be no more than about 500,000 years old.

Although the two populations overlap in time, the Chinese fossils are, on the whole, not quite so old as those from Java. Not surprisingly, Chinese *H. erectus* is a bit less "primitive" looking. Its average cranial capacity is about 1,000 cubic centimeters, compared to 900 cc for Javanese *H. erec-*

tus (Figure 8.2). The smaller teeth, short jaw, and lack of diastema in the lower dentition—a gap in the teeth to accommodate a large upper canine when the jaws are closed—of the Chinese are further evidence of their more modern status.

HOMO ERECTUS FROM AFRICA

Although our samples of *H. erectus* from Asia remain among the best, several important specimens are now known from Africa. Fossils assigned to this species were discovered there as long ago as 1933, but the better-known finds have been made since 1960, at Olduvai and at Lake Turkana. Among them is the most complete *H. erectus* skeleton ever found, that of a boy who died 1.6 million years ago at about the age of 12. Another partial skeleton, that of an adult, had diseased bones, possibly the result of a massive overdose

One of the oldest and certainly the most complete *Homo erectus* fossil is the Strapping Youth from Lake Turkana. The remains are those of a boy who died in his early teens.

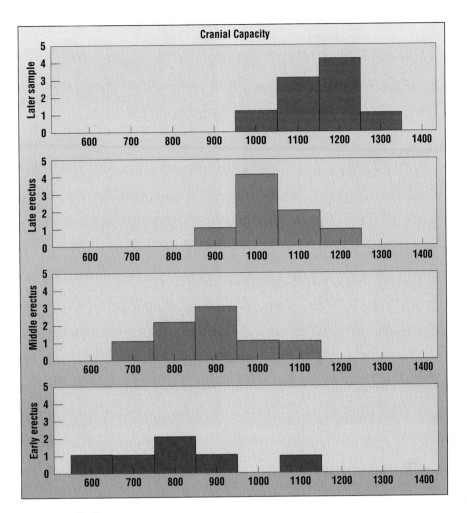

FIGURE 8.2

Cranial capacity in *Homo erectus* increased over time, as illustrated by these bar graphs, shown in cubic centimeters. The top graph depicts cranial capacity in skulls transitional from *erectus* to *sapiens*.

of Vitamin A. This excess could have come from eating the livers of carnivorous animals, for they accumulate Vitamin A in their livers at levels that are poisonous to human beings. Another possibility might have been heavy consumption of bee brood and other immature insects, producing the same result.

Generally speaking, African *H. erectus* skulls are quite similar to those from Asia; one difference is that their bones aren't quite as thick, another is that some Africans had smaller brow ridges. It may be, too, that individuals living in China were shorter and stockier, on the whole,

than those living in Africa. Although some anthropologists have argued that the African fossils represent a separate species *(H. ergaster)* and would restrict *H. erectus* to Asia, neither detailed anatomical comparisons nor measurements support such a separation.[2] Such differences as exist are minor and approximate the variation seen in

---

[2]Rightmire, G. P. (1998). Evidence from facial morphology for similarity of Asian and African representatives of *Homo erectus*. *American Journal of Physical Anthropology, 106,* 61.

This photo is of a late *H. erectus* skull from Zhoukoudian, China. It may be compared with the earlier African *erectus* skull shown at right.

This photo is of an early *H. erectus* skull from East Africa. It may be compared with the later *erectus* skull shown at left.

H. sapiens. Consistent with this is the fact that a mandible almost 1.8 million years old from Dmanisi, Georgia, a region that lies between Africa on the one hand and Indonesia on the other, shows a mix of characters seen in African and Asian *erectus* populations.[3] Overall, it seems the Africans reveal no more significant physical variations from their Asian counterparts than are seen if modern human populations from East and West are compared. As in Asia, the most recent African fossils are less "primitive" in appearance, and the oldest fossils (up to 1.8 million years old) display features reminiscent of the earlier *Homo habilis.* In-

deed, one of the problems is distinguishing early *H. erectus* from late *H. habilis*; precisely what one would expect if the one evolved from the other.

HOMO ERECTUS FROM EUROPE

Although Europe seems to have been inhabited by at least 780,000 years ago, few fossils attributable to *H. erectus* have so far been found there. A robust shinbone from Boxgrove, England, and a large lower jaw from Mauer, Germany, may be close to half a million years old. The jaw certainly came from a skull wide at the base, as is that of *H. erectus.* Older yet are fragments of four individuals from Atapuerca Hill, in north-central Spain, and a skull from Ceprano in southern Italy. As might be expected, these remains are quite similar to contemporary *erectus* material from North

---

[3]Rosas, A., & Bermdez de Castro, J. M. (1998). On the taxonomic affinities of the Dmanisi mandible (Georgia). *American Journal of Physical Anthropology, 107,* 159.

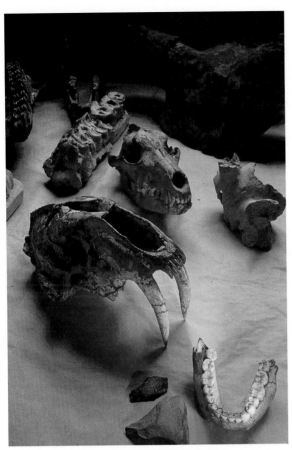

Shown here is a mandible assigned to *Homo erectus*, along with other mammalian fossils from the same site in Dmanisi, Georgia. All are about 1.8 million years old.

Africa. This finding, and the fact that the earliest evidence of hominines in Europe comes from Spain and Italy, suggests that they arrived there by crossing from North Africa. Since there was no land connection, this migration required crossing open water, but evidence from Indonesia (discussed later in this chapter) demonstrates that *H. erectus* was capable of doing this by 800,000 years ago. And all of this evidence, in turn, undermines arguments made by some European researchers that the early Europeans represent a separate species from *H. erectus*. Such speciation would require isolation of Europeans from other populations, but if ancient humans could cross between North Africa and southern Europe at least once, if not twice,

they could do it any number of times, and thus maintain at least a modicum of gene flow between populations.

Other European fossils are not as old as the Mauer and Boxgrove remains, and display a mosaic of features characteristic of both *H. erectus* and subsequent archaic *H. sapiens*. Here, as in Africa and Asia, a distinction between late *erectus* and early *sapiens* is difficult to make.

PHYSICAL CHARACTERISTICS OF *HOMO ERECTUS*

Apart from its skull, the skeleton of *H. erectus* differs only subtly from that of modern humans. Although its bodily proportions are like ours, it was more heavily muscled, its rib cage was conical rather than barrel-shaped, and its hips were narrower. With a small birth canal, gestation must have been short, with infants born in a relatively immature (and dependant) state. This implies prolongation of early growth, which is important in humans, as it allows for production of more synaptic connections in the brain. Stature seems to have been in the modern range, as the youth from Lake Turkana was about 5 feet 3 inches tall. Long legs and short toes made for effective long-distance walking. Compared to *Homo habilis*, *H. erectus* was notably larger, but displayed significantly less sexual dimorphism.

Cranial capacity in *H. erectus* ranged from 700 to 1,225 cubic centimeters (average about 1,000 cc), which compares with 752 cc for the nearly 2-million-year-old KNM ER 1470 skull from East Africa, and 1,000 to 2,000 cc (average 1,300 cc) for modern human skulls (Figure 8.2). The cranium itself had a low vault, and the head was long and narrow. When viewed from behind, its width was greater than its height, with its greatest width at the base. The skulls of modern humans when similarly viewed are higher than they are wide, with the widest dimension in the region above the ears. The shape of the inside of *H. erectus'* brain case showed near-modern development of the brain, especially in the speech area. Although some anthropologists argue that the vocal apparatus was not adequate for speech, others argue that asymmetries of the brain suggest the same pattern of right-handedness with left cerebral

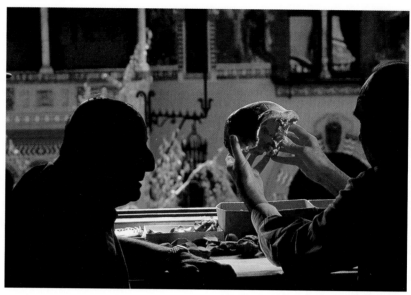

This skull, from Ceprano, Italy, is one of the oldest fossils *of H. erectus* from Europe. It is close to 800,000 years old.

dominance that, in modern peoples, is correlated with the capacity for language.[4]

Massive ridges over the eyes gave this early hominine a somewhat simian, "beetle-browed" appearance. *H. erectus* also possessed a sloping forehead and a receding "chin." Powerful jaws with large teeth, a protruding mouth, and huge neck muscles added to the generally rugged appearance. Nevertheless, the face, teeth, and jaws of this hominine are smaller than those of *Homo habilis*.

RELATIONSHIP BETWEEN *HOMO ERECTUS* AND *HOMO HABILIS*

The smaller teeth and larger brains of *H. erectus* seem to mark continuation of a trend first seen in *Homo habilis*. What is new is the increased body size, reduced sexual dimorphism, and more "human" body form of *erectus*. Nonetheless, there

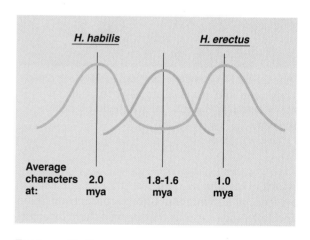

FIGURE 8.3

To understand the evolution of any species, the full range of variation must be considered, not merely typical representatives. The fact that fossils seemingly attributed to *H. habilis* and *H. erectus* coexisted between 1.8 and 1.6 million years ago (mya) need not mean coexistence of two separate species. If one evolved from the other, we would expect that at some point, the full range of variation included some individuals that still resembled *habilis,* while some others were increasingly taking on the appearance of *erectus.*

[4]Holloway, R. L. (1981). The Indonesian *Homo erectus* brain endocasts revisited. *American Journal of Physical Anthropology, 55,* 521.

is some resemblance to *habilis*, for example, in the conical shape of the rib cage, the long neck and low neck angle of the thighbone, the long low vault and marked constriction of the skull behind the eyes, and smaller brain size in the earliest *erectus* fossils. Indeed, as already noted, it is very difficult to distinguish between the earliest *erectus* and the latest *habilis* fossils (Figure 8.3). Presumably the one form evolved from the other, evidently fairly abruptly, in the period between 1.8 and 1.6 million years ago.

▲▽▲▽▲▽▲▽▲▽▲▽▲▽▲▽▲▽▲▽▲▽▲▽▲▽▲▽▲▽▲▽▲

THE CULTURE OF *HOMO ERECTUS*

As one might expect given its larger brain, *H. erectus* outstripped its predecessors in cultural development. In Africa, Europe, and Asia, there was refinement of the stone toolmaking technology begun by the makers of earlier flake and chopper tools. At some point, fire began to be used for protection, warmth, and cooking, though precisely when is still a matter for debate. Finally, there is indirect evidence that the organizational abilities of *H. erectus,* or at least the later ones, were improved over those of their predecessors.

THE ACHEULEAN TOOL TRADITION

Associated with the remains of *Homo erectus* in Africa, Europe, and Southwest Asia are tools of the **Acheulean tradition.** Characteristic of this are hand axes: pear-shaped tools pointed at one end with a sharp cutting edge all around. In East Africa, the earliest hand axes are about 1.4 million years old; those found in Europe and Southwest Asia are no older than about 750,000 years. Since the spread of the genus *Homo* from Africa took place before the invention of the hand axe,

it is not surprising to find that different forms of tools were developed in East Asia.

That the Acheulean grew out of the Oldowan tradition is indicated by an examination of the evidence discovered at Olduvai. In Bed I, the lowest level, chopper tools were found along with remains of *Homo habilis.* In lower Bed II, the first crude hand axes were found intermingled with chopper tools. Acheulean hand axes having a more "finished" look about them appear in middle Bed II, together with *H. erectus* remains.

Early Acheulean tools represent a definite step beyond the generalized cutting, chopping, and scraping tools of the Oldowan tradition. Like chopper tools, the hand axes were probably general-purpose implements for food procurement, processing, and defense. However, they were more standardized in form, having been shaped by regular blows rather than by random strikes. In this way, sharper points and more regular cutting edges were produced, and more cutting edge was available from the same amount of stone.

During this part of the **Paleolithic,** or Old Stone Age, tool cultures began to diversify (Figure 8.4). Besides hand axes, *H. erectus* used tools that functioned as cleavers (these were hand axes with

Homo erectus made a variety of Acheulean hand axes.

Acheulean tradition.   The toolmaking tradition of *Homo erectus* in Africa, Europe, and Southwest Asia in which hand axes were developed from the earlier Oldowan chopper. **> Paleolithic.**   The Old Stone Age, characterized by manufacture and use of chipped stone tools.

FIGURE 8.4

Ten % of the shaped tools in a typical Acheulean assemblage are the forms drawn here.

a straight edge where the point would otherwise be), and flake tools (generally smaller tools made by hitting a flint core with a hammerstone, thus knocking off flakes with sharp edges). Many flake tools were byproducts of hand axe and cleaver manufacture. Their sharp edges made them useful as is, but many were retouched to make points, scrapers, borers, and other sorts of tools. Diversification of tool kits is also indicated by the smaller numbers of hand axes in northern and eastern Europe, where people relied more on simply flaked choppers, a wide variety of unstandardized flakes, and supplementary tools of bone, antler, and wood. In eastern Asia, by contrast,

people developed a variety of choppers, scrapers, points, and burins (chisel-like tools) different from those in the West. Besides direct percussion, anvil (striking the raw material against a stationary stone) and bipolar percussion (holding the raw material against an anvil, but striking it at the same time with a hammerstone) were used to make them. While tens of thousands of stone tools have been found with *H. erectus* remains at Zhoukoudian, stone implements are not at all common in Southeast Asia. Here, favored materials likely were bamboo and other local woods, from which excellent knives, scrapers, and the like can be made.

Homo erectus and the Use of Bamboo[5]

▲▽

Bamboo provides, I believe, the solution to a puzzle first raised in 1943, when the late archaeologist Hallam Movius of Harvard began to publish his observations on Paleolithic (Old Stone Age) cultures of the Far East. In 1937 and 1938 Movius had investigated a number of archeological localities in India, Southeast Asia, and China. Although most of the archeological "cultures" that he recognized are no longer accepted by modern workers, he made another, more lasting contribution. This was the identification of the "Movius line" (which his colleague Carleton Coon named in his honor): a geographical boundary, extending through northern India, that separates two long-lasting Paleolithic cultures. West of the line are found collections of tools with a high percentage of symmetrical and consistently proportioned hand axes (these are called Acheulean tools, after the French site of Saint Acheul). More or less similar tool kits also occur in Mongolia and Siberia, but with few exceptions (which are generally relatively late in time), not in eastern China or Southeast Asia, where more crudely made tools known as choppers and chopping tools prevail [Figure 8.5].

My own research on the Movius line and related questions evolved almost by accident. During the course of my work in Southeast Asia, I excavated many sites, studied a variety of fossil faunal collections, and reviewed the scientific literature dealing with Asia. As part of this research I compared fossil mammals from Asia with those recovered from other parts of the world. In the beginning, my purpose was biostratigraphic—to use the animals to estimate the most likely dates of various sites used by early hominines. On the basis of the associated fauna, for example, I estimate that Kao Pah Nam [a site in Thailand] may be as old as 700,000 years. After years of looking at fossil collections and faunal lists, I realized that something was very strange about the collections from Southeast Asia: There were no fossil horses of Pleistocene age or for a considerable time before that. The only exceptions were a few horse fossils from one place in southern China, the Yuanmou Basin which was and is a special small grassland habitat in a low, dry valley within the Shan-Yunnan Massif.

To mammalian biostratigraphers this is unusual, since members of the horse family are so common in both the Old and New World that they are a primary means of dating various fossil localities. Fossil horses have been reported from western Burma, but the last one probably lived there some 20 million years ago. Not a single fossil horse turns up later than that in Southeast Asia, although they are known from India to the west and China to the north and every other part of Europe and Asia.

I then began to wonder what other normally common animals might be missing. The answer soon became apparent: camels—even though they too were once widespread throughout the world—and members and relatives of the giraffe family. Pleistocene Southeast Asia was shaping up as a kind of "black hole" for certain fossil mammals! These animals—horses,

---

[5]Adapted from G. C. Pope. (1989). Bamboo and human evolution. *Natural History*, 10, 50–54.

FIGURE 8.5
Choppers and flakes like these were used by *Homo erectus* at
Zhoukoudian, China.

camels, and giraffids—all dwell in open country. Their absence on the Southeast Asian mainland and islands (all once connected, along with the now inundated Sunda Shelf) is indicative of a forested environment. The mammals that are present—orangutans, tapirs, and gibbons—confirm this conclusion.

The significance of this is that most reconstructions of our evolutionary past have emphasized the influence of savanna grassland habitats, so important in Africa, the cradle of hominine evolution. Many anthropologists theorize that shrinking forests and spreading grasslands encouraged our primarily tree-dwelling ancestors to adapt to ground-dwelling conditions, giving rise to the unique bipedal gait that is the hallmark of hominines. Bipedalism, in turn, freed the hands for tool use and ultimately led to the evolution of a large-brained, cultural animal. Tropical Asia, instead, apparently was where early hominines had to readapt to tropical forest.

In studying the record, I noticed that the forested zone—the zone that lacked open-dwelling mammals—coincided generally with the distribution of the chopper-chopping tools. The latter appeared to be the products of a forest adaptation that, for one reason or another, deemphasized the utilization of standardized stone tools. At least this held for Southeast Asia; what at first I could not explain was the existence of similar tools in northern China, where fossil horses, camels, and giraffids were present. Finally, I came upon the arresting fact that the distribution of naturally occurring bamboo coincided almost directly with the distribution of chopper-chopping tools. The only exceptions that may possibly be of real antiquity—certain hand axe collections from Kehe and Dingcun, in China, and Chonggok-Ni, in Korea—fall on the northernmost periphery of the distribution of bamboo and probably can be attributed to fluctuation of the boundary.

Today there are, by various estimates, some 1,000 to 1,200 species of bamboo. This giant grass is distributed worldwide, but more than 60 percent of the species are from Asia. Only 16% occur in Africa, and those on the Indian subcontinent—to an unknown extent the product of human importation and cultivation—are discontinuous in distribution and low in diversity. By far, the greatest diversity occurs in East and Southeast Asia.

Based on these observations, I hypothesized that the early Asians relied on bamboo for much of their technology. At first I envisioned bamboo simply as a kind of icon representing all nonlithic technology. I now think bamboo specifically must have been an extremely important resource. This was not, in my opinion, because appropriate rock was scarce but because bamboo tools would have been efficient, durable, and highly portable.

There are few useful tools that cannot be constructed from bamboo. Cooking and storage containers, knives, spears, heavy and light projectile points, elaborate traps, rope, fasteners, clothing, and even entire villages can be manufactured from bamboo. In addition to the stalks, which are a source of raw material for the manufacture of a variety of artifacts, the seeds and shoots of many species can be eaten. In historical times, bamboo has been to Asian civilization what the olive tree was to the Greeks. In the great cities of the Far East, bamboo is still the preferred choice for the scaffolding used in the construction of skyscrapers. This incomparable resource is also highly renewable. One can actually hear some varieties growing, at more than 1 foot per day.

Some may question how bamboo tools would have been sufficient for killing and processing large and medium-size animals. Lethal projectile and stabbing implements can in fact be fashioned from bamboo, but their importance may be exaggerated. Large game accounts for a relatively small proportion of the diet of many modern hunters and gatherers. Furthermore, animals are frequently trapped, collected, killed, and then thrown on a fire and cooked whole prior to using bare hands to dismember the roasted carcass. There are many ethnographic examples among forest peoples of this practice.

The only implements that cannot be manufactured from bamboo are axes or choppers suitable for the working of hard woods. More than a few archaeologists have suggested that the stone choppers and resultant "waste" flakes of Asia were created with the objective of using them to manufacture and maintain nonlithic tools. Bamboo can be easily worked with stone flakes resulting from the manufacture of choppers (many choppers may have been a throwaway component in the manufacture of flakes).

The greater variety of tools found in the Acheulean and contemporary traditions is indicative of *H. erectus'* increased ability to deal with the environment. The greater the range of tools used, the greater the range of natural resources capable of being exploited in less time, with less effort, and with a higher degree of efficiency. For example, hand axes may have been used to kill game and dig up roots; cleavers to butcher; scrapers to process hides for bedding and clothes; and flake tools to cut meat and shape wooden objects. As argued in the Original Study, the differences between tool kits from the Far East and West are likely indicative of adaptation to specific regions. The same may be indicated by the differences between the tool kits of northern and eastern Europe on the one hand, and southern and western Europe on the other. One suggested explanation for this is that certain resources were scarcer in the latter region, which was more heavily forested than the former, and

that this scarcity was a spur to increasing the efficiency of technology.[6]

The improved technological efficiency of *H. erectus* is also evident in the selection of raw materials. While Oldowan toolmakers frequently used coarse-grained stone such as basalt, their Acheulean counterparts generally used such stone only for their heavier implements, preferring flint or other stones with a high silica content for the smaller ones. During later Acheulean times, two techniques were developed which produced thinner, more sophisticated axes with straighter, sharper cutting edges. The **baton method** of percussion manufacture involved using a bone or antler punch to strike the edge of the flint core. This method produced shallow flake scars, rather than

---

[6]Gamble, C. (1986). *The paleolithic settlement of Europe* (p. 310). Cambridge, England: Cambridge University Press.

Baton method. The technique of stone tool manufacture performed by striking the raw material with a bone or antler "baton" to remove flakes.

Experimentation on an elephant that died of natural causes demonstrates the effectiveness of Acheulean tools. Simple flint flakes easily slice through the thick hide, while hand axes sever large muscles. With such tools, two men working together can each butcher 100 pounds of meat in an hour.

the crushed edge that the hammerstone method produced on the earlier Acheulean hand axes. In later Acheulean times, the striking-platform method was also used to create sharper, thinner axes; the toolmakers would often strike off flakes to create a flat surface near the edge. These flat surfaces, or striking platforms, were set up along the edge of the tool perpendicular to its sides, so that the toolmaker could remove long, thin flakes stretching from the edge across each side of the tool.

USE OF FIRE

Another sign of *H. erectus*' developing technology is evidence of fires and cooking. Compelling evidence comes from the 700,000-year-old Kao Poh Nam rock shelter in Thailand, where a roughly cir-

cular arrangement of fire-cracked basalt cobbles was found in association with artifacts and animal bones. Since such rocks are not native to the rock shelter, and are quite heavy, they probably had to have been carried in by hominines. The reason more readily available limestone rocks were not used for hearths is that, when burned, they produce a quicklime, which causes itchy and burning skin rashes.[7] The bones associated with the hearth (which was located near the rock shelter entrance, away from the deeper recesses favored by denning animals) show clear evidence of cut marks from butchering, as well as burning.

---

[7]Pope, G. C. (1989). Bamboo and human evolution. *Natural History, 10,* 56.

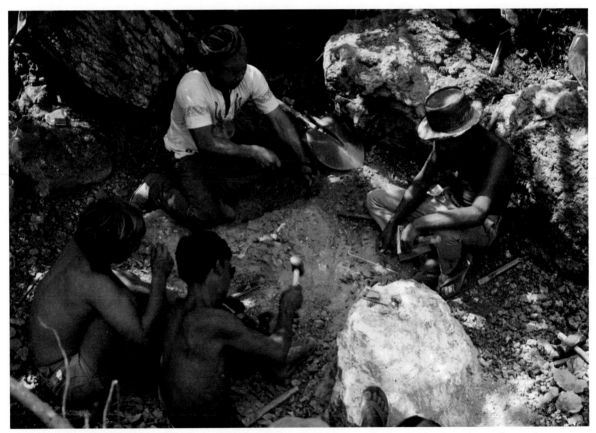

Archaeologists excavate a hearth at a rock shelter in Kao Poh Nam, Thailand. This hearth testifies to human use of fire 700,000 years ago.

Homo erectus may have been using fire even earlier, based on evidence from Swartkrans, in South Africa. Here, in deposits estimated to date between 1.3 and 1 million years ago, bones have been found which had been heated to temperatures far in excess of what one would expect as the result of natural fires. Natural grass fires in the region will not heat bones above 212 degrees Fahrenheit, whereas coals in campfires reach temperatures from 900° to 1200°F. Consequently, bones thrown into such fires reach temperatures higher than 212°F. Furthermore, the burned bones do not occur in deeper deposits, even though natural grass fires would have been no less common. South African paleoanthropologists Andrew Sillen and C. K. Brain suggest that the purpose of the Swartkrans fires was protection from predators, as the bones were heated to such high temperatures that any meat on them would have been inedible.[8] Thus, fire may not have been "tamed" initially for cooking or to keep people warm; such uses may have come later.

Whatever the reason for *Homo erectus'* original use of fire, it proved invaluable to populations that spread out of the tropics into regions with cooler climates. Not only did it provide warmth, but it may have assisted in the quest for food. In places like Europe and China, food would have been hard to come by in the long, cold winters, as edible plants were unavailable and the large herds of animals, whose mobility exceeded the potential of humans to maintain contact, dispersed and migrated. One solution would have been to search out the frozen carcasses of animals that had died naturally in the late fall and winter, using long wooden probes to locate them beneath the snow, wooden scoops to dig them out, and fire to thaw them so that they could be butchered and eaten.[9] Furthermore, such fire-assisted scavenging would have made available meat and hides of wooly mammoths, wooly rhinoceroses, and bison, which were probably beyond the ability of *H. erectus* to kill, at least until late in the species' career.

Perhaps it was the use of fire to thaw carcasses that led to the idea of cooking food, thereby altering the forces of natural selection, which previously favored individuals with heavy jaws and large, sharp teeth (food is tougher and needs more chewing when it is uncooked), thus promoting further reduction in tooth size as well as supportive facial architecture. So we find that, between early and late *H. erectus*, chewing-related structures undergo reduction at a rate markedly above the fossil vertebrate average.[10] Cooking did more than soften food, though. Cooking detoxifies a number of otherwise poisonous plants; alters digestion-inhibiting substances so that important vitamins, minerals, and proteins can be absorbed while in the gut, rather than just passing through it unused; and makes complex carbohydrates like starch—high-energy foods—digestible. With cooking, the basic resources available to humans were substantially increased and made more secure. The partial predigestion of food by cooking also may have caused a reduction in the size of the digestive tract. Despite its overall similarity of form to those of apes, the digestive tract of modern humans is substantially smaller. The advantage of this gut reduction is that it draws less energy to operate, thereby competing less with the high energy requirements of a larger brain. (Although a mere 2% of body weight, the brain accounts for about 20% to 25% of energy consumed at resting metabolism in modern human adults.[11])

Like tools, then, fire gave people more control over their environment. Possibly, *H. erectus* in Southeast Asia used fire, as have more recent populations living there, to keep areas in the forest clear for foot traffic. Certainly, the resistance to burning characteristic of many hardwood trees in this forest today indicates that fire has for a long time been important in their evolution. Fire may

[8]Sillen, A., & Brain, C. K. (1990). Old flame. *Natural History, 4,* 10.

[9]Gamble, 387.

[10]Wolpoff, M. H. (1993). Evolution in *Homo erectus*: The question of stasis. In R. L. Ciochon & J. G. Fleagle (Eds.), *The human evolution source book* (p. 396). Englewood Cliffs, NJ: Prentice Hall.

[11]Leigh, S. R., & Park, P. B. (1998). Evolution of human growth prolongation. *American Journal of Physical Anthropology, 107,* 347.

also have been used by *H. erectus*, as it was by subsequent hominines, not just for protection from animals out in the open, but to frighten away cave-dwelling predators so that the fire-users might live in the caves themselves; and fire could then be used to provide warmth and light in these otherwise cold and dark habitations. Even more, it modified the natural succession of day and night, perhaps encouraging *H. erectus* to stay up after dark to review the day's events and plan the next day's activities. That *H. erectus* was capable of at least some planning is implied by the existence of populations in temperate climates, where the ability to anticipate the needs of the winter season by preparing in advance to protect against the cold would have been crucial to survival.[12]

▲▽▲▽▲▽▲▽▲▽▲▽▲▽▲▽▲▽▲▽▲▽▲▽▲▽▲

OTHER ASPECTS OF *HOMO ERECTUS'* CULTURE

There is no evidence that populations of *H. erectus* lived anywhere outside the Old World tropics prior to a million years ago. Presumably, control of fire was a key element in permitting them to move into cooler regions like Europe and China. In cold winters, however, a fire is of little use without adequate shelter, and *H. erectus'* increased sophistication in the construction of shelters is suggested by three circular foundations of bone and stone 9 to 13 feet across at a 350,000-year-old site in Bilzingsleben, Germany. These could mark the bases of shelters of poles and grass similar to those used in recent times by people like the Bushmen of southern Africa. In the middle of one foundation was found a long elephant tusk, possibly used as a center post. Adjacent to these possible huts were hearths.

Keeping warm by the hearth is one thing, but keeping warm away from the hearth when procuring food or other necessities is another. Studies of modern humans indicate that they can remain reasonably comfortable down to 50°F with a mini-

mum of clothing so long as they are active; below that temperature, the extremities cool to the point of pain;[13] thus the dispersal of early humans into regions where winter temperatures regularly went below 50°, as they must have in China and Europe, was probably not possible without more in the way of clothing than hominines had hitherto worn. Unfortunately, we have no direct evidence as to the kind of clothing worn by *H. erectus*; we only know that it must have been more sophisticated than before.

That *H. erectus* developed the ability to organize in order to hunt live animals is suggested by remains such as those from the 400,000-year-old sites of Ambrona and Torralba, in Spain. At the latter site, in what was an ancient swamp, were found the remains of several elephants, horses, red deer, wild oxen, and rhinoceroses. Since their skeletons were dismembered, rather than in proper anatomical order, a fact that cannot be explained as a result of any natural geological process, it is clear that these animals did not accidently get mired in a swamp where they simply died and decayed.[14] In fact, the bones are closely associated with a variety of stone tools—a few thousand of them. Furthermore, there is very little evidence of carnivore activity, and none at all for the really big carnivores. Clearly, hominines were involved, not just in butchering the animals, but evidently in killing them as well. In fact, it is likely that the animals were actually driven into the swamp so that they could be easily dispatched. The remains of charcoal and carbon, widely but thinly scattered in the vicinity, raises the possibility that grass fires were used to drive the animals into the swamp. In any event, what we have here is evidence for more than opportunistic scavenging; not only was *H. erectus* able to hunt, but considerable organizational and communicative skills are implied as well.

[12]Goodenough, W. H. (1990). Evolution of the human capacity for beliefs. *American Anthropologist, 92,* 601.

[13]Whiting, J. W. M., Sodergem, J. A., & Stigler, S. M. (1982). Winter temperature as a constraint to the migration of preindustrial peoples. *American Anthropologist, 84,* 289.

[14]Freeman, L. G. (1992). *Ambrona and Torralba: New evidence and interpretation.* Paper presented at the 91st Annual Meeting, American Anthropological Association, San Francisco.

At some point, *H. erectus* ceased relying on scavenging as a source of meat, in favor of hunting live animals. One of those animals was the elephant hunted at Ambrona, Spain, where the tusk remains.

Additional evidence for hunting 400,000 years ago was discovered accidently in 1995 in the course of strip mining at Schöningen in northern Germany. Here were found five well-made and finely balanced spears made entirely of wood, the longest one measuring more than 7 feet in length. These are sophisticated weapons made by hunters who clearly knew what they were doing; no novices were they! The effectiveness of their weapons is attested by the thousands of butchered horse bones nearby.

There is no reason to suppose that *H. erectus* became an accomplished hunter all at once. Presumably, the most ancient members of this species, like *Homo habilis* before them, got the bulk of their meat through scavenging. As their cultural capabilities increased, however, they could have devised ways of doing their own killing, rather than waiting for animals to die or be killed by other predators. As they became more proficient predators over time, they would have been able to count on a more reliable supply of meat.

Yet other evidence of *H. erectus'* capabilities comes from the island of Flores, in Indonesia. This island lies east of a deepwater strait which has acted as a barrier to the passage of animals to and from Southeast Asia. To get to Flores requires crossing open water; at minimum 25 kilometers from Bali to Sumbawa, with a further 19 kilometers to Flores. That early humans did just this is indicated by the presence of 800,000-year-old stone tools.[15] Precisely how they navigated across the deep, fast-moving water is not known, but at the least it required some sort of substantial raft.

Evidence for a developing symbolic life comes from several sites in Europe, where deliberately marked objects of stone, bone, and ivory have been found in Acheulean contexts (see p. 221). These include several objects from Bilzingsleben, Germany, among them an elephant bone with a series of regular lines that appear to have been deliberately engraved. Though a far cry from the later Paleolithic cave art of France and Spain, these are among the earliest Paleolithic artifacts which

---

[15]Gibbons, A. (1998). Ancient island tools suggest *Homo erectus* was a seafarer. *Science, 279,* 1635.

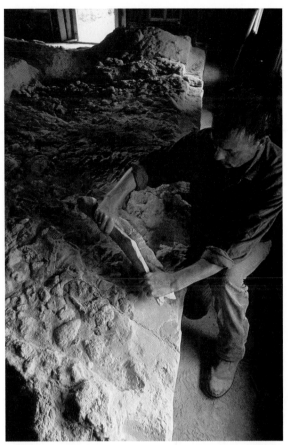

Shown here are wooden spears made by *Homo erectus* 400,000 years ago. Found in a bog in northern Germany, they are anything but crude, testifying to the sophisticated tool making and hunting skills developed by then.

At Bilzingsleben, Germany, archaeologists have uncovered an arrangement of stones and bones suggesting pavement of an area, perhaps for group rituals.

have no obvious utility or model in the natural world. Such apparently symbolic artifacts became more common in later phases of the Paleolithic, as more modern forms of the genus *Homo* appeared on the scene. Similarly, the world's oldest known rock carvings are associated with Acheulean tools in a cave in India.[16] Alexander Marshack argues that the use of such symbolic images requires some sort of spoken language, not only to assign meaning to the images but to main-

tain the tradition they seem to represent.[17] That such a symbolic tradition did exist is suggested by similar motifs on later Paleolithic artifacts. It is also in late Acheulean contexts on three continents that we have our earliest evidence for the use of red ochre, a pigment that more modern forms of *Homo* employed to color symbolic as well as utilitarian artifacts, to stain the bodies of the dead, to paint the bodies of the living, and (ultimately) to make notations and paint pictures.

---

[16]Bednarik, R. G. (1995). Concept-mediated marking in the lower Paleolithic. *Current Anthropology, 36,* 610–611.

[17]Marshack, A. (1976). Some implications of the paleolithic symbolic evidence for the origin of language. *Current Anthropology, 17,* 280.

We do not, of course, know anything definitive about *H. erectus'* linguistic abilities, but this evidence of a developing symbolic life, as well as the need to plan for seasonal changes and to coordinate hunting activities (and cross bodies of open water?), implies improving linguistic competence. In fact, the vocal tract and brain of *erectus* are intermediate between those of *H. sapiens* and earlier *Australopithecus*. Another clue is the size of the **hypoglossal canal,** the opening in the skull through which the nerve that controls tongue movements, so important for spoken language, passes from the skull (Figure 8.6). In modern humans this is twice the size that it is in any ape. It is in the skulls of late *H. erectus,* about 500,000 years ago, that we first see this characteristic in fossil remains.[18] Possibly, a changeover from gestural to spoken language was a driving force in these evolutionary changes. Certainly, the advantages of a spoken language over a gestural one seem to be obvious; not only does one *not* have to stop whatever one is doing with one's hands to "talk" (useful to a species increasingly dependent on tool use), but it is possible to talk in the dark, past opaque objects, or among people whose gaze is concentrated on something else (potential prey, for example).

With *H. erectus,* then, we find a clearer manifestation of the interplay among cultural, physical, and environmental factors than ever before. However slowly, social organization, technology, and communication developed along with an increase in brain size and complexity. In fact, the cranial capacity of late *H. erectus* is 31% greater than the mean for early *erectus,* a rate of increase more rapid than the average fossil vertebrate rate.[19] As a consequence of these, *H. erectus'* resource base was enlarged significantly;

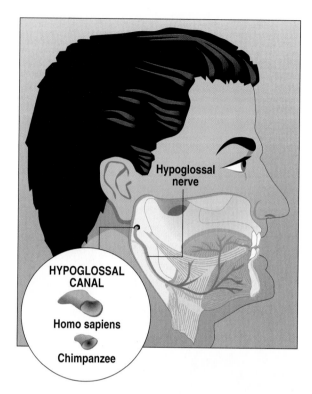

FIGURE 8.6

The size of the hypoglossal canal is much larger in humans than in chimpanzees. The nerve that passes through this canal controls tongue movement, and complex tongue movements are involved in spoken language. All homonines after about 500,000 years ago have this enlarged hypoglossal canal.

the supply of meat could be increased by hunting as well as by scavenging, and the supply of plant foods was increased as cooking allowed the consumption of previously toxic or indigestible vegetables. This, along with an increased ability to modify the environment in advantageous ways—for example, by using fire to provide warmth—undoubtedly contributed to a population increase and territorial expansion. In humans, as in other mammals, any kind of adaptation that makes life significantly easier reduces

---

[18]Cartmill, M. (1998). The gift of gab. *Discover 19*(11), 64.
[19]Wolpoff, pp. 392, 396.

Hypoglossal canal. The opening in the skull through which the tongue-controlling hypoglossal nerve passes.

This 300,000-year-old ox rib from a site in France is one of several from the Lower Paleolithic that exhibit engraved designs.

selective pressures, makes reproduction easier, helps more offspring to survive, and so causes population growth. This growth causes fringe populations to "spill over" into neighboring regions previously uninhabited by the species.

Thus, *Homo erectus* was able to move into areas that had never been inhabited by hominines before; first into the warm, southern regions of Asia, and ultimately into the cooler regions of China and Europe.

CHAPTER SUMMARY

The remains of *Homo erectus* have been found at several sites in Africa, Europe, China, and Java. The earliest is 1.6 million years old, and the species endured until about 400,000 years ago, by which period fossils exhibit a mosaic of features characteristic of both *H. erectus* and *H. sapiens*. *Erectus* appears to have evolved, rather abruptly, from *Homo habilis*. From the neck down, the body of *H. erectus* was essentially modern in appearance. The brain, although small by modern standards, was larger than that of *H. habilis*. The skull was generally low, with maximum breadth near its base, and massive brow ridges. Powerful teeth and jaws added to a generally rugged appearance.

With *H. erectus* we find a greater interaction among cultural, physical, and environmental factors than ever before. Social organization and improved technology developed along with an increase in brain size. The Oldowan chopper evolved into the Acheulean hand axe. These tools, the earliest of which are about 1.4 million years old, are pear-shaped, with pointed ends and sharp cutting edges. Like the chopper, they served a general purpose. During Acheulean times, tool cultures began to diversify. Along with hand axes, tool kits included cleavers, scrapers, and flakes. Further signs of *H. erectus*' developing technology was the selection of different stone for different tools and the use of fires to provide protection, warmth, and light; thawing frozen carcasses; and cooking. Cooking is a significant cultural adaptation because it took the place of certain physical adaptations such as large, heavy jaws and teeth, since cooked food is easier to chew. Because it detoxifies various substances in plants, cooking also increased the food resources available and allowed reduction in the size of the digestive tract. During later Acheulean times, *H. erectus* used the baton and striking-platform methods to make thinner axes with straighter, sharper cutting edges. From Germany comes evidence of the building of huts and the making of nonutilitarian artifacts; from Spain comes evidence of cooperative efforts to kill large amounts of game.

H. erectus' improved organizational, technological, and communicative abilities led to more effective hunting and a greater ability to modify the environment in advantageous ways. As a result, the populations of these early hominines increased and they expanded into new geographic areas.

POINTS FOR CONSIDERATION

1. Why was fire perhaps the single most important tool first utilized by *Homo erectus*? Why was it so important? What physical consequences resulted? What was its effect on diet?

2. What is the significance of travel to southwestern Europe and Eastern Indonesia by *Homo erectus*?

3. What are the dietary ramifications associated with improving tool kits? How might this demonstrate important patterns of thinking? What important facet of hominine behavior does this indicate?

4. What is so significant about *Homo erectus'* material selection in tool use?

5. What does the presence of purely nonfunctional artifacts indicate about *Homo erectus*?

SUGGESTED READINGS

Campbell, B. G., & Loy, J. D. (1995). *Humankind emerging* (7th ed.). New York: Harper Collins.

This well-illustrated book has three good up-to-date chapters on *Homo erectus* and their way of life.

Ciochon, R. L., & Fleagle, J. G. (Eds.). (1993). *The Human evolution source book.* Englewood Cliffs, NJ: Prentice Hall.

Part V of this book reproduces eight articles that deal with a variety of topics on the history of recovery, diversity, tempo, and mode of evolution and culture of *H. erectus*. An introduction by the editors puts the articles in context.

Gamble, C. (1986). *The Paleolithic settlement of Europe.* Cambridge, England: Cambridge University Press.

Although it does not deal exclusively with *Homo erectus*, this work does discuss material from Europe associated with this species. In doing so, it takes a critical stance as to conventional interpretations and offers novel explanations of *H. erectus'* behavior based on a better understanding of the process of archeological site formation.

Rightmire, G. P. (1990). *The evolution of Homo erectus: Comparative anatomical studies of an extinct human species.* Cambridge, England: Cambridge University Press.

This is the standard work on our current understanding of *Homo erectus*.

White, E., & Brown, D., et al., and the editors of Time-Life (1973). *The first men.* New York: Time-Life.

This magnificently illustrated volume in the Time-Life *Emergence of Man* series deals with *Homo erectus*. Its drawbacks are that it is not up-to-date, and it portrays early *H. erectus* as too much of a "big game hunter"; otherwise, it remains a good introduction to many of the fossils, sites, and tools associated with this hominine.

Chapter 9
ARCHAIC *HOMO SAPIENS* AND THE MIDDLE PALEOLITHIC

NO EXAMPLES OF ARCHAIC *HOMO SAPIENS* ARE
BETTER KNOWN THAN THE NEANDERTALS OF
EUROPE AND WESTERN ASIA. THOUGH DIFFERENT
IN MANY WAYS FROM MODERN HUMANS, THEY
HAD MODERN-SIZED BRAINS AND, SOME
ANTICIPATE, OTHER MODERN FEATURES. SHOWN
HERE IS ONE SUCH—A NEANDERTAL SKULL FROM
LA FERRASSIE, IN FRANCE, ONE OF SEVERAL
NEANDERTALS WITH A CHIN.

Chapter Preview

Who Was "Archaic" *Homo sapiens?*

"Archaic" *Homo sapiens* is the name used for members of this species who lived prior to about 35,000 years ago. Included are the Neandertals, descendants of *Homo erectus*, who lived in Europe and western Asia between about 130,000 and 35,000 years ago, and other populations somewhat like them who lived in Africa, China, and Southeast Asia. All had essentially modern-sized brains in skulls that still retained a number of primitive features.

What Was the Culture of Archaic *Homo sapiens* Like?

By 200,000 years ago, the human brain had reached its modern size, and by then human culture had become rich and varied. People not only made a wide variety of tools for special purposes, but they also made objects for purely symbolic purposes, engaged in ceremonial activities, and cared for the old and disabled.

What Became of the Neandertals?

Although there is some debate, the most likely explanation is that their contemporaries, and at least some of the Neandertals themselves, evolved into anatomically modern versions of *Homo sapiens*. This seems to have happened as features of modern anatomy arose in different regional populations and were carried to others through gene flow. Thus, human populations on all three continents of the Old World seem to have contributed to the making of modern humans.

The anthropologist attempting to piece together the innumerable parts of the puzzle of human evolution must be as good a detective as a scholar, for the available evidence is often scant, enigmatic, or full of misleading clues. The quest for the origin of modern humans from more ancient representatives of the genus *Homo* has some of the elements of a detective story, for it contains a number of mysteries concerning the emergence of humanity, none of which has been completely solved to this day. The mysteries involve the appearance of the first fully sapient humans, the identity of the Neandertals, and the relationship of both to more modern forms.

▲▽▲▽▲▽▲▽▲▽▲▽▲▽▲▽▲▽▲▽▲▽▲▽▲▽▲

THE APPEARANCE OF
HOMO SAPIENS

At various sites in Europe and Africa, a number of hominine fossils, primarily skulls, jaws, and jaw fragments, have been found which seem to date roughly between 400,000 and 200,000 years ago. Most consist of parts of one or a very few individuals, the one exception consisting of 300,000-year-old bones and teeth from the Sierra de Ata-

puerca in northern Spain. Here, the remains of at least 32 individuals of both sexes, juveniles as well as adults, were deliberately dumped (after defleshing their skulls) by their contemporaries into a deep cave shaft known today as Sima de los Huesos ("Pit of the Bones"). This makes it the best population sample from this time period anywhere in the world. As expected of any population, this one displays a significant degree of variation; cranial capacity ranges, for example, from 1,125 to 1,390 cubic centimeters, overlapping the upper end of the range for *H. erectus* and the lower end of the range for *H. sapiens*. Overall, the bones display a mix of features, some typical of *erectus*, others of *sapiens*, including some incipient Neandertal characteristics. Of interest is the fact that, varied as it is, the sample shows no more sexual dimorphism than displayed by modern humans.[1]

Other remains from Africa and Europe dating between 400,000 and 200,000 years ago have

---

[1]Lorenzo, C., Carretero, J. M., Arsuaga, J. L., Gracia, A., & Martinez, I. (1998). Intrapopulational body size variation and cranial capacity variation in middle Pleistocene humans: The Sima de los Huesos sample (Sierra de Atapuerca, Spain). *American Journal of Physical Anthropology, 106,* 30.

These two skulls are from the 300,000-year-old site of Sima de los Huesos in Spain and represent the transition from *H. erectus* to archaic *H. sapiens* in Europe.

This skull from Dali, China, is representative of archaic *H. sapiens* in East Asia.

This skull, from Ethiopia, is one of several from Africa indicative of a transition from *Homo erectus* to *Homo sapiens.*

sometimes been classified as *H. sapiens*—for example skulls from Ndutu in Tanzania, Swanscombe in England, and Steinheim in Germany—and sometimes as *H. erectus,* as in the case of skulls from several African sites as well as Arago, France; Bilzingsleben, Germany; and Petralona, Greece. Yet all have cranial capacities that fit within the range exhibited by the Sima de los Huesos skulls, and display the same mosaic of *erectus* and *sapiens* features. Compared to us, for instance, the Swanscombe and Steinheim skulls are large and robust, with their maximum breadth lower on the skull, and they had more prominent brow ridges, larger faces, and bigger teeth. Similarly, the face of the Petralona skull resembles European Neandertals, but its back looks like *H. erectus.* Conversely, a skull from Salé in Morocco, which had

a rather small brain for *H. sapiens* (930–960 cc), looks surprisingly modern from the back. Finally, various jaws from Morocco and France seem to combine features of *H. erectus* with those of the European Neandertals.

A similar situation exists in East Asia, where skulls from several sites in China exhibit the same sort of mix of *erectus* and *sapiens* characteristics. Whether one chooses to call any of these early humans early *H. sapiens* or late *H. erectus* seems to be a matter of taste; whichever one calls them does not alter their apparently transitional status. Despite their retention of a number of features of *H. erectus,* their brain size shows a clear increase over that of even late representatives of that species (see Figure 8.2).

LEVALLOISIAN TECHNIQUE

The culture of the hominines transitional between *H. erectus* and *H. sapiens* seems little changed from that of their predecessors. Early *sapiens* (or late *H. erectus,* if that is what one wishes to call them), for example, employed the kinds of heavy-duty tools such as hand axes and smaller flake tools used by *H. erectus* for thousands of years; however, by 200,000 years ago, the **Levalloisian technique** of tool manufacture had come into use. Levalloisian flake tools have been found widely in

---

Levalloisian technique. Toolmaking technique developed about 200,000 years ago by which three or four long triangular flakes were detached from a specially prepared core.

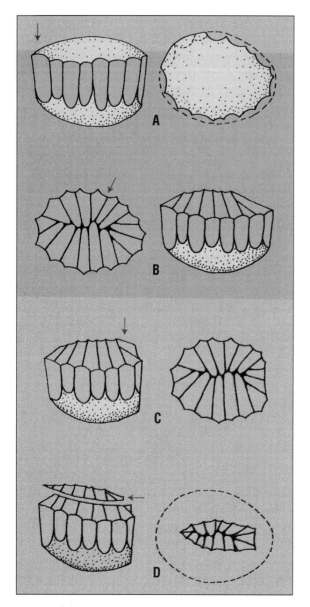

FIGURE 9.1

These drawings show top and side views of the steps in the Levalloisian technique. Drawing A shows the preparatory flaking of the stone core; B, the same of the top surface; C, the striking platform; and D, the final step of detaching a flake of a size and shape predetermined by the preceding steps.

Africa, Europe, the Middle East, and even China, where practically no hand axes have been uncovered. This could be a case of independent invention, since eastern Asia is quite distinct culturally

from the west. Or, it could represent the spread of ideas from one part of the inhabited world to another. In the Levalloisian technique, the core was shaped by removal of small waste flakes over its surface, following which a striking platform was set up by a crosswise blow at one end of the core of stone (Figure 9.1). Then the platform was struck, removing three or four long flakes, whose size and shape had been predetermined by the preceding preparation. What was left, besides the waste flakes, was a nodule that looked like a tortoise shell. This method produced a longer edge for the same amount of flint than the previous ones. The edges were sharper and could be produced in less time.

Also around 200,000 years ago in Africa, another technological breakthrough took place. This was the invention of hafting—the affixing of small stone bifaces and flakes in handles of wood—to make improved spears and knives. At about the same time, also in Africa, the use of yellow and red pigments of iron oxide picks up, becoming especially common by 130,000 years ago.[2] This may signal a rise in ritual activity, as may the deliberate deposition of the human remains in the Sima de los Heusos, already discussed. One possibility is that this involved ritual activity that presaged burial of the dead, a practice that became common after 100,000 years ago.

ARCHAIC *HOMO SAPIENS*

In 1856, three years before publication of Darwin's *On the Origin of Species*, the skeletal remains of an early man were discovered in the Neander Valley—Neandertal in German—near Dusseldorf, Germany. Although the discovery was of considerable interest, the experts were generally at a loss as to what to make of it. Examination of the fossil skull, a few ribs, and some limb bones revealed that the individual was a human being, showing primitive and modern characteristics. Cranial capacity had reached modern size, but the skull was still primitive looking. Some people believed the bones were those of a sickly and deformed contemporary. Others thought the skele-

---

[2]Barham, L. S. (1998). Possible early pigment use in south-central Africa. *Current Anthropology, 39,* 703–710.

ton belonged to a soldier who had succumbed to "water on the brain" during the Napoleonic Wars. One prominent anatomist thought the remains were those of an idiot suffering from malnutrition, whose violent temper had gotten him into many scrapes, flattening his forehead and making his brow ridges bumpy.

The idea that **Neandertals** were somehow deformed or aberrant was given impetus by an analysis of a Neandertal skeleton found in 1908 near La Chapelle-Aux-Saints in France. The analysis mistakenly concluded that the specimen's brain was apelike and that it walked like an ape. Although a team of North American investigators subsequently proved that this French Neandertal specimen was that of an elderly *H. sapiens* who had suffered from malnutrition, arthritis of the spine, and other deformities, the apelike image has persisted. To many nonanthropologists, Neandertal has become the quintessential "caveman," portrayed by imaginative cartoonists as a slant-headed, stooped, dim-witted individual clad in animal skins and carrying a big club as he plods across the prehistoric landscape, perhaps dragging behind him an unwilling female or a dead leopard. In a best-selling novel of the 1970s, *Clan of the Cave Bear*, Neandertals were depicted as bow-legged and barrel-chested with extra-long arms (more like those of apes than humans and incapable of the full range of human arm movements), muzzlelike jaws, and a body covering of coarse brown hair; not quite a pelt but not far from it. This brutish image was completed by portraying Neandertals as incapable of spoken language, abstract or innovative thinking, or even thinking ahead.

With the discovery that Neandertals were nowhere near as brutish and apelike as originally portrayed, some scholars began to see them as no more than "less finished" versions of the anatomically modern populations that held exclusive sway in Europe and the Middle East after 30,000 years

In spite of their distinctive features, Neandertals did not differ all that much from modern Europeans, as this reconstruction in a German museum shows.

Neandertals. Representatives of "archaic" *Homo sapiens* in Europe and western Asia, living from about 130,000 years ago to about 35,000 years ago.

Skull of archaic *Homo sapiens* from Kabwe (Broken Hill), Zambia.

ago. For example, C. Loring Brace of the University of Michigan observes that such "classic" Neandertal features as a sloping forehead, a bunlike back of the skull, and a distinctively small, inward-sloping mastoid process (behind the ear) are commonly present in medieval skulls from Denmark and Norway.[3] Nevertheless, recent work has shown that Neandertals are distinctive, when compared to anatomically modern populations. Although they held modern-sized brains (average cranial capacity 1,400 cc, versus 1,300 cc for modern *H. sapiens*), Neandertal skulls are distinctive in the projection of their noses and teeth, and the swollen appearance of the mid-facial region. This is due at least in part to the large size of their front teeth, which were heavily used for tasks other than chewing. In many individuals, front teeth were worn down to the stubs of their roots by 35 to 40 years of age. The large noses, for their part, prob-

ably were necessary to warm frigid air to prevent damage to the lungs and brain, and to moisten and clean the dry, dusty air of the glacial climate. The eye sockets were also positioned well forward, with prominent brow ridges above them. At the back of the skull, a bunlike bony mass provided for attachment of powerful neck muscles, needed to counteract the weight of a heavy face.

Both sexes were extraordinarily muscular, with extremely robust and dense limb bones. Details of the shoulder blades indicate the importance of overarm and downward thrusting movements; their arms were exceptionally powerful, and pronounced attachments on their hand bones attest to a remarkably strong grip. It has been suggested that a healthy Neandertal could lift an average NFL linebacker over his head and throw him through the goalposts.[4] Their massive foot and leg

[3]Ferrie, H. (1997). An interview with C. Loring Brace. *Current Anthropology, 38,* 861.

[4]Shreeve, J. (1995). *The Neandertal enigma: Solving the mystery of modern human origins* (p. 5). New York: William Morrow.

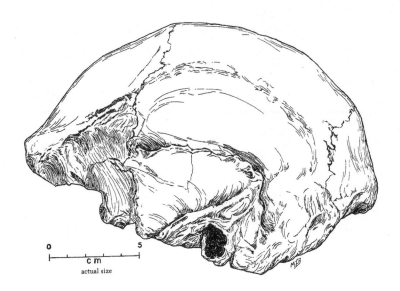

0   5

c m

actual size

In the 1930s, 11 skulls were found at Ngandong, Java. Though their dating was not precisely known, they were generally considered to be Southeast Asian equivalents of the Neandertals with modern-sized brains (from 1013 to 1252 ccs), while on the exterior they retained features of earlier Javanese *H. erectus.* With time, opinion on their dating changed, regarding them as considerably earlier than the Neandertals. This insight focused attention on their resemblance to *erectus,* so that when their dating was recently pinned down (to sometime between 53,000 and 27,000 years ago), some assumed that this proved a late survival of *erectus* in Asia, contemporary with *H. sapiens* elsewhere. But the skulls remain what they always were: representatives of archaic *sapiens,* with modern brains in otherwise primitive-looking skulls.

bones (their shin bones, for example, were twice as strong as those of any recent human population) suggests a high level of endurance; evidently, Neandertals spent long hours walking and scrambling about. Since brain size is related to overall body mass as well as intelligence, the large average size of the Neandertal brain (compared to that of modern humans) is accounted for by their heavy, robust bodies.

The Neandertal pelvis, too, shows differences from that of anatomically modern humans, but these do not support suggestions that obstetric requirements were different for Neandertals than they are for modern humans. Although the pelvic outlet is small by modern standards, it is still within the present-day range of variation, and the size of the pelvic inlet is virtually

the same.[5] Differences in pelvic shape are easily accounted for as a consequence of posture-related biomechanics and deviation in modern humans from a shape characteristic of earlier hominines. Once born, however, Neandertal infants did mature more rapidly than do our own, as the characteristic Neandertal robustness can be discerned in the bones even of children who died before the age of 5. Furthermore, their teeth erupted earlier, and their brains grew more rapidly after birth than do our own.

---

[5]Togue, R. G. (1992). Sexual dimorphism in the human bony pelvis, with a consideration of the Neandertal pelvis from Kebara Cave, Israel. *American Journal of Physical Anthropology, 88,* 1–21.

In China, the Maba skull is the one most like the Neandertals. Its round eye orbits are without precedent in the Far East and suggest mixture with Western populations.

African, Chinese, and Javanese Populations

Because Neandertal fossils are so numerous, have been known for so long, and are relatively well dated (30,000 to 130,000 years ago), they have received much more attention than have other populations of archaic *H. sapiens*. Nevertheless, outside Europe and western Asia, a number of skulls have been found in Africa, China, and Java, which date to roughly the same time period. They differ from the Neandertals primarily in their lack of midfacial projection and massive muscle attachments on the back of the skull. Thus, the Neandertals represent an extreme form of archaic *sapiens*. Elsewhere, the archaics look like robust versions of the early modern populations that lived in the same regions or, if one looks backward, somewhat less primitive versions of the *H. erectus* populations that preceded them. All had fully modern-sized brains in skulls that still looked primitive on the outside.

THE CULTURE OF ARCHAIC *HOMO SAPIENS*

As the first hominines to possess brains of modern size, archaic *H. sapiens* had, as we would expect, greater cultural capabilities than their near ancestors. Such a brain made possible technological advancements as well as conceptual thought of considerable sophistication and, almost surely, communication by speech. In short, Neandertals and others like them were a fully sapient species of human being, relatively successful in surviving and thriving even in environments that would seem to us impossibly cold and hostile.

MIDDLE PALEOLITHIC

The improved toolmaking capabilities of archaic *H. sapiens* are represented by various **Middle Paleolithic** traditions, of which the best known are the Mousterian and Mousterianlike traditions of Europe, western Asia, and North Africa. These date between about 166,000 and 40,000 years ago, and represent a technological advance over Acheulean and even Levalloisian tools. The 16 inches of working edge that an Acheulean flint worker could get from a 2-pound core compares with the 6 feet the Mousterian could get from the same core.

The Mousterian Tradition

The **Mousterian tradition** is named after the Neandertal site of Le Moustier, France. The presence of Acheulean hand axes at Mousterian sites is one indication that this culture was ultimately rooted in the older Acheulean tradition. Neandertals and their contemporaries improved upon Levalloisian techniques; Mousterian flake tools are lighter and smaller than those of the Levalloisian. Whereas Levalloisian toolmakers obtained only two or three flakes from one core, Mousterian toolmak-

---

Middle Paleolithic.   The middle part of the "Old Stone Age" characterized by the emergence of archaic *H. sapiens* and the development of the Mousterian tradition of toolmaking. **>** **Mousterian tradition.**   Toolmaking tradition of the Neandertals and their contemporaries of Europe, western Asia, and northern Africa, featuring flake tools lighter and smaller than Levalloisian flake tools.

ers obtained many more smaller flakes, which were then skillfully retouched and sharpened for special purposes.

The Mousterian tool kits contained a much greater variety of tool types than the previous traditions: hand axes, flakes, scrapers, borers, gravers, notched flakes for sawing and shredding wood, and many types of points that could be attached to wooden shafts to form thrusting spears. Many other tools also were hafted in handles of wood or bone, and some populations were experimenting with bitumen as a glue. With this new and varied tool kit, humans intensified their utilization of food resources and increased the availability and quality of clothing and shelter. For the first time, people could cope with the nearly arctic conditions that became prevalent in Europe as the glaciers began to expand about 70,000 years ago.

Tools such as 5, 6, and 7 are characteristic of the Mousterian tradition (1–4 are earlier, 8–13 later).

People likely came to live in cold climates as a result of a slow but steady population increase during the Paleolithic era. As this caused populations to "spill over" into previously uninhabited colder regions, humans developed a series of cold-climate adaptations that increased their cultural variability. Under near arctic conditions vegetable foods are only rarely or seasonally available, and meat is the staff of life. In particular, animal fats, rather than carbohydrates, become the chief source of energy on account of their slower rate of metabolism. Abundant animal fat in the diets of cold-climate meat eaters provides them with the extra energy needed for full-time hunting, as well as needed body heat. Insufficient fat in the diet produces lower resistance to disease, lassitude, and a loss of the will to work.

That meat was important to the makers of Mousterian tools is indicated by an abundance of associated animal bones, often showing clear cut marks. Frequently, the remains consist almost entirely of very large game—wild cattle (including bison), wild horses, and even mammoths and woolly rhinoceroses. At several sites there is striking evidence that particular species were singled out for the hunt. For example, at one site in the French Pyrenees, well over 90% of the faunal assemblage (representing at least 108 animals) consists of large members of the cattle family. These bones accumulated at the foot of a steep riverside escarpment, over which the animals were evidently stampeded. Similar mass hunting techniques are documented at other Mousterian sites: At La Quina in western France, a dense accumulation of cattle, horse, and reindeer bones (many with clear cut marks from butchering) occurred at the base of a steep cliff; at another site in the Channel Islands, dense deposits of mammoth and woolly rhinoceros bones indicate use of a deep coastal ravine for cliff-fall hunting. Clearly, the Neandertals were not mere unstructured or opportunistic hunters, but engaged in a great deal of deliberate hunting of very large game.[6] This required deliberate planning, forethought, and logistical organization.

[6]Mellars, P. (1989). Major issues in the emergence of modern humans. *Current Anthropology, 30*, 356–357.

anthropology *applied*   Forensic Archaeology

Although the fields of Paleolithic and forensic archaeology might appear to have little in common, the two do share common techniques of data recovery. The difference is that in one case what is recovered is evidence to be used in legal proceedings involving cases of murder, human rights abuses, and the like; in the other, the evidence is used to reconstruct ancient human behavior.

Forensic archaeologists commonly work closely with forensic anthropologists (Chapter 1). The relation between them is rather like that between a forensic pathologist, who examines a corpse to establish time and manner of death, and a crime scene investigator who searches the site for clues. While the forensic anthropologist deals with the human remains—often only bones and teeth—the forensic archaeologist controls the site, recording the position of all relevant finds and recovering any clues associated with the remains. In Rwanda, for example, a team assembled in 1995 to investigate a mass atrocity for the United Nations included archaeologists from the U.S. National Park Service's Midwest Archaeological Center. They performed the standard archaeological procedures of mapping the site, determining its boundaries, photographing and recording all surface finds, and excavating, photographing, and recording buried skeletons and associated materials in mass graves.*

As another example, Karen Burns of the University of Georgia was part of a team sent to northern Iraq after the Gulf War to investigate alleged atrocities. On a military base where there had been many executions, she excavated the remains of a man's body found lying on its side facing Mecca, conforming to Islamic practice. Although there was no intact clothing, two threads of polyester used for sewing clothing were found along the sides of both legs. Although they survived, the clothing, because it was made of natural fiber, had decayed. "Those two threads at each side of the leg just shouted that his family didn't bury him," says Burns.** Proper though his position was, no Islamic family would bury their own in a garment sewn with polyester thread; proper ritual would require a simple shroud.

---

*Connor, M. (1996). The archaeology of contemporary mass graves. *SAA Bulletin*, 14 (4), 6 and 31.

**Cornwell, T. (1995, November 10). Skeleton staff. *Times Higher Education*, p. 20.

The importance of hunting to Mousterian peoples may also be reflected in their hunting implements, which are more standardized with respect to size and shape than are their domestic and maintenance implements (for maintaining necessary equipment). The complexity of the tool kit needed for survival in a cold climate may have played a role in lessening the mobility of the users of all these possessions. That they were less mobile is suggested by the greater depth of deposits at Mousterian sites compared with those from the earlier ("lower") Paleolithic. Similarly, evidence for long sequences of production, resharpening and discarding of tools, and large-scale butchering and cooking of game, along with evidence of efforts to improve accommodations in some caves and rock shelters through pebble paving, constructing simple walls, and digging postholes and artificial pits, all suggest that Mousterian sites were more than mere stopovers in peoples' constant quest for food. The large number of Mousterian sites uncovered in Europe and western Asia, as well as clear differences between them, is closely related to Neandertal's improved hunting techniques, based on superior technology in weapon and toolmaking and more efficient social organization than before. These, in turn, were closely related to Neandertal's increased brain size.

Neandertal society had developed, evidence shows, even to the point of being able to care for physically disabled members of the group. For the first time, the remains of "oldsters"—individuals well past their prime—are well represented in the fossil record. Furthermore virtually every elderly Neandertal skeleton that is reasonably complete shows evidence of trauma having been treated, with extensive healing of wounds and little or no infection.[7] Particularly dramatic examples include the remains of a blind amputee discovered in Shanidar Cave in Iraq and a man badly crippled by arthritis unearthed at La Chapelle. Whether or not this evidence indicates true "compassion" on the part of these early people is not known; what is certain is that culture had become more than barely adequate to ensure survival.

One powerful selective force that might have favored empathy (not to mention cooperation and communication) among Neandertals was childbirth. Earlier in this chapter, we noted that the obstetric requirements for these people were no different than they are for modern humans. This is significant, for among humans, unlike all other primates, childbirth is a difficult business. Because of the remodeling of the pelvis for bipedal locomotion, to get a large-headed fetus down the birth canal, it must enter the canal facing sideways, and then rotate so that when it emerges, it faces down. In other primates, it enters the canal facing up and exits that way as well. The consequence of this, for humans, is that not only does it take longer to traverse the canal, prolonging the pain, but because babies do not bend backward, mothers cannot pull them out without serious injury. Nor can they clear their newborns' airways if they are in trouble. The upshot is, human mothers need help from others to deliver a baby successfully, so that empathy as well as cooperation and communication would clearly enhance reproductive success. In earlier hominines, the problem may not have been as great, as infants were likely delivered sideways, without need of the final rotation. But as the first hominines with really big heads, Neandertals and other archaic *sapiens* would have had to cope with the full pain and risk.[8]

THE SYMBOLIC LIFE OF NEANDERTALS

Although earlier reports of evidence for some sort of "cave bear cult" have turned out to be far-fetched, indications of some sort of symbolic life do exist. At several sites, there is clear evidence for deliberate burial of the dead. This is important, for the intentional positioning of dead hominine bodies by other hominines, whatever the specific reason, nonetheless constitutes evidence of symbolism.[9] To date, about 17 sites in Europe, South Africa, and Southwest Asia include Middle Paleolithic burials. To cite but two examples, at Kebara Cave, in Israel, sometime between 64,000 and 59,000 years ago, a Neandertal male aged between 25 and 35 years was placed in a pit on his back, with his arms folded over his chest and abdomen. Some time later, after complete decay of attaching ligaments, the grave was reopened and the skull removed (a practice that, interestingly, is sometimes seen in burials in the same region roughly 50,000 years later). Another example is from Shanidar Cave in Iraq, where evidence was found of a burial accompanied by funeral ceremonies. In the back of the cave a Neandertal was buried in a pit. Pollen analysis of the soil around the skeleton indicated that flowers had been placed below the body and in a wreath about the head. (The possibility that the pollen blew into the cave has been effectively ruled out.) The flowers in question consist solely of varieties valued in historic times for their medicinal properties.

Other evidence for symbolic behavior in Mousterian culture comes from the use of two different naturally occuring pigments: manganese dioxide and red ocher. Finds of these in human trash reveal clear evidence of scraping to produce

---

[7]Conroy, G. C. (1997). *Reconstructing human origins: A modern synthesis* (p. 427). New York: W. W. Norton.

[8]Fischman, J. (1994). Putting a new spin on the birth of human birth. *Science, 264,* 1082–1083.

[9]Schepartz, L. A. (1993). Language and modern human origins. *Yearbook of Physical Anthropology, 36,* 113.

powder, as well as crayonlike facets from use. Thus, Mousterian peoples were clearly using these for applying color to things. An example is the carved and shaped section of a mammoth tooth, illustrated below, that was worked by Mousterian peoples about 50,000 years ago. One of a number of carved and engraved objects that may have been made for purely symbolic purposes, it is similar to a number of plaques of bone and ivory made by later Paleolithic peoples, and it is also similar to the *churingas* made of wood by historic Australian aborigines for ritual purposes. The Mousterian object, which was once smeared with red ocher, has a highly polished face as if from long handling. Microscopic examination reveals that it was never provided with a working edge for any utilitarian purpose. As Alexander Marshack observes: "A number of researchers have indicated that the Neandertals did in fact have conceptual models and maps as well as problem-solving capacities comparable to, if

not equal to, those found among anatomically modern humans."[10]

NEANDERTALS AND SPOKEN LANGUAGE

Among modern humans, the sharing of thoughts and ideas, as well as the transmission of culture from one generation to the next, is dependent upon a spoken language. Since the Neandertals had modern-sized brains and a tool kit comparable to that being used in historic times by Australian aborigines, it might be supposed that they had some form of spoken language. Nevertheless, some have argued that the Neandertals lacked the physical features necessary for spoken language.

[10]Marshack, A. (1989). Evolution of the human capacity: the symbolic evidence. *Yearbook of Physical Anthropology, 32,* 22.

This carved symbolic plaque or *churinga* made from a section of a mammoth molar was excavated at the Mousterian site of Tata, Hungary. The edge is rounded and polished from long handling. The plaque has been symbolically smeared with red ocher. The reverse face of the plaque (right) shows the beveling and shaping of the tooth.

For example, the larynx was thought to be higher in the throat than it is in modern humans, a reconstruction we now know to be faulty. In the skeleton from the Kebara Cave burial, for instance, the shape and position of the hyoid bone (the "wish bone," associated with the larynx) show that the vocal tract was quite adequate for speech. This is especially noteworthy, for humans pay a high price for the way their vocal tract is positioned. With the lowered position of our larynx, it is far easier for us to choke to death than it is for other mammals. (Before the Heimlich maneuver, choking on food was the sixth leading cause of accidental death in the United States.)[11] The only advantage worth such a price seems to be the ability to speak.

With respect to the brain, paleoneurologists, working from endocranial casts, are agreed that Neandertals had the neural development necessary for language. Indeed, they argue that the changes associated with speech began even before the appearance of archaic *Homo sapiens*.[12] Consistent is the size of the hypoglossal canal, which in Neandertals is like that of modern humans and unlike that of apes.[13] As discussed in the last chapter, this feature is apparent in hominine fossils that are at least 400,000 years old, and indicates an ability to make the tongue movements necessary for articulate speech. Nor do arguments that a relatively flat skull base would have prevented speech have merit, as some modern adults show as much flattening as the Neandertals, yet have no trouble talking. Talking Neandertals make a good deal of sense in view of the evidence for the manufacture of objects of apparently symbolic significance. Objects such as the mammoth tooth "churinga" already described would seem to have required some

form of linguistic explanation. Clearly, the burden of proof is now on those who would deny these ancients the ability to speak.

ARCHAIC *HOMO SAPIENS* AND MODERN HUMAN ORIGINS

One of the hot debates in paleoanthropology today is over the question: Did populations of archaic *H. sapiens* in most, if not all, parts of the Old World evolve simultaneously into anatomically modern humans, (the "multiregional hypothesis") or was there a single, geographic place of origin, from which anatomically modern *H. sapiens* spread to replace existing populations of the archaic species everywhere else (The "Eve" or "Out of Africa" hypothesis)? Based on the fossil evidence from Africa and some parts of Asia, a good case can be made for the former, as opposed to the latter, hypothesis. As several anthropologists have noted, African, Chinese, and Southeast Asian fossils of archaic *H. sapiens* imply local population continuity from *Homo erectus*, through archaic, to modern *Homo sapiens*,[14] lending strong support to the interpretation that there was genetic continuity in these regions. For example, in China, hominine fossils consistently have flatter faces than their contemporaries elsewhere, as is still true today. Instead of evolving extremely "puffy" faces and massive neck musculature, as did the Neandertals, other archaic *sapiens* populations experienced a reduction in total facial protrusion as facial robusticity decreased, while the backs of their skulls took on a more modern form.

One possible exception to this scenario consists of the Neandertals of Europe. About 35,000 to 40,000 years ago a new technology, known as the **Aurignacian tradition** spread into Europe from Southwest Asia, where its appearance marks the start of the **Upper Paleolithic** period. In both

---

[11]Shreeve, J. (1995). *The Neandertal enigma: Solving the mystery of modern human origins* (p. 273). New York: William Morrow.

[12]Schepartz, p. 98.

[13]Cartmill, M. (1998). The gift of gab. *Discover, 19* (11), 62.

---

[14]Wolpoff, M. H., & Caspari, R. (1997). *Race and human evolution.* New York: Simon and Schuster.

Aurignacian tradition.   Toolmaking tradition of anatomically modern *H. sapiens* in Europe and western Asia at the beginning of the Upper Paleolithic. **> Upper Paleolithic.**   The last part of the "Old Stone Age," characterized by the emergence of anatomically modern hominines and an emphasis on the blade technique of toolmaking.

Franz Weidenreich *(1873–1948)*

Franz Weidenreich was born and educated in Germany, where he later held professorships in anatomy, first at Strassburg and then at Heidelberg. Although his early work was primarily in hematology (the study of blood), his scientific work shifted to the study of bones and related tissues, and in 1926 he published his first study of a human fossil, an archaic *Homo sapiens* cranium from Ehringsdorf. Two years later, he was appointed professor of anthropology at the University of Frankfurt.

In 1935, he was sent by the Rockefeller Foundation to take up the study of fossils of *Homo erectus* from Zhoukoudian, China, following the death of their discoverer, Davidson Black. When the Japanese invasion of China forced Weidenreich to leave, he took with him to the United States several painstakingly prepared casts, as well as detailed notes on the actual fossils. From these he was able to prepare a major monograph which set new standards for paleoanthropological reports. For this alone, anthropology owes him a great debt, for the fossils themselves were among the casualties of World War II.

Unlike many physical anthropologists of his time or ours, Weidenreich had an extensive firsthand knowledge of extant human fossils from several parts of the Old World: Europe (where he had worked before going to China), China, and Southeast Asia (he collaborated in the 1930s study of *Homo erectus* and later fossils from Java). What struck him about the fossils in each of these regions was the evident continuity from the earliest to the latest specimens. From this observation, he developed his polycentric theory of human evolution, which received its first clear statement in a 1943 publication. In it, he argued the thesis that human populations of common ancestry thereafter evolved in the same direction in four different geographical regions (Africa was the fourth). Although some have (mis)understood this as the completely separate but parallel evolution of four lineages, Weidenreich was quite clear about the continued operation of gene flow in the process. As the number of human fossils has increased, and our knowledge of evolutionary processes has grown, Weidenreich's ideas have been taken up by others and developed into the modern multiregional theory of human evolution.

---

regions, human skeletons associated with Aurignacian tools are typically modern in their features (but a notable exception is the Central European site of Vindija, where Neandertals are associated with an Aurignacian split-bone point).[15] Nevertheless, fossils identified as Neandertals are known from sites in western Europe that date to 35,000 to 33,000 years ago, in which case coexistence between the modern and archaic forms of *sapiens* would seem to be indicated. Given the striking

anatomical differences between the two, some form of population replacement, rather than simple evolution from one to the other, may have occurred.

An alternate explanation is possible, however. If we think in terms of varied populations—as we should[16]—instead of ideal types, we find that features reminiscent of modern humans can be discerned in some of the latest Neandertals. A spec-

---

[15]Conroy, p. 436.

[16]Gould, S. J. (1996). *Full house: The spread of excellence from Plato to Darwin* (pp. 72–73). New York: Harmony Books.

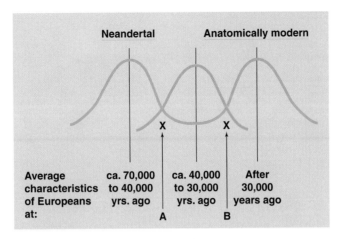

FIGURE 9.2

Graphically portrayed here is a shift in average characteristics of an otherwise varied population over time from Neandertal to more modern features. Between 40,000 and 30,000 years ago, we would expect to find individuals with characteristics such as those of the Saint Césaire "Neandertal" (A) and the almost (but not quite) modern Cro-Magnon (B; this fossil is discussed in Chapter 10).

imen from Saint Césaire in France, for example, has a higher forehead and chin. The Vindija fossils, too, show incipient chin development (as do a number of other Neandertals) as well as reduced facial protrusion and thinning of the brow ridges. Conversely, the earliest anatomically modern human skulls from Europe often exhibit features reminiscent of Neandertals (see Chapter 10). Accordingly, we might view the population of this region between 40,000 and 30,000 years ago as a varied one, with some individuals retaining a stronger Neandertal heritage than others, in whom modern characteristics are more prominent (Figure 9.2).

Nothing in the physical or mental makeup of Neandertals seems to have prevented them from leading a "typical" Upper Paleolithic way of life, as in fact the final Neandertals of western, central and eastern Europe did.[17] Out of the earlier Mousterian, they created their own Upper Paleolithic cultures (see Figure 9.3). In some respects, they outdid their Aurignacian contemporaries, as in the use of red ocher, a substance less frequently used by the Aurignacians than by their late Neandertal neighbors.[18] Although some have suggested that this represents a case of borrowing ideas and techniques from Aurignacians, this now seems unlikely.[19]

Another often cited case of coexistence of the two forms is in Southwest Asia. While Neandertal skeletons are clearly present at sites such as Kebara and Shanidar caves, skeletons from some older sites have been described as anatomically modern. At Qafzeh, in Israel, for example, 90,000-year-old skeletons are said to show none of the Neandertal hallmarks; although their faces and bodies are large and heavily built by today's standards, they are nonetheless claimed to be within the range of living peoples. Yet, a statistical study comparing a number of measurements among Qafzeh, Upper Paleolithic, and Neandertal skulls

---

[17]Mellars, p. 378.

[18]Bednarik, R. G. (1995). Concept-mediated marking in the lower Paleolithic. *Current Anthropology, 36,* 606.

[19]d'Errico, F., Zilhão, J., Julien, M., Baffier, D., and Pelegrin, J. (1998). Neanderthal acculturation in Western Europe? *Current Anthropology, 39,* 521.

FIGURE 9.3

Between 40,000 and 30,000 years ago, Upper Paleolithic industries developed from the Mousterian by descendants of European Neandertals coexisted with the Aurignacian industry, usually associated with anatomically modern humans.

found those from Qafzeh to fall in between the Aurignacian and Neandertal norms, though slightly closer to the Neandertals.[20]

Furthermore, an individual from the nearby site of Skuhl, whose skeleton was similar to those from Qafzeh, was part of a population whose continuous range of variation included individuals with markedly Neandertal characteristics. Nor does the idea of two distinctly different but coexisting populations receive any support from cultural remains, inasmuch as the people living at Skuhl and Qafzeh were making and using the same Mousterian tools as those at Kebara and Shanidar. Thus, there are no indications of groups with different cultural traditions coexisting in the same region. For that matter, the actual behaviors represented by Middle Paleolithic and early Upper Paleolithic cultures were not significantly different. In Kebara Cave, for example, the Upper Paleolithic people who used the cave continued to live in exactly the same way as their Neandertal predecessors: They procured the same foods, processed them in the same way, used similar hearths, and disposed of their trash in the same way. The only evident difference is that the Neandertals did not bank their fires for warmth with small stones or cobbles as did their Upper Paleolithic successors.[21]

THE "EVE" OR "OUT OF AFRICA" HYPOTHESIS

This alternative to the multiregional hypothesis states that anatomically modern humans are descended from one specific population of *H. sapiens*, replacing not just the Neandertals, but other populations of archaic *H. sapiens* as our ancestors spread out of their original homeland. The idea for this hypothesis came not from fossils, but from

[20]Corruccini, R. S. (1992). Metrical reconsideration of the Skhul IV and IX and Border Cave I crania in the context of modern human origins. *American Journal of Physical Anthropology, 87,* 433–445.

[21]Bar-Yosef, O., Vandermeesch, B., Arensburg, B., Belfer-Cohen, A., Goldberg, P., Laville, H., Meignen, L., Rak, Y., Speth, J. D., Tchernov, E., Tillier, A. M., & Weiner, S. (1992). The excavations in Kebara Cave, Mt. Carmel. *Current Anthropology, 33,* 534.

Showing a strikingly modern appearance, this *H. sapiens* skull from Qafzeh, Israel, is 90,000 years old. Measurements taken on the skull, however, fall slightly closer to those of the Neandertals than they do to those of anatomically modern Upper Paleolithic people.

a relatively new technique which uses mitochondrial DNA to reconstruct family trees. Unlike the DNA in the cell nucleus, mitochondrial DNA is located elsewhere in the cell, in compartments that produce the energy needed to keep cells alive. Since the male sperm does not contribute mitochondrial DNA to the fertilized egg, it is inherited only from one's mother and is not "rescrambled" with each succeeding generation. Therefore, it should be altered only by mutation. By comparing the mitochondrial DNA of living individuals from diverse geographical populations, anthropologists and molecular biologists seek to determine when and where modern *H. sapiens* originated. As widely reported in the popular press (including a cover story in *Newsweek*), preliminary results suggested that the mitochondrial DNA of all living humans could be traced back to a "Mitochondrial Eve" who lived in Africa (though some argued for Asia) some 200,000 years ago. If so, all

other populations of archaic *H. sapiens,* as well as non-African *H. erectus,* would have to be ruled out of the ancestry of modern humans.

Although most scholars accept that fossils from Africa exhibit the transition from *H. erectus* through archaic to anatomically modern *sapiens* on that continent, this by itself offers no confirmation of the "Out of Africa" hypothesis. After all, proponents of the multiregional model also argue that the transition took place here, as in other parts of the Old World. If, however, anatomically modern fossils could be shown to be significantly older in Africa than elsewhere, this would bolster the argument for an African homeland for modern humanity. To date, the strongest candidates for such fossils consist of a skull from Border Cave and fragments of jaws of at least 10 people from a cave at the Klasies River mouth. Both sites are in South Africa. Unfortunately, the Border cave skull is not adequately dated, nor is it as similar to modern African skulls as is often claimed.[22] The Klasies River material is well dated to between 120,000 and 90,000 years ago, but is too fragmentary (they were cut and burned anciently, suggesting cannibalism) to permit categorical statements as to its modernity. Although one mandible displays what looks like a well-developed chin, this could be a result of loss of the front teeth, something that leads to resorption of supporting bone. This does not affect the bottom of the jaw, however, leaving it to protrude and appear more chinlike than it may have been.[23] Apart from this, chins are not entirely unknown in archaic *sapiens* (for example, some European Neandertals, as already discussed). Certainly, the Klasies remains are not inconsistent with the sort of wide variation just discussed for Southwest Asia.

It is true that the people of Klasies River were culturally precocious. For one thing, they are the first people we know of to augment resources of the land with those from the sea; their gathering of shellfish led to the buildup of middens comparable to those left by later Upper Paleolithic peoples. Their technology was also advanced in the common production of blades—long parallel-sided flakes of a sort not commonly made in Europe until some 40,000 years ago. By 70,000 years ago, the people

[22]Corruccini, p. 436.

[23]Wolpoff and Caspari, p. 331.

Because of its chin, this mandible from the Klasies River in South Africa has often been called "modern." Yet a number of archaic *sapiens* skulls, including Neandertals, have this feature.

at Klasies River were blunting the backs of blades, much as later Europeans did, for hafting in composite tools. Some take these signs of cultural "advancement" as indicative of anatomically modern status. The fallacy of such argument, however, is revealed by the evidence from Europe and Southwest Asia that the cognitive abilities of archaic and modern *H. sapiens* were the same.

The fossil evidence presents other problems for the "Out of Africa" hypothesis as well. For one thing, we would expect an early replacement of archaic *sapiens* in Southwest Asia as more anatomically modern humans moved up out of Africa but, as we have already seen, we have no clear evidence for such a replacement. Nor is such evidence available for East Asia, where evidence for continuity from regional *H. erectus,* through archaic, to anatomical *H. sapiens* populations is as good as, if not better than, the evidence for such continuity in Africa. Consistent with this, the archaeological record of East Asia, though distinctly

Even older than the blades from the Klasies River mouth are these, from a site in Kenya. Struck from preshaped cores, they are about 240,000 years old, predating any known or possible fossils of anatomically modern humans.

different from Europe, Africa, and western Asia, shows the same kind of continuity as do the fossils.[24] There is no sign of invasion by people possessing a superior, or even different, technology, as an "Out of Africa" scenario would require.

Given the problems in reconciling the "Out of Africa" hypothesis with the archaeological and fossil records, one may ask, what about the DNA analysis that gave birth to the hypothesis? Here, things are not as certain as proponents of "Out of Africa" maintain.

---

[24]Pope, G. C. (1992). Craniofacial evidence for the origin of modern humans in China. *Yearbook of Physical Anthropology, 35,* 291.

African Origin or Ancient Population Size Differences?[25]

The Eve theory depends on genetic evidence indicating an African origin for modern humanity, because . . . the fossil evidence is quite equivocal on this issue. But there is no particular reason to suggest Africa was the place of origin for the current mtDNA [mitochondrial DNA] lineages. The original studies suggesting an African origin were invalid because the computer program used in the analysis was not applied correctly. Then the greater genetic variability in Africans was taken to mean humans evolved there longer: The variation was thought to reflect more mutations and therefore a longer time span for their accumulation. Templeton [a geneticist] has argued that no statistical analysis shows that the genetic variation of Africans actually is greater than that of other populations; but even if it is, there is another, more compelling explanation.

Ancient population sizes expanded first and are larger in Africa than in other regions, which would have the same effect, creating more African variation. Consider what happens in an expanding population. Average family size is greater than two, and all variations have a good chance of being passed on; at least, if they are not selected against, they will probably not get lost by accident. But if a population is decreasing, drift can play a very active role since average family size is less than two. The role of drift is greatly amplified for mtDNA, because for transmission of this molecule the number of *female* offspring is important. Decreasing populations stand an excellent chance of losing mtDNA lineages.

Now, consider a small but stable population, neither increasing nor decreasing. Here, existing variations may each occur in only one individual. If it is a woman, and she has no female offspring, which can happen one fourth of the time in a stable population, her unique variation is lost, her mtDNA lineage terminated. But in a large stable population with the same amount of genetic variability, it is likely each mtDNA variant is shared by many individuals. The odds are the same against one woman having no female offspring, but it is very unlikely all the women with a certain mtDNA variant will lack female offspring. It is much harder for mtDNA lines to end by accident in large populations.

---

[25]Ibid., pp. 305–307.

These comparisons show that prehistoric population demography, how large or small populations were in the past and how much they fluctuated, can affect mtDNA evolution. Small, fluctuating populations will lose many mtDNA lines. The last common ancestor for the remaining mtDNA variations will be more recent because there is less remaining variation. Large or increasing populations will retain more variation. For them, the roots will be deeper and the last common ancestor will be farther in the past since more variations are retained.

Thus, ancient population size can dictate how long genetic lineages have existed, and therefore when they arose. Because ancient population size differences are an alternate explanation that unlinks the origin of genetic lineages from the origin of a population, it seems as though genetic analysis cannot help solve the problem of whether today's variation reflects African origin or ancient population size differences.

However, genetic analysis can indicate ancient population expansions. Henry Harpending and colleagues studied the probability distributions of pairwise mtDNA comparisons within populations for evidence of past population structure and size expansions. They conclude: "Our results show human populations are derived from separate ancestral populations that were relatively isolated from each other before 50,000 years ago." These studies clearly reveal there have been a series of recent, very significant, population expansions. Some of these are without question associated with the development and spread of agricultural revolutions. But others are earlier.

This means population size history by itself can explain the pattern of mtDNA variation. If, as we believe and as the archaeological record seems to show,

♦ there were more people living in Africa for most of human prehistory, and

♦ human populations outside of Africa were smaller and fluctuated more because of the changing ice-age environments,

we would expect just what we do see—African mtDNA has deeper roots, while in other places the coalescent time is more recent. *But this explanation does not mean the* **populations** *living out of Africa have a more recent origin, or that they originated in Africa.* MtDNA history, in other words, is not population history.

John Relethford and Henry Harpending examined the consequences of the possibility that greater African population size, and not greater time depth for modern humans in Africa, may account for their greater variation.

> Our results support our earlier contention that regional differences in population size can explain the genetic evidence pertaining to modern human origins. Our work thus far has involved examination of the classic genetic markers and craniometrics, but it also has implications for mitochondrial DNA. The greater mtDNA diversity in sub-Saharan African populations could also be a reflection of a larger long-term African population.

Moreover, they write, a unique African ancestry implies there was a bottleneck for the human species, as moderns would be able to trace their ancestry to only a small portion of humanity, as it existed then.

While this seems at first glance a reasonable notion, it soon becomes apparent that the actual effect of such a [bottleneck] event depends on both the magnitude and duration of a shift in population size. Rogers and Jorde show that given reasonable parameters for our species, the bottleneck would have to be more severe and long-lasting than considered plausible. We have to think of a population of 50 females for 6,000 years, for example.

Other assumptions made by DNA analysts are problematic. For example, it is assumed that rates of mutation are steady, when in fact they can be notoriously uneven. Another assumption is that mtDNA is not subject to selection, when in fact variants have been implicated in epilepsy and a disease of the eye.[26] A third is that DNA is seen as traveling exclusively *from* Africa, when it is known that, over the past 10,000 years, there has been plenty of movement the other way. In fact, a recent study of DNA carried on the Y chromosome and inherited exclusively in the male line suggests that some DNA seen on the Y chromosome of some Africans was introduced from Asia, where it originated some 200,000 years ago.[27] Finally, mention might be made of a 1997 study of mtDNA extracted from the original German Neandertal.

This was reported to differ too greatly from that of modern Europeans for there to be an ancestor-descendant relationship. But as a geneticist at the Australian National University points out, chimpanzees and other primates display more within-species variation in their mtDNA than do modern humans, and the amount of diversity between Neandertals and us is not exceptional.[28]

In short, it is definitely premature to read out of the modern human ancestry all populations of archaic *sapiens* save those of Africa. Not even the case for exclusion of Neandertals is clear; but even if it were, this by itself would not be sufficient to rule out the multiregional hypothesis. We shall return to this problem in the next chapter, but at the moment, the evidence seems to favor a multiregional emergence of anatomically modern humans. Still, the debate is by no means resolved.

---

[26]Shreeve, p. 121.

[27]Gibbons, A. (1997). Ideas on human origins evolve at anthropology gathering. *Science, 276,* 535–536.

[28]Wong, K. (January 1998). Ancestral quandary: Neandertals not our ancestors? Not so fast. *Scientific American,* 32.

CHAPTER   SUMMARY

At various sites in Europe, Africa, and East Asia, a number of fossils have been found that date between about 400,000 and 200,000 years ago, and which show a mixture of traits of both *H. erectus* and *H. sapiens.* They are indicative of evolution from the older into the younger species. Their culture was much like that of *H. erectus,* until about

200,000 years ago, when they developed a new technique of tool manufacture known as the Levalloisian.

By 200,000 years ago, populations of archaic *H. sapiens* lived in all parts of the inhabited world. Although some Neandertals of Europe and western Asia are said to have survived until at least 35,000 years ago, they may be members of varied populations in which some individuals show modern characteristics more strongly than others.

The brains of archaic *H. sapiens* were no different in size and organization than our own, although their skulls retained some primitive characteristics. With a larger brain, they were able to utilize culture as a means of environmental adaptation to a far greater extent than any of their predecessors; they were capable of an advanced technology and sophisticated conceptual thought.

The cultures of archaic *H. sapiens* are known as Middle Paleolithic, and the best known is the Mousterian of Europe, northern Africa, and western Asia. Mousterian tools included hand axes, flakes, scrapers, borers, wood shavers, and spears. These flake tools were lighter and smaller than those of the Levalloisian. Mousterian tools increased the availability and quality of food, shelter, and clothing. Archaeological evidence indicates that Mousterian peoples buried their dead, cared for the disabled, and made a number of objects for purely symbolic purposes.

All populations of archaic *H. sapiens* are easily derivable from earlier populations of *H. erectus* from the same regions. With the possible (but not certain) exception of the Neandertals, all populations of archaic *H. sapiens* could be ancestral to more modern populations in the same regions. An alternative hypothesis is that the transition from archaic to anatomically modern *H. sapiens* took place in one specific population, probably in Africa. From here, people spread to other regions, replacing older populations as they did so.

POINTS FOR CONSIDERATION

1. What indications are there of organized funerary traditions among archaic *Homo sapiens*? What does this say about the cultural values/beliefs of the individuals involved? How does this compare with early assumptions about Neandertal?

2. How does the evidence regarding the transitions from *Homo erectus* and archaic *Homo sapiens,* and then between Neandertal and modern *Homo sapiens,* support: A) direct descent of the latter from the former (in both cases), and B) multiregional development of modern *Homo sapiens*? For example: Why is it more likely, given the fossil evidence, that modern *Homo sapiens* in Asia is descended from archaic *Homo sapiens* in Asia, rather than in Europe or Africa?

3. What evidence is present for the practice of some form of medicine by archaic *Homo sapiens*? What does this reveal about cognitive abilities?

SUGGESTED READINGS

Shreeve, J. (1995). *The Neandertal enigma: Solving the mystery of modern human origins.* New York: William Morrow.

Shreeve is a science writer who has written extensively about human evolution. This book is engagingly written and covers most of the major issues in the Neandertal-Modern debate.

Stringer, C. B., & McKie, R. (1996). *African exodus: The origins of modern humanity.* London: Jonathan Cape.

Chris Stringer of the British Museum is a leading champion of the "Out of Africa" hypothesis, and in this book one will find a vigorous presentation of his arguments.

Trinkaus, E., & Shipman, P. (1992). *The Neandertals: Changing the image of mankind.* New York: Alfred A. Knopf.

The senior author of this book is a long-time specialist on the Neandertals. Eminently readable, the book chronicles the changing interpretations of these fossils since the first recognized find in 1856. For a good look at what is known about the Neandertals, there is no better place to go than this.

Wolpoff, M., & Caspari, R. (1997). *Race and human evolution*. New York: Simon and Schuster.

One of the problems in evaluating the multiregional and "Out of Africa" hypotheses is that many writers misrepresent the former. That is no problem in this book, written by the leading champion of multiregionalism and his wife. The hypothesis is presented and defended in a straightforward and thorough way so that anyone can understand it.

Chapter 10
HOMO SAPIENS AND THE
UPPER PALEOLITHIC

WITH THE EMERGENCE OF ANATOMICALLY
MODERN HUMANS, EVIDENCE OF HUMAN
CREATIVITY BECOMES BOTH WIDESPREAD AND
DRAMATIC, AS THIS 32,000-YEAR-OLD PAINTING
FROM THE RECENTLY DISCOVERED CHAUVET
CAVE IN FRANCE SHOWS. EQUALLY OLD, AND IN
SOME CASES OLDER, ART IS KNOWN AS WELL
FROM AFRICA AND AUSTRALIA.

Chapter Preview

When Did Anatomically Modern Forms of *Homo sapiens* Appear?

Although some fossils as old as 100,000 years from Africa and Southwest Asia have been interpreted as essentially modern in appearance, there is now reason to question this. Fossils of *Homo sapiens* that are unequivocally modern in their anatomy had the world to themselves after 30,000 years ago.

What Was the Culture of Anatomically Modern Peoples Like?

Anatomically modern people are associated with Upper Paleolithic cultures. These generally include a greater diversity of tools than before. Techniques of toolmaking previously used to limited degrees came into widespread use, including the making of blades, pressure flaking, and using of chisel-like tools called burins to fashion implements of bone and antler. In Europe, large game hunting was improved by invention of the spear thrower, while net hunting allowed effective "harvesting" of small game. In Africa the bow and arrow were invented but did not spread to Europe until about 12,000 years ago, the end of the Old and the beginning of the Middle Stone Age, or Mesolithic. Technological improvements in the Mesolithic included the invention of ground stone axes and adzes for woodworking as well as widespread use of a variety of composite tools made by inserting microlithic blades into handles of wood, bone, or antler.

What Were the Consequences of the New Upper Paleolithic and Mesolithic Technologies?

First Upper Paleolithic and then Mesolithic technologies improved peoples' abilities to adapt through the medium of culture. This resulted in increased regionalism, as people refined their adaptations to local conditions, and further population growth caused "spillover" into new regions, most dramatically Australia and the Americas. Biological consequences included final reduction of the human face to modern proportions, and the new hunting technologies led to reduction of body mass.

Although scholars continue to argue about earlier populations, they agree that, by 30,000 years ago, anatomically modern peoples with Upper ("late") Paleolithic cultures had the world to themselves. The remains of these ancient peoples, who looked much like us, were first discovered in 1868 at Les Eyzies in France in a rock shelter called Cro-Magnon, and so European remains from the Upper Paleolithic are often referred to as **Cro-Magnons.** Between 1872 and 1902, the fossils of 13 other specimens were unearthed in the caves of the Côte d'Azur near the Italian Riviera. Since then, other Cro-Magnon skeletons have been recovered from various parts of Europe. Equivalent remains have been unearthed in Africa and Asia, even if in not such great numbers.

Though the original Cro-Magnon skull shows some resemblance to modern European skulls, it is not identical.

UPPER PALEOLITHIC PEOPLES: THE FIRST MODERN HUMANS

The Cro-Magnons of Europe have suffered their share of idealization on the part of physical anthropologists; at one time they were depicted as having a somewhat godlike appearance, in contrast to the Neandertals, who supposedly stood just a step ahead of the ape. The idea found its way into popular culture, as in a best-selling novel of the 1970s, *The Clan of the Cave Bear.* In this book, the heroine is portrayed as a tall, slender, blonde-haired, blue-eyed beauty. As more Upper Paleolithic remains have been found, in various parts of Africa and Asia as well as Europe, it has become clear that the differences from earlier populations have been greatly exaggerated. In the case of Europeans, for example, there is some resemblance between Cro-Magnons and later populations: in braincase shape, high broad forehead, narrow nasal openings, and common presence of chins. But Cro-Magnon faces were shorter and broader than those of modern Europeans, their brow ridges were a bit more prominent, and their teeth and jaws were as large as those of Neandertals. Some (a skull from the original Cro-

Magnon site, for instance) even display the distinctive "occipital bun" of the Neandertals on the back of the skull.[1] Nor were they particularly tall, as their height of 5 feet 7 or 8 inches does not fall outside the Neandertal range.

Although we refer to the Upper Paleolithic people as anatomically modern, it is surprisingly hard to be precise about what we mean by this. We think of people with brains the size of modern people, but this had already been achieved by archaic *H. sapiens,* among whom brain size actually peaked at 10% larger than ours. The reduction to today's size correlates with a reduction in brawn, as bodies have become less massive overall. Modern faces and jaws are, by and large, less massive as well, but there are exceptions. For example, anthropologists Wolpoff and Caspari have pointed out that any definition of "modernity" that excludes Neandertals also excludes substantial numbers of recent and living native Australians, in spite of the fact that they are, quite obviously, a modern people. The fact is, no multidimensional diagnosis of modern humans

---

[1]Brace, C. L. (1997). Cro-Magnons "Я" us? *Anthropology Newsletter, 38*(8), 1.

Cro-Magnons. The first anatomically modern Europeans, of Upper Paleolithic times.

can be both exclusive of archaic populations and inclusive of all contemporary humans.[2]

The appearance of modern-sized brains in archaic *H. sapiens* no doubt was a consequence of increased reliance on cultural adaptation. Ultimately, this emphasis on cultural adaptation led to the development of more complex tool kits. Among Upper Paleolithic peoples, as specialized tools increasingly took over the cutting, softening, and clamping functions once performed by the front teeth, there followed a reduction in the size of the teeth and, eventually, the jaws. The cooking of food (which began with *H. erectus)* had already favored

some reduction in size of the teeth and muscles involved in chewing; consequently, the jaws diminished in size, and robust sites for muscle attachment disappeared along with features like brow ridges that buttress the skull from the stresses and strains imposed by massive jaw muscles.

Technological improvements also reduced the intensity of selective pressures favoring especially massive, robust bodies. With new emphasis on elongate tools with greater mechanical advantages, more effective techniques of hafting, a switch from thrusting to throwing spears, and development of net hunting, there was a marked reduction in overall muscularity. Moreover, the skeletons of Upper Paleolithic peoples show far less evidence of trauma than do those of archaic *H. sapiens*, whose bones almost always show evidence of injury.

---

[2]Wolpoff, M., & Caspari, R. (1997). *Race and human evolution* (p. 344–345, 393). New York: Simon and Schuster.

 Stone Tools for Modern Surgeons

When anthropologist Irven DeVore of Harvard University was to have some minor melanomas removed from his face, he did not leave it up to the surgeon to supply his own scalpels. Instead, he had graduate student John Shea make a scalpel. Making a blade of obsidian (a naturally-occurring volcanic "glass") by the same techniques used by Upper Paleolithic people to make blades, he then hafted this in a wooden handle, using melted pine resin as glue and then lashing it with sinew. After the procedure, the surgeon reported that the obsidian scalpel was superior to metal ones.*

DeVore was not the first to undergo surgery in which stone scalpels were used. In 1975, Don Crabtree, then at Idaho State University, prepared the scalpels that his surgeon would use in Crabtree's heart surgery. In 1980, Payson Sheets at the University of Colorado prepared obsidian scalpels that were used suc-

cessfully in eye surgery. And in 1986, David Pokotylo of the Museum of Anthropology at the University of British Columbia underwent reconstructive surgery on his hand with blades he himself had made (the hafting was done by his museum colleague, Len McFarlane).

The reason for these uses of scalpels modeled on ancient stone tools is that the anthropologists realized that obsidian is superior in almost every way to materials normally used to make scalpels: It is 210 to 1,050 times sharper than surgical steel, 100 to 500 times sharper than a razor blade, and three times sharper than a diamond blade (which not only costs many times more, but cannot be made with more than 3 mm of cutting edge). Obsidian blades are easier to cut with, and do less damage in the process (under a microscope, incisions made with the sharpest steel blades show torn ragged edges and are littered with bits of displaced flesh).** As a consequence,

---

*Shreeve, J. (1995). *The Neandertal enigma: Solving the mystery of modern human origins* (p. 134). New York: William Morrow.

**Sheets, P. D. (1987). Dawn of a New Stone Age in eye surgery. In R. J. Sharer and W. Ashmore (Eds.), *Archaeology: Discovering our past* (p. 231). Palo Alto, CA: Mayfield.

These microphotographs of an obsidian blade (bottom photo) and a modern steel scalpel (top photo) illustrate the superiority of the obsidian.

the surgeon has better control over what she or he is doing and the incisions heal faster with less scarring and pain. Because of the superiority of obsidian scalpels, Sheets went so far as to form a corporation in partnership with Boulder, Colorado, eye surgeon Dr. Firmon Hardenbergh. Together, they developed a means of producing cores of uniform size from molten glass, as well as a machine to detach blades from the cores.

Upper Paleolithic peoples also tended to live longer than their archaic predecessors. Furthermore, the prolonged period of development characteristic of the human species today, which allows people to learn so much before they are responsible for themselves as adults, was associated with the evolution of anatomically modern peoples. Perhaps both have something to do with the burst of creativity that was a part of Upper Paleolithic culture. Being too old for most day-to-day subsistence activities, but able to recall events beyond the experience of younger adults, elders could have spent more time passing on a greater store of wisdom to youngsters who were capable of absorbing it all.

UPPER PALEOLITHIC TOOLS

The typical Upper Paleolithic tool was the blade, a flint flake at least twice as long as it is wide. Although Middle Paleolithic toolmakers, especially

in Africa, also made blades, they did not do so to the extent that their Upper Paleolithic successors did. What made this possible were new techniques of core preparation that allowed more intensive production of highly standardized blades. The toolmaker formed a cylindrical core, struck the blade off near the edge of the core, and repeated this procedure, going around the core in one direction until finishing near its center (Figure 10.1). The procedure is analogous to peeling long leaves off an artichoke. With this **blade technique,** an Upper Paleolithic flint knapper could get 75 feet of working edge from a 2-pound core; his Mousterian counterpart could get only 6 feet from the same-sized core.

Other efficient techniques of tool manufacture also came into common use at this time. One such method was **pressure flaking,** in which a bone, antler, or wooden tool was used to press rather than strike off small flakes as the final step in stone

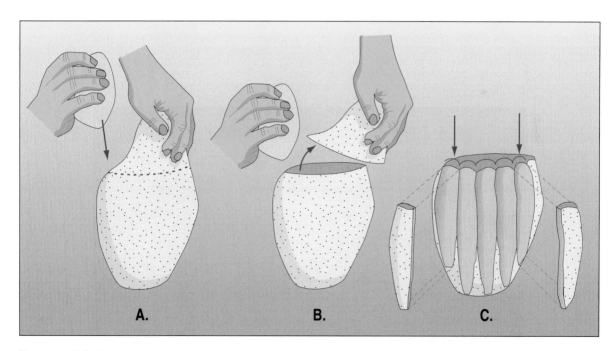

FIGURE 10.1
During the Upper Paleolithic, a new technique was used to manufacture blades. The stone is flaked to create a striking platform, then long, almost parallel-sided flakes are struck around the sides, providing sharp-edged blades.

Blade technique.   A technique of stone tool manufacture by which long, parallel-sided flakes are struck off the edges of a specially prepared core. **> Pressure flaking.**   A technique of stone tool manufacture in which a bone, antler, or wooden tool is used to press, rather than strike off, small flakes from a piece of flint or similar stone.

FIGURE 10.2
Two methods used for pressure flaking.

tool manufacture (Figure 10.2). The advantage of this technique was that the toolmaker had greater control over the final shape of the tool than is possible with percussion flaking. The so-called Solutrean laurel leaf blades found in Spain and France are examples of this technique. The longest of these blades is 13 inches in length but only about a quarter of an inch thick. Pressure flaking also provided great precision in retouching cutting edges for extra sharpness.

Another common Upper Paleolithic tool was the **burin,** although it too was invented earlier, in the Middle Paleolithic. These implements, with their chisel-like edges, facilitated the working of bone, horn, antler, and ivory into such useful things as fishhooks, harpoons, and eyed needles, all of which made life easier for *H. sapiens,* especially in northern regions. The spear-thrower, too, appeared at this time. Spear-throwers are wooden devices, one end of which is gripped in the hunter's hand, while the other end has a hole or hook, in or against which the end of the spear is placed (see Figure 10.3, lower right). It is held so as to effectively extend the length of the hunter's arm, thereby increasing the velocity of the spear when thrown. Using a spear-thrower greatly added to the efficiency of the spear as a hunting tool. With handheld spears, hunters had to get close to their quarry to make the kill, and since many of the animals they hunted were quite large and fierce, this was a dangerous business. The need to approach closely, and the improbability of an instant kill, exposed the spear hunter to considerable risk. But with the spear-thrower, the effective killing distance was increased; experiments demonstrate that the effective killing distance of a spear when

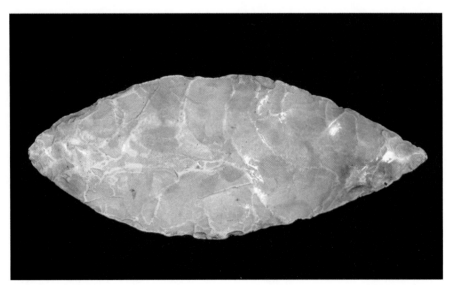

Shown here is one of the Solutrean laurel leaf bifaces from Europe. Such fine flint work requires a high degree of skill.

Burins.   Stone tools with chisel-like edges used for working bone and antler.

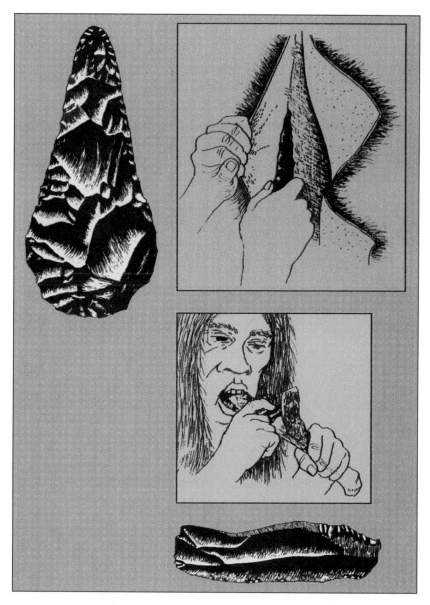

FIGURE 10.3(a)
This figure, which continues on the next two pages, shows a variety of tools found in Upper Paleolithic tool kits, along with an artist's reconstruction of the way they were used.

used with a spear-thrower is between 18 and 27 meters (as opposed to 2 or 3 feet without).[3]

Another important innovation, net hunting, appeared sometime between 29,000 and 22,000 years ago.[4] Knotted nets, made from the fibers

---

[3]Frayer, D. W. (1981). Body size, weapon use, and natural selection in the European Upper Paleolithic and Mesolithic. *American Anthropologist, 83,* 58.

[4]Pringle, H. (1997). Ice Age communities may be earliest known net hunters. *Science, 277,* 1203.

FIGURE 10.3(b)

of wild plants such as hemp or nettle, left their impression on the clay floors of huts when people walked on them. These impressions were then baked in when the huts burned, which is how we know that nets existed. Their use accounts for the high number of hare, fox, and other small mammal bones at archaeological sites. Like historically known net hunters, everyone—men, women, and children—probably participated, frightening animals with loud noises to drive them to where hunters were stationed with their nets. In this way, large amounts of

FIGURE 10.3(c)

meat could be amassed in ways that did not put a premium on speed or strength.

A further improvement of hunting techniques came with the invention of the bow and arrow, which appeared first in Africa, but not until the end of the Upper Paleolithic in Europe. The greatest advantage of the bow is that it increases the distance between hunter and prey; beyond 18 to 27 meters, the accuracy and penetration of a spear thrown with a spear-thrower is quite poor, whereas even a poor bow will shoot an arrow farther, with greater accuracy and penetrating power. A good bow is effective even at 91 meters. Thus, hunters were able to maintain an even safer distance between themselves and dangerous prey, dramatically decreasing their chances of being seriously injured by an animal fighting for its life.

These changes in hunting weaponry and techniques had important consequences for human biology. Spear hunting, particularly where large, fierce animals are the prey as they often were in Upper Paleolithic Europe, demands strength, power, and overall robusticity on the part of the hunter. Without them, the hunter is poorly equipped to withstand the rigors of close-quarter killing. A high nutritional price must be paid, however, for large, powerful, and robust bodies. Therefore, as speed and strength become less important for success, people tended to become weaker and less robust as a form of nutritional conservation.

The invention of the bow did more than merely improve hunting techniques. Long before anyone thought of beating swords into plowshares, some genius discovered that bows could be used not just for killing, but to make music as well. Just when and where this discovery was made we do not know, but we do know that there was music in the lives of Upper Paleolithic peoples, for bone flutes and whistles as many as 30,000 years old have been found. We also know that the musical bow is the oldest of all the stringed instruments, and its invention ultimately made possible the development of all of the stringed instruments with which we are familiar today.

Upper Paleolithic peoples not only had better tools but also a greater diversity of types than earlier peoples. The highly developed Upper Paleolithic kit included tools for use during different seasons, and regional variation in tool kits was greater than ever before (see Figure 10.3 for some examples of Upper Paleolithic tools). Thus, it is really impossible to speak of an Upper Paleolithic culture, even in a relatively small peripheral region like Europe; instead, one must make note of the many different traditions that made it possible for people to adapt ever more specifically to the various environments in which they were living. Just how proficient (and even wasteful) people had become at securing a livelihood is indicated by boneyards containing thousands of skeletons. At Solutré in France, for example, Upper Paleolithic hunters killed 10,000 horses; at Predmost in Czechoslovakia, they were responsible for the deaths of 1,000 mammoths. The favored big game of European hunters, however, was reindeer, which they killed in even greater numbers.

UPPER PALEOLITHIC ART

Although the creativity of Upper Paleolithic peoples is evident in the tools and weapons they made, it is nowhere more evident than in their outburst of artistic expression. Some have argued that this was made possible by a newly evolved biological ability to manipulate symbols and make images, but in view of the modern-sized brains of archaic *sapiens* and increasingly compelling evidence that even the Neandertals were capable of speech, such an idea is hard to maintain. Like agriculture, which came later (see Chapter 11), the artistic explosion may have been no more than a consequence of innovations made by a people who were capable of them tens of thousands of years earlier.

In fact, just as many of the distinctive tools that were commonly used in Upper Paleolithic times first appear in the Middle Paleolithic, so too do objects of art. In Southwest Asia, a crude figurine of volcanic tuff is some 250,000 years old.[5] Although it is unusual, the fact that it exists at all indicates that people had the ability to carve all sorts of things from wood, a substance easier to

---

[5]Appenzeller, T. (1998). Art: Evolution or revolution? *Science, 282,* 1452.

Crude though it may be, this piece of tuff, carved some 250,000 years ago, looks like a woman if viewed from the right angle. It was found in 1980 on the Golan Heights in the Middle East.

work than volcanic tuff, but rarely preserved for long periods of time. Furthermore, ocher "crayons" from the Middle Paleolithic contexts in various parts of the world must have been used to decorate or mark something. In southern Africa, for example, regular use of yellow and red ocher goes back 130,000 years, with some evidence as old as 200,000 years.[6] Perhaps pigments were used on people's bodies, as well as objects, as the

50,000-year-old mammoth-tooth "churinga," discussed in the last chapter, might suggest.

The earliest evidence of figurative pictures goes back 32,000 years in Europe and is probably equally old in Africa. Both engravings and paintings are known from many rock shelters and outcrops in southern Africa, where they continued to be made by Bushman peoples up until about 100 years ago. Scenes feature both humans and animals, depicted with extraordinary skill, often in association with geometric and other abstract motifs.

Because this rock art tradition continued unbroken into historic times, it has been possible to discover what this art means. There is a close connection between the art and shamanism, and many scenes depict visions seen in a state of trance. Distortions in the art, usually of human figures, represent sensations felt by individuals in a state of trance, while the geometric designs depict illusions that originate in the central nervous system in altered states of consciousness. These **entoptic phenomena** are luminous grids, dots, zigzags, and other designs that seem to shimmer, pulsate, rotate, and expand, and are seen as one enters a state of trance (sufferers of migraines experience similar hallucinations). The animals depicted in this art, often with startling realism, are not the ones most often eaten. Rather, they are powerful beasts like the eland, and this power is important to shamans—individuals skilled at manipulating supernatural powers and spirits for human benefit—who try to harness it for their rain-making and other rituals.

Rock art in Australia goes back at least 45,000 years, with the earliest examples consisting entirely of entoptic motifs. But the Upper Paleolithic art that is most famous—largely because most students of prehistoric art are themselves of European background—is that of Europe. The earliest of this art took the form of sculpture and engravings often portraying such animals as reindeer, horses, bears, and ibexes, but there are also numerous portrayals of voluptuous women with exaggerated sexual and reproductive characteristics. Many appear to be pregnant, and some are shown in birthing postures. These so-called "Venus" figures have been

---

[6]Barham, L. S. (1998). Possible early pigment use in south-central Africa. *Current Anthropology, 39*, 709.

Entoptic phenomena. Bright pulsating forms that are generated by the central nervous system and "seen" in states of trance.

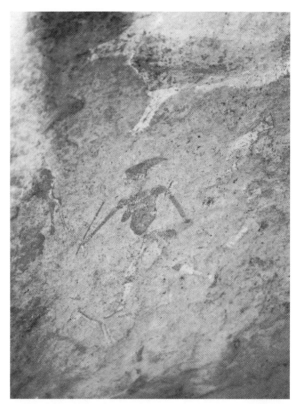

In South Africa, rock art, like these engravings and paintings from Namibia, depict things seen by dancers while in states of trance.

found at sites from southwestern France as far east as Siberia. Made of stone, ivory, antler, or baked clay, they differ little in style from place to place, testifying to the sharing of ideas over vast distances. Although some have interpreted the Venuses as objects associated with a fertility cult, others suggest that they may have been exchanged to cement alliances between groups.

Most spectacular are the paintings on the walls of 200 or so caves in southern France and northern Spain, the oldest of which date from about 32,000 years ago. Most common are visually accurate portrayals of ice-age mammals, including bison, bulls, horses, mammoths, and stags, often painted one on top of another. Although well represented in other media, humans are not commonly portrayed in cave paintings, nor are scenes or depictions of events at all common. Instead, the animals are usually abstracted from nature and rendered two-dimensionally without regard to the

conformations of the surfaces they are on—no small achievement for these early "artists." Sometimes, though, the artists made use of bulges and other features of the rock to impart a more three-dimensional feeling. Often, the paintings are in hard-to-get-at places while suitable surfaces in more accessible places remain untouched. In some caves, the lamps by which the artists worked have been found; these are spoon-shaped objects of sandstone in which animal fat was burned. Experimentation has shown that such lamps would have provided adequate illumination over several hours.

The techniques used by Upper Paleolithic people to create their cave paintings have recently been unraveled through the experimental work of Michel Lorblanchet. Interestingly, they turn out to be the same ones used by native rock painters in Australia. Lorblanchet's experiments are described in the following Original Study by science writer Roger Lewin.

Upper Paleolithic art was quite varied: a carved antler spear-thrower ornamented by two headless ibexes (from Enlene Cave, France); a female Venus figurine of yellow steatite (from a cave at Liguria, Italy); and one of the sandstone lamps by which artists worked in caves (from Lascaux Cave, France).

Paleolithic Paint Job[7]

▲▽

Lorblanchet's recent bid to re-create one of the most important Ice Age images in Europe was an affair of the heart as much as the head. "I tried to abandon my skin of a modern citizen, tried to experience the feeling of the artist, to enter the dialogue between the rock and the man," he explains. Every day for a week in the fall of 1990 he drove the 20 miles from his home in the medieval village of Cajarc into the hills above the river Lot. There, in a small, practically inaccessible cave, he transformed himself into an Upper Paleolithic painter. And not just any Upper Paleolithic painter, but the one who 18,400 years ago crafted the dotted horses inside the famous cave of Pech Merle.

You can still see the original horses in Pech Merle's vast underground geologic splendor. You enter through a narrow passageway and soon find

[7]Lewin, R. (1993). Paleolithic paint job. *Discover, 14*(7), 67–69.

yourself gazing across a grand cavern to where the painting seems to hang in the gloom. "Outside, the landscape is very different from the one the Upper Paleolithic people saw," says Lorblanchet. "But in here, the landscape is the same as it was more than 18,000 years ago. You see what the Upper Paleolithic people experienced." No matter where you look in this cavern, the eye is drawn back to the panel of horses.

The two horses face away from each other, rumps slightly overlapping, their outlines sketched in black. The animal on the right seems to come alive as it merges with a crook in the edge of the panel, the perfect natural shape for a horse's head. But the impression of naturalism quickly fades as the eye falls on the painting's dark dots. There are more than 200 of them, deliberately distributed within and below the bodies and arcing around the right-hand horse's head and mane. More cryptic still are a smattering of red dots and half-circles and the floating outline of a fish. The surrealism is completed by six disembodied human hands stenciled above and below the animals.

Lorblanchet began thinking about re-creating the horses after a research trip to Australia over a decade ago. Not only is Australia a treasure trove of rock art, but its aboriginal people are still creating it. "In Queensland I learned how people painted by spitting pigment onto the rock," he recalls. "They spat paint and used their hand, a piece of cloth, or a feather as a screen to create different lines and other effects. Elsewhere in Australia people used chewed twigs as paintbrushes, but in Queensland the spitting technique worked best." The rock surfaces there were too uneven for extensive brushwork, he adds—just as they are in Quercy.

When Lorblanchet returned home he looked at the Quercy paintings with a new eye. Sure enough, he began seeing the telltale signs of spit-painting—lines with edges that were sharply demarcated on one side and fuzzy on the other, as if they had been airbrushed—instead of the brushstrokes he and others had assumed were there. Could you produce lines that were crisp on both edges with the same technique, he wondered, and perhaps dots too? Archeologists had long recognized that hand stencils, which are common in prehistoric art, were produced by spitting paint around a hand held to the wall. But no one had thought that entire animal images could be created this way. Before he could test his ideas, however, Lorblanchet had to find a suitable rock face—the original horses were painted on a roughly vertical panel 13 feet across and 6 feet high. With the help of a speleologist, he eventually found a rock face in a remote cave high in the hills and set to work.

Following the aboriginal practices he had witnessed, Lorblanchet first made a light outline sketch of the horses with a charred stick. Then he prepared black pigment for the painting. "My intention had been to use manganese dioxide, as the Pech Merle painter did," says Lorblanchet, referring to one of the minerals ground up for paint by the early artists. "But I was advised that manganese is somewhat toxic, so I used wood charcoal instead." (Charcoal was used as pigment by Paleolithic painters in other caves, so Lorblanchet felt he could justify his concession to safety.) To turn the charcoal into paint, Lorblanchet ground it with a limestone block, put the powder in

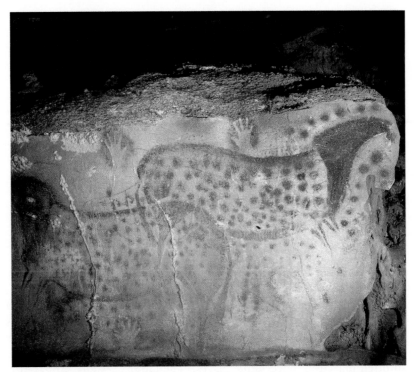

This spotted horse in the French cave of Pech Merle was painted by an Upper Paleolithic artist.

his mouth, and diluted it to the right consistency with saliva and water. For red pigment he used ocher from the local iron-rich clay.

He started with the dark mane of the right hand horse. "I spat a series of dots and fused them together to represent tufts of hair," he says, unself-consciously reproducing the spitting action as he talks. "Then I painted the horse's back by blowing the pigment below my hand held so"—he holds his hand flat against the rock with his thumb tucked in to form a straight line—"and used it like a stencil to produce a sharp upper edge and a diffused lower edge. You get an illusion of the animal's rounded flank this way."

He experimented as he went. "You see the angular rump?" he says, pointing to the original painting. "I reproduced that by holding my hand perpendicular to the rock, with my palm slightly bent, and I spat along the edge formed by my hand and the rock." He found he could produce sharp lines, such as those in the tail and in the upper hind leg, by spitting into the gap between parallel hands. The belly demanded more ingenuity; he spat paint into a V-shape formed by his two splayed hands, rubbed it into a curved swath to shape the belly's outline, then finger-painted short protruding lines to suggest the animals' shaggy hair. Neatly outlined dots, he found, could not be made by blowing a thin jet of charcoal onto the wall. He had to spit pigment through a hole made in an animal skin. "I spent seven hours a day for a week," he says. "Puff . . . puff . . . puff. . . . It was exhausting, particularly because there was carbon monoxide in the cave. But you experience something special, painting like that. You feel you are breathing the image onto the rock—projecting your spirit from the deepest part of your body onto the rock surface."

Was that what the Paleolithic painter felt when creating this image? "Yes, I know it doesn't sound very scientific," Lorblanchet says of his highly personal style of investigation, "but the intellectual games of the structuralists haven't got us very far, have they? Studying rock art shouldn't be an intellectual game. It is about understanding humanity. That's why I believe the experimental approach is valid in this case."

Hypotheses to account for the early European cave art are difficult because they so often depend on conjectural and subjective interpretations. Some have argued that it is art for art's sake; but if that is so, why were animals so often painted over one another, and why were they so often placed in inaccessible places? The latter might suggest that they were for ceremonial purposes and that the caves served as religious sanctuaries. One suggestion is that the animals were drawn to ensure success in the hunt, another that their depiction was seen as a way to promote fertility and increase the size of the herds on which humans depended. Some support for this comes from a major reassessment of the art of Altimira Cave in northern Spain. Here, the art shows a pervasive concern for the sexual reproduction of the bison.[8] In cave art generally, though, the animals painted bear little relationship to those most frequently hunted. Furthermore, there are few depictions of animals being hunted or killed, nor are there depictions of animals copulating or with exaggerated sexual parts as there are in the Venus figures. Another suggestion is that rites by which youngsters were initiated into adulthood took place in the painted galleries. In support of this idea, footprints, most of which are small, have been found in the clay floors of

several caves, and in one, they even circle a modeled clay bison. The animals painted, so this argument goes, may have had to do with knowledge being transmitted from the elders to the youths. Furthermore, the transmission of information might be implied by countless so-called signs, apparently abstract designs that accompany much Upper Paleolithic art. Some have interpreted these as tallies of animals killed, a reckoning of time according to a lunar calendar, or both.

These abstract designs, including such ones as the spots on the Pech Merle horses, suggest yet another possibility. For the most part, these are just like the entoptic designs seen by subjects in experiments dealing with altered states of consciousness, and which are so consistently present in the rock art of southern Africa. Furthermore, the rock art of southern Africa shows the same painting of new images over older ones, as well as the same sort of fixation on large, powerful animals instead of the ones most often eaten. Thus, the cave art of Europe may well represent the same depictions of trance experiences, painted after the fact. Consistent with this interpretation, the caves themselves are conducive to the sort of sensory distortion that can induce trance.

Artistic expression, whatever its purpose may have been, was not confined to rock surfaces and portable objects alone. Upper Paleolithic peoples also ornamented their bodies with necklaces of perforated animal teeth, shells,

---

[8]Halverson, J. (1989). Review of the book *Altimira revisited and other essays on early art*. American Antiquity, 54, 883.

Dots are a common entoptic form, and in art depicting visions seen in trance, lines of dots are not uncommon, as on this 24,000-year-old ivory pendant from Sungir, Russia.

beads of bone, stone, and ivory; rings; bracelets; and anklets. Clothing, too, was adorned with beads. This should alert us to the probability that quite a lot of art was executed in perishable materials—wood carving, paintings on bark or animal skins, and the like. Thus, the rarity or absence of Upper Paleolithic art in some parts of the inhabited world may be more apparent than real, as people elsewhere worked with materials unlikely to survive so long in the archeological record.

OTHER ASPECTS OF UPPER PALEOLITHIC CULTURE

Upper Paleolithic peoples lived not only in caves and rock shelters, but also in structures built out in the open. In Ukraine, for example, the remains have been found of sizable settlements, in which huts were built on frameworks of intricately stacked mammoth bones. Where the ground was frozen, cobblestones were heated and placed in the earth to sink in, thereby providing sturdy, dry floors. Their hearths, no longer shallow depressions or flat surfaces that radiated back little heat,

These 40,000-year-old beads made from ostrich eggshells, found at a site in Kenya, are among the earliest undisputed items of personal adornment.

were instead stone-lined pits that conserved heat for extended periods and made for more efficient cooking. For the outdoors, they had the same sort of tailored clothing worn in historical times by the natives of Siberia, Alaska, and Canada. And they engaged in long-distance trade, as indicated, for example, by the presence of seashells and Baltic amber at sites several hundred kilometers from the sources of these materials. Although Middle Paleolithic peoples made use of rare and distant materials, they did not do so with the regularity seen in the Upper Paleolithic.

THE SPREAD OF UPPER PALEOLITHIC PEOPLES

Such was the effectiveness of their cultures that Upper Paleolithic peoples were able to expand into regions previously uninhabited by their archaic forebears. Colonization of Siberia began about 42,000 years ago, although it took some-

thing like 10,000 years before they reached the northeastern part of that region. Much earlier, by 60,000 years ago, people managed to get to Australia and New Guinea. To do this, they had to use some kind of watercraft to make the difficult crossing of at least 90 kilometers of water that separated Australia and New Guinea (then a single landmass) from the Asian continent throughout Paleolithic times. Once in Australia, these people created some of the world's earliest sophisticated rock art, some 10,000 to 15,000 years earlier than the more famous European cave paintings. Other evidence for sophisticated ritual activity in early Australia is provided by 26,000-year-old cremation burials associated with red ochre. It may be that this pigment had more than symbolic value; for example, its iron salts have antiseptic and deodorizing properties, and there are recorded instances in which red ochre is associated with prolonging life and is used medicinally to treat particular conditions or infections.

Reconstruction of an Upper Paleolithic hut with walls of interlocked mammoth mandibles.

One historically known native Australian society is reported to use ochre to heal wounds, scars, and burns, and a person with internal pain is covered with the substance and placed in the sun to promote sweating. What is especially interesting in view of the impressive accomplishments of native Australians is that the tools used by these people are remarkably similar to those of the Eurasian Middle Paleolithic. Clearly, simplicity of tool kits does not bespeak absence of sophisticated intellectual capabilities.

To get to the Americas, voyages of the sort undertaken by the first Australians were not necessary. With much of the world's water supply taken up by the great continental glaciers, there was a worldwide lowering of sea levels, causing an emergence of land joining Siberia to Alaska. With expanding populations in Asia, brought about by increasingly effective cultural adaptations, it was only a matter of time before human populations began to spread gradually eastward over this dry land. Thus, their arrival in Alaska was probably not the result of an actual migration. The precise timing of their first arrival is still

debated, but securely dated remains from Monte Verde, a site in south-central Chile indicate that populations had spread as far as the southern part of South America by 12,500 years ago, if not earlier. Linguist Johanna Nichols, looking at the time it took various languages to spread from their homelands—Celtic languages in Europe, Eskimo languages in the Arctic, and Athabaskan languages from interior western Canada to New Mexico and Arizona (Navajo)—estimates it would have taken at least 7,000 years for people to reach south-central Chile.[9] This would mean that the first people to arrive in North America did so by 20,000 years ago. But until they were cut off from other Siberians, probably by expanding ice sheets of the last glacial maximum, they could not be considered Americans, as opposed to a peripheral group of Siberian people (Figure 10.4).

---

[9]The first Americans, ca. 20,000 B.C. (1998). *Discover, 19*(6), 24.

FIGURE 10.4

As this map shows, the land connecting Siberia and Alaska at the height of the last glaciation was not so much a bridge for people to cross into North America as it was a peripheral portion of a region into which human populations in the Upper Paleolithic spread.

Fluted points, such as these, tipped the spears of Paleoindian hunters.

Paleoindians, like their Upper Paleolithic contemporaries in Eurasia, were such accomplished hunters that they, too, could kill more animals than could possibly be used at one time. These bones are the remains of some 200 bison that Paleoindian hunters stampeded over a cliff 8,500 years ago.

Although the earliest technologies in the Americas remain poorly known, they gave rise in North America, about 12,000 years ago, to the distinctive fluted spear points of **Paleoindian** hunters of big game, such as mammoths, caribou, and now extinct forms of bison. Fluted points are finely made, with large channel flakes removed from one or both surfaces. This thinned section was inserted into the notched end of a spear shaft for a sturdy haft. Fluted points are found from the Atlantic seaboard to the Pacific coast, and from Alaska down into Panama. So efficient were the hunters who made these points that they may have hastened the extinction of the mammoth and other large Pleistocene mammals. By driving large numbers of animals over cliffs, they killed many more than they could possibly use, thus wasting huge amounts of meat.

WHERE DID UPPER PALEOLITHIC PEOPLE COME FROM?

As noted in Chapter 9, scholars still debate whether the transition from archaic to anatomi-

---

Paleoindian. The earliest inhabitants of North America.

cally modern *H. sapiens* took place in one specific population or was the result of in situ evolution on the part of populations living in Africa, Asia, and even Europe between 100,000 and 40,000 years ago. At the moment, though, the odds seem to favor the latter hypothesis. Even in Europe, where the argument for replacement of archaic by modern *sapiens* has been most strongly made, the most recent Neandertals display modern features, whereas the most ancient moderns show what appear to be Neandertal holdovers. For example, the Saint Césaire skull has the high forehead and chin of moderns. Similarly, a late Neandertal from Vindija, northern Croatia, shows a thinning of brow ridges towards their outer margins. Conversely, anatomically modern skulls from Brno, Mladec, and Predmosti, in the Czech Republic, retain heavy brow ridges and Neandertal-like muscle attachments on their backs.[10] As noted early in this chapter, some of the skulls from the Cro-Magnon rock shelter look Neandertal-like from the back. Of course, these features could all be the result of interbreeding between two populations that overlapped in time, rather than simple evolution from one into the other. Or, they could represent a single, varied population whose average characters were shifting in a more "modern" direction. In either case, they do not fit with the idea of the complete extinction of the older population.

Looking at the larger picture, what we see in all regions of the Old World, since the time of *H. erectus*, is more and more emphasis placed on cultural, as opposed to biological, adaptation. To handle environmental stress, reliance was placed increasingly on the development of appropriate tools, clothes, shelter, use of fire, and so forth, as opposed to alteration of the hu-

The bulge on the back of this Upper Paleolithic skull from Predmosti in the Czech Republic, along with its still prominent brow ridges, is reminiscent of the earlier Neandertals.

man organism itself. This was true whether human populations lived in hot or cold, wet or dry, forest or grassland areas. Since culture is learned and not carried by genes, it is ultimately based on what might loosely be called "brain power" or, more formally, **cognitive capacity**. While this includes intelligence in the IQ sense, it is broader than that, for it also includes such skills as educability, concept formation, self-awareness, self-evaluation, reliability of performance under stress, attention span, sensitivity in discrimination, and creativity.

The major thrust in the evolution of the genus *Homo*, then, has been toward improved cognitive capacity through the evolution of the brain regardless of the environmental and climatic differences between the regions in which populations of the genus lived. Hence, there has been a certain similarity of selective pressures in all regions. In

[10]Bednarik, R. G. (1995). Concept-mediated marking in the Lower Paleolithic. *Current Anthropology, 36,* 627. Minugh-Purvis, N. (1992). The inhabitants of Ice Age Europe. *Expedition, 34*(3), 33–34.

Cognitive capacity. A broad concept including intelligence, educability, concept formation, self-awareness, self-evaluation, attention span, sensitivity in discrimination, and creativity.

These Upper Paleolithic skulls from China (left) and Africa (right) are easily derivable from earlier archaic *sapiens* skulls in the same regions.

addition, this evolution of all populations of the genus *Homo* would have been helped along by a certain amount of gene flow between populations. In an evolving species, genes having survival value anywhere tend to spread from one population to another. In the case of the human species, these would be whatever genes happen to relate to cognitive capacity.

It is impossible to know just how much gene flow took place among ancient human populations, but that some took place is consistent with the sudden appearance of novel traits in one region later than their appearance somewhere else. For example, Upper Paleolithic remains from North Africa exhibit the kind of midfacial flatness previously seen only in East Asian fossils; similarly, various Cro-Magnon fossils from Europe show the short upper jaws, horizontally oriented cheek bones, and rectangular eye orbits previously seen in East Asians. Conversely, the round orbits, large frontal sinuses and thin cranial bones seen in some archaic *sapiens* skulls from China represent the first appearance there of traits that have greater

antiquity in the west.[11] What appears to be happening, then, is that genes from the east are being introduced into western gene pools and vice versa. Support for this comes from studies of the Y chromosome in humans (found only in males). These studies indicate that some DNA carried by this chromosome originated in Asia at least 200,000 years ago, and spread from there to Africa.[12] Not only is such gene flow consistent with the remarkable tendency historically known humans have to "swap genes" between populations, even in the face of cultural barriers to gene flow, it is also consistent with the tendency of other primates to produce hybrids when two subspecies (and sometimes even species) come into contact.[13] Moreover, without such gene

[11]Pope, G. C. (1992). Craniofacial evidence for the origin of modern humans in China. *Yearbook of Physical Anthropology, 35,* 287–288.

[12]Gibbons, A. (1997). Ideas on human origins evolve at anthropology gathering. *Science, 276,* 535–536.

[13]Simons, E. L. (1989). Human origins. *Science, 245,* 1349.

flow, multiregional evolution inevitably would have resulted in the appearance of multiple species of modern humans, something that clearly has *not* happened. In fact, the low level of genetic differentiation among modern humans can be explained easily as a consequence of high levels of gene flow.[14]

THE MESOLITHIC ERA

By 12,000 years ago, glacial conditions in the world were moderating, causing changes in human habitats. Throughout the world, sea levels were on the rise, ultimately flooding many areas that had been above sea level during periods of glaciation, such as the Bering Straits, parts of the North Sea, and an extensive area that had joined Indonesia to Southeast Asia. In northern regions, milder climates brought about marked changes as tundras were ultimately replaced by hardwood forests. In the process, the herd animals upon which northern Paleolithic peoples had depended for much of their food, clothing, and shelter disappeared from many areas. Some, like the reindeer and musk ox, moved to colder climates; others, like the mammoths, died out completely. Thus, the northerners especially were forced to adapt to new conditions. In the new forests, animals were more solitary in their habits and so not as easy to hunt as they had been, and large, cooperative hunts were less productive than before. However, plant food was more abundant, and there were new and abundant sources of fish and other food around lake shores, bays, and rivers. Hence, human populations developed new and ingenious ways to catch and kill animals, while at the same time they devoted more energy to fishing and the collection of wild plant foods. This new way of life marks the end of the Paleolithic and the start of the **Mesolithic,** or Middle Stone Age. In a sense, it marks a return to more typical hominine subsistence patterns.

MESOLITHIC TOOLS AND WEAPONS

New technologies were developed for the changed postglacial environment (Figure 10.5). Ground stone tools, shaped and sharpened by grinding the tool against sandstone (often using sand as an additional abrasive), made effective axes and adzes. Such implements, though they do take longer to make, are less prone to breakage under heavy-duty usage than are those made of chipped stone. Thus, they were helpful in clearing forest areas and in the woodwork needed for the creation of dugout canoes and skin-covered boats. Although some kind of water craft had been developed early enough to get humans to the island of Flores (and probably Italy and Spain) by 800,000 years ago, boats become prominent only in Mesolithic sites, indicating that human foraging for food frequently took place on the water as well as the land. Thus, it was possible to make use of deep-water resources as well as those of coastal areas.

The characteristic Mesolithic tool was the **microlith,** a small but hard, sharp blade. Although a microlithic tradition existed in the Democratic Republic of Congo by about 40,000 years ago,[15] such tools did not become common elsewhere until the Mesolithic. Microliths could be mass-produced because they were small, easy to make, and could be fashioned from materials other than flint. Also, they could be attached to

[14]Relethford, J. H., & Harpending, H. C. (1994). Craniometric variation, genetic theory, and modern human origins. *American Journal of Physical Antropology, 95,* 265.

[15]Bednarik, p. 606.

Mesolithic.   The Middle Stone Age of Europe and Southwest Asia. Began about 12,000 years ago. **> Microlith.**   A small blade of flint or similar stone widespread in the Mesolithic, several of which were hafted together in wooden handles to make tools.

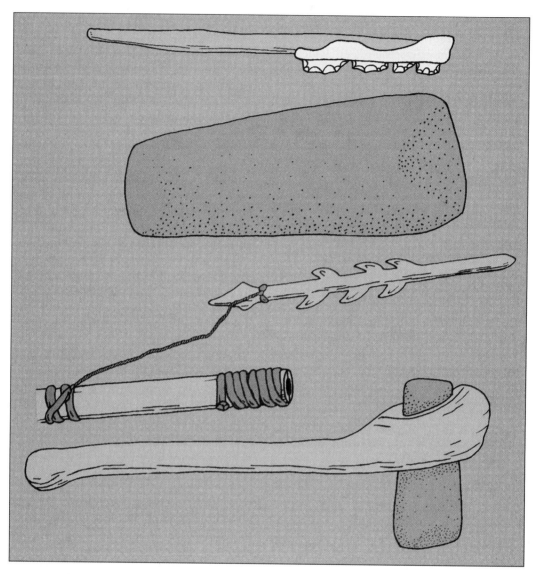

FIGURE 10.5

This drawing shows a Mesolithic tool consisting of a wooden or bone handle with microliths set into it. Below it is a ground stone axe blade; how such blades could be hafted is shown at the bottom. Between the axes is a bone harpoon head and the end of its wooden shaft. Harpoons actually come into use somewhat before the Mesolithic.

arrow shafts by using melted resin as a binder. Thus, the bow and arrow with the microlith arrowhead became the deadliest and most common weapon of the Mesolithic.

The reliance of Mesolithic peoples on microliths provided them with an important advantage over their Upper Paleolithic forebears: The small size of the microlith enabled them to devise a wider array of composite tools made out of stone and wood or bone (see Figure 10.5, top). Thus, they could make sickles, harpoons, arrows, and daggers by fitting microliths into grooves in wood or bone handles. Later experimentation with these forms led to more sophisticated tools and weapons.

It is possible that the Mesolithic was a more sedentary period for humans than earlier eras. Dwellings from this period seem more substantial, an indication of permanency. Indeed, this is a logical development: Most hunting cultures, and especially those depending on herd animals are nomadic. To be successful, one must follow the game. This is not necessary for peoples subsisting on a diet of seafood and plants, as the location of shore and vegetation remains relatively constant.

CULTURAL DIVERSITY IN THE MESOLITHIC

In the warmer parts of the world, the collection of wild plant foods had been more of an equal partner with hunting in subsistence activities in the Upper Paleolithic than had been the case in the colder north. Hence, in areas like Southwest Asia,

the Mesolithic represents less of a changed way of life than was true in Europe. Here, the important **Natufian culture** flourished.

The Natufians were a people who lived between 12,500 and 10,200 years ago at the eastern end of the Mediterranean Sea in caves, rock shelters, and small villages with stone- and mud-walled houses. Nearby, their dead were buried in communal cemeteries, usually in shallow pits without grave goods or decorations. A small shrine is known from one of their villages, a 10,500-year-old settlement at Jericho. Basin-shaped depressions in the rocks found outside homes at Natufian sites are thought to have been storage pits. Plastered storage pits beneath the floors of the houses were also found, indicating that the Natufians were the earliest Mesolithic people known to have stored plant foods. Certain tools found among Natufian remains bear evidence that they were used to cut grain. These

At Nulliak, Labrador, maritime archaic people lived in large, long houses with stone foundations. The alignments of stones seen in this photo are all that remain of one such house.

Natufian culture.   A Mesolithic culture of Israel, Lebanon, and western Syria, between about 12,500 and 10,200 years ago.

Mesolithic sickles, for that is what they were, consisted of small stone blades set in straight handles of wood or bone.

In the Americas, cultures comparable to Mesolithic cultures of the Old World developed, but here they are referred to as **Archaic cultures.** Outside of the Arctic, microlithic tools are not prominent in them, as they are in parts of the Old World, but ground stone tools such as axes, adzes, gouges, plummets, and spear-thrower weights are common. Archaic cultures were widespread in the Americas; one of the more dramatic was the **Maritime archaic,** which began to develop about 7,000 years ago around the Gulf of St. Lawrence. These people developed an elaborate assortment of bone and ground slate tools with which they hunted a wide variety of sea mammals, including whales; fish, including swordfish; and sea birds. To get some of these, they regularly paddled their dugout canoes far off shore. To appreciate the skills this required, one need only recognize the difficulty of landing a 500-pound swordfish, as these are very aggressive fish. They are known historically to have driven their swords through the hulls of substantial wooden vessels. The Maritime Archaic people also developed the first elaborate burial cult in North America, involving the use of red ochre ("red paint") and the placement of finely made grave goods with the deceased.

MAJOR PALEOLITHIC AND MESOLITHIC TRENDS

Certain trends stand out from the information anthropologists have gathered about the Old and Middle Stone ages. These are general progressions that occurred from one culture to the next in most parts of the world.

One trend was toward increasingly more sophisticated, varied, and specialized tool kits.

Tools became progressively lighter and smaller, resulting in the conservation of raw materials and a better ratio between length of cutting edge and weight of stone. Tools became specialized according to region and function. Instead of crude all-purpose tools, more effective particularized devices were made to deal more effectively with the differing conditions of savanna, forest, and shore.

This more efficient tool technology enabled human populations to increase and spill over into more diverse environments; it also was responsible for the loss of heavy physical features, favoring instead decreased size and weight of face and teeth, the development of larger and more complex brains, and ultimately a reduction in body size and robusticity. This dependence on intelligence rather than bulk provided the key for peoples' increased reliance on cultural rather than physical adaptation. As the brain became modernized, conceptual thought developed, as evidenced by symbolic artifacts and signs of magico-religious ceremonies.

By the Upper Paleolithic, the amount of sexual dimorphism, too, was greatly reduced, as size differences between men and women were relatively slight compared to what they were in *Australopithecus, Homo habilis,* or (to a lesser extent) *Homo erectus.* This has important implications for gender relations. As noted in earlier chapters, among primates marked sexual dimorphism is associated with male dominance over females. Lack of sexual dimorphism, by contrast, correlates with a lack of such dominance. In evolving humans, it appears that a loss of male dominance went hand in hand with the ever increasing importance of cooperative relationships.

Through Paleolithic times, at least in the colder parts of the world, there appeared a trend toward the importance of and proficiency in hunting. People's intelligence enabled them to develop tools that exceeded other animals' physical equipment, as well as the improved social organization and cooperation so important for survival and population growth. This trend was reversed during the Mesolithic, when hunting lost its preeminence and the gathering of wild plants and seafood became increasingly important.

As human populations grew and spread, regionalism also became more marked. Tool assemblages developed in different ways at different times in different areas. General differences appeared between north and south, east and west. Although there are some indications of cultural contact and intercommunication, such as the development of long-distance trade in the Upper Paleolithic, regionalism was a dominant characteristic of Paleolithic and Mesolithic times. The persistence of regionalism is probably due to two factors: a perceived need to distinguish symbolically one's own people from others, and the need to adapt to differing environments. Paleolithic peoples eventually spread over all the continents of the world, including Australia and the Americas, and as they did so, changes in climate and environment called for new kinds of adaptations. Thus Paleolithic and Mesolithic tool kits had to be altered to meet the requirements of many varying locations. In forest environments, people needed strong axes for working wood; on the open savanna and plains, they used the bow and arrow to hunt the game they could not stalk closely; the people in settlements that grew up around lakes and along rivers and coasts developed harpoons and hooks; in the subarctic regions they needed tools to work the heavy skins of seals and caribou; in the grasslands they needed tools for harvesting grain and separating the usable part from the chaff. The fact that culture is first and foremost an adaptive mechanism meant that it was of necessity a regional thing.

CHAPTER SUMMARY

The Cro-Magnons and the other anatomically modern peoples that held exclusive sway in the world after 30,000 years ago, in addition to a full-sized brain, possessed a physical appearance somewhat similar to our own. The modernization of the face of Upper Paleolithic peoples is a result of a reduction in the size of the teeth and the muscles involved in chewing as a consequence of the fact that teeth were no longer being used as tools. Similarly, bodies became somewhat less massive and robust as improved technology reduced the need for brute strength.

The emphasis in evolution of the genus *Homo* in all parts of the world was toward increasing cognitive capacity through development of the brain. This progression took place regardless of environmental or climatic conditions under which the genus lived. In addition, evolution of the genus *Homo* undoubtedly was aided by gene flow between populations. Lack of much genetic differentiation between human populations today bespeaks high levels of gene flow between populations in the past.

Upper Paleolithic cultures evolved out of the Middle Paleolithic cultures of Africa, Asia, and Europe. The typical Upper Paleolithic tool was the blade. The blade technique of toolmaking saved much more flint than Middle Paleolithic methods. Other efficient Upper Paleolithic toolmaking techniques were pressure flaking of stone and using chisel-like tools called burins to fashion bone, antler horn, and ivory into tools. The cultural adaptation of Upper Paleolithic peoples became specific; they developed different tools for different seasons. There is no one Upper Paleolithic culture, as people living in different environments produced different cultures. Northern Upper Paleolithic cultures supported themselves by the hunting of large herd animals and catching smaller animals in nets. Upper Paleolithic cultures are the earliest in which pictorial art is common.

The end of the glacial period caused great physical changes in human habitats. Sea levels were raised, vegetation changed, and herd animals disappeared from many areas. The European Mesolithic period marked a return to more typical hominine ways of subsistence, as big game hunters returned to more of a balance between hunting and gathering. Increased reliance on seafood and plants made the Mesolithic a more sedentary period for people. Ground stone tools, including axes and adzes, answered postglacial needs for new technologies. The characteristic Mesolithic tool in the Old World was made with microliths, small, hard, sharp blades of flint or similar stone which could be mass-produced and hafted with others to produce implements like sickles. Widespread reliance on the bow and arrow to hunt generally smaller, less aggressive animals resulted in a reduction of the size and robusticity of men, at least in Europe.

Three trends emerged from the Paleolithic and Mesolithic periods. First was a trend toward more sophisticated, varied, and specialized tool kits. This trend enabled people to increase their population and spread to new environments. It also was adaptive, leading to decreased size and weight of face and teeth, the development of larger, more complex brains, and ultimately a reduction in body size, mass, and degree of sexual dimorphism. Second was a trend toward the importance of and proficiency in hunting. The importance of hunting was somewhat reversed during the Mesolithic period, as hunting large game became less important than hunting smaller game and gathering plants and seafood. Third was a trend toward regionalism, as people's technology and life habits increasingly reflected their association with a particular environment.

POINTS FOR CONSIDERATION

1. Why, if *Homo sapiens* developed simultaneously throughout Asia, Africa, and Europe, is there so little genetic differentiation between these groups? Wouldn't this indicate a single point of origin, instead? What other factors have to be considered?

2. What is the significance of new toolmaking techniques? What correlation might there be between new tool types and greater variety and physical traits in modern *Homo sapiens*? How is this a continuation of a trend in hominines in general? What is the benefit of the new physical type over the old?

3. What are the benefits of greater control in toolmaking resulting from pressure flaking? Does it extend beyond merely "more edge per pound"? What are the nonfunctional implications? How might this be related to the "explosion" of artwork found in the upper Paleolithic?

4. How is longevity of youth in hominines, particularly in modern *Homo sapiens*, useful to the species? How might this relate to overall longevity of life? How does this compare with other mammals' patterns of development? What do the differences reflect?

SUGGESTED READINGS

Campbell, B. G., and Loy, J. D. (1995). *Humankind emerging* (7th ed.). New York: HarperCollins.

Adapted in part from Time-Life's *Emergence of Man* and *Life Nature Library,* this is a richly illustrated, up-to-date account of the Paleolithic. In it, Campbell integrates paleontological and archaeological data with ethnographic data on modern food foragers to present a rich picture of evolving Paleolithic ways of life.

Pfeiffer, J. E. (1985). *The creative explosion.* Ithaca, NY: Cornell University Press.

A fascinating and readable discussion of the origins of art and religion. Its main drawback is its focus on European art.

Prideaux, T., et al. (1973). *Cro-Magnon man*. New York: Time-Life.

This beautifully illustrated volume in the Time-Life *Emergence of Man* series covers the period between 40,000 and 10,000 years ago. A whole chapter is devoted to "The Subtle Mind of Cro-Magnon."

Wolpoff, M., & Caspari, R. (1997). *Race and human evolution*. New York: Simon and Schuster.

This book is a detailed but readable presentation of the multiregional hypothesis of modern human origins. Among its strengths is a discussion of the problem of defining what "anatomically modern" means.

PART IV

HUMAN BIOLOGICAL AND CULTURAL EVOLUTION SINCE THE OLD STONE AGE

Chapter 11
CULTIVATION AND DOMESTICATION

Chapter 12
THE RISE OF CITIES AND CIVILIZATION

Chapter 13
MODERN HUMAN DIVERSITY

Introduction

In the Upper Paleolithic, by 30,000 years ago, anatomically modern varieties of humans, with cultures comparable to those of historic and existing food-foraging peoples, had sole possession of the inhabited parts of the world. The story of human evolution in the Paleolithic is one of a close interrelation between developing culture and developing humanity. The critical importance of culture as the human adaptive mechanism seems to have imposed selective pressures favoring a bigger, more elaborate brain, and this greater cognitive power made possible improved cultural adaptation. Indeed, it seems fair to say that modern humans look the way they do today because cultural adaptation came to play such an important role in the survival of our ancient ancestors. Because cultural adaptation worked so well, human populations were able to grow, probably rather slowly, with a consequent expansion into previously uninhabited parts of the world. And this, too, affected cultural adaptation, as adjustments were made to meet new conditions.

Although food foraging served humans well for hundreds of thousands of years in the Paleolithic, far-reaching changes began to take place in some parts of the world as many as 11,000 years ago. This second major cultural revolution consisted of the emergence of food production, the subject of Chapter 11. Eventually, most of the world's people became food producers, even though food foraging remained a satisfactory way of life for some. At the present time, no more than a quarter of a million people—less than 0.00005% of a world population of almost 6 billion—remain food foragers. Just as the emergence of food foraging was followed by modifications and improvements leading to regional variants of this pattern, so the advent of food production opened the way for new cultural variants based upon it. Chapter 12 discusses the result: further cultural diversity, out of which developed civilization, the basis of modern life.

In spite of the increasing effectiveness of culture as the primary mechanism by which humans adapt to diverse environments, our species has continued to evolve biologically. In the course of their movement into other parts of the world, humans had already developed a certain amount of biological variation from one population to another. On top of this, populations of food producers were exposed to selective pressures of a different sort than those affecting food foragers, thereby inducing further changes in human gene pools. Such changes continue to affect the human species today, even though it remains the same species now as it was at the end of the Paleolithic. Chapter 13 discusses how the variation to be seen in *Homo sapiens* today came into existence as the result of forces altering the frequencies of alleles in human gene pools, and why such variation probably has nothing to do with intelligence. The chapter concludes with a look at forces apparently active today to produce further changes in those same gene pools.

Chapter 11
CULTIVATION AND DOMESTICATION

BEGINNING ABOUT 11,000 YEARS AGO, SOME OF
THE WORLD'S PEOPLE EMBARKED ON A NEW WAY
OF LIFE BASED ON FOOD PRODUCTION. ONE PLACE
THIS HAPPENED WAS IN CHINA. AT AN
ARCHAEOLOGICAL SITE IN DIATONGHUAN CAVE,
ARCHAEOLOGISTS RECOVER EVIDENCE OF THE
TRANSITION FROM WILD TO DOMESTIC RICE.

Chapter Preview

When and Where Did the Change From Food Foraging to Food Production Begin?

Centers of early plant and animal domestication exist in Africa, China, Mesoamerica, North and South America, as well as Southwest and Southeast Asia. From these places, food production spread to most other parts of the world. It began at more or less the same time in these different places; perhaps a bit earlier in Southwest Asia, but a bit later in Southeast Asia.

Why Did the Change Take Place?

Since food production by and large requires more work than hunting and gathering, is not necessarily a more secure means of subsistence, and requires people to eat more of the foods that food foragers eat only when they have no other choice, it can be assumed that people probably did not become food producers through choice. Of various theories that have been proposed, the most likely is that food production came about as a consequence of a chance convergence of separate natural events and cultural developments.

What Were the Consequences of the Change to Food Production?

Although food production generally provides less leisure time than food foraging, it does permit some reallocation of the workload. Some people can produce enough food to allow others to spend more time at other tasks, and so a number of technological developments, such as weaving and pottery-making, generally accompany food production. In addition, it facilitates a sedentary way of life in villages, with more substantial housing. Finally, the new modes of work and resource allocation require new ways of organizing people, generally into lineages, clans, and common-interest associations.

Throughout the Paleolithic, people depended exclusively on wild sources of food for their survival. In cold northern regions, they came to rely on the hunting of large animals such as mammoth, bison, and horses, but especially reindeer, as well as smaller animals such as hares and foxes. Elsewhere, they hunted, fished, or gathered whatever nature provided. There is no evidence in Paleolithic remains to indicate that livestock was kept or plants cultivated. Paleolithic people followed wild herds and gathered wild plant foods, relying on their wits and muscles to acquire what nature provided. Whenever favored sources of food became scarce, as sometimes happened, people adjusted by increasing the variety of food eaten, and incorporating less favored food into their diets.

About 12,000 years ago, the subsistence practices of some people began to change in ways that were to transform radically their way of life, although no one involved had any way of knowing it at the time. Not until these changes were well advanced could people become aware that their mode of subsistence differed from that of other cultures—that they had become farmers, rather than food foragers.[1] This change in the means of obtaining food had important implications for human development, for it meant that by taking matters into their own hands, people could become more sedentary. Moreover, by reorganizing the workload, some of them could be freed from the food quest to devote their energies to other sorts of tasks. With good reason, the **Neolithic period,** when this change took place, has been called a revolutionary one in human history. This period, and the changes that took place within it, are the subjects of this chapter.

---

[1]Rindos, D. (1984). *The origins of agriculture: An evolutionary perspective* (p. 99). Orlando, FL: Academic Press.

In spite of all the innovations that have happened since, it remains a fact that all of the crops we rely on today were invented by Neolithic farmers.

Neolithic period. The New Stone Age, which began about 11,000 years ago in Southwest Asia.

THE MESOLITHIC ROOTS OF FARMING AND PASTORALISM

The Mesolithic may be viewed either as the final stage of the Paleolithic (sometimes called the Epipaleolithic) or as the beginning of the Neolithic. During this period, which began around 12,000 years ago, people turned increasingly toward the abundant food supplies to be found in rivers, lakes, and oceans. These waterways were teeming with aquatic life because of the rising seas brought about by warmer temperatures and melting glaciers. In addition, people gathered a broad spectrum of plant foods on land and hunted a variety of birds and smaller mammals. Generally, this new way of life offered more secure supplies of food and therefore an increased margin of survival. In some parts of the world, people started living in larger and more sedentary groups and cooperating with others outside the sphere of family or hunting band. They became settled village-dwellers, and some of these settlements were shortly to expand into the first farming villages, towns, and (ultimately) cities.

THE NEOLITHIC REVOLUTION

The Neolithic, or New Stone Age, was characterized by the transition from foraging for food to dependence upon domesticated plants and animals. It was by no means a smooth or rapid transition; in fact, the switch to food production spread over many centuries—even millennia—and was a direct outgrowth of the preceding Mesolithic. Where to draw the line between the two periods is not always clear.

The term *New Stone Age* is derived from the polished stone tools that are characteristic of this period. But more important than the presence of these tools is the transition from a hunting, gathering, and fishing economy to one based on food production, representing a major change in the subsistence practices of early peoples. One of the first regions to undergo this transition, and certainly the most intensively studied, was Southwest Asia. The remains of domesticated plants and animals are known from parts of Israel, Jordan, Syria, Turkey, Iraq, and Iran, all before 8,000 years ago.

DOMESTICATION: WHAT IS IT?

Domestication is an evolutionary process whereby humans modify, either intentionally or unintentionally, the genetic makeup of a population of plants or animals, sometimes to the extent that members of the population are unable to survive and/or reproduce without human assistance. As such, it constitutes a special case of a kind of relationship between different species frequently seen in the natural world, as in the case of one species that has come to depend for its protection and reproductive success on some other that feeds upon it. A particularly dramatic example is offered by species of New World ants that grow fungi in their nests, providing the ants with most of their nutrition. Like human farmers, the ants add manure to stimulate fungal growth and eliminate competing weeds both mechanically and through use of antibiotic herbicides. They propagate their crops vegetatively, as do humans for some of their crops (bananas, for example), and even share crops, as when one ant species borrows from another's nest or when several nests become disturbed and mixed. Finally, like human farming, ant farming did not develop just once, but at least five different times.[2]

Looked at from the perspective of the fungi, the benefit gained is protection and ensured reproductive success. Turning from fungi to plants, we find that there are numerous species that rely

------

[2]Diamond, J. (1998). Ants, crops, and history. *Science, 281,* 1974–1975.

Domestication. An evolutionary process whereby humans modify, either intentionally or unintentionally, the genetic makeup of a population of plants or animals, sometimes to the extent that members of the population are unable to survive and/or reproduce without human assistance.

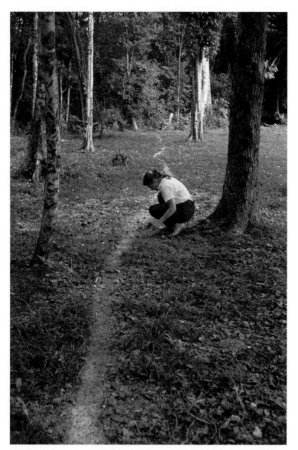

In this photo, worker ants have made a path as they go out to cut pieces of leaf that they bring back to their nest to make the soil in which they plant their fungus gardens.

on some type of animal—in some cases birds, in others mammals, and in yet others insects—for protection and dispersal of their seeds. The important thing is that both parties benefit from the arrangement; reliance on animals for seed dispersal ensures that the latter will be carried farther afield than would otherwise be possible, thereby cutting down on competition for sun and nutrients between young and old plants and reducing the likelihood that any diseases or parasites harbored by one will be transmitted to the others. Added vigor is apt to come to plants that are freed from the need to provide themselves with built-in

defensive mechanisms such as thorns, toxins, or chemical compounds that make them taste bad. This enhanced vigor may be translated into larger and more tasty edible parts to attract the animals that feed upon them, thereby cementing the relationship between the protected and protector.

EVIDENCE OF EARLY PLANT DOMESTICATION

The characteristics of plants under human domestication that set them apart from their wild ancestors and have made them attractive to those who eat them include increased size, at least of edible parts; reduction or loss of natural means of seed dispersal; reduction or loss of protective devices such as husks or distasteful chemical compounds; loss of delayed seed germination (important to wild plants for survival in times of drought or other adverse conditions of temporary duration); and development of simultaneous ripening of the seed or fruit. Many of these characteristics can be seen in plant remains from archaeological sites; thus, paleobotanists can often tell the fossil of a wild plant species from a domesticated one, for example, by studying the seed of cereal grasses, such as barley, wheat, and maize (corn). Wild cereals have a very fragile stem, whereas domesticated ones have a tough stem. Under natural conditions, plants with fragile stems scatter their seed for themselves, while those with tough stems do not.

The structural change from a soft to a tough stem in early domesticated plants involves a genetic change, undoubtedly the result of what Darwin referred to as **unconscious selection:** the preservation of valued individuals and the destruction of less valued ones, with no thought as to long-range consequences.[3] When the grain stalks were harvested, their soft stem would shatter at the touch of sickle or flail, and many of their seeds would be lost. Inevitably, most of the seeds

_____

[3]Rindos, p. 86.

_____

Unconscious selection.   The preservation of valued variants of a plant or animal species and the destruction of less valued ones, with no thought as to the long-range consequences.

Wild wheat kernels from a site in Syria (left) are compared with those of a domestic variety grown in Greece 2,000 to 3,000 years later (right). Increased size of edible parts is a common feature of domestication.

that people harvested would have been taken from the tough plants. Early domesticators probably also tended to select seed from plants having few husks or none at all—eventually breeding them out—because husking prior to pounding the grains into meal or flour was much too time consuming. Size of plants is another good indicator of the presence of domestication. For example, the large ear of corn we know today is a far cry from the tiny ears (about an inch long) characteristic of early corn. In fact, the ear of corn may have arisen as a simple gene mutation transformed male tassel spikes of the wild grass *teosinte* into small and primitive versions of the female corn ear.[4] Small and primitive though these were (an entire ear contained less nourishment than a single kernel of modern corn), they were radically different in structure from the ears of Teosinte.

EVIDENCE OF EARLY ANIMAL DOMESTICATION

Domestication also produced changes in the skeletal structure of some animals. For example, the horns of wild goats and sheep differ from those of their domesticated counterparts (domesticated female sheep have none). Another structural change that occurred in domestication involves the size of

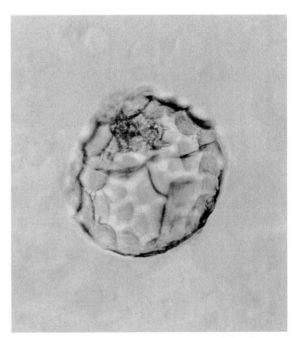

Shown here is a magnification of a phytolith of squash. Phytoliths are microscopic silica bodies formed as plants take up silica from ground water. As the silica gradually fills plant cells, it assumes their distinctive size and shape. They are important for archaeologists, as they survive in humid climates where organic remains rapidly decay.

the animal or its parts. For example, certain teeth of domesticated pigs are smaller than those of wild ones.

---

[4]Gould, S. J. (1991). *The flamingo's smile: Reflections in natural history* (p. 368). New York: Norton.

Teosinte (A), compared to the 5,500-year-old maize (B) and modern maize (C). The wild grass from which maize originated, teosinte is far less productive than maize and doesn't taste very good. Like most plants that were domesticated, it was not a first- or even second-choice food for foraging people.

A study of age and sex ratios of butchered animals at a site may indicate whether or not animal domestication was practiced. Investigators have assumed that if the age and/or sex ratios at the site

differ from those in wild herds, the imbalances are due to conscious selection. For example, at the site of Zawi Chemi Shanidar, in northern Iraq, about 50% of the sheep killed were under 1 year of age. Evidently, the occupants of Zawi Chemi Shanidar were slaughtering the young males for food and saving the females for breeding. Although such herd management does not prove that the sheep were fully domesticated, it does suggest a first step in the domestication process.

In Peru, the prominence of bones of newborn llamas at archaeological sites (up to 72% at some), dating to around 6,300 years ago, is probably indicative of at least incipient domestication. Such high mortality rates for newborn animals are uncommon in wild herds, but are common where animals are penned up. Under confined conditions, the inevitable buildup of mud and filth harbors bacteria that cause diarrhea and enterotoxemia, both of which are fatal to newborn animals.

BEGINNINGS OF DOMESTICATION

Over the past 30 years, a good deal of information has accumulated about the beginnings of domestication, primarily in Southwest Asia as well as Central and South America. We still do not have all the answers about how and why it took place. Nonetheless, some observations of general validity can be made which help us to understand how the switch to food production may have taken place.

The first of these observations is that the switch to food production was not the result of such discoveries that seeds, if planted, grow into plants. Food foragers are far from ignorant about the forces of nature and are perfectly aware of the role of seeds in plant growth, that plants grow better under certain conditions than others, and so forth. In fact, they frequently put their knowledge to work so as to manage actively the resources on which they depend. For example, Indians living in the northern part of Canada's Alberta Province put to use a sophisticated knowledge of the effects of fire to create local environments of their own design. Similarly, Indians in California used fire to perpetuate oak woodland savanna, to promote hunting and the collection of acorns. And in northern Australia, runoff channels of creeks were deliberately altered so as to flood extensive tracts of land, converting them into fields of wild grain. People do not remain food foragers through ignorance, but through choice.

A second observation is that a switch from food foraging to food production does not free people from hard work. The available ethnographic data indicate just the opposite—that farmers, by and large, work far longer hours than do most food foragers. Furthermore, it is clear that early farming required people not only to work longer hours but also to eat more "third choice" food. Typically, food foragers divide potentially edible food resources into first-, second-, and third-choice categories; third-choice foods are eaten only by necessity, when there is no other option. And in Southwest Asia and Mexico, at least, the plants that were brought under domestication were clearly third choice plants.

A final observation is that food production is not necessarily a more secure means of subsistence than food foraging. Seed crops in particular, of the sort domesticated in Southwest Asia, Mexico, and Peru, are highly productive but very unstable on account of low species diversity. Without constant human attention, their productivity suffers.

From all of this, it is little wonder that food foragers do not necessarily regard farming and animal husbandry as superior to hunting, gathering, and fishing. Thus, there are some people in the world who have remained food foragers down into the 1990s, although it has become increasingly difficult for them as food-producing peoples have deprived them of more and more of the land base necessary for their way of life. But as long as existing practices worked well, there was no felt need to abandon them. After all, their traditional way of life gave them all the food they needed and an eminently satisfactory way of living in small, intimate groups. Free from tedious routine, their lives were often more exciting than those of farmers. Food could be hunted, gathered, or fished for as needed, but in most environments they could relax when they had enough to eat. Why raise crops through backbreaking work when the whole family could camp under a tree bearing tasty and nutritious nuts? Farming brings with it a whole new system of human relationships that offers no easily understood advantages, and disturbs an age-

old balance between humans and nature as well as the people who live together.

WHY HUMANS BECAME FOOD PRODUCERS

In view of what has been said so far, we may well ask: Why did any human group abandon food foraging in favor of food production?

Several theories have been proposed to account for this change in human subsistence practices. One older theory, championed by V. Gordon Childe, is the desiccation, or oasis, theory based on climatic determinism. Its proponents advanced the idea that the glacial cover over Europe and Asia caused a southern shift in rain patterns from Europe to northern Africa and Southwest Asia. When the glaciers retreated northward, so did the rain patterns. As a result, northern Africa and Southwest Asia became dryer, and people were forced to congregate at oases for water. Because of the scarcity of wild animals in such an environment, people were driven by necessity to collect the wild grasses and seeds growing around the oases. Eventually they had to cultivate the grasses to provide enough food for the community. According to this theory, animal domestication began because the oases attracted hungry animals, such as wild goats, sheep, and also cattle, which came to graze on the stubble of the grain fields. People, finding these animals too thin to kill for food, began to fatten them up.

In spite of its initial popularity, evidence in support of the oasis theory was not immediately forthcoming. Moreover, as systematic fieldwork into the origins of domestication began in the late 1940s, other theories gained favor. One of the pioneers in this work was Robert Braidwood of the University of Chicago, who proposed what is sometimes called the "hilly flanks" theory. Contrary to Childe, Braidwood argued that plants and animals were domesticated by people living in the hill country surrounding the Fertile Crescent (Figure 11.1). They had reached the point in their evolutionary development where they were beginning to "settle in"—that is, become more sedentary—a consequence of which was that they could become intimately familiar with the plants and animals around their settlements. Given the human

V. Gordon Childe *(1892–1957)*

This distinguished Australian, once the private secretary to the premier of New South Wales, became one of the most eminent British archaeologists. His knowledge of the archaeological sequences of Europe and the Middle East was unsurpassed, enabling him to write two of the most popular and influential descriptions of prehistory ever written: *Man Makes Himself* in 1936 and *What Happened in History*. In these, he described two great "revolutions" which added measurably to the capacity of humans to survive: the Neolithic and urban revolutions. The first of these transformed food foragers into farmers and brought with it a drastic reordering of society; populations increased, a cooperative group spirit arose, trade began on a large scale, and new religions arose to ensure the success of crops. This set the stage for the urban revolution, which transformed society from one of egalitarianism with a simple age-sex division of labor into one of social classes and organized political bodies. The result of these ideas was to generate a whole new interest in the evolution of human culture in general.

capacity and enthusiasm for experimentation, it was inevitable that they would have experimented with grasses and animals, bringing them under domestication. Problems with this theory include the ethnocentric notion that nonsedentary food foragers are not intimately familiar with the plants and animals on which they rely for survival, and its projection onto all human cultures of the great value Western culture places on experimentation and innovation for its own sake. In short, the theory was culture bound, strongly reflecting the notions of progress in which people in the Western world had such faith in the period following World War II.

Yet another theory that became popular in the 1960s is one in which population growth played a key role. In Southwest Asia, so this theory goes, people adapted to the cool, dry conditions of the last glacial period by developing a mixed pattern of resource utilization: They hunted such animals as were available, harvested wild cereal grasses, gathered nuts, and collected a wide variety of birds, turtles, snails, crabs, and mussels. They did so well that their populations grew, requiring the development of new ways of providing sufficient food. The result, especially in marginal situations where wild foods were least abundant, was to improve productivity through the domestication of plants and animals.

Just as there are problems with Braidwood's theory, so are there problems with this one. The most serious is that it requires an intentional decision on the part of the people involved to become producers of domestic crops, whereas, as we have already seen, domestication (as illustrated by ant farmers) does not require intentional design. Furthermore, prior to domestication, people could have had no way of knowing that plants and animals could be so radically transformed as to permit a food-producing way of life (even today, the long-term outcome of plant breeding cannot be predicted). Finally, even if people had wanted to become producers of their own food, there is no way such a decision could have had an immediate and perceptible effect; in fact, a complete switch to food production took more than a thousand years to accomplish. Although this may seem a relatively short period of time compared to the 200,000 or 300,000 years since the appearance of *H. sapiens,*

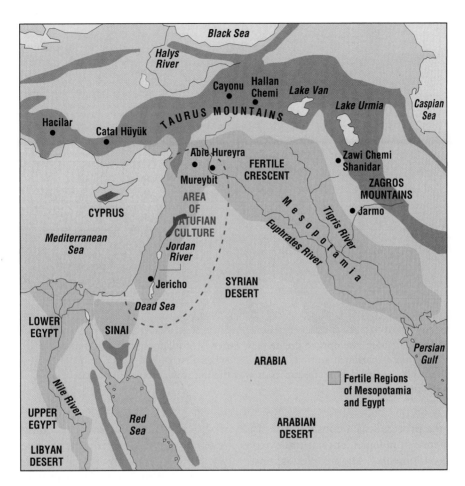

FIGURE 11.1

In Southwest Asia, early domestication of plants began in the area of Natufian culture, whereas animal domestication began in the Taurus and Zagros Mountains.

it was still too long to have made any difference to people faced with immediate food shortages. Under such conditions, the usual response among food foragers is to make use of a wider variety of foods than before, which acts as a brake on domestication by diverting attention from potential domesticates, while alleviating the immediate problem.

Another theory, in accord with the evidence as we now know it, but also more in accord with the role played by chance both in evolution (Chapter 3) and in cultural innovation, takes us back to some of the ideas of Childe, who, as it turns out, guessed what the environmental circumstances were, even though he didn't fully understand the

process. We now know that the earliest plant domestication took place in the lands just east of the Mediterranean Sea (Figure 11.1). As early as 13,000 years ago people living at a site (Abu Hureyra) east of Aleppo, Syria, were growing domestic rye, although they otherwise continued to rely heavily on wild plants and animals for food. Not until 3 millennia later did they become full-fledged farmers.[5] By 10,300 years ago, however, others in the region were also domesticating plants.

---

[5]Pringle, H. (1998). The slow birth of agriculture. *Science, 282,* 1449.

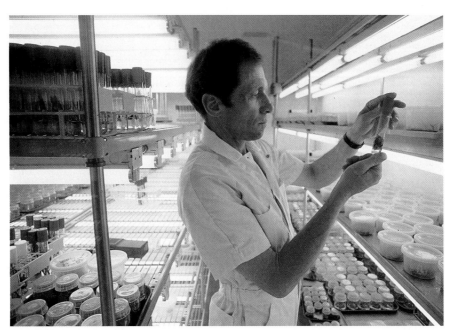

Today, deliberate attempts to create new varieties of plants take place in many a greenhouse, experiment station, or lab. But when first begun, the creation of domestic plants was not deliberate; rather, it was the unforeseen outcome of traditional food foraging activities.

Evidently, the process was a consequence of a chance convergence of independent natural events and cultural developments.[6] The people responsible were the Natufians, whose culture we looked at briefly in the preceding chapter. These people lived at a time of dramatically changing climates in the region. With the end of the last glaciation, climates not only became significantly warmer, but markedly seasonal as well. Between 12,000 and 6,000 years ago, the region experienced the most extreme seasonality in its history, with summer aridity significantly longer and more pronounced than today. As a consequence of increased evaporation, many shallow lakes dried up, leaving just three in the Jordan River Valley. At the same time, the region's plant cover changed dramatically. Those plants best adapted to environmental instability and seasonal aridity were annuals, including wild cereal grains and legumes (plants that

fix nitrogen in the soil, including peas, lentils, chickpeas, and bitter vetch). Such plants can evolve very quickly under unstable conditions, since they complete their life cycle in a single year. Moreover, they store their reproductive abilities for the next wet season in abundant seeds, which can remain dormant for prolonged periods.

The Natufians, who lived where these conditions were especially severe, adapted by modifying their subsistence practices in two ways: They probably regularly fired the landscape to promote browsing by red deer and grazing by gazelles, the main focus of their hunting activities; and they placed greater emphasis on the collection of wild seeds from the increasingly abundant annual plants that could be effectively stored to see people through the dry season. The importance of stored foods, coupled with the scarcity of reliable water sources, promoted more sedentary living patterns, reflected in the substantial villages of late Natufian times. The greater importance of seeds in Natufian subsistence was made possible by the fact that they already possessed sickles for harvesting grain and grinding stones for processing seeds. The grinding

---

[6]McCorriston, J., & Hole, F. (1991). The ecology of seasonal stress and the origins of agriculture in the Near East. *American Anthropologist, 93,* 46–69.

Stands of wild wheat are still to be found in parts of the Middle East.

stones were used originally to process a variety of wild foods, while the sickles may originally have served to procure nonfood plants such as sedges or reeds used to make baskets and mats (Natufian sites yielding large numbers of sickles tend to be located near coastal marshes and swamps).[7] Thus, these implements were not invented to enable people to become farmers, even though they turned out to be useful for that purpose.

The use of sickles to harvest grain turned out to have important consequences, again unexpected, for the Natufians. In the course of harvesting, it was inevitable that many easily dispersed seeds would be "lost" at the harvest site, whereas those from plants that did not readily scatter their seeds would mostly be carried back to where people processed and stored them.[8] Genetic mutations against easy dispersal would inevitably arise in the wild stocks, but would be at a competitive disadvantage compared to variants

that could readily disperse their seeds. Moreover, the rate of this and other mutations potentially useful to human consumers might have been unknowingly increased by the periodic firing carried out to promote the deer and gazelle herds, for heat is known to be an effective mutagenic agent, and fire can drastically and quickly change gene frequencies. In any event, with seeds for nondispersing variants being carried back to settlements, it was inevitable that some lost seeds would germinate and grow there on dump heaps and other disturbed sites (latrines, areas cleared of trees, or burned over). As it turns out, many of the plants that became domesticated were colonizers, which do particularly well in disturbed habitats. Moreover, with people becoming increasingly sedentary, disturbed habitats became more extensive as resources in proximity to settlements were depleted over time; thus variants of plants particularly susceptible to human manipulation had more and more opportunity to flourish where people were living and where they would inevitably attract attention. Under such circumstances, it was inevitable that people sooner or later would begin to actively promote their growth, even by deliberately sowing them, especially as people otherwise had to travel farther afield to procure the resources

[7]Olszewski, D. I. (1991). Comment. *Current Anthropology, 32,* 43.

[8]Blumer, M. A., & Byrne, R. (1991). The ecological genetics and domestication and the origins of agriculture. *Current Anthropology, 32,* 30.

that were depleted near their villages. An inevitable consequence of increased human manipulation would be the appearance of other mutant strains of particular benefit. For example, barley, which in its wild state can be tremendously productive but difficult to harvest and process, had developed the tougher stems that make it easier to harvest by 9,000 years ago; by 8,000 years ago "naked" barley, which is easier to process, was common, and by 7,500 years ago six-row barley, which is more productive than the original two-row, was widespread. Sooner or later, people realized that they could play a more active role in the process by deliberately trying to breed more useful strains. With this, domestication may be said to have shifted from a process that was unintentional to one that was intentional.

The development of animal domestication in Southwest Asia seems to have proceeded along somewhat similar lines but in the hilly country of Southeast Turkey, northern Iraq, and the Zagros Mountains of Iran (Figure 11.1). In the latter two regions were to be found large herds of wild sheep and goats, as well as much environmental diversity. From the low, alluvial plains of the valley of the Tigris and Euphrates rivers, for example, travel to the north or east takes one into the high country through three other zones: first steppe, then oak and pistachio woodlands, and, finally high plateau country with grass, scrub, or desert vegetation. Valleys that run at right angles to the mountain ranges afford relatively easy access between these zones. Today, a number of pastoral peoples in the region practice a pattern of **transhumance,** in which they graze their herds of sheep and goats on the low steppe in the winter and move to high pastures on the plateaus in the summer.

Moving 12,000 years backward in time to the Mesolithic, we find that the region was inhabited by peoples whose subsistence pattern, like that of the Natufians, was one of food foraging. Different plants were found in different ecological zones and, because of the difference in altitude, plant foods matured at different times in different zones. The animals hunted for meat and hides by these people included several species, among them bear, fox, boar, and wolf. Most notable, though, were the hoofed animals: deer, gazelles, wild goats, and wild sheep. Their bones are far more common in

Although sheep and goats were first valued for their meat, hides, and sinew, the changes wrought by domestication made them useful for other purposes as well. This impression, from a 4,500-year-old seal, shows a goat being milked.

Transhumance. Among pastoralists, the grazing of sheep and goats in low steppe lands in the winter and then moving to high pastures on the plateaus in the summer.

human refuse piles than those of other animals. This is significant, for most of these animals are naturally transhumant in the region, moving back and forth from low winter pastures to high summer pastures. People followed these animals in their seasonal migrations, making use along the way of other wild foods in the zones through which they passed: dates in the lowlands; acorns, almonds, and pistachios higher up; apples and pears higher still; wild grains maturing at different times in different zones; woodland animals in the forested zone between summer and winter grazing lands. All in all, it was a rich, varied fare.

There was in hunting, then, a concentration on hoofed animals, including wild sheep and goats, which provided meat and hides. At first, animals of all ages and sexes were hunted. But, beginning about 11,000 years ago, the percentage of immature sheep eaten, for example, increased to about 50% of the total. At the same time, the percentage frequency of females among animals eaten decreased. Apparently, people were learning that they could increase yields by sparing the females for breeding, while feasting on ram lambs.

This marks the beginning of human management of sheep. As this management of flocks became more and more efficient, sheep were increasingly shielded from the effects of natural selection. Eventually, they were introduced into areas outside their natural habitat. So we find sheep and goats being kept by farmers at ancient Jericho, in the Jordan River Valley, 8,000 years ago (by which time farming, too, had spread from its original homeland far to the north into Turkey and far to the east into the Zagros Mountains). As a consequence of this human intervention, variants that usually were not successful in the wild were able to survive and reproduce. Although variants that were perceived as being of immediate advantage would have attracted peoples' attention, they did not arise out of need, but independently of it at random, as mutations do. In such a way did those features characteristic of domestic sheep, such as greater fat and meat production, excess wool (Figure 11.2), and so on, begin to develop. By 9,000 years ago, the bones of domestic sheep had become distinguishable from those of wild sheep.

FIGURE 11.2
Domestication of sheep resulted in evolutionary changes that created more wool. Drawing A shows a section, as seen through a microscope, of skin of wild sheep, showing the arrangement of primary (hair) and secondary (wool) follicles. Drawing B shows a section of similarly enlarged skin of domestic sheep, showing the changed relationship and the change in size of follicles that accompanied the development of wool.

At about the same time that these events were happening, similar developments were taking place in southeastern Turkey, where pigs were the focus of attention.[9] Here, an increase in pig bones in human trash, coupled with a heavy bias in favor of very young animals, is indicative of a taste for suckling pigs and the beginning of stock management by 10,500 years ago.

To sum up, the domesticators of plants and animals sought only to maximize the food sources available to them. They were not aware of the revolutionary consequences their actions were to have. But as the process continued, the productivity of the domestic species increased relative to wild species. Thus they became increasingly more important to subsistence, resulting in further intensification of interest in, and management of, the domesticates. Inevitably, the result would be further increases in productivity.

OTHER CENTERS OF DOMESTICATION

In addition to Southwest Asia, the domestication of plants and, in some cases, animals took place independently in Southeast Asia, parts of the Americas (southern Mexico, Peru, the tropical forests of South America, and eastern North America), northern China, and Africa (Figure 11.3). In China, domestication of rice was underway along the middle Yangtze River, by about 11,000 years ago.[10] It was not until 4,000 years later, however, that domestic rice dominated wild rice to become the dietary staple.

In Southeast Asia the oldest domestic plant so far identified is rice, in pottery dated to sometime

---

[9]Pringle, p. 1448.

[10]Ibid., p. 1449.

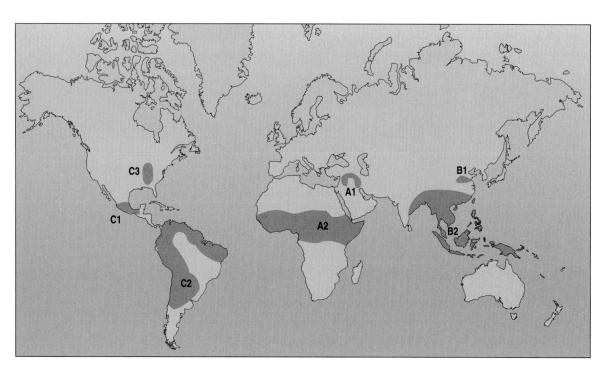

FIGURE 11.3

Early plant and animal domestication took place in such widely scattered areas as Southwest Asia (A1), Central Africa (A2), China (B1), Southeast Asia (B2), Mesoamerica (C1), South America (C2), and North America (C3).

between 8,800 and 5,000 years ago. What was distinctive in this region, however, was domestication of root crops, most notably yams and taro. Root crop farming, or **vegeculture**, typically involves the growing of many different species together in a single field. Because this approximates the complexity of the natural vegetation, vegeculture tends to be more stable than seed crop cultivation. Propagation (as in the case of the fungi-farming ants discussed earlier) is by vegetative means—the planting of cuttings—rather than the planting of seeds.

In the Americas, the domestication of plants began about as early as it did in these other regions. One species of domestic squash may have been grown as early as 10,000 years ago in the coastal forests of Ecuador at the same time another species was being grown in an arid region of highland Mexico.[11] Evidently, these developments were independent of one another. Other crops were eventually added later; the earliest occurrence of maize, for example, is from deposits in Panama dated 7,700 years ago. Since its place of origin lies somewhere in the highlands of western Mexico, it must have appeared somewhat earlier there. Ultimately, native Americans domesticated over three hundred food crops, including two of the four most important ones in the world today: potatoes and maize (the other two are wheat and rice). In fact, 60% of the crops grown in the world today were invented by American Indians, who not only remain the developers of the world's largest array of nutritious foods, but are also the primary contributors to the world's varied cuisines.[12] After all, where would Italian cuisine be without tomatoes? Thai cooking without the peanut? Northern European cooking without the potato? Or Chinese cooking without the sweet potato, which became the daily food of peasants but is also used to make noodles rivaling in popularity those made of wheat? Small wonder American Indians have been called the world's greatest farmers.[13]

[11]Ibid., p. 1447.

[12]Weatherford, J. (1988). *Indian givers: How the Indians of the Americas transformed the world* (pp. 71 and 115). New York: Fawcett Columbine.

[13]Ibid., p. 95.

CULTIGENS		Hunting	Horti-culture	Wild plant use	BC
Squash Chili Amaranth Avocado	Cotton Maize Beans Gourd Sapote	29%		31%	1000 1500 2000
Squash Chili Amaranth Avocado	Maize Beans Gourd Sapote	25%		50%	2500 3000
Squash Chili Amaranth Avocado	Maize Beans Gourd Sapote	34%		52%	3500 4000 4500
Squash Chili Amaranth Avocado		54%		40%	5000 5500 6000 6500

FIGURE 11.4

Subsistence trends in Tehuacan Valley show that here, as elsewhere, dependence on horticulture came about gradually, over a prolonged period of time.

Archaeological evidence for the beginning of farming in Mexico comes from the highland valleys of Oaxaca, Puebla, and Tamaulipas. In the Tehuacan Valley of Puebla, for example, crops such as maize, beans, and squash very gradually came to make up a greater percentage of the food eaten (see Figure 11.4). Like the hill country of Southwest Asia, the Tehuacan Valley is environmentally diverse, and the people living there had a cyclical pattern of hunting and gathering that made use of the resources of different environmental zones. In the course of their seasonal movements, people carried the wild precursors of future domesticates out of their native habitat, exposing them to different selective pressures. Under

Vegeculture. The cultivation of domesticated root crops, such as yams and taro.

anthropology applied   Archaeology for and by Native Americans

In the Americas, the practice of archaeology is closely tied to Native Americans because it is their ancestors who were responsible for the record those archaeologists seek to investigate. Yet, relationships between native people and archaeologists have not always been easy. Part of the problem has to do with power relationships: Archaeologists have been members of a dominant society with a long record of appropriating native lands and resources while denying native people political and even human rights. To have nonnative scholars appropriate their cultural heritage, while collecting their sacred objects and even the bodies of their ancestors, was the last straw. This is not to say that all archaeologists were insensitive to native concerns, but all too often the aims of the discipline and the interests of those whose past was being studied were at odds.

As a consequence, some native people today want nothing to do with archaeology and those who practice it. Others, however, recognize that archaeology can serve their own interests. Today, there are more than 43 tribes or native communities in 23 states that conduct their own archaeological research. At the same time, nonnative archaeologists have become more sensitive to native concerns, and have been actively working to reconcile those interests with those of science. The result is that opportunities have been opened for fruitful collaboration. Today, a number of archaeologists are actually employed by native organizations, and programs have been set up to train native people themselves in archaeology.

One archaeologist who has worked for native organizations, including the Hopi tribe and the Pueblo of Zuni in Arizona and New Mexico is T. J. Ferguson.* He points out that there are many reasons that American Indians need archaeology. A major one is that archeologists are needed to implement the National Historic Preservation Act and other federal legislation governing archaeological research. Many natives, too, are genuinely interested in uncovering their own history, using archaeological evidence to litigate land and water claims, attaining intellectual parity with non-Indian researchers, facilitating development on Indian lands, retaining financial benefits from mandated archaeology, and maintaining tribes' political sovereignty by controlling the management and protection of their own cultural resources and burials. There are benefits for the archaeologist as well. Ferguson has found working for native people to be personally rewarding, as it has resulted in modification of scientific values he learned in graduate school. This has not, however, prevented him from making important contributions to the profession. Moreover, it generates all sorts of new and fruitful research questions to pursue.

---

*Ferguson, T. J. (1996, November). *Archaeology for and by Native Americans.* Paper presented at the 95th Annual Meeting of the American Anthropological Association, San Francisco, CA.

---

such circumstances, potentially useful (to humans) variants that did not do well in the native habitat would, by chance, do well in novel settings, again (as in Southwest Asia) attracting human attention.

The change to food production also took place in South America, including the highlands of Peru; again, an environmentally diverse region. While a number of crops first grown in Mexico eventually came to be grown here, there was greater emphasis on root crops, the best known being potatoes (of which about 3,000 varieties were grown, versus the mere 250 grown today in North America), sweet potatoes, and manioc (originally developed in the tropics). South Americans domesticated guinea pigs, llamas, alpacas, and ducks, whereas the Mexicans never did much with domestic livestock. They limited themselves to dogs, turkeys, and bees.

Domestic plants were useful for purposes other than food. This illustration from a 16th-century Aztec manuscript shows a woman threatening her child with punishment by being exposed to smoke from chili peppers. Chili smoke was also used as a kind of chemical weapon in warfare.

Although the Native Americans living north of Mexico ultimately adopted several crops, such as maize and beans, from their southern neighbors, this occurred after they developed some of their own, indigenous domesticates. These included local varieties of squash and sunflower (today, grown widely in Russia as a reliable source of edible oil). Other native crops such as lambsquarter and sumpweed reverted to the wild as preferred foods appeared from Mexico.

Considering all of the separate innovations of domestic plants, it is interesting to note that in all cases people developed the same categories of foods. Everywhere, starchy grains (or root crops) are accompanied by one or more legumes; wheat and barley with peas, chickpeas, bitter vetch, and lentils in Southwest Asia; or maize with various kinds of beans in Mexico, for example. The starchy grains are the core of the diet, and are eaten at every meal in the form of bread, some sort of food "wrapper" (like a tortilla), or a gruel or thickening agent in a stew along with one or more legumes. Being rather bland, these sources of carbohydrates and proteins are invariably combined with flavor-giving substances that help the food go down. In Mexico, for example, the flavor enhancer par excellence is the chili pepper; in other cuisines it may be a bit of meat, a dairy product, mushrooms, or whatever. Anthropologist Sidney Mintz refers to this as the core-fringe-legume pattern (CFLP), noting that only recently has it been upset by the worldwide spread of processed sugars and high-fat foods.[14]

THE SPREAD OF FOOD PRODUCTION

Although population growth and the need to feed more people cannot explain the origin of the food-producing way of life, it does have a lot to do with its subsequent spread. As already noted, domestication inevitably leads to higher yields, and higher yields make it possible to feed more people. In addition, unlike most food foragers, farmers have available a variety of foods that are soft enough to be fed to infants. Hence, farmers do not need

[14]Mintz, S. (1996). A taste of history. In W. A. Haviland and R. J. Gordon (Eds.), Talking about people (2nd ed., pp. 81–82). Mountain View, CA: Mayfield.

to nurse their children so intensively nor for so many years. In humans, prolonged nursing, so long as it involves frequent stimulation of the nipple by the infant, has a dampening effect on ovulation. As a result, women in food-foraging societies are less likely to become fertile as soon after childbirth as they are in food-producing societies. Coupled with this, having too many children to care for at once interferes with the foraging activities of women in hunting, gathering, and fishing societies. Among farmers, however, numerous children are frequently seen as assets, to help out with the many household chores. Small wonder, then, that increased dependence on farming is associated with increased fertility across human populations.[15]

Paradoxically, while domestication increases productivity, so does it increase instability. This is so because those varieties with the highest yields become the focus of human attention, while other varieties are less valued and ultimately ignored. As a result, farmers become dependent on a rather narrow range of resources, compared to the wide range utilized by food foragers. Modern agriculturists, for example, rely on about 20 crops, versus the more than 100 species regarded as edible by the Bushmen of Africa's Kalahari Desert. This

dependence upon fewer varieties means that when a crop fails, for whatever reason, farmers have less to fall back on than do food foragers. Furthermore, the likelihood of failure is increased by the common farming practice of planting crops together in one locality, so that a disease contracted by one plant can easily spread to others. Moreover, by relying on seeds from the most productive plants of a species to establish next year's crop, farmers favor genetic uniformity over diversity. The result is that if some virus, bacterium, or fungus is able to destroy one plant, it will likely destroy them all. This is what happened in the famous Irish potato famine of 1845–1846, which sent waves of Irish immigrants to the United States.

The Irish potato famine illustrates how the combination of increased productivity and vulnerability may contribute to the geographical spread of farming. Time and time again in the past, population growth followed by crop failures has triggered movements of people from one place to another, where they have reestablished the subsistence practices with which they were familiar. Thus, once farming came into existence, it was more or less guaranteed that it would spread to neighboring regions (see Figure 11.5). From Southwest Asia, for instance, it spread to southeastern Europe by 8,000 years ago, reaching Central Europe and the Netherlands by 4,000 years ago, and England between 4,000 and 3,000 years ago.

---

[15]Sellen, D. W., & Mace, R. (1997). Fertility and mode of subsistence: A phylogenetic analysis. *Current Anthropology, 38*, 886.

FIGURE 11.5
Population growth has a tendency to follow increases in farming yields. Inevitably, this results in too large a population to be fed when crops fail, as they periodically do. The result is an outward migration of people to other regions.

Those who brought crops to Europe brought other things as well, including new alleles for human gene pools. As a consequence, those modern Europeans who most resemble their Upper Paleolithic predecessors are to be found around the northern fringes of the region.[16] Early farmers likely introduced languages ancestral to most of today's European languages as well, leaving Basque (spoken today on the Atlantic coast where France and Spain meet) as the sole survivor of languages once spoken by earlier Mesolithic people.

From Southwest Asia, farming also spread westward in North Africa and eastward to India. Here, crops domesticated in the west met those spreading from Southeast Asia, some of which spread farther west. Facilitating this east-west exchange was the fact that localities shared the same seasonal variations in day length and more or less the same diseases, temperature, and rainfall.

In sub-Saharan Africa, a similar spread occurred, and accounts for the modern distribution of speakers of Bantu languages. Crops including sorghum (so valuable today it is grown in hot, dry areas on all continents), pearl millet, watermelon, black-eyed peas, African yams, oil palms, and kola nuts (source of modern cola drinks) were first domesticated in West Africa, but began spreading east by 5,000 years ago.

Between 3,000 and 2,000 years ago Bantu speakers with their crops reached the east coast, and a few centuries later, reached the Great Fish River, 500 miles east of Capetown. Being well adapted to summer rains, African crops spread no farther, for the Cape has a Mediterranean climate with winter rains.

In some instances, farming appears to have been adopted by food foragers from food-producing neighbors. By way of illustration, a crisis developed on the coast of Peru some 4,500 years ago as continental uplift caused lowering of the water table and destruction of marine habitats at a time of growing population; the result was an increasing shortage of the wild food resources on which people depended. Their response was to be-

---

[16]Brace, C. L. (1997). Cro-Magnons "Я" us? *Anthropology Newsletter*, 38(8), 2.

In coastal Peru, the earliest domesticates were the nonedible bottle gourd (like the one shown here) and cotton. They were used to make nets and floats to catch fish, which was an important source of food.

gin growing along the edges of rivers many of the domestic plants that their highland neighbors to the east had begun to cultivate a few thousand years earlier. Here, then, farming appears to have been a subsistence practice of last resort, which a food-foraging people took up only because they had no real choice.

CULTURE OF NEOLITHIC SETTLEMENTS

A number of Neolithic settlements have been excavated, particularly in Southwest Asia. The structures, artifacts, and food debris found at these sites have revealed much about the daily activities of their former inhabitants as they pursued the business of making a living.

EARLIEST FULL-FLEDGED FARMING SETTLEMENTS

The earliest known sites containing domesticated plants and animals found in Southwest Asia date mostly between 10,300 and 9,000 years ago. These sites occur in a region extending from the Jordan Valley northward across the Taurus Mountains into Turkey, eastward across the flanks of the Taurus Mountains into northeastern Iran, and southward into Iraq and Iran along the hilly flanks of the Zagros Mountains. The sites contain evidence of domesticated barley, wheat, peas, chickpeas, bitter vetch, lentils, flax, goats, sheep, dogs, and pigs.

These sites are generally the remains of small village farming communities—small clusters of houses built of mud, each with its own storage pit and clay oven. Their occupants continued to use stone tools of Mesolithic type, plus a few new types of use in farming. Probably the people born into these communities spent their lives in them in a common effort to make their crops grow and their animals prosper. At the same time, they participated in long-distance trade networks. Obsidian found at Jarmo, Iraq, for instance, was imported from 300 miles away.

JERICHO: AN EARLY FARMING COMMUNITY

At the Neolithic settlement which later grew to become the biblical city of Jericho, excavation has revealed the remains of a sizable farming community occupied as early as 10,350 years ago. Located in the Jordan River Valley, what made the site attractive was the presence of a bounteous spring and the rich soils of an Ice Age lake that had dried up some 3,000 years earlier. Here, crops could be grown almost continuously, since the fertility of the

soil was regularly renewed by flood-borne deposits originating in the Judean Highlands, to the west.

Neolithic farming communities, such as Jericho in the Jordan River Valley, were made possible by the result of the domestication of plants and animals. Jericho was surrounded by a stone wall as protection against floods. The wall included a tower (left). People lived in substantial houses (right).

To protect their settlement against these floods and associated mudflows, the people of Jericho built massive walls of stone around it.[17] Within these walls, an estimated 400 to 900 people lived in houses of mud brick with plastered floors arranged around courtyards. In addition to these houses, a stone tower that would have taken 100 people 104 days to build was located inside one corner of the wall, near the spring. A staircase inside it probably led to a mud brick building on top. Nearby were mud brick storage facilities as well as peculiar structures of possible ceremonial significance. A village cemetery also reflects the sedentary life of these early people; nomadic groups, with few exceptions, rarely buried their dead in a single central location.

Evidence of domestic plants and animals is scant at Jericho. However, indirect evidence in the form of harvesting tools and milling equipment has been uncovered at the site, and wheat, barley, and other domestic plants are known from sites of similar age in the region. We do know that the people of Jericho were keeping sheep and goats by 8,000 years ago, although some hunting still went on. Some of the meat from wild animals may have been supplied by food-foraging peoples whose campsites have been found everywhere in the desert of the Arabian peninsula. Close contacts between these people and the farmers of Jericho and other villages are indicated by common features in art, ritual, use of prestige goods, and burial practices. Other evidence of trade consists of obsidian and turquoise from Sinai as well as marine shells from the coast, all discovered inside the walls of Jericho.

NEOLITHIC TECHNOLOGY

Early harvesting tools were made of wood or bone into which serrated flints were inserted. Later tools continued to be made by chipping and flaking stone, but during the Neolithic period, stone that was too hard to be chipped was ground and polished for tools (Figure 11.6). People developed scythes, forks, hoes, and plows to replace their

simple digging sticks. Pestles and mortars were used for preparation of grain. Plows were later redesigned when, after 8,000 years ago, domesticated cattle became available for use as draft animals.

Pottery

In addition to the domestication of plants and animals, one of the characteristics of the Neolithic period is the extensive manufacture and use of pottery. In food-foraging societies, most people are involved in the food quest. In food-producing societies, even though people have to work as long—if not longer—at subsistence activities than food foragers, the whole community need not be involved in the food quest. Hard work on the part of those producing the food may free other members of the society to devote their energies to other craft specialties. One such craft is pottery making, and different forms of pottery were created for transporting and storing food, artifacts, and other material possessions. Because pottery vessels are impervious to damage by insects, rodents, and dampness, they could be used for storing small grain, seeds, and other materials. Moreover, food can be boiled in pottery vessels directly over the fire rather than by such ancient techniques as dropping stones heated directly in the fire into the food being cooked. Pottery is also used for pipes, ladles, lamps, and other objects, and some cultures

In the Middle East, pigs were under domestication as early as 10,500 to 11,000 years ago in southeastern Turkey. This pottery vessel, also from Turkey, was made much later, around 7,600 years ago.

---

[17]Bar-Yosef, O. (1986). The walls of Jericho: An alternative interpretation. *Current Anthropology, 27,* 160.

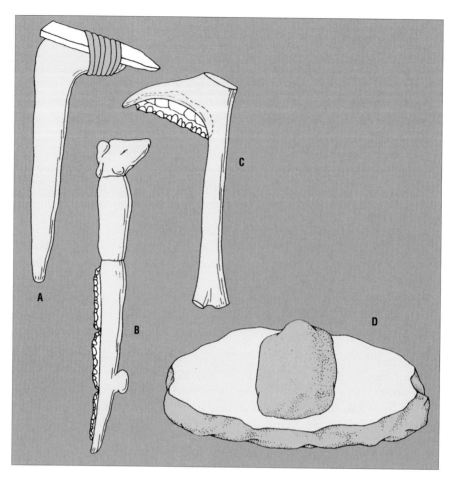

FIGURE 11.6

In Southwest Asia, many tools fabricated by Neolithic peoples made use of flint microliths in bone or wood handles, as had been done in the Mesolithic, but some tools were made of ground and polished stone.

used large vessels for burial of the dead. Significantly, pottery containers remain important for much of humanity today.

Widespread use of pottery, which is manufactured of clay and fired, is a good, though not foolproof, indication of a sedentary community. It is found in abundance in all but a few of the earliest Neolithic settlements. At ancient Jericho, for example, the earliest Neolithic people lacked pottery. Its fragility and weight make it impractical for use by nomads and hunters, who use baskets and hide containers. Nevertheless, there are some modern nomads who make and use pottery, just as there are farmers who lack it. In fact, food for-

agers in Japan were making pottery by 13,000 years ago, long before it was being made in Southwest Asia.

The manufacture of pottery is a difficult art and requires a high degree of technological sophistication. To make a useful vessel requires knowledge of clay and the techniques of firing or baking. Neolithic pots, for example, are often coarse and ill-made because of improper clay mixture or faulty firing technique.

Pottery is decorated in various ways. For example, designs can be engraved on the vessel before firing, or special rims, legs, bases, and other details may be made separately and fastened to the finished pot. Painting is the most common form of pottery decoration, and there are literally thousands of painted designs found among the pottery remains of ancient cultures.

Housing

Food production and the new sedentary lifestyle engendered another technological development—house building. Permanent housing is of limited interest to food foragers who usually are on the move. Cave shelters, pits dug in the earth, and simple lean-tos made of hides and tree limbs serve their purpose of keeping the weather out. In the Neolithic, however, dwellings became more complex in design and more diverse in type. Some, like Swiss Lake Dwellings, were constructed of wood, housed several families per building, had doors, and contained beds, tables, and other furniture. More elaborate shelters were made of stone, sundried brick, or branches plastered together with mud or clay.

Although permanent housing frequently goes along with food production, there is evidence that one can have substantial houses without food pro-

duction. For example, on the northwest coast of North America, people lived in substantial houses made of heavy planks hewn from cedar logs. Yet their food consisted entirely of wild plants and animals, especially fish.

Clothing

During the Neolithic, for the first time in human history, clothing was made of woven textiles. The raw materials and technology necessary for the production of clothing came from three sources: flax and cotton from farming, wool from domesticated sheep, and the spindle for spinning and the loom for weaving from the inventive human mind.

SOCIAL STRUCTURE

Evidence of all the economic and technological developments listed thus far has enabled archaeologists to draw certain inferences concerning the organization of Neolithic society. The general absence of elaborate buildings in all but a few settlements may suggest that neither religion nor government was yet a formally established institution

New ways of living based on food production included new attitudes toward the earth and forces of nature, sometimes reflected in monumental construction. One such is Stonehenge, the famous ceremonial and astronomical center in England, which dates back to about 2,500 B.C.

able to wield real social power. Although there is evidence of ceremonial activity, little evidence of a centrally organized and directed religious life has been found. Burials, for example, show a marked absence of patterning; variation seems to have been common. Since early Neolithic graves were rarely constructed of or covered by stone slabs and rarely included grave goods, it is believed that no person had attained the superior social status that would have required an elaborate funeral. The smallness of most villages suggests that the inhabitants knew each other very well, so that most of their relationships were probably highly personal ones, charged with emotional significance.

The general picture that emerges is one of an egalitarian society with little division of labor and probably little development of new and more specialized social roles. Villages seem to have been made up of several households, each providing for its own needs. The organizational needs of society beyond the household level were probably met by kinship groups and common-interest associations.

NEOLITHIC CULTURE IN THE NEW WORLD

Outside Mesoamerica (southern Mexico and northern Central America) and Peru, hunting, fishing, and the gathering of wild plant foods remained important elements in the economy of Neolithic peoples in the New World. Apparently, most American Indians never made a complete change from a food-foraging to a food-producing mode of life, even though maize and other domestic crops came to be cultivated just about everywhere that climate permitted. Farming developed independently of Europe and Asia, and the crops differed because of different natural conditions and cultural traits.

The Neolithic developed even more slowly in the New World than in the Old. For example, Neolithic agricultural villages were common in Southwest Asia between 9,000 and 8,000 years ago, but similar villages did not appear in the New World until about 4,500 years ago, in Mesoamerica and Peru. Moreover, pottery, which

arose in the Old World shortly after plant and animal domestication, did not develop in the New World until about 4,500 years ago. Neither the potter's wheel nor the loom and spindle were used by early Neolithic people in the New World. Both pottery and textiles were manufactured by hand; evidence of the loom and spindle does not appear in the New World until 3,000 years ago. None of these absences indicate any "backwardness" on the part of New World peoples, who, as we have already seen, were highly sophisticated farmers and plant breeders. Rather, older practices continued to be satisfactory for relatively long periods of time.

Textiles like this one, produced in Peru sometime between 500 and 200 B.C., remain unsurpassed anywhere in the world, even though weaving began later in the Americas than in some parts of the Old World.

THE NEOLITHIC AND HUMAN BIOLOGY

Although we tend to think of the invention of food production in terms of its cultural impact, it obviously had a biological impact as well. From studies of human skeletons from Neolithic burials, physical anthropologists have found evidence for a somewhat lessened mechanical stress on peoples' bodies and teeth. Although there are exceptions, the teeth of Neolithic peoples show less wear, their bones are less robust, and osteoarthritis (the result of stressed joint surfaces) is not as marked as in the skeletons of Paleolithic and Mesolithic peoples. On the other hand, there is clear evidence for a marked deterioration in health and mortality. Anthropologist Anna Roosevelt sums up our knowledge of this in the following Original Study.

History of Mortality and Physiological Stress[18]

Although there is a relative lack of evidence for the Paleolithic stage, enough skeletons have been studied that it seems clear that seasonal and periodic physiological stress regularly affected most prehistoric hunting-gathering populations, as evidenced by the presence of enamel hypoplasias [horizontal linear defects in tooth enamel] and Harris lines [horizontal lines near the ends of long bones]. What also seems clear is that severe and chronic stress, with high frequency of hypoplasias, infectious disease lesions, pathologies related to iron-deficiency anemia, and high mortality rates, is not characteristic of these early populations. There is no evidence of frequent, severe malnutrition, and so the diet must have been adequate in calories and other nutrients most of the time. During the Mesolithic, the proportion of starch in the diet rose, to judge from the increased occurrence of certain dental diseases, but not enough to create an impoverished diet. At this time, diets seem to have been made up of a rather large number of foods, so that the failure of one food source would not be catastrophic. There is a possible slight tendency for Paleolithic people to be healthier and taller than Mesolithic people, but there is no apparent trend toward increasing physiological stress during the Mesolithic. Thus, it seems that both hunter-gatherers and incipient agriculturalists regularly underwent population pressure, but only to a moderate degree.

During the periods when effective agriculture first comes into use, there seems to be a temporary upturn in health and survival rates in a few regions: Europe, North America, and the eastern Mediterranean. At this stage, wild foods are still consumed periodically and a variety of plants are cultivated, suggesting the availability of adequate amounts of different nutrients. Based on the increasing frequency of tooth disease related to high carbohydrate consumption, it seems that cultivated plants probably increased the storable calorie supply, removing for a time any seasonal or periodic

---

[18]Roosevelt, A. C. (1984). Population, health, and the evolution of subsistence: Conclusions from the conference. In M. N. Cohen & G. J. Armelagos (Eds.) *Paleopathology at the origins of agriculture* (pp. 572–574). Orlando, FL: Academic Press.

Harris lines near the ends of these youthful thigh bones, found in a prehistoric farming community in Arizona, are indicative of recovery after growth arrest, caused by famine or severe disease.

Enamel hypoplasias such as those shown on these teeth are indicative of arrested growth caused by severe disease or famine. The teeth are from an adult who lived in an ancient farming community in Arizona.

problems in food supply. In most regions, however, the development of agriculture seems not to have had this effect, and there seems to have been a slight increase in physiological stress.

Stress, however, does not seem to have become *common* and widespread until after the development of high degrees of sedentism, population density, and reliance on intensive agriculture. At this stage in all regions the incidence of physiological stress increases greatly, and average mortality rates increase appreciably. Most of these agricultural populations have high frequencies of porotic hyperostosis and cribra orbitalia [bone deformities indicative of chronic iron-deficiency anemia], and there is a substantial increase in the number and severity of enamel hypoplasias and pathologies associated with infectious disease. Stature in many populations appears to have been considerably lower than would be expected if genetically determined height maxima had been reached, which suggests that the growth arrests documented by pathologies were causing stunting. Accompanying these indicators of poor health and nourishment, there is a universal drop in the occurrence of Harris lines, suggesting a poor rate of full recovery from the stress. Incidence of carbohydrate-related tooth disease increases, apparently because subsistence by this time is characterized by a heavy emphasis on a few starchy food crops. Populations seem to have grown beyond the point at which wild food resources could be a meaningful dietary supplement, and even domestic animal resources were commonly reserved for farm labor and transport rather than for diet supplementation.

It seems that a large proportion of most sedentary prehistoric populations under intensive agriculture underwent chronic and life-threatening malnutrition and disease, especially during infancy and childhood. The causes of the nutritional stress are likely to have been the poverty of the staple crops in most nutrients except calories, periodic famines caused by the instability of the agricultural system, and chronic lack of food due to both population growth and economic expropriation by elites. The increases in infectious disease probably reflect both a poorer diet and increased interpersonal contact in crowded settlements, and it is, in turn, likely to have aggravated nutritional problems.

For the most part, the crops on which Neolithic peoples came to depend were selected for their higher productivity and storability rather than their nutritional value. Moreover, as already noted, their nutritional shortcomings would have been exacerbated by their susceptibility to periodic failure, particularly as populations grew in size. Thus, the worsened health and mortality of Neolithic peoples is not surprising. Some have gone so far as to assert that the switch from food foraging to food production was the worst mistake that humans ever made!

The chicken pox from which this child suffers is a direct consequence of the domestication of animals thousands of years earlier. Close and continuing contact with domestic stock allowed for the transfer of many animal diseases to humans.

Another key contributor to the increased incidence of disease and mortality was probably the new mode of life in Neolithic communities. Sedentary life in fixed villages brings with it sanitation problems that do not exist for small groups of people who move about from one campsite to another. Moreover, airborne diseases are more easily transmitted in such villages. Another factor, too, seems to have been close association between humans and their domestic animals, a situation conducive to the transmission of some animal diseases to humans. A host of life-threatening diseases, including smallpox, chicken pox, and in fact all of the infectious diseases of childhood that were not overcome by medical science until the latter half of the 20th century, were transmitted to humans through their close association with domestic animals.

Another example of the biological impact of food production on human biology is that of the abnormal hemoglobin responsible for sickle-cell anemia, discussed in Chapter 3. Other abnormal hemoglobins are associated with the spread of farming from Southwest Asia westward around the Mediterranean as well as eastward to India, and also with the spread of farming in Southeast Asia. In all these regions, changes in human gene pools took place as a biological response to malaria, which had become a problem as a result of farming practices.

Higher mortality rates in Neolithic villages were offset by increased fertility, for population growth accelerated dramatically at precisely the moment that health and mortality worsened. The factors responsible for this increased natality have already been discussed in this chapter.

THE NEOLITHIC AND THE IDEA OF PROGRESS

One of the more deeply held biases of Western culture is that human history is basically a record of steady progress over time. The transition from food foraging to food production is generally viewed as a great step upward on a supposed "ladder of progress." To be sure, farming allowed people to increase the size of their populations, to live together in substantial sedentary communities, and to reorganize the workload in ways that permitted craft specialization. If one chooses to regard this as "progress," that is fine—progress is, after all, whatever it is defined as, and different cultures define it differently.

Whatever the benefits of food production, however, a substantial price was paid. As anthropologists Mark Cohen and George Armelagos put it:

> Taken as a whole, indicators fairly clearly suggest an overall decline in the quality—and probably in the length—of human life associated with the adoption of agriculture. This decline was offset in some regions, but not in others, by a decline in physical demands on the body. The studies support recent ethnographic statements and theoretical arguments about the relatively good health and nutrition of hunter-gatherers. They also suggest that hunter-gatherers were relatively well buffered against episodic stress. These data call in question simplistic popular ideas about human progress. They also call in question models of human population growth that are based on assumed progressive in-

creases in life expectancy. The data suggest that the well documented expansion of early farming populations was accomplished in spite of general diminution of both child and adult life expectancy rather than being fueled by increased survivorship.[19]

Rather than imposing ethnocentric notions of progress on the archaeological record, it is best to view the advent of food production as but one more factor contributing to the diversification of cultures, something that had begun in the Paleolithic. While some societies continued to practice hunting, gathering, and fishing, others became **horticultural**—small communities of gardeners working with simple hand tools and using neither irrigation nor the plow. Horticulturists typically cultivate different varieties of crops in small gardens they have cleared by hand. Some horticultural societies, however, developed **intensive agriculture**. Technologically more complex than the horticulturalists, intensive agriculturalists employ such techniques as irrigation, fertilizers, and the wooden or metal plow pulled by two harnessed draft animals, such as oxen or water buffalo, to produce food on larger plots of land. The distinction between horticulturalist and intensive agriculturalist is not always an easy one to make. For example, the Hopi Indians of the North American Southwest traditionally employed irrigation in their farming, while at the same time using simple hand tools.

Some societies became specialized **pastoralists** in environments that were too dry, too grassy, too steep, or too cold for effective horticulture or intensive agriculture. For example, the Russian steppes, with their heavy grass cover, were not

---

[19]Cohen, M. N., & Armelagos, G. J. (1984). Paleopathology at the origins of agriculture: Editors' summation. In *Paleopathology at the origins of agriculture* (p. 594). Orlando FL: Academic Press.

Horticulture.   Cultivation of crops carried out with hand tools such as digging sticks or hoes. **> Intensive agriculture.**   Intensive farming of large plots of land, employing fertilizers, plows, and/or extensive irrigation. **> Pastoralists.**   People who rely on herds of domestic animals for their subsistence.

suitable to farming without a plow, but they were ideal for herding. Thus, a number of peoples living in the arid grasslands and deserts that stretch from North Africa into Central Asia kept large herds of domestic animals, relying on their neighbors for plant foods. Finally, some societies went on to develop civilizations—the subject of the next chapter.

CHAPTER SUMMARY

Throughout the Paleolithic, people were strictly food foragers moving from place to place as the food supply became exhausted. The change to food production, which (in Southwest Asia) was becoming widespread by 10,300 years ago, took place as people were becoming more sedentary, and allowed reorganization of the work load, freeing some people from the food quest to pursue other tasks. From the end of the Mesolithic, human groups became larger and more permanent as people turned to animal breeding and crop growing.

A domesticated plant or animal is one which has become genetically modified as an intended or unintended consequence of human manipulation. Analysis of plant and animal remains at a site will usually indicate whether or not its occupants were food producers. Wild cereal grasses, for example, usually have fragile stems, whereas cultivated ones have tough stems. Domesticated plants can also be identified because their edible parts are usually larger than those of their wild counterparts. Domestication produces skeletal changes in some animals. The horns of wild goats and sheep, for example, differ from those of domesticated ones. Age and sex imbalances in herd animals may also indicate manipulation by human domesticators.

Several theories have been proposed to account for the changes in the subsistence patterns of early humans. One theory, the "oasis" or "desiccation" theory, is based on climatic determination. Domestication began because the oasis attracted hungry animals, which were domesticated instead of killed by early humans. Although once popular, this theory fell out of favor as systematic studies of the origins of domestication were begun in the late 1940s. One alternative idea was that domestication began in the hilly flanks of the Fertile Crescent because culture was ready for it.

This somewhat culture-bound idea was replaced by theories, popular in the 1960s, that saw domestication as a response to population growth. However, this would require a deliberate decision on the part of people who could have had no prior knowledge of the long-range consequences of domestication. The most probable theory is that domestication came about as a consequence of a chance convergence of separate natural events and cultural developments. This happened independently even if at more or less similar times in Southwest and Southeast Asia, highland Mexico and Peru, South America's Amazon forest, eastern North America, China, and Africa. In all cases, however, people developed food complexes based on starchy grains and/or roots, which were consumed with protein-containing legumes plus some other flavor enhancers.

Two major consequences of domestication are that crops become more productive but also more vulnerable. This combination periodically causes population to outstrip food supplies, whereupon people are apt to move into new regions. In this way, farming has often spread from one region to another, as into Europe from Southwest Asia. Sometimes, food foragers will adopt the cultivation of crops from neighboring peoples, in response to the shortage of wild foods, as happened in ancient coastal Peru.

Among the earliest known sites containing domesticated plants and animals, about 10,300 to 9,000 years old, are those of Southwest Asia. These sites were mostly small villages of mud huts with individual storage pits and clay ovens. There is evidence not only of cultivation and domestication but also of trade. At ancient Jericho, remains of tools, houses, and clothing indicate the oasis was occupied by Neolithic people as early as 10,350 years ago. At its height, Neolithic

Jericho had a population of 400 to 900 people. Comparable villages developed independently in Mexico and Peru by about 4,500 years ago.

During the Neolithic, stone that was too hard to be chipped was ground and polished for tools. People developed scythes, forks, hoes, and plows to replace simple digging sticks. The Neolithic was also characterized by the extensive manufacture and use of pottery. The widespread use of pottery is a good indicator of a sedentary community; it is found in all but a few of the earliest Neolithic settlements. The manufacture of pottery requires a knowledge of clay and the techniques of firing or baking. Neolithic pottery is often coarse. Other technological developments that accompanied food production

and the sedentary life were the building of permanent houses and the weaving of textiles.

Archaeologists have been able to draw some inferences concerning the social structure of Neolithic society. No evidence has been found indicating that religion or government was yet a centrally organized institution. Society was probably egalitarian, with little division of labor and little development of specialized social roles.

The development of food production had biological, as well as cultural, consequences. New diets, living arrangements, and farming practices led to increased incidence of disease and higher mortality rates. Increased fertility of women, however, more than offset mortality.

POINTS FOR CONSIDERATION

1. Is food production more or less efficient as a lifestyle than food gathering? Why did it persist? What are the benefits?

2. What were the health implications of early food production? Are they all directly linked to diet? What other factors might a sedentary lifestyle create?

3. Why does domestication often lead to less hardy species? Why are domestic crops and livestock more vulnerable to hardship? What are the consequences? What are the benefits to the domesticated species?

4. What new opportunities did a sedentary life allow? What was the impact of agriculture on technology?

SUGGESTED READINGS

Childe, V. G. (1951). *Man makes himself*. New York: New American Library.

In this classic, originally published in 1936, Childe presented his concept of the "Neolithic Revolution." He places special emphasis on the technological inventions that helped transform humans from food gatherers to food producers.

Coe, S. D. (1994). *America's first cuisines*. Austin: University of Texas Press.

Writing in an accessible style, Coe discusses some of the more important crops grown by Native Americans, and explores their early history and domestication. Following this she

describes how these foods were prepared, served, and preserved by the Aztec, Maya, and Incas.

MacNeish, R. S. (1992). *The origins of agriculture and settled life*. Norman: University of Oklahoma Press.

MacNeish's work in Mexico is responsible for much of our knowledge of the beginning of food production in the New World. In this book, he reviews the evidence from around the world in order to develop general laws about the development of agriculture and evolution of settled life.

Rindos, D. (1984). *The origins of agriculture: An evolutionary perspective*. Orlando, FL: Academic Press.

This is the most important book on agricultural origins to appear in recent times. After identifying the weaknesses of existing theories, Rindos presents his own evolutionary theory of agricultural origins.

Wernick, R., et al. (1973). *The monument builders*. New York: Time-Life.

This volume of the Time-Life *Emergence of Man* series deals with the spread of the Neolithic to Europe and the emergence there of distinctive patterns of this way of life. Like all volumes in this series, it is richly illustrated and contains a useful bibliography.

Zohary, D., & Hopf, M. (1993). *Domestication of plants in the Old World* (2nd ed.). Oxford: Clarenden Press.

This book deals with the origin and spread of domestic plants in western Asia, Europe, and the Nile Valley. Included is a species-by-species discussion of the various crops, an inventory of remains from archaeological sites, and a conclusion summarizing present knowledge.

Chapter 12
THE RISE OF CITIES AND CIVILIZATION

ONE OF THE LARGEST CITIES OF THE ANCIENT WORLD
WAS TEOTIHUACAN IN CENTRAL MEXICO. AT ITS
HEIGHT, JUST BEFORE ITS VIOLENT END IN THE
8TH CENTURY A.D., A POPULATION OF 125,000 PEOPLE
MAY HAVE LIVED THERE. THIS PHOTO LOOKS
SOUTH DOWN THE CITY'S PRINCIPAL AVENUE, AN
URBAN AXIS UNEQUALLED IN ITS SCALE UNTIL
CONSTRUCTION OF SUCH MODERN-DAY AVENUES AS
THE CHAMPS ELYSÉES IN PARIS.

Chapter Preview

When and Where Did the World's First Cities First Develop?

Cities—urban settlements with well-defined nuclei, populations that are large, dense, and diversified both economically and socially—are characteristic of civilizations which developed initially in China, the Indus and Nile valleys, Mesopotamia, Mesoamerica, and Peru. The world's oldest cities were those of Mesopotamia, but one of the world's largest was located in Mesoamerica.

What Changes in Culture Accompanied the Rise of Cities?

Four basic culture changes mark the transition from Neolithic village life to that in civilized urban centers. These are agricultural innovation, as new farming methods were developed; diversification of labor, as more people were freed from food production to pursue a variety of full-time craft specialties; the emergence of centralized governments to deal with the new problems of urban life; and the emergence of social classes as people were ranked according to the work they did or the position of the families into which they were born.

Why Did Civilizations Develop in the First Place?

A number of theories have been proposed to explain why civilizations develop. Most have emphasized the interrelation of people and what they do on the one hand and their environment on the other. For example, some civilizations may have developed as populations grew, causing competition for space and scarce resources, which favored the development of centralized authority to control resources and organize warfare. Some civilizations, though, appear to have developed as a result of certain beliefs and values which brought people together into large, heavily populated centers, again encouraging centralized authority to manage the problems—of which there are many—of living in such a way. In some cases, too, the actions of powerful individuals to promote their own interests may have played a role. Thus, it may be that civilizations arose in different places for somewhat different reasons.

A walk down a street of a busy North American city brings us in contact with numerous activities that are essential to the well-being of North American society. The sidewalks are crowded with people going to and from offices and stores. The traffic of cars, taxis, and trucks is heavy, sometimes almost at a standstill. In a brief two-block stretch, there may be a department store, shops selling clothing, appliances, or books, a restaurant, a newsstand, a gasoline station, and a movie theater. Perhaps there will also be a museum, a police station, a school, a hospital, or a church. That is quite a number of services and specialized skills to find in such a small area.

Each of these services or places of business is dependent on others. A butcher shop, for instance, depends on slaughterhouses and beef ranches. A clothing store depends on designers, farmers who produce cotton and wool, and workers who manufacture synthetic fibers. Restaurants depend on refrigerated trucking and vegetable and dairy farmers. Hospitals depend on a great variety of other institutions to meet their more complex needs. All institutions, finally, depend on the public utilities—the telephone, gas, water, and electric companies. Although interdependence is not immediately apparent to the passerby, it is an important aspect of modern cities.

The interdependence of goods and services in a big city is what makes so many products readily available to people. For example, refrigerated air transport makes it possible to buy fresh California artichokes on the East Coast. This same interdependence, however, has undesirable effects if one service stops functioning, for example, because of strikes or bad weather. Thus, every so often, major North American cities have had to do without services as vital as newspapers, subways, schools, and trash removal. The question is not so much "Why does this happen?" but rather "Why doesn't it happen more often, and why does the city continue to function as well as it does when one of its services stops?" The answer is that services are not only interdependent, but they are also adaptable. When one breaks down, others take over its functions. During a long newspaper strike

in New York City in the 1960s, for example, several new magazines were launched and television expanded its coverage of news and events.

On the surface, city life seems so orderly that we take it for granted; but a moment's pause reminds us that the intricate fabric of city life did not always exist, and the goods which are widely accessible to us were once simply not available.

WHAT CIVILIZATION MEANS

This complicated system of goods and services available in such a small space is a mark of civilization itself. The history of civilization is intimately bound up with the history of cities. This does not mean that civilization is to be equated with modern industrial cities or with present-day North American society. People as diverse as the ancient preindustrial Aztecs of Mexico and the industrial North Americans of today are included in the term "civilization," but each represents a very different kind. It was with the development of the earliest preindustrial cities, however, that civilization first developed (Figure 12.1). In fact, the word comes from the Latin *civis*, which refers to one who is an inhabitant of a city, and *civitas*, which refers to the community in which one dwells. The word "civilization" contains the idea of "citification," or "the coming-to-be of cities."

Today, the term **civilization** has a very specific meaning in anthropology; it refers to societies in which one finds large numbers of people living in cities, who are socially stratified and are governed by centrally organized political systems called states. We shall elaborate on all of these points in the course of this chapter.

The world's first cities sprang up in some parts of the world as Neolithic villages of the sort discussed in Chapter 11 grew into towns, some of which in turn grew into cities. This happened first in Mesopotamia (in modern-day Iraq), then in Egypt and the Indus Valley, between 6,000 and 4,500 years ago. The inhabitants of Sumer, in southern Mesopotamia,

---

Civilization.   A type of society marked by the presence of cities, social classes, and the state.

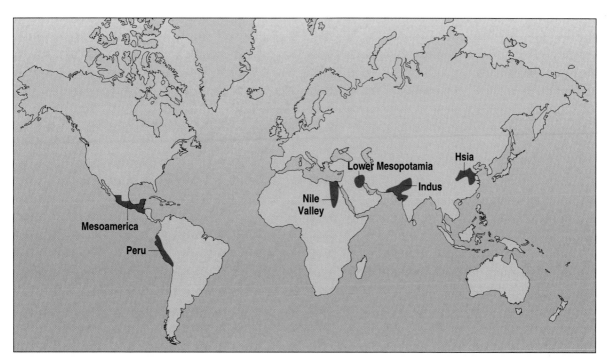

FIGURE 12.1

The major early civilizations sprang from Neolithic villages in various parts of the world. Those of North and South America developed wholly independently of those in Africa and Asia; Chinese civilization seems to have developed independently of Southwest Asia (including the Nile and Indus) civilizations.

developed the world's first civilization about 5,500 years ago. In China, civilization was under way by 5,000 years ago. Independent of these developments in the Old World, the first cities appeared in Mesoamerica and Peru between 3,000 and 2,000 years ago.

What characterized these first cities? Why are they called the birthplaces of civilization? The first characteristic of cities—and of civilization—is their large size and population. But is this all that a city is? Consider the case of Çatal Hüyük, a 9,000-year-old settlement in south-central Turkey (Figure 11.1). Home to 10,000 people, its houses were so tightly packed together in an area of roughly 12 hectares that one had to go in and out of them through openings in their roofs. Yet, in spite of their similar plans, there is great individual variation in the way they were built, and there is no known public architecture or any other evidence of centralized authority. Furthermore, there was little division of labor, or even evidence of intensive agriculture, as residents relied heavily on

wild food. It is as if a number of what otherwise would be separate Neolithic villages were all crammed together in one place.[1]

One may compare Çatal Hüyük with Teotihuacan, America's first great experience in urbanism (Figure 12.2). Located in central Mexico, in the first 400 years after its founding 2,200 years ago, its population grew rapidly, until it reached perhaps 80,000 people. Slower growth thereafter brought this figure to around 100,000, all packed

---

[1]Balter, M. (1998). Why settle down? The mystery of communities. *Science, 282,* 1442–1444.

Çatal Hüyük in Turkey was a compact village, as suggested by this photo, but it was not a true city.

FIGURE 12.2

The founders of Teotihuacan imposed an audacious plan on several square kilometers of landscape in central Mexico. At the center is the Avenue of the Dead, running from the Temple of the Moon (near top), past the Temple of the Sun and, south of the Río San Juan, the palace compound. Note the gridded layout of surrounding apartment compounds.

within an area of about 20 km². One reason for the early rapid growth was that the population of the entire 5,000 km² Basin of Mexico (where modern Mexico City is located today) was removed and relocated to Teotihuacan. Furthermore, the layout of the city was planned from the very start. At its center is what is known as the "Street of the Dead," a grand north-south axis along which are located the huge Sun and Moon pyramids as well as a royal palace compound (associated with the planet Venus) and other monumental construction (see the photograph that opens this chapter). The Sun pyramid was built above a cave, seen as a portal to the underworld, home of deities associated with death. The street itself was deliberately oriented to an astronomical alignment 15.5° east of true north. Surrounding this core were thousands of apartment compounds, separated from each other by narrow streets laid out in a grid, maintaining the 15.5°-east-of-north orientation throughout the city. Key linear dimensions of construction and distance between them seem to have translated calendrical numbers into a unified spatial pattern. So rigid was this layout that the Río San Juan, where it runs through the city, was channelized to conform with the grid. Finally, there is clear evidence for both social and economic diversity. Some six levels of society can be recognized by variation in size and quality of apartment rooms. Those at and near the top of the social scale lived on or near the Street of the Dead. Exotic goods and raw materials were imported from afar to be worked by Teotihuacano artisans, and at least two enclaves housed people with foreign affiliations, one to Oaxaca, the other ("merchant's barrio") to the Gulf and Maya lowlands. Also resident in the city were farmers, whose labor in fields (some of them irrigated) supplied the food on which the city dwellers relied.[2]

As this comparison shows, early cities were far more than expanded Neolithic villages. The changes that took place in the transition from village to city were so great that the emergence of urban living is considered by some to be one of the great "revolutions" in human culture. The following case study gives us a glimpse of another of

the world's ancient cities, how it was studied by archaeologists, and how it may have grown from a smaller farming community.

TIKAL: A CASE STUDY

The ancient city of Tikal, one of the largest lowland Maya centers in existence, is situated in Central America about 200 miles by air north of Guatemala City. Tikal was built on a broad limestone terrace in a rain forest. Here the Maya settled in the 1st millennium B.C., and their civilization flourished until about A.D. 869.

At its height, Tikal covered about 120.5 km², and its nucleus, or "epicenter," was the Great Plaza, a large, paved area surrounded by about 300 major structures and thousands of houses. Starting from a small, dispersed population, the population of Tikal swelled to large proportions. By A.D. 550, the density of Tikal was on the order of 600 to 700 persons per km², six times that of the surrounding regions.

From 1956 through the 1960s, Tikal and the surrounding region were intensively explored under the joint auspices of the University of Pennsylvania Museum and the Guatemalan government. Until 1959, the Tikal Project had investigated only major temple and palace structures found in the vicinity of the Great Plaza, at the site's epicenter. It became evident, however, that in order to gain a balanced view of Tikal's development and composition, considerable attention would have to be devoted to hundreds of small mounds, thought to be the remains of dwellings, which surround the larger buildings. Just as one cannot get a realistic view of Washington, D.C., by looking at its monumental public buildings alone, so one cannot obtain a realistic view of Tikal without examining the full range of ruins in the area.

[2]Cowgill, G. L. (1997). State and society at Teotihuacan, Mexico. *Annual Review of Anthropology, 26,* 129–161.

It became evident that a long-range program of excavation of small structures, most of which were probably houses, was necessary at Tikal. Such a program would provide some basis for an estimate of the city's population size and density—information critical for testing the traditional assumption that the Maya could not have sustained large concentrations of population because their subsistence practices were not adequate. Extensive excavation would also provide a sound basis for a reconstruction of the everyday life of the Maya, previously known almost entirely through a study of ceremonial remains. Moreover, the excavation might shed light on the social organization of the Maya. For example, differences in house construction and in the quality and quantity of associated remains might suggest social class differences; or features of house distribution might reflect the existence of extended families or other types of kin groups. The excavation of both large and small structures could reveal the variations in architecture and associated artifacts and burials; such variations might reflect the social structure of the total population of Tikal.[3]

SURVEYING THE SITE

By the time the first excavations of small structures were undertaken, 6 km^2 surrounding the Great Plaza had already been extensively surveyed by mapping crews (see Figure 2.1). For this mapping, aerial photography was worthless because the tree canopy in this area is often 100 feet above the ground and obscures all but the tallest temples; many of the small ruins are practically invisible even to observers on the ground. The only effective way to explore the region is on foot. Once a ruin is found, it is not easy to mark its exact location. Even after 4 years of careful mapping, the limits of the site still had not been revealed. Ancient Tikal was far larger than the 6 km^2 surveyed till

---

[3]Coe, W. R., & Haviland, W. A. (1982). *Introduction to the archaeology of Tikal.* Philadelphia: University Museum.

The buildings shown here make up the civic and ceremonial heart of Tikal. In the foreground are the palaces where the city's rulers lived and carried out their administrative tasks. Beyond are the temples erected over the tombs of past kings.

then. More time and money were required to continue surveying the area in order to define the city's boundaries. To simplify this problem, straight survey trails oriented toward the four cardinal directions, with the Great Plaza as the center point, were cut through the forest, measured, and staked by government surveyors. The distribution of ruins was plotted, using the trails as reference points, and the overall size of Tikal was calculated.[4]

The area selected for the first small-structure excavation was surveyed in 1957 while it was still covered by forest. A map was drafted, and 2 years later the first excavations were undertaken.[5] Six structures, two plazas, and a platform were investigated. The original plan was to strip each of the structures to bedrock in order to obtain every bit of information possible. Three obstacles prevented this procedure, however. First was the discovery of new structures not visible before excavation; second, the structures turned out to be much more complex architecturally than anyone had expected; and, finally, the enormous quantity of artifacts found then had to be washed and cataloged, a time-consuming process. Consequently, not every structure was completely excavated, and some remained uninvestigated.

EVIDENCE FROM THE EXCAVATION

Following this initial work, over 100 additional small structures were excavated in different parts of the site in order to ensure that a representative sample was investigated. Numerous test pits were sunk in various other small structure groups to supplement the information gained from more extensive excavations.

Excavation at Tikal revealed evidence of trade in nonperishable items. Granite, quartzite, hematite, pyrite, jade, slate, and obsidian all were imported, either as raw materials or finished products. Marine materials came from Caribbean and Pacific coastal areas. Tikal itself is located on a source of abundant flint, which may have been ex-

ported in the form of raw material and finished objects. The site also happens to be located between two river systems to the east and west, and so may have been on a major overland trade route between the two. There is indirect evidence that trade went on in perishable goods such as textiles, feathers, salt, and cacao. We can safely conclude that there were full-time traders among the Tikal Maya.

In the realm of technology, specialized woodworking, pottery, obsidian, and shell workshops have been found. The skillful stone carving displayed on stone monuments suggests that this was done by occupational specialists. The same is true of the fine artwork exhibited on ceramic vessels. Those who painted these had to envision what their work would look like after their pale, relatively colorless slips had been fired. The complex Maya calendar required astronomers, and in order to control the large population, estimated to have been at least 50,000 people, there must have been some form of bureaucratic organization. We do know that the government was headed by a hereditary ruling dynasty. Although we do not have direct evidence, there are clues to the

This painting from Cacaxtla in southern Mexico shows a deity with the typical backpack of a Maya merchant.

[4]Puleston, D. E. (1983). *The settlement survey of Tikal.* Philadelphia: University Museum.

[5]Haviland, W. A., et al. (1985). *Excavations in small residential groups of Tikal: Groups 4F-1 and 4F-2.* Philadelphia: University Museum.

Carved monuments like this were commissioned by Tikal's rulers to commemorate important events in their reigns. Portrayed on this one is a king who ruled between A.D. 768 and A.D. 790 or a bit later. Such skilled stone carving could only have been accomplished by a specialist. (For a translation of the inscription on the monument's left side, see Figure 12.4.)

existence of textile workers, dental workers, makers of bark cloth "paper," scribes, masons, and other occupational specialists.

The religion of the Tikal Maya probably developed initially as a means to cope with the uncertainties of agriculture. When people are faced with problems unsolvable by technological or organizational means, they resort to manipulation of magic and the supernatural. Soils at Tikal are thin, and there is no water except that which can be collected in ponds. Rain is abundant in season, but its onset tends to be unreliable. Once the wet season arrives, there may be dry spells of varying duration which can seriously affect crop productivity. Or there may be too much rain, so that crops

rot in the fields. Other risks include storm damage, locust plagues, and incursions of wild animals. To this day, the native inhabitants of the region display great concern about these very real risks involved in agriculture over which they have no direct control.

The Maya priesthood devoted much of its time to calendrical matters; the priests tried not only to placate the deities in times of drought but also to propitiate them in times of plenty. They determined the most auspicious time to plant crops and were concerned with other agricultural matters. The dependence of the population in and around Tikal upon their priesthood to manipulate supernatural beings and forces in their behalf, in order that their crops would not fail, tended to keep them in or near the city, in spite of the fact that a slash-and-burn method of agriculture, which was probably the prevailing method early in Tikal's history, requires the constant shifting of plots and consequently tended to disperse the population over large areas.

As the population increased, land for agriculture became scarcer, and the Maya were forced to find new methods of food production that could sustain the dense population concentrated at Tikal. To slash-and-burn agriculture as their main form of subsistence, they added the planting and tending of fruit trees and other crops that could be grown around their houses in soils enriched by human waste (unlike houses at Teotihuacan, those at Tikal were not built close to one another). Along with increased reliance on household gardening went the construction of artificially raised fields in areas that were flooded each rainy season. In these fields, crops could be intensively cultivated year after year, so long as they were carefully maintained. Measures also were taken to maximize catchment for the dry season, by converting low areas into reservoirs and constructing channels to carry runoff from plazas and other architecture into these reservoirs. As these changes were taking place, a class of artisans, craftspeople, and other occupational specialists emerged to serve the needs first of religion, then of an elite consisting of the priesthood and a ruling dynasty. The arts flourished, and numerous temples, public buildings, and houses were built.

For several hundred years, Tikal was able to sustain its ever-growing population. Then the pressure for food and land reached a critical point, and population growth was halted. At the same time, warfare with other cities was becoming increasingly destructive. All of this is marked archaeologically by abandonment of houses on prime land in rural areas, by the advent of nutritional problems as evidenced by the bones from burials, and by the construction of a system of defensive ditches and embankments. In other words, a period of readjustment set in, which must have been directed by an already strong central authority. Activities then continued as before, but without further population growth for another 250 years or so.

CITIES AND CULTURAL CHANGE

If someone who grew up in a small village of Maine, Wyoming, or Mississippi were to move to Chicago, Detroit, or Los Angeles, that person would experience a number of marked changes in his or her way of life. Some of the same changes in daily life would have been felt 5,000 years ago by a Neolithic village dweller upon moving into one of the world's first cities in Mesopotamia. Of course, the differences would be less extreme today. In the 20th century, every North American village, however small, is part of civilization; back when cities first developed, *they* were civilization, and the villages for the most part represented a continuation of Neolithic life.

Four basic culture changes mark the transition from Neolithic village life to life in the first urban centers.

AGRICULTURAL INNOVATION

The first culture change characteristic of life in cities—hence, of civilization itself—occurred in farming methods. The ancient Sumerians, for example, built an extensive system of dikes, canals, and reservoirs to irrigate their farmlands. With such a system, they could control water resources at will; water could be held and then run off into the fields as necessary. Irrigation was an important factor affecting an increase of crop yields. Because farming could now be carried on independently of the seasons, more crops could be harvested in one year. On the other hand, this intensification of agri-

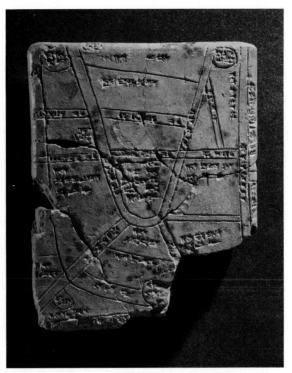

This clay tablet map of farmland outside of the Mesopotamian city of Nippur dates to 1300 B.C. Shown are irrigation canals separating the various fields, each of which is identified with the name of the owner.

culture did not necessarily mean that people ate better than before. Under centralized governments, intensification was generally carried out with less regard for human health than when such governments did not exist.[6]

The ancient Maya who lived at Tikal developed systems of tree cultivation and constructed raised fields in seasonally flooded swamplands to supplement their earlier slash-and-burn farming. The resultant increase in crop yields provided for a higher population density. Increased crop yields, resulting from agricultural innovations such as those of the ancient Maya and Sumerians, were undoubtedly a factor contributing to the high population densities of all civilized societies.

---

[6]Roosevelt, A. C. (1984). Population, health, and the evolution of subsistence: Conclusions from the conference. In M. N. Cohen & G. J. Armelagos (Eds.), *Paleopathology at the origins of agriculture* (p. 568). Orlando, FL: Academic Press.

One technique of agricultural intensification used by the Maya reclaimed swampland by constructing raised fields surrounded by canals. Traces of these raised fields can still be seen, as shown here in Pulltrouser Swamp, Belize.

DIVERSIFICATION OF LABOR

The second culture change characteristic of civilization is diversification of labor. In a Neolithic village that possessed neither irrigation nor plow farming, the members of every family were primarily concerned with the raising of crops. The high crop yields made possible by new farming methods and the increased population freed more and more people from farming. For the first time, a sizable number of people were available to pursue nonagricultural activities on a full-time basis. In the early cities, some people still farmed (as at Tikal and Teotihuacan), but a large number of the inhabitants were skilled workers or craftspeople.

Ancient public records indicate there was a considerable variety of such skilled workers. For example, an early Mesopotamian document from the city of Lagash lists the artisans, craftspeople, and others paid from crop surpluses stored in the temple granaries. Among them were coppersmiths, silversmiths, sculptors, merchants, potters, tanners, engravers, butchers, carpenters, spinners, barbers, cabinetmakers, bakers, clerks, and brewers. At the ancient Maya city of Tikal we have evidence for traders, potters, woodworkers, obsidian workers, painters, scribes and sculptors, and perhaps textile workers, dental workers, shell workers, and paper makers.

With specialization came the expertise that led to the invention of new and novel ways of making and doing things. In the Old World, civilization ushered in what archaeologists often refer to as the **Bronze Age,** a period marked by the production of tools and ornaments of this metal. Metals were in great demand for the manufacture of farmers' and artisans' tools, as well as for weapons. Copper and tin—the raw materials from

---

Bronze Age.   In the Old World, the period marked by the production of tools and ornaments of bronze; began about 3000 B.C. in China and Southwest Asia and about 500 years earlier in Southeast Asia.

THE RISE OF CITIES AND CIVILIZATION

anthropology applied Economic Development and Tropical Forests

Prime targets for development in the world today, in the eyes of governments and private corporations alike, are vast tracts of tropical forests. On a global basis, forests are being rapidly cleared for lumber and fuel, as well as to make way for farms, ranches, mines, and other forms of economic development. The world's largest uninterrupted tracts are the forests of the Amazon and Orinoco watersheds of South America, which are being destroyed at about the rate of 4% a year. Just what the rate is for the world as a whole no one is quite sure, but it is clearly accelerating. And already there are signs of trouble, as extensive tracts of once-lush growth have been converted to semidesert. Essential nutrients are lost, either through erosion (which increases by several orders of magnitude under deforestation) or by leaching too deeply, as soils are exposed to the direct force of the heavy tropical rains.

The problem is that developers, until recently, have lacked reliable models by which the long-term impact of their actions might be assessed. Such a model now exists, thanks to the efforts of archaeologists unraveling the mystery of how the ancient Maya, in a tropical rainforest setting, carried out large-scale urban construction and sustained huge numbers of people successfully for two millennia. The key to the Maya success was their implementation of sophisticated practices to

reduce regionwide processes of nutrient loss, deterioration of soil structure, destabilization of water flows, soil erosion, and loss of productive components of their environment.* These included construction of terraces, canals, and raised fields, the fertility of which was maintained through mulching with water plants and the addition of organic wastes. Coupled with all this, crops were planted in such a way as to produce complex patterns of foliage distribution, canopy heights, and nutrient demands. Far different from "modern" monocrop agriculture, this reduced the impact on the soils of intensive farming, while making maximum use of nutrients and enhancing their cycling in the system.

In Mexico, where population growth has threatened the country's ability to provide sufficient food for its people, archaeologists and agriculturalists are already cooperating to apply our knowledge of ancient Maya techniques to the problems of modern food production in the tropics. Application of these techniques in other tropical forested countries, like Brazil, could do much to alleviate food shortages.

---

*Rice, D. S., & Rice, P. M. (1984). Lessons from the Maya. *Latin American Research Review, 19*(3), 24–28.

---

which bronze is made—and eventually iron were smelted, separating them from their ores, then purified, and cast to make plows, swords, axes, and shields. In wars over border disputes or to extend a state's territory, stone knives, spears, and slings could not stand up against bronze spears, arrowheads, swords, or armor.

The native civilizations of the Americas also used metals—in South America, for tools as well as ceremonial and ornamental objects, but in Mesoamerica, mostly for ceremonial and orna-

mental objects. Why people like the Aztecs and Maya continued to rely on stone for their everyday tools has puzzled those who assume that metal is inherently superior. The answer, however, is simple: The ready availability of obsidian (a glass formed by volcanic activity), its extreme sharpness (many times sharper than the finest steel), and the ease with which it could be worked made it perfectly suited to their needs. With obsidian, these people fabricated tools with the sharpest cutting edges ever made.

The earliest objects of bronze, such as this one, come from Ban Chiang, Thailand.

In order to procure the raw materials needed for their technologies, extensive trade systems were developed by the early civilizations. The city of Teotihuacan, for example, controlled most of the obsidian trade in central Mexico. Trade agreements were maintained with distant peoples, not only to secure basic raw materials but to provide luxury items as well.

Boats gave greater access to trade centers; they could easily carry back to cities large loads of imports at less cost than if they had been brought back overland. A one-way trip from Egypt to the northern city of Byblos in Phoenicia (now Lebanon) took only four to eight days by rowboat. With a sailboat, it took even less.

Egyptian pharaohs sent expeditions to the Sinai Peninsula for copper; to Nubia for gold; to Arabia for spices and perfumes; to Asia for lapis lazuli (a blue semiprecious stone) and other jewels; to Lebanon for cedar, wine, and funerary oils; and to central Africa for ivory, ebony, ostrich feathers, leopard skins, cattle, and slaves.

Bronze tools and weapons were more durable than their stone counterparts, which were more easily broken. The bronze sword (above) comes from Mycaenae, Greece, dating to about 1200 B.C. The ear pendant from Greece of about the same age is a fine example of the artistry that became possible with the introduction of bronze.

With technological innovation, along with increased contact with foreign peoples through trade, came new knowledge. It was within the early civilizations that sciences such as geometry and astronomy were first developed. Geometry was used by the Egyptians for such purposes as measuring the area of a field or staking off an accurate right angle at the corner of a building.

Astronomy grew out of the need to know when to plant and harvest crops or to hold religious observances and to find exact bearings on voyages. Astronomy and mathematics were used to devise calendars. The Maya calculated that the solar year was 365 days (actually, it is $365\frac{1}{4}$ days), accurately predicted the appearances of the planet Venus as morning and evening "star," predicted eclipses, and tracked other astronomical events. As one scholar comments: "Maya science, in its representation of numbers, and its empirical base, is in many respects superior to the science of their European contemporaries."[7]

Aztec spears tipped and edged with obsidian blades are shown in this 16th-century drawing of a battle with the Aztecs' Spanish conquerors. Though superior to steel for piercing, cutting, and slashing, the brittleness of obsidian placed the Aztecs at a disadvantage when faced with Spanish swords.

---

[7]Frake, C. O. (1992). Lessons of the Mayan sky: A perspective from medieval Europe. In A. F. Aveni (Ed.), *The sky in Mayan literature* (p. 287). New York: Oxford University Press.

Paper making, invented in China 2,000 years ago, is an example of technological innovation by which farming societies evolved into civilizations.

Central Government

The third culture change characteristic of civilization is the emergence of a governing elite, a strong central authority required to deal with the many problems arising within the new cities because of their size and complexity. The new governing elite saw to it that different interest groups, such as farmers, craft specialists, or moneylenders, provided the services that were expected of them and did not infringe on each other's rights. It ensured that the city was safe from its enemies by constructing walls and raising an army. It levied taxes and appointed tax collectors so that construction workers, the army, and other public expenses could be paid. It saw to it that merchants, carpenters, or farmers who made legal claims received justice. It guaranteed safety for the lives and property of ordinary people and assured that any harm done one person by another would be justly handled. In addition, surplus food had to be stored for times of scarcity, and public works such as extensive irrigation systems or fortifications had to be supervised by competent, disinterested individuals. The mechanisms of government served all these functions.

Evidence of Centralized Authority

Evidence of a centralized authority in ancient civilizations comes from such sources as law codes, temple records, and royal chronicles. Excavation of the city structures themselves provides further evidence. For example, archaeologists believe that the cities of Mohenjodaro and Harappa in the Indus Valley were governed by a centralized authority because they show definite signs of city planning. Both cities are over 3 miles long; their main streets are laid out in a rectangular grid pattern; and both contain city-wide drainage systems. Similar evidence for centralized planning comes from Teotihuacan where, in addition, the forced relocation of people from the Basin of Mexico also attests to strong, centralized control.

Monumental buildings and temples, palaces, and large sculptures are usually found in civilizations. The Maya city of Tikal contained over 300 major structures, including temples, ball courts, and "palaces" (residences of the aristocracy). The Pyramid of the Sun in the pre-Aztec city of Teotihuacan (see chapter opener) is 700 feet long and more than 200 feet high. Its interior is filled by more than 1 million cubic yards of sun-dried

Construction of such large-scale public works as the Great Wall of China reflects the power of a centralized government to mobilize and supervise the labor necessary to carry out such monumental undertakings.

bricks. The tomb of the Egyptian pharaoh Khufu, known as the Great Pyramid, is 755 feet long and 481 feet high. It contains about 2,300,000 stone blocks, each with an average weight of 2.5 tons. The Greek historian Herodotus reports that it took 100,000 men 20 years to build this tomb. Such gigantic structures could be built only because the considerable labor force, engineering skills, and raw materials necessary for their construction could be harnessed by a powerful central authority.

Another indicator of the existence of centralized authority is writing, or some form of recorded information (Figure 12.3). In the Old World, early governments found it useful to keep records of state affairs, such as accounts of their food surplus, tribute records, and other business receipts. The earliest documents appear to be just such records—lists of vegetables and animals bought and sold, tax lists, and storehouse inventories. Be-

ing able to record information was an extremely important invention, because governments could keep records of their assets instead of simply relying upon the memory of administrators.

Prior to 5,000 years ago, records consisted of pictures drawn or carved on stone, bone, or shell to commemorate a notable event, such as a hunt, a military victory, or the deed of some king. The earliest "picture writing"—called pictographs—functioned much like historical paintings or newspaper photos.

The figures in such pictures gradually became simplified and generalized and stood for ideas of things, rather than for the things themselves. Thus, a royal palace could be represented by a simple stick drawing of a house with a crown placed above it. This representation of the idea of a palace is called an ideogram. In the older pictographic "writing," it would have been necessary to draw

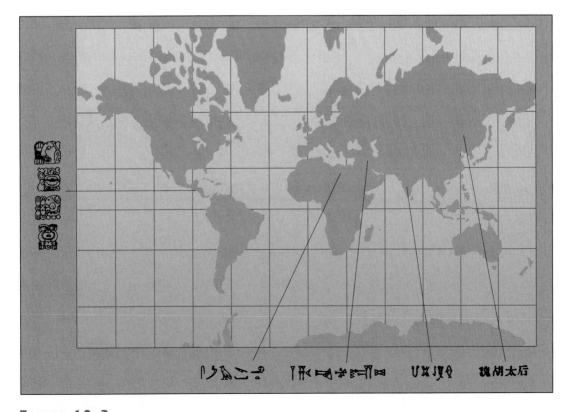

FIGURE 12.3
The impermanence of spoken words contrasts with the relative permanence of written records. In all of human history, writing has been independently invented no more than five times.

a likeness of an actual palace in order to convey the message effectively. Ideographic writing was faster, simpler, and more flexible than the pictographic system. Over the centuries the ideograms became more simplified and, although their meaning was clear to their users, they looked less and less like the natural objects they had originally depicted.

In Mesopotamia, about 6,000 years ago, a new writing technique emerged, which used a stylus to make wedge-shaped markings on a tablet of damp clay. Originally, each marking stood for a word. Since most words in this language were monosyllabic, the markings came, in time, to stand for syllables. There were about 600 signs, half of them ideograms, the others functioning either as ideograms or as syllables.

In the New World, systems of writing came into use among various Mesoamerican peoples, but the most sophisticated was that of the Maya. Their hieroglyphic system had less to do with keeping track of state belongings than with "dynastic bombast." Maya lords glorified themselves by recording their dynastic genealogies, important conquests, and royal marriages, by using grandiose titles to refer to themselves and by associating their actions with important astrological events (Figure 12.4). Often, the latter involved complicated mathematical calculations.

The Earliest Governments

The government organization of the earliest cities was typically headed by a king and his special advisers. In addition, there were sometimes councils of lesser advisers. Formal laws were enacted and courts sat in judgment over the claims of rival litigants or the criminal charges brought by the government against an individual.

FIGURE 12.4

The translation of the text on the monument on p. 320 gives some indication of the importance of dynastic genealogy to Maya rulers. The "scattering" mentioned may refer to bloodletting as part of the ceremonies associated with the end of one 20-year period, or Katun, and the beginning of the next.

The day 13 Ahau
Eighteenth day of the month, Cumku,

End of the seventeenth Katun.
The completion of its period.

(Part of the ruler's name?)
Chitam

In the dynastic line, lord of Tikal,
From Yax Moch Xoc
(an early Tikal king)

The ninth plus twenty,
In the count of the rulers

(Successor to ?)
His lord father,

Yax Kin Caan Chac
(A probable title,)

In the dynastic line, lord of Tikal,
In his fourth katun (period of 20 tuns,
or 360 day years)

The leader (*batab*)
Sixteen days plus one period
of twenty days,

Plus two tuns (back to),
The day 11 Kan,

Twelfth day of the month
of the parrot, Kayab,
He took the throne,

At the place of leadership,
He who scatters blessings.

Of the many ancient kings known, one stands out as truly remarkable for the efficient government organization and highly developed legal system that characterized his reign. This is Hammurabi, the Babylonian king who lived sometime between 1950 and 1700 B.C. He promulgated a set of laws for his kingdom, known as the Code of Hammurabi, which is important because of its thorough detail and standardization. It prescribes the correct form for legal procedures and determines penalties for perjury, false accusation, and injustice done by judges. It contains laws applying to property rights, loans and debts, family rights, and damages paid for malpractice by a physician. There are fixed rates to be charged in various trades and branches of commerce. The poor, women, children, and slaves are protected against injustice. The code was publicly displayed on huge stone slabs so that no one accused could plead ignorance. Even the poorest citizen was supposed to know his or her rights.

Some civilizations flourished under a ruler with extraordinary governing abilities, such as Hammurabi. Other civilizations possessed a widespread governing bureaucracy that was very efficient at every level. Teotihuacan was probably of this sort, but the government of the Inca civilization is better known.

The Inca empire of Peru reached its zenith in the 16th century A.D., just before the arrival of the Spanish. In the mid-1400s, the Inca kingdom probably did not extend more than 20 miles beyond the modern-day city of Cuzco, which was then its center. Within a 30-year period, in the late 1400s, the Inca kingdom enlarged a thousand times its original size. By A.D. 1525, it stretched 2,500 miles from north to south and 500 miles from east to west, making it at the time the greatest empire on the face of the earth. Its population numbered in the millions, composed of people of various ethnic groups. In the achievements of its governmental and political system, Inca civilization surpassed every other civilization of the New World and most of those of the Old World. At the head of the government was the emperor, regarded as semidivine, followed by the royal family, the aristocracy, imperial administrators, the lower nobility, and the masses of artisans, craftspeople, and farmers.

The empire was divided into four administrative regions, further subdivided into provinces, and so on down to villages and families. Planting, irrigation, and harvesting were closely supervised by government agricultural and tax officials. Teams of professional relay runners could carry messages up to 250 miles in a single day over a network of roads and bridges that remains impressive even today. The Inca are unusual in that they had no writing that we know about; public records and historical chronicles were kept in the form of an ingenious system of colored beads, knots, and ropes.

SOCIAL STRATIFICATION

The rise of large, economically diversified populations presided over by centralized governing authorities brought with it the fourth culture change characteristic of civilization: social stratification, or the emergence of social classes. Thus, we note that symbols of special status and privilege appeared in the ancient cities of Mesopotamia, and people were ranked according to the kind of work they did or the family into which they were born.

People who stood at or near the head of government were the earliest holders of high status. Although economic specialists of one sort or another—metal workers, tanners, traders, or the like—generally outranked farmers, such specialization did not necessarily bring with it high status. Rather, people engaged in economic activity were either of the lower class or outcasts.[8] The exception was those merchants who were in a position to buy their way into some kind of higher class. With time, the possession of wealth, and the influence it could buy, became in itself a requisite for high status.

Evidence of Social Stratification

How do archaeologists know that there were different social classes in ancient civilizations? One way they are revealed is by burial customs. Graves excavated at early Neolithic sites are mostly

---

[8]Sjoberg, G. (1960). *The preindustrial city* (p. 325). New York: Free Press.

simple pits dug in the ground, containing few, if any, grave goods. Grave goods consist of things such as utensils, figurines, and personal possessions, which are placed in the grave in order that the dead person might use them in the afterlife. The lack of much variation between burials in terms of the wealth implied by grave goods in Neolithic sites indicates an essentially classless society. Graves excavated in civilizations, by contrast, vary widely in size, mode of burial, and the number and variety of grave goods. This indicates a stratified society—one divided into social classes. The graves of important persons contain not only a great variety of artifacts made from precious materials, but sometimes, as in some early Egyptian

burials, even the remains of servants evidently killed to serve their masters in their afterlives. The skeletons from the burials may also give evidence of stratification. At Tikal, skeletons from elaborate tombs indicate that the subjects of these tombs had longer life expectancy, ate better food, and enjoyed better health than the bulk of that city's population. In stratified societies, the elite usually live longer, eat better, and enjoy an easier life than other members of society.

As an example of what upper-class burials may look like, and what more they can tell us about the customs of the people placed in them, we may look at a spectacular tomb from one of the civilizations that preceded that of the Incas in Peru.

Finding the Tomb of a Moche Priestess[9]

The Moche kingdom flourished on the north coast of Peru between A.D. 100 and 800. Although the Moche had no writing system, they left a vivid artistic record of their beliefs and activities on beautifully modeled and painted ceramic vessels. Because of the realism and detail of these depictions we are able to reconstruct various aspects of Moche society such as religious ceremonies and mythology, as well as activities like hunting, weaving, and combat rarely preserved in the archaeological record.

During the past 20 years we have developed a major photographic archive of Moche art at the University of California, Los Angeles, which serves as an important resource for the study of their culture. Our goal has been to reconstruct aspects of Moche culture by combining systematic studies of their art with archaeological fieldwork in Peru. Our analyses of sites, including residential compounds, palaces, temples, and cemeteries, and the artifacts associated with them have allowed us to document archaeologically some of the complex scenes illustrated in Moche art, and to understand aspects of their culture that are not portrayed in the art.

During the past 10 years our research has focused on the Jequetepeque Valley, located in the northern portion of the territory occupied by the Moche. In this region we have undertaken several lines of research, concentrating our efforts on the relationship between Moche ceremonial activities and socioeconomic organization. In June 1991, UCLA began excavations at San José de Moro, a major ceremonial center in the lower Jequetepeque Valley. It was clear from its various ceramic styles that the site had a long history of occupation and thus would be ideal for answering questions about the cultural sequence of the region. Moreover, the quantity and variation in monumental construction at the site strongly suggested that it had served as a major ceremonial

[9]Donnan, C. B., & Castillo, L. J. (1992). Finding the tomb of a Moche priestess. *Archaeology, 45*(6), 38–42.

A silver-copper alloy mask (left) was found near the priestess's skull. Her body (right) was covered with hammered metal arms and legs.

center through most of its occupation and thus could provide us with good insights about the nature of Moche ceremonial activity.

During our first field season we excavated three complex late-Moche tombs—each consisting of a room-sized burial chamber made of mud bricks. The tomb chambers had originally been roofed with large wooden beams. The principal occupant of each tomb was lying face up in an extended position, with the remains of complete llamas, humans, or both, at their feet. In two of the tombs the principal occupants were flanked by other individuals. Hundreds of ceramic vessels and metal objects, including ceremonial knives, lance points, sandals, cups, masks, and jewelry, had been placed in the tombs as offerings.

The most elaborate of the three tombs was that of a high-status adult female. It is the richest Moche female burial ever scientifically excavated and clearly demonstrates that in Moche society extraordinary wealth and power were not the exclusive domain of males. The tomb chamber was approximately $7\frac{1}{2}$ by 14 feet. The walls, which were made of mud brick, had niches— six on each side and four at the head of the tomb—in which ceramic vessels and parts of llamas had been placed. Additional ceramic vessels had been stacked on the floor of the tomb chamber.

Some of the artifacts associated with this burial provide clear evidence that the Moche were involved in long-distance trade and that their elite expended a great deal of effort to obtain precious materials. Included among the offerings were three imported ceramic vessels—a plate of Cajamarca style, which must have been brought to San José de Moro from the highland area located more than 70 miles to the east, and two exotic ceramic bottles of Nieveria style, a type of pottery that was made in the area of Lima, more than 350 miles to the south. Two other kinds of materials associated with the tomb provide further evidence of long-distance trade. Over the woman's chest and hands were *Spondylus princeps* shells that had been brought from Ecuador to the north, and around her neck were cylindrical beads of lapis lazuli that had been brought from Chile to the south.

The most remarkable aspect of this woman's tomb, however, was that the objects buried with her allow us to identify her as a specific priestess who is depicted in Moche art. This priestess was first identified in the Moche Archive at UCLA in 1975, at which time she was given the name "Figure C." Five years later, Anne Marie Hocquenghem and Patricia Lyon convincingly demonstrated that this individual was female. She was one of the principal participants in the "Sacrifice Ceremony," an event depicted in Moche art where prisoners of war were sacrificed and their blood ritually consumed in tall ceremonial goblets.

Figure C is always depicted with her hair in wrapped braids that hang across her chest, and wearing a long dresslike garment. Also characteristic of Figure C is her headdress, which is unique in having two prominent tassels. The tomb of the woman at San José de Moro contained an identical headdress with two huge tassels made of a silver copper alloy.

In one corner of the tomb was a large blackware ceramic basin containing cups and a tall goblet. An identical blackware basin with cups in it is shown associated with Figure C in a famous mural at the site of Pañamarca, a ceremonial center located in the Nepeña Valley. Furthermore, the tall goblet contained in the ceramic basin was of the type used in the Sacrifice Ceremony. It is decorated with a scene of anthropomorphized clubs and shields drinking blood from similar goblets. The tall goblet is a prominent feature in all depictions of the Sacrifice Ceremony, and it is often seen being presented by Figure C. Finding the tall goblet in her grave thus supports her identification as Figure C.

The tomb of Figure C at San José de Moro has profound implications for Moche studies. Excavations by Walter Alva at Sipán, located in a valley to the north of San José de Moro, have revealed the tombs of two other participants, Figure A and Figure B, in the Sacrifice Ceremony. The richest of these tombs is that of the Lord of Sipán, Figure A. He was buried with his characteristic crescent-shaped headdress, crescent-shaped nose ornament, large circular ear ornaments, and warrior's backflap, and was holding a rattle like that shown in representations of Figure A. The occupant of another tomb appears to be Figure B, a bird warrior who is frequently shown as companion to Figure A. He was found wearing a headdress adorned with an owl. Although no grave of Figure C has yet been excavated at Sipán, it seems likely that someone who performed this role was also buried at that site.

How do the tombs at Sipán relate to the tomb of Figure C at San José de Moro? First, it should be noted that the two tombs at Sipán date to approximately A.D. 300, and those at San José de Moro at least 250 years later— sometime after A.D. 550. Clearly, the Sacrifice Ceremony had a long duration in Moche culture, with individuals consistently dressing in traditional garments and headdresses to perform the roles of specific members of the priesthood.

The Sacrifice Ceremony was also widespread geographically. The Pañamarca mural, which clearly depicts this ceremony, was found in the Nepeña Valley, in the southern part of the Moche kingdom. San José de Moro is more than 150 miles to the north of Pañamarca, and Sipán is another 40 miles further north. Moreover, in the 1960s rich tombs containing artifacts with Sacrifice Ceremony iconography were looted from the site of Loma Negra in the Piura Valley, more than 300 miles north of Pañamarca.

The Moche Sacrifice Ceremony

The Sacrifice Ceremony, an event at which prisoners of war are sacrificed and their blood ritually consumed, is a common iconographic theme in Moche art. One of the better known representations of this ceremony appears on a stirrup spout bottle. The scene, center, shows four principal figures and attendants. Below them are bound captives having their throats slashed. During recent excavations at San José de Moro and at Sipán, the remains of several people who participated in this ceremony have been identified. Figure C, a priestess, was discovered at San José de Moro, while Figure A, a warrior-priest, and Figure B, a bird-warrior, were excavated at Sipán.

A goblet, recovered during the excavation of the priestess's tomb at San José de Moro, is decorated with a scene of anthropomorphic war clubs and shields drinking the blood of captives from tall goblets. A similar goblet is being passed between Figure A and Figure B in the drawing below.

Silver-copper alloy tassels worn by the principal occupant of the tomb allowed her to be identified as the priestess depicted in the Sacrifice Ceremony. The tassels are identical to those worn by Figure C in both the drawing and the Pañamarca mural, bottom.

The Pañamarca mural, right, painted on an adobe wall at a Moche ceremonial center in the Nepeña Valley, shows Figure C accompanied by several attendants bearing goblets. Pictured too are three bound captives with their throats slashed and a ceramic basin containing cups. A similar basin, below, was found in the priestess's tomb.

The four sites where evidence of the Sacrifice Ceremony has been found have certain characteristics in common. Each is located on an elevated area that rises naturally above the intensively cultivated valley floor and is near, but not immediately adjacent to, a river. Each was a major ceremonial complex, with multiple pyramids that for centuries served as staging areas for religious activities. Perhaps each of the other river valleys that made up the Moche kingdom also had a central ceremonial precinct where the Sacrifice Ceremony was enacted.

The fact that the Sacrifice Ceremony was so widespread in both time and space strongly implies that it was part of a state religion, with a priesthood in each part of the kingdom comprised of individuals who dressed in prescribed ritual attire. When members of the priesthood died, they were buried at the temple where the Sacrifice Ceremony took place, wearing their ceremonial paraphernalia and accompanied by the objects they had used to perform the ritual. Subsequently, other men and women were chosen to replace them, to dress like them, and to perform the same ceremonial role.

The careful excavation of the tomb of Figure C at San José de Moro has provided important new insights into the nature of Moche religious practices. As our excavations continue at this remarkable site, we expect to find additional archaeological evidence that will refine and improve upon these insights.

In addition to burials, there are three other ways by which archaeologists may recognize the stratified nature of ancient civilizations:

1. The Size of Dwellings In early Neolithic sites, dwellings tended to be uniformly small in size. In the oldest excavated cities, however, some dwellings were notably larger than others, well spaced, and located together in one district, whereas dwellings in other parts of the city were much smaller, sometimes little more than hovels. In the city of Eshnunna in Mesopotamia, archaeologists excavated houses that occupied an area of 200 meters situated on main thoroughfares, and huts of but 50 meters located along narrow back alleys. The rooms in the larger houses often contained impressive artwork, such as friezes or murals. At Tikal, and other Maya cities, the elite lived in large, multiroomed, masonry houses, mostly in the city's center, while lower-class people lived in small, peripherally scattered houses of one or two rooms, built partly or wholly of pole and thatch materials.

This "palace," which housed members of Tikal's ruling dynasty, may be compared with the lower-class house in the next photo.

2. Written Documents Preserved records of business transactions, royal chronicles, or law codes of a civilization reveal much about the social status of its inhabitants. Babylonian and Assyrian texts reveal three main social classes—

Lower-class residents of Tikal lived in the same sort of houses in which most Maya live today.

aristocrats, commoners, and slaves. The members of each class had different rights and privileges. This stratification was clearly reflected by the law. If an aristocrat put out another's eye, then that person's eye was to be put out too; hence, the saying "an eye for an eye." If the aristocrat broke another's bone, then the first aristocrat's bone was to be broken in return. If the aristocrat put out the eye or broke the bone of a commoner, however, the punishment was to pay a mina of silver.[10]

Even in the absence of written information, people may record much about their society in other ways. As the Original Study demonstrates, the Moche recorded much information about their society in their art. The stratified nature of this ancient society is clearly revealed by the scenes painted on ceramic vessels.

3. CORRESPONDENCE European documents describing the aboriginal cultures of the New World as seen by early European explorers and adventurers also offer evidence of social stratifi-

cation. Letters written by the Spanish conquistadors about the Aztec empire indicate that they found a social order divided into three main classes: nobles, commoners, and serfs. The nobles operated outside the lineage system on the basis of land and serfs allotted them by the ruler from conquered peoples. The commoners were divided into lineages, on which they were dependent for land. Within each of these, individual status depended on the degree of descent from the founder; those more closely related to the lineage founder had higher status than those whose kinship was more distant. The third class in Aztec society consisted of serfs bound to the land and porters employed as carriers by merchants. Lowest of this class were the slaves. Some had voluntarily sold themselves into bondage; others were captives taken in war.

Informative though written records may be, they are not without their problems. For example, European explorers did not always understand what they saw; moreover, they had their own interests (or those of their sponsors) to look out for, and were not above falsifying information to further those interests. These points are of

[10]Moseati, S. (1962). *The face of the ancient orient* (p. 90). New York: Doubleday.

major importance, given the tendency of Western peoples, with their long tradition of literacy, to assume that written documents are reliable. In fact, they are not always reliable, and must be checked for accuracy against other sources of information. The same is true of ancient documents written by other people about themselves, for they, too, had their particular agendas. Ancient Maya inscriptions, for example, were often propagandistic in their intent, which was to impress people with particular rulers' importance.

▲▽▲▽▲▽▲▽▲▽▲▽▲▽▲▽▲▽▲▽▲▽▲▽▲▽▲▽▲

THE MAKING OF CIVILIZATION

From Mesopotamia to China to the South American Andes, we witness the enduring achievements of the human intellect: magnificent palaces built high above ground; sculptures so perfect as to be unrivaled by those of contemporary artists; engineering projects so vast and daring as to awaken in us a sense of wonder. Looking back to the beginnings of written history, we can see a point at which humans transform themselves into "civilized" beings; they begin to live in cities and to expand the scope of their achievements at a rapid pace. How is it, then, that humans at a certain moment in history became consummate builders, harnessing mighty rivers so that they could irrigate crops, developing a system whereby their thoughts could be preserved in writing? The fascinating subject of the development of civilization has occupied the minds of philosophers and anthropologists alike for a long time. We do not yet have the answers, but a number of theories have been proposed.

THEORIES OF CIVILIZATION'S EMERGENCE

Each of the theories sees the appearance of centralized government as the point at which there is no longer any question whether or not a civiliza-

tion exists. So, the question they pose is: What brought about the appearance of a centralized government? Or, stated another way: What caused the transition from a small, egalitarian farming village to a large urban center in which population density and diversity of labor required a centralized government?

Irrigation Systems

One popular theory concerning the emergence of civilization was given its most forceful statement by Karl Wittfogel[11], and variants of this theory are still held by some anthropologists. Simply put, the irrigation theory, or **hydraulic theory**, holds that Neolithic farmers in ancient Mesopotamia and Egypt, and later in the Americas, noticed that the river valleys that were periodically flooded contained better soils than those that were not; but they also noted that violent floods destroyed their planted fields and turned them into swamps. So the farmers built dikes and reservoirs to collect the floodwater and save it until it was needed. Then they released it into canals and ran it over the fields. At first, these dikes and canals, built by small groups of neighboring farmers, were very simple. The success of this measure led to larger, more complex irrigation systems, which eventually necessitated the emergence of a group of "specialists"—people whose sole responsibility was managing the irrigation system. The centralized effort to control the irrigation process blossomed into the first governing body and elite social class, and civilization was born.

There are several objections to this theory. One of them is that some of the earliest large-scale irrigation systems we know about anywhere in the world developed in highland New Guinea, where strong centralized governments never emerged. Conversely, actual field studies of ancient Meso-

---

[11]Wittfogel, K. A. (1957). *Oriental despotism, a comparative study of total power*. New Haven: Yale University Press.

Hydraulic theory. The theory that sees civilization's emergence as the result of the construction of elaborate irrigation systems, the functioning of which required full-time managers whose control blossomed into the first governing body and elite social class.

potamian irrigation systems reveal that by the year 2000 B.C., by which time many cities had already flourished, irrigation was still carried out on a small scale, consisting of small canals and diversions of natural waterways. If there were state-managed irrigation, it is argued, such a system would have been far more extensive than excavations show it really was. Moreover, documents indicate that in about 2000 B.C. irrigation was regulated by officials of local temples and not by centralized government. Irrigation systems among the American Indian civilizations of Central and South America began on so small a scale as to suggest they were built and run by families, or, at most, by small groups of local farmers. It can just as well be argued that more extensive irrigation works were a consequence of civilization's development, rather than a cause.

Trade Networks

Some anthropologists argue that trade was a decisive factor in the development of civilizations. In regions of ecological diversity, so the argument goes, trade mechanisms are necessary to procure scarce resources. In Mexico, for example, maize was grown just about everywhere; but chilis were grown in the highlands, cotton and beans were planted at intermediate elevations, certain animals were found only in the river valleys, and salt was found along the coasts.

This theory holds that some form of centralized authority was necessary in order to organize trade for the procurement of these and other commodities. Once procured, some system was necessary in order to redistribute commodities throughout the population. Redistribution, like procurement, must have required a centralized authority, promoting the growth of a centralized government.

While trade may have played an important role in the development of some civilizations, it did not invariably do so. For example, the native peoples of northeastern North America traded widely with each other for at least 6,000 years without developing civilizations comparable to those of Mexico or Peru. In the course of this trade, copper from deposits around Lake Superior wound up in such faraway places as New England, as did chert from Labrador and marine shells from the Gulf of Mexico. Wampum, made on the

shores of Long Island Sound, was carried westward, and obsidian from the Yellowstone region has been found in mounds in Ohio.[12]

Environmental and Social Circumscription

In a series of papers, Robert Carneiro[13] has advanced the theory that civilization develops where populations are hemmed in by such things as mountains, seas, or other human populations. As such populations grow, they have no space in which to expand, and so they begin to compete for increasingly scarce resources. Internally, this results in the development of social stratification, in which an elite controls important resources to which lower classes have limited access. Externally, this leads to warfare and conquest, which, to be successful, require elaborate organization under a centralized authority.

Religion

The three theories just summarized exemplify ecological approaches to explaining the development of civilization. Such theories emphasize the interrelation between people and what they do on the one hand and the environment in which they live on the other. Theories of the emergence of civilization have commonly taken some such approach. While few anthropologists would deny the importance of the human-environment interrelationship, a growing number of them are dissatisfied with theories that do not take into account the beliefs and values which regulate the interaction between people and their environment.

An example of a theory that does take into account the role of beliefs is one which seeks to explain the emergence of Maya civilization in Mesoamerica.[14] This theory holds that Maya

[12]Haviland, W. A., & Power, M. W. (1994). *The original Vermonters*, (2nd. ed., Chapters 3 and 4). Hanover, NH: University Press of New England.

[13]Carneiro, R. L. (1970). A theory of the origin of the state. *Science, 169*, 733–738.

[14]Haviland, W. A. (1975). The ancient Maya and the evolution of urban society. *University of Colorado Museum of Anthropology, Miscellaneous Series*, No. 37.

civilization was the result of a process of urbanization that occurred at places like Tikal. In the case study on Tikal earlier in this chapter, it is suggested that Maya religion probably developed initially as a means of coping with the uncertainties of agriculture. In the last millennium B.C., Tikal seems to have been an important religious center. Because of its religious importance, people sought to settle there, with the result that its population grew in size and density. Because this was incompatible with the prevailing slash-and-burn agriculture, which tends to promote dispersed settlement, new subsistence techniques were developed. By chance, these were sufficiently productive to permit further population growth and, by A.D. 550, Tikal had become an urban settlement of at least 50,000 people. Craft specialization also developed, at first in the service of religion but soon in the service of an emerging social elite as well. This social elite was concerned at first with calendrical ritual, but through the control of ritual it developed into the centralized governing elite needed to control a population growing larger and more diversified in its interests.

Developing craft specialization served as another factor to pull people into Tikal, where their crafts were in demand. It also required further development of trade networks, if only to provide exotic raw materials. More long-distance trade contacts, of course, brought more contact with outside ideas, including some from as far afield as Teotihuacan. In other words, what we seem to have is a complex system with several factors acting upon each other, with religion playing a central role in getting the system started in the first place.

A criticism that may be leveled at all of the above theories is that they fail to recognize the capacity of aggressive, charismatic leaders to shape the course of human history. Accordingly, anthropologists Joyce Marcus and Kent Flannery have developed what they call "**action theory.**"[15] This

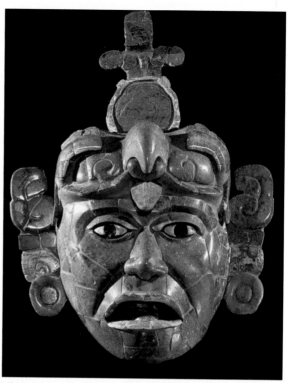

This mosaic death mask of greenstone, pyrite, and shell was worn by a king of the Maya city of Tikal who died ca. A.D. 527. Obviously the product of skilled craft work, such specialization developed first to serve the needs of religion, but soon served the needs of an emerging elite as well.

recognizes the systemic nature of society and the impact of the environment in shaping social and cultural behavior, but recognizes as well that forceful leaders in any society strive to advance their material or political positions through self-serving actions. In so doing, they may create change. Applying this to the Maya, for example, local leaders, who once relied on personal charisma for the economic and political support needed to sustain them in their positions, may have seized upon religion to solidify their grip on power. They did this by developing an ideology endowing them and their descendants with supernatural ancestry. Only they were seen as having the kind of access to the gods on which their followers depended. In this

[15]Marcus, J., & Flannery, K. V. (1996). *Zapotec civilization: How urban society evolved in Mexico's Oaxaca Valley.* New York: Thames & Hudson.

Action theory. The theory that self-serving actions by forceful leaders play a role in civilization's emergence.

case, the nature of the existing system presented a situation in which certain individuals could monopolize power and emerge as divine kings, using their power to subjugate any rivals.

As the above example makes clear, the context in which a forceful leader operates is critical. In the case of the Maya, it was the combination of cultural and ecological factors in existence that opened the way for emergence of political dynasties. Thus, explanations of civilization's emergence are likely to involve multiple causes, rather than just one. Furthermore, we may also have the cultural equivalent of what biologists call convergent evolution, where somewhat similar forms come about in quite different ways. Consequently, a theory that accounts for the rise of civilization in one place may not account for its rise in another.

CIVILIZATION AND STRESS

Living in the context of civilization ourselves, we are inclined to view its development as a great step upward on some sort of ladder of progress. Whatever benefits civilization has brought, though, the cultural changes it represents seem to have produced new sorts of problems. Among them is the problem of waste disposal. Actually, waste disposal probably began to be a problem in settled, farming communities even before the emergence of civilization. But as villages grew into towns and towns grew into cities, the problem became far more serious, as the buildup of waste created optimum environments for such diseases as bubonic plague.

Quite apart from sanitation problems, the rise of towns and cities brought with it a problem of acute, infectious diseases. In a small population, such diseases, which include influenza, measles, mumps, polio, rubella, and smallpox, will kill or immunize so high a proportion of the population that the virus cannot continue to propagate. Hence, such diseases, when introduced into small populations, spread immediately to the whole population and then die out. Their continued existence depends upon the presence of large population aggregates, such as towns and cities provide.

In essence, early cities tended to be disease-ridden places, with relatively high death rates. At

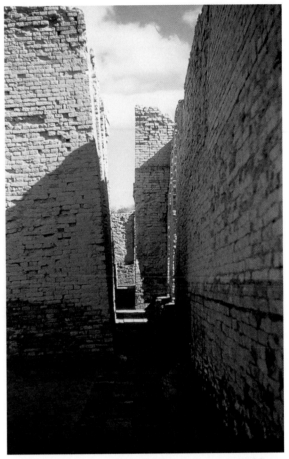

Unlike most ancient cities, Mohenjo-Daro, a 4,000-year-old metropolis in the Indus River Valley, had an extensive system of drains. Lack of adequate drains in cities contributed to poor public health.

Teotihuacan, for instance, very high infant and child mortality rates set a limit to the city's growth. Not until relatively recent times did public health measures reduce the risk of living in cities, and had it not been for a constant influx of rural peoples, they would have been hard pressed to maintain their population size, let alone increase it. One might wonder, then, what would have led people to go live in such unhealthy places? The answer is, they were attracted by the same sorts of things that lure people to cities today: they are vibrant, exciting places that also provide people with opportunities not available in rural communities. Of course, their experience in the cities did not always

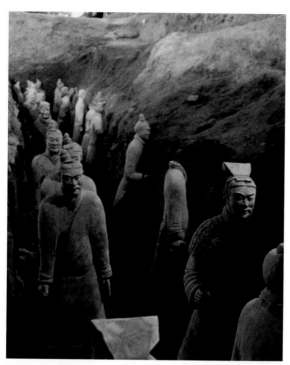

Signs of warfare are common in ancient civilizations. China's first emperor wanted his army to remain with him—in the form of 7,000 life-sized terra-cotta figures of warriors.

live up to advance expectations, anymore than is true today.

Early cities faced social problems strikingly similar to those found in modern North America. Dense population, class systems, and a strong centralized government created internal stress. The slaves and the poor saw that the wealthy had all the things that they themselves lacked. It was not just a question of luxury items; the poor did not have enough space in which to live with comfort and dignity.

Evidence of warfare in early civilizations is common. Cities were fortified; documents list many battles, raids, and wars between groups; cylinder seals, paintings, and sculpture depict battle scenes, victorious kings, and captured prisoners of war. Increasing population and the accompanying scarcity of good farming land often led to boundary disputes and quarrels over land between civilized states or between tribal peoples and a state. Open warfare often developed. People tended to crowd into walled cities for protection and to be near irrigation systems.

The class system also caused internal stress. As time went on, the rich became richer and the poor poorer. In early civilizations one's place in society was relatively fixed. Wealth was based on free slave labor. For this reason there was little or no impetus for social reform. Records from the Mesopotamian city of Lagash indicate that social unrest due to exploitation of the poor by the rich grew during this period. Members of the upper class received tracts of farmland some 20 times larger than those granted the lower class. An upper-class reformer, Urukaginal saw the danger and introduced changes to protect the poor from exploitation by the wealthy, thus preserving the stability of the city.

Given the problems associated with civilization, it is perhaps not surprising that a recurring phenomenon is their collapse. Nonetheless, the rise of cities and civilization laid the basis for modern life. It is sobering to note that many of the problems associated with the first civilizations are still with us. Waste disposal, pollution-related health problems, crowding, social inequities, and warfare continue to be serious problems. Through the study of past civilizations, we now stand a chance of understanding why such problems persist. Such an understanding will be required if the problems are ever to be overcome. It would be nice if the next cultural revolution saw the human species transcending these problems. If this comes about, anthropology, through its comparative study of civilizations, will have played a key role.

CHAPTER SUMMARY

The world's first cities grew out of Neolithic villages between 6,000 and 4,500 years ago, first in Mesopotamia, then in Egypt and the Indus Valley. In China, the process was under way by 5,000 years ago. Somewhat later, and completely independently, similar changes took place in

Mesoamerica and Peru. Four basic culture changes mark the transition from Neolithic village life to life in civilized urban centers. The first culture change is agricultural innovation as new farming methods were developed. For example, the ancient Sumerians built an irrigation system that enabled them to control their water resources and thus increase crop yields.

The second culture change is diversification of labor. With the growth of large populations in cities, some people were freed from agricultural activities to develop skills as artisans and craftspeople. With specialization came the development of new technologies, leading to the beginnings of extensive trade systems. An outgrowth of technological innovation and increased contact with foreign people through trade was new knowledge; within the early civilizations sciences such as geometry and astronomy were first developed.

The third culture change that characterized urban life is the emergence of central government with authority to deal with the complex problems associated with cities. Evidence of a central governing authority comes from such sources as law codes, temple records, and royal chronicles. With the invention of writing, governments could keep records of their transactions and/or boast of their own power and glory. Further evidence of centralized government comes from archeological excavations of city structures.

Typically, the first cities were headed by a king and his special advisers. The reign of the Babylonian King Hammurabi, sometime between 1950 and 1700 B.C., is well known for its efficient government organization and the standardization of its legal system. In the New World the Inca empire in Peru reached its culmination in the 16th century A.D. With a population of several million people, the Inca state, headed by an emperor, possessed a widespread governing bureaucracy that functioned with great efficiency at every level.

The fourth culture change characteristic of civilization is social stratification, or the emergence of social classes. In the early cities of Mesopotamia, symbols of status and privilege appeared for the first time, and individuals were ranked according to the work they did or the position of their families. Archaeologists have been able to verify the existence of social classes in ancient civilizations in four ways: by studying burial customs, as well as skeletons, through grave excavations; by noting the size of dwellings in excavated cities; by examining preserved records in writing and art; and by studying the correspondence of Europeans who described the great civilizations that they destroyed in the New World.

A number of theories have been proposed to explain why civilizations developed. The irrigation, or hydraulic, theory holds that the effort to build and control an irrigation system required a degree of social organization that eventually led to civilization. There are several objections to this theory, however. One might argue simply that sophisticated irrigation systems were a result of the development of civilization rather than a cause. Another theory suggests that in the multicrop economies of both the Old and New Worlds, some kind of system was needed to distribute the various food products throughout the population. Such a procedure would have required a centralized authority, leading to the emergence of a centralized government. A third theory holds that civilization develops where populations are circumscribed by environmental barriers or other societies. As such populations grow, competition for space and scarce resources leads to the development of centralized authority to control resources and organize warfare.

These theories all emphasize the interrelation of people and what they do on the one hand and the environment in which they live on the other. A theory that lays greater stress on the beliefs and values which regulate the interaction between people and their environment seeks to explain the emergence of Maya civilization in terms of the role religion may have played in keeping the Maya in and about cities like Tikal. Finally, action theory focuses attention on the actions of forceful leaders, whose efforts to promote their own interests may play a role in social change.

Sanitation problems in early cities, coupled with large numbers of people living in close proximity, created environments in which infectious diseases were rampant. Early urban centers also faced problems strikingly similar to our own. Dense population, class systems, and a strong centralized government created internal stress. Warfare was common; cities were fortified, and armies served to protect the state. Nevertheless, a recurrent phenomenon in all civilizations has been their ultimate collapse.

POINTS FOR CONSIDERATION

1. What is the importance of planned cities and monumental architecture to centralized authorities? What can it reveal about the culture, beliefs, and values of the builders? How is this demonstrated in ancient cities like Tikal? How is it demonstrated in modern cities like New York, Washington D.C., London, Moscow, Beijing, etc.?

2. What is the importance of the public display of the Code of Hammurabi? What does it mean in terms of the process of justice? How does it affect the power of those issuing judgment relative to those who might be judged?

3. Why is a centralized government less effective in a nomadic rather than an agricultural culture? What tools to create and reinforce authority might it have less access to?

4. Another concern raised by economic development in tropical areas is the displacement of indigenous peoples. Often the argument is raised that these people will benefit from their introduction to "civilization." Is this true? Is "civilized" life measurably better or worse than the food gathering or early agricultural lifestyles of many of these people? What are the social and biological consequences of their displacement?

SUGGESTED READINGS

Marcus, J., & Flannery, K.V. (1996). *Zapote civilization: How urban society evolved in Mexico's Oaxaca Valley*. New York: Thames & Hudson.

With its lavish illustrations, this looks like a book for coffee table adornment, but it is in fact a thoughtful and serious work on the rise of a pristine civilization. In it, the authors present their action theory.

Meltzer, D., Fowler, D., & Sabloff, J. (Eds.). (1986). *American archaeology: Past and future*. Washington, D.C.: Smithsonian Institution Press.

This collection of articles contains one by Henry Wright, "The Evolution of Civilization," an excellent comparative consideration of the subject.

Pfeiffer, J. E. (1977). *The emergence of society*. New York: McGraw-Hill.

This is a comprehensive survey of the origins of food production and the world's first cities. In order to write the book, the author traveled to archaeological sites throughout the world and consulted with numerous investigators. The book is notable for its readability.

Redman, C. E. (1978). *The rise of civilization: From early farmers to urban society in the ancient Near East*. San Francisco: Freeman.

One of the best-documented examples of the rise of urban societies is that of Greater Mesopotamia in the Middle East. This clearly written textbook focuses on that development, presenting the data, discussing interpretations of those data, as well as problems.

Sabloff, J. A. (1997). *The cities of ancient Mexico* (Rev. ed.). New York: Thames & Hudson.

This well-written and lavishly illustrated book describes the major cities of the Olmecs, Zapotecs, Maya, Teotihuacanos, Toltecs, and Aztecs. Following the descriptions, Sabloff discusses the question of origins, the problems of archaeological reconstruction, and the basis on which he provides vignettes of life in the ancient cities. The book concludes with a gazetteer of fifty sites in Mesoamerica.

Sabloff, J. A., & Lamberg-Karlovsky, C. C. (Eds.). (1974). *The rise and fall of civilizations, mod-* *ern archaeological approaches to ancient cultures*. Menlo Park, CA: Cummings.

The emphasis in this collection of articles is theoretical or methodological rather than purely descriptive. Special emphasis is on Mesopotamia and Mesoamerica, but papers are included on Peru, Egypt, the Indus Valley, China, and Europe.

Chapter 13
MODERN HUMAN DIVERSITY

ONE OF THE NOTABLE CHARACTERISTICS OF THE
HUMAN SPECIES TODAY IS ITS GREAT VARIABILITY.
HUMAN DIVERSITY HAS LONG FASCINATED
PEOPLE, BUT UNFORTUNATELY, IT ALSO HAS LED
TO DISCRIMINATION AND EVEN BLOODSHED.

Chapter Preview

What Are the Causes of Physical Variability in Modern Animals?

In the gene pool of a species like *Homo sapiens,* there are various alleles for any given physical characteristic. When such a species is divided into geographically dispersed populations, as is the human species, forces such as drift and natural selection operate in slightly different ways, causing the store of genetic variability to be unevenly expressed. Thus, for example, alleles for dark skin pigmentation are found in high frequency in human populations native to regions of heavy ultraviolet radiation, while alleles for light skin pigmentation have a high incidence in populations native to regions of reduced ultraviolet radiation.

Is the Concept of Race Useful for Studying Human Physical Variation?

No. Because races are arbitrarily defined, it is impossible to agree on any specific classification. The problem is compounded by the tendency for "racial" characteristics to occur in gradations from one population to another without sharp breaks. Furthermore, while one characteristic may be distributed in a north-south gradient, another may occur in an east-west gradient. For these and other reasons, most anthropologists have found it most productive to study the distribution and significance of specific characteristics.

Are There Differences in Intelligence From One Population to Another?

Probably not, in spite of the fact that some populations receive lower average scores on IQ tests than others. Even so, many individuals in "low-scoring" populations score higher than some in the "higher-scoring" populations. Part of the problem is that there is no agreement on what intelligence really is, except that it is made up of several different talents and abilities. Certainly, there are genes affecting these, but they may be independently assorted, and their expression is known to be affected significantly by environmental factors. Whatever genes may be involved, it is clear that environmental factors are critically important.

W hat a piece of work is man," said Hamlet. "How noble in reason, how infinite in faculties, in form and moving how express and admirable, in action how like an angel, in apprehension how like a god: the beauty of the world, the paragon of animals! And yet to me what is this quintessence of dust?"

What people are to each other is the province of anthropology: Physical anthropology reveals what we are; cultural anthropology reveals what we think we are. Our dreams of ourselves are as varied as our languages and our physical bodies. We are the same, but we differ. We speak English or French, our hair is curly or straight, our skin is lightly to heavily pigmented, and in height we range from short to tall. Human genetic variation generally is distributed in such a continuous range, with varying clusters of frequency. The significance we give our variations, the way we perceive them—in fact, whether or not we perceive them at all—is determined by our culture. For example, in many Polynesian countries, where skin color is not a determinant of social status, people really pay little attention to this physical characteristic; in the United States and South Africa, it is one of the first things people do notice.

▲▽▲▽▲▽▲▽▲▽▲▽▲▽▲▽▲▽▲▽▲▽▲▽▲▽▲▽▲
VARIATION AND EVOLUTION

Many behavioral traits—reading, for instance—are learned or acquired by living in a society; other characteristics, such as blue eyes, are passed on physically by heredity. Environment affects both. A person growing up surrounded by books learns to read. If the culture insists that brown-eyed people watch TV and blue-eyed people read, the brown-eyed people may end up making videotapes while the blue-eyed people are writing books. These skills or tastes are acquired characteristics. Changes in such things within one population but not another are capable of making the two distinct in learned behavioral characteristics within relatively few generations.

PHYSICAL VARIABILITY

The physical characteristics of both populations and individuals, as we saw in Chapter 3, are a product of the interaction between genes and environments. Thus, one's genes predispose one to a particular skin color, for example, but the skin color one actually has is strongly affected by environmental factors such as the amount of solar radiation. In this case, phenotypic expression is strongly influenced by environment; in some others, such as one's ABO blood type, phenotypic expression closely reflects genotype.

For most characteristics, there are within the gene pool of *Homo sapiens* variant forms of genes, known as alleles. In the color of an eye, the shape of a hand, the texture of skin, many variations can occur. This kind of variability, found in many animal species, signifies a rich potential for new combinations of characteristics in future generations. Such a species is called **polymorphic.** Our blood types, determined by the alleles for Types A, B, and O blood, are an example of a polymorphic trait, which in this case may appear in any of four distinct phenotypic forms. A polymorphic species faced with changing environmental conditions has within its gene pool the possibility of producing individuals with traits appropriate to its altered life. Many may not achieve reproductive success, but those whose physical characteristics enable them to do well in the new environment will usually reproduce, so that their genes will become more common in subsequent generations. Thus, humankind, being polymorphic, has been able to occupy a variety of environments.

A major expansion into new environments was under way by the time *Homo erectus* appeared on the scene (Chapter 8). Populations of this species were living in Africa, Southeast Asia, Europe, and China. Each of these places constitutes a different **faunal region,** which is to say that each possesses its own distinctive assemblage of animal life, not precisely like that of other regions. This differentiation of animal life is the result of selective pressures that, through the Pleistocene,

---

Polymorphic. A species in the gene pool of which there are alternative forms (alleles) for particular genes. **>** **Faunal region.** A geographic region with its own distinctive assemblage of animal life, not precisely like that of other regions.

differed from one region to another. For example, the conditions of life were quite different in China, which lies in the temperate zone, than they were in tropical Southeast Asia. Coupled with differing selective pressures were geographical features that restricted or prevented gene flow between populations of different faunal regions.

When a polymorphic species is divided into geographically dispersed populations, it usually is **polytypic;** that is, the store of genetic variability is unevenly expressed. Genetic variants will be expressed in different frequencies in different populations. For example, in the Old World, populations of *H. sapiens* living in the tropics have a higher frequency of genes for dark skin color than do those living in more northerly regions. In blood type, *H. sapiens* is polymorphic, with four distinct groups (A, B, O, or AB). In the distribution of

these types, the polytypic nature of the species is again revealed. The frequency of the O allele is highest in American Indians, especially among some populations native to South America; the highest frequencies of the allele for Type A blood tend to be found among certain European populations (although the highest frequency of all is found among the Blackfoot and Blood Indians of North America); the highest frequencies of the B allele are found in some Asian populations (see Figure 13.1). We would expect the earlier species, *H. erectus*, with populations in the four faunal regions of the Old World, to have been polytypic. This appears to have been the case, for the fossils from each of the four regions show some differences from those in the others. African *Homo erectus*, for example, had the tall linear body build often seen in some modern African populations,

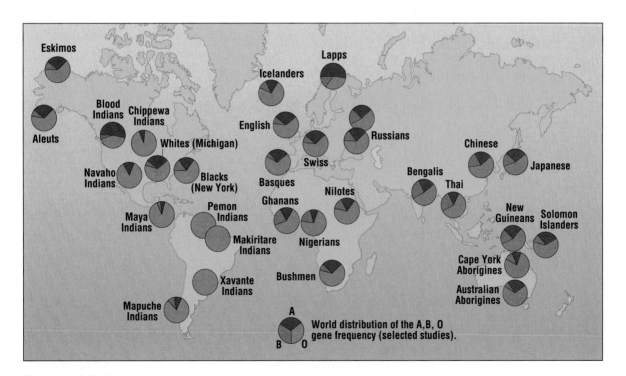

FIGURE 13.1

Frequencies of the three alleles for the A, B, and O blood groups for selected populations around the world demonstrate the polytypic nature of *H. sapiens*.

Polytypic.   The expression of genetic variants in different frequencies in different populations of a species.

whereas Chinese *erectus*, like the modern Chinese, seems to have been shorter of stature. It seems, then, that the human species has been polytypic since at least the time of *H. erectus*.

THE MEANING OF RACE

Early anthropologists tried to explore the polytypic nature of the human species by systematically classifying *H. sapiens* into subspecies, or **races,** based on geographic location and phenotypic (physical) features such as skin color, body size, head shape, and hair texture. Such classifications were continually being challenged by the presence of individuals who did not fit the categories, such as light-skinned Africans or dark-skinned "Caucasoids"; to get around the problem, it was assumed that these individuals were hybrids or the product of racial mixtures. Lack of concordance between traits—for example, the fact that long prominent noses are not only common among Europeans but have a high frequency in various East African populations as well—was usually explained away in a similar manner. The fact is, generalized references to human types such as "Asiatic" or "Mongoloid," "European" or "Caucasoid," and "African" or "Negroid" were at best mere statistical abstractions about populations in which certain physical features appeared in higher frequencies than in other populations; no example of "pure" racial types could be found. These categories turned out to be neither definitive nor particularly helpful. The visible traits were found to occur not in abrupt shifts from population to population, but in a continuum that changed gradually, with few sharp breaks. To compound the problem, one trait might change gradually over a north-south gradient, while another might show a similar change from east to west. Human skin color, for instance, becomes progressively darker as one moves from northern Europe to central Africa, while blood type B becomes progressively more common as one moves from western to eastern Europe.

Finally, there were many variations within each group, and those within groups were often greater than those between groups. In Africa, the skin color of someone from the Kalahari Desert might more closely resemble that of a person of East Indian extraction than the darkly pigmented Nilotic Sudanese who was supposed to be of the same race.

The Negroid was characterized as having dark skin, thick lips, a broad nose, and tightly curled hair; the Mongoloid, straight hair, a flat face, a flat nose, and spread nostrils; and the Caucasoid, pale skin, a narrow nose, and varied eye color and hair form. The classification then expanded to take in American Indians, Australians, and Polynesians, but even the expanded system failed to account for dramatic differences in appearance among individuals, or even populations, in each racial category; for example, Europeans, Arabs, and East Indians were all lumped together as Caucasoids.

In an attempt to encompass such variations, schemes of racial classification proliferated. In 1926, J. Deniker classified 29 races according to texture of hair, presumably improving upon Roland B. Dixon's 1923 classification based on three indexes of body measures. Hair texture and body build were the characteristics used for another set of racial categories proposed in 1930. By 1947, Earnest Hooton had proposed three new composite races resulting from the interbreeding of "primary" races. Despite these classificatory attempts on the part of Western anthropologists, no definitive grouping of distinct, discontinuous biological groups was found for modern humanity.

A turning point is represented by the publication in 1950 of a book called *Races* by Carleton Coon, Stanley Garn, and Joseph Birdsell. Like their predecessors, they too tried to classify modern humans into a number of racial groups—30 in this case—but they rejected a trait-list approach. Instead, they recognized races as popula-

---

Race.   A population of a species that differs in the frequency of the variants of some gene or genes from other populations of the same species.

Among the tallest people in the world are the Tutsi (left), while among the smallest are the Efe (right). Both are from central Africa and illustrate the wide range of variation seen in a (supposedly) single racial category.

tions that owed certain common characteristics to environmental, primarily climatic, adaptation, which continued to change in response to evolutionary forces such as gene flow and altered selective pressures. While this book certainly had its weaknesses, it did represent a significant departure from previous attempts at racial classification and was influential in paving the way for a sounder understanding of human variation.

RACE AS A BIOLOGICAL CONCEPT

To understand why the racial approach to human variation has been so unproductive, we must first understand the race concept in strictly biological terms. In biology, a race is defined as a popula-

tion of a species that differs in the frequency of different variants of some gene or genes from other populations of the same species. Simple and straightforward though such a definition may seem, there are three very important things to note about it. First, it is arbitrary; there is no agreement on how many genetic differences it takes to make a race. For some who are interested in the topic, different frequencies in the variants of one gene are sufficient; for others, differences in frequencies involving several genes were necessary. The number of genes and precisely which ones are the more important for defining races are still open to debate.

The arbitrariness of racial classification is well illustrated by the following Original Study.

Race Without Color[1]

What Could Be More Objective?

Science often violates simple common sense. Our eyes tell us that the Earth is flat, that the sun revolves around the Earth, and that we humans are not animals. But we now ignore that evidence of our senses. We have learned that our planet is in fact round and revolves around the sun, and that humans are slightly modified chimpanzees. The reality of human races is another commonsense "truth" destined to follow the flat Earth into oblivion.

The commonsense view of races goes somewhat as follows. All native Swedes differ from all native Nigerians in appearance: There is no Swede whom you would mistake for a Nigerian, and vice versa. Swedes have lighter skin than Nigerians do. They also generally have blond or light brown hair, while Nigerians have very dark hair. Nigerians usually have more tightly coiled hair than Swedes do, dark eyes as opposed to eyes that are blue or gray, and fuller lips and broader noses.

In addition, other Europeans look much more like Swedes than like Nigerians, while other peoples of sub-Saharan Africa—except perhaps the Khoisan peoples of southern Africa—look much more like Nigerians than like Swedes. Yes, skin color does get darker in Europe toward the Mediterranean, but it is still lighter than the skin of sub-Saharan Africans. In Europe, very dark or curly hair becomes more common outside Scandinavia, but European hair is still not as tightly coiled as in Africa. Since it's easy then to distinguish almost any native European from any native sub-Saharan African, we recognize Europeans and sub-Saharan Africans as distinct races, which we name for their skin colors: Whites and Blacks, respectively.

As it turns out, this seemingly unassailable reasoning is not objective. There are many different, equally valid procedures for defining races, and those different procedures yield very different classifications. One such procedure would group Italians and Greeks with most African blacks. It would classify Xhosas—the South African "black" group to which President Nelson Mandela belongs—with Swedes rather than Nigerians. Another equally valid procedure would place Swedes with Fulani (a Nigerian "black" group) and not with Italians, who would again be grouped with most other African blacks. Still another procedure would keep Swedes and Italians separate from all African blacks but would throw the Swedes and Italians into the same race as New Guineans and American Indians. Faced with such differing classifications, many anthropologists today conclude that one cannot recognize any human races at all.

If we were just arguing about races of nonhuman animals, essentially the same uncertainties of classification would arise. But the debates would remain polite and would never attract attention outside the halls of academia. Classification of humans is different "only" in that it shapes our views of other peoples, fosters our subconscious differentiation between "us" and "them," and is invoked to justify political and socioeconomic discrimination. On this basis, many anthropologists therefore argue that even if one *could* classify humans into races, one should not.

---

[1]Diamond, J. (1994). Race without color. *Discover, 15*(11), 83–88.

To understand how such uncertainties in classification arise, let's steer clear of humans for a moment and instead focus on warblers and lions, about which we can easily remain dispassionate. Biologists begin by classifying living creatures into species. A species is a group of populations whose individual members would, if given the opportunity, interbreed with individuals of other populations of that group. But they would not interbreed with individuals of other species that are similarly defined. Thus all human populations, no matter how different they look, belong to the same species because they do interbreed and have interbred whenever they have encountered each other. Gorillas and humans, however, belong to two different species because—to the best of our knowledge—they have never interbred despite their coexisting in close proximity for millions of years.

We know that different populations classified together in the human species are visibly different. The same proves true for most other animal and plant species as well, whenever biologists look carefully. For example, consider one of the most familiar species of bird in North America, the yellow-rumped warbler. Breeding males of eastern and western North America can be distinguished at a glance by their throat color: white in the east, yellow in the west. Hence they are classified into two different races, or subspecies (alternative words with identical meanings), termed the myrtle and Audubon races, respectively. The white-throated eastern birds differ from the yellow-throated western birds in other characteristics as well, such as in voice and habitat preference. But where the two races meet, in western Canada, white-throated birds do indeed interbreed with yellow-throated birds. That's why we consider myrtle warblers and Audubon warblers as races of the same species rather than different species.

Racial classification of these birds is easy. Throat color, voice, and habitat preference all vary geographically in yellow-rumped warblers, but the variation of those three traits is "concordant"—that is, voice differences or habitat differences lead to the same racial classification as differences in throat color because the same populations that differ in throat color also differ in voice and habitat.

Racial classification of many other species, though, presents problems of concordance. For instance, a Pacific island bird species called the golden whistler varies from one island to the next. Some populations consist of big birds, some of small birds; some have black-winged males, others green-winged males; some have yellow-breasted females, others gray-breasted females; many other characteristics vary as well. But, unfortunately for humans like me who study these birds, those characteristics don't vary concordantly. Islands with green-winged males can have either yellow-breasted or gray-breasted females, and green-winged males are big on some islands but small on other islands. As a result, if you classified golden whistlers into races based on single traits, you would get entirely different classifications depending on which trait you chose.

Classification of these birds also presents problems of "hierarchy." Some of the golden whistler races recognized by ornithologists are wildly different from all other races, but some are very similar to one another. They can therefore be grouped into a hierarchy of distinctness. You start by establishing the most distinct population as a race separate from all other populations.

You then separate the most distinct of the remaining populations. You continue by grouping similar populations, and separating distinct populations or groups of populations as races or groups of races. The problem is that the extent to which you continue the racial classification is arbitrary, and it's a decision about which taxonomists disagree passionately. Some taxonomists, the "splitters," like to recognize many different races, partly for the egotistical motive of getting credit for having named a race. Other taxonomists, the "lumpers," prefer to recognize few races. Which type of taxonomist you are is a matter of personal preference.

How does that variability of traits by which we classify races come about in the first place? Some traits vary because of natural selection: That is, one form of the trait is advantageous for survival in one area, another form in a different area. For example, northern hares and weasels develop white fur in the winter, but southern ones retain brown fur year-round. The white winter fur is selected in the north for camouflage against the snow, while any animal unfortunate enough to turn white in the snowless southern states would stand out from afar against the brown ground and would be picked off by predators.

Other traits vary geographically because of sexual selection, meaning that those traits serve as arbitrary signals by which individuals of one sex attract mates of the opposite sex while intimidating rivals. Adult male lions, for instance, have a mane, but lionesses and young males don't. The adult male's mane signals to lionesses that he is sexually mature, and signals to young male rivals that he is a dangerous and experienced adversary. The length and color of a lion's mane vary among populations, being shorter and blacker in Indian lions than in African lions. Indian lions and lionesses evidently find short black manes sexy or intimidating; African lions don't.

Finally, some geographically variable traits have no known effect on survival and are invisible to rivals and to prospective sex partners. They merely reflect mutations that happened to arise and spread in one area. They could equally well have arisen and spread elsewhere—they just didn't.

Nothing that I've said about geographic variation in animals is likely to get me branded a racist. We don't attribute higher IQ or social status to black-winged whistlers than to green-winged whistlers. But now let's consider geographic variation in humans. We'll start with invisible traits, about which it's easy to remain dispassionate.

Many geographically variable human traits evolved by natural selection to adapt humans to particular climates or environments—just as the winter color of a hare or weasel did. Good examples are the mutations that people in tropical parts of the Old World evolved to help them survive malaria, the leading infectious disease of the Old World tropics. One such mutation is the sickle-cell gene, so-called because the red blood cells of people with that mutation tend to assume a sickle shape. People bearing the gene are more resistant to malaria than people without it. Not surprisingly, the gene is absent from northern Europe, where malaria is nonexistent, but it's common in tropical Africa, where malaria is widespread. Up to 40% of Africans in such areas carry the sickle-cell gene. It's also common in the malaria-ridden Arabian Peninsula and southern India, and rare or absent in the southernmost parts of South Africa, among the Xhosas, who live mostly beyond the tropical geographic range of malaria.

The geographic range of human malaria is much wider than the range of the sickle-cell gene. As it happens, other antimalarial genes take over the protective function of the sickle-cell gene in malarial Southeast Asia and New Guinea and in Italy, Greece, and other warm parts of the Mediterranean basin. Thus human races, if defined by antimalarial genes, would be very different from human races as traditionally defined by traits such as skin color. As classified by antimalarial genes (or their absence), Swedes are grouped with Xhosas but not with Italians or Greeks. Most other peoples usually viewed as African blacks are grouped with Arabia's "whites" and are kept separate from the "black" Xhosas.

Antimalarial genes exemplify the many features of our body chemistry that vary geographically under the influence of natural selection. Another such feature is the enzyme lactase, which enables us to digest the milk sugar lactose. Infant humans, like infants of almost all other mammal species, possess lactase and drink milk. Until about 6,000 years ago most humans, like all other mammal species, lost the lactase enzyme on reaching the age of weaning. The obvious reason is that it was unnecessary—no human or other mammal drank milk as an adult. Beginning around 4000 B.C., however, fresh milk obtained from domestic mammals became a major food for adults of a few human populations. Natural selection caused individuals in these populations to retain lactase into adulthood. Among such peoples are northern and central Europeans, Arabians, northern Indians, and several milk-drinking black African peoples, such as the Fulani of West Africa. Adult lactase is much less common in southern European populations and in most other African black populations, as well as in all populations of east Asians, aboriginal Australians, and American Indians.

Once again races defined by body chemistry don't match races defined by skin color. Swedes belong with Fulani in the "lactase-positive race," while most African "blacks," Japanese, and American Indians belong in the "lactase-negative race."

Not all the effects of natural selection are as invisible as lactase and sickle cells. Environmental pressures have also produced more noticeable differences among peoples, particularly in body shapes. Among the tallest and most long-limbed peoples in the world are the Nilotic peoples, such as the Dinkas, who live in the hot, dry areas of East Africa. At the opposite extreme in body shape are the Inuit, or Eskimo, who have compact bodies and relatively short arms and legs. The reasons have to do with heat loss. The greater the surface area of a warm body, the more body heat that's lost, since heat loss is directly proportional to surface area. For people of a given weight, a long-limbed, tall shape maximizes surface area, while a compact, short-limbed shape minimizes it. Dinkas and Inuit have opposite problems of heat balance: The former usually need desperately to get rid of body heat, while the latter need desperately to conserve it. Thus natural selection molded their body shapes oppositely, based on their contrasting climates.

Other visible traits that vary geographically among humans evolved by means of sexual selection. We all know that we find some individuals of the opposite sex more attractive than other individuals. We also know that in sizing up sex appeal, we pay more attention to certain parts of a prospective sex partner's body than to other parts. Men tend to be inordinately interested in women's breasts and much less concerned with women's toenails. Women, in turn, tend to be turned on by the shape of a man's buttocks or the details of a man's beard and body hair, if any, but not by the size of his feet.

But all those determinants of sex appeal vary geographically. Khoisan and Andaman Island women tend to have much larger buttocks than most other women. Nipple color and breast shape and size also vary geographically among women. European men are rather hairy by world standards, while Southeast Asian men tend to have very sparse beards and body hair.

What's the function of these traits that differ so markedly between men and women? They certainly don't aid survival: It's not the case that orange nipples help Khoisan women escape lions, while darker nipples help European women survive cold winters. Instead, these varying traits play a crucial role in sexual selection. Women with very large buttocks are a turn-on, or at least acceptable, to Khoisan and Andaman men but look freakish to many men from other parts of the world. Bearded and hairy men readily find mates in Europe but fare worse in Southeast Asia. The geographic variation of these traits, however, is as arbitrary as the geographic variation in the color of a lion's mane.

There is a third possible explanation for the function of geographically variable human traits, besides survival or sexual selection—namely, no function at all. A good example is provided by fingerprints, whose complex pattern of arches, loops, and whorls is determined genetically. Fingerprints also vary geographically: For example, Europeans' fingerprints tend to have many loops, while aboriginal Australians' fingerprints tend to have many whorls.

If we classify human populations by their fingerprints, most Europeans and black Africans would sort out together in one race, Jews and some Indonesians in another, and aboriginal Australians in still another. But those geographic variations in fingerprint patterns possess no known function whatsoever. They play no role in survival: Whorls aren't especially suitable for grabbing kangaroos, nor do loops help bar mitzvah candidates hold on to the pointer for the Torah. They also play no role in sexual selection: While you've undoubtedly noticed whether your mate is bearded or has brown nipples, you surely haven't the faintest idea whether his or her fingerprints have more loops than whorls. Instead it's purely a matter of chance that whorls became common in aboriginal Australians, and loops among Jews. Our rhesus factor blood groups and numerous other human traits fall into the same category of genetic characteristics whose geographic variation serves no function.

Fingerprints' patterns of loops, whorls, and arches are genetically determined. Grouping people on this basis would place most Europeans, sub-Saharan Africans, and East Asians together as "loops," Australian aborigines and the people of Mongolia together as "whorls," and Central Europeans and the Bushmen of southern Africa together as "arches."

The "openness" of races to gene flow is illustrated by this picture of an Asian and African-American couple with their children.

After arbitrariness, the second thing to note about the biological definition of race is that it does not mean that any one race has exclusive possession of any particular variant of any gene or genes. In human terms, the frequency of the allele for blood group O may be high in one population and low in another, but it is present in both. Races are genetically "open," meaning that gene flow takes place between them. Because they are genetically "open," they are apt to be impermanent and subject to reamalgamation. Thus, one can easily see the fallacy of any attempt to identify "pure" races; if gene flow cannot take place between two populations, either directly or indirectly through intermediate populations, then they are not races, but are separate species.

The third thing to note about the biological definition of race is that individuals of one race will not necessarily be distinguishable from those of another. In fact, as we have just noted with respect to humans, the differences between individuals within a population are generally greater than the differences between populations. As the science writer James Shreeve puts it, "most of what separates me genetically from a typical African or Eskimo also separates me from another average American of Eu-

ropean ancestry."[2] This follows from the genetic "openness" of races; no one race has an exclusive claim to any particular gene or allele.

THE CONCEPT OF HUMAN RACES

As a device for understanding polytypic variation in humans, the biological race concept has serious drawbacks. One is that the category is arbitrary to begin with, which makes agreement on any given classification difficult, if not impossible. For example, if one researcher emphasizes skin color, while another emphasizes blood group differences, they will not classify people in the same way. Perhaps if the human species were divided into a number of relatively discrete breeding populations, this wouldn't be such a problem, but even this is open to debate. What has happened, though, is that human populations have grown in the course of human evolution, and with this growth have come increased opportunities for contact and gene flow between populations. Since the advent of food

---

[2]Shreeve, J. (1994) Terms of estrangement. *Discover, 15*(11), 60.

production, the process has accelerated as higher birth rates and periodic food shortages (discussed in Chapter 11) have prompted the movement of farmers from their homelands to other places. In East Asia, for example, the development of farming, followed by the invention of bronze and a host of other technologies in China resulted in expansion of northern Chinese populations and displacements of southern Chinese peoples into Southeast Asia. This expansion effectively "swamped" the original populations of this region, except in a few out-of-the-way places like the Andaman Islands.[3] As a consequence of such movements, differences between human populations today are probably less clear-cut than back in the days of *H. erectus*, or even archaic *H. sapiens*.

If this isn't enough of a problem, things are complicated even more because humans are so complicated genetically. Thus, the genetic underpinnings of the phenotypic traits upon which traditional racial classifications are usually based are poorly understood. To compound the problem,

"race" exists as a cultural, as well as a biological, category. In various different ways, cultures define religious, linguistic, and ethnic groups as races, thereby confusing linguistic and cultural traits with physical traits. For example, in many Central and South American countries, people are commonly classified as "Indian," "Mestizo" (mixed), or "Ladino" (of Spanish descent). But in spite of the biological connotations of these terms, the criteria used for assigning individuals to these categories consist of such things as whether they wear shoes, sandals, or go barefoot; speak Spanish or some Indian language; live in a thatched hut or a European-style house; and so forth. Thus, an Indian, by speaking Spanish, wearing Western-style clothes, and living in a house in a non-Indian neighborhood, ceases to be an Indian, no matter how many "Indian genes" he or she may possess.

This sort of confusion of nonbiological characteristics with what are spoken of as biological categories is by no means limited to Central and South American societies. To one degree or another, such confusion is found in most Western societies, including those of Europe and North America. Take, for example, the racial categories used by the U.S. Census Bureau: White, Black, American Indian, Asian, and Pacific Islander are

---

[3]Diamond, J. (1996). Empire of uniformity. *Discover, 17*(3), 83–84.

The Andaman Islanders (left) are a remnant of the original inhabitants of Southeast Asia; the Vietnamese (right) are descendants of people from South China who spread into the region after the invention of agriculture. In the process there was mixing of gene pools.

large catchall categories that include diverse people. *Asian,* for example, includes such different people as Chinese and East Indians (to which Indians, at least, take exception), whereas *Eskimo* (a term these people, the Inuit, find offensive) and *Aleut* are far more restrictive. Addition of slots for native Hawaiians, Middle Easterners, and people who consider themselves multiracial does nothing to improve the situation. To compound the confusion, inclusion in one or another of these categories is usually based on self-identification. In short, what we are dealing with here are not biological categories at all, but rather social constructs.

To make matters even worse, this confusion of social with biological factors is frequently combined with attitudes that are then taken as excuses to exclude whole categories of people from certain roles or positions in society. In the United States, for example, the idea of race originated in the 18th century to refer to the diverse peoples—European settlers, conquered Indians, and Africans imported as slaves—that were brought together in colonial North America. This racial worldview assigned some groups to perpetual low status on the basis of their supposedly biological inferiority, while access to privilege, power, and wealth was reserved for favored groups of European descent.[4]

Different ways in which this discrimination plays out may be illustrated with two quite different examples. An old stereotype is that "blacks are born with rhythm," which somehow is thought to give them a "natural affinity" for jazz, "soul music," rap, and similar forms of musical expression. The corollary of this myth is that African Americans are unsuited "by nature" for symphonic music. Hence, until recently, one did not find an African American at the head of any major symphony orchestra in the United States, even though African American conductors such as James de Priest, Paul Freeman, and Dean Dixon made distinguished careers for themselves in Canada and Europe. A particularly evil consequence of the racial worldview occurred when the Nazis declared the superiority of the "Aryan race" (which is really a linguistic grouping and not a

race at all), and the inferiority of the Gypsy and Jewish "races" (really ethno-religious categories), and then used this distinction as an excuse to exclude Gypsies and Jews from life altogether. In all, 11 million people (Jews, Gypsies, Africans, homosexuals, and other supposedly "inferior" people) were deliberately put to death.

Tragically, such programs of extermination of one group by another continue to occur in many parts of the world today, including parts of South America, Africa, Europe, and Asia. "Holocausts" are by no means things of the past, nor are Gypsies and Jews their only victims. The well-meant vow "never again" contrasts with the reality of "frequently again."

Considering all the problems, confusion, and evil consequences, it is small wonder that there has been a lot of debate not just about how many human races there may be, but about what "race" is and is not. Often forgotten is the fact that a race, even if it can be defined biologically, is the result of the operation of evolutionary processes. Because it is these processes rather than racial categories themselves in which we are really interested, most anthropologists have abandoned the race concept as being of no particular utility. Instead, they prefer to study the distribution and significance of specific, genetically based characteristics, or else the characteristics of small breeding populations that are, after all, the smallest units in which evolutionary change occurs.

SOME PHYSICAL VARIABLES

Not only have attempts to classify people into races proven futile and counterproductive, it has also become apparent that the amount of genetic variation in humans is relatively low, compared to that of other primate species. Nonetheless, human biological variation is a fact of life, and physical anthropologists have learned a great deal about it. Much of it is related to climatic adaptation. For example, a correlation has been noted between body build and climate. Generally, people native to regions with cold climates tend to have greater body bulk (not to be equated with fat) relative to their extremities (arms and legs) than do people native to regions with hot climates, who tend to be long and slender. Interestingly, these differences

---

[4]American Anthropological Association (1998). Statement on "race." Available at www.ameranthassn.org.

Far from being a thing of the past, genocide continues to occur in the world today, as this picture taken in 1998 in the Yugoslav province of Kosovo vividly illustrates.

show up as early as the time of *Homo erectus,* as already noted. Anthropologists generally argue that such differences of body build represent a climatic adaptation; certain body builds are better suited to particular living conditions than others. A person with larger body bulk and shorter extremities may suffer more from summer heat than someone whose extremities are long and whose body is slender. But they will conserve needed body heat under cold conditions. The reason is that a bulky body tends to conserve more heat than a less bulky one, since it has less surface relative to volume. People living in hot, open country, by contrast, benefit from a body build that can get rid of excess heat quickly so as to keep from overheating; for this, long extremities and a slender body, which increase surface area relative to volume, are advantageous.

Studies of body build and climatic adaptation are complicated by the intervening effects on physique of diet, since dietary differences will cause variation in body build. Another complicating factor is clothing. Thus, much of the way people adapt to cold is cultural, rather than biological. For example, Inuit peoples (the proper name

for "Eskimos") live in a region where it is cold much of the year. To cope with this, they long ago developed efficient clothing to keep the body warm. Because of this, the Inuit are provided with what amount to artificial tropical environments inside their clothing. In spite of such considerations, it remains true that in northerly regions of the world, bulky body builds predominate, whereas the reverse is true in the tropics.

Anthropologists have also studied such body features as nose and eye shape and hair textures in relation to climate. A wide flaring nose, for example, is common in populations living in tropical forests; here the air is warm and damp, and so the warming and humidifying functions of the nose are secondary. Longer, more prominent noses, common among cold dwellers, are helpful in humidifying and warming cold air before it reaches the lungs. They are also useful in cleaning and humidifying dry, dusty air in hot climates, which is why long prominent noses are not restricted to places like Europe. Coon, Garn, and Birdsell once proposed that the "Mongoloid face," common in populations native to East and Central Asia, as well as arctic North America, exhibits features flat facial profile generally goes with a round head. A significant percentage of body heat may be lost from the head; however, a round head, having less surface area relative to volume, loses less heat than a longer, more elliptical head. As one would predict from this, long-headed populations are generally found in hotter climates; round-headed ones are more common in cold climates.

SKIN COLOR: A CASE STUDY IN ADAPTATION

In the United States, race is most commonly equated with skin color. Perhaps this is not surprising, since it is such a highly visible trait. Skin color is subject to great variation, and there are at least four main factors associated with it: transparency or thickness of the skin, a copper-colored pigment called carotene, reflected color from the blood vessels, and the amount of **melanin** found in a given area of skin. Exposure to sunlight increases the amount of melanin and, hence, the skin darkens. Melanin is known to protect skin against damaging ultraviolet solar radiation;[5] consequently, darkly pigmented peoples are less susceptible to skin cancers and sunburn than are those whose skin has less melanin. They also seem to be less susceptible to photo-destruction of certain vitamins. Since the highest concentration of dark-skinned people tends to be found in the tropical regions of the world, it appears that natural selection has favored heavily pigmented skin as a protection against the strong solar radiation of equatorial latitudes, where ultraviolet radiation is most intense. Because skin cancers generally do not develop until later in life, they are unlikely to have interfered with the reproductive success of lightly pigmented individuals in the tropics, and so are unlikely to have been the agent of selection. On the other hand, severe sunburn, which is

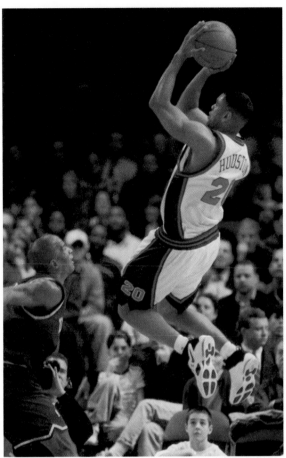

African Americans are disproportionately represented among professional basketball players in part because of the prevalence of tall, linear body shapes among them. This does not mean, however, that "Whites can't jump" or that the anatomy of Blacks necessarily makes them better basketball players. In fact, one reason there are so many African American basketball players has nothing to do with biology, but is due rather to socioeconomic opportunities available to them in a society that still discriminates on the basis of skin color.

adapted to life in very cold environments. The **epicanthic eye fold,** which minimizes eye exposure to the cold, a flat facial profile, and extensive fatty deposits may help to protect the face against frostbite. Although experimental studies have failed to sustain the frostbite hypothesis, it is true that a

[5]Neer, R. M. (1975). The evolutionary significance of vitamin D, skin pigment, and ultraviolet light. *American Journal of Physical Anthropology, 43,* 409–416.

Epicanthic eye fold. A fold of skin at the inner corner of the eye that covers the true corner of the eye; common in Asiatic populations. **> Melanin.** The chemical responsible for dark skin pigmentation, which helps protect against damage from ultraviolet radiation.

The epicanthic eye fold is common among people native to East Asia. Still, a comparison of this individual with those shown on p. 356 shows the absurdity of lumping all Asians in a single category.

FIGURE 13.2

The outline of a normal pelvic inlet (A) compared with that of a woman with rickets (B), which would interfere with her capacity to give birth. Rickets is caused by a deficiency of Vitamin D. In the absence of artificial sources of this vitamin among people living in northern latitudes, lightly pigmented people are least likely to contract rickets.

especially dangerous to infants, causes the body to overheat and interferes with its ability to sweat, by which it might rid itself of excess heat. Furthermore, it makes one susceptible to other kinds of infection. In addition to all this, decomposition of folate, an essential vitamin sensitive to heavy doses of ultraviolet radiation, can cause anemia, spontaneous abortion, and infertility.[6]

While dark skin pigmentation has enjoyed a selective advantage in the tropics, the opposite is true in northern latitudes, where skins have generally been lightly pigmented. This lack of heavy amounts of melanin enables the weak ultraviolet radiation of northern latitudes to penetrate the skin and stimulate formation of Vitamin D. Dark pigmentation interferes with this process. Without access to external sources of Vitamin D, once provided by cod liver oil but now more often provided in Vitamin D-fortified milk, individuals incapable of synthesizing enough of this vitamin in their own bodies were selected against, for they contracted rickets, a disease that seriously deforms children's bones. At its worst, rickets prevents children from reaching reproductive age; at the least, it interferes with a woman's ability to give birth if she does reach reproductive age (see Figure 13.2).

Given what we know about the adaptive significance of human skin color, and the fact that, until 800,000 years ago, hominines were exclusively creatures of the tropics, it is likely that lightly pigmented skins are a recent development in human history. Darkly pigmented skins likely are quite ancient. Consistent with this, the enzyme tyrosinase, which converts the amino acid tyrosine into the compound that forms melanin, is present in lightly pigmented peoples in sufficient quantity to make them very "black." The reason it does not is that they have genes that inactivate or inhibit it.[7] Human skin is more liberally endowed

[6]Branda, R. F., & Eatoil, J. W. (1978). Skin color and photolysis: An evolutionary hypothesis, *Science, 201,* 625–626.

[7]Wills, C. (1994). The skin we're in. *Discover, 15*(11), 79.

with sweat glands than is the skin of other mammals; in combination with our lack of heavy body hair, this makes for effective elimination of excess body heat in a hot climate. This would have been especially advantageous to early hominines on the savanna, who could have avoided confrontations with carnivorous animals by carrying out most of their activities in the heat of the day. For the most part, carnivores rest during this period, being active from dusk until early morning. Without much hair to cover early hominine bodies, selection would have favored dark skins; hence all humans appear to have had a "Black" ancestry, no matter how "White" some of them may be today.

One should not conclude that, because it is newer, lightly pigmented skin is better, or more highly evolved, than heavily pigmented skin. The latter is clearly more highly evolved to the conditions of life in the tropics, although with protective clothing, hats, and sunscreen lotions, lightly pigmented peoples can survive there. Conversely, the availability of supplementary sources of Vitamin D allows heavily pigmented peoples to do quite well away from the tropics. In both cases, culture has rendered skin color differences largely irrelevant.

An interesting question is how long it took for light pigmentation to develop in populations living outside the tropics. We now know that the first people to reach Australia did so about 60,000 years ago. They came there from tropical Southeast Asia, and, as we would expect, had darkly pigmented skin. In Australia, those populations that spread south of the tropics (where, as in northern latitudes, ultraviolet radiation is less intense), underwent some reduction of pigmentation. But for all that, their skin color is still far darker than that of Europeans or East Asians (remember that most of today's Southeast Asian population spread there from southern China following the invention of farming; hence their relatively light pigmentation). The obvious conclusion is that 60,000 years is not enough to produce advanced

These photos of people from Spain, Scandinavia, Senegal, and Indonesia illustrate the range of variation in human skin color. Generally, the closer to the equator populations live, the darker the skin color.

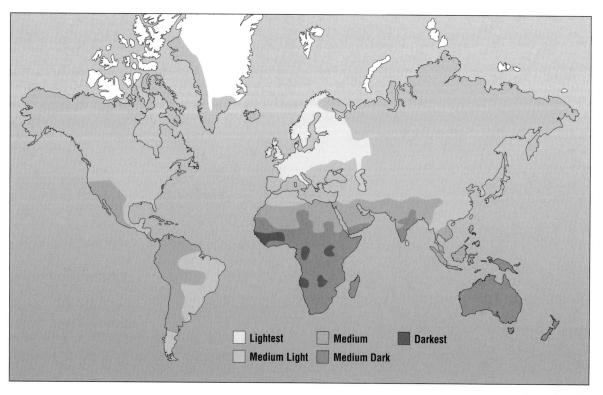

FIGURE 13.3

This map illustrates the distribution of dark and light human skin pigmentation before A.D. 1492. Medium-light skin color in Southeast Asia reflects the spread into that region of people from southern China, while the medium darkness of people native to southern Australia is a consequence of their tropical Southeast Asian ancestry. Lack of a dark skin pigmentation among tropical populations of native Americans reflects their ancestry in Northeast Asia a mere 20,000 years ago.

depigmentation, and that Europeans and East Asians lived outside the tropics for a far longer period.[8]

The inheritance of skin color is not well understood, except that several genes (rather than variants of a single gene), each with several alleles, must be involved. Nevertheless, its geographical distribution, with few exceptions, tends to be continuous, like that of other human traits (see Figure 13.3). The exceptions have to do with the movement of certain populations from their original homelands to other regions or the practice of selective mating, or both. For example, there have

been repeated invasions of the Indian subcontinent by peoples from the north, who were then incorporated into the Hindu caste system. Still today, the higher the caste, the lighter its skin color. This skin color gradient is maintained by strict in-group marriage rules. In the United States, statistical studies have shown that there has been a similar trend among African Americans, with African American women of higher status choosing to marry lighter-skinned males, reflecting the culture's emphasis on the supposed superiority of people with light skin. It is quite possible that the "black pride" movement, which places positive value on features common among those of West African descent, such as dark skins, tightly curled hair, and broad, flat noses, is leading to a reversal of this cultural selection factor.

[8]Ferrie, H. (1997). An interview with C. Loring Brace. *Current Anthropology, 38,* 864.

Although Tasmania is as far south of the equator as Europe is north of it, native Tasmanians were more darkly pigmented. Although the ancestors of both Europeans and Tasmanians lived in tropical regions, populations did not arrive in Tasmania until a good deal later than they reached Europe. Consequently, Tasmanians have not been subject to selection for light pigmentation for as long as have Europeans.

▲▼▲▼▲▼▲▼▲▼▲▼▲▼▲▼▲▼▲▼▲▼▲▼▲▼▲▼

THE SOCIAL SIGNIFICANCE OF RACE: RACISM

Scientific facts do not seem to change what people think about race. **Racism** can be viewed solely as a social problem, although at times it has been used by politicians as a purportedly "scientific" tool. It is an emotional phenomenon best explained in terms of collective psychology. Racial conflict results from long-suppressed resentments and hostilities. The racist responds to social stereotypes, not to known scientific facts.

RACE AND BEHAVIOR

The assumption that there are behavioral differences among human races remains an issue of contemporary society, not easily argued away. Throughout history, certain "races" have been attributed certain characteristics, which assume a variety of names—"national character," "spirit," "temperament"—all of them vague and standing for a number of concepts totally unrelated to any biological concept of race. Common myths involve the "coldness" of Scandinavians or the "martial" character of the Germanics or the "indolent" nature of Africans. These generalizations serve to characterize a people unjustly; German citizens do not necessarily advocate genocide, nor do Africans necessarily hate to work. The term "race" has a precise biological meaning, but in popular usage, as we have already seen, the term often acquires a meaning unrelated to that given by scientists, often with disastrous results.

To date, no innate behavioral characteristic can be attributed to any group of people that the nonscientist would most probably term a "race" that cannot be explained in terms of cultural practices. If the Chinese happen to be especially successful mathematicians, it can probably be explained in terms of emphasis within their culture on abstract concepts, learned ways of perceiving the universe, and their philosophies. If African Americans are not as well represented in managerial positions as their fellow citizens, it is because for a long time they were allowed neither the necessary training nor the opportunity (nor is the problem fully rectified today). The list could go on, and all such differences or characteristics can be explained in terms of culture.

Similarly, high crime rates among certain groups can be explained with reference to culture and not biology. Individuals alienated and demoralized by poverty, injustice, and inequality of opportunity tend to display what the dominant

Racism. A doctrine of racial superiority by which one group asserts its superiority over another.

These photos show how important the environment is in the expression of genetic traits. The same strain of corn that flourishes in one set of circumstances may do quite poorly in another.

members of society regard as antisocial behavior more frequently than those who are culturally well-integrated. For example, American Indians, when they have been equipped and allowed to compete on an equal footing with other North Americans, have not suffered from the high rate of alcoholism and criminal behavior exhibited by Indians living under conditions of poverty, whether on or off reservations.

RACE AND INTELLIGENCE

A question frequently asked by those unfamiliar with the deficiencies of the race concept is whether or not some races are inherently more intelligent than others. Intelligence tests carried on in the United States by European American investigators among people of European and African descent have often shown that European Americans attain higher scores. During World War I, a series of IQ tests known as Alpha and Beta were regularly given to draftees. The results showed that the average score attained by European Americans was higher than that obtained by African Americans. Even though many African Americans scored higher than some European Americans, and some African Americans scored higher than most European Americans (African Americans from the north, for instance, score better on average than southern Whites), many people took this as proof of the intellectual superiority of "White people." But all the tests really showed was that, on the av-

erage, European Americans outperformed African Americans in certain social situations. The tests did not measure "intelligence" per se, but the ability, conditioned by culture, of certain individuals to respond to certain socially conditioned problems. These tests had been conceived by European Americans for comparable middle-class European Americans. While people of color coming from similar backgrounds generally did well (Chinese and Japanese Americans, for example, generally out-perform "Whites"), African Americans as well as people of color coming from other backgrounds to meet the challenge of these tests were clearly at a disadvantage. It would be unrealistic to expect individuals unfamiliar with European American middle-class values and linguistic behavior to respond to a problem based on a familiarity with these.

Many large-scale intelligence tests continue to be administered in the United States. Notable among these are several series which attempt to hold environmental factors constant. Where this is done, African and European Americans tend to score equally well.[9] Nor is this surprising; since genes assort themselves independently of one another, there is no reason to suppose that whatever

---

[9]Sanday, P. R. (1975). On the causes of IQ differences between groups and implications for social policy. In M. F. A. Montagu (Ed.) *Race and IQ* (pp. 232–238). New York: Oxford.

On one IQ test designed to be "fair" to both Black and White American students, they are asked to identify either of two famous scientists, Albert Einstein or George Washington Carver. Unfortunately, Carver is mostly a White person's Black hero, so a White is more likely to identify either than is a Black (see Mark Cohen, 1995, "Anthropology and race: The Bell Curve phenomenon," *General Anthropology* 2(1), p. 3).

alleles may be associated with intelligence are likely to be concordant with the ones for skin pigmentation. Intelligence tests, however, have increasingly become the subject of controversy. There are many psychologists as well as anthropologists who believe that their use is overdone. Intelligence tests, they say, are of limited use, since they are applicable only to particular cultural circumstances. Only when these circumstances are carefully met can any meaningful generalizations be derived from the use of tests.

Notwithstanding the foregoing, there continue to be some who insist that there are significant differences in intelligence between human populations. Recent proponents of this view are the psychologist Richard Herrenstein and Charles Murray, a social scientist who is a fellow of the American Enterprise Institute, a conservative think tank. Their argument, in a lengthy (and highly publicized) book entitled *The Bell Curve,* is that

a well-documented 15-point difference in IQ exists between African and European Americans, with the latter scoring higher, though not quite as high as Asian Americans. Furthermore, they assert that these differences are mostly determined by genetic factors, and are therefore immutable.

Herrenstein and Murray's book has been justly criticized on many grounds, including violation of all sorts of rules of statistics and their practice of utilizing studies, no matter how flawed, that appear to support their thesis while ignoring or barely mentioning those that contradict it. But does this mean that they are wrong? On purely theoretical grounds, could we not suppose that, just as we see a spectrum of inherited variations in physical traits—skin color, hair texture, height, or whatever—might not there be similar variation in innate intellectual potential of different populations? It is likely that just as there are genes affecting the development of such things as blue eyes, curly hair, or heavily pigmented skin, there are others affecting the development of intelligence. Of course, even if genes affecting intelligence do exist, we would still need to ask why their distribution should be any more concordant with those for skin color than with ones that determine whether one has A, B, or O blood, normal or abnormal (antimalarial) hemoglobin, sufficient lactase to digest raw milk, or whatever.

A number of studies have appeared to indicate an appreciable degree of hereditary control of intelligence. First, there is a general tendency for those pairs of individuals who are most genetically similar (identical twins) to be most similar in intelligence, even when reared in different environments. Furthermore, the scores on IQ tests of biological parents and their children are correlated and tend to be similar, while foster parents and their foster children show less of this tendency. There are, however, enormous problems in attempting to separate genetic components from environmental contributors.[10] As biologists Richard Lewontin and Steven Rose and psychologist Leon Kanin observe, twin studies are plagued by a host of problems: inadequate sample sizes, biased subjective judgments, failure to make sure that "separated twins" really were raised separately, unrepresentative samples of adoptees to serve as controls, untested assumptions about similarity of environments. In fact, children reared by the same mother resemble her in IQ to the same degree, whether or not they share her genes.[11] Clearly, we do not know what the heritability of intelligence really is.[12]

Whatever the degree of heritability may be, it is clear that the effects of environment are important for intelligence. This should not surprise us, as even traits of high heritablity are strongly influenced by environmental factors. Height in humans, for example, is genetically determined while being dependent both upon nutrition and health status (severe illness in childhood arrests growth,

and renewed growth never makes up for this loss). With respect to intelligence, in the early 1900s, new immigrants to the United States, many of whom were Jews, scored lower on IQ tests than U.S.-born Whites. Today, the descendants of those Jewish immigrants score 10 points higher on average than Whites. In fact, IQ scores of all groups have risen some 15 points in the last 40 years, some faster than others. The gap between African and European Americans, for example, is narrower today than in the past. Nor is this surprising, for there are studies showing impressive IQ scores for African American children from poor backgrounds who have been adopted into affluent and intellectual homes. It is now known that disadvantaged children adopted into affluent and stable families can boost their IQs by 20 points. It is also well known that IQ scores rise with the amount of schooling the test-takers have. More such cases could be cited, but these suffice to make the point: The assertion that IQ is fixed and immutable is clearly false. Just as millions of people routinely overcome deficiencies of vision that are far more heritable than *anyone* claims intelligence to be, so may enriched education increase intelligence.

INTELLIGENCE: WHAT IS IT?

A question that must now be asked is: What do we mean by the term *intelligence*? The answer, to some, is that which is measured by IQ tests. Unfortunately, there is no general agreement as to what abilities or talents actually make up the trait of intelligence, even though there are some psychologists who insist that it is a single quantifiable thing. Many more psychologists believe intelligence to be the product of the interaction of different sorts of cognitive abilities: verbal, mathematical-logical, spatial, linguistic, musical, bodily kinesthetic, social, and personal.[13] Each may be thought of as a particular kind of intelligence, unrelated to the others. This being so, they must be independently inherited (to the degree they are inherited), just as height, blood type, skin color, and

[10]Andrews, L. B., & Nelkin, D. (1996). The bell curve: A statement. *Science, 271,* 13.

[11]Lewontin, R. C., Rose, S., & Kamin, L. J. (1984). *Not in our genes* (pp. 100, 113, 116). New York: Pantheon.

[12]Ibid., pp. 9, 121.

[13]Jacoby, R., & Glauberman, N. (Eds.). (1995). *The bell curve debate* (pp. 7, 55–56, 59). New York: Random House.

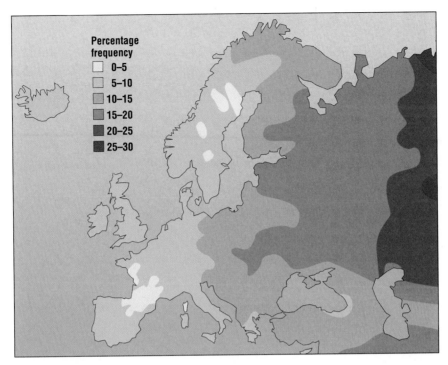

FIGURE 13.4

The east-west gradient in the frequency of the Type B blood in Europe contrasts with north-south gradient in skin color show in Figure 13.3. Whatever genes are involved in the various abilities lumped together as "intelligence" must be independently assorted as well.

so forth are independently inherited. Thus, the various abilities that constitute "intelligence" may be independently distributed as are, for example, the previously discussed skin color and blood type (compare Figures 13.3 and 13.4).

The next question is: If we are not exactly sure what IQ tests are measuring, how can we be sure of the validity of such tests—that is, can we be sure an IQ test measures what it is supposed to measure? The answer, of course, is that we cannot be sure. But even at best, an IQ test measures performance (something that one does) rather than genetic disposition (something that lies within the individual). Reflected in one's performance are one's past experiences and present motivational state, as well as one's innate ability. In sum, it is fair to say that an IQ test is not a reliable measure of innate intelligence.

Attempts to prove the existence of significant differences in intelligence between human populations have been going on as long as people have been talking about race. But in spite of all, the hypothesis remains unproven. Nor is it ever likely to be proven, in view of what we saw in Chapter 10 as the major thrust in the evolution of the genus *Homo*. Over the past 2.5 million years, in all populations of this genus, the emphasis has been on cultural adaptation—actively inventing solutions to the problems of existence, rather than passively relying on biological adaptation. Thus, we would expect a comparable degree of intelligence in all present-day human populations. But even if this were not the case, it would mean only that "dull" and "bright" people are to be found in all human populations, though in different frequencies. Remember: Within-group variation generally is greater than between-group variation. Thus, geniuses can and do appear in any population, regardless of what that population's "average" intelligence may be. The fact of the matter is that

This photo of African, Asian, Native American, and other winners of the Nobel Peace Prize was taken in 1998. It illustrates the point that individuals of exceptional ability can and do appear in any human population.

the only way to be sure that individual human beings develop their innate abilities and skills, whatever they may be, to the fullest is to make sure they have access to the necessary resources and the opportunity to do so. This certainly cannot be accomplished if whole populations are assumed at the outset to be inferior.

▲▽▲▽▲▽▲▽▲▽▲▽▲▽▲▽▲▽▲▽▲▽▲▽

CONTINUING HUMAN BIOLOGICAL EVOLUTION

In the course of their evolution, humans in all parts of the world came to rely on cultural rather than biological adaptation for their survival. Nevertheless, as they spread beyond their tropical homeland into other parts of the world, they did develop considerable physical variation from one population to another. The forces responsible for this include genetic drift—especially at the margins of their range where small populations were easily isolated for varying amounts of time—and biological adaptation to differing climates.

Although much of this physical variation can still be seen in human populations today, the increasing effectiveness of cultural adaptation has often reduced its importance. For instance, the consumption of cod liver oil or Vitamin D-fortified milk has canceled out the selective advantage of lightly pigmented skins in northern peoples. At the same time, culture has also imposed its own selective pressures, as we have seen in preceding chapters. Just as the invention of the spear thrower was followed by a reduction in overall muscularity, or just as the transition to food production was followed by worsened health and mortality, so cultural practices today are affecting the human organism in important, often surprising, ways.

The probability of alterations in human biological makeup induced by culture raises a number of important questions. By trying to eliminate genetic variants for balanced polymorphic traits, such as the sickle-cell trait discussed in

Chapter 3, are we also removing alleles that have survival value? Are we weakening the gene pool by allowing people with hereditary diseases and defects to reproduce? Are we reducing chances for genetic variation by trying to control population size?

We are not sure of the answers to all of these questions. If we are able to wipe out sickle-cell anemia, we also may be able to wipe out malaria; thus, we would have eliminated the condition that made the sickle-cell trait advantageous. On the other hand, antimalarial campaigns have had at most limited success, as the disease afflicts some 270 million people around the world. In 1997, 1.5 million to 2.7 million deaths were caused by malaria, making it the fifth largest infectious killer in the world. Moreover, as a consequence of global warming, the disease could spread (with a number of others) into more northerly regions. While it is not certain, it is at least possible that over the next century, an average temperature increase of 3°C could result in 50 million to 80 million new malaria cases per year.[14] Nor is it strictly true that medical science is weakening the gene pool by letting those with disorders for which there may be a genetic predisposition, such as diabetes, reproduce. In the present environment, where medication is easily available, such people are as fit as anyone else. However, if such people are denied access to the needed medication, their biological fitness is lost and they die out. In fact, one's financial status affects one's access to medication, and so, however unintentional it may be, one's biological fitness in North American society may be decided by one's financial status.

The effects of culture in enabling individuals to reproduce even though they suffer from genetic disorders are familiar. Perhaps less familiar are the cases in which medical technology selects against some individuals by removing them from the reproducing population. One example can be seen in South Africa. About 1% of South Africans of Dutch descent have a gene which, in its dominant form, causes porphyria, a disorder that renders the skin of its victims sensitive to light and causes skin abrasions. If these Afrikaners remain in a rural environment, they suffer only minor skin abrasions as a result of their condition. However, the allele renders them very sensitive to modern medical treatment, such as they might receive in a large urban center like Johannesburg. If they are treated for some problem quite unrelated to porphyria, with barbiturates or similar drugs, they suffer acute attacks and very often die. In a relatively quiet rural environment where medical services are less readily accessible the Afrikaners with this peculiar condition are able to live normal lives; it is only in an urban context, where they are more likely to receive medical attention, that they suffer physical impairment or loss of life.

Another example of culture acting as an agent of biological selection has to do with lactose tolerance: The ability to assimilate **lactose**, the primary constituent of fresh milk. This ability depends on the presence of a particular enzyme, **lactase**, in the small intestine. Failure to retain lactase into adulthood, although controlled by recessive alleles, is characteristic of mammals in general, as well as most human populations—especially Asian, native Australian, Native American, and many (but not all) African populations. Hence, only 10 to 30% of Americans of African descent, and 0 to 30% of adult Asians, retain lactase into adulthood and so are lactose tolerant.[15] By contrast, lactase retention and lactose tolerance are normal for over 80% of adults of northern European descent. Eastern Europeans, Arabs, and some East Africans are closer to northern Europeans in lactase retention than they are to Asians

[14]Stone, R. (1995). If the mercury soars, so may health hazards. *Science, 267,* 958.

[15]Harrison, G. G. (1975). Primary adult lactase deficiency: A problem in anthropological genetics. *American Anthropologist, 77,* 815–819.

Lactose. The primary constituent of fresh milk. > **Lactase.** An enzyme in the small intestine which enables humans to assimilate lactose.

and other Africans. Generally speaking, a high retention of lactase is found in populations with a long tradition of fresh milk as an important dietary item. In such populations, selection has in the past favored those individuals with the dominant allele that confers the ability to assimilate lactose, selecting out those without this allele.

In developing countries, milk supplements are used in the treatment of acute protein-calorie malnutrition. Tube-fed diets of milk are used in connection with other medical procedures. Quite apart from medical practices, powdered milk has long been a staple of economic aid to other countries. Such practices in fact discriminate against the members of populations in which lactase is not commonly retained into adulthood. At the least, those individuals who are not lactose tolerant will fail to utilize the nutritive value of milk; frequently they will suffer diarrhea, abdominal cramping, and

even bone degeneration, with serious results. In fact, the shipping of powdered milk to victims of South American earthquakes in the 1960s caused many deaths among them.

Among Europeans, the evolution of lactose tolerance is linked with evolution of a nonthrifty genotype.[16] Until about 6,000 years ago all humans were characterized by a **thrifty genotype.** This permitted efficient storage of fat to draw on in times of food shortage, and in times of scarcity conserved glucose (a simple sugar) for use in brain and red blood cells (as opposed to other tissues such as muscle), as well as nitrogen (vital for growth and health) through the body's diminished exertion. Regular access to lactose, a source of glucose, led to selection for

---

[16]Allen, J. S., & Cheer, S. M. (1996). The non-thrifty genotype. *Current Anthropology, 37,* 831–842.

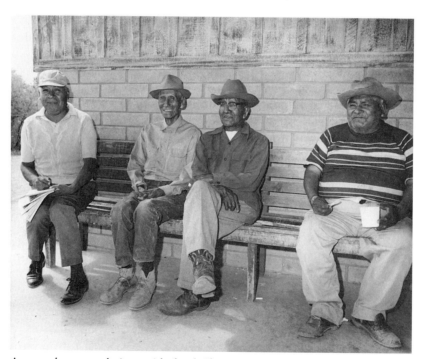

Among those populations with the thrifty genotype are Pima Indians. As with other such populations, exposure to Westernized diets high in calories leads to high rates of adult-onset diabetes; in the case of the Pima, as high as 50.25%.

Thrifty genotype.   Human genotype that, in times of food shortage, permits efficient storage of fat to draw on and conservation of glucose and nitrogen.

the nonthrifty genotype as protection against adult-onset diabetes, or at least its onset relatively late in life (at a nonreproductive age). By contrast, populations that are lactose intolerant retain the thrifty genotype. As a consequence, when they are introduced to Western-style diets, characterized by abundance, particularly of foods high in sugar content, the incidence of diabetes skyrockets.

In recent years, there has been considerable concern about human activities that damage the earth's ozone layer. A major contributor to the ozone layer's deterioration has been the use of chlorofluorocarbons in aerosol sprays, refrigeration and air conditioning, and the manufacture of Styrofoam. Since the ozone layer screens out some of the sun's ultraviolet rays, its continued deterioration will expose humans to increased ultraviolet radiation. As we saw earlier in this chapter, some ultraviolet radiation is necessary for the production of Vitamin D, but excessive amounts lead, among other things, to an increased incidence of skin cancers. Hence a rising incidence of skin cancers is not surprising, as the ozone layer continues to deteriorate.

Although a ban on the use of chlorofluorocarbons in aerosol sprays was imposed some years ago, the destruction of the ozone layer continued about twice as fast as scientists had predicted it would, even without the ban. Subsequently, an international treaty further limiting the use of chlorofluorocarbons was negotiated, but this ban has merely slowed, rather than halted, further deterioration. In fact, the ozone hole over Antarctica in October of 1994 was the severest ever recorded in 35 years. Most immediately affected by the consequent increase in ultraviolet radiation are the world's lightly pigmented peoples, but ultimately, all will be affected.

Ozone depletion is merely one of a host of problems confronted by humans today that ultimately have an impact on human gene pools. In view of the consequences for human biology of such seemingly benign innovations as dairying or (as discussed in Chapter 11) farming, we may wonder about many recent practices; for example, the effects of increased exposure to radiation from increased use of X-rays, more nuclear accidents, increased production of radioactive wastes, and the like. To be sure, we are constantly

reassured by various experts that we are protected by adequate safety regulations, but one is not reassured by discoveries, such as the one announced by the National Academy of Sciences in 1989, that what were accepted as safe levels of radiation were in fact too high; or the earlier discovery that the supposedly safe treatment of sinus disorders in the 1940s by massive doses of x-ray radiation produced a bumper crop of thyroid cancers in the late 1960s. But it is not just increased exposure to radiation that we confront, but increased exposure to other known mutagenic agents, including a wide variety of chemicals, such as pesticides. In spite of repeated assurances about their safety, there have been tens of thousands of cases of poisonings in the United States alone (probably more in so-called "underdeveloped" countries, where controls are even less effective than in the United States and where substances banned for use in the United States are routinely used), and thousands of cases of cancer related to the manufacture and use of pesticides. All this on top of the several million birds killed each year (many of which would otherwise have been happily gobbling down bugs and other pests), serious fish kills, honey bee kills (bees are needed for the efficient pollination of many crops), and the like. In all, pesticides alone (never mind other agricultural chemicals) are responsible for an estimated $8 *billion* worth of environmental and public health damage in the United States each year.[17]

Beyond pesticides are other substances, like the hormone-disrupting chemicals. In 1938, a synthetic estrogen known as DES was developed and subsequently prescribed for a variety of ailments ranging from acne to prostate cancer. Moreover, tons of it are routinely added to animal feeds. It was not until 1971, however, that the first indication that DES causes vaginal cancer in young women came to light. Subsequent research has shown that DES causes problems with the male reproductive system, and causes deformities of the female reproductive tract. DES mimics the natural hormone, binding with appropriate receptors

[17]Pimentel, D. (1991). Response. *Science, 252,* 358.

in and on cells and thereby turns on biological activity associated with the hormone. As one group of scientists observes:

> The synthetic hormone has two troublesome traits. First, it triggers certain parts of the reproductive system more effectively than does estradiol, one of the body's own estrogens. . . . Even more important, it manages to circumvent a mechanism that protects the fetus from the developmentally disruptive effects of excessive estrogen exposure. Normally, special maternal and fetal blood proteins soak up almost all excess circulating estrogen. But they do not recognize DES. As a consequence, DES in the fetal blood supply remains biologically active.[18]

DES is not alone in its effects: At least 51 chemicals—many of them in common use—are now known to disrupt hormones, and even this could be the "tip of the iceberg." Some of these chemicals mimic hormones in the manner of DES, while others interfere with other parts of the endocrine system, such as thyroid and testosterone metabolism. Included are such supposedly benign and inert substances as plastics widely used in laboratories, and chemicals added to polystyrene and polyvinyl chloride (PVCs) to make them more stable and less breakable. These plastics are widely used in plumbing, food processing, and food packaging. Hormone disrupting chemicals are also found in many detergents and personal care products, contraceptive creams, the giant jugs used to bottle drinking water, and plastic linings in cans (about 85% of food cans in the United States are so lined).

The implications of all these developments are sobering. We know that pathologies result from extremely low levels of exposure to harmful chemicals. Yet, besides those used domestically, millions of pounds are exported to the rest of the world (40 million pounds in 1991 alone).[19] It is quite possible that hormone disruptions are at least partially responsible for certain trends that have recently become causes for concern among scientists.

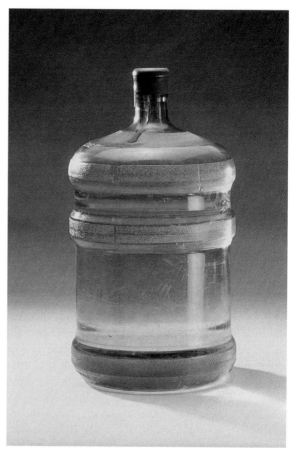

Hormone-disrupting chemicals are present in so many things, including this plastic water jug, that it is virtually impossible to avoid exposure to them.

These range from increasingly early onset of puberty in human females to dramatic declines in human sperm counts. With respect to the latter, some 61 separate studies confirm that sperm counts have dropped almost 50% from 1938 to 1990 (Figure 13.5). Most of these studies were carried out in the United States and Europe, but some from Africa, Asia, and South America show that this is essentially a worldwide phenomenon. If this trend continues, it will have profound results.

It is not that the experts who assure us of the safety of such things are deliberately misleading us. (Although there are cases of that too, one notorious example being the case of asbestos. As early as 1902 it was included in a list

---

[18]Colburn, T., Dumanoski, D., & Myers, J. P. (1996). Hormonal sabotage. *Natural History*, (3), 45–46.

[19]Colburn et al., 47.

anthropology
applied Studying the Emergence
of New Diseases*

Ever since the Neolithic, humans have had to cope with a host of new diseases that got their start as a consequence of changes in human behavior. This has become a renewed source of concern following the recent appearance and spread of a host of new and lethal diseases, of which perhaps the best known is AIDS. This has now become number 4 among infectious killers of humans, with 5.8 million people infected in 1998 alone.** But there are others—like ebola, which causes victims to hemorrhage to death, blood pouring from every orifice; other hemorrhagic fevers like dengue fever, lassa fever, and Hantavirus, Invasive Streptococcus A, which consumes the victims' flesh, Legionnaire's disease, and Lyme disease. What has sparked the appearance and spread of these and other new diseases has been a considerable mystery, but one theory is that some are the result of human activities. In particular, the intrusion of people into new ecological settings, such as rain forests, along with construction of roads allows viruses and other infectious microbes to spread rapidly to large numbers of people.

To test this theory anthropologist Carol Jenkins, whose specialty is medical anthropology, obtained a grant from the MacArthur Foundation in 1993. From her base at the Papua New Guinea Institute of Medical Research, she is following what happens to the health of local people in the wake of a massive logging operation, begun in 1993. From this should come a better understanding of how disease organisms spread from animal hosts to humans. Since most of

the "new" viruses that have suddenly afflicted humans are in fact old ones that have been present in animals like monkeys, rodents, and insects, it appears that something new has enabled them to jump from their animal hosts to humans. A recent example comes from the Democratic Republic of Congo. Here civil war created a situation where villagers in the central part of the country were faced with starvation. Their response was to increase the hunting of animals, including monkeys, squirrels, and rats that carry a disease called monkey pox. Related to smallpox, the disease transfers easily to humans, resulting in the largest outbreak of this disease ever seen among humans. What makes this outbreak even more serious is an apparently new strain of the infection, enabling it to spread from person to person, instead of only from an animal host.***

Large-scale habitat disturbance is an obvious candidate for such disease transfers, but this needs to be confirmed and the process understood. So far, it is hard to make more than a circumstantial case, by looking back after a disease outbreak. The work of Jenkins and her team is unique, in that she was able to get baseline health data on local people before their environment was disturbed. Thus, she is in a position to follow events as they unfold.

It will be some time before conclusions can be drawn from Jenkins's study. Its importance is obvious; in an era when more and more tropical diseases are spreading beyond the tropics, we need a fuller understanding of how viruses interact with their hosts if we are to devise effective preventive and therapeutic strategies to deal with them.

---

*Gibbons, A. (1993). Where are new diseases born? *Science*, *261*, 680–681.

**Balter, M. (1998). On world AIDS day, a shadow looms over southern Africa. *Science, 282*, 1790.

***Cohen, J. (1997). Is an old virus up to new tricks? *Science, 277*, 312–313.

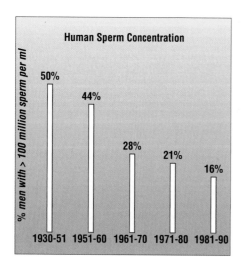

Human Sperm Concentration

% men with > 100 million sperm per ml

- 50% — 1930-51
- 44% — 1951-60
- 28% — 1961-70
- 21% — 1971-80
- 16% — 1981-90

FIGURE 13.5

A documented decline in human male sperm counts worldwide may be related to widespread exposure to hormone-disrupting chemicals.

The denial by corporate executives of the known health hazards of asbestos is, unfortunately, an example of an all too common phenomenon. The heads of U.S. tobacco companies shown here taking an oath before a congressional subcommittee deliberately denied the known harmful effects of their product, and in a similar vein, executives of energy corporations are now trying to discredit scientists concerned with global warming.

of dusts known to be hazardous. By 1933 it was well-documented as a cause of lung cancer, yet in the 1960s, corporate executives denied ever hearing of the dangers). For the most part, experts are convinced of the validity of what they say; the difficulty is that serious problems, such as those having to do with radiation or exposure to various chemicals, have a way of not being apparent until years, or even decades later. By then, of course, serious financial interests are at stake.

What is clear, then, is that cultural practices, probably as never before, are currently having an impact on human gene pools. Unquestionably, this impact is deleterious to those individuals who suffer the effects of negative selection, whose misery and death are the price paid for many of the material benefits of civilization we enjoy today. It remains to be seen just what the long-term effects on the human species as a whole will be. If the promise of "genetic engineering" offers hope of alleviating some of the misery and death that result from our own practices, it also raises the specter of removing genetic variants that might turn out to be of future adaptive value, or that might turn out to make us immediately susceptible to new problems that we don't even know about today.

CHAPTER SUMMARY

In humans, most behavioral attitudes are culturally learned or acquired. Other characteristics are determined by an interaction between genes and environment. The gene pools of populations contain various alternative alleles. When the environment changes, their gene pool gives them the possibility of the appropriate physical alteration to meet the change.

When a polymorphic species is separated into different faunal regions, it is usually polytypic; that is, populations differ in the frequency with which genetic variability is expressed. It appears that the human species has been polytypic at least since the time of *Homo erectus.*

Early anthropologists classified *Homo sapiens* into subspecies, or races, based on geographical location and such phenotypic features as skin color, body size, head shape, and hair texture. The presence of atypical individuals and the nonconcordance of traits continually challenged these racial classifications. No examples of "pure" racial types could be found. The visible traits were found to occur in a worldwide continuum. No definite grouping of distinct, discontinuous biological groups has been found in modern humans.

A biological race is a population of a species that differs in the frequency of genetic variants from other populations of the same species. Three observations must be made concerning this biological definition: (1) It is arbitrary; (2) it does not mean that any one race has exclusive possession of any particular allele(s); and (3) individuals of one race will not necessarily be distinguishable from those of another. As a means for understanding human variation, the concept of race has several limitations. First, race is an arbitrary category, making agreement on any particular classification difficult; second, humans are so complex genetically that often the genetic basis of traits on which racial studies are based is itself poorly understood; and finally, race exists as a cultural as well as a biological category. Most anthropologists now view the race concept as useless for an understanding of human variation, preferring to study the distribution and significance of specific, genetically based characteristics, or else the characteristics of small breeding populations.

Physical anthropologists have determined that much of human physical variation appears related to climatic adaptation. People native to cold climates tend to have greater body bulk relative to their extremities than individuals who live in hot climates; the latter tend to be long and slender. Studies involving body build and climate are complicated by such other factors as the effects on physique of diet and of clothing.

In the United States, race is commonly thought of in terms of skin color. Subject to tremendous variation, skin color is a function of four factors: transparency or thickness of the skin, distribution of blood vessels, and amount of carotene and melanin in a given area of skin.

Exposure to sunlight increases the amount of melanin, darkening the skin. Natural selection has favored heavily pigmented skin as protection against the strong solar radiation of equatorial latitudes. In northern latitudes, natural selection has favored relatively depigmented skins, which can utilize relatively weak solar radiation in the production of Vitamin D. Selective mating, as well as geographical location, plays a part in skin color distribution.

Racism can be viewed solely as a social problem. It is an emotional phenomenon best explained in terms of collective psychology. The racist individual reacts on the basis of social stereotypes and not established scientific facts.

Notwithstanding the impossibility of defining valid human races, many people have assumed that there are behavioral differences among human races. The innate behavioral characteristics attributed by these people to race can be explained in terms of enculturation rather than biology. Those intelligence tests that have been interpreted to indicate that European Americans are intellectually superior to African Americans are designed by European Americans for European Americans from similar backgrounds. It is not realistic to expect individuals who are not familiar with European American middle-class values to respond to items based on knowledge of these values. African and European Americans both, if they come from different types of backgrounds, are thus at a disadvantage. At present, it is not possible to separate the inherited components of intelligence from those that are culturally acquired. Furthermore, there is still no agreement on what intelligence really is, but it is made up probably of several different talents and abilities.

Although the human species has come to rely on cultural rather than biological adaptation for survival, human gene pools still continue to change in response to external factors. Many of these changes are brought about by cultural practices; for example, the shipment of powdered milk to human populations which are low in the frequency of the allele for lactase retention into adulthood may contribute to the death of large numbers of people. Those who survive are most likely to be those with the allele for lactase retention. Unquestionably, this kind of selection is deleterious to those individuals who are "selected out" in this way. Just what the long-term effects will be on the human species as a whole remains to be seen.

POINTS FOR CONSIDERATION

1. There is great hope that advances in genetic engineering will allow humans to cure previously devastating diseases, and correct genetic disorders before an individual is even born. Given the example of genetic control exercised on domestic species, and the concept of *unconscious selection*, what might the ramifications be to such a practice? Is it possible to rule out negative consequences with the positive?

2. Race, as it is usually used, is a cultural construct, often associated with stereotypes of behavior and ability. While there is also a biological definition for **race**, what are the social consequences of using it to define different peoples? Why is it unlikely that certain specific genetic traits will or will not be present in or absent from certain phenotypes, exclusively?

3. What is the importance of understanding how the concept of race functions? Why is it important to exercise extra care in discussing the idea of race, biologically or socially?

4. What is significant about the fact that two individuals from two different phenotypes may display less genetic variation than two individuals from the same phenotype? What does this demonstrate about human mechanisms for adapting to different environments in comparison and in contrast with other animals? What does it indicate regarding the cultural definition of race?

SUGGESTED READINGS

Cohen, M. N. (1998). *Culture of intolerance: Chauvinism, class and racism in the United States.* New Haven, CT: Yale.

This very readable book was written to counter political propaganda claiming that science affirms the need to shape the political order on the basis of inherent inequality and mutual disdain. In it, Cohen summarizes what scientific data *really* say about biological differences between humans; explores the depth, power, beauty and potential value of cultural differences; shows how the cultural blinders of U.S. culture cause people in this country to misunderstand others as well as themselves; and looks at questionable assumptions in U.S. culture that promote intolerance and generate problems where none need exist.

Gould, S. J. (1996). *The mismeasure of man* (2nd ed.). New York: Norton.

This is an updating of a classic critique of supposedly scientific studies that attempt to rank all people on a linear scale of intrinsic and unalterable mental worth. The revision was prompted by what Gould refers to as the "latest cyclic episode of biodeterminism" represented by the publication of the widely discussed book, *The Bell Curve.*

Jacoby, R., & Glauberman, N. (Eds.). (1995). *The Bell Curve debate.* New York: Random House.

This is a collection of articles by a wide variety of authors including biologists, anthropologists, psychologists, mathematicians, essayists, and others critically examining the claims and issues raised in the widely read and much discussed book, *The Bell Curve.* Included are pieces written to address many of the same issues as they were raised by earlier writers. For anyone who hopes to understand the "race and intelligence" debate, this book is a must.

Marks, J. (1995). *Human biodiversity: Genes, race and history.* Hawthorne, NY: Aldine de Gruyter.

In this book, Marks shows how genetics has undermined the fundamental assumptions of racial taxonomy. In addition to its presentation of the nature of human biodiversity, the book also deals with the history of cultural attitudes towards "race" and diversity.

Molnar, S. (1992). *Human variation: Races, types, and ethnic groups* (3rd ed). Englewood Cliffs, NJ: Prentice Hall.

Key questions examined here are: How does biological diversity relate to the classical racial divisions? Are these divisions useful in the study of our species? How would human environmental relationships affect humanity's future?

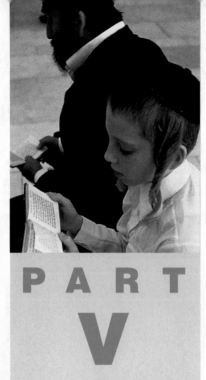

PART

V

CULTURE AND SURVIVAL: COMMUNICATING, RAISING CHILDREN, AND STAYING ALIVE

Chapter 14
THE NATURE OF CULTURE

Chapter 15
LANGUAGE AND COMMUNICATION

Chapter 16
GROWING UP HUMAN

Chapter 17
PATTERNS OF SUBSISTENCE

Chapter 18
ECONOMIC SYSTEMS

Introduction

All living creatures face a fundamental problem in common: Simply put, unless they adapt themselves to some available environment, they cannot survive. Adaptation requires the development of behaviors that will help an organism use the environment to its advantage—to find food and sustenance, avoid hazards, and (if the species is to survive) reproduce its own kind. In turn, organisms need to have the biological equipment that allows development of appropriate patterns of behavior. For the hundreds of millions of years of life on earth, biological adaptation has been the primary means of solving the problem of survival. This is accomplished as organisms of a particular kind whose biological equipment is best suited to a particular way of life produce more offspring than those whose equipment is not as well suited. In this way, advantageous characteristics become more common in succeeding generations, while less advantageous ones become less common.

One characteristic that ultimately became common among mammals, to one degree or another, was the ability to learn new patterns of behavior to solve at least limited problems of existence. This problem-solving ability became particularly well developed among the last common ancestors of both apes and humans, and by 2.5 million years ago (long after the human and ape lines of evolution had diverged) early members of the genus *Homo* began to rely increasingly on what their minds could invent, rather than on what their bodies were capable of. Although the human species has not freed itself entirely, even today, from the forces of biological adaptation, it has come to rely primarily on culture—a body of learned traditions that, in essence, tells people how to live—as the medium for solving the problems of human existence. The consequences of this reliance are profound. As the evolving genus *Homo* unconsciously came to depend more on cultural as opposed to biological solutions to its problems, its chances of survival improved. As a consequence, culture became basic to human survival.

To do its job, culture must deal successfully with certain basic problems. Because culture is learned and not inherited biologically, its transmission from one person to another, and from one generation to the next, depends on an effective communication system that must be far more complex than any other animal's. Thus, a first requirement for any culture is providing a means of communication among individuals. All cultures do this through some form of language, one of the most distinctive of human possessions and the subject of Chapter 15.

In human societies each generation must learn its culture anew. The learning process itself is thus crucial to a culture's survival. A second requirement of culture, then, is the development of reliable means for individuals to learn the behavior expected of them as members of their community, and how children learn appears to be as important as what they learn. Since an adult's personality is shaped by life experiences, the ways children are raised and educated play a major part in the shaping of their later selves: The ability of individuals to function properly as adults depends, to an important degree, upon how effectively their personalities have been shaped to fit their culture. As we will see in Chapter 16, findings have emerged from anthropological investigations of these areas that have implications for human behavior beyond anthropology.

Important as effective communication and education are for the survival of a culture, they are of no avail unless the culture can satisfy the basic needs of the individuals who live by its rules. A third requirement of culture, therefore, is the ability to provide its members with food, water, and protection from the elements. Chapter 17 discusses the ways cultures handle people's basic needs and the ways societies adapt to the environment through culture. Since this leads to the production, distribution, and consumption of goods—the subject matter of economic anthropology—we conclude this section with a chapter (Chapter 18) on economic systems.

Chapter 14
THE NATURE OF CULTURE

THE POWER OF CULTURE IS ILLUSTRATED BY THIS
PICTURE OF CHINESE AND UNITED STATES LEADERS
AT A STATE DINNER. WHILE FOOD PROVIDES
NUTRIENTS HUMANS NEED TO SURVIVE, IT IS GIVEN
ADDITIONAL, CULTURAL MEANING. HERE, THE
SHARING OF FOOD IS USED TO PROMOTE POLITICAL
DIALOGUE BETWEEN DIFFERENT PEOPLE AND TO
SYMBOLIZE A DESIRE FOR PEACEFUL RELATIONS.

Chapter Preview

What Is Culture?

Culture consists of the abstract values, beliefs, and perceptions of the world that lie behind people's behavior and that are reflected by their behavior. These are shared by members of a society, and when they are acted upon, these elements produce behavior that is intelligible to other members of that society. Cultures are learned, rather than inherited biologically, and they are learned largely through the medium of language. The parts of a culture function as an integrated whole.

How Is Culture Studied?

Anthropologists, like children, learn about a culture by experiencing it and talking about it with those who live by its rules. Of course, anthropologists have less time to learn but are more systematic in the way they learn. Through careful observation and discussion with informants who are particularly knowledgeable in the ways of their culture, the anthropologist abstracts a set of rules to explain how people behave in a particular society.

Why Do Cultures Exist?

People maintain cultures to deal with problems or matters that concern them. To survive, a culture must satisfy the basic needs of those who live by its rules, must provide for its own continuity, and must furnish an orderly existence for the members of its society. In doing so, a culture must strike a balance between the self-interests of individuals and the needs of society as a whole. And, finally, a culture must have the capacity to change so it can adapt to new circumstances or to altered perceptions of existing circumstances.

Students of anthropology are bound to find themselves studying a seemingly endless variety of human societies, each with its own distinctive system of politics, economics, and religion. Yet for all this variation, these societies have one thing in common. Each is a collection of people cooperating to ensure their collective survival and well-being. For this to work, some degree of predictable behavior is required of each individual within the society, for group living and cooperation are impossible unless individuals know how others are likely to behave in any given situation. For humans, it is culture that sets the limits of behavior and guides it along predictable paths.

THE CONCEPT OF CULTURE

The concept of **culture** was first developed by anthropologists toward the end of the 19th century. The first really clear and comprehensive definition was that of the British anthropologist Sir Edward Burnett Tylor. Writing in 1871, Tylor defined culture as "that complex whole which includes knowledge, belief, art, law, morals, custom and any other capabilities and habits acquired by man as a member of society." Since Tylor's time, definitions of culture have proliferated, so by the early 1950s North American anthropologists A. L. Kroeber and Clyde Kluckhohn were able to collect more than a hundred definitions of culture from the literature. Recent definitions tend to distinguish more clearly between actual behavior on the one hand and the abstract values, beliefs, and perceptions of the world that lie behind that behavior on the other. To put it another way, culture is not observable behavior but, rather, the shared ideals, values, and beliefs people use to interpret experience and generate behavior and that are reflected by their behavior.

CHARACTERISTICS OF CULTURE

Through the comparative study of many different cultures, anthropologists have arrived at an understanding of the basic characteristics all cultures share. A careful study of these helps us to see the importance of and the function of culture itself.

CULTURE IS SHARED

As stated earlier, culture is a set of shared ideals, values, and standards of behavior; it is the common denominator that makes the actions of individuals intelligible to other members of their society. Because they share a common culture, people can predict how others are most likely to behave in a given circumstance and can react accordingly. A group of people from different cultures, stranded for a period on a desert island, might appear to become a society of sorts. They would have a common interest—survival—and would develop techniques for living and working together. Each of the group members, however, would retain his or her own identity and cultural background, and the group would disintegrate without further ado as soon as its members were rescued from the island. The group would have been merely a temporary aggregate and not a cultural entity. **Society** may be defined as a group of people who have a common homeland, who are dependent on each other for survival, and who share a common culture. The way these people depend upon each other can be seen in such things as their economic systems and their family relationships; moreover, members of a society are held together by a sense of common identity. The relationships that hold a society together are known as its **social structure**.

Culture and society are two closely related concepts, and anthropologists study both. Obvi-

---

Culture.   The ideals, values, and beliefs members of a society share to interpret experience and generate behavior and that are reflected by their behavior. ＞ **Society.**   A group of people who have a common homeland, are interdependent, and share a common culture. ＞ **Social structure.**   The relationships of groups within a society that hold it together.

ously, no culture can exist without a society, just as no society can exist without individuals. Conversely, no known human societies exist, or have existed, that do not exhibit culture. Some other species of animals, however, do lead a social existence without culture. Ants and bees, for example, instinctively cooperate in a manner that clearly indicates a degree of social organization, yet this instinctual behavior is not a culture. Therefore, a society (but not a *human* society) can exist without a culture, even though a culture cannot exist without a society. Whether or not animals other than humans exist that exhibit cultural *behavior* is a question that will be dealt with shortly.

Although a culture is shared by members of a society, it is important to realize that all is not uniformity. For one thing, no member has the exact same version of his or her culture as another. Beyond such individual variation, however, some further variation is bound to occur within a given culture. At the very least, in any human society some differences between the roles of men and women exist. These stem from the facts women give birth but men do not, and male and female anatomy and physiology differ in obvious ways. Every culture gives meaning to these differences by explaining them and specifying what to do about them. Every culture, as well, specifies how the two kinds of people resulting from the differ-

ences should relate to one another and to the world at large. Since each culture does this in its own way, tremendous variation occurs from one society to another. Anthropologists use the term **gender** to refer to the cultural elaborations and meanings assigned to the biological differentiations between the sexes. Thus, though one's sex is biologically determined, one's sexual identity or gender is culturally constructed.

The distinction between sex, which is biological, and gender, which is cultural, is an important one. Presumably, gender differences are as old as human culture—about 2.5 million years—and arose from the biological differences between early human males and females. Back then, males were about twice the size of females, as they are today among such species as gorillas, orangutans, and baboons, all of which are closely related to humans. As humans evolved, however, the biological differences between the two sexes were radically reduced. Thus, apart from differences directly related to reproduction, whatever biological basis that once existed for gender role differences largely has disappeared.

Nevertheless, cultures have maintained some differentiation of gender roles ever since, although these are far greater in some societies than others. Paradoxically, gender differences were far more extreme in late 19th and early 20th century

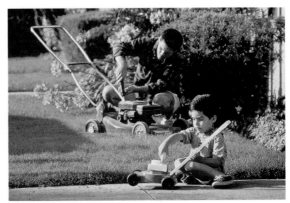

In all human societies, children's play is used both consciously and unconsciously to teach gender roles.

Gender.   The elaborations and meanings cultures assign to the biological differentiation of the sexes.

Western (European and European derived) societies, when women were expected to submit unquestioningly to male authority, than they are among most historically known food-foraging peoples whose ways of life, though not unchanged, are more like those of the late Stone Age ancestors of Western peoples. Among food foragers, relations between men and women tend to be relatively egalitarian, and, although the two sexes may not typically carry out the same tasks, such arrangements tend to be flexible. In other words, differences between the behavior of men and of women in North American and Western societies today, differences thought by many to be rooted in human biology, are not so rooted at all. Rather, they appear to have been elaborated recently in the course of history.

In addition to cultural variation along lines of sex, cultural variation related to age occurs. In any society, children are not expected to behave as adults, and the reverse is equally true. Also, variation between subgroups exists in societies. These may be occupational groups, where a complex division of labor exists, or social classes in a stratified society, or ethnic groups in some other societies. When there are such groups within a society, each functioning by its own distinctive standards of behavior while at the same time sharing some standards in common, we speak of **subcultures.** The word *subculture,* it should be noted, carries no connotation of lesser status relative to the word *cultural.*

One example of a subculture in the United States can be seen in the Amish.[1] The old-order Amish originated in Austria and Moravia during the Reformation; today members of this order number about 60,000 and live mainly in Pennsylvania, Ohio, and Indiana. They are pacifistic, agrarian people whose lives focus on their religious beliefs. They value simplicity, hard work, and a high degree of neighborly cooperation. The Amish dress in a distinctive plain garb and even today rely on the horse for transportation as well as agricultural work. They mingle as little as possible with the non-Amish.

The goal of Amish education is to teach reading, writing, and arithmetic and to instill Amish values in their children. They reject what they regard as "worldly" knowledge and the idea of schools producing good citizens for the state. The Amish insist that their children attend school near home and that teachers be committed to Amish values. Their nonconformity to many standards of the larger culture has caused frequent conflict with state authorities, as well as legal and personal harassment. The Amish have resisted all attempts to force their children to attend regular public schools. Some compromise has been necessary, and "vocational training" has been introduced beyond the elementary school level to fulfill state requirements. The Amish have succeeded in gaining con-

[1]Hostetler, J., & Huntington, G. (1971). *Children in Amish society.* New York: Holt, Rinehart and Winston.

New Houses for Apache Indians

The United States, in common with the other industrialized countries of the world, has within it a number of more or less separate subcultures. Those who live by the standards of one particular subculture have their closest relationships with one another, receiving constant reassurance that their perceptions of the world are the only correct ones and taking it for granted that the whole culture is as they see it. As a consequence, members of one subcultural group frequently have trouble understanding the needs and as-

---

Subculture.   A distinctive set of standards and behavior patterns that a group within a larger society operates by.

pirations of other such groups. For this reason anthropologists, with their special understanding of cultural differences, are frequently employed as go-betweens in situations requiring interaction between peoples of differing cultural traditions.

As an example, George S. Esber Jr., while still a graduate student in anthropology, was hired to work with architects and a band of Apache Indians on designing a new community for the Apaches.* Although architects began with an awareness that cross-cultural differences in the use of space exist, they had no idea how to get relevant information from the Indians. For their part, the Apaches had no explicit awareness of their needs, for these were based on unconscious patterns of behavior. Moreover, the idea that patterns of behavior could be acted out unconsciously was an alien idea to them.

Esber's task was to persuade the architects to hold back on their planning long enough for him to gather, through fieldwork and review of written records, the kind of data needed to abstract Apache housing needs. At the same time, he had to overcome Apache anxieties over an outsider coming into their midst to learn about matters as personal as their daily lives. After these tasks were accomplished, Esber identified and successfully communicated to the architects features of Apache

life with important implications for community design. In addition, discussions of his findings with the Apaches enhanced their awareness of their own unique needs.

As a result of Esber's work, in 1981 the Apaches could move into houses that had been designed with *their* participation for *their* specific needs. Among other things, account was taken of the Indians' need to ease into a social situation, rather than jumping right in. Apache etiquette requires that all people be in full view of one another, so each can assess from a distance the behavior of others to act appropriately with them. This requires a large, open living space. In addition, hosts must be able to offer food to guests as a prelude to further social interaction. Thus, cooking and dining areas cannot be separated from living space. Nor can standard middle-class Anglo kitchen equipment be installed; the need for handling large quantities of food requires large pots and pans, for which extra large sinks and cupboards are necessary. In such ways the new houses were made to accommodate long-standing native traditions.

*See Esber, G. (1987). Designing Apache houses with Apaches. In R. M. Wulff & S. J. Fiske (Eds.), *Anthropological praxis: Translating knowledge into action.* Boulder, CO: Westview.

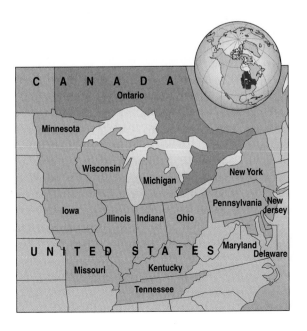

trol of their schools and maintaining their way of life, but they are a beleaguered, defensive culture, more distrustful than ever of the larger culture around them.

The experience of the Amish is one example of the way a subculture may be dealt with by the larger culture it functions within. Different as they are, the Amish actually practice many values citizens of the United States respect in the abstract: thrift, hard work, independence, and a close family life. The degree of tolerance accorded to them is also due in part to the fact the Amish are white-skinned Europeans. American Indian subcultures have been treated differently by Whites, who came as conquerors and who defined Indian values as "savage." For some 500 years, Europeans and their descendants in what is now the United States have generally accepted the notion the Indian cultures were doomed to disappear; yet they are still very much with us, even if in altered form.

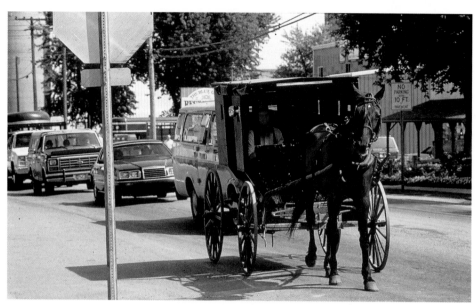

The Amish people have maintained a distinctive agrarian way of life in the midst of industrialized North American society. By maintaining their own schools to instill Amish values in their children, prohibiting mechanized vehicles and equipment, and dressing in their distinctive plain clothing, the Amish proclaim their own special identity.

Implicit in the discussion thus far is the fact subcultures may develop in different ways. On the one hand, the Amish subculture emerged as the product of the way these people have communicated and interacted in pursuit of their common goals within the wider society. On the other hand, American Indian subcultures are the result of once independent cultures having been forcibly brought under the control of the United States. Although all Indian cultures have undergone change as a result, many of them have remained different enough from European American culture so that it is difficult to decide whether they remain as distinct cultures as opposed to subcultures. In this sense, *culture* and *subculture* represent opposite ends of a continuum, with no clear dividing line in the "gray area" between.

Raised here is the issue of so-called **pluralistic societies** in which cultural variation is especially marked and few standards, if any, are held in common. Pluralistic societies are, in effect, multicul-tural, and could not have existed before the first politically centralized states arose a mere 5,000 years ago. With the rise of the state, it became possible to politically unify two or more formerly independent societies, each with its own culture, thereby creating what amounts to a higher order social entity that transcends the theoretical one culture-one society linkage. Pluralistic societies, which are common in the world today (Figure 14.1), are characterized by a particular problem: The groups within them, by virtue of their high degree of cultural variation, are all essentially operating by different sets of rules. This can create problems, given that social living demands predictable behavior. In a culturally plural society, it may become difficult for the members of any one subgroup to comprehend the different standards the others operate under. At the least, this can lead to major misunderstandings, as in the following case reported in the *Wall Street Journal* (May 13, 1983):

Pluralistic societies. Societies that have a diversity of cultural patterns.

FIGURE 14.1
Shown here are a few of the ethnic groups of the
Russian Federation. Contrary to popular belief, the
ethnic conflicts that have broken out since the collapse of the Soviet Union stem not from a supposedly
conflictive nature of ethnicity but from Stalin's policy
of emphasizing ethnicity while preventing its expression and forcibly removing populations from their
homelands to new localities.

Salt Lake City—Police called it a cross-cultural misunderstanding. When the man showed up to buy
the Shetland pony advertised for sale, the owner
asked what he intended to do with the animal.

"For my son's birthday," he replied, and the
deal was closed.

The buyer thereupon clubbed the pony to
death with a two-by-four, dumped the carcass in
his pickup truck and drove away. The horrified
seller called the police, who tracked down the
buyer. At his house they found a birthday party in
progress. The pony was trussed and roasting in a
luau pit.

We don't ride horses, we eat them, explained
the buyer, a recent immigrant from Tonga.

Members of one subgroup within a pluralistic society may have difficulty understanding the
standards members of others operate under. Unfortunately, sometimes this difficulty can go far beyond mere misunderstanding, and violence and
bloodshed may result. Many cases might be cited,
but one we shall look at in some detail in a later
chapter (27) is Guatemala, where a government
distrustful of its Indian population unleashed a
reign of terror against it.

In every culture are persons whose idiosyncratic behavior has earned them the label of

The difficulties of making pluralistic societies work is illustrated by the
continuing tragedy of Bosnia. Here, a long tradition of different people
living together peacefully was overwhelmed by the passions of nationalism.

"eccentric," "crazy," or "queer." Such persons are looked upon with disapproval by most members of their society, and if their behavior becomes too idiosyncratic, they are sooner or later excluded from participating in group activities. Such exclusion acts to keep what is defined as deviant behavior outside groups. Yet what is regarded as deviant in one society may not be in another. In many Native American societies, for example, individuals were permitted to assume for life the role normally associated with people of the opposite sex. Thus, a man could dress as a woman and engage in what were conventionally defined as "female" activities; conversely, women could achieve renown in activities normally in the masculine domain. In effect, four different gender identities were available: masculine men, feminine men, feminine women, and masculine women. Furthermore, masculine women and feminine men were not merely accepted but were highly respected.

Because individuals who share a culture tend to marry within their society and thus to share certain physical characteristics, some people mistakenly believe a direct relationship exists between culture and race. This idea has two problems, one of them being that the human species cannot be divided into biological races. The reason is that physical traits of humans do not co-vary; hence, a classification based on differential skin color, for example, will be quite different from one based on some other characteristic. The second problem is that so-called racial characteristics represent biological adaptations to climate and have nothing to do with differences in intelligence or cultural superiority. Some African Americans have argued they have more in common with dark-skinned Africans than they do with light-skinned North Americans. Yet if they suddenly had to live in a traditional Bantu society, they would find themselves lacking the cultural knowledge to be successful members of this group. The culture they share with White North Americans is more significant than the physical traits they share with the Black Africans.

CULTURE IS LEARNED

All culture is learned rather than biologically inherited, prompting anthropologist Ralph Linton

In the United States, a man dressing as a woman has been regarded traditionally as abnormal behavior, but in some other cultures, such behavior is regarded as perfectly normal. Not only does culture define what is abnormal as well as normal, but also such definitions may change over time, as when women in the United States wear men's clothing without being regarded as at all odd.

to refer to it as humanity's "social heredity." People learn their culture by growing up with it, and the process whereby culture is transmitted from one generation to the next is called **enculturation.**

Most animals eat and drink whenever the urge arises. Humans, however, do most of their eating and drinking at certain culturally prescribed times and feel hungry as those times approach. These eating times vary from culture to culture, as does what is eaten and how it is eaten. To add complexity, food is used to do more than merely satisfy nutritional requirements. When used to celebrate rituals and religious activities, food

---

Enculturation.   The process that transmits a society's culture from one generation to the next.

"establishes relationships of give and take, of co-operation, of sharing, of an emotional bond that is universal."[2]

Through enculturation one learns the socially appropriate way to satisfy one's biologically determined needs. It is important to distinguish between the needs themselves, which are not learned, and the learned ways they are satisfied. Thus, a North American's idea of a comfortable way to sleep will vary greatly from that of a Japanese. The biological needs of humans are the same as those of other animals: besides food and sleep, they include shelter, companionship, self-defense, and sexual gratification. Each culture determines in its own way how these needs will be met.

Not all learned behavior is cultural. A pigeon may learn tricks, but this behavior is reflexive, the result of conditioning by repeated training, not the product of enculturation. Learned behavior is exhibited to one degree or another by most, if not all, mammals. Moreover, several species may be said to have culture, in that local populations share patterns of behavior that, just like humans, each generation learns from the one before and that differ from one population to another. Elizabeth Marshall Thomas, for example, has described a distinctive pattern of behavior among lions of southern Africa's Kalahari Desert that each generation passed on to the next and that regulated interaction with the region's native people.[3] She has shown as well how that culture changed over the past 30 years in response to new circumstances.

Among nonhuman primates, examples of cultural behavior are particularly evident. A chimpanzee, for example, will take a twig, strip it of all leaves, and smooth it down in order to fashion a tool for extracting termites from their nest. Such toolmaking, which juveniles learn from their elders, is unquestionably a form of cultural behavior once thought exclusively human. In Japan, macaques that learned the advantages of washing sweet potatoes before eating them passed the practice on to the next generation. And so it goes; it is interesting that within any given primate species, the culture of one population often differs from

that of others, just as it does among humans. Beyond this, we have discovered both in captivity and in the wild that primates in general and apes in particular "possess a near-human intelligence generally, including the use of sounds in representational ways, a rich awareness of the aims and objectives of others, the ability to engage in tactical deception, and the ability to use symbols in communication with humans and each other."[4]

Given the degree of biological similarity between apes and humans (discussed in Chapter 4), it should come as no surprise to find they are like us in other ways as well. In all respects the differences between apes and humans are differences of degree, rather than kind (although the degree does make a difference). This knowledge has shocked many, as it contradicts a belief deeply embedded in Western cultures: that a deep and unbridgeable gap between humans and animals is supposed to exist. It has not been easy to overcome this bias, and, indeed, we still have not come to grips fully with the moral implications with respect to the way we treat primates in research laboratories.

CULTURE IS BASED ON SYMBOLS

When anthropologist Leslie White observed that all human behavior originates in the use of symbols, he expressed an opinion all anthropologists share. Art, religion, and money involve symbols. We are all familiar with the fervor and devotion religion can elicit from a believer. A Christian cross, an Islamic crescent, a Jewish Star of David, or any object of worship may bring to mind centuries of struggle and persecution or may stand for a whole philosophy or creed. The most important symbolic aspect of culture is language—the substitution of words for objects.

Through language humans are able to transmit culture from one generation to another. In particular, language makes it possible to learn from cumulative shared experience. Without it, one could not inform others about events they were not a party to. We shall consider the important relationship between language and culture in greater detail in Chapter 15.

[2]Caroulis, J. (1996). Food for thought. *Pennsylvania Gazette, 95* (3), 16.

[3]Thomas, E. M. (1994). *The tribe of the tiger* (pp. 109–186). New York: Simon and Schuster.

[4]Reynolds, V. (1994). Primates in the field, primates in the lab. *Anthropology Today, 10* (2), 4.

Leslie A. White   (1900–1975)

Leslie White was a major theoretician in North American anthropology who saw culture as consisting of three essential components, which he referred to as techno-economic, the social, and the ideological. White defined the techno-economic aspect of a culture as the way members of the culture deal with their environment, and this aspect then determines the culture's social and ideological aspects.

Although he acknowledged the importance of symbols, White considered how culture harnessed energy the most significant factor in its development. Hence, in his "culturological" approach, he saw culture (in this case, technology) determining culture, and extracultural phenomena were deemed irrelevant. In *The Evolution of Culture*

(1959), White stated his basic law of evolution, that culture evolves in proportion to the amount of energy harnessed for each individual, or to the increased efficiency with which that energy is put to work. In other words, culture develops in direct response to technological "progress."

A problem with White's position is his equation of "evolution" with "progress," the latter being a concept Europeans (and European Americans) invented in the 18th century to rationalize the transformation taking place in their societies with the advent of the industrial revolution. In this respect, his theories were heavily culture bound. Yet he did alert anthropologists to the importance technological changes may have for the rest of culture.

CULTURE IS INTEGRATED

For comparison and analysis, anthropologists customarily break a culture down into many seemingly discrete parts, even though such distinctions are arbitrary. The anthropologist who examines one aspect of a culture invariably finds it necessary to examine others as well. This tendency for all aspects of a culture to function as an interrelated whole is called **integration**.

The integration of the economic, political, and social aspects of a culture can be illustrated by the Kapauku Papuans, a mountain people of western New Guinea studied in 1955 by North American anthropologist Leopold Pospisil.[5] The Kapauku economy relies on plant cultivation, along with pig

---

[5]Pospisil, L. (1963). *The Kapauku Papuans of west New Guinea*. New York: Holt, Rinehart and Winston.

breeding, hunting, and fishing. Although plant cultivation provides most of the people's food, men achieve political power and positions of legal authority through pig breeding.

Among the Kapauku, pig breeding is a complex business. Raising lots of pigs, obviously, requires a lot of food to feed them. This consists primarily of sweet potatoes grown in garden plots. Kapauku culture defines some essential gardening activities as women's work. Furthermore, pigs must be cared for by women. So, to raise many pigs, a man must have many women in the household. He accomplishes this by marrying them. In Kapauku society, multiple wives (polygyny) are not only permitted but are highly desired as well. For each wife, however, a man must pay a bride price, which can be expensive. Furthermore, wives have to be compensated for their care of pigs. Put simply, it takes pigs, by which wealth is measured,

---

Integration.   The tendency for all aspects of a culture to function as an interrelated whole.

A. R. Radcliffe-Brown   *(1881–1955)*

British anthropologist A. R. Radcliffe-Brown was the originator of what has come to be known as the structural-functionalist school of thought. He and his followers maintained that each societal custom and belief has a specific function that serves to perpetuate that society's structure—its ordered arrangement of parts—so that the society's continued existence is possible. The anthropologist's job, therefore, was to study the ways customs and beliefs function to solve the problem of maintaining the system. From such studies should emerge universal laws of human behavior.

The value of the structural-functionalist approach is that it caused anthropologists to analyze societies and their cultures as systems and to examine the interconnections between their various parts. It also gave a new dimension to comparative studies, as present-day societies were compared in terms of structural-functional similarities and differences rather than their presumed historical connections. Radcliffe-Brown's universal laws have not emerged, however, and these questions remain: Why do particular customs arise in the first place, and how do cultures change? To answer these questions, other approaches are necessary.

to get wives, which are necessary to raise pigs in the first place. Needless to say, this requires considerable entrepreneurship. It is this ability that produces leaders in Kapauku society.

The interrelatedness of the various parts of Kapauku culture is even more complex than this. For example, one condition conducive to polygyny is a surplus of adult women. In the Kapauku case, warfare is endemic, regarded as a necessary evil. By the rules of Kapauku warfare, men get killed but women do not. This system works to promote the kind of imbalance of sexes that facilitates polygyny. Polygyny also tends to work best if wives come to live in their husband's village, rather than the other way around, and this is the case among the Kapauku. Thus, the men of a village are "blood" relatives of one another. Given this, a patrilineal (descent reckoned through men) emphasis in Kapauku culture is not unexpected.

These examples by no means exhaust the interrelationships found in Kapauku culture. For example, both patrilineality and endemic warfare tend to promote male dominance, so it is not surprising to find that positions of leadership in Kapauku society are held exclusively by men, who appropriate the products of women's labor in order to play their political "games." Assertions to the contrary notwithstanding, male dominance is by no means characteristic of all human societies. Rather, as with the Kapauku, it arises only under particular circumstances that, if changed, would alter the way men and women relate to one another.

From what has been said so far, one might suppose the various parts of a culture must operate in perfect harmony at all times. The analogy would be that of a machine; all parts must be compatible and complementary or it won't run. Try putting diesel fuel in the tank of a car that runs on gasoline and you've got a problem; one part of the system is no longer compatible with the rest. To a degree, this is true of all cultures. A change in one part of a culture usually will affect other parts, sometimes in rather dramatic ways. This point, which we will return to later in this chapter, is particularly important today as diverse agents seek to introduce changes of all sorts into societies around the world.

While we must recognize that a degree of harmony is necessary in any properly functioning culture, we should not assume complete harmony is required. Because no two individuals experience the enculturation process in precisely the same way, no two individuals perceive their culture in exactly the same way, so always some potential for change exists in any culture. We should speak, instead, of a strain to consistency in culture. So long as the parts are reasonably consistent, a culture will operate reasonably well. If, however, that strain to consistency breaks down, a situation of cultural crisis ensues.

STUDYING CULTURE IN THE FIELD

Armed, now, with some understanding of what culture is, we next address this question: How does an anthropologist study culture in the field? Culture, being a set of rules or standards, cannot itself be directly observed; only actual behavior is observable. The anthropologist must abstract a set of rules from what is seen and heard in order to explain social behavior, much as a linguist, from the way people speak a language, tries to develop a set of rules to account for the ways those speakers combine sounds into meaningful phrases.

To pursue this further, consider the following discussion of exogamy—marriage outside one's own group—among the Trobriand Islanders, as described by Bronislaw Malinowski.

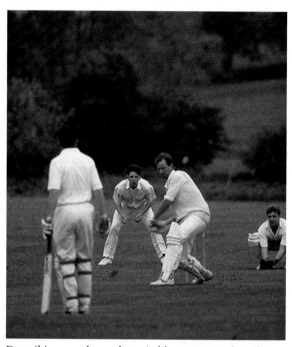

Describing another culture is like trying to describe a new game. The people in this picture look as though they are playing baseball, but they are playing cricket. To describe cricket in the language of baseball would be at best a caricature of the game as the British know it. The problem in anthropology is how to describe another culture for an audience unfamiliar with it, so that the description is not a caricature.

If you were to inquire into the matter among the Trobrianders, you would find that . . . the natives show horror at the idea of violating the rules of exogamy and that they believe that sores, diseases, even death might follow clan incest. [But] from the viewpoint of the native libertine, *suvasova* (the breach of exogamy) is indeed a specially interesting and spicy form of erotic experience. Most of my informants would not only admit but did actually boast about having committed this offense.[6]

Malinowski himself determined that although such breaches did occasionally occur, they were much less frequent than gossip would have it. Had Malinowski relied solely on what the Trobrianders told him, his description of their culture would have been inaccurate. The same sort of discrep-

---

[6]Malinowski, B. (1922). *Argonauts of the western Pacific.* New York: Dutton.

Bronislaw Malinowski *(1884–1942)*

The Polish-born Bronislaw Malinowski argued that people everywhere share certain biological and psychological needs and that the ultimate function of all cultural institutions is to fulfill those needs. Everyone, for example, needs to feel secure in relation to the physical universe. Therefore, when science and technology are inadequate to explain certain natural phenomena—such as eclipses or earthquakes—people develop religion and magic to account for those phenomena and to restore a feeling of security. The nature of the institution, according to Malinowski, is determined by its function.

Malinowski outlined three fundamental levels of needs that he claimed had to be resolved by all cultures:

1. A culture must provide for biological needs, such as food and procreation.

2. A culture must provide for instrumental needs, such as law and education.

3. A culture must provide for integrative needs, such as religion and art.

If anthropologists could analyze the ways a culture fulfills these needs for its members, Malinowski believed they also could deduce the origin of cultural traits. Although this belief was never justified, the quality of data Malinowski's approach called for set new standards for ethnographic fieldwork. He himself showed the way with his work in the Trobriand Islands between 1915 and 1918. Never before had such in-depth fieldwork been done, nor had such insights been gained into the workings of another culture. Such was the quality of Malinowski's Trobriand research that with it ethnography can be said to have come of age as a scientific enterprise.

ancy between cultural ideals and the way people really do behave can be found in any culture. Chapter 1 had an example from contemporary North America in the Garbage Project discussion.

From these examples, it is obvious anthropologists must be cautious if they are to give a realistic description of a culture. To play it safe, data drawn in three different ways ought to be considered. First, the people's own understanding of the rules they share—that is, their notion of the way their society *ought* to be—must be examined. Second, the extent people believe they are observing those rules—that is, how they think they actually do behave—needs to be investigated. Third, the behavior that can be directly observed should be considered—in the Trobrianders example, whether or not the rule of *suvasova* is actually violated. As we see here, and as shown in the Garbage Project discussion, the way people think they *should* behave, the way they think they *do* behave, and the way they *actually* behave may be three distinctly different versions. By carefully examining these elements, anthropologists can draw up a set of rules that actually may explain the acceptable behavior within a culture.

Of course, the anthropologist is only human. As discussed in Chapter 1, it is difficult to completely cast aside one's personal feelings and biases, which have been shaped by one's own culture. Yet it is important to make every effort to do just this, for otherwise anthropologists may seriously misinterpret what they see. As a case in point, consider how the male bias of the European culture Malinowski came from caused him to miss important factors in his pioneering study of the Trobriand Islanders.

The Importance of Trobriand Women[7]

▲▽

Walking into a village at the beginning of fieldwork is entering a world without cultural guideposts. The task of learning values that others live by is never easy. The rigors of fieldwork involve listening and watching, learning a new language of speech and actions, and most of all, letting go of one's own cultural assumptions in order to understand the meanings others give to work, power, death, family, and friends. As my fieldwork in the Trobriand Islands of Papua New Guinea was no exception, I wrestled doggedly with each of these problems. Doing research in the Trobriand Islands created one additional obstacle. I was working in the footsteps of a celebrated anthropological ancestor, Bronislaw Kasper Malinowski. . . .

In 1971, before my first trip to the Trobriands, I thought I understood many things about Trobriand customs and beliefs from having read Malinowski's exhaustive writings. Once there, however, I found that I had much more to discover about what I thought I already knew. For many months I worked with these discordant realities, always conscious of Malinowski's shadow, his words, his explanations. Although I found significant differences in areas of importance, I gradually came to understand how he reached certain conclusions. The answers we both received from informants were not so dissimilar, and I could actually trace how Malinowski had analyzed what his informants told him in a way that made sense and was scientifically significant—given what anthropologists generally then recognized about such societies. Sixty years separate our fieldwork, and any comparison of our studies illustrates not so much Malinowski's mistaken interpretations but the developments in anthropological knowledge and inquiry from his time to mine.

This important point has been forgotten by those anthropologists who today argue that ethnographic writing can never be more than a kind of fictional account of an author's experiences. Although Malinowski and I were in the Trobriands at vastly different historical moments and there also are many areas in which our analyses differ, a large part of what we learned in the field was similar. From the vantage point that time gives to me, I can illustrate how our differences, even those that are major, came to be. Taken together, our two studies profoundly exemplify the scientific basis that underlies the collection of ethnographic data. Like all such data, however, whether researched in a laboratory or a village, the more we learn about a subject, the more we can refine and revise earlier assumptions. This is the way all sciences create their own historical developments. Therefore, the lack of agreement between Malinowski's ethnography and mine must not be taken as an adversarial attack against an opponent. Nor should it be read as an example of the writing of ethnography as "fiction" or "partial truths." Each of our differences can be traced historically within the discipline of anthropology.

My most significant point of departure from Malinowski's analyses was the attention I gave to women's productive work. In my original research plans, women were not the central focus of study, but on the first day I took up residence in a village I was taken by them to watch a distribution of their

---

[7]Weiner, A. B. (1988). *The Trobrianders of Papua New Guinea* (pp. 4–7). New York: Holt, Rinehart and Winston.

own wealth—bundles of banana leaves and banana fiber skirts—which they exchanged with other women in commemoration of someone who had recently died. Watching that event forced me to take women's economic roles more seriously than I would have from reading Malinowski's studies. Although Malinowski noted the high status of Trobriand women, he attributed their importance to the fact that Trobrianders reckon descent through women, thereby giving them genealogical significance in a matrilineal society. Yet he never considered that this significance was underwritten by women's own wealth because he did not systematically investigate the women's productive activities. Although in his field notes he mentions Trobriand women making these seemingly useless banana bundles to be exchanged at a death, his published work only deals with men's wealth.

My taking seriously the importance of women's wealth not only brought women as the neglected half of society clearly into the ethnographic picture but also forced me to revise many of Malinowski's assumptions about Trobriand men. For example, Trobriand kinship as described by Malinowski has always been a subject of debate among anthropologists. For Malinowski, the basic relationships within a Trobriand family were guided by the matrilineal principle of "mother-right" and "father-love." A father was called "stranger" and had little authority over his own children. A woman's brother was the commanding figure and exercised control over his sister's sons because they were members of his matrilineage rather than their father's matrilineage.

According to Malinowski, this matrilineal drama was played out biologically by the Trobrianders' belief that a man has no role as genitor. A man's

In the Trobriand Islands, women's wealth consists of skirts and banana leaves, large quantities of which must be given away on the death of a relative.

wife is thought to become pregnant when an ancestral spirit enters her body and causes conception. Even after a child is born, Malinowski reported, it is the woman's brother who presents a harvest of yams to his sister so that her child will be fed with food from its own matrilineage, rather than its father's matrilineage. In this way, Malinowski conceptualized matrilineality as an institution in which the father of a child, as a member of a *different* matrilineage, was excluded not only from participating in procreation but also from giving any objects of lasting value to his children, thus provisioning them only with love.

In my study of Trobriand women and men, a different configuration of matrilineal descent emerged. A Trobriand father is not a "stranger" in Malinowski's definition, nor is he a powerless figure as the third party to the relationship between a woman and her brother. The father is one of the most important persons in his child's life, and remains so even after his child grows up and marries. Even a father's procreative importance is incorporated into his child's growth and development. A Trobriand man gives his child many opportunities to gain things from his matrilineage, thereby adding to the available resources that he or she can draw upon. At the same time, this giving creates obligations on the part of a man's children toward him that last even beyond his death. Therefore, the roles that men and their children play in each other's lives are worked out through extensive cycles of exchanges, which define the strength of their relationships to each other and eventually benefit the other members of both their matrilineages. Central to these exchanges are women and their wealth.

That Malinowski never gave equal time to the women's side of things, given the deep significance of their role in societal and political life, is not surprising. Only recently have anthropologists begun to understand the importance of taking women's work seriously. In some cultures, such as the Middle East or among Australian aborigines, it is extremely difficult for ethnographers to cross the culturally bounded ritual worlds that separate women from men. In the past, however, both women and men ethnographers generally analyzed the societies they studied from a male perspective. The "women's point of view" was largely ignored in the study of gender roles, since anthropologists generally perceived women as living in the shadows of men—occupying the private rather than the public sectors of society, rearing children rather than engaging in economic or political pursuits.

CULTURE AND ADAPTATION

In the course of their evolution, humans, like all animals, have been continually faced with the problem of adapting to their environment. The term **adaptation** refers to a natural (rather than willful) process organisms undergo to achieve a beneficial adjustment to an available environment and the results of that process—the characteristics possessed by organisms that permit them to overcome the hazards of and to secure the resources they need for the particular environments they live in. With the exception of humans, organisms have

---

Adaptation. A process organisms undergo to achieve a beneficial adjustment to an available environment and the results of that process: characteristics that fit them to the particular conditions of the environment they are generally found in.

generally adapted as natural selection has provided them with advantageous anatomical and physiological characteristics. For example, a body covering of hair, coupled with certain other physiological mechanisms, protects mammals from extremes of temperature; specialized teeth help them to procure the kinds of food they need; and so on. Humans, however, have come to depend more and more on cultural adaptation. For example, biology has not provided them with built-in fur coats to protect them in cold climates, but it has provided them with the ability to make their own coats, build fires, and erect shelters to protect themselves against the cold. More than this, culture enables people to use a wide diversity of environments. By manipulating environments through cultural means, people have been able to move into the Arctic and the Sahara and have even set foot on the moon. Through culture the human species has secured not just its survival but its expansion as well.

This does not mean humans do everything *because* it is adaptive to a particular environment. For one, people do not just react to an environment as given; rather, they react to it as they perceive it, and different groups of people may perceive the same environment in radically different ways. They also react to things other than the environment: their own biological natures, for one, and their beliefs, attitudes, and the consequences of their own behavior, for others. All of these present them with problems, and people maintain cultures to deal with problems, or matters that concern them. To be sure, their cultures must produce behavior that is generally adaptive, or at least not maladaptive, but this is not the same as saying cultural practices necessarily arise because they are adaptive in a given environment. The fact is, current utility of a custom is an unreliable guide to its origin.

A further complication is the relativity of any given adaptation: What is adaptive in one context may be seriously maladaptive in another. For example, the sanitation practices of food-foraging peoples—their toilet habits and methods of garbage disposal—are appropriate to contexts of low population levels and some degree of residential mobility. These same practices, however, become serious health hazards in the context of

What is adaptive at one time may not be at another. In the United States, the principal source of fruits, vegetables, and fiber is the Central Valley of California, where irrigation works have made the desert bloom. As happened in ancient Mesopotamia, evaporation concentrates salts in the water, but here pollution is made even worse by chemical fertilizers. These poisons are now accumulating in the soil and threaten to make the valley a desert again.

large, fully sedentary populations. Similarly, behavior that is adaptive in the short run may be maladaptive in the long run. For example, the development of irrigation in ancient Mesopotamia (modern-day Iraq) made it possible in the short run to increase food production, but in the long run it favored the gradual accumulation of salts in the soils. This, in turn, contributed to the collapse of civilization there after 2000 B.C. Similarly, the development of prime farmland today in places such as the eastern United States for purposes other than food production makes us increasingly dependent on food raised in marginal environments. High yields are presently possible through the application of expensive technology, but continuing loss of topsoil, increasing salinity of soils from the evaporation of irrigation waters, and silting of irrigation works, not to mention impending shortages of water and fossil fuels, make continuing high yields over the long term unlikely.

FUNCTIONS OF CULTURE

From what has been said so far, it is clear a culture cannot survive if it does not successfully deal with basic problems. A culture must provide for the production and distribution of goods and services considered necessary for life. It must provide for biological continuity through the reproduction of its members. It must enculturate new members so that they can become functioning adults. It must maintain order among its members, as well as between them and outsiders. It must motivate its members to survive and to engage in activities necessary for survival. On top of all of these, it must be able to change if it is to remain adaptive under changed conditions.

CULTURE AND CHANGE

All cultures change over time, although not always as rapidly or as massively as many are doing today. Changes occur in response to events such as environmental crises, the intrusion of outsiders, or the modification of behavior and values within the culture. In North American culture, clothing fashions change frequently. In the past few decades it has become culturally permissible for men and women alike to bare more of their bodies not just in swimming but in dress as well. Along with this has come greater permissiveness about the body in photographs and movies. Finally, the sexual attitudes and practices of North Americans have become less restrictive. Obviously, these changes are interrelated, reflecting an underlying change in attitudes toward cultural rules regarding sex.

Although cultures must be able to change to remain adaptive, culture change also can bring unexpected and often disastrous results. A case in point are the droughts that periodically afflict so many peoples living in Africa just south of the Sahara Desert. Native to this region are some 14 million pastoral nomadic peoples whose lives are centered on cattle and other livestock, which are herded from place to place as required for pasturage and water. For thousands of years these people went about their business, efficiently using vast areas of arid lands in ways that allowed them to survive severe droughts many times in the past. Unfortunately for them, their nomadic lifestyle, which makes it difficult to impose controls upon them and takes them across international boundaries at will, makes them a source of annoyance to the governments of the postcolonial states of the region. Seeing nomads as a challenge to their

Though pastoral nomadic peoples are often blamed for causing the sort of environmental degradation evident here, the fault is not theirs. Rather, it lies with the governments of countries that restrict their movements, thereby causing overgrazing.

authority, these governments have gone all out to convert them into sedentary villagers. Overgrazing has resulted from this loss of mobility, and the problem has been compounded by governmental efforts to involve the pastoralists in a market economy by encouraging them to raise many more animals than required for their own needs in order to have a surplus to sell. The resultant devastation, where previously no significant overgrazing or erosion had occurred, now makes droughts far more disastrous than they would otherwise be and places the former nomads' very existence in jeopardy.

▲▼▲▼▲▼▲▼▲▼▲▼▲▼▲▼▲▼▲▼▲▼▲▼▲▼▲

CULTURE, SOCIETY, AND THE INDIVIDUAL

Ultimately, a society is no more than a union of individuals, all of whom have their own special needs and interests. If a society is to survive, it must succeed in balancing the self-interests of its members against the demands of the society as a whole. To accomplish this, a society offers rewards for adherence to its cultural standards. In most cases, these rewards assume the form of social acceptance. In contemporary North American society, a man who holds a good job, is faithful to his wife, and goes to church, for example, may be elected "Model Citizen" by his neighbors. In order to ensure the survival of the group, each person must learn to postpone certain immediate satisfactions. Yet the needs of the individual cannot be suppressed too far, lest stress levels become too much to bear. Hence, a delicate balance always exists between personal interests and the demands the group makes on each individual.

Take, for example, the matter of sex, which, like anything people do, is shaped by culture. Sex is important in any society, for it helps to strengthen cooperative bonds between men and women and ensures the perpetuation of the society itself. Yet sex can be disruptive to social living; if who has sexual access to whom is not clearly spelled out, competition for sexual privileges can destroy the cooperative bonds human survival depends upon. Uncontrolled sexual activity, too, can result in reproductive rates that cause a society's population to outstrip its resources. Hence, as they shape sexual behavior, every culture must balance the needs of society against the need for sufficient individual gratification, lest frustration build until it causes disruption. Of course, cultures vary widely in the way they resolve this dilemma. Resolutions range all the way from the quite restrictive approach of British and United States society in the late 19th and early 20th century, which specified no sex out of wedlock, to practices among the Canela (who live in eastern Brazil) that guarantee that, sooner or later, everyone in a given village has had sex with just about everyone of the opposite sex. But permissive though the latter sit-

In the United States, the rise of private militia groups reflects the frustration of people whose needs are poorly satisfied by the culture.

uation may seem, nonetheless, strict rules specify how the system operates.[8]

Not just in sex, but in all things, cultures must strike a balance between the needs of individuals and those of society. When the needs of society take precedence, people experience excessive stress. Symptomatic of this are increased levels of mental illness and behavior regarded as antisocial: violence, crime, abuse of alcohol and other drugs, suicide, and simply alienation. If not corrected, the situation can result in cultural breakdown. But just as problems develop if the needs of society take precedence over those of individuals, so do they develop if the balance is upset in the other direction.

EVALUATION OF CULTURE

Humans know of diverse cultural solutions to the problems of their existence. This question often arises: Which is best? In the 19th century, Europeans (and European Americans) had no doubts

[8]Crocker, W. A., & Crocker, J. (1994). *The Canela, bonding through kinship, ritual and sex* (pp. 143–171). Fort Worth, TX: Harcourt Brace.

about the answer—they saw their civilization as the peak of human development. At the same time, though, anthropologists were intrigued to find that all cultures they had any familiarity with saw themselves as the best of all possible worlds. Commonly, this was reflected in a name for the society that, roughly translated, meant "we human beings," as opposed to outsiders as "you subhumans." Anthropologists now know that any culture functioning adequately regards itself as the best, a view reflecting a phenomenon known as **ethnocentrism.** Hence, the 19th-century Europeans and European Americans were merely displaying their own ethnocentrism.

Anthropologists have been engaged actively in the fight against ethnocentrism ever since they started to live among so-called "savage" peoples and discovered they were just as human as anyone else. As a consequence, anthropologists began to examine each culture on its own terms, asking whether or not the culture satisfied its people's needs and expectations. If a people practiced human sacrifice, for example, anthropologists asked about the circumstances that made the taking of human life acceptable according to native values. The idea that one must suspend judgment on other peoples' practices in order to understand them in their own cultural terms is called **cultural relativism.** Only through such an approach can one gain an undistorted view of another people's ways, as well as insights into the practices of one's own society.

Take, for example, the 16th-century Aztec practice of sacrificing humans for ritual purposes. Few (if any) North Americans today would condone such practices, but by suspending judgment one can get beneath the surface and understand how it functioned to reassure the populace that the Aztec state was healthy and that the sun would remain in the heavens. Beyond this, one can understand how the death penalty functions in the same way in the United States today. Numerous studies by a variety of social scientists have shown clearly that the death penalty does not deter violent crime, any more than Aztec sacrifice really provided sustenance for the sun. In fact, cross-cultural studies show that homi-

cide rates mostly decline after its abolition.[9] Just like Aztec human sacrifice, capital punishment is an institutionalized magical response to perceived disorder. As anthropologists Anthony Parades and Elizabeth D. Purdum point out: It "reassures many that society is not out of control after all, that the majesty of the law reigns and that God is indeed in his heaven."[10]

Essential though cultural relativism is as a research tool, it does not require suspension of judgment forever or that we must defend the right of any people to engage in any practice, no matter how reprehensible. All that is necessary is that we avoid *premature* judgment until we have a proper understanding of the culture we are interested in. Then, and only then, may one adopt a critical stance. As David Maybury-Lewis emphasizes: "One does not avoid making judgements, but rather postpones them in order to make informed judgements later."[11]

While anthropologists avoid the "anything goes" position of cultural relativism pushed to absurdity, they also must avoid the pitfall of judging the practices of other cultures in terms of ethnocentric criteria. A still useful formula for this was devised more than 40 years ago by anthropologist Walter Goldschmidt.[12] In his view the important question to ask is: How well does a given culture satisfy the physical and psychological needs of those whose behavior it guides? Specific indicators are found in the nutritional status and general physical and mental health of its population; the incidence of violence, crime, and delinquency; the demographic structure; the stability and tranquil-

---

[9]Ember, C. J., & Ember, M. (1996). What have we learned from cross-cultural research? *General Anthropology, 2* (2), 5.

[10]Parades, J. A., & Purdum, E. D. (1990). Bye, bye Ted . . . *Anthropology Today, 6* (2), 9.

[11]Maybury-Lewis, D. H. P. (1993). A special sort of pleading. In W. A. Haviland & R. J. Gordon (Eds.), *Talking about people* (2nd ed., p. 17). Mountain View, CA: Mayfield.

[12]Bodley, J. H. (1990). *Victims of progress* (3rd ed., p. 138). Mountain View, CA: Mayfield.

Ethnocentrism. The belief that one's own culture is superior to all others. > **Cultural relativism.** The thesis that one must suspend judgment on other peoples' practices to understand them in their own cultural terms.

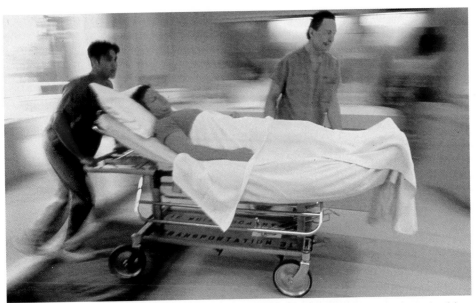

Although citizens of the United States are fond of boasting that theirs is the finest health care system in the world, they are merely reflecting the ethnocentrism of their own culture. Objective measures show that, while the U.S. system is better than many, it is far from being "number one."

ity of domestic life; and the group's relationship to its resource base. The culture of a people who experience high rates of malnutrition, violence, crime, delinquency, suicide, emotional disorders and despair, and environmental degradation may be said to be operating less well than that of another people who exhibit few such problems. In a well-working culture, people "can be proud, jealous, and pugnacious, and live a very satisfactory life without feeling 'angst,' 'alienation,' 'anomie,' 'depression,' or any of the other pervasive ills of our own inhuman and civilized way of living."[13] When people feel helpless to effect their own lives in their own societies and when traditional ways of coping no longer seem to work, the symptoms of cultural breakdown become prominent.

A culture is essentially a system to ensure the continued well-being of a group of people; therefore, it may be termed successful so long as it secures the survival of a society in a way that its members recognize as reasonably fulfilling. What complicates matters is that any society is made up

One sign that a culture is not adequately satisfying the needs and expectations of those who live by its rules is a high incidence of crime and delinquency. It is, therefore, sobering to note that the United States has a higher percentage of its population in prison than any other country in the world, yet it still has insufficient space to hold all those convicted of crimes.

---

[13]Fox, R. (1968). *Encounter with anthropology* (p. 290). New York: Dell.

of groups with different interests, raising the possibility that some people's interests may be served better than others. Therefore, a culture that is quite fulfilling for one group within a society may be less so for another. For this reason, anthropologists always must ask this: Whose needs, and whose survival, are best served by the culture in question? Only by examining the overall situation can a reasonably objective judgment be made as to how well a culture is working.

CHAPTER SUMMARY

Culture, to anthropologists, consists of the shared ideals, values, and beliefs members of a society use to interpret experience and to generate behavior and that are reflected by their behavior.

All cultures share certain basic characteristics; studying these sheds light on culture's nature and function. Culture cannot exist without society: a group of people sharing a common homeland who are dependent on each other for survival. Society is held together by relationships determined by social structure or social organization. It is possible to have a society, as do creatures such as ants and bees, without culture. All is not uniform within a culture; one reason is that some differences exist between male and female roles in any human society. Anthropologists use the term *gender* to refer to the elaborations or meanings cultures assign to the biological differences between men and women. Age variation is also universal, and in some cultures other subcultural variations occur as well. A subculture shares certain overarching assumptions of the larger culture while observing a distinctively different set of rules. One example of a subculture in the United States is that of the Amish. Pluralistic societies are those with particularly marked cultural variation. They are characterized by a number of groups operating under different sets of rules.

In addition to being shared, all cultures are learned. Individual members of a society learn the accepted norms of social behavior through the process of enculturation. Another characteristic is that culture is based on symbols. It is transmitted through the communication of ideas, emotions, and desires expressed in language. Finally, culture is integrated, so all aspects of a culture function as an integrated whole. In a properly functioning culture, though, total harmony of all elements is approximated, rather than completely achieved.

The job of anthropologists is to abstract a set of rules from what they observe to explain the social behavior of a people. To arrive at a realistic description of a culture free from personal and cultural biases, anthropologists must (1) examine a people's notion of the way their society ought to function; (2) determine how a people think they behave; and (3) compare these with how a people actually do behave. Anthropologists also must be as free as possible of biases of their own culture.

Cultural adaptation has enabled humans, in the course of evolution, to survive and expand in a variety of environments. Sometimes, though, what is adaptive in one set of circumstances, or in the short run, is maladaptive in another set of circumstances, or in the long run.

To survive, a culture must satisfy the basic biological needs of its members, provide for their continuity, and maintain order among them and between them and outsiders.

All cultures change over time, sometimes because the environment they must cope with has changed, sometimes as the result of the intrusion of outsiders, or sometimes because values within the culture have undergone modification. Although cultures must change to adapt to new circumstances, sometimes the unforeseen consequences of change are disastrous for a society.

A society must strike a balance between the self-interests of individuals and the needs of the group. If one or the other becomes paramount, the result may be cultural breakdown.

Ethnocentrism is the belief that one's own culture is superior to all others. To avoid making ethnocentric judgments, anthropologists adopt the approach of cultural relativism, which requires examination of each culture in its own terms and according to its own standards. The least biased measure of a culture's success, however, employs criteria indicative of the culture's effectiveness at securing the survival of a society in a way its members see as reasonably fulfilling.

POINTS FOR CONSIDERATION

1. Have you ever had an experience that made you aware of profound cultural differences? How did you react? How did any other parties react?

2. Cultural anthropologists generally conduct fieldwork, which is very different from the research methods of other social and behavioral scientists. Is fieldwork really necessary for the kinds of research topics anthropologists are interested in? How might other research methods provide different data?

3. Consider the problem of ancient Mesopotamian agriculture mentioned in the text. The same set of farming practices both led to the rise of a series of civilizations and, in time, helped to undermine those cultures. In the past 2 centuries, Europeans and North Americans often have felt tension between preexisting cultural practices and changes new technology prompts. What kinds of cultural traits seem to have become nonadaptive in recent decades in North America? How do you know which are now adaptive?

SUGGESTED READINGS

Brown, D. E. (1991). *Human universals.* New York: McGraw-Hill.

The message of this book is that we should not let our fascination with the diversity of cultural practices interfere with the study of human universals: those aspects all cultures share in spite of their differences. Important though the differences are, the universals have special relevance for our understanding of the nature of all humanity and raise issues that transcend the boundaries of biological and social science, as well as the humanities.

Gamst, F. C., & Norbeck, E. (1976). *Ideas of culture: Sources and uses.* New York: Holt, Rinehart and Winston.

This is a book of selected writings, with editorial comments, about the concept of culture. From these selections one can see how the concept has grown, as well as how it has given rise to narrow specializations within anthropology.

Goodenough, W. H. (1970). *Description and comparison in cultural anthropology.* Chicago: Aldine.

The major question Goodenough addresses is how anthropologists can avoid ethnocentric bias when studying culture. His approach relies on models of descriptive linguistics. A large part of the book covers kinship and terminology, with a discussion of the problems of a universal definition of marriage and the family. This is a particularly lucid discussion of culture, its relation to society, and the problem of individual variance.

Hatch, E. (1983). *Culture and morality: The relativity of values in anthropology.* New York: Columbia University Press.

This book is about cultural relativism, often used as a cover term for the quite different concepts of relativity of knowledge, historical relativism, and ethical relativism. It traces the attempts of anthropologists to grapple with these concepts, beginning with the rise of the discipline in the 19th century.

Linton, R. (1963). *The study of man: An introduction.* New York: Appleton.

Linton wrote this book in 1936 with the intention of providing a general survey of anthropology. His study of social structure is still illuminating today. This book is regarded as a classic and is an important source historically.

Chapter 15
LANGUAGE AND COMMUNICATION

THE RICHNESS OF HUMAN CULTURE IS MADE
POSSIBLE BY LANGUAGE, ONE OF OUR MOST
DISTINCTIVE CHARACTERISTICS. ALTHOUGH WE
ARE GENETICALLY PROGRAMMED TO SPEAK, WHAT
WE SPEAK IS DETERMINED BY OUR CULTURE.

Chapter Preview

What Is Language?

Language is a system of sounds or gestures that, when put together according to certain rules, results in meanings intelligible to all speakers. Although humans rely primarily on language to communicate with one another, it is not their sole means of communication. Language is embedded in a gesture-call system that consists of paralanguage—extralinguistic noises that accompany language—and kinesics, body motions that convey messages.

How Is Language Related to Culture?

Languages are spoken by people, who are members of societies, which have their own distinctive cultures. Social variables, such as the class, gender, and status of the speaker, influence people's language use. Moreover, people communicate what is meaningful to them, and what is or is not meaningful is defined by their particular culture. In fact, our language use affects, and is affected by, our culture.

How Did Language Begin?

Many theories have been proposed to account for the origin of language, several of them quite far-fetched. One theory anthropologists today hold is that human language began as a system of gestures with rudimentary syntax. As such, it represents an outgrowth of abilities the great apes also possessed. A key factor in its elaboration may have been the importance of planning ahead for future contingencies by our ancient ancestors. Since speech, like gestures, is a product of muscular movements, spoken language may have emerged as the muscles of the mouth and vocal tract were favored so that people could use their hands for other things as they talked and could communicate with others without having to be in full view.

All normal humans have the ability to talk, and in many societies they spend a considerable part of each day doing so. Indeed, **language** is so much a part of our lives that it permeates everything we do, and everything we do permeates language. No one doubts that our ability to speak, whether it be through sounds or gestures (sign languages, such as the American Sign Language the hearing impaired use, are fully developed languages in their own right), rests squarely upon our biological organization. We are "programmed" to speak, although only in a general way. Beyond the cries of babies, which are not learned but which do communicate, humans must learn how to speak. We must be taught to speak a particular language, and any normal child from anywhere in the world readily learns whatever language is spoken where she or he happens to be reared.

Language is a system for the communication, in **symbols,** of any kind of information. In the sense that nonhuman animals also communicate certain kinds of information systematically, we may speak of animal language. "Symbol" in our definition, however, means any kind of sound or gesture cultural tradition has assigned meaning to as standing for something, and not a symbol that has a natural or self-evident meaning, which language specialists call a **signal.** A tear is a signal of crying, and crying is a signal of some kind of emotional or physical state; the word *crying*, however, is a symbol, a group of sounds we have learned to assign the meaning of a particular action to and that we can use to communicate that meaning whether or not anyone around us is actually crying.

Currently, language experts are not certain how much credit to give to animals, such as dolphins or chimpanzees, for the ability to use symbols as well as signals, even though these animals and many others have been found to communicate in remarkable ways. Several apes have been taught American Sign Language, with results such as those noted in the Original Study for Chapter

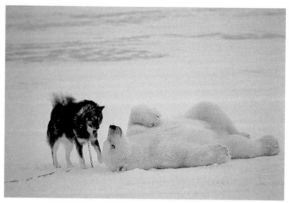

This example of animal communication shows a young polar bear in a submissive posture to the dog.

3. Even among vervet monkeys, at least 10 different calls are used for communication, nor are these mere indexes of degree of arousal or fear. As primatologist Allison Jolly notes:

> They mean something in the outside world; they include which direction to look in or where to run. There is an audience effect: calls are given when there is someone appropriate to listen . . . monkey calls are far more than involuntary expressions of emotion.[1]

What are the implications of this nonhuman ability for our understanding of the nature and evolution of language? No final answer will be evident until we have a better understanding of animal communication than we now have. What is clear is that animal communication cannot be dismissed as a set of simple reflexes or fixed action patterns, even though debate continues over just how human and animal communication relate to one another.[2] The fact is, human culture, as we

---

[1]Jolly, A. (1991). Thinking like a vervet. *Science, 251,* 574.
[2]Armstrong, D. F., Stokoe, W. C., & Wilcox, S. E. (1994). Signs of the origin of syntax. *Current Anthropology, 35,* 349–368. Burling, R. (1993). Primate calls, human language, and nonverbal communication. *Current Anthropology, 34,* 25–53.

Language. A system of communication using sounds or gestures put together in meaningful ways according to a set of rules. **> Symbols.** Sounds or gestures that stand for meanings among a group of people. **> Signal.** A sound or gesture that has a natural or self-evident meaning.

FIGURE 15.1

The price humans pay for spoken language is an increased risk of choking to death, caused by a lower position of larynx and epiglottis.

know it, is ultimately dependent on a system of communication far more complex than that of any other animal. The reason is the sheer amount of what each individual must learn from other individuals to control the knowledge and rules for behavior necessary for full participation in his or her society. Of course, learning can and does occur in the absence of language by observation and imitation, guided by a limited number of signs or symbols. All known cultures, however, are so rich in content that they require communication systems that not only can give precise labels to various classes of phenomena but also permit people to think and talk about their own and others' experiences in the past and future as well as the present. The central and most highly developed human system of communication is language. So important to us is spoken language that we have paid a significant price for it: To speak as we do, our vocal-respiratory tract has been modified in a way that greatly increases our chances of both choking to death and having impacted teeth, the latter condition generally being fatal until the 19th century

(Figure 15.1). Knowledge of the workings of language, then, is essential to a full understanding of culture.

THE NATURE OF LANGUAGE

Any human language—English, Chinese, Swahili, or whatever—is obviously a means of transmitting information and sharing with others both cultural and individual experiences. Because we tend to take language for granted, it is perhaps not so obvious that language is also a system that enables us to translate our concerns, beliefs, and perceptions into symbols others can understand and interpret. In spoken language, this is done by taking a few sounds—no language uses more than about 50—and developing rules for putting them together in meaningful ways. Sign languages, such as American Sign Language, do the same thing but with gestures rather than sounds. The many languages presently existing all over the world—some

6,000 or so different ones—may well astound and mystify us by their great variety and complexity; but this should not blind us to the fact all languages, as far back as we can trace them, are organized in the same basic way.

The roots of **linguistics**, the modern scientific study of language, go back a long way, to the works of ancient grammarians in India more than 2,000 years ago. In the age of exploration and discovery, the scientific study of language was given impetus by the accumulation of facts: the collection of sounds, words, and sentences from all sorts of different languages, chiefly those European explorers, invaders, and missionaries encountered in exotic lands. The great contribution of the 19th century was the discovery of system, regularity, and relationships in the data and the tentative for-

mulation of some laws and regular principles. In the 20th century, although researchers are still collecting data, they have made considerable progress in the reasoning process, testing and working from new and improved theories. Insofar as language theories and facts are verifiable by independent researchers looking at the same materials, a science of linguistics now can be said to exist.

THE SOUND AND SHAPE OF LANGUAGE

How can an anthropologist, a missionary, a social worker, or a medical worker approach and make sense of a language that has not already been analyzed and described or that is not covered in immediately available materials? Hundreds of such

For the linguist studying another language in the field, the tape recorder has become an indispensable tool.

Linguistics.   The modern scientific study of all aspects of language.

languages exist in the world; fortunately, some effective methods have been developed to help with the task. It is a painstaking process to unravel a language, but it is ultimately rewarding and often even fascinating for its own sake.

For a spoken language, the process requires first a trained ear and a thorough understanding of the way speech sounds are produced. Otherwise, it would be extremely difficult to write out or make intelligent use of any data. To satisfy this preliminary requirement, most people need special training in **phonetics,** or the systematic study of the production, transmission, and reception of speech sounds.

Phonology

To analyze and describe any new language, a researcher needs an inventory of all of its sounds and an accurate way of writing them down. Some sounds of other languages may be much like the sounds of English; others (such as the "clicks" in

Bushman languages) may be sounds English speakers have never consciously produced. Yet since all people have the same vocal equipment, we all can, with practice, reproduce all the sounds anyone else makes. Once a researcher knows all the possible sounds in a language, he or she can study the patterns these sounds take as they are used to form words. From this, the person can discover the underlying rules that tell which combinations of sounds are permissible in the language and which are not.

The first step in studying any language, once a number of utterances have been collected, is to isolate the **phonemes,** or the smallest classes of sound that make a difference in meaning. This isolation and analysis may be done by a process called the minimal-pair test: The linguist tries to find two short words that appear to be exactly alike except for one sound, such as *bit* and *pit* in English. If the substitution of *b* for *p* in this minimal pair makes a difference in meaning, which it does in English, then those two sounds have been

TABLE 15.1	Phonetic Vowel Symbols (Sapir System)*				
i (Fr. *fini*)	*ü* (Fr. *lune*)	*i*	*u̇* (Swed. *hus*)	*ï*	*u* (Ger. *gut*)
ɩ (Eng. *bit*)	*ü̇* (Ger. *Mütze*)	ɩ	*v̇*	*ü̈*	*v* (Eng. *put*)
e (Fr. *été*)	*ö* (Fr. *peu*)	—	*ȯ*	α (Eng. *but*)	*o* (Ger. *so*)
ɛ (Eng. *men*)	*ȫ* (Ger. *Götter*)	—	*ɔ́*	*a* (Ger. *Mann*)	ɔ (Ger. *Volk*)
—	ω (Fr. *peur*)	—	ω	—	ω (Eng. *law*)
ä (Eng. *man*)	—	*à* (Fr. *patte*)	—	—	—

*The symbol ə is used for an "indeterminate" vowel.
SOURCE: G. L. Trager. (1972). *Language and languages* (p. 304). San Francisco: Chandler Publishing Company.

Phonetics. The study of the production, transmission, and reception of speech sounds. **> Phonemes.** In linguistics, the smallest classes of sound that make a difference in meaning.

identified as distinct phonemes of the language and will require two different symbols to record. If, however, the linguist finds two different pronunciations, as when *butter* is pronounced "budder," and then finds that their meaning is the same for a native speaker, the sounds represented will be considered variants of the same phoneme. In such cases, for economy of representation, only one of the two symbols will be used to record that sound wherever it is found. For greater accuracy and to avoid confusion with the various sounds of the researcher's language, the symbols of a phonetic alphabet, such as was developed by Edward Sapir for the American Anthropological Association (Table 15.1), can be used to distinguish the sounds of most languages in a way comprehensible to anyone who knows the system.

Morphology

The process of making and studying an inventory of sounds may, of course, be a lengthy task; concurrently, the linguist may begin to work out all groups of or combinations of sounds that seem to have meaning. These are called **morphemes,** and they are the smallest units that have meaning in the language (unlike phonemes, which, while making a difference in meaning, have no meaning by themselves). They may consist of words or parts of words. A field linguist can abstract morphemes and their meanings from speakers of a language by pointing or gesturing to elicit words and their meanings, but the ideal situation is to have an informant, a person who knows enough of a common second language to help the linguist make approximate translations more efficiently and confidently. It is pointless to write down data without any suggestion of meaning for them. *Cat* and *dog* would, of course, turn out to be morphemes, or meaningful combinations of phonemes, in English. By pointing to two of either of these animals, the linguist could elicit *cats* and *dogs*. This indi-

cates that another unit carries meaning, an -*s*, that may be added to the original morpheme to mean "plural." When the linguist finds that this -*s* cannot occur in the language unattached, it will be identified as a **bound morpheme;** because *dog* and *cat* can occur unattached to anything, they are called **free morphemes.** Because the sound represented in writing as *s* is actually different in the two words (*s* in *cats* and *z* in *dogs*), the linguist will conclude that the sounds *s* and *z* are two varieties of the same morpheme (even though they may be two different phonemes) occurring in different contexts but with no difference in meaning.

Grammar and Syntax

The next step is to put morphemes together to form phrases or sentences. This process is known as identifying the *syntactic units* of the language, or the way morphemes are combined into larger chains or strings that have meaning. One way to do this is to use a method called **frame substitution.** By proceeding slowly at first, and relying on pointing or gestures, the field linguist can elicit strings such as *my cat, your cat,* or *her cat, I see your cat* and *she sees my cat.* This begins to establish the rules or principles of phrase and sentence making, the **syntax** of the language.

Further success of this sort of linguistic study depends greatly on individual ingenuity, tact, logic, and experience with language. A language may make extensive use of kinds of utterances not found at all in English and that an English-speaking linguist may not, therefore, even think of asking for. Furthermore, some speakers may pretend they cannot say (or may truly not be able to say) certain words their culture considers impolite, taboo, or inappropriate for mention to outsiders. It even may be unacceptable to point, so the linguist may have to devise roundabout ways to elicit words for objects.

Morphemes. In linguistics, the smallest units of sound that carry a meaning. **> Bound morpheme.** A sound that can occur in a language only in combination with other sounds, as *s* in English does to signify the plural. **> Free morphemes.** Morphemes that can occur unattached in a language; for example, *dog* and *cat* are free morphemes in English. **> Frame substitution.** A method used to identify the syntactic units of language. For example, a category called *nouns* may be established as anything that will fit the substitution frame "I see a . . . " **> Syntax.** In linguistics, the rules or principles of phrase and sentence making.

The **grammar** of the language ultimately will consist of all observations about its morphemes and syntax. Further work may include the establishment, by substitution frames, of all the **form classes** of the language: that is, the parts of speech or categories of words that work the same way in any sentence. For example, a linguist may establish a category called *nouns,* defined as anything that will fit the substitution frame "I see a . . . " The researcher simply makes the frame, tries out a number of words in it, and has a native speaker indicate "yes" or "no" for whether the words work. In English, the words *house* and *cat* will fit this frame and can be said to belong to the same form class, but the word *think* will not. Another possible substitution frame for nouns might be "The _____ died," in which the word *cat* will fit, but not the word *house.* Thus the linguist can identify subclasses of English nouns: in this case, "animate" or "inanimate" subclasses. The same procedure can be followed for all the words of the language, using as many different frames as necessary, until a lexicon, or dictionary, can be created that accurately describes the possible uses of all the words in the language.

One of the strengths of modern descriptive linguistics is the objectivity of its methods. A descriptive linguist does not approach a language with the idea that it must have nouns, verbs, prepositions, or any other of the form classes identifiable in English. The linguist instead sees what turns up in the language and makes an attempt to describe it in terms of its own inner workings. For convenience, morphemes that behave approximately like English nouns and verbs may be labeled as such, but if the terms would be misleading, the linguist instead might call them "x-words" and "y-words," or "form class A" and "form class B."

▲▽▲▽▲▽▲▽▲▽▲▽▲▽▲▽▲▽▲▽▲▽▲▽▲▽▲▽▲▽▲

THE GESTURE-CALL SYSTEM

Efficient though languages are at naming and talking about things, all are deficient to some degree in communicating certain kinds of information people need to know to understand what is being said. For this reason, human language is always embedded within a *gesture-call system* of a type we share with monkeys and apes. The various sounds and gestures of this system serve to "key" speech, providing listeners with the appropriate frame for interpreting what a speaker is saying. Through it, we learn information such as the age and sex of the speaker, as well as his or her individual identity if it is someone we already know. Moreover, subtle messages about emotions and intentions are conveyed. Is the speaker happy, sad, enthusiastic, tired, or in some other emotional state? Is he or she requesting information, denying something, reporting factually, or lying? Very little of this information is conveyed by spoken language alone. In English, for example, at least 90% of emotional information is transmitted not by the words spoken but by "body language" and tone of voice. One (but not the only) reason English has become the *lingua franca* of business is because of how easily deception can be carried out in written English. Not all languages are as rich in mechanisms for evasion or as impoverished in mechanisms for truth as English.[3] None, including English, communicate peoples' emotions and intentions as effectively as the gesture-call system.

As features we have inherited from our primate ancestors, many sounds and gestures of our gesture-call system are subject to greater genetic determination than language. This accounts for the universality of various cries and facial expressions, as well as for the great difficulty people have bluffing or especially lying through gesture-calls. This does not mean the system is entirely immune to deliberate control, for it is not; it is merely less subject to control than spoken language.

---

[3]Elgin, S. H. (1994). I am not scowling fiercely as I write this. *Anthropology Newsletter, 35* (9), 44.

Grammar. The entire formal structure of a language consisting of all observations about the morphemes and syntax.
> **Form classes.** The parts of speech or categories of words that work the same way in any sentence.

Humans talk, while much communication among other primates is done through gestures. Still, humans have not abandoned gestural communication altogether, as we see here.

KINESICS

The gestural component of the gesture-call system consists of postures, facial expressions, and bodily motions that convey messages. The method for notating and analyzing this body language is known as **kinesics**. Kinesic messages may be communicated directly, such as gestures do. For example, in North America scratching one's scalp, biting one's lip, or knitting one's brows are ways of conveying doubt. More complex examples are the gender signals North American men and women send. Although some regional and class variation occurs, women when standing generally bring their legs together, at times to the point the upper legs cross, either in a full leg cross with feet still together, the outer sides of the feet parallel to each other, or in standing knee over knee. The pelvis is carried rolled slightly forward. The upper arms are held close to the body, and in movement the entire body from neck to ankle is presented as a moving whole. Men, by contrast, hold their legs apart, with the upper legs at a 10° or 15° angle.

Their pelvis is carried in a slightly rolled-back position. The arms are held out at 10° to 15° from the body, and they are moved independently of the body. Finally, a man may subtly wag his hips with a slight right and left presentation, with a movement involving a twist at the base of the rib cage and at the ankles.

Such gender markers should not be mistaken for invitations to sexual activity. Rather, they are conventions inscribed on the body through imitation and subtle training. In any culture, as little girls grow up, they imitate their mothers or other older women; little boys do the same with their fathers or other older men. In North American culture, by the time individuals become adults, they have acquired a host of gender markers that intrude into every moment of their lives, so much so that they are literally at a loss if they do not know the sex of someone they must interact with. This is easily verified, as the philosopher Marilyn Frye suggests:

> To discover the differences in how you greet a woman and how you greet a man, for instance, just

---

Kinesics.   A system of notating and analyzing postures, facial expressions, and body motions that convey messages.

The body language shown in this photo of Senator Robert Dole and First Lady Hillary Rodham Clinton speaks volumes about gender relations in the United States. The senator's discomfort in the presence of Clinton's confident assertiveness is obvious.

observe yourself, paying attention to the following sorts of things: frequency and duration of eye contact, frequency and type of touch . . . physical distance maintained between bodies, how and whether you smile . . . whether your body dips into a shadow curtsey or bow. That I have two repertories for handling introductions to people was vividly confirmed for me when a student introduced me to his friend, Pat, and I really could not tell what sex Pat was. For a moment I was stopped cold, completely incapable of action. I felt myself helplessly caught between two paths—the one I would take if Pat were female and the one I would take if Pat were male. Of course the paralysis does not last. One is rescued by one's ingenuity and good will: one can invent a way to behave as one says "How do you do?" to a human being. But the habitual ways are not for humans: they are one way for women and another for men.[4]

Often, kinesic messages complement spoken messages, such as nodding the head while affirming

something verbally. Other examples are punching the palm of the hand for emphasis, raising the head and brows when asking a question, or using the hands to illustrate the subject being talked about. Such gestures are rather like bound morphemes; they have meaning but do not stand alone, except in particular situations, such as a nodded response to a question.

Although little scientific notice was taken of body language prior to the 1950s, since then a great deal of research, particularly among North Americans, has occurred. Cross-cultural research has shown, however, many similarities around the world for such basic facial expressions as smiling, laughing, crying, and variations of anger. Such smirks, frowns, and so forth that we have inherited from our primate ancestry require little learning and are harder to fake than conventional gestures. Great similarity, too, exists around the world in the routine for greeting over a distance. Europeans, Balinese, Papuans, Samoans, Bushmen, and at least some South American Indians all smile and nod, and if the individuals are especially friendly, they will raise their eyebrows with a rapid movement, keeping them raised for a

[4]Frye, M. (1983). Sexism. *The politics of reality* (p. 20). New York: The Crossing Press.

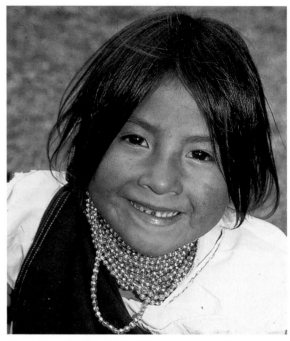

There is a great deal of similarity around the world in such basic expressions as smiling, laughing, crying, and anger, as one can see from the expressions of these children from Asia, Africa, and South America. Basic expressions like these are part of the human inheritance from their primate ancestry.

fraction of a second. By doing so, they signal a readiness for contact. The Japanese, however, suppress the eyebrow flash, regarding it as indecent, which shows that important differences, as well as similarities, occur cross-culturally. This point can be further demonstrated by gestural expressions for "yes" and "no." In North America, one nods the head for "yes" or shakes it for "no." The people of Sri Lanka, also, will nod to answer "yes" to a factual question, but if they are asked to do something, a slow sideways movement of the head means "yes." In Greece, the nodded head means "yes," but "no" is indicated by jerking the head back so as to lift the face, while the eyes are often closed and the eyebrows lifted. Body movements and gestures such as these, which vary cross-culturally and have to be learned, are known as conventional gestures.

Learned gestures different cultures assign different meanings to are known as conventional gestures. An example is this sign, which in North America means "OK." In Brazil, it is an obscene gesture.

PARALANGUAGE

The second component of the gesture-call system is **paralanguage,** consisting of cries and other sounds that are not part of language but always accompany it. The importance of paralanguage is suggested by this remark: "It's not so much *what* was said as *how* it was said." Recent studies have shown, for example, that subliminal messages communicated by seemingly minor differences in phraseology, tempo, length of answers and the like are far more important in courtroom proceedings than even the most perceptive trial lawyer may have realized. Among other things, how a witness gives testimony alters the reception it gets from jurors, and bears on the witness' credibility where inconsistencies exist in testimony.[5]

Voice Qualities

Although it is not always easy for the linguist to distinguish between the sounds of language and paralinguistic noises, two different kinds of the latter have been identified. The first has to do with **voice qualities,** which operate as the background characteristics of a speaker's voice. These involve pitch range (from low to high pitched); lip control (from closed to open); glottis control (sharp to smooth transitions in pitch); articulation control (forceful and relaxed speech); rhythm control (smooth or jerky setting off of portions of vocal activity); resonance (from resonant to thin); and tempo (an increase or decrease from the norm).

Voice qualities are capable of communicating much about the state of being of the speaker, quite apart from what is said. An obvious example of this is slurred speech, which may indicate the speaker is intoxicated. Or if someone says rather languidly, coupled with a restricted pitch range, that she or he is delighted with something, it probably indicates the person is not delighted at all. The same words said more rapidly, with increasing pitch, might indicate the speaker is genuinely excited about the matter. While the speaker's state of being is affected by his or her anatomical and physiological status, it is also markedly affected by the individual's overall self-image in the given situation. If a person is made to feel anxious by

Paralanguage.   The extralinguistic noises that accompany language, such as crying or laughing. > **Voice qualities.**   In paralanguage, the background characteristics of a speaker's voice.

being crowded in some way or by some aspects of the social situation, for example, this anxiety probably will be conveyed by certain voice qualities.

Vocalizations

The second kind of paralinguistic noises consists of **vocalizations**. Rather than background characteristics, these are actual identifiable noises that, unlike voice qualities, are turned on and off at perceivable and relatively short intervals. They are, nonetheless, separate from language sounds. One category of vocalizations is **vocal characterizers:** the sounds of laughing or crying, yelling or whispering, yawning or belching, and the like. Many combine sounds with gestures. Speakers "talk" through vocal characterizers, which generally indicate their attitude. If a person yawns while speaking to someone, for example, this may indicate an attitude of boredom. *Breaking,* an intermittent tensing and relaxing of the vocal musculature that produces a tremulousness while speaking, may indicate great emotion on the part of the speaker.

Another category of vocalizations consists of **vocal qualifiers.** These are of briefer duration than vocal characterizers, limited generally to the space of a single intonation, rather than over whole phrases. They modify utterances in terms of intensity—loud versus soft; pitch—high versus low; and extent—drawl versus clipping. These indicate the speaker's attitude toward specific phrases, such as "Get out!" The third category consists of **vocal segregates.** Sometimes called "*oh oh* expressions," these are somewhat like the actual sounds of language, but they do not appear in the kinds of sequences that can be called words. Examples of vocal segregates besides *oh oh* that are familiar to English-speaking peoples are such substitutes for language as *shh, uh-uh,* or *uh-huh.* Unlike such paralinguistic sounds as sobs, giggles, and screams, "*oh oh* expressions" are conventional, learned, and far more variable from culture to culture.

LINGUISTIC CHANGE

In our discussion of the sound and shape of language, we looked briefly at the internal organization of language—its phonology, morphology, syntax, and grammar. Of various approaches to linguistics, *descriptive linguistics* is concerned with registering and explaining all the features of a particular language at any one time in its history. This approach concentrates, for example, on the way modern French or Spanish functions now, as if it were a separate system, consistent within itself, without any reference to historical reasons for its development. Yet languages, like the rest of culture, have histories. The Latin *ille* ("that") is identifiable as the origin of both the French *le* ("the") and the Spanish *el* ("the"), even though the descriptive linguist treats *le* and *el* only as they function in the modern language, where the meaning "that" is no longer relevant and very few native speakers are aware they are speaking modern derivatives of Latin.

A second approach, *historical linguistics,* by contrast, investigates relationships between earlier and later forms of the same language, antecedents in older languages for developments in modern ones, and questions of relationships between older languages. Historical linguists, for example, attempt to identify and explain the development of early medieval spoken Latin into later medieval French and Spanish by investigating both natural change in the original language and the influence of contacts with invaders from the north. No conflicts exist between historical and descriptive linguists; the two approaches are recognized as interdependent. Even a modern language is constantly changing; consider, for example, the changed meaning of the word *gay* in English, which today is used to refer to homosexual persons. Its meaning in the title of the 1942 play *Our Hearts Were Young and Gay* illustrates the word's

---

Vocalizations. Identifiable paralinguistic noises turned on and off at perceivable and relatively short intervals. > **Vocal characterizers.** In paralanguage, sound productions such as laughing or crying that humans "speak" through. > **Vocal qualifiers.** In paralanguage, sound productions of brief duration that modify utterances in terms of intensity. > **Vocal segregates.** In paralanguage, sound productions that are similar to the sounds of language but do not appear in sequences that can be properly called words.

different usage as recently as that time. Such changes occur according to principles that can be established only historically.

Historical linguists have achieved considerable success working out the genealogical relationships between different languages, and these are reflected in classification schemes. For example, English is one of a number of languages classified in the Indo-European **language family** (Figure 15.2). This family is subdivided into 11 subgroups, which reflect the long period (8,000 years or so) of **linguistic divergence** from an ancient unified language (referred to as Proto-Indo-European) into separate "daughter" languages. English is one of a number of languages in the Germanic subgroup (Figure 15.3); all are more closely related to one another than to the languages of any other subgroup of the Indo-European family. So, in spite of the differences among them, the languages of one subgroup share certain features when compared to other subgroups. As an illustration, the word for *father* in the Germanic languages always starts with an *f* or closely related *v* sound (Dutch *vader,* German *Vater,* Gothic *Fadar*). Among the Romance languages, by contrast, the comparable word always starts with a *p:* French *père,* Spanish and Italian *padre,* and all derived from the Latin *pater.* The original Indo-European word for *father* was *p'tēr,* so in this case, the Romance languages have retained the earlier pronunciation, whereas the Germanic languages have diverged. Thus many words that begin with *p* in the Romance languages, such as the Latin *piscis* and *pes,* become words like the English *fish* and *foot* in the Germanic languages.

Historical linguists have successfully described the changes that have occurred as languages have diverged from more ancient parent languages. They also have developed means of estimating when certain migrations, invasions, and contacts of peoples have taken place, on the basis of linguistic similarities and differences. The concept of

FIGURE 15.2
The Indo-European languages.

linguistic divergence, for example, is used to guess when one group of speakers of a language separated from another group. A more complicated technique, known as **glottochronology,** was developed by Swadesh and Lees in the early 1950s to try to date the divergence of related languages, such as Latin and Greek, from an earlier common language. The technique is based on the assumption that changes in a language's **core vocabulary** —pronouns, lower numerals, and names for body parts and natural objects—change at a more or less constant rate. By applying a logarithmic formula to two related core vocabularies, linguists should be able to determine how many years the languages have been separated. Although not as precise as this might suggest, glottochronology provides a useful way to estimate when languages may have separated.

While many of the changes that have occurred in the course of linguistic divergence are well

---

Language family. A group of languages ultimately descended from a single ancestral language. ▸ **Linguistic divergence.** The development of different languages from a single ancestral language. ▸ **Glottochronology.** In linguistics, a method of dating divergence in branches of language families. ▸ **Core vocabulary.** In language, pronouns, lower numerals, and names for body parts and natural objects.

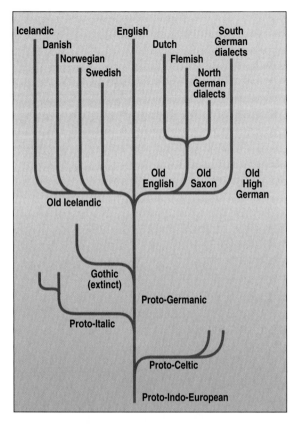

FIGURE 15.3

English is one of a group of languages in the Germanic subgroup of the Indo-European family. This diagram shows its relationship to other languages in the same subgroup. The root was Proto-Indo-European, a language spoken by a people who spread westward over Europe, bringing with them both their customs and their language.

known, their causes are not. One force for linguistic change is borrowing from another language, something speakers readily do when in a position to do so; but if borrowing were the sole force for change, linguistic differences would be expected to become less pronounced through time. By studying modern languages in their cultural settings, linguists can begin to understand the forces for change. One such force is novelty, pure and simple. Humans tend to admire the person who comes up with a new and clever idiom, a new and

useful word, or a particularly stylish pronunciation, so long as these do not seriously interfere with communication. Indeed, in linguistic matters, complexity tends to be admired, while simplicity seems dull. Hence, about as fast as a language is simplified, purged of needlessly complex constructions or phrases, new ones arise.

Group membership also plays a role in linguistic change. Part of this is functional: professions, sects, or other groups in a society often need special vocabularies to communicate effectively about their special interests. Beyond this, special vocabularies may serve as labeling devices; those who use such vocabularies are set off as a group from those who do not. Here, we have the paradox of language acting to *prevent* communication, in this case between members of different groups. Such linguistic barriers serve to create a strong sense of group identity.

When a military officer speaks of "incontinent ordinance" and "collateral damage," a physician of "exsanguination," a dentist of "oral cavity," or an anthropologist of "the structural implications of matrilateral cross-cousin marriage," they express, in part at least, their membership in a profession and their command of its language. For insiders, professional terminology reinforces their sense of belonging to a select in-group; to outsiders it often seems an unneeded and pretentious use of "bafflegab" where perfectly adequate and simple words would do as well. Whether needed or not, professional terminology does serve to differentiate language and to set the speech of one group apart from that of others. Therefore, it is a force for stylistic divergence.

Phonological differences between groups may be regarded in the same light as vocabulary differences. In a class-structured society, for example, members of the upper class may try to keep their pronunciation distinct from that of lower classes. An example of a different sort involves coastal communities in Maine, in particular, though it may be seen to varying degrees elsewhere along the New England coast. In the past, people in these communities developed a regional dialect with a pronunciation style quite distinct from those of "inlanders." More recently, as outsiders have moved into these coastal communities, either as summer people or as permanent residents, the traditional coastal style has come to identify those who adhere to traditional coastal values, as opposed to those who do not.

One other far-reaching force for linguistic change is **linguistic nationalism,** an attempt by whole countries to proclaim their independence by purging their vocabularies of "foreign" terms. This phenomenon is particularly characteristic of the former colonial countries of Africa and Asia today. It is by no means limited to those countries, however, as shown by periodic French attempts to purge their language of such Americanisms as *le hamburger*. Also in the category of linguistic na-

tionalism are revivals of languages long out of common use, by ethnic minorities and sometimes even whole countries. In the latter group is the successful revival of Hebrew as Israel's first language, though not without a bitter campaign against its competitor, Yiddish. In the former group is the Ute's attempt to revive their language, as discussed in the nearby Anthropology Applied.

For ethnic minorities, the revival of lost languages or the maintenance of those not lost is important for their sense of identity and self-worth. Furthermore, it serves as an effective barrier to penetration by outsiders, allowing people to

anthropology applied Language Renewal Among the Northern Ute

On April 10, 1984, the Northern Ute Tribe became the first community of American Indians in the United States to affirm the right of its members to regain and maintain fluency in their ancestral language, as well as their right to communicate in it throughout their lives. Like many other Native Americans, these people had experienced a decline in fluency in their native tongue as they were forced to interact more and more intensively with outsiders who spoke only English. Once the on-reservation boarding school was closed in 1953, Ute children had to attend schools where teachers and most other students were ignorant of the Ute language. Outside the classroom as well, children and adults alike were increasingly bombarded by English as they sought employment off the reservation, traded in non-Indian communities, or were exposed to television and other popular media. By the late 1960s, although Ute language fluency was still highly valued, many community members could no longer speak it.

Alarmed by this situation, the group of Ute parents and educators that supervises federally funded tutorial services to Indian students decided action needed to be taken, lest their native language be lost altogether.

With the assistance of other community leaders, they launched discussions on what they could do about the situation and invited anthropologist William L. Leap to join in these discussions. Previously, Leap had worked on language education with other tribes, and the Utes subsequently hired him to assist them in their efforts at linguistic renewal. One result of his work was the official policy statement by the tribe's governing body, noted earlier.

Leap began work for the Northern Utes in 1978, and his first task was to carry out a first-ever reservation-wide language survey.* This found, among other facts, that inability to speak Ute did not automatically imply loss of skill; evidently, many nonspeakers retained a "passive fluency" in the language and could understand it, even though they could not speak it. Furthermore (and quite contrary to expectations), children who still could speak Ute had fewer problems with English in school than did nonspeakers.

For the next few years, Leap helped set up a Ute language renewal program within the tribe's Division of Education, wrote several grants to provide funding, led staff training workshops in linguistic transcription and

---

Linguistic nationalism.   The attempt by ethnic minorities, and even countries, to proclaim independence by purging their languages of foreign terms or reviving unused languages.

grammatical analysis, provided technical assistance in designing a practical writing system for the language, and supervised data-gathering sessions with already fluent speakers of the language. With the establishment in 1980 of an in-school program to provide developmental Ute and English instruction to Indian and other interested children, he became staff linguist. In this capacity he helped train the language teachers (all of whom were Ute and none of whom had degrees in education); carried out research that resulted in numerous technical reports, publications, and in-service workshops; helped prepare a practical Ute language handbook for home use so that parents and grandparents might enrich the children's language learning experience; prepared the preliminary text for the tribe's policy statement on language; and helped persuade the governing body to accept this policy. By 1984, not only did this policy become "official," but also several (not just one) language development projects were in place on the reservation, all monitored and coordinated by

a tribally sanctioned language and culture committee. Supported by both tribal and federal funds, these involved the participation of persons with varying degrees of familiarity with the language. Although literacy was not a goal, down-to-earth needs resulted in the development of practical writing systems, and a number of people in fact became literate in Ute. One important reason for all this success was the involvement of the Ute people in all stages of development. Not only did these projects originate in response to their own expressed needs, but also they were active participants in all discussions and made decisions at each stage of the activities, participating not just as individuals but also as members of family, kin, community, and band.

---

*Leap, W. L. (1987). Tribally controlled culture change: The Northern Ute language renewal project. In R. M. Wulff & S. J. Fiske (Eds.), *Anthropological praxis: Translating knowledge into action.* Boulder, CO: Westview.

---

pursue the livelihoods and interests they choose for themselves. By the same token, a prime means countries use to try to assert their dominance over minorities living within their borders is to suppress their languages. A good illustration of this was the policy pursued in the United States of taking Indian children away from their parents and putting them in boarding schools, where use of Indian languages was absolutely forbidden and punished with physical abuse and humiliation. Not until 1934 did the government begin to ease up on this harsh policy, but it was only as recently as 1990 that Congress passed the Native American Languages Act, encouraging Indians to use their own languages.

In spite of such changes, the United States remains uneasy about linguistic diversity. This is reflected in a reluctance to learn foreign languages. In many human societies, it is not unusual for people to be fluent in two, three, or even four languages, but to become so it is important to begin learning them as children—not as high school or college students, as is traditional in the United States. More dramatically, it is illustrated by efforts to make "English only" a national policy. Proponents of such a policy argue that multilingualism is divisive and often cite the example of French sep-

aratism in Canada. What they do not cite are examples such as the former Yugoslavia or Northern Ireland, both instances where speaking a single language has not prevented violent fighting between factions. Nor do they mention countries such as Finland, where three languages are spoken, or Switzerland, where four exist without people being at one another's throats. The fact is, where linguistic diversity is divisive, it is often *because* of official policies in favor of monolingualism.

LANGUAGE IN ITS CULTURAL SETTING

As the preceeding discussion suggests, language is not simply a matter of combining sounds according to certain rules to come up with meaningful utterances. It is important to remember that languages are spoken by people, who are members of societies, each of which has its own distinctive culture. Individuals tend to vary in the ways they use language, and influences include social variables such as class, ethnicity, and status. Moreover, people choose words and sentences to communicate

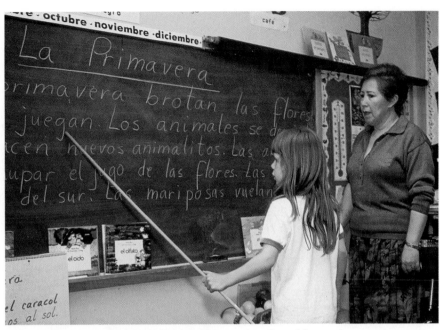

The linguistic nationalism of the United States is reflected by a reluctance to encourage bilingualism in Spanish, the language spoken by more people in the Americas than English or any other language. Some even go so far as to lobby for an "English only" policy.

meaning, and what is meaningful in one culture may not be in another. In other words, our use of language affects, and is affected by, the rest of our culture.

The whole question of the relationships between language and other aspects of culture is the province of **ethnolinguistics,** an outgrowth of both ethnology and descriptive linguistics, which has become almost a separate field of inquiry. Ethnolinguistics is concerned with every aspect of the structure and use of language that has anything to do with society, culture, and human behavior.

LANGUAGE AND THOUGHT

An important ethnolinguistic concern of the 1930s and 1940s was the question of whether language might actually determine other aspects of culture.

Do we see and react differently to the colors blue and green, with different cultural symbolism for each color, only because our language has different names for these two neighboring parts of the unbroken color spectrum? When anthropologists noticed that some cultures lump together blue and green with one name, they began to wonder about this question. American linguist Edward Sapir had earlier formulated the problem, and his student Benjamin Lee Whorf, drawing on his experience with the Hopi Indian language, developed a full-fledged theory, sometimes called the **Sapir-Whorf hypothesis.** Whorf proposed that a language is not simply an encoding process for voicing our ideas and needs but, rather, is a shaping force, which, by providing habitual grooves of expression that predispose people to see the world in a certain way, guides their thinking and behavior. The problem

---

Ethnolinguistics. The study of the relation between language and culture. **> Sapir-Whorf hypothesis.** The hypothesis, proposed by linguist B. L. Whorf, that states that language, by providing habitual grooves of expression, predisposes people to see the world in a certain way and thus guides their thinking and behavior.

is a little like the old question of the chicken or the egg. Some later formulations of Whorf's theory about which came first, thinking and behavior or language, have since been criticized as both logically unsound and not amenable to any experimentation or proof. The idea's primary value is that it focused attention on the relationships between language and the rest of culture.

The opposite point of view is that language reflects reality. In this view, because language mirrors cultural reality, as the latter changes, so too will language. Some support for this is provided by studies of blue-green color terms. It has been shown that eye pigmentation acts to filter out the shorter wavelengths of solar radiation. Color vision is thus limited by a reduced sensitivity to blue and confusion of the short visible wavelengths. The effect shows up in color-naming behavior, where green may be identified with blue, blue with black, or both green and blue with black. The severity of the visual limitation, as well as the extent of the lumping of color terms, depends on the density of eye pigmentation characteristic of the people in a given society.

These findings do not mean language merely reflects reality, any more than thinking and behavior are determined by language. The truth is more as anthropologist Peter Woolfson has put it:

> Reality should be the same for us all. Our nervous systems, however, are being bombarded by a continual flow of sensations of different kinds, intensities, and durations. It is obvious that all of these sensations do not reach our consciousness; some kind of filtering system reduces them to manageable propositions. The Whorfian hypothesis suggests that the filtering system is one's language. Our language, in effect, provides us with a special pair of glasses that heightens certain perceptions and dims others. Thus, while all sensations are received by the nervous system, only some are brought to the level of consciousness.[6]

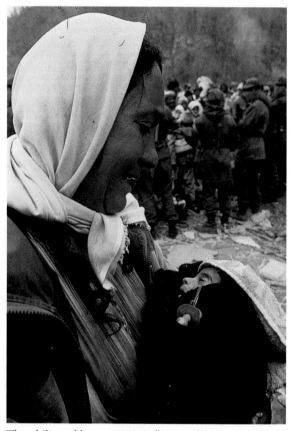

The ability of language to influence the way we think is illustrated by the bland phrase "collateral damage," by which the military in the 1991 Gulf War referred to civilian casualties from raids on Iraqi cities.

Linguists have found that although language is generally flexible and adaptable, once a terminology is established, it tends to perpetuate itself and to reflect and reveal the social structure and a group's common perceptions and concerns. For example, English is richly endowed with words having to do with war, the tactics of war, and the hierarchy of officers and fighting men. Militaristic metaphors also abound, as when we speak of "conquering" space, "fighting" the budget "battle," carrying out a "war" on poverty, making a "killing" on the stockmarket, "shooting down" an argument, or "bombing" out on an exam, to mention just a few. An observer from an entirely different and perhaps warless culture could understand a great deal about the importance of warfare

---

[6]Woolfson, P. (1972). Language, thought, and culture. In V. P. Clark, P. A. Escholz, & A. F. Rosa (Eds.), *Language* (p. 4). New York: St. Martin's.

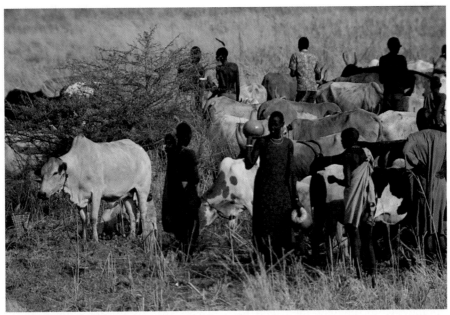

So important are cattle to the Nuer of southern Sudan that they have more than 400 words to describe them.

in our lives, as well as how we conduct it, simply from what we have found necessary to name and how we talk. Similarly, anthropologists have noted that the language of the Nuer, a nomadic people of southern Sudan, is rich in words and expressions having to do with cattle; not only are more than 400 words used to describe cattle, but also Nuer boys actually take their names from them. Thus, by studying the language we can determine the importance of cattle to Nuer culture, attitudes toward cattle, and the whole etiquette of human and cattle relationships.

A people's language does not, however, prevent them from thinking in new and novel ways. If this leads to important changes in common perceptions and concerns, then language can be expected to change accordingly.

Kinship Terms

In the same connection, anthropologists have paid considerable attention to the way people name their relatives in various societies, as we will see in Chapter 21. In English we have terms to identify brother, sister, mother, father, grandmother, grandfather, granddaughter, grandson, niece, nephew, mother-in-law, father-in-law, sister-in-law, and brother-in-law. Some people also distinguish first and second cousin and great-aunt and great-uncle. Is this the only possible system for naming relatives and identifying relationships? Obviously not. We could have separate terms, as some cultures do, for younger and older brothers, for mother's sister and father's sister, and so on. What we can describe in English with a phrase, if pressed to do so, other languages make explicit from the outset, and vice versa: A number of languages use the same word to denote both a brother and a cousin, and a mother's sister also may be called by the same term as the mother.

What do kinship terms reveal? They certainly can give a good idea of how the family is structured, what relationships are considered especially important, and sometimes what attitudes toward relationships may prevail. Caution is required, however, in drawing conclusions from kinship terms. Just because English speakers do not distinguish linguistically between their mother's parents and their father's parents (both are simply grandmother and grandfather), does that mean they do not know or care about which is which? Certainly not. Nevertheless, nonanthropologists, when confronted with a kinship system that applies the same term for father's brother to father, frequently make the mistake of assuming "these people don't know who their own father is."

LANGUAGE AND GENDER

Throughout history, human beings have handled the relationship between men and women in many different ways, and here again language can be revealing. In English-speaking societies, for example, men and women use the language in different ways, revealing a deep-seated bias against women. For example, women frequently use the expression "I'm sorry" to indicate sympathy and concerns, rather than apology. Unfortunately, men tend to accept it in the literal sense, as an apology, instead of in its intended figurative sense. In so doing, whether purposeful or not, men place women in a position of subordination. Similarly, words spoken by or about women imply, sometimes subtly and sometimes not, a lesser status. For example, behavior described as "forceful" for a man might be described as "pushy" for a woman. Or, while a man "passes out" (falling directly to the ground), a woman "faints" (as if giving way to weakness). While a man is "a fighter," a woman is "spunky" or "feisty," words suggestive of lesser power. In innumerable ways the traditional inequality of men and women in North American society receives linguistic expression.

SOCIAL DIALECTS

In our previous discussion of linguistic change, phonological and vocabulary differences among groups were noted as important forces for linguistic change. Varying forms of a language similar enough to be mutually intelligible are known as **dialects**, and the study of dialects is a concern

of **sociolinguistics**. Technically, all dialects are languages—they have nothing partial or sublinguistic about them—and at the point two dialects become distinctly different languages is roughly where speakers of one are almost totally unable to communicate with speakers of the other. Boundaries may be psychological, geographic, social, or economic, and they are not always very clear. Regional dialects frequently have a transitional territory, or perhaps a buffer zone, where features of both are found and understood, as between central and southern China. But if you learn the Chinese of Beijing, you cannot communicate with someone who comes from Canton or Hong Kong, although both languages—or dialects—are conventionally called Chinese.

A classic example of the kind of dialect that may set one group apart from others within a single society is one spoken by many inner-city African Americans. Technically known as African American Vernacular English, it often has been referred to as Black English and (more recently) as Ebonics.

Unfortunately, a widespread perception among upper- and middle-class Whites and Blacks alike is that this dialect is somehow substandard or defective, which it is not. A basic principle of linguistics is that the selection of a prestige dialect—in this case, what we may call Standard English as opposed to Ebonics—is determined by accidental extralinguistic forces and is not dependent on indirect virtues of the dialects themselves. In fact, African American Vernacular English is a highly structured mode of speech, capable of expressing anything its speakers care to express, often in extremely creative ways (as in "rapping"). Many of its distinctive features stem from the retention of sound patterns, grammatical devices, and even words of the West African languages spoken by the ancestors of today's African Americans. Compared to the richness of Black English, the Standard English dialect lacks certain sounds; contains some unnecessary sounds that others may serve for just as well; doubles and drawls some of its vowel sounds in unusual sequences that are dif-

---

Dialects. Varying forms of a language that reflect particular regions or social classes and that are similar enough to be mutually intelligible. **> Sociolinguistics.** The study of the structure and use of language as it relates to its social setting.

ficult to imitate; lacks a method of forming an important tense (the habitual); requires more ways than necessary to indicate tense, plurality, and gender; and does not mark negatives so as to make a strong negative statement.

Because their dialect differs so much from Standard English and has been stigmatized so often, speakers of African American Vernacular English frequently find themselves at a disadvantage outside their communities. In schools, for example, African American children often have been judged by teachers as deficient in verbal skills and even have been diagnosed—quite wrongly—as

"learning impaired." The great challenge for U.S. schools is to find ways to teach these children how to use Standard English in situations where it is to their advantage to do so, without denigrating them or affecting their ability to use their community dialect. Unfortunately, the general public's misunderstandings and prejudices are so great that a recent attempt by the school board of Oakland, California, to deal with the problem stirred up a firestorm of criticism. In the accompanying Original Study, anthropologist Leila Monaghan and two colleagues discuss the controversy and the Oakland School Board's proposal.

The Great Ebonics Controversy[7]

Leanne Hinton (Linguistics, California-Berkeley)

▲▽▲

Ebonics raised a storm of protest from around the country. The very names for this dialect reflect the diversity of views. What the Oakland school board refers to as Ebonics has also been known over time as Black English Vernacular (BEV), Black English (BE), African American Vernacular English (AAVE) and African American English (AAE). English used by African Americans ranges from distinctive styles of master orators like Martin Luther King and Jesse Jackson, through urban and rural vernaculars influenced by Southern roots and the language of recent Caribbean and African immigrants, to standard and local Englishes identical to those used by members of other communities. This diversity also makes us question how to designate what white Americans speak. In this piece we refer to Standard English (SE), which is strongly associated with written forms taught in school. There are, of course, numerous English vernacular forms, which have received less discussion.

The furor over Oakland's recently adopted resolution regarding Ebonics is based in large part on two issues: (1) there is a misunderstanding that the Oakland school system wants to teach BE in the schools; and (2) there is a sense of outrage among some that a stigmatized variety of English would be treated as a valid way of talking.

When I attended the school board meeting at which the Ebonics resolution was adopted, all discussion in support of the resolution by board members, parents and teachers was centered around the importance of teaching SE to children. This resolution is not about teaching BE but about the best way to teach SE. The children whom the board is concerned about have learned BE at home, a linguistic variety that has many differences from SE. To teach SE the board has rightfully concluded that teachers need to understand BE to teach children the differences between these two linguis-

---

[7]Monaghan, L., Hinton, L., & Kephart, R. (1997). Can't teach a dog to be a cat? The dialogue on Ebonics. *Anthropology Newsletter, 38* (3), 1, 8, 9.

The passions aroused by peoples' ideas about language are illustrated by the protests for and against the Oakland, California, School Board's recognition of "Ebonics" for what it is: a rich and complex language spoken by many inner-city African Americans.

tic varieties. It has also rightfully concluded that BE is not just some random form of "broken-down English" intrinsically inferior to SE but is a speech variety with its own long history, logical rules of grammar, discourse practices traceable to West African languages and a vibrant oral literature worthy of respect. BE has also been one of the major contributors of vocabulary to American English in general.

Whether Ebonics is a separate language in any technical sense is not what I think educators are concerned with here. What they are after is elevating the status of African American English (AAE). While from a linguistic point of view, these notions are being carried to an unscientific extreme, proponents of Ebonics are battling an even more unscientific set of extreme prejudices against AAE. The Oakland board is trying to promulgate a new set of political ideas about AAE as a legitimate form of speech, partly for the sake of African American pride but mainly for the sake of teaching SE in an emotionally positive way.

The notion that there is something just plain "bad" about nonstandard varieties of English is so deeply imbedded in the minds of many people that they tend to believe that children speak BE out of contrariness and need to be corrected by punishment. Educators have known better for a long time and don't want to be disrespectful of African American children's ways of speech, but that very respect has left them without a way of teaching SE. The method being embraced by the Oakland school board fills that void. By escaping the trap of thinking of nonstandard BE as a set of "errors" and instead treating it as it really is—a different system, not a wrong one—SE can be taught by helping children develop an awareness of the contrast between their two speech varieties and learning to use one without losing pride in the other.

Ron Kephart (Linguistic Anthropology and English, U North Florida)

My take on the Ebonics issue has to do with being a linguistic anthropologist and having conducted research on reading in Creole English on Carriacou, Grenada. In both cases, one of the hardest problems seems to be making people understand what you are doing.

A major criticism of the Oakland proposal which I have heard is that teachers will be wasting time "teaching" AAVE when the kids should be learning SE. On Carriacou I often found it necessary to explain that I didn't have to "teach" children Creole; they were already native speakers when they got to school. I was giving them access to literacy through Creole and then attempting to test the extent this helped them acquire literacy in SE.

On Carriacou, "educational experts" claimed that taking children out of their SE classes and working with them in Creole would slow them down and confuse them. I found neither to be the case: working in Creole they continued to improve in reading SE as fast as others working entirely in SE and never seemed to confuse the two. (It helped, no doubt, that I wrote Creole with a broadly phonemic spelling system that made it look different.)

My research was interrupted by the coup and subsequent US invasion of Grenada and Carriacou in 1983. As a result, I was unable to draw the strong conclusions I would have liked. Still, I showed that working on Creole did not slow down or confuse the children and was able to present some evidence that reading Creole helped their reading of SE. On a more qualitative note, they enjoyed it. Other teachers told me they had never seen children fight over who was going to read to the class. And they had rarely taken schoolbooks home to read before getting the little booklets in Creole we produced. Even children not in the Creole class asked for booklets.

Ultimately, this is a political issue. My experience on Grenada suggests that recognition of AAVE in Oakland can't hurt. Surely it can't hurt children to discover that what they bring with them to school—as a realization of the universal human potential for language and culture—is worthy of respect, worthy enough to be valued and used in their formal education. And it can't hurt teachers to learn this either. How much will it help? We have research from all over the world on the positive effects of native-language first-literacy acquisition and early schooling. Since it can't hurt, it seems worth finding out whether these results can be replicated in Oakland, and elsewhere, for AAVE.

We must also remain aware that simply gaining greater command of the standard language will not help unless society is willing to adjust its attitudes toward those involved. Otherwise, discrimination and exploitation will continue as before; racists will have one less justification to trot out, that's all. Perhaps this is where anthropologists and linguists have their most important work to do: raising public awareness and understanding of what linguistic, cultural and biological differences mean and, most importantly, what they don't mean.

Beneath all the rhetoric, the Oakland School Board proposal is no different from what several other countries are doing with considerable success. In Scotland, for example, Scots English is recognized in the schools as a valid and valued way of speaking, and it is used in teaching Standard English. As a consequence, individuals become skilled at switching back and forth between the two dialects, depending on the situation. Without being conscious of it, we all do something similar when we switch from formality to informality in our speech, depending upon where we are and whom we are talking to. The process of changing from one level of language to another as the situation demands, whether from one language to another or from one dialect of a language to another, is known as **code switching,** and it has been the subject of a number of sociolinguistic studies.

Martin Luther King, Jr. Part of his effectiveness as a civil rights leader was his skill at code switching between Standard and African American Vernacular English.

THE ORIGINS OF LANGUAGE

Realization of language's central importance to human culture leads inevitably to speculation about how language might have started. The question of the origin of language has long been a popular subject, and some reasonable and many not-so-reasonable ideas have been proposed: Exclamations became words, sounds in nature were imitated, or people simply got together and assigned sounds to objects and actions. The main trouble with past ideas about language origins is that so little evidence existed that attempts to explain them often amounted to not much more than wild speculation. The result was a reaction against such speculation, exemplified by the ban the Société de Linguistique de Paris imposed in 1866 against papers on linguistic origins. Now researchers have more evidence to work with—better knowledge of primate brains, new studies of primate communication, more information on the development of linguistic competence in children, more human fossils that can be used to tentatively reconstruct what ancient brains and vocal tracts were like, and a better understanding of early hominine ways of life. They still cannot prove how and when human language developed, but they can speculate much less wildly than was once the case.

Attempts to teach other primates to talk like humans have not been successful. In one famous experiment in communication that went on for 7 years, for example, the chimpanzee Viki learned to voice only a few words, such as *up, mama,* and *papa.* This inability to speak is not the result of any obvious sensory or perceptual deficit, and apes can in fact produce many of the sounds used in speech. Evidently, their failure to speak has to do with either a lack of motor control mechanisms to articulate speech or the virtually complete preoccupation of their vocal apparatus for expressing emotional states.

Better results have been achieved through nonvocal methods. Chimpanzees and gorillas in the wild make a variety of vocalizations, but these are

Code switching. The process of changing from one level of language to another.

Owing to our common ancestry, some of the gestures humans use are shared with other primates.

often emotional, rather than propositional. In this sense, they are equivalent to human paralanguage. Much of their communication occurs by kinesics —specific gestures and postures. Indeed, some of these, such as grimacing, kissing, and embracing, are in virtually universal use today among humans as well as apes. Recognizing the importance of gestural communication to apes, psychologists Allen and Beatrice Gardner began teaching the American Sign Language, used by the deaf, to their young chimpanzee Washoe, the first of several who have since learned to sign. With vocabularies of more than 400 signs, chimps have shown they can transfer each sign from its original referent to other appropriate objects and even pictures of objects. Their vocabularies include verbs, adjectives, and words such as *sorry* and *please*. Furthermore, they can string signs together properly to produce original sentences, even inflecting their signs to indicate person, place, and instrument. More impressive still, Washoe has been observed spontaneously teaching her adopted offspring Loulis how to sign by deliberately manipulating his hand. For 5 years, humans refrained from signing when in sight of Loulis, while he learned no fewer than 50

signs. Today, Loulis and Washoe live with three other signing chimpanzees, all of whom have shown via remote videotaping they use signs to communicate among themselves when no humans are present.

Other chimpanzees have been taught to communicate by other means. One named Sarah learned to converse using pictographs—designs such as squares and triangles—on brightly colored plastic chips. Each pictograph stands for a noun or a verb. Sarah also can produce new sentences of her own. Another chimpanzee, Lana, learned to converse via a computer with a keyboard somewhat like that of a typewriter, but with symbols rather than letters. One of the most adept with this system is a bonobo named Kanzi who, rather than being taught by a human, learned it as an infant from its mother and soon went on to surpass her abilities.

Chimps have not been the only subjects of ape language experiments. Gorillas and orangutans also have been taught American Sign Language with results that replicate those obtained with chimps. As a consequence, there is now a growing consensus that all of the great apes can develop language skills at least to the level of a 2- to 3-year-old human.[8] Not only are comprehension skills similar, but so is acquisition order: What and where, what-to-do and who, as well as how questions are acquired in that order by both apes and humans. Like humans, apes are capable of referring to events removed in time and space, a phenomenon known as **displacement** and one of the distinctive features of human language.

In view of apes' demonstrated abilities in sign language, it is not surprising that a number of anthropologists, psychologists, and other linguists have shown new interest in an old hypothesis, that human language began as a gestural, rather than vocal, system. Certainly, the potential to communicate through gestures must have been as well developed among the earliest hominines as it is among today's apes, since they share it as a consequence of a common ancestry that predates the divergence of human evolution. Moreover, the bipedalism of our earliest ancestors would have enabled them to use their hands more freely to gesture. Now, human manual signing and gesturing are skilled activities with hand preference playing a major role, and evidence for the pronounced "handedness" found only among humans is provided by the external configuration of the *Homo habilis* brain, as well as by the stone tools this hominine made. Furthermore, among modern children learning American Sign Language, hand preference appears in signing *before* it does in object manipulation. Thus, not only is it likely that *Homo habilis* used gestures to communicate, but this may have played a role in the development of the manual dexterity involved in early stone toolmaking.

One of the most difficult problems for students dealing with the origin of language is the origin of syntax, which was necessary to enable our ancestors to articulate and communicate complex thought. Here, a look at the physical nature of gestures is helpful, for, in fact, they can be construed not just as words but also as sentences. This is illustrated with the modern gesture meaning *seize*: The hand begins fully open or slightly bent, the elbow is slightly flexed, and the upper arm rotates at the shoulder to bring the forearm and hand across the body until the moving hand closes around the upright forefinger of the other hand. This is not just the word *seize* but also a complete transitive sentence with a verb and a direct object or, in semantic terms, an agent, an action, and a patient.[9] In this case, the sign and what is signified are clearly related, suggesting that syntax could have its origin in signs that mimic what they stand for.

Another conceptual problem involves the shift from manual gestures to spoken language. Two facts to keep in mind here are that (a) the manual signs of a sign language are typically accompanied by facial gestures, and (b) just as a sign is the outcome of a particular motor act, so is speech the outcome of a series of motor acts, in this case concentrated in the mouth and throat. In other words, *all* language, signed or spoken, can be analyzed as gesture. Furthermore, research on hearing-impaired users of American Sign Language suggests that the brain areas critical for speech may be critical to signing as well. Thus, continuity exists between gestural and spoken language, and the latter could have emerged from the former through increasing emphasis on finely controlled movements of the mouth and throat. This scenario is consistent with the appearance of neurological structures underlying language in the earliest representatives of the genus *Homo* and the steady enlargement of the human brain *before* the vocal tract alteration that allows us to speak the way we do.

The advantage of spoken over gestural language to a species increasingly dependent on tool use for survival is obvious. To talk with their hands, people must stop whatever else they are doing with them; speech does not interfere with that.

---

[8]Miles, H. L. W. (1993). Language and the orang-utan: The old 'person' of the forest. In P. Cavalieri & P. Singer (Eds.), *The Great Ape Project* (p. 46). New York: St. Martin's Press.

[9]Armstrong, D. F., Stokoe, W. C., & Wilcox, S. E. (1994). Signs of the origin of syntax. *Current Anthropology, 35,* 355.

Displacement.   The ability to refer to objects and events removed in time and space.

Other benefits include ability to talk in the dark, past opaque objects, or among speakers whose attention is diverted. Just when the changeover to spoken language occurred is not known, though all would agree that spoken languages are at least as old as anatomically modern *Homo sapiens*. What's more, no anatomical evidence exists to support arguments that Neanderthals and other representatives of archaic *H. sapiens* were incapable of speech. Perhaps its emergence began with *Homo erectus*, the first hominine to live in regions with cold climates. The ability to plan ahead for changes in seasonal conditions was crucial for survival and would not have been possible without a grammatically structured language, either gestural or vocal. We do know that having the use of fire, *H. erectus* would not have had to cease all activity when darkness fell. We also know that the vocal tract and brain of *H. erectus* were intermediate between that of *H. sapiens* and earlier *Australopithecus*. It may be that the changeover from gestural to spoken language was a driving force in these evolutionary changes.

The once popular search for a truly primitive language spoken by a living people that might show the processes of language just beginning or developing now has been abandoned. The reason is that no such thing as a primitive language exists in the world today, or even in the recent past. So far, all human languages that have been described and studied, even among people with something approximating a Stone Age technology,

are highly developed, complex, and capable of expressing infinite meanings. The truth is, people have been talking in this world for an extremely long time, and every known language, wherever it is, now has a long history and has developed subtleties and complexities that do not permit any label of "primitivism." What a language may or may not express is not a measure of its age but of its speakers' way of life, reflecting what they want or need to share and communicate with others.

Far from being "simple" or "primitive," the languages of non-literate people are often the opposite. For example, in World War II, the complexity of Navajo was such that, when used for a code by U.S. Marines in the Pacific, it defied all attempts by the Japanese to decipher it.

CHAPTER SUMMARY

Anthropologists need to understand the workings of language, because it is language that enables people in every society to share their experiences, concerns, and beliefs, in the past and in the present, and communicate these to the next generation. Language makes communication of infinite meanings possible by employing a few sounds or gestures that, when combined according to certain rules, result in meanings intelligible to all speakers.

Linguistics is the modern scientific study of all aspects of language. Phonetics focuses on the production, transmission, and reception of speech

sounds, or phonemes. Phonology studies the sound patterns of language to extract the rules that govern the way sounds are combined. Morphology is concerned with the smallest units of meaningful combinations of sounds—morphemes—in a language. Syntax refers to the principles phrases and sentences are built with. The entire formal structure of a language, consisting of all observations about its morphemes and syntax, constitutes its grammar.

Human language is embedded in a gesture-call system inherited from our primate ancestors that serves to "key" speech, providing the appropriate frame for interpreting linguistic form. The gestural component of this system consists of body motions used to convey messages; the system of notating and recording these motions is known as kinesics. The call component is represented by paralanguage, consisting of extralinguistic noises involving various voice qualities and vocalizations.

Descriptive linguistics registers and explains the features of a language at a particular time in its history. Historical linguistics investigates relationships between earlier and later forms of the same language. A major concern of historical linguists is to identify the forces behind the changes that have occurred in languages in the course of linguistic divergence. Historical linguistics also provides a means of roughly dating certain human migrations, invasions, and contacts with other people.

Ethnolinguistics deals with language as it relates to society, the rest of culture, and human behavior. Some linguists, following Benjamin Lee Whorf, have proposed that language shapes the way people think and behave. Others have argued that language reflects reality. Although linguists find language flexible and adaptable, they have found that once a terminology is established, it tends to perpetuate itself and to reflect much about the speakers' beliefs and social relationships. Kinship terms, for example, help reveal how a family is structured, what relationships are considered close or distant, and what attitudes are held toward relationships. Similarly, gender language reveals how the men and women in a society relate to one another.

A social dialect is the language of a group of people within a larger group, all of whom may speak more or less the same language. Sociolinguists are concerned with whether dialect differences reflect cultural differences. They also study code switching—the process of changing from one level of language to another as the situation demands—for much the same reason.

One theory of language origins is that early hominines, by developing potentials exhibited also by apes and monkeys, with their hands freed by their bipedalism, began using gestures as a tool to communicate and implement intentions within a social setting. With the movement of *Homo erectus* out of the tropics, the need to plan for future needs in order to survive seasons of cold temperatures required grammar and syntax to communicate information about events removed in time and space. By the time archaic *Homo sapiens* appeared, emphasis on finely controlled movements of the mouth and throat had probably given rise to spoken language.

For some time linguists searched for a truly primitive language spoken by some living group that would reveal language in its very early state. This search has been abandoned. All languages that have been studied, including those of people with supposedly "primitive" cultures, are complex, highly developed, and able to express a wide range of experiences. What a language is capable of expressing is anything its speakers wish to talk about and has nothing to do with its age.

POINTS FOR CONSIDERATION

1. Music and the visual arts often are spoken of as if they have their own "language." Is this a language in the same sense as spoken or written language? Would your interpretation change if you distinguished between improvised music (such as some jazz) and written and rehearsed music (such as classical or pop music)? between highly formal, professional painting and a child's scribblings? What do music and the visual arts communicate to an audience?

2. How does your vocabulary reflect your interests? your opinions? the groups and culture you belong to? How does your language change in the classroom? when you are shopping or are with your family? Is your vocabulary larger or smaller than 5 years ago? 15 years ago?

3. Do you know of any new languages? If so, how did they originate? What is new about them—vocabulary? grammar? syntax? How might they differ from an "older" language such as English? Can languages die? Are Latin and Sanskrit dead?

4. Consider native Spanish or Chinese speakers. What is the difference between language and culture? How can language and culture be confused?

SUGGESTED READINGS

Birdwhistell, R. L. (1970). *Kinesics and context: Essays in body motion communication.* Philadelphia: University of Pennsylvania Press.

Kinesics was first delineated as an area for anthropological research by Birdwhistell, so this book is particularly appropriate for those who wish to know more about the phenomenon.

Crane, L. B., Yeager, E. & Whitman, R. L. (1981). *An introduction to linguistics.* Boston: Little, Brown.

This book gives balanced coverage to all subfields of linguistics, including topics traditionally ignored in textbooks.

Eastman, C. M. (1990). *Aspects of language and culture* (2nd ed.). Novato, CA: Chandler and Sharp.

The bulk of this book is devoted to the subjects of worldview, ethnography of communication, nonverbal behavior, animal communication, discourse pragmatics, conversational analysis, semiotics, and ethnicity. A single chapter deals with linguistics as a field tool.

Gardner, R A., Gardner, B. T., & Van Cantfort, T. E. (Eds.). (1989). *Teaching sign language to chimpanzees.* Albany, NY: State University of New York Press.

In 10 jargon-free chapters, easily accessible to the interested layperson as well as professionals, the methods and results of the Gardners and their students are laid out in great detail. Psychologists and anthropologists who reviewed the book agree it represents a milestone in ape language research and, as one put it, should be read by all interested in the evolution of human behavior.

Hickerson, N. P. (1980). *Linguistic anthropology.* New York: Holt, Rinehart and Winston.

A description and explanation of what anthropological linguistics is all about, written so beginning students understand it.

Ruhlen, M. (1994). *The origin of language: Tracing the evolution of the mother tongue.* New York: John Wiley and Sons.

Scholarly in substance but written for a popular audience, this book makes a good introduction to comparative linguistics for beginning anthropology students. With an evolutionary theme, it cuts through the difficult problems of our linguistic ancestors with plausible though still controversial results.

Trager, G. L. (1964). Paralanguage: A first approximation. In D. Hymes (Ed.), *Language in culture and society* (pp. 274–279). New York: Harper & Row.

The author was the pioneer in paralinguistic research, and in this article he discusses what paralanguage is, why it should be studied, and how.

Chapter 16
GROWING UP HUMAN

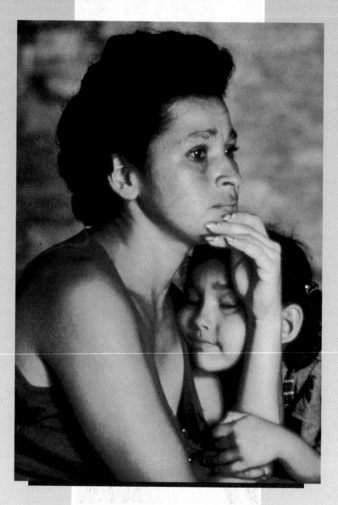

ETHNOGRAPHIC RESEARCH HAS REVEALED A WIDE
RANGE OF APPROACHES TO THE RAISING OF
CHILDREN. THESE DIFFERENCES AND THEIR
POSSIBLE EFFECTS ON ADULT PERSONALITIES HAVE
LONG BEEN OF INTEREST TO ANTHROPOLOGISTS.

Chapter Preview

What Is Enculturation?

Enculturation is the process by which culture is passed from one generation to the next. It begins soon after birth, as self-awareness—the ability to perceive oneself as an object in time and space and to judge one's actions—starts to develop. For self-awareness to function, the individual must be provided with a behavioral environment. First, one learns about a world of objects other than the self, and these always are perceived in terms the culture he or she grows up in specifies. Along with this, one is provided with spatial, temporal, and normative orientations.

What Is the Effect of Enculturation on Adult Personality?

Studies have shown some kind of nonrandom relationship between enculturation and personality development, although it is also clear that each individual begins with certain genetically inherited broad potentials and limitations. In some cultures specific child-rearing practices seem to promote the development of compliant personalities, while in others different practices seem to promote more independent, self-reliant personalities.

Are Different Personalities Characteristic of Different Cultures?

Although cultures vary a great deal in terms of the personality traits that are looked upon with admiration or disapproval, it is difficult to characterize cultures in terms of particular personalities. Of the several attempts made, the modal personality concept is the most satisfactory. This recognizes that any human society has a range of individual personalities but some will be more "typical" than others.

Do Cultures Differ in What They Regard as Abnormal Personalities?

A normal personality may be thought of as one that approximates the modal personality of a particular culture. Since modal personalities may differ from one culture to another and since cultures may differ in the range of variation they will accept, it is clear abnormal personality is a relative concept. A particular personality regarded as abnormal in one culture may not be regarded as so in another.

435

In 1690 John Locke presented his *tabula rasa* theory in his book *An Essay Concerning Human Understanding*. This notion held that the newborn human was like a blank slate, and what the individual became in life was written on the slate by his or her life experiences. The implication is that all individuals are biologically identical at birth in their potential for personality development and that their adult personalities are exclusively the products of their postnatal experiences, which differs from culture to culture. Stated in these terms, the theory is not acceptable, for we know now that each person is born with unique inherited tendencies that will help determine his or her adult personality. It is also known, however, that genetic inheritance sets certain broad potentials and limitations and that life experiences, particularly in the early years, are also important in the shaping of individual personalities. Since different cultures handle the raising and education of children in varied ways, these practices and their effects on personalities are important subjects of anthropological inquiry. Such studies gave rise to the subfield of psychological anthropology and are the subjects of this chapter.

▲▼▲▼▲▼▲▼▲▼▲▼▲▼▲▼▲▼▲▼▲▼▲▼▲▼▲▼▲▼

THE SELF AND THE BEHAVIORAL ENVIRONMENT

Since culture is created and learned rather than biologically inherited, all societies must somehow ensure that their culture is adequately transmitted from one generation to the next. This transmission process is known as **enculturation,** and it begins soon after birth. The first agents of enculturation in all societies are the members of the household a person is born into. At first, the most important member of this household is the newborn's mother, but other household members soon play roles in the process. Just who these others are depends on how households are structured in the particular society (Chapter 20). In the United

States, they ideally include the father or stepfather and the child's siblings. In other societies the father may seldom have contact with his children in their early years; indeed, in some societies men do not even live with the mothers of their children. In such instances, brothers of the child's mother usually have important responsibilities toward their nieces and nephews. In many societies, grandparents, other wives of the father, brothers of the father or sisters of the mother, not to mention their children, also are likely key players in the enculturation process.

As the young person matures, individuals outside the household are brought into the process. These usually include other kin, and certainly the individual's peers. The latter may be included informally in the form of play groups or formally in age associations, in which children actually teach other children. In some societies, and that of the United States is a good example, professionals are brought into the enculturation process to provide formal instruction. In many societies, however, children are pretty much allowed to learn through observation and participation at their own speed.

THE SELF

Enculturation begins with the development of **self-awareness**—the ability to identify oneself as an object, to react to oneself, and to appraise or evaluate oneself. People do not have this ability at birth, even though it is essential for existence in human societies. Self-awareness permits individuals to assume responsibility for their conduct, to learn how to react to others, and to assume a variety of roles. An important aspect of self-awareness is the attachment of positive value to the self. Without this, individuals cannot be motivated to act to their advantage rather than disadvantage; self-identification alone is not sufficient.

Self-awareness does not come all at once. In modern North American society, for example, self and nonself are not clearly distinguished until about 2 years of age. This development of self-

---

Enculturation. The process by which a society's culture is transmitted from one generation to the next. **> Self-awareness.** The ability to identify oneself as an object, to react to oneself, and to appraise oneself.

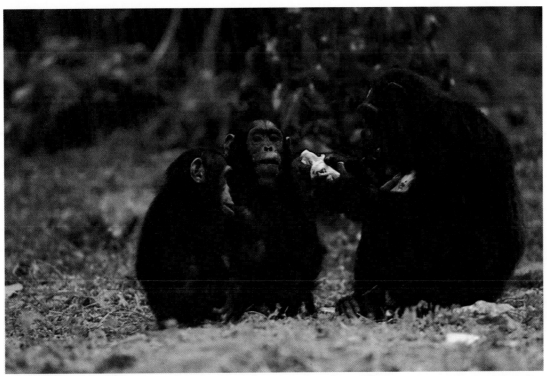

A chimpanzee mother with her offspring. The basic primate child-rearing unit consists of a mother and her offspring; to this humans have added an adult male. In some societies, this is the mother's husband; in others, it is her brother.

awareness in North American children, however, may lag somewhat behind other cultures. Self-awareness develops in concert with neuromotor development, which is known to proceed at a slower rate in infants from North America than in infants in many, perhaps even most, non-Western societies. The reasons for this slower rate are not yet clear, although the amount of human contact and stimulation infants receive seems to play an important role. In the United States, for example, infants generally do not sleep with their parents, most often being put in rooms of their own. This deprives them of a steady stream of stimuli, including touch, smell, movement, and warmth, they would receive by cosleeping. It also deprives them of the opportunity for frequent nursing through the night.

In traditional societies, infants routinely sleep with their parents, or at least their mothers. What's more (again unlike practices in the United States), they are carried or held most other times, usually in an upright position. The mother usually responds to a cry or "fuss" literally within seconds, usually offering the infant her breast. Thus, among traditional Ju/'hoansi (of whom more in a moment) of southern Africa's Kalahari Desert, infants are nursed about four times an hour, for 1 or 2 minutes at a time. Overall, a 15-week-old Ju/'hoansi infant is in close contact with its mother about 70% of the time, compared to 20% for home-reared infants in the United States. Moreover, their contacts are not usually limited to their mothers; they include numerous other adults and children of virtually all ages. In the United States and Canada, day-care centers now approximate these same conditions. The catch here is that their personnel must remain stable and (ideally) be recruited from the same neighborhood as the child if these centers are to have a positive effect on the cognitive and social development of the very

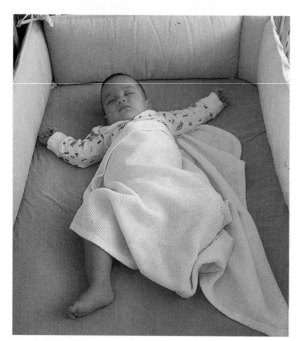

In traditional societies around the world, infants are never left by themselves and so receive constant stimulation, an important element in their development. In the United States, by contrast, infants spend a great deal of time in isolation, without such stimulation.

young children enrolled in them. Unfortunately, these conditions all too often are not met.

From the above it is obvious that infants in traditional societies are far more constantly exposed to a variety of stimuli than they are in North American (and most other industrialized) societies. This is important, for recent studies show that stimulation plays a key role in the "hard wiring" of the brain; stimulation is necessary for development of the neural circuitry. Nor should the role of frequent nursing be overlooked, as studies show that the longer a child is breast-fed, the higher it will score on cognitive tests and the lower its risk of attention deficit (hyperactivity) disorder. Furthermore, breast-fed children have fewer allergies, fewer ear infections, less diarrhea, and are at less risk of sudden infant death syndrome.[1]

As a child develops self-awareness, *perception* —a kind of vague awareness of one's existence— precedes *conception*, or more specific knowledge of the interrelated needs, attitudes, concerns, and

_____

[1]Dettinger, K. A. (1997, October). When to wean. *Natural History*, 49.

interests that define what one is. This involves a cultural definition of self, and in this definition language plays a crucial role. This is why in all cultures individuals become competent at using personal and possessive pronouns at an early age. Personal names, too, are important devices for self-identification in all cultures. Then, as infancy gives way to early childhood, the "I" or "me" is increasingly separated from the environment.

THE BEHAVIORAL ENVIRONMENT

For self-awareness to emerge and function, basic orientations are necessary to structure the psy-

chological field the self is prepared to act in. Thus, each individual must learn about a world of objects other than the self. The basis of this world of other-than-self is what we would think of as the physical environment of things. The physical environment, though, is organized culturally and mediated symbolically through language. Putting this another way, we might say the world around us is perceived through cultural glasses. Culturally significant attributes of the environment are singled out for attention and labeled; those that are not significant may be ignored or lumped together in broad categories. Culture, however, also *explains* the perceived environment. This is impor-

 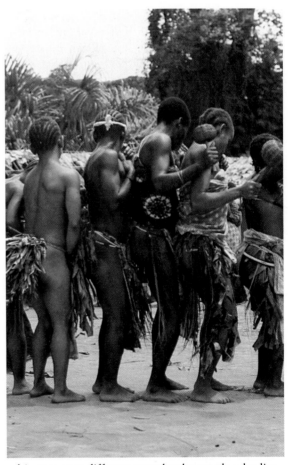

The Ituri forest, in the geographical heart of Africa, is viewed in two very different ways by the people who live there. Mbuti foragers view it with affection; like a benevolent parent, it provides them with all they ask for: sustenance, protection, and security. Village-dwelling farmers, by contrast, view the forest with a mixture of fear, hostility, and mistrust—something they must constantly struggle to control.

tant, for it provides the individual an orderly, rather than chaotic, universe in which to act. Behind this lies a powerful psychological drive to reduce uncertainty, the product of a universal human need for a balanced and integrated perspective on the relevant universe. When confronted with ambiguity and uncertainty, people invariably strive to clarify and give structure to the situation; they do this, of course, in ways their particular culture tells them are appropriate. Indeed, the greater the lack of structure and certainty, the greater individual suggestibility and persuadability tend to be. Thus, we should not be surprised to find that explanations of the universe are never entirely objective in nature.

The behavioral environment the self acts in involves more than *object orientation*. Action requires *spatial orientation,* or the ability to get from one object, or place, to another. In all societies, names and significant features of places are important means of discriminating and representing points of reference for spatial orientation. Individuals must know where they have been and will be to get from one place to another. They also need to maintain a sense of self-continuity so that past actions are connected with those in the present and future. Hence, temporal orientation is also part of the behavioral environment. Just as the perceived environment is organized in cultural terms, so too are time and space.

A final aspect of the behavioral environment is the *normative orientation*. Values, ideals, and standards, which are purely cultural in origin, are as much a part of an individual's behavioral environment as are trees, rivers, and mountains. Without them people would have nothing to judge their actions or those of others against. In short, the self-appraisal aspect of self-awareness could not be made functional.

Like any aspect of culture, conceptions of the self vary considerably from one society to another. The Penobscot Indians, a people who at one time relied on fishing, hunting, and the gathering of wild plants (food foraging) for subsistence, and whose descendants still live today in the woodlands of northeastern North America, serve as an example.[2]

The Penobscot

When first encountered by Europeans, the Penobscot conceived of each individual as being made of two parts—the body and a personal spirit. The latter was dependent on the body yet could have "out of body" experiences—that is, disengaging itself from the body and travel about for short periods to perform overt acts and to interact with other spirits. Such activity by one's personal spirit was thought to occur in dreams or in states of trance. As long as one's spirit returned to the body before the passage of too much time, the individual remained in good health; if, however, the spirit was prevented from returning to the body, then the individual sickened and died. Along with this dual nature of the self went a potential for every person to work magic. Theoretically, it was possible to send one's personal spirit out to work mischief on others, just as it was possible for others to lure one's own spirit away from the body, resulting in sickness and eventual death.

To many people today, the traditional Penobscot concept of self may seem strange. The British colonists of New England regarded such ideas as false and shot through with superstition, even though their own concept of self at the time was

---

[2]Speck, F. G. (1920). Penobscot shamanism. *Memoirs of the American Anthropological Association, 6,* 239–288.

every bit as supernaturalistic. To the Indians their concept made sense, for it adequately accounted for their experience, regardless of its rightness or wrongness in any objective sense. Furthermore, the Penobscot view of self is relevant for anyone who wishes to understand Penobscot behavior in the days when the British and French first tried to settle in North America. For one thing, it was responsible for an undercurrent of suspicion and distrust of strangers, as well as for the individual secretiveness that characterized Penobscot society at the time. This propensity for individual secretiveness made it difficult for a potentially malevolent stranger to gain control of an individual's spirit. Also, the belief that dreams are real experiences, rather than expressions of unconscious desires, could impose burdens of guilt and anxiety on individuals who dreamed of doing things not accepted as proper. Finally, individuals indulged in acts that would strike many people today as quite mad. In one case a Penobscot Indian spent the night literally fighting for his life with a fallen tree. To the Indian, this was a metamorphosed magician who was out to get him, and it would have been madness *not* to try to overcome his adversary.

The behavioral environment the Penobscot self operated in consisted of a flat world, which these people believed was surrounded by saltwater. They could actually see the latter downstream, where the Penobscot River met the sea. The river was the spatial reference point and also was the main artery for canoe travel in the region. The largest of a number of watercourses, it flowed through forests abounding with game. Like humans, each animal also was composed of a body and a spirit. Along with the animals were various quasi-human supernatural beings that inhabited bodies of water and mountains or roamed freely through the forest. One of these, *Gluskabe*, created the all-important Penobscot River by deceiving a greedy giant frog that had monopolized the world's water supply. Gluskabe also was respon-

sible for a number of other natural features of the world, often as a by-product of punishment for moral-code transgressions such as that of the giant frog. Indeed, individuals had to be concerned about their behavior vis-à-vis both the animals and these quasi-human beings or they, too, would come to various kinds of grief. Hence, these supernaturals not only explained many otherwise unexplainable natural phenomena to the Penobscot but also were important for structuring the Penobscot moral order. To the Penobscot, all of this was quite believable; the lone hunter, for example, off for extended periods in the forest, could hear in the night what sounded like the cry of *Pskedemus*, the swamp woman. And a Penobscot accepted as fact that his or her spirit routinely traveled about while the body slept, interacting with various of these supernatural beings.

Penobscot concepts of the self and behavioral environment have changed considerably since the 17th century, though no less so than those of the descendants of the Europeans who first came to New England. Both groups now may be said to hold more modern beliefs about the nature of their selves and the world they live in. Still, in both cases, aspects of the old beliefs remain. Associated with them were **patterns of affect**—how people *feel* about themselves and others—which differed considerably in Indian and European cultures. As Chinese-born anthropologist Francis Hsu has pointed out, patterns of affect are likely to persist over thousands of years, even in the face of far-reaching changes in all other cultural aspects.[3] To illustrate, consider the following Original Study, written by Rhonda Kay Williamson while an undergraduate student of philosophy at Bryn Mawr College.

---

[3]Hsu, F. L. K. (1977). Role, affect, and anthropology. *American Anthropologist, 79*, 807.

Patterns of affect. How people feel about themselves and others.

The Blessed Curse[4]

A Foot in Both Worlds

▲▼.

One morning not so long ago, a child was born. This birth, however, was no occasion for the customary celebration. Something was wrong: something very grave, very serious, very sinister. This child was born between sexes, an "intersexed" child. From the day of its birth, this child would be caught in a series of struggles involving virtually every aspect of its life. Things that required little thought under "ordinary" circumstances were, in this instance, extraordinarily difficult. Simple questions now had an air of complexity: "What is it, a girl or a boy?"; "What do we name it?"; "How shall we raise it?"; "Who (or what) is to blame for this?"

The child referred to in the introductory paragraph is myself. As I was born the great-granddaughter of a Cherokee woman, I was exposed to the Native American view of people who were born intersexed, as I was, and individuals who exhibited transgendered characteristics. This view, unlike the Euro-American one, sees such individuals in a very positive and affirming light.

Yet my immediate family (mother, father, and brothers) were firmly fixed in the Christian Euro-American point of view. As a result, from a very early age I was presented with two different and conflicting views of myself. As might be expected, this resulted in a lot of confusion within me about what I was, how I came to be born the way I was, and what my intersexuality meant in terms of my spirituality as well as my place in society.

I remember, even as a small child, getting mixed messages about my own value and worth as a human being. My grandmother, in keeping with Native American ways, would tell me stories about my birth. She would tell me how she knew when I was born that I had a special place in life, given to me by God, the Great Spirit, and that I had been given "a great strength that girls never have, yet a gentle tenderness that boys never know" and that I was "too pretty and beautiful to be a boy only and too strong to be a girl only." She rejoiced at this "special gift" and taught me that it meant that the Great Spirit had "something important for me to do in this life." I remember how good I felt inside when she told me these things and how I soberly contemplated, even at the young age of five, that I must be diligent and try to learn and carry out the purpose designed just for me by the Great Spirit.

My parents, however, had a completely different view of my birth, of me as a human being, and of the origin of my intersexuality. My parents were so repulsed by it that they would never speak of it directly. They would just refer to it as "the work of Satan." To them, I was not at all blessed with a "special gift" from some "Great Spirit," but was "cursed and given over to the Devil" by God. I was treated with contempt by my father, and my mother wavered between contempt and distant indifference. I was taken from one charismatic church to another in order to have the "demon of mixed sex" cast out of me. At some of these "deliverance" services I was even given a napkin to cough out the demon into!

---

[4]Adapted from Williamson, R. K. (1995). The blessed curse: Spirituality and sexual difference as viewed by Euro-American and Native American cultures. *The College News, 17* (4).

In the end, no demon ever popped out of me. Still, I grew up believing that there was something inherent within me that caused God to hate me, that my intersexuality was a punishment for this something, a mark of condemnation.

There were periods in my life when I stayed at my grandmother's house for extensive amounts of time. During these stays, my fears would be allayed, for she would once again remind me that I was fortunate to have been given this special gift. She was distraught that my parents were treating me cruelly and pleaded with them to let me live with her, but they would not let me stay at her home permanently.

Nevertheless, they did let me spend a significant portion of my childhood with her. Had it not been for that, I might not have been able to survive the tremendous trials that awaited me in my walk through life.

Blessed Gift: The Native American View

It is now known that most, if not all, of the Native American societies had certain individuals which fell between the categories of "man" and "woman." The various nations had different names for this type of individual, but a term broadly used and recognized is "berdache," a term of French origin that designated a male, passive homosexual. [The preferred term today is "two-spirit."]

Some of these individuals were born physically intersexed. Others appeared to be anatomically normal males, who exhibited the character and the manners of women, and vice versa. The way native people treated such individuals reveals some interesting insights into the Native American belief system.

The Spirit

The extent to which Native Americans see spirituality is reflected in their belief that all things have a spirit: "Every object—plants, rocks, water, air, the moon, animals, humans, the earth itself—has a spirit. The spirit of one thing (including a human) is not superior to the spirit of any other. . . . The function of religion is not to try to condemn or to change what exists, but to accept the realities of the world and to appreciate their contributions to life. Everything that exists has a purpose."

This paradigm is the core of Native American thought and action. Because everything has a spirit, and no spirit is superior to that of another, there is no "above" or "below," no "superior" or "inferior," no "dominant" and "subordinate." These are only illusions which arise from unclear thinking. Thus, an intersexed child is not derided or viewed as a "freak of nature" in traditional Native American culture. Intersexuality (as well as masculinity in a female or effeminacy in a male) is seen as the manifestation of the spirit of the child, so an intersexed child is respected as much as a girl child or a boy child.

It is the spirit of the child which determines what the gender of the child will ultimately be. According to a Lakota, Lame Deer, "the Great Spirit made them winktes [two-spirit] and we accepted them as such." In this sense, the child has no control over what her or his gender will be. It follows that where there is no choice, there can be no accountability on the part of the child. Indeed, the child who is given the spirit of a winkte is unable to resist becoming one.

"When an Omaha boy sees the Moon Being [Moon Being is a feminine Spirit] on his vision quest, the spirit holds in one hand a man's bow and

Shown here is the famous Zuni Indian two-spirit named We'wha, who once had the experience of meeting President Grover Cleveland. For a man to assume a feminine identity was not regarded as abnormal by the Zuni; in fact, such individuals were regarded as special in that they bridged the gap between the purely feminine and purely masculine. European-Americans, by contrast, regarded such individuals with aversion.

arrow and in the other a woman's pack strap. 'When the youth tried to grasp the bow and arrows the Moon Being crossed [the boy's] hands very quickly, and if the youth was not very careful he seized the pack strap instead of the bow and arrows, thereby fixing his lot in later life. In such a case he could not help acting [like a] woman, speaking, dressing, and working just as . . . women . . . do.'"

Sacred Role

The Europeans were not only aghast, but amazed and dumbfounded as to why two-spirits were considered sacred. In the Native American view, because two-spirits were considered to have received their intersex spirit from the Great Spirit, and were different from the norm by the feminine/masculine combination of their nature, they were considered to be especially blessed by the Great Spirit. To be a two-spirit was considered to be a special gift from the Great Spirit.

The Curse: The Euro-American View

In contrast to the view of respect and admiration of physical intersexuality and transgendered behavior held by Native Americans, the Europeans who came to "Turtle Island" (the Cherokee name for North America) brought with them their world view, which was shaped primarily by their Judaeo-Christian beliefs. According to this religion, there had to be, by mandate of God, a complete dichotomy of the sexes. The Christian religion was also to be the basis by which Europeans claimed "divine right" to take from Native Americans both their home and their culture.

Will Roscoe, in *The Zuni Man-Woman,* reports (pp. 172–173): "Spanish oppression of 'homosexual' practices in the New World took brutal forms.

In 1513, the explorer Balboa had some forty berdaches thrown to his dogs [to be eaten alive]—'a fine action by an honorable and Catholic Spaniard,' as one Spanish historian commented. In Peru, the Spaniards burned 'sodomites,' 'and in this way they frightened them in such a manner that they left this great sin.'"

It is abundantly clear that Christian Euro-Americans exerted every effort to destroy Native American culture: "In 1883, the U.S. Office of Indian Affairs issued a set of regulations that came to be known as the Code of Religious Offenses" or Religious Crimes Code. . . . Indians who refused to adopt the habits of industry, or to engage in 'civilized pursuits or employments' were subject to arrest and punishment. . . . By interfering with native sexuality [and culture], the agents of assimilation effectively undermined the social fabric of entire tribes." (Ibid, p. 176).

The Role of Education

Any paradigm necessarily involves education. Here we have two paradigms which are based on completely opposed ideologies. The Native American view holds that each thing or person has its own spirit that is not condemned nor to be changed, but is respected and even encouraged. This paradigm has inherent in it an education wherein every part of the universe, every star, every tree, every creature, every grain of sand is considered to be sacred and holy.

Native Americans learned through stories told to the younger generation by the older generation. At first the stories seemed to have different themes when the telling of them (the education) began for the child, but in the end it became clear that the stories had an interdependence on one another. Over the years, a great Web of Life was woven. Each story, or strand in the Web, connected to another to make a beautiful weaving of the nature of all the world. No part of the Web was more important or less important than any other part. In sex and gender roles, man, woman, intersex, effeminate man and masculine woman were equally valid and necessary.

In contrast is the Christian, Euro-American paradigm within which there is *no* flexibility. There is one God and one way, only, to worship the Christian God (at least in theory). One wise Iroquois leader, Red Jacket, pointed out the fallacy of this theory in a speech to the Boston Missionary Society. In this speech he said: "Brother! You say there is but one way to worship and serve the Great Spirit. If there is but one religion, why do you white people differ so much about it? Why do you not all agree, as you can all read the book?"

The problem Christianity poses for any culture other than its own is the condemnation and destruction of it. It seeks to impose the moral and social ideology of one culture onto all the other cultures of the entire world. Moreover, the culture that it sets out to impose is an ancient one that was reported by a handful of men whose identity is not even known in many cases. Yet, the words from these unknown men are presented as "the divinely inspired word of God." Christianity is purportedly the most widespread religion in the world. Is this a wonder, though, when nearly all who have been opposed to its self-proclaimed manifest destiny ("Every knee shall bow and every tongue confess that Jesus Christ is Lord."—Revelation) have been all but obliterated in its founder's name?

A Personal Resolution

For me, the resolution to the dual message I was receiving was slow in coming, largely due to the fear and self-hatred instilled in me by Christianity. Eventually, though, the Spirit wins out. I came to adopt my Grandmother's teaching about my intersexuality. Through therapy, and a new, loving home environment, I was able to shed the constant fear of eternal punishment I felt for something I had no control over. After all, I did not create myself.

Because of my own experience, and drawing on the teaching of my grandmother, I am now able to see myself as a wondrous creation of the Great Spirit—but not only me. All creation is wondrous. There is a purpose for everyone in the gender spectrum. Each person's spirit is unique in her or his or her-his own way. It is only by living true to the nature that was bestowed upon us by the Great Spirit, in my view, that we are able to be at peace with ourselves and be in harmony with our neighbor. This, to me, is the Great Meaning and the Great Purpose . . . to be at peace with ourselves and to live in harmony with our neighbor.

PERSONALITY

In the process of enculturation, we have seen that each individual is introduced to the concepts of self and the behavioral environment characteristic of his or her culture. The result is that a kind of cognitive or mental map of the operating world is built, in terms of which the individual will think and act. It is each person's "map" of how to run the "maze" of life. This cognitive map is an integrated, dynamic system of perceptual assemblages, including the self and its behavioral environment. When we speak of an individual's **personality,** we are generalizing about that individual's cognitive map over time. Hence, personalities are products of enculturation, as experienced by individuals, each with his or her distinctive genetic makeup. "Personality" does not lend itself to a formal definition, but for our purposes we may take it as the distinctive way a person thinks, feels, and behaves.

THE DEVELOPMENT OF PERSONALITY

Although *what* one learns is important to personality development, most anthropologists assume that *how* one learns is no less important. Along with the psychoanalytic theorists, anthropologists view early childhood experiences as strongly influencing adult personality. Indeed, many anthropologists have been seriously attracted to Freudian psychoanalytic theory, but with a critical eye. Psychoanalytic literature tends to be long on concepts, speculation, and clinical data but short on less culture-bound studies. Anthropologists, for their part, are most interested in studies that seek to prove, modify, or at least shed light on the role of early childhood experiences in shaping personality. For example, the traditional ideal in Western societies has been for men to be tough, aggressive, assertive, dominant, self-reliant, and achievement oriented, whereas women have been expected to be passive, obedient, compliant, loyal, and caring. To many, these perceived personality differences between the sexes seem so "natural" that they must be biologically grounded and therefore inescapable, unchangeable, and universal. But are they? Have anthropologists identified any psychological or personality characteristics that universally differentiate men and women?

As Margaret Mead's pioneering studies suggested, and subsequent cross-cultural studies have confirmed, whatever biological differences may exist between men and women, they are extremely

---

Personality.   The distinctive way a person thinks, feels, and behaves.

malleable. Among the Arapesh of New Guinea it is not just the women but the men, too, who are gentle and nonaggressive, while among the Mundugamor (also of New Guinea), both sexes are angry and aggressive. Although biological differences in male-female behavior cannot be entirely ruled out (although debate continues about the role biology plays), it is nonetheless clear that each culture has different expectations for male-female behavior. The criteria of differentiation in one may bear no relation to those in another and may in fact be poles apart. From this we may conclude that the physical, political, and economic dominance men have traditionally exerted over women in Western societies is not inevitable and that other arrangements are possible.

To understand the importance of child-rearing practices in the development of gender-related personality characteristics, we may look briefly at how children grow up among the Ju/'hoansi (pronounced zhutwasi), a people native to the Kalahari Desert of Namibia and Botswana. The Ju/'hoansi are one of a number of people traditionally referred to as Bushmen who once were widespread through much of southern Africa. In recent times, anthropologists have referred to these people as the San, thinking the word *Bushman* insulting. Unfortunately, San, a Nama word, has highly pejorative associations. Moreover, anthropologists misunderstood the derivation of the word *Bushman,* which comes from the Dutch *Bossiesman,* meaning "bandit" or "outlaw." This designation the people earned for their refusal to knuckle under to colonial domination, so to refer to them as Bushman honors their long and valiant, if costly, record of resistance to colonialization. But most important, Bushman is the term they themselves prefer as a generic word covering all groups.[5]

Traditionally food foragers, in the past 3 decades many Ju/'hoansi have adopted a more sedentary lifestyle, tending small herds of goats

and planting gardens for their livelihood.[6] Among those who forage for a living, dominance and aggressiveness are not tolerated in either sex, men are as mild mannered as the women, and women are as energetic and self-reliant as the men. In the villages, by contrast, men and women exhibit personality characteristics approximating those traditionally thought of as typically masculine and feminine in Western societies. Among the food foragers, children of both sexes receive lengthy, intensive care from their mother, whose attention is not diverted by the birth of new offspring until after the passage of many years. This does not mean mothers are constantly with their children, for they are not; when they go off to gather wild plant foods in the bush, they do not always take their offspring with them. At such times, the children are supervised by their fathers or other community adults, one third to one half of whom are always found in camp on any given day. Because these include men as well as women, children are as much habituated to the male as to the female presence.

Fathers, too, spend much time with their offspring, interacting with them in nonauthoritarian ways. Although they may correct their children's behavior, so may women who neither defer to male authority nor use the threat of paternal anger.

[5]Gordon, R. J. (1992). *The Bushman myth* (p. 6). Boulder, CO: Westview. Griffin, B. (1994). CHAGS 7. *Anthropology Newsletter, 35,* (1), 13. Lewis-Williams, J. D., Dowson, T. A., & Deacon, J. (1993). Rock art and changing perceptions of Southern Africa's past: Ezeljagdspoort reviewed. *Antiquity, 67,* 273.

[6]Draper, P. (1975). !Kung women: Contrasts in sexual egalitarianism in foraging and sedentary contexts. In R. Reiter (Ed.), *Toward an anthropology of women* (pp. 77–109). New York: Monthly Review Press.

In traditional Ju/'hoansi society, children are shown great indulgence by adults of both sexes and do not grow up to fear or respect one sex more than the other.

Thus, among Ju/'hoansi foragers, no one grows up to respect or fear male authority any more than that of women. In fact, instead of being punished, a child who misbehaves will be simply carried away and interested in some other more inoffensive activity. Nor are boys or girls assigned tasks to do; both sexes do equally little work, instead spending much of their time in play groups that include members of both sexes of widely different ages. Thus, Ju/'hoansi children have few experiences that set one sex apart from another. Although older ones do amuse and monitor younger ones, this is done spontaneously rather than as an assigned chore, and the burden does not fall any more heavily on girls than boys.

Among the sedentary villagers, women spend much of their time in and around the home preparing food and attending to other domestic chores, as well as tending the children. The work of men, by contrast, requires them to spend many hours outside the household. As a result, children are less habituated to their presence. This remoteness of the men, coupled with their more extensive knowledge of the outside world, tends to enhance their influence within the household.

Within village households, sex role typing begins early as girls, as soon as they are old enough, are expected to attend to many of the needs of their younger siblings, thereby allowing the mother more time to attend to her other domestic tasks. This not only shapes but also limits the behavior of girls, who cannot range as widely or explore as freely and independently as they could without little brothers and sisters in tow. Indeed, they must stay close to home and be more careful, more obedient, and more sensitive to the wishes of others than they otherwise might be. Boys, by contrast, have little to do with the handling of infants, and when they are assigned work, it generally takes them away from the household. Thus, the space girls occupy becomes restricted, and they are trained in behaviors that promote passivity and nurturance, whereas boys begin to become the distant, controlling figures they will be as adults.

From this comparison, we may begin to understand how a society's economy helps structure the way a child is brought up and how this, in turn, influences the adult personality. It also shows that alternatives to the way children are raised in Western societies exist and that by changing the conditions our children grow up in, we might make it significantly easier for men and women to interact on an equal basis than has been the case so far. Thus, child rearing emerges as not only an anthropological problem but a practical one as well.

Dependence Training

Although Margaret Mead compared sex and temperament in three different societies in the early 1930s, most cross-cultural studies of child rearing

Margaret Mead   *(1901–1978)*

Although all of the natural and social sciences can look back and pay homage to certain "founding fathers," anthropologists take pride in the fact they have a number of "founding mothers" they pay homage to. One is Margaret Mead, who was encouraged by her teacher Franz Boas to pursue a career in anthropology when most other academic disciplines rarely accepted women into their ranks. In 1925, she set out for Samoa to test the theory (then widely accepted) that the biological changes of adolescence could not be accomplished without a great deal of stress, both social and psychological. In her book *Coming of Age in Samoa: A Psychological Study of Primitive Youth for Western Civilization*, she concluded that adolescence does not have to be a time of stress and strain but cultural conditions may make it so. Published in 1928, this book is generally credited as marking the beginning of the culture and personality field.

Pioneering works are never without their

faults, and *Coming of Age* is no exception. For one, it is not clear that Mead's time in the field (9 months) was sufficient for her to understand fully the nuances of native speech and body language necessary to comprehend the innermost feelings of her informants. Furthermore, her sample of Samoan adolescents was a mere 50, half of whom had not yet passed puberty. That she exaggerated her findings is suggested by her dismissal of girls who did not fit her ideal as "deviant" and by inconsistencies with data collated elsewhere in Polynesia. But despite its faults, Mead's book stands as a landmark for several reasons: Not only was it a deliberate test of a Western psychological hypothesis, but it also showed psychologists the value of modifying intelligence tests so that they are appropriate for the population under study. Furthermore, by emphasizing the lesson to be drawn for Mead's own society, it laid the groundwork for the popularization of anthropology and advanced the cause of applied anthropology.

effects on personality have been carried out more recently by John and Beatrice Whiting and Irving L. Child or their associates. Their work has demonstrated a number of apparent regularities. For example, it is possible to distinguish between two different patterns of child rearing at a broad level of generalization, which we may label for convenience "dependence training" and "independence training."[7]

Dependence training promotes compliance in the performance of assigned tasks and favors

---

[7]Wolf, E. (1966). *Peasants* (pp. 69–70). Englewood Cliffs, NJ: Prentice-Hall.

Dependence training.   Child-rearing practices that foster compliance in the performance of assigned tasks and dependence on the domestic group, rather than reliance on oneself.

The White Man's Bad Medicine, by American Indian artist Jerome Tiger (1941–1967). In the 1950s, in an effort to end its special relationship with the American Indians, the federal government terminated its establishment of, and aid to, some Indian reservations. This termination policy led many Indians to relocate to urban areas. Because they were a people whose definition of self springs from the group they were born into, separation from family and kin led many to severe depression and related problems.

keeping individuals within the group. This pattern is typically associated with extended families, which consist of several husband-wife-children units within the same household and which are most apt to be found in societies with an economy based on subsistence farming. Such families are important, for they provide the large labor force necessary to till the soil, tend whatever flocks are kept, and carry out other part-time economic pursuits considered necessary for existence. These large families, however, have built into them certain potentially disruptive tensions. For example, one of the adults typically makes the important family decisions, which must be followed by all other family members. In addition, the in-marrying spouses—husbands and/or wives—must subordinate themselves to the group's will, which may not be easy for them.

Dependence training helps to keep these potential problems under control and involves both supportive and punitive aspects. On the support-

ive side, indulgence is shown to young children, particularly in the form of prolonged oral gratification. Nursing continues for several years and is virtually on demand. This may be interpreted as rewarding the child for seeking support within the family, the main agent in meeting the child's needs. Also on the supportive side, children at a relatively early age are assigned a number of child-care and domestic tasks, all of which make significant and obvious contributions to the family's welfare. Thus, family members all actively work to help and support one another. On the punitive side, behavior the adults interpret as aggressive or sexual is apt to be actively discouraged. Moreover, the adults tend to be quite insistent on overall obedience, which is seen as rendering the individual subordinate to the group. This combination of encouragement and discouragement ideally produces individuals who are obedient, supportive, noncompetitive, and generally responsible and who will stay within the fold and not do anything potentially disruptive. Indeed, their very definition of *self* comes from their affiliation with a group, rather than from the mere fact of their individual existence.

Independence Training

By contrast, **independence training** emphasizes individual independence, self-reliance, and personal achievement. It is typically associated with societies whose nuclear families, consisting of a husband, wife, and their offspring, are independent rather than a part of a larger household group. Independence training is particularly characteristic of industrial societies such as that of the United States, where self-reliance and personal achievement, especially for men, are important traits for survival.

Again, this pattern of training involves both encouragement and discouragement. On the negative side, little emphasis is placed on prolonged oral gratification, and feeding is prompted more by schedule than demand. In the United States, for example, people like to establish a schedule as soon as possible, and it is not long before they start feeding infants baby food and even try to get them to feed themselves. Many parents are delighted if they can prop up their infants in the crib or playpen so that the infants can hold their own bottles. Moreover, as soon after birth as possible, children are given their own private space away from their parents. As already noted, infants do not receive the amount of attention they so often do in nonindustrialized societies. In the United States a mother may be very affectionate with her 15-week-old infant during the 20% of the time she is in contact with it, but for the other 80% of the time the infant is more or less on its own. Collective responsibility is not encouraged in children; they are not given responsible tasks to perform until later in childhood, and these are generally few. Furthermore, the contribution of the tasks to the family's welfare is often not immediately apparent to the child, to whom the tasks appear arbitrary as a result. Indeed, children often are encouraged to perform tasks for play, rather than as contributions to the family's welfare.

Displays of aggression and sexuality are encouraged or at least tolerated to a greater degree than where dependence training is the rule. In schools, and even in the family, competition is emphasized. In the United States, we have gone to the extreme of turning the biological functions of infancy—eating, sleeping, crying, and elimination—into contests between parents and offspring. In our schools, considerable resources are devoted to competitive sports, but competition is fostered within the classroom as well: overtly, through devices such as spelling bees and competition for prizes, and covertly, through devices such as grading on a curve. The latter practice, widely used, especially for heavily enrolled courses, on some college campuses, condemns some students to failure, irrespective of how well they actually do, if most of the class does better. This puts students in competition with one another, for they soon learn that their chances for a decent grade depend, as much as anything, on other class members not doing well. If the stakes are high, students may devote considerable effort to placing obstacles in the way of classmates so that they are prevented from doing too well. Thus, by the time individuals have grown up in U.S. society, regardless of what they may think about it, they have received a clear message: Success comes at someone else's expense. As anthropologist Colin Turnbull observed: "Even the team spirit, so loudly touted" in school athletics (or out of school in Little League baseball and the like), "is merely a more efficient way, through limited cooperation, to 'beat' a greater number of people more efficiently."[8]

In sum, independence training generally encourages individuals to seek help and attention, rather than to give it, and to try to exert individual dominance. Such qualities are useful in societies with social structures that emphasize personal

---

[8]Turnbull, C. M. (1983). *The human cycle* (p. 74). New York: Simon & Schuster.

Independence training. Child-rearing practices that promote the child's independence, self-reliance, and personal achievement.

In North American society, independence training pits individuals against one another through games and other forms of competition.

achievement and where individuals are expected to look out for their own interests.

Combined Dependence/Independence Training

In actuality, dependence and independence training represent extremes along a continuum, and actual situations may partake of elements of both. In food-foraging societies, for example, child-rearing practices combine elements of both. "Share and share alike" is the order of the day, so competitive behavior, which can interfere with the co-operation all else depends on, is discouraged. Thus, infants receive much positive, affectionate attention from adults, along with prolonged oral gratification. This, as well as low pressure for compliance and a lack of emphasis on competition, encourages individuals to be more supportive of one another than is often the case in modern industrial societies. At the same time, personal achievement and independence are encouraged, for the individuals most capable of self-reliance are apt to be the most successful in the food quest.

In the United States the argument sometimes has been made (not by anthropologists) that "permissive" child rearing produces irresponsible adults. Yet the practices of food foragers seem to be about as "permissive" as they can get, and socially responsible adults are produced. The fact is, no particular system of child rearing is inherently better or worse than any other; what matters is whether the system is functional or dysfunctional

in the context of a particular society. If compliant adults, who are accepting of authority, are required, then independence training will not work well in that society. Nor will dependence training serve very well a society whose adults are expected to be independent, self-reliant, and questioning authority.

Sometimes, however, inconsistencies develop, and here we may look again at the situation in North America. As shown, independence training generally tends to be stressed in the United States, where people often speak in glowing terms of the worth of personal independence, the dignity of the individual, and so on. Their pronouncements, however, do not always suit their actions. In spite of the professed desire for personal independence and emphasis on competition, a strong underlying desire for compliance seems to exist. This is reflected, for example, in decisions handed down over the past 2 decades or so by the Supreme Court, which, as observers of the Court have noted, often have favored the rights of authority over those of individuals. It is reflected, too, by the fate of "whistle blowers" in both government and industry, who if they don't lose their jobs are at least shunted to one side and passed by when the rewards are handed out. In business as well as in government, the rewards tend to be given to those who go along with the system, while criticism, no matter how constructive, is a risky business. In corporate, as well as government, bureaucracies, the ability to please, not shake up the system, is required for success. Yet, in spite of pressures for compliance, which would be most effectively served by dependence training, we continue to raise our children to be independent and then wonder why they so often refuse to behave in ways adults would have them behave.

GROUP PERSONALITY

From studies such as those reviewed here, it is clear that personality, child-rearing practices, and other aspects of culture are interrelated in a nonrandom way. Whiting and Child argued that the child-rearing practices of a society originate in basic customs surrounding nourishment, shelter, and protection and that these child-rearing practices in turn produce particular kinds of adult personalities.[9] The trouble is that correlations do not prove cause and effect. We still are left with the fact, however logical it may seem, such a causal chain remains an unproven hypothesis.

The existence of a close, if not causal, relationship between child-rearing practices and personality, coupled with variation in child-rearing practices from one society to another, have led to a number of attempts to characterize whole societies in terms of particular kinds of personalities. Indeed, common sense suggests that personalities appropriate for one culture may be less appropriate for others. For example, an egocentric, aggressive personality would be out of place where cooperation and sharing are the keys to success. Or, in the context of traditional Penobscot Indian culture, examined briefly earlier in this chapter, an open and extroverted personality would seem inappropriate, given its inconsistency with the prevailing conception of the self.

Unfortunately, common sense, like conventional wisdom in general, is not always the truth. A question worth asking is: Can we describe a group personality without falling into stereotyping? The answer appears to be a qualified yes; in an abstract way, we may speak of a generalized "cultural personality" for a society, as long as we do not expect to find a uniformity of personalities within that society. Put another way, each individual develops certain personality characteristics that, from common experience, resemble those of other people. Yet, because each individual is exposed to unique experiences as well, may react to common experiences in novel ways, and brings to these experiences a unique (except for the case of identical twins) genetic potential, each also acquires distinct personality traits. Because individual personalities differ, the organization of diversity is important to all cultures.

As an example of the fact individual personalities in traditional societies are far from uniform, consider the Yanomami, who live in the forests of northern Brazil and southern Venezuela. Among them, individual men strive to achieve a reputation for fierceness and aggressiveness they are willing to defend at the risk of serious personal injury and death. And yet some men among the Yanomami are quiet and somewhat retiring. In any gathering of these people, the quiet ones are all too easily overlooked by outsiders, when so many others are in the front row pushing and demanding attention.

MODAL PERSONALITY

Obviously, any fruitful approach to the problem of group personality must recognize that each individual is unique to a degree in both inheritance and life experiences and must expect a range of personality types in any society. In addition, personality traits that may be regarded as appropriate in men may not be so regarded in women and vice versa. Given all this, we may focus our attention on the **modal personality** of a group, defined as the personality typical of a culturally bounded population, as indicated by the central

---

[9]Whiting, J. W. M., & Child, I. L. (1953). *Child training and personality: A cross-cultural study.* New Haven, CT: Yale University Press.

Modal personality. The personality typical of a society as indicated by the central tendency of a defined frequency distribution.

Yanomami men display their fierceness. While flamboyant, belligerent personalities are especially compatible with the Yanomami ideal that men should be fierce, some are quiet and retiring.

tendency of a defined frequency distribution. Modal personality is a statistical concept, and, as such, it opens for investigation the questions of how societies organize diversity and how diversity relates to culture change. Such questions are easily overlooked if one associates a particular personality type with a particular culture, as older approaches (like that of Ruth Benedict, described in the nearby biography) tended to do. Also, modal personalities of different groups can be compared.

Data on modal personality are best gathered with psychological tests administered to a sample of the population in question. Those most often used include the Rorschach, or inkblot test, and the Thematic Apperception Test (TAT). The latter consists of pictures the individual tested is asked to explain or describe. Other sorts of projective tests have been used as well at one time or an-

other; all have in common a purposeful ambiguity so that the individual tested has to structure the situation before responding. The idea is that one's personality is projected into the ambiguous situation. Along with such tests, observations recording the frequency of certain behaviors, the collection and analysis of life histories and dreams, and the analysis of oral literature are helpful for eliciting data on modal personality.

While having much to recommend it, the concept of modal personality as a means of dealing with group personality nevertheless presents certain difficulties. One of these is the complexity of the measurement techniques, which may be difficult to implement in the field. For one, an adequate representative sample of subjects is necessary. The problem here is twofold: making sure the sample is genuinely representative and having

Ruth Fulton Benedict   *(1887–1947)*

Ruth Benedict came late to anthropology; after her graduation from Vassar College, she taught high school English, published poetry, and tried her hand at social work. For anthropology, she developed the idea that culture was a projection of the personality of those who created it. In her most famous book, *Patterns of Culture* (1934), she compared the cultures of three peoples—the Kwakiutl of western Canada, the Zuni of the southwestern United States, and the Dobuans of Melanesia. She held that each was comparable to a great work of art, with an internal coherence and consistency of its own. Seeing the Kwakiutl as egocentric, individualistic, and ecstatic in their rituals, she labeled their cultural configuration "Dionysian"; the Zuni, whom she saw as living by the golden mean, wanting no part of excess or disruptive psychological states, and distrusting of individualism, she characterized as "Apollonian." The Dobuans, whose culture seemed to her magic ridden, with everyone fearing and hating everyone else, she characterized as "paranoid."

Although *Patterns of Culture* still enjoys popularity in some nonanthropological circles, anthropologists long since have abandoned its approach as impressionistic and not susceptible to replication. To compound the problem, Benedict's characterizations of cultures are misleading (the supposedly "Apollonian" Zunis, for example, indulge in such seemingly "Dionysian" practices as sword swallowing and walking over hot coals), and using such value-laden terms as "paranoid" prejudices others against the culture. Nonetheless, the book did have an enormous and valuable influence by focusing attention on the problem of the interrelation between culture and personality and by popularizing the reality of cultural variation.

the time and personnel necessary to administer the tests, conduct interviews, and so on, all of which can be lengthy proceedings. Also, the tests themselves constitute a problem, for those devised for one cultural setting may not be appropriate for another. This is more of a problem with the TAT than with some other tests, although different pictures have been devised for other cultures. Still, to minimize any hidden cultural bias, it is best not to rely on projective tests alone. In addition to all this, language differences often lead to problems, such as misinterpretation. Furthermore, the field investigator may be in conflict with cultural values. A people such as the Penobscot, whose concept of self we surveyed earlier, would not take kindly to revealing their dreams to strangers. Finally, what is being measured must be questioned.

Just what, for example, is aggression? Does everyone define it the same way? Is it a legitimate entity, or does it involve other variables?

NATIONAL CHARACTER

No discussion of group personality would be complete without considering national character, which popular thought all too often ascribes to the citizens of various countries. Henry Miller epitomizes this view when he says, "Madmen are logical—as are the French," suggesting that Frenchmen, in general, are overly rational. A Parisian, in contrast, might view North Americans as maudlin and unsophisticated. Similarly, we all have in mind some image, perhaps not well defined, of the "typical" Russian or Japanese or English citizen.

Essentially, these are simply stereotypes. We might well ask, however, if these stereotypes have any basis in fact. In reality, does such a thing as national character exist?

Some anthropologists have thought the answer, maybe, is yes. Accordingly, national character studies were begun that sought to discover basic personality traits the majority of the peoples of modern countries shared. Along with these went an emphasis on child-rearing practices and education as the factors theoretically responsible for such characteristics. Margaret Mead, Ruth Benedict, Weston LaBarre, and Geoffrey Gorer conducted pioneering studies of national character using relatively small samples of informants. During World War II, techniques were developed for studying "culture at a distance" through the analysis of newspapers, books, photographs, and interviews with expatriates from the country in question. By investigating memories of childhood and cultural attitudes and by examining graphic material for the appearance of recurrent themes and values, researchers attempted to portray national character.

The Japanese

At the height of World War II, Geoffrey Gorer attempted to determine the underlying reasons for the "contrast between the all-pervasive gentleness of family life in Japan, which has charmed nearly every visitor, and the overwhelming brutality and sadism of the Japanese at War." Strongly influenced by Freud, Gorer sought his causes in the toilet-training practices of the Japanese, which he believed were severe and threatening. He suggested that because Japanese infants were forced to control their sphincters before they had acquired the necessary muscular or neurological development, they grew up filled with repressed rage. As adults, the Japanese could express this rage through their ruthlessness in war.[10]

In the midst of war Gorer could not do field-

---

[10]Gorer, G. (1943). Themes in Japanese culture. *Transactions of the New York Academy of Sciences, Series II, 5.*

work in Japan. After the war was over, though, the toilet-training hypothesis was tested, and it was found that the severity of Japanese toilet training was a myth. Children were not subject to threats of severe punishment. Nor were all Japanese soldiers brutal and sadistic in war; some were, but then so were some North Americans. Also, the participation of many Japanese in postwar peace movements in the Far East hardly conformed to the wartime image of brutality.

Gorer's study, along with others by Benedict and LaBarre, was most important not for revealing the importance of Japanese sphincters to the national character but for pointing out the dangers of generalizing from insufficient evidence and employing simplistic individual psychology to explain complex social phenomena.

Objections to National Character Studies

Critics of national character theories have emphasized the tendency for such work to be based on unscientific and overgeneralized data. The concept of modal personality has a certain statistical validity, they argue, but to generalize the qualities of a complex country on the basis of such limited data is to lend insufficient recognition to the countless individuals who vary from the generalization. Further, such studies tend to be highly subjective; for example, the tendency during the late 1930s and 1940s for anthropologists to characterize the German people as aggressive paranoids was obviously a reflection of wartime hostilities rather than scientific objectivity. Finally, it has been pointed out that occupational and social status tend to cut across national boundaries. A French farmer may have less in common with a French factory worker than with a German farmer.

An alternative approach to national character—one that allows for the fact not all personalities conform to cultural ideals—is that of anthropologist Francis Hsu. His approach was to study the **core values** of a country's culture and related personality traits. The Chinese, he suggested, value kin ties and cooperation above all else. To them, mutual dependence is the very essence of personal relationships

---

Core values. The values a particular culture especially promotes.

The core values of Chinese culture promote the integration of the individual into a larger group. By contrast, the core values of Anglo-American culture promote the separation of the individual from the group.

and has been for thousands of years. Compliance and subordination of one's will to that of family and kin transcends all else, while self-reliance is neither promoted nor a source of pride. Following the 1949 revolution, Mao Tse-tung sought to expand the sphere of affect to the country as a whole, with himself as the "father" of all citizens.

Perhaps the core value North Americans of European descent hold in highest esteem is "rugged individualism," at least for men (only recently has this become recognized as a valid ideal for women). Each individual is supposed to be able to achieve anything he or she likes alone, given a willingness to work hard enough. From their earliest years, individuals are subjected to relentless pressures to excel, and, as we have already noted, competition and winning are seen as crucial to this. Undoubtedly, this value contributes to the "restlessness" and "drivenness" of North American society, and to the degree it motivates individuals to work hard and to go where the economy needs them, it fits well with the needs of an industrial society. Thus, while individuals in Chinese society are firmly bound into a larger group they have lifelong obligations to, North Americans are isolated from all other kin save husband or wife, and even here commitment to marriage has lessened.[11] More couples live together without either marriage or future plans for marriage. When couples do marry, prenuptial agreements are made to protect their assets, and something like 50% of

---

[11]This and most of the following observations on North American culture are drawn from Natadecha-Sponsal, P. (1993). The young, the rich and the famous: Individualism as an American cultural value. In P. R. DeVita & J. D. Armstrong (Eds.), *Distant mirrors: America as a foreign culture* (pp. 46–53). Belmont, CA: Wadsworth.

marriages do end in divorce. Even parents and children have no legal obligations to one another, once the latter have reached the age of majority. Indeed, many North American parents seem to "lose" their children in their teenage years. As for relations with nonkin, these tend to remain at an abbreviated and superficial level.

NORMAL AND ABNORMAL PERSONALITY

The concept of modal personality holds that a range of personalities exists in any society. The modal personality itself may be thought of as normal for that society but in fact may be shared by less than half the population. What of personalities that differ from the norm? The Dobuans of New Guinea and Indians of the North American Great Plains furnish examples of abnormal and normal behavior strikingly different from that of nonnative North Americans.

The individual in Dobu the other villagers considered neurotic and thoroughly disoriented was a man who was naturally friendly and found activity an end in itself. He was a pleasant person who did not seek to overthrow his fellows or to punish them. He worked for anyone who asked him, and he was tireless in carrying out their commands. In any other Dobuan, this would have been scandalous behavior, but in him it was regarded as merely silly. The village treated him in a kindly fashion, not taking advantage of him nor making sport of or ridiculing him, but he was definitely regarded as one who stood outside the normal conventions of behavior.

To return to the subject of the Original Study earlier in this chapter, among North American Indians, a man, compelled by supernatural spirits, could assume women's attire and perform women's work; he even could marry another man, although not all men who adopted a female identity were homosexuals, nor did all homosexuals behave in this way (most Indian societies allowed individuals ways to engage in homosexual behavior without altering their gender status). Under this institution of the "two-spirit," an individual could live in a dramatically different manner from most

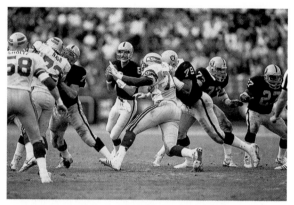

In the United States, traditional attitudes toward homosexuality have been largely negative. Paradoxically, football, a game so loaded with homosexual symbolism that anthropologist/folklorist Alan Dundes has compared it to homosexual initiation rituals in New Guinea, has been immensely popular.

men; yet, although the two-spirit was rare among Indians, it was *not* looked upon as deviant behavior.[12] Quite the contrary, for the two-spirit often was sought out as a curer, artist, matchmaker, and companion of warriors because of the great spiritual power he was thought to possess.

In Western societies such as the United States, behavior like that of the Indian two-spirits traditionally has been regarded as deviant. If a man dresses as a woman, it is still widely considered a cause for concern and is likely to lead to psychiatric intervention. Nor have jobs women traditionally filled been seen as desirable for men. By contrast, women have more freedom to wear masculine-style clothing and to assume jobs men traditionally held, even though to do so may cause others to brand them as somehow "unfeminine." Lying behind these views are traditional values (jobs customarily associated with men have been more highly valued than those associated with women) and a pattern of child rearing that creates gender identity problems for both sexes, although of a different sort for each sex.

---

[12]Although the European term *berdache* has been widely used in the literature, it carries a pejorative connotation, so it has been abandoned for the term *two-spirit* favored by Native Americans. See Jacobs, S. E. (1994). Native American two-spirits. *Anthropology Newsletter, 35* (8), 7.

Nancy Chodorow, a sociologist with a strong background in anthropology, has argued that in United States society, girls traditionally have been raised by women, usually their mothers, and most still are. Thus, feminine role models are constantly available and easily understandable. Very early, girls begin to do what women do and gradually and continuously acquire the identity deemed appropriate for their sex. Once they enter school, however, they learn that women are not all-powerful and prestigious and that it is men who generally are in charge and who are portrayed as the ones who have most advanced human progress. As a consequence, a girl finds that the feminine identity, which has become so easy for her, leaves much to be desired. Under the circumstances, she is bound to feel a certain resentment toward it.

Boys have a different problem; like girls they too begin their lives in a feminine world. With adult men out of the house working, not only is a male model rarely present, but also the mother seems to be all-powerful. Under these conditions, boys begin to develop a feminine identity with its expected compliant personality. In keeping with all this, boys used to be even dressed as girls (dresses for little boys were not dropped from the Sears catalog until 1940) until the age thought proper to "graduate" into less feminine attire arrived. Once out of the house and in school, boys learn they must switch from a female to male identity; in a sense, they must renounce femininity and prove their maleness in a way that girls do not have to prove their femaleness. Generally speaking, the more distant a boy's father (or other male companion of his mother) is, the greater the boy's insecurity is in his male identity and the greater his compulsion is to be seen as really masculine. To do this, he must strive all the harder to be aggressive and assert his dominance, particularly over women.

Nancy Chodorow sums up the consequences of this situation as follows:

> Sex-role ideology and socialization for these roles seem to ensure that neither boys nor girls can attain both stable identity and meaningful roles. The tragedy of woman's socialization is not that she is left unclear, as is the man, about her basic sexual identity. This identity is ascribed to her, and she does not need to prove to herself or to society that she has earned it or continues to have it. Her problem is that this identity is clearly devalued in the society in which she lives. This does not mean that women too should be required to compete for identity, to be assertive and to need to achieve—to "do" like men. Nor does it suggest that it is not crucial for everyone, men and women alike, to have a stable sexual identity. But until male "identity" does not depend upon men's proving themselves, their "doing" will be a reaction to insecurity, not a creative exercise of their humanity, and woman's "being," far from being an easy and positive acceptance of self, will be a resignation to inferiority. And as long as women must live through their children, and men do not genuinely contribute to socialization and provide easily accessible role models, women will continue to bring up sons whose sexual identity depends upon devaluing femininity inside and outside themselves, and daughters who must accept this devalued position and resign themselves to producing more men who will perpetuate the system that devalues them.[13]

This example shows how a culture itself actually may induce certain kinds of psychological conflicts with important consequences for the entire society. Although the conditions children are raised under in United States society are now changing, they have a long way to go before the conflicts just described become part of the past. Still, what has seemed "normal" in the past could become "abnormal" in the future.

The standards that define normal behavior for any culture are determined by that culture itself. Take, for example, attitudes toward individuals who enter into altered states of consciousness. Among the Melemchi of Nepal, to effect a cure the healer must call the gods into his body to let them speak through him.[14] To do this, he must ride into their world. Through drumming and chanting, sometimes accompanied by use of

---

[13]Chodorow, N. (1971). Being and doing: A cross-cultural examination of the socialization of males and females. In V. Gornick & B. K. Moran (Eds.), *Woman in sexist society* (p. 193). New York: Basic Books.

[14]Womack, M. (1994). Program 5: Psychological anthropology. *Faces of culture*. Fountain Valley, CA: Coast Telecourses, Inc.

anthropology
applied Anthropologists
and Mental Health

One consequence of development in the newly emerged states of Africa, Asia, and Central and South America is a rising incidence of mental disturbances among their people. Similarly, mental health problems abound among ethnic minorities living within industrialized countries. Unfortunately, orthodox approaches to mental health have not been successful at dealing with these problems for a number of reasons. For one, the various ethnic groups have different attitudes toward mental disorders than do medical practitioners (who are, after all, products of Western culture). For another, the diverse conditions different ethnic groups live under produce culturally patterned health conditions, including culture-bound syndromes the orthodox medical profession does not recognize. Among Puerto Ricans, for example, a widely held belief is that spirits are active in the world and that they influence human behavior. Thus, for someone with a psychiatric problem, it makes sense to go to a native spiritist for help, rather than to a psychiatrist. In a Puerto Rican community, going to a spiritist is "normal." Not only does the client not understand the symbols of psychiatry, but also going to a psychiatrist implies that he or she is "crazy" and requires restraint or removal from the community.

Although practitioners of Western medicine traditionally have regarded spiritists and other folk healers as "ignorant," if not "charlatans," efforts in the 1950s began experimentation with community-based treatment in which psychiatrists cooperated with traditional

healers. Since then, this approach has gained widespread acceptance in many parts of the world, as when (in 1977) the World Health Organization advocated cooperation between health professionals and native specialists (including herbalists and midwives). As a consequence, many anthropologists have found work as cultural brokers, studying the cultural system of the client population and explaining this to the health professionals while also explaining the world of the psychiatrists to the folk healers and the client population.

To cite one example, as a part of the Miami Community Mental Health Program, a field team led by an anthropologist was set up to work with the Puerto Rican community of Dade County.* Like other ethnic communities in the area, this one was characterized by low incomes, high rents, and a plethora of health (including mental health) problems, yet health facilities and social service agencies were underused. Working in the community, the team successfully built support networks among the Puerto Ricans, involving extended families, churches, clubs, and spiritists. At the same time, they gathered information about the community, providing it to the appropriate social service agencies. At the Dade County Hospital, team members acted as brokers between the psychiatric personnel and their Puerto Rican clients, and a training program was implemented for the mental health staff.

---

*See Willigan, J. V. (1986). *Applied anthropology* (pp. 128–129, 133–139). South Hadley, MA: Bergin and Garvey.

---

hallucinogenic drugs and intoxicants, he enters an altered state of consciousness, or trance. This allows him to see and communicate with the gods. To outsiders, it appears the curer is hallucinating: seeing visions, smelling smells, hearing sounds, and experiencing bodily sensations that seem real but are not seen, smelled, heard, or felt by others who are present but have not entered into trance. In modern North American society, behavior like that of the Melemchi curer generally is regarded

as deviant, and the practice of entering altered states is apt to be seen as a sign of mental instability, or even unlawful activity if it involves the use of hallucinogenic substances.

The negative attitude of North American culture notwithstanding, nothing is abnormal *per se* about the ability to enter trancelike states and experience a wide range of hallucinations. To the contrary, "The desire to alter consciousness periodically is an innate, normal drive analogous to

Although the ability to enter trance is a consequence of having a normal human nervous system, some societies, such as that of the United States, define entering trance as abnormal, while many others accept it as normal. Among the Ju/'hoansi of Namibia, men enter trance in a dance, accompanied by the rhythmic clapping and singing of women. By entering trance, these men can summon supernatural power to heal, bring rain, and control animals.

not just human, nervous system.[16] Thus, the ability to enter altered states and experience visions and other sensations appears to predate the appearance of *Homo sapiens,* and it is not surprising that the ability to enter trance is a human universal. Although some societies try to suppress the practice, the vast majority (such as the Melemchi) accept trancing and shape it to their own ends. One study, for example, found that as many as 437 of a sample of 488 historically known societies had some form of *institutionalized* altered states of consciousness.[17]

Is all this to suggest that "normalcy" is a meaningless concept when applied to personality? Within the context of a given culture, the concept of normal personality is quite meaningful. A. I. Hallowell,

hunger or the sexual drive."[15] There is even good evidence that chimpanzees, baboons, other monkeys, cats, dogs, and other animals hallucinate and that the ability is a function of the mammalian,

[15]Furst, P. T. (1976). *Hallucinogens and culture* (p. 7). Novato, CA: Chandler and Sharp.

[16]Lewis-Williams, J. D., & Dowson, T. A. (1988). Signs of all times: Entoptic phenomena in Upper Paleolithic art. *Current Anthropology, 29,* 202.

[17]Lewis-Williams, J. D., & Dowson, T. A. (1993). On vision and power in the Neolithic: Evidence from the decorated monuments. *Current Anthropology, 34,* 55.

TABLE 16.1	Ethnic Psychoses and Other Culture-Bound Psychological Disorders	
Name of Disorder	**Culture**	**Description**
Amok	Malaya (also observed in Java, Philippines, Africa, and Tierra del Fuego)	A disorder characterized by sudden, wild outbursts of homicidal aggression in which the afflicted person may kill or injure others. The rage disorder is usually found in males who are rather withdrawn, quiet, and inoffensive prior to the onset of the disorder. Stress, sleep deprivation, extreme heat, and alcohol are among the conditions thought to precipitate the disorder. Several stages have been observed: Typically in the first stage the person becomes more withdrawn; then a period of brooding follows in which a loss of reality contact is evident. Ideas of persecution and anger predominate. Finally, a phase of automatism, or *amok*, occurs, in which the person jumps up, yells, grabs a knife, and stabs people or objects within reach. Exhaustion and depression usually follow, with amnesia for the rage.
Anorexia nervosa	Western countries	A disorder occurring most frequently among young women in which a preoccupation with thinness produces a refusal to eat. This condition can result in death.
Latah	Malay	A fear reaction often occurring in middle-aged women of low intelligence who are subservient and self-effacing. The disorder is precipitated by the word *snake* or by tickling. It is characterized by *echolalia* (repetition of the words and sentences of others). The disturbed individual may also react with negativism and the compulsive use of obscene language.

a major figure in the development of psychological anthropology, somewhat ironically observed that it is normal to share the delusions traditionally accepted by one's society. Abnormality involves the development of a delusional system the culture does not sanction. The individual who is disturbed because he or she cannot adequately measure up to the norms of society and be happy may be termed *neurotic*. When a person's delusional system is so different that it in no way reflects his or her society's norms, the individual may be termed *psychotic*.

Culturally induced conflicts not only can, if severe enough, produce psychosis but can determine the form of the psychosis as well. To a culture that encourages aggressiveness and suspicion, the insane person is the individual who is passive and trusting. To a culture that encourages passivity and trust, the insane person is the individual who is aggressive and suspicious. Just as each society establishes its own norms, each individual is unique in his or her perceptions. Many anthropologists see the only meaningful criterion for personality evaluation as the correlation between personality and social conformity.

Although it is true that culture defines what is and is not normal behavior, the situation is complicated by findings suggesting that major categories of mental disorders may be universal types of human affliction. Take, for example, schizophrenia, probably the most common of all psychoses and one found in any culture, no matter how it manifests itself. Individuals afflicted by schizophrenia experience distortions of reality that impair their ability to function adequately, so they withdraw from the social world into their own psychological shell, from which they do not emerge. Although environmental factors play a role, evidence exists that schizophrenia is caused by a biochemical disorder for which there is an inheritable tendency. One of its

Name of Disorder	Culture	Description
Koro	Southeast Asia (particularly Malay Archipelago)	A fear reaction or anxiety state in which the person fears that his penis will withdraw into his abdomen and he will die. This reaction may appear after sexual overindulgence or excessive masturbation. The anxiety is typically very intense and of sudden onset. The condition is "treated" by having the penis held firmly by the patient or by family members or friends. Often the penis is clamped to a wooden box.
Windigo	Algonkian Indians of Canada and northern United States	A fear reaction in which a hunter becomes anxious and agitated, convinced that he is bewitched. Fears center on his being turned into a cannibal by the power of a monster with an insatiable craving for human flesh.
Kitsunetsuki	Japan	A disorder in which victims believe that they are possessed by foxes and are said to change their facial expressions to resemble foxes. Entire families are often possessed and banned by the community. This reaction occurs in rural areas of Japan where people are relatively uneducated.
Pibloktoq and other arctic hysterias	Circumpolar peoples from Lapland eastward across Siberia, northern Alaska, and Canada to Greenland	A disorder brought on by fright, which is followed by a short period of bizarre behavior; victim may tear clothes off, jump in water or fire, roll in snow, try to walk on the ceiling, throw things, thrash about, and "speak in tongues." Outburst followed by return to normal behavior.

Based on Carson, R. C., Butcher, J. N., & Coleman, J. C. (1990). (8th ed.) (p. 85). Glenview, Il: Scott Foresman.

more severe forms is paranoid schizophrenia. Those suffering from it fear and mistrust almost everyone; they hear voices that whisper dreadful things to them, and they are convinced someone is "out to get them." Acting on this conviction, they engage in bizarre behaviors, which leads to their removal from society, usually to a mental institution.

A precise image of paranoid schizophrenia is one of the so-called **ethnic psychoses** known as *Windigo*. Such psychoses involve symptoms of mental disorder specific to particular ethnic groups (Table 16.1). Windigo psychosis is limited to northern Algonkian Indian groups such as the Chippewa, Cree, and Ojibwa. In their traditional belief systems, these northern Indians recognized the existence of cannibalistic monsters called Windigos. In-

dividuals afflicted by the psychosis developed the delusion that, falling under control of these monsters, they themselves were being transformed into Windigos, with a craving for human flesh. Meanwhile, they saw people around them turning into various edible animals—fat, juicy beavers, for instance. Although no instances where sufferers of Windigo psychosis actually ate another human being are known, they nonetheless developed an acute fear of doing so. Furthermore, other members of their group genuinely feared they might.

At first, Windigo psychosis seems quite different from European-American clinical cases of paranoid schizophrenia, but a closer look suggests otherwise; the disorder was merely expressed in ways compatible with traditional northern Algonkian

Ethnic psychoses. Mental disorders specific to particular ethnic groups.

culture. Ideas of persecution, instead of directed toward other humans, are directed toward supernatural beings (the Windigo monsters); cannibalistic panic replaces homosexual panic; and the like. The northern Algonkian Indian, like the European-American, expresses his or her problem in terms compatible with the appropriate view of the self and its behavioral environment. The northern Algonkian, though, was removed from society not by commitment to a mental institution but by being killed.

Windigo behavior has seemed exotic and dramatic to the European-American. When all is said and done, however, the imagery and symbolism a psychotic person has to draw upon are what his or her culture has to offer, and in northern Algonkian culture these involve myths in which cannibal giants figure prominently. By contrast, the delusions of Irish schizophrenics draw on the images and symbols of Irish Catholicism and feature Virgin and Savior motifs. Anglo-Americans, on the other hand, tend toward secular or electromagnetic persecution delusions. The underlying structure of the mental disorder is the same in all cases, but its expression is culturally specific.

CHAPTER SUMMARY

Enculturation, the process by which culture is passed from one generation to the next, begins soon after birth. Its first agents are the members of an individual's household, but later, in some societies, this role is assumed by professionals. For enculturation to proceed, individuals must possess self-awareness, or the ability to perceive themselves as objects in time and space and to judge their own actions. A major facet of self-awareness is a positive view of the self, for this is what motivates persons to act to their advantage rather than disadvantage.

Several requirements involving a person's behavioral environment need to be met for emerging self-awareness to function. The individual first needs to learn about a world of objects other than the self; this environment is perceived in terms compatible with the values of the culture he or she is born into. Also required is a sense of both spatial and temporal orientation. Finally, the growing individual needs a normative orientation, or an understanding of the values, ideals, and standards that constitute the behavioral environment.

Personality is a product of enculturation and refers to the distinctive ways a person thinks, feels, and behaves. Along with the psychoanalysts, most anthropologists believe adult personality is shaped by early childhood experiences. A prime goal of anthropologists has been to produce objective studies that test this theory. Cross-cultural studies of gender-related personality characteristics, for example, show that whatever biologically based personality differences may exist between men and women are extremely malleable. A society's economy helps structure the way children are brought up, which in turn influences their adult personalities.

Anthropologists John and Beatrice Whiting and Irvin Child, on the basis of cross-cultural studies, have established the interrelation of personality, child-rearing practices, and other cultural aspects. One practice, for example, is dependence training. Usually associated with traditional farming societies, it tries to ensure that society members will willingly and routinely work for the benefit of the group by performing the jobs assigned to them. At the opposite extreme, independence training, typical of societies characterized by independent nuclear families, puts a premium on self-reliance and independent behavior. Although a society may emphasize one sort of behavior over the other, it may not emphasize it to the same degree in both sexes. Whiting and Child believe that child-rearing practices have their roots in a society's customs for meeting the basic physical needs of its members; these practices, in turn, develop particular kinds of adult personalities.

Anthropologists early on began to work on the problem of whether it is possible to delineate a group personality without falling into stereotyping. Each culture chooses, from the vast array of possibilities, traits it sees as normative or ideal. Individuals who conform to these traits are rewarded; the rest are not. The modal personality of a group is the personality typical of a culturally bounded population, as indicated by the central tendency of a defined frequency distribution. As a statistical concept, it opens for investigation how societies organize the diverse personalities of their members, some of whom conform more than others to the modal "type."

National character studies have focused on the modal characteristics of modern countries. They then have attempted to determine the child-rearing practices and education that shape such a group personality. Investigators during World War II interviewed foreign-born nationals and analyzed other sources in an effort to depict national character. Many anthropologists believe national character theories are based on unscientific and overgeneralized data. Others have chosen to focus on the core values promoted in particular societies while recognizing that success in instilling these values in individuals may vary considerably.

What defines normal behavior in any culture is determined by the culture itself, and what may be acceptable, or even admirable, in one may not be in another. Abnormality involves developing a delusional system the culture does not accept. Culturally induced conflicts not only can produce psychological disturbance but can determine the form of the disturbance as well. Similarly, mental disorders that have a biological cause, such as schizophrenia, will be expressed by symptoms specific to the culture of the afflicted individual.

POINTS FOR CONSIDERATION

1. Why might a clinical psychologist—someone who treats patients or clients directly—value the enculturation concept when working with a patient from the same culture as the psychologist? from a different culture?

2. What cultural forces in your childhood have made you different from your parents? from friends who grew up in different environments? Were these forces more important than the individual qualities of your home?

3. Do you believe cultures have different "personalities"? Why or why not? Does the modal personality concept still have meaning for societies with numerous subcultures, such as those in Canada or the United States?

SUGGESTED READINGS

Barnouw, V. (1985). *Culture and personality* (4th ed.). Homewood, IL: Dorsey Press.

This is a revision of a well-respected text designed to introduce students to psychological anthropology.

Furst, P. T. (1976). *Hallucinogens and culture.* Novato, CA: Chandler and Sharp.

For those interested in altered states of consciousness, this book is the best place to start. This important cross-cultural study of mind-altering substances is thorough yet easily read by those with no previous knowledge.

Suárez-Orozoco, M. M., Spindler, G., & Spindler, L. (1994). *The making of psychological anthropology II.* Fort Worth, TX: Harcourt Brace.

This collection of articles consists of firsthand accounts of the objectives, accomplishments, and failures of well-known specialists in psychological anthropology.

Wallace, A. F. C. (1970). *Culture and personality* (2nd ed.). New York: Random House.

The logical and methodological foundations of culture and personality as a science form the basis of this book. The study is guided by the assumptions that anthropology should develop a scientific theory about culture and that a theory pretending to explain or predict cultural phenomena must reckon with noncultural phenomena (such as personality) as well.

Whiting, J. W. M., & Child, I. (1953). *Child training and personality: A cross-cultural study.* New Haven, CT: Yale University Press.

How culture is integrated though the medium of personality processes is the main concern of this classic study. It covers the influence of both culture on personality and personality on culture. It is oriented toward testing general hypotheses about human behavior in any and all societies, rather than toward a detailed analysis of a particular society.

Chapter 17
PATTERNS OF SUBSISTENCE

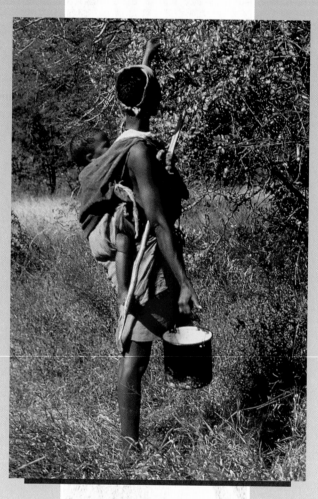

A BUSHMAN WOMAN IN SOUTHERN AFRICA
GATHERS FOOD. THE BASIC BUSINESS OF
CULTURE IS SECURING THE SURVIVAL OF THOSE
WHO LIVE BY ITS RULES, AND SO THE STUDY OF
SUBSISTENCE IS AN IMPORTANT ASPECT OF
ANTHROPOLOGICAL STUDY.

Chapter Preview

What Is Adaptation?

Adaptation refers to the interaction process between changes an organism makes in its environment and changes the environment makes in the organism. This kind of two-way adjustment is necessary for the survival of all life forms, including human beings.

How Do Humans Adapt?

Humans adapt through the medium of culture as they develop ways of doing things compatible with the resources they have available to them and within the limitations of the environment they live in. In a particular region, people living in similar environments tend to borrow from one another customs that seem to work well in those environments. Once achieved, adaptations may be remarkably stable for long periods, even thousands of years.

What Sorts of Adaptations Have Humans Achieved Through the Ages?

Food foraging is the oldest and most universal type of human adaptation. To it we owe such important elements of social organization as the sexual division of labor, food sharing, and a home base as the center of daily activity and where food sharing is accomplished. Quite different adaptations, involving farming and animal husbandry, began to develop in some parts of the world between 9,000 and 11,000 years ago. Horticulture—the cultivation of domestic plants with simple hand tools—made possible more permanent settlements and a reorganization of the division of labor. Under pastoralism—reliance on raising herds of domestic animals—nomadism continued, but new modes of interaction with other peoples were developed. Urbanism began to develop as early as 5,000 years ago in some places as intensive agriculture produced sufficient food to support various full-time specialists. With this went a further transformation of the social fabric.

Several times today you will interrupt your activities to eat or drink. You may take this very much for granted, but if you went totally without food for as long as a day, you would begin to feel the symptoms of hunger: weakness, fatigue, headache. After a month of starvation, your body would probably never repair the damage. A mere week to 10 days without water would be enough to kill you.

All living beings, and people are no exception, must satisfy certain basic needs in order to stay alive. Among these needs are food, water, and shelter. Humans may not "live by bread alone," but nobody can live for long without any bread at all; and no creature could survive long if its relations with its environment were random and chaotic. Living beings must have regular access to a supply of food and water and a reliable means of obtaining and using it. A lion might die if all its prey disappeared, if its teeth and claws grew soft, or if its digestive system failed. Although people face these same sorts of problems, they have an overwhelming advantage over other creatures: People have culture. If our meat supply dwindles, we can turn to a vegetable, such as the soybean, and process it to taste like meat. When our tools fail, we replace them or invent better ones. Even when our stomachs are incapable of digesting food, we can predigest food by boiling or pureeing. We are, however, subject to the same needs and pressures as all living creatures, and it is important to understand human behavior from this point of view. The crucial concept that underlies such a perspective is *adaptation,* that is, how humans manage to deal with the contingencies of daily life. Dealing with these contingencies is the basic business of all cultures.

▲▽▲▽▲▽▲▽▲▽▲▽▲▽▲▽▲▽▲▽▲▽▲▽▲▽▲

ADAPTATION

The adaptation process establishes a moving balance between the needs of a population and the potential of its environment. This process can be illustrated by the Tsembaga, New Guinea, high-landers, who support themselves chiefly through **horticulture**—the cultivation of crops carried out with simple hand tools.[1] Although they also raise pigs, they eat them only under conditions of illness, injury, warfare, or celebration. At such times the pigs are sacrificed to ancestral spirits, and their flesh is ritually consumed by the people involved in the crisis. (This guarantees a supply of high-quality protein when it is most needed.)

In precolonial times the Tsembaga and their neighbors were bound together in a unique cycle of pig sacrifices that served to mark the end of hostilities between groups. Frequent hostilities were set off by a number of ecological pressures, with pigs playing a significant role. Since very few pigs normally were slaughtered and their food requirements were great, they could very quickly literally eat a local group out of house and home. The need to expand food production to support the prestigious but hungry pigs put a strain on the land best suited for farming. Therefore, when one group had driven another off its land, hostilities ended, and the new residents celebrated their victory with a pig festival. Many pigs were slaughtered, and the pork was widely shared among allied groups. Even without hostilities, festivals were held whenever the pig population became un-

---

[1] Rappaport, R. A. (1969). Ritual regulation of environmental relations among a New Guinea people. In A. P. Vayda (Ed.), *Environment and cultural behavior* (pp. 181–201). Garden City, NY: Natural History Press.

Horticulture.   Cultivation of crops using hand tools such as digging sticks or hoes.

manageable, every 5 to 10 years, depending on the groups' success at farming. Thus the cycle of fighting and feasting kept the balance among humans, land, and animals.

The term *adaptation* also refers to the interaction process between changes an organism makes in its environment and changes the environment makes in the organism. The spread of the gene for sickle-cell anemia is a case in point. Long ago, in the tropics of central Africa, a genetic mutation appeared in human populations, causing the manufacture of red blood cells that take on a sickle shape under conditions of low oxygen pressure. Since persons who receive a gene for this trait from each parent usually develop severe anemia and die in childhood, selective pressure was exerted

against the spread of this gene in the local gene pool. Then slash-and-burn horticulture was introduced into this region, creating a change in the natural environment by removal—through cutting (slashing) and burning—of the natural vegetative cover. This was conducive to the breeding of mosquitos that carry the parasite causing falciparum malaria. When transmitted to humans, the parasites live in the red blood cells and cause a disease that is always debilitating and very often fatal. Individuals who received the gene for the sickle-cell trait from only one parent, however (receiving one "normal" gene from the other), turned out to have a specific natural defense against the parasite. The gene's presence caused only some of the cells to take on a sickle shape; when those cells circulated

Human adaptations impact environments in various ways. In California, native food foragers regularly burned over vast areas, thereby favoring the growth of oak trees (acorns were a staple food) and deer browse. Once "White" settlers stopped the practice, highly flammable brush and conifers flourished at the expense of oaks. As a consequence, disastrous outbreaks of wildfires periodically sweep through parts of the state, causing millions of dollars in property loss.

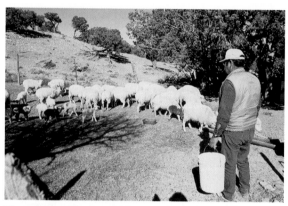

Though the Hopi and Navajo share the same environment, their cultures are quite different. Originally food foragers, Navajos became pastoral nomads, while the Hopi are village-dwelling farmers. Environments do not determine culture but do set certain potentials and limitations.

through the spleen, which routinely screens out all damaged or worn red blood cells, the infected cells and the parasites along with them were destroyed. Since these individuals did not succumb to malaria, they were favored by selection, and the sickling trait became more and more common in the population. Thus, while people changed their environment, their environment also changed them. Nor is this an isolated example; analogous forms of heredity anemias that protect against malaria followed the spread of farming from southwest Asia and Southeast Asia as well.

Sickle-cell and similar anemias are a neat illustration of the relativity of any adaptation. In malarial areas, the genes responsible for these conditions are adaptive for human populations, even though some individuals suffer as a result of their presence. In nonmalarial regions, however, they are highly maladaptive, for not only do such genes confer no advantages at all on human populations living under such conditions, but some individuals die as a result of their presence.

THE UNIT OF ADAPTATION

The unit of adaptation includes both organisms and the environment. Organisms exist as members of populations; populations, in turn, must have the flexibility to cope with variability and change within the environment. In biological terms, this means different organisms within the population have somewhat differing genetic endowments. In cultural terms, it means variation occurs among individual skills, knowledge, and personalities. Organisms and environments form interacting systems. People might as easily be farmers as fisherfolk, but we do not expect to find farmers north of the Arctic Circle or people who fish for a living in the Sahara Desert. In other words, although environments do not determine culture, they do present certain possibilities and limitations.

Consider the example of a group of lakeside people who live off fish. The fish in turn live off smaller organisms, which in turn consume green plants; plants liberate minerals from water and mud, and, with energy from sunlight, transform them into proteins and carbohydrates. Dead plant and animal matter is decomposed by bacteria, returning chemicals to the soil and water. Some energy escapes from this system in the form of heat. Evaporation and rainfall constantly recirculate the water. People add chemicals to the system in the form of their wastes, and, if they are judicious, they may help to regulate the balance of animals and plants.

Some anthropologists have borrowed the ecologists' concept of **ecosystem.** An ecosystem is composed of both the physical environment and the organisms living within it. The system is bound by the activities of the organisms, as well as by such physical processes as erosion and evaporation.

Human ecologists generally are concerned with detailed microstudies of particular human ecosystems; they emphasize that all aspects of human culture must be considered, not just the most obvious technological ones. The Tsembaga's attitude toward pigs and the cycle of sacrifices have important economic functions; outsiders may see them in this way, but the Tsembaga do not. They are motivated by their belief in the power and needs of their ancestral spirits. Although the pigs are consumed *by* the living, they are sacrificed *for* ancestors. Human ecosystems often must be interpreted in cultural terms.

EVOLUTIONARY ADAPTATION

Adaptation also must be understood from a historical point of view. For organisms to fit into an ecosystem, they must have the potential to adjust

Shown here are Indians of the North American plains hunting bison they have driven into the Missouri River. Plains Indians such as the Cheyenne, Comanche, Crow, and Sioux developed similar cultures, as they had to adapt to similar environmental conditions (for a map of Native American culture areas, see Figure 17.1).

Ecosystem. A system, or a functioning whole, composed of both the physical environment and the organisms living within it.

to or become a part of it. The Comanche, whose history began in the harsh, arid country of southern Idaho, provide a good example.[2] In their original home they subsisted on wild plants, small animals, and occasionally larger game. Their material equipment was simple and limited to what their women could transport. The size of their groups was restricted, and what little social power could develop was in the hands of the shaman, who was a combination of healer and spiritual guide.

At some point in their nomadic history, the Comanche moved onto the Great Plains, where buffalo were abundant and the Indians' potential as hunters could be fully developed. As larger groups could be supported by the new food supply, the need arose for a more complex political organization. Hunting ability thus became a means to acquire political power.

Eventually the Comanche acquired horses and guns from Whites, which greatly enhanced their hunting prowess, and the great hunting chiefs became powerful indeed. The Comanche became raiders in order to get horses, which they did not breed for themselves, and their hunting chiefs evolved into war chiefs. The once "poor" and peaceful hunter-gatherers of the Great Basin became wealthy and warlike, dominating the Southwest from the borders of New Spain (Mexico) in the south to those of New France (Louisiana) to the fledgling United States in the east and north. In moving from one environment to another, and in evolving from one way of life to a second, the Comanche were able to capitalize on existing cultural capabilities to flourish in their new situation.

Sometimes societies that have developed independently find similar solutions to similar problems. For example, another group that moved onto the Great Plains and took up a form of Plains Indian culture, similar in many ways to that of the Comanche, were the Cheyenne. Yet their cultural background was quite different; formerly, they were settled farmers with social, political, and religious institutions quite unlike those of the Comanche in their ancestral homeland. This kind of development of similar cultural adaptations to

Saying that a society is stable is not saying that it is changeless. These Western Abenakis are descendants of people who maintained a stable way of life for 5,000 years, even though they frequently incorporated new elements into their culture. Even today, 400 years after the Abenakis' first contact with Europeans, many traditional values and practices endure.

[2]Wallace, E., & Hoebel, E. A. (1952). *The Comanches*. Norman: University of Oklahoma Press.

similar environmental conditions by peoples whose ancestral cultures were quite different is called **convergent evolution**. Especially interesting is that the Cheyenne switch was from a farming to a food-foraging way of life. Contrary to Western notions of "progress," change in subsistence practices does not inevitably go from dependence on wild food to farming; it may go the other way as well.

Somewhat similar to the phenomenon of convergent evolution is **parallel evolution**, the difference being that similar adaptations are achieved by peoples whose ancestral cultures were already somewhat similar. For example, the development of farming in southwest Asia and Mesoamerica took place independently, as people in both places, whose ways of life were already alike, became dependent on a narrow range of plant foods that depended upon human intervention for their protection and reproductive success.

It is important to recognize that stability as well as change is involved in evolutionary adaptation and that once a satisfactory adaptation is achieved, too much change may cause it to break down. Thus, episodes of major change may be followed by long periods of relative stability. For example, by 3500 B.C., a way of life had evolved in northwestern New England and southern Quebec that was well attuned to the environmental conditions of the times.[3] Since those conditions remained more or less stable for the next 5,000 years or so, it is understandable that people's lifeways also remained stable. This does not mean change was entirely absent. (*Stable* does not mean *static.*) Periodically, people refined and enhanced their way of life—for example, improving hunting methods by replacing spears and spear throwers with bows and arrows; improving cooking by substituting pottery vessels for containers made from

animal hide, wood, or bark; improving transport by replacing heavy and cumbersome dugouts with sturdy yet lightweight birchbark canoes; and improving yields by supplementing the products of hunting, gathering, and fishing with limited cultivation of corn, beans, and squash. In spite of these changes, however, the native peoples of the region still retained the basic structure of their culture and tended toward a balance with their resource base well into the 17th century, when the culture had to adjust to pressures associated with the European invasion of North America. Such long-term stability by no means implies "stagnation," "backwardness," or "failure to progress"; rather, it indicates success. Had this culture not effectively satisfied people's physical and psychological needs, it never would have endured as it did for thousands of years.

CULTURE AREAS

The aboriginal **culture area** of the Great Plains (Figure 17.1) was a geographic region where a number of societies with similar ways of life existed. Thirty-one politically independent peoples (the aforementioned Cheyenne and Comanche were but two of them) faced a common environment, in which the buffalo was an obvious and practical source of food as well as materials for clothing and shelter. Living close by each other, the nations could share new inventions and discoveries. They reached a common and shared adaptation to a particular ecological zone.

The Indians of the Great Plains were, at the time of contact with Europeans, invariably buffalo hunters, dependent upon this animal for food, clothing, shelter, and bone tools. Each nation was organized into a number of warrior societies, and prestige came from hunting and fighting skills. Their camps typically were arranged in a distinctive circular pattern. Many religious rituals, such as the Sun Dance, were practiced throughout the plains region.

Sometimes geographic regions are not uniform in climate and topography, so new discoveries do

---

[3]Haviland, W. A., & Power, M. W. (1994). *The original Vermonters* (Rev. and exp. ed.). Hanover, NH: University Press of New England.

Convergent evolution. In cultural evolution, the development of similar adaptations to similar environmental conditions by peoples whose ancestral cultures were quite different. > **Parallel evolution.** In cultural evolution, the development of similar adaptations to similar environmental conditions by peoples whose ancestral cultures were similar. > **Culture area.** A geographic region where numerous different societies follow similar patterns of life.

FIGURE 17.1

The culture-area concept was developed by North American anthropologists in the early part of the 20th century. This map shows the culture areas that have been defined for North and Central America. Within each, there is an overall similarity of native cultures, as opposed to the differences that distinguish the cultures of one area from those of all others.

not always spread from one group to another. Moreover, within a culture area, variations between local environments exist, and these favor variations in adaptation. The Great Basin of the western United States—an area embracing Nevada and Utah, with adjacent portions of California, Oregon, Wyoming, and Idaho—is a case in point.[4]

---

[4]Steward, J. H. (1972). *Theory of culture change: The methodology of multilinear evolution.* Urbana: University of Illinois Press.

The Great Basin Shoshone Indians were divided into a northern and a western group, both primarily nomadic hunters and gatherers. In the north, a relative abundance of game animals provided for the maintenance of large populations, requiring a great deal of cooperation among local groups. The western Shoshone, in contrast, were almost entirely dependent upon the gathering of wild plants for their subsistence, and as these varied considerably in their seasonal and local availability, the western Shoshone were forced to cover vast distances in search of food. Under such conditions, it was most efficient to travel in groups of but a few families, only occasionally coming together with other groups, and not always with the same ones.

The Shoshone were not the only inhabitants of the Great Basin. To the south lived the closely related Paiutes. They, too, were hunter-gatherers living under the same environmental conditions as the Shoshone, but the Paiutes managed their food resources more actively by diverting small streams to irrigate wild crops. They did not plant and cultivate these, but they could secure higher yields than their northern neighbors. Hence, their populations were larger than those of the Shoshone, and they led a less nomadic existence.

To deal with variations within a given region, anthropologist Julian Steward proposed the concept of **culture type,** or consideration of a culture in terms of a particular technology and its relationship with the environmental features that technology is equipped to deal with. The example of the Great Plains shows how technology helps decide just which environmental features will be useful. Those same prairies that once supported buffalo hunters now support grain farmers. The Indians were prevented from farming the plains not for environmental reasons, nor for lack of knowledge about farming, since some of them, such as the Cheyenne, had been farmers before they moved onto the plains. They did not farm because the buffalo herds provided abundant food without farming and because farming would have been difficult without the steel-tipped plow that

---

Culture type   The concept of viewing a culture in terms of the relation of its particular technology to the environment that technology exploits.

Julian H. Steward *(1902–1972)*

North American anthropologist Julian H. Steward developed an approach he called **cultural ecology**—that is, the interaction of specific cultures with their environments. Initially, Steward was struck by a number of similarities in the development of urban civilizations in both Peru and Mesoamerica and noted that certain developments were paralleled in the urban civilizations of the Old World. He identified the constants and abstracted from this his laws of cultural development. Steward proposed three fundamental procedures for cultural ecology:

1. The interrelationship of a culture's technology and its environment must be analyzed. How effectively does the culture take advantage of available resources to provide food and housing for its members?
2. The patterns of behavior associated with a culture's technology must be analyzed. How do members of the culture perform the work necessary for their survival?
3. The relation between those behavioral patterns and the rest of the cultural system must be determined. How does the work people do to survive affect their attitudes and outlooks? How is their survival behavior linked to their social activities and their personal relationships?

was needed to break up the compact prairie sod. The farming potential of the Great Plains was simply not a relevant feature of the environment, given the available resources and technology before the Europeans arrived.

CULTURE CORE

Environment and technology are not the only factors that determine a society's way of subsistence; social and political organization also affect the application of technology to the problem of staying alive. To understand the rise of irrigation agriculture in the great centers of ancient civilization, such as China, Mesopotamia, and Mesoamerica, it is important to note not only the technological and environmental factors that made the building of large-scale irrigation works possible but also the social and political organization that made it possible to mobilize the many workers necessary to

build and maintain the systems. Researchers must examine the monarchies and priesthoods that organized the work and decided where the water would be used and how the agricultural products of this collective venture would be distributed.

The cultural features that play a part in the society's way of making its living are called its **culture core**. This includes the society's productive techniques and its knowledge of the resources available to it. It encompasses the patterns of labor involved in applying those techniques to the local environment. For example, do people work every day for a fixed number of hours, or is most work concentrated during certain times of the year? The culture core also includes other aspects of culture that bear on the production and distribution of food. Examples of the way ideology can indirectly affect subsistence can be seen in a number of cultures where religion may lead to failure to use both locally available and nutritionally

---

Cultural ecology. The study of the interaction of specific human cultures with their environment. **>** **Culture core.** The features of a culture that play a part in matters relating to the society's way of making a living.

valuable foods. One example is the taboo of the Tutchone, a people native to the Yukon territory of northwestern Canada, against eating otters, young ravens, or crows, even though their meat is perfectly edible. In their northern forest homeland, seasonal food shortages are always a threat, but even when faced with famine, the Tutchone adhere to their taboo. Instead of eating these animals, they resort to techniques such as lighting a fire over an area mice previously used to melt the frozen soil to gain access to bare roots the mice had stored.[5]

A number of anthropologists, known as **ethnoscientists,** are actively attempting to understand the principles behind folk ideologies and the way these principles usually help keep a people alive. The Tsembaga, for example, avoid certain low-lying, marshy areas, because they believe those areas are inhabited by red spirits who punish trespassers. Western science, by contrast, interprets those areas as the home of mosquitos and the "punishment" as malaria. Whatever Western people may think of the Tsembaga's belief in red spirits, it is a perfectly useful and reasonable one; it keeps them away from marshy areas just as surely as does a belief in malaria. To understand why people in other cultures behave the way they do, one must understand their system of thought from their point of view as well as from one's own. Not all such beliefs are as easy to translate as that of the Tsembaga red spirits.

THE FOOD-FORAGING WAY OF LIFE

At present, perhaps a quarter of a million people —less then 0.00005% of a world population of almost 6 billion—support themselves chiefly through hunting, fishing, and gathering wild plant foods. Yet, before the domestication of plants and animals, which began a mere 10,000 years ago, all

people supported themselves through some combination of wild plant collection, hunting, and fishing. Of all the people who have *ever* lived, 90% have been food foragers, and it was as food foragers that we became truly human, acquiring the basic habits of dealing with one another and with the world around us that still guide the behavior of individuals, communities, and nations. Thus, if we want to know who we are and how we came to be, if we want to understand the relationship between environment and culture, and if we want to comprehend the institutions of the food-producing societies that have arisen since the development of farming and animal husbandry, we should turn first to the oldest and most universal of fully human lifestyles, the food-foraging adaptation. The beginnings of this were examined in Chapter 7.

When food foragers had the world to themselves some 10,000 years ago, they had their pick of the best environments. These long since have been appropriated by farming and, more recently, by industrial societies. Today, most food foragers are found only in the world's marginal areas— frozen Arctic tundra, deserts, and inaccessible forests. These habitats, although they may not support large or dense agricultural societies, provide a good living for food-foraging peoples.

Until recently it was assumed that a food-foraging life in these areas was difficult and that one had to work hard just to stay alive. Behind this view lies the Western notion of progress, which, although widely accepted as a fact of nature, is actually nothing more than a culturally conditioned bias. This predisposes one to see what is new as generally preferable to what is old and to read human history as a more-or-less steady climb up an evolutionary ladder of progress. Thus, many assume that because food foraging as a way of life is much older than industrial civilization, the latter must be intrinsically better than the former. Hence, food-foraging societies are referred to as "primitive," "backward," or "undeveloped," labels economists, politicians, and other members of industrial or would-be industrial societies use to express their disapproval. In reality, food-foraging

---

[5]Legros, D. (1997). Comment. *Current Anthropology, 38,* 617.

Ethnoscientists. Anthropologists who seek to understand the principles behind folk ideologies and the way these ideologies help a people survive.

societies are very highly developed, but in a way quite different from industrial societies.

Detailed studies have revealed that life in food-foraging societies is far from "solitary, poor, nasty, brutish, and short," as philosopher Thomas Hobbes asserted more than 300 years ago. Rather, food foragers' diets are well balanced and ample, and these people are less likely to experience severe famine than are farmers. While their material comforts are limited, so are their desires. They also have plenty of leisure time for concentrating on family ties, social life, and spiritual development. The Ju/'hoansi, a Bushman people of southern Africa's Kalahari Desert (see Chapter 16)—scarcely what one would call a "lush" environment—obtain a diet in an average workweek of about 20 hours that surpasses internationally recommended levels of nutrients. If one adds to this the time spent making and repairing equipment, the total rises to just a bit more than 23 hours, while the equivalent of Western housework adds another 19 hours. The grand total, just over 42 hours (44.5 for men, 40.1 for women), is still less than the time spent on the job (currently 41 hours for manufacturing jobs, just under 44 hours for white-collar jobs), on maintenance tasks, and on housework in North America today.[6] Their lives are rich in human warmth and aesthetic experience, displaying a balance of work and love, ritual, and play many of us might envy. Small wonder some anthropologists have gone so far as to label this "the original affluent society." The Ju/'hoansi are not exceptional among food foragers today; one can only wonder about the level of affluence their ancient counterparts who lived in lusher environments achieved with more secure and plentiful supplies of food.

All modern food foragers have had some degree of interaction with neighbors whose ways of life often differ radically from their own. Bushman people such as the Ju/'hoansi, for example, have interacted for at least 2,000 years with Bantu farmers who kept cattle and sheep. Likewise, the food-foraging Mbuti of the Republic of Congo's

---

[6]Cashdan, E. (1989). Hunters and gatherers: Economic behavior in bands. In S. Plattner (Ed.), *Economic anthropology* (pp. 23–24). Stanford, CA: Stanford University Press.

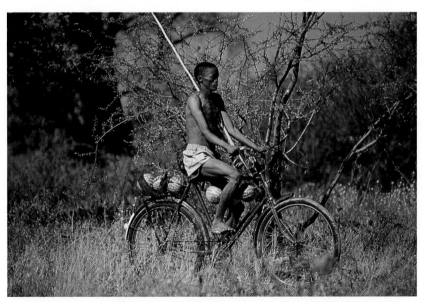

Human groups (including food foragers) do not exist in isolation except occasionally, and even then not for long. The bicycle this Bushman of southern Africa is riding is indicative of his links with the wider world. For 2,000 years, Bushmen have been interacting regularly with farmers and pastoralists, and much of the ivory used for the pianos so widely sought in 19th-century North America came from the Bushmen.

Food foraging has by no means disappeared, even in industrial societies such as that of the United States. Some do it occasionally for pleasure, as the author and his brother-in-law are shown doing in the top photo—gathering wild mussels. Some, such as commercial fishers, forage full-time, as do many homeless people in order to survive.

Ituri rain forest live in a complex patron-client relationship with their neighbors, Bantu- and Sudanic-speaking peoples who are farmers. They exchange meat and other products of the forest for farm produce and manufactured goods. During part of the year, they live in their patron's village and are incorporated into his kin group, even to the point of allowing him to initiate their sons.

Although some modern food foragers, such as the Mbuti, have continued to maintain traditional ways while adapting to neighbors and traders, various other groups turned to this way of life after giving up other modes of subsistence. Some, such as the Cheyenne of the Great Plains, were once farmers, while others, such as some of the Bushmen of southern Africa, have at times been farmers and at others pastoral nomads. Nor are such transformations only of the past. In the 1980s, when a world economic recession led to the abandonment of many sheep stations in the Australian outback, a number of Aboriginal peoples returned to food foraging, thereby emancipating themselves

from a dependency on the government they had been forced into.

An important point that emerges from the preceding discussion is this: People in the world today who subsist by hunting, fishing, and gathering wild plants are not following an ancient way of life because they do not know any better; they are doing it either because they have been forced by circumstances into a situation where foraging is the best means of survival or because they simply prefer to live this way. In many cases, they find such satisfaction in living the way they do that, like the Hadza of northern Tanzania, they go to great lengths to avoid adopting other ways of life.[7] The fact is, foraging constitutes a rational response to particular ecological, economic, and sociopolitical realities. Moreover, for at least 2,000 years, a need has existed for specialist "commercial" hunter-gatherers to supply the wild forest commodities that have helped feed east-west trade since ancient times.[8]

---

[7]Hawkes, K., O'Connell, J. F., & Blurton Jones, N. G. (1997). Hadza women's time allocation, offspring provisioning, and the evolution of long postmenopausal life spans. *Current Anthropology, 38,* 552.

[8]Stiles, D. (1992). The hunter-gatherer 'revisionist' debate. *Anthropology Today,* 8 (2), 15.

CHARACTERISTICS OF THE FOOD-FORAGING LIFE

Food foragers are by definition people who do not farm or practice animal husbandry. Hence, they must accommodate their places of residence to naturally available food sources. Thus, it is no wonder they move about a great deal. Such movement is not aimless wandering but is done within a fixed territory or home range. Some groups, such as the Ju/'hoansi, who depend on the reliable and highly drought-resistant Mongongo nut, may keep to fairly fixed annual routes and cover only a restricted territory. Others, such as the Great Basin Shoshone, had to cover a wider territory; their course was determined by the local availability of the erratically productive pine nut. A crucial factor in this mobility is water availability. The distance between the food supply and water must not be so great that more energy is required to fetch water than can be obtained from the food.

Another characteristic of the food-foraging adaptation is the small size of local groups, which usually include fewer than 100 people. Although no completely satisfactory explanation of group size has yet been offered, it seems certain that both ecological and social factors are involved. Among those suggested are the **carrying capacity** of the land, or the number of people who the available resources can support at a given level of food-getting techniques, and the **density of social relations**, or roughly the number and intensity of interactions among camp members. More people means a higher social density, which, in turn, means more opportunities for conflict.

Both carrying capacity and social density are complex variables. Carrying capacity involves not only the immediate presence of food and water but also the tools and work necessary to secure them, as well as short- and long-term fluctuations in their availability. Social density involves not only the number of people and their interactions but also the circumstances and quality of those interactions, as well as the mechanisms for regulating them. A mob of a hundred angry strangers has a different social density than the same number of neighbors enjoying themselves at a block party.

Among food-foraging populations, social density always seems in a state of flux as people spend more or less time away from camp and as they move to other camps, either on visits or more permanently. Among the Ju/'hoansi, for example, exhaustion of local food resources, conflict within the group, or the desire to visit friends or relatives living elsewhere cause people to leave one group for another. As Richard Lee notes: "Ju love to go visiting, and the practice acts as a safety valve when tempers get frayed. In fact, the Ju usually move, not when their food is exhausted, but rather when only their patience is exhausted."[9] If a camp has so many children as to create a burden for the working adults, some young families may be encouraged to join others where fewer children live. Conversely, groups with few children may actively recruit families with young children in order to ensure the group's survival. Redistribution of people, then, is an important mechanism for regulating social density, as well as for assuring that the size and composition of local groups is suited to local variations in resources. Thus, cultural adaptations help transcend the limitations of the physical environment.

In addition to seasonal or local adjustments, food foragers must make long-term adjustments to resources. Most food-foraging populations seem to stabilize at numbers well below the carrying capacity of their land. In fact, the home ranges of most food foragers could support from three to five times as many people as they typically do. In the long run, it may be more adaptive for a group to keep its numbers low, rather than to expand indefinitely and risk destruction by a sudden and unexpected natural reduction in food resources. The population density of food-foraging groups rarely exceeds one person per square

---

[9]Lee, R. (1993). *The Dobe Ju/'hoansi* (p. 65). Fort Worth, TX: Harcourt Brace.

Carrying capacity.   The number of people the available resources can support at a given technological level. > **Density of social relations.**   Roughly, the number and intensity of interactions among the members of a camp or other residential unit.

mile, a very low density, even though their resources could support greater numbers.

How food-foraging peoples regulate population size relates to how they care for their children. Typically, they nurse their infants several times each hour, even at night, over a period of as many as 4 or 5 years. The constant stimulation of the mothers' nipples suppresses the hormones that promote ovulation, making conception unlikely, especially if their work keeps them physically active and they do not have large stores of body fat to draw on for energy.[10] By continuing to nurse

---

[10]Small, M. F. (1997). Making connections. *American Scientist, 85,* 503.

Frequent nursing of children over as many as 4 or 5 years acts to suppress ovulation among food foragers such as Bushmen. As a consequence, women give birth to relatively few offspring at widely spaced intervals.

for several years, women give birth only at widely spaced intervals, and the total number of offspring remains low.

THE IMPACT OF FOOD FORAGING ON HUMAN SOCIETY

Although much has been written on the theoretical importance of hunting for shaping the supposedly competitive and aggressive nature of the human species, most anthropologists are unconvinced by these arguments. To be sure, warlike food-foraging people are known, but their behavior is most often a response to pressure from expansionist states, a recent phenomenon in human history (see Chapter 23). In the absence of such pressures, food-foraging peoples are remarkably unaggressive and place more emphasis on cooperation than they do on competition. It does seem likely, however, that three crucial elements of human social organization developed with food foraging. The first of these is the sexual division of labor. Some form of this, however modified, has been observed in all human societies and is probably as old as human culture (see Chapter 7). Contemporary Western society is somewhat tending to do away with such division, as we shall see in the next chapter. One may ask what the implications are for future cooperative relationships between men and women, a problem we will discuss further in Chapters 19 and 20.

Subsistence and Gender

The hunting and butchering of large game as well as the processing of hard or tough raw materials are almost universally masculine occupations. Women's work, by contrast, usually consists of gathering and processing a variety of vegetal foods, as well as other domestic chores. Historically, this pattern appears to have its origin in an earlier era, when males, who were twice the size of females, got meat by scavenging from the carcasses of dead animals, butchered it with stone tools, and shared it with females (see Chapter 7). The latter, for their part, gathered wild plant foods, probably using digging sticks and carrying devices made of soft, perishable materials. As the hunting of live animals replaced scavenging as a source of meat and the biological differences between the sexes were reduced to minor proportions, the essence of the original division of labor was maintained nonetheless.

Among food foragers today, the work of women is no less arduous than that of men. Ju/'hoansi women, for example, may walk as many as 12 miles a day two or three times a week to gather food, carrying not only their children but also, on the return home, anywhere from 15 to 33 pounds of food. Still, they do not have to travel quite so far afield as do men on the hunt, nor is their work usually quite so dangerous. Finally, their tasks require less rapid mobility, do not need complete and undivided attention, and are readily resumed after interruption. All of this is compatible with the biological differences that remain between the sexes. Certainly women who are pregnant, or have infants to nurse, cannot as easily travel long distances in pursuit of game as men can. In addition to wide-ranging mobility, the successful hunter also must be able to mobilize rapidly high bursts of energy. Although some women certainly can run faster than some men, it is a fact that in general men can run faster than women,

even when the latter are not pregnant or encumbered with infants. Because human females must be able to give birth to infants with relatively large heads, their pelvic structure differs from that of human males to a greater degree than the male/female structures differ among most other species of mammals. As a consequence, the human female is not as well equipped as the human male for rapid and prolonged mobility.

To say differing sex roles among food foragers are compatible with the biological differences between men and women is *not* to say they are biologically determined. Among the Great Plains Indians of North America, for example, are numerous reported cases of women who gained fame as hunters and warriors, both regarded as men's activities. One case even involves a Gros Ventre girl the Crow captured who became one of their chiefs, so accomplished was she at what were considered masculine pursuits. Conversely, any young man who found masculine pursuits uncongenial could assume the dress and demeanor of women, provided he had the necessary skills to achieve success in feminine activities. Although sexual preference might enter into the decision to assume a feminine

Food foragers like the Ju/'hoansi have a division of labor in which women gather and prepare "bush" food (here an ostrich egg omelette), but hunting is usually done by men.

identity, not all such individuals were homosexuals, nor did all homosexuals assume a female role. Clearly, sexual preference was less important than occupation and appearance. In fact, the sexual division of labor is often far less rigid among food foragers than it is in most other types of societies. Thus, Ju/'hoansi men, willingly and without embarrassment, as the occasion demands, will gather wild plant foods, build huts, and collect water, even though all are regarded as women's work.

The nature of women's work in food-foraging societies is such that women can do it while taking care of children. They also can do it in company with other women, which helps alleviate somewhat the monotony of the work. In the past, the cultural gender biases of European and North American anthropologists caused them to underestimate the contributions the food-gathering activities of women made to the survival of their group. We now know that modern food foragers may obtain up to 60 or 70% of their diets from plant foods, with perhaps some fish and shellfish women provide (the exceptions tend to be food foragers living in the far north, where plant foods are not available for much of the year).

Although women in food-foraging societies may spend some time each day gathering plant food, men do not spend all or even the greatest part of their time hunting. The amount of energy expended in hunting, especially in hot climates, is often greater than the energy return from the kill. Too much time spent searching out game actually might be counterproductive. Energy itself is derived primarily from plant carbohydrates, and it is usually the female gatherer who brings in the bulk of the calories. A certain amount of meat in the diet, though, guarantees high-quality protein that is less easily obtained from plant sources, for meat contains exactly the right balance of all the amino acids (the building blocks of protein) the human body requires. No single plant food does this, and in order to get by without meat, people must hit on exactly the right combination of plants to provide the essential amino acids in the correct proportions.

Food Sharing

A second key feature of human social organization associated with food foraging is the sharing of food between adults, something quite rare among nonhuman primates. It is easy enough to see why sharing takes place, with women supplying one kind of food and men another. Among the Ju/'hoansi, women have control over the food they collect and can share it with whomever they choose. Men, by contrast, are constrained by rules that specify how much meat is to be distributed and to whom. Thus, a hunter has little effective control over the meat he brings into camp. For the individual hunter, meat sharing is really a way of storing it for the future; his generosity, obligatory though it might be, gives him a claim on the future kills of other hunters. As a cultural trait, food sharing has the obvious survival value of distributing resources needed for subsistence.

Although carnivorous animals often share food, the few examples of food sharing among nonhuman primate adults all involve groups of male chimpanzees cooperating in a hunt and later sharing the spoils, frequently with adult females as well as juveniles. This suggests that the origins of food sharing and the division of labor are related to a shift in food habits from infrequent to more frequent meat eating. This change seems to have occurred with the appearance of the earliest members of the genus *Homo* some 2.5 million years ago.

A final distinctive feature of the food-foraging economy is the importance of the camp as the center of daily activity and the place where food sharing actually occurs. Among nonhuman primates, and probably among human ancestors until they controlled the use of fire, activities tend to be divided between feeding areas and sleeping areas, and the latter tend to be shifted each evening. Historically known food-foraging people, however, live in camps of some permanence, ranging from the dry-season camps of the Ju/'hoansi that serve for the entire winter to the wet-season camps of the Hadza, oriented to berry picking and honey collecting, that serve for a few weeks at most. Moreover, human camps are more than sleeping areas; people are in and out all day, eating, working, and socializing in camps to a greater extent than any other primates.

Cultural Adaptations and Material Technology

The mobility of food-foraging groups may depend on the availability of water, as among the

Ju/'hoansi; of pine nuts, as in the Shoshone example; or of game animals and other seasonal resources, as among the Hadza. Hunting styles and equipment also may play a role in determining population size and movement. Some Mbuti hunt with nets. This requires the cooperation of 7 to 30 families; consequently, their camps are relatively large. The camps of Mbuti who hunt with bow and arrow number from 3 to 6 families. Too many archers in the same locale means each must travel a great distance daily to keep out of another's way. Only during midsummer do the archers collect into larger camps for religious ceremonies, matrimonial arrangements, and social exchange. At this time the bowmen turn to communal beat-hunts. Without nets they are less effective than their neighbors, and only when the net hunters are widely dispersed in the pursuit of honey (and not competing for meat) can the archers come together and still hunt.

Egalitarian Society

An important characteristic of the food-foraging society is its egalitarianism. Food foragers are usually highly mobile, and, lacking animal or mechanical transportation, they must be able to travel without many encumbrances, especially on food-getting expeditions. The average weight of an individual's personal belongings among the Ju/'hoansi, for example, is just under 25 pounds. The material goods of food foragers must be limited to the barest essentials, which include implements for hunting, gathering, fishing, building, and making tools, cooking utensils, traps, and nets. They have little chance to accumulate luxuries or surplus goods, and the fact no one owns significantly more than others helps to limit status differences. Age and sex are usually the only sources of significant status differences.

It is important to realize that status differences by themselves do not imply any necessary inequality, a point that all too often has been misunderstood, especially where relations between men and women are concerned. In traditional food-foraging societies, nothing necessitated special deference of women to men. To be sure, women may be excluded from some rituals males participate in, but the reverse is also true. Moreover, the fruits of women's labor are not controlled by men but by the women themselves. Nor do women sacrifice their autonomy, even in societies in which male hunting, rather than female gathering, brings in the bulk of the food. Such was the case, for example, among the Montagnais and Naskapi people of Labrador. The hunt was overwhelmingly important in their society. For their part, women manufactured clothing and other necessities but provided much less of the food than is common among food foragers. Until recently, women as well as men could be shamans. Nevertheless, women were excluded from ritual feasts having to do with hunting, but men were excluded from ritual feasts held by women. Basically, each sex carried out its own activities, with neither meddling in those of the other. Early missionaries to the Montagnais and Naskapi lamented that men had no inclination to make their wives obey them and worked long and hard to convince the Indians that civilization required men to impose their authority on women. But after 300 years of trying, they still have achieved only limited success.

Food foragers make no attempt to accumulate surplus foodstuffs, often an important source of status in agrarian societies. This does not mean, however, they live constantly on the verge of starvation. Their environment is their storehouse, and, except in the coldest climates (where a surplus must be stored to see people through the lean season) or in times of acute ecological disaster, some food is always to be found in a group's territory.

Because food resources are typically distributed equally throughout the group (share and share alike is the order of the day), no one achieves the wealth or status that hoarding might bring. In such a society, wealth is a sign of deviance rather than a desirable characteristic.

The food forager's concept of territory contributes as much to social equality as it does to the equal distribution of resources. Most groups use home ranges where access to resources is open to all members: What is available to one is available to all. If a Mbuti hunter discovers a honey tree, he has first rights; but when he has taken his share, others have a turn. In the unlikely possibility he does not take advantage of his discovery, others will. No one owns the tree; the system is first come, first served. Therefore, knowledge of the existence of food resources circulates quickly throughout the entire group.

Families move easily from one group to another, settling in any group where they have a previous kinship tie. (Although the idea of food foragers being patrilocal—that is, a wife moving to her husband's group—is still held by some, as discussed in Chapter 1, this represents a historic response to European exploration and colonization.) As noted earlier, the composition of groups among food foragers is always shifting. This loose attitude toward group membership promotes the widest access to resources while maintaining a balance between populations and resources.

The food-forager pattern of generalized exchange, or sharing without any expectation of a direct return, also serves the ends of balancing resource distribution and social equality. A Ju/'hoansi man or woman spends as much as two thirds of his or her day visiting others or receiving guests; during this time, many exchanges of gifts occur. Refusing to share—hoarding—would be morally wrong. By sharing whatever is at hand, the Ju/'hoansi achieve social leveling and assure their right to share in others' windfalls.

▲▽▲▽▲▽▲▽▲▽▲▽▲▽▲▽▲▽▲▽▲▽▲▽▲▽▲▽▲

FOOD-PRODUCING SOCIETY

As we saw in Chapter 7, it was toolmaking that allowed humans to consume significant amounts of meat as well as plant foods. The next truly momentous event in human history was the domestication of plants and animals (Figure 17.2). The transition from food forager to food producer (the available evidence suggests this change began 9,000 to 11,000 years ago) has been termed revolutionary. By changing the way they provided for their subsistence, people changed the very nature of human society.

Just why this change occurred is one of the important questions in anthropology. Since food production by and large requires more work than food foraging, is more monotonous, is often a less secure means of subsistence, and requires people to eat more of the types of foods foragers eat only when they have no other choice, it is unlikely people voluntarily became food producers. Initially, it appears food production arose as a largely unintended by-product of existing food-management practices. By chance, these promoted the development of new varieties of particular plants and animals, which came to take on increasing importance for peoples' subsistence. Later on, many populations adopted farming out of necessity in situations where population growth outstripped peoples' ability to sustain themselves through food foraging. For them, food production became a subsistence option of last resort.

THE SETTLED LIFE OF FARMERS

Whatever the causes, one of the most significant correlates of this new way of life was the development of permanent settlements where families of farmers lived together. As food foragers stay close to their food by moving around, farmers stay close to their food by staying near their gardens. The task of food production lent itself to a different kind of social organization; the hard work of some group members could provide food for all, thus freeing some people to devote their time to inventing and manufacturing the equipment needed for a new sedentary way of life. Harvesting and digging tools, pottery for storage and cooking, clothing made of woven textiles, and housing made of stone, wood, or sun-dried bricks were some of the results of this combination of new sedentary living conditions and altered division of labor.

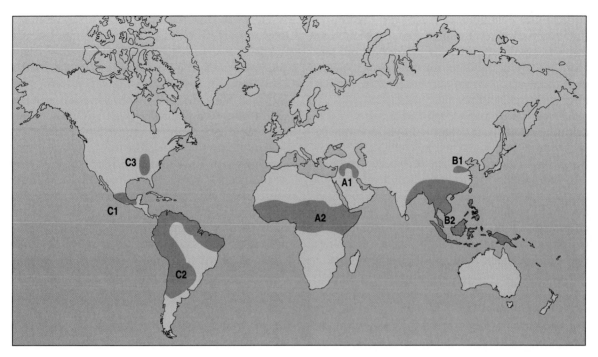

FIGURE 17.2

Early plant and animal domestication occurred in such widely scattered places as southwest Asia (A1), central Africa (A2), China (B1), Southeast Asia (B2), Mesoamerica (C1), South America (C2), and eastern North America (C3).

The transition also brought important changes in social structure. At first, social relations were egalitarian and hardly different from those that prevailed among food foragers. As settlements grew, however, and large numbers of people began to share the same important resources, such as land and water, society became more elaborately structured. Multifamily kinship groups such as lineages, which people belong to by virtue of descent from a common ancestor but which do not commonly play a large part in the social order of food foragers, were probably the organizing units. As will be discussed in Chapter 21, they provide a convenient way to handle the distinctive problems of land use and ownership that arise in food-producing societies.

Humans adapted to this new settled life in a number of ways. For example, some societies became horticultural—small communities of gardeners working with simple hand tools and using neither irrigation nor the plow. Horticulturists usually cultivate several varieties of crops together in small gardens they have cleared by hand. Be-

While it supports larger and more sedentary populations than food foraging, farming generally requires longer and more monotonous work.

cause these gardeners typically used a given garden plot for only a few years before abandoning it in favor of a new one, horticulture may be said to constitute an *extensive* form of agriculture. Production is for subsistence, rather than to produce a surplus for sale; however, the politics of horticultural communities commonly involve periodic feasts, when substantial amounts of produce and other gifts are given away to gain prestige. Such prestige is the basis for the political power of leaders, who play important roles in production, exchange, and resource allocation.

One of the most widespread forms of horticulture, especially in the tropics, is slash and burn, or **swidden farming**. Unfortunately, widespread use of fire to clear vast tracts of Amazonian or Indonesian forest for cattle raising and other development schemes has led many people to see slash-and-burn farming in a negative light. In fact, it is an ecologically sophisticated and sustainable way of raising food, especially in the tropics, when carried out under the right conditions: low population densities and adequate amounts of land. Only when pursued in the absence of these conditions does the practice lead to environmental degradation and destruction. Properly carried out, swidden farming mimics the diversity of the natural ecosystem; moreover, growing several crops together in the same field makes them less vulnerable to pests and plant diseases than growing single crops. Not only is the system ecologically sound, but also it is far more energy efficient than farming as carried out in developed countries such as the United States, which requires the input of more energy than comes out of the system. By contrast, for every unit of energy expended, slash-and-burn farming produces between 10 and 20 units in return. A good example of how such a system works is provided by the Mekranoti Kayapo Indians of Brazil's Amazon forest.

Swidden farming.   An extensive form of horticulture in which the natural vegetation is cut, the slash is subsequently burned, and crops then are planted among the ashes.

Gardens of the Mekranoti Kayapo[11]

The planting of a Mekranoti garden always follows the same sequence. First, men clear the forest and then burn the debris. In the ashes, both men and women plant sweet potatoes, manioc, bananas, corn, pumpkins, papaya, sugar cane, pineapple, cotton, tobacco, and annatto, whose seeds yield achiote, the red dye used for painting ornaments and people's bodies. Since the Mekranoti don't bother with weeding, the forest gradually invades the garden. After the second year, only manioc, sweet potatoes, and bananas remain. And after three years or so there is usually nothing left but bananas. Except for a few tree species that require hundreds of years to grow, the area will look like the original forest twenty-five or thirty years later.

This gardening technique, known as slash-and-burn agriculture, is one of the most common in the world. The early European settlers in North America adopted the method from the surrounding Indians, although it had been used in an earlier period in Europe as well. At one time critics condemned the technique as wasteful and ecologically destructive, but today we know that, especially in the humid tropics, slash-and-burn agriculture may be one of the best gardening techniques possible.

Anthropologists were among the first to note the possibly disastrous consequences of U.S.-style agriculture in the tropics. Continuous high temperatures encourage the growth of the microorganisms that cause rot, so

[11]Adapted from Werner, D. (1990). *Amazon journey* (pp. 105–112). Englewood Cliffs, NJ: Prentice Hall.

organic matter quickly breaks down into simple minerals. The heavy rains dissolve these valuable nutrients and carry them deep into the soils, out of the reach of plants. The tropical forest maintains its richness because the heavy foliage shades the earth, cooling it and inhibiting the growth of the decomposers. A good deal of the rain is captured by leaves before ever reaching the ground. When a tree falls in the forest, and begins to rot, other plants quickly absorb the nutrients that are released. With open-field agriculture, the sun heats the earth, the decomposers multiply, and the rains quickly leach the soils of their nutrients. In a few years a lush forest, if cleared for open one-crop agriculture, can be transformed into a barren wasteland.

Slash-and-burn agriculture is less of a problem than open-field agriculture. A few months after planting, banana and papaya trees shade the soil, just as the larger forest trees do. The mixing of different kinds of plants in the same area means that minerals can be absorbed as soon as they are released—corn picks up nutrients very fast, while manioc is slow. Also, the small and temporary clearings mean that the forest can quickly reinvade its lost territory.

Because decomposers need moisture as well as warmth, the long Mekranoti dry season could alter this whole picture of soil ecology. But soil samples from recently burned Mekranoti fields and the adjacent forest floor showed that, as in most of the humid tropics, the high fertility of the Indians' garden plots comes from the trees that are burned there, not from the soil, as in temperate climes.

Getting a good burn is a tricky operation. Perhaps for this reason its timing was left to the more experienced and knowledgeable members of the community. If the burn is too early, the rains will leach out the minerals in the ash before planting time. If too late, the debris will be too wet to burn properly. Then, insects and weeds that could plague the plants will not die and few minerals will be released into the soil. If the winds are too weak, the burn will not cover the entire plot. If they are too strong, the fire can get out of hand. In the past, the Mekranoti accidentally burned down villages several times because of fires that spread too fast.

Ronaldo remembered an incident when a garden fire caught some of the houses in the village. Fearing the flames would spread from one rooftop to the next until the entire village circle was ablaze, the Indians ran inside their homes and gathered their belongings to set them in the center of the village plaza. In the past, this reaction made good sense. Constructions were simpler, and people had fewer belongings to lose. Since moves were frequent anyway, destroying a village in smoke was not very serious. A fire could even get rid of insect pests that infest villages after many years. But this time people were more concerned. Ronaldo finally persuaded some of the Indians to chop down some of the houses next to the burning structures and the village was saved.

Shortly after the burning of the garden plots and the clearing away of some of the charred debris, people began the long job of planting, which took up all of September and lasted into October. Tákákngo returned in time to help Kaxti and his wife with their garden. Although he could not walk well enough to work, Kaxti could accompany his wife, Nhákkamro, to the garden and take care of their children, while she did most of the planting.

In the center of the circular garden plot the women dug holes and threw in a few pieces of sweet potatoes. After covering the tubers with dirt they usually asked a male—one of their husbands or anyone else who happened to be nearby—to stomp on the mound and make a ritual noise resembling a Bronx cheer. This magic would ensure a large crop, I was told. Forming a large ring around the sweet potatoes, the Indians rapidly thrust pieces of manioc stems into the ground, one after the other.

When grown, the manioc stems form a dense barrier to the sweet potato patch, and some of the plants must be cut down to gain entrance. Outside of the ring of manioc, the women plant yams, cotton, sugar cane, and annatto. Banana stalks and papaya trees, planted by simply throwing the seeds on the ground, form the outermost circle. The Indians also plant corn, pumpkins, watermelons, and pineapple throughout the garden. These grow rapidly and are harvested long before the manioc matures. The garden appears to change magically from corn and pumpkins to sweet potatoes and manioc without replanting.

Mekranoti gardens grew well. A few Indians complained now and then about a peccary that had eaten a watermelon they were looking forward to eating, or that had reduced their corn harvest. Capybara, large rodents usually found near the river banks, were known for their love of sugar cane, but in general the animals seemed to leave the crops alone. Even the leaf-cutting ants that are problems in other areas did not bother the Mekranoti. Occasionally a neighbor who had not planted a new garden would make off with a prized first-year crop, such as pumpkin, watermelon, or pineapple. But even these thefts were rare. In general, the Mekranoti could depend on harvesting whatever they planted.

Eventually, I wanted to calculate the productivity of Mekranoti gardens. Agronomists knew very little about slash-and-burn agriculture. They were accustomed to experiments in which a field was given over to one crop only, and in which the harvest happened all at once. Here, the plants were all mixed together, and people harvested piecemeal whenever they needed something. The manioc could stay in the ground, growing for several years before it was dug up.

I began measuring off areas of gardens to count how many manioc plants, ears of corn, or pumpkins were found there. The women thought it strange to see me struggling through the tangle of plants to measure off areas, 10 meters by 10 meters, placing string along the borders, and then counting what was inside. Sometimes I asked a woman to dig up all of the sweet potatoes within the marked-off area. The requests were bizarre, but the women cooperated just the same, holding on to the ends of the measuring tapes, or sending their children to help. For some plants, like bananas, I simply counted the number of clumps of stalks in the garden, and the number of banana bunches I could see growing in various clumps. By watching how long it took the bananas to grow, from the time I could see them until they were harvested, I could calculate a garden's total banana yield per year.

After returning from the field, I was able to combine the time allocation data with the garden productivities to get an idea of how hard the Mekranoti need to work to survive. The data showed that for every hour of gardening one Mekranoti adult produces almost 18,000 kilocalories of food. (As a basis for comparison, people in the United States consume approximately 3,000 kilocalories of food per day.) As insurance against bad years, and in case they receive visitors from other villages, they grow far more produce than they need. But even so, they don't need to work very hard to survive. A look at the average amount of time adults spend on different tasks every week shows just how easy going life in horticultural societies can be:

8.5 hours	Gardening
6.0 hours	Hunting
1.5 hours	Fishing
1.0 hour	Gathering wild foods
33.5 hours	All other jobs

Altogether, the Mekranoti need to work less than 51 hours a week, and this includes getting to and from work, cooking, repairing broken tools, and all of the other things we normally don't count as part of our work week.

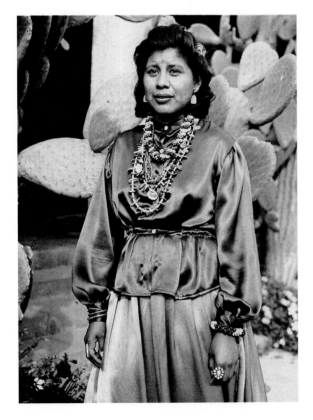

Although we tend to think of people as either food foragers or food producers, there are numerous examples of people like the Papago, shown here, who rely on a mix of wild and domesticated resources.

Technologically more complex than the horticulturists are intensive agriculturalists, whose practices usually result in far more modification of the landscape and ecology than those of horticulturalists. Employed are techniques such as irrigation, fertilizers, and the wooden or metal plow harnessed draft animals pull or, in the so-called developed countries of the world, tractors to produce food on large plots of land. Such farmers can grow sufficient food to provide not just for their own needs but for those of various full-time specialists as well. This surplus may be sold for cash, or it may be coerced out of the farmers through taxes or rent paid to landowners. These landowners and other specialists typically reside in substantial towns or cities where political power is centralized in the hands of a socially elite class of people. The distinction between horticulturalist and intensive agriculturalist is not always an easy one to make. For example, the Hopi Indians of the North American Southwest traditionally employed irrigation in their farming while using simple hand tools. Moreover, they produced for their own immediate needs and lived in towns without centralized political government.

As food producers, people have developed several major crop complexes: two adapted to seasonal uplands and two to tropical wetlands. In the dry uplands of southwest Asia, for example,

This swidden plot in Chiapas, Mexico, shows what such gardens look like after slash has been burned but before the crops have begun to grow. Although it looks destructive, if properly carried out, swidden farming is an ecologically sound way of growing crops in the tropics.

they time their agricultural activities with the rhythm of the changing seasons, cultivating wheat, barley, flax, rye, and millet. In the tropical wetlands of Southeast Asia, rice and tubers such as yams and taro are cultivated. In the Americas, people have adapted to environments similar to those of the Old World but have cultivated different plants. Maize, beans, squash, and the potato are typically grown in drier areas, whereas manioc is extensively grown in the tropical wetlands.

Pastoralism: The Bakhtiari

Before continuing about agriculturalists, we should examine one of the more striking examples of human adaptation to the environment, that of the **pastoralist**. Pastoralists live in societies that view animal husbandry as the proper way to make a living and consider movement of all or part of the society a normal and natural part of life. This cultural aspect is vitally important, for although

some (but not all) pastoral nomads are dependent on nearby farmers for some of their supplies, and may even earn more from nonpastoral sources than from their own herds, the concept of nomadic pastoralism remains central to their identities. These societies are built around a pastoral economic specialization but imbued with values far beyond just doing a job. This distinguishes them from American ranchers, who likewise have a pastoral economic specialization but identify culturally with a larger society.[12] It also sets them apart from food foragers, migrant farm workers, corporate executives, and others who are nomadic but not pastoralists.

Pastoralism is an effective way of living in places that are too dry, too cold, too steep, or too rocky for farming, such as the arid grasslands that stretch eastward from North Africa through the

[12]Barfield, T. J. (1984). Introduction. *Cultural Survival Quarterly, 8,* 2.

Pastoralist. Member of a society that regards animal husbandry as the ideal way of making a living and considers movement of all or part of the society a normal and natural way of life.

Pastoral nomadism is an adaptation that works in many parts of the world that are too hot, too cold, or too dry for farming. In high elevations in Peru and Bolivia, the Incas and other native people relied on the herding of llamas and alpacas.

Arabian Desert, across the plateau of Iran and into Turkestan and Mongolia. In Africa and southwest Asia alone, more than 21 million people follow pastoral nomadic ways of life. One group living in this belt of arid lands is the Bakhtiari, a fiercely independent people who live in the south Zagros Mountains of western Iran, where they tend herds of goats and fat-tailed sheep.[13] Although some of the Bakhtiari own horses and most own donkeys, they use these only for transport; the animals these people's lives revolve around are the sheep and goat.

[13]Material on the Bakhtiari is drawn mainly from the following: Barth, F. (1960). Nomadism in the mountain and plateau areas of south west Asia. *The problems of the arid zone* (pp. 341–355). Paris: UNESCO. Coon, C. S. (1958). *Caravan: The story of the Middle East* (2nd ed., Chap. 13). New York: Holt, Rinehart and Winston. Salzman, P. C. (1967). Political organization among nomadic peoples. *Proceedings of the American Philosophical Society, III,* 115–131.

The harsh, bleak environment dominates the lives of the Bakhtiari: It determines when and where they move their flocks, the clothes they wear, the food they eat, and even their dispositions —they have been called "mountain bears" by Iranian townspeople. In the Zagros are ridges that

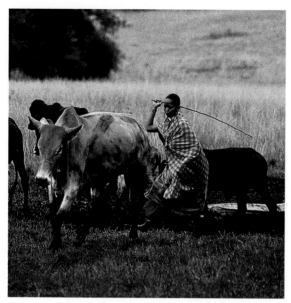

In East Africa, pastoral peoples are not dependent on farmers the way that pastoralists of the Middle East are.

reach altitudes of 12,000 to 14,000 feet. Their steep, rocky trails and escarpments challenge the hardiest and ablest climbers; jagged peaks, deep chasms, and watercourses with thunderous torrents also make living and traveling hazardous.

The pastoral life of the Bakhtiari revolves around two seasonal migrations to find better grazing lands for the flocks. Twice a year the people move: in the fall from their summer quarters in the mountains and in the spring from their winter quarters in the lowlands. This pattern of strict seasonal movement is known as **transhumance**. In the fall, before the harsh winter comes to the mountains, the nomads load their tents and other belongings on donkeys and drive their flocks down to the warm plains that border Iraq in the west; grazing land here is excellent and well watered in the winter. In the spring, when the low-lying pastures dry up, the Bakhtiari return to the mountain valleys, where a new crop of grass is sprouting. For this trek, they split into five groups, each

containing about 5,000 individuals and 50,000 animals.

The return trip north is the more dangerous because the mountain snows are melting and the gorges are full of turbulent, ice-cold water rushing down from the mountain peaks. This long trek is further impeded by the kids and lambs born in the spring, just before migration. Where the watercourses are not very deep, the nomads ford them. Deeper channels, including one river a half-mile wide, are crossed with the help of inflatable goatskin rafts, which they place infants, the elderly and infirm, and lambs and kids on; the rafts are then pushed by the men swimming alongside in the icy water. If they work from dawn to dusk, the nomads can get all of the people and animals across the river in 5 days. Not surprisingly, dozens of sheep are drowned each day at the river crossing.

In the mountain passes, where a biting wind numbs the skin and brings tears to the eyes, the Bakhtiari must make their way through slippery unmelted snow. Climbing the steep escarpments is dangerous, and the stronger men often must carry their own children and the newborn animals on their shoulders as they make their way over the ice and snow to the lush mountain valley that is their destination. During each migration the people may cover as many as 200 miles, and the trek can take weeks, because the flocks travel slowly and require constant attention. The nomads have fixed routes and a somewhat definite itinerary; generally, they know where they should be and when they should be there. On the drive the men and boys herd the sheep and goats, while the women and children along with the tents and other equipment ride the donkeys.

When they reach their destination, the Bakhtiari live in black tents of goat-hair cloth the women wove. The tents have sloping tops and vertical sides held up by wooden poles. Inside, the furnishings are sparse: Rugs the women wove or heavy felt pads cover the floor. Against one side of the tent are blankets; containers made of goatskin, copper utensils, clay jugs, and bags of

Transhumance. Pattern of strict seasonal movement between different environmental zones.

grain line the opposite side. Bakhtiari tents provide an excellent example of adaptation to a changing environment. The goat-hair cloth retains heat and repels water during the winter and keeps out heat during the summer. These portable homes are very easy to erect, take down, and transport.

Sheep and goats are central to Bakhtiari subsistence. The animals provide milk, cheese, butter, meat, hides, and wool, which is woven into clothes, tents, storage bags, and other essentials by the women or sold in towns. The people also engage in very limited horticulture; they own lands that contain orchards, and the nomads consume the fruit or sell it to townspeople. The division of labor is according to sex. The men, who take great pride in their marksmanship and horsemanship, engage in a limited amount of hunting on horseback, but their chief task is the tending of the flocks. The women cook, sew, weave, care for the children, and carry fuel and water.

The Bakhtiari have their own system of justice, including laws and a penal code. They are governed by tribal leaders, or *khans,* men who are elected or inherit their office. Because men own and control the livestock, women lack control of the economy and are relegated to the domestic sphere. This prominence of men in both economic and political affairs is common among pastoral nomads; theirs is very much a man's world. Thus, women typically occupy subordinate positions vis-à-vis men, even though elderly women eventually may gain a good deal of power. Most of the Bakhtiari *khans* grew wealthy when oil was discovered in their homeland around the start of the 20th century, and many of them are well educated, having attended Iranian or foreign universities. Despite this, and although some of them own houses in cities, the *khans* spend much of their lives among their people.

INTENSIVE AGRICULTURE AND NONINDUSTRIAL CITIES

With the intensification of agriculture, some farming communities grew into cities (Figure 17.3), where individuals who previously had been engaged in farming were freed to specialize in other activities. Thus, craft specialists such as carpenters, blacksmiths, sculptors, basketmakers, and stonecutters contribute to the vibrant, diversified life of the city.

Unlike horticulturalists and pastoralists, city dwellers are only indirectly concerned with adapting to their natural environment. Far more important is the need to adapt to living with and getting along with their fellow urbanites. To an important degree, this is true as well for the farmers who provide the city dwellers with their food. Under the political control of an urban elite, much of what the farmers do is governed by economic forces they have little, if any, control over. Urbanization brings with it a new social order: Marked inequality develops as society becomes stratified and people are ranked according to their gender, the kind of work they do, or the family they are born into. As social institutions cease to operate in simple, face-to-face groups of relatives, friends, and acquaintances, they become more formal and bureaucratic, with specialized political institutions.

With urbanization came a sharp increase in the tempo of human cultural evolution. Writing was invented, trade intensified and expanded, the wheel and the sail were invented, and metallurgy and other crafts were developed. In many early cities, monumental buildings, such as royal palaces and temples, were built by thousands of men, often slaves taken in war; these feats of engineering still amaze modern architects and engineers. The inhabitants of these buildings—the ruling class

anthropology applied
Agricultural Development and the Anthropologist

High up in the Andes mountains of South America, at an elevation of 2 miles above sea level, lies the vast intermontane plain known as the Bolivian Altiplano. On this plain, not far from where the modern countries of Bolivia, Chile, and Peru meet, is Lake Titicaca, the world's highest navigable body of water. A kilometer or so from this lake's south end stands the elaborate, monumental architecture of Tiwanaku, one of the most impressive archaeological sites in the region that, 500 years ago, constituted the southern quarter of the Inca Empire. Today, the region is a bleak and barren landscape, where some 20,000 Aymara Indians have a hard time producing enough food for their own survival.

Once thought to be strictly a ceremonial center with a small resident population, to which pilgrimages were made periodically from vast distances, we now know Tiwanaku was a major city, inhabited during its Classic Period (A.D. 375 to 725) by between 20,000 and 40,000 people. Another 200,000 or so people inhabited the surrounding Titicaca basin, all under the political control of Tiwanaku, a true imperial city that controlled a vast empire centuries before the Incas were anything but a relatively insignificant people living in the mountains some distance north of Tiwanaku. Its political control stretched well beyond the Altiplano into northern Chile and southern Peru, where administrative centers, satellite cities, and even colonies were established.

To support the huge population of the Altiplano, Tiwanaku carried out massive land reclamation, constructing an extensive system of raised and ridged fields where hardy crops could be intensively grown. These fields have been studied by anthropologist Alan Kolata of the University of Chicago. Built up to a height of 3 to 5 feet, the constituent materials of cobblestones, clay, gravel, and topsoil were carefully layered to prevent the buildup of crop-killing salt that leaches into the ground. Between the fields ran canals that filled with groundwater. (The water table here is but a few feet beneath the surface.) These 5-foot-wide trenches were oriented to soak up the maximum amount of solar heat during the day, thus acting as a kind of solar sump. One reason Altiplano agriculture today is so difficult is because of periodic frost; as much as 90% of a harvest can be lost as a result. In Tiwanaku times, however, the heat stored in the canals radiated over the fields' surface, raising the ambient temperatures as much as 2°C or 3°C, which is more than enough to prevent frost. In addition, the canals functioned as fertilizer factories. Organic sediments that settled in the canals could be scooped out at the end of each growing season and dumped on the fields, thereby renewing their fertility.

Having figured out how the system worked, in 1988, Kolata began to put his knowledge to work in the service of the Aymara farmers living in the region today.* In selected communities, Kolata has secured the cooperation of native farmers by guaranteeing a harvest, even if their experimental fields fail. Planting onions, beets, and potatoes, they have increased their yields significantly; not only do they get up to twice as many potatoes per plant, for instance, but also the potatoes are bigger and of better quality. Moreover, the farmers do not have to use scarce funds for fertilizer, since canal muck is free, and they are not causing pollution through use of chemical fertilizer.

By reintroducing an ancient technology that was lost following disintegration of the Tiwanaku empire some 1,000 years ago, Kolata is now improving the quality of life for countless Aymara Indians, reversing the poor harvests that have driven many men from the Altiplano to valleys south and east, where coca is grown to be turned into cocaine. Given the technique's success, Kolata predicts that, by the end of the 1990s, the ancient raised-field technology will be widely used not just in Bolivia but also in many other parts of South and Central America where it is suitable.

---

*Straughan, B. (1996). The secrets of ancient Tiwanaku are benefitting today's Bolivia. In W. A. Haviland & R. J. Gordon (Eds.), *Talking about people* (2nd ed., pp. 76–78). Mountain View, CA: Mayfield.

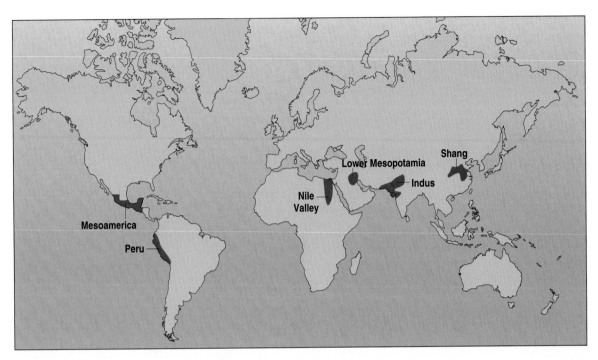

FIGURE 17.3

Locations of major early civilizations. Those of North and South America developed wholly independently of those in Africa and Asia. Chinese civilization may have developed independently of southwest Asian (including the Nile and Indus) civilization.

composed of nobles and priests—formed a central government that dictated social and religious rules; in turn, the merchants, soldiers, artisans, farmers, and other citizens carried out the rules.

Aztec City Life

The Aztec empire, which flourished in Mexico in the 16th century, is a good example of a highly developed urban society among non-Western peoples.[14] The capital city of the empire, Tenochtitlán (modern-day Mexico City), was located in a fertile valley 7,000 feet above sea level. Its population, along with that of its sister city, Tlatelolco, was about 200,000 in 1519, when Cortes first saw it. This makes it five times more populous than London at the same time. The Aztec metropolis

sat on an island in the middle of a lake, which has since dried up, and two aqueducts brought in fresh water from springs on the mainland. A 10-mile dike rimmed the eastern end of the city to prevent nearby salty waters from entering the lake around Tenochtitlán.

As in the early cities of southwest Asia, the foundation of Aztec society was intensive agriculture. Corn was the principal crop. Each family, allotted a plot of land by its lineage, cultivated any of a number of crops, including beans, squash, gourds, peppers, tomatoes, cotton, and tobacco. Unlike Old World societies, however, only a few animals were domesticated; these included dogs and turkeys (both for eating). Many of the crops were grown in around Tenochtitlán in plots actually constructed artificially in the shallow waters of the surrounding lake. Canals between these *chinampas* not only facilitated transport but were also a source of water plants used for heavy mulching. In addition, muck rich in fish feces was periodically dredged from the

[14]Most of the following information is taken from Berdan, F. F. (1982). *The Aztecs of central Mexico.* New York: Holt, Rinehart and Winston.

One form of intensive agriculture, the *chinampa*, was perfected in ancient Mexico. This picture is of a modern *chinampa* garden on the Gulf Coast of Mexico.

canals and spread over the gardens to maintain their fertility. Because they were incredibly productive as well as sustainable, *chinampas* still can be found today at Xochimilco on the outskirts of Mexico City.

Aztec agricultural success provided for an increasingly large population and the diversification of labor. Skilled artisans, such as sculptors, silversmiths, stone workers, potters, weavers, feather workers, and painters, could make good livings by pursuing these crafts exclusively. Since religion was central to the Aztec social order, these craftspeople were engaged continuously in the manufacture of religious artifacts, clothing, and decorations for buildings and temples. Other nonagricultural specialists included some of the warriors, the traveling merchants or *pochteca*, the priests, and the government bureaucracy of nobles.

As specialization increased, both among individuals and cities of the Aztec empire, the market became an extremely important economic and social institution. In addition to the daily markets in each city, larger markets were held in the various cities at different times of year. Buyers and sellers traveled to these from the far reaches of the empire. The market at Tlatelolco, Tenochtitlán's sister city, was so huge that the Spanish compared it to those of Rome and Constantinople. At the Aztec markets barter was the primary means of exchange. At times, however, cacao beans, gold dust, crescent-shaped knives, and copper were used as a kind of currency. In addition to its obvious economic use, the market served social functions: People went there not only to buy or to sell but also to meet other people and to hear the latest news. A law actually required that each person go to market at least once within a specified number of days; this ensured that the citizenry was kept informed of all important news. The other major economic institution, trade networks between the Aztec capital and other cities, brought goods such as chocolate, vanilla beans, and pineapples into Tenochtitlán.

The Aztec social order was stratified into three main classes: nobles, commoners, and serfs. The nobles, among whom gender inequality was most marked, operated outside the lineage system on the basis of land and serfs the ruler allotted them from conquered peoples. The commoners were divided into lineages they were dependent on for land. Within each of these, individual status depended on the degree of descent from the founder: Those more closely related to the lineage founder had higher status than those whose kinship was more distant. The third class in Aztec society consisted of serfs bound to the land and porters merchants employed as carriers. Lowest of this class were the slaves. Some voluntarily had sold themselves into bondage; others were captives taken in war.

The Aztecs were governed by a semidivine king, whom a council of nobles, priests, and leaders chose from among candidates of royal lineage.

Although the king was an absolute monarch, the councilors advised him on affairs of state. A vast number of government officials oversaw various functions, such as maintenance of the tax system and the courts of justice, management of government storehouses, and control of military training.

The typical Aztec city was rectangular and reflected the way the land was divided among the lineages. In the center was a large plaza containing the temple and the house of the city's ruler. At Tenochtitlán, with a total area of about 20 square miles, a huge temple and two lavish palaces stood in the central plaza, also called the Sacred Precinct. Surrounding this area were other ceremonial buildings belonging to each lineage.

As in a modern city, housing in Tenochtitlán ranged from squalid to magnificent. On the outskirts of the city, on *chinampas,* were the farmers' huts, built of wooden posts, thatched straw, and wattle plastered with mud. In the city proper were the houses of the middle class—graceful, multiroomed, single- and two-story stone and mortar buildings, each surrounding a flower-filled patio and resting on a stone platform for protection against floods. It is estimated Tenochtitlán

Model of the center of Tenochtitlán, the Aztec capital city.

The modern industrial city is a very recent human development, although its roots lie in the so-called preindustrial city. The widespread belief that preindustrial cities are things of the past and that industrial cities are things of the future is based upon culture-bound assumptions rather than established facts.

had about 60,000 houses. The focal points of the city were the *teocallis,* or pyramidal temples, where religious ceremonies, including human sacrifice, were held. The 100-foot-high double temple dedicated to the war god and the rain god was made of stone and featured a steep staircase leading to a platform with an altar, a chamber containing shrines, and an antechamber for the priests.

The palace of the emperor Moctezuma boasted numerous rooms for attendants and concubines, a menagerie, hanging gardens, and a swimming pool. Since Tenochtitlán sat in the middle of a lake, it was unfortified and connected to the mainland by three causeways. Communication among different parts of the city was easy, and people could travel either by land or by water. A series of canals, with footpaths beside them, ran throughout the city. The Spaniards who came to the Aztec capital reported that thousands of canoes plied the canals, carrying passengers and cargo around the city; these Europeans were so impressed by the communication network that they called Tenochtitlán the Venice of the New World.

NONINDUSTRIAL CITIES IN THE MODERN WORLD

Tenochtitlán is a good example of the kind of urban settlement characteristic of most ancient, nonindustrial civilizations. Commonly termed **preindustrial cities,** they are apt to be thought of as part of the past or as little more than stages in some sort of inevitable progression toward the kinds of industrial cities found today in places such as Europe and North America. This essentially ethnocentric view obscures the fact "preindustrial" cities are far from uncommon in the world today—

Preindustrial cities.   The kinds of urban settlements characteristic of nonindustrial civilizations.

especially in the so-called underdeveloped countries of the world. Furthermore, industrial cities have not yet come close to demonstrating they have the long-term viability shown by nonindustrial cities, which in some parts of the world have been around for not just hundreds but thousands of years.

CHAPTER SUMMARY

To meet their requirements for food, water, and shelter, people must adjust their behavior to suit their environment. This adjustment, which involves both change and stability, is a part of adaptation. Adaptation means a moving balance exists between a society's needs and its environmental potential. Adaptation also refers to the interaction between an organism and its environment, with each causing changes in the other. Adaptation is a continuing process, and it is essential for survival. An ecosystem is bound by the activities of organisms and by physical forces such as erosion. Human ecosystems must be considered in terms of all aspects of culture.

To fit into an ecosystem an organism must be able to adapt or become a part of it. Once such a fit is achieved, stability may serve the organism's interest more than change.

A culture area is a geographic region where various societies follow similar life patterns. Since geographic regions are not always uniform in climate and topography, new discoveries do not always spread to every group. Environmental variation also favors variation in technology, since needs may be quite different from area to area.

Julian Steward used the concept of culture type to explain variations within geographic regions. In this view a culture is considered in terms of a particular technology and of the particular environmental features that technology is best suited for.

The social and political organization of a society are other factors that influence how technology can be used to ensure survival. The features of a culture that play a part in the way the society makes a living are its culture core. Anthropologists can trace direct relationships between types of culture cores and types of environments.

The food-foraging way of life, the oldest and most universal type of human adaptation, requires that people move their residence according to changing food sources. For as yet unknown ecological and social factors, local group size is kept small. One explanation contends that small sizes fit the land capacity to sustain the groups. Another states that the fewer the people, the less the chance of social conflict. The primary mechanism for regulating population size among food foragers is frequent stimulation of female nipples, which prevents ovulation, as infants nurse several times an hour for several years.

Three important elements of human social organization probably developed along with scavenging and hunting for meat. These are a sexual division of labor, food sharing, and the camp as the center of daily activity and the place where food sharing occurs.

A characteristic of food-foraging societies is their egalitarianism. Since this way of life requires mobility, people accumulate only the material goods necessary for survival, so status differences are limited to those based on age and sex. Status differences associated with sex, however, do not imply subordination of women to men. Food resources are distributed equally throughout the groups; thus no individual can achieve the wealth or status hoarding might bring.

The reason for the transition from food foraging to food production, which began about 11,000 to 9,000 years ago, was likely the unforeseen result of increased management of wild food resources. One correlate of the food-producing revolution was the development of permanent settlements as people practiced horticulture using simple hand tools. One common form of horticulture is slash-and-burn, or swidden, farming. Intensive agriculture, a more complex activity, requires irrigation, fertilizers, and draft animals.

Pastoralism is a means of subsistence that relies on raising herds of domesticated animals, such as cattle, sheep, and goats. Pastoralists are usually nomads, moving to different pastures as required for grass and water.

Cities developed as intensified agricultural techniques created a surplus, freeing individuals to specialize full-time in other activities. Social structure becomes increasingly stratified with the development of cities, and people are ranked according to gender, the work they do, and the family they are born into. Social relationships grow more formal, and centralized political institutions are formed.

One should not conclude that the sequence from food-foraging to horticultural/pastoral to intensive agricultural to nonindustrial urban and then industrial societies is inevitable, even though these did appear in that order. Where older adaptations continue to prevail, it is because conditions are such that they continue to work so well and provide such satisfaction that the people who maintain them prefer them to the alternatives, which they are aware of. It is not because of any "backwardness" or ignorance. Modern food-foraging, horticultural, pastoral, nonindustrial, and industrial urban societies are all highly evolved adaptations, each in its own particular way.

POINTS FOR CONSIDERATION

1. Is change always adapative? What are examples of nonadaptive change within North American culture?

2. The Incas of South America did not have or widely use the wheel or the concept of zero. Does this mean Incan culture might have been nonadaptive?

3. Is cultural change or increasing technical complexity the same as progress? Why or why not? Do you believe in human "progress"? If so, in what sense do we progress?

SUGGESTED READINGS

Bates, D. G., & Plog, F. (1991). *Human adaptive strategies*. New York: McGraw-Hill.

This book takes an ecological approach to understanding human cultural diversity. A chapter each is devoted to hunting and gathering, horticultural, pastoral, intensive agricultural, and industrial societies, with a final chapter devoted to change and development. Theoretical issues are made easy to grasp through use of readable ethnographic cases.

Lustig-Arecco, V. (1975). *Technology: Strategies for survival*. New York: Holt, Rinehart and Winston.

Although the early anthropologists devoted a good deal of attention to technology, the subject fell into neglect early in the 20th century. This is one of the few more recent studies of the subject. The author's particular interest is the technoeconomic adaptation of hunters, pastoralists, and farmers.

Oswalt, W. H. (1972). *Habitat and technology*. New York: Holt, Rinehart and Winston.

The author develops a taxonomy that permits precise cross-cultural comparisons of the complexity of manufactures. The research is based on a systematic analysis of the known manufactures of non-Western peoples. Shelters, tools, clothing, implements, and cultivated foodstuffs are considered.

Schrire, C. (Ed.). (1984). *Past and present in hunter gatherer studies*. Orlando, FL: Academic Press.

This collection of papers demolishes many a myth (including several anthropologists hold) about food-foraging societies. Especially recommended is the editor's introduction, "Wild Surmises on Savage Thoughts."

Vayda, A. (Ed.). (1969). *Environment and cultural behavior: Ecological studies in cultural anthropology.* Garden City, NY: Natural History Press.

The focus of the studies collected here is the interrelationship between cultural behavior and environmental phenomena. The writers attempt to make cultural behavior intelligible by relating it to the material world it develops in. This volume includes articles concerning population, divination, ritual, warfare, food production; climate, and diseases.

Chapter 18
ECONOMIC SYSTEMS

THE FUNDAMENTAL CHARACTERISTIC OF THE
MARKET IN NON-WESTERN SOCIETIES IS THAT IT
ALWAYS MEANS A LITERAL MARKETPLACE, WHERE
ACTUAL GOODS ARE EXCHANGED. AT THIS
MARKET IN THAILAND, PEOPLE EXCHANGE ITEMS
THEY HAVE PRODUCED FOR THINGS THEY NEED
BUT CAN ONLY GET FROM OTHERS.

Chapter Preview

How Do Anthropologists Study Economic Systems?

Anthropologists study how goods are produced, distributed, and consumed in the context of the total culture of particular societies. Although they have borrowed theories and concepts from economists, most anthropologists feel principles derived from the study of Western market economies have limited applicability to economic systems where people do not produce and exchange goods for profit.

How Do the Economies of Nonindustrial Peoples Work?

In non-Western, nonindustrial societies, there is always a division of labor by age and sex, with some additional craft specialization. Land and other valuable resources usually are controlled by groups of relatives, such as bands or lineages, and individual ownership is rare. Production takes place in the quantity and at the time required, and most goods are consumed by the group that produces them. Leveling mechanisms ensure that no one accumulates significantly more goods than anyone else.

How and Why Are Goods Exchanged in Nonindustrial Societies?

Nonindustrial peoples exchange goods through the processes of reciprocity, redistribution, and market exchange. *Reciprocity* involves the exchange of goods and services of roughly equivalent value, and it is often undertaken for ritual purposes or in order to gain prestige. *Redistribution* requires some sort of government and/or religious elite to collect and then reallocate resources in the form of either goods or services. *Market exchange,* which in nonindustrial societies means going to a specific place for direct exchange of goods, also serves as entertainment and as a way to exchange important information. The latter two are frequently primary motivating forces bringing people into the marketplace.

An economic system may be defined as a means of producing, distributing, and consuming goods. Since a people, in pursuing a particular means of subsistence, necessarily produces, distributes, and consumes goods, it is obvious that our earlier discussion of subsistence patterns (Chapter 17) involved economic matters. Yet economic systems encompass much more than we so far have covered. This chapter will look at aspects of economic systems—specifically systems of production, exchange, and redistribution—that require more discussion than possible in the previous chapter.

ECONOMIC ANTHROPOLOGY

It is in the study of the economies of nonliterate peoples that we are perhaps most apt to fall prey to interpreting anthropological data in terms of our own technologies, our own values of work and property, and our own determination of what is rational. Take, for example, the following statement from just one respected textbook in economics: "In all societies, the prevailing reality of life has been the inadequacy of output to fill the wants and needs of the people."[1] This ethnocentric assertion fails to realize that in many societies people's wants are maintained at levels that can be fully and continuously satisfied, and without jeopardizing the environment. In such societies, goods and services are produced in the quantity and at the time required, and to do more than this makes no sense at all. Thus, no matter how hard people may work when hard work is called for, at other times they will have available hours, days, or even weeks on end to devote to "unproductive" (in the economic sense) activities. To Western observers, such people are apt to appear lazy (Figure 18.1); "instead of disciplined workers, they are reluctant and untrained laborers."[2] If the people happen to be hunters and gatherers, even the hard work is likely to be misinterpreted. In Western culture hunting is defined as a "sport"; hence, the men in

food-foraging societies often are perceived as spending virtually all of their time in "recreational pursuits," while the women are seen as working themselves to the bone.

The point here is that to understand how the schedule of wants or demands of a given society is balanced against the supply of goods and services available, it is necessary to introduce a noneconomic variable—the anthropological variable of culture. In any given economic system, economic processes cannot be interpreted without culturally defining the demands and understanding the conventions that dictate how and when they are satisfied. The fact is, the economic sphere of behavior is *not* separate from the social, religious, and political spheres and thus not free to follow its own purely economic logic. To be sure, economic behavior and institutions can be analyzed in purely economic terms, but to do so is to ignore crucial noneconomic considerations.

As a case in point, we may look briefly at yam production among the Trobriand Islanders, who inhabit a group of coral atolls that lie north of New Guinea's eastern end.[3] Trobriand men spend a great deal of their time and energy raising yams, not for themselves or their own households but to give to others, normally their sisters and married daughters. The purpose of this yam production is not to provision the households they are given to, because most of what people eat they grow for themselves in gardens where they plant taro, sweet potatoes, tapioca, greens, beans, and squash, as well as breadfruit and banana trees. The reason a man gives yams to a woman is to show his support for her husband and to enhance his own influence.

Once received by the woman, they are loaded into her husband's yam house, symbolizing his worth as a man of power and influence in his community. Some of these yams he may use to purchase a variety of things, including arm shells, shell necklaces and earrings, betel nuts, pigs, chickens, and locally produced goods such as wooden bowls, combs, floor mats, lime pots, and even magic spells. Some he must use to discharge obligations, as in the presentation of yams to the rel-

[1]Heilbroner, R. L., & Thurow, L. C. (1981). *The economic problem* (6th ed., p. 327). Englewood Cliffs, NJ: Prentice-Hall.
[2]Ibid., p. 609.
[3]Weiner, A. B. (1988). *The Trobrianders of Papua New Guinea*. New York: Holt, Rinehart and Winston.

The Chief Registrar of Natives,
NAIROBI.

N.A.D. Form No 54/_____

COMPLAINT OF DESERTION OF REGISTERED NATIVE

Native's Certificate No. _____ Name _____

The above native deserted from my employ_____
                                                                    (date)

He was engaged _____ on _____ days verbal contract
                    (date)
                                         _____ months written contract

at _____
                          (place)   *(Contract No.)*

    I wish to prosecute him for this offence and hereby agree to appear as a witness or
to produce evidence if and when called upon.

                                                    _____
                                                    Signature of Employer

Address _____

Date _____

FIGURE 18.1

People with industrial economies frequently misunderstand the work ethic in so-
called tribal societies. Thus the British in colonial Kenya thought it necessary to
teach natives "the dignity of labor" and made it a crime for a tribal person to quit
work without authorization.

atives of his daughter's husband when she marries
or making required payments following the death
of a member of his lineage (an organized group of
relatives descended, in this case through women,
from a common ancestor). Finally, any man who
aspires to high status and power is expected to
show his worth by organizing a yam competition,
in the course of which he gives away huge quantities of yams to invited guests. As anthropologist
Annette Weiner explains: "A yam house, then, is
like a bank account; when full, a man is wealthy
and powerful. Until yams are cooked or they rot,
they may circulate as limited currency. That is why,
once harvested, the usage of yams for daily food
is avoided as much as possible."[4]

By giving yams to his sister or daughter, a man
not only expresses his confidence in the woman's
husband, but he also makes the latter indebted to
him. Although the recipient rewards the gardener

and his helpers by throwing a feast, at which they
are fed cooked yams, taro, and—what everyone
especially looks forward to—ample pieces of pork,
this in no way pays off the debt. Nor does the gift
of a stone axe blade (another valuable in the Trobriand system), which may reward an especially
good harvest. The debt can be repaid only in
women's wealth, which consists of bundles of banana leaves and skirts made of the same material
dyed red.

Although the bundles are of no utilitarian
value, extensive labor is invested in their production, and large quantities of them, along with
skirts, are regarded as essential for paying off all
the members of other lineages who were close to
a recently deceased relative in life and who assisted
with the funeral. Also, the wealth and vitality of
the dead person's lineage is measured by the quality and quantity of the bundles and skirts so distributed. Because a man has received yams from
his wife's brother, he is obligated to provide his
wife yams for purchasing the necessary bundles

[4]Ibid., p. 86.

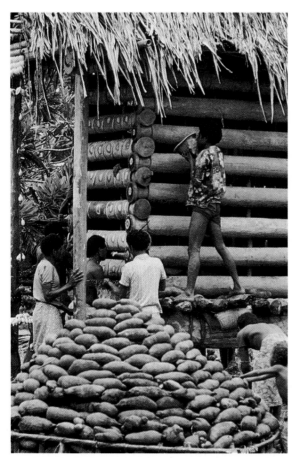

Trobriand Island men devote a great deal of time and energy to raising yams, not for themselves but to give to others. These yams, which have been raised by men related through marriage to a chief, are about to be loaded into the chief's yam house.

and skirts, beyond those she has produced, to help with payments following the death of a member of her lineage. Because deaths are unpredictable, a man must have yams available for his wife when she needs them. This, and the fact she may require all of his yams, acts as an effective check on a man's wealth.

Like people the world over, the Trobriand Islanders assign meanings to objects that make the objects worth far more than their cost in labor or materials. Yams, for example, establish long-term relationships that lead to other advantages, such as access to land, protection, assistance, and other kinds of wealth. Thus, yam exchanges are as much

social and political transactions as they are economic transactions. Banana leaf bundles and skirts, for their part, are symbolic of the political state of lineages and of their immortality. In their distribution, which is related to rituals associated with death, we see how men in Trobriand society are ultimately dependent on women and their valuables. So important are these matters to the Trobrianders that even in the face of Western money, education, religion, and law, these people remain as committed today as in the past to yam cultivation and the production of women's wealth. Viewed in terms of Western economics, these activities appear to make little sense, but viewed in terms of Trobriand values and concerns, they make a great deal of sense.

RESOURCES

In every society customs and rules govern the kinds of work done, who does the work, who controls the resources and tools, and how the work is accomplished. Raw materials, labor, and technology are the productive resources a social group may use to produce desired goods and services. The rules surrounding the use of these resources are embedded in the culture and determine the way the economy operates.

PATTERNS OF LABOR

Every human society always has a division of labor by both sex and age categories; such division is an elaboration of patterns found among all higher primates. Dividing by sex increases the chances that the learning of necessary skills will be more efficient, since only half the adult repertoire needs to be learned by any individual. Dividing by age provides sufficient time for developing those skills.

Sexual Division of Labor

Anthropologists have studied extensively the sexual division of labor in human societies of all sorts, and we discussed some aspects of it in Chapter 17, as well as in Chapter 7. Whether men or women do a particular job varies from group to group,

Often, work that is considered inappropriate for men (or for women) in one society is performed by them in another. Here, a laudryman works in Bangalore, India, and Indian women work on construction.

but much work has been set apart as the work of either one sex or the other. For example, we have seen that the tasks most often regarded as "women's work" tend to be those that can be carried out near home and that are easily resumed after interruption. The tasks most often regarded as "men's work" tend to be those that require physical strength, rapid mobilization of high bursts of energy, frequent travel at some distance from home, and assumption of high levels of risk and danger. However, plenty of exceptions occur, as in societies where women regularly carry burdensome loads or put in long hours of hard work cultivating crops in the fields. In some societies, women perform almost three quarters of all work, and there are even societies where women serve as warriors. In the 19th-century kingdom of Dahomey, in West Africa, thousands of women served in the armed forces of the Dahomean king and in the eyes of some observers were better fighters than their male counterparts. Also, references to women warriors in ancient Ireland exist, archae-

ological evidence indicates their presence among the Vikings, and among the Abkhasians of Georgia women were trained in weaponry until quite recently. In modern guerilla uprisings, women frequently fight. Clearly, the sexual division of labor cannot be explained simply as a consequence of male strength, expendability, or female reproductive biology.

Instead of looking for biological imperatives to explain the sexual division of labor, a more productive strategy is to examine the kinds of work men and women do in the context of specific societies to see how the work relates to other cultural and historical factors. Researchers find three configurations, one featuring flexibility and sexual integration, another involving rigid segregation by sex, and a third combining elements of the other two.[5] The flexible/integrated pattern is

[5]Sanday, P. R. (1981). *Female power and male dominance: On the origins of sexual inequality* (pp. 79–80). Cambridge, England: Cambridge University Press.

In nonindustrial societies, households produce much of what they consume. Among the Maya, men work in the fields to produce foods for the household; women prepare the food and take care of other chores that can be performed in or near the house.

exemplified by people such as the Ju/'hoansi (whose practices we examined in Chapters 16 and 17) and is seen most often among food foragers and subsistence farmers. In such societies, both sexes perform up to 35% of activities with approximately equal participation, while tasks deemed appropriate for one sex may be performed by the other, without loss of face, as the situation warrants. Where these practices prevail, boys and girls grow up in much the same way, learn to value cooperation over competition, and become equally habituated to adult men and women, who interact with one another on a relatively equal basis.

Sexually segregated societies rigidly define almost all work as either masculine or feminine, so men and women rarely engage in joint efforts of any kind. In such societies, it is inconceivable someone would even think of doing something considered the work of the opposite sex! This pattern is frequently seen in pastoral nomadic, intensive agricultural, and industrial societies, where men's work keeps them outside the home for much of the time. Thus, boys and girls alike are raised primarily by women, who encourage compliance in their charges. At some point, however, boys

must undergo a role reversal to become like men, who are supposed to be tough, aggressive, and competitive. To do this they must prove their masculinity in ways women do not to prove their feminine identity. Commonly, this involves assertions of male superiority, and hence authority, over women. Historically, sexually segregated societies often have imposed their control on societies featuring sexual integration, upsetting the egalitarian nature of the latter.

In the third, or dual sex, configuration, men and women carry out their work separately, as in sexually segregated societies, but the relationship between them is one of balanced complementarity, rather than inequality. Although competition is a prevailing ethic, each sex manages its own affairs, and the interests of both men and women are represented at all levels. Thus, as in sexually integrated societies, neither sex exerts dominance over the other. The dual sex orientation may be seen among certain Native American peoples whose economies were based on subsistence farming, as well as among several West African kingdoms, including that of the aforementioned Dahomeans.

Age Division of Labor

Dividing labor according to age is also typical of human societies. Among the Ju/'hoansi, for example, children are not expected to contribute significantly to subsistence until they reach their late teens. Indeed, until they possess adult levels of strength and endurance, many "bush foods"—edible tubers, for example—are not readily accessible to them. The Ju/'hoansi equivalent of "retirement" comes somewhere around the age of 60. Elderly people, although they usually will do some foraging for themselves, are not expected to contribute much food. However, older men and women alike play an essential role in spiritual matters; freed from food taboos and other restrictions that apply to younger adults, they may handle ritual substances considered dangerous to those still involved with hunting or having children. By virtue of their old age, they also remember things that happened far in the past. Thus, they are repositories of accumulated wisdom—the "libraries" of a nonliterate people—and can suggest solutions to problems younger adults have never before had to face. Thus, they are far from being unproductive members of society.

In some food-foraging societies, women do continue to make a significant contribution to provisioning in their older years. Among the Hadza of Tanzania, their contribution is critical to their daughters, whose foraging abilities are significantly impaired when they have new infants to nurse. Lactation is energetically expensive, while holding, carrying, and nursing an infant interfere with the mother's foraging efficiency. Those most immediately affected by this are a woman's weaned children who are not yet old enough to forage effectively for themselves. The problem is overcome, however, by the foraging efforts of grandmothers, whose time spent foraging is greatest when their infant grandchildren are youngest and their weaned grandchildren receive the least food from their mothers.[6]

In many nonindustrial societies, not just older people but children as well may make a greater contribution to the economy in terms of work and responsibility than is common in modern North America. For instance, in Maya communities in southern Mexico and Guatemala, young children not only look after their younger brothers and sisters but help with housework as well. Girls begin to make a substantial contribution to household work by age 7 or 8 and by age 11 are constantly busy grinding corn, making tortillas, fetching wood and water, sweeping the house, and so forth. Boys have less to do but are given small tasks, such as bringing in the chickens or playing with a baby; by age 12, however, they are carrying toasted tortillas to the men out working in the fields and returning with loads of corn.[7]

Similar situations are not unknown in industrial societies. In Naples, Italy, children play a significant role in the economy. At a very young age, girls begin to take on responsibilities for housework, freeing the labor of their mothers and older sisters for earning money for the household. Nor is it long before girls are apprenticed out to neighbors and kin, who teach them skills that enable them, by age 14, to enter a small factory or workshop. The wages earned are typically turned over to the girls' mothers. Boys, too, are also apprenticed out at an early age, though they may achieve more freedom from adult control by becoming involved in various street activities not available to girls.[8]

The use of child labor has become a matter of increasing concern as large corporations rely more frequently on the manufacture of goods in the world's poorer countries. Although reliable figures are hard to come by, it is estimated that there are some 15 million indentured child laborers in south Asia alone, including some as young as 4 years old. Each year, the United States imports at least $100 million worth of products children manufacture, ranging from rugs and carpets to clothing

---

[6]Hawkes, K., O'Connell, J. F., & Blurton Jones, N. G. (1997). Hadza women's time allocation, offspring, provisioning, and the evolution of long postmenopausal life spans. *Current Anthropology, 38,* 551–577.

[7]Vogt, E. Z. (1990). *The Zinacantecos of Mexico, a modern Maya way of life* (2nd ed., pp.83–87). Fort Worth: Holt, Rinehart and Winston.

[8]Goddard, V. (1993). Child labor in Naples. In W. A. Haviland & R. J. Gordon (Eds.), *Talking about people* (pp. 105–109). Mountain View CA: Mayfield.

This Thai girl exemplifies the use of child labor in many parts of the world, often by large corporations. Even in Western countries, child labor plays a major economic role.

and soccer balls.[9] In 1990, President Clinton signed into law legislation that would prevent importation of products made by children who are indentured servants, but how effectively it can be enforced still remains to be seen.

Cooperation

Cooperative work groups can be found everywhere in nonliterate as well as literate and in nonindustrial as well as industrial societies. Often, if the effort involves the whole community, a festive spirit permeates the work. Jomo Kenyatta, the anthropologist who later became a respected statesman and "father" of an independent Kenya, described the time of enjoyment after a day's labor in his country:

If a stranger happens to pass by, he will have no idea that these people who are singing and dancing have completed their day's work. This is why most Europeans have erred by not realizing that the African in his own environment does not count hours or work by the movement of the clock, but works with good spirit and enthusiasm to complete the tasks before him.[10]

In some parts of East Africa, work parties begin with the display of a pot of beer to be consumed after the tasks have been finished. Yet, the beer is not payment for the work; indeed, the labor involved is worth far more than the beer consumed. Rather, the beverage is more of a symbol, whereas recompense comes as individuals sooner or later participate in work parties for others.

Among the Ju/'hoansi, women's work is frequently highly social. About three times a week, they go out to gather wild plant foods away from the camp. Although they may do this alone, they more often go out in groups, talking loudly all the while. This not only turns what might otherwise seem a monotonous task into a social occasion, but it also causes large animals—potential sources of danger—to move elsewhere.

In most human societies, the basic cooperative unit is the household. It is both a unit of production and consumption; only in industrial societies have these two activities been separated. The Maya farmer, for example, unlike his North American counterpart (but like peasant and subsistence farmers everywhere), is not so much running a commercial enterprise as he is a household. He is motivated by a desire to provide for the welfare of his own family; each family, as an economic unit, works as a group for its own good. Cooperative work may be undertaken outside the household, however, for other reasons, though not always voluntarily. It may be part of fulfilling duties to inlaws, or it may be performed for political officials or priests by command. Thus, institutions of family, kinship, religion, and the state all may act as organizing elements that define the nature and condition of each worker's cooperative obligations.

[9]It's the law: Child labor protection. (1997, November/December). *Peace and Justice News,* 11.

[10]Herskovits, M. (1952). *Economic anthropology: A study in comparative economics* (2nd ed., p.103). New York: Knopf.

Craft Specialization

In nonindustrial societies, where division of labor occurs along lines of age and sex, each person in the society has knowledge and competence in all aspects of work appropriate to his or her age and sex. In modern industrial societies, by contrast, a greater diversity of more specialized tasks to be performed exists, and no individual even can begin to know all those appropriate for his or her age and sex. Yet even in nonindustrial societies some specialization of craft occurs. This is often minimal in food-foraging societies, but even here the arrow points of one man may be in some demand because of his particular skill at making them. Among people who produce their own food, specialization is more apt to occur. In the Trobriand Islands, for example, if a man wanted stone

In industrial societies, people do not have unrestricted access to the means of production, nor do they generally produce directly for their own consumption. Instead, they work for strangers, often at monotonous tasks done in a depersonalized setting. Such conditions contribute to alienation, a major problem in industrial societies.

to make axe blades, he had to travel some distance to a particular island where the appropriate kind of stone was quarried; clay pots, however, were made by people living on yet another island.

One example of specialization is afforded by the Afar people of Ethiopia's Danakil Depression. Afar men are miners of salt, which since ancient times has been widely traded in East Africa. It is mined from the crust of an extensive salt plain in the north part of the depression, and to get it is a risky and difficult business. L. M. Nesbitt, the first European to successfully traverse the depression, labeled it "the hell-hole of creation."[11] The heat is extreme during the day, with shade temperatures between 140°F and 156°F not unusual. Shade is not found on the salt plain, however, unless a shelter of salt blocks is built. Nor is there food or water for man or beast. To add to the difficulty, until recently the Muslim Afars and the Christian Tegreans, highlanders who also mine salt, were mortal enemies.

Successful mining, then, requires specialized skills at planning and organization, as well as physical strength and the will to work under the most trying conditions.[12] Pack animals to carry the salt have to be fed in advance, for carrying sufficient fodder for them interferes with their ability to carry out salt. Food and water must be carried for the miners, who usually number 30 to 40 per group. Travel is planned to take place at night to avoid the intense heat of day. In the past, measures to protect against attack had to be taken. Finally, timing is critical; a party has to return to sources of food and water before these supplies are too long exhausted and before the animals are unable to continue farther.

CONTROL OF LAND

All societies have regulations that determine the way valuable land resources will be allocated. Food foragers must determine who can hunt game

---

[11]Nesbitt, L. M. (1935). *Hell-hole of creation.* New York: Knopf.

[12]Mesghinua, H. M. (1966). Salt mining in Enderta. *Journal of Ethiopian Studies, 4* (2). O'Mahoney, K. (1970). The salt trade. *Journal of Ethiopian Studies, 8* (2).

and gather plants and where these activities take place. Horticulturists must decide how their farmland is to be acquired, worked, and passed on. Pastoralists require a system that determines rights to watering places and grazing land, as well as the right of access to land they move their herds over. Full-time or intensive agriculturalists must have some means of determining title to land and access to water supplies for irrigation. In industrialized Western societies, a system of private ownership of land and rights to natural resources generally prevails. Although elaborate laws have been enacted to regulate the buying, owning, and selling of land and water resources, if individuals wish to reallocate valuable farmland, for instance, to some other purpose, they generally can.

In nonindustrial societies, land is often controlled by kinship groups such as the lineage (discussed in Chapter 21) or band, rather than by individuals. For example, among the Ju/'hoansi, each band of anywhere from 10 to 30 people lives on roughly 250 square miles of land, which they consider their territory—their own country. These territories are defined not in terms of boundaries but in terms of water holes located within them. The land is said to be "owned" by those who have lived the longest in the band, usually a group of brothers and sisters or cousins. Their ownership, however, is more symbolic than real. They cannot sell (or buy) land, but outsiders must ask their permission to enter the territory. To refuse such permission, though, would be unthinkable.

The practice of defining territories on the basis of core features, be they water holes (as among the Ju/'hoansi), distinctive landscape features where ancestral spirits are thought to dwell (as among Australian Aborigines), watercourses (as among Indians of the northeastern United States), or whatever, is typical of food foragers. Territorial boundaries are left vaguely defined at best. The adaptive value of this is clear: The size of band territories, as well as the size of the bands, can adjust to keep in balance with availability of resources in any given place. Such adjustment would be more difficult under a system of individual ownership of clearly bounded land.

Among some West African farmers, a feudal system of land ownership prevails: All land is said to belong to the head chief. He allocates it to various subchiefs, who in turn distribute it to lineages; lineage leaders then assign individual plots to each farmer. Just as in medieval Europe, these African people owe allegiance to the subchiefs (or nobles) and the principal chief (or king). The people who work the land must pay taxes and fight for the king when necessary. Yet these people do not really own the land; rather, it is a form of lease. As long as the land is kept in use, rights to such use will pass to their heirs. No user, however, can give away, sell, or otherwise dispose of a plot of land without approval from the elder of the lineage. When an individual no longer uses the allocated land, it reverts to the lineage head, who reallocates it to some other member of the lineage. The important operative principle here is that the system extends the individual's right to use land for an indefinite period, but the land is not "owned" outright. This serves to maintain the integrity of valuable farmland as such, preventing its loss through subdivision and conversion to other uses.

TECHNOLOGY

All societies have some means of creating and allocating the tools and other artifacts used for producing goods and passed on to succeeding generations. The number and kinds of tools a society uses—which, together with knowledge about how to make and use them, constitute its **technology**—are related to the lifestyles of its members. Food foragers and pastoral nomads, who are frequently on the move, are apt to have fewer and simpler tools than the more sedentary farmer, in part because a great number of complex tools would decrease their mobility.

Food foragers make and use a variety of tools, and many are ingenious in their effectiveness. Some of these they make for their individual use, but codes of generosity are such that a person may not refuse giving or loaning what is requested. Thus, tools may be given or loaned to others in exchange for the products resulting from their use.

Technology. Tools and other material equipment, together with the knowledge of how to make and use them.

Among the Ju/'hoansi, game "belongs" to the man whose arrow killed it. But because arrows are freely loaned or given, the man who "owns" the kill may not even have been present on the hunt.

For example, a Ju/'hoansi who gives his arrow to another hunter has a right to a share in any animals the hunter kills. Game is considered to "belong" to the man whose arrow killed it, even when he is not present on the hunt.

Among horticulturists, the axe, machete, and digging stick or hoe are the primary tools. Since these are relatively easy to produce, every person can make them. Although the maker has first rights to their use, when that person is not using them, any family member may ask to use them and usually is granted permission to do so. Refusal would cause people to treat the tool owner with scorn for this singular lack of concern for others. If a relative helps another raise the crop traded for a particular tool, that relative becomes part owner of the implement, and it may not be traded or given away without his or her permission.

In sedentary communities, which farming makes possible, tools and other productive goods are more complex and more difficult and costlier to make. Where this happens, individual ownership usually is more absolute, as are the conditions

persons may borrow and use such equipment under. It is easy to replace a knife lost by a relative during palm cultivation but much more difficult to replace an iron plow or a power-driven threshing machine. Rights to the ownership of complex tools are more rigidly applied; generally, the person who has funded the purchase of a complex piece of machinery is considered the sole owner and may decide how and by whom it will be used.

LEVELING MECHANISMS

In spite of the increased opportunities in sedentary farming communities for people to accumulate belongings, limits on property acquisition may be as prominent in them as among nomadic peoples. In such communities, social obligations compel people to divest themselves of wealth, and no one is permitted to accumulate too much more than others. Greater wealth simply brings greater obligation to give. Anthropologists refer to such obligations as **leveling mechanisms**.

Leveling mechanism.   A societal obligation compelling a family to distribute goods so that no one accumulates more wealth than anyone else.

Leveling mechanisms are found in communities where property must not be allowed to threaten a more-or-less egalitarian social order, as in many Maya villages and towns in the highlands of Mexico and Guatemala. In these communities, *cargo systems* function to siphon off any excess wealth people may accumulate. A cargo system is a civil-religious hierarchy, which, on a revolving basis, combines most of a community's civic and ceremonial offices. All offices are open to all men, and eventually virtually every man has at least one term in office, each term lasting for 1 year. The scale is pyramidal, which means more offices exist at the lower levels, with progressively fewer toward the top. For example, a community of about 8,000 people may have four levels of offices, with 32 on the lowest level, 12 on the next one up, 6 on the next, and 2 at the apex. Positions at the lowest level include those for the performance of various menial chores, such as sweeping and carrying messages. The higher offices are councilmen, judges, mayors, and ceremonial positions. All offices are regarded as burdens for which the holders are not paid. Instead, the officeholder is expected to pay for the food, liquor, music, fireworks, or whatever is required for community festivals or for banquets associated with the transmission of that office. For some cargos, the cost is as much as a man can earn in 4 years! After holding a cargo position, a man usually returns to normal life for a period, when he may accumulate sufficient resources to campaign for a higher office. Each male citizen of the community is socially obligated to serve in the system at least once, and social pressure to do so is such that it drives individuals who have once again accumulated excess wealth to apply for higher offices in order to raise their social status. Ideally, although some individuals gain appreciably more prestige than others in their community, no one has appreciably more wealth in a material sense than anyone else. In actuality, the ideal is not always achieved, so service in the cargo system functions to legitimize wealth differences, thereby preventing disruptive envy.

In addition to equalizing (or legitimizing) wealth, the cargo system accomplishes other results. Through its system of offices, it ensures that necessary services within the community are performed. It also keeps goods in circulation, rather than sitting around gathering dust. Moreover, members are pressured into investing their resources in their own community, rather than elsewhere. Likewise, the costs of holding office require participants to produce and sell a surplus or seek work outside the community to secure sufficient funds, thereby benefiting outside interests. To the degree outsiders can control the goods and wages cargo holders require, the system's basic function may be subverted to serve as a means of drawing wealth and labor *out* of the community.

DISTRIBUTION AND EXCHANGE

The money economy of industrial societies involves a two-step process between labor and consumption. The money received for labor must be translated into something else before it is directly consumable. In societies with no such medium of exchange, the rewards for labor are usually direct. The workers in a family group consume what they harvest, they eat what the hunter or gatherer brings home, and they use the tools they themselves make. But even where no formal exchange medium exists, some distribution of goods occurs. Karl Polanyi, an economist, classified the cultural systems of distributing material goods into three modes: reciprocity, redistribution, and market exchange.[13]

RECIPROCITY

Reciprocity refers to a transaction between two parties whereby goods and services of roughly equivalent value are exchanged. This may involve gift giving, but in non-Western societies pure al-

---

[13]Polanyi, K. (1968). The economy as instituted process. In E. E. LeClair, Jr., & H. K. Schneider (Eds.), *Economic anthropology: Readings in theory and analysis* (pp. 127–138). New York: Holt, Rinehart and Winston.

Reciprocity. The exchange of goods and services of approximately equal value between two parties.

truism in gift giving is as rare as it is in the United States or any other Western society. The overriding motive is to fulfill social obligations and perhaps to gain a bit of prestige in the process. It might be best compared in North American society to someone who gives a party. The person may go to great lengths to impress others by the excellence of the food and drink served, not to mention the quality of wit and conversation of those in attendance. The expectation is that, sooner or later, the individual will be invited to similar parties by some, although perhaps not all, of the guests.

Social customs dictate the nature and occasion of exchange. When an animal is killed by a group of Aboriginal hunters in Australia, the meat is divided among the hunters' families and other relatives. Each person in the camp gets a share, the size depending on the nature of the person's kinship tie to the hunters. The least desirable parts may be kept by the hunters themselves. When one hunter kills a kangaroo, for example, the left hind leg goes to the brother of the hunter, the tail to his father's brother's son, the loins and the fat to his father-in-law, the ribs to his mother-in-law, the forelegs to his father's younger sister, the head to his wife, and the entrails and the blood to the hunter. If arguments were to arise over the apportionment, it would be because the principles of distribution were not followed properly. The hunter and his family seem to fare badly in this arrangement, but they have their turn when another man makes a kill. The giving and receiving is obligatory, as is the particularity of the distribution. Such sharing of food reinforces community bonds and ensures that everyone eats. It also might be viewed as a way of saving perishable goods. By giving away part of his kill, the hunter gets a social IOU for a similar amount of food in the future. It is a little bit like putting money in a time-deposit savings account.

The food-distribution practices just described for Australian Aboriginal hunters constitute an example of **generalized reciprocity**. This may be

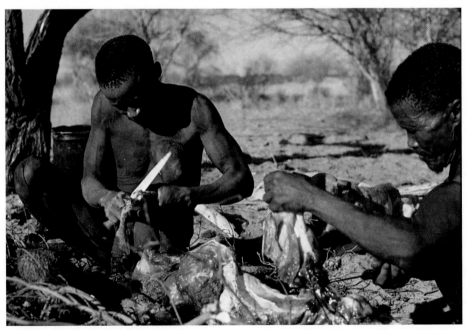

Ju/'hoansi cutting up meat, which will be shared by others in the camp. The food distribution practices of such food foragers are an example of generalized reciprocity.

Generalized reciprocity.   A mode of exchange in which the value of the gift is not calculated, nor is the time of repayment specified.

Political fund-raising in the United States involves elements of both balanced and negative reciprocity. Large contributors expect that their "generosity" will buy influence with a candidate, resulting in considerations and benefits of equal value. The recipient of the contribution, however, may seek to do as little as possible in return, but not so little as to jeopardize future contributions.

defined as an exchange in which the value of what is given is not calculated, nor is the time of repayment specified. Gift giving, in the altruistic sense, also falls in this category. So, too, does the act of a Good Samaritan who stops to help a stranded motorist or someone else in distress and refuses payment with the admonition "Pass it on to the next person in need." Most generalized reciprocity, though, occurs among close kin or people who otherwise have very close ties with one another. Typically, participants will deny that the exchanges are economic and will couch them explicitly in terms of kinship and friendship obligations.

Balanced reciprocity differs in that it is not part of a long-term process. The giving and receiving, as well as the time involved, are more specific; a person has a direct obligation to recipro-

cate promptly in equal value for the social relationship to continue. Examples of balanced reciprocity in North American society include practices such as trading baseball cards or buying drinks when one's turn comes at a gathering of friends or associates. Examples from a non-Western society include those anthropologist Robert Lowie related in his classic account of the Crow Indians.[14] A woman skilled in the tanning of buffalo hides might offer her services to a neighbor who needed a new cover for her tepee. It took an expert to design a tepee cover, which required from 14 to 20 skins. The designer might need as many as 20 collaborators, whom she instructed on the

[14]Lowie, R. (1956). *Crow Indians* (p.75). New York: Holt, Rinehart and Winston. (Original work published 1935)

Balanced reciprocity. A mode of exchange whereby the giving and the receiving are specific as to the value of the goods and the time of their delivery.

sewing together of the skins and whom the tepee owner might remunerate with a feast. The designer herself would be given some kind of property by the tepee owner. In another example from the Crow, Lowie relates that if a married woman brought her brother a present of food, he might reciprocate with a present of 10 arrows for her husband, which rated as the equivalent of a horse.

Giving, receiving, and sharing as so far described constitute a form of social security or insurance. A family contributes to others when they have the means and can count on receiving from others in time of need. A leveling mechanism is at work in the process of generalized or balanced reciprocity, promoting an egalitarian distribution of wealth over the long run.

Negative reciprocity is a third form of reciprocity exchange, in which the giver tries to get the better end of the deal. The parties involved have opposing interests, usually are members of different communities, and are not closely related. The ultimate form of negative reciprocity is to take something by force. Less extreme forms involve guile and deception or, at the least, hard bargaining. In the United States, an example would be the stereotype of the car salesperson who claims a car was "driven by a little old lady to church" when in fact it was not and is likely to develop problems soon after it leaves the sales lot. Among the Navajo, according to anthropologist Clyde Kluckhohn, "to deceive when trading with foreign peoples is morally accepted."[15]

Barter and Trade

Exchanges that occur within a group of people generally take the form of generalized or balanced reciprocity. When they occur between two groups, at least a potential for hostility and competition is apt to exist. Therefore, such exchanges may well take the form of negative reciprocity, unless some sort of arrangement has been made to ensure at least

an approach to balance. *Barter* is one form of negative reciprocity, involving the exchange of scarce items from one group for desirable goods from another group. Relative value is calculated, and despite an outward show of indifference, sharp trading is more the rule, when compared to the more balanced nature of exchanges within a group.

An arrangement that combined elements of balanced reciprocity as well as barter existed between the Kota, in India, and three neighboring peoples who traded their surplus goods and certain services with the Kota. The Kota were the musicians and artisans for the region. They exchanged their iron tools with the other three groups and provided the music essential for ceremonial occasions. The Toda furnished to the Kota ghee (a kind of butter) for certain ceremonies and buffalo for funerals; relations between the two peoples were amicable. The Badaga were agricultural and traded their grain for music and tools. Between the Kota and Badaga was a feeling of great competition, which sometimes led to one-sided trading practices; usually the Kota procured the advantage. The forest-dwelling Kurumba, who were renowned as sorcerers, had honey, canes, and occasionally fruits to offer, but their main contribution was protection against the supernatural. The Kota feared the Kurumba, and the Kurumba took advantage of this in their trade dealings, so they always got more than they gave. Thus great latent hostility existed between these two peoples.

Silent trade is a specialized form of barter with no verbal communication. In fact, it may involve no actual face-to-face contact at all. Such cases often have characterized the dealings between food-foraging peoples and their food-producing neighbors, as the former have supplied for the past 2,000 or so years various commodities in demand by the world economy. A classic description of such trade follows:

> The forest people creep through the lianas to the trading place, and leave a neat pile of jungle products, such as wax, camphor, monkeys' gall bladders, birds' nests for Chinese soup. They creep back a certain distance, and wait in a safe place. The

---

[15]Kluckhohn, C. (1972). Quoted in Sahlins, M. (1972). *Stone Age economics* (p. 200). Chicago: Aldine.

Negative reciprocity. A form of exchange whereby the giver tries to get the better of the exchange. > **Silent trade.** A form of barter with no verbal communication.

partners to the exchange, who are usually agriculturalists with a more elaborate and extensive set of material possessions but who cannot be bothered stumbling through the jungle after wax when they have someone else to do it for them, discover the little pile, and lay down beside it what they consider its equivalent in metal cutting tools, cheap cloth, bananas, and the like. They too discreetly retire. The shy folk then reappear, inspect the two piles, and if they are satisfied, take the second one away. Then the opposite group comes back and takes pile number one, and the exchange is completed. If the forest people are dissatisfied, they can retire once more, and if the other people want to increase their offering they may, time and again, until everyone is happy.[16]

The reasons for silent trade only can be postulated, but in some situations trade may be silent for lack of a common language. More often it may serve to control situations of distrust so as to keep relations peaceful. In a very real sense, good relations are maintained by preventing relations. Another possibility, which does not exclude the others, is that it makes exchange possible where problems of status might make verbal communication unthinkable. In any event, it provides for the exchange of goods between groups in spite of potential barriers.

THE KULA RING

Although we tend to think of trade as something undertaken for purely practical purposes, in order to gain access to desired goods and services, not all trade is motivated by economic considerations. A classic case of this is the Kula ring (also referred to as the Kula), a Trobriand Island interisland trading system whereby prestige items are ceremoniously exchanged. Malinowski first described the Kula in 1920, but it is still going strong today.[17] From their coral atolls, men periodically set sail in their canoes to exchange shell valuables with their

Kula partners, who live on distant islands. These voyages take men away from their homes for weeks, even months, at a time and may expose them to various hardships along the way. The valuables are red shell necklaces, which always circulate in trade in a clockwise direction, and ornate white arm shells, which move in the opposite direction (Figure 18.2). These objects are ranked according to their size, their color, how finely polished they are, and their particular histories. Such is the fame of some that, when they appear in a village, they create a sensation. No one man holds these valuables for very long—at most, perhaps 10 years. Holding onto an arm shell or necklace too long risks disrupting the "path" it must follow as it is passed from one partner to another.

Although men on Kula voyages may use the opportunity to trade for other goods, this is not the reason for such voyages, nor is the Kula even necessary for trade to occur. In fact, overseas trade is regularly undertaken without the exchange of shell valuables. Instead, Trobriand men seek to create history through their Kula exchanges. By circulating armbands and necklaces that accumulate the histories of their travels and names of those who have possessed them, men proclaim their individual fame and talent, gaining considerable

[16]Coon, C. S. (1948). *A reader in general anthropology* (p. 594). New York: Holt, Rinehart and Winston.

[17]Weiner, A. B. (1988). *The Trobrianders of Papua New Guinea* (pp. 139–157). New York: Holt, Rinehart and Winston.

FIGURE 18.2
The ceremonial trading of necklaces and arm shells in the Kula ring encourages trade throughout Melanesia.

These photos show Kula valuables and a canoe used for Kula voyages.

influence for themselves in the process. Although the idea is to match the size and value of one shell for another, men draw on all their negotiating skills, material resources, and magical expertise to gain access to the strongest partners and most valuable shells; thus, an element of negative reciprocity arises when a man diverts shells from their proper "paths" or entices others to compete for whatever necklaces and armbands he may have to offer. But when all is said and done, success is limited, for although a man may keep a shell for 5 or 10 years, sooner or later it must be passed on to others.

The Kula is a most elaborate complex of ceremony, political relationships, economic exchange, travel, magic, and social integration. To see it only in its economic aspects is to misunderstand it completely. The Kula demonstrates once more how inseparable economic matters are from the rest of culture and shows that economics is not a realm unto itself. This is just as true in modern indus-

trial societies as it is in Trobriand society; when the United States stopped trading with Cuba, Haiti, Iran, Iraq, and Serbia, for instance, it was for political rather than economic reasons. Indeed, economic embargoes are increasingly popular as political weapons both governments and special interest groups wield. On a less political note, consider how retail activity in the United States peaks in December for a combination of religious and social, rather than purely economic, reasons.

REDISTRIBUTION

In societies with a sufficient surplus to support some sort of government, income flows into the public coffers in the form of gifts, taxes, and the spoils of war; then it is distributed again. The chief, king, or whoever the agent of redistribution may be has three motives for disposing of this income: The first is to maintain a position of superiority through a display of wealth; the second is to assure those who support the agent an adequate standard of living; and the third is to establish alliances outside the agent's territory.

The administration of the Inca empire in Peru was one of the most efficient the world has ever known, both in the collection of taxes and methods of control.[18] A census was kept of the

[18]Mason, J. A. (1957). *The ancient civilizations of Peru*. Baltimore, MD: Penguin.

population and resources. Tributes in goods and, more important, in services were levied. Each craft specialist had to produce a specific quota of goods from materials overseers supplied. Forced labor was used for some agricultural work or work in the mines. Forced labor was also employed in a program of public works, which included a remarkable system of roads and bridges throughout the mountainous terrain, aqueducts that guaranteed a supply of water, and storehouses that held surplus food for times of famine. Careful accounts were kept of income and expenditures. A governmental bureaucracy had the responsibility for ensuring production was maintained and commodities were distributed according to the regulations the ruling powers set forth.

Through the activities of the government, **redistribution** took place. The ruling class lived in great luxury, but goods were redistributed to the common people when necessary. Redistribution is a pattern of distribution in which the exchange is not between individuals or between groups, but, rather, a proportion of the products of labor is funneled into one source and is parceled out again as directed by a central administration. Commonly, it involves an element of coercion. Taxes are a form of redistribution in the United States. People pay taxes to the government, some of which support the government itself while the rest are redistributed either in cash, such as welfare payments and government loans or subsidies to business, or in services, such as food and drug inspection, construction of highways, support of the military, and the like. With the growth of the federal deficit after 1980, wealth in the United States increasingly has been redistributed from middle-

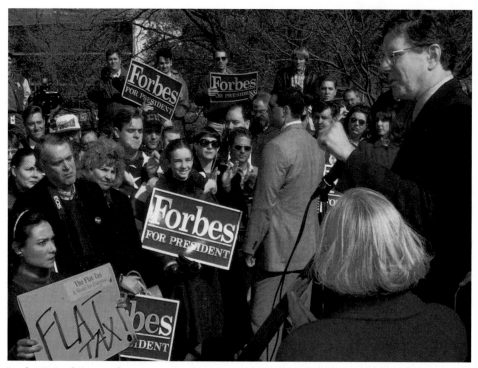

In the United States, the progressive income tax acts to redistribute wealth from more- to less-wealthy people. Some, like presidential candidate Steve Forbes, propose replacing this with a flat tax. Yet, by favoring accumulation of wealth by the already wealthy, this, too, would act to redistribute the wealth, as taxes invariably do.

Redistribution. A form of exchange in which goods flow into a central place where they are sorted, counted, and re-allocated.

income taxpayers to wealthy holders of government securities. For redistribution to be possible, a society must have a centralized system of political organization, as well as an economic surplus beyond people's immediate needs.

DISTRIBUTION OF WEALTH

In societies where people devote most of their time to subsistence activities, gradations of wealth are small, kept that way through leveling mechanisms and systems of reciprocity that serve to distribute in a fairly equitable fashion what little wealth exists.

Display for social prestige, what economist Thorstein Veblen called **conspicuous consumption,** is a strong motivating force for the distribution of wealth in societies where a substantial surplus is produced. It has, of course, long been recognized that conspicuous consumption plays a prominent role in Western societies as individuals compete with one another for prestige. Indeed, many North Americans spend much of their lives trying to impress others, and this requires the display of items symbolic of prestigious positions in life. This all fits very nicely into an economy based on consumer wants:

> In an expanding economy based on consumer wants, every effort must be made to place the standard of living in the center of public and private consideration, and every effort must therefore be lent to remove material and psychological impediments to consumption. Hence, rather than feelings of restraint, feelings of letting-go must be in the ascendant, and the institutions supporting restraint must recede into the background and give way to their opposite.[19]

[19]Henry, J. (1974). A theory for an anthropological analysis of American culture. In J. G. Jorgensen & M. Truzzi (Eds.), *Anthropology and American life* (p. 14). Englewood Cliffs, NJ: Prentice-Hall.

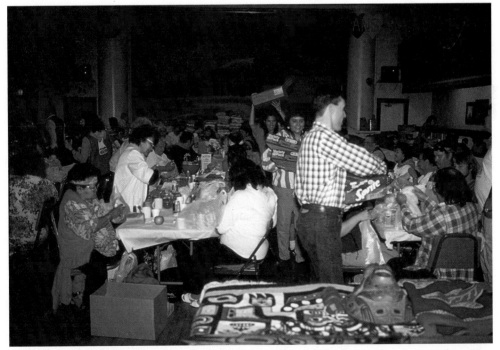

The giving of gifts at a potlatch on the Northwest Coast of North America. Among these Native Americans, one gains prestige by giving away valuables at the potlatch.

Conspicuous consumption.   A term Thorstein Veblen coined to describe the display of wealth for social prestige.

A form of conspicuous consumption also occurs in some nonindustrial societies, as illustrated by the potlatches Indians on the Northwest Coast of North America give or the lavish feasts Big Men in many societies of Papua New Guinea give. In both cases, food and various other items of wealth, laboriously accumulated over several preceding months, are all given away to others. Western observers are apt to see such grandiose displays as wasteful in the extreme, which is one reason why the Canadian government sought for many decades to suppress potlatches. To the people involved, however, these giveaways accomplish important social and political goals, as the following analysis demonstrates.

Prestige Economics in Papua New Guinea[20]

The average Enga patrilineage group [people who trace their descent through men to a particular male ancestor] numbers about 33 and . . . [constitutes a] . . . close knit extended family. . . . At the next level, however, is the Enga subclan, a [larger order patrilineal descent] group numbering about 90 members that owns a sacred dance ground and a sacred grove of trees. Members of a subclan are required to pool wealth for bride payments whenever any of their members marries and in support of one of their members who is striving to become a Big Man. A subclan is in competition with other subclans for prestige, which affects its members' ability to obtain wives and their desirability as partners in regional alliances. An individual householder is motivated to contribute to his subclan's political and economic activities, therefore, because his immediate family's self-interest is intimately bound with that of the subclan.

The Enga subclan is a unit approximately the size of the largest corporate kin groups in societies occupying the less densely populated highland fringe of New Guinea, such as the Tsembaga [see Chapter 17]. But the Enga are organized into a still higher level grouping [also based on patrilineal descent], the clan, which averages about 350 members and is the ultimate owner and defender of the territory of the clan, from which all clan members ultimately derive their subsistence. Clans own carefully defined territories and defend them both in battle and on ceremonial occasions. They are led by Big Men who speak for their clans in interclan relations and who work within their clans to mobilize the separate households for military, political, and ceremonial action.

Like the subclan, the clan is an arena for dramatic public activities. The clan owns a main dance ground and an ancestral cult house. At these ceremonial centers, public gatherings take place that emphasize the unity of the group as against other clans. Sackschewsky . . . sees this as an essential tactic to overcome the fierce independence of Enga households, where "each man makes his own decisions." Such familistic independence creates problems for Big Men, who encourage interfamily unity in the effort to enhance the strength of their own clans in a fiercely competitive and dangerous social environment.

Let us imagine the problems faced by the members of an Enga clan. They are trying to make an adequate subsistence from small amounts of

---

[20]Johnson, A. (1989). Horticulturists: Economic behavior in tribes. In S. Plattner (Ed.), *Economic anthropology* (pp. 63–67). Stanford, CA: Stanford University Press.

intensely utilized land. Surrounding them is a world of enemies ready to drive them from their land and seize it at the first sign of weakness. They must attempt to neutralize this external threat by several means: (1) by maintaining a large, unified group, they show strength in numbers, making others afraid to attack them; (2) by collaborating in the accumulation of food and wealth to be generously given away at ceremonies, they make themselves attractive as feasting partners; and (3) by being strong and wealthy, they become attractive as allies for defensive purposes, turning their neighbors either into friends or into outnumbered enemies. These three goals can be achieved only if each member of a clan is willing to fight on behalf of other members, to avoid fighting within the clan (even though it is with his clan members that a man is most directly in competition for land, since they are his most immediate neighbors), and to give up a share of his precious household accumulation of food and wealth objects in order that his Big Man may host an impressive feast.

This dependence of the household on the economic and political success of the clan is the basis of the Big Man's power. A Big Man is a local leader who motivates his followers to act in concert. He does not hold office and has no ultimate institutional power, so he must lead by pleading and bullyragging. His personal characteristics make him a leader. . . . He is usually a good speaker, convincing to his listeners; he has an excellent memory for kinship relations and for past transactions in societies where there is no writing; he is a peacemaker whenever possible, arranging compensatory payments and fines in order to avoid direct violent retribution from groups who feel they have been injured; and, when all else fails, he leads his followers into battle.

Of great importance in this system is the exchange of brides between patrilineal groups, for which payments of food, especially pigs, and wealth objects are required. An individual's political position—which affects his access to land, pigs, and other necessities—depends on alliances formed via his own marriage and those of his close kin. A Big Man, skilled as a negotiator and extremely knowledgeable about the delicate web of alliances created across the generations by a myriad of previous marriages and wealth payments, can help a group to marry well and maintain its competitive edge. By arranging his own marriages, of course, the Big Man can not only increase the number of alliances in which he is personally involved, but he can also bring more women, which is to say, more production of sweet potatoes and pigs, under his control. Hence, as he strengthens his group, he does not neglect his own personal power, as measured by his control of women, pigs, and wealth objects. His efforts both public and personal come together most visibly when he succeeds in hosting a feast.

Among the most dramatic economic institutions on earth, the Melanesian feasts have fascinated economic anthropologists. The Big Man works for months, painfully acquiring food and wealth from his reluctant followers, only to present them in spectacular accumulations—as *gifts* to his allies. But the generosity has an edge, as the Kawelka Big Man Ongka put it: "I have won. I have knocked you down by giving so much . . ." And the Big Man expects that his turn will come to be hosted by his allies, when they will be morally bound to return his gift with an equivalent or larger one. The "conspicuous consumption" and underlying competitiveness of these displays of generosity have been regarded as so similar to philanthropy in our own economy as to seem to close the gap between "primitive" and "modern" economies.

But the Big Man feast must be understood in context. Similar to the famous potlatch of the Northwest Coast of North America, these feasts do not exist merely as arenas for grandiose men to flaunt their ambition. As analyzed for the Northwest Coast, the competitive feast is the most dramatic event in a complex of interactions that maintain what Newman . . . calls "the intergroup collectivity." We must remember that, beyond the Enga clan, there is no group that can guarantee the rights of the individual, in the sense that the modern state does for us. Beyond the clan are only allies, strangers, and enemies. Many of them covet the desirable lands of other clans, and, if they sense weakness, they will strike. Small groups—weak in numbers and vulnerable to attack—must seek to swell their numbers and to attract allies in other clans. Thus an individual family's access to the means of subsistence depends on the success of its clan in the political arena, ultimately in the size of fighting force that can be mounted from within the clan and recruited from allied clans.

In the absence of courts and constitutions regulating intergroup relations, the Big Men assume central importance. It is they who maintain and advertise their group's attractiveness as allies (hence the bragging and showmanship that accompany Big Man feasts), who mediate disputes to avoid the dangerous extremity of homicidal violence, who remember old alliances and initiate new ones. Despite the public competitiveness between Big Men as they attempt to humiliate one another with generosity, over time they develop relationships of a predictable, even trustworthy, nature with other Big Men, lending intergroup stability in an unstable world.

A good example of this stabilizing effect is seen in the *Te* cycle, a series of competitive exchanges that link many Central Enga clans. Starting at one end of the chain, initiatory gifts of pigs, salt, and other valuables are given as individual exchanges from one partner to the next down the chain of clans. Big Men do not have to be directly involved, since such individual exchanges follow personal lines of alliance. But because the gifts are flowing in one direction down the chain of clans, after a time the giving clans begin to demand repayment. As this signal passes through the system, individuals amass pigs for larger feasts at the opposite, or receiving end, of the chain. These larger interclan ceremonies are full of oratory and display that serve to advertise the size and wealth of individual clans. Over a period of months a series of large gifting ceremonies move back up the chain of clans toward the beginning. The emphasis on prestige in these ceremonies is certainly gratifying to the participants, but it serves larger purposes: to maintain peace by substituting competitive feasting for open warfare, to establish and reinforce alliances, and to advertise a clan's attractiveness as an ally and fearsomeness as an enemy.

The central points to note from this example are the following:

1. The high population density of the Enga . . . implies two related developments: First, there is little wild forest left and virtually no supply of wild foods for the diet; and, second, the best horticultural land is fully occupied and in permanent use. These two primary consequences of population growth have further implications.

2. One is an intensive mode of food production that does not rely so much on regeneration of natural soil fertility through fallowing as upon mounding and the addition of green manure to soils. Because of the Enga's reliance on pigs, these fields must support not only the human population but also that of the pigs, who consume as much garden produce as humans do. The labor costs of pigs therefore include both producing their food and building fences to control their predation of gardens. Although the Enga populations are able to provide their basic nutritional needs in this manner, other highland groups with similar economies do show some signs of malnutrition, suggesting that overall production is not much more than adequate.

3. Furthermore, with land scarce, warfare shows a clear emphasis on territorial expansion and displacement. In response to this basic threat to their livelihood, families participate, albeit somewhat reluctantly, in the political activities of the lineage and clan. Although these activities often appear belligerent and can lead to warfare by deflecting hostilities outside the clan or local alliance of clans, it remains true that they have the primary function of preventing violence and stabilizing access to land.

The three major paths for creating alliances are marriage exchanges, sharing of food at feasts (commensality), and an intricate web of debt and credit established through exchanges of food and wealth objects. All of these together constitute the prestige economies for which such groups are famous. Crucial junctures in the prestige economy are occupied by Big Men, who earn their status by personally managing the complex alliances that provide a degree of security to otherwise vulnerable groups of closely related kin.

For these Big Man feasts, a surplus is created for the express purpose of gaining prestige through a display of wealth and generous giving of gifts. But, unlike conspicuous consumption in Western societies, the emphasis is not on the hoarding of goods, which would make them unavailable to others. Instead, the emphasis is on giving away, or at least getting rid of, one's wealth goods. Thus, these feasts serve as a leveling mechanism, preventing some individuals from accumulating too much wealth at the expense of other society members.

MARKET EXCHANGE

To an economist, **market exchange** has to do with the buying and selling of goods and services, with prices set by the powers of supply and demand. Loyalties and values are not supposed to play a role, but they often do. Just where the buying and selling takes place is largely irrelevant, so we must distinguish between market *exchange* and the *marketplace*. Although some modern market transactions do occur in a specific identifiable location—much of the trade in cotton, for example, happens in the New Orleans Cotton Exchange—it is also quite possible for North Americans to buy or sell goods without ever being on the same side of the continent as the other party. When people talk about a market in today's world, the particular place where something is sold is often not important at all. For example, think of the way people speak of a "market" for certain types of automobiles or for mouthwash.

Until well into the 20th century, market exchange typically was carried out in specific places, as it still is in much of the non-Western world. In

Market exchange. The buying and selling of goods and services, with prices set by the powers of supply and demand.

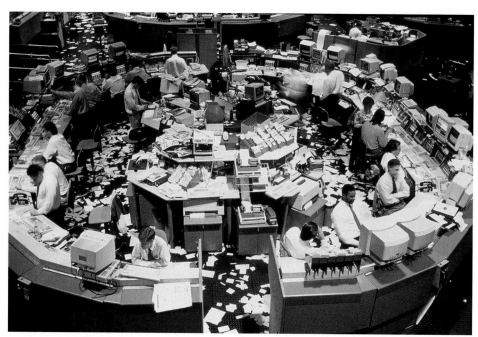

The Chicago Commodities Exchange, where people are buying and selling, even though no goods are physically present.

peasant or agrarian societies, marketplaces overseen by a centralized political authority provide the opportunity for farmers living in rural regions to exchange some of their livestock and produce for needed items manufactured in factories or the workshops of craft specialists living (usually) in towns and cities. Thus, some sort of complex division of labor as well as centralized political organization is necessary for the appearance of markets. In the marketplace land, labor, and occupations are not bought and sold as they are through the Western market economy. In other words, what happens in these marketplaces has little to do with the price of land, the amount paid for labor, or the cost of services. The market is local, specific, and contained. Prices are apt to be set on the basis of face-to-face bargaining (buy cheap and sell dear is the order of the day), rather than by faceless "market forces" wholly removed from the transaction itself. Nor need some form of money be involved; instead, goods may be directly exchanged through some form of reciprocity between the specific individuals involved.

In non-Western societies, marketplaces have much of the excitement of a fair; they are vibrant

places where one's senses are assaulted by a host of colorful sights, sounds, and smells. Indeed, many of the large urban and suburban malls built in the United States and other industrialized countries over the past few decades have tried to recreate, though in a more contrived manner, some of the interest and excitement of more traditional marketplaces. In the latter, noneconomic activities may even overshadow the economic. Social relationships are as important there as they are anywhere else. As anthropologist Stuart Plattner observes, the marketplace is where friendships are made, love affairs begun, and marriages arranged.[21] Dancers and musicians may perform, and the end of the day may be marked by drinking, dancing, and fighting. At the market, too, people gather to hear news. In ancient Mexico, under the Aztecs, people were required by law to go to market at specific intervals to keep informed about current events. Government officials held court and settled judicial disputes at the market. Thus,

[21]Plattner, S. (1989). Markets and market places. In S. Plattner (Ed.), *Economic anthropology* (p. 171). Stanford, CA: Stanford University Press.

In non-Western societies, the market is an important focus of social as well as economic activity, as typified by this market in Guatemala.

the market is a gathering place where people renew friendships, see relatives, gossip, and keep up with the world while procuring needed goods they cannot produce for themselves.

Although marketplaces can exist without money exchange of any sort, no one doubts that money facilitates trade. **Money** may be defined as something used to make payments for other goods and services as well as to measure their value. Its critical attributes are durability, portability, divisibility, recognizability, and fungibility (ability to substitute any item of money for any other monetary item of the same value, as when four quarters are substituted for a dollar bill). The wide range of things that have been used as money in one or another society includes salt, shells, stones, beads, feathers, fur, bones, teeth, and of course metals, from iron to gold and silver. Among the Aztecs of Mexico, both cacao beans and cotton cloaks served as money. The beans could be used to purchase merchandise and labor, though usually as a supplement to barter; if the value of the items exchanged was not equal, cacao beans could

be used to make up the difference. Cotton cloaks represented a higher denomination in the monetary system, with 65 to 300 beans equivalent to one cloak, depending on the latter's quality. Cloaks could be used to obtain credit, to purchase land, as restitution for theft, and to ransom slaves, whose value in any case was measured in terms of cloaks. Interestingly, counterfeiting was not unknown to the Aztecs—unscrupulous people sometimes carefully peeled back the outer skin of cacao beans, removed the contents, and then substituted packed earth!

Among the Tiv of West Africa, brass rods might be exchanged for cattle, with the cattle seller then using the rods to purchase slaves (the economic value of the cattle being converted into the rods and then reconverted into slaves). In both the Aztec and Tiv cases, the money in question is (or was) only used for special purposes. To a Tiv, the idea of exchanging a brass rod for subsistence foods is repugnant, and most market exchanges involve direct barter. Special-purpose monies usually have more moral restrictions on their use than

---

Money.   Anything used to make payments for goods or labor as well as to measure their value; may be special purpose or multipurpose.

Ancient Lydian money: the world's first coins. Lydia was located in Anatolia, which is now Turkey.

United States it is considered immoral, as well as illegal, to exchange money for sexual and political favors, even though infractions against these constraints occur.

The United States, as part of a reaction to the increasingly "face-to-faceless" nature of the modern economic system, is having something of a revival and proliferation of "flea markets" (Figure 18.3), where anyone, for a small fee, may display and sell handicrafts, secondhand items, farm produce, and paintings in a face-to-face setting. Excitement is felt in the search for bargains and an opportunity for haggling. A carnival atmosphere prevails, with eating, laughing, and conversation, and items even may be bartered without any cash passing hands. These flea markets, including fairs, festivals, and farmers' markets, are similar to the marketplaces of non-Western societies.

Flea markets also raise the issue of the distinction between the informal and formal sectors of the market economy. The **informal economy**

do general-purpose monies, which can be used to purchase just about anything. Even the latter category, however, has limits. For example, in the

FIGURE 18.3

Marketplace structure and function may range from formal to informal and from economic to festive, as this diagram suggests.

Informal economy. The production of marketable commodities that for various reasons escape enumeration, regulation, or any other sort of public monitoring or auditing.

may be defined as the system whereby producers of goods and services provide marketable commodities that for various reasons escape enumeration, regulation, or other type of public monitoring or auditing. Such enterprises may encompass just about anything: market gardening, making and selling beer or other alcoholic beverages, doing repair or construction work, begging, selling things on the street, performing ritual services, lending money, dealing drugs, picking pockets, and gambling, to mention just a few. These sort of "off the books" activities have been known for a long time but generally have been dismissed by economists as aberrant and therefore more of an annoyance than anything of importance. It is also difficult for them to track; yet, in many countries of the world, the informal economy is, in fact, more important than the formal economy. In many places, large numbers of under- and unemployed peoples who have only limited access to the formal sector in effect improvise as best they can various means of "getting by" on scant resources. Meanwhile, more affluent society members may evade various regulations to maximize returns and to vent their frustrations at their perceived loss of self-determination in the face of increasing government regulation.

Steve Barnett, who earned his Ph.D. in anthropology from the University of Chicago, was for several years head of a consulting firm that served several large corporations. He is now a vice president at Citibank in Long Island City, New York, where he studies long-term cultural trends in patterns of consumption worldwide.

ECONOMICS, CULTURE, AND THE WORLD OF BUSINESS

At the start of this chapter, we noted that when studying the economies of nonliterate peoples we perhaps are most apt to fall prey to our ethnocentric biases. The misunderstandings that result from our failure to overcome these biases are of major importance to us in the modern world in at least two ways. For one, they encourage development schemes for countries that, by Western economic standards, are regarded as "underdeveloped" (a comfortably ethnocentric term), schemes that all too often result in poverty, poor health, discontent, and a host of other ills. In northeastern Brazil, for example, development of large-scale plantations to grow sisal for export to the United States took over numerous small farms where peasants grew food to feed themselves. With this

change, peasants were forced into the ranks of the unemployed. Because the farmers were unable to earn enough money to satisfy their minimal nutritional needs, the incidence of malnutrition rose dramatically. Similarly, development projects in Africa, designed to initiate changes in local hydrology, vegetation, and settlement patterns—and even programs aimed at reducing certain diseases—frequently have led directly to *increased* disease rates.[22] Fortunately, now awareness is growing among development officials that future projects are unlikely to succeed without the expertise anthropologically trained people can bring to bear.

Secondly, achieving an understanding of the economic systems of other peoples that is not bound by the hopes and expectations of one's own culture also has become important for corporate executives in today's world. At least, recognition of how embedded such systems are within the

---

[22]Bodley, J. H. (1990). *Victims of progress* (3rd ed., p. 141). Mountain View, CA: Mayfield.

anthropology
applied   Anthropology and the World
of Business

When people hear of anthropologists working for, and sometimes running, private-sector businesses ranging from major financial institutions to consulting firms for large corporations, their reaction is usually surprise. In the public mind, anthropologists are supposed to work in exotic, faraway places such as remote islands, deep forests, hostile deserts, or arctic wastes —not in the world of business. After all, when anthropology makes the pages of the *New York Times,* is it not to report the "discovery" of a "last surviving Stone Age tribe," the uncovering of some ancient "lost city," or the recovery of bones of some remote human ancestor, usually in some out-of-the-way part of the world?

Not only have anthropologists found niches for themselves in the business world, but also since 1972 the number of them going into business has grown five-fold. The reason for their success is they have skills to offer the corporate world other social and behavioral scientists do not. One example is the discovery of anthropology by the market-research and product industry, as reported by Susan Squires:*

The October/November 1996 issue of *Fast Company,* a magazine devoted to cutting-edge business practice, introduced its readers to the newest innovation in the market-research and design industry: ethnography. What companies in the forefront of market research and design are learning is that "nearly all the tools of conventional marketing—

focus groups, customer surveys' segmentation— are designed to measure what people think. But the secret to breakthrough innovation . . . is understanding how people behave: what they do and how they live."

Companies that are serious about ethnography are recruiting and hiring anthropologists like Christina Wasson, a linguist who received her PhD from Yale in 1996. Christina Wasson joined E-Lab, the company featured in the *Fast Company* article, after graduation. At E-Lab, Christina Wasson uses methods to collect data that include participant observation, in-depth interviewing, and video-taping.

While many market-research and design companies are beginning to advertise themselves as having "ethnographers" and "doing ethnography," most do not have anthropologists on staff and are not really "doing ethnography." Some of these companies would like to hire an anthropologist to legitimize their claims and improve their methods. This means that there is a potential job market for anthropologists in the market-research and design area. But to be considered for available positions, the successful applicant must have some knowledge of business.

Christina Wasson is a good example of the combination of skills and knowledge sought. She was recruited not only for her anthropological background but also for her business knowledge. Her dissertation, *Covert Causation: Linguistic Traces of Effective Organizational Control,* is based on lengthy fieldwork conducted at Motorola in Chicago.

*Squires, S. (1997). The market research and product industry discovers anthropology. *Anthropology Newsletter, 38* (4), 31.

---

cultures they are parts of could avoid problems of the sort a large New York City-based cosmetics manufacturer experienced. About to release an ad in Italy featuring a model holding some flowers,

it was discovered the flowers were the kind traditionally given at Italian funerals. Along the same lines, the Chevrolet NOVA did not sell well in Spanish-speaking countries because in Spanish

"No Va" means "No Go." Anthropologists Edward and Mildred Hall describe another case of the same sort:

> José Ybarra and Sir Edmund Jones are at the same party and it is important for them to establish a cordial relationship for business reasons. Each is trying to be warm and friendly, yet they will part with mutual distrust and their business transaction will probably fall through. José, in Latin fashion, moved closer and closer to Sir Edmund as they spoke, and this movement was miscommunicated as pushiness to Sir Edmund, who kept backing away from this intimacy, and this was miscommunicated to José as coldness.[23]

[23]Hall, E. T., & Hall, M. R. (1986). The sounds of silence. In E. Angeloni (Ed.), *Anthropology 86/87* (p. 65). Guilford CT: Dushkin.

When the so-called underdeveloped countries of Africa, Asia, and South and Central America are involved, the chances for cross-cultural misunderstandings increase dramatically. The executives of major corporations realize their dependency on these countries for raw materials, they are increasingly inclined to manufacture their products in them, and they see their best potential for market expansion as lying outside North America and Europe. That is why business recruiters on college campuses in the United States are on the lookout for job candidates with the kind of understanding of the world anthropology provides.

In Africa, much of the farming is the job of women. Failure to accept this fact is responsible for the failure of many development schemes, since outside experts design projects that usually assume the men in the society are the farmers.

CHAPTER SUMMARY

An economic system is a means of producing, distributing, and consuming goods. Studying the economics of nonliterate, nonindustrial societies can be undertaken only in the context of the total culture of each society. Each society solves the problem of subsisting by allocating raw materials, land, labor, and technology and by distributing goods according to its own priorities.

The work people do is a major productive resource, and the allotment of work is always governed by rules according to sex and age. Only a few broad generalizations can be made covering the kinds of work men and women perform. Instead of looking for biological imperatives to explain the sexual division of labor, a more productive strategy is to examine the kinds of work men and women do in the context of specific societies to see how it relates to other cultural and historical factors. The cooperation of many people working together is a typical feature of both nonliterate and literate societies. Specialization of craft is important even in societies with very simple technologies.

All societies regulate the allocation of land and its valuable resources. In nonindustrial societies, individual ownership of land is rare; generally, land is controlled by kinship groups, such as the lineage or band. This system provides greater flexibility of land use, since the size of the bands and their territories can be adjusted according to the availability of resources in any particular place. The technology of a people, in the form of the tools they use and associated knowledge, is related to their mode of subsistence. In food-foraging societies, codes of generosity promote free access to tools, even though individuals may have made them for their own use. Sedentary farming communities offer greater opportunities to accumulate material belongings, and inequalities of wealth may develop. In many such communities, though, a relatively egalitarian social order may be maintained through leveling mechanisms.

Nonliterate people consume most of what they produce themselves, but they do exchange goods. The processes of distribution may be distinguished as reciprocity, redistribution, and market exchange. Reciprocity is a transaction between individuals or groups, involving the exchange of goods and services of roughly equivalent value. Usually it is prescribed by ritual and ceremony.

Barter and trade occur between groups. Trading exchanges have elements of reciprocity, but they involve a greater calculation of the relative value of goods exchanged. Barter is one form of negative reciprocity, whereby scarce goods from one group are exchanged for desirable goods from another group. Silent trade, which need not involve face-to-face contact, is a specialized form of barter with no verbal communication. It allows control of the potential dangers of negative reciprocity. A classic example of exchange between groups that partakes of both reciprocity and sharp trading is the Kula ring of the Trobriand Islanders.

Strong, centralized political organization is necessary for redistribution to occur. The government assesses each citizen a tax or tribute, uses the proceeds to support the governmental and religious elite, and redistributes the rest, usually in the form of public services. The collection of taxes and delivery of government services and subsidies in the United States is a form of redistribution.

Display for social prestige is a motivating force in societies that produce some surplus of goods. In the United States, goods accumulated for display generally remain in the hands of those who accumulated them, whereas in other societies they are generally given away; the prestige comes from publicly divesting oneself of valuables.

Exchange in the marketplace serves to distribute goods in a region. In nonindustrial societies, the marketplace is usually a specific site where produce, livestock, and material items the people produce are exchanged. It also functions as a social gathering place and a news medium. Although market exchanges may occur without money through bartering and other forms of reciprocity, some form of money at least for special transactions makes market exchange more efficient.

In market economies, the informal sector may become more important than the formal sector as large numbers of under- and unemployed people with marginal access to the formal economy seek to survive. The informal economy consists of economic activities that escape official scrutiny and regulation.

The anthropological approach to economics has taken on new importance in today's world of international development and commerce. Without it, development schemes for so-called underdeveloped countries are prone to failure, and international trade is handicapped due to crosscultural misunderstandings.

POINTS FOR CONSIDERATION

1. What parts of North American or European economies are comparable to nonindustrial societies' economies? Are these parts changing?

2. Imagine you run a word processing service for other students or you work at a fast-food resturaunt part-time. How might your personal economic valuation of your labor appear to someone from another culture with a foraging economic system? to someone from North America with a foraging economic system, such as a homeless person?

3. Do you see examples of nonindustrial forms of market exchange in your neighborhood? Do North American consumers or sellers make use of nonindustrial forms? How and why?

SUGGESTED READINGS

Dalton, G. (1971). *Traditional tribal and peasant economies: An introductory survey of economic anthropology.* Reading, MA: Addison-Wesley.

This is just what the title says it is, by a major specialist in economic anthropology.

LeClair, E. E., Jr., & Schneider, H. K. (Eds.). (1968). *Economic anthropology: Readings in theory and analysis.* New York: Holt, Rinehart and Winston.

This book is a selection of significant writings in economic anthropology from the preceding 50 years. In the first section are theoretical papers covering major points of view, and in the second are case materials selected to show the practical application of the various theoretical positions.

Nash, M. (1966). *Primitive and peasant economic systems.* San Francisco: Chandler.

Heavily theoretical, this book studies the problems of economic anthropology, especially the dynamics of social and economic change in terms of primitive and peasant economic systems. It draws on the author's fieldwork in Guatemala, Mexico, and Burma.

Plattner, S. (Ed.). (1989). *Economic anthropology.* Stanford, CA: Stanford University Press.

This is the first comprehensive text in economic anthropology to appear since the 1970s. Twelve scholars in the field contributed chapters on a variety of issues ranging from economic behavior in foraging, horticultural, preindustrial-state, peasant, and industrial societies to sex roles, common-property resources, informal economics in industrial societies, and mass marketing in urban areas.

PART
VI

THE FORMATION OF GROUPS:
SOLVING THE PROBLEM OF
COOPERATION

Chapter 19
SEX AND MARRIAGE

Chapter 20
FAMILY AND HOUSEHOLD

Chapter 21
KINSHIP AND DESCENT

Chapter 22
GROUPING BY SEX, AGE,
COMMON INTEREST, AND CLASS

Introduction

One important insight to come from anthropological study is how fundamental cooperation is to human survival. Through cooperation, humans handle even the most basic problems of existence—the need for food and protection not just from the elements but from predatory animals and even one another. To some extent, this is true not only for humans but for other primates. But what really sets humans apart from other primates is some form of regular cooperation between adults in subsistence activities. At the least, this takes the form of the sexual division of labor as seen among food-foraging peoples. Such cooperation is not usual among nonhuman primates; adult chimpanzees, for example, may cooperate to get meat, and share it when they get it, but they don't get meat very often, and they don't normally share other kinds of food the way humans regularly do.

Just as cooperation is basic to human nature, the organization of groups is basic to cooperation. Humans form many kinds of groups, each geared toward solving different kinds of problems people must cope with. Social groups are important to humans also because they give identity and support to their members. The basic building block of human societies is the household, where economic production, consumption, inheritance, child rearing, and shelter are organized. Usually, the core of the household consists of some form of family, a group of relatives that stems from the parent-child bond and the interdependence of men and women. Although it may be structured in many different ways, the family always provides for economic cooperation between men and women while furnishing the kind of setting required for child rearing. Another problem all human societies face is the need to control sexual activity, and this is the job of marriage. Given the inevitable connection between sexual activity and the production of children, who then must be nurtured, a close interconnection between marriage and family is to be expected.

Many different marriage and family patterns exist the world over, but all societies have some form of marriage, and most have some form of family organization. As shown in Chapters 19 and 20, the forms of family and marriage organization are to a large extent shaped by the specific kinds of problems people must solve in particular situations.

Solutions to some organizational challenges are beyond the scope of family and household. These include defense, allocation of resources, and provision of labor for tasks too large for single households. Nonindustrial societies frequently meet these challenges through kinship groups, discussed in Chapter 21. These large, cohesive groups of individuals base their loyalty to one another on descent from a common ancestor or their relationship to a living individual. In cases where a great many people are linked by kinship, these groups serve the important function of precisely defining the social roles of their members. In this way they reduce the potential for tension that might arise from an individual's sudden unexpected behavior. They also provide their members with material security and moral support through ritual activities.

Other important forms of human social groups are the subjects of Chapter 22. Where kinship ties do not provide for all of a society's organizational needs, grouping by age and sex are forces societies may use to create groups. In North America, as well as in many non-Western countries, today and in the past, the organization of persons by age is common. In many cases, too, social groups based on the common interests of their members serve a vital function. In developing countries, they may help ease the transition of rural individuals into urban settings. Finally, groups based on social rank—social classes—are characteristic of the world's civilizations, past and present. Class structure involves inequalities between classes and is the means one group may use to dominate large numbers of other people. To the extent social class membership cuts across lines of kinship, residence, age, or other group membership, it may counteract tendencies for a society to fragment into discrete special-interest groups. Paradoxically, it does so in a divisive way, in that class distinctions systematically deprive people of equal access to important resources. Thus, class conflict has been a recurrent phenomenon in class-structured societies, in spite of the existence of political and religious institutions that function to maintain the status quo.

Chapter 19
SEX AND MARRIAGE

THE WEDDING CEREMONY OF NELSON
MANDELA'S DAUGHTER ZINZI. IN ALL SOCIETIES,
MARRIAGE ESTABLISHES A CONTINUING SEXUAL
RELATIONSHIP BETWEEN TWO INDIVIDUALS,
BACKED BY LEGAL, ECONOMIC, AND SOCIAL
FORCES. THUS, UNLIKE MATING (WHICH IS
BIOLOGICAL), MARRIAGE IS DISTINCTLY CULTURAL.

Chapter Preview

What Is Marriage?

Marriage is a relationship between one or more men (male or female) and one or more women (female or male) who are recognized by society as having a continuing claim to the right of sexual access to one another. Because gender is culturally defined, the "man" may be a female or the "woman" a male. Although in many societies, husbands and wives live together as members of the same household, this is not true in all societies. And though most marriages around the world tend to involve one spouse, most societies permit, and regard as most desirable, marriage of an individual to multiple spouses.

What Is the Difference Between Marriage and Mating?

All animals, including humans, mate—that is, they form a sexual bond with individuals of the opposite sex. In some species, the bond lasts for life, but in some others it lasts no longer than a single sex act. Thus, some animals mate with a single individual, while others mate with several. Only marriage, however, is backed by social, legal, and economic forces. Consequently, while mating is biological, marriage is cultural.

Why Is Marriage Universal?

A problem universal to all human societies is the need to control sexual relations so that competition over sexual access does not introduce a disruptive, combative influence into society. Because the problem marriage deals with is universal, it follows that marriage should be universal. The specific form marriage takes is related to who has rights to offspring that normally result from sexual intercourse, as well as how property is distributed.

Among the Trobriand Islanders, whose yam exchanges and Kula voyages we examined in Chapter 18, children who have reached age 7 or 8 begin playing erotic games with each other and imitating adult seductive attitudes. Within another 4 or 5 years they begin to pursue sexual partners in earnest, changing partners often, experimenting sexually first with one and then another. By the time they are in their midteens, meetings between lovers take up most of the night, and affairs between them are apt to last for several months. Ultimately, lovers begin to meet the same partner again and again, rejecting the advances of others. When the couple is ready, they appear together one morning outside the young man's house as a way of announcing their intention to be married.

For young Trobrianders, attracting sexual partners is an important business, and they spend a great deal of time making themselves look as attractive and seductive as possible. Youthful conversations during the day are loaded with sexual innuendos, and magical spells as well as small gifts are employed to entice a prospective sex partner to the beach at night or to the house where boys sleep apart from their parents. Because girls, too, sleep apart from their parents, youths and adolescents have considerable freedom to arrange their love affairs. Boys and girls play this game as equals, with neither sex having an advantage over the other.

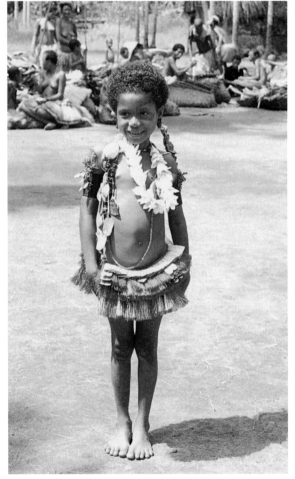

To attract lovers, young Trobriand Islanders must look as attractive and seductive as possible. The young men shown here have decorated themselves with Johnson's Baby Powder, while the young girl's beauty has been enhanced by decorations given by her father.

As anthropologist Annette Weiner points out, all of this sexual activity is not a frivolous, adolescent pastime. Attracting lovers:

> is the first step toward entering the adult world of strategies, where the line between influencing others while not allowing others to gain control of oneself must be carefully learned. . . . Sexual liaisons give adolescents the time and occasion to experiment with all the possibilities and problems that adults face in creating relationships with those who are not relatives. Individual wills may clash, and the achievement of one's desire takes patience, hard work, and determination. The adolescent world of lovemaking has its own dangers and disillusionments. Young people, to the degree they are capable, must learn to be both careful and fearless.[1]

The Trobriand attitude toward adolescent sexuality stands in marked contrast to that of North American society. Theoretically, North Americans are not supposed to have sexual relations outside of wedlock, although, as is well known, a considerable discrepancy between theory and practice exists. Nonetheless, premarital sexual activity in North American society cannot be conducted with the openness and approval that characterizes the Trobriand situation. As a consequence, it is not subject to the kind of social pressures from the community at large that prepare traditional Trobriand youths for the adult world after marriage.

CONTROL OF SEXUAL RELATIONS

One distinctively human characteristic is the ability of the human female, like the human male, to engage in sexual relations at any time she wants to or whenever her culture deems it appropriate. Although this ability to perform at any time when provided with the appropriate cue is not unusual for male mammals in general, it is not usual for females. Female primates, whose offspring are weaned but who have not yet become pregnant again, are likely to engage in sexual activity around the time of ovulation (approximately once

Unlike chimpanzees and other female apes that signal their fertility through highly visible swelling of their skin, the human female gives no such signal. Thus, males do not know when females are fertile, an inducement for them to hang around for successful reproduction.

a month), at which time they advertise their availability through highly visible physical signs. Otherwise, they are little interested in such activity. By contrast, the human female displays no visible sign of ovulation and may be willing to engage in sex at any point in her cycle or even when she is pregnant. In some societies, intercourse during pregnancy is thought to promote the growth of the fetus. Among Trobriand Islanders, for example, a child's identity is thought to come from its mother, but it is the father's job to build up and nurture the child, which he begins to do before birth through frequent intercourse with its mother.

On the basis of clues from the behavior of other primates, anthropologists have speculated about the evolutionary significance of this human female sexuality. The best current explanation is that it arose as a side effect of persistent bipedal locomotion in early hominines.[2] The energetic requirements of this form of locomotion are such that endurance is impossible without a significantly greater hormone output than other primates have. These hormones catalyze the steady release of muscular energy required for endurance;

[1]Weiner, A. B. (1988). *The Trobrianders of Papua New Guinea* (p. 71). New York: Holt, Rinehart and Winston.

[2]Spuhler, J. N. (1979). Continuities and discontinuities in anthropoid-hominid behavioral evolution: Bipedal locomotion and sexual reception. In N. A. Chagnon & William Irons (Eds.), *Evolutionary biology and human social behavior* (pp. 454–461). North Scituate, MA: Duxbury Press.

likewise, they make us the "sexiest" of all primates. This does not mean either men or women are simply at the mercy of their hormones where sex is concerned, for in the human species both males and females have voluntary control over sex. People engage in it when it suits them to do so and when it is deemed appropriate.

anthropology applied　Anthropology and AIDS

An irony of human life is that sexual activity, necessary for perpetuation of the species as well as a source of pleasure and fulfillment, also can be a source of danger. The problem lies in sexually transmitted diseases, which in recent years have been spreading and increasing in variety. Among these is acquired immune deficiency syndrome or AIDS, although intravenous drug use and blood transfusions also contributed to its spread. Recent reports specify 16,000 new cases of AIDS arise in the world *every day!* (See Figure 19.1.) What follows is A. M. Williams's account of what she and other anthropologists have to contribute to our understanding and control of this disease.

After a decade and a half, it is hard to deny that AIDS is a pandemic experienced in significant ways at local levels. The World Health Organization (WHO) estimates 18.5 million adults are infected with HIV (the virus present in most people with AIDS) worldwide, with 4.5 million of those people diagnosed with AIDS. While HIV and AIDS has hit areas of Sub-Saharan Africa and Southeast Asia hardest, as of June 1996, the Centers for Disease Control report a cumulative total of 548,102 AIDS cases in the United States, with 343,000 deaths. Where I work in San Francisco, California, a city of less than 800,000 people, there have been 24,509

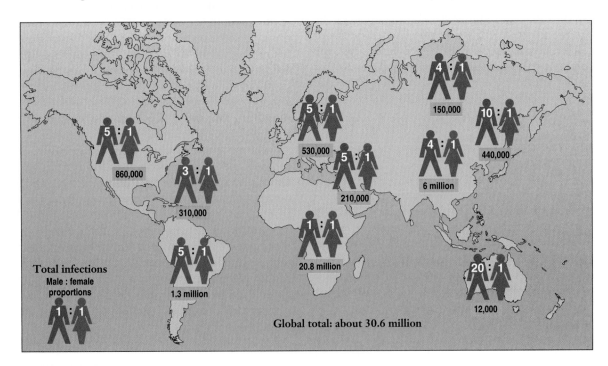

FIGURE 19.1
Estimated global distribution of adult HIV infections, December 1997.

AIDS cases and 16,838 deaths from AIDS reported since 1980. Of these cases, 22,161 are among gay and bisexual men in the city.*

To grasp the proportions of the pandemic, public health perspectives, epidemiological models, biomedical information, and psychological interpretations are used to help figure out who is infected, who will become infected, and where these infections are most likely to occur. However, anthropology takes a different approach, one that helps to clarify the dynamic relationship between people, who are infected or at risk for infection, and their social, cultural, political and economic surroundings. Such research is important because it can provide rich explanations of why people become infected or progress rapidly in HIV disease. This in turn can assist all manner of institutions in addressing a wide variety of local issues for those who need their services and support. Moreover, anthropological analyses often help describe the dynamic links between individual practices, social and cultural systems, and larger structural forces, all of which may combine in ways that encourage the problems of HIV.

Working alone or as part of teams to collect and analyze data, most anthropologists enter into an extended engagement with groups of people who are dealing with numerous aspects of HIV and AIDS. Since anthropology begins from the premise that circumstances and phenomena are complex within different populations, we employ a variety of methods and theoretical frameworks to reach our understandings. As a result, we do not develop monolithic models for explaining HIV and AIDS. For example, anthropologist Richard Parker's work in Brazil provided the formative research on sexual practices and their relationship to local systems of power and inequality needed to create more appropriate responses to the increasing spread of HIV/AIDS there. Others, like Paul Farmer, demonstrate how political economy and constructions of sickness among people in Haiti can negatively influence the quality of life of those infected in ways that encourage the further spread of the virus. And some, like Emily Martin, show that within the relationships between science, clinical research, and people affected by HIV and AIDS there emerge new concepts of body and AIDS that can reveal dynamics about society and the authoritative role of experts in shaping public awareness.[†]

These anthropological studies and many others contribute to a very broad research and theoretical literature on HIV and AIDS, which can be drawn upon by community-based organizations, policy makers, and other researchers. However, some anthropologists like myself work more directly with groups and organizations on problems posed by primary prevention (preventing HIV transmission) and secondary prevention (slowing the disease's progression). Here anthropology is well-suited for both formative research and conducting evaluations of programs and services. As the anthropologist on a multi-disciplinary research team at the Center for AIDS Prevention Studies, University of California San Francisco, I work directly with local gay male populations and such local AIDS organizations as the San Francisco AIDS Foundation and the STOP AIDS Project. While the team uses many strategies of inquiry, I specifically employ anthropological methods of investigation such as living and participating in the community, conducting a variety of in-depth interviews, and studying archival materials. I also rely on anthropological perspectives that require descriptions of the links between historical contexts, larger structural phenomena, and local practices and understandings.

Recently, by examining the relationship between HIV and drug use in two local groups of gay men who engage in unprotected sex, I was able to describe how groups of poorer gay male drug users in the city may be subjected to physical violence from their homophobic peers. This influences their ability to use condoms or openly seek HIV prevention education or support. At the same time, groups of more middle-class gay male drug users did not seek education or support because their social location and values encouraged them to believe that they did not need these resources because they had everything under control.[‡] With a greater clarity regarding local social and cultural barriers to HIV prevention, some local HIV prevention program designers rapidly developed more culturally appropriate prevention programs for these groups of men. Because HIV and AIDS are a dynamic part of lived experiences, learning about how people conceptualize and shape their ideas and practices around the virus, selfhood, sex practices, collective life, and institutions is important.

And when these concepts become part of a foundation for HIV/AIDS programs, the services are better able to respond to people's needs since the programs make better sense within the contexts of people's lived realities.

As we head into the next century, bio-technology's advances are beginning to reconfigure the HIV/AIDS pandemic. While this is good news, it also means the meanings of HIV and AIDS become more complex and difficult to navigate. Moreover while new pharmaceutical therapies are providing hope for many enfranchised people in the West, infection rates climb and many more people remain unable to access these treatments. For most of us, culturally specific education and services will still be the most effective means to prevent infection or stem disease progression in many communities. In this light, the variety of perspectives offered by anthropology becomes even more crucial. This is because the foundations of these prevention efforts and services need to be developed with considerable understanding of how HIV and AIDS are constructed and shaped in a dynamic relationship with local complexities and concerns.

---

*Centers For Disease Control Semi-Annual AIDS Report (through June 1996). 1997. Centers For Disease Control. Atlanta, Georgia, and AIDS Monthly Surveillance Summary (through July 1997). 1997. San Francisco Department of Public Health AIDS Office, Seroepidemiology and Surveillance Branch. San Francisco, CA. The earliest circumstances for tracking HIV and AIDS were problematic, and many people today still do not know their HIV status. Therefore, the cases reported in San Francisco or anywhere in the world must be understood to be under counted.

†See for example, Parker, Richard. 1991. Bodies, Pleasures, and Passions: Sexual Culture in Contemporary Brazil; Farmer, Paul. 1992. AIDS and Accusation: Haiti and the Geography of Blame; and Martin, Emily. 1994. Flexible Bodies: Tracking Immunity in American Culture—from the days of polio to the age of AIDS.

‡See Williams, A. M. 1996. Sex, Drugs and HIV: A Sociocultural Analysis of Two Groups of Gay and Bisexual Male Substance Users Who Practice Unprotected Sex. Unpublished manuscript.

Although developed as an accidental by-product of something else, a common phenomenon in evolution, the ability of females as well as males to engage in sex at any time would have been advantageous to early hominines to the extent that it acted, not alone but with other factors, to tie members of both sexes more firmly to the social groups so crucial to their survival. However, while sexual activity can reinforce group ties, it also can be disruptive. This stems from the common primate characteristic of male dominance. On the average, males are bigger and more muscular than females, although this differentiation has become drastically reduced in modern *Homo sapiens* compared to the earliest hominines. Among other primates, the males' larger size allows them to try to dominate females when the latter are at the height of their sexuality. This trait can be seen among baboons, gorillas, and, though less obviously, chimpanzees (significantly, the size difference between male and female chimpanzees is not as great as among baboons or gorillas, but it is still substantially greater than among modern humans). With early hominine females potentially ready for sexual intercourse at any time, dominant males may have attempted to monopolize females; an added inducement could have been the prowess of the female at food gathering. (In food-foraging societies, women usually provide the bulk of the food by their gathering activities.) In any event, a tendency to monopolize females would introduce the kind of competitive, combative element into hominine groupings seen among many other primate species —an element that cannot be allowed to disrupt harmonious social relationships. The solution to this problem is to bring sexual activity under cultural control. Thus, just as a culture tells people what, when, and how they should eat, so does it tell them when, where, how, and with whom they should have sex.

RULES OF SEXUAL ACCESS

We find that everywhere societies have cultural rules that seek to control sexual relations. In the United States and Canada, the official ideology has been that all sexual activity outside of wedlock is taboo. One is supposed to establish a family

Attempts by males to dominate females may introduce a competitive, combative element into social relations. Among gorillas, male silverbacks maintain absolute breeding rights over females in their group. All other adult males must acknowledge this dominance or leave the group and attempt to lure females from other groups.

through marriage. With *marriage,* a person establishes a continuing claim to the right of sexual access to another person. Actually very few known societies—only about 5%—prohibit all sexual involvement outside of marriage, and even North American society has become less restrictive. Among other peoples, as we already have seen, practices are often quite different. As a further example, we may look at the Nayar peoples of India.[3]

The Nayar constitute a landowning, warrior caste (rather than an independent society) from southwest India. Among them, estates are held by corporations of sorts made up of kinsmen related in the female line. These kinsmen all live together in a large household, with the eldest male serving as manager.

Three Nayar transactions are of interest here. The first occurs shortly before a girl undergoes her

first menstruation. It involves a ceremony that joins together in a temporary union the girl with a young man. This union, which may or may not involve sexual relations, lasts for a few days and then breaks up. Neither individual has any further obligation, although the woman and her future children probably will mourn for the man when he dies. This transaction establishes the girl's eligibility for sexual activity with men her household approves. With this, she is officially an adult.

The second transaction occurs when a girl enters into a continuing sexual liaison with an approved man. This is a formal relationship, which requires the man to present her with gifts three times each year until the relationship is terminated. In return, the man may spend the nights with her. In spite of continuing sexual privileges, however, the man has no obligation to support his sex partner economically, nor is her home regarded as his home. In fact, she may have such an arrangement with more than one man at the same time. Regardless of how many men are involved with one woman, this second Nayar transaction, their version of marriage, clearly specifies who has sexual rights to whom so as to avoid conflict. We may define **marriage** as a relationship between one or

---

[3]My interpretation of the Nayar follows W. H. Goodenough (1970), *Description and comparison in cultural anthropology* (pp. 6–11). Chicago: Aldine.

Marriage. A relationship between one or more men (male or female) and one or more women (female or male) recognized by society as having a continuing claim to the right of sexual access to one another.

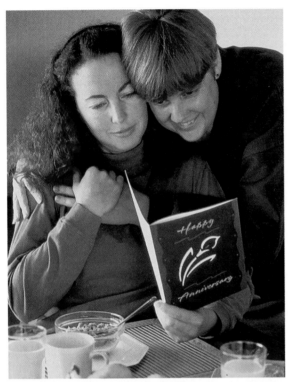

In the United States, gay or lesbian couples who wish to marry have met with considerable resistance, in spite of the fact that there is nothing abnormal, in any scientific sense, about such unions. In a number of other societies, same-sex marriages are regarded as perfectly appropriate.

more men (male or female) and one or more women (female or male) recognized by society as having a continuing claim to the right of sexual access to one another.[4] Thus defined, marriage is universal, presumably because the problems it deals with are universal. As the Nayar case demonstrates, however, marriage need not have anything to do with starting a new family or even establishing a cooperative economic relationship between people of opposite gender.

---

[4]This definition of marriage is adapted from D. Bell (1997), Defining marriage and legitimacy, *Current Anthropology, 38,* 241; and R. K. Jain (1997), Comment, *Current Anthropology, 38,* 248.

The qualification in our definition of marriage—that the man actually may be a female or the woman actually may be a male—is an important one. It stems from the fact gender does not automatically follow from biological sex but is culturally defined (as discussed in Chapters 2 and 5). Thus we find that, in many societies, same-sex marriages are regarded as appropriate and normal in particular circumstances, even though opposite-sex marriages are far more common. We shall return to this point later in the chapter.

In the absence of effective birth-control devices, the usual outcome of sexual activity between individuals of opposite sex is that, sooner or later, the woman becomes pregnant. When this happens among the Nayar, some man must formally acknowledge paternity, the third transaction. He does this by making gifts to the woman and the midwife. Though he may continue to take much interest in the child, he has no further obligations, for the child's education and support are the responsibility of the child's mother's brothers, whom the child and its mother live with. This transaction establishes the child's legitimacy. In this sense, it is the counterpart of the registration of births in North American culture that spells out motherhood and fatherhood. In Western societies generally, the father is supposed to be the mother's husband, but he does not have to be. In the United States, the child of an unwed mother may be spoken of as "illegitimate," yet its citizenship rights, as well as those of inheritance, are not denied. Nor does legitimacy require the father to be married to the mother. In numerous other societies—for example, among the Pueblo peoples (such as the Hopi) of the North American Southwest—fatherhood is utterly irrelevant to the child's legitimacy. In their societies legitimacy comes automatically from one's mother, regardless of whether or not she is married.

Before we leave the Nayar, it is important to note that nothing in this society is comparable to the family as we know it in North America. The group that forms the household does not include **affinal kin,** or individuals joined by a **conjugal bond** established by marriage. As will be shown

---

Affinal kin. Relatives by marriage. > **Conjugal bond.** The bond between a man and a woman who are married.

in Chapter 20, a household group does not have to be a family as we know it. Among the Nayar the household is composed wholly of what we often call "blood" relatives, technically known as **consanguineal kin.** Sexual relations are with those who are not consanguineal kin and thus live in other households. This brings us to another supposed human universal, the incest taboo.

THE INCEST TABOO

A cultural rule that long has fascinated anthropologists as well as other students of human behavior is the **incest taboo.** This prohibits sexual relations at least between parents and children of opposite sex and usually siblings as well. Once thought to be universal, save for a few exceptions involving siblings, the taboo has became something of a challenge for anthropologists to explain, both regarding this supposed universality and why incest commonly should be regarded as such loathsome behavior.

Many explanations have been given. Of those that have gained some popularity at one time or another, the simplest and least satisfactory is based on "human nature"—that is, some instinctive horror of incest. It has been documented that human beings raised together have less sexual attraction for one another, but by itself this "familiarity breeds contempt" argument simply may substitute the result for the cause. The incest taboo ensures that children and their parents, who are constantly in intimate contact, avoid regarding one another as sexual objects. Besides this, if an instinctive horror of incest exists, we would be hard pressed to account for the far from rare violations of the incest taboo, such as occur in North American society (an estimated 10%–14% of children under 18 years of age in the United States have been involved in incestuous relations[5]), or for cases of institutionalized incest, such as requiring the head

of the Inca empire in Peru to marry his own sister.

Various psychological explanations of the incest taboo have been advanced at one time or another. Sigmund Freud tried to account for it in his psychoanalytic theory of the unconscious. According to him, the son desires the mother (familiarity breeds attempt), creating a rivalry with the father. (Freud called this the Oedipus complex.) The son must suppress these feelings or earn the wrath of the father, who is far more powerful than he. Similarly, the attraction of the daughter to the father (the Electra complex) places her in rivalry with her mother. From this, we might expect a same-sex bias in the case of intrafamily homicides—mother versus daughter or son versus father—but in fact no such bias exists. Some psychologists have argued that young children can be emotionally scarred by sexual experiences, which they may interpret as violent and frightening acts of aggression. The incest taboo thus protects children against sexual advances by older members of the family. A closely related theory is that the incest taboo helps prevent girls who are socially and emotionally too young for motherhood from becoming pregnant.

Early students of genetics argued that the incest taboo precluded the harmful effects of inbreeding. Although this is so, it is also true that, as with domestic animals, inbreeding can increase desired characteristics as well as detrimental ones. Furthermore, undesirable effects show up sooner than without inbreeding, so whatever genes are responsible for them are quickly eliminated from the population. However, a preference for a genetically different mate does tend to maintain a higher level of genetic diversity within a population, and in evolution this generally works to a species' advantage. Without genetic diversity a species cannot adapt biologically to a changed environment when and if this becomes necessary.

A truly convincing explanation of the incest taboo has yet to be advanced. Certainly, there are persistent hints that it may be a cultural elaboration of an underlying biological tendency toward

[5]Whelehan, P. (1985). Review of incest, a biosocial view. *American Anthropologist, 87,* 678.

Consanguineal kin. Relatives by birth; that is, "blood" relatives. **> Incest taboo.** The prohibition of sexual relations between specified individuals, usually parent-child and sibling relations at a minimum.

Although children raised together on an Israeli kibbutz rarely marry one another, it is not because of any instinctive desire to avoid mating with people who are close. Rather, they marry outside their group because service in the military takes them out of their kibbutz, where they meet new people, precisely when they are most likely to begin thinking about marriage.

avoidance of inbreeding. Studies of animal behavior have shown such a tendency to be common among relatively large, long-lived, slow-to-mature, and intelligent species. Humans qualify for membership in this group on all counts. So do a number of other primates, including those most closely related to humans—chimpanzees. Although they exhibit few sexual inhibitions, chimpanzees do tend to avoid inbreeding between siblings and between females and their male offspring. This suggests that the tendency for human children to look for sexual partners outside the group they have been raised in is not just the result of a cultural taboo. Studies that might seem to support this show that children raised together on an Israeli kibbutz, although not required or even encouraged to do so, almost invariably marry outside their group. In this case, however, appearances seem to be deceiving. There is hardly a kibbutz, for example, without a report of heterosexual relationships between adolescents who have grown up to-

gether since infancy.[6] As for actual marriage, most Israeli youths leave the kibbutz in their late teens for service in the armed forces. Thus, they are away from the kibbutz precisely when they are most ready to consider marriage. Consequently, those most available as potential spouses are from other parts of the country.

An even greater challenge to the "biological avoidance" theory, however, is raised by detailed census records made in Roman Egypt that conclusively demonstrate that brother-sister marriages were not only common but also preferred by ordinary members of the farming class.[7] Moreover, anthropologist Nancy Thornhill found that, in a sample of 129 societies, only 57 had specific rules

---

[6]Leavitt, G. C. (1990). Sociobiological explanations of incest avoidance: A critical review of evidential claims. *American Anthropologist, 92,* 973.

[7]Ibid., p. 982.

against parent-child or sibling incest (so much for the universality of the incest taboo!). Twice that number, 114, had explicit rules to control activity with cousins, in-laws, or both.[8]

If indeed a biological basis for inbreeding avoidance exists among humans, it clearly is far from completely effective in its operation. Nor is its mechanism understood. Moreover, it still leaves us with questions such as these: Why do some societies have an explicit taboo while others do not? And why do some societies not only condone certain kinds of incest but also even favor them?

ENDOGAMY AND EXOGAMY

Whatever its cause, the utility of the incest taboo can be seen by examining its effects on social structure. Closely related to prohibitions against incest are rules against **endogamy,** or marriage within a particular group of individuals (cousins and in-laws, for example). If the group is defined as one's immediate family alone, then societies generally prohibit or at least discourage endogamy and practice or at least encourage **exogamy,** or marriage outside the group. Yet a society that practices exogamy at one level may practice endogamy at another. Among the Trobriand Islanders, for example, each individual has to marry outside of his or her own clan and lineage (exogamy). However, since eligible sex partners are to be found within one's own community, village endogamy, though not obligatory, is commonly practiced. Interestingly, a wide variety exists among societies as to which relatives are or are not covered by exogamy rules. In Europe, for example, the Catholic Church has long had a prohibition on marriages to first cousins, and in the 19th century such marriages were illegal in most of the United States. In numerous other societies, however, first cousins are preferred spouses.

In the 19th century, Sir Edward Tylor advanced a proposition that alternatives to inbreeding were either "marrying out or being killed out."[9] Our ancestors, he suggested, discovered the advantage of intermarriage to create bonds of friendship. Claude Lévi-Strauss elaborated on this premise. He saw exogamy as the basis of a distinction between early hominine life in isolated endogamous groups and the life of *Homo sapiens* in a supportive society with an accumulating culture. Alliances with other groups, established and strengthened by marriage ties, make possible a sharing of culture. Building on Lévi Strauss's work, anthropologist Yehudi Cohen suggests exogamy was an important means of promoting trade between groups, thereby ensuring access to needed goods and resources not otherwise available. Noting that incest taboos necessitating exogamy are generally most widely extended in the least complex of human societies but do not extend beyond parents and siblings in industrialized societies, he argues that as formal governments and other institutions have come to control trade, the need for extended taboos has been removed. Indeed, he suggests that this may have reached the point where the incest taboo is becoming obsolete altogether.

In a roundabout way, exogamy also helps to explain some exceptions to the incest taboo, such as that of obligatory brother and sister marriage within the royal families of ancient Egypt, the Inca empire, and Hawaii. Members of these royal families were considered semidivine, and their very sacredness kept them from marrying mere mortals. The brother and sister married so as *not* to share their godliness, thereby maintaining the "purity" of the royal line, not to mention control of royal property. By the same token, in Roman Egypt, where property was inherited by women as well as men and where the relationship between land

[8]Thornhill, N. (1993). Quoted in W. A. Haviland & R. J. Gordon (Eds.), *Talking about people* (p. 127). Mountain View, CA: Mayfield.

[9]Quoted in R. M. Keesing (1976), *Cultural anthropology: A contemporary perspective* (p. 286). New York: Holt, Rinehart and Winston.

Endogamy. Marriage within a particular group or category of individuals. **> Exogamy.** Marriage outside the group.

Claude Lévi-Strauss   *(1908–)*

Claude Lévi-Strauss is the leading exponent of French structuralism, which sees culture as a surface representation of underlying mental structures that have been affected by a group's physical and social environment as well as its history. Thus, cultures may vary considerably, even though the structure of the human thought processes responsible for them is the same for all people everywhere.

Human thought processes are structured, according to Lévi-Strauss, into contrastive pairs of polar opposites, such as light versus dark, good versus evil, nature versus culture, and raw versus cooked. The ultimate contrastive pair is that of "self" versus "others," which is necessary for true symbolic communication to occur and which culture depends on. Communication is a reciprocal exchange, which is extended to include goods and marital partners. Hence, the incest taboo stems from this fundamental contrastive pair of "self" versus "others." From this universal taboo are built the many and varied marriage rules ethnographers have described.

and people was particularly tight, brother-sister marriages among the farming class acted to prevent fragmentation of a family's holdings.

THE DISTINCTION BETWEEN MARRIAGE AND MATING

Having defined marriage in terms of sexual access, we must at this point make clear the distinction between systems of marriage and mating. All animals, including humans, mate—some for life and some not, some with a single individual of the opposite sex, and some with several. Mates are secured and held solely through individual effort, as opposed to marriage, which is a right society confers. Only marriage is backed by legal, economic, and social forces. Even among the Nayar, where marriage seems to involve little else than a sexual relationship, a woman's husband is legally obligated to provide her with gifts at specified intervals. Nor may a woman legally have sex with a man she is not married to. Thus, while mating is biological, marriage is cultural.

In the United States, as in most Western countries, monogamy is the only legally recognized form of marriage. Nevertheless, about 50 percent of all marriages end in divorce, and most divorced people remarry at least once. Thus, serial monogamy is far from uncommon.

The distinction between marriage and mating may be seen by looking, briefly, at practices in contemporary North American society, where **monogamy**—the taking of a single spouse—is the

---

Monogamy.   Marriage in which an individual has one spouse.

only legally recognized form of marriage. Not only are other forms not legally sanctioned, but also systems of inheritance, whereby property and wealth are transferred from one generation to the next, are predicated upon the institution of monogamous marriage. Mating patterns, by contrast, are frequently *not* monogamous. Not only is adultery far from rare in the United States and Canada, but also it has become increasingly acceptable for individuals of the opposite sex—particularly young people who have not yet married—to live together outside of wedlock. None of these arrangements, however, are legally sanctioned. Frequently, even individuals who do not engage in sexual activity outside of wedlock mate with more than one person of the opposite sex in their lifetime; this follows from the fact that more than 50% of first marriages in the United States end in divorce and most divorced people ultimately remarry.

Among primates in general, monogamous mating patterns are not common. Although some smaller species of South American monkeys, a few island-dwelling populations of leaf-eating Old World monkeys, and all of the smaller apes (gibbons and siamangs) do mate for life with but one individual of the opposite sex, none of these are closely related to human beings. Nor do "monogamous" primates ever display the degree of anatomical differences between males and females characteristic of our closest primate relatives or of our own ancient ancestors. Thus it is not likely the human species began its career as one with monogamous mating patterns. Certainly, we cannot say (as some have tried to assert) the human species is, by nature, monogamous in its mating behavior.

MARRIAGE AND THE FAMILY

Although, as shown in the discussion of the Nayar, marriage need not involve establishment of a new family, it easily can serve this purpose, in addition to its main function of indicating who has continuing sexual access to whom. Creating a family through marriage is precisely what most human societies do. Consequently, some mention of family organization—otherwise discussed in Chapter 20—is necessary before we proceed further with the discussion of marriage. If we were to define the family in familiar terms, as requiring fathers, mothers, and children, then we would have to say people like the Nayar (who, as we shall see in Chapter 20, do not constitute a unique case) do not have families. We can, however, define the **family** in a less ethnocentric way as a group composed of a woman and her dependent children and at least one adult male joined through marriage or blood relationship.[10] The Nayar form a **consanguine family,** consisting as it does of women, their dependent offspring, and the women's brothers. In such societies, men and women get married but do not live together as members of one household. Rather, they spend their lives in the households they grew up in, with the men "commuting" for sexual activity with their wives. Economic cooperation between men and women occurs between sisters and brothers, rather than husbands and wives.

Conjugal, as opposed to consanguine, families are formed on the basis of marital ties between husband and wife. Minimally, a conjugal family consists of a married couple with their dependent children, otherwise known as the **nuclear family;** other forms of conjugal families are *polygynous* and *polyandrous* families, which may be thought of as aggregates of nuclear families with one spouse in common. A polygynous family includes the multiple wives of a single husband, while a polyandrous family includes the multiple husbands of a single wife. Both are often lumped together under the heading of polygamous families.

---

[10]Goodenough, W. H. (1970). *Description and comparison in cultural anthropology* (p. 19). Chicago: Aldine.

Family. A residential kin group composed of a woman, her dependent children, and at least one adult male joined through marriage or blood relationship. **> Consanguine family.** A family consisting of related women, their offspring, and the women's brothers **> Nuclear family.** A family unit consisting of husband, wife, and dependent children.

FORMS OF MARRIAGE

Monogamy is the form of marriage North Americans are most familiar with. It is also the most common, but for economic rather than moral reasons. In many polygynous societies, a man must be fairly wealthy to afford **polygyny,** or marriage to more than one wife. Among the Kapauku of western New Guinea, the ideal is to have as many wives as possible, and a woman actually urges her husband to spend money on acquiring additional wives.[11] She even has the legal right to divorce him if she can prove he has money for bride-prices and refuses to remarry. As we saw in Chapter 14, wives are desirable because they work in the fields and care for pigs, by which wealth is measured, but

[11]Pospisil, L. (1963). *The Kapauku Papuans of west New Guinea.* New York: Holt, Rinehart and Winston.

not all men are wealthy enough to afford bride-prices for multiple wives.

Among the Turkana, a pastoral nomadic people of northern Kenya, the number of animals at a family's disposal is directly related to the number of adult women available to care for them. The more wives a man has, the more women there are looking after the livestock and the more substantial are the family's holdings. Thus, it is not uncommon for a man's existing wife to actively search for another woman to marry her husband. Again, however, a substantial bride-price is involved in marriage, and only men of wealth and prominence can afford large numbers of wives.

Although monogamy may be the commonest form of marriage around the world, it is not the most preferred. That distinction goes to polygyny, which is favored by about 80% to 85% of the world's societies. Even in the United States, an estimated 50,000 people in the Rocky Mountain states live in households made up of a man with

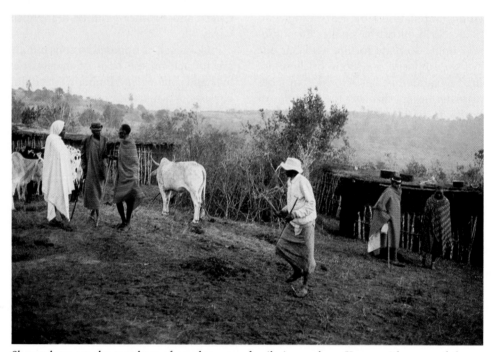

Shown here are the members of a polygynous family in northern Kenya with some of the dwellings that make up their household compound.

Polygyny. The marriage custom of a man having two or more wives simultaneously; a form of polygamy.

two or more wives. In spite of its illegality, regional law enforcement officials have adopted a "live and let live" attitude toward polygyny. Nor are those involved in such marriages uneducated. One woman—a lawyer and one of nine cowives—expresses her attitude as follows:

> I see it as the ideal way for a woman to have a career and children. In our family, the women can help each other care for the children. Women in monogamous relationships don't have that luxury. As I see it, if this life style didn't already exist, it would have to be invented to accommodate career women.[12]

Polygyny is particularly common in societies that support themselves by growing crops and where women do the bulk of the farmwork. Under these conditions, women are valued both as workers and as childbearers. Because the labor of wives in polygynous households generates wealth and little support is required from husbands, the wives have a strong bargaining position within the household. Often, they have considerable freedom of movement and some economic independence from the sale of crops. Commonly, each wife within the household lives with her children in her own dwelling, apart from her cowives and husband who occupy other houses within some sort of larger household compound (note that the terms *house* and *household* need not be synonymous; a household may consist of several houses together, as here). Because of this residential autonomy, fathers are usually remote from their sons, who grow up among women. As noted in Chapter 16, this is the sort of setting conducive to the development of aggressiveness in adult males, who must prove their masculinity. As a consequence, a high value is often placed on military glory, and one reason for going to war is to capture women, who then may become a warrior's cowives. This wealth-increasing pattern is found in its fullest elaboration in sub-Saharan Africa, though it is known elsewhere as well (the Kapauku are another case). Moreover, it is still intact in the world today, because its wealth-generating properties at the household level make it an economically productive system.[13]

In societies practicing wealth-generating polygyny, most men and women do enter into polygynous marriages, although some can do this earlier in life than others. This practice is made possible by a female-biased sex ratio and/or by a mean age at marriage for females significantly below that for males (this creates a cohort of women looking for husbands larger than the cohort of men looking for wives). By contrast, in societies where men are more heavily involved in productive work, generally only a small minority of marriages are polygynous. Under these circumstances, women are more dependant on men for support, so they are valued as childbearers more than for the work they do. This is commonly the case in pastoral nomadic societies where men are the primary owners and tenders of livestock. This makes women especially vulnerable if they prove incapable of bearing children, which is one reason a man may seek another wife. Another reason for a man to take on secondary wives is to demonstrate his high position in society. But where men do most of the productive work, they must work exceptionally hard to support more than one wife, and few actually do so. Usually, it is the exceptional hunter, a male shaman ("medicine man") in a food-foraging society, or a particularly wealthy man in an agricultural or pastoral society who is most apt to practice polygyny. When he does, it is usually of the *sororal* type, with the cowives being sisters. Having already lived together before marriage, the sisters continue to do so with their husband, instead of occupying separate dwellings of their own.

Although monogamy and polygyny are the most common forms of marriage in the world today, other forms do occur, however rarely. **Polyandry**, the marriage of one woman to two or

---

[12]Johnson, D. (1996). Polygamists emerge from secrecy, seeking not just peace but respect. In W. A. Haviland & R. J. Gordon (Eds.), *Talking about people* (2nd ed., pp. 129–131). Mountain View, CA: Mayfield.

[13]White, D. R. (1988). Rethinking polygyny: Co-Wives, codes and cultural systems. *Current Anthropology, 29,* 529–572.

Polyandry.   The marriage custom of a woman having two or more husbands simultaneously; a form of polygamy.

more men simultaneously, is known in only a few societies, perhaps in part because men's life expectancy is shorter than women's, and male infant mortality is high, so a surplus of men in a society is unlikely. Where sex ratios are balanced, as in Ladakh, many women are likely to remain unmarried. Another reason for polyandry's rarity is that it limits a man's descendants more than any other pattern. Fewer than a dozen societies are known to have favored this form of marriage, but they involve people as widely separated from one another as the eastern Inuit (Eskimos), Marquesan Islanders of Polynesia, and Tibetans. In Tibet, where inheritance is in the male line and arable land is limited, the marriage of brothers to a single woman averts the danger of constantly subdividing farmlands among all the sons of any one landholder. Unlike monogamy, it also restrains population growth, thereby avoiding increased pressures on resources. Finally, it provides the household with an adequate pool of male labor. For tripartite economies of farming, herding, and trading, trifraternal polyandry is highly valued, as it allows the three brothers who are cohusbands to pursue all three options at once.[14]

Group marriage, in which several men and women have sexual access to one another, also occurs rarely. Even in recent communal groups, among young people seeking alternatives to modern marriage forms, group marriage seems a transitory phenomenon, despite the publicity it sometimes has received.

THE LEVIRATE AND THE SORORATE

If a husband dies, leaving a wife and children, it is often the custom that the wife marry one of the brothers of the dead man. This custom, called the **levirate,** not only provides social security for the widow and her children but also is a way for the husband's family to maintain their rights over her sexuality and her future children: It acts to preserve relationships previously established. When a man marries the sister of his dead wife, it is called the **sororate;** in essence, a family of "wife givers" supplies one of "wife takers" with another spouse to take the place of the one who died. In societies that have the levirate and sororate, the relationship between the two families thus is maintained even after a spouse's death; and in such societies, an adequate supply of brothers and sisters is generally ensured by the structure of the kinship system (discussed in Chapter 21), whereby individuals North Americans would call "cousins" are classified as brothers and sisters.

SERIAL MONOGAMY

A form of marriage increasingly common in North American society today is **serial monogamy,** whereby the man or the woman marries or lives with a series of partners in succession. Currently, more than 50% of first marriages end in divorce, and some experts project that two thirds of recent marriages will not last.[15] Upon dissolution of a marriage, the children more often than not remain with the mother. This pattern is an outgrowth of one sociologists and anthropologists first described among West Indians and lower-class urban blacks in the United States. Early in life, women begin to bear children by men who are not married to them. To support themselves and their children, the women must look for work outside the household, but to do so they must seek help from other kin, most commonly their mother. As a consequence, households are frequently headed by women (on the average, about 32% are so headed in the West Indies). After a number of years, however, an unmarried woman usually does marry a man, who may or may not be the father of some

---

[14]Levine, N. E., & Silk, J. B. (1997). Why polyandry fails. *Current Anthropology, 38,* 375–398.

[15]Stacey, J. (1990). *Brave new families* (pp.15, 286, n. 46). New York: Basic Books.

Group marriage. Marriage in which several men and women have sexual access to one another. > **Levirate.** The marriage custom whereby a widow marries a brother of her dead husband. > **Sororate.** The marriage custom whereby a widower marries his dead wife's sister. > **Serial monogamy.** A marriage form in which a man or a woman marries or lives with a series of partners in succession.

or all of her children. Under poverty conditions, where this pattern has been most common, women are driven to seek this male support, owing to the difficulties of supporting themselves and their children while fulfilling their domestic obligations.

In the United States, with the rise of live-in premarital arrangements by couples, the increasing necessity for women to seek work outside the home, and rising divorce rates, a similar pattern is becoming more common among middle-class whites. In 90% of divorce cases, it is the women who assume responsibility for any children; furthermore, of all children born in the United States today, fully 25% are born out of wedlock. Frequently isolated from kin or other assistance, women in single-parent households (which now outnumber nuclear family households) commonly find it difficult to cope. Within a year following divorce, the standard of living for women drops some 73%, whereas that of men *increases* by about 42%.[16] To be sure, fathers of children are usually expected to provide child support, but in 50% of the cases of children born out of wedlock, paternity cannot be established. Furthermore, failure of fathers to live up to their obligations is far from rare. One solution for unmarried women is to marry (often, to remarry) to get the assistance of another adult.

CHOICE OF SPOUSE

The Western egalitarian ideal that an individual should be free to marry whomever he or she chooses is an unusual arrangement, certainly not universally embraced. However desirable such an ideal may be in the abstract, it is fraught with difficulties and certainly contributes to the apparent instability of marital relationships in modern North American society. Part of the problem is the great emphasis the culture places on the importance of youth and glamour—especially of women —for romantic love. Female youth and beauty are perhaps most glaringly exploited by the women's wear, cosmetics, and beauty parlor industries, but

movies, television, and the recorded-music business generally do not lag far behind, nor do advertisements for cigarettes, hard and soft drinks, beer, automobiles, and a host of other products that make liberal use of young, glamorous women. As anthropologist Jules Henry once observed, "even men's wear and toiletries could not be marketed as efficiently without an adoring, pretty woman (well under thirty-five years of age) looking at a man wearing a stylish shirt or sniffing at a man wearing a deodorant."[17] By no means are all North Americans taken in by this, but it does

---

[17]Henry, J. (1966). The metaphysic of youth, beauty, and romantic love. In S. Farber & R. Wilson (Eds.), *The challenge to women.* New York: Basic Books.

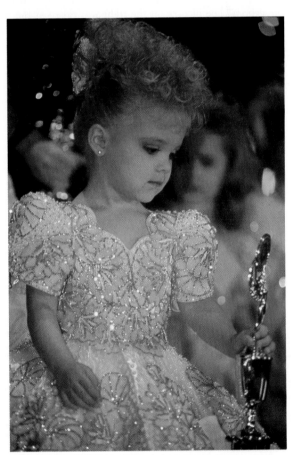

The obsession with a particular idea of feminine beauty in the United States is reflected in the beauty pageants organized for very young girls.

---

[16]Weitzman, L. J. (1985). *The divorce revolution: The unexpected social and economic consequences for women and children in America* (p. 338). New York: The Free Press.

Marriage is a means of creating alliances between groups of people. Since such alliances have important economic and political implications, the decision cannot be left in the hands of the two young and inexperienced people. At the left is shown a Indian bride, whose marriage has been arranged between her parents and those of the groom. The picture on the right was taken at the wedding of Prince Charles and Lady Diana in England.

tend to nudge people in such a way that marriages all too easily may be based on trivial and transient characteristics. In no other part of the world are such chances taken with something as momentous as marriage.

In many societies, marriage and the establishment of a family are considered far too important to be left to the whims of young people. The marriage of two individuals expected to spend their whole lives together and raise their children together is incidental to the more serious matter of making allies of two families through the marriage bond. Marriage involves a transfer of rights between families, including rights to property and rights over the children, as well as sexual rights.

Thus, marriages tend to be arranged for the economic and political advantage of the family unit.

Arranged marriages, needless to say, are not commonplace in North American society, but they do occur. Among ethnic minorities, they may serve to preserve traditional values people fear might otherwise be lost. Among families of wealth and power, marriages may be arranged by segregating their children in private schools and carefully steering them toward "proper" marriages. A careful reading of announced engagements in the society pages of the *New York Times* provides clear evidence of such family alliances. The following Original Study illustrates how marriages may be arranged in societies where such practices are commonplace.

Arranging Marriage in India[18]

Sister and doctor brother-in-law invite correspondence from North Indian professionals only, for a beautiful, talented, sophisticated, intelligent sister, 5'3", slim, M.A. in textile design, father a senior civil officer. Would prefer immigrant doctors, between 26–29 years. Reply with full details and returnable photo.

[18]Nanda, S. (1992). Arranging a marriage in India. In P. R. De Vita (Ed.), *The naked anthropologist* (pp. 139–143). Belmont, CA: Wadsworth.

A well-settled uncle invites matrimonial correspondence from slim, fair, educated South Indian girl, for his nephew, 25 years, smart, M.B.A., green card holder, 5'6". Full particulars with returnable photo appreciated.
—*Matrimonial Advertisements*, India Abroad

Six years [after my first field trip] I returned to India to again do fieldwork, this time among the middle class in Bombay (now known as Mumbai), a modern, sophisticated city. From the experience of my earlier visit, I decided to include a study of arranged marriages in my project. By this time I had met many Indian couples whose marriages had been arranged and who seemed very happy. Particularly in contrast to the fate of many of my married friends in the United States who were already in the process of divorce the positive aspects of arranged marriages appeared to me to outweigh the negatives. In fact, I thought I might even participate in arranging a marriage myself. I had been fairly successful in the United States in "fixing up" many of my friends, and I was confident that my matchmaking skills could be easily applied to this new situation, once I learned the basic rules. "After all," I thought, "how complicated can it be? People want pretty much the same things in a marriage whether it is in India or America."

An opportunity presented itself almost immediately. A friend from my previous Indian trip was in the process of arranging for the marriage of her eldest son. In India there is a perceived shortage of "good boys," and since my friend's family was eminently respectable and the boy himself personable, well educated, and nice looking, I was sure that by the end of my year's fieldwork, we would have found a match.

The basic rule seems to be that a family's reputation is most important. It is understood that matches would be arranged only within the same caste and general social class, although some crossing of subcastes is permissible if the class positions of the bride's and groom's families are similar. Although dowry is now prohibited by law in India, extensive gift exchanges took place with every marriage. Even when the boy's family do not "make demands," every girl's family nevertheless feels the obligation to give the traditional gifts, to the girl, to the boy, and to the boy's family. Particularly when the couple would be living in the joint family—that is, with the boy's parents and his married brothers and their families, as well as with unmarried siblings—which is still very common even among the urban, upper-middle class in India, the girl's parents are anxious to establish smooth relations between their family and that of the boy. Offering the proper gifts, even when not called "dowry," is often an important factor in influencing the relationship between the bride's and groom's families and perhaps, also, the treatment of the bride in her new home.

In a society where divorce is still a scandal and where, in fact, the divorce rate is exceedingly low, an arranged marriage is the beginning of a lifetime relationship not just between the bride and groom but between their families as well. Thus, while a girl's looks are important, her character is even more so, for she is being judged as a prospective daughter-in-law as much as a prospective bride. Where she would be living in a joint family, as was the case with my friend, the girl's ability to get along harmoniously in a family is perhaps the single most important quality in assessing her suitability.

My friend is a highly esteemed wife, mother, and daughter-in-law. She is religious, soft-spoken, modest, and deferential. She rarely gossips and never quarrels, two qualities highly desirable in a woman. A family that has the reputation for gossip and conflict among its womenfolk will not find it easy to get good wives for their sons. Parents will not want to send their daughter to a house in which there is conflict.

My friend's family were originally from North India. They had lived in Bombay, where her husband owned a business, for forty years. The family had delayed in seeking a match for their eldest son because he had been an Air Force pilot for several years, stationed in such remote places that it had seemed fruitless to try to find a girl who would be willing to accompany him. In their social class, a military career, despite its economic security, has little prestige and is considered a drawback in finding a suitable bride. Many families would not allow their daughters to marry a man in an occupation so potentially dangerous and which requires so much moving around.

The son had recently left the military and joined his father's business. Since he was a college graduate, modern, and well traveled, from such a good family, and, I thought, quite handsome, it seemed to me that he, or rather his family, was in a position to pick and choose. I said as much to my friend.

While she agreed that there were many advantages on their side, she also said, "We must keep in mind that my son is both short and dark; these are drawbacks in finding the right match." While the boy's height had not escaped my notice, "dark" seemed to me inaccurate; I would have called him "wheat" colored perhaps, and in any case, I did not realize that color would be a consideration. I discovered, however, that while a boy's skin color is a less important consideration than a girl's, it is still a factor.

An important source of contacts in trying to arrange her son's marriage was my friend's social club in Bombay. Many of the women had daughters of the right age, and some had already expressed an interest in my friend's son. I was most enthusiastic about the possibilities of one particular family who had five daughters, all of whom were pretty, demure, and well educated. Their mother had told my friend, "You can have your pick for your son, whichever one of my daughters appeals to you most."

I saw a match in sight. "Surely," I said to my friend, "we will find one there. Let's go visit and make our choice." But my friend held back; she did not seem to share my enthusiasm, for reasons I could not then fathom.

When I kept pressing for an explanation of her reluctance, she admitted, "See, Serena, here is the problem. The family has so many daughters, how will they be able to provide nicely for any of them? We are not making any demands, but still, with so many daughters to marry off, one wonders whether she will even be able to make a proper wedding. Since this is our eldest son, it's best if we marry him to a girl who is the only daughter, then the wedding will truly be a gala affair." I argued that surely the quality of the girls themselves made up for any deficiency in the elaborateness of the wedding. My friend admitted this point but still seemed reluctant to proceed.

"Is there something else," I asked her, "some factor I have missed?" "Well," she finally said, "there is one other thing. They have one daughter already married and living in Bombay. The mother is always complaining to me that the girl's in-laws don't let her visit her own family often enough. So it makes me wonder, will she be that kind of mother who always wants her daughter at her own home? This will prevent the girl from adjusting to our house. It is not a good thing." And so, this family of five daughters was dropped as a possibility.

Somewhat disappointed, I nevertheless respected my friend's reasoning and geared up for the next prospect. This was also the daughter of a woman in my friend's social club. There was clear interest in this family and I could see why. The family's reputation was excellent; in fact, they came from a sub-caste slightly higher than my friend's own. The girl, who was an only daughter, was pretty and well educated and had a brother studying in the United States. Yet, after expressing an interest to me in this family, all talk of them suddenly died down and the search began elsewhere.

"What happened to that girl as a prospect?" I asked one day. "You never mention her any more. She is so pretty and so educated, what did you find wrong?"

"She is too educated. We've decided against it. My husband's father saw the girl on the bus the other day and thought her forward. A girl who 'roams about' the city by herself is not the girl for our family." My disappointment this time was even greater, as I thought the son would have liked the girl very much. But then I thought, my friend is right, a girl who is going to live in a joint family cannot be too independent or she will make life miserable for everyone. I also learned that if the family of the girl has even a slightly higher social status than the family of the boy, the bride may think herself too good for them, and this too will cause problems. Later my friend admitted to me that this had been an important factor in her decision not to pursue the match.

The next candidate was the daughter of a client of my friend's husband. When the client learned that the family was looking for a match for their son, he said, "Look no further, we have a daughter." This man then invited my friends to dinner to see the girl. He had already seen their son at the office and decided that "he liked the boy." We all went together for tea, rather than dinner—it was less of a commitment—and while we were there, the girl's mother showed us around the house. The girl was studying for her exams and was briefly introduced to us.

After we left, I was anxious to hear my friend's opinion. While her husband liked the family very much and was impressed with his client's business accomplishments and reputation, the wife didn't like the girl's looks. "She is short, no doubt, which is an important plus point, but she is also fat and wears glasses." My friend obviously thought she could do better for her son and asked her husband to make his excuses to his client by saying that they had decided to postpone the boy's marriage indefinitely.

By this time almost six months had passed and I was becoming impatient. What I had thought would be an easy matter to arrange was turning out to be quite complicated. I began to believe that between my friend's desire for a girl who was modest enough to fit into her joint family, yet attractive and educated enough to be an acceptable partner for her son, she would not find anyone suitable. My friend laughed at my impatience: "Don't be so much in a hurry," she said. "You Americans want everything done so quickly. You get married quickly and then just as quickly get divorced. Here we take marriage more seriously. We must take all the factors into account. It is not enough for us to learn by our mistakes. This is too serious a business. If a mistake is made we have not only ruined the life of our son or daughter, but we have spoiled the reputation of our family as well. And that will make it much harder for their brothers and sisters to get married. So we must be very careful."

What she said was true and I promised myself to be more patient, though it was not easy. I had really hoped and expected that the match would be made before my year in India was up. But it was not to be. When I left India my friend seemed no further along in finding a suitable match for her son than when I had arrived.

Two years later, I returned to India and still my friend had not found a girl for her son. By this time, he was close to thirty, and I think she was a little worried. Since she knew I had friends all over India, and I was going to be there for a year, she asked me to "help her in this work" and keep an eye out for someone suitable. I was flattered that my judgment was respected, but knowing now how complicated the process was, I had lost my earlier confidence as a matchmaker. Nevertheless, I promised that I would try.

It was almost at the end of my year's stay in India that I met a family with a marriageable daughter whom I felt might be a good possibility for my friend's son. The girl's father was related to a good friend of mine and by coincidence came from the same village as my friend's husband. This new family had a successful business in a medium-sized city in central India and were from the same subcaste as my friend. The daughter was pretty and chic; in fact, she had studied fashion design in college. Her parents would not allow her to go off by herself to any of the major cities in India where she could make a career, but they had compromised with her wish to work by allowing her to run a small dress-making boutique from their home. In spite of her desire to have a career, the daughter was both modest and home-loving and had had a traditional, sheltered upbringing. She had only one other sister, already married, and a brother who was in his father's business.

I mentioned the possibility of a match with my friend's son. The girl's parents were most interested. Although their daughter was not eager to marry just yet, the idea of living in Bombay—a sophisticated, extremely fashion-conscious city where she could continue her education in clothing design—was a great inducement. I gave the girl's father my friend's address and suggested that when they went to Bombay on some business or whatever, they look up the boy's family.

Returning to Bombay on my way to New York, I told my friend of this newly discovered possibility. She seemed to feel there was potential but, in spite of my urging, would not make any moves herself. She rather preferred to wait for the girl's family to call upon them. I hoped something would come of this introduction, though by now I had learned to rein in my optimism.

A year later I received a letter from my friend. The family had indeed come to visit Bombay, and their daughter and my friend's daughter, who were near in age, had become very good friends. During that year, the two girls had frequently visited each other. I thought things looked promising.

Last week I received an invitation to a wedding: My friend's son and the girl were getting married. Since I had found the match, my presence was particularly requested at the wedding. I was thrilled. Success at last! As I prepared to leave for India, I began thinking, "Now, my friend's younger son, who do I know who has a nice girl for him . . . ?"

COUSIN MARRIAGE

In some societies, preferred marriages are a man marrying his father's brother's daughter. This is known as **patrilateral parallel-cousin marriage** (Figure 19.2; a parallel cousin is the child of a father's brother or a mother's sister). Although not obligatory, such marriages have been favored historically among Arabs, the ancient Israelites, and also in ancient Greece and traditional China. All of these societies are hierarchical in nature—that is, some people have more property than others—

and although male dominance and descent are emphasized, property of interest to men is inherited by daughters as well as sons. Thus, when a man marries his father's brother's daughter (or from the woman's point of view, her father's brother's son), property is retained within the male line of descent. In these societies, generally speaking, the greater the property, the more this form of parallel-cousin marriage is apt to occur.

Matrilateral cross-cousin marriage (Figure 19.2)—that is, of a man to his mother's brother's

FIGURE 19.2
Anthropologists use diagrams of this sort to illustrate kinship relationships. Shown in this one is the distinction between cross and parallel cousins. In such diagrams, males are always shown as triangles, females as circles, martial ties by a =, sibling relationships as a horizontal line, and parent-child relationships as a vertical line. Terms are given from the perspective of the individual labeled *ego,* who can be female or male.

Patrilateral parallel-cousin marriage.   Marriage of a man to his father's brother's daughter or of a woman to her father's brother's son (i.e., to a parallel cousin on the paternal side). **> Matrilateral cross-cousin marriage.**   Marriage of a woman to her father's sister's son or of a man to his mother's brother's daughter (her cross cousin on the paternal side, his cross cousin on the maternal side).

daughter or of a woman to her father's sister's son (a cross cousin is the child of a mother's brother or a father's sister)—is a preferred form of marriage in a variety of societies ranging from food foragers (Australian Aborigines, for example) to intensive agriculturists (such as among various peoples of South India). Among food-foraging peoples, who inherit relatively little property, such marriages help establish and maintain ties of solidarity between social groups. In agricultural societies, however, the transmission of property is an important determinant. Societies that trace descent exclusively in the female line, for instance, usually pass property and important rights from a man to his sister's son; under cross-cousin marriage, the sister's son is also the man's daughter's husband.

MARRIAGE EXCHANGES

In the Trobriand Islands, when a young couple decides to get married, they sit in public on the veranda of the young man's adolescent retreat, where all may see them. Here they remain until the bride's mother brings the couple cooked yams, which they then eat together, making their marriage official. This is followed a day later by the presentation of three long skirts to the bride by the husband's sister, a symbol of the fact the sexual freedom of adolescence is now over for the newly wed woman. This is followed up by a large presentation of uncooked yams by the bride's father and her mother's brother, who represent both her father's and her own lineages.

Meanwhile, the groom's father and mother's brother—representing his father's and his own lineages—collect such valuables as stone axe blades, clay pots, money, and the occasional Kula shell to present to the young wife's maternal kin and father. After the first year of the marriage, during which the bride's mother continues to provide the couple's meals of cooked yams, each of the young husband's relatives who provided valuables for his father and mother's brother to present to the bride's relatives will receive yams from her maternal relatives and father. All of this gift giving back and forth between the lineages the husband and

On the day her marriage is announced, the Trobriand bride must give up the provocative miniskirts she has worn until then in favor of longer skirts, the first of which the groom's sister provides. This announces that her days of sexual freedom are gone.

wife belong to, as well as those of their fathers, serve to bind the four parties together so that people respect and honor the marriage and to create obligations for the woman's kin to take care of her husband in the future.

As among the Trobriand Islanders, marriages in many human societies are formalized by some sort of economic exchange. Among the Trobrianders, this takes the form of a gift exchange, as just described. Far more common is **bride-price**,

---

Bride-price. Compensation the groom or his family pays to the bride's family on marriage.

In many African societies, bride price takes the form of cattle, which are paid by the groom's family to the bride's family.

sometimes called bride wealth. This involves payments of money or other valuables to a bride's parents or other close kin. This usually happens in societies where the bride will become a member of the household where her husband grew up; this household will benefit from her labor, as well as the offspring she produces. Thus, her family must be compensated for their loss.

Not only is bride-price *not* a simple "buying and selling" of women, but also the bride's parents may use the money to buy jewelry or household furnishings for her or to finance an elaborate and costly wedding celebration. It also contributes to the stability of the marriage, because it usually must be refunded if the couple separates. Other forms of compensation are an exchange of women between families—"my son will marry your daughter if your son will marry my daughter"—

In some societies when a woman marries, she receives her share of the family inheritance (her dowry), which she brings to her new family (unlike bride-price, which passes from the groom's family to the bride's family). Shown here are Slovakian women carrying the objects of a woman's dowry.

or **bride service,** a period of time during which the groom works for the bride's family.

In a number of societies more or less restricted to the western, southern, and eastern margins of Eurasia, where the economy is based on intensive agriculture, women often bring a **dowry** with them at marriage. A form of dowry in the United States is the custom of the bride's family paying the wedding expenses. In effect, a dowry is a woman's share of parental property that, instead of passing to her upon her parents' death, is distributed to her at the time of her marriage. This does not mean she retains control of this property after marriage. In a number of European countries, for example, a woman's property falls exclusively under her husband's control. Having benefited by what she has brought to the marriage, however, he is obligated to look out for her future well-being, even after his death. Thus, one of the functions of dowry is to ensure a woman's support in widowhood (or after divorce), an important consideration in a society where men carry out the bulk of productive work and women are valued for their reproductive potential, rather than for the work they do. In such societies, women incapable of bearing children are especially vulnerable, but the dowry they bring with them at marriage helps protect them against desertion. Another dowry function is to reflect the economic status of the woman in societies where differences in wealth are important. Thus, the property a woman brings with her at marriage demonstrates that the man is marrying a woman whose standing is on a par with his own. It also permits women, with the aid of their parents and kin, to compete through dowries for desirable (that is, wealthy) husbands.

SAME-SEX MARRIAGE

As noted earlier in this chapter, although marriage is defined in terms of a continuing sexual relationship between a man and woman, the cultural nature of gender is such that the "man" may in fact be a female or the "woman" a male. Thus, marriages between individuals of the same sex may be regarded as proper and normal. Such marriages provide a way to deal with problems opposite-sex marriage offers no satisfactory solution for. This is true for the woman/woman marriage practice sanctioned in many societies of sub-Saharan Africa, although in none does it involve more than a small minority of all women.

Although details differ from one society to another, woman/woman marriages among the Nandi of western Kenya may be taken as reasonably representative of such practices in Africa.[19] The Nandi are a pastoral people who also do considerable farming. Control of most significant property and the primary means of production—livestock and land—is exclusively in the hands of men, and may only be transmitted to their male heirs, usually their sons. Since polygyny is the preferred form of marriage, a man's property is normally divided equally among his wives for their sons to inherit. Within the household, each wife has her own house in which she lives with her children, but all are under the authority of the woman's husband, who is a remote and aloof figure within the household. In such situations, the position of a woman who bears no sons is difficult; not only does she not help perpetuate her husband's male line—a major concern among the Nandi—but also she has no one to inherit the proper share of her husband's property.

To get around these problems, a woman of advanced age who bore no sons may become a female husband by marrying a young woman. The purpose of this arrangement is for the wife to provide the male heirs her female husband could not. To accomplish this, the woman's wife enters into a sex-

---

[19]The following is based on R. S. Obler (1980), Is the female husband a man? Woman/woman marriage among the Nandi of Kenya. *Ethnology, 19,* 69–88.

Bride service.   A designated period after marriage when the groom works for the bride's family.   > **Dowry.**   Payment of a woman's inheritance at the time of her marriage, either to her or to her husband.

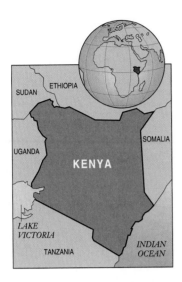

ual relationship with a man other than her female husband's male husband; usually it is one of his male relatives. No other obligations exist between this woman and her male sex partner, and her female husband is recognized as the social and legal father of any children born under these conditions.

In keeping with her role as female husband, this woman is expected to abandon her female gender identity and, ideally, dress and behave as a man. In practice, the ideal is not completely achieved, for the habits of a lifetime are difficult to reverse. Generally, it is in the context of domestic activities, which are most highly symbolic of female identity, that female husbands most completely assume a male identity.

The individuals who are parties to woman/woman marriages enjoy several advantages. By assuming a male identity, a barren or sonless woman raises her status considerably and even achieves near equality with men, who otherwise occupy a far more favored position in Nandi society than women. A woman who marries a female husband is usually one who is unable to make a good marriage, often because she has lost face as a consequence of premarital pregnancy. By marrying a female husband, she too raises her status and also secures legitimacy for her children. Moreover, a female husband is usually less harsh and

demanding, spends more time with her, and allows her a greater say in decision making than a male husband does. Her one prohibition is engaging in sexual activity with her marriage partner; in fact, female husbands are expected to abandon sexual activity altogether, even with their male husband, to whom they remain married even though the women now have their own wives.

DIVORCE

Like marriage, divorce in non-Western societies is a matter of great concern to the couple's families. Since marriage is less often a religious than an economic matter, divorce arrangements can be made for a variety of reasons and with varying degrees of difficulty.

Among the Gusii of Kenya, sterility or impotence were grounds for a divorce. Among the Chenchu of Hyderabad and certain Indians of northern Canada, divorce was discouraged after children were born, and couples usually were urged by their families to adjust their differences. By contrast, in the southwestern United States, a Hopi woman might divorce her husband at any time merely by placing his belongings outside the door to indicate he was no longer welcome. Divorce was fairly common among the Yahgan, who lived at the southernmost tip of South America, and was seen as justified if the husband was considered cruel or failed as a provider.

Divorce in these societies seems familiar and even sensible, and, in one way or another, the children are taken care of. An adult unmarried woman is almost unheard of in most non-Western societies; a divorced woman soon remarries. In many societies, economic considerations are often the strongest motivation to marry. On the island of New Guinea, a man does not marry because of sexual needs, which he can readily satisfy out of wedlock, but because he needs a woman to make pots and cook his meals, to fabricate nets, and to weed his plantings. A man without a wife among the Australian Aborigines is in an unsatisfactory position, since he

In Europe, where both men and women inherit family wealth, the "marriage" of women to the Church as nuns passed wealth that might otherwise have gone to husbands and offspring to the Church instead.

has no one to supply him regularly with food or firewood.

Although divorce may be high in some non-Western societies, notably matrilineal societies such as that of the Hopi, they have become so high in Western societies as to cause many North Americans to worry about the future of marriage and the family in the contemporary world. Undoubtedly, the causes of divorce in the United States are many and varied. Among them are the trivial

and transient characteristics we have already mentioned that marriages may all too easily be based upon. Beyond this, a U.S. marriage is supposed to involve an enduring, supportive, and intimate bond between a man and woman, full of affection and love. In this relationship, people are supposed to find escape from the pressures of the competitive workaday world, as well as from the legal and social constraints that so affect their behavior outside the family. Yet in a society where people are brought up to seek individual gratification, where this often is seen to come through competition at someone else's expense (see Chapter 5), and where women traditionally have been expected to be submissive to men, it should not come as a surprise to find that the reality of marriage does not always live up to the ideal. Harsh treatment and neglect of spouses—usually of wives by husbands—in the United States is neither new nor rare; furthermore, people are more tolerant of violence directed against spouses and children than they are against outsiders. As anthropologists Collier, Rosaldo, and Yanagisako have observed: "A smaller percentage of homicides involving family members are prosecuted than those involving strangers. We are faced with the irony that in our society the place where nurturance and noncontingent [unconditional] affection are supposed to be located is simultaneously the place where violence is most tolerated."[20] However, what has happened in recent years is that people have become less inclined toward moral censure of those—women especially—who seek escape from unsatisfactory marriages. No longer are people as willing to "stick it out at all costs" no matter how intolerable the situation may be. Thus, divorce is increasingly exercised as a sensible reaction to marriages that do not work.

---

[20]Collier, J., Rosaldo, M. Z., & Yanagisako, S. (1982). Is there a family? New anthropological views. In B. Thorne & M. Yalom (Eds.), *Rethinking the family: Some feminist problems* (p. 36). New York: Longman.

CHAPTER SUMMARY

Among primates, the human female is unique in her ability to engage in sexual behavior whenever she wants to or whenever her culture tells her it is appropriate, irrespective of whether or not she is fertile. Although such activity may reinforce social bonds between men and women, competition for sexual access also can be disruptive, so every society has rules that govern such access. The near universality of the incest taboo, which forbids sexual relations between parents and their children, and usually between siblings, long has interested anthropologists, but a truly convincing explanation of the taboo has yet to be advanced. Related to incest are the practices of endogamy and exogamy. Endogamy is marriage within a group of individuals; exogamy is marriage outside the group. If the group is limited to the immediate family, almost all societies can be said to prohibit endogamy and practice exogamy. Likewise, societies that practice exogamy at one level may practice endogamy at another. Community endogamy, for example, is a relatively common practice. In a few societies, royal families are known to have practiced endogamy rather than exogamy among siblings to preserve intact the purity of the royal line.

Although defined in terms of a continuing sexual relationship between a man and woman, marriage should not be confused with mating. Although mating occurs within marriage, it often occurs outside of it as well. Unlike mating, marriage is backed by social, legal, and economic forces. In some societies, new families are formed through marriage, but this is not true for all societies.

Monogamy, or the taking of a single spouse, is the most common form of marriage, primarily for economic reasons. A man must have a certain amount of wealth to afford polygyny, or marriage to more than one wife at the same time. Yet in societies where women do most of the productive work, polygyny may serve as a means of generating wealth for a household. Although few marriages in a given society may be polygynous, it is regarded as an appropriate, and even preferred, form of marriage in the majority of the world's societies. Since few communities have a surplus of men, polyandry, or the custom of a woman having several husbands, is uncommon. Also rare is group marriage, in which several men and several women have sexual access to one another. The levirate ensures the security of a woman by providing that a widow marry her husband's brother; the sororate provides that a widower marry his wife's sister.

Serial monogamy is a form in which a man or woman marries a series of partners. In recent decades, this pattern has become increasingly common among middle-class North Americans as individuals divorce and remarry.

In the United States and many of the other industrialized countries of the West, marriages run the risk of being based on an ideal of romantic love that emphasizes youthful beauty. In no other parts of the world would marriages based on such trivial and transitory characteristics be expected to work. In non-Western societies economic considerations are of major concern in arranging marriages. Love follows rather than precedes marriage. The family arranges marriages in societies where it is the most powerful social institution. Marriage serves to bind two families as allies.

Preferred marriage partners in many societies are particular cross cousins (a mother's brother's daughter if a man, a father's sister's son if a woman) or, less commonly, parallel cousins on the paternal side (a father's brother's son or daughter). Cross-cousin marriage is a means of establishing and maintaining solidarity between groups. Marriage to a paternal parallel cousin serves to retain property within a single male line of descent.

In many human societies, marriages are formalized by some sort of economic exchange. Sometimes, this takes the form of reciprocal gift exchange between the bride's and groom's relatives. More common is bride-price, the payment of money or other valuables from the groom's to the bride's kin; this is characteristic of societies where the women both work and bear children for the husband's family. An alternative arrangement is for families to exchange daughters. Bride service occurs when the groom is expected to work for a period for the bride's family. A dowry is the payment of a woman's inheritance at the time of marriage to her or her husband; its purpose is to ensure support for women in societies where men do most of the productive work and women are valued for their reproductive potential alone.

In some societies, marriage arrangements exist between individuals of the same sex. An example is woman/woman marriage as practiced in many African societies. Such marriages provide a socially approved way to deal with problems marriages between individuals of opposite sex offer no satisfactory solution for.

Divorce is possible in all societies, though reasons for divorce as well as its frequency vary widely from one society to another. In the United States, factors contributing to the breakup of marriages include the trivial and transitory characteristics many marriages are based on and the difficulty of establishing a supportive, intimate bond in a society where people are brought up to seek individual gratification, often through competition at someone else's expense, and where women traditionally have been expected to be submissive to men.

POINTS FOR CONSIDERATION

1. Why do the forms and rules surrounding marriage vary so much across cultures? Does this variation weaken or reinforce the anthropological understanding of marriage? Why or why not?

2. Is it possible for humans to develop a culture without marriage? If not, why not? If so, how could sexual access be governed in other ways?

3. Assuming marriage is a cross-cultural institution, why don't all humans get married? Why is marriage often prohibited for certain categories of people, as in the case of Roman Catholic and Eastern Orthodox priests and nuns?

SUGGESTED READINGS

duToit, B. M. (1991). *Human sexuality: Cross cultural readings.* New York: McGraw Hill.

Of the numerous texts that deal with most aspects of human sexuality, this is the only one that gives adequate recognition to the fact most peoples in the world do things differently from North Americans. This reader deals cross-culturally with such topics as menstrual cycle, pair bonding, sexuality, pregnancy and childbirth, childhood, puberty, birth control, sexually transmitted diseases, sex roles, and the climacteric.

Goodenough, W. H. (1970). *Description and comparison in cultural anthropology.* Chicago: Aldine.

This book illustrates the difficulties anthropologists confront when describing and comparing social organization cross-culturally. The author begins with an examination of marriage and family, clarifying these and related concepts in important ways.

Goody, J. (1976). *Production and reproduction: A comparative study of the domestic domain.* Cambridge: Cambridge University Press.

This book is especially good in its discussion of the interrelationship between marriage, property, and inheritance. Although cross-cultural in its approach, readers will be fascinated by the many insights into the history of marriage in the Western world.

Mair, L. (1971). *Marriage*. Baltimore: Penguin.

Dr. Mair traces the evolution of marriage and such alternative relationships as surrogates and protectors. Commenting on marriage as an institution and drawing her examples from "tribal" cultures, Dr. Mair deals with the function, rules, symbolic rituals, and economic factors of marriage. She also cites the inferior status of women and discusses the self-determining behavior of "serious free women" as an important factor in social change.

Chapter 20
FAMILY AND HOUSEHOLD

A FAMILY GROUP IN NORTHERN THAILAND. ONE
OF THE BASIC FUNCTIONS OF THE FAMILY IS
RAISING CHILDREN.

Chapter Preview

What Is the Family?

The human family is a group composed of a woman, her dependent children, and at least one adult man joined through marriage or blood relationship. The family may take many forms, ranging all the way from one married couple with their children, as in North American society, to a large group composed of several brothers and sisters with the sisters' children, as in southwest India among the Nayar. The specific form the family takes is related to particular social, historical, and ecological circumstances.

What Is the Difference Between Family and Household?

Households are task-oriented residential units where economic production, consumption, inheritance, child rearing, and shelter are organized and implemented. In the vast majority of human societies, households either consist of families or their core members constitute families, even though some household members may not be relatives of the family the household is built around. In some societies, although households are present, families are not. Furthermore, in some societies where families are present, they may be less important in peoples' thinking than the households they are parts of.

What Are Some of the Problems of Family and Household Organization?

Although families and households exist to solve in various ways the problems all peoples must deal with, the different forms families and households may take are all accompanied by their own characteristic problems. Where families and households are small and relatively independent, as they are in North American society, individuals are isolated from the aid and support of kin and must fend for themselves in many situations. By contrast, families that include several adults within the same large household must find ways to control various kinds of tensions that invariably exist among their members.

The family, long regarded by North Americans as a critically necessary core social institution, today has become a matter of controversy and discussion. Women taking jobs outside the home rather than staying home with children, couples living together without the formality of marriage, soaring divorce rates, and increasing numbers of households headed by a single parent have raised questions about the functions of the family in North American society and its ability to survive in a period of rapid social change. Evidence of the widespread interest in these questions was seen in the convening, in 1980, of a White House Conference on Families. Since then, scarcely a political campaign for national office has passed without frequent reference to what candidates like to call "traditional family values."

Does the family, as presently constituted in North America, offer the best environment for bringing up children? Does it impose an inferior status on the woman, confined and isolated in the home performing household and child-raising chores? Does the man, locked into an authoritarian role, suffer unduly in his personal development from bearing the primary responsibility for the family's financial support? Do adequate substitutes exist for people who have no family to care for them, such as old people and orphans? If the family as people in the United States know it today is found wanting, what are the alternatives?

Historical and cross-cultural studies of the family offer as many different family patterns as the fertile human imagination can invent. The one considered "normal" or "natural" to most North Americans—a discrete and independent living unit consisting of the nuclear family (Figure 20.1)—is in fact no more normal or natural than any other and cannot be used as the standard for measuring other forms. Neither universal nor even common among human societies, the independent nuclear family emerged only recently in human history. Its roots go back to a series of regulations the Roman Catholic Church imposed in the 4th century A.D. that prohibited close marriages, discouraged adoption, and condemned polygyny, concubinage, divorce, and remarriage (all of which previously had been perfectly respectable, as the Old Testament of the Bible, among other sources, makes clear). Not only did this prohibition strengthen the conjugal tie between one man and one woman, at the expense of consanguineal or "blood" ties, but it also ensured that large numbers of people would be left with no male heirs. It is a biological fact that 20% of all couples will have only daughters, and another 20% will have no children at all. By eliminating polygyny, concubinage, divorce, and remarriage and by discouraging adoption, the

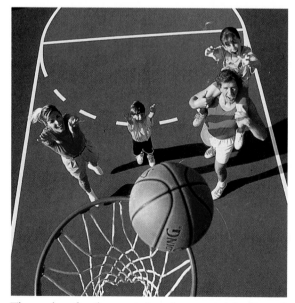

The nuclear family, consisting of a married family and dependent offspring, is held up as the ideal in the United States.

FIGURE 20.1

This diagram shows the relationships in a nuclear family, such as those found in North American society.

The Holy Family of Christianity. Mary's husband Joseph was her father's brother's son and was himself the product of a leviratic marriage. Even though both kinds of marriage were considered proper in the early days of Christianity, they were not allowed by the Church after the 4th century.

Church removed the means for people to overcome these odds and to make sure they would have male heirs. The result of all this was to facilitate the transfer of property from families to the Roman Catholic Church, which rapidly became the largest landowner in most European countries, a position it has retained to this day. By insinuating itself into the very fabric of domestic life, heirship, and marriage, the Church gained tremendous control over the grass roots of society, enriching itself in the process.[1]

With the industrialization of Europe and North America, the nuclear family became further isolated from other kin. One reason is that industrial economies require a mobile labor force; peo-

ple must be prepared to move where the jobs are, which they do most easily without excess kin in tow. Another reason is that the family came to be seen as a kind of refuge from a public world people saw as threatening to their sense of privacy and self-determination.[2] Within the family, relationships were supposed to be enduring and noncontingent, entailing love and affection, based upon cooperation, and governed by feeling and morality. Outside the family, where people sold their work and negotiated contracts, relationships increasingly were seen as competitive, temporary, and contingent upon performance, requiring buttressing by law and legal sanction. Such views were held most widely in the late 19th and early 20th centuries, and in the United States independent nuclear family households reached their highest frequency around 1950, when 60% of all households conformed to this model.[3] Since then, the situation has changed, and a mere 26% of U.S. households now conform to the independent nuclear family ideal. More are now headed by divorced, separated, and never-married individuals. This situation has arisen as increasingly large numbers of people find more intimacy and emotional support in relationships outside the family and are less inclined to tolerate the harsh treatment and neglect of children and spouses, especially wives, that all too commonly occur within families. (In the United States, more than 2 million women experience abuse from the men in their families, and at least an equal number of children are also abused.)

The family as it has emerged in Europe and North America, then, is the product of particular historical and social circumstances; where these have differed, so have family forms. Thus, how men and women in other societies live together must be studied, not as bizarre and exotic forms of human behavior but as logical outcomes of peoples' experience living in particular times, places, and social situations.

[1]Goody, J. (1983). *The development of the family and marriage in Europe* (pp. 44–46). Cambridge: Cambridge University Press.

[2]Collier, J., Rosaldo, M. Z., & Yanagisako, S. (1982). Is there a family? New anthropological views. In B. Thorne and M. Yalom (Eds.), *Rethinking the family: Some feminist questions* (pp. 34–35). New York: Longman.

[3]Stacey, J. (1990). *Brave new families* (pp. 5, 10). New York: Basic Books.

FAMILY AND SOCIETY

Although many North Americans continue to think of families as standing in opposition to the rest of society, the truth is that they are affected by, and in turn affect, the values and structure of the society they are embedded in. To clarify this, we will take a more detailed look at the rise and fall of nuclear families in the United States.

The Ephemeral Modern Family[4]

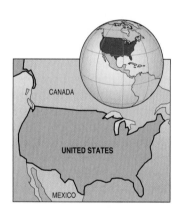

Now that the "modern" [i.e., independent nuclear] family system has almost exited from its historical stage, we can perceive how peculiar, ephemeral, and internally contradictory was this once-revolutionary gender and kinship order. Historians place the emergence of the modern [North] American family among white middle-class people in the late eighteenth century; they depict its flowering in the nineteenth century and chart its decline in the second half of the twentieth. Thus, for white Americans, the history of modern families traverses the same historical trajectory as that of modern industrial society. What was modern about upper-middle-class family life in the half century after the American Revolution was the appearance of social arrangements governing gender and kinship relationships that contrasted sharply with those of "traditional," or premodern, patriarchal corporate units.

The premodern family among white Colonial Americans, an institution some scholars characterize as "the Godly family," was the constitutive element of Colonial society. This integrated economic, social, and political unit explicitly subordinated individual to corporate family interests and women and children to the authority of the household's patriarchal head. Decisions regarding the timing and crafting of premodern marriages served not the emotional needs of individuals but the economic, religious, and social purposes of larger kin groups, as these were interpreted by patriarchs who controlled access to land, property, and craft skills. Nostalgic images of "traditional" families rarely recall their instability or diversity. Death visited Colonial homes so frequently that second marriages and blended households composed of stepkin were commonplace. With female submission thought to be divinely prescribed, conjugal love was a fortuitous bonus, not a prerequisite of such marriages. Similarly the doctrine of innate depravity demanded authoritarian parenting to break the will and save the souls of obstinate children, a project that required extensive paternal involvement in child rearing. Few boundaries between family and work impeded such patriarchal supervision, or segregated the sexes who labored at their arduous and interdependent tasks in close proximity. Boundaries between public and private life were equally permeable. Communities regulated proper family conduct, intervening actively to enforce disciplinary codes, and parents exchanged their children as apprentices and servants.

Four radical innovations differentiate modern from premodern family life among white Americans: (1) Family work and productive work became separated, rendering women's work invisible as they and their children became

---

[4]Ibid., pp. 6–11.

economically dependent on the earnings of men. (2) Love and companionship became the ideal purposes of marriages that were to be freely contracted by individuals. (3) A doctrine of privacy emerged that attempted to withdraw middle-class family relationships from public scrutiny. (4) Women devoted increased attention to nurturing fewer and fewer children as mothering came to be exalted as both a natural and demanding vocation.

The rise of the modern American family accompanied the rise of industrial capitalist society, with its revolutionary social, spatial, and temporal reorganization of work and domestic life. The core premises and practices of the new family regime were far more contradictory than those of the premodern family order. Coding work as masculine and home as feminine modern economic arrangements deepened the segregation of the sexes by extracting men from, and consigning white married women to, an increasingly privatized domestic domain. The institutionalized subordination of these wives to their husbands persisted; indeed, as factory production supplanted domestic industry, wives became increasingly dependent on their spouse's earnings. The doctrine of separate gender spheres governing the modern family order in the nineteenth century was so potent that few married women among even the poorest of native white families dared to venture outside their homes in search of income.

The proper sphere of working-class married white women also was confined to the home. Yet few working-class families approximated the modern family ideal before well into the twentieth century. Enduring conditions of poverty, squalor, disease, and duress rivaling those in industrializing England, most immigrant and native white working-class families in nineteenth-century America depended on supplementary income. Income from women's out work, child labor, lodgers, and the earnings of employed unmarried sons and daughters supplemented the meager and unreliable wages paid to working men. Not until the post–World War II era did substantial numbers of working-class households achieve the "modern family" pattern.

If the doctrine of separate, and unequal, gender spheres limited women's domain and rendered their work invisible, it also enhanced their capacity to formulate potent moral and political challenges to patriarchy. Men ceded the domains of child rearing and virtue to "moral" mothers who made these responsibilities the basis for expanding their social influence and political rights. This and the radical ideologies of individualism, democracy, and conjugal love, which infused modern family culture, would lead ultimately to its undoing. It is no accident, historians suggest, that the first wave of American feminism accompanied the rise of the modern family.

With rearview vision one glimpses the structural fragility of the modern family system, particularly its premise of enduring voluntary commitment. For modern marriages, unlike their predecessors, were properly affairs not of the purse but of the heart. A romantic "until death do us part" commitment volunteered by two young adults acting largely independent of the needs, interests, or wishes of their kin was the vulnerable linchpin of the modern family order. It seems rather remarkable, looking back, that during the first century of the modern family's cultural ascendancy, death did part the vast majority of married couples. But an ideology of conjugal love and companionship implies access to divorce as a safety valve for failures of youthful judgment or the vagaries of adult affective development. Thus, a statistical omen of the internal instability of this form of marriage lies in the unprecedented rise of divorce rates that accompanied the spread of the modern family. Despite severe legal and social restrictions, divorce rates began to climb at least as early as the 1840s. They have continued their ascent ever since, until by the middle of the 1970s divorce outstripped death as a source of marital dissolution. A crucial component of the modern family system, divorce would ultimately prove to be its Achilles' heel.

For a century, as the cultural significance of the modern family grew, the productive and even the reproductive work performed within its domain contracted. By the end of the "modern" industrial era in the 1950s, virtually all productive work had left the home. While advances in longevity stretched enduring marriages to unprecedented lengths, the full-time homemaker's province had been pared to the chores of housework, consumption, and the cultivation of a declining number of progeny during a shortened span of years.

Those Americans, like myself, who came of age at that historic moment were encouraged to absorb a particularly distorted impression of the normalcy and timelessness of the modern family system. The decade between the late 1940s and the late 1950s represents an aberrant period in the history of this aberrant form of family life. Fueled in part, as historian Elaine May has suggested, by the apocalyptic Cold War sensibilities of the post–World War II nuclear age, the nation indulged in what would prove to be a last-gasp orgy of modern nuclear family domesticity. Three-fifths of American households conformed to the celebrated breadwinner-fulltime homemaker modern form in 1950, as substantial sectors of working-class men began at long last to secure access to a family wage. A few years later Walt Disney opened the nation's first family theme park in southern California, designed to please and profit from the socially conservative fantasies of such increasingly prosperous families.

The aberrant fifties temporarily reversed the century's steady decline in birth rates. The average age of first-time visitors to the conjugal altar also dropped to record lows. Higher percentages of Americans were marrying than ever before or since, and even the majority of white working-class families achieved coveted home ownership status. It was during this time that Talcott Parsons provided family sociology with its most influential theoretical elaboration of the modern American family, of how its nuclear household structure and complementary division of roles into female "expressive" and male "instrumental" domains was sociologically adaptive to the functional demands of an industrial society. Rare are the generations, or even the sociologists, who perceive the historical idiosyncrasies of the normal cultural arrangements of their time.

The postwar baby boom was to make the behaviors and beliefs of that decade's offspring disproportionately significant for the rest of their lives. The media, the market, and all social and political institutions would follow their development with heightened interest. Thus, a peculiar period in U.S. family history came to set the terms for the waves of rebellion against, and nostalgia for, the passing modern family and gender order that have become such prominent and disruptive features of the American political landscape.

The world's first generation of childhood television viewers grew up, as I did, inundated by such weekly paeans to the male breadwinner nuclear household and modern family ideology as *Father Knows Best, Leave It to Beaver,* and *Ozzie and Harriet.* Because unusual numbers of us later pushed women's biological "clock" to its reproductive limits, many now find ourselves parenting (or choosing not to) in the less innocent age of *Thirtysomething, Kate and Allie,* and *Who's the Boss?* For beneath the sentimental gloss that the fifties enameled onto its domestic customs, forces undermining the modern family of the 1950s accelerated while those sustaining it eroded. In the midst of profamily pageantry, nonfamily households proliferated. As the decade drew to a close, the nation entered what C. Wright Mills, with characteristic prescience, termed its "postmodern period." The emergent postindustrial economy shifted employment from heavy industries to nonunionized clerical, service, and new industrial sectors. Employers found themselves irresistibly attracted to the nonunionized, cheaper labor of women and, thus, increasingly to that of married women and mothers.

One glimpses the ironies of class and gender history here. For decades industrial unions struggled heroically for a socially recognized male breadwinner wage that would allow the working class to participate in the modern gender order. These struggles, however, contributed to the cheapening of female labor that helped gradually to undermine the modern family regime. Escalating consumption standards, the expansion of mass collegiate coeducation, and the persistence of high divorce rates then gave more and more women ample cause to invest a portion of their identities in the "instrumental" sphere of paid labor. Thus, middle-class women began to abandon their confinement in the modern family just as working-class women were approaching its access ramps. The former did so, however, only after the wives of working-class men had pioneered the twentieth-century revolution in women's paid work. Entering employment during the catastrophic 1930s, participating in defense industries in the 1940s, and raising their family incomes to middle-class standards by returning to the labor force rapidly after child rearing in the 1950s, working-class women quietly modeled and normalized the postmodern family standard of employment for married mothers. Whereas in 1950 the less a man earned, the more likely his wife was to be employed, by 1968 wives of middle-income men were the most likely to be in the labor force.

FUNCTIONS OF THE FAMILY

Among humans, reliance on group living for survival is a basic characteristic. They have inherited this from their primate ancestors, though they have developed it in their own distinctively human ways. Even among monkeys and apes, group living requires the participation of adults of both sexes. Among species that, like us, have taken up life on the ground, as well as among species most closely related to us, adult males are normally much larger and stronger than females, and their teeth are usually more efficient for fighting. Thus, they are essential for the group's defense. Moreover, the close and prolonged relationship between infants and their mothers, without which the infants cannot survive, renders the adult primate females less well suited than the males to handle defense.

NURTURANCE OF CHILDREN

Taking care of the young is primarily the job of the adult primate female. Primate babies are born relatively helpless and remain dependent upon their mothers for a longer time than any other animals (a chimpanzee, for example, cannot survive without its mother until it reaches age 4 or even 5). This dependence is not only for food and physical care, but also, as numerous studies have shown, primate infants deprived of normal maternal attention will not grow and develop normally, if they survive at all. The protective presence of adult males shields the mothers from both danger and harassment from other troop members, allowing them to give their infants the attention they require.

Among humans, the sexual division of labor has developed beyond that of other primates. Until the recent advent of synthetic infant formulas, human females more often than not had been occupied much of their adult lives with child rearing. And human infants need no less active "mothering" than do the young of other primates. For one thing, they are even more helpless at birth, and, for another, the period of infant dependency is longer in humans. Besides all this, studies have shown that human infants, no less than other primates, need more than just food and physical care if they are to develop normally. But among humans, unlike other primates, the infant's biological mother does not have to provide all this "mothering." Not only may other women provide the child with much of the attention it needs, but so may men. In many societies children are handled and fondled as much by men as by women, and in some societies men are more nurturing to children than are women.

ECONOMIC COOPERATION

In all human societies, even though women may be the primary providers of child care, women have other responsibilities as well. Although several of the economic activities they traditionally have engaged in have been compatible with their child-rearing role and have not placed their off-

A female baboon with her infant and male friend. Baboon males are protective of their female friends, even though they are not always the fathers of their friends' infants. Thus shielded from danger and harassment from other troop members, females can give their infants the attention they require to survive.

spring at risk, this cannot be said of all their activities. Consider how the common combination of child care with food preparation, especially if cooking is done over an open fire, creates a potentially hazardous situation for children. With the mother (or other caregiver) distracted by some other task, the child all too easily may receive a severe burn or bad cut, with serious consequences. What can be said is that the economic activities of women generally have complemented those of men, even though, in some societies, individuals may perform tasks normally assigned to the opposite sex, as the occasion dictates. Thus, men and women could share the results of their labors on a regular basis, as was discussed in Chapters 17 and 18.

An effective way both to facilitate economic cooperation between the sexes and to provide for a close bond between mother and child at the same time is through the establishment of residential groups that include adults of both sexes. The differing nature of male and female roles, as these are defined by different cultures, requires a child to have an adult of the same sex available to serve as a proper model for the appropriate adult role. The presence of adult men and women in the same

residential group provides for this. As defined in Chapter 19, a family is a residential group composed of a woman, her dependent children, and at least one man joined through marriage or consanguineal ("blood") relationship. Again (see Chapter 19), because gender roles are culturally defined, the man may in some cases be a female.

One alternative to the family as a child-rearing unit is the Israeli kibbutz. Here, children of a kibbutz are shown in a supervised session of creative play.

Well suited though the family may be for these tasks, we should not suppose it is the only unit capable of providing such conditions. In fact, other arrangements are possible, such as the Israeli kibbutz, where paired teams of male and female specialists raise groups of children. In many food-foraging societies (the Ju/'hoansi and Mbuti, discussed in Chapters 16 and 17, are good examples), all adult members of a community share in the responsibilities of child care. Thus, when parents go off to hunt or to collect plants and herbs, they may leave their children behind, secure in the knowledge they will be looked after by whatever adults remain in the camp. Yet another arrangement may be seen among the Mundurucu, a horticultural people of South America's Amazon forest. Their children live in houses with their mothers, apart from all men until age 13, whereupon the boys leave their mothers' houses to go live with the village men. Because Mundurucu men and women do not live together as members of discrete residential units, it cannot be said their society has families.

FAMILY AND HOUSEHOLD

Although it is often stated that some form of family is present in all human societies, the Mundurucu case just cited demonstrates this is not so. In Mundurucu villages, the men all live together in one house with all boys over age 13; women live with others of their sex as well as younger boys in two or three houses grouped around the men's house. As among the Nayar (discussed in Chapter 19), married men and women are members of separate households, meeting periodically for sexual activity.

Although the family is not universally present in human societies, the **household,** defined as the basic residential unit where economic production,

A celebration at the palace in the Yoruba city of Oyo, Nigeria. As is usual in societies where royal households are found, that of the Yoruba includes many individuals not related to the ruler, as well as the royal family.

Household. The basic residential unit where economic production, consumption, inheritance, child rearing, and shelter are organized and implemented; may or may not be synonymous with family.

consumption, inheritance, child rearing, and shelter are organized and implemented, is universally present. Among the Mundurucu, the men's house constitutes one household, and the women's houses constitute others. Although, in this case as in many, each house is in effect a household, a number of societies have households made up of two or more houses together, as we shall see later in this chapter.

In many human societies, most households in fact constitute families, although other sorts of households may be present as well (single-parent households, for example, in the United States and many Caribbean countries). Often, a household may consist of a family along with some more distant relatives of family members. Or coresidents may be unrelated, such as the service personnel in an elaborate royal household, apprentices in the household of craft specialists, or low-status clients in the household of rich and powerful patrons. In such societies, even though people may think in terms of households, rather than families, the households are built around the latter. Thus, even though the family is not universal, in the vast majority of human societies the family is the basic core of the household.

▲▽▲▽▲▽▲▽▲▽▲▽▲▽▲▽▲▽▲▽▲▽▲▽▲▽▲▽▲▽▲
FORM OF THE FAMILY

As suggested earlier in this chapter, the family may take any one of a number of forms in response to particular social, historical, and ecological circumstances. At the outset, a distinction must be made between **conjugal families,** which are formed on the basis of marital ties, and consanguineal families, which are not. As defined in Chapter 19, consanguineal families consist of related women, their brothers, and the women's offspring. Such families are not common; the classic case is the Nayar household group. The Nayar are not unique, however, and consanguineal families are found elsewhere—for example, among the Tory Islanders, a Roman Catholic, Gaelic-speaking fish-

erfolk living off the coast of Ireland. These people do not marry until they are in their late 20s or early 30s and thus experience tremendous resistance to breaking up existing household arrangements. The Tory Islanders look at it this way: "Oh well, you get married at that age, it's too late to break up arrangements that you have already known for a long time. . . . You know, I have my sisters and brothers to look after, why should I leave home to go live with a husband? After all, he's got his sisters and his brothers looking after him."[5] Because the community numbers only a few hundred people, husbands and wives are within easy commuting distance of each other.

THE NUCLEAR FAMILY

The form of conjugal family most familiar to most North Americans is the independent nuclear family, which in spite of its precipitous decline is still widely regarded as the "standard" in the United States and Canada. In these countries it is not considered desirable for young people to live with their parents beyond a certain age, nor is it considered a moral responsibility for a couple to take their aged parents into their home when the parents no longer can care for themselves. Retirement communities and nursing homes provide these services, and to take aged parents into one's home is commonly regarded as not only an economic burden but also a threat to the household's privacy and independence.

The nuclear family is also apt to be prominent in societies such as the Inuit that live in harsh environments. In the winter the Inuit husband and wife, with their children, roam the vast Arctic wilderness in search of food. The husband hunts and makes shelters. The wife cooks, is responsible for the children, and makes the clothing and keeps it in good repair. One of her chores is to chew her

---

[5]Fox, R. (1981, December 3). [Interview for Coast Telecourses, Inc.]. Los Angeles.

Conjugal Family.   A family consisting of one (or more) man (who may be a female) married to one (or more) woman (who may be a male) and their offspring.

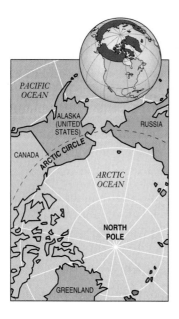

husband's boots to soften the leather for the next day so that he can resume his search for game. The wife and her children could not survive without the husband, and life for a man is unimaginable without a wife.

Certain parallels can be drawn between the nuclear family in industrial societies and families living under especially harsh environmental conditions. In both cases, the family is an independent unit that must be prepared to fend for itself; this creates for individual members a strong dependence on one another. Minimal help is available from outside in the event of emergencies or catastrophes. When their usefulness ends, the elderly are cared for only if it is feasible. In the event of the mother or father's death, life becomes precarious for the child. Yet this form of family is well adapted to a life that requires a high degree of geographic mobility. For the Inuit, this mobility permits the hunt for food; for North Americans, the hunt for jobs and improved social status requires a mobile form of family unit.

Not even among the Inuit, however, is the nuclear family as isolated from other kin as it has become among most nonnative North Americans. When Inuit families are off by themselves, it is regarded as a matter of temporary expediency; most of the time, they are found in groups of at least a few families together, with members of one group

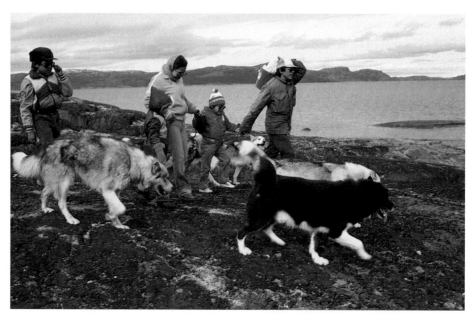

Among the Inuit, nuclear families such as the one shown here are the norm, although they are not as isolated from other kin as are nuclear families in the United States.

Extended families like this one are still found in parts of rural North America.

having relatives in all of the others.[6] Thus families cooperate with one another on a daily basis, sharing food and other resources, looking out for the children, and sometimes even eating together. The sense of shared responsibility for one another's children and for the general welfare in Inuit multifamily groups contrasts with families in the United States, which are basically "on their own." Here the state has assigned sole responsibility to the family for child care and the welfare of family members, with relatively little assistance from outside.[7] To be sure, families can and often do help one another out, but they are under no obligation

to do so. In fact, once children reach the age of majority (18), parents have no further legal obligation to them, nor do the children to their parents. When families do have difficulty fulfilling their assigned functions—as is increasingly the case—even if it is through no fault of their own, less support is available to them from the community at large than in most of the world's stateless societies, including that of the Inuit.

THE EXTENDED FAMILY

In North America, nuclear families have not always had the degree of independence they came to have with the rise of industrialism. In an earlier more agrarian era, the small nuclear family commonly was part of a larger **extended family.** This kind of family, in part conjugal and in part consanguine, might include grandparents, mother and father, brothers and sisters, perhaps an uncle and aunt, and a stray cousin or two. All these peo-

---

[6]Graburn, N. H. H. (1969). *Eskimos without igloos: Social and economic development in Sugluk* (pp. 56–58). Boston: Little Brown.

[7]Collier, R., Rosaldo, M. Z., & Yanagisako, S. (1982). Is there a family? Some new anthropological views. In B. Thorne and M. Yalom (Eds.), *Rethinking the family: Some feminist problems* (pp. 28–29). New York: Longman.

Extended family.   A collection of nuclear families, related by ties of blood, that live together in one household.

ple, some related by blood and some by marriage, lived and worked together. Because members of the younger generation brought their spouses (husbands or wives) to live in the family, extended families, like consanguine families, had continuity through time. As older members died off, new members were born into the family.

In the United States, such families have survived until recently in some communities, as along the Maine coast.[8] There they developed in response to a unique economy featuring a mix of farming and seafaring, coupled with an ideal of self-sufficiency. Because family farms were incapable of providing self-sufficiency, seafaring was taken up as an economic alternative. Seagoing commerce, however, was periodically afflicted by depression, so family farming remained important as a cushion against economic hard times. The need for a sufficient labor pool to tend the farm, while furnishing officers, crew, or (frequently) both for locally owned vessels, was satisfied by the practice of a newly married couple settling on the farm of either the bride's or the groom's parents. Thus, most people spent their lives cooperating on a day-to-day basis in economic activities with close relatives, all of whom lived together (even if in separate houses) on the same farm.

The Maya of Guatemala and southern Mexico also live in extended family households.[9] In many of their communities, sons bring their wives to live in houses built on the edges of a small open plaza, where on one edge their father's house already stands (Figure 20.2). Numerous household activities occur on this plaza; here women may weave, men may receive guests, and children play together. The head of the family is the sons' father, who makes most of the important decisions.

All family members work together for the common good and deal with outsiders as a single unit.

Extended families living together in single households were and often still are important social units among the Hopi Indians of Arizona.[10] Ideally, the household head was an old woman; her married daughters, their husbands, and their children lived with her. The household women owned land, but the men (usually their husbands) tilled it. When extra help was needed during the harvest, for example, other male relatives, friends, or persons local religious organizations designated formed work groups and turned the hard work into a festive occasion. The women performed household tasks, such as processing food or making pottery, together.

The 1960s saw a number of attempts by young people in the United States to reinvent a form of extended family living. Their families (often called communes) were groups of unrelated nuclear families that held property in common and lived together. It is further noteworthy that the lifestyle of these modern families often emphasized the kinds of cooperative ties found in the rural North American extended family of old, which provided a labor pool for the many tasks required for economic survival. In some of them the members even reverted to traditional gender roles; the women took care of the child rearing and household chores, while the men took care of tasks that took people outside of the household itself.

RESIDENCE PATTERNS

Where some form of conjugal or extended family is the norm, family exogamy requires that either the husband or wife, if not both, must move to a new household upon marriage. A newly married couple may adopt one of five common patterns of residence whose prime determinants are ecological circumstances, although other factors enter in as well. One option is **patrilocal residence;** as just

---

[8]Haviland, W. A. (1973). Farming, seafaring and bilocal residence on the coast of Maine. *Man in the Northeast, 6,* 31–44.

[9]Vogt, E. Z. (1990). *The Zinacantecos of Mexico, A modern Maya way of life* (2nd ed., pp. 30–34). Fort Worth, TX: Holt, Rinehart and Winston.

---

[10]Forde, C. D. (1950). *Habitat, economy and society* (pp. 225–245). New York: E. P. Dutton.

Patrilocal residence. A pattern in which a married couple lives in the locality associated with the husband's father's relatives.

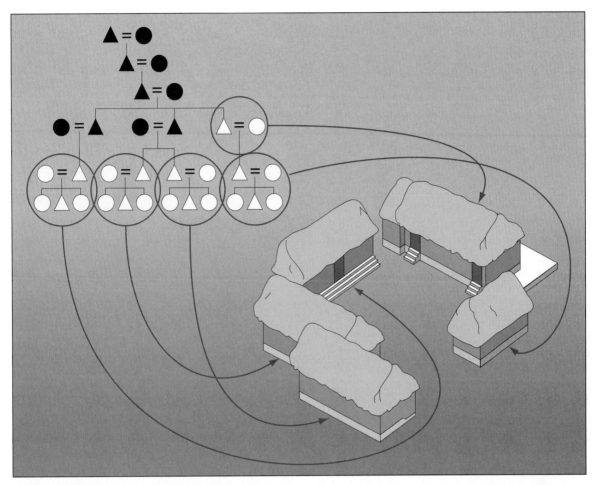

FIGURE 20.2
This diagram shows the living arrangements and relationships in a patrilocal extended family. Deceased household members are blacked out.

Members of modern Maya extended families carry out various activities on the household plaza; here, for example, women weave and family members interact with outsiders.

described for the Maya, a woman goes to live with her husband in the household he grew up in. Favoring this arrangement are societies with a predominant role for men in subsistence, particularly if they own property that can be accumulated, if polygyny is customary, if warfare is prominent enough to make cooperation among men especially important, and if an elaborate political organization in which men wield authority exists. These conditions are most often found together in societies that rely on animal husbandry and/or intensive agriculture for their subsistence. Where patrilocal residence is customary, the bride often must move to a different band or community. In such cases, her parents' family is not only losing the services of a useful family member, but they are losing her potential offspring as well. Hence, some kind of compensation to her family, most commonly bride-price, is usual.

Matrilocal residence, where the man leaves the family he grew up with to go live with his wife in her parents' household, is a likely result if ecological circumstances make the women's role predominant in subsistence. It is found most often in horticultural societies, where political organization is relatively uncentralized and where cooperation among women is important. The Hopi Indians provide one example; although the men do the farming, the women control access to land and "own" the harvest. Indeed, men are not even allowed in the granaries. Under matrilocal residence, men usually do not move very far from the family they were raised with, so they are available to help out there from time to time. Therefore, marriage usually does not involve compensation to the groom's family.

Ambilocal residence is particularly well suited to situations where economic cooperation of more people than are available in the nuclear family is needed but where resources are limited in some way. Because the couple can join either the bride's or the groom's family, family membership is flexible, and the two can live where the resources look best or where their labor is most needed. This was once the situation on the peninsulas and islands

This old photo shows members of a Hopi Indian matrilocal extended family in front of their house. Traditionally, women who were sisters and daughters lived with their husbands in adjacent rooms of a single tenement.

along the Maine coast, where, as already noted, extended family households were based upon ambilocal residence. The same residential pattern is particularly common among food-foraging peoples, as among the Mbuti of Africa's Ituri forest. Typically, a Mbuti marries someone from another band, so one spouse has in-laws who live elsewhere. Thus, if foraging is bad in their part of the forest, the couple has somewhere else to go where food may be more readily available. Ambilocality greatly enhances the Mbutis' opportunity to find food. It also provides a place to go if a dispute breaks out with someone in the band where the couple is currently living. Consequently, Mbuti camps are constantly changing their composition as people split off to go live with their in-laws, while others are joining from other groups. For a people like food foragers, who find their food in nature and who maintain an egalitarian social order, ambilocal residence can be a crucial factor in both survival and conflict resolution.

Matrilocal residence.   A pattern in which a married couple lives in the locality associated with the wife's relatives
> **Ambilocal residence.**   A pattern in which a married couple may choose either matrilocal or patrilocal residence.

Although Hopi society is matrilocal, it is men's labor that provides the food. In the past, however, it is probable that women were the farmers, with men taking over the task as irrigation became more important.

Under **neolocal residence,** a married couple forms a household in an independent location. This occurs where the independence of the nuclear family is emphasized. In industrial societies such as the United States, where most economic activity occurs outside rather than inside the family and where it is important for individuals to be able to move where jobs are found, neolocal residence is better suited than any of the other patterns.

Avunculocal residence, in which a married couple goes to live with the groom's mother's brother (Figure 20.3) is favored by the same factors

Groom = Bride

FIGURE 20.3
Under avunculocal residence, a newly married couple goes to live with the husband's mother's brother.

Neolocal residence.   A pattern in which a married couple establishes their household in a location apart from either the husband's or the wife's relatives. **>** **Avunculocal residence.**   A pattern in which a married couple lives with the husband's mother's brother.

that promote patrilocal residence, but only in societies where descent through women is deemed crucial for the transmission of important rights and property. Such is the case among the people of the Trobriand Islands, where each individual is a member from birth of a group of relatives who trace their descent back through their mother, their mother's mother, and so on to the one woman all others are descended from. Each of these descent groups holds property, consisting of hamlet sites, bush and garden lands, and, in some cases, beachfronts members have access rights to. These properties are controlled each generation by a male chief or other leader who inherits these rights and obligations, but because descent is traced exclusively through women, a man cannot inherit these from his father. Thus, succession to positions of leadership passes from a man to his sister's son. For this reason, a man who is in line to take control of his descent group's assets will take his wife to live with the one he will succeed—his mother's brother. This enables him to observe how the older man takes care of his hamlet's affairs, as well as to learn the oral traditions and magic he will need to be an effective leader.

Although Trobriand leaders and chiefs live avunculocally, most married couples in this society live patrilocally. This allows sons to fulfill their obligations to their fathers, who helped build up and nurture them when they were small; in return, the sons will inherit personal property such as clay pots and valuable stone axe blades from their fathers. This also gives men access to land their father's descent groups control in addition to their own, enabling them to improve their own economic and political position in Trobriand society. In short, here, as in any human society, practical considerations play a central role in determining where people will live following marriage.

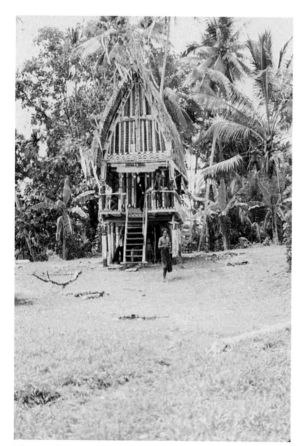

This Trobriand Island chief, shown in front of his house, will be succeeded by his sister's son. Hence, men who will become chiefs live avunculocally.

PROBLEMS OF FAMILY AND HOUSEHOLD ORGANIZATION

Effective though the family may be at organizing economic production, consumption, inheritance, and child rearing, at the household level relationships within the family inevitably involve a certain amount of conflict and tension. This does not mean they may not also involve a great deal of warmth and affection. Nevertheless, at least the potential for conflict is always there and must be dealt with lest families become dysfunctional. Different forms of families are associated with different sorts of tensions, and the means employed to manage these tensions differ accordingly.

POLYGAMOUS FAMILIES

A major source of tension within polygamous families is the potential for conflict that exists between the multiple spouses of the individual they are married to. For example, under polygyny (the most common form of polygamy), the several wives of a man must be able to get along with a minimum of bickering and jealousy. One way to handle this is through sororal polygyny, or marriage to women who are sisters. Presumably, women who have grown up together can get along as cowives of a man more easily than can women who grew up in different households and have never had to live together before. Another mechanism is to provide each wife with a separate apartment or house within a household compound and perhaps require the husband to adhere to a system of rotation for sleeping purposes. The latter at least prevents the husband from playing obvious favorites among his wives. Although polygyny can be difficult for the women involved, this is not always the case (recall the comments of women in polygynous marriages in the Rocky Mountains discussed in the previous chapter). In some polygynous societies, women enjoy considerable economic autonomy, and in societies where women's work is hard and boring, polygyny allows sharing of the workload and alleviating boredom through sociability.

A Bakhtiari man, his wives, and his children. In polygamous families, tensions may arise between cowives, or (in the case of polygyny), the man and his wives.

In polyandrous families, two distinctive structural characteristics may cause difficulty. One is that a woman's older husbands are apt to dominate the younger ones. The other is that, under conditions of fraternal polyandry (where cohusbands are brothers), the most common kind, the youngest brothers are likely to be considerably younger than their wives, whose reproductive years are limited. Hence, a young husband's chances of reproducing successfully are reduced, compared to older husbands. Not surprisingly, when polyandrous families in Tibet break up, it is usually the younger husbands who depart. Moreover, large family groups are more prone to discord than smaller ones.[11]

EXTENDED FAMILIES

Extended families too, no matter how well they may work, have their own potential areas of stress. Decision making in such families usually rests with an older individual, and other family members must defer to the elder's decisions. Among a group of siblings, an older one usually has the authority. Another possible problem involves in-marrying spouses, who must adjust their ways to conform to the expectations of the family they have come to live with. To combat these problems, cultures rely on various techniques to enforce harmony, including dependence training and the concept of "face" or "honor." Dependence training, discussed in Chapter 16, is typically associated with extended family organization and involves raising people who are more inclined to be compliant and accept their lot in life than are individuals raised to be independent. One of the many problems young people in North American society who have experimented with extended family living face is that they generally have been raised to be independent, making it hard to defer to others' wishes when they disagree.

The concept of "face" may constitute a particularly potent check on the power of senior members of extended families. Among pastoral nomads of North Africa, for example, young men can escape

---

[11]Levine, N. E., & Silk, J. B. (1997). Why polyandry fails. *Current Anthropology, 38*, 385–387.

Some young North Americans have attempted to re-create the extended family in the formation of communes. These attempts sometimes run into trouble as members cope with stress associated with extended family organization they are unprepared for.

from ill treatment by a father or older brother by leaving the patrilocal extended family to join the family of his maternal relatives, in-laws, or even an unrelated family willing to take him in.[12] Because men lose face if their sons or brothers flee in this way, they are generally at pains to control their behavior to prevent this from happening. Women, who are the in-marrying spouses, also may return to their natal family if they are mistreated in their husband's family. A woman who does this exposes her husband and his family to scolding by her kin, again causing loss of face.

Effective though such techniques may be in societies that stress the importance of the group over the individual, and where loss of face is to be avoided at almost any cost, not all conflict is avoided. When all else fails to restore harmony, siblings may be forced to demand their share of family assets to set up separate households, and in this way new families arise. Divorce, too, may be possible, although how easily this may be accomplished varies considerably from one society to another. In societies that practice matrilocal residence, divorce rates tend to be high, reflecting how easily unsatisfactory marriages can be terminated. In some (not all) societies with patrilocal residence, by contrast, divorce may be all but impossible, at least for women (the in-marrying spouses). This was the case in traditional China, for example, where women were raised to be cast out of their families.[13] When they married, they exchanged their dependence on fathers and brothers for absolute dependence on husbands and, later in life, sons. Without divorce as an option, to protect themselves against ill treatment women went to great lengths to develop the strongest bond possible between themselves and their sons so that the latter would rise to their mother's defense when necessary. So single-minded were many women toward developing such relationships with their sons that they often made life miserable for their daughters-in-law, who were seen as competitors for their sons' affections.

NUCLEAR FAMILIES

Just as extended families have built into them particular sources of stress and tensions, so too do nuclear families, especially in modern industrial societies where the family has lost one of its chief reasons for being: its economic function as a basic unit of production. Instead of staying within the fold, working with and for each other, one or both adults in a marriage must seek work outside the family. Furthermore, their work may keep them away for prolonged periods. If both spouses are employed, (as is increasingly the case, since couples find it ever more difficult to maintain their

[12]Abu-Lughod, L. (1986). *Veiled sentiments: Honor and poetry in a Bedouin society* (pp. 99–103). Berkeley, CA: University of California Press.

[13]Wolf, M. (1972). *Women and the family in rural Taiwan* (pp. 32–35). Stanford, CA: Stanford University Press.

desired standard of living on one income), the requirement for workers to go where their jobs take them may pull the husband and wife in different directions. On top of all this, neolocal residence tends to isolate husbands and wives from both sets of kin. Because clearly established patterns of responsibility no longer exist between husbands and wives, couples must work these out for themselves. Two factors make this difficult, one being women's traditional dependence on men that for so long has been a feature of Western society. In spite of recent progress toward greater equality between men and women, all too often the partners to a marriage do not come to it as equals. The other problem is the great emphasis North American society places on the pursuit of individual gratification through competition, often at someone else's expense. The problem is especially acute if the husband and wife grew up in households with widely divergent outlooks on life and ways of operating. Furthermore, their isolation from kin means no one is on hand to help stabilize the new marriage; for that matter, intervention of kin likely would be regarded as interference.

anthropology applied   Dealing With Infant Mortality

In 1979 Dr. Margaret Boone, an anthropologist who now works as a social science analyst with the Program Evaluation and Methodology Division of the United States government's General Accounting Office, began a residency on the staff of Washington, D.C.'s only public hospital. Her task was to gain an understanding of the sociocultural basis of poor maternal and infant health among inner-city Blacks—something little was known about at the time—and to communicate that understanding to the relevant public and private agencies, as well as to a wider public. As Dr. Boone put it:

> The problem was death—the highest infant death rate in the United States. In Washington, D.C., babies were dying in their first years of life at the highest rate for any large American city, and nobody could figure out why.[*]

In Washington, as in the rest of the United States, infant mortality is mainly an African American health problem because of the large and increasing number of disadvantaged Black women; their infants die at almost twice the rate of White infants. The hospital where Boone worked served an overwhelmingly impoverished and African American population.

For the next year and a half, Boone worked intensively reviewing medical, birth, and death records; doing statistical analyses; and interviewing women whose infants had died, as well as nurses, physicians, social workers, and administrators. As she points out, no matter how important the records review and statistical analyses were (and they were important), her basic understanding of reproduction in the inner-city Black community came from the daily experience working in the "community center" for birth and death (the hospital)—classic anthropological participant observation.

Boone found out that infant death and miscarriage are associated with absence of prenatal care, smoking, alcohol consumption, psychological distress during pregnancy and hospitalization, evidence of violence, ineffective contraception, rapid childbearing in the teens (average age at first pregnancy was 18), and combining several harmful drugs. Contrary to everyone's expectations, heroin abuse was less important a factor than alcohol abuse, and drug abuse in general was no higher among women whose infants died than among those whose infants did not. Cultural factors found important include a belief in a birth for every death, a high value placed on children, a value on gestation without necessarily any causal or sequential understanding of the children it will produce, a lack of planning ability,

---

[*]Boone, E. S. (1987). Practicing sociomedicine: Redefining the problem of infant mortality in Washington, D.C. In R. M. Wulff & S. J. Fiske (Eds.), *Anthropological praxis: Translating knowledge into action* (p. 56). Boulder, CO: Westview Press.

distrust of both men and women, and a separation of men's roles from family formation (indeed, three quarters of the women in Boone's study were unmarried at the time of delivery). Of course, some of these factors already were known to be related to infant mortality, but many were not.

As a consequence of Boone's work, important changes in policies and programs relating to infant mortality have been implemented. It is now widely recognized that the problem goes beyond mere medicine and that medical solutions have gone about as far as they can go. Only by dealing with the social and cultural factors connected to the poor health of inner-city African Americans will further progress be made, and new service delivery systems are slowly emerging to reflect this fact.

Isolation from kin also means that a young mother-to-be must face pregnancy and childbirth without the direct aid and support of female kin she already has a relationship with and who have been through pregnancy and childbirth themselves. Instead, for regular advice and guidance she must turn to physicians (who are more often men than women), books, and friends and neighbors who themselves often are inexperienced. The problem continues through motherhood, in the absence of experienced women within the family as well as a clear model for child rearing. So reliance on physicians, books, and mostly inexperienced friends for advice and support continues. The problems are exacerbated because families differ widely in how they deal with their children. In the competitive society of the United States, the children themselves recognize this and often use such differences against their parents to their own ends.

Women who have devoted themselves entirely to raising children confront a further problem: What will they do when the children are gone? One answer to this, of course, is to pursue an outside career, but this, too, may present problems. She may have a husband with traditional values who thinks "a woman's place is in the home." Or it may be difficult to begin a career in middle age. To begin a career earlier, though, may involve difficult choices: Should she have her career at the expense of having children, or should she have both simultaneously? If the latter, she is not likely to find kin available to look after the children, as would be possible in an extended family, so arrangements must be made with people who are not kin. And, of course, all of these thorny decisions must be made without nearby aid and support of kin.

Louise Woodward, the *au pair* found guilty in 1997 by a Massachusetts jury of causing the death of the child in her care. Her case illustrates the danger inherent in the separation between child and parent in the United States that inevitably results as adults pursue careers or other interests.

The impermanence of the nuclear family itself may constitute a problem, in the form of anxieties over old age. Once the children are gone, who will care for the parents in their old age? In North American society, no *requirement* exists for their children to do so. The problem does not arise in an extended family, where one is cared for from womb to tomb.

FEMALE-HEADED HOUSEHOLDS

In North America, as increasing numbers of adults have sought escape from dysfunctional nuclear families through divorces and as young adults have become more sexually active outside of wedlock, a dramatic rise in the incidence of single-parent households headed by women has occurred. By the 1990s, twice as many households in the United States were headed by divorced, separated, and never-married individuals as those occupied by supposedly "normal" nuclear families.[14] In the vast majority of cases, as shown in Chapter 19, any children remain with their mother, who then faces the problem of having to provide for them as well as for herself. In divorce cases, fathers are usually required to pay child support, but they are not always able or willing to do this, and when they are the amount is often not sufficient to pay for all the necessary food, clothes, and medical care, let alone the cost of child care so that the woman can seek or continue income-producing work outside the house to support herself. One of the problems here is that support payments determined in court are based not so much on the needs of the woman and her children as on her "earning potential," which, if she has been true to middle-class values by staying at home rather than going out to earn money, is seen as low given that she has not brought income into the family. What is ignored, of course, is the fact her unpaid work at home contributed to her husband's ability to pursue a financially rewarding career, but since she is not paid for her work at home, no value is set for it.

As also in the case of working women who remain with their husbands, kin may not be available to look after the single mother's children, so outside help must be sought and (usually) paid for, thereupon making it even more difficult for the mother to support herself adequately. To compound the problem, women frequently lack the skills necessary to secure more than menial and low-paying jobs, not having acquired such skills earlier due to raising children. Even when they do have skills, it is still a fact women are not paid as much as men who hold the same jobs.

In the United States, single mothers who are heads of households are often placed in no-win situations: If they work to support the household, they are seen as unfit mothers; if they stay home with the children, they are labeled "deadbeats."

Not surprisingly, as the number of female-headed households has increased, so has the number of women (and, of course, their children) who live below the poverty line. More than one third of all female-headed households in the United States now fall into this category, and one quarter of all children are poor (Figure 20.4). Moreover, these women and children are the ones most severely affected by cutbacks made in social welfare programs since 1980. Even before then, the purchasing power of women was declining, and, ever since, the programs that most assisted women and children have suffered the deepest cuts. One reason for this is a flawed assumption that is nonetheless entrenched in public policy: that the poverty seen in so many female-headed households is caused by the supposedly deviant nature of such households. This deviation is allegedly caused in part by women wanting to go outside the home

---

[14]Stacey, J. (1990). *Brave new families* (pp. 5, 15). New York: Basic Books.

Median family income
(in constant 1987 dollars)

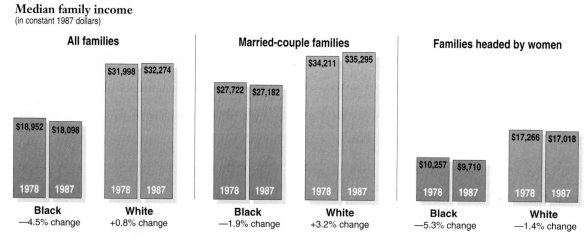

FIGURE 20.4

Median family income: married-couple families and female-headed families compared. Though the figures have changed some since 1987, the disparities have not altered significantly.

to earn money instead of finding husbands to support them so that they can stay home and bring up the children, as women are "supposed" to do. In fact, women have participated in the labor force throughout United States history, whereas only a limited proportion of the population ever possessed the resources to support "proper" nonworking "ladies."[15] Far from "pathological," female-headed households are in fact a rational response to economic constraints in a society that defines gender roles in ways that put women at a disadvantage.

Single-parent households headed by women are neither new nor restricted to industrialized societies such as the United States. They have been known and studied for a long time in the countries of the Caribbean basin, where men historically have been exploited as a cheap source of labor on plantations. Under such conditions, men have no power and few economic rewards; hence they are tenuously attached at best to any particular household. These are held together by women, who as producers of subsistence foods

provide the means of economic survival for households. Similar female-headed households are becoming increasingly common in other "underdeveloped" countries, too, as development projects increasingly restrict women's ability to earn a living wage (reasons for this are discussed in Chapters 26 and 27).

Thus, women constitute the majority of the poor, the underprivileged, and the economically and socially disadvantaged in most of the world's societies, just as is becoming true in the United States. In underdeveloped countries, the situation has been made worse by "reforms" the International Monetary Fund (IMF) requires to renegotiate payment of foreign debts. Cutbacks in government education, health, and social programs for debt service have their most direct (and negative) impact on women and children, while further development designed to increase foreign exchange (for debt repayment and the financing of more industrialization) also comes at women and children's expense. Meanwhile, the prices people must pay for basic life necessities increase (to cut down on unfavorable trade balances). If a woman is *lucky*, the wage she earns to buy bread for herself and her children remains constant, even if low, while the price she must pay for that bread continues to rise.

[15]Mullings, L. (1989). Gender and the application of anthropological knowledge to public policy in the United States. In S. Morgen (Ed.), *Gender and anthropology* (pp. 362–365). Washington: American Anthropological Association.

In North America, families are widely believed to be places of refuge from the rough-and-tumble outside world. Yet, domestic violence is far from rare, and women and children are its usual victims. Shown here is O.J. Simpson and his wife Nicole, whose "wrongful death" he was found guilty of by a civil court.

At the start of this chapter we posed a number of questions relating to the effectiveness of the family, as it is known today in North America, in meeting human needs. From what we have just discussed, it is obvious neolocal nuclear families impose considerable anxiety and stress upon the individuals in such families. Deprived of the security and multiplicity of emotional ties found in polygamous, extended, or consanguineal families, these nuclear families find that if something goes wrong, it is potentially more devastating to the individuals involved. Yet it is also obvious that alternative forms of family and household organization come complete with their distinctive stresses and strains. To the question of which alternative is preferable, we must answer that it depends on what problems one wishes to overcome and what price one is willing to pay.

In the United States, it is clear the problems inherent in the "traditional" nuclear family have led to a marked decline in the percentage of households such families occupy. Meanwhile, the conditions that gave rise to these families in the first place have changed. So far, no single family structure or ideology has arisen to supplant the nuclear family, nor can we predict which (if any) of the alternatives will gain preeminence in the future. The only certainty is that family and household arrangements, not just in the United States but throughout the world, will continue to evolve, as they always have, as the conditions they are sensitive to change.

CHAPTER SUMMARY

Dependence on group living for survival is a basic human characteristic. Nurturing children traditionally has been the adult female's job, although men also may play a role, and in some societies men are even more involved with their children than are women. In addition to at least some child care, women also carry out other economic tasks that complement those of men. The presence of adults of both sexes in a residential group is advantageous, in that it provides children with adult models of the same sex, from whom they can learn the gender-appropriate roles as defined in that society.

A definition of the family that avoids Western ethnocentrism sees it as a group composed of a woman and her dependent children, with at least one adult man joined through marriage or blood relationship. In most human societies, families either constitute households or households are built around families. Although families are not universally present in human societies, households are. Households are defined as the basic residential units where economic production, consumption, inheritance, child rearing, and shelter are organized and implemented.

Far from being a stable, unchanging entity, the family may take any one of a number of forms in response to particular social, historical, and ecological circumstances. Conjugal families are those formed on the basis of marital ties. The smallest conjugal unit of mother, father, and their dependent children is called the nuclear family. Contrasting with the conjugal is the consanguineal family, consisting of women, their dependent children, and their brothers. The nuclear family, which became the ideal in North American society, is also found in societies that live in harsh environments, such as the Inuit. In industrial societies as well as societies in particularly harsh environments, the nuclear family must be able to look after itself. The result is that individual members are strongly dependent on very few people. This form of family is well suited to the mobility required both in food-foraging groups and in industrial societies where job changes are frequent. Among food foragers, however, the nuclear family is not as isolated from other kin as in modern industrial society.

Characteristic of many nonindustrial societies is the large extended, or conjugal-consanguineal, family. Ideally, some of an extended family's members are related by blood, others are related by marriage, and all live and work together as members of one household. Conjugal or extended families are based upon five basic residential patterns: patrilocal, matrilocal, ambilocal, neolocal, and avunculocal.

Different forms of family organization are accompanied by their distinctive problems. Polygamous families endure the potential for conflict among the several spouses of the individual they are married to. One way to ameliorate this problem is through sororal polygyny or fraternal polyandry. Under polyandry, an added difficulty for the youngest husbands is reduced opportunity for reproduction. In extended families, the matter of decision making may be the source of stress, resting as it does with an older individual whose views may not coincide with those of the younger family members. In-marrying spouses in particular may have trouble complying with the demands of the family they must now live in.

In neolocal nuclear families, individuals are isolated from the direct aid and support of kin, so husbands and wives must work out their own solutions to the problems of living together and having children. The problems are especially difficult in North American society, owing to the inequality that still persists between men and women, the great emphasis placed on individualism and competition, and an absence of clearly understood patterns of responsibility between husbands and wives, as well as a clear model for child rearing.

In North America, an alternative to the independent nuclear family, and which is now twice as common, is the single-parent household, usually headed by a woman. Female-headed households are also common in underdeveloped countries. Because the women in such households are hard pressed to provide adequately for themselves as well as for their children, more women than ever in the United States and abroad find themselves sinking deeply into poverty.

POINTS FOR CONSIDERATION

1. Why do families take on particular forms?

2. Why might families in a culture stop being households? Why might families evolve into households? How flexible and diverse have North American families been regarding their roles as households?

3. Many individuals in North America have strong feelings about families with adult members involved in a homosexual relationship. Indeed, legislation as of yet has not been an adequate solution in the United States. How can this controversy be resolved? How will its resolution affect the status of families in North American culture?

SUGGESTED READINGS

Fox, R. (1967). *Kinship and marriage in an anthropological perspective.* Baltimore: Penguin.

Fox's book is a good introduction to older, orthodox theories about the family.

Goody, J. (1983). *Development of the family and marriage in Europe.* Cambridge: Cambridge University Press.

This historical study shows how the nature of the family changed in Europe in response to regulations the Catholic Church introduced to weaken the power of kin groups and gain access to property. It explains how European patterns of kinship and marriage came to differ from those of the ancient circum-Mediterranean world and from those that succeeded them in the Middle East and North Africa.

Netting, R. M., Wilk, R. R., & Arnold, E. J. (Eds.). (1984). *Households: Comparative and historical studies of the domestic group.* Berkeley, CA: University of California Press.

This collection of essays by 20 anthropologists and historians focuses on how and why households vary within and between societies and over time within single societies.

Stacey, J. (1990). *Brave new families.* New York: Basic Books.

Written by a sociologist, this book (subtitled *Stories of Domestic Conflict in Late Twentieth Century America*) takes an anthropological approach to understanding the changes affecting family structure in the United States. Her conclusion is that "the family" is *not* here to stay, nor should we wish otherwise. For all the difficulties attendant to "the family's demise," alternative arrangements do open hopeful possibilities for the future.

Thorne, B., & Yalom, M. (Eds.). (1982). *Rethinking the family: Some feminist questions.* New York: Longman.

As anthropologists have paid more attention to how institutions and practices work from a woman's perspective, they have had to reexamine existing assumptions about families in human societies. The 12 original essays in this volume, by scholars in economics, history, law, literature, philosophy, psychology, and sociology, as well as anthropology, examine topics such as the idea of the monolithic family, the sexual division of labor and inequality, motherhood, parenting, and mental illness and relations between family, class, and state. Especially recommended is the essay "Is There a Family? New Anthropological Views."

Chapter 21
KINSHIP AND DESCENT

AMONG PEOPLE OF SCOTTISH ANCESTRY, CLAN
AFFILIATION IS STILL A MATTER OF INTEREST,
THOUGH THE IMPORTANCE OF SUCH KIN GROUPS
HAS DIMINISHED. IN MANY HUMAN SOCIETIES,
HOWEVER, CLANS AND OTHER KIN GROUPS
REMAIN STRONG.

Chapter Preview

What Are Descent Groups?

A descent group is a kind of kinship group whereby being a lineal descendant of a particular real or mythical ancestor is a criterion of membership. Descent may be reckoned exclusively through men, exclusively through women, or through either at the individual's discretion. In some cases, two different means of reckoning descent are used at the same time to assign individuals to different groups for different purposes.

What Functions Do Descent Groups Serve?

Descent groups of various kinds—lineages, clans, phratries, and moieties—are convenient devices for solving a number of problems human societies commonly confront: how to maintain the integrity of resources that cannot be divided without destruction; generating workforces for tasks that require a labor pool larger than households can provide; and allowing members of one sovereign local group to claim support and protection from members of another. Not all societies have descent groups; in many food-foraging and industrial societies, some of these problems often are handled by the kindred, a group of people with a living relative in common. The kindred, however, does not exist in perpetuity, as does the descent group, nor is its membership as clearly and explicitly defined. Hence, it is generally a weaker unit than the descent group.

How Do Descent Groups Evolve?

Descent groups arise from extended family organization, as long as problems of organization exist that such groups help to solve. This is most apt to happen in food-producing as opposed to food-foraging societies. First to develop are localized lineages, followed by larger, dispersed groups such as clans and phratries. With the passage of time kinship terminology itself is affected by and adjusts to the kinds of descent or other kinship groups important to a society.

All societies have found some form of family and/or household organization a convenient way to deal with problems all human groups face: how to facilitate economic cooperation between the sexes, how to provide a proper setting for child rearing, and how to regulate sexual activity. Efficient and flexible though family and household organization may be in rising to challenges connected with such problems, the fact is many societies confront problems beyond the coping ability of family and household organization. For one, members of one sovereign local group often need some means of claiming support and protection from individuals in another group. This can be important for defense against natural or human-made disasters; if people have the right of entry into local groups other than their own, they can secure protection or critical resources when their own group cannot provide them. For another, a group frequently needs to share rights to some means of production that cannot be divided without its destruction. This is often the case in horticultural societies, where division of land is impractical beyond a certain point. The problem can be avoided if land ownership is vested in a corporate group that exists in perpetuity. Finally, people often need some means of providing cooperative workforces for tasks that require more participants than households alone can provide.

Many ways to deal with these sorts of problems exist. One is by developing a formal political system, with personnel to make and enforce laws, keep the peace, allocate resources, and perform other regulatory and societal functions. A more common way in nonindustrial societies—especially horticultural and pastoral societies—is by developing kinship groups.

DESCENT GROUPS

A common way of organizing a society along kinship lines is by creating what anthropologists call

On this altar, King Yax-Pac of the ancient Maya city of Copan portrays himself and his predecessors, thereby tracing his descent back to the founder of the dynasty. In many human societies, such genealogical connections are used to define each individual's rights, privileges, and obligations.

descent groups. A **descent group** is any publicly recognized social entity requiring lineal descent from a particular real or mythical ancestor for membership. Members of a descent group trace their connections back to a common ancestor through a chain of parent-child links. This feature may explain why descent groups are found in so many human societies. They appear to stem from the parent-child bond, which is built upon as the basis for a structured social group. This is a convenient relationship to seize upon, and the addition of a few nonburdensome obligations and avoidances acts as a kind of glue to help hold the group together.

To operate most efficiently, descent groups ought to clearly define membership. Otherwise, membership overlaps and it is not always clear where one's primary loyalty belongs. Membership can be restricted in a number of ways. It can be based on where people live; for example, if your parents live patrilocally, you automatically might be assigned to your father's descent group. Another way is through choice; each individual might be presented with a number of options. This, though, introduces a possibility of competition and conflict as groups vie for members. The most common way to restrict membership is by making sex jurally relevant. Instead of tracing membership back to the common ancestor, through men and sometimes through women, a society does it exclusively through one sex. In this way, each individual is automatically assigned from the moment of birth to his or her mother's or father's group and to that group only.

UNILINEAL DESCENT

Unilineal descent (sometimes called *unilateral descent*) establishes descent group membership exclusively through the male or the female line. In non-Western societies, unilineal descent groups are quite common. The individual is assigned at birth to

membership in a specific descent group, which may be traced either by **matrilineal descent,** through the female line, or by **patrilineal descent,** through the male line, depending on the society. In patrilineal societies the males are far more important than the females, for they are considered responsible for the group's perpetuation. In matrilineal societies, this responsibility falls on the female group members, whose importance is thereby enhanced.

A close relation between the descent system and a society's economy seems to exist. Generally, patrilineal descent predominates where the man is the breadwinner, as among pastoralists and intensive agriculturalists, where male labor is a prime factor. Matrilineal descent is important mainly among horticulturists in societies where women are the breadwinners. Numerous matrilineal societies are found in south Asia, one of the cradles of food production in the Old World. These include societies in India, Sri Lanka, Indonesia, Sumatra, Tibet, south China, and many Indonesian islands. Matrilineal systems also were prominent in parts of aboriginal North America and still are in parts of Africa.

It is now recognized that in all societies, the kin of both mother and father are important components of the social structure. Just because descent may be reckoned patrilineally, for example, does not mean maternal relatives are unimportant. It simply means that, for purposes of *group membership,* the mother's relatives are excluded. Similarly, under matrilineal descent, the father's relatives are excluded for purposes of group membership. For example, we already have seen in the two preceding chapters how important paternal relatives are among the matrilineal Trobriand Islanders. Although children belong to their mother's descent groups, fathers play an important role in nurturing and building them up. Upon marriage, the bride's and groom's paternal relatives contribute to the required exchange of gifts, and, throughout life, a man may expect his paternal

Descent group. Any publicly recognized social entity requiring lineal descent from a particular real or mythical ancestor for membership. > **Unilineal descent.** Descent that establishes group membership exclusively through either the mother's or the father's line. > **Matrilineal descent.** Descent traced exclusively through the female line to establish group membership. > **Patrilineal descent.** Descent traced exclusively through the male line to establish group membership.

kin to help him improve his economic and political position in society. Eventually, sons may expect to inherit personal property from their fathers.

Patrilineal Descent and Organization

Patrilineal descent (sometimes called *agnatic* or *male descent*) is the more widespread of the two unilineal descent systems. The male members of a patrilineal descent group trace through other males their descent from a common ancestor (Figure 21.1). Brothers and sisters belong to the descent group of their father's father, their father, their father's siblings, and their father's brother's children. A man's son and daughter also trace their descent back through the male line to their common ancestor. In the typical patrilineal group, the responsibility for training the children rests with the father or his elder brother. A woman belongs to the same descent group as her father and his brothers, but her children cannot trace their descent through them. A person's paternal aunt's children, for example, trace their descent through the patrilineal group of her husband.

Traditional China: A Patrilineal Society Until World War II, rural Chinese society was strongly patrilineal. Since then, considerable changes have occurred, although vestiges of the old system persist to varying degrees in different regions. Traditionally, the basic unit for economic cooperation was the large extended family, typically including aged parents, their sons, and their sons' wives and sons' children.[1] Residence, therefore, was patrilocal, as defined in Chapter 9. As in most patrilocal societies, then, children grew up in a household their father and his male relatives dominated. The father was a source of discipline a child would maintain a respectful social distance from. Often, the father's brother and his sons were members of the same household. Thus, the paternal uncle was rather like a second father and was treated with obedience and respect, while his sons were like one's brothers. Accordingly, the kinship term applied to a father was extended to the father's brother, as the term for a brother was extended to the father's brother's sons. When families became too large and unwieldy, as frequently

---

[1]Most of the following is from F. Hsiaotung (1939), *Peasant life in China*. London: Kegan, Paul, Trench and Truber.

Figure 21.1

How patrilineal descent is traced. Only the individuals symbolized by a filled-in circle or triangle are in the same descent group as ego. The abbreviation *F* stands for father, *B* for brother, *H* for husband, *S* for son, *M* for mother, *Z* for sister, *D* for daughter, and *W* for wife.

absorbed by that of her husband, whom she went to live with after marriage. Nonetheless, members of her natal *tsu* retained some interest in her after her departure. Her mother, for example, would assist her in the birth of her children, and her brother or some other male relative would look after her interests, perhaps even intervening if her husband or other members of his family treated her badly.

The function of the *tsu* was to assist its members economically and to gather on ceremonial occasions such as weddings and funerals or to make offerings to the ancestors. Recently deceased ancestors, up to about three generations back, were given offerings of food and paper money on the anniversaries of their births and deaths, while more distant ancestors were collectively worshiped five times a year. Each *tsu* maintained its own place for storage of ancestral tablets on which the names of all members were recorded. In addition to its economic and ritual functions, the *tsu* also functioned as a legal body, passing judgment on errant members.

happened, one or more sons would move elsewhere to establish separate households; when a son did so, however, the tie to his natal household remained strong.

Important though family membership was for each individual, it was the *tsu* that was regarded as the primary social unit. Each *tsu* consisted of men who traced their ancestry back through the male line to a common ancestor, usually within about five generations. Although a woman belonged to her father's *tsu*, for all practical purposes she was

Just as families periodically split into new ones, so would the larger descent groups periodically splinter along the lines of their main family branches. Causes included disputes among brothers over management of land holdings and suspicion of unfair division of profits. When such

In patrilineal and other societies that promote the dominance of men over women, this practice sometimes goes to the extreme of inflicting physical, as well as social, disabilities on women. In the 19th century, Chinese women had their feet tightly bound, while in North America women often were tightly corseted. The result in both cases was actual physical impairment.

separation occurred, a representative of the new *tsu* would return periodically to the ancestral temple to pay respect to the ancestors and record recent births and deaths in the official genealogy. Ultimately, though the tie to the old *tsu* still would be recognized, a copy of the old genealogy would be made and brought home to the younger *tsu*, and then only its births and deaths would be recorded. In this way, for many centuries a whole hierarchy of descent groups developed, with all persons having the same surname considering themselves members of a great patrilineal clan. With this went surname exogamy, which is still widely practiced today even though clan members no longer carry on ceremonial activities together.

The patrilineal system reached throughout rural Chinese social relations. Children owed obedience and respect to their fathers and older patrilineal relatives in life and had to marry whomever their parents chose for them. It was the duty of sons to care for their parents when they

became old and helpless, and even after death sons had ceremonial obligations to them. Inheritance passed from fathers to sons, with an extra share going to the eldest, since he ordinarily made the greatest contribution to the household and had the greatest responsibility toward his parents after their deaths. Women, by contrast, had no claims on their families' heritable property. Once married, a woman was in effect cast off by her patrilineal kin (even though they might continue to take an interest in her) to produce children for her husband's family and *tsu*.

As the preceding suggests, a patrilineal society is very much a man's world; no matter how valued women may be, they inevitably find themselves in a difficult position. Far from resigning themselves to a subordinate position, however, they actively manipulate the system to their own advantage as best they can. To learn how they may do so, let us look more closely at the way women relate to one another in traditional Chinese society.

Coping as a Woman in a Man's World[2]

Women in rural Taiwan do not live their lives in the walled courtyards of their husbands' households. If they did, they might be as powerless as their stereotype. It is in their relations in the outside world (and for women in rural Taiwan that world consists almost entirely of the village) that women develop sufficient backing to maintain some independence under their powerful mothers-in-law. A successful venture into the men's world is no small feat when one recalls that the men of a village were born there and are often related to one another, whereas the women are unlikely to have either the ties of childhood or the ties of kinship to unite them. All the same, shared interests, and common problems of women are reflected in every village in a loosely knit society that can when needed be called on to exercise considerable influence.

Women carry on as many of their activities as possible outside the house. They wash clothes on the riverbank, clean and pare vegetables at a communal pump, mend under a tree that is a known meetingplace, and stop to rest on a bench or group of stones with other women. There is a continual moving back and forth between kitchens, and conversations are carried on from open doorways through the long, hot afternoons of summer. The shy young girl who enters the village as a bride is examined as frankly and suspiciously by the women as an animal that is up for sale. If she is deferential to her elders, does not criticize or compare her new world unfa-

---

[2]Wolf, M. (1972). *Women and the family in rural Taiwan* (pp. 37–41). Stanford, CA: Stanford University Press.

vorably with the one she has left, the older residents will gradually accept her presence on the edge of their conversations and stop changing the topic to general subjects when she brings the family laundry to scrub on the rocks near them. As the young bride meets other girls in her position, she makes allies for the future, but she must also develop relationships with the older women. She learns to use considerable discretion in making and receiving confidences, for a girl who gossips freely about the affairs of her husband's household may find herself always on the outside of the group, or worse yet, accused of snobbery. I described in *The House of Lim* the plight of Lim Chui-ieng, who had little village backing in her troubles with her husband and his family as a result of her arrogance toward the women's community. In Peihotien the young wife of the storekeeper's son suffered a similar lack of support. Warned by her husband's parents not to be too "easy" with the other villagers lest they try to buy things on credit, she obeyed to the point of being considered unfriendly by the women of the village. When she began to have serious troubles with her husband and eventually his family, there was no one in the village she could turn to for solace, advice, and most important, peacemaking.

Once a young bride has established herself as a member of the women's community, she has also established for herself a certain amount of protection. If the members of her husband's family step beyond the limits of propriety in their treatment of her—such as refusing to allow her to return to her natal home for her brother's wedding or beating her without serious justification—she can complain to a woman friend, preferably older, while they are washing vegetables at the communal pump. The story will quickly spread to the other women, and one of them will take it upon herself to check the facts with another member of the girl's household. For a few days the matter will be thoroughly discussed whenever a few women gather. In a young wife's first few years in the community, she can expect to have her mother-in-law's side of any disagreement given fuller weight than her own —her mother-in-law has, after all, been a part of the community a lot longer. However, the discussion itself will serve to curb many offenses. Even if the older woman knows that public opinion is falling to her side, she will be somewhat more judicious about refusing her daughter-in-law's next request. Still, the daughter-in-law who hopes to make use of the village forum to depose her mother-in-law or at least gain herself special privilege will discover just how important the prerogatives of age and length of residence are. Although the women can serve as a powerful protective force for their defenseless younger members, they are also a very conservative force in the village.

Taiwanese women can and do make use of their collective power to lose face for their menfolk in order to influence decisions that are ostensibly not theirs to make. Although young women may have little or no influence over their husbands and would not dare express an unsolicited opinion (and perhaps not even a solicited one) to their fathers-in-law, older women who have raised their sons properly retain considerable influence over their sons' actions, even in activities exclusive to men. Further, older women who have displayed years of good judgement are regularly consulted by their husbands about major as well as minor economic and social projects. But even men who think themselves free to ignore the opinions of their women are never free of their own concept, face. It is much easier to lose face than to have face. We once asked a male friend in Peihotien just what "having face" amounted to. He replied, "When no one is talking about a family, you can say it has face." This is precisely where women wield their power. When a man behaves in a way that they consider wrong, they talk about him—not only among themselves, but to their sons and husbands. No one "tells him how to mind his own business," but it becomes abundantly clear that he is losing face and by continuing in this manner may bring shame to the family of his ancestors and descendants. Few men will risk that.

The rules that a Taiwanese man must learn and obey to be a successful member of his society are well developed, clear, and relatively easy to stay within. A Taiwanese woman must also learn the rules, but if she is to be a successful woman, she must learn not to stay within them, but to appear to stay within them; to manipulate them, but not to appear to be manipulating them; to teach them to her children, but not to depend on her children for her protection. A truly successful Taiwanese woman is a rugged individualist who has learned to depend largely on herself while appearing to lean on her father, her husband, and her son. The contrast between the terrified young bride and the loud, confident, often lewd old woman who has outlived her mother-in-law and her husband reflects the tests met and passed by not strictly following the rules and by making purposeful use of those who must. The Chinese male's conception of women as "narrow-hearted" and socially inept may well be his vague recognition of this facet of women's power and technique.

Matrilineal Descent and Organization

In one respect, matrilineal descent is the opposite of patrilineal: It is reckoned through the female line (Figure 21.2). The matrilineal pattern differs from the patrilineal, however, in that descent does not automatically confer authority. Thus, although patrilineal societies are patriarchal, matrilineal societies are not matriarchal. Although descent passes through the female line and women may have considerable power, they do not hold exclusive authority in the descent group: They share it with men. These are the brothers, rather than the husbands, of the women descent is reckoned through. Apparently, the adaptive purpose of the matrilineal system is to provide continuous female solidarity within the female work group. Matrilineal systems are usually found in farming societies where women perform much of the productive work. Because women's work is regarded as so important to the society, matrilineal descent prevails.

In the matrilineal system, brothers and sisters belong to the descent group of the mother's mother, the mother, the mother's siblings, and the mother's sister's children. Males belong to the same descent group as their mother and sister, but their children cannot trace their descent through them. For example, the children of a man's maternal uncle are considered members of the uncle's wife's matrilineal descent group. Similarly, a man's children belong to his wife's, but not his, descent group.

Although not true of all matrilineal systems, a common feature is the weakness of the tie between husband and wife. The wife's brother, and not the husband/father, distributes goods, organizes work, settles disputes, administers inheritance and succession rules, and supervises rituals. The husband has legal authority not in his household but in that of his sister. Furthermore, his property and status are inherited by his sister's son, rather than by his son. Thus, brothers and sisters

FIGURE 21.2

This diagram, which traces descent matrilineally, can be compared with that in Figure 21.1, showing patrilineal descent. The two patterns are virtually mirror images. Note that a man cannot transmit descent to his own children.

maintain lifelong ties with one another, whereas marital ties are easily severed. In matrilineal societies, unsatisfactory marriages are more easily ended than in patrilineal societies.

THE HOPI: A MATRILINEAL SOCIETY

In northeastern Arizona are the villages, or pueblos, of the Hopi Indians, a farming people whose ancestors have lived in the region for at least 2,000 years. Their society is divided into a number of named clans based strictly on matrilineal descent.[3] Each individual is assigned from birth to his or her mother's clan, and so important is this affiliation that, in a very real sense, a person has no identity apart from it. Two or more clans together constitute larger, supraclan units, or *phratries,* of which nine exist in Hopi society. Within each of these, member clans are expected to support one another and to observe strict exogamy. Because members of all nine phratries live in any given pueblo, marriage partners always can be found in one's home

community. This same dispersal of membership provides individuals with entry rights into villages other than their own.

Although clans are the major units in Hopi thinking, the functional units consist of subclans, or lineages, and each village has several. Each is headed by a senior woman—usually the eldest, although it is her brother or maternal uncle who

---

[3]Most of the following is from J. C. Connelly (1979), Hopi social organization. In A. Ortiz (Ed.), *Handbook of North American Indians* (Vol. 9, Southwest, pp. 539–553). Washington, DC: Smithsonian Institution.

keeps the sacred "medicine bundle" and plays an active role in running lineage affairs. The woman, however, is not a mere figurehead; she may act as mediator to help resolve disputes among group members, nor does she yield any authority to her brother or uncle. Although these men have the right to offer her advice and criticism, they are equally obligated to listen to what she has to say. Most female authority, however, is exerted within the household, and here men clearly take second place. These households consist of the women of the lineage with their husbands and unmarried sons, all of whom used to live in sets of adjacent rooms in single large tenements. Nowadays, nuclear families often live (frequently with a maternal relative or two) in separate houses, but pickup trucks and other vehicles enable related households to maintain close contacts and to cooperate as before.

Lineages function as landholding corporations, allocating land for the support of member households. These lands are farmed by "outsiders," the husbands of the women whose lineage owns the land, and the harvest belongs to these women. Thus, Hopi men spend their lives laboring for alien lineages (their wives'), and in return they are given food and shelter (by their wives). Although sons learn from their fathers how to farm, a man has no real authority over his son (the two belong to different lineages). Thus, when parents have difficulty with an unruly child, the mother's brother is called upon to mete out discipline. Male loyalties are therefore divided between their wives' households on the one hand and their sisters' on the other. If, at any time, a man is perceived as an unsatisfactory husband, his wife merely has to place his belongings outside the door, and the marriage is over.

In addition to their economic and legal functions, lineages play a role in Hopi ceremonial activities. Although membership in the associations that actually perform ceremonies is open to all who have the proper qualifications, clans own and manage all the associations, and in each village a leading lineage acts as its clan's representative. This lineage owns a special house where the clan's religious paraphernalia are stored and cared for by the "clan mother." Together with her brother, the clan's Big Uncle, she helps manage ceremonial

Many of the things that Hopi women do are done in the company of other women; thus, they have ample opportunity to discuss issues of importance to them.

activity. Although men control most of the associations that do the actual performing, women still have vital roles to play. For example, they provide the cornmeal, symbolic of natural and spiritual life that is a necessary ingredient in virtually all ceremonies.

Prior to the United States government's imposition in 1936 of a different system, each Hopi pueblo was politically autonomous, with its own chief and village council. Here again, however, descent group organization made itself felt, for the council was made up of men who inherited their positions through their clans. Moreover, the powers of the chief and his council were limited; the chief's major job was to maintain harmony between his village and the spiritual world, and whatever authority he and his council wielded was directed at coordination of community effort, not enforcement of unilateral decrees. Decisions were made on a consensual basis, and women's views had to be considered, as well as those of men. Once again, although men held positions of authority, women had considerable control over their decisions in a behind-the-scene way. These men, after all, lived in households women controlled, and their position within them depended largely on how well they got along with the senior women. Outside the household, women's refusal to play their part in the performance of ceremonies gave them veto power. Small wonder, then, that Hopi men readily admit that "women usually get their way."[4]

DOUBLE DESCENT

Double descent, or double unilineal descent, whereby descent is reckoned both patrilineally and matrilineally at the same time, is very rare. In this system descent is matrilineal for some purposes and patrilineal for others. Generally, where double descent is reckoned, the matrilineal and patrilineal groups take action in different spheres of society.

For example, among the Yakö of eastern Nigeria, property is divided into both patrilineal line possessions and matrilineal line possessions.[5] The patrilineage owns perpetual productive resources, such as land, whereas the matrilineage owns consumable property, such as livestock. The legally weaker matrilineal line is somewhat more important in religious matters than the patrilineal line. Through double descent, a Yakö might inherit grazing lands from the father's patrilineal group and certain ritual privileges from the mother's matrilineal line.

AMBILINEAL DESCENT

Unilineal descent provides an easy way of restricting descent group membership to avoid prob-

lems of divided loyalty and the like. A number of societies, many of them in the Pacific and in Southeast Asia, accomplish the same task in other ways, though perhaps not quite so neatly. The resultant descent groups are known as *ambilineal, nonunilineal,* or *cognatic.* **Ambilineal descent** provides a measure of flexibility not normally found under unilineal descent; each individual has the option of affiliating with either the mother's or the father's descent group. In many of these societies, an individual is allowed to belong to only one group at a time, regardless of how many groups he or she may be eligible to join. Thus, the society may be divided into the same sorts of discrete and separate groups of kin as in a patrilineal or matrilineal society. Other cognatic societies, however, such as the Samoans of the South Pacific or the Bella Coola and the southern branch of the Kwakiutl of the Pacific Northwest Coast of North America, allow overlapping membership in a number of descent groups. As anthropologist George Murdock observed, too great a range of individual choice interferes with the orderly functioning of any kin-oriented society:

An individual's plural membership almost inevitably becomes segregated into a primary membership, strongly activated by residence, and one or more secondary memberships with only partial or occasional participation.[6]

Ambilineal Descent Among New York City Jews

For an example of ambilineal organization, we easily might turn to a traditional non-Western society, as we have for patrilineal and matrilineal organization. Instead, we shall turn to contemporary North American society to dispel the common (but false) notion that descent groups are necessarily incompatible in structure and function with the demands of modern industrial society. In fact,

---

[4]Schlegel, A. (1977). Male and female in Hopi thought and action. In A. Schlegel (Ed.), *Sexual stratification* (p. 254). New York: Columbia University Press.

[5]Forde, C. D. (1968). Double descent among the Yakö. In P. Bohannan and J. Middleton (Eds.), *Kinship and social organization* (pp. 179–191). Garden City, NY: Natural History Press.

[6]Murdock, G. P. (1960). Cognatic forms of social organization. In G. P. Murdock, *Social structure in Southeast Asia* (p. 11). Chicago: Quadrangle Books.

Double descent. A system tracing descent matrilineally for some purposes and patrilineally for others. **> Ambilineal descent.** Descent in which the individual may affiliate with either the mother's or the father's descent group.

large corporate descent groups that hold assets in common and exist in perpetuity are found in New York City, as well as in every large city in the United States where a substantial Jewish population of eastern European background is found.[7] Furthermore, these descent groups are not survivals of an old eastern European descent-based organization. Rather, they represent a social innovation designed to restructure and preserve the

---

[7]Mitchell, W. E. (1978). *Mishpokhe: A study of New York City Jewish family clubs.* The Hague: Mouton.

traditionally close affective family ties of the old eastern European Jewish culture in the face of continuing immigration to the United States, subsequent dispersal from New York City, and the development of significant social and even temperamental differences among their descendants. The earliest of these descent groups did not develop until the end of the first decade of the 1900s, some 40 years after the immigration of eastern European Jews began in earnest. Although some groups have disbanded, they generally have remained alive and vital right down to the present.

The original Jewish descent groups in New York City are known as *family circles.* The potential members of a family circle consist of all living descendants, with their spouses, of an ancestral pair. In actuality, not all who are eligible actually join, so an element of voluntarism exists. But eligibility is explicitly determined by descent, using both male and female links, without set order, to establish the connection with the ancestral pair. Thus, individuals are normally eligible for membership in more than one group or "circle." To activate a membership, one simply pays the required dues, attends meetings, and participates in the group's affairs. Individuals can, and frequently do, belong at the same time to two or three groups they are eligible for. Each family circle bears a name, usually including the surname of the male

Close family ties have always been important in eastern European Jewish culture. To maintain such ties in the United States, the descendants of eastern European Jews developed ambilineal descent groups.

ancestor; each has elected officers; and each meets regularly throughout the year rather than just once or twice. At the least, the family circle as a corporation holds funds in common, and some hold title to burial plots for members. Originally, they functioned as mutual-aid societies, as well as had the purpose of maintaining family solidarity. Now, as the mutual-aid functions have been taken over by outside agencies, the promotion of solidarity has become their primary goal. It will be interesting to see if reduced government funding for these agencies leads to a resurgence of the mutual-aid function of family circles.

In the years just prior to World War II, an interesting variant of the ambilineal descent group developed among younger-generation descendants of east European Jewish immigrants. Being more assimilated into North American culture, some of them sought to separate themselves somewhat from members of older generations, who were perceived as a bit old-fashioned. Yet they still wished to maintain the traditional Jewish ethic of family solidarity. The result was the *cousins club,* which

consists of a group of first cousins who share a common ancestry, their spouses, and their descendants. Excluded are parents and grandparents of the cousins, with their older views and lifestyles. Ambilineal descent remains the primary organizing principle, but it has been modified by a generational principle. Otherwise, cousins clubs are organized and function in many of the same ways as family circles.

FORMS AND FUNCTIONS OF DESCENT GROUPS

Descent groups with restricted membership, regardless of how descent is reckoned, are usually more than mere groups of relatives providing warmth and a sense of belonging; in nonindustrial societies they are tightly organized working units providing security and services in what can be a difficult, uncertain life. The tasks descent groups perform are manifold. Besides acting as economic

Anthropologist Peggy Reeves Sanday with members of a matrilineal clan among the Minangkabau of Sumatra gathered for a house-raising ceremony. The one adult male is the brother of the senior female leader (the woman on Sanday's left); he is the clan's male leader. Absence of other men reflects the predominance of women in this society.

units providing mutual aid to their members, they may support the aged and infirm and help with marriages and deaths. Often, they play a role in determining who an individual may or may not marry. The descent group also may act as a repository of religious traditions. Ancestor worship, for example, is a powerful force acting to reinforce group solidarity.

Lineage

A **lineage** (such as those of the Hopi or the Chinese *tsu*) is a corporate descent group composed of consanguineal kin who trace descent genealogically through known links back to a common ancestor. The term is usually employed where a form of unilineal descent is the rule, but some ambilineal groups are similar, such as the Jewish family circles just discussed.

The lineage is ancestor oriented; membership in the group is recognized only if relationship to a common ancestor can be traced and proved. In many societies an individual has no legal or political status except as a lineage member. Since "citizenship" is derived from lineage membership and legal status depends on it, political and religious power are derived from it as well. Important religious and magical powers, such as those associated with the cults of gods and ancestors, also may be bound to the lineage.

The lineage, like General Motors or IBM, is a corporate group. Because it endures after the deaths of members with new members continually born into it, it has a perpetual existence that enables it to take corporate actions, such as owning property, organizing productive activities, distributing goods and labor power, assigning status, and regulating relations with other groups. The lineage is a strong, effective base of social organization.

A common feature of lineages is their exogamy. This means lineage members must find their marriage partners in other lineages. One advantage of lineage exogamy is that potential sexual competition within the group is curbed, promoting the group's solidarity. Lineage exogamy also means each marriage is more than an arrangement between two individuals; it amounts as well to a new alliance between lineages. This helps to maintain them as components of larger social systems. Finally, lineage exogamy supports open communication within a society by promoting the diffusion of knowledge from one lineage to another.

Clan

In the course of time, as generation succeeds generation and new members are born into the lineage, its membership may become unmanageably large or too much for the lineage's resources to support. When this happens, as we have seen with the Chinese *tsu*, **fission** occurs; that is, the lineage splits into new, smaller lineages. When fission occurs, usually the members of the new lineages continue to recognize their ultimate relationship to one another. The result of this process is the appearance of a second kind of descent group, the **clan**. The term *clan* and its close relative, the term *sib*, have been used differently by various anthropologists, and a certain amount of confusion exists about their meaning. The clan (or sib) will be defined here as a noncorporate descent group whose members assume descent from a common ancestor (who may be real or fictive) but are unable to trace the actual genealogical links back to that ancestor. This stems from the great genealogical depth of the clan, whose founding ancestor lived so far in the past that the links must be assumed rather than known in detail. A clan differs from a lineage in another respect: It lacks the residential unity generally—though not invariably—characteristic of a lineage's core members. As with the lineage, descent may be patrilineal, matrilineal, or ambilineal.

Because clan membership is dispersed rather than localized, it usually does not hold tangible property corporately. Instead, it tends to be more a unit for ceremonial matters. Only on special occasions will the membership gather for specific

---

Lineage. A corporate descent group whose members trace their genealogical links to a common ancestor. **> Fission.** The splitting of a descent group into two or more new descent groups. **> Clan.** A noncorporate descent group whose members claim descent from a common ancestor without actually knowing the genealogical links to that ancestor.

anthropology applied Federal Recognition for Native Americans

Esoteric though research on kinship organization may sometimes seem, it is important for the kind of applied anthropology described here by anthropologist Harald Prins.*

In autumn 1981, Dutch anthropologist Harald Prins drove through Maine's vast woodlands to the small town of Houlton near the Canadian border. He'd come to check out a job at the Association of Aroostook Indians (AAI), which needed a research and development director. Founded by a group of Indian activists in 1970 to deal with a host of serious problems, AAI served 1,200 off-reservation Mi'kmaqs and Maliseets in Aroostook County. Crushed by chronic poverty and suffering from poor health, most resided in shacks or run-down apartments. Few had more than an eighth-grade education, many were alcoholics and almost all felt victimized by racial discrimination. The AAI tried to ease their burdens by providing social services. Moreover, it tackled political problems, including reclamation of traditional rights to freely hunt, trap, and fish.

Fresh from fieldwork in the Argentine pampas and frustrated by an anthropology that had little practical use for the people being studied, Prins welcomed the opportunity to be an activist in Maine's backlands. The elders on AAI's Board hired him, saying his main task was to help Aroostook Mi'kmaqs gain federal recognition as a tribal community. That would make them eligible for federal assistance (health, housing, education and child welfare) and loan guarantees for economic development.

Prins quickly realized the difficulty of the task. A year earlier, Maine's other three Indian groups (including the Maliseet) had negotiated a land claims settlement with the US government and the State of Maine, winning federal recognition and money to buy back about 300,000 acres of land. Mi'kmaqs had been left out because no one had done the research needed to ensure their inclusion. Worse, Mi'kmaqs had lost the right to put together their own claim because the settlement extinguished all aboriginal titles held by any Indian tribe to all lands in Maine.

Since Maliseets had already gained federal status as a "tribe," Prins helped Mi'kmaqs reorganize based on their ethnic identity. Newly incorporated as the Aroostook Band of Micmacs (ABM), they abandoned the AAI (which then dissolved) and set up new headquarters in Presque Isle. As staff anthropologist, Prins sought funding for ABM, worked closely with Mi'kmaq leaders to define political strategies and helped generate broad popular support for the effort. Considering

The Sanipass-Lafford family cluster in Chapman, Maine, represents a traditional Mi'kmaq residential kin-group. Such extended families typically include grandchildren and bilaterally related family members such as in-laws, uncles and aunts. Taken from the Sanipass family album, this picture shows a handful of members in the mid-1980s: Marline Sanipass Morey with two of her nephews and uncles.

---

*By Harald Prins, now a professor of anthropology at Kansas State University who also serves on the land claims team of Newfoundland's Miawpukek Band of Mi'kmaqs. For further information, see his case study (1996), *The Mi'kmaq: Resistance, accommodation, and cultural survival.* Fort Worth, TX: Harcourt Brace.

the importance of informing the public and politicians as well as government agencies about their cultural identity and their struggle for native rights, he coproduced a documentary film, *Our Lives in Our Hands* (D.E.R. 1986), which aired on television and had dozens of public screenings. Most important, he gathered detailed ethnographic and historical documentation to address government requirements for federal recognition. Groups seeking this special status must present an elaborate document that includes: (1) Historical and *genealogical records* of its existence as a distinct community from ancient times to the present, (2) Evidence that the group has maintained political influence over its members on a continual basis, (3) Proof that its members are descendants of a tribe historically inhabiting the area.

Aroostook Mi'kmaqs faced many obstacles in meeting these requirements: (1) Band members lived widely dispersed in small family groups throughout the huge county, so they didn't fill the conventional definition of community, (2) They didn't have a clearly defined membership and lacked formally appointed political leaders, (3) Scholars had described them as "Canadian Indians" without historic ties to Maine. They did this on the basis of a widely accepted "riverine model" of tribal territoriality which tied each tribe to a particular river. This given, Mi'kmaqs dwelling in the St. John River drainage area in northern Maine were considered recent interlopers on traditional Maliseet lands.

Several years of research yielded the data needed to counter these problems. Prins (with the help of others) unearthed genealogical documentation showing that most Mi'kmaq adults were at least "half-blood" (having two of their grandparents officially recorded as Mi'kmaq Indians). He discovered that the loosely-structured ABM, with its informal system of political leadership, actually matched that of traditional Mi'kmaq hunting bands. And, finding historical evidence that Mi'kmaqs were no strangers to northern Maine, he showed that the region fell within the aboriginal range of their ancestors who were historically allied with Maine's other three tribes in the Wabanaki Confederacy. Based on this evidence, Mi'kmaqs argued that they would have been able to claim aboriginal title to jointly used lands in the region and should not have been left out of the earlier settlement. Supported by Maine's recognized tribes, ABM convinced the state's Congressional delegation in Washington, D.C. to introduce a special bill to acknowledge their tribal status and settle their land claims. When formal hearings were held, Prins testified as expert witness for the Mi'kmaqs. In 1991 President George Bush signed the Aroostook Band of Micmacs Settlement Act into federal law. Since then, the band has received assistance available to all federally recognized tribes, plus funding to buy a 5,000-acre tribal land base. Although their cultural survival is not guaranteed, Aroostook's Mi'kmaqs have witnessed vital improvements in their community.

---

purposes. Clans, however, may handle important integrative functions. Like lineages, they may regulate marriage through exogamy. Because of their dispersed membership, they give individuals entry rights into local groups other than their own. Members usually are expected to give protection and hospitality to others in the clan. Hence, these can be expected in any local group that includes people who belong to a single clan.

Clans, lacking the residential unity of lineages, frequently depend on symbols—of animals, plants, natural forces, and objects—to provide members with solidarity and a ready means of identification. These symbols, called *totems*, are often associated with the clan's mythical origin and reinforce for clan members an awareness of their common descent with what the totems represent. The word *totem* comes from the Ojibwa American Indian word *ototeman*, meaning "he is a relative of mine." **Totemism** was defined by British anthropologist A. R. Radcliffe-Brown as a set of "customs and beliefs by which there is set up a special system of relations between the society and the plants, animals, and other natural objects that are important in the social life."[8] Hopi Indian matriclans, for example, bear such totemic

---

[8]Radcliffe-Brown, A. R. (1931). Social organization of Australian tribes. *Oceania Monographs, 1,* 29. Melbourne: Macmillan.

Totemism.   The belief that people are related to particular animals, plants, or natural objects by virtue of descent from common ancestral spirits.

names as Bear, Bluebird, Butterfly, Lizard, Spider, and Snake.

Totemism is a changing concept that varies from clan to clan. A kind of watered-down totemism may be found even in modern North American society, where baseball and football teams are given the names of such powerful wild animals as bears, tigers, and wildcats. This extends to the Democratic Party's donkey and the Republican Party's elephant, the Elks, the Lions, and other fraternal and social organizations. These animal emblems, however, do not involve the same notions of descent and strong sense of kinship that clans have toward what the totems represent nor are they linked with the various ritual observances associated with clan totems.

PHRATRIES AND MOIETIES

Other kinds of descent group are phratries and moieties (Figure 21.3). A **phratry,** such as those of the Hopi we already have discussed, is a unilineal descent group composed of at least two clans that supposedly share a common ancestry, whether or not they really do. Like clan individuals, phratry members cannot trace accurately their descent links to a common ancestor, though they firmly believe such an ancestor existed.

If the entire society is divided into only two major descent groups, whether they are equivalent to clans or phratries or involve an even more all-inclusive level, each group is called a **moiety** (after the French word for "half"). Moiety members also believe they share a common ancestor but cannot prove it through definite genealogical links. As a rule, the feelings of kinship among members of lineages and clans are stronger than those of members of phratries and moieties. This may be due to the larger size and more diffuse nature of the latter groups.

Like clans and lineages, phratries and moieties are often exogamous and thus are bound together by marriages between their members. And like clans, they provide members rights of access to other communities, as among the Hopi. In a community that does not include one's clan members, one's phratry members will still be there to turn to for hospitality. Finally, moieties may perform reciprocal services for one another, as among the Mohawks and other Iroquoian nations of what is now New York State. Among them, individuals turned to members of the opposite moiety for the necessary rituals when a member of their own moiety died. Such interdependence between moieties, again, served to maintain the integrity of the entire society.

BILATERAL DESCENT AND THE KINDRED

Important though descent groups are in many societies, they are not found in all societies nor are they the only kinds of nonfamilial kinship groups found. *Bilateral descent,* a characteristic of Western society as well as a number of food-foraging societies, affiliates a person with close relatives through both sexes; in other words, the individual traces descent through both parents, all four grandparents, and so forth, recognizing multiple ancestors. Theoretically, a person is associated equally with all consanguineal relatives on both the mother's and father's sides of the family. Thus, this principle relates an individual lineally to all

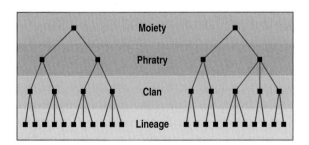

FIGURE 21.3

This diagram shows how lineages, clans, phratries, and moieties form an organizational hierarchy. Each moiety is subdivided into phratries, each phratry is subdivided into clans, and each clan is subdivided into lineages.

Phratry. A unilineal descent group composed of two or more clans that claim to be of common ancestry. If only two such groups exist, each is a moiety. **> Moiety.** Each group that results from a division of a society into two halves on the basis of descent.

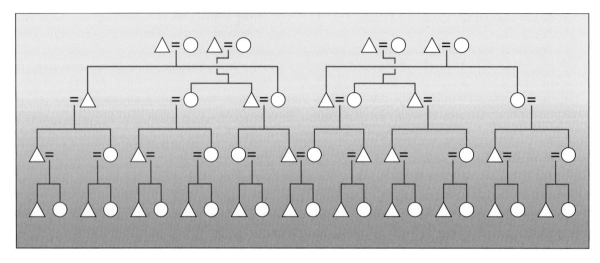

FIGURE 21.4

The kinship pattern of the kindred. These people are related not to a common ancestor but, rather, to a living relative, here the sister and brother shown at the center of the bottom row.

eight great-grandparents and laterally to all third and fourth cousins. Since such a huge group is too big to be socially practical, it is usually reduced to a small circle of paternal and maternal relatives, called the **kindred.** The kindred may be defined as a group of people closely related to one living individual through both parents. Since the kindred is laterally rather than lineally organized—that is, ego, or the focal person the degree of each relationship is reckoned from, is the center of the group (Figure 21.4)—it really is not a descent group, even though it occurs in societies with bilateral descent.

North Americans are all familiar with the kindred; those who belong are simply called relatives. It includes the relatives on both sides of the family who are seen on important occasions, such as family reunions and funerals. Most people in the United States can identify the members of their kindred up to grandparents and first, if not always second, cousins. The limits of the kindred, however, are variable and indefinite; no one ever can be absolutely certain which relatives to invite to every important function and which to exclude.

Inevitably, situations arise that require some debate about whether to invite particular, usually distant, relatives. Kindreds are thus not clearly bounded and lack the discreteness of unilineal or ambilineal descent groups. (They also are temporary, lasting only as long as the functions they are assembled for.)

Because of its bilateral structure, a kindred is never the same for any two persons except siblings (brothers and sisters). Thus, no two people (except siblings) belong to the same kindred. The kindred of ego's first cousin on the father's side, for example, includes not only the father's sister (or brother), as does ego's, but the father's sister's (or brother's) spouse, as well as consanguineal relatives of the latter. As for the kindreds of ego's parents, these range from grandparents lineally to cousins too distant laterally for ego to know, and the same is true of ego's aunts and uncles. Thus, the kindred is not composed of people with an ancestor in common but with a living relative in common—ego. Furthermore, as ego goes through life, the kindreds he or she is affiliated with will change. When young, individuals belong to the kindreds

---

Kindred.   A group of consanguineal kin linked by their relationship to one living individual; includes both maternal and paternal kin.

Members of the groom's personal kindred shown here are his new wife, father, mother, two brothers, sister-in-law, aunt, and niece.

of their parents; ultimately, they belong to the kindreds of their sons and daughters as well as their nieces and nephews.

Thus, because of its vagueness, temporary nature, and changing affiliation, the kindred cannot function as a group except in relation to ego. Unlike descent groups, it is not self-perpetuating—it ceases with ego's death. It has no constant leader, nor can it easily hold, administer, or pass on property. In most cases, it cannot organize work, nor can it easily administer justice or assign status. It can, however, be turned to for aid. In non-Western societies, for example, raiding or trading parties may be composed of kindred groups. The group is assembled, does what it was gathered to do, shares the results, and then disbands. It also can act as a ceremonial group for rites of passage: initiation ceremonies and the like. Thus, as noted, kindreds assemble only for specific purposes. Finally, they too can regulate marriage through exogamy.

Kindreds are frequently found in industrial societies such as that of the United States, where mobility weakens contact with relatives. Individuality is emphasized in such societies, and strong kinship organization is usually not as important as it is among non-Western peoples. In contrast, bilateral kindred groups also may be found in so-

cieties where kinship ties are important, and in some instances they even occur alongside descent groups.

EVOLUTION OF THE DESCENT GROUP

Just as various types of families occur in different societies, so do various kinds of nonfamilial kin groups. Descent groups, for example, are *not* a common feature of food-foraging societies, where marriage acts as the social mechanism for integrating individuals within communities. In horticultural, pastoral, or many intensive agricultural societies, however, the descent group usually provides the structural framework upon which the fabric of the society rests.

It is generally agreed that lineages arise from extended-family organization, as long as organizational problems exist that such groups help solve. All that is required, really, is that as members of existing extended families find it necessary to split off and establish new households elsewhere, they not move too far away; that the core members of such related families (men in patrilocal, women in matrilocal, and members of both sexes in ambilocal extended families) explicitly acknowledge their descent from a common ancestor; and that they continue to participate in common activities in an organized way. As these divisions proceed, lineages will develop, and these may with time give rise to clans and ultimately phratries.

Another way clans may arise is as legal fictions to integrate otherwise autonomous units. The five Iroquoian Indian nations of what now is New York State, for example, developed clans by simply behaving as if lineages of the same name in different villages were related. Thus, their members became fictitious brothers and sisters. By this device, members of, say, a "Turtle" lineage in one village could travel to another and be welcomed in and hosted by members of another "Turtle" lineage. In this way, the "Five Nations" achieved a wider unity than had previously existed.

Iroquoian clans were a legal fiction that allowed people to travel back and forth between villages of the "Five Nations" in what is now New York State. This portrait, done in 1710, shows a member of the Mohawk Nation. Behind him stands a bear, which represents his clan.

As larger, dispersed descent groups develop, the conditions that gave rise to extended families and lineages may change. For example, economic diversity and the availability of alternative occupations for individuals may conflict with the residential unity of extended families and (usually) lineages. Or, lineages may lose their economic bases if developing political institutions take control of resources. In such circumstances, lineages would be expected to disappear as important organizational units. Clans, however, might survive, if they continue to provide an important integrative function. In this sense, the Jewish family circles and cousins clubs discussed earlier have become essentially clanlike in their function. This helps explain their continued strength and vitality in the United States today: They perform an integrative function among kin who are geographically dispersed as well as socially diverse but in a way that does not conflict with the mobility characteristic of North American society.

In societies where the small domestic units—nuclear families or single-parent households—are of primary importance, bilateral descent and kindred organization are apt to result. This can be seen in modern industrial societies, in newly emerging societies in the underdeveloped world, and in many food-foraging societies throughout the world.

KINSHIP TERMINOLOGY AND KINSHIP GROUPS

Any system of organizing people who are relatives into different kinds of groups, whether descent based or ego oriented, is bound to have an important effect upon the ways relatives are labeled in any given society. The fact is, the kinship terminologies of other peoples are far from what Western people all too often interpret as arbitrary and even capricious ways of labeling relatives. Rather, they reflect the positions individuals occupy within their society. In particular, kinship terminology is affected by, and adjusts to, the kinds of kinship groups that exist in a society. However, other factors also are at work in each system of kinship terminology that help differentiate one kin from another. These factors may be sex, generational differences, or genealogical differences. In the various systems of kinship terminology, any one of these factors may be emphasized at the expense of others, and sometimes they are qualified by distinguishing younger from older individuals in a particular category or by emphasizing the sex of the person who is referring to a particular relative. But regardless of the factors emphasized, all kinship terminologies accomplish two important tasks. First, they classify similar kinds of persons into specific categories; second, they separate different kinds of persons into distinct categories. Generally, two or more kin are merged under the same term when the individuals share similar status, which then emphasizes these similarities.

Six different systems of kinship terminology result from the application of the principles mentioned: the Eskimo, Hawaiian, Iroquois, Crow, Omaha, and Sudanese or descriptive systems, each identified according to the way cousins are classified.

ESKIMO SYSTEM

The **Eskimo system** of kinship terminology, comparatively rare among all the world's systems, is the one used by Anglo Americans, as well as by a

number of food-foraging peoples (including the Inuit, once called Eskimos—hence the name). The Eskimo or lineal system emphasizes the nuclear family by specifically identifying the mother, father, brother, and sister while lumping together all other relatives into a few gross categories (Figure 21.5). For example, the father is distinguished from the father's brother (*uncle*), but the father's brother is not distinguished from the mother's brother (both are called *uncle*). The mother's sister and father's sister are treated similarly, both called *aunt*. In addition, all the sons and daughters of aunts and uncles are called *cousin*, thereby making a generational distinction but without indicating the side of the family they belong to or even their sex.

Unlike other terminologies, the Eskimo system provides separate and distinct terms for each nuclear family member. This is probably because the Eskimo system generally is found in societies where the dominant kin group is the bilateral kindred, in which only immediate family members are important in day-to-day affairs. This is especially true of modern North American society, where the family is independent, living apart from, and not directly involved with, other kin except on ceremonial occasions. Thus, people in the United States distinguish between their closest kin

FIGURE 21.5
The Eskimo system of kinship terminology emphasizes the nuclear family (surrounded by the red line). Ego's father and mother are distinguished from ego's aunts and uncles, and siblings from cousins.

Eskimo system. System of kinship terminology, also called *lineal system,* that emphasizes the nuclear family by specifically identifying the mother, father, brother, and sister while lumping together all other relatives into broad categories such as *uncle, aunt,* and *cousin.*

(parents and siblings) but lump together (as aunts, uncles, cousins) other kin on both sides of the family.

HAWAIIAN SYSTEM

The **Hawaiian system** of kinship terminology, common (as its name implies) in Hawaii and other Malayo-Polynesian-speaking areas but found elsewhere as well, is the least complex system, in that it uses the fewest terms. The Hawaiian system is also called the generational system, since all relatives of the same generation and sex are referred to by the same term (Figure 21.6). For example, in one's parents' generation, the term used to refer to one's father is used as well for the father's brother and mother's brother. Similarly, one's mother, her sister, and one's father's sister are all lumped under a single term. In ego's generation, male and female cousins are distinguished by sex and are equated with brothers and sisters.

The Hawaiian system reflects the absence of strong unilineal descent and is usually associated with ambilineal descent. Because ambilineal rules allow individuals the option of tracing their an-

cestry back through either side of the family and members on both the father's and the mother's side are viewed as more-or-less equal, a certain degree of similarity is created among the father's and the mother's siblings. Thus, they are all simultaneously recognized as being similar relations and are merged under a single term appropriate for their sex. In like manner, the children of the mother's and father's siblings are related to ego in the same way brothers and sisters are. Thus, they are ruled out as potential marriage partners.

IROQUOIS SYSTEM

In the **Iroquois system** of kinship terminology, the father and father's brother are referred to by a single term, as are the mother and mother's sister; however, the father's sister and mother's brother are given separate terms (Figure 21.7). In one's own generation, brothers, sisters, and parallel cousins (offspring of parental siblings of the same sex, that is, the children of the mother's sister or father's brother) of the same sex are referred to by the same terms, which is logical enough considering they are the offspring of people who are clas-

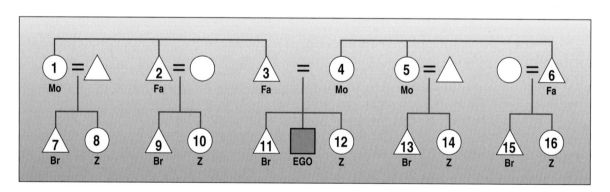

FIGURE 21.6

The Hawaiian kinship system. The men numbered 2 and 6 are called by the same term as father (3) by ego; the women numbered 1 and 5 are called by the same term as mother (4). All cousins of ego's own generation (7–16) are considered brothers and sisters.

Hawaiian system. Kinship reckoning in which all relatives of the same sex and generation are referred to by the same term. > **Iroquois system.** Kinship terminology wherein a father and father's brother are given a single term, as are a mother and mother's sister, but a father's sister and mother's brother are given separate terms. Parallel cousins are classified with brothers and sisters, while cross cousins are classified separately but (unlike Crow and Omaha kinship) not equated with relatives of some other generation.

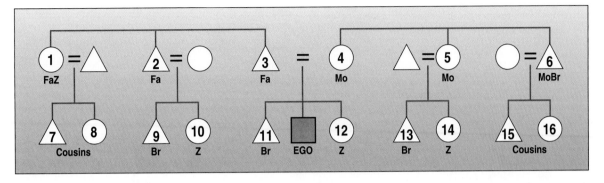

FIGURE 21.7

According to the Iroquois system of kinship terminology, the father's brother (2) is called by the same term as the father (3); the mother's sister (5) is called by the same term as the mother (4); but the people numbered 1 and 6 have separate terms for themselves. Those people numbered 9–14 are all considered siblings, but 7, 8, 15, and 16 are cousins.

sified in the same category as ego's actual mother and father. Cross cousins (offspring of parental siblings of opposite sex, that is, the children of the mother's brother or father's sister) are distinguished by terms that set them apart from all other kin. In fact, cross cousins are often preferred as spouses, for marriage to them reaffirms alliances between related lineages.

Iroquois terminology, named for the Iroquoian Indians of northeastern North America who employ such terminology, is in fact widespread and is usually found with unilineal descent groups. It was, for example, the terminology in use until recently in rural Chinese society.

CROW SYSTEM

In the preceding systems of terminology, some relatives were grouped under common terms, while others of the same generation were separated and

Lewis Henry Morgan *(1818–1881)*

Lewis Henry Morgan, a major theoretician of 19th-century North American anthropology, has been regarded as the founder of kinship studies. In *Systems of Consanguinity and Affinity of the Human Family* (1871), he classified and compared the kinship systems of peoples around the world in an attempt to prove the Asiatic origin of American Indians. In doing so, he developed the idea that the human family had evolved through a series of evolutionary stages, from primitive promiscuity on the one hand to the monogamous, patriarchal family on the other.

Although subsequent research proved Morgan was wrong about this and a number of other ideas, his work showed the potential value of studying the distribution of different kinship systems for framing hypotheses of a developmental or historical nature and, by noting the connection between terminology and behavior, showed the value of kinship for sociological study. Besides his contributions to kinship and evolutionary studies, he produced an ethnography of the Iroquois, which still stands as a major source of information.

In matrilineal societies with Crow kinship, sisters remain close to one another throughout their lives. Such a people are the Hopi, in whose traditional housing sisters lived in adjacent rooms. Under these circumstances, very little differentiates a mother and her sister or siblings and the children of the mother's sister. The mother's brother and his children, however, live elsewhere.

given different labels or terms. In the Crow system, another variable enters the picture: The system ignores the distinction that occurs between generations among certain kin.

The **Crow System** (named for the Crow Indians of Montana), found in many parts of the world, is the one used by the Hopi Indians, who were discussed earlier in this chapter. Associated with strong

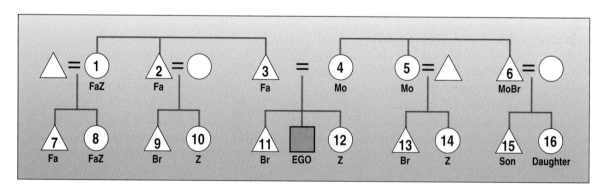

FIGURE 21.8

The Crow system is the obverse of the Omaha system, shown in Figure 21.9. Those numbered 4 and 5 are merged under a single term, as are 2 and 3. Ego's parallel cousins (9, 10, 13, 14) are considered siblings, while the mother's brother's children are equated with the children of a male ego and his brother.

Crow system. Kinship classification usually associated with matrilineal descent in which a father's sister and father's sister's daughter are called by the same term, a mother and mother's sister are merged under another, and a father and father's brother are given a third. Parallel cousins are equated with brothers and sisters.

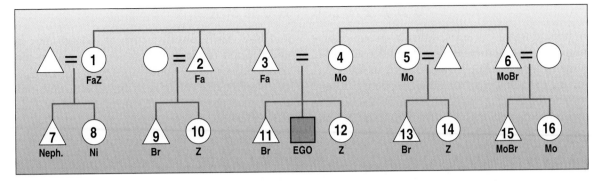

FIGURE 21.9

In the Omaha system, 2 is called by the same term as father (3); 5 is called by the same term as mother (4); but 1 and 6 have separate terms. In ego's generation 9–14 are all considered siblings, but 7 and 8 are equated with the generation of ego's children, while 15 and 16 are equated with the generation of ego's parents.

matrilineal descent organization, it groups differently the relations on the father's side and mother's side (Figure 21.8). Cross cousins on the father's side are equated with relatives of the parental generation, while those on the mother's side are equated with ego's children's generation. Otherwise, the system is much like Iroquois terminology.

To those unfamiliar with it, the Crow system seems terribly complex and illogical. Why does it exist? In societies such as that of the Hopi, where individual identity is dependent on descent group affiliation and descent is matrilineal, it makes sense to merge the father's sister, her daughter, and even her mother together under a single term, regardless of generation. These are women descent is traced through in the lineage that sired ego, just as a male ego's children, along with those of his mother's brother, were sired by men of ego's lineage. Thus, it is perfectly logical for ego to equate his maternal cross cousins with his children's generation.

OMAHA SYSTEM

The **Omaha System** (named for the Omaha Indians of Nebraska) is the patrilineal equivalent of the matrilineal Crow system. Thus, a mother and

her sister are designated by a single term, the father and his brother are merged under another, and parallel cousins are merged with brothers and sisters (Figure 21.9). Cross cousins on the maternal side are raised a generation, while those on the paternal side are equated with ego's children's generation. Thus, children born of women from one patrilineage for the men of another patrilineage are lowered by one generation.

SUDANESE OR DESCRIPTIVE SYSTEM

The **Sudanese or descriptive system** is found among the peoples of southern Sudan in Africa—hence the name Sudanese. Otherwise, it is found among few of the world's societies, although it has come to replace Iroquois terminology among rural Chinese. In this system, the mother's brother is distinguished from the father's brother, who is distinguished from the father; the mother's sister is distinguished from the mother, as well as from the father's sister. Each cousin is distinguished from all others, as well as from siblings. It is therefore more precise than any of the other systems (including that used by Anglo Americans), which may be one reason it is so rare. In few societies are all aunts, uncles, cousins, and siblings treated differently from one another.

Omaha system. The patrilineal equivalent of the Crow system; the line of a mother's patrilineal kin are equated across generations. > **Sudanese or descriptive system.** System of kinship terminology whereby a father, father's brother, and mother's brother are distinguished from one another as are a mother, mother's sister, and father's sister; cross and parallel cousins are distinguished from each other as well as from siblings.

CHAPTER SUMMARY

In nonindustrial societies, kinship groups commonly deal with problems families and households alone cannot handle: problems such as those involving defense, the allocation of property, and the pooling of other resources. As societies become larger and more complex, formal political systems take over many of these matters.

A common form of kinship group is the descent group, which has as its criterion of membership descent from a common ancestor through a series of parent-child links. Unilineal descent establishes kin group membership exclusively through the male or female line. Matrilineal descent is traced through the female line; patrilineal, through the male.

The descent system is closely tied to a society's economic base. Generally, patrilineal descent predominates where the male is the breadwinner and matrilineal where the female is the breadwinner. Anthropologists now recognize that in all societies the kin of both mother and father are important elements in the social structure, regardless of how descent group membership is defined.

The male members of a patrilineage trace their descent from a common male ancestor. A female belongs to the same descent group as her father and his brother, but her children cannot trace their descent through him. Typically, authority over the children lies with the father or his elder brother. The requirement for younger men to defer to older men and for women to defer to men, as well as to the women of a household they marry into, are common sources of tension in a patrilineal society.

In one respect, matrilineal is the opposite of patrilineal descent, with descent traced through the female line. Unlike the patrilineal pattern, which confers authority on men, matrilineal descent does not necessarily confer authority on women, although women usually have more of a say in decision making than they do in patrilineal societies. The matrilineal system is common in societies where women perform much of the productive work. This system may be a source of family tension, since the husband's authority is not in his own household but in that of his sister. This

and how easily unsatisfactory marriages may be ended often result in higher divorce rates in matrilineal than in patrilineal societies.

Double descent is matrilineal for some purposes and patrilineal for others. Ambilineal descent provides a measure of flexibility in that an individual has the option of affiliating with either the mother's or father's descent group.

Descent groups are often highly structured economic units that provide aid and security to their members. They also may be repositories of religious tradition, with group solidarity enhanced by worship of a common ancestor. A lineage is a corporate descent group made up of consanguineal kin who can trace their genealogical links to a common ancestor. Since lineages are commonly exogamous, sexual competition within the group is largely avoided. In addition, marriage of a group member represents an alliance of two lineages. Lineage exogamy also serves to maintain open communication within a society and fosters the exchange of information among lineages.

Fission is the splitting up of a large lineage group into new, smaller ones, with the original lineage becoming a clan. Clan members claim descent from a common ancestor but without actually knowing the genealogical links to that ancestor. Unlike lineages, clan residence is usually dispersed rather than localized. In the absence of residential unity, clan identification is often reinforced by totems, usually symbols from nature that remind members of their common ancestry. A phratry is a unilineal descent group of two or more clans that supposedly share a common ancestry. If there are but two such groups, they are called moieties.

Bilateral descent, characteristic of Western, modernizing, and many food-foraging societies, is traced through both parents simultaneously and recognizes several ancestors. An individual is affiliated equally with all relatives on both the mother's and father's sides. Such a large group is socially impractical and is usually reduced to a small circle of paternal and maternal relatives called the kindred. A kindred is never the same for any two persons except siblings.

Different types of descent systems appear in different societies. In societies where the nuclear family is paramount, bilateral kinship and kindred organization are likely to prevail.

In any society cultural rules dictate the way kinship relationships are defined. Factors such as sex and generational or genealogical differences help distinguish one kin from another. The Hawaiian system is the simplest system of kinship terminology. All relatives of the same generation and sex are referred to by the same term. The Eskimo system, used by Anglo Americans, emphasizes the nuclear family and merges all other relatives in a given generation into a few large, generally undifferentiated categories. In the Iroquois system, a single term is used for a father and his brother and another term for a mother and her sister. Parallel cousins are equated with brothers and sisters but distinguished from cross cousins. The same is true in the Omaha and Crow systems, except they equate cross cousins with relatives of other generations. The relatively rare Sudanese or descriptive system treats all aunts, uncles, cousins, and siblings as different from one another.

POINTS FOR CONSIDERATION

1. How do you define your family? Through direct descent? Through "adopted" or fictive descent? Through some combination?

2. When in your life has the ability to trace your descent been the most important or obvious? When are you made aware of your kin group? Do you find your kindred or a descent group more relevant to your daily life? Why?

3. How are changes in North American families altering how North Americans view descent? How do these changes contrast with those occurring in other cultures?

SUGGESTED READINGS

Fox, R. (1967). *Kinship and marriage in an anthropological perspective.* Baltimore: Penguin.

An excellent introduction to the concepts of kinship and marriage, this book outlines some of the methods of analysis used in the anthropological treatment of kinship and marriage. It updates Radcliffe-Brown's *African Systems of Kinship and Marriage* and features a perspective focused on kinship groups and social organization.

Goodenough, W. H. (1970). *Description and comparison in cultural anthropology.* Chicago: Aldine.

This is an important contribution to the study of social organization that confronts the problem of describing kinship organization—kindred and clan, sibling and cousin—in such a way that meaningful cross-cultural comparisons can be made.

Keesing, R. M. (1975). *Kin groups and social structure.* New York: Holt, Rinehart and Winston.

This is a high-level introduction to kinship theory suitable for advanced undergraduate students. A strong point of the work is the attention given to nonunilineal, as well as unilineal, systems.

Schusky, E. L. (1975). *Variation in kinship.* New York: Holt, Rinehart and Winston.

This book is an introduction to kinship, descent, and residence for the beginner. A reliance on a case-study approach leads the reader from basic data to generalizations, a strategy that helps remove some of the abstraction students of kinship organization sometimes find confusing.

Schusky, E. L. (1983). *Manual for kinship analysis* (2nd ed.). Lanham, MD: University Press of America.

This useful book discusses the elements of kinship, diagramming, systems classification, and descent with specific examples.

Chapter 22
GROUPING BY SEX, AGE, COMMON INTEREST, AND CLASS

THESE GIRL SCOUTS EXEMPLIFY THE PHENOMENA
OF GROUPING BY SEX, AGE, AND COMMON
INTEREST, SOME OF THE MEANS BY WHICH PEOPLE
MAY BE ORGANIZED INTO GROUPS WITHOUT
RECOURSE TO KINSHIP OR DESCENT.

Chapter Preview

What Principles, Besides Kinship and Marriage, Do People Use to Organize Societies?

People group themselves by sex, age, common interest, and position within a ranked hierarchy (class stratification) to deal with problems not conveniently handled by marriage, the family and/or household, descent groups, or kindred. In addition, certain groups within society use stratification to enjoy preferential treatment for themselves at the expense of other groups.

What Is Age Grading?

Age grading—the formation of groups on an age basis—is a widely used means of organizing people in human societies, including those of Europe and North America. In industrial societies, or nonindustrial societies with relatively large populations, age grades may be broken down into age sets—people of approximately the same age who move as groups through the series of age grades.

What Are Common-Interest Associations?

Common-interest associations are formed to deal with specific problems. They acquire their members as individuals act to join them. Such actions may range all the way from fully voluntary to compulsory. Common-interest associations have been a feature of human societies since the advent of the first farming villages several thousand years ago, but they have become especially prominent in modern industrial or industrializing societies.

What Is Social Stratification?

Stratification is the division of society into two or more classes of people that do not share equally in basic resources, influence, or prestige. Such class structure is characteristic of all of the world's societies having large and heterogeneous populations with centralized political control. Among others, these include the ancient civilizations of the Middle East, Asia, Mexico, and Peru, as well as modern industrial societies, including the United States.

Social organization based on kinship and marriage has received an extraordinary amount of attention from anthropologists, and the subject usually is quite prominent in anthropological writing. There are several reasons for this: In one way or another, kinship and marriage operate as organizing principles in all societies, and in the small stateless societies anthropologists so often study, they are usually the most important organizational principles. There is, too, a certain fascination in the almost mathematical way kinship systems at least appear to work. To the unwary, all this attention to kinship and marriage may convey the impression that these are the only principles of social organization that really count. Yet it is obvious from viewing modern industrial societies that other principles of social organization not only exist but also may be quite important. Principles we will examine in this chapter are the grouping by gender, age, common interest, and class (stratification).

▲▽▲▽▲▽▲▽▲▽▲▽▲▽▲▽▲▽▲▽▲▽▲▽▲▽▲▽▲

GROUPING BY GENDER

As shown in preceding chapters, some division of labor along gender lines is characteristic of all human societies. Although in some—the Ju/'hoansi, for example (Chapter 17)—many tasks men and women undertake may be shared, and people may perform work normally assigned to the opposite sex without loss of face, in some other societies, men and women are rigidly segregated in what they do. For instance, among the Mohawk, Oneida, Onondaga, Cayuga, and Seneca Indians of New York—the famous Five Nations Iroquois—society was divided into two parts consisting of sedentary women on the one hand and nomadic men on the other. Living in villages were the women, who were "blood" relatives of one another and whose job was to grow the corn, beans, and squash the Iroquois relied on for subsistence. Although houses and the palisades that protected villages were built by men, who also helped women clear their fields, the most important of men's work was pursued at some distance from their villages. This consisted of hunting, fishing, trading, warring, and diplomacy. As a consequence, men were transients in the villages, being present for only brief periods.

Although masculine activities were considered more prestigious than those of women, the latter were explicitly acknowledged by all as the sustainers of life. Moreover, women headed the longhouses (dwellings matrilocal extended families occupied), descent and inheritance passed through women, and ceremonial life centered on women's activities. Although men held all leadership positions outside households, on the councils of the villages, tribes, and the league of Five Nations, the women of their lineages nominated them for these

Among the Iroquoians of New York, society was divided into sedentary women, whose work was carried out in or near the village, and nomadic men, whose work was carried out away from the village. This pattern still holds today, as men leave their villages for extended periods to do much of the high steel work in the cities of North America.

positions and held veto power over them. Thus, male leadership was balanced by female authority. Overall, the phrase "separate but equal" accurately describes relations between the sexes in Five Nations Iroquoian society, with members of neither sex dominant or submissive to the other. Related to this seems to have been a low incidence of rape, at least among the Five Nations. Outside observers in the 19th century widely commented upon an apparent absence of rape within Iroquoian communities. Even in warfare, sexual violation of female captives was virtually unheard of; as General James Clinton observed in 1779: "Bad as the savages are, they never violate the chastity of any women of their prisoners."[1]

Although Iroquoian men often were absent from the village, when present they ate and slept with women. Among the Mundurucu of the Amazon, discussed briefly in Chapter 20, men not only work apart from women but eat and sleep separately as well. All men from age 13 on live in a large house of their own, while women with their young children occupy two or three houses grouped around that of the men. For all intents and purposes, men associate with men, and women with women. The relation between the sexes is, rather than harmonious, one of opposition. According to Mundurucu belief, sex roles were once reversed: Women ruled over men and controlled the sacred trumpets that are the symbols of power and represent the generative capacities of women. But because women could not hunt, they could not supply the meat demanded by the ancient spirits contained within the trumpets, enabling the men to take the trumpets from the women, establishing their dominance in the process. Ever since, the trumpets have been kept carefully guarded and hidden in the men's house, and no woman can see them under penalty of gang rape. Thus, Mundurucu men express fear and envy toward women, whom they seek to control by force. For their part, the women neither like nor accept a submissive status, and even though men occupy all formal positions of political and religious leadership, women are autonomous in the economic realm.

Although important differences exist, there are nonetheless interesting similarities between Mundurucu beliefs and those of traditional European (including European-American) culture. The idea of rule by men replacing an earlier state of matriarchy (rule by women), for example, was held by many 19th-century intellectuals. Moreover, the idea that men may use force in order to control women is deeply embedded in both Judaic and Christian traditions (and even today, in spite of changing attitudes, one out of three women in the United States is sexually assaulted at some time in her life). A major difference between Mundurucu and traditional European society is that, in the latter, women have not had control of their economic activities. Although this is now

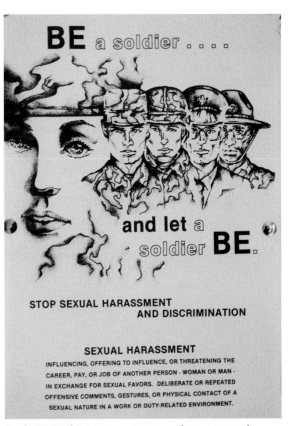

In the United States, women were long expected to submit to male authority, but in recent decades, there has been a major effort to achieve more egalitarian gender relations. That the change has not been completed is illustrated by this poster.

---

[1]Kolodday, A. (1993, January 31). Among the Indians: The uses of captivity. *New York Times Review of Books, 28.*

changing, women in North America and other Western countries still have a considerable distance to go before they achieve economic parity with men.

▲▼▲▼▲▼▲▼▲▼▲▼▲▼▲▼▲▼▲▼▲▼▲▼▲▼▲▼▲▼▲

AGE GROUPING

Age grouping is so familiar and so important that it and sex sometimes have been called the only universal factors for determining a person's position in society. In North America today, one's first friends generally are children one's own age. Together they are sent off to school, where together they remain until their late teens. At specified ages they finally are allowed to do things reserved for adults, such as driving a car, voting, and drinking alcoholic beverages, and (if they are males) are required to go off to war if asked to do so. Ultimately, North Americans retire from their jobs at a specified age and, more than ever, live the final years of their lives in "retirement communities," segregated from the rest of society. As North Americans age, they are labeled "teen-agers," "middle-aged," and "senior citizens" whether they like it or not and for no other reason than their age.

Age grading in modern North American society is exemplified by the educational system, which specifies that at 6 years of age all children must enter the first grade.

The pervasiveness of age grouping in North American society is further illustrated by its effects on the Jewish descent groups discussed in Chapter 21. Until well into the 1930s, these always took on a more-or-less conventional ambilineal structure, which united relatives of all generations from the very old to the very young, with no age restrictions. By the late 1930s, however, young generations of Jews of eastern European background were becoming assimilated into North American culture to such a degree that some of them began to form new descent groups that deliberately excluded any kin of the parental and grandparental generations. In these new cousins clubs, as they are called, descendants of the cousins are eligible for membership, but not until they reach legal majority or are married, whichever comes first. Here, again, these new descent groups contrast with the older family circles, which allowed membership activation at any age, no matter how young.

Age classification also plays a significant role in non-Western societies, which at least make a distinction among the immature, mature, and older people whose physical powers are waning. Old age often has profound significance, bringing with it the period of greatest respect (for women it may mean the first social equality with men); rarely are the elderly shunted aside or abandoned. Even the Inuit, who often are cited as a people who quite literally abandon their aged relatives, do so only in truly desperate circumstances, when the group's physical survival is at stake. In all nonliterate societies, the elders are the repositories of accumulated wisdom; they are the "living libraries" for their people. In keeping with this, and given their freedom from many subsistence activities, they play a major role in passing cultural traditions to their grandchildren. For a nonliterate society to cast them aside would be analogous to closing down all the schools, archives, and libraries in a modern industrial state.

In the United States people rely on the written word, rather than on their elders, for long-term memory. Moreover, people have become so accustomed to rapid change that they tend to assume the experiences of their grandparents and others of their generation are hardly relevant to them in "today's world." Indeed, retirement from earning a living implies one has nothing further to offer society and should stay out of the way of those who are younger. "The symbolism of the traditional gold watch is all too plain: you should have made your money by now, and your time has run out. The watch will merely tick off the hours that remain between the end of adulthood and death."[2] The status of the elderly is even more problematic because they now constitute so large (and growing) a part of the overall population. Thus, the achievement of old age seems less an accomplishment than it once did and so commands less respect. Furthermore, the elderly begin to be seen as not just unproductive but also as a serious economic burden. The ultimate irony is that in the United States all of the ingenuity of modern science is used to keep alive the bodies of individuals who, in virtually every other way, society has shunted aside.

In the institutionalization of age, cultural rather than biological factors are of prime importance for determining social status. All human societies recognize a number of life stages; precisely how they are defined varies from one culture to another. Out of this recognition they establish patterns of activity, attitudes, prohibitions, and obligations. In some instances, these are designed to help the transition from one age to another, to teach needed skills, or to lend economic assistance. Often they are taken as the basis for forming organized groups.

INSTITUTIONS OF AGE GROUPING

An organized class of people with membership based on age is known as an **age grade**. Theoretically speaking, membership in an age grade ought to be automatic: One reaches the appropriate age and thus is included, without question, in the particular age grade. Just such situations exist, for ex-

ample, among the East African Tiriki, whose system we will examine shortly. Sometimes, though, individuals have to buy their way into the age grade they are eligible for. This was the case among some of the Indians of the North American plains, who required boys to purchase the appropriate costumes, dances, and songs for age-grade membership. In societies where entrance fees are expensive, not all people eligible for membership in a particular age grade can actually join.

Entry into and transfer out of age grades may be accomplished individually, either by a biological distinction, such as puberty, or by a socially recognized status, such as marriage or childbirth. Whereas age-grade members may have much in common, may engage in similar activities, may cooperate with one another, and may share the same orientation and aspirations, their membership may not be entirely parallel with physiological age. A specific time is often ritually established for moving from a younger to an older grade. Although members of senior groups commonly expect deference from and acknowledge certain responsibilities to their juniors, this does not necessarily mean one grade is better or worse or even more important than another. Standardized competition (opposition) between age grades can occur, such as that traditionally between first-year students and sophomores on U.S. college campuses. Individuals can, comparably, accept the realities of being a teenager without feeling the need to "prove" anything.

In some societies, age grades are subdivided into **age sets**. An age set is a group of persons initiated into an age grade who move through the system together. For example, among the Tiriki of East Africa, the age group consisting of those initiated into an age grade for a 15-year period amounts to an age set. Age sets, unlike age grades, do not cease to exist after a specified number of years; the members of an age set usually remain closely associated throughout their lives, or at least through much of their lives.

[2]Turnbull, C. M. (1983). *The human cycle* (p. 229). New York: Simon & Schuster.

Age grade. An organized category of people based on age; every individual passes through a series of such categories during a lifetime. **>** **Age sets.** Groups of persons initiated into age grades simultaneously who move through the series of categories together.

In many societies it is common for children of the same age to play, eat, and learn together, such as these Masai boys, who are gathering for the first time to receive instruction for their initiation into an age grade.

A certain amount of controversy has arisen among anthropologists over the relative strength, cohesiveness, and stability that subdividing by age suggests. The age-set notion implies strong feelings of loyalty and mutual support. Because such groups may possess property, songs, shield designs, and rituals and are internally organized for collective decision making and leadership, a distinction is called for between them and simple age grades. Researchers also may distinguish between transitory age grades—which initially concern young men (sometimes women too) but become less important and disintegrate as the members grow older—and the comprehensive age-related systems that affect people throughout their lives.

AGE GROUPING IN AFRICAN SOCIETIES

Although age is a criterion for group membership in many parts of the world, its most varied and elaborate use is found in Africa, south of the Sahara. An example may be seen among the Tiriki, one of several pastoral nomadic groups living in Kenya.[3] In this society, each boy born during a 15-year period becomes a member of a particular age set then open for membership. Seven of such named age sets exist, and only one is open for membership at a time; when membership in one is closed, the next one is open for a 15-year period and so on until the passage of 105 years (7 × 15), when the first set once again takes in new "recruits."

Members of Tiriki age sets remain together for life as they move through four age grades: Advancement occurs at 15-year intervals at the same time one age set closes and another opens for membership. Each age grade has its particular duties and responsibilities. The first, or "Warrior" age grade, traditionally served as the country's guardians, and members gained renown through fighting. Since colonial times, however, this traditional function has been lost with cessation of war-

---

[3]Sangree, W. H. (1965). The Bantu Tiriki of Western Kenya. In J. L. Gibbs Jr. (Ed.), *Peoples of Africa* (pp. 69–72). New York: Holt, Rinehart and Winston.

fare, and members of this age grade now find excitement and adventure by leaving their community for extended employment or study elsewhere.

The next age grade, the "Elder Warriors," traditionally had few specialized tasks but learned skills they would need later on by assuming an increasing share of administrative activities. For example, they would chair the postfuneral gatherings held to settle property claims after someone's death. Elder Warriors also served as envoys between elders of different communities. Nowadays, Elder Warriors hold nearly all of the administrative and executive roles opened up by the creation and growth of a centralized Tiriki administrative bureaucracy.

"Judicial Elders," the third age grade, traditionally handled most tasks connected with the administration of and settlement of local disputes. Today, they still serve as the local judiciary body. Members of the "Ritual Elders," the senior age grade, presided over the priestly functions of ancestral shrine observances at households, at subclan meetings, at semiannual community appeals, and at rites of initiation into the various age grades. They also were credited with access to special magical powers. With the decline of ancestor worship over the past several decades, many of

these traditional functions have been lost and no new ones have arisen to take their places. Nonetheless, Ritual Elders continue to hold the most important positions in the initiation ceremonies, and their power as sorcerers and expungers of witchcraft are still recognized.

COMMON-INTEREST ASSOCIATIONS

The proliferation of **common-interest associations,** whether out of individual predilection or community need, is a theme intimately associated with world urbanization and its attendant social upheavals; the fondness people in modern societies feel for joining all sorts of organizations is incontestably related to these societies' complexity. This fondness for joining no doubt reflects the reality that individuals often are separated by physical distance from their brothers, sisters, and age mates. They obviously cannot obtain regular help from one another in learning to cope with life in a new and bewildering environment, such as learning a new language or the mannerisms necessary for the change from village to city or even from city to city or from city to different country. But such needs somehow must be met. Because common-interest associations are by nature quite flexible, they are increasingly, both in cities and in traditional villages, filling this gap in the social structure. Common-interest associations are not, however, restricted to modernizing societies alone. They also are found in many traditional societies, and there is reason to believe they arose with the emergence of the first horticultural villages. Furthermore, associations in traditional societies may be just as complex and highly organized as those of countries such as the United States and Canada.

Common-interest associations often have been referred to in the anthropological literature as voluntary associations, but this term is misleading. The act of joining may range from a fully voluntary act to one required by law. For example, in

---

Common-interest associations.   Associations not based on age, kinship, marriage, or territory but that result from the act of joining.

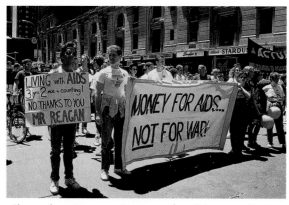

The diversity of common-interest association is astounding. Shown here is an environmental activist organization and an AIDS advocacy group.

the United States, under the draft laws individuals often became members of the armed forces without choosing to join. It is not really compulsory to join a labor union, but unless potential employees do, they cannot work in a union shop. The term *voluntary association* really refers to associations not based on sex, age, kinship, marriage, or territory that result from the act of joining. Therefore, the act often may be voluntary, but it does not have to be.

KINDS OF COMMON-INTEREST ASSOCIATIONS

The diversity of common-interest associations is astonishing. In the United States, they include such diverse entities as women's clubs of all sorts, street gangs, private militias, Kiwanis clubs, Rotary clubs, Parent Teacher Associations, religious organizations, political parties, and labor unions—the list could go on and on. Their goals may include the pursuit of friendship, recreation, and promotion of certain values, as well as governing and the pursuit or defense of economic interests. Associations also serve to preserve traditional songs, history, language, and moral beliefs among various ethnic minorities; the Tribal Unions of West Africa, for example, continue to serve this purpose. Similar organizations, often operating clandestinely, have kept traditions alive among North American Indians, who are undergoing a resurgence of ethnic pride despite generations of

schooling designed to stamp out their cultural identity. Another significant force in the formation of associations may be a supernatural experience common to all members; the Crow Indian Tobacco Society, the secret associations of the Kwakiutl Indians of British Columbia with cycles of rituals known only to initiates, and the Kachina cults of the Hopi Indians are well-known examples. Among other traditional forms of association are military, occupational, political, and entertainment groups that parallel such familiar organizations as the American Legion, labor unions, block associations, and college fraternities and sororities, not to mention co-ops of every kind.

In nonindustrial societies, such organizations are frequently exclusive, but a prevailing characteristic is their concern for the general well-being of an entire village or group of villages. The rain that falls as a result of the work of Hopi rainmakers nourishes the crops of members and nonmembers alike.

Men's and Women's Associations

For many years, scholars dismissed women's contributions to common-interest associations as less developed than men's. The reason is that men's associations attracted more notice around the world than did women's. Heinrich Schurtz's theory, published in 1902, that underlying the differentiation between kinship and associational groups is a profound difference in the psychology of the sexes, was widely accepted for years. Schurtz regarded

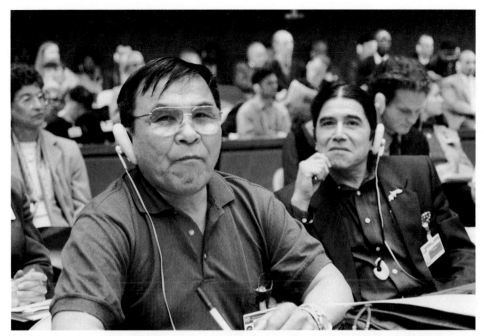

Non-governmental organizations such as the International Indian Treaty Council are common-interest associations that have arisen to promote the rights of indigenous peoples. Shown here are Antonio Gonzales of the Council and Chief Gideon James of Venetie, Alaska, testifying at the 54th session of the UN Commission on Human Rights at Geneva in 1998.

women as unsocial beings who preferred remaining in kinship groups based on sexual relations and the reproductive function rather than forming units based on commonly held interests. Men, by contrast, were said to view sexual relations as isolated episodes, an attitude that fostered the purely social factor that makes "birds of a feather flock together."

In the past few decades, scholars of both sexes have shown this kind of thinking to be culture bound. In some societies women have not formed associations to the extent men have because the demands of raising a family and their daily activities have not permitted it and because men have not always encouraged them to do so. Given the plethora of women's clubs of all kinds in the United States for several generations, however, one wonders how this belief in women as unsocial beings survived as long as it did. Earlier in this country's history, of course, when women were stuck at home in rural situations with no near neighbors, they had little chance to participate in common-interest associations. Moreover, some functions of men's associations—such as military duties—often are culturally defined as purely for men or repugnant to women. In a number of the world's traditional societies, however, the opportunities for female sociability are so great that little need may exist for women's associations. Among the Indians of northeastern North America (including the Five Nations Iroquois discussed earlier), the men spent extended periods off in the woods hunting, either by themselves or with a single companion. The women, by contrast, spent most of their time in and around their village, in close, everyday contact with all the other women of the community. Not only did they find many people to talk to, but also they always found someone available to help with whatever tasks required assistance.

Still, as cross-cultural research makes clear, women do play important roles in associations of their own and even in those where men predominate. Among the Crow Indians, women

Common-interest associations are not limited to modern industrial societies. This 1832 picture shows a Mandan Indian Bull Dance. The Bulls were one of several common-interest groups concerned with both social and military affairs.

participated even in the secret Tobacco Society, as well as in their own exclusive groups. Throughout Africa women's social clubs complement the men's and are concerned with educating women, with crafts, and with charitable activities. In Sierra Leone, where once-simple dancing societies have developed under urban conditions into complex organizations with a set of new objectives, the dancing *compin* is made up of young women as well as men who together perform plays based on traditional music and dancing and raise money for various mutual-benefit causes.

Women's rights organizations, consciousness-raising groups, and professional organizations for women are examples of associations arising directly or indirectly out of today's social climate. These groups cover the entire range of association formation, from simple friendship and support

groups to political, guildlike, and economic (the publication of magazines, groups designed to influence advertising) associations on a national scale. If an unresolved point does exist in the matter of women's participation, it is in determining why women are excluded from associations in some societies, while in others their participation is essentially equal to that of men.

SOCIAL STRATIFICATION

The study of social stratification involves the examination of distinctions that, when we think about them, impress us as unfair and even outrageous, but social stratification is a common and powerful phenomenon in some of the world's societies. Civilizations, in particular, with their large and heterogeneous populations, are invariably stratified.

Basically, a **stratified society** is one divided into two or more categories of people ranked high and low relative to one another. When the people in one such stratum are compared with those in another, marked differences in privileges, rewards, restrictions, and obligations become apparent. Members of low ranked strata tend to have fewer privileges and less power than those in higher ranked strata. In addition, they tend not to be rewarded to the same degree and are denied equal access to basic resources. Their restrictions and obligations, too, are usually more onerous, although members of high ranked strata usually have their own distinctive restrictions and obligations to attend to. In short, social stratification amounts to institutionalized inequality. Without ranking—high versus low—no stratification ex-

ists; social differences without this do not constitute stratification.

Stratified societies stand in sharp contrast to **egalitarian societies.** As we saw in Chapter 17, societies of food-foraging peoples are characteristically egalitarian, although some exceptions occur. Such societies have as many valued positions as people capable of filling them. Hence, individuals depend mostly on their abilities alone for their positions in society. A poor hunter may become a good hunter if he has the ability; he is not excluded from such a prestigious position because he comes from a group of poor hunters. Poor hunters do not constitute a social stratum. Furthermore, they have as much right to their society's resources as any other of its members. No one can deny a poor hunter a fair share of food, the right to be heard when important decisions are to be made, or anything else a man is entitled to.

 Anthropologists and Social-Impact Assessment

A kind of policy research anthropologists frequently do is a social-impact assessment, which entails collection of data about a community or neighborhood for planners of development projects. Such an assessment seeks to determine a project's effect by determining how and upon whom its impact will fall and whether the impact is likely to be positive or negative. In the United States, any project requiring a federal permit or license, or using federal funds, by law must be preceded by a social impact assessment as part of the environmental review process. Examples of such projects include highway construction, urban renewal, water diversion schemes, and land reclamation. Often, projects of these sorts are sited so that their impact falls most heavily on neighborhoods or communities inhabited by people of low socioeconomic strata, sometimes

because the projects are seen as ways of improving the lives of impoverished people and sometimes because these people are seen as having less political power to block proposals others conceive as (sometimes rightly, sometimes wrongly) in "the public interest."

As an illustration of this kind of work, consider how anthropologist Sue Ellen Jacobs was hired to do a social impact assessment of a water diversion project in New Mexico the Bureau of Land Reclamation planned in cooperation with the Bureau of Indian Affairs. This project proposed construction of a diversion dam and an extensive canal system for irrigation on the Rio Grande River. Affected by this would be 22 communities inhabited primarily by Spanish Americans, as well as two Indian pueblos. In the region, unemployment was high (19.1% in June 1970), and the project was seen as

---

Stratified society.   The division of society into two or more categories of people who do not share equally in the basic resources that support life, influence, and prestige. **> Egalitarian societies.**   Social systems that have as many valued positions as persons capable of filling them.

a way to promote a perceived trend toward urbanism (which theoretically would be associated with industrial development) while bringing new land into production for intensive agriculture.

However, the planners failed to take into account that both the Hispanic and Indian populations were heavily committed to farming for household consumption, with some surpluses raised for the market, using a system of irrigation canals established as many as 300 years ago. These *acequias* (aqueducts) are maintained by elected supervisors who know the communities as well as the requirements of the land and crops, water laws, and ditch management skills. Such individuals can allocate water equitably in times of scarcity and can prevent and resolve conflict in the realm of water and land use, as well as in community life beyond the ditches. Under the proposed project, this system was to be given up in favor of one in which fewer people would control larger tracts of land and water allocation would be in the hands of a government technocrat. One of the strongest measures of local government would be lost.

Not surprisingly, Jacobs discovered widespread community opposition to this project, and her report helped convince Congress that any positive impact was far outweighed by negative effects.

"One of the major objections to the construction of the project is that it would result in the obliteration of the three-hundred-year-old irrigation system structures. Project planners did not seem to recognize the antiquity and cultural significance of the traditional irrigation system. These were referred to as 'temporary diversion structures.' The fact that the old dams associated with the ditches were attached to local descent groups was simply not recognized by the official documents."*

Other negative effects of the project, besides loss of local control, would be problems associated with population growth and relocation, loss of fishing and other river-related resources, and new health hazards, including increased threat of drowning, insect breeding, and airborne dust. Finally, physical transformation of the communities' life space was seen likely to result in changes in the context of the informal processes of enculturation that occur within the communities.

*Van Willigen, J. (1986). *Applied anthropology* (p. 169). South Hadley, MA: Bergin and Garvey.

CLASS AND CASTE

A **social class** may be defined as a category of individuals of equal or nearly equal prestige according to the system of evaluation. The qualification "nearly equal" is important, for a certain amount of inequality may occur even within a given class. If this is so, to an outside observer low ranking individuals in an upper class may not seem much different from the highest ranking members of a lower class. Yet marked differences exist when the classes are compared as wholes with one another. The point here is that class distinctions are not clear-cut and obvious in societies such as those of North America that have a continuous range of differential privileges, for example, from virtually none to several. Such a continuum can be divided into classes in a variety of ways. If fine distinctions are made, then many classes may be recognized. If, however, only a few gross distinctions are made, then only a few classes will be recognized. Thus, some speak of North American society as divided into three classes: lower, middle, and upper. Others speak of several classes: lower lower, middle lower, upper lower, lower middle, and so forth.

A **caste** is a particular kind of social class with a fairly fixed or impermeable membership. Castes are strongly endogamous, and offspring are automatically members of their parents' caste. The classic case is the caste system of India. Coupled with strict endogamy and membership by descent in Indian castes is an association of particular castes with specific occupations and customs, such

Social class. A category of individuals who enjoy equal or nearly equal prestige according to the evaluation system. >
Caste. A special form of social class in which membership is determined by birth and remains fixed for life.

Despite their close association, the clothing worn by these two individuals and the way they interact clearly indicate they are of different social classes.

as food habits and styles of dress, along with rituals involving notions of purity and impurity. The literally thousands of castes are organized into a hierarchy of four named categories, at the top of which are the priests or *Brahmans*, the bearers of universal order and values and of highest ritual purity. Below them are the powerful—though less pure—warriors. Dominant at the local level, besides fulfilling warrior functions, they control all village lands. Furnishing services to the landowners, and owning the tools of their trade, are two lower ranking, landless caste groups of artisans and laborers. At the bottom of the system, owning neither land nor the tools of their trade, are the outcasts or "untouchables." In India, these considered most impure of all people constitute a large labor pool at the beck and call of those con-

trolling economic and political affairs, the landholding warrior caste.

Although some argue that the term *caste* should be restricted to the Indian situation, others find this much too narrow a usage, since castelike situations are known elsewhere in the world. In South Africa, for example, although the situation is now changing, Blacks traditionally were relegated to a low ranking stratum in society, until recently were barred by law from marrying non-Blacks, and could not hold property except to a limited degree in specified "black homelands." Most Blacks still perform menial jobs for Whites, but even the small cadre of "middle class" Blacks that existed were until recently prohibited from living where Whites do, or even swimming in the same water or holding the hand of someone who is White. All of this brings to mind the concepts of ritual purity and pollution so basic to the Indian caste system. In South Africa, Whites feared pollution of their purity through improper contact with Blacks.

In India and South Africa, untouchables and Blacks comprised categories of landless or near-landless people who served as a body of mobile laborers always available for exploitation by those in political control. A similar mobile labor force of landless men at the state's disposal emerged in China as many as 2,200 years ago (caste, in India, is at least as old). Paradoxically, at the very same time South Africa is trying to change its system, a similar castelike underclass has emerged in United States society as automation reduces the need for unskilled workers and downsizing occurs. Its members consist of unemployed, unemployable, or drastically underemployed people who own little, if any, property and who live "out on the streets" or—at best—in urban or rural slums. Lacking both economic and political power, they have no access to the kinds of educational facilities that would enable them or their children to improve their lot. Rather than providing a cheap labor pool for the state, this new underclass has served the economy by ensuring a significant incidence of permanent unemployment, thereby making the employed feel less secure in their jobs. As a consequence, the employed are apt to be less demanding of wages and benefits from their employers.

Outcast groups such as India's untouchables are a common feature of stratified societies; the United States, for example, has in recent years seen the growth of a castelike underclass.

India, South Africa, China, and the United States—all very different countries, in different parts of the world, with different ideologies—and yet a similar phenomenon has emerged in each. Does something in the structure of socially stratified states sooner or later produce a sort of exploitable, impoverished outcast group? The answer to this is clearly unknown, but the question is deserving of the attention of anthropologists and other social scientists.

The basis of social class structure is role differentiation. Some role differentiation, of course, exists in any society, at least along the lines of sex and age. Furthermore, any necessary role always will be valued to some degree. In a food-foraging society, the role of "good hunter" will be valued. The fact one man already may play that role does not, however, prevent another man from playing it, too, in an egalitarian society. Therefore, role differentiation by itself is not sufficient for stratification. Two more ingredients are necessary: formalized evaluation of roles, involving attitudes such as like/dislike, or admiration/revulsion, and restricted access to the more highly valued roles. Obviously, the greater the diversity of roles in a society, the more complex evaluation and restriction can become. Since great role diversity is most characteristic of civilizations, it is not surprising they provide the most opportunities for stratifica-

tion. Furthermore, the large size and heterogeneity of populations in civilizations create a need for classifying people into a manageable number of social categories. Small wonder, then, that social stratification is one of the defining characteristics of a true civilization.

Social classes are manifested in several ways. One is through **verbal evaluation**—what people say about others in their own society. For this, anything can be singled out for attention and spoken of favorably or unfavorably: political, military, religious, economic, or professional roles; wealth and property; kinship; personal qualities (skin color, for example); community activity; linguistic dialect; and a host of other traits. Cultures do this differently, and what may be spoken of favorably in one may be spoken of unfavorably in another and ignored in a third. Furthermore, cultural values may change, so something regarded favorably at one time may not be at another. This is one reason why a researcher may be misled by verbal evaluation, for what people say may not correspond completely with social reality. As an example, the official language of Egypt is Classical Arabic, the language of the Qur'an (the most holy of Islamic texts). Though it is highly valued, no one in Egypt uses this language in daily interaction; rather, it is used for official documents or on formal occasions. Those most proficient in it are not of the

---

Verbal evaluation.   The way people in a stratified society evaluate society members.

upper class but, rather, of the lower-middle classes. These are the people educated in the public schools (where Classical Arabic is the language of schooling) and who hold jobs in the government bureaucracy (which requires the most use of Classical Arabic). Upper-class Egyptians, by contrast, go to private schools, where they learn the foreign languages essential for success in diplomacy and (in the global economy) business and industry.[4]

Social classes also are manifested through patterns of association: not just who interacts with whom but also how and in what context. In Western society, informal, friendly relations take place mostly within one's own class. Relations with members of other classes tend to be less informal and occur in the context of specific situations. For example, a corporate executive and a janitor normally are members of different social classes. They may have frequent contact with each other, but it occurs in the setting of the corporate office and usually requires certain stereotyped behavioral patterns.

A third way social classes are manifested is through **symbolic indicators.** Included here are activities and possessions indicative of class. For example, in North American society, occupation (a garbage collector has different class status than a physician); wealth (rich people generally are in a higher social class than poor people); dress (we have all heard the expression "white collar" versus "blue collar"); form of recreation (upper-class people are expected to play golf rather than shoot pool down at the pool hall—but they can shoot pool at home or in a club); residential location (upper-class people do not ordinarily live in slums); kind of car; and so on. The fact is, all sorts of status symbols indicate class position, including such measures as how many bathrooms in an individual's house. At the same time, symbolic indicators may be cruder reflections of class position than verbal indicators or patterns of associa-

tion. One reason is that access to wealth may not be wholly restricted to upper classes, so individuals can buy symbols suggestive of upper-class status whether or not this really is their status. To

Symbolic indicators of class or caste include factors of lifestyle, such as the kind of housing one lives in.

[4]Haeri, N. (1997). The reproduction of symbolic capital: Language, state and class in Egypt. *Current Anthropology, 38,* 795–816.

Symbolic indicators. In a stratified society, activities and possessions indicative of social class.

take an extreme example, the head of an organized crime ring may display more of the symbols of high-class status than may some members of old, established upper-class families. For that matter, someone from an upper class deliberately may choose a simpler lifestyle than is customary. Instead of driving a Mercedes, he or she may drive a beat-up Volkswagen.

Symbolic indicators involve factors of lifestyle, but differences in life chances also may signal differences in class standing. Life is apt to be less hard for members of an upper class as opposed to a lower class. This shows up in a tendency for lower infant mortality and longer life expectancy for the upper class. Another tendency is for greater physical stature and robustness among upper-class people, the result of better diet and protection from serious illness in their juvenile years.

MOBILITY

All stratified societies offer at least some **mobility**, and this helps to ease the strains in any system of inequality. Even the Indian caste system, with its guiding ideology that pretends all arrangements within it are static, has a surprising amount of flexibility and mobility, not all of it associated with the recent changes "modernization" has brought to India. As a rather dramatic case in point, in the state of Rajasthan, those who own and control most land and who are wealthy and politically powerful are not of warrior caste, as one would expect, but are of the lowest caste. Their tenants and laborers, by contrast, are Brahmans. Thus, the group ritually superior to all others finds itself in the same social position as untouchables, whereas the landowners who are the Brahmans' ritual in-

In the United States, the ability to "move up" in the system of stratification is increasingly dependent upon access to higher education.

Mobility.   The ability to change one's class position.

feriors are superior in all other ways. Meanwhile, a group of leather workers in the untouchable category, who have gained political power in India's new democracy, are trying to better their position by claiming they are Brahmans who were tricked in the past into doing defiling work. Although individuals cannot move up or down the caste hierarchy, whole groups can do so depending on claims they can make for higher status and on how well they can manipulate others into acknowledging their claims. Interestingly, the people at the bottom of India's caste system traditionally have not questioned the validity of the system itself so much as their particular position within it.

With their limited mobility, caste-structured societies exemplify **closed-class societies.** Those that permit a great deal of mobility are referred to as **open-class societies.** Even here, however, mobility is apt to be more limited than one might suppose. In the United States, in spite of its "rags to riches" ideology, most mobility involves a move up or down only a notch, although if this continues in a family for several generations, it may add up to a major change. Generally, the culture makes much of those relatively rare examples of great upward mobility consistent with its cultural values and does its best to ignore, or at least downplay, the numerous cases of little or no upward, not to mention downward, mobility.

The degree of mobility in a stratified society is related to the prevailing kind of family organization. In societies where the extended family is the usual form, mobility is apt to be difficult, because each individual is strongly tied to the large family group. Hence, for a person to move up to a higher social class, his or her family must move up as well. Mobility is easier for independent nuclear families where the individual is closely tied to fewer persons. Moreover, under neolocal residence, individuals normally leave the family they were born into. So it is, then, that through careful marriage, occupational success, and disassociating themselves from the lower-class family they grew up in, all of which are made possible by res-

idential mobility, individuals can more easily "move up" in society.

GENDER STRATIFICATION

Closely associated with class and caste stratification is the related phenomenon of gender stratification. For instance, in our earlier discussion of sex as an organizing principle, we saw that in some (but not all) societies, men and women may be regarded as unequal, with the former outranking the latter. Generally speaking, sexual inequality is characteristic of societies stratified in other ways as well; thus women historically have occupied a position of inferiority to men in the class-structured societies of the Western world. Nevertheless, sexual inequality sometimes may be seen in societies not otherwise stratified; in such instances, men and women are always physically as well as conceptually separated from one another. Yet, as the Iroquoian case cited earlier in this chapter demonstrates, not all societies that separate men and women exhibit gender stratification.

The rise of gender stratification often seems to be associated with the development of strongly centralized states. For example, among the Maya of Central America the basic social unit in the past and today is the complementary gender pair. On the household level, men raise the crops and bring in the other raw materials the women transform into food, textiles, and other cultural objects. The same complementarity existed in public ritual and politics, but in the last century B.C. at the Maya city of Tikal, this situation began to change. With the development of strong dynastic rule by men, women began to be excluded from favored places for burial, their graves were not as richly stocked with material items as were those of important men, they all but disappeared from public art, and they were rarely mentioned in inscriptions. When women were portrayed or mentioned, it was on account of their relationship to a particular male ruler. Clearly, women came to hold a lesser place in Maya society than did men, although gender

---

Closed-class societies. Stratified societies that severely restrict social mobility. > **Open-class societies.** Stratified societies that permit a great deal of social mobility.

At the ancient Maya city of Tikal, in Central America, one reflection of gender stratification is the rarity of the portrayals of women, compared to men, in the city's public art. The woman shown in this drawing was portrayed on a wooden lintel only because of her relationship to the king who commissioned the temple of which the lintel is a part.

stratification was not nearly as marked at the grass roots of society as it was among the elite. When the Tikal state collapsed, as it did in the 9th century A.D., the relationship of equality between men and women returned to what it had been 8 or 9 centuries before.[5]

DEVELOPMENT OF STRATIFICATION

Because social stratification of any kind tends to make life oppressive for large segments of a population, the lower classes are usually placated with religion, which promises them a better existence in the hereafter. If they have this to look forward to, they are more likely to accept an existing disadvantaged position. In India, for example, belief in reincarnation and in the existence of an incor-

ruptible supernatural power that assigns people to a particular caste position as a reward or punishment for the deeds and misdeeds of past lives justifies one's position in this life. If, however, individuals perform the duties appropriate to their caste in this lifetime, then they can expect to be reborn into a higher caste in a future existence. Truly exemplary performance of their duties may even release them from the cycle of rebirth, to be reunited with the divinity all existence springs from. In the minds of orthodox Hindus, then, one's caste position is something earned (an achieved status), rather than the accident of birth (ascribed) it appears to outside observers. Thus, although the caste system explicitly recognizes (and accepts as legitimate) inequality among people, it is underlain by an implicit assumption of ultimate equality. This contrasts with the situation in the United States, where the equality of all people is proclaimed while various groups are clearly regarded as unequal.

When considering the origin of social stratification, we must reckon with such common tendencies as the human desire for prestige, either for oneself or one's group. Although the impulse need not result inevitably in the ranking of individuals or groups relative to one another, it sometimes may. Among the Iroquois and Hopi Indians and the Sherente and Ugandan peoples, the superiority of some kinship lineages over others is recognized by electing chiefs, performing sacred rituals, and other special tasks, whether or not membership entails any economic advantages.

This sort of situation easily could develop into full-fledged stratification. Just such a development may have arisen among the Maya of Central America.[6] These people began as horticulturists with a relatively egalitarian, kinship-based organization. In the last centuries B.C., elaborate rituals developed for dealing with the very serious

---

[5]Haviland, W. A. (1997). The rise and fall of sexual inequality: Death and gender at Tikal, Guatemala. *Ancient Mesoamerica, 8,* 1–12.

[6]Haviland, W. A. (1975). The ancient Maya and the evolution of urban society. *University of Colorado Museum of Anthropology Miscellaneous Series,* no. 37; and Haviland, W. A., & Moholy-Nagy, H. (1992). Distinguishing the high and mighty from the hoi polloi at Tikal, Guatemala. In A. F. & D. Z. Chase (Eds.), *Mesoamerican elites: An archaeological assessment.* Norman: University of Oklahoma Press.

The high status of the two Maya kings shown in this painting from a pottery vessel is revealed by their jewelry, elaborate headdress, and the fact they sit on thrones. Among these people, stratification arose as certain lineages monopolized important offices.

problems of agriculture, such as uncertain rains, vulnerability of crops to a variety of pests, and periodic devastation from hurricanes. As these changes occurred, a full-time priesthood arose, along with some craft specialization in the service of religion. Out of the priesthood developed, in the last century B.C., the hereditary ruling dynasties mentioned earlier. In this developmental process, certain lineages seem to have monopolized the important civic and ceremonial positions

and thus came to be ranked above other lineages, forming the basis of an upper class.

Just as lineages may come to be ranked differentially relative to one another, so may ethnic groups. In South Africa, for example, Europeans came as conquerors, establishing a social order whereby they could maintain their favored position. In the United States, the importation of African slaves produced a severely disadvantaged castelike group at the bottom of the social order.

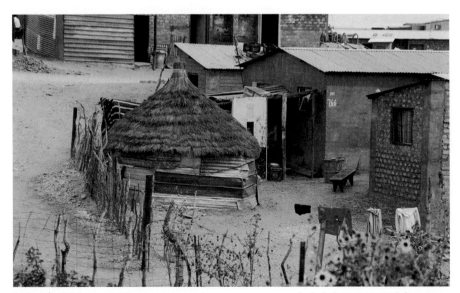

In South Africa, stratification emerged as conquerors excluded the conquered from positions of importance and restricted their access to basic resources. Shown here is the Black township outside the capital of Namibia, until recently ruled from South Africa.

Not only was it nearly impossible for such individuals to rise above this group, but also downward mobility into it was possible, owing to the belief that "a single drop of Black blood" was enough to define one as Black (a belief similar to South African concepts of purity and pollution). In the United States, it has taken a long time for African Americans to move up in the class system, though the legacy persists, as they are still disproportionately represented in the low ranks of society. Even without conquest and/or slavery, ethnic differences often are a factor in the definition of social classes and castes, as not only African Americans but also members of other North American minorities have experienced through the

racial stereotyping that leads to social and economic disadvantages.

Sometimes, rather than providing the basis for stratification, ethnicity comes to serve as a metaphor for what began as nothing more than class distinctions. A dramatic example of this can be found in the African state of Rwanda where what began simply as class distinctions were misinterpreted by Belgian colonial authorities as differences in ethnicity. Ultimately, they were magnified until the whole country erupted in a bloodbath, illustrating how class systems have built into them the seeds of their own destruction. In Rwanda, this happened through an intersection of class differences with the interests of particular common-interest associations.

Genocide in Rwanda[7]

The genocide in Rwanda is a crime, perpetrated by a known group of individuals associated with two extremist parties, the National Republican Movement for Development of Democracy (MRND) and the Coalition for the Defense of the Republic (CDR). The first targets were members of opposition parties, journalists and human rights activists, both Hutu and Tutsi. As the killing spread to the rural areas, it has become a programme of genocide specifically targeted at the Tutsi, who before the killing represented about ten percent of Rwanda's seven million people. Over 200,000 have died so far [June 1994], and the killing continues. [After this piece was written, an uneasy peace was established under international supervision.]

A crime requires motive, means, and opportunity. The motive of those responsible was to continue to monopolize power and to seek a "final solution" to the political opposition, both civilian and armed. Attempts by President Juvenal Habyarimana to stall on the implementation of agreements for power sharing were not succeeding, owing to domestic and international pressure.

The primary means for perpetuating genocide is mobilization of the militias that had been established by the MRND and CDR since late 1971. Use of the civil administration to encourage ordinary people to participate in killings is a supplementary strategy. Army units, especially from the Presidential Guard, and death squads have also helped direct the killings, especially in the towns. Radio broadcasts have been used to incite the population.

The genocide against rural Tutsi in Rwanda is particularly traumatic because the killers are largely people from the same community as their victims. People are murdered by their neighbors, their schoolteachers, their local shopkeepers. Such mass mobilization of killers was necessary because of the particular nature of Rwandese society.

[7]de Waal, A. (1994). Genocide in Rwanda. *Anthropology Today, 10* (3), 1–2.

Although the killing is supposed to have stopped, outbreaks of violence in Rwanda still occur, as in this 1997 massacre.

Rwanda has long been known as a true nation in Africa, containing three groups: Twa, Hutu and Tutsi. German and Belgian colonists characterized them as respectively aboriginal Pygmies, Bantu peasants and Nilo-Hamitic aristocrats. The truth is that they were three different strata of the same group, differentiated by occupational and political status. There is some analogy with the Indian caste system, though individuals could and did move with difficulty between the categories; and the Twa are victims of some of the worst discrimination in Africa.

The reciprocity in Hutu-Tutsi relations that had diluted the latter's dominance in precolonial days was destroyed by Belgian rule. Instead a rigid system of tribute and exploitation was imposed, creating deep grievances that underlie today's violence. In the northwest, formerly an anomalous region of Hutu kingdoms, the Belgians dismantled the precolonial political system, and imposed Tutsi overlords. The modern Hutu extremists—the late President Habyarimana and his clan—derive from this area.

The differences in physical stature between the groups have been widely exaggerated: it is rarely possible to tell whether an *individual* is a Twa, Hutu or Tutsi from his or her height. Speaking the same language, sharing the same culture and religion, living in the same places, they are in no sense "tribes," nor even distinct "ethnic groups."

Two things enable one to identify an individual as Twa, Hutu or Tutsi: knowledge of the person's ancestry, and the possession of an identity card which, since 1926, has by law specified which group he or she belongs to. The latter is a legacy of Belgian rule: those with ten or more cows were classified as Tutsi, those with less as Hutu—and a tiny minority of those recognized as Twa has their status as an ethnographic curiosity confirmed in perpetuity. But checking every identity card is time-consuming, and the killings needed to be carried out rapidly to be successful, so those planning the killing needed to mobilize militiamen from every community in the country, who knew every Tutsi family personally. In 1991, the government began to implement a system known as "Nyumba Kumi" (literally "ten houses")—one man from every ten houses was mobilized and armed. Such are the logistical challenges facing those who contemplate genocide.

The killers were able to practise their methods on various occasions since 1990, killing perhaps 3,000 people, mainly Tutsi. This is well-documented in the 1993 report of an international human rights commission.

The opportunity was provided by a conjunction of circumstances, which allowed the hardliners to confuse the international community for sufficiently long to be able to perpetuate the crime with extraordinarily little international response. The sowing of confusion was the key to the killers' success. Because President Habyarimana himself was the first casualty, his acolytes were able to present themselves as victims of the plot, rather than the perpetrators. The deaths of ten Belgians serving on the UN force focused international attention on the plight of foreigners. The renewed offensive by the Rwandan Patriotic Front (RPF)—motivated in part by the desire to rescue Tutsi civilians from the militias—enabled the government to speak of aggression and the need for a ceasefire. But above all, the killers portrayed the situation as one of uncontrollable spontaneous ethnic violence.

Prompt international condemnation of the coup in Burundi in October 1993 prevented political extremists from seizing and holding on to power. The absence of such condemnation in Rwanda last month [May 1994] allowed the killers to carry out their task undisturbed. This was largely because the crime of genocide was misdiagnosed as a spontaneous ethnic violence. The Secretary General of the United Nations, Boutros Boutros-Ghali, spoke in late April of "Hutus killing Tutsi and Tutsi killing Hutus" and proposed sending troops to bring about a ceasefire between the (Tutsi-dominated) RPF and the (Hutu-dominated) army. This was precisely what the militias wanted: a chance to stop the RPF advance so they could complete the genocide of unarmed Tutsi away from the battle lines.

Although the cost is great—social classes do, after all, make life oppressive for large numbers of people—classes may nevertheless perform an integrative function in society. By cutting across some or all lines of kinship, residence, occupation, and age group, depending on the particular society, they counteract potential tendencies of a society to fragment into discrete entities. In India diverse national groups were incorporated into the larger society by certification of their leaders as warriors and by marriage of their women to Brahmans. The problem is that stratification, by its very nature, provides a means for one, usually small, group of people to dominate and make life miserable for large numbers of others, as in the just-cited case of Rwanda or as in South Africa, where 4.5 million Whites dominated 25 million non-Whites. In India a succession of conquerors was able to move into the caste hierarchy near its top as warriors.

In any system of stratification, those who dominate proclaim their supposedly superior status, which they try to convert into respect, or at least acquiescence, from the lower classes. As anthropologist Laura Nader points out: "Systems of thought develop over time and reflect the interests of certain classes or groups in the society who manage to universalize their beliefs and values."[8]

_____

[8]Nader, L. (1997). Controlling processes: Tracing the dynamic components of power. *Current Anthropology, 38,* 271.

One sees this, for example, in religious ideologies that assert the social order is divinely fixed and therefore not to be questioned. Thus, they hope members of the lower classes will thereby "know their place" and not contest their domination by the "chosen elite." If, however, this domination is contested, the elite usually control the power of the state, which they use to protect their privileged position.

CHAPTER SUMMARY

Grouping by sex separates men and women to varying degrees in different societies; in some they may be together much of the time, while in others they may spend much of their time apart, even to the extreme of eating and sleeping separately. Although men perceive women as their inferiors in some sexually segregated societies, in others men perceive women as equals.

Age grouping is another form of association that may augment or replace kinship grouping. An age grade is a category of persons, usually of the same sex, organized by age. Age grades in some societies are broken up into age sets, which include individuals initiated into an age grade at the same time who move together through a series of life stages. A specific time is often ritually established for moving from a younger to an older age grade.

The most varied use of age grouping is found in African societies south of the Sahara. Among the Tiriki of East Africa, for example, seven named age sets pass through four successive age grades. Each age set embraces a 15-year age span and thus opens to accept new initiates every 105 years. In principle, the system resembles U.S. college classes, where (say) the "Class of 1990" (an age set) will move through the four age grades: first year, sophomore, junior, senior.

Common-interest associations are linked with rapid social change and urbanization. They are increasingly assuming the roles kinship or age groups formerly played. In urban areas they help new arrivals cope with the changes demanded by the move from the village or previous city or country to the new city. Common-interest associations are also seen in traditional societies, and their roots are probably found in the first horticultural villages. Membership may range from voluntary to legally compulsory.

For a long time social scientists mistakenly viewed women's common-interest associations as less developed than men's, largely because of culture-bound assumptions. A question that remains to be resolved is why women are barred from associations in some societies, while in others they participate on an equal basis with men.

A stratified society is divided into two or more categories of people who do not share equally in basic resources, influence, and prestige. This form contrasts with the egalitarian society, which has as many valued positions as persons capable of filling them. Societies may be stratified in various ways, such as by gender, age, social class, or caste. Members of a class enjoy equal or nearly equal access to basic resources and prestige (according to the way the latter is defined). Class differences are not always clear and obvious. Where fine distinctions are made in privileges, the result is a multiplicity of classes. In societies where only gross distinctions are made, only a few social classes may be recognized.

Caste is a special form of social class in which membership is determined by birth and fixed for life. Endogamy is particularly marked within castes, and children automatically belong to their parents' caste. Social class structure is based on role differentiation, although this by itself is not sufficient for stratification. Also necessary are formalized positive and negative attitudes toward roles and restricted access to the more valued ones.

Social classes are given expression in several ways. One is through verbal evaluation, or what people say about other people in their society.

Another is through patterns of association—who interacts with whom, how, and in what context. Social classes also are manifest through symbolic indicators: activities and possessions indicative of class position. Finally, they are reflected by differences in life chances, as high-status people generally live longer and in better health than low-status people.

Mobility is present to a greater or lesser extent in all stratified societies. Open-class societies are those with the easiest mobility. In most cases, however, the move is limited to one rung up or down the social ladder. The degree of mobility is related to the type of family organization that prevails in a society. Where the extended family is the norm, mobility tends to be severely limited. The independent nuclear family provides an easier situation for mobility.

Social stratification can be based on many criteria, such as wealth, legal status, birth, personal qualities, and ideology. A rigidly stratified society with limited mobility normally makes life particularly oppressive for large segments of a population.

POINTS FOR CONSIDERATION

1. Are you a part of an *age group* as described in this chapter? If so, how does it define itself, and what are its functions? What are the functions of similar such groups in industrial societies? Do these differ from their functions in other cultures? Explain.

2. Why have specialized formations such as *common-interest associations* and *age groups* developed in addition to kinship and marriage groups? What needs do such associations serve? How are they important in industrial societies? in *stratified societies*?

3. How might the concept of "race" be reflected in the various groupings discussed in this chapter? How might race function in an insider's definition of such categories within a society? in an outsider's definition?

4. Have you had an experience that made you aware of certain behaviors stemming from *social stratification*? Where did this occur? What was your role in the encounter? How aware of it were you at the time? Did it seem out of place, or was it an appropriate interaction?

SUGGESTED READINGS

Bernardi, B. (1985). *Age class systems: Social institutions and policies based on age.* New York: Cambridge University Press.

This is a cross-cultural analysis of age as a device for organizing society and for distributing and rotating power.

Bradfield, R. M. (1973). *A natural history of associations.* New York: International Universities Press.

This two-volume work is the first major anthropological study of common-interest associations since 1902. It attempts to provide a comprehensive theory of the origin of associations and their role in kin-based societies.

Hammond, D. (1972). *Associations* (p. 14). Reading, MA: Addison-Wesley Modular Publications.

This is a brief first-rate review of anthropological thinking and of the literature on common-interest associations and age groups.

Lenski, G. E. (1966). *Power and privilege: A theory of social stratification.* New York: McGraw-Hill.

Who gets what and why is explained by the distributive process and systems of social stratification in industrial nations: the United States, Russia, Sweden, and Britain. With a broadly comparative approach, the author makes heavy use of anthropological and historical materials, as well as the usual sociological materials on modern industrial societies. The basic approach is theoretical and analytical; the book builds on certain postulates about the nature of humans and society, seeking to develop in a systematic manner an explanation of a variety of patterns of stratification. The theory presented is a synthesis of the two dominant theoretical traditions of the past and present, currently represented in both Marxist and functionalist theory.

Price, T. D., & Feinman, G. M. (Eds.). (1995). *Foundations of social inequality*. New York: Plenum.

This book is a collection of essays by various contributors that examines the emergence of social inequality.

Sanday, P. R. (1981). *Female power and male dominance: On the origins of sexual inequality*. Cambridge: Cambridge University Press.

In this cross-cultural study, Professor Sanday reveals the various ways male-female relations are organized in human societies and demonstrates that male dominance is not inherent in those relations. Rather, it appears to emerge in situations of stress as a result of such things as chronic food shortages, migration, and colonial domination.

PART VII

THE SEARCH FOR ORDER: SOLVING THE PROBLEM OF DISORDER

Chapter 23
POLITICAL ORGANIZATION AND THE MAINTENANCE OF ORDER

Chapter 24
RELIGION AND THE SUPERNATURAL

Chapter 25
THE ARTS

Introduction

An irony of human life is that something as fundamental to our existence as cooperation should contain within it the seeds of its own destruction. It is nonetheless true that the groups people form to fulfill important organizational needs do not just facilitate cooperation among the members of those groups, but they also create conditions that may lead to the disruption of society. A case in point is the escalating gang violence seen in many North American cities. The attitude that "my group is better than your group" is not confined to any one of the world's cultures and it not infrequently takes the form of rivalry between groups: descent group against descent group, men against women, age grade against age grade, social class against social class, and so forth. This does not mean such rivalry has to be disruptive; indeed, it may function to ensure that the members of groups perform their jobs well so as not to "lose face" or be subject to ridicule. Rivalry, however, can become a serious problem if it develops into conflict.

The fact is, social living inevitably entails a certain amount of friction—not just between groups but between individual members of groups as well. Thus, any society can count on a degree of disruptive behavior by some of its members at one time or another. Yet no one can know precisely when such outbursts will occur or what form they will take. Not only does this uncertainty go against the predictability social life demands, but it also goes against the deep-seated psychological need each individual has for structure and certainty, which we discussed in Chapter 16. Therefore, every society must have a means of resolving conflicts and preventing a breakdown of the social order. Control of peoples' behavior and political systems, which primarily function to maintain social order, are the subjects of Chapter 23.

Religion and politics may seem like strange bedfellows, but both fulfill the same goal: to protect society against the unexpected and unwanted. Effective though a culture may be in equipping, organizing, and controlling a society to provide for its members' needs, certain problems always defy existing technological or organizational solutions. The response of every culture is to devise a set of rituals, with a set of beliefs to explain them, aimed at solving these problems through the manipulation of supernatural beings and powers. In short, religion and magic exist to transform the uncertainties of life into certainties. In addition, they may serve as powerful integrative forces through commonly held values, beliefs, and practices. Also important is religion's rationalization of the existing social order, which thereby becomes a moral order as well. Thus, a link exists between religion and magic on the one hand and political organization and social control on the other. Religion and magic are, then, appropriate subjects for discussion in Chapter 24 of this section on the search for order.

Like religion and magic, the arts also contribute to human well-being and help give shape and significance to life. Indeed, the relationship between art and religion goes deeper than this, for much of what we call art has been created in the service of religion: myths to explain ritual practices, objects to portray important deities, music and dances for ceremonial use, pictorial art to record religious experiences and/or to serve as objects of supernatural power in their own right, and the like. In a very real sense, music, dance, and any other form of art, like magic, exploit psychological predispositions so as to enchant other people and cause them to perceive social reality in a way favorable to the interests of the enchanter. And, like religion, art of any kind expresses the human search for order, in that the artist gives form to some essentially formless raw material. Accordingly, a chapter on the arts follows that on religion, concluding this section.

Chapter 23
POLITICAL ORGANIZATION
AND THE MAINTENANCE OF ORDER

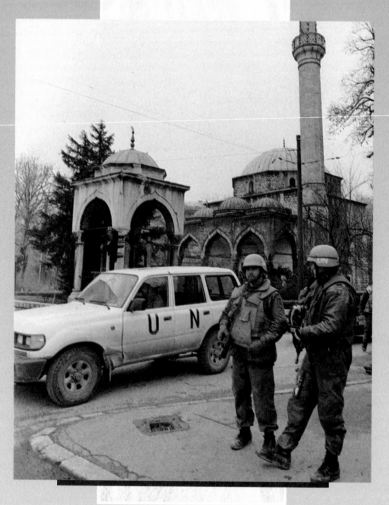

POLITICAL ORGANIZATION IN HUMAN SOCIETIES TAKES MANY
FORMS, OF WHICH THE STATE IS BUT ONE. ONE REASON
STATES GENERALLY DO NOT LAST VERY LONG IS THAT THEY
ARE OFTEN CONTROLLED BY MEMBERS OF ONE NATIONALITY
WHO TRY TO REPRESS (OR EVEN EXTERMINATE) OTHER
NATIONALITIES WITHIN THE STATE. THIS IS WHAT SERBS TRIED
TO DO IN BOSNIA, EVEN IN THE FACE OF UN INTERVENTION.

Chapter Preview

What Is Political Organization?

Political organization refers to the means a society uses to maintain order internally and manage its affairs with other societies externally. Such organization may be relatively uncentralized and informal, as in bands and tribes, or centralized and formal, as in chiefdoms and states.

How Is Order Maintained Within a Society?

Social controls may be internalized—"built into" individuals—or externalized in the form of sanctions. Built-in controls rely on deterrents such as personal shame and fear of supernatural punishment. Sanctions, by contrast, rely on actions other members of society take toward specifically approved or disapproved behavior. Positive sanctions encourage approved behavior, while negative sanctions discourage disapproved behavior. Negative sanctions an authorized political body formalizes and enforces are called laws. Consequently, we may say laws are sanctions, but not all sanctions are laws. Similarly, societies do not maintain order through law alone.

How Is Order Maintained Between Societies?

Just as the threatened or actual use of force may be employed to maintain order within a society, it also may be used to manage affairs among bands, lineages, clans, or whatever the largest autonomous political units may be. Not all societies, however, rely on force, because some do not practice warfare as we know it. Such societies generally have views of themselves and their place in the world quite different from those characteristic of centrally organized states.

How Do Political Systems Obtain People's Allegiance?

No form of political organization can function without the loyalty and support of those it governs. To a greater or lesser extent, political organizations the world over use religion to legitimize their power. In uncentralized systems people freely give loyalty and cooperation because everyone participates in making decisions. Centralized systems, by contrast, rely more heavily on force and coercion, although in the long run these may lessen the system's effectiveness.

653

L ouis XIV proclaimed, "I am the state." With this sweeping statement, the king declared absolute rule over France; he held himself to be the law, the lawmaker, the court, the judge, jailer, and executioner—in short, the seat of all political power in France.

Louis XIV took a great deal of responsibility on his royal shoulders; had he actually performed each of these functions, he would have done the work of thousands of people, the number required to keep the machinery of a large political organization such as a state running at full steam. As a form of political organization, the 17th-century French state was not much different from those that exist in modern times. All large states require elaborate centralized structures, involving hierarchies of executives, legislators, and judges who initiate, pass, and enforce laws that affect large numbers of people.

Such complex structures, however, have not always been in existence: The oldest European states, for instance, are not much older than the United States, and many are in fact younger. Even today some societies depend on far less formal means of organization. In these societies, flexible and informal kinship systems with leaders who lack real power prevail. Problems, such as homicide and theft, are perceived as serious "family quarrels," rather than affairs that affect the entire community. Between these two polarities of political organization lies a world of variety, including societies with chiefs, Big Men, or charismatic leaders and segmented tribal societies with multicentric authority systems. Such disparity prompts this question: What is political organization?

The term *political organization* refers to the way power is distributed and embedded in society, whether in organizing a giraffe hunt or raising an army. In other words, political organization has to do with the way power is used to coordinate and regulate behavior so that order is maintained. Government, on the other hand, consists of an administrative system having specialized personnel that may or may not form a part of the political organization, depending on the so-ciety's complexity. Some form of political organization exists in all societies, but it is not always a government.

KINDS OF POLITICAL SYSTEMS

Political organization is the means a society uses to maintain social order and reduce social disorder. It assumes a variety of forms among the peoples of the world, but scholars have simplified this complex subject by identifying four basic kinds of political systems: bands, tribes, chiefdoms, and states. The first two are uncentralized systems; the latter two are centralized.

UNCENTRALIZED POLITICAL SYSTEMS

Until recently, many non-Western peoples have had neither chiefs with established rights and du-ties nor any fixed form of government, as the cit-izens of modern states understand the term. In-stead, marriage and kinship form the principal means of social organization among such peoples. The economies of these societies are of a subsis-tence type, and populations are typically quite small. Leaders do not have real power to force compliance with the society's customs or laws, but if individual members do not conform, they may become the target of scorn and gossip or even os-tracized. Important decisions are usually made in a democratic manner by a consensus of adults, of-ten including women as well as men; dissenting members may decide to act with the majority, or they may choose to adopt some other course of action, if they are willing to risk the social conse-quences. This form of political organization pro-vides great flexibility, which in many situations confers an adaptive advantage.

Band Organization

The **band** is a small group of politically indepen-dent, though related, households and is the least complicated form of political organization. Bands

---

Band. A small group of related households occupying a particular region that gather periodically on an ad hoc basis but that do not yield their sovereignty to the larger collective.

usually are found among food foragers and other nomadic societies where people organize into politically autonomous extended-family groups that usually camp together, although the members of such families may frequently split into smaller groups for periods to forage for food or visit other relatives. Bands are thus kin groups, composed of men and/or women who are related (or assumed to be) and their spouses and unmarried children. Bands may be characterized as associations of related families who occupy a common (often vaguely defined) territory and who live there together, so long as environmental and subsistence circumstances are favorable. The band is probably the oldest form of political organization, since all humans were once food foragers and remained so until the development of farming and pastoralism over the past 10,000 years.

Since bands are small, numbering at most a few hundred people, no real need exists for formal, centralized political systems. In egalitarian groups, where everyone is related to—and knows on a personal basis—everyone else with whom dealings are required and where most everyone values "getting along" with the natural order of life, the potential for conflicts to develop is re-

duced in the first place. Many of those that do arise are settled informally through gossip, ridicule, direct negotiation, or mediation. In the latter instances, the emphasis is on achieving a solution considered just by most parties concerned, rather than conforming to some abstract law or rule. Where all else fails, disgruntled individuals have the option of leaving the band to go live in another where they have relatives.

Decisions affecting a band are made with the participation of all its adult members, with an emphasis on achieving consensus, rather than a simple majority. Leaders become such by virtue of their abilities and serve in that capacity only as long as they retain the community's confidence. Thus, they neither have a guaranteed hold on their position for a specified length of time nor the power to force people to abide by their decisions. People will follow them only as long as they consider it in their best interests, and a leader who exceeds what people are willing to accept quickly loses followers.

An example of the informal nature of leadership in the band is found among the Ju/'hoansi Bushmen of the Kalahari Desert, whom we met in Chapters 16 and 17. Each Ju/'hoansi band is

Toma, a Ju/'hoansi headman known to many North Americans through the documentary film *The Hunters*.

656 PART VII THE SEARCH FOR ORDER: SOLVING THE PROBLEM OF DISORDER

composed of a group of families who live together, linked to one another and to the headman or, less often, headwoman through kinship. Although each band has rights to the territory it occupies and the resources within it, two or more bands may range over the same territory. The head, called the *kxau* or "owner," is the focal point for the band's theoretical ownership of the territory. The headman or headwoman does not really own the land or resources but symbolically personifies the rights of band members to them. If the head leaves a territory to live elsewhere, he or she ceases to be the band's head, and people turn to someone else to lead them.

The head coordinates the Ju/'hoansi band's movements when resources are no longer adequate for subsistence in a particular territory. This leader's chief duty is to plan when and where the group will move; when the move begins, his or her position is at the head of the line. The leader chooses the site for the new settlement and has the first choice of a spot for his or her own fire. The head has no other rewards or duties. For example, a head does not organize hunting parties, trading expeditions, the making of artifacts, or gift giving, nor does this leader make marriage arrangements. Instead, individuals instigate their own activities. The headman or headwoman is not a judge and does not punish other band members. Wrongdoers are judged and regulated by public opinion, usually expressed by gossip among band members. A prime technique for resolving disputes, or even avoiding them in the first place, is mobility. Those unable to get along with others of their group simply move to another group where kinship ties give them entry rights.

Tribal Organization

The second type of uncentralized or multicentric authority system is the **tribe**, a word that, unfortunately, is used in different ways by different people. Among the general public, it is used commonly to label any people who are not organized into states, irrespective of whether or not they consti-

tute what anthropologists would call bands, tribes, or chiefdoms. Sometimes, the term even is applied to non-Western peoples who in fact had strongly centralized states (the Aztecs, for example), a practice no more warranted than calling the Chinese people a tribe. Historically, Europeans coined the term to contrast people they regarded as inferior with supposedly superior, "civilized" Europeans. The word often is still used in a derogatory way, as when political unrest in many parts of the world is blamed on "tribalism," which is not accurate (usually, the strife is the direct consequence of the creation of multinational states that make it possible for a governing elite of one nationality to exploit others for their own benefit).[1] To complicate matters, the term *tribe* also has a distinct legal meaning in the United States; it refers to a centralized political organization imposed upon American Indian communities that traditionally were organized in a variety of ways—some as bands, some as tribes (in the anthropological sense), and some as chiefdoms.

So what, then, do anthropologists have in mind when they speak of tribal organization? To them, a tribal system involves separate bands or villages integrated by factors such as clans that unite people in separate communities or age grades or associations that crosscut kinship or territorial boundaries. In such cases people sacrifice a degree of household autonomy to a larger-order group in return for greater security against enemy attacks or starvation. Typically, though not invariably, a tribe has an economy based on some form of farming or herding. Since these production methods usually yield more food than those of the food-foraging band, tribal membership is usually larger than band membership. Compared to bands, where population densities are usually less than 1 person per square mile, tribal population densi-

---

[1]Whitehead, N. L., & Ferguson, R. B. (1993, November 10). Deceptive stereotypes about tribal warfare (p. A48). *Chronicle of Higher Education*. Van Den Berghe, P. L. (1992). The modern state: Nation builder or nation killer? *International Journal of Group Tensions, 92* (3), 199–200.

Tribe. A group of nominally independent communities occupying a specific region and sharing a common language and culture integrated by some unifying factor.

Shown here is a meeting of the Navajo Tribal Council, a non-traditional governing body created in response to requirements set by the U.S. government in order for the Navajo to exercise national sovereignty.

ties always exceed 1 person per square mile and may be as high as 250 per square mile. Greater population density in tribes than in bands brings a new set of problems to be solved as opportunities for bickering, begging, adultery, and theft increase markedly, especially among people living in sedentary villages.

Each tribe consists of one or more small, autonomous local communities, which then may form alliances with one another for various purposes. As in the band, political organization in the tribe is informal and temporary. Whenever a situation requiring political integration of all or several groups within the tribe arises—perhaps for defense, to carry out a raid, to pool resources in times of scarcity, or to capitalize on a windfall that must be distributed quickly lest it spoil—they join to deal with the situation in a cooperative manner. When the problem is satisfactorily solved, each group then returns to its autonomous state.

Leadership among tribes is also informal. The Navajo Indians, for example, did not think of government as something fixed and all-powerful, and

leadership was not vested in a central authority. A local leader was a man respected for his age, integrity, and wisdom. His advice therefore was sought frequently, but he had no formal means of control and could not force any decision on those who asked for his help. Group decisions were made by public consensus, although the most influential man usually played a key role in reaching a decision. Among the social mechanisms that induced members to abide by group decisions were withdrawal of cooperation, gossip, criticism, and the belief antisocial actions caused disease.

Another example of tribal leadership is the Melanesian Big Man. Such men are leaders of localized descent groups or of a territorial group. The Big Man combines a small amount of interest in his tribe's welfare with a great deal of self-interested cunning and calculation for his own gain. His authority is personal; he does not come to office in any formal sense, nor is he elected. His status is the result of acts that raise him above most other tribe members and attract to him a band of loyal followers.

Typical of this form of political organization are the Kapauku of west New Guinea. Among them, the Big Man is called the *tonowi,* or "rich one." To achieve this status, one must be male, wealthy, generous, and eloquent; physical bravery and skills in dealing with the supernatural also are frequent characteristics of a *tonowi,* but they are not essential. The *tonowi* functions as the headman of the village unit.

Kapauku culture places a high value on wealth, so it is not surprising that a wealthy man is considered successful and admirable. Yet the possession of wealth must be coupled with the trait of generosity, which in this society means not gift giving but willingness to make loans. Wealthy men who refuse to lend money to other villagers may be ostracized, ridiculed, and, in extreme cases, actually executed by a group of warriors. This social pressure ensures that economic wealth is rarely hoarded but instead is distributed throughout the group.

Through the loans he makes the *tonowi* acquires his political power. Other villagers comply with his requests because they are in his debt (often without paying interest), and they do not want to have to repay their loans. Those who have not yet borrowed from the *tonowi* may wish to do so in the future, so they, too, want to keep his goodwill.

Other sources of support for the *tonowi* are apprentices he has taken into his household for training. They are fed, housed, given a chance to learn the *tonowi's* business wisdom, and given a loan to get a wife when they leave; in return, they act as messengers and bodyguards. Even after they

This Big Man from New Guinea is wearing his "official" regalia.

leave his household, these men are tied to the *tonowi* by bonds of affection and gratitude. Political support also comes from the *tonowi's* kinsmen, whose relationship brings with it varying obligations.

The *tonowi* functions as a leader in a wide variety of situations. He represents his group when dealing with outsiders and other villages; he acts as negotiator and/or judge when disputes break out among his followers. Leopold Pospisil, who studied the Kapauku, notes:

> The multiple functions of a *tonowi* are not limited to the political and legal fields only. His word also carries weight in economic and social matters. He is especially influential in determining proper dates for pig feasts and pig markets, in inducing specific individuals to become co-sponsors at feasts, in

sponsoring communal dance expeditions to other villages, and in initiating large projects, such as extensive drainage ditches and main fences or bridges, the completion of which requires a joint effort of the whole community.[2]

The *tonowi's* wealth comes from his success at pig breeding (as we discussed in Chapter 14), for pigs are the focus of the entire Kapauku economy. Like all kinds of cultivation and domestication, raising pigs requires a combination of strength, skill, and luck. It is not uncommon for a *tonowi* to lose his fortune rapidly due to bad management or bad luck with his pigs. Thus the Kapauku political structure shifts frequently; as one man loses wealth and consequently power, another gains it and becomes a *tonowi*. These changes confer a degree of flexibility on the political organization and prevent any one *tonowi* from holding political power for too long.

Kinship Organization

In many tribal societies (as among the Kapauku) the organizing unit and seat of political authority is the clan, an association of people who believe themselves to share a common ancestry. Within the clan, elders or headmen regulate members' affairs and represent their clan in relations with other clans. As a group, the elders of all the clans may form a council that acts within the community or for the community in dealings with outsiders. Because clan members usually do not all live together in one community, clan organization facilitates joint action with members of other communities when necessary.

Another form of tribal kinship bond that provides political organization is the **segmentary lineage system.** This system is similar in operation to the clan, but it is less extensive and is relatively rare. The best known examples are East African

societies such as the Somali and the Dinka or Nuer of the Sudan: pastoral nomads who are highly mobile and widely scattered over large territories. Unlike other East African pastoralists (the Maasai, for example), they lack the age grading organization that cuts across descent group membership.

The economy of the segmentary tribe is generally just above subsistence level. Production is small scale, and the labor pool is just large enough to provide necessities. Since each lineage in the tribe produces the same goods, none depends on another for goods or services. Political organization among segmentary lineage societies is usually informal: They have neither political offices nor chiefs, although older tribal members may exercise some personal authority. In his classic study of segmentary lineage organization, Marshall Sahlins describes how this works among the Nuer.[3] According to Sahlins, segmentation is the normal process of tribal growth. It is also the social means for temporary unification of a fragmented tribal society to join in a particular action. The segmentary lineage may be viewed as a substitute for the fixed political structure, which a tribe cannot maintain.

Among the Nuer, who number some 200,000 people living in the swampland and savanna of Sudan, at least 20 clans exist. Each is patrilineal and is segmented into maximal lineages; each of these is in turn segmented into major lineages, which are segmented into minor lineages, which in turn are segmented into minimal lineages. The minimal lineage is a group descended from one great-grandfather or great-great-grandfather (Figure 23.1).

The lineage segments among the Nuer are all equal, and no real leadership or political organization at all exists above the level of the autonomous minimal or primary segments. The lineage's entire superstructure is nothing more than an alliance, active only during conflicts between

[2]Pospisil, L. (1963). *The Kapauku Papuans of west New Guinea* (pp. 51–52). New York: Holt, Rinehart and Winston.

[3]Sahlins, M. (1961). The segmentary lineage: An organization of predatory expansion. *American Anthropologist, 63,* 322–343.

Segmentary lineage system. A form of political organization in which a large group is broken up into clans that are further divided into lineages.

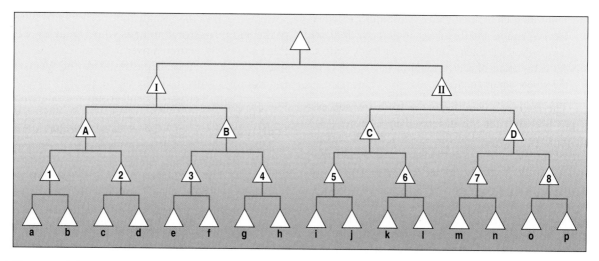

FIGURE 23.1

Segmentary lineage organization: a and b represent minimal lineages of 1; 1 and 2 represent minor lineages of A; A and B represent major lineages of I; and I and II represent maximal lineages of a single clan. In a serious dispute between (say) a and e, members of b, c, and d will join forces against e because they are more closely related to a than any are to e.

any of the minimal segments. In any serious dispute between members of different minimal lineage segments, members of all other segments take the side of the contestant they are most closely related to, and the issue is then joined between the higher-order lineages involved to address the issue. Such a system of political organization is known as *complementary* or *balanced opposition*.

Disputes among the Nuer are frequent, as they are among other groups with similar organization, and under the segmentary lineage system, they can lead to widespread feuds. This possible source of social disruption is minimized by the actions of the "leopard-skin chief," not really a chief but a holder of a ritual conciliation office. The leopard-skin chief has no political power and is viewed as standing outside the lineage network. All he can do is try to persuade feuding lineages to accept payment in "blood cattle" rather than taking another life. His mediation gives each side the chance to back down gracefully before too many people are killed; but if the participants are for some reason unwilling to compromise, the leopard-skin chief has no authority to enforce a settlement.

Age-Grade Organization

Age-grade systems provide a tribal society with a means of political integration beyond the kin group. Under this system, youths are initiated into an age grade, and then they pass as sets from one age grade to another at appropriate ages. Age grades and sets cut across territorial and kin groupings and thus may be important means of political organization. This is the case with the

Among the Nuer, the leopard-skin chief tries to settle disputes between lineages.

Tiriki of East Africa, whose age grades and sets we examined in Chapter 22. Among them, the warrior age grade guards the country, while judicial elders resolve disputes. Between these two age grades are elder warriors, who are in a sense understudies to the judicial elders. The oldest age grade, the ritual elders, advise on matters involving the well-being of all the Tiriki people. Thus, the tribe's political affairs are in the hands of the age grades and their officers. Among East African pastoralists, those like the Tiriki with age-grading organization generally experience less feuding than those with segmentary lineage organization.

Association Organization

Common-interest associations that function as politically integrative systems within tribes are found in many areas of the world, including Africa, Melanesia, and India. A good example of associ-

ation organization functioned during the 19th century among the Plains Indians of the United States, such as the Cheyenne, whom we will talk about again later in this chapter. The basic Cheyenne territorial and political unit was the band, but seven military societies, or warriors' clubs, were common to the entire tribe; the clubs functioned in several areas. A boy might be invited to join one of these societies when he achieved warrior status, whereupon he became familiar with the society's particular insignia, songs, and rituals. In addition to military functions, the warriors' societies also had ceremonial and social functions.

The Cheyenne warriors' routine daily tasks consisted of overseeing movements in the camp, protecting a moving column, and enforcing rules against individual hunting when the whole tribe was on a buffalo hunt. In addition, each warrior society had its own repertoire of dances the members performed on special ceremonial occasions. Since each Cheyenne band had identical military societies bearing identical names, the societies served to integrate the entire tribe for military and political purposes.[4]

CENTRALIZED POLITICAL SYSTEMS

In bands and tribes, authority is uncentralized, and each group is economically and politically autonomous. Political organization is vested in kinship, age, and common-interest groups. Populations are small and relatively homogeneous, with people engaged mostly in the same sorts of activities throughout their lives. As a society's social life becomes more complex, however, as population rises and technology becomes more complex, and as specialization of labor and trade networks produce surpluses of goods, the opportunity for some individuals or groups to exercise control increases. In such societies, political authority and power are concentrated in a single individual—the chief—or in a body of individuals—the state. The state is a form of organization found in societies where each individual must interact on a regular basis with large numbers of people with diversified interests who are neither kin nor close acquaintances.

---

[4]Hoebel, E. A. (1960). *The Cheyennes: Indians of the Great Plains.* New York: Holt, Rinehart and Winston.

Chiefdoms

A **chiefdom** is a regional polity in which two or more local groups are organized under a single ruling individual—the chief—who is at the head of a ranked hierarchy of people. An individual's status in such a polity is determined by his or her closeness of relationship to the chief. Those closest are officially superior and receive deferential treatment from those in lower ranks.

The office of the chief is usually hereditary, passing from a man to his own or his sister's son, depending on whether descent is reckoned patrilineally or matrilineally. Unlike the headmen in bands and lineages, the chief is generally a true authority figure, and his authority serves to unite his people in all affairs and at all times. For example, a chief can distribute land among his community members and recruit people into his military service. Chiefdoms have a recognized hierarchy consisting of major and minor authorities who control major and minor subdivisions. Such an arrangement is, in effect, a chain of command, linking leaders at every level. It serves to bind tribal groups in the heartland to the chief's headquarters, be it a mud and dung hut or a marble palace.

The chief controls the economic activities of his people. Chiefdoms are typically redistributive systems; the chief has control over surplus goods and perhaps even over the community labor force. Thus, he may demand a quota of rice from farmers, which he will redistribute to the entire community. Similarly, he may recruit laborers to build irrigation works, a palace, or a temple.

The chief also may amass a great amount of personal wealth and pass it on to his heirs. Land, cattle, and luxury goods specialists produce can be collected by the chief and become part of his power base. Moreover, high-ranking families of the chiefdom may engage in the same practice and use their possessions as evidence of status.

An example of people using this form of political organization is the Kpelle of Liberia in West Africa.[5] Among them is a class of paramount chiefs, each of whom presides over one of the Kpelle chiefdoms (each of which is now a district of the Liberian state). The paramount chiefs' traditional tasks are hearing disputes, preserving order, seeing to the upkeep of trails, and maintaining "medicines." In addition, they now are salaried officials of the Liberian government, mediating between it and their people. Other rewards a paramount chief receives include a commission on taxes collected within his chiefdom, a commission for laborers furnished for the rubber plantations, a portion of court fees collected, a stipulated amount of rice from each household, and gifts from people who come to request favors and intercessions. In keeping with his exalted station in life, a paramount chief has at his disposal uniformed messengers, a literate clerk, and the symbols of wealth: many wives, embroidered gowns, and freedom from manual labor.

In a ranked hierarchy beneath each Kpelle paramount chief are several lesser chiefs: one for each district within the chiefdom, one for each town

---

[5]Gibbs, J. L., Jr. (1965). The Kpelle of Liberia. In J. L. Gibbs Jr. (Ed.), *Peoples of Africa* (pp. 216–218). New York: Holt, Rinehart and Winston.

Chiefdom. A regional polity in which two or more local groups are organized under a single chief, who is at the head of a ranked hierarchy of people.

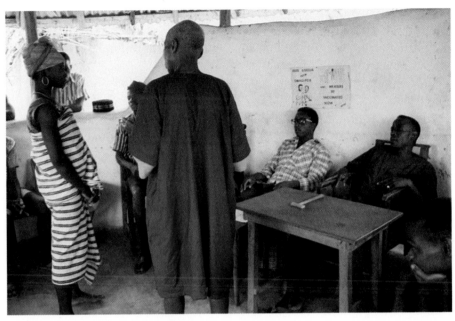

A Kpelle town chief settles a dispute.

within a district, and one for each quarter of all but the smallest towns. Each acts as a kind of lieutenant for his chief of the next higher rank and also serves as a liaison between him and those of lower rank. Unlike paramount or district chiefs, who are comparatively remote, town and quarter chiefs are readily accessible to people at the local level.

Stable though the Kpelle political system may be today, traditionally chiefdoms in all parts of the world have been highly unstable. This happens as lesser chiefs try to take power from higher ranking chiefs or as paramount chiefs vie with one another for supreme power. In precolonial Hawaii, for example, war was the way to gain territory and maintain power; great chiefs set out to conquer one another in an effort to become paramount chief of all the islands. When one chief conquered another, the loser and all his nobles were dispossessed of all property and were lucky if they escaped alive. The new chief then appointed his own supporters to positions of political power. As a consequence, governmental or religious administration had very little continuity.

State Systems

The **state**, the most formal of political organizations, is (like stratification) one of the hallmarks of civilization. In the state, political power is centralized in a government, which may legitimately use force to regulate the affairs of its citizens, as well as its relations with other states. As anthropologist Bruce Knauft observes:

> It is likely . . . that coercion and violence as systematic means of organizational constraint developed especially with the increasing socioeconomic complexity and potential for political hierarchy afforded by substantial food surplus and food production.[6]

Associated with increased food production is increased population. Together, these lead to a filling in of the landscape, improvements such as

---

[6]Knauft, B. M. (1991). Violence and sociality in human evolution. *Current Anthropology, 32,* 391.

State. In anthropology, a centralized political system with the power to coerce.

Reflecting the state's ability to force people to abide by its decisions are institutions to administer force, like police.

irrigation and terracing, carefully managed rotation cycles, intensive competition for clearly demarcated lands, and rural populations large enough to support market systems and a specialized urban sector. Under such conditions, corporate groups that stress exclusive membership proliferate, ethnic differentiation and ethnocentrism become more pronounced, and the potential for social conflict increases dramatically. Given these circumstances, the state institutions, which minimally involve a bureaucracy, a military, and (usually) an official religion, provide a means for numerous and diverse groups to function together as an integrated whole.

Although their guiding ideology pretends they are permanent and stable, the fact is, since their first appearance some 5,000 years ago, states have been anything but permanent. Whatever stability they have achieved has been short term at best; over the long term, they show a clear tendency toward instability and transience. Nowhere have

states even begun to show the staying power exhibited by more uncentralized political systems, the longest lasting social forms invented by humans.

An important distinction to make at this point is between **nation** and state. Today, there are roughly 181 states in the world, and most did not exist before the end of World War II. By contrast, probably about 5,000 nations exist in the world today. "What makes each a nation is that its people share a language, culture, territorial base, and political organization and history."[7] Today, states commonly have living within their boundaries people of more than one nation; for example, the Yanomami are but one of many nations within the state of Brazil (other Yanomami live within the state of Venezuela). Rarely do state and nation co-

---

[7]Clay, J. W. (1996). What's a nation? In W. A. Haviland & R. J. Gordon (Eds.), *Talking about people* (2nd ed., p. 188). Mountain View, CA: Mayfield.

Nation. Communities of people who see themselves as "one people" on the basis of common ancestry, history, society, institutions, ideology, language, territory, and (often) religion.

incide, as they do, for example, in Iceland, Japan, Somalia, and Swaziland. By contrast, some 73% of the world's states are multinational.[8]

An important aspect of the state is its delegation of authority to maintain order within and outside its borders. Police, foreign ministries, war ministries, and other bureaucracies function to control and punish disruptive acts of crime, terror, and rebellion. By such agencies the state asserts authority impersonally and in a consistent, predictable manner.

Western forms of government, such as that of the United States (in reality, a mega state), of course, are state governments, and their organization and workings are undoubtedly familiar to most everyone. An example of a not-so-familiar state is that of the Swazi of Swaziland (one of the world's few true nation-states), a Bantu-speaking people who live in southeast Africa.[9] They are primarily farmers, but cattle raising is more highly valued than farming: the ritual, wealth, and power of their authority system are all intricately linked with cattle. In addition to farming and cattle raising, some specialization of labor occurs; certain people become specialists in ritual, smithing, wood carving, and pottery. Their goods and services are traded, although the Swazi do not have elaborate markets.

The Swazi authority system is characterized by a highly developed dual monarchy, a hereditary aristocracy, and elaborate kinship rituals, as well as by statewide age sets. The king and his mother are the central figures of all national activity, linking all the people of the Swazi state: They preside over higher courts, summon national gatherings, control age classes, allocate land, disburse national wealth, take precedence in ritual, and help organize important social events.

Advising the Swazi king are the senior princes, who are usually his uncles and half-brothers. Between the king and the princes are two specially

created *tinsila,* or "blood brothers," who are chosen from certain common clans. These men are his shields, protecting him from evildoers and serving him in intimate personal situations. In addition, the king is guided by two *tindvuna,* or counselors, one civil and one military. The people of the state make their opinions known through two councils: the *liqoqo,* or privy council, composed of senior princes, and the *libanda,* or council of state, composed of chiefs and headmen and open to all adult males of the state. The *liqoqo* may advise the king, make decisions, and carry them out. For example, they may rule on questions about land, education, traditional ritual, court procedure, and transport.

Swazi government extends from the smallest local unit—the homestead—upward to the central administration. The head of a homestead has legal and administrative powers; he is responsible for the crimes of those under him, controls their property, and speaks for them before his superiors. On the district level, political organization is similar to that of the central government. The relationship between a district chief, however, and his subjects is personal and familiar; he knows all the families in his district. The main check on any autocratic tendencies he may exhibit rests in his subjects' ability to transfer their allegiance to a more responsive chief. Swazi officials hold their positions for life and are dismissed only for treason or witchcraft. Incompetence, drunkenness, and stupidity are frowned upon, but they are not considered sufficient grounds for dismissal.

[8]Van Den Berghe, P. L. (1992). The modern state: Nation builder or nation killer? *International Journal of Group Tensions, 92* (3), 193.

[9]Kuper, H. (1965). The Swazi of Swaziland. In J. L. Gibbs Jr. (Ed.), *Peoples of Africa* (pp. 475–512). New York: Holt, Rinehart and Winston.

POLITICAL LEADERSHIP AND GENDER

Irrespective of cultural configuration, or type of political organization, women rarely hold important positions of political leadership. Furthermore, when they do occupy publicly recognized offices, their power and authority rarely exceed those of men. Nevertheless, exceptions occur, and recent ones are Corazon Aquino, Sirimavo Badaranaike, Benazir Bhutto, Gro Harlem Brundtland, Indira Ghandi, Janet Jagan, Golda Meir, and Margaret Thatcher, who do head or have headed governments of the Philippines, Sri Lanka, Pakistan, Norway, India, Guyana, Israel, and Great Britain, respectively. Historically, one might cite the occasional "squaw sachems" (woman chiefs) mentioned in early accounts of New England Indians, the last native monarch of Hawaii, and powerful queens such as Elizabeth I of England or Catherine the Great of Russia. When women do hold high office, it is often because of their relationship to men. Thus, a queen is either the wife of a reigning monarch or else the daughter of a king who died without a male heir to succeed him. Moreover, women in focal positions frequently must adopt many of the characteristics of temperament normally deemed appropriate for men in their societies. For instance, in her role as prime minister, Margaret Thatcher displayed the toughness and assertiveness that, in Western societies, long have been considered desirable masculine qualities, rather than the nurturance and compliance Westerners traditionally have expected of women.

In spite of all this, in a number of societies, women regularly enjoy as much political power as men. In band societies, it is common for them to have as much of a say in public affairs as men, even though the latter more often than not are the nominal leaders of their groups. Among the Iroquoian nations of New York State (discussed in Chapter 22), all leadership positions above the household level were, without exception, filled by men. Thus they held all positions on the village and tribal councils, as well as on the great council of the league of Five Nations. However, they were completely beholden to women, for only the latter could appoint men to high office. Moreover, women actively lobbied the men on the councils

This Seneca chief, Cornplanter, participated in three treaties with the United States in the late 18th century. Although Iroquoian chiefs were always men, they served strictly at the pleasure of women, whose position in society was equal to that of men.

and could remove someone from office whenever it suited them.

As these cases make clear, low visibility of women in politics does not necessarily exclude them from the realm of social control nor does it mean men have more power in political affairs. Sometimes, though, women may play more visible roles, as in the dual-sex systems of West Africa. Among the Igbo of Nigeria, in each political unit, separate political institutions for men and women give each sex their autonomous spheres of authority, as well as an area of shared responsibility.[10] At the head of each was a male *obi*, consid-

[10]Okonjo, K. (1976). The dual-sex political system in operation: Igbo women and community politics in midwestern Nigeria. In N. Hafkin & E. Bay (Eds.), *Women in Africa*. Stanford, CA: Stanford University Press.

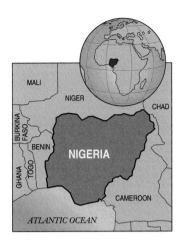

ATLANTIC OCEAN

ered the head of government though in fact he presided over the male community, and a female *omu,* the acknowledged mother of the whole community but in practice concerned with the female section. Unlike a queen (though both she and the *obi* were crowned), the *omu* was neither the *obi's* wife nor the previous *obi's* daughter.

Just as the Igbo *obi* had a council of dignitaries to advise him and to act as a check against any arbitrary exercise of power, the *omu* was served by a council of women in equal number to the *obi's* male councilors. The duties of the *omu* and her councilors involved tasks such as establishing rules and regulations for the community market (marketing was a women's activity) and hearing cases involving women brought to her from throughout the town or village. If such cases also involved men, then she and her council would cooperate with the *obi* and his council. Widows also went to the *omu* for the final rites required to end their period of mourning for dead husbands. Since the *omu* represented all women, she had to be responsive to her constituency and would seek their approval and cooperation in all major decisions.

In addition to the *omu* and her council, the Igbo women's government included a representative body of women chosen from each quarter or section of the village or town on the basis of their ability to think logically and speak well. In addition, acting at the village or lineage level, were political-pressure groups of women who acted to stop quarrels and prevent wars. These were of two types: women born into a community, most of

whom lived elsewhere since villages were exogamous and residence was patrilocal, and women who had married into their community. Their duties included helping companion wives in times of illness and stress and meting out discipline to lazy or recalcitrant husbands.

In the Igbo system, then, women managed their own affairs, and their interests were represented at all levels of government. Moreover, they had the right to enforce their decisions and rules with sanctions similar to those men employed. Included were strikes, boycotts, and "sitting on a man" or woman. Political scientist Judith Van Allen describes the latter:

> To "sit on" or "make war on" a man involved gathering at his compound, sometimes late at night, dancing, singing scurrilous songs which detailed the women's grievances against him and often called his manhood into question, banging on his hut with the pestles women used for pounding yams, and perhaps demolishing his hut or plastering it with mud and roughing him up a bit. A man might be sanctioned in this way for mistreating his wife, for violating the women's market rules, or for letting his cows eat the women's crops. The women would stay at his hut throughout the day, and late into the night if necessary, until he repented and promised to mend his ways. . . . Although this could hardly have been a pleasant experience for the offending man, it was considered legitimate and no man would consider intervening.[11]

Given the high visibility of women in the Igbo political system, it may come as a surprise to learn that when the British imposed colonial rule upon these people, they failed to recognize the autonomy and power those women possessed. The reason is the British were blinded by their Victorian values, which then were at their height. To them, a woman's mind was not strong enough for such supposedly masculine subjects as science, business, and politics; her place was clearly in the home. Hence, it was inconceivable women might play important roles in politics. As a consequence, the

---

[11]Van Allen, J. (1979). Sitting on a man: Colonialism and the lost political institutions of Igbo women. In S. Tiffany (Ed.), *Women in society* (p. 169). St. Albans, VT: Eden Press.

British introduced "reforms" that destroyed women's traditional forms of autonomy and power without providing alternative forms in exchange. Far from enhancing women's status, as Western people like to think their influence does, in this case, women lost their equality and became subordinate to men. Nor is the Igbo situation unusual in this regard. Historically, in state-organized societies, women usually have been subordinate to men. Hence, when states impose their control on societies where the sexes are equal to each other, the situation almost invariably changes so that women become subordinate to men.

▲▽▲▽▲▽▲▽▲▽▲▽▲▽▲▽▲▽▲▽▲▽▲▽▲▽▲

POLITICAL ORGANIZATION AND THE MAINTENANCE OF ORDER

Whatever form a society's political organization may take, and whatever else it may do, it is always involved in one way or another with maintaining social order. Always it seeks to ensure that people behave in acceptable ways and defines the proper action to take when they do not. In chiefdoms and states, some sort of authority has the power to regulate the affairs of society. In bands and tribes, however, people behave generally as they are expected to, without the direct intervention of any centralized political authority. To a large degree, gossip, criticism, fear of supernatural forces, and the like serve as effective deterrents to antisocial behavior.

As an example of how such seemingly informal considerations serve to keep people in line, we may look at the Wape people of Papua New Guinea, who believe the ghosts of dead ancestors roam lineage lands, protecting them from trespassers and helping their hunting descendants by driving game their way.[12] These ghosts also punish those who have wronged them or their descendants by preventing hunters from finding

game or by causing them to miss their shots, thereby depriving people of much needed meat. Nowadays, the Wape hunt with shotguns, which the community purchases for the use of one man, whose job it is to hunt for all the others. The cartridges used in the hunt, however, are invariably supplied by individual community members. Not always is the gunman successful; if he shoots and misses, it is because the owner of the fired shell, or some close relative, has quarreled or wronged another person whose ghost relative is securing revenge by causing the hunter to miss. Or, if the gunman cannot even find game, it is because vengeful ghosts have chased the animals away. As a proxy hunter for the villagers, the gunman is potentially subject to ghostly sanctions in response to collective wrongs by those he hunts for.

For the Wape, then, successful hunting depends upon avoiding quarrels and maintaining tranquility within the community so as not to antagonize anybody's ghost ancestor. Unfortunately, complete peace and tranquility are impossible to achieve in any human community, and the Wape are no exception. Thus, when hunting is poor, the gunman must discover what quarrels and wrongs have occurred within his village to identify the proper ancestral ghosts to appeal to for renewed success. Usually, this is done in a special meeting where confessions of wrongdoing may be forthcoming. If not, questioning accusations are bandied about until resolution occurs, but even with no resolution, the meeting must end amicably to prevent new antagonisms. Thus, everyone's behavior comes under public scrutiny, reminding everyone of what is expected of them and encouraging everyone to avoid acts that will cast them in an unfavorable light.

INTERNALIZED CONTROLS

The Wape concern about ancestral ghosts is a good example of internalized, or cultural, controls—beliefs so thoroughly ingrained that each person becomes personally responsible for his or her own conduct. **Cultural control** may be thought of as control by the mind, as opposed to **social control,**

---

[12]Mitchell, W. E. (1973, December). A new weapon stirs up old ghosts. *Natural History Magazine*, 77–84.

Cultural control. Control through beliefs and values deeply internalized in the minds of individuals. **> Social control.** Control over groups through open coercion.

which involves overt coercion. Examples of cultural control also can be found in North American society; for instance, people refrain from committing incest not so much from fear of legal punishment as from a sense of deep disgust at the thought of the act and from the shame they would feel in performing it. Obviously, not all members of North American society feel this disgust, or such a high incidence of incest would not occur, especially between fathers and daughters, but, then, no deterrent to misbehavior is ever 100% effective. Cultural controls are built in, or internalized, and rely on such deterrents as fear of supernatural punishment—ancestral ghosts sabotaging the hunting, for example—and magical retaliation. Like the devout Christian who avoids sinning for fear of hell, the individual expects some sort of punishment, even though no one in the community may be aware of the wrongdoing.

EXTERNALIZED CONTROLS

Because internalized controls are not wholly sufficient even in bands and tribes, every society develops customs designed to encourage conformity to social norms. These institutions are referred to as **sanctions;** they are externalized controls and involve varying mixes of cultural and social control. According to Radcliffe-Brown, "A sanction is a reaction on the part of a society or of a considerable number of its members to a mode of behavior which is thereby approved (positive sanctions) or disapproved (negative sanctions)."[13] Sanctions also may be either formal or informal and may vary significantly within a given society.

Sanctions operate within social groups of all sizes. Moreover, they need not be enacted into law to play a significant role in regulating peoples' behavior: "They include not only the organized sanctions of the law but also the gossip of neighbors or the customs regulating norms of production that

[13]Radcliffe-Brown, A. R. (1952). *Structure and function in primitive society* (p. 205). New York: Free Press.

are spontaneously generated among workers on the factory floor. In small scale communities . . . informal sanctions may become more drastic than the penalties provided for in the legal code."[14] If, however, a sanction is to be effective, it cannot be arbitrary. Quite the opposite: Sanctions must be consistently applied, and the society's members must know generally of their existence.

Social sanctions may be categorized as either positive or negative. Positive sanctions consist of incentives to conformity, such as awards, titles, and recognition by one's neighbors. Negative sanctions consist of threats, such as imprisonment, corporal

[14]Epstein, A. L. (1968). Sanctions. *International Encyclopedia of Social Sciences* (Vol. 14, p. 3).

Jody Williams, who in 1997 was awarded the Nobel Peace Prize for her work to ban the use of land mines. Awards such as the Nobel Prize are examples of positive sanctions, by which societies promote approved behavior.

Sanctions.   Externalized social controls designed to encourage conformity to social norms.

punishment, or ostracism from the community for violation of social norms. One example of a negative sanction discussed earlier is the Igbo practice of "sitting on a man." If some individuals are not convinced of the advantages of social conformity, they are still more likely to obey society's rules than to accept the consequences of not doing so.

Sanctions also may be categorized as either formal or informal, depending on whether or not a legal statute is involved. In the United States, the man who wears tennis shorts to a church service may be subject to a variety of informal sanctions, ranging from disapproving glances from the clergy to the chuckling of other parishioners. If, however, he were to show up without any trousers at all, he would be subject to the formal negative sanction of arrest for indecent exposure. Only in the second instance would he have been guilty of breaking the **law.**

Formal sanctions, such as laws, are always organized, because they attempt to precisely and explicitly regulate people's behavior. Other examples of organized sanctions include, on the positive side, military decorations and monetary rewards. On the negative side are loss of face, exclusion from social life and its privileges, seizure of property, imprisonment, and even bodily mutilation or death.

Informal sanctions emphasize cultural control and are diffuse in nature, involving spontaneous expressions of approval or disapproval by members of the group or community. They are, nonetheless, very effective in enforcing a large number of seemingly unimportant customs. Because most people want to be accepted, they are willing to acquiesce to the rules that govern dress, eating, and conversation, even in the absence of actual laws.

To show how informal sanctions work, we will examine them in the context of power relationships among the Bedouins of Egypt's western desert. The example is especially interesting, for it shows how sanctions not only act to control peoples' behavior but also act to keep individuals in their place in a hierarchical society.

Negative sanctions may involve some form of regulated combat, seen here as armed dancers near Mount Hagen in New Guinea demand redress for murder.

Law. Formal negative sanctions.

Limits on Power in Bedouin Society[15]

▲▽

Where individuals value their independence and believe in equality, those who exercise authority over others enjoy a precarious status. In Bedouin society, social precedence or power depends not on force but on demonstration of the moral virtues that win respect from others. Persons in positions of power are said to have social standing (*gíma*), which is recognized by the respect paid them. To win the respect of others, in particular dependents, such persons must adhere to the ideals of honor, provide for and protect their dependents, and be fair, taking no undue advantage of their positions. They must assert their authority gingerly lest it so compromise their dependents' autonomy that it provoke rebellion and be exposed as a sham.

Because those in authority are expected to treat their dependents, even children, with some respect, they must draw as little attention as possible to the inequality of their relationships. Euphemisms that obscure the nature of such relationships abound. For example, Sa'ádi [free tribes] individuals do not like to call Mrábit [client tribes] associates Mrábtín in their presence. My host corrected me once when I referred to his shepherds by the technical word for shepherd, saying, "We prefer to call them 'people of the sheep' [*hal il-ghanam*]. It sounds nicer." The use of fictive kin terms serves the same function of masking relations of inequality, as for example in the case of patrons and clients.

Those in authority are also expected to respect their dependents' dignity by minimizing open assertion of their power over them. Because the provider's position requires dependents, he risks losing his power base if he alienates them. When a superior publicly orders, insults, or beats a dependent, he invites the rebellion that would undermine his position. Such moments are fraught with tension, as the dependent might feel the need to respond to a public humiliation to preserve his dignity or honor. Indeed, refusal to comply with an unreasonable order, or an order given in a compromising way, reflects well on the dependent and undercuts the authority of the person who gave it.

Tyranny is never tolerated for long. Most dependents wield sanctions that check the power of their providers. Anyone can appeal to a mediator to intervene on his or her behalf, and more radical solutions are open to all but young children. Clients can simply leave an unreasonable patron and attach themselves to a new one. Young men can always escape the tyranny of a father or paternal uncle by leaving to join maternal relatives or, if they have them, affines, or even to become clients to some other family. For the last twenty years or so, young men could go to Libya to find work.

Younger brothers commonly get out from under difficult elder brothers by splitting off from them, demanding their share of the patrimony and setting up separate households. The dynamic is clear in the case of four brothers who constituted the core of the camp in which I lived. Two had split off and lived in separate households. Another two still shared property, herds,

---

[15]Abu-Lughod, L. (1986). *Veiled sentiments: Honor and poetry in a Bedouin society* (pp. 99–103). Berkeley: University of California Press.

and expenses. While I was there, tensions began to develop. Although the elder brother was more important in the community at large, and the younger brother was slightly irresponsible and less intelligent, for the most part they worked various enterprises jointly and without friction. The younger brother deferred to his older brother and usually executed his decisions.

But one day the tensions surfaced. The elder brother came home at midday in a bad mood only to find that no one had prepared him lunch. He went to one of his wives and scolded her for not having prepared any lunch, asserting that his children had complained that they were hungry. He accused her of trying to starve his children and threatened to beat her. His younger brother tried to intervene, but the elder brother then turned on him, calling him names. Accusing him of being lazy (because he had failed to follow through on a promise involving the care of the sheep that day), he then asked why the younger brother let his wife get away with sitting in her room when there was plenty of work to be done around the household. Then he went off toward his other wife carrying a big stick and yelling.

The younger brother was furious and set off to get their mother. The matriarch, accompanied by another of her sons, arrived and conferred at length with the quarreling men. The younger son wished to split off from his elder brother's household; the other brother scolded him for being so sensitive about a few words, reminding him that this was his elder brother, from whom even a beating should not matter. His mother disapproved of splitting up the households. Eventually everyone calmed down. But it is likely that a few more incidents such as that will eventually lead the younger brother to demand a separate household.

Even a woman can resist a tyrannical husband by leaving for her natal home "angry" (mughtáóa). This is the approved response to abuse, and it forces the husband or his representatives to face the scolding of the woman's kin and, sometimes, to appease her with gifts. Women have less recourse against tyrannical fathers or guardians, but various informal means to resist the imposition of unwanted decisions do exist. As a last resort there is always suicide, and I heard of a number of both young men and women who committed suicide in desperate resistance to their fathers' decisions, especially regarding marriage. One old woman's tale illustrates the extent to which force can be resisted, even by women. Náfla reminisced:

> My first marriage was to my paternal cousin [ibn 'amm]. He was from the same camp. One day the men came over to our tent. I saw the tent full of men and wondered why. I heard they were coming to ask for my hand [yukhultú fiyya]. I went and stood at the edge of the tent and called out, "If you're planning to do anything, stop. I don't want it." Well, they went ahead anyway, and every day I would cry and say that I did not want to marry him. I was young, perhaps fourteen. When they began drumming and singing, everyone assured me that it was in celebration of another cousin's wedding, so I sang and danced along with them. This went on for days. Then on the day of the wedding my aunt and another relative caught me in the tent and suddenly closed it and took out the washbasin. They wanted to bathe me. I screamed. I screamed and screamed; every time they held a pitcher of water to wash me with, I knocked it out of their hands.

His relatives came with camels and dragged me into the litter and took me to his tent. I screamed and screamed when he came into the tent in the afternoon [for the defloration]. Then at night, I hid among the blankets. Look as they might, they couldn't find me. My father was furious. After a few days he insisted I had to stay in my tent with my husband. As soon as he left, I ran off and hid behind the tent in which the groom's sister stayed. I made her promise not to tell anyone I was there and slept there.

But they made me go back. That night, my father stood guard nearby with his gun. Every time I started to leave the tent, he would take a puff on his cigarette so I could see that he was still there. Finally I rolled myself up in the straw mat. When the groom came, he looked and looked but could not find me.

Finally I went back to my family's household. I pretended to be possessed. I tensed my body, rolled my eyes, and everyone rushed about, brought me incense and prayed for me. They brought the healer [or holyman, *fgih*], who blamed the unwanted marriage. Then they decided that perhaps I was too young and that I should not be forced to return to my husband. I came out of the seizure, and they were so grateful that they forced my husband's family to grant a divorce. My family returned the bride-price, and I stayed at home.

Náfla could not oppose her father's decision directly, but she was nevertheless able to resist his will through indirect means. Like other options for resistance by dependents unfairly treated, abused, or humiliated publicly, her rebellion served as a check on her father's and, perhaps, more important, her paternal uncle's power.

Supernatural sanctions, which seem to be associated with the weak and with dependents, provide the final check on abuse of authority. Supernatural retribution is believed to follow when the saintly lineages of Mrábtín are mistreated, their curses causing death or the downfall of the offender's lineage. In one Bedouin tale, when a woman denied food to two young girls, she fell ill, and blood appeared on food she cooked—a punishment for mistreating the helpless. Possession, as Náfla's tale illustrates, may also be a form of resistance. . . .

All these sanctions serve to check the abuse of power by eminent persons who have the resources to be autonomous and to control those who are dependent upon them. At the same time, moreover, figures of authority are vulnerable to their dependents because their positions rest on the respect these people are willing to give them.

Another agent of control in societies, whether or not they possess centralized political systems, may be witchcraft. An individual naturally would hesitate to offend a neighbor when that neighbor might retaliate by resorting to black magic. Similarly, individuals may not wish to be accused of practicing witchcraft, so they behave with greater circumspection. Among the Azande of the Sudan, people who think they have been bewitched may consult an oracle, who, after performing the appropriate mystical rites, then may establish or confirm the identity of the offending witch.[16] Confronted with this evidence, the accused witch usually will agree to cooperate in order to avoid any additional trouble. Should the victim die, the relatives of the deceased may choose to make magic against the witch, ultimately accepting the death of some villager both as evidence of guilt and of the efficacy of their magic. For the Azande, witchcraft provides not only a sanction against antisocial behavior but also a means of dealing with natural hostilities and death. No one wishes to be thought of as a witch, and surely no one wishes to be victimized by one. By institutionalizing their emotional responses, the Azande successfully maintain social order. (For more on witchcraft, see Chapter 24.)

SOCIAL CONTROL THROUGH LAW

Among the Inuit of northern Canada, all offenses are considered to involve disputes between individuals; thus, they must be settled between the disputants themselves. One way they may do so is through a song duel, in which they heap insults upon one another in songs specially composed for the occasion. Although society does not intervene, its interests are represented by spectators, whose applause determines the outcome. If, however, social harmony cannot be restored—and that, rather than assigning and punishing guilt, is the goal— one or the other disputant may move to another band. Among the Inuit, the alternative to peaceful settlement is to leave the group. Ultimately, no binding legal authority exists.

In Western society, by contrast, someone who commits an offense against another person is subject to a series of complex legal proceedings. In criminal cases the primary concern is to assign and punish guilt, rather than to help out the victim. The offender will be arrested by the police; tried before a judge and, perhaps, a jury; and, if the crime is

serious enough, may be fined, imprisoned, or even executed. Rarely does the victim receive restitution or compensation. Throughout this chain of events, the accused party is dealt with by (presumably) disinterested police, judges, jurors, and jailers, who may have no personal acquaintance whatsoever with the plaintiff or the defendant. How strange this all seems from the standpoint of traditional Inuit culture! Clearly, the two systems operate under distinctly different assumptions.

DEFINITION OF LAW

Once two Inuit settle a dispute by engaging in a song contest, the affair is considered closed; no further action is expected. Would we choose to describe the outcome of such a contest as a legal decision? If every law is a sanction but not every sanction is a law, how are we to distinguish between social sanctions in general and those we apply the label of law to?

The definition of *law* has been a lively point of contention among anthropologists in the 20th century. In 1926, Malinowski argued that the rules of law are distinguished from the rules of custom in that "they are regarded as the obligation of one person and the rightful claim of another, sanctioned not by mere psychological motive, but by a definite social machinery of binding force based . . . upon mutual dependence."[17] In other words, laws exemplify social control because they employ overt coercion. An example of one rule of custom in contemporary North American society might be the dictate that guests at a dinner party should repay the person who gave the party with entertainment in the future. A host or hostess who does not receive a return invitation may feel cheated of something thought to be owed but has no legal claim against the ungrateful guest for the $22.67 spent on food. If, however, an individual was cheated of the same sum by the grocer when shopping, the law could be invoked. Although Malinowski's definition introduced several important elements of law, his failure to distinguish adequately between legal and nonlegal sanctions left

[16]Evans-Pritchard, E. E. (1937). *Witchcraft, oracles and magic among the Azande.* London: Oxford University Press.

[17]Malinowski, B. (1951). *Crime and custom in savage society* (p. 55). London: Routledge.

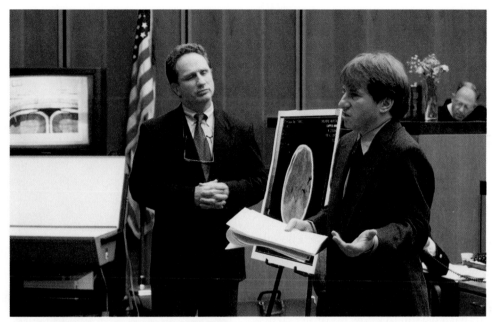

In Western society, someone who commits an offense against someone else is subject to a series of complex proceedings, in which the emphasis is on assigning and punishing guilt. In non-Western societies, by contrast, the emphasis is often on finding a solution that both parties can live with.

the problem of formulating a workable definition of *law* in the hands of later anthropologists.

An important pioneer in the anthropological study of law was E. Adamson Hoebel, according to whom "a social norm is legal if its neglect or infraction is regularly met, in threat or in fact, by the application of physical force by an individual or group possessing the socially recognized privilege of so acting."[18] In stressing the legitimate use of physical coercion, Hoebel de-emphasized the traditional association of law with a centralized court system. Although judge and jury are fundamental features of Western jurisprudence, they are not the universal backbone of human law. Some anthropologists have proposed that a precise definition of *law* is an impossible—and perhaps even undesirable—undertaking. When we speak of "the law," are we not inclined to fall back on our familiar Western conception of rules enacted by an authorized legislative body and enforced by the judicial mechanisms of the state? Can any concept of law be applied to such societies as the Nuer or the Inuit, for whom the notion of a centralized judiciary is virtually meaningless? How shall we categorize duels, song contests, and other socially condoned forms of self-help that seem to meet some but not all of the criteria of law?

Ultimately, it is always of greatest value to consider each case within its cultural context. Nonetheless, a working definition of *law* is useful for purposes of discussion and cross-cultural comparison, and for this *law* is adequately characterized as formal negative sanctions.

FUNCTIONS OF LAW

In *The Law of Primitive Man* (1954), Hoebel writes of a time when the notion that private property should be generously shared was a fundamental precept of Cheyenne Indian life. Subsequently,

---

[18]Hoebel, E. A. (1954). *The law of primitive man: A study in comparative legal dynamics* (p. 28). Cambridge, MA: Harvard University Press.

however, some men assumed the privilege of borrowing other men's horses without bothering to obtain permission. When Wolf Lies Down complained of such unauthorized borrowing to the members of the Elk Soldier Society, the Elk Soldiers not only had his horse returned to him but also secured an award for damages from the offender. The Elk Soldiers then announced that, to avoid such difficulties in the future, horses no longer could be borrowed without permission. Furthermore, they declared their intention to retrieve any such property and to administer a whipping to anyone who resisted their efforts to return improperly borrowed goods.

The case of Wolf Lies Down and the Elk Soldier Society clearly illustrates three basic functions of law. First, it defines relationships among society members, determining proper behavior under specified circumstances. Knowledge of the law permits each person to know his or her rights and duties in respect to every other society member. Second, law allocates the authority to employ coercion in the enforcement of sanctions. In societies with centralized political systems, such authority is generally vested in the government and its judiciary system. In societies that lack centralized political control, the authority to employ force may be allocated directly to the injured party. Third, law functions to redefine social relations and to ensure social flexibility. As new situations arise, law must determine whether old rules and assumptions retain their validity and the extent to which they must be altered. Law, if it is to operate efficiently, must allow room for change.

In practice, law is rarely the smooth and well-integrated system described here. In any given society, various legal sanctions may apply at various levels. Because the people in a society are usually members of numerous subgroups, they are subject to the dictates of these diverse groups. For example, each Kapauku is simultaneously a member of a family, a household, a sublineage, and a confederacy and is subject to all their laws. In some cases it may be impossible for an individual to submit to contradictory legal indications:

> In one of the confederacy's lineages, incestuous relations between members of the same clan were

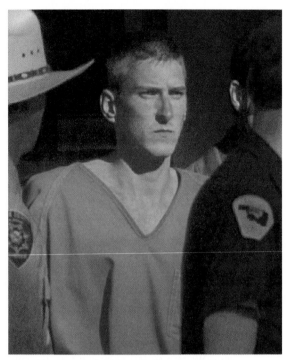

This picture of Timothy McVeigh, convicted of bombing the federal building in Oklahoma City, illustrates the role of overt coercion in law.

punished by execution of the culprits, and in another by severe beating, in the third constituent lineage such a relationship was not punishable and . . . was not regarded as incest at all. In one of the sublineages, it became even a preferred type of marriage.[19]

Furthermore, the power to employ sanctions may vary from level to level within a given society. The head of a Kapauku household may punish a household member by slapping or beating, but the authority to confiscate property is vested exclusively in the headman of the lineage. Analogous distinctions exist in the United States among municipal, state, and federal jurisdictions. The complexity of legal jurisdiction within each society makes any easy generalization about law difficult.

---

[19]Pospisil, L. (1971). *Anthropology of law: A comparative theory* (p. 36). New York: Harper & Row.

CRIME

As we have observed, an important function of sanctions, legal or otherwise, is to discourage the breach of social norms. A person contemplating theft is aware of the possibility of being caught and punished. Yet, even in the face of severe sanctions, individuals in every society sometimes violate the norms and subject themselves to the consequences of their behavior. What is the nature of crime in non-Western societies?

Western society makes a clear distinction between offenses against the state and offenses against an individual. *Black's Law Dictionary* tells us:

> The distinction between a crime and a tort or civil injury is that the former is a breach and violation of the public right and of duties due to the whole community considered as such, and in its social and aggregate capacity; whereas the latter is an infringement or privation of the civil rights of individuals merely.[20]

Thus, a reckless driver who crashes into another car may be guilty of a crime by endangering public safety. The same driver also may be guilty of a tort by causing damages to the other car, and the other driver can sue for their cost.

Many non-Western societies, however, have no conception of a central state. Consequently, all offenses are viewed as against individuals, rendering the distinction between crime and tort of no value. Indeed, a dispute between individuals may seriously disrupt the social order, especially in small groups where the number of disputants, though small in absolute numbers, may be a large percentage of the total population. Although the Inuit have no effective domestic or economic unit beyond the family, a dispute between two people will interfere with the ability of members of separate families to come to one another's aid when necessary and is consequently a matter of wider social concern. The goal of judicial proceedings in most cases is to restore social harmony, instead of punishing an offender. When distinguishing between offenses of concern to the community as a whole and those of concern only to a few individuals, we may refer to offenses as public or private, rather than distinguishing between criminal and civil law. In this way we may avoid values and assumptions irrelevant to a discussion of non-Western systems of law.

Basically, disputes are settled in either of two ways. First, disputing parties may, via argument and compromise, voluntarily arrive at a mutually satisfactory agreement. This form of settlement is referred to as **negotiation** or, if it involves an unbiased third party's assistance, **mediation.** In bands and tribes a third-party mediator has no coercive power and thus cannot force disputants to abide by such a decision, but as a person who commands great personal respect, the mediator frequently may effect a settlement through these judgments.

Second, in chiefdoms and states, an authorized third party may issue a binding decision the disputing parties will be compelled to respect. This process is referred to as **adjudication.** The difference between mediation and adjudication is basically a difference in authorization. In a dispute settled by adjudication, the disputing parties present their positions as convincingly as they can, but they do not participate in the ultimate decision making.

Although the adjudication process is not universally characteristic, every society employs some form of negotiation to settle disputes. Often negotiation acts as a prerequisite or an alternative to adjudication. For example, in the resolution of U.S. labor disputes, striking workers may first negotiate with management, often with the mediation of a third party. If the state decides the strike constitutes a threat to the public welfare, the disputing parties may be forced to submit to adjudication. In this case, the responsibility for resolving the dispute is transferred to a presumably impartial judge.

[20]Black, H. C. (1968). *Black's law dictionary.* St. Paul, MN: West.

Negotiation.   The use of direct argument and compromise by the parties to a dispute to arrive voluntarily at a mutually satisfactory agreement. > **Mediation.**   Settlement of a dispute through negotiation assisted by an unbiased third party. > **Adjudication.**   Mediation with an unbiased third party making the ultimate decision.

anthropology applied
Dispute Resolution and the Anthropologist

In an era when the peaceful resolution of disputes is increasingly valued, the field of dispute management is one of growing anthropological involvement (and employment). One practitioner is William L. Ury, an independent negotiations specialist who earned his PhD at Harvard University. His 1982 dissertation was titled *Talk Out or Walk Out: The Role and Control of Conflict in a Kentucky Coal Mine.*

At Harvard, Ury cofounded—with Roger Fisher of the law school—the Program on Negotiation. Together, the two also authored what has become the negotiator's "bible": *Getting to Yes: Negotiating Agreement Without Giving In* (published in 1981, it has been translated into 21 languages). In 1980, Ury helped the United States and Soviet Union replace their obsolete "hot line" with fully equipped nuclear crisis centers in each capital.

Ury now runs regular workshops on dealing with difficult people and situations. Among those who have enlisted his services is the Ford Motor Company, whose 6,000 top executives worldwide have taken his seminars. As one put it: "His influence on the company is incalculable. He inoculated a whole culture with a new way of looking at things."* Now, he specializes in ethnic and secessionist disputes, including those between White and Black South Africans, Serbs and Croats, and Turks and Kurds. One of his toughest jobs has been to mediate a peace between the Russians and Chechens, a task that has brought together other adversaries from the former Soviet Union as well: Tatars, Crimeans, Moldovans, and Georgians.

In his most recent book, *Getting Past No: Negotiating Your Way From Confrontation,* Ury praises the perspective of Japan's "home-run king" who viewed opposing "pitchers" not as enemies trying to do him in but as partners offering repeated opportunities to hit another ball out of the park. In dealing with the Chechens, one of his techniques was to have them imagine the speech Russian President Boris Yeltsin could give that would help his people accept the Chechens' goal. The Russians were asked to do the same: What kind of speech could the Chechen president give that would persuade his followers to remain in the Russian Federation?

Ury and others are helping to create a culture of negotiation in a world where adversarial, win-lose attitudes are out of step with the increasingly interdependent relations among people.

---

*Stewart, D. (1997). Expanding the pie before you divvy it up. *Smithsonian, 28,* 82.

The judge's work is difficult and complex. Not only must the evidence presented be sifted through, but also the judge must consider a wide range of norms, values, and earlier rulings to arrive at a decision intended to be considered just not only by the disputing parties but by the public and other judges as well.

In the United States, for the past 3 decades a significant movement away from the courts in favor of outside negotiation and mediation to resolve a wide variety of disputes has been occurring. Many jurists see this as a means to clear overloaded court dockets so as to concentrate on more important cases. A correlate of this move is a change in ideology, elevating order and harmony to positive values and replacing open coercion (seen as "undemocratic") with control through persuasion. In the abstract, this seems like a good change and suggests a return to a system of cultural control characteristic of band and tribal societies. However, a crucial difference exists. In tribal and band societies, consensus is less likely to be coercive, because all concerned individuals can negotiate and mediate on relatively equal terms. The United States, by contrast, has great disparities in power, and evidence indicates that it is the stronger parties that prefer mediation and negotiation. As anthropologist Laura Nader points out, now less emphasis is given on justice and on concern with the causes of disputes than on smoothing things over in ways that tend to be pacifying and restrictive; an emphasis that produces order of a repressive sort.[21]

In many politically centralized societies, incorruptible supernatural, or at least nonhuman, powers are thought to make judgments through trial by ordeal. Among the Kpelle of Liberia, for example, when guilt is in doubt an ordeal operator licensed by the government may apply a hot knife to a suspect's leg. If the leg is burned, the suspect is guilty; if not, innocence is assumed. But the operator does not merely heat the knife and apply it. After massaging the suspect's legs and determining the knife is hot enough, the operator then strokes his own leg with it without being burned, demonstrating that the innocent will escape injury. The knife is then applied to the suspect. Up to this point—consciously or unconsciously—the operator has read the suspect's

nonverbal cues: gestures, the degree of muscular tension, amount of perspiration, and so forth. From this the operator can judge whether or not the accused is showing enough anxiety to indicate probable guilt; in effect, a psychological stress evaluation has been made. As the knife is applied, it is manipulated to either burn or not burn the suspect, once this judgment has been made. The operator easily does this manipulation by controlling how long the knife is in the fire, as well as the pressure and angle at which it is pressed against the leg.[22]

Similar to this is the use of the lie detector (polygraph) in the United States, although the guiding ideology is scientific rather than supernaturalistic. Nevertheless, an incorruptible nonhuman agency is thought to establish who is lying and who is not, whereas in reality the polygraph operator cannot just "read" the needles of the machine. He or she must judge whether or not they are registering a high level of anxiety brought on by the testing situation, as opposed to the stress of guilt. Thus, the polygraph operator has much in common with the Kpelle ordeal operator.

---

[21]Nader, L. (1997). Controlling processes: Tracing the dynamic components of power. *Current Anthropology, 38,* 714–715.

[22]Gibbs, J. L., Jr. (1983). [Interview.] *Faces of culture: Program 18.* Fountain Valley, CA: Coast Telecourses.

Two means of psychological evaluation: a Kpelle trial by ordeal and a Western polygraph ("lie detector").

POLITICAL ORGANIZATION AND EXTERNAL AFFAIRS

Although the regulation of internal affairs is an important function of any political system, it is by no means the sole function. Another is the management of external or international affairs—relations not just between states but also between different bands, lineages, clans, or whatever the largest autonomous political unit may be. And just as threatened or actual force may be used to maintain order within a society, it also may be used in the conduct of external affairs.

WAR

One of the state's responsibilities is the organization and execution of war. Throughout the past few thousand years of history, people have engaged in a seemingly endless chain of wars and intergroup hostilities. Why do wars occur? Is the need to wage war an instinctive feature of the human personality? What are the alternatives to violence as a means of settling disputes between societies?

War is not a universal phenomenon, for in various parts of the world societies do not practice warfare as we know it. Examples include people as diverse as the Bushmen of southern Africa, the Arapesh of New Guinea, and the Hopi of North America. Among societies that do practice warfare, levels of violence may differ dramatically. Of warfare in New Guinea, for example, anthropologist Robert Gordon notes:

> It's slightly more "civilized" than the violence of warfare which we practice insofar as it's strictly between two groups. And as an outsider, you can go up and interview people and talk to them while they're fighting and the arrows will miss you. It's quite safe and you can take photographs. Now, of course, the problem with modern warfare is precisely that it kills indiscriminately and you can't do much research on it, but at the same time, you can learn a lot talking to these people about the dynamics of how violence escalates into full-blown warfare.[23]

We have ample reason to suppose war has become a problem only in the past 10,000 years, since the invention of food-production techniques and especially centralized states. It has reached crisis proportions in the past 200 years, with the invention of modern weaponry and increased direction of violence against civilian populations. In contemporary warfare, we have reached the point where casualties not just of civilians but also of *children* outnumber those of soldiers. Thus, war is not so much an age-old problem, as some have supposed, as it is a relatively recent one.

Among food foragers, with their uncentralized political systems, warfare is all but unknown, although violence emerges sporadically. Because territorial boundaries and membership of food-foraging bands are usually fluid and loosely defined, a man who hunts with one band today may hunt with a neighboring band tomorrow. Warfare is further rendered impractical by the systematic interchange of marriage partners among food-foraging groups—it is likely someone in each band will have a sister, a brother, or a cousin in a neighboring band. Moreover, absence of a food surplus does not permit prolonged combat. Where populations are small, food surpluses absent, property ownership minimal, and no state organization exists, the likelihood of organized violence by one group against another is minimal.[24]

Although peaceful farmers exist and despite the traditional view of the farmer as a gentle tiller of the soil, it is among such people, along with pastoralists, warfare becomes prominent. One reason may be that food-producing peoples are far more prone to population growth than are food foragers, whose numbers generally are maintained well below carrying capacity. This population growth, if unchecked, can lead to resource depletion, one solution to which may be seizure of some other people's resources. In addition, the commitment to a fixed piece of land inherent in farming makes such societies somewhat less fluid in their membership than those of food foragers. In rigidly matrilocal or patrilocal societies, each new generation is bound to the same territory, no matter how small it may be or how large the group trying to live within it.

[23]Gordon, R. J. (1981, December). [Interview.] Los Angeles: Coast Telecourses.

[24]Knauft, B. (1991). Violence and sociality in human evolution. *Current Anthropology, 32,* 391–409.

In Mexico, as in many countries of the world, armed conflict has become commonplace as governments controlled by one ethnic group seek to control members of other once autonomous ethnic groups in order to benefit from their resources and labor. Shown here are police of the Mexican state of Chiapas, with local Maya Indians and (in the bags) the bodies of sympathizers of the Zapatista rebel movement, 45 of whom were massacred in late 1997. The Zapatista movement is a largely Indian uprising following 500 years of exploitation by the Spanish and their descendants in Mexico.

The availability of virgin land may not serve as a sufficient detriment to the outbreak of war. Among slash-and-burn horticulturists, for example, competition for land cleared of virgin forest frequently leads to hostility and armed conflict. The centralization of political control and the possession of valuable property among farming people provide many more stimuli for warfare. When such peoples are organized into states, the violence of warfare is most apt to result in indiscriminate killing. This development has reached its peak in modern states. Indeed, much (but not all) of the warfare observed in stateless societies (so-called tribal warfare) has been induced by states, as a reaction to their colonial expansion.[25]

[25]Whitehead, N. L., & Ferguson, R. B. (1993, November). Deceptive stereotypes about tribal warfare. *Chronicle of Higher Education*, A48.

Another difference between food-gathering and food-producing populations lies in their different **worldviews**. As a general rule, food foragers tend to conceive of themselves as a part of the natural world and in some sort of balance with it. This is reflected in their attitudes toward the animals they kill. Western Abenaki hunters, for example, thought animals, like humans, were composed of both a body and a personal spirit. Although Abenakis hunted and killed animals to sustain their own lives, they clearly recognized that animals were entitled to proper respect. Thus, when beaver, muskrat, or waterfowl were killed, the hunters could not just toss their bones into the nearest garbage pit. Proper respect required that their bones be returned to the water, with a request that the species be continued. Such attitudes may be referred to as part of a naturalistic worldview.

Worldviews. The conceptions, explicit and implicit, an individual or a society has of the limits and workings of its world.

The Abenaki's respect for nature contrasts sharply with the kind of worldview prevalent among farmers and pastoralists, who do not find their food in nature but impose their dominance upon it to produce food for themselves. The attitude that nature exists only for human use may be referred to as an exploitative worldview. With such an outlook, it is a small step from dominating the rest of nature to dominating other societies for the benefit of one's own. The exploitative worldview, prevalent among food-producing peoples, is an important contributor to intersocietal warfare.

A comparison between the Western Abenakis and their Iroquoian neighbors to the west is instructive. Among the Abenakis warfare was essentially a defensive activity. These food foragers, with their naturalistic worldview, believed they could not operate in someone else's territory, since they did not control the necessary supernatural powers. Furthermore, operating far below carrying capacity, they had no need to prey upon the resources of others. The Iroquois, by contrast, were slash-and-burn horticulturists who engaged in predatory warfare. Evidence indicates significant environmental degradation around their settlements, suggesting overutilization of resources. Although the Iroquois went to war to replace men lost in previous battles, the main motive was to achieve dominance by making their victims acknowledge Iroquoian superiority. The relation between victim and victor, however, was subjection, rather than outright subordination. The payment of tribute purchased "protection" from the Iroquois, no doubt helping to offset the depletion of resources near the village of the would-be protectors. The price of protection went further than this, though; it included constant and public ceremonial deference to the Iroquois, free passage for their war parties through the subjugated group's country, and the contribution of young men to Iroquoian war parties.

A comparison between the Iroquois and Europeans is also instructive. Sometime in the 16th century, five Iroquoian nations—the Mohawks, Oneidas, Onondagas, Cayugas, and Senecas—determined to end warfare among themselves by the simple device of directing their predatory activities against outsiders, rather than each other. In this way the famous League of the Iroquois

came into being. Similarly, in the year 1095, Pope Urban II launched the Crusades with a speech urging European barons to end their ceaseless wars against each other by directing their hostilities outward against the Turks and Arabs. In that same speech he also alluded to the economic benefits to be realized by seizing the resources of the infidels. Although rationalized as a "holy war," the Crusades clearly were motivated by more than religious ideology.

Although the Europeans never did "liberate" the Holy Land, at least some of them did benefit from the booty obtained in battle, lending credence to the idea people could live better than they had before by locating and seizing the resources of others. Thus, the state formation that occurred in Europe in the centuries after A.D. 1000 was followed by colonial expansion into other parts of the world. Proceeding in concert with this growth and outward expansion was the development of the technology and organization of warfare.

The idea that warfare is an acceptable way to gain economic benefits is still a part of the European cultural tradition, as the following from a quite serious letter that appeared in New Hampshire's largest daily newspaper several years ago illustrates: "If a war is necessary to stabilize the economy, then we shall have a war. It affects the everyday lives of most of us so little that we need hardly acknowledge the fact that it is going on. Surely the sacrifice of a son, husband or father by a hundred or so of our citizens every week is not that overwhelming. They will forget their losses in time."[26] Certainly, we would like to think this kind of attitude is not widespread in the United States, and perhaps it is not, but we do not know this for a fact. Nor do we really know the extent it is or is not held by members of those segments of U.S. society that tend to influence the setting of public policy. These unknowns obviously raise important questions, and we need to find out more about them.

As the examples show, the causes of warfare are complex; economic, political, and ideological factors are all involved. With the emergence of states (not just in Europe but in other parts of the

---

[26]Quoted in MacNeil, R. (1982). *The right place at the right time* (p. 263). Boston: Little, Brown.

Shown here are U.S. soldiers in Haiti, where intervention to restore President Aristide to power fortunately turned out to be relatively peaceful. Since World War II, no state has gone to war as often as the United States.

world as well) has come a dramatic increase in the scale of warfare. Perhaps this is not surprising, given the state's acceptance of force as a legitimate tool for regulating human affairs and its ability to organize large numbers of people. In the modern world, we are as far (and probably further) from the elimination of war as humanity ever has been, a fact reflected in the 120-odd shooting wars going on in the mid-1990s. Moreover, value systems seem to be as crucial as any element to the continued existence of warfare.

POLITICAL SYSTEMS AND THE QUESTION OF LEGITIMACY

Whatever form a society's political system may take and however the society may go about its business, it always must find some way to obtain the people's allegiance. In uncentralized systems, where every adult participates in all decision making, loyalty and cooperation are freely given, since each person is considered a part of the political system. As the group grows larger, however, and the organization becomes more formal, the problems of obtaining and keeping public support become greater.

In centralized political systems, increased reliance is placed upon coercion as a means of social control. This, however, tends to lessen the effectiveness of a political system. For example, the staff needed to apply force often must be large and may itself grow to be a political power. The emphasis on force also may create resentment from those it is applied to, which lessens cooperation. Thus, police states are generally short-lived; most societies choose less-extreme forms of social coercion. In the United States, this is reflected in the increasing emphasis placed on cultural, as opposed to social, control.

Also basic to the political process is the concept of legitimacy, or the right of political leaders to rule. Like force, legitimacy is a form of support for a political system; unlike force, legitimacy is based on the values a particular society believes most important. For example, among the Kapauku the legitimacy of the *tonowi's* power comes from his wealth; the kings of Hawaii, and of England and France before their revolutions, were thought to have a divine right to rule; and the head of the Dahomey state of West Africa acquires legitimacy through his age, as he is always the oldest living male.

Legitimacy grants the right to hold, use, and allocate power. Power based on legitimacy, a form of cultural control, may be distinguished from power based on force alone (social control): Obedience to the former results from the belief obedience is "right"; compliance to power based on force results from fear of the deprivation of liberty, physical well-being, life, and material property. Thus, power based on legitimacy is symbolic and depends not upon any intrinsic value but upon the positive expectations of those who recognize and accede to it. If the expectations are not met regularly (if the head of state fails to deliver "eco-

In the United States, in spite of an official separation of church and state, the president is always sworn in over a Christian Bible.

nomic prosperity" or the leader is continuously unsuccessful in preventing horse or camel theft), the legitimacy of the recognized power figure is minimized and may collapse altogether.

▲▼▲▼▲▼▲▼▲▼▲▼▲▼▲▼▲▼▲▼▲▼▲▼▲▼▲
RELIGION AND POLITICS

Religion is intricately connected with politics. Religious beliefs may influence laws: Acts people believe to be sinful, such as sodomy and incest, are often illegal as well. Frequently, it is religion that legitimizes the political order.

In both industrial and nonindustrial societies, belief in the supernatural is important and is reflected in people's governments. The effect of religion on politics was perhaps best exemplified in medieval Europe. Holy wars were fought over the smallest matter; labor was mobilized to build immense cathedrals in honor of the Virgin and other saints; and kings and queens ruled by "divine right," pledged allegiance to the pope, and asked his blessing in all important ventures, were they marital or martial. In the pre-Columbian Americas the Aztec state was a religious state, or theocracy, that thrived in spite of more-or-less constant warfare carried out to procure captives for human sacrifices to assuage or please the gods. In Peru the Inca emperor proclaimed absolute authority based on the proposition he was descended from the sun god. Modern Iran was proclaimed an "Islamic republic," and its first head of state was the most holy of all Shiite Muslim holy men.

In the United States the Declaration of Independence, which is an expression of the country's social and political values, stresses a belief in a supreme being. The document states that "all men are created [by God] equal," a tenet that gave rise to American democracy, because it implied all people should participate in governing themselves. The fact the president of the United States takes the oath of office by swearing on the Bible is another instance of the use of religion to legitimize political power, as is the phrase "one nation, under God" in the Pledge of Allegiance. On U.S. coins is the phrase "In God We Trust," many meetings of government bodies begin with a prayer or invocation, and the phrase "so help me God" is routinely used in legal proceedings. In spite of an official separation of church and state, religious legitimization of government lingers on.

CHAPTER SUMMARY

Political organization and control are the ways power is distributed and embedded in society. Through political organization, societies maintain social order, manage public affairs, and reduce social disorder. No group can live together without persuading or coercing its members to conform to agreed-upon rules of conduct. To properly understand a society's political organization, one needs to view it in the light of its ecological, social, and ideological context.

Four basic types of political systems may be identified. In order of complexity, these range from uncentralized bands and tribes to centralized chiefdoms and states. The band, characteristic of foraging and some other nomadic societies, is an association of politically independent but related families or households occupying a common territory. Political organization in bands is democratic, and informal control is exerted by public opinion in the form of gossip and ridicule. Band leaders are older men, or sometimes women, whose personal authority lasts only as long as members believe they are leading well and making the right decisions.

The tribe is composed of separate bands or other social units tied together by such unifying factors as descent groups, age grading, or common interest. With an economy usually based on farming or herding, the tribe's population is larger than that of the band, although family units within the tribe are still relatively autonomous and egalitarian. As in the band, political organization is transitory, and leaders have no formal means of maintaining authority.

Many tribal societies vest political authority in the clan, an association of people who consider themselves descended from a common ancestor. A group of elders or headmen or headwomen regulate the affairs of members and represent their group in relations with other clans. Another variant of authority in tribes in Melanesia is the Big Man, who builds up his wealth and political power until he must be reckoned with as a leader. The segmentary lineage system, similar in operation to the clan, is a rare form of tribal organization based on kinship bonds.

Tribal age-grade systems cut across territorial and kin groupings. Leadership is vested in men in the group who were initiated into the age grade at the same time and passed as a set from one age grade to another until reaching the proper age to become elders. Common-interest associations wield political authority in some tribes. A boy joins one club or another when he reaches warrior status. These organizations administer the tribe's affairs.

As societies include larger numbers of people and become more heterogeneous socially, politically, and economically, leadership becomes more centralized. Chiefdoms are ranked societies in which every member has a position in the hierarchy. Status is determined by the individual's position in a descent group and distance of relationship to the chief. Power is concentrated in a single chief whose true authority serves to unite his community in all matters. The chief may accumulate great personal wealth, which enhances his power base and which he may pass on to his heirs.

The most centralized of political organizations is the state. It has a central power that legitimately can use force to administer a rigid code of laws and to maintain order, even beyond its borders. A large bureaucracy functions to uphold the central power's authority. The state is found only in soci-

eties with numerous diverse groups. Typically, it is a stratified society where economic functions and wealth are distributed unequally. Although thought of as stable and permanent, it is, in fact, inherently unstable and transitory. States differ from nations, which are communities of people who see themselves as "one people" with a common culture but who may or may not have a centralized form of political organization.

Historically women rarely have held important positions of political leadership, and when they have, it sometimes has been for lack of a qualified man to hold the position. Nonetheless, in a number of societies, women have enjoyed political equality with men, as among the Iroquoian tribes of New York State. In these tribes, all men held office at the pleasure of women, who not only appointed them but could remove them as well. Among the Igbo of midwestern Nigeria, women held positions in an administrative hierarchy that paralleled and balanced that of the men. Under centralized political systems, women are most apt to be subordinate to men, and when states impose their control on societies marked by sexual egalitarianism, the relationship changes so that men dominate women.

Two kinds of societal control exist: internalized and externalized. Internalized controls are self-imposed by individuals. These are purely cultural in nature, as they are built into the peoples' minds. They rely on such deterrents as personal shame, fear of divine punishment, and magical retaliation. Although bands and tribes rely heavily upon them, internalized controls are generally insufficient by themselves. Every society develops externalized controls, called sanctions, that mix cultural and social control. The latter involves overt coercion. Positive sanctions, in the form of rewards or recognition by one's neighbors, is the position a society, or a number of its members, takes toward approved behavior; negative sanctions, such as threat of imprisonment, corporal punishment, or "loss of face," reflect societal reactions to disapproved behavior.

Sanctions also may be classified as either formal, including actual laws, or informal, involving norms but not legal statutes. Formal sanctions are organized and reward or punish behavior through a rigidly regulated social procedure. Informal sanctions are diffuse, involving immediate reactions of approval or disapproval by individual community members to a compatriot's behavior. Other important agents of social control are witchcraft beliefs and religious sanctions.

Sanctions serve to formalize conformity to group norms, including actual law, and to maintain each social faction in a community in its "proper" place. An adequate working definition of law is that it consists of formal negative sanctions.

Law serves several basic functions. First, it defines relationships among a society's members and thereby dictates proper behavior under different circumstances. Second, law allocates authority to employ coercion to enforce sanctions. In centralized political systems, this authority rests with the government and court system. Uncentralized societies may give this authority directly to the injured party. Third, law redefines social relations and aids its own efficient operation by ensuring it allows for change.

Western societies clearly distinguish offenses against the state, called crimes, from offenses against individuals, called torts. Uncentralized societies may view all offenses as against individuals. One way to understand the nature of law is to analyze individual dispute cases against their cultural background. A dispute may be settled in two ways: negotiation and adjudication. All societies use negotiation to settle individual disputes. In negotiation the parties to the dispute reach an agreement themselves, with or without the help of a third party. In adjudication, not found in some societies, an authorized third party issues a binding decision. The disputing parties present their petitions but play no part in the decision making.

In addition to regulating internal affairs, political systems also attempt to regulate external affairs, or relations between politically autonomous units. In doing so they may resort to the threat or use of force.

War is not a universal phenomenon, since some societies do not practice warfare as we know it. Usually, these are stateless societies that have some kind of naturalistic worldview, an attitude that until recently had become nearly extinguished in modern industrial societies.

A major problem any form of political organization faces is obtaining and maintaining people's loyalty and support. Reliance on force and coercion usually tends in the long run to lessen a political system's effectiveness. A basic instrument of political implementation is legitimacy, or the right of political leaders to exercise authority. Power based on legitimacy stems from the belief of a society's members that obedience is "right" and therefore stems from the positive expectations of those who obey. It may be distinguished from compliance based on force, which stems from fear and thus from negative expectations.

Religion is so intricately woven into the life of the people in both industrial and nonindustrial countries that its presence is inevitably felt in the political sphere. To a greater or lesser extent, most governments the world over use religion to legitimize political power.

POINTS FOR CONSIDERATION

1. In this chapter we read about the use of informal *sanctions* (as opposed to formalized, codified *laws*) to control individual behavior in a group. What are examples of such sanctions? How do they operate in large societies that do have more codified laws? Are the two necessarily in total accord? In your experience, which takes precedence, and under what circumstances?

2. In many countries the press has taken on the role of watching and reporting on the behavior of powerful individuals. How can this serve as a sanction? What are the potential benefits of such publications and broadcastings? the potential drawbacks?

3. Do informal sanctions operate in the political sphere at the state level? Do they operate between states? How effective are they at these various levels?

SUGGESTED READINGS

Cohen, R., & Middleton, J. (Eds.). (1967). *Comparative political systems*. Garden City, NY: Natural History Press.

The editors have selected some 20 studies in the politics of nonindustrial societies by such well-known scholars as Lévi-Strauss, S. F. Nadel, Marshall Sahlins, and S. N. Eisenstadt.

Fried, M. (1967). *The evolution of political society: An essay in political anthropology*. New York: Random House.

The author attempts to trace the evolution of political society through a study of simple egalitarian societies. The character of the state and how this organizational form takes shape are considered in terms of pristine and secondary states, formed because preexisting states supplied the stimuli or models for organization.

Gordon, R. J., & Meggitt, M. J. (1985). *Law and order in the New Guinea highlands*. Hanover, NH: University Press of New England.

This ethnographic study of the resurgence of tribal fighting among the Mae-Enga addresses two issues of major importance in today's world: the changing nature of law and order in "underdeveloped" countries and the nature of violence in human societies.

Johnson, A. W., & Earle, T. (1987). *The evolution of human societies, from foraging group to agrarian state*. Stanford, CA: Stanford University Press.

Although written as a synthesis of economic and ecological anthropology, this is also a book on the evolution of political organization in human societies. Proceeding from family-level up through state organization, the authors discuss nine levels, illustrating each with specific case studies, and specify the conditions that give rise to each level.

Nader, L. (Ed.). (1980). *No Access to law: Alternatives to the American judicial system*. New York: Academic Press.

This is an eye-opening study of how consumer complaints are resolved in U.S. society. After 10 years of study, Nader found repeated and documented offenses by business that cannot be handled by present complaint mechanisms, either in or out of court. The high cost exacted includes a terrible sense of apathy and loss of faith in the system.

Whitehead, N., & Ferguson, R. B. (Eds.). (1992). *War in the tribal zone*. Santa Fe: School of American Research Press.

The central point of this book is that both the transformation and intensification of war, as well as the formation of tribes, result from complex interaction in the "tribal zone" that begins where centralized authority makes contact with stateless people it does not rule. In such zones, newly introduced plants, animals, diseases, and technologies often spread widely, even before colonizers appear. These and other changes disrupt existing social and political relationships, fostering new alliances and creating new kinds of conflicts.

Chapter 24
RELIGION AND THE SUPERNATURAL

RITUAL IS RELIGION IN ACTION; AND TRANCE, DANCE, AND SACRIFICE ARE FREQUENTLY PART OF RITUAL. SHOWN HERE IS A BALINESE CREMATION RITUAL.

Chapter Preview

What Is Religion?

Religion may be regarded as the beliefs and patterns of behavior by which humans try to deal with what they view as important problems that cannot be solved with known technology or organizational techniques. To overcome these limitations, people turn to the manipulation of supernatural beings and powers.

What Are Religion's Identifying Features?

Religion consists of various rituals—prayers, songs, dances, offerings, and sacrifices—people enact to try to manipulate supernatural beings and powers to their advantage. These beings and powers may consist of gods and goddesses, ancestral and other spirits, or impersonal powers, either by themselves or in various combinations. In all societies certain individuals are especially skilled at dealing with these beings and powers and assist other society members in their ritual activities. A body of myths rationalizes or "explains" the system in a manner consistent with people's experience in the world in which they live.

What Functions Does Religion Serve?

Whether or not a particular religion accomplishes what people believe it does, all religions serve a number of important psychological and social functions. They reduce anxiety by explaining the unknown and making it understandable, as well as provide comfort with the belief supernatural aid is available in times of crisis. They sanction a wide range of human conduct by providing notions of right and wrong, setting precedents for acceptable behavior, and by transferring the burden of decision making from individuals to supernatural powers. Through ritual, religion may be used to enhance the learning of oral traditions. Finally, religion plays an important role in maintaining social solidarity.

According to their origin myth, the Tewa Indians of New Mexico emerged from a lake far to the north of where they now live. Once on dry land, they divided into two groups, the Summer People and the Winter People, and migrated south along the Rio Grande. During their travels they made 12 stops before finally reuniting into a single community.

For the Tewa all existence is divided into six categories, three human and three supernatural. Each of the human categories, which are arranged in a hierarchy, is matched by a spiritual category so that when people die, they immediately pass into their proper spiritual role. Not only are the supernatural categories identified with human categories, but they also correspond to divisions in the natural world.

To those of some other religious persuasions, such beliefs may seem, at best, irrational and arbitrary, but in fact they are neither. The late Alfonso Ortiz, an anthropologist who was also a Tewa, showed that his native religion is not only logical and socially functional but also the very model of Tewa society.[1] These people have a society that is divided into two independent moieties, each with its own economy, rituals, and authority. The individual is introduced into one of these moieties (which in this case are *not* based on kinship), and his or her membership is regularly reinforced

---

[1] Ortiz, A. (1969). *The Tewa world* (p.43). Chicago: University of Chicago Press.

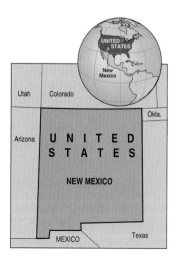

through a series of life-cycle rituals that correspond to the stops on the mythical journey down the Rio Grande. The rites of birth and death are shared by the whole community; other rites differ in the two moieties. The highest status of the human hierarchy belongs to the priests, who also help integrate this divided society; they mediate not only between the human and spiritual world but between the two moieties as well.

Tewa religion enters into virtually every aspect of Tewa life and society. It is the basis of the simultaneously dualistic and unified worldview of the individual Tewa. It provides numerous points of mediation so that the two moieties can continue to exist together as a single community. It sanctifies the community by linking its origin with the realm of the supernatural, and it offers divine sanction to *rites of passage* that soften life's major transitions. By providing an afterworld that is the mirror image of human society, it answers the question of death in a manner that reinforces social structure. In short, Tewa religion, by weaving all elements of Tewa experience into a single pattern, gives a solid foundation for the stability and continuity of Tewa society.

All religions fulfill numerous social and psychological needs. Some of these—the need to confront and explain death, for example—appear to be universal; indeed, we know of no group of people anywhere on the face of the earth who, at any time over the past 100,000 years, have been without religion. Unbound by time, religion gives meaning to individual and group life, drawing power from "the time of the gods in the Beginning" and offering continuity of existence beyond death. It can provide the path by which people transcend their arduous earthly existence and attain, if only momentarily, spiritual selfhood. The social functions of religion are no less important than the psychological ones. A traditional religion reinforces group norms, provides moral sanctions for individual conduct, and furnishes the substratum of common purpose and values upon which the equilibrium of the community depends.

In the 19th century, the European intellectual tradition gave rise to the idea that science ultimately would destroy religion by showing people the irrationality of their myths and rituals. Indeed, many still believe that as scientific explanations replace those of religion, the latter will wither on the vine. Yet an opposite tendency has occurred; not only do traditional mainline religions continue to thrive, but also fundamentalist religions are having a strong resurgence. Examples include Islamic fundamentalism in countries such as Afghanistan, Algeria, and Iran; Jewish fundamentalism in Israel; and Hindu fundamentalism in India. Christian fundamentalism is represented in the dramatic growth of evangelical denominations in the United States (Table 24.1). Often, these have a strong antiscience bias. Other religions continue to grow in North America as well, including Islam (at least 3.5 million in the United States, comparable to the number of Presbyterians), Buddhism (750,000 in the United States), Hinduism (800,000 in the United States, up from ca. 70,000 in 1977), not to mention the various "New Age" options. Of approximately 1,600 religions and denominations in the United States, about 800 were founded after 1965.[2]

Science, far from destroying religion, may have contributed to the creation of a veritable religious boom. In the United States, the latter is worth billions of tax-free dollars each year, and

some religious leaders even go so far as to flaunt luxurious lifestyles as proof they enjoy God's favor. Science has fostered this religious boom by

Far from causing the death of religion, the growth of scientific knowledge, by producing new anxieties and raising new questions about human existence, may have contributed to the continuing practice of religion in modern life. North Americans continue to participate in traditional religions, such as Judaism (top), as well as imported sects, such as the new Vrindaban (middle) and evangelism (bottom).

[2]Shorto, R. (1997, December 7). Belief by the numbers. *New York Times Magazine,* 60.

TABLE 24.1	Increase or Decrease of Selected Christian Denominations for the Past 30 Years as a Proportion of the U.S. Population
Episcopal	−44%
Methodist	−38
Roman Catholic	−3
Southern Baptist	+8
Mormon	+96
Jehovah's Witnesses	+119
Assemblies of God	+211
Church of God in Christ	+863

SOURCE: [1]Shorto, R. (1997, December 7). Belief by the numbers. *New York Times Magazine,* 60.

removing many traditional psychological props while creating, in its technological applications, a host of new problems: threat of nuclear catastrophe; health threats from pollution; unease about the consequences of new developments in biotechnology, such as the cloning of animals, production of new strains of genetically engineered organisms, and ability to store human sperm and eggs for future fertilization; fear of loss of economic security as machines replace workers; and fear of loneliness in a society that isolates us from our kin and places impediments in the way of establishing deep and lasting friendships, to list but a few issues people now must deal with. In the face of these new anxieties, religion offers social and psychological support.

The continuing strength of religion in the face of Western rationalism clearly reveals it is a powerful and dynamic force in society. Although anthropologists are not qualified to pass judgment on the metaphysical truths of any particular religion, they can show how each religion embodies a number of "truths" about humans and society.

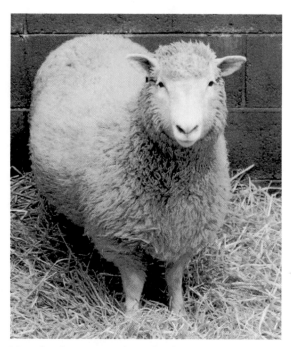

New developments in biotechnology, such as cloning, which produced the sheep Dolly (shown here) have been a source of new anxieties. Answers to these anxieties are often sought in religion.

THE ANTHROPOLOGICAL APPROACH TO RELIGION

Anthropologist Anthony F. C. Wallace defined **religion** as "a set of rituals, rationalized by myth, which mobilizes supernatural powers for the purpose of achieving or preventing transformations of state in man and nature."[3] Behind this definition is a recognition that people, when they cannot "fix" through technological or organizational means serious problems that cause them anxiety, try to do so through the manipulation of supernatural beings and powers. This requires ritual, which Wallace sees as the primary phenomenon of religion, or "religion in action." Its major functions are to reduce anxiety and keep confidence high, which serve to keep people in some sort of shape to cope with reality. It is this that gives religion its survival value.

Religion, then, may be regarded as the beliefs and patterns of behavior by which people try to control aspects of the universe otherwise beyond their control. Since no known culture, including those of modern industrial societies, has achieved complete certainty in controlling the universe, religion is a part of all known cultures. However, considerable variability exists here. At one end of the human spectrum are food-foraging peoples, whose technological ability to manipulate their environment is limited and who tend to see themselves more as part, rather than masters, of nature. This is what we referred to in Chapter 23 as a naturalistic worldview. Among food foragers

---

[3]Wallace, A. F. C. (1966). *Religion: An anthropological view* (p. 107). New York: Random House.

Religion. A set of rituals, rationalized by myth, that mobilizes supernatural powers to achieve or prevent transformations of state in people and nature.

religion is apt to be inseparable from the rest of daily life. It also mirrors and confirms the egalitarian nature of social relations in their societies, in that individuals do not plead for aid to high-ranking deities the way members of stratified societies do. At the other end of the human spectrum is Western civilization, with its ideological commitment to overcoming problems through technological and organizational skills. Here religion is less a part of daily activities and is restricted to more specific occasions. Moreover, with its hierarchy of supernatural beings—for instance, God, the angels, and the saints of Christianity—it reflects and confirms the stratified nature of the society in which it is embedded.

Even so, variation exists between these two extremes. Religious activity may be less prominent in the lives of social elites, who see themselves as more in control of their own destinies, than it is in the lives of peasants or members of lower classes. Among the latter, religion may afford some compensation for a subordinate position in society. Yet religion is still important to elite members

of a society, in that it rationalizes the system in such a way that less advantaged people are not as likely to question the existing social order as they might otherwise be. After all, with hope for a better existence after death, one may be more willing to put up with a disadvantaged position in life. Thus, religious beliefs serve to influence and perpetuate conceptions, if not actual relations, between different classes of people.

THE PRACTICE OF RELIGION

Much of religion's value comes from the activities its practice calls for. Participation in religious ceremonies may bring a sense of personal transcendence—a wave of reassurance, security, and even ecstasy—or a feeling of closeness to fellow participants. Although the rituals and practices of religions vary considerably, even rites that seem to us most bizarrely exotic can be shown to serve the same basic social and psychological functions.

The huge public participation in the funeral of Princess Diana, as in all collective rituals, created a sense of communion that encouraged a belief in shared values.

SUPERNATURAL BEINGS AND POWERS

One of the hallmarks of religion is a belief in supernatural beings and forces. When attempting to control by religious means what cannot be controlled in other ways, humans turn to prayer, sacrifice, and other religious rituals. This presupposes a world of supernatural beings who have an interest in human affairs and to whom people may turn for aid. For convenience we may divide these beings into three categories: major deities (gods and goddesses), ancestral spirits, and other sorts of spirit beings. Although the variety of deities and spirits the world's cultures recognize is tremendous, certain generalizations about them are possible.

Gods and Goddesses

Gods and goddesses are the great and more remote beings. They usually are seen as controlling the universe, or, if several are recognized (known as **polytheism**), each has charge of a particular part of the universe. Such was the case of the gods and goddesses of ancient Greece: Zeus was lord of the sky, Poseidon was ruler of the sea, and Hades was lord of the underworld and ruler of the dead. Besides these three brothers were a host of other deities, female as well as male, each similarly concerned with specific aspects of life and the universe.

Pantheons, or collections of gods and goddesses such as those of the Greeks, are common in non-Western states as well. Since states usually have grown through conquest, their pantheons often have developed as local deities of conquered peoples were incorporated into the official state pantheon. Although creators of the present world may be included, this is not always the case; the Greeks, to cite but one example, did not include them. Another frequent though not invariable feature of pantheons is the presence of a supreme deity, who may be all but totally ignored by humans. The Aztecs of Mexico, for instance, recognized a supreme pair to whom they paid little attention. After all, being so remote, the deities were unlikely to be interested in human affairs. The sensible practice, then, was to focus attention on less-remote deities who therefore were more directly concerned with human matters.

Whether or not a people recognize gods, goddesses, or both has to do with how men and women relate to one another in everyday life. Generally speaking, societies that subordinate women to men define the godhead in exclusively masculine terms. Such societies are mainly those with economies based upon the herding of animals or intensive agriculture carried out by men, who as fathers are distant and controlling figures to their children.

Goddesses, by contrast, are apt to be most prominent in societies where women make a major contribution to the economy and enjoy relative equality with men and where men are more involved in their children's lives. Such societies are most often those that depend upon farming, much or all of which women do. As an illustration, the early Hebrews, like other pastoral nomadic tribes of the Middle East, described their god in masculine, authoritarian terms. By contrast, goddesses played central roles in religious ritual and the popular consciousness of the region's agricultural peoples. Associated with these goddesses were concepts of light, love, fertility, and procreation. Around 1300 B.C., the Hebrew tribes entered the land of Canaan and began to practice agriculture, requiring them to establish a new kind of relationship with the soil. As they became dependent upon rainfall and the rotation of seasons for crops and concerned about fertility (as the Canaanites already were), they adopted many of the Canaanite goddess cults. Although diametrically opposed to the original Hebrew cult, belief in the Canaanite goddesses catered to the human desire for security by seeking to control the forces of fertility in the interest of peoples' well-being.

Later on, when the Israelite tribes sought national unity in the face of a military threat by the Philistines and when they strengthened their identity as a "chosen people," the goddess cults lost out to followers of the old masculine tribal god.

Polytheism. Belief in several gods and/or goddesses (as contrasted with monotheism—belief in one god). > **Pantheon.** The several gods and goddesses of a people.

The patriarchal nature of Western society is expressed in its theology, in which a masculine God gives life to the first man, as depicted here on the ceiling of the Sistine Chapel. Only after this is the first woman created from the first man.

This ancient masculine-authoritarian concept of god has been perpetuated down to the present, not just in the Judaic tradition but also by Christians and Muslims, whose religions stem from the old Hebrew religion. As a consequence, this masculine-authoritarian model has played an important role in perpetuating a relationship between men and women in which the latter traditionally have been expected to submit to the "rule" of men at every level of Jewish, Christian, and Islamic society.

Ancestral Spirits

A belief in ancestral spirits is consistent with the widespread notion that human beings are made up of two parts, a body and some kind of vital spirit. For example, the Penobscot Indians, whom we met in Chapter 16, maintained that each person had a personal spirit that could detach itself and travel about apart from the body, while the latter remained inert. Given such a concept, the idea of the spirit being freed from the body by death and having a continued existence seems quite logical.

Where a belief in ancestral spirits exists, these beings frequently are seen as retaining an active interest and even membership in society. In Chapter 23, for instance, we saw how ghost ancestors of the Wape acted to provide or withhold meat from their living descendants. Like living persons, ancestral spirits may be benevolent or malevolent, but no one is ever quite sure what their behavior will be. The same feeling of uncertainty—"How will they react to what I have done?"—may be displayed toward ancestral spirits that tends to be displayed toward people of a senior generation who hold authority over individuals. Beyond this, ancestral spirits closely resemble living humans in their appetites, feelings, emotions, and behavior. Thus, they reflect and reinforce social reality.

A belief in ancestral spirits of one sort or another is found in many parts of the world, especially among people with unilineal descent systems. In several such African societies, the concept is especially elaborate. Here one frequently finds ancestral spirits behaving just like humans. They are able to feel hot, cold, and pain, and they may be capable of dying a second death by drowning or burning. They even may participate in family and lineage affairs, and seats will be provided for them, even though the spirits are invisible. If they are annoyed, they may send sickness or even death. Eventually, they are reborn as new members of their lineage, and, in societies that hold such beliefs, adults need to observe infants closely to determine just who has been reborn.

Deceased ancestors were also important in the patrilineal society of traditional China. For the gift of life, a boy was forever indebted to his parents, owing them obedience, deference, and a comfortable old age. Even after their death, he had to provide for them in the spirit world, offering food, money, and incense to them on the anniversaries of their births and deaths. In addition, people collectively worshiped all lineage ancestors periodically throughout the year. This society even regarded the birth of sons as an obligation to the ancestors, because this ensured the latter's needs would continue to be attended to even after their own sons' death. To satisfy ancestors' needs for descendants (and a man's own need to be respectable in a culture that demanded he satisfy his ancestors' needs), a man would go so far as to marry a girl who had been adopted into his family as an infant to be raised as a dutiful wife for him, even when this arrangement went against the wishes of both parties. Furthermore, a man readily would force his daughter to marry a man against her will. In fact, a female child was raised to be cast out by her natal family yet might not find acceptance in her husband's family for years. Not until after death, when her soul was carried in a tablet and placed in the shrine of her husband's family, was she an official member of it. As a consequence, once a son was born to her, a woman worked long and hard to establish the strongest possible tie between herself and her son to ensure she would be looked after in life.

Strong beliefs in ancestral spirits are particularly appropriate in a society of descent-based groups with their associated ancestral orientation. More than this, though, these beliefs provide a strong sense of continuity that links the past, present, and future.

Animism

One of the most widespread beliefs about supernatural beings is **animism,** which sees nature as animated by all sorts of spirits. In reality, the term masks a wide range of variation. Animals and plants, like humans, all may have their individual spirits, as may springs, mountains, or other natural features. So too may stones, weapons, ornaments, and so on. In addition, the woods may be full of a variety of unattached or free-ranging spirits. The various spirits involved are a highly diverse lot. Generally speaking, though, they are less remote from people than gods and goddesses and are more involved in daily affairs. They may be benevolent, malevolent, or just plain neutral. They also may be awesome, terrifying, lovable, or even mischievous. Since they may be pleased or irritated by human actions, people are obliged to be concerned about them.

Animism is typical of those who see themselves as a part of nature rather than superior to it. This takes in most food foragers, as well as food-producing peoples who recognize little difference between a human life and that of any growing thing. Among such societies, gods and goddesses are relatively unimportant, but the woods are full of all sorts of spirits. (For a good example, see the discussion of the Penobscot behavioral environment in Chapter 16.) Gods and goddesses, if they exist at all, may be seen as having created the world and perhaps making it fit to live in; but it is spirits individuals turn to for curing, who help or hinder the shaman, and whom the ordinary hunter may meet when off in the woods.

Animism. A belief in spirit beings thought to animate nature.

Sir Edward B. Tylor   *(1832–1917)*

The concept of animism was first brought to the attention of anthropologists by the British scholar Sir Edward B. Tylor.

Though not university educated himself, Tylor was the first person to hold a chair in anthropology at a British university, with his appointment first as lecturer, then as reader, and finally (in 1895) as professor at Oxford. His interest in anthropology developed from travels that took him as a young man to the United States (where he visited an Indian pueblo), Cuba, and Mexico, where he was especially impressed by the achievements of the ancient Aztec and the contemporary blend of Indian and Spanish culture.

Tylor's numerous publications covered such diverse topics as the possible historical connection between the games of pachisi and patolli (played in India and ancient Mexico); the origin of games of Cat's Cradle; and the structural connections between postmarital residence, descent, and certain other customs such as in-law avoidance and the couvade (the confinement of a child's father following birth).

Tylor also formulated the first widely accepted definition of culture (see Chapter 14). The considerable attention he paid to religious concepts and practices in his writings stemmed from a lifelong commitment to combat the idea, still widely held in his time, that so-called savage people had degenerated more than civilized people from an original state of grace. To Tylor, "savages" were intellectuals just like anyone else, grappling with their problems but handicapped (as was Tylor in his intellectual life) by limited information.

Native Indians carved these faces into a rock along the Connecticut River to depict spirit beings they saw here while in states of trance.

Animatism

Although supernatural power is often thought of as being vested in supernatural beings, it does not have to be. The Melanesians, for example, think of *mana* as a force inherent in all objects. It is not in itself physical, but it can reveal itself physically. A warrior's success in fighting is not attributed to his own strength but to the *mana* contained in an amulet that hangs around his neck. Similarly, a farmer may know a great deal about horticulture, soil conditioning, and the correct time for sowing and harvesting but nevertheless depends upon *mana* for a successful crop, often building a simple altar to this power at the end of the field. If the crop is good, it is a sign the farmer has in some way appropriated the necessary *mana*. Far from being a personalized force, *mana* is abstract in the extreme, a power lying always just beyond reach of the senses. As R. H. Codrington described it, "Virtue, prestige, authority, good fortune, influence, sanctity, luck are all words which, under certain conditions, give something near the meaning. . . . *Mana* sometimes means a more than natural virtue or power attaching to some person or thing."[4] This concept of impersonal power also was widespread among North American Indians. The Iroquois called it *orenda, to* the Sioux it was *wakonda,* and to the Algonquians it was *manitu.* Though found on every continent, the concept is not necessarily universal, however.

R. R. Marett called this concept of impersonal power **animatism.** The two concepts, animatism (which is inanimate) and animism (a belief in spirit beings), are not mutually exclusive. They often are found in the same culture, as in Melanesia, and also in the Indian societies just mentioned.

People trying to comprehend beliefs in the supernatural beings and powers others recognize frequently ask how such beliefs are maintained. In part, the answer is through manifestations of power. This means, given a belief in animatism and/or the powers of supernatural beings, one is predisposed to see what appear to be results of the application of such powers. For example, if a Melanesian warrior is convinced of his power because he possesses the necessary *mana* and he is successful, he is likely to interpret this success as proof of the power of *mana.* "After all, I would have lost had I not possessed it, wouldn't I?" Beyond this, because of his confidence in his *mana,* he may be willing to take more chances in his fighting, and this indeed could mean the difference between success or failure.

Failures, of course, do occur, but they can be explained. Perhaps a prayer was not answered because a deity or spirit was still angry about some past insult. Or perhaps our Melanesian warrior lost his battle—the obvious explanation is that he was not as successful in bringing *mana* to bear as he thought, or else his opponent had more of it. In any case, humans generally emphasize successes over failures, and, long after many of the latter have been forgotten, tales probably still will be told of striking cases of the workings of supernatural powers.

Another feature that tends to perpetuate beliefs in supernatural beings is that the beings have attributes people are familiar with. Allowing for the fact supernatural beings are in a sense larger than life, they generally are conceived of as living the way people do and as having the same sorts of interests. For example, the Penobscot Indians believed in a quasi–human being called Gluskabe. Like ordinary mortals, Gluskabe traveled about in a canoe, used snowshoes, lived in a wigwam, and made stone arrowheads. The gods and goddesses of the ancient Greeks had all the familiar human lusts and jealousies. Such features serve to make supernatural beings believable.

The role of mythology in maintaining beliefs should not be overlooked. *Myths,* which are discussed in some detail in Chapter 25, are explanatory narratives that rationalize religious beliefs and practices. To European Americans, the word *myth*

---

[4]Quoted by G. Leinhardt (1960), Religion. In H. Shapiro (Ed.), *Man, culture, and society* (p. 368). London: Oxford University Press.

Animatism. A belief that the world is animated by impersonal supernatural powers.

immediately conjures up the idea of a story about imaginary events, but the people responsible for a particular myth usually do not see it that way. To them myths are true stories, analogous to historical documents in modern North American culture. Even so, myths exist even in literate societies, as in the Judaic and Christian account of creation in the Bible's Book of Genesis. Myths invariably are full of accounts of the doings of various supernatural beings and thus serve to reinforce beliefs in them.

RELIGIOUS SPECIALISTS

Priests and Priestesses

In all human societies there exist individuals whose job it is to guide and supplement the religious practices of others. Such individuals are highly skilled at contacting and influencing supernatural beings and manipulating supernatural forces. Their qualification for this is that they have undergone special training. In addition, they may display certain distinctive personality traits that particularly suit them for their job. Societies with the resources to support full-time occupational specialists give the role of guiding religious practices and influencing the supernatural to the **priest** or **priestess.** He or she is the socially initiated, ceremonially inducted member of a recognized religious organization, with a rank and function that belongs to him or her as the tenant of an office others have held before. The sources of power are the society and the institution the priest or priestess functions within.

The priest, if not the priestess, is a familiar figure in Western societies; he is the priest, minister, pastor, rector, rabbi, or whatever the official title may be in an organized religion. With the Judaic, Christian, and Islamic god defined in masculine-authoritarian terms, it was not surprising that traditionally men have filled the most important positions in these religions . Only in societies where women make a major contribution to the economy and that recognize goddesses as well as gods are female religious specialists likely to be found.

Shamans

Societies that lack full-time occupational specialization have existed far longer than those with such specialization, and the former always have had individuals who acquired religious power individually, usually in solitude and isolation, when the Great Spirit, the Power, the Great Mystery, or whatever is revealed to them. These persons become the recipients of certain special gifts, such as healing or divination; when they return to society, they frequently are given another kind of religious role, that of the **shaman.**

In the United States millions of people have learned something about shamans through reading the popular autobiography of Black Elk, a traditional Oglala Sioux Indian "medicine man," or Carlos Castaneda's apparently fictional accounts of his experiences with Don Juan, the Yaqui Indian shaman. Numerous other books have emerged in the past decade. Few may realize, however, that the faith healers and many other evangelists in their own society conform in every respect to our definition of the shaman. Thus, one should not get the idea shamans are not found in modern, industrial societies, for they are. Shamanism is particularly popular among so-called "New Age" enthusiasts.

Typically, one becomes a shaman by passing through difficult stages commonly set forth in many myths. These stages are often thought to involve torture and violent dismemberment of the body; scraping away of the flesh until the body is reduced to a skeleton; substitution of the viscera and renewal of the blood; a period spent in a nether region, or land of the dead, during which the shaman is taught by the souls of dead shamans and other spirit beings; and an ascent to a sky realm. Among the Crow Indians, for example, any man could become a shaman, since no ecclesiastical organization provided rules and regulations to guide religious consciousness. The search for shamanistic visions was pursued by most adult Crow males, who would engage in bodily

---

Priest or **Priestess.**   A full-time religious specialist. > **Shaman.**   A part-time religious specialist who has unique power acquired through his or her initiative; such individuals are thought to possess exceptional abilities for dealing with supernatural beings and powers.

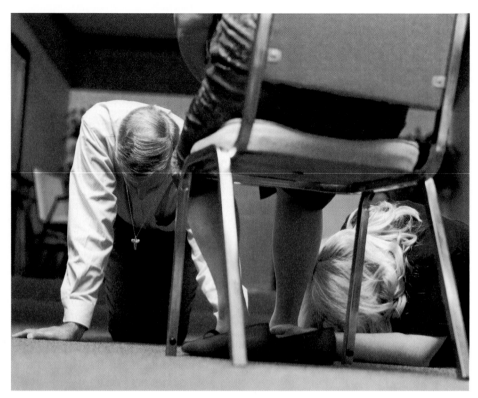

Two Christian evangelists working to heal an arthritis sufferer. Such faith healers in the United States and elsewhere correspond in every respect to our definition of the shaman; hence, shamanism is by no means absent in modern industrial societies.

deprivation, even self-torture, to induce such visions. Not all seekers were granted a vision, but failure carried no social stigma. Although those who claimed supernatural vision would be expected to manifest some special power in battle or wealth, the sincerity of the seeker carried the essential truth of the experience.

Many of the elements of shamanism, such as transvestism, trance states, and speaking in undecipherable languages, just as easily can be regarded as abnormalities, and it has been frequently pointed out that those regarded as specially gifted in some societies would be outcasts or worse in others. The position of shaman can provide a socially approved role for those who in other circumstances might be labeled as having unstable personalities.

The shaman is essentially a religious entrepreneur who acts on behalf of some human client,

often to effect a cure or foretell some future event. To do so, the shaman intervenes to influence or impose his or her will on supernatural powers. The shaman can be contrasted with the priest or priestess, whose "clients" are the deities. Priests and priestesses frequently tell people what to do; the shaman tells the supernatural what to do. In return for services rendered, the shaman may collect a fee—fresh meat, yams, or a favorite possession. In some cases, the added prestige, authority, and social power attached to the shaman's status are reward enough.

When a shaman acts for a client, he or she may put on something of a show—one that heightens the basic drama with a sense of danger. Frequently, the shaman must enter a trancelike state, in which he or she experiences the sensation of traveling to the spirit world, seeing and interacting with spirit beings there. (For more on trance, see Chapters 16 and 25.) The shaman tries to impose his or her will upon these spirits, an inherently dangerous contest, considering the superhuman powers spirits are usually thought to possess. One example of this is afforded by the trance dances of the Ju/'hoansi Bushmen of Africa's Kalahari Desert. Among these people shamans constitute, on average, about half the men and a third of the older women in any group. The most common reasons for their going into trance are to bring rain, control animals, and—as in the present example—to heal the sick (always an important activity of shamans, wherever they are found).

Healing Among the Ju/'hoansi of the Kalahari[5]

Ju/'hoansi healers, when entering trance, are assisted by others among the trance dancers.

One way the spirits affect humans is by shooting them with invisible arrows carrying disease, death, or misfortune. If the arrows can be warded off, illness will not take hold. If illness has already penetrated, the arrows must be removed to enable the sick person to recover. An ancestral spirit may exercise this power against the living if a person is not being treated well by others. If people argue with her frequently, if her husband shows how little he values her by carrying on blatant affairs, or if people refuse to cooperate or share with her, the spirit may conclude that no one cares whether or not she remains alive and may "take her into the sky."

Interceding with the spirits and drawing out their invisible arrows is the task of (Ju/'hoansi) healers, men and women who possess the powerful healing force called n/um (the Ju/'hoansi equivalent of mana). N/um generally remains dormant in a healer until an effort is made to activate it. Although an occasional healer can accomplish this through solo singing or instrumental playing, the usual way of activating n/um is through the medicinal curing ceremony or trance dance. To the sound of undulating melodies sung by women, healers dance around and around the fire, sometimes for hours. The music, the strenuous dancing, the smoke, the heat of the fire, and the healers' intense concentration cause their n/um to heat up. When it comes to a boil, trance is achieved.

At this moment the n/um becomes available as a powerful healing force, to serve the entire community. In trance, a healer lays hands on and ritually cures everyone sitting around the fire. His hands flutter lightly beside each person's head or chest or wherever illness is evident; his body trembles; his breathing becomes deep and coarse; and he becomes coated with a thick sweat—also considered to be imbued with power. Whatever "badness" is discovered in the person is drawn into the healer's own body and met by the n/um coursing up his spinal column. The healer gives a mounting cry that culminates in a soul-wrenching shriek as the illness is catapulted out of his body and into the air.

While in trance, many healers see various gods and spirits sitting just outside the circle of firelight, enjoying the spectacle of the dance. Sometimes the spirits are recognizable—departed relatives and friends—at other times they are "just people." Whoever these beings are, healers in trance usually

[5]Shostak, M. (1983). *Nisa: The life and words of a !Kung woman* (pp. 291–293). New York: Vintage.

blame them for whatever misfortune is being experienced by the community. They are barraged by hurled objects, shouted at, and aggressively warned not to take any of the living back with them to the village of the spirits.

To cure a very serious illness, the most experienced healers may be called upon, for only they have enough knowledge to undertake the dangerous spiritual exploration that may be necessary to effect a cure. When they are in a trance, their souls are said to leave their bodies and to travel to the spirit world to discover the cause of the illness or the problem. An ancestral spirit or a god is usually found responsible and asked to reconsider. If the healer is persuasive and the spirit agrees, the sick person recovers. If the spirit is elusive or unsympathetic, a cure is not achieved. The healer may go to the principal god, but even this does not always work. As one healer put it, "Sometimes, when you speak with God, he says, 'I want this person to die and won't help you make him better.' At other times, God helps; the next morning, someone who has been lying on the ground, seriously ill, gets up and walks again."

These journeys are considered dangerous because while the healer's soul is absent his body is in half-death. Akin to loss of consciousness, this state has been observed and verified by medical and scientific investigators. The power of other healers' n/um is all that is thought to protect the healer in this state from actual death. He receives lavish attention and care—his body is vigorously massaged, his skin is rubbed with sweat, and hands are laid on him. Only when consciousness returns—the signal that his soul has been reunited with his body—do the other healers cease their efforts.

In many human societies trancing is accompanied by sleight-of-hand tricks and ventriloquism. Among Arctic peoples, for example, a shaman may summon spirits in the dark and produce all sorts of flapping noises and strange voices to impress the audiences. Some Western observers regard this kind of trickery as evidence of the fraudulent nature of shamanism, but is this so? The truth is that shamans know perfectly well they are pulling the wool over people's eyes with their tricks. Yet virtually everyone who has studied them agrees shamans really believe in their power to deal with supernatural powers and spirits. It is this power that gives them the right as well as the ability to fool people in minor technical matters. In short, the shaman regards his or her ability to perform tricks as proof of effective powers.

The importance of shamanism in a society should not be underestimated. For individual members, it promotes, through the drama of performance, a feeling of ecstasy and release of tension. It provides psychological assurance, through the manipulation of supernatural powers and spirits otherwise beyond human control, of such things as invulnerability from attack, success at love, or the return of health. In fact, a frequent reason for a shamanistic performance is to cure illness. Although the treatment may not be medically effective, the state of mind induced in the patient may be critical to his or her recovery.

What shamanism provides for society is a focal point of attention. This is not without danger to the shaman. Someone with so much skill and power has the ability to work evil as well as good and so is potentially dangerous. The group may interpret too much nonsuccess from a shaman as evidence of malpractice and may drive out or even kill the shaman. Likewise, the shaman may help maintain social control through the ability to detect and punish evildoers.

The benefits of shamanism for the shaman are that it provides prestige and perhaps even wealth. It also may be therapeutic, in that it provides an approved outlet for the outbreaks of what otherwise might seem an unstable personality. An individual who is psychologically unstable (and not all shamans are) actually may get better by becoming intensely involved with the problems of others. In this respect, shamanism is a bit like self-analysis. Finally, shamanism is a good outlet for the self-expression of those who might be described as endowed with an "artistic temperament."

RITUALS AND CEREMONIES

Although not all rituals are religious in nature (graduation ceremonies in North America, for example), those that are play a crucial role in religious activity. Religious ritual is the means through which persons relate to the sacred; it is religion in action. Not only is ritual a means for reinforcing a group's social bonds and for relieving tensions, but it is also one way many important events are celebrated and crises, such as death, made less socially disruptive and less difficult for individuals to bear. Anthropologists have classified several different types of ritual, among them **rites of passage,** which pertain to stages in the individual's life cycle, and **rites of intensification,** which occur during a crisis in the life of the group, serving to bind individuals together.

Rites of Passage

In one of anthropology's classic works, Arnold Van Gennep analyzed the rites of passage that help individuals through the crucial crises of their lives, such as birth, puberty, marriage, parenthood, advancement to a higher class, occupational specialization, and death.[6] He found it useful to divide ceremonies for all of these life crises into three stages: **separation, transition,** and **incorporation.** The individual first would be ritually removed

---

[6]Van Gennep, A. (1960). *The rites of passage.* Chicago: University of Chicago Press.

from the society as a whole, then isolated for a period, and finally incorporated back into society in his or her new status.

Van Gennep described the male initiation rites of Australian Aborigines. When the elders decide the time for the initiation, the boys are taken from the village (separation), while the women cry and make a ritual show of resistance. At a place distant from the camp, groups of men from many villages gather. The elders sing and dance, while the initiates act as though they are dead. The climax of this part of the ritual is a bodily operation, such as circumcision or the knocking out of a tooth. Anthropologist A. P. Elkin says:

> This is partly a continuation of the drama of death. The tooth-knocking, circumcision or other symbolical act "killed" the novice; after this he does not return to the general camp and normally may not be seen by any woman. He is dead to the ordinary life of the tribe.[7]

---

[7]Elkin, A. P. (1964). *The Australian Aborigines.* Garden City, NY: Doubleday/Anchor Books.

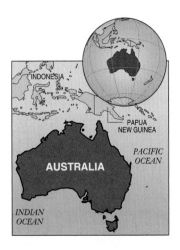

Rites of passage.   Rituals, often religious in nature, marking important stages in the lives of individuals, such as birth, marriage, and death. > **Rites of intensification.**   Religious rituals enacted during a group's real or potential crisis. > **Separation.**   In rites of passage, the ritual removal of the individual from society. > **Transition.**   In rites of passage, a stage where the individual is isolated following separation and prior to incorporation into society. > **Incorporation.** In rites of passage, reincorporation of the individual into society in his or her new status.

In this transitional stage, the novice may be shown secret ceremonies and receive some instruction, but the most significant element is his complete removal from society. In the course of these Australian puberty rites, the initiate must learn the lore all adult men are expected to know; he is given, in effect, a "cram course." The trauma of the occasion is a pedagogical technique that ensures he will learn and remember everything; in a nonliterate society the perpetuation of cultural traditions requires no less, so effective teaching methods are necessary.

On his return to society (incorporation) the novice is welcomed with ceremonies, as though he had returned from the dead. This alerts the society at large to the individual's new status—that people can expect him to act in certain ways and in return they must act in the appropriate ways toward him. The individual's new rights and duties are thus clearly defined. He is spared, for example, the problems of American teenagers, a time when an individual is neither adult nor child but a person whose status is ill defined.

In the Australian case just cited, boys are prepared not just for adulthood but also for *manhood*. In their society, for example, fortitude is considered an important masculine virtue, and the pain of tooth-knocking or circumcision helps instill this in initiates. In a similar way, female initiation rites help prepare Mende girls in West Africa for womanhood. After they have begun to menstruate, the girls are removed from society to spend weeks, or even months, in seclusion. There they discard the clothes of childhood, smear their bodies with white clay, and dress in brief skirts and many strands of beads. Shortly after entering this transitional stage, they undergo surgery that excises their clitoris and part of the labia minora, something they believe enhances their procreative potential. Until their incorporation back into society, they are trained in the moral and practical responsibilities of potential childbearers by experienced women in the Sande association, an organization the initiates will belong to once their training has ended. This training is not all harsh, however, for it is accompanied by a good deal of singing, dancing, and storytelling, and the initiates are very well fed. Thus, they acquire both a positive image of womanhood and a strong sense of

sisterhood. Once their training is complete, a medicine made by brewing leaves in water is used for a ritual washing, removing the magical protection that has shielded them during the period of their confinement.

Mende women emerge from their initiation, then, as women in knowledgeable control of their sexuality, eligible for marriage and childbearing. The pain and danger of the surgery, endured in the context of intense social support from other women, serves as a metaphor for childbirth, which may well take place in the same place of seclusion, again with the support of Sande women. It also has been suggested that, symbolically, excision of the clitoris (as the female version of the male penis) removes sexual ambiguity.[8] Once it is done, a woman *knows* she is "all woman." Thus we have symbolic expression of gender as something important in peoples' cultural lives.

In the case just cited, the anthropological commitment to cultural relativism permits an understanding of the practice of clitoridectomy (removal of the clitoris) in the Mende female initiation rites. But as discussed earlier in this book (see Chapter 14), cultural relativism does not preclude the anthropologist from criticizing a given practice. In this case, removal of the clitoris (like male circumcision) is a form of genital mutilation, and a particularly dangerous one at that. Some form of genital mutilation, ranging from the removal of the clitoris to the removal of the entire external female genitalia, including the partial closing of the vaginal opening (surgically opened for intercourse and closed again after a birth until the male again desires intercourse), affects an estimated 80 million women in the world today and is particularly widespread in Africa, where it occurs in 28 countries.[9] The custom is found also among some groups outside Africa: in Oman, Yemen, the United Arab Emirates (but not Iran, Iraq, Jordan, Libya, or Saudi Arabia), and among some Muslims in Malaya and Indonesia. As this listing sug-

---

[8]MacCormack, C. P. (1977). Biological events and cultural control. *Signs, 3,* 98.

[9]Armstrong, S. (1991). Female circumcision: Fighting a cruel tradition. *New Scientist,* 42.

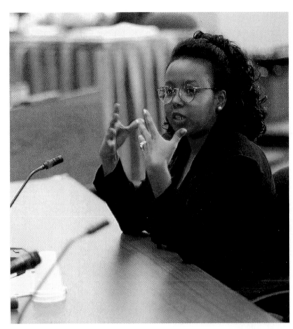

Soraya Mire, a Somalian film maker who underwent genital mutilation at age 13, speaks to Nevada lawmakers in support of a bill that would make the practice a felony.

gests, female genital mutilation is not required by Islamic religion; where it is practiced by Muslims (not to mention the occasional Christian and Jewish group), it functions as a means for men to control women's sexuality (unlike among the Mende).

Quite apart from the pain involved, and the operation's effect on a woman's future sexual satisfaction, significant numbers of young women die from excessive bleeding, shock, or infection or (later on) when giving birth as scar tissue tears. As a consequence, the practice has been widely condemned in recent years, and committees to end such practices have been set up in 22 African countries.

Rites of Intensification

Rites of intensification are rituals that mark occasions of crisis in the life of the group, rather than an individual. Whatever the precise nature of the crisis—a severe lack of rain that threatens crops in the fields, the sudden appearance of an enemy war party, the onset of an epidemic, or some other event that disturbs everyone—mass ceremonies are performed to allay the danger to the group.

This unites people in a common effort so that fear and confusion yield to collective action and a degree of optimism. The balance in the relations of all concerned, which has been upset, is restored to normal, and the community values are celebrated and affirmed.

While an individual's death might be regarded as the ultimate crisis in that individual's life, it is, as well, a crisis for the entire group, particularly if the group is small. A member of the group has been removed, so its equilibrium has been upset. The survivors, therefore, must readjust and restore balance. They also need to reconcile themselves to the loss of someone to whom they were emotionally tied. Funerary ceremonies, then, can be regarded as rites of intensification that permit the living to express in nondisruptive ways their upset over the death while providing for social readjustment. A frequent feature of such ceremonies is an ambivalence toward the dead person. For example, one of the parts of the funerary rites of certain Melanesians was the eating of the dead person's flesh. This ritual cannibalism, witnessed by anthropologist Bronislaw Malinowski, was performed with "extreme repugnance and dread and usually followed by a violent vomiting fit. At the same time it is felt to be a supreme act of reverence, love and devotion."[10] This custom and the emotions accompanying it clearly reveal the ambiguous attitude toward death: On the one hand, the survivors desire to maintain the tie to the dead person, and, on the other hand, they feel disgust and fear at the transformation wrought by death. According to Malinowski, funeral ceremonies provide an approved collective means for individuals to express these feelings while maintaining social cohesiveness and preventing disruption of society.

The performance of rites of intensification does not have to be limited to times of overt crisis. In regions where the seasons differ enough that human activities must change accordingly, they take the form of annual ceremonies. These are particularly common among horticultural and

---

[10]Malinowski, B. (1954). *Magic, science and religion, and other essays* (p. 50). Garden City, NY: Doubleday/Anchor Books.

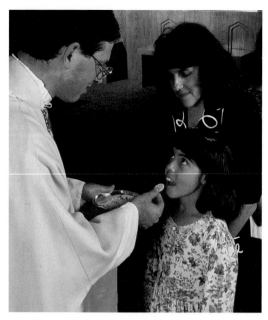

Ritual cannibalism appears in various societies in diverse forms. In Christianity, it is symbolic rather than actual, although some Christians believe the communion wafer actually becomes the body of Christ.

agricultural people, with their planting, first-fruit, and harvest ceremonies. For these critical times in the lives of people in such societies, the ceremonies express a reverent attitude toward nature's forces of generation and fertility that peoples' very existence depends on. If all goes well, as it often does at such times, participation in a happy situation reinforces group involvement. It also serves as a kind of dress rehearsal for serious crisis situations; it promotes a habit of reliance on supernatural forces through ritual activity, which can be easily activated under stressful circumstances when it is important not to give way to fear and despair.

RELIGION, MAGIC, AND WITCHCRAFT

Among the most fascinating of ritual practices is application of the belief that supernatural powers can be compelled to act in certain ways for good or evil purposes by recourse to particular specified formulas. This is a classical anthropological no-

Queen Elizabeth II of England presides at the launching of a ship. Magic plays an important part in British ship-launching ceremonies, involving symbolic classification of the ship, the reincarnating power of the ship's name, and the relationship between women and ships. All play an important role in how sailors, including their officers, believe and act.

tion of magic. Many societies have magical rituals to ensure good crops, the replenishment of game, the fertility of domestic animals, and the avoidance or cure of illness in humans.

Although most Western peoples today, seeking to objectify and demythologize their world, often have tried to suppress the existence of these fantastic notions in their own consciousness, they continue to be fascinated by them. Not only are books and films about demonic possession and witchcraft avidly devoured and discussed, but also by 1967 (after some 40 years of poor sales) sales of Ouija boards in the United States passed the 2 million mark. Thirty years ago about 100 newspapers carried horoscope columns, but by 1970 1,200 of a total of 1,750 daily newspapers regularly carried such columns. Anthropologist Lauren Kendall notes that "Many witches, wizards, druids, Cabalists, and shamans . . . practice modern magic in contemporary England and the United States, where their ranks are comfortably reckoned in the tens of thousands." Furthermore, "The usual magician is ordinary, generally middle class, and often highly intelligent—a noticeable number of them have something to do with computers."[11] Al-

though it is certainly true non-Western and peasant peoples tend to endow their world quite freely with magical properties, so do many highly educated Western peoples.

In the 19th century Sir James George Frazer, author of one of the most widely read anthropological books of all time, *The Golden Bough*, made a strong distinction between religion and magic. Religion he saw as "a propitiation or conciliation of powers superior to man which are believed to direct and control the course of nature and human life."[12] Magic, by contrast, he saw as an attempt to manipulate certain perceived "laws" of nature. The magician never doubts the same causes always will produce the same effects. Thus, Frazer saw magic as a sort of pseudoscience, differing from modern science only in its misconception of the

---

[11]Kendall, L. (1990, October). In the company of witches. *Natural History*, 92.

[12]Frazer, J. G. (1931). Magic and religion. In V. F. Calverton (Ed.), *The making of man: An outline of anthropology* (p. 693). New York: Modern Library.

What these two pictures have in common is that both are examples of institutionalized magical responses to concerns many harbor in their societies. In death-penalty states, executing criminals does no more to deter violent crimes than Aztec human sacrifices did to keep the sun in the sky.

nature of the particular laws that govern the succession of events.

Useful though Frazer's characterization of magic has been, anthropologists no longer accept his distinction between it and religion. Far from being separate, magical procedures frequently are part of religious rituals, and both magic and religion deal directly with the supernatural. In fact, Frazer's distinction seems to be no more than a bias of Western culture, which regards magic as quite separate from religion.

Frazer did make a useful distinction between two fundamental principles of magic. The first principle, that "like produces like," he called **imitative magic**. In Burma, for example, a rejected lover might engage a sorcerer to make an image of his would-be love. If this image were tossed into water, to the accompaniment of certain charms, the hapless girl would go mad. Thus, the girl would suffer a fate similar to that of her image.

Frazer's second principle was called **contagious magic**—the concept that things or persons once in contact can afterward influence one another. The most common example of contagious magic is the permanent relationship between an individual and any part of his or her body, such as hair, fingernails, or teeth. Frazer cites the Basutos of Lesotho, in southern Africa, who were careful to conceal their extracted teeth, because these might fall into the hands of certain mythical beings who could harm the owners of the teeth by working magic on them. Related to this is the custom, in Western societies, of treasuring objects that have been touched by special people.

WITCHCRAFT

In Salem, Massachusetts, 200 suspected witches were arrested in 1692; of these, 19 were hanged and 1 was hounded to death. Despite the awarding of damages to descendants of some of the victims 19 years later, not until 1957 were the last of the Salem witches exonerated by the Massachusetts legislature. Although many North Americans suppose **witchcraft** is something that belongs to a less enlightened past, in fact, it is alive and well in the United States today. Indeed, starting in the 1960s, witchcraft began to undergo something of a boom in this country. North Americans are by no means alone in this; for example, as the Ibibio of Nigeria have become increasingly exposed to modern education and scientific training, their reliance on witchcraft as an explanation for misfortune has increased.[13] Furthermore, it is often the younger, more educated members of Ibibio society who accuse others of bewitching them. Frequently, the accused are the older, more traditional members of society; thus we have an expression of the intergenerational hostility that often exists in fast-changing traditional societies.

---

[13]Offiong, D. (1985). Witchcraft among the Ibibio of Nigeria. In C. Lehmann and J. E. Myers (Eds.), *Magic, witchcraft and religion* (pp. 152–165). Palo Alto, CA: Mayfield.

Imitative magic.   Magic based on the principle that like produces like. > **Contagious magic.**   Magic based on the principle that beings once in contact can influence one another after separation. > **Witchcraft.**   An explanation of events based on the belief certain individuals possess an innate psychic power capable of causing harm, including sickness and death. Also includes beliefs and practices of benevolent magic.

Ibibio Witchcraft

Among the Ibibio, as among most peoples of sub-Saharan Africa, witchcraft beliefs are highly developed and long standing. A rat that eats up a person's crops is not really a rat but a witch that changed into one; if a young and enterprising man cannot get a job or fails an exam, he has been bewitched; and if someone's money is wasted away or if the person becomes sick, is bitten by a snake, or is struck by lightning, the reason is always the same—witchcraft. Indeed, virtually all misfortune, illness, and death are attributed to the malevolent activities of witches. The Ibibio's modern knowledge of such discoveries as the role microorganisms play in disease has little impact; after all, it says nothing about why these were sent to the afflicted individual. Although Ibibio religious beliefs provide alternative explanations for misfortune, they carry negative connotations and do not elicit nearly as much sympathy from others. Thus, if evil befalls a person, witchcraft is a far more satisfying explanation than something such as filial disobedience or violation of some taboo.

Who are these Ibibio witches? They are thought to be males or females who have within them a special substance acquired from another established witch. This substance is made up of red, white, and black threads, needles, and other ingredients, and one gets it by swallowing it. From it comes a special power that causes harm, up to and including death, irrespective of whether its possessor intends to cause harm or not. The power is purely psychic, and Ibibio witches do not perform rites nor make use of "bad medicine." It gives them the ability to change into animals, to travel any distance at incredible speed to get at their victims, whom they may torture or kill by transferring the victim's soul into an animal, which is then eaten.

To identify a witch, an Ibibio looks for any person whose behavior is out of the ordinary. Specifically, any combination of the following may cause someone to be labeled a witch: not being fond of greeting people; living alone in a place apart from others; charging too high a price for something; enjoying adultery or committing incest; walking about at night; not showing sufficient grief upon the death of a relative or other community member; taking improper care of one's parents, children, or wives; and hardheartedness. Witches are apt to look and act mean and to be socially disruptive people in the sense that their behavior too far exceeds the range of variance considered acceptable.

Neither the Ibibio in particular nor Africans in general are alone in attributing most malevolent happenings to witchcraft. Similar beliefs can be found in any human society, including—as already noted—that of the United States. As among the Ibibio, the powers (however they may be gained) are generally considered innate and uncontrollable; they result in activities that are the antithesis of proper behavior, and persons displaying undesirable personality characteristics (however these may be defined) are generally the ones accused of being witches.

In North America, interest in and practice of witchcraft have grown significantly over the past 30 years, often among highly educated segments of society. Contrary to popular belief, witchcraft (sometimes called Wicca) is *not* concerned exclusively, or even primarily, with working evil.

The Ibibio make a distinction between "black witches"—those whose acts are especially diabolical and destructive—and "white witches," whose witchcraft is relatively benign, even though their powers are thought to be greater than those of their black counterparts. This exemplifies a common distinction between what Lucy Mair, a British anthropologist, has dubbed "nightmare witches" and "everyday witches."[14] The nightmare witch is the very embodiment of a society's conception of evil, a being that flouts the rules of sexual behavior and disregards every standard of decency. Nightmare witches, being almost literally the product of dreams and repressed fantasies, have much in common wherever they appear: The modern Navajo and the ancient Roman, for example, like the Ibibio, conceived of witches who could turn themselves into animals and gather to feast on their victims. Everyday witches are often the community's nonconformists, who are morose, who eat alone, who are arrogant and unfriendly, but who otherwise cause little trouble. Such witches may be dangerous when offended and retaliate by causing sickness, death, crop failure, cattle disease, or any number of lesser ills; people thought to be witches are usually treated very courteously.

THE FUNCTIONS OF WITCHCRAFT

Why witchcraft? We might better ask, why not? As Mair aptly observed, in a world where there are few proven techniques for dealing with everyday crises, especially sickness, a belief in witches is not foolish; it is indispensable. No one wants to resign oneself to illness, and if the malady is caused by a witch's hex, then magical countermeasures should cure it. Not only does the idea of personalized evil answer the problem of unmerited suffering, but it also provides an explanation for many happenings no cause can be discovered for. Witchcraft, then, cannot be refuted. Even if we could convince a person that his or her illness was due to natural causes, the victim would still ask, as the Ibibio do, Why me? Why now? Such a view

leaves no room for pure chance; everything must be assigned a cause or meaning. Witchcraft provides the explanation and, in so doing, also provides both the basis and the means for taking counteraction.

Nor is witchcraft always malevolent; even during the Spanish Inquisition, church officials recognized a benevolent or "white" variety. The positive functions of even malevolent witchcraft may be seen in many African societies in which people believe sickness and death are caused by witches. The ensuing search for the perpetrator of the misfortune becomes, in effect, a communal probe into social behavior.

A witch-hunt is, in fact, a systematic investigation, through a public hearing, into all social relationships involving the victim of the sickness or death. Was her husband unfaithful or her son lacking in the performance of his duties? Were her friends uncooperative, or was the victim guilty of any of these wrongs? Accusations are reciprocal, and before long just about every unsocial or hostile act that has occurred in that society since the last outbreak of witchcraft (sickness or death) is brought into the open.[15]

Through such periodic public scrutiny of everyone's behavior, people are reminded of what their society regards as both strengths and weaknesses of character. This encourages individuals to suppress as best they can those personality traits looked upon with disapproval, for if they do not, they at some time may be accused of being a witch. A belief in witchcraft thus serves a function of social control.

Psychological Functions of Witchcraft Among the Navajo

Widely known among American Indians are the Navajo, who possess a detailed concept of witchcraft. Several types of witchcraft are distinguished. *Witchery* encompasses the practices of witches, who are said to meet at night to practice cannibalism and kill people at a distance. *Sorcery* is distinguished from witchery only by the methods

---

[14]Mair, L. (1969). *Witchcraft* (p. 37). New York: McGraw-Hill.

[15]Turnbull, C. M. (1983). *The human cycle* (p. 181). New York: Simon & Schuster.

anthropology applied

Reconciling Modern Medicine With Traditional Beliefs in Swaziland

Although the biomedical germ theory is generally accepted in Western societies today, this is not the case in many other societies around the world. In southern Africa's Swaziland, for example, all types of illnesses are generally thought to be caused by sorcery or by loss of ancestral protection. Even where the effectiveness of Western medicine is recognized, the ultimate question remains: Why was the disease sent in the first place? Thus, for the treatment of disease, the Swazi traditionally have relied upon herbalists, diviner mediums ancestral spirits are thought to work through, and Christian faith healers. Unfortunately, such individuals usually have been regarded as quacks and charlatans by the medical establishment, even though the herbal medicines traditional healers use are effective in several ways, and the reassurance provided patient and family alike through rituals that reduce stress and anxiety plays an important role in the patient's recovery. In a country with 1 traditional healer for every 110 people but only 1 physician for every 10,000, the potential benefit of cooperation between physicians and healers seems self-evident. Nevertheless, it was unrecognized until proposed by anthropologist Edward C. Green.*

Green, who is now senior research associate with a private firm, went to Swaziland in 1981 as a researcher for a Rural Water-Borne Disease Control Project, funded by the United States Agency for International Development. Assigned the task of finding out about knowledge, attitudes, and practices related to water and sanitation, and aware of the serious deficiencies of conventional surveys that rely on precoded questionnaires (see Chapter 1), Green used instead the traditional anthropological techniques of open-ended interviews with key informants, along with participant observation. The key informants were traditional healers, patients, and rural health motivators (individuals communities chose to receive 8 weeks of training in preventive health care in regional clinics). Without such work, Green would have found it impossible to design and interpret a reliable survey instrument, but the added payoff was that he learned a great deal about Swazi theories of disease and its treatment.

Disposed at the outset to recognize the positive value of many traditional practices, Green also could see how cooperation with physicians might be achieved. For example, traditional healers already recognized the utility of Western medicines for the treatment of diseases not indigenous to Africa, and traditional medicines routinely were given to children through inhalation and a kind of vaccination. Thus, nontraditional medicines and vaccinations might be accepted, if presented in traditional terms.

Realizing the suspicion existing on both sides, Green and his Swazi associate Lydia Makhubu (a chemist who had studied the properties of native medicines) recommended to the Minister of Health a cooperative project focused on a problem of concern to health professionals and native healers alike: infant diarrheal diseases. These recently had become a health problem of high concern to the general public; healers wanted a way to prevent such diseases, and a means of treatment existed—oral rehydration therapy—that was compatible with traditional treatments for diarrhea (herbal preparations taken orally for a period). Packets of oral rehydration salts, along with instructions, were provided healers in a pilot project, with positive results. This helped convince health professionals of the benefits of cooperation, while the healers saw the distribution of packets to them as a gesture of trust and cooperation from the Ministry of Health.

Since then, further steps toward cooperation have been taken. All of this demonstrates the importance of finding how to work in ways compatible with existing belief systems. Directly challenging traditional beliefs, as all too often happens, does little more than create stress, confusion, and resentment among a people.

---

*Green, E. C. (1987). The planning of health education strategies in Swaziland; and The integration of modern and traditional health sectors in Swaziland. In R. M. Wulff & S. J. Fiske (Eds.), *Anthropological praxis: Translating knowledge into action* (pp. 15–25; 87–97). Boulder, CO: Westview.

used by the sorcerer, who casts spells on individuals using the victim's fingernails, hair, or discarded clothing. *Wizardry* is not distinguished so much by its effects as by its manner of working: Wizards kill by injecting a cursed substance, such as a tooth from a corpse, into the victim's body.

Whether or not a particular illness results from Navajo witchcraft is determined by **divination,** a magical procedure that also reveals the witch's identity. Once a person is charged with witchcraft, he or she is publicly interrogated, possibly even tortured, until there is a confession. It is believed the witch's own curse will turn against the witch once this happens, so it is expected the witch will die within a year. Some confessed witches have been allowed to live in exile.

According to Clyde Kluckhohn, Navajo witchcraft served to channel anxieties, tensions, and frustrations caused by the pressures from Anglo Americans.[16] The rigid rules of decorum among the Navajo allow little means for expression of hostility, except through accusations of witchcraft. Such accusations funnel pent-up negative emotions against individuals without upsetting the wider society. Another function of witchcraft accusations is that they permit the direct expression of hostile feelings against people one ordinarily would be unable to express anger or enmity toward. On a more positive note, individuals strive to behave in ways that will prevent their being accused of witchcraft. Since excessive wealth is believed to result from witchcraft, individuals are encouraged to redistribute their assets among friends and relatives, thereby leveling economic differences. Similarly, because Navajos believe uncared-for elders will turn into witches, people are strongly motivated to take care of aged relatives. And because leaders are thought to be witches, people are understandably reluctant to go against their wishes, lest they suffer supernatural retribution.

Analyses such as these demonstrate that witchcraft, in spite of its often negative image, frequently functions in a very positive way to manage tensions within a society. Nonetheless, events may get out of hand, particularly in crisis situations, when widespread accusations may cause great suffering. This certainly was the case in the Salem witch trials, but even those pale in comparison to the something like half a million individuals executed as witches in Europe from the 15th through 17th centuries. This was a time of profound change in European society, marked by a good deal of political and religious conflict. At such times, it is all too easy to search out scapegoats to place the blame on for what people believe are undesirable changes.

---

[16]Kluckhohn, C. (1944). Navajo witchcraft. *Papers of the Peabody Museum of American Archaeology and Ethnology,* 22 (2).

THE FUNCTIONS OF RELIGION

Just as a belief in witchcraft may serve a variety of psychological and social functions, so too do religious beliefs and practices in general. Here we will summarize these functions in a more systematic way. One psychological function is to provide an orderly model of the universe; its importance for orderly human behavior is discussed in Chapter 16. Beyond this, by explaining the unknown and making it understandable, religion reduces the

---

Divination. A magical procedure for determining the cause of a particular event, such as illness, or foretelling the future.

Members of the same religion may engage in, as well as suffer, persecution. In the former Yugoslavia, Roman Catholic Croats and Eastern Orthodox Serbs fought each other, while both fought Islamic Bosnians. In the Sudan, Islamic fundamentalists routinely direct violence against Christians and Pagans. In the Middle East, at the same time that Jews are the victims of violence from Islamic fundamentalists, fundamentalist Jews have directed violence against Muslims.

fears and anxieties of individuals. As we have seen, the explanations usually assume the existence of various sorts of supernatural beings and powers, which people potentially may appeal to or manipulate. This being so, a means is provided for dealing with crises: Divine aid is, theoretically, available when all else fails.

A social function of religion is to sanction a wide range of conduct. In this context, religion plays a role in social control, which, as we saw in Chapter 23, does not rely on law alone. This is done through notions of right and wrong. Right actions earn the approval of whatever supernatural powers a particular culture recognizes. Wrong actions may cause retribution through supernatural agencies. In short, by deliberately *raising* peoples' feelings of guilt and anxiety about their actions, religion helps keep them in line.

Religion does more than this, though; it sets precedents for acceptable behavior. We already have noted the connection between myths and religion. Usually, myths are full of tales of supernatural beings that in various ways illustrate the society's ethical code in action. So it is that Gluskabe, the Penobscot culture hero, is portrayed in the Penobscot myths as tricking and punishing those who mock others, lie, are greedy, or go in for extremes of behavior. Moreover, the specific situations serve as precedents for human behavior in similar circumstances. The Bible's Old and New Testaments are rich in the same sort of material. Related to this, by the models religion presents and the morals it espouses, religion serves to justify and perpetuate a particular social order. Thus, in the Jewish, Christian, and Islamic traditions, a masculine-authoritarian godhead along with a creation story that portrays a woman as responsible for a fall from grace serves to justify a social order where men exercise control over women.

A psychological function also is tied up in all this. A society's moral code, since it is considered divinely fixed, lifts the burden of responsibility for conduct from the shoulders of the society's individual members, at least in important situations. It can be a tremendous relief to individuals to know that the responsibility for the way things are rests with the gods, rather than with themselves.

Another social function of religion is its role

in the maintenance of social solidarity. In our discussion of shamans, we saw how such individuals provide focal points of interest, thus supplying one ingredient of assistance for maintaining group unity. In addition, common participation in rituals, coupled with a basic uniformity of beliefs, helps to bind people together and reinforce their identification with their group. Particularly effective may be their participation together in rituals, when the atmosphere is charged with emotion. The exalted feelings people may experience in such circumstances serve as a positive reinforcement in that they feel good as a result. Here, once again, we find religion providing psychological assurance while providing for the needs of society.

One other area where religion serves a social function is education. In our discussion of rites of passage, we noted that Australian puberty rites served as a kind of cram course in tribal lore. By providing a memorable occasion, initiation rites can enhance learning and thus help ensure the perpetuation of a nonliterate culture. And as we saw for the female initiation rites among the Mende, they can serve to ensure individuals have the knowledge they will need to fulfill their adult roles in society. Education also may be served by rites of intensification. Frequently, such rites involve dramas that portray matters of cultural importance. For example, among a food-foraging people dances may imitate the movement of game and techniques of hunting. Among farmers a fixed round of ceremonies may emphasize the steps necessary for good crops. These rites help preserve knowledge important to a people's material well-being.

RELIGION AND CULTURAL CHANGE

Although the subject of culture change is taken up in a later chapter, no anthropological consideration of religion is complete without some mention of *revitalization movements*. In 1931, at Buka in the Solomon Islands, a native religious cult suddenly emerged, its prophets predicting a deluge would soon engulf all Whites. This would be followed by the arrival of a ship laden with European goods. The believers were to construct a storehouse for the goods and to prepare themselves to repulse the colonial police. Because the ship would arrive only after the natives had used up all their own supplies, they ceased working in the fields. Although the cult leaders were arrested, the movement continued for some years.

This was not an isolated instance. Such "cargo cults"—and many other movements promising the resurrection of the dead, the destruction or enslavement of Europeans, and the coming of utopian riches—have sporadically appeared throughout Melanesia ever since the beginning of this century. Since these cults are widely separated in space and time, their similarities are apparently the result of similarities in social conditions. In these

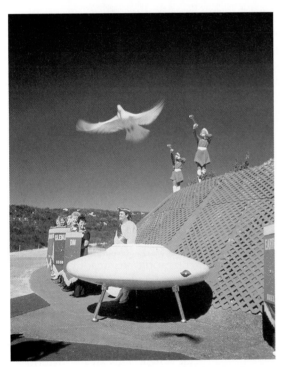

Shown here are members of the Unarias Academy of Science, a "New Age" Revitalization movement that believes in the future arrival of wise space beings who will inspire a new spiritual awareness in human beings.

areas the traditional cultures of the indigenous peoples have been uprooted. Europeans, or European-influenced natives, hold all political and economic power. Natives are employed unloading and distributing Western-made goods but have no practical knowledge of how to attain these goods. When cold reality offers no hope from the daily frustrations of cultural deterioration and economic deprivation, religion offers the solution.

REVITALIZATION MOVEMENTS

From the 1890 Ghost Dance of many North American Indians to the Mau Mau of Kenya to the "cargo cults" of Melanesia, extreme and sometimes violent religious reactions to European domination are so common that anthropologists have sought to formulate their underlying causes and general characteristics. Yet **revitalization movements,** as they are now called, are by no means restricted to the colonial world, and in the United States alone hundreds of such movements have sprung up. Among the more widely known are Mormonism, which began in the 19th century; the more recent Unification Church of the Reverend Sun Myung Moon; the Branch Davidians whose "prophet" was David Koresh; and the Heaven's Gate cult led by Marshall Herf Applewhite and Bonnie Lu Trousdale Nettles. As these four examples suggest, revitalization movements show a great deal of diversity, and some have been much more successful than others.

A revitalization movement is a deliberate effort by members of a society to construct a more satisfying culture. The emphasis in this definition is on the reformation not just of the religious sphere of activity but also of the entire cultural system. Such a drastic solution is attempted when a group's anxiety and frustration have become so intense that the only way to reduce the stress is to overturn the entire social system and replace it with a new one.

Given the numerous sources of anxiety in North American society today, ranging from those related to science and technology, noted earlier in

---

Revitalization movements.   Social movements, often of a religious nature, with the purpose of totally reforming a society.

A fascination with numbers and calendrical calculations is not restricted to North Americans and others at the end of the millennium. Shown here are pages from a Maya Indian book that predates Columbus; they consist of Venus tables that track the movement of this planet over a period of several centuries. The information was important for deciding auspicious times to make war.

this chapter, to what many regard as a breakdown of the family and morality (see Chapters 19 and 20), coupled with the turn of the millennium in the year 2001 (the year 2000 is the last year of the 20th century), we may expect to see a number of millenarian revitalization movements for the next few years. Although periods of 1,000 years (millennia) have no relationship whatever to any astronomical cycle, numbers have their own fascination in the seemingly magical ways they can be manipulated. In this case, the completely arbitrary unit of 1,000 years is fused with apocalyptic Christian beliefs to predict an imminent destruction of the present world. (The same fears occurred before the previous millennium.) Precisely such a mix of bits and pieces of Christian belief with folk myths of contemporary North American culture—UFOlogy in particular—and the end of the millennium cost the followers of Heaven's Gate their lives.[17]

Anthropologist Anthony Wallace has outlined a sequence common to all expressions of the revitalization process.[18] First is the normal state of society, in which stress is not too great and sufficient cultural means of satisfying needs exist. Under certain conditions, such as domination by a more powerful group or severe economic depression, stress and frustration are steadily amplified; this ushers in the second phase, or the period of increased individual stress. If there are no significant adaptive changes, a period of cultural distortion follows, in which stress becomes so chronic that socially approved methods of releasing tension begin to break down. This steady deterioration of the culture may be checked by a period of revitalization, during which a dynamic cult or religious movement grips a sizable proportion of the population. Often the movement will be so out of touch with reality that it is doomed to failure from

[17]Gould, S. J. (1997). *Questioning the millennium*. New York: Crown.

[18]Wallace, A. F. C. (1970). *Culture and personality* (2nd ed., pp. 191–196). New York: Random House.

In the United States, Mormonism is an example of a revitalization movement that is enormously successful in gaining acceptance in the wider society. By contrast, the Branch Davidians so antagonized elements of mainstream society that a confrontation occurred, ending with the mass immolation of many cult members.

the beginning. This was the case with the Heaven's Gate cult, because its followers self-destructed from suicide based on a conviction their spiritual essences would reunite with extraterrestrial higher bodies in a spaceship that awaited them behind the tail of the Hale-Bopp comet to take them "home." This self-destruction was the case also with the Branch Davidians, when the suspicions of government authorities led to an assault on the cult's compound. In reaction, cult members committed mass suicide by deliberately immolating themselves in their headquarters.

More rarely, a movement may tap long-dormant adaptive forces underlying a culture, and an enduring religion may result. Such is the case with Mormonism. Though heavily persecuted at first and hounded from place to place, Mormons adapted to the point that their religion thrives in the United States today. Indeed, revitalization movements lie at the root of all known religions, Judaism, Christianity, and Islam included. We shall return to revitalization movements in Chapter 26.

CHAPTER SUMMARY

Religion is a part of all cultures. It consists of beliefs and behavior patterns by which people try to control areas of the universe otherwise beyond their control. Among food-foraging peoples, religion is a basic ingredient of everyday life. As societies become more complex, religion is less a part of daily activities and tends to be restricted to particular occasions.

Religion is characterized by a belief in supernatural beings and forces. Through prayer, sacrifice, and other religious rituals, people appeal to the supernatural world for aid. Supernatural beings may be grouped into three categories: major deities (gods and goddesses), ancestral spirits, and other sorts of spirit beings. Gods and goddesses are the greatest but most remote beings. They are usually thought of as controlling the universe or a specific part of it. Whether or not people recognize gods, goddesses, or both has to do with how men and women relate to one another in everyday life. Animism is a belief in spirit beings, other than ancestors, who are believed to animate all of nature. These spirit beings are closer to humans than gods and goddesses and are intimately concerned with human activities. Animism is typical of peoples who see themselves as a part of nature rather than as superior to it. A belief in ancestral spirits is based on the idea that human beings are made up of a body and soul. At death the spirit is freed from the body and continues to participate in human affairs. Belief in ancestral spirits is particularly characteristic of descent-based groups with their associated ancestral orientation. Animatism may be found with animism in the same culture. Animatism is a force or power directed to a successful outcome and may make itself manifest in any object.

Beliefs in supernatural beings and powers are maintained, first, through what are interpreted as manifestations of power. Second, they are perpetuated because supernatural beings possess attributes familiar to people. Finally, myths serve to rationalize religious beliefs and practices.

All human societies have specialists—priests and priestesses and/or shamans—to guide religious practices and to intervene with the supernatural world. Shamanism, with its often dramatic ritual, promotes a release of tension among individuals in a society. The shaman provides a focal point of attention for society and can help to maintain social control. The benefits of shamanism for the shaman are prestige, sometimes wealth, and an outlet for artistic self-expression.

Religious rituals are religion in action. Through ritual acts, social bonds are reinforced. Times of life crises are occasions for ritual. Arnold Van Gennep divided such rites of passage into rites of separation, transition, and incorporation. Rites of intensification are rituals to mark crisis occasions in the life of the group rather than the individual. They serve to unite people, allay fear of the crisis, and prompt collective action. Funerary ceremonies are rites of intensification that provide for social readjustment after the loss of the deceased. Rites of intensification also may involve annual ceremonies to seek favorable conditions surrounding critical activities such as planting and harvesting.

Ritual practices of peasant and non-Western peoples are often an expression of the belief they can make supernatural powers act in certain ways with certain prescribed formulas. This is the classic anthropological notion of magic. Sir James Frazer differentiated two principles of magic— "like produces like," or imitative magic, and the law of contagion.

Witchcraft functions as an effective way for people to explain away personal misfortune without having to shoulder any of the blame. Even malevolent witchcraft may function positively in the realm of social control. It also may provide an outlet for feelings of hostility and frustration without disturbing the norms of the larger group.

Religion (including magic and witchcraft) serves several important social functions. First, it sanctions a wide range of conduct by providing notions of right and wrong. Second, it sets precedents for acceptable behavior and helps perpetuate an existing social order. Third, religion serves to lift the burden of decision making from individuals and places responsibility with the gods. Fourth, religion plays a large role in maintaining social solidarity. Finally, religion serves education. Ritual ceremonies enhance learning of tribal lore and thus help to ensure the perpetuation of a nonliterate culture.

Domination by Western society has been the cause of revitalization movements in non-Western societies. In the islands of Melanesia, these take the form of cargo cults that have appeared spontaneously at different times since the beginning of the century. Anthony Wallace has interpreted revitalization movements as attempts, sometimes successful, to change the society. Regardless of the society they appear in, revitalization movements all follow a common sequence, and all religions stem from such movements.

POINTS FOR CONSIDERATION

1. Many have felt that with the advance of technology and Western scientific investigation, "irrational" religious beliefs gradually would fade away to be replaced by "logical knowledge." Has this been the case? Is it ever likely to occur? Why or why not?

2. Are religion and science necessarily opposed? What is your own experience with these two worlds?

3. What is the purpose of myths? What is their relationship to social organization? How do the functions of myths compare with those of "history" in various societies?

4. Religion is often called "irrational" or "illogical" in comparison with science. Is this a fair assessment? Why or why not? What is required for an argument to be "logical" and "rational"? Recalling the Anthropology Applied section dealing with Swaziland, what are the potential consequences of such a position? How possible and how rewarding is compromise?

SUGGESTED READINGS

Kalwet, H. (1988). *Dreamtime and inner space: The world of the shaman.* New York: Random House.

Written by an ethnopsychologist, this book surveys the practices and paranormal experiences of healers and shamans from Africa, the Americas, Asia, and Australia.

Lehmann, A. C., & Myers, J. E. (Eds.). (1993). *Magic, witchcraft and religion: An anthropological study of the supernatural* (3rd ed.). Mountain View, CA: Mayfield.

This anthology of readings is cross-cultural in scope, covering traditional as well as nontraditional themes. Well represented are both "tribal" and "modern" religions. It is a good way to discover the relevance and vitality of anthropological approaches to the supernatural.

Malinowski, B. (1954). *Magic, science and religion, and other essays.* Garden City, NY: Doubleday/Anchor Books.

The articles collected here provide a discussion of the Trobriand Islanders as illustrative of conceptual and theoretical knowledge of humankind. The author covers such diversified topics as religion, life, death, character of "primitive" cults, magic, faith, and myth.

Norbeck, E. (1974). *Religion in human life: Anthropological views.* New York: Holt, Rinehart and Winston.

The author presents a comprehensive view of religion based on twin themes: the description of religious events, rituals, and states of mind and the nature of anthropological aims, views, procedures, and interpretations.

Wallace, A. F. C. (1966). *Religion: An anthropological view.* New York: Random House.

This is a classic textbook treatment of religion by an anthropologist who has specialized in the study of revitalization movements.

Chapter 25
The Arts

No known culture is without some
form of art, even though that art
may be applied to purely utilitarian objects.
These carpets, on display in Morocco,
are one expression of the universal urge
for artistic creation.

Chapter Preview

What Is Art?

Art is the creative use of the human imagination to interpret, understand, and enjoy life. Although the idea of art serving nonuseful, nonpractical purposes seems firmly entrenched in the thinking of modern Western peoples, in other cultures art often serves what are regarded as important, practical purposes.

Why Do Anthropologists Study Art?

Anthropologists have found that art reflects a people's cultural values and concerns. This is especially true of the verbal arts—myths, legends, and tales. From these the anthropologist may learn how a people order their universe and may discover much about a people's history as well. Also, music and the visual arts may provide insights into a people's worldview and, through distributional studies, may suggest things about a people's history.

What Are the Functions of the Arts?

Aside from adding pleasure to everyday life, the various arts serve a number of functions. Myths, for example, set standards for orderly behavior, and the verbal arts generally transmit and preserve a culture's customs and values. Songs, too, may do this within the restrictions musical form imposes. And any art form, to the degree it is characteristic of a particular society, may contribute to the cohesiveness or solidarity of that society.

In the United States, the arts often are seen as something of a frill, something to be engaged in for personal enjoyment apart from more productive pursuits or to provide pleasure for others, or both. This attitude becomes apparent whenever public funds are in short supply; on the local level, for example, in battles over school budgets, art programs are often the first to be cut. Unlike sports, which usually are supported more than the arts because they are perceived as providing skills thought to be essential to success in a competitive world, the arts are seen as nonessential: pleasurable and worthwhile but expensive, with little practical payoff. On the national level, fiscal conservatives labor to cut back funds for the arts, on the premise the arts lack the practical importance of defense, economic, or other governmental activities. Indeed, artists and their supporters are seen as something of an elite, subsidized at the expense of hard-working "practical" people. Yet one might ask, why in recent years has the National Endowment for the Arts so often been the center of such hot political controversy? If art really is such an unimportant diversionary activity, why has so much legislative time and energy been devoted to often bitter fights to cut off funding or at least to impose controls on the kinds of work artists may engage in?

The fact is artistic behavior is far from unimportant and is as basic to human beings as talking. Just as speech is used to communicate feelings, to make statements, so too is artistic expression. Moreover, it is not simply a special category of persons called "artists" who do this; for example, all human beings adorn their bodies in certain ways and by doing so make a statement about who they are, both as individuals and as members of social groups of various sorts. Similarly, all people tell stories, in which they express their values, their hopes, and their concerns and thus reveal much about themselves and the nature of the world as they see it. In short, all peoples engage in artistic behavior as they use their imagination creatively to interpret, understand, and even enjoy life. What's more, they have been doing this for at least 40,000 years, if not longer. Far from a luxury afforded or appreciated by a minority of aesthetes or escapists, art is a necessary kind of social behavior every normal and active human being participates in.

The idea of art serving nonuseful, nonpractical purposes seems firmly entrenched in the thinking of modern Western peoples. Today, for example, the objects from the tomb of the young Egyptian king Tutankhamen are on display in a museum, where they may be seen and admired as the exquisite works of art they are. They were made,

Perhaps the oldest means of artistic expression is body decoration. Shown here is a Moroccan woman whose hands and feet are dyed with henna (to celebrate a royal wedding) and a tattooed Asian man.

however, to be hidden away from human eyes, where they were to guarantee the eternal life of the king and to protect him from evil forces that might enter his body and gain control over it. Or we may listen to the singing of a sea chantey purely for aesthetic pleasure, as a form of entertainment. In fact, in the days of sail, sea chanteys served very useful and practical purposes. They set the appropriate rhythm for performance of specific shipboard tasks, and the same qualities that make them pleasurable to listen to today served to relieve the boredom of those tasks. Such links between art and other aspects are common in human societies around the world. Only in the West—and recently at that—has *fine art* become less accessible to members of the society at large, as wealthy collectors commission and purchase artworks for their personal enjoyment in the privacy of their homes. Yet *pop art* or *folk art*—call it what you will—continues to thrive. Because art, like any aspect of culture, is inextricably intertwined with everything else people do, it affords us glimpses into other aspects of peoples' lives, including their values and worldview.

To people today, making exquisite objects of gold and precious stones to place in a tomb might seem like throwing them away. Yet, something similar happens when a Navajo Indian creates an intricate sand painting as part of a ritual act, only to destroy it once the ritual is over. Johann Sebastian Bach did the very same thing when, almost

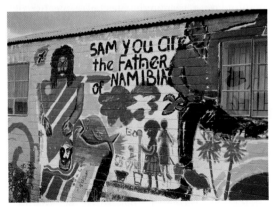

Much of the world's art is created for functional rather than aesthetic purposes. Shown here, counterclockwise, are examples of art used to cure sickness (a Navajo sand painting), to express cultural identity (the Mardi Gras costume of one of New Orleans' "Black Indians"), and for political purposes (graffiti from Katatura, Namibia).

300 years ago, he composed his cantatas for church services. These were "throwaway" music, meant to be discarded after the services they were written for. That many of them are still performed today is something of an accident, for Bach did not compose them for posterity. In many human societies, creating the art is often of greater importance than the final product itself.

Whether a particular work of art is intended to be appreciated purely as such or (as in the examples just noted) to serve some practical purpose, it will in every case require the same special combination of the symbolic representation of form and the expression of feeling that constitute the creative imagination. Insofar as the creative use of the human ability to symbolize is universal and both expresses and is shaped by cultural values and concerns, it is an important subject for anthropological study.

As an activity or kind of behavior that contributes to human well-being and that helps give shape and significance to life, art must be related to, yet differentiated from, religion. The dividing line between the two is not distinct: It is not easy to say, for example, precisely where art stops and religion begins in an elaborate ceremony involving ornamentation, masks, costumes, songs, dances, and effigies. And like magic, music, dance, and other arts may be used to "enchant"—to exploit the innate or psychological biases of another person or group so as to cause them to perceive social reality in a way favorable to the interests of the "enchanter." Indeed, the arts may be used to manipulate a seemingly inexhaustible list of human passions, including desire, terror, wonder, cupidity, fantasy, and vanity.[1]

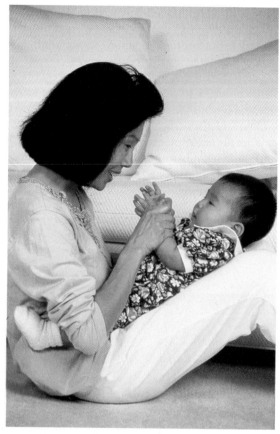

Use of art to enchant: By singing to her child, this mother soothes and at the same time promotes the kind of behavior she wants from her child.

▲▽▲▽▲▽▲▽▲▽▲▽▲▽▲▽▲▽▲▽▲▽▲▽▲▽▲

THE ANTHROPOLOGICAL STUDY OF ART

When approaching art as a cultural phenomenon, anthropologists have the pleasant task of cataloging, photographing, recording, and describing all possible forms of imaginative activity in any

particular culture. An enormous variety of forms and modes of artistic expression exist in the world. Because people everywhere continue to create and develop in new directions, no point of diminishing returns is foreseeable for the interesting process of collecting and describing the world's ornaments, body decorations, variations in clothing, blanket and rug designs, pottery and basket styles, architectural embellishments, monuments, ceremonial masks, legends, work songs, dances, and other art forms. The collecting process, however, eventually must lead to some kind of analysis and generalizations about relationships between art and the rest of culture.

A good way to begin a study of the relationships between art and the rest of culture is to examine critically some of the generalizations already made about specific arts. Since it is impos-

[1]Gell, A. (1988). Technology and magic. *Anthropology Today, 4* (2), 7.

Among the Inuit, the artist does not impose his or her will on the medium, but rather seeks to help what is already there to emerge from hiding.

 Protecting Cultural Heritages

In these last years of the 20th century, the time is long past when the anthropologist could go out and describe small tribal groups in out-of-the-way places that had not been "contaminated" by contact with Western people. Not only do few such groups exist in the world today, but also those that do remain face strong pressures to abandon their traditional ways in the name of "progress." All too often, tribal peoples are made to forfeit their indigenous identity and are pressed into a mold that allows them neither the opportunity nor the motivation to rise above the lowest rung of the social ladder. From an autonomous people able to provide for their own needs, with pride and a strong sense of identity as a people, they are transformed into a deprived underclass with neither pride nor a sense of identity,

often despised by more fortunate members of some multinational state in which they live.

The basic rights of groups of people to be themselves and not to be deprived of their distinctive cultural identities are and should be our paramount consideration and will be dealt with in the final two chapters of this book. However, anthropologists have additional reasons to be concerned about the disappearance of the societies and traditions they study. For one thing, the need for information about them has become steadily more apparent. If we are ever to have a realistic understanding of that elusive thing called human nature, we need reliable data on all humans. More is involved than this, though; once a traditional society is gone, it is lost to humanity, unless an adequate record of it exists. When a culture is lost without records of it, humanity is the poorer for the loss. Hence, anthropologists have in a sense rescued many such societies from oblivion. This not only helps to preserve the human heritage, but it also may be important to an ethnic group that, having become Westernized, wishes to rediscover and reassert its past cultural identity. Better yet, of course, is to find ways to prevent the loss of cultural traditions and societies in the first place.

To the Pomo Indians of California, the art of basket making has been important for their sense of who they are since before the coming of European settlers. Recognized for their skilled techniques and aesthetic artistry, Pomo baskets—some of the finest in the world—are prized by museums and private collectors alike. Nevertheless, the art of Pomo basket making was threatened in the 1970s by the impending construction of the Warm Springs Dam-Lake Sonoma Project to the north of San Francisco. The effect of this project would be to wipe out virtually all existing habitat for a particular species of sedge essential for the weaving of Pomo baskets.

Accordingly, a coalition of archaeologists, Native Americans, and others with objections to the project brought suit in federal district court. As it happened, the U.S. Army Corps of Engineers had recently hired anthropologist Richard N. Lerner for its San Francisco

District Office to advise on sociocultural factors associated with water resources programs in northwestern California. One of Lerner's first tasks, therefore, was to undertake studies of the problem and to find ways to overcome it.*

After comprehensive archaeological, ethnographic, and other studies were completed in 1976, Lerner succeeded in having the Pomo basketry materials recognized by the National Register of Historic Places as "historic property," requiring the Corps of Engineers to find ways to mitigate the adverse impact dam construction would have. The result was a complex ethnobotanical project developed and implemented by Lerner. Working in concert with Pomo Indians as well as botanists, Lerner relocated 48,000 sedge plants onto nearly 3 acres of suitable lands downstream from the dam. By the fall of 1983, the sedge was doing well enough to be harvested and proved to be of excellent quality. Since this initial harvest, groups of weavers have returned each year, and the art of Pomo Indian basket making appears to be safe for the time being.

*Lerner, R. N. (1987). Preserving plants for Pomos. In R. M. Wulff & S. J. Fiske (Eds.), *Anthropological praxis: Translating knowledge into action* (pp. 212–222). Boulder CO: Westview.

---

sible to cover all art forms in the space of a single chapter, we shall concentrate on just a few: verbal arts, music, and pictorial art. We will start with the verbal arts, for we have already touched upon them in earlier discussions of religion (Chapter 24) and worldview (Chapters 16 and 23).

VERBAL ARTS

The term **folklore** was coined in the 19th century to denote the unwritten stories, beliefs, and customs of European peasantry, as opposed to the

traditions of the literate elite. The subsequent study of folklore, **folkloristics,** has become a discipline allied to but somewhat independent of anthropology, working on cross-cultural comparisons of themes, motifs, genres, and structures from a literary as well as ethnological point of view. Many linguists and anthropologists prefer to speak of a culture's oral traditions and verbal arts rather than its folklore and folktales, recognizing that creative verbal expression takes many forms and that the implied distinction between folk and "fine" art is a projection of the recent attitude of European (and European-derived) cultures onto others.

Folklore. A 19th-century term first used to refer to the traditional oral stories and sayings of the European peasant and later extended to traditions preserved orally in all societies. > **Folkloristics.** The study of folklore (as linguistics is the study of language).

The verbal arts include narratives, dramas, poetry, incantations, proverbs, riddles, word games, and even naming procedures, compliments, and insults, when these take structured and special forms. Narratives seem to be one of the easiest kinds of verbal arts to record or collect. Perhaps because they also are the most publishable, with popular appeal in North American culture, they have received the most study and attention. Generally, narratives have been divided into three basic and recurring categories: myth, legend, and tale.

MYTH

The word *myth,* in popular usage, refers to something that is widely believed to be true but probably is not. Actually, a true **myth** is basically religious, in that it provides a rationale for religious beliefs and practices. Its subject matter is the ultimates of human existence: where we and everything in our world came from, why we are here, and where we are going. As was noted in Chapter 24, the myth has an explanatory function; it depicts and describes an orderly universe, which sets the stage for orderly behavior. A typical origin myth traditional with the Western Abenaki of northwestern New England and southern Quebec follows.

> In the beginning, *Tabaldak,* "The Owner," created all living things but one—the spirit being who was to accomplish the final transformation of the earth. Man and woman *Tabaldak* made out of a piece of stone, but he didn't like the result, their hearts being cold and hard. This being so, he broke them up, and their remains today can be seen in the many stones that litter the landscape of the Abenaki homeland. But Tabaldak tried again, this time using living wood, and from them came all later Abenakis. Like the trees from which the wood came, these people were rooted in the earth and (like trees when being blown by the wind) could dance gracefully. The one living thing not created by *Tabaldak* was *Odzihózo,* "He Makes Himself from Something." This being seems to have created

himself out of dust, but since he was more transformer than creator, he wasn't able to accomplish it all at once. At first, he managed only his head, body, and arms; the legs came later, growing slowly as legs do on a tadpole. Not waiting until his legs were grown, he set out to change the shape of the earth. He dragged his body about with his hands, gouging channels that became the rivers. To make the mountains, he piled dirt up with his hands. Once his legs grew, *Odzihózo's* task was made easier; by merely extending his legs, he made the tributaries of the main streams.

> *Odzihózo,* then, was the Abenaki transformer who laid out the river channels and lake basins and shaped the hills and mountains. Just how long he took is a subject which Abenakis have discussed for as long as any can remember. Once he was finished, like Jehovah in Genesis, he surveyed his handiwork and found it was good. The last work he made was Lake Champlain and this he found especially good. He liked it so well that he climbed onto a rock in Burlington Bay and changed himself into stone so that he could sit there and enjoy his masterpiece through the ages. He still likes it, because he is still there and he is still given offerings of tobacco as Abenakis pass this way. The Abenaki call the rock *Odzihózo,* since it is the Transformer himself.[2]

Such a myth, insofar as it is believed, accepted, and perpetuated in a culture, may be said to express a part of a people's worldview: the unexpressed but implicit conceptions of their place in nature and of the limits and workings of their world. (We discussed this concept in Chapters 16 and 23.) Extrapolating from the details of the Abenaki myth, we might arrive at the conclusion that these people recognize a kinship among all living things; after all, they were all part of the same creation, and humans even were made from living wood. Moreover, an attempt to make them

[2]Haviland, W. A., & Power, M. W. (1994). *The Original Vermonters: Native inhabitants, past and present* (rev. and exp. ed., p. 193). Hanover, NH: University Press of New England.

Myth. A sacred narrative explaining how the world came to be in its present form.

To the Abenaki, these rocks in a northern New England blueberry field are the remains of the first man and woman, who were broken up by the Creator as their hearts were cold and hard.

of nonliving stone was not satisfactory. This idea of a closeness among all living things led the Abenaki to show special respect to the animals they hunted to sustain themselves. For example, after killing a beaver, muskrat, or waterfowl, one could not unceremoniously toss its bones into the nearest garbage pit. Proper respect required that the bones be returned to the water, with a request to continue its kind. Similarly, before eating meat, an Abenaki placed an offering of grease on the fire to thank *Tabaldak*. More generally, waste was to be avoided so as not to offend the animals. Failure to respect their rights would result in their unwillingness to continue sacrificing their lives that people might live.

By transforming himself into stone to enjoy his work for all eternity, *Odzihózo* may be seen as setting an example for people; they should see the beauty in things as they are and not seek to alter what is already so good. To question the goodness of existing reality would be to question the judgment of a powerful deity. A characteristic of explanatory myths, such as this one, is that the un-

known is simplified and explained in terms of the known. This myth, in terms of human experience, accounts for the existence of rivers, mountains, lakes, and other features of the landscape, as well as of humans and all other living things. It also sanctions particular attitudes and behaviors. It is a product of creative imagination, and it is a work of art, as well as a potentially religious statement.

One aspect of mythology that has attracted a good deal of interest over the years is the similarity of certain themes in the stories of peoples living in separate parts of the world. One of these themes is the myth of matriarchy, or one-time rule by women. In a number of societies, stories tell about a time when women ruled over men. Eventually, so these stories go, men were forced to rise up and assert their dominance over women to combat their tyranny or incompetence (or both). In the 19th century, a number of European scholars interpreted such myths as evidence of an early stage of matriarchy in the evolution of human culture, an idea some feminists recently have revived. Although a number of societies are known where the two sexes relate to one another as equals (western Abenaki society was one), never have anthropologists found one where women rule over or dominate men. The interesting thing about myths of matriarchy is that they generally are found in societies where men dominate women, while the latter also have considerable autonomy.[3] Under such conditions, male dominance is insecure, and a rationale is needed to justify it. Thus, myths of men overthrowing women and taking control mirror an existing paradoxical relationship between the two sexes.

The analysis and interpretation of myths have been carried to great lengths, becoming a field of study almost unto itself. It is certain that myth making is an extremely important kind of human creativity, and the study of the myth-making process and its results can give valuable clues to the way people perceive and think about their world. The dangers and problems of interpretation, however, are great. Several questions arise: Are myths literally believed or perhaps accepted symbolically or emotionally as a different kind of truth? To what extent do myths actually determine or reflect human behavior? Can an outsider discover the meaning a myth has in its own culture? How do we account for contradictory myths in the same culture? New myths arise and old ones die. Is it then the myth's content or structure that is important? All of these questions deserve, and currently receive, serious consideration.

LEGEND

Less problematic, but perhaps more complex, than the myth is the legend. **Legends** are stories told as true and set in the postcreation world. An example of a modern urban legend in the United States is one Ronald Reagan often told when he was president about an African American woman on welfare in Chicago. Supposedly, her ability to collect something like 103 welfare checks under different names enabled her to live lavishly. Although proven to be false, the story was told as if true (by the president even after he was informed it was not true), as all legends are. This particular legend illustrates a number of features all such narratives share: They cannot be attributed to any known author; they always exist in multiple versions, but, in spite of variation, they are told with sufficient detail to be plausible; and they tell us something about the societies they are found in. In this case, we learn something about the existence of racism in U.S. society (the story is told by Whites, who identify the woman as an African American), social policy (the existence of governmental policies to help the poor), and attitudes toward the poor (distrust, if not dislike).

As this illustration shows, legends (no more than myths) are not confined to nonliterate, nonindustrialized societies. Commonly, legends consist of pseudo-historical narratives that account for the deeds of heroes, the movements of peoples, and the establishment of local customs, typically with a mixture of realism and the supernatural or extraordinary. As stories, they are not necessarily believed or disbelieved, but they usually serve to entertain, as well as to instruct and to inspire or bolster pride in family, community, or nation.

To a degree, in literate states (such as the United States), the function of legends has been taken over by history. Yet much of what passes for history, to paraphrase one historian, consists of the legends we develop to make ourselves feel better about who we are.[4] The trouble is that history does not always tell people what they want to hear about themselves, or, conversely, it tells them things that they would prefer not to hear. By projecting their culture's hopes and expectations onto the record of the past, they seize upon and even

---

[3]Sanday, P. R. (1981). *Female power and male dominance: On the origins of sexual inequality* (p. 181). Cambridge: Cambridge University Press.

[4]Stoler, M. (1982). To tell the truth. *Vermont Visions, 82* (3), 3.

Legends. Stories told as true and set in the postcreation world.

Part of an ancient Aztec manuscript. In the reign of King Itzcoatl, the Aztecs rewrote their history in a way to better glorify their past. In politically centralized states, such rewriting of history is a common practice.

exaggerate some past events while ignoring or giving scant attention to others. Although this often occurs unconsciously, so strong is the motivation to transform history into legend that states often have gone so far as to deliberately rewrite it, as when the Aztecs in the reign of their 15th-century king Itzcoatl rewrote their history in a way more flattering to their position of dominance in ancient Mexico. An example from the United States may be seen in the way conventional histories of New England were written. King Philip's War, an uprising of Indians in 1675, is protrayed as a treacherous uprising (rather than the desperate bid for survival in the face of English provocation it was) after which Indians disappeared from the region (in spite of clear evidence to the contrary).[5] In modern times, the Soviet Union was particularly

well known for similar practices. Historians, when attempting to separate fact from fiction, frequently incur the wrath of people who will not willingly abandon what they wish to believe is true, whether or not it really is. This may be seen in recent debates in the United States over the "proper" teaching of history.

Long legends, sometimes in poetry or in rhythmic prose, are known as **epics**. In parts of West and central Africa, people hold remarkably elaborate and formalized recitations of extremely long legends, lasting several hours and even days. These long narratives have been described as veritable encyclopedias of a culture's most diverse aspects, with direct and indirect statements about history, institutions, relationships, values, and ideas. Epics typically are found in nonliterate societies with a form of state political organization; they serve to transmit and preserve a culture's legal and political precedents and practices.

Legends may incorporate mythological details, especially when they make an appeal to the supernatural, and are therefore not always clearly distinct from myth. The Mwindo epic of the Nyanga people follows him through the earth, the atmosphere, the underworld, and the remote sky and gives a complete picture of the Nyanga people's view of their world's organization and limits. Legends also may incorporate proverbs and incidental tales and thus may be related to other forms of verbal art as well. A recitation of the Kambili epic of the Mande, for example, has been said to include as many as 150 proverbs.

An example of a short legend that instructs, traditional with the Western Abenakis of northwestern New England and southern Quebec, follows.

> This is a story of a lonesome little boy who used to wander down to the riverbank at Odanak or downhill toward the two swamps. He used to hear someone call his name but when he got to the swamp pond, there was no one to be seen or heard. But when he went back, he heard his name called again. As he was sitting by the marshy bank wait-

[5]Calloway, C. (1997). Introduction: Surviving the Dark Ages. In C. G. Calloway (Ed.), *After King Philip's War: Presence and persistence in Indian New England* (pp. 1–28). Havover, NH: University Press of New England.

Epics.   Long oral narratives, sometimes in poetry or rhythmic prose, recounting the glorious events in the life of a real or legendary person.

ing, an old man came and asked him why he was waiting. When the boy told him, the old man said that the same thing happened long ago. What he heard was the Swamp Creature and pointed out the big tussocks of grass where it hid; having called out it would sink down behind them. The old man said: "It just wants to drown you. If you go out there you will sink in the mud. You better go home!"[6]

The moral of this story is quite simple: Swamps are dangerous places; stay away from them. When told well, the story is a lot more effective in keeping children away from swamps than just telling them, "Don't go near swamps."

For the anthropologist, a major significance of the secular and apparently realistic portions of legends, whether long or short, is the clues they provide to what constitutes a culture's approved or ideal ethical behavior. The subject matter of legends is essentially problem-solving, and the content is likely to include combat, warfare, confrontations, and physical and psychological trials of many kinds. Certain questions may be answered explicitly or implicitly. Does the culture justify homicide? What kinds of behavior are considered brave or cowardly? What is the etiquette of combat or warfare? Does the culture honor or recognize a concept of altruism or self-sacrifice? Here again, however, pitfalls occur in the process of interpreting art in relation to life. It is always possible certain kinds of behavior are acceptable or even admirable, with the distance or objectivity art affords, but are not at all approved for daily life. In European American culture, murderers, charlatans, and rakes sometimes have become popular heroes and the subjects of legends; North Americans would object, however, to an outsider's inference that they necessarily approved or wanted to emulate the morality of Billy the Kid or Jesse James.

---

[6]Day, G. M. (1972). Quoted in *Prehistoric life in the Champlain Valley* [film], by Thomas C. Vogelman (Director) and others. Burlington, VT: Department of Anthropology (Producer), University of Vermont.

TALE

The term **tale** is a nonspecific label for a third category of creative narratives: those purely secular, nonhistorical, and recognized as fiction for entertainment, though they may draw a moral or teach a practical lesson, as well. Consider this brief summary of a tale from Ghana, known as "Father, Son, and Donkey":

> A father and his son farmed their corn, sold it, and spent part of the profit on a donkey. When the hot season came, they harvested their yams and prepared to take them to storage using their donkey. The father mounted the donkey, and they all three proceeded on their way until they met some people. "What? You lazy man!" the people said to the father. "You let your young son walk barefoot on this hot ground while you ride on a donkey? For shame!" The father yielded his place to the son, and they proceeded until they came to an old woman. "What? You useless boy!" said the old woman. "You ride on the donkey and let your poor father walk barefoot on this hot ground? For shame!" The son dismounted, and both father and son walked on the road, leading the donkey behind them until they came to an old man. "What? You foolish people!" said the old man. "You have a donkey and you walk barefoot on the hot ground instead of riding?" And so it goes. Listen: when you are doing something and other people come along, just keep on doing what you like.

This is precisely the kind of tale of special interest in traditional folklore studies. It is an internationally popular "numbskull" tale; versions of it have been recorded in India, the Middle East, the Balkans, Italy, Spain, England, and the United States, as well as in West Africa. It is classified or cataloged as exhibiting a basic **motif** or story situation—father and son trying to please everyone —one of the many thousands found to recur in world folktales. Despite variations in detail, every version has about the same basic structure in the sequence of events, sometimes called the *syntax* of the tale: a peasant father and son work together, a beast of burden is purchased, the three set out

---

Tale. A creative narrative recognized as fiction for entertainment. > **Motif.** A story situation in a folktale.

on a short excursion, the father rides and is criticized, the son rides and is criticized, both walk and are criticized, and a conclusion is drawn.

Tales of this sort with an international distribution sometimes raise more problems than they solve: Which one is the original? What is the path of its diffusion? Could it be sheer coincidence that different cultures have come up with the same motif and syntax, or are independent inventions of similar tales developing in similar situations in response to like causes? A surprisingly large number of motifs in European and African tales are traceable to ancient sources in India. Is this good evidence of a spread of culture from a "cradle" of civilization, or is it an example of diffusion of tales in contiguous areas? Of course, purely local tales exist, as well as the tales with such wide distribution. Within any particular culture, anthropologists probably could categorize local types of tales: animal, human experience, trickster, dilemma, ghost, moral, scatological, and nonsense tales, and so on. In West Africa there is a remarkable prevalence of animal stories, for example, with creatures such as the spider, the rabbit, and the hyena as the protagonists. Many were carried to the slave-holding areas of the Americas; the Uncle Remus stories about Brer Rabbit, Brer Fox, and other animals may be a survival of this tradition.

The significance of tales for anthropologists rests partly in this matter of their distribution. The tales provide evidence of either cultural contacts or cultural isolation and of limits of influence and cultural cohesion. Debated for decades now, for example, has been the extent to which the culture of West Africa was transmitted to the southeastern United States. As far as folktales are concerned, one school of folklorists always has found and insisted on European origins; another school, somewhat more recently, points to African prototypes. Anthropologists are interested, however, in more than these questions of distribution. Like legends, tales very often illustrate local solutions to universal human ethical problems, and in some sense they state a moral philosophy. Anthropologists see that whether the tale of the father, the son, and the donkey originated in West Africa or arrived there from Europe or the Middle East, the very fact it is told in West Africa suggests it states something valid for that culture. The tale's lesson of a neces-

sary degree of self-confidence in the face of arbitrary social criticism is therefore something that can be read into the culture's values and beliefs.

OTHER VERBAL ARTS

Myths, legends, and tales, prominent as they are in anthropological studies, in many cultures turn out to be no more important than the other verbal arts. In the culture of the Awlad 'Ali Bedouins of Egypt's western desert, for example, poetry is a lively and active verbal art, especially as a vehicle for personal expression and private communication. These people use two forms of poetry, one being the elaborately structured and heroic poems men chant or recite only on ceremonial occasions and in specific public contexts. The other is the *ghinnáwa*, or "little songs" that punctuate everyday conversations. Simple in structure, these deal with personal matters and feelings more appropriate to informal social situations, and older men regard them as the unimportant productions of women and youths. Despite this official devaluation in the male-dominated society of the Bedouins, however, they play a vital part in peoples' daily lives. In their "little songs" individuals are shielded from the consequences of making statements and expressing sentiments that contravene the moral system. Paradoxically, by sharing these "immoral" sentiments only with intimates

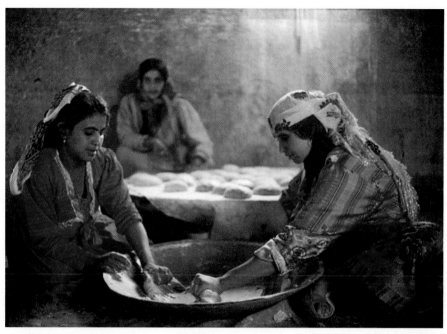

The "little songs" of the Awlad 'Ali Bedouins punctuate conversations carried out while the people perform everyday chores, such as making bread, as these young women are doing. Through these "little songs," they can express what otherwise are taboo topics.

and veiling them in impersonal traditional formulas, those who recite them demonstrate they have a certain control, which actually enhances their moral standing.

As is often true of folklore in general, the "little songs" of the Awlad 'Ali provide a sanctioned outlet for otherwise taboo thoughts or opinions. Disaster jokes are an example of this in contemporary North American society. As anthropologist Lila Abu-Lughod points out:

> What may be peculiar to Awlad 'Ali is that their discourse of rebellion is both culturally elaborated and sanctioned. Although poetry refers to personal life, it is not individual, spontaneous, idiosyncratic, or unofficial but public, conventional, and formulaic—a highly developed art. More important, this poetic discourse of defiance is not condemned, or even just tolerated, as well it might be given all the constraints of time and place and form that bind it. Poetry is a privileged discourse in Awlad 'Ali society. Like other Arabs, and perhaps like many oral cultures, the Bedouins cherish poetry and other verbal arts. . . . They are drawn to *ghinnáwas*, and at the same time they consider them risqué, against religion, and slightly improper. . . . This ambivalence about poetry is significant, and it makes sense only in terms of the cultural meaning of opposition. Because ordinary discourse is informed by the values of honor and modesty, the moral correlates of the ideology that upholds the Awlad 'Ali social and political system, we would expect the antistructural poetic discourse, with its contradictory messages, to be informed by an opposing set of values. This is not the case. Poetry as a discourse of defiance of the system symbolizes freedom—the ultimate value of the system and the essential entailment of the honor code.[7]

In all cultures the words of songs constitute a kind of poetry. Poetry and stories recited with gesture,

---

[7]Abu-Lughod, L. (1986). *Veiled sentiments: Honor and poetry in a Bedouin society* (p. 252). Berkeley, CA: University of California Press.

movement, and props become drama. Drama combined with dance, music, and spectacle becomes a public celebration. The more we look at the individual arts, the clearer it becomes that they often are interrelated and interdependent. The verbal arts are, in fact, simply differing manifestations of the same creative imagination that produces music and the other arts.

THE ART OF MUSIC

The study of music in specific cultural settings, beginning in the 19th century with the collection of folk songs, has developed into a specialized field, called **ethnomusicology**. Like the study of folktales for their own sake, ethnomusicology is both re-

---

Frederica de Laguna *(1906–)*

A concern with the arts of non-Western people always has been an important part of anthropology, and the work of anthropologist Frederica de Laguna is representative. Educated at Bryn Mawr College and Columbia University, where she was awarded her PhD, she made her first trip into the field with a Danish expedition to Greenland in 1929. A year later, she began work in southeastern Alaska, a region she has returned repeatedly to since. Her first work there was archaeological, and she was the pioneer in southeastern Alaskan prehistory. But as her interest in native people grew, she became more and more involved with ethnographic work as well. She found out that to understand the past, one had to know what it led to, just as to understand the present native people, one had to know their past.

After many seasons of work in different localities, de Laguna began in 1949 a project to trace the beginnings of the way of life of the Tlingit Indians of Yakutat through a combination of archaeological and ethnographic work. This resulted in a monumental three-volume work, published in 1972, *Under Mount St. Elias*. It amounted to no less than a holistic picture of Tlingit culture through their eyes. Since songs and stories are important

parts of any nonliterate culture, much space was devoted to their transcriptions just as they were related and performed by elders now long dead (one whole volume is devoted to the words and music of songs). The importance of this work goes far beyond anthropology and has been enormously significant to the Tlingit themselves.

When de Laguna began to work at Yakutat, the children were being sent to government boarding schools, where they were told nothing of their own culture and were severely punished for even speaking their own language. The aim was to stamp out native culture to facilitate assimilation into "mainstream American" culture. Thus, as the elders died out, many traditions were being lost. But with the publication of *Under Mount St. Elias* (copies of which were avidly snapped up by the Tlingit), as well as "Freddy" de Laguna's continuing participation in the community, the people regained much they were in danger of losing. As de Laguna says, songs and stories are for giving back, and in 1997 the Tlingit of Yakutat honored her for what she gave back to them. As they acknowledge, the new vigor shown by Tlingit culture and their renewed pride in who they are owes much to their "Grandmother Freddy's" work.

Ethnomusicology. The study of a society's music in terms of its cultural setting.

lated to and somewhat independent of anthropology. Nevertheless, it is possible to sort out several concepts of interest to general anthropology from the field's various concerns.

To begin, we may ask these questions: How does a culture conceive of music? What is considered of primary importance when distinguishing music from other modes of expression? What is music to one person is mere noise to another. Music is a form of communication that includes a nonverbal component. The information transmitted is often abstract emotion rather than concrete ideas, and it is experienced in a variety of ways by different listeners. This, and music's communication of something that is verbally incommunicable, makes it very difficult to discuss music. In fact, not even a single definition of music can be agreed upon, because different peoples may include or exclude different ideas within that category. Ethnomusicologists often must rely upon a working definition as the basis for their investigations and often distinguish between "music" and that which is "musical." The way to approach an unfamiliar kind of musical expression is to define it either in indigenous terms or in orthodox musicological terms such as melody, rhythm, and form.

Much of the historical development of ethnomusicology has been based upon musicology, which is primarily the study of Western European music. One problem has been the tendency to discuss music in terms of elements considered important in European music (tonality, rhythm, melody, etc.), when these may be of little importance to the practitioner. European music is defined, primarily, in terms of the presence of melody and rhythm. Melody is a function of tonality, and rhythm is an organizing concept involving tempo, stress, and measured repetition. Although these can be addressed in non-European musics, they may not be the defining characteristics of a performance.

Early investigators of non-European songs were struck by the apparent simplicity of *pentatonic* (five-tone) scales and a seemingly endless repetition of phrases. They often did not give sufficient credit to the formal function of repetition

Even among food-foraging peoples, music plays an important role. Shown here is a native Australian playing a digeridoo.

in such music, confusing repetition with lack of invention. A great deal of complex, sophisticated non-European music was dismissed as "primitive" and formless and typically treated as trivial. Repetition, nevertheless, is a fact of music, including European music, and a basic formal principle.

In general, human music is said to differ from natural music—the songs of birds, wolves, and whales, for example—by being almost everywhere perceived in terms of a repertory of tones at fixed or regular intervals: in other words, a scale. Scale systems and their modifications comprise what is known as **tonality** in music. Humans make closed systems out of a formless range of possible sounds by dividing the distance between a tone and its first *overtone* or sympathetic vibration (which always has exactly twice as many vibrations as the basic tone) into a series of measured steps. In the Western or European system, the distance between the basic tone and the first overtone is called the *octave*; it consists of seven steps: 5 *whole* tones and 2 *semitones*. The whole tones are further divided into semitones for a total working scale of 12 tones. Western people learn at an early age to recognize and imitate this arbitrary system and its conventions, and it comes to sound natural (Table 25.1).

Tonality. In music, scale systems and their modifications.

TABLE 25.1   Two different ways of dividing the octave into seven steps

Pipe Scale		Just Scale
A′		A′
		$16/15$
	$10/9$	G#
G		
	$27/25$	$9/8$
F		F#
	$10/9$	$10/9$
E		E
	$10/9$	$9/8$
D		
	$27/25$	D
C		$16/15$
	$10/9$	C#
B		$10/9$
	$9/8$	B
A		$9/8$
		A

The conventional scale of Western music is represented graphically on the right, that used by bagpipers on the left. Neither is a variation of the other. All the notes are out of tune, but only slightly so; once heard often enough, they sound just fine.

Yet the overtone series it is partially based on is the only part of it that can be considered a wholly natural phenomenon.

One of the most common alternatives to the semitonal system is the pentatonic system, which, as noted, divides the scale into five nearly equidistant tones. Such scales may be found all over the world, including in much European folk music. In Java people use scales of both 5 and 7 equal steps, which have no relation to the intervals Europeans and European Americans hear as "natural." Arabic and Persian music have smaller units of a third of a tone with scales of 17 and 24 steps in the octave. Even quarter-tone scales are used in India with subtleties of shading nearly indistinguishable to a Western ear. Small wonder, then, that even when Western people can hear what sounds like melody and rhythm in these systems, the total result may sound peculiar to them or "out of tune." Anthropologists need a very practiced ear to learn to appreciate—perhaps even to tolerate—some of the music they hear, and only some of the most skilled folk-song collectors have attempted to notate and analyze the music of nonsemitonal systems.

As another organizing factor in music, whether regular or irregular, rhythm may be more important than tonality. Traditional European music is most often measured into recurrent patterns of 2, 3, and 4 beats, with combinations of weak and strong beats to mark the division and form patterns. Non-European music is likely to move in patterns of 5, 7, or 11 beats, with complex arrangements of internal beats and sometimes polyrhythms: one instrument or singer going in a pattern of 3 beats, for example, while another is in a pattern of 5 or 7. Polyrhythms are frequent in the drum music of West Africa, which shows remarkable precision in the overlapping of rhythmic lines. Non-European music also may contain shifting rhythms: a pattern of 3 beats, for example, followed by a pattern of 2 or 5 beats with little or no regular recurrence or repetition of any one pattern, though the patterns are fixed and identifiable as units.

Although anthropologists do not necessarily need to untangle these complicated technical matters, they will want to know enough to be aware of the degree of skill involved in a performance. This allows a measure of the extent people in a culture have learned to practice and respond to this often important creative activity. Moreover, the distribution of musical forms and instruments can reveal much about cultural contact or isolation.

FUNCTIONS OF MUSIC

Even without concern for technical matters, anthropologists can profitably investigate the function of music in a society. First, rarely has a culture been reported to lack any kind of music. Bone flutes and whistles as much as 40,000 years old have been found by archaeologists, nor have historically known food-foraging peoples been without their music. In the Kalahari Desert, for example, a Ju/'hoansi hunter off by himself would play a tune on his bow simply to help while away the time. (Long before anyone thought of beating swords into plowshares, some genius discovered —when and where we do not know—that bows could be used not just to kill but to make music as well.) In northern New England, Abenaki shamans used cedar flutes to call game, lure enemies, and attract women. In addition, a drum with two rawhide strings stretched over it to produce a buzzing sound, thought to represent singing, gave the shaman the power to communicate with the spirit world.

Music is also a powerful identifier. Many marginalized groups have used music for purposes of self-identification, bringing the group together and in many cases contraposing their own forms against the onslaught of a dominant culture or voicing social and political commentary. Examples of this include so-called punk groups such as Rage Against the Machine and rap groups such as Public Enemy or L. L. Cool J, as well as ethnic groups sponsoring musical festivals. Potlatches and powwows, among other occasions, allow certain Native American groups to reaffirm and celebrate their ethnic identity, as well as fulfilling other functions. Music plays an important part at these events, thus becoming closely bound to the group identity, both from without and from within the group. It should be understood, too, that these associations of music with groups are not dependent upon words alone but also upon particular tonal, rhythmic, and instrumental conventions. For example, Scottish gatherings would not be "Scottish" without the sound of the Highland bagpipes and the fiddle.

This power of music to shape identity has been recognized everywhere, with varying consequences. The English recognized the power of the bagpipes for creating an esprit de corps among the Highland regiments of the British army and encouraged it within certain bounds, even while surpressing piping in Scotland itself under the Disarming Act. Over time, the British military piping tradition was assimilated into the Scottish

Although much music performed by Scottish pipers is of English origin, it has been so thoroughly absorbed that most people think of it as purely Scottish.

piping tradition, so the blend was accepted and spread by Scottish pipers. As a result, much of the supposedly Scottish piping one hears today consists of marches written within the conventions of the English musical tradition, though shaped to fit the physical constraints of the instrument. Less often heard is the "classical" music known as pibroch, or *ceol mor*. The latter, however, has been undergoing a series of revivals over the past century and is now often associated with rising nationalist sentiments.

The English adoption of the Highland bagpipe into Scottish regiments is an instance of those in authority employing music to further a political agenda. So too in Spain, the dictator Francisco Franco (who came to power in the 1930s) established community choruses in even the smallest towns to promote the singing of patriotic songs. Similarly, in Ireland Comhaltas Ceoltoiri Eireann has promoted the collection and performance of traditional Irish music; in Brittany and Galicia, music is playing an important role in attempts to revive the spirits of the indigenous Celtic cultures in these regions; and the list goes on. But, however played or for whatever reason, music (like all art) is an individual creative skill one can cultivate and be proud of, whether from a sense of accomplishment or from the sheer pleasure of performing; and it is a form of social behavior promoting a communication or sharing of feelings and life experience with other humans. Moreover, because individual creativity is constrained by the traditions of a particular culture, each society's art is distinctive and helps to define its members' sense of identity.

The social function of music is perhaps most obvious in songs, since these contain verbal text. This is probably why many earlier studies concentrated upon them. Songs, like other verbal forms, express a group's values, beliefs, and concerns, but they do so with an increased formalism resulting from adherence to the restrictions of systematic "rules," or conventions, of pitch, rhythm, timbre, and musical genre.

Songs serve many purposes, entertainment being only one of these. Work songs long have played an important part in manual labor, serving to coordinate heavy or dangerous labor, such as weighing anchor and furling sail on board ships and making ax or hammer strokes, and serving to pass time and relieve tedium, such as with oyster shucking songs. Songs also have been used to soothe babies to sleep, to charm animals into giving more milk or to keep witchcraft at bay, to advertise goods, and much more. Songs also may serve social and political purposes, spreading particular ideas swiftly and effectively by giving them a special form involving poetic language and rhythm and by attaching a pleasing and appropriate tune, be it solemn or light.

In the United States numerous examples exist of marginalized social and ethnic groups attempting to gain a larger audience and more compassion for their plight through song. Perhaps most familiar are performers such as Joan Baez and Pete Seeger who gained great visibility when supporting civil and human rights causes. Indeed, both performers' celebrity status led to the broader dissemination of their social and political beliefs. Such celebrity status comes from skill in performing and communicating with the intended audience. So powerful a force was music in the civil rights and peace movements of the '50s and '60s that Seeger was targeted by Senator Joseph McCarthy and his investigating committee, becoming one of many performers the entertainment industry blacklisted.

In Australia, traditional Aboriginal songs have taken on a new legal function, as they are being introduced into court as evidence of early settlement patterns. This helps the native peoples claim more extensive land ownership, thus allowing them greater authority to use the land, as well as to negotiate and profit from the sale of natural resources. This had been impossible before. The British, upon their annexation of Australia, declared the land ownerless (Terra Nullius). Although the Aborigines had preserved their records of ownership in song and story, these were not admissible in the British courts. In the early '70s, however, the Aboriginal peoples exposed the injustice of the situation, and the Australian government began responding in a more favorable, if somewhat limited, fashion, granting the claims of traditional ownership to groups in the Northern Territory. In 1992 the concept of Terra Nullius was overturned, and native claims are now being presented in the other

Folk singer Pete Seeger sings in celebration of anti-war priest Philip Berrigan's release from prison.

territories, as well. These newer claimants are granted equal partnership with developers and others. Sacred sites are being recognized, and profits are being shared with the traditional owners. Proof of native ownership includes recordings of traditional songs indicating traditional settlement and travel patterns and land use.[8]

Music gives a concrete form, made memorable and attractive with melody and rhythm, to basic human ideas. Whether the song's content is didactic, satirical, inspirational, religious, political, or purely emotional, the important thing is that the formless has been given form and that feelings hard to express in words alone are communicated in a symbolic and memorable way that can be repeated and shared. The group is consequently united and has the sense their shared experience, whatever it may be, has shape and meaning. This, in turn, shapes and gives meaning to the community.

---

[8]Koch, G. (1997). Songs, land rights and archives in Australia. *Cultural Survival Quarterly, 20* (4).

PICTORIAL ART

To many Europeans and European Americans, the first image that springs to mind in connection with the word *art* is some sort of picture, be it a painting, drawing, sketch, or whatever. And indeed, in many parts of the world, people have been making pictures in one way or another for a very long time—etching them in bone; engraving them in rock; painting them on cave walls and rock faces; carving and painting them on wood, gourds, or pots; or painting them on textiles, bark, bark cloth, animal hide, or even their own bodies. As with musical art, some form of pictorial art is a part of every historically known human culture.

As a type of symbolic expression, pictorial art may be representational, imitating closely the forms of nature, or abstract, drawing from natural forms but representing only their basic patterns or arrangements. Actually, the two categories are not mutually exclusive, for even the most naturalistic portrayal is partly abstract to the extent it generalizes from nature and abstracts patterns of ideal beauty, ugliness, or typical expressions of emotion. But between the most naturalistic and the most schematic or symbolic abstract art lies a continuum. In some of the Indian art of North America's Northwest Coast, for example, animal figures may be so highly stylized as to be difficult for an outsider to identify. Although the art is abstract, the artist has drawn on nature, even though he or she has exaggerated and deliberately transformed some of its shapes to express a particular feeling toward them. Because the artists do these exaggerations and transformations according to the canons of Northwest Coast Indian culture, their meanings are understood not just by the artist but by other community members as well.

Southern African Rock Art

The rock art of southern Africa, which has been described and studied in considerable detail, especially over the past 3 decades, is a rich non-Western tradition that helps illustrate different ways of approaching the study of art. This rock art is one of the world's oldest traditions, extending unbroken from at least 27,000 years ago until a mere 100 years ago. It came to an end only with the destruction of the Bushman people responsible for it, at the hands of European colonizers. Those (such as the Ju/'hoansi) who have survived in places such as Namibia and Botswana did not themselves produce rock art but do share the same general belief system the rock art expresses.

Bushman rock art consists of both paintings and engravings on the faces of rock outcrops as well as on the walls of rock shelters. Depicted are a variety of animals as well as humans in highly sophisticated ways, sometimes in static poses but often in highly animated scenes. Associated with these figures are a variety of abstract signs, including dots, zigzags, nested curves, and the like. Until fairly recently, the significance of these latter was not understood by non-Bushmen; equally puzzling was the frequent presence of new pictures painted or engraved directly over existing ones.

In spite of its puzzling aspects, southern African rock art long has been considered worthy of being viewed and admired. The paintings, especially, generally are seen as quite beautiful and a source of pleasure to look at. Consequently, it is not surprising the earliest study of the art was

This stylized painting on a ceremonial shirt represents a bear. Though the art of the Northwest Coast Indians often portrays actual animals, they are not depicted in a naturalistic style. To identify them, one must be familiar with the conventions of this art.

in the aesthetic approach, one also well developed in the study of European and other Western art. Thus, the art could be studied for its use of pigments: charcoal and specularite for black, silica, china clay and gypsum for white, and ferric oxide for red and reddish-brown hues. These were mixed with fat, blood, and perhaps water and applied to the rough rock with consummate artistry. The

Bushman rock paintings and engravings from southern Africa often depict animals
thought to possess great supernatural power. Shamans appear as well: In the painted
example at the top, we see rain shamans with swallowtails acting in the spirit realm to
protect people from the dangers of storms. Like modern Bushman shamans, several of
these hold paired dance sticks. The idea of shamans transforming into birds, as well as
being greatly elongated (note one figure's long, undulating body above the lower row
of shamans), is based on sensations experienced in trance. Other undulating lines and
dots in the picture are entoptic phenomena.

economy of line and the way shading is used to
mold the contours of animal bodies elicits admiration, as does the rendering of all sorts of realistic details. One of the more popular animals depicted was the eland, shown with such details as
the tuft of red hair on its forehead, the black line
running along its back, the darkening of its snout,
its cloven hoofs, the folds of skin on its shoulders,
and the twist of its horns.

Similar anatomical details of humans are
shown, including the details of dress, headgear,
and body ornamentation, including leather bands

and ostrich eggshell beads. Meanwhile, human figures appear more as caricatures, rather than as literal depictions; features such as fatness and thinness may be exaggerated, and the figures are sometimes elongated and sometimes in positions suggestive of flying across the rock face. Sometimes, too, the feet take on the appearance of a swallowtail or a fish tail. Even more puzzling are figures that appear to be part human/part animal (therianthropes).

Another obvious approach to studying Bushman rock art, the narrative, focuses on *what* it depicts, supplementing the focus of the aesthetic approach on *how* things are depicted. Certainly, aspects of Bushman life are shown, as in several hunting scenes depicting men with bows, arrows, quivers, and hunting bags. Occasional depictions show nets used in the hunt and also fish traps. Women are also shown—identifiable by their primary sexual characteristics and the stone-weighted digging sticks they carry, but they are rarely shown gathering food. Considering the importance of food women gather for the Bushman diet, this seems rather odd. Of course, it might merely reflect the importance Bushmen attach to the hunt, but the fact is hunting scenes are not at all common, either. Furthermore, the animals shown in the art are *not* representative of the meat eaten; animals commonly depicted (such as the eland) are not commonly eaten. Thus, a narrative approach can lead to a distorted view of Bushman life.

Other scenes portrayed in the art clearly relate to the trance dance, still the most important ritual today among Bushmen (see the Original Study in Chapter 24). This is clearly indicated by the numbers of people shown, the arrangement of hand-clapping women surrounding dancing men, whose bodies are bent forward in the distinctive posture the cramping of abdominal muscles causes as they go into trance, whose noses are shown bleeding (common today when Bushmen trance), whose arms are stretched behind their backs (modern Bushmen do this to gather more of the supernatural potency—*n/um*), who are wearing dance rattles, and who carry fly whisks (used to extract invisible arrows of sickness). As it turns out, we have here a significant clue to what the art is really all about, though we cannot discern this from the narrative and aesthetic

approaches alone. For this we need the third, or *interpretive,* approach.

The distinctions among the aesthetic, narrative, and interpretive approaches become clear if we pause for a moment to consider a famous work of Western art, Leonardo da Vinci's painting *The Last Supper.*[9] A non-Western person viewing this mural will see what appear to be 13 ordinary men at a table, apparently enjoying an ordinary meal. Although one of the men appears a bit clumsy, knocking over the salt, and clutches a bag of money, nothing else here indicates the scene is anything out of the ordinary. Aesthetically, our non-Western observer may admire the way the composition fits the space available, the way the attitudes of the men are depicted, and the way the artist conveys a sense of movement. As a narrative, the painting may be seen as a record of customs, table manners, dress, and architecture. But to know the real meaning of this picture, the viewer must be aware that, in Western culture, spilling the salt is a symbol of impending disaster and that money symbolizes the root of all evil. But even this is not enough; for a full understanding of this work of art, one must know something of the beliefs of Christianity. Moving to the interpretive level, then, requires knowledge of the symbols and beliefs of the people responsible for the art.

Applying the interpretive approach to southern African rock art requires knowledge of two subjects: Bushman ethnography and the nature of trance. With respect to the latter, a clear understanding comes from a combination of ethnographic data and data gained experimentally in laboratories. Because all human beings have essentially the same nervous system, whether they are urban dwellers from the United States, food foragers from southern Africa, horticulturalists from the Amazon forest, or whoever, they all progress through the same three stages when going into trance. In the first stage, the nervous system generates a variety of luminous, pulsating, re-

---

[9]This example is drawn from J. D. Lewis-Williams (1990), *Discovering southern African rock art* (p. 9). Cape Town and Johannesburg: David Philip.

Leonardo da Vinci's *The Last Supper.*

volving, and constantly shifting geometric patterns known as **entoptic phenomena** (anyone who has suffered from migraine headaches is familiar with these). Typical forms include grids, parallel lines, zigzags, dots, nested curves, and filigrees, often in a spiral pattern.

As one goes into deeper trance, the brain tries to "make sense" of these abstract forms, just as it does of sensations received when in an unaltered state of consciousness. This process is known as **construal,** and here differences in culture and experience come into play. Commonly, a Bushman in trance will construe a grid pattern as the markings on a giraffe's skin, nested curves as a honeycomb (honey is a Bushman delicacy, and the auditory sensation of buzzing that often accompanies trance promotes the illusion), and dots as *nu/m,* the potency only shamans in trance see. Obviously, we would not expect an Inuit or someone from Los Angeles to construe these patterns in the same way.

In the third and deepest trance stage, subjects cease to be observers of their hallucinations but seem to become part of them. As this happens, they feel themselves passing into a rotating tunnel or vortex with latticelike sides and on which appear images of animals, humans, and monsters of various sorts. In the process, the entoptic forms of the earlier stages become integrated into these **iconic images,** as they are called. The entoptics may be hard to discern apart from the main image, although sometimes they appear as a kind of background. Iconic images are culture specific; individuals "see" what their culture disposes them to see; often these images have high emotional content. In the case of Bushmen, they often see the eland, an animal thought to be imbued with specially strong potency, particularly for rain making. Given this, one of the things shamans try to do in trance is to "capture" elands—"rain animals"—to make rain.

Entoptic phenomena. Bright, pulsating geometric forms the central nervous system generates and "seen" in trance states. > **Construal.** In the second stage of trance, the process the brain uses when trying to "make sense" of entoptic images. > **Iconic images.** Hallucinations of people, animals, and monsters "seen" in the deepest trance stage.

The zigzags and curves in two of these pictures, drawn by migraine sufferers, are classic entoptic phenomena seen in early stages of trance. The "tunnel" with lattice walls in the third picture is representative of those seen when passing from the second to third stage of trance.

From all of this, we begin to understand why elands are so prominent in the rock art. Moreover, it reveals the significance of the zigzags, dots, grids, and so forth that are so often a part of the compositions. It also leads to an understanding of other puzzling features of the art. For example, sensations in the third trance stage include such feelings as being stretched out or elongated, weightlessness as in flight or in the water, and difficulty breathing as when under water. Hence we find depictions in the art of humans who appear to be abnormally long, as well as individuals who appear to be swimming or flying. Another well-documented trance phenomenon is the sense of being transformed into some sort of animal. Such

sensations are triggered in the deepest stage of trance if the individual sees or thinks of an animal, and the sensation accounts for the part human/part animal therianthropes in the art. Finally, the superpositioning of one artwork over another becomes comprehensible; not only are the visions seen in trance commonly superimposed on one another as they rotate and move, but if the trancer stares at a painting or engraving of an earlier vision, the new one will appear as if projected on the old.

The interpretive approach makes clear, then, that the rock art of southern Africa—even compositions that otherwise might appear to be scenes of everyday life—is intimately connected with the

This late Stone Age painting from the Peche-Merle cave in France incorporates dot entoptics over and near the body of a bull, one indication the artist was painting something seen in a state of trance. An association of rock art with trance experience has been noted in many parts of the world.

practices and beliefs of shamanism. After shamans came out of trance and reflected on their visions, they then proceeded to paint or engrave their recollections of them on the rock faces. But these were more than records of important visions; they had their own innate power, owing to their supernatural origin. This being so, when the need arose for a new trance experience, it might be held where the old vision was recorded to draw power from it.

With the fuller understanding the interpretive approach provides, we now may look at the broader significance of what the Bushmen did with their art. For this, we turn to the writings of the two South African anthropologists who are the leading authorities on the rock art.

Bushman Rock Art and Political Power[10]

Whatever may be said about Bushman rock art, its images are not the "banal, meaningless artefacts" into which exhibits can so easily transform them. "Meaning" is, of course, an elusive concept. Like all art, the Bushman images did not have a single, one-to-one "meaning" that they unequivocally transmitted from maker to viewer. "Meaning" was historically and complexly constituted; Bushman viewers shared with the makers of the art in the construction of "meaning." Similarly, modern viewers who engage the images will inevitably bring with them their own contribution to their "meaning." If all the original viewers did not "read" the images identically, each viewer having

[10]Adapted from T. A. Dowson & J. D. Lewis-Williams (1993, November), Myths, museums, and Southern African rock art. *South African Historical Journal, 29,* 52–56.

had his or her own socially constituted perspective, how much less likely is it that modern viewers will share identical responses? None the less, some general observations on the art's "meaning" and its role in Bushman communities can be made in the hope that they will challenge the current trivialising stereotypes.

The "ideas which most deeply moved the Bushman mind" were rooted in what our reading of the nineteenth-century accounts suggests was a three-tiered, though not strictly demarcated, view of the cosmos: the level of daily life, the realm above and the realm below. These levels were mediated by shamans. Amongst the Kalahari groups of the 1950s and 1960s, about half of the men and a third of the women were shamans. Entering an altered state of consciousness during a communal dance or in more solitary circumstances, these shamans were believed to activate a supernatural potency so that they could move between the cosmological levels as they performed such diverse tasks as curing the sick, making rain and controlling animals.

The making of rock art was associated with these shamanistic practices in ways not fully understood. The images comprise: representations of animals that were believed to possess supernatural potency; privileged views of communal dances that show not only what ordinary people saw but also elements, such as potency, that were seen by shamans only; conflicts in the spiritual realm between benign shamans and shamans of illness; rain-animals that shamans killed so that their blood and milk would fall as rain; therianthropic figures showing the blending of a shaman with a power-animal; geometric images derived from entoptic phenomena (bright pulsating forms "seen" in certain altered states of consciousness); and a range of other fantastic experiences.

The images were not, however, simply records of religious experiences. There is reason to believe that at least some of them were reservoirs of potency that could be tapped by trancing shamans. They were not just pictures, but powerful things in themselves that could be implicated in effecting alterations in the shamans' states of consciousness, that is, in facilitating the mediation of the cosmological realms.

Even this brief outline shows that the art can be presented as a challenge to the popular belief that the making of art was, for the Bushmen, an idle pastime. The artists' manipulation of metaphors and symbols was far more complex and subtle than many modern viewers realize. The painted and engraved images explore unknown and unsuspected realms in often idiosyncratic ways. In the past the images were active; today they are made static by being separated from their highly charged ritual, social and conceptual contexts.

The activity of the images, however, extended beyond the generation of religious experience to the negotiation of political power. Especially in the last two hundred years of the Bushmen's occupation of the south-eastern part of the subcontinent, major and escalating changes were taking place. For many hundreds of years the Bushmen had interacted in various and changing ways with Bantu-speaking agropastoralists, but these, for the most part amicable, exchanges were disrupted by colonial expansion. New social relations began to develop. Shamans, who were already being paid with cattle and a share of the crops by the agropastoralists for whom they made rain, found that they had access to new resources. As the colonists shot out the game and the Bushman territories became more and more restricted, relations with the agropastoralists increased in importance, and political and economic struggles developed between competing shamans and between shamans and ordinary people. The "egalitarian" values that militated against development of political power by shamans were eroded.

Rock painting was implicated in these changes. To illustrate the artistic dynamics of, largely, the nineteenth century, we mention three types of painting. One type shows groups of people, some of whom are identifiable by various features as shamans, in which no one is larger or more elaborately painted than another. A second type shows groups of people in which two or three shaman figures are more elaborately and individually depicted. The third type shows an elaborately painted central shaman with sometimes, facial features, surrounded by "lesser" figures. The historical record from parts of the Kalahari combines with these three types of paintings to suggest that the art became a site of struggle. As social circumstances changed, shamans translated their supernatural potency into political power and vied with one another for control of resources that were, in the final decades, increasingly derived from rain-making for agropastoralists.

The artists who made these types of paintings were not merely painting historical events, chronicling social changes. Such an understanding would be related to the close-to-nature stereotype—simple people painting what was happening around them. Rather, the making of each painting was a sociopolitical intervention that negotiated the artist's (or artists') political status. The art did not simply reflect social relations: in some instances it transformed those relations; in other instances it worked to reproduce them. Each painting was more than an image of the way things were, or even of the way artists wished they would become. Because the images were themselves charged with the supernatural potency that mediated the levels of the cosmos and made shamanistic activity possible, they exercised a coercive, persuasive influence that was founded in their factuality.

In specific and diverse historical circumstances, the artists invoked this coercive function in their responses to the colonial invasion. Unlike the agropastoralists, the colonists were not intended to be among the viewers of the art, but their threatening presence implicated them in the social production of the art none the less. As the shamans had, for centuries, battled in the spiritual realm with marauding shamans of illness, who often took feline forms, so, the art suggests, did they battle in the spiritual realm with the colonists. The shamans tried to deploy their powers in such a way as to thwart the advance of the colonists. As we know, their efforts were fruitless; the colonists' rifles were, in the end, invincible. At times prosecuting a policy of calculated genocide, at other times mounting ad hoc but nevertheless vicious "retaliatory" commandos, the colonists all but wiped out the Bushman communities south of the Orange River. Many Bushmen, it is true, intermarried with agropastoralists and others went to live with them, but, all in all, the unpalatable truth of the matter is that genocide was the finality.

Although southern African rock art is all too often dismissively labeled as "primitive" or "simple," the discussion here shows that it is anything but. Neither the art itself nor the belief system it was embedded in can be described as remotely "simple." Understanding such art requires a good deal more than simply staring at a picture, but the effort is well worth making.

CHAPTER SUMMARY

Art is the creative use of the human imagination to interpret, understand, and enjoy life. It stems from the uniquely human ability to use symbols to give shape and significance to the physical world for more than just a utilitarian purpose. Anthropologists are concerned with art as a reflection of people's cultural values and concerns.

Oral traditions denote a culture's unwritten stories, beliefs, and customs. Verbal arts include narratives, dramas, poetry, incantations, proverbs, riddles, and word games. Narratives, which have received the most study, have been divided into three categories: myths, legends, and tales.

Myths are basically sacred narratives that explain how the world came to be as it is. By describing an orderly universe, myths function to set standards for orderly behavior. Legends are stories told as if true that often recount the exploits of heroes, the movements of people, and the establishment of local customs. Epics, which are long legends in poetry or prose, typically are found in nonliterate societies with some form of state political organization. They serve to transmit and preserve a culture's legal and political practices. In literate states, history has taken over these functions to one degree or another. Anthropologists are interested in legends because they provide clues about what constitutes model ethical behavior in a culture. Tales are fictional, secular, and nonhistorical narratives that instruct as they entertain. Anthropological interest in tales centers in part on the fact their distribution provides evidence of cultural contacts or cultural isolation.

The study of music in specific cultural settings has developed into the specialized field of ethnomusicology. Almost everywhere human music is perceived in terms of a scale. Scale systems and their modifications comprise tonality in music. Tonality determines the possibilities and limits of melody and harmony. Rhythm is an organizing factor in music. Traditional European music is measured into recurrent patterns of two, three, and four beats.

The social function of music is most obvious in song. Like tales, songs may express a group's concerns, but with greater formalism because of the restrictions closed systems of tonality, rhythm, and musical form impose. Music also serves as a powerful way for a social or ethnic group to assert its distinctive identity. As well, it may be used to advance particular political, economic, and social agendas or for any one of a number of other purposes.

Pictorial art may be regarded as either representational or abstract, though in truth these categories represent polar ends of a continuum. The rock art of southern Africa illustrates three ways the study of art may be approached. The aesthetic and narrative approaches focus on *how* and *what* things are depicted. By themselves they reveal little about what the art is all about and may convey a distorted view of the people responsible for it. Only the interpretive approach can reveal the meaning of another people's art. This approach requires drawing on a rich body of ethnography and often other sets of data. The effort is worthwhile, as it may reveal the art to be far more complex than one might otherwise expect. Applied to southern African rock art, it shows, among other aspects of the culture, how paintings and engravings were actually part of Bushman strategy for negotiating changing power relations as colonists invaded their lands.

POINTS FOR CONSIDERATION

1. In this chapter the Navajo tradition of sand painting is used to illustrate how sometimes the "art" is the process of creation, rather than what is produced. What other traditions stress the

act over the product? Why would Western people think more in terms of the resulting object than the act of creation? What does this tell observers about Western values?

2. Why is art perceived as elitist and nonproductive in Western society? Is this a valid viewpoint? How does it differ from other societies' opinions, and how might Western culture itself belie such a statement?

3. How does art participate in politics? Why are various art forms (music, graphic arts, literature, etc.) so important to nationalist or ethnic groups existing under the influence of foreign dominant cultures?

SUGGESTED READINGS

Dundes, A. (1980). *Interpreting folk lore*. Bloomington: Indiana University Press.

A collection of articles that assess the materials folklorists have amassed and classified, this book seeks to broaden and refine traditional assumptions about the proper subject matter and methods of folklore.

Hannah, J. L. (1988). *Dance, sex and gender*. Chicago: University of Chicago Press.

Like other art forms, dances are social acts that contribute to the continuation and emergence of culture. One of the oldest—if not the oldest—art forms, dance shares the same instrument, the human body, with sexuality. This book, written for a broad nonspecialist audience, explicitly examines sexuality and the construction of gender identities as they are played out in the production and visual imagery of dance.

Hatcher, E. P. (1985). *Art as culture: An Introduction to the anthropology of art*. New York: University Press of America.

This handy, clearly written book does a nice job of relating the visual arts to other aspects of culture. Topics include "The Technological Means," "The Psychological Perspective," "Social Contexts and Social Functions," "Art as Communication," and "The Time Dimension." Numerous line drawings help the reader understand the varied art forms in non-Western societies.

Layton, R. (1991). *The anthropology of art* (2nd ed.). Cambridge: Cambridge University Press.

This readable introduction to the diversity of non-Western art deals with questions of aesthetic appreciation, the use of art, and the big question: What *is* art?

Merriam, A. P. (1964). *The anthropology of music*. Chicago: Northwestern University Press.

This book focuses upon music as a complex of behavior that resonates throughout all of culture: social organization, aesthetic activity, economics, and religion.

Otten, C. M. (1971). *Anthropology and art: Readings in cross-cultural aesthetics*. Garden City, NY: Natural History Press.

This is a collection of articles by anthropologists and art historians with emphasis on the functional relationships between art and culture.

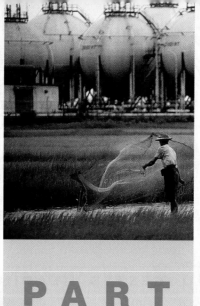

PART
VIII

CHANGE AND THE FUTURE: SOLVING THE PROBLEM OF ADJUSTING TO CHANGED CONDITIONS

Chapter 26
CULTURAL CHANGE

Chapter 27
ANTHROPOLOGY AND THE FUTURE

Introduction

Understanding the processes of change, the subject of Chapter 26, is one of the most important and fundamental of anthropological goals. Unfortunately, the task is made difficult by the cultural biases of most modern North Americans, which predispose them to see change as a progressive process leading in a predictable and determined way to where they are now, and even beyond to a future where they lead the way. So pervasive is this notion of progress that it motivates the thinking of North Americans in a great many ways they are hardly aware of. Among other ideas, it leads them to view cultures not like their own as "backward" and "underdeveloped." Of course, they are no such thing; as we saw in Chapter 17, no culture is static, and cultures may be very highly developed in quite different ways.

A simple analogy with the world of nature may be helpful here. In the course of evolution, simple bacteria appeared long before vertebrate animals, and land vertebrates such as mammals are relative latecomers indeed. Yet bacteria abound in the world today, not as relics of the past but as organisms highly adapted to situations mammals are totally unsuited for. Just because mammals got here late does not mean dogs, for example, are "better" or "more progressive" than bacteria.

Belief in "progress" and its inevitability has important implications for North Americans as well as others. For people in the United States, it means change has become necessary for its own sake, for whatever is old is, by virtue of that fact alone, inadequate and should be abandoned, no matter how well it seems to be working. Toward others, the logic runs like this: If the old inevitably must give way to the new, then societies North Americans perceive as "old" or "out of the past" also must give way to the new. Since the U.S. way of life is a recent development in human history, it must represent the new. "Old" societies therefore must become like that of the United States, or else it is their fate to disappear altogether. This idea amounts to a charter for massive intervention into the lives of others, whether they want this or not; the outcome, more often than not, is the destabilization and even destruction of other societies in the world.

A conscious attempt to identify and eliminate the biases of North American culture allows us to see change in a very different way. It allows us to recognize that, although people can change their ways in response to particular problems, much change occurs accidentally. The fact is the historical record is quirky and full of random events. And although it is true that without change cultures could never adapt to changed conditions, we also must recognize that too much large-scale, continuing change may place a culture in jeopardy. It conflicts with the social need for predictability, discussed in Chapter 14; individuals' needs for regularity and structure, discussed in Chapter 16; and a population's need for an adaptive "fit" with its environment, discussed in Chapter 6.

The more anthropologists study change and learn about the various ways people solve their problems of existence, the more aware they become of a great paradox of culture. Although the basic business of culture is to solve problems, in doing so, inevitably, new problems are created that demand solutions. Throughout this book we have seen examples of this—the problems of forming groups to cooperate in solving the problems of staying alive, the problem of overcoming the stresses and strains on individuals as a consequence of their group memberships, and the structural problems inherent in dividing society into a number of smaller groups, to mention a few. It is apparent every solution to a problem has its price, but as long as culture can keep at least a step ahead of the problems, all is reasonably well.

When we see all the problems the human species today faces (Chapter 27), most of them the result of cultural practices, we may wonder if we have passed some critical threshold where culture has begun to fall a step behind the problems. This does not mean the future necessarily has to be bleak for the generations that follow, but it would be irresponsible to project a rosy science-fiction-type of future as inevitable, at least on the basis of present evidence.

To prevent a bleak future, humans will have to rise to the challenge of changing their behavior and ideas to conquer the large problems that threaten to annihilate them: overpopulation and unequal access to basic resources with their concomitant starvation, poverty, and squalor; environmental pollution and poisoning; and the culture of discontent and bitterness that arises from the widening economic gap separating industrialized from nonindustrialized countries and the "haves" from the "have nots" within countries.

Chapter 26
CULTURAL CHANGE

The ability to change has always been important to human cultures. Probably at no time has the pace of change equaled that of today, as traditional peoples all over the world are pressured to "change their ways" or be "run over" by "progress." But indigenous peoples are fighting back and gaining the world's attention. Here, Aymara and Quechua Indians protest efforts to stamp out native American peoples and cultures that began with Columbus and have continued for over 500 years since.

Chapter Preview

Why Do Cultures Change?

All cultures change at one time or another for a variety of reasons. Although people deliberately may change their ways in response to some perceived problem, much change is accidental, including the unforeseen outcome of existing events. Or contact with other peoples may introduce "foreign" ideas, leading to changes in existing values and behavior. This even may involve the massive imposition of foreign ways through conquest of one group by another. Through change, cultures can adapt to altered conditions; however, not all change is adaptive.

How Do Cultures Change?

The mechanisms of change are innovation, diffusion, cultural loss, and acculturation. Innovation occurs when someone within a society discovers something new that is then accepted by other society members. Diffusion is the borrowing of something from another group, and cultural loss is the abandonment of an existing practice or trait, with or without replacement. Acculturation is the massive change that comes about with the sort of intensive firsthand contact that has occurred under colonialism.

What Is Modernization?

Modernization is an ethnocentric term referring to a global process of change by which traditional, nonindustrial societies seek to acquire characteristics of industrially "advanced" societies. Although modernization generally has been assumed to be a good thing, and some successes have occurred, it frequently has led to the development of a new "culture of discontent," a level of aspirations far exceeding the bounds of an individual's local opportunities. Sometimes it leads to the destruction of cherished customs and values people had no desire to abandon.

Culture is the medium through which the human species solves the problems of existence, as these are perceived by members of the species. Various cultural institutions, such as kinship and marriage, political and economic organization, and religion, mesh to form an integrated cultural system. Because systems generally work to maintain stability, cultures are often fairly stable and remain so unless either the conditions they are adapted to or human perceptions of those conditions change. Archaeological studies have revealed how elements of a culture may persist for long periods. In Chapter 17, for example, we saw how the culture of the native inhabitants of northwestern New England and southern Quebec remained relatively stable for thousands of years.

Although stability may be a striking feature of many cultures, none are ever changeless, as the cultures of food foragers, subsistence farmers, and pastoralists are all too often assumed to be. In a stable society, change may occur gently and gradually, without altering in any fundamental way the culture's underlying logic. Sometimes, though, the pace of change may increase dramatically, causing a radical cultural alteration in a relatively short period. The modern world is full of examples as diverse as the disintegration of the Soviet Union and what is happening to the native peoples of the Amazon forest as Brazil presses ahead to "develop" this vast region.

The causes of change are many and include the unexpected outcome of existing activities. To cite an example from U.S. history, the settlement of what we now call New England by English-speaking people had nothing to do with their culture being "better" or "more advanced" than those of the region's native inhabitants (one might argue it was just the reverse, as, at the time, New England's Indians had higher quality diets, enjoyed better health, and experienced less violence in their lives than did most Europeans[1]). Rather, the new settlement was the outcome of a series of unrelated events that happened to coincide at a critical time. In England, economic and political developments that drove large numbers of farmers

off the land, occurring at a time of population growth, forced an outward migration of people; it was purely chance that this happened shortly after the European discovery of the Americas.

Even at that, attempts to establish British colonies in New England ended in failure, until an epidemic of unprecedented scope resulted in the sudden death of about 90% of the native inhabitants of coastal New England. This epidemic did not occur because the British could not settle unless the land were cleared of its original occupants but, rather, because the Indians had been in regular contact with European fishermen and fur traders—whose activities were independent of British attempts at colonization—from whom they contracted the disease. For centuries, up to this time, Europeans had been living under conditions that were ideal for the incubation and spread of all sorts of infectious diseases, but the Indians had not. Consequently, the Europeans had developed over time a degree of resistance to such diseases, which Indians lacked altogether. To be sure, the consequences were inevitable, once direct contact between these people occurred; nonetheless, differential immunity did not occur to clear the coast of New England for English settlement. And even once those settlements were established, it is unlikely the colonists could have dispossessed the remaining natives from their land had they not come equipped with the political and military techniques for dominating other peoples, tactics previously used to impose their control upon the Scots, Irish, and Welsh.

In sum, had not a number of otherwise unrelated phenomena come together by chance at just the right time, English might very well not be the language most North Americans speak today.

Not just the unexpected outcome of existing activities but other sorts of accidents, too, may bring about changes if people perceive them as useful. Of course, people also may respond deliberately to altered conditions, thereby correcting the perceived problem that made the cultural modification seem necessary. Change also may be forced upon one group by another, as happened in colonial New England and as is happening in so much of the world today in the course of especially intense contact between two societies. Progress and adaptation, by contrast, are *not* causes of change; the latter is

[1]Stannard, D. E. (1992). *American holocaust* (pp. 57–67). Oxford: Oxford University Press.

a consequence of it that happens to work well for a population, and the former is a judgment of those consequences in terms of the group's cultural values. Progress is however it is defined.

▲▼▲▼▲▼▲▼▲▼▲▼▲▼▲▼▲▼▲▼▲▼▲▼▲▼▲

MECHANISMS OF CHANGE

INNOVATION

The ultimate source of all change is innovation: any new practice, tool, or principle that gains widespread acceptance within a group. Those that involve the chance discovery of a new principle we refer to as **primary innovations;** those that result from the deliberate applications of known principles are **secondary innovations.** The latter corresponds most closely to Western culture's model of

change as predictable and determined, while the former involves accidents of one sort or another.

An example of a primary innovation is the discovery that the firing of clay makes it permanently hard. Presumably, accidental firing of clay occurred frequently in ancient cooking fires. An accidental occurrence is of no account, however, unless someone perceives an application of it. This perception first took place about 25,000 years ago, when people began making figurines of fired clay. Pottery vessels were not made, however, nor did the practice of making objects of fired clay reach southwest Asia; at least if it did, it failed to take root. Not until sometime between 7000 and 6500 B.C. did people living in southwest Asia recognize a significant application of fired clay, when they began using it to make cheap, durable, and easy-to-produce containers and cooking vessels.

A Hopi woman firing pottery vessels. The discovery that firing clay vessels makes them indestructible (unless they are dropped or otherwise smashed) probably came about when clay-lined basins next to cooking fires in the Middle East were accidentally fired.

Primary innovation. The chance discovery of a new principle. **> Secondary innovation.** Something new that results from the deliberate application of known principles.

As nearly as we can reconstruct it, the development of the earliest known pottery vessels came about in the following way.[2] By 7000 B.C., cooking areas in southwest Asia included clay-lined basins built into the floor, clay ovens, and hearths, making the accidental firing of clay inevitable. Moreover, people were already familiar with the working of clay, which they used to build houses, line storage pits, and model figurines. For containers, however, they still relied upon baskets and upon bags made of animal hides.

Once the significance of fired clay—the primary innovation—was perceived, then the application of known techniques to it—secondary innovation—became possible. Clay could be modeled in the familiar way but now into the known shapes of baskets, bags, and stone bowls and then fired, either in an open fire or in the same facilities used for cooking food. In fact, the earliest known southwest Asian pottery imitates leather and stone containers, and the decoration consists of motifs transferred from basketry, even though they were ill suited to the new medium. Eventually, potters developed shapes and decorative techniques more suited to the new technology.

Since men are never the potters in traditional societies unless the craft has become more a commercial operation, women probably made the first pottery. The vessels they produced were initially handmade, and the earliest kilns were the same ovens used for cooking. As people became more adept at making pottery, they made further technological refinements. The clay could be modeled on a mat or other surface, which the woman could move as work progressed, to aid production. Hence, she could sit in one place while she worked, rather than getting up to move around the piece. A further refinement was to mount the movable surface on a vertical rotating shaft—an application of a known principle used for drills—creating the potter's wheel and permitting mass production. Kilns, too, were improved for better heat circulation by separating the firing chamber from the fire itself. By chance, these improved kilns produced enough heat to smelt ores such as copper, tin, gold, silver, and lead. Presumably, this discovery was made by accident—another primary innovation—and the stage was set for the eventual development of the forced-draft furnace from the earlier pottery kiln.

The accidents responsible for primary innovations are not generated by environmental change or some other need, nor are they preferentially oriented in an adaptive direction (see Figure 26.1). They are, however, given structure by their cultural context. Thus, the outcome of the discovery of fired clay by mobile food foragers 25,000 years ago was very different from what it was when discovered later on by more sedentary farmers in southwest Asia, where it set off a veritable chain reaction as one invention led to another. Indeed, given certain sets of cultural goals, values, and knowledge, particular innovations are almost bound to be made, such as penicillin. This antibiotic was discovered in 1928 when a mold blew in through the window of Sir Alexander Fleming's lab and landed on a microbial colony of staphylococcus, which it then dissolved. Fleming recog-

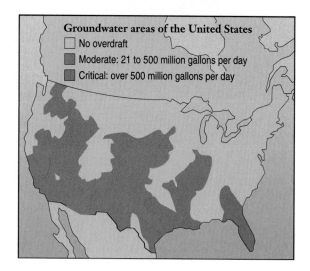

FIGURE 26.1

Human practices may or may not be adaptive. In the United States, for example, it is not adaptive over the long run to deplete groundwater in regions of fast-growing populations, yet people do this.

[2]Amiran, R. (1965). The beginnings of pottery-making in the Near East. In F. R. Matson (Ed.), *Ceramics and man* (pp. 240–247). Viking Fund Publications in Anthropology (No. 41). Chicago: Aldine.

nized the importance of this accident, because he was sensitive to the need for more than antiseptics and immunization, the mainstays of medicine at the time, to fight infection. Of course, he was not alone in his awareness, nor was this accident at all unusual. Any physician who studied medicine in the early part of this century had stories about having to scrub down laboratories when their studies in bacteriology were brought to a halt by molds that persisted in contaminating cultures and killing off the bacteria. To them, it was an annoyance; to Fleming, it was a "magic bullet" to fight infection. Under the circumstances, however, had he not made the discovery, someone else would have before long.

Although a culture's internal dynamics may encourage certain innovative tendencies, they may discourage others, or even remain neutral with respect to yet others. Indeed, Copernicus's discovery of the rotation of the planets around the sun and Mendel's discovery of the basic laws of heredity

are instances of genuine creative insights out of step with the established needs, values, and goals of their times and places. In fact, Mendel's work remained obscure until 16 years after his death, when three scientists working independently rediscovered, all in the same year (1900), the same laws of heredity. Thus, in the context of turn-of-the-century Western culture, Mendel's laws were bound to be discovered, even had Mendel not hit upon them earlier.

Although an innovation must be reasonably consistent with a society's needs, values, and goals if it is to be accepted, this is not sufficient to assure its acceptance. Force of habit tends to be an obstacle to acceptance; people generally will tend to stick with what they are used to, rather than adopt something new that will require some adjustment on their part. An example of this is the continued use of the QWERTY keyboard for typewriters and computers (named from the starting arrangement of letters). Devised in 1874, the

In the face of the AIDS epidemic sweeping southern Africa, the beliefs of several million Christian Zionists, such as the one being baptized here, are highly adaptive in that they militate against the kind of sexual practices that spread the disease. That these beliefs are adaptive, however, is a consequence of, rather than reason for, their origin.

arrangement minimized jamming of type bars and was combined with other desirable mechanical features to become the first commercially successful typewriter. Yet, the QWERTY keyboard has a number of serious drawbacks. The more typing one can do in the "home row" (2nd from bottom) of keys, the faster one can type, with the fewest errors and least strain on the fingers. But with QWERTY, only 32% of the strokes are done on the home row, versus 52% on the upper row and 16% on the (hardest) bottom row. What's more, it requires overuse of the weaker (left) hand (for the right-handed majority) and the weakest (fifth) finger.

In 1932, after extensive study, August Dvorak developed a keyboard that avoids the defects of QWERTY (Figure 26.2). Tests consistently show that the Dvorak keyboard can be learned in one

Once one's reflexes become adjusted to doing something one way, it becomes difficult to do it differently. Thus, when a North American or European goes to Great Britain, learning to drive on the "wrong" side of the road is difficult.

FIGURE 26.2

Dvorak and QWERTY keyboards, compared. Though superior to the latter in virtually every way, Dvorak has not been adopted owing to the head start enjoyed by QWERTY.

third the time, and, once learned, typists increase their accuracy by 68% and their speed by 74%, and they experience significantly less fatigue. So why hasn't Dvorak replaced QWERTY? The answer is commitment. Because QWERTY had a head start, by the time Dvorak came along manufacturers, typists, teachers, salespeople, and office managers were committed to the old keyboard; it was what they were used to.[3]

Obviously, being markedly better than the thing or idea an innovation replaces is not necessarily sufficient to ensure its acceptance. Much may depend on the prestige of the innovator and potential adopters. If the innovator's prestige is high, this will help gain acceptance for the innovation. If it is low, acceptance is less likely, unless the innovator can attract a sponsor who has high prestige.

DIFFUSION

When the Pilgrims established their colony of New Plymouth in North America, they very likely would have starved to death had the Indian Squanto not showed them how to grow the native American crops—corn, beans, and squash. The borrowing of cultural elements from one society by members of another is known as **diffusion,** and the donor society is, for all intents and purposes, the "inventor" of that element. So common is borrowing that the late Ralph Linton, a North American anthropologist, suggested that borrowing accounts for as much as 90% of any culture's content. People are creative about their borrowing, however, picking and choosing from multiple possibilities and sources. Usually their selections are limited to those compatible with the existing culture. In modern-day Guatemala, for example, Maya Indians, who make up more than half of that country's population, will adopt Western ways if the value of what they adopt is self-evident

and does not conflict with traditional ways and values. The use of metal hoes, shovels, and machetes became standard long ago, for they are superior to stone tools and yet compatible with the cultivation of corn in the traditional way by men using hand tools.

Yet certain other "modern" practices that might appear advantageous to the Maya tend to be resisted if they are perceived as running counter to Indian tradition. Thus, in the early 1960s, a young man in one community who tried his hand at truck gardening, using chemical fertilizers and pesticides to grow cash crops with market value only in the city—vegetables never eaten by the Maya—could not secure a "good" woman for a wife (a "good" woman has never had sex with another man and is skilled at domestic chores, not lazy, and willing to attend to her husband's needs). After he abandoned his unorthodox ways, however, his community accepted him as a "real" man, no longer different from the rest of them and therefore conspicuous (a "real" man will work steadily to provide his household with what they need to live by farming and making charcoal in the traditional ways). Before long, he was well married.[4]

Although the tendency toward borrowing is so great it led Robert Lowie to comment, "Culture is a thing of shreds and patches," the borrowed traits usually undergo sufficient modifications to make this wry comment more colorful than critical. Moreover, existing cultural traits may be modified to accommodate a borrowed one. An awareness of the extent of borrowing can be eye opening. Take, for example, the numerous things European Americans have borrowed from American Indians. Domestic plants developed ("invented") by the Indians—"Irish" potatoes, avocados, corn, beans, squash, tomatoes, peanuts, manioc, chili peppers, chocolate, and sweet potatoes, to name a few, furnish a major portion of the world's food supply. In fact, American Indians

---

[3]Diamond, J. (1997). The curse of QWERTY. *Discover, 18* (4), 34–42.

[4]Reina, R. E. (1966). *The law of the saints* (pp. 65–68). Indianapolis: Bobbs-Merrill.

Diffusion. The spread of customs or practices from one culture to another.

remain the developers of the world's largest array of nutritious foods and the primary contributors to the world's varied cuisine.[5] Among drugs and stimulants, tobacco is the best known (Figure 26.3), but others include coca in cocaine, ephedra in ephedrine, datura in pain relievers, and cascara in laxatives. Early on, European physicians recognized that Indians had the world's most sophisticated pharmacy, and Indians used all but a handful of drugs known today made from plants native to the Americas. More than 200 plants and herbs they used for medicinal purposes have at one time or another been included in the *Pharmacopeia of the United States* or in the *National Formulary*. Varieties of cotton Indians developed supply much of the world's clothing needs, while the woolen poncho, the parka, and moccasins are universally familiar items. Not only has Anglo

American literature been permanently shaped by such works as Longfellow's *Hiawatha* and James Fenimore Cooper's *Leatherstocking Tales,* but also American Indian music has contributed to world music such ultramodern devices as unusual intervals, arbitrary scales, conflicting rhythms, and hypnotic monotony. These borrowings are so well integrated into modern North American culture that few people are aware of their source.

Despite the obvious importance of diffusion, accepting an innovation from another culture probably has more obstacles than accepting a "homegrown" one. In addition to the same obstacles that stand in the way of homegrown inventions is the fact a borrowed one is, by its very nature, foreign. In the United States, for example, this is one reason why people have been so reluctant to abandon completely the awkward and cumbersome old English system of weights and measures for the far more logical metric system, which has been adopted by just about everyone else on the face of the earth. (The only holdouts besides the United States are South Yemen

---

[5]Weatherford, J. (1988). *Indian givers: How the Indians of the Americas transformed the New World* (p. 115). New York: Ballantine.

FIGURE 26.3

The diffusion of tobacco. Having spread from the tropics of the Western hemisphere to much of the rest of North and South America, it rapidly spread after 1492 to the rest of the world.

and Liberia.) Hence, the ethnocentrism of the potential borrowing culture may act as a barrier to acceptance.

CULTURAL LOSS

Most often people tend to think of change as an accumulation of innovations: adding new things to those already there. They think so because this seems so much a part of the way they live. A little reflection, however, leads to the realization that frequently the acceptance of a new innovation leads to the loss of an older one. This sort of replacement is not just a feature of Western civilization. For example, back in biblical times, chariots and carts were in widespread use in the Middle East, but by the 6th century A.D. wheeled vehicles had virtually disappeared from Morocco to Afghanistan. They were replaced by camels, not because of some reversion to the past by the region's inhabitants but because camels, used as pack animals, worked better. By the 6th century Roman roads had deteriorated, but camels, as long as they were not used as draft animals, were not bound to them. Not only that, their longevity, endurance, and ability to ford rivers and traverse rough ground without people having to build roads in the first place made pack camels admirably suited for the region. Finally, they were laborsaving: A wagon required a man for every two draft animals, whereas a single person can manage from three to six pack camels. Stephen Jay Gould comments:

> We are initially surprised . . . because wheels have come to symbolize in our culture the sine qua non of intelligent exploitation and technological progress. Once invented, their superiority cannot be gainsaid or superseded. Indeed, "reinventing the wheel" has become our standard metaphor for deriding the repetition of such obvious truths. In an earlier era of triumphant social Darwinism, wheels stood as an ineluctable stage of human progress. The "inferior" cultures of Africa slid to defeat; their conquerors rolled to victory. The "advanced" cultures of Mexico and Peru might have repulsed Cortés and Pizarro if only a clever artisan had thought of turning a calendar stone into a cartwheel. The notion that carts could ever be replaced

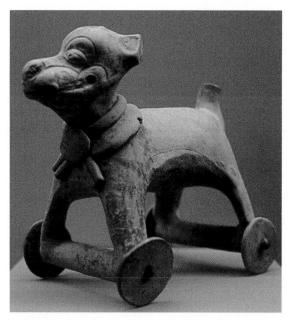

Although the wheel has become a symbol of progress in Western cultures, wheeled transport is not always superior to other forms. Such was the case in pre-Columbian Mexico, where wheels were used on toys but not for transport. The existence of adequate alternatives made wheeled vehicles unnecessary.

by pack animals strikes us not only as backward but almost sacrilegious.

> The success of camels reemphasizes a fundamental theme. . . . Adaptation, be it biological or cultural, represents a better fit to specific, local environments, not an inevitable stage in a ladder of progress. Wheels were a formidable invention, and their uses are manifold (potters and millers did not abandon them, even when cartwrights were eclipsed). But camels may work better in some circumstances. Wheels, like wings, fins, and brains, are exquisite devices for certain purposes, not signs of intrinsic superiority.[6]

Often overlooked is another facet of losing apparently useful traits: loss without replacement. An example of this is the absence of boats among the inhabitants of the Canary Islands, an archipelago

---

[6]Gould, S. J. (1983). *Hens' teeth and horses' toes* (p. 159). New York: Norton.

isolated in the stormy seas off the coast of West Africa. The ancestors of these people must have had boats, for without them they could never have transported themselves and their domestic livestock to the islands in the first place. Later, without boats, they had no way to communicate between islands. The cause of this loss of something useful was that the islands contain no stone suitable for making polished stone axes, which in turn limited the islanders' carpentry.[7]

FORCIBLE CHANGE

Innovation, diffusion, and cultural loss all may occur among peoples who are free to decide what changes they will accept. Not always, however, are people free to make their own choices; frequently, changes they would not willingly make themselves have been forced upon them by some other group, usually in the course of conquest and colonialism. A direct outcome in many cases is a phenomenon anthropologists call acculturation.

ACCULTURATION

Acculturation occurs when groups having different cultures come into intensive firsthand contact, with subsequent massive changes in the original cultural patterns of one or both groups. It always involves an element of force, either directly, as in conquests, or indirectly, as in the implicit or explicit threat that force will be used if people refuse to make the changes those in the other group expect them to make. Other variables include the degree of cultural difference; circumstances, intensity, frequency, and hostility of contact; relative status of the agents of contact; who is dominant and who is submissive; and whether the nature of the flow is reciprocal or nonreciprocal. It should

be emphasized that acculturation and diffusion are not equivalent terms; one culture can borrow from another without being in the least acculturated.

In the course of acculturation, any one of a number of things may happen. Merger or fusion occurs when two cultures lose their separate identities and form a single culture, as expressed by the "melting pot" ideology of Anglo American culture in the United States. Sometimes, though, one of the cultures loses its autonomy but retains its identity as a subculture in the form of a caste, class, or ethnic group; this is typical of conquest or slavery situations, and the United States has examples despite its melting-pot ideology. One need look no farther afield than the nearest Indian reservation. Today, in virtually all parts of the world, people are faced with the indignity of forced removal from their traditional homelands as entire communities are uprooted to make way for hydroelectric projects, grazing lands for cattle, mining operations, or highway construction. In Brazil's rush to develop the Amazon basin, for instance, whole villages have been relocated to "national parks," where resources are inadequate for so many people and where former enemies are often forced to live in close proximity.

Extinction is the phenomenon whereby so many carriers of a culture die that those who survive become refugees living among peoples of other cultures. Examples of this may be seen in many parts of the world today; the closest examples are found in many parts of South America, again as in Brazil's Amazon basin. One particularly well-documented case occurred in 1968, when hired killers tried to wipe out several Indian groups, including the Cinta-Larga. For this they used arsenic, dynamite, and machine guns from light planes; in the case of the Cinta-Largas, the killers chose a time when an important native ceremony was taking place to attack a village seen as an obstacle to development. Violence continues to be used in Brazil as a means of dealing with native people. For example, as a conservative estimate, at least 1,500 Yanomami died in the 1980s, often as victims of deliberate massacres, as cattle

[7]Coon, C. S. (1954). *The story of man* (p. 174). New York: Knopf.

Acculturation. Major cultural changes people are forced to make due to intensive firsthand contact between societies.

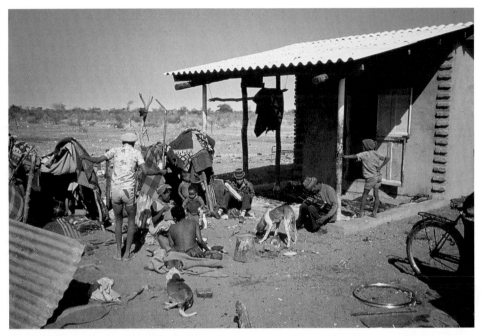

In Namibia, Bushmen from the Kalahari Desert were collected in settlements like Tsumkwe, shown here. Deprived of the means to secure their own necessities in life, such people commonly lapse into apathy and depression.

ranchers and miners poured into northern Brazil. By 1990, 70% of the Yanomami's land in Brazil had been unconstitutionally expropriated; their fish supplies were poisoned by mercury contamination of rivers; and malaria, venereal disease, and tuberculosis were running rampant. The Yanomami were dying at the rate of 10% a year, and their fertility had dropped off to near zero. Many villages were left with no children or old people, and the survivors awaited their fate with a profound terror of extinction.[8]

The usual Brazilian attitude to such situations is illustrated by the reaction of their government when two Kayapó Indians and an anthropologist traveled to the United States, where they spoke with members of several congressional committees, as well as officials of the Department of State, the Treasury, and the World Bank, about the destruction of their land and way of life caused by internationally financed development projects. All three were charged with violating Brazil's Foreign Sedition Act. Fortunately, international expressions of outrage at these and other atrocities has

---

[8]Turner, T. (1991). Major shift in Brazilian Yanomami policy. *Anthropology Newsletter, 32* (5), 1, 46.

brought positive changes from Brazilian authorities, but whether the Brazilians' recommendations will be sufficient, or even acted upon fully, remains to be seen. We will return to this problem later in this chapter.

GENOCIDE

The Brazilian Indian case just cited raises the issue of **genocide**—the extermination of one group of people by another, often deliberately and in the name of "progress." Genocide is not new in the world, as we need look no farther than North American history to see. In 1637, for example, a deliberate attempt was made to destroy the Pequot Indians by setting afire their village at Mystic, Connecticut, and then shooting down all those—primarily women and children—who sought to escape from being burned alive. To try to ensure that even their very memory would be stamped out, colonial authorities forbade even the mention of the Pequot's name. Several other massacres of Indian peoples occurred thereafter, until the last one at Wounded Knee, South Dakota, in 1890. Of course, such acts were by no means restricted to North America. One of the most famous 19th-century acts of genocide was the extermination of the Aboriginal inhabitants of Tasmania, a large island just south of Australia. In this case, the use of military force failed to achieve the complete elimination of the Tasmanians, but what the military could not achieve, a missionary could. George Augustus Robinson was able to round up the surviving natives, and at his mission station the deadly combination of psychological depression and European diseases brought about the demise of the last full-blooded Tasmanians in time for Robinson to retire to England a moderately wealthy man.

The most widely known act of genocide in recent history was the Nazi German attempt to wipe out European Jews and gypsies in the name of racial superiority. Unfortunately, the common practice of referring to this as "*the* holocaust"—

as if it were something unique or at least exceptional—tends to blind us to the fact this thoroughly monstrous act is simply one more example of an all too common phenomenon. From 1945 to 1987, a minimum of 6.8 million, but perhaps as many as 16.3 million, people were victims of internal (within state) genocide, as compared to the 3.34 million people who have died in wars between different countries from 1945 to 1980.[9] Moreover, genocide continues to occur in the world today in places such as Iraq, where in 1988 the government began to use poison gas against Kurdish villagers, and (as we will see in Chapter 27) Guatemala, to mention but two cases.

If such ugly practices are ever to be ended, we must gain a better understanding of them than currently exists. Anthropologists are actively engaged in this, carrying out cross-cultural as well as individual case studies. One finding to emerge is the regularity that religious, economic, and political interests are allied in cases of genocide. In Tasmania, for example, wool growers wanted Aborigines off the land so that they could have it for their sheep. The government advanced their interests through its military campaigns against the natives, but it was Robinson's missionary work that finally secured Tasmania for the wool interests. In the 1960s and 1970s, the Ju/'hoansi living in Namibia found themselves in a situation remarkably similar to that the Tasmanians experienced earlier. A combination of religious (Dutch Reformed church), political (Namibia's Department of Nature Conservation), and economic (agricultural/pastoral and touristic) interests forced the people's confinement to a reserve where disease and apathy caused death rates to outstrip birthrates. This case is important for another reason: It clearly illustrates that genocide is not al-

---

[9]Van Den Berghe, P. (1992). The modern state: Nation builder or nation killer? *International Journal of Group Tensions, 22* (3), 198.

Genocide.   The extermination of one people by another, often in the name of "progress," either as a deliberate act or as the accidental outcome of one people's activities done with little regard for their impact on others.

Genocide is not new in the world; this 1638 illustration shows English colonists with their Narragansett allies (the outer ring of bowmen) shooting down Pequot Indian women, children, and unarmed men attempting to flee their homes, which have been set afire.

ways a deliberate act. It also occurs as the unforeseen outcome of activities carried out with little regard for their impact on other peoples. For the people whose lives are snuffed out, however, it makes no difference whether the genocide is deliberate or not; for them, the outcome is the same.

Two examples (out of many) of attempted genocide in the 20th century: Hitler's Germany against Jews and gypsies, during the 1930s and the 1940s; and Saddam Hussein's Iraq against the Kurds, beginning in the 1980s.

DIRECTED CHANGE

The most extreme cases of acculturation usually occur as a result of military conquest and displacement of traditional political authority by conquerors who know or care nothing about the culture they control. The indigenous people, unable to resist imposed changes and prevented from carrying out many of their traditional social, religious, and economic activities, may be forced into new activities that tend to isolate individuals and tear apart the integration of their societies. Such a people are the Ju/'hoansi of Namibia, who were rounded up in the early 1960s and confined to a reserve where they could not possibly provide for their own needs. In this situation, the government provided them with insufficient rations to meet their nutritional needs. In poor health and prevented from developing meaningful alternatives to traditional activities, the people became argumentative and depressed, and, as already noted, their death rate came to exceed birthrates. After a visit to the reserve in 1980, anthropologist Robert J. Gordon commented: "I had never been in a place where one could literally smell death and decay, as in Tsumkwe."[10] In the 1980s, however, the Ju/'hoansi began to take matters into their own hands, returning to water holes in the back country, where, assisted by anthropologists and others concerned with their welfare, they are trying to sustain themselves by raising livestock. Whether this will succeed or not remains to be seen, as they have still many obstacles to success.

One by-product of colonial dealings with indigenous peoples has been the growth of **applied anthropology** and the use of anthropological tech-

---

[10]Gordon, R. J. (1992). *The Bushman myth: The making of a Namibian underclass* (p. 3). Boulder, CO: Westview.

A common agent of change in many nonindustrial societies is the religious missionary. Although they see themselves as bringing enlightenment to indigenous peoples, such missionaries seek to subvert the beliefs that lie at the heart of such cultures and that make life within them meaningful.

Applied anthropology.　The use of anthropological knowledge and techniques for solving "practical" problems, often for a specific "client."

anthropology applied   Growing Trees in Haiti

When foreigners go to Haiti, one of the sights that impresses them is the massive deforestation. Since colonial times, this country's population has swelled from fewer than half a million to more than 6 million—too many people for too little arable land. In their quest for fields, peasants eventually cut down all but a few stands of trees in remote areas. The resultant erosion, coupled with overuse of cropland, resulted in catastrophic declines in yields, sending many peasants into the capital, Port au Prince, in search of other work. This, in turn, created a growing demand for construction wood and charcoal in that city, which the rural poor were all too happy to satisfy by going after the country's few remaining trees. Responding to this crisis, international development organizations poured millions of dollars into studies of the problem, as well as into reforestation schemes, all to no avail. Not only were very few seedlings planted, but also those that were planted quickly became forage for the goats of peasants, and these people were reluctant to devote any of their scarce landholdings to the growing of state-owned trees.

Faced with failure, the United States Agency for International Development (AID) in Haiti invited anthropologist Gerald F. Murray to develop an alternative approach to reforestation and subsequently hired him as Project Director. Already familiar with peasant land usage in Haiti, Murray knew that typical reforestation projects, such as the planting of fruit trees by government agents for purposes of soil conservation, would not work. To peasants, fruit trees were of little commercial or nutritional value, especially if they were perceived as state owned. They needed a cash crop that was theirs to do with as they wished. Accordingly, Murray made available, through nongovernmental organizations rather than state agencies, seedlings of leucaena, ocassia, and eucalyptus, fast-growing wood trees good for charcoal and basic construction material that attracted a ready market. Moreover, the trees could be cut in some instances as early as 4 years after planting and could be grown along borders of fields or even intercropped among other plants, rather than in large, unbroken, uncropped stands. Thus, their growth was compatible with continued subsistence farming. Moreover, any potential loss from decreased food production was far offset by income the trees would generate.

The idea that trees were meant to be cut, while heretical to the international development "establishment," was extremely popular with the peasants. As Murray observes, "Though it had taken AID two years to decide about the project; it took about twenty minutes with any group of skeptical but economically rational peasants to generate a list of enthusiastic potential tree planters. . . . Cash-flow dialogues and ownership . . . were a far cry from the finger-wagging ecological sermons to which many peasant groups had been subjected on the topic of trees."* When first conceived, the planting of 3 million trees on the land of 6,000 peasants was set as the project's 4-year goal. In fact, by the end of the 4th year, 20 million trees had been planted by 75,000 peasants.

Unlike bureaucratically conceived projects, this anthropologically conceived and implemented agroforestry project was reasonably successful, until a military coup ousted the president. Unfortunately, one of the means the military regime used to show the rural population who was in control was to wantonly cut down trees. What will happen now that civilian power has been restored still remains to be seen.

---

*Murray, G. F. (1989). The domestication of wood in Haiti: A case study in applied evolution. In A. Podolefsky & P. J. Brown (Eds.), *Applying anthropology, an introductory reader* (pp. 151–152). Mountain View, CA: Mayfield.

niques and knowledge for certain "practical" ends. For example, British anthropology often has been considered the "handmaiden" of that country's colonial policy, for it typically provided information needed for maintaining effective colonial rule. In the United States, the Bureau of American Ethnology was founded toward the end of the 19th century to gather reliable data the government might base its Indian policies on. At the time, North American anthropologists were convinced of the practicality of their discipline, and many who did ethnographic work among Indians devoted a great deal of time, energy, and even money toward assisting their informants, whose interests were frequently threatened from outside.

In the present century, the scope of applied anthropology has broadened. Early on, the applied work of Franz Boas, who almost single-handedly trained a generation of anthropologists in the United States, was instrumental in reforming the country's immigration policies. In the 1930s, anthropologists with avowedly applied goals did a number of studies in industrial and other institutional settings in the United States. With World War II came the first efforts at colonial administration beyond U.S. borders, especially in the Pacific, by officers trained in anthropology. The rapid recovery of Japan was due in no small measure to the influence of anthropologists on structuring the U.S. occupation. Anthropologists continue to play an active role today in administering the U.S. trust territories in the Pacific.

Today, applied anthropologists are in some demand in international development because of their specialized knowledge of social structure, value systems, and the functional interrelatedness of cultures targeted for development. The role of the applied anthropologists, however, is far from easy; as anthropologists, they are bound to respect other peoples' dignity and cultural integrity, yet they are asked for advice on how to change certain aspects of those cultures. If the request comes from the people themselves, that is one thing, but more often than not the request comes from an outside "expert." Supposedly, the proposed change is for the good of the targeted population, yet the people do not always see it that way. Just how far applied anthropologists should go when advising how people—especially ones without the power to resist—can be made to embrace changes proposed for them is a serious ethical question.

Despite such difficulties, applied anthropology is flourishing today as never before. As the several Anthropology Applied boxes spaced throughout this book illustrate, anthropologists now practice their profession in many different nonacademic

Franz Boas *(1858–1942)*

Born in Germany, where he studied physics and geography, Franz Boas came to the United States to live in 1888. His interest in anthropology began a few years earlier with a trip to Baffinland, where he met his first so-called primitive people. Thereafter, he and his students came to dominate anthropology in North America for the first 3 decades of the 1900s.

Through meticulous and detailed fieldwork, which set new standards for excellence, Boas and his students exposed the shortcomings of the grandiose, culture-bound schemes of cultural evolution earlier social theorists had proposed. His thesis that a culture must be understood according to its own standards and values, rather than those of the investigator, represented a tremendously liberating philosophy in his time. (The photo shows Boas posing as a Kwakiutl *hanatsa* dancer for a National Museum diorama, 1895).

Applied anthropologist Tekle Haile Selassie of Ethiopia speaks with women of the village of Mai Misham about water improvement systems.

settings, both at home and abroad, in a wide variety of ways.

REACTIONS TO FORCIBLE CHANGE

The reactions of indigenous peoples to the changes outsiders have thrust upon them have varied considerably. Some have responded by moving to the nearest available forest, desert, or other inhospitable place in hopes of being left alone. In Brazil, a number of communities once located near the coast took this option a few hundred years ago and were successful until the great push to develop the Amazon forest began in the 1960s. Others, such as the Indians of North America, tried to fight back but were ultimately defeated and reduced to an impoverished underclass in their own land. Sometimes, though, people have managed to keep faith with their traditions by inventing creative and

ingenious ways to express them in the face of powerful foreign domination. This blending of indigenous and foreign elements into a new system is known as **syncretism,** and a fine illustration of it is the game of cricket as played by the Trobriand Islanders, some of whose practices we looked at in Chapters 18, 19, and 20.

Under British rule, the Trobrianders were introduced by missionaries to the rather staid British game of cricket to replace the erotic dancing and open sexuality that normally followed yam harvests. Traditionally, this was when chiefs sought to spread their fame by hosting nights of dancing, providing food for the hundreds of young married people who participated. For 2 months or so, night after night of provocative dancing would occur, accompanied by chanting and shouting full of sexual innuendo, each night ending as couples disappeared off into the bush together. Since no chief wished to be outdone by any other (to be outdone reflected on the strength of one's magic), all of this dancing had a strong competitive element, and

Syncretism.   In acculturation, the blending of indigenous and foreign traits to form a new system.

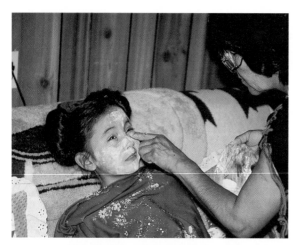

An example of syncretism. Although the Hopi Indians have adopted a number of items from European Americans (note the glasses and electrical outlet), such "borrowed" things are combined with traditional ones, as in the ritual use of cornmeal, here being applied to a young girl as required by ancient tradition.

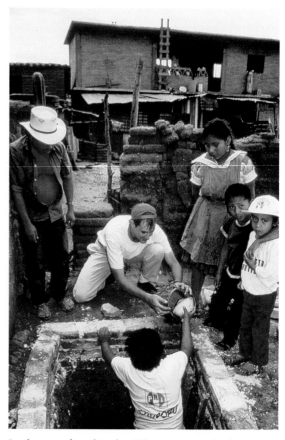

In the past few decades, Western countries have sent technological "missionaries" to teach people in other places new ways of doing old tasks. Unless they have had anthropological training, however, such "missionaries" are apt to be unaware of the side effects their new ways will have.

fighting sometimes erupted. To the missionaries, cricket seemed a good way to end all of this, encouraging conformity to "civilized" comportment in dress, religion, and "sportsmanship." The Trobrianders, however, were determined to "rubbish" (throw out) the British game and turned it into the same kind of distinctly Trobriand event their dance competitions had once been.

The Trobrianders made cricket their own by adding battle dress and battle magic and by incorporating erotic dancing into the festivities. Instead of inviting dancers each night, chiefs now arrange games of cricket. Pitching has been modified from the British style to one closer to their old way of throwing a spear. Following the game, they hold massive feasts, where wealth is displayed to enhance their prestige. Cricket, in its altered form, has been made to serve traditional systems of prestige and exchange. Neither "primitive" nor passively accepted in its original form, Trobriand cricket was thoughtfully and creatively adapted into a sophisticated activity reflecting the importance of basic indigenous cultural premises. Exuberance and pride are displayed by everyone associated with the game, and the players are as much concerned with conveying the full meaning of who they are as with scoring well. From the

sensual dressing in preparation for the game to the team chanting of songs full of sexual metaphors to erotic chorus-line dancing between the innings, observers have little doubt each player is playing for his own importance, for the fame of his team, and for the hundreds of attractive young women who usually watch the game.

REVITALIZATION MOVEMENTS

Another common reaction to forcible change is revitalization, a process already touched upon in Chapter 24. Revitalization may be looked upon as a deliberate attempt by some members of a society to construct a more satisfactory culture by the rapid acceptance of a pattern of multiple innovations. Once primary ties of culture, social relationships, and activities are broken and meaningless activity is imposed by force, individuals and groups characteristically react with fantasy, withdrawal, and escape.

Examples of revitalization movements have been common in the history of the United States whenever significant population segments have found their conditions in life to be at odds with the values of "the American Dream." For example, in the 19th century, periodic depression and the disillusionment of the decades after the Civil War produced a host of revitalization movements, the most successful being that of the Mormons. In the 20th century, movements repeatedly arose in the slums of major cities, as well as in depressed rural areas such as Appalachia. By the 1960s, a number of movements were less inward looking and more activist, a good example being the rise of the Black Muslim movement. The 1960s also saw the rise of revitalization movements among the young of middle-class and even upper-class families. In their case, the professed values of peace, equality, and individual freedom were seen to be at odds with the realities of persistent war, poverty, and constraints on individual action imposed by a variety of impersonal institutions. Their reactions to these realities were expressed by their drug use; in their outlandish or "freaky" clothes, hairstyles, music, and speech; and in their behavior toward authority and authority figures.

By the 1980s revitalization movements were becoming prominent even among older, more affluent segments of society, as in the rise of the so-called religious right. In these cases, the reaction is not so much against a perceived failure of the American Dream as it is against perceived threats to that dream by dissenters and activists within their society, by foreign governments, by new ideas that challenge other ideas they like to believe, and by the sheer complexity of modern life.

Clearly, when value systems get out of step with existing realities, for whatever reason, a condition of cultural crisis is likely to build up that may breed some forms of reactive movements. Not all suppressed, conquered, or colonized people eventually rebel against established authority, although why they do not is still a debated issue. When they do,

Revitalization movements that attempt to revive traditional ways of the past are not restricted to "underdeveloped" countries; in the United States, the Reverend Pat Robertson is a leader in such a movement.

however, resistance may take one of several forms, all of which are varieties of revitalization movements. A culture may seek to speed up the acculturation process to share more fully in the supposed benefits of the dominant cultures. Melanesian cargo cults of the post–World War II era generally have been of this sort, although earlier ones stressed a revival of traditional ways. Sometimes, a movement tries to reconstitute a destroyed but not forgotten way of life, as did many Plains Indians with the Ghost Dance in the 19th century and as do movements on the "religious right" today. Sometimes, a suppressed pariah group, which long has suffered in an inferior social standing and which has its own special subcultural ideology, attempts to create a new social order; the most familiar examples of this to Western peoples are prophetic Judaism and early Christianity. If the movement's aim is directed from within primarily at the ideological system and the attendant social structure of a cultural system, it is then called **revolutionary.**

▲▽▲▽▲▽▲▽▲▽▲▽▲▽▲▽▲▽▲▽▲▽▲▽▲▽▲
REBELLION AND REVOLUTION

When the scale of discontent within a society reaches a certain level, the possibilities for rebellion and revolution—such as the Iranian Revolution, the Sandinista Revolution in Nicaragua, or the Zapatista uprising in Mexico—are high.

The question of why revolutions erupt, as well as why they frequently fail to live up to the expectations of the people initiating them, is a problem. It is clear, however, that the colonial policies of countries such as England, France, Spain, Portugal, and the United States during the 19th and early 20th centuries have created a worldwide situation in which revolution is nearly inevitable. Despite the political independence most colonies have gained since World War II, more powerful countries continue to exploit many for their natural resources and cheap labor, causing a deep resentment of rulers beholden to foreign powers. Further discontent has been caused by the governing elite of newly independent states attempting to assert their control over peoples living within their boundaries who, by virtue of a common ancestry, possession of distinct cultures, persistent occupation of their own territories, and traditions of self-determination, identify themselves as distinct nations and refuse to recognize the sovereignty of what they regard as a foreign government. Thus, in many a former colony, large numbers of people have taken up arms to resist annexation and absorption by imposed state regimes run by people

A leading cause of rebellion and revolution in the world today is the refusal of governing elites to recognize the cultural, economic, and political rights of people of other nationalities whom the state has unilaterally asserted its authority over. A recent illustration is the Zapatista uprising in Mexico in response to continued repressive control by Ladinos (non-Indians).

Revolutionary.   A revitalization movement from within directed primarily at a culture's ideological system and the attendant social structure.

of other nationalities. While attempting to make their states into nations, governing elites of one nationality endeavor to strip the peoples of other nations within their states of their lands, resources, and sense of identity as a people. The phenomenon is so common as to lead anthropologist Pierre Van Den Berghe to label what modern states refer to as "nation building" as, in fact, "nation killing."[11] One of the most important facts of our time is that the vast majority of the distinct peoples of the world have never consented to rule by the governments of states they find themselves living within.[12] In many a newly emerged country, such peoples feel they have no other option than to fight.

On the basis of an examination of four revolutions of the past—English, American, French, and Bolshevik—the following conditions have been offered as precipitators of rebellion and revolution:

1. Loss of prestige of established authority, often from the failure of foreign policy, financial difficulties, dismissals of popular ministers, or alteration of popular policies.
2. Threat to recent economic improvement. In France and Russia, sections of the population (professional classes and urban workers) whose economic fortunes previously had taken an upward swing were radicalized by unexpected setbacks, such as steeply rising food prices and unemployment.
3. Indecisiveness of government, as exemplified by lack of consistent policy; such governments appear to be controlled by, rather than in control of, events.
4. Loss of support of the intellectual class. Such a loss deprived the prerevolutionary governments of France and Russia of philosophical support, thus leading to their lack of popularity with the literate public.
5. A leader or group of leaders with charisma enough to mobilize a substantial part of the population against the establishment.

Apart from resistance to internal authority, such as in the English, French, and Russian Revolutions, many revolutions in modern times have been struggles against an authority outsiders impose on them. Such resistance usually takes the form of independence movements that wage campaigns of armed defiance against colonial powers. The Algerian struggle for independence from France and the American Revolution are typical examples. Of the 120 or so armed conflicts in the world today, 98% are in the economically poor countries of Africa, Asia, and Central and South America, almost all of which were at one time under European colonial domination. Of these wars, 75% are between the state and one or more peoples within the state's borders who are seeking to maintain or regain control of their persons, communities, lands, and resources in the face of what they regard as subjugation by a foreign power.[13]

Not all revolts are truly revolutionary in their consequences. According to Max Gluckman, rebellions

> ". . . throw the rascals out" and substitute another set, but there is no attempt to alter either the cultural ideology or the form of the social structure. In political revolution, attempts are made to seize the offices of power in order to change social structure, belief systems, and their symbolic representations. Political revolutions are usually turbulent, violent, and not long-lasting. A successful revolution soon moves to re-establish a stable, though changed, social structure; yet it has far-reaching political, social and sometimes economic and cultural consequences.[14]

Not always are revolutions successful about accomplishing what they set out to do. One of the stated goals of the Chinese Revolution, for example, was to liberate women from the oppression of a strongly patriarchal society where a woman owed lifelong obedience to some man or another—first her father, later her husband, and, after his death,

---

[11]Van Den Berghe, P. (1992). The modern state: Nation builder or nation killer? *International Journal of Group Tensions, 22* (3), 191–207.

[12]Nietschmann, B. (1987). The third world war. *Cultural Survival Quarterly, 11* (3), 3.

[13]Ibid., 7.

[14]Hoebel, E. A. (1972). *Anthropology: The study of man* (4th ed., p. 667). New York: McGraw-Hill.

her sons. Although some progress has been made, the effort overall has been frustrated by the cultural lens the revolutionaries view their work through. A tradition of extreme patriarchy extending back at least 22 centuries is not easily overcome and has unconsciously influenced many of the decisions China's leaders since 1949 have made. In rural China today, as in the past, a woman's life is still usually determined by her relationship to some man, be it her father, husband, or son, rather than by her own efforts or failures. What's more, women are being told more frequently that their primary roles are as wives and mothers. When they work outside the house, it is generally at jobs with low pay, low status, and no benefits. Indeed, the 1990s have seen a major outbreak of the abduction and sale of women from rural areas as brides and workers. Their no-wage labor for their husbands' household or low-wage labor outside (which goes back to the household) has been essential to China's economic expansion, which relies on the allocation of labor by the heads of patrilineal households.[15] Thus despite whatever autonomy women may achieve for

a while, they become totally dependent in their old age on their sons.

This situation shows that the subversion of revolutionary goals, if it occurs, is not necessarily by political opponents. Rather, it may be a consequence of the revolutionaries' own cultural background. In rural China, as long as women marry out and their labor is controlled by male heads of families, women always will be seen as something of a commodity.

It should be pointed out that revolution is a relatively recent phenomenon, occurring only during the past 5,000 years or so. The reason is that political rebellion requires a centralized political authority (chiefdom or state) to rebel against, and states (if not chiefdoms) have been in existence for only 5,000 years. Obviously, then, in societies typified by tribes and bands, and in other nonindustrial societies lacking central authority, rebellion or political revolution could not have occurred.

---

[15]Gates, H. (1996). Buying brides in China—again. *Anthropology Today, 12* (4), 10.

In China, women's labor has become critical to economic expansion. Much of this labor is controlled by male heads of families, who act as agents of the state in allocating labor.

MODERNIZATION

One of the most frequently used terms to describe social and cultural changes as they are occurring today is **modernization**. This is most clearly defined as an all-encompassing global process of cultural and socioeconomic change, whereby developing societies seek to acquire some of the characteristics common to industrial societies. Looking closely at this definition's meaning reveals that "becoming modern" really means "becoming like us" ("us" being the United States and other industrial societies), with the very clear implication that not being like us is to be antiquated and obsolete. Not only is this ethnocentric, but it also fosters the notion that these other societies must be *changed* to be more like us, irrespective of other considerations. It is unfortunate that the term *modernization* continues to be so widely used. Since we seem to be stuck with it, the best we can

do at the moment is to recognize its inappropriateness, even though we continue to use it.

The process of modernization may be best understood as consisting of four subprocesses, of which one is *technological development*. In the course of modernization, traditional knowledge and techniques give way to the application of scientific knowledge and techniques borrowed mainly from the West. Another subprocess is *agricultural development*, represented by a shift in emphasis from subsistence farming to commercial farming. Instead of raising crops and livestock for their own use, people turn more frequently to the production of cash crops, with greater reliance on a cash economy and on markets for selling farm products and purchasing goods. A third subprocess is *industrialization*, with a greater emphasis placed on inanimate forms of energy—especially fossil fuels—to power machines. Human and animal power become less important, as do handicrafts in general. The fourth subprocess is *urbanization*, marked particularly by population movements from rural settlements into cities. Although all four subprocesses are interrelated, they follow no fixed order of appearance.

Structural differentiation. Whereas most items for daily use were once made at home, such as butter (left), almost everything we use today is the product of specialized production, as is the butter we buy in the food store.

Modernization. The process of cultural and socioeconomic change, whereby developing societies acquire some of the characteristics of Western industrialized societies.

As modernization occurs, other changes are likely to follow. In the political realm, political parties and some sort of electoral machinery frequently appear, along with the development of a bureaucracy. In education, learning opportunities expand, literacy increases, and an indigenous educated elite develops. Religion becomes less important in many areas of thought and behavior as traditional beliefs and practices are undermined. The traditional rights and duties connected with kinship are altered, if not eliminated, especially where distant kin are concerned. Finally, where stratification is a factor, mobility increases as ascribed status becomes less important and achievement counts more.

Two other features of modernization go hand in hand with those already noted. One, **structural differentiation,** is the division of single traditional roles, which embrace two or more functions, into two or more separate roles, each with a single specialized function. This represents a kind of fragmentation of society, which must be counteracted by new **integrative mechanisms** if the society is not to disintegrate into a number of discrete units. These new mechanisms take such forms as formal governmental structures, official state ideologies, political parties, legal codes, and labor and trade unions as well as other common-interest associations. All of these crosscut other societal divisions and thus serve to oppose differentiating forces. These two forces, however, are not the only ones in opposition in a situation of modernization; to them must be added a third, the force of **tradition.** This opposes the new forces of both differentiation and integration. Yet the conflict does not have to be total. Traditional ways may on occasion facilitate modernization. For example, traditional kinship ties may assist rural people as they move into cities if they have relatives already there they may turn to for aid. One's relatives, too, may provide the financing necessary for business success.

One aspect of modernization, the technological explosion, has made it possible to transport human beings and ideas from one place to another with astounding speed and in great numbers. Formerly independent cultural systems have been brought into contact with others. The cultural differences between New York and Pukapuka are declining, while the differences between fishers and physicists are increasing. No one knows whether this implies a net gain or net loss in cultural diversity, but the worldwide spread of anything, whether it is DDT (an environmentally toxic insecticide) or a new idea, should be viewed with at least caution. That human beings and human cultural systems are different is the most exciting aspect about them, yet the destruction of diversity is implicit in the worldwide spread of rock-and-roll, socialism, capitalism, or anything else. When a song is forgotten or a ceremony ceases to be performed, a part of the human heritage is destroyed forever.

An examination of two traditional cultures that have felt the impact of modernization or other cultural changes will help to pinpoint some of the problems such cultures have met. The cultures are the Skolt Lapps, a division of the Saami people whose homeland straddles the Arctic Circle in Norway, Sweden, Finland, and Russia, and the Shuar Indians of Ecuador.

SKOLT LAPPS AND THE SNOWMOBILE REVOLUTION

The Skolt Lapps, whose homeland is in northern Finland, traditionally supported themselves by fishing and herding reindeer.[16] Although they depended on the outside world for certain material goods, the resources crucial for their system were

---

[16]Pelto, P. J. (1973). *The snowmobile revolution: Technology and social change in the Arctic.* Menlo Park, CA: Cummings.

Structural differentiation. The division of single traditional roles, which embrace two or more functions (for example, political, economic, and religious), into two or more roles, each with a single specialized function. ▷ **Integrative mechanisms.** Cultural mechanisms that oppose a society's differentiation forces; in modernizing societies, they include formal governmental structures, official state ideologies, political parties, legal codes, and labor and trade unions and other common-interest associations. ▷ **Tradition.** In a modernizing society, old cultural practices that may oppose new differentiation and integration forces.

found locally and were for all practical purposes available to all. No one was denied access to critical resources, and little social and economic differentiation existed among the people. Theirs was basically an egalitarian society.

Of particular importance to the Skolt Lapps was reindeer herding. Indeed, herd management is central to their definition of themselves as a people. These animals were a source of meat for home consumption or for sale to procure outside goods. They were also a source of hides for shoes and clothing, sinews for sewing, and antlers and bones for making certain objects. Finally, reindeer were used to pull sleds in the winter and as pack animals when no snow was on the ground. Understandably, the animals were the objects of much attention. The herds were not large, but without a great deal of attention, productivity suffered. Hence, most winter activities centered on reindeer. Men, operating on skis, were closely associated with their herds, intensively from November to January and periodically from January to April.

In the early 1960s these reindeer herders speedily adopted snowmobiles on the premise the new machines would make herding physically easier and economically more advantageous. The first machine arrived in Finland in 1962; by 1971 the Skolt Lapps and non-Lapps in the same area owned 70 operating machines. Although men on skis still carry out some herding activity, their importance and prestige are now diminished. As early as 1967 only four people were still using reindeer sleds for winter travel; most had gotten rid of draft animals.

Those who had not converted to snowmobiles felt disadvantaged compared to the rest.

The consequences of this mechanization were extraordinary and far reaching. The need for snowmobiles, parts and equipment to maintain them, and a steady supply of gasoline created a dependency on the outside world unlike anything that had previously existed. As snowmobile technology replaced traditional skills, the ability of the Lapps to determine their own survival without dependence on outsiders, should this be necessary, was lost. Snowmobiles are also expensive, costing several thousand dollars in the Arctic. Maintenance and gasoline expenses must be added to this initial cost. Accordingly, a sharp rise in the need for cash occurred. To get this, men must go outside the Lapp community for wage work more than just occasionally, as had once been the case, or else rely on such sources as government pensions or welfare.

The argument may be made that dependency and the need for cash are prices worth paying for an improved system of reindeer herding, but has it improved? In truth, snowmobiles have contributed in a significant way to a disastrous decline in reindeer herding. By 1971 the average size of the family herd had declined from 50 to 12. Not only is this too small a number to be economically viable, but also it is too small to maintain at all. The reason is that the animals in such small herds will take the first opportunity to run off to join another larger one. The old close, prolonged, and largely peaceful relationship between

A Saami man separating his reindeer from those of other herds.

herdsman and beast has changed to a noisy, trau-matic relationship. Now, when men appear, it is to come speeding out of the woods on snarling, smelly machines that invariably chase the animals, often for long distances. Instead of helping the reindeer in their winter food quest, helping females with their calves, and protecting them from predators, men appear either to slaughter or castrate them. Naturally enough, the reindeer have become suspi-cious. The result has been actual de-domestication, with reindeer scattering and running off to more in-accessible areas, given the slightest chance. More-over, indications are that snowmobile harassment has adversely effected the number of viable calves added to the herds. This is a classic illustration of the fact change is not always adaptive.

The cost of mechanized herding—and the de-cline of the herds—has led many Lapps to aban-don herding altogether. Now, the majority of males are no longer herders at all. This constitutes a serious economic problem, since few economic alternatives are available. The problem is com-pounded by the fact participation in a cash-credit economy means most people, employed or not, have payments to make. This is more than just an economic problem, for in the traditional culture of this people, being a herder of reindeer is the very essence of manhood. Hence, today's non-herders are not only poor in a way they could not be in previous times, but also they are in a sense inadequate as "men" quite apart from this.

This economic differentiation with its reeval-uation of roles has led to the development of a stratified society out of the older egalitarian one. Differences have arisen in terms of wealth and, with this, in lifestyles. It is difficult to break into reindeer herding now, for one needs a substantial cash outlay. And herding now requires skills and knowledge that were not a part of traditional cul-ture. Not everyone has these, and those without them are dependent on others if they are to par-ticipate. Hence, access to critical resources is now restricted where once it had been open to all.

THE SHUAR SOLUTION

Although the Skolt Lapps have not escaped many negative aspects of modernization, the choice to modernize or not was essentially theirs. The Shuar

(sometimes called Jivaro) Indians, by contrast, de-liberately avoided modernization, until they felt they had no other option if they were to fend off the same outside forces that elsewhere in the Ama-zon basin have destroyed whole societies. Threat-ened with the loss of their land base as more and more Ecuadoran colonists intruded into their ter-ritory, the Shuar in 1964 founded a fully inde-pendent corporate body, the Shuar Federation, to take control of their own future. Recognized by Ecuador's government, albeit grudgingly, the Fed-eration is officially dedicated to promotion of the social, economic, and moral advancement of its members and to coordination of development with official governmental agencies.

Since its founding, the Federation has secured title to more than 96,000 hectares of communal land; has established a cattle herd of more than 15,000 head as the peoples' primary source of in-come; has taken control of their education, using their language and mostly Shuar teachers; and has established their own bilingual broadcasting station and a bilingual newspaper. Obviously, all this has required enormous changes by the Shuar, but they have been able to maintain a variety of distinctive cultural markers, including their language, commu-nal land tenure, cooperative production and distri-bution, a basically egalitarian economy, and kin-based communities that retain maximum autonomy. Thus, for all the changes, they feel they are still Shuar and quite distinct from other Ecuadorans.[17]

---

[17]Bodley, J. H. (1990). *Victims of progress* (3rd ed., pp. 160–162). Mountain View, CA: Mayfield.

The Shuar case shows that Amazonian Indian nations are capable of taking control of their own destinies even in the face of intense outside pressures, *if* allowed to do so. Unfortunately, until recently, few have had that option. Prior to European invasions of the Amazon, more than 700 distinct groups inhabited the region. By 1900 in Brazil, the number was down to 270, and today something like 180 remain.[18] Many of these survivors find themselves in situations not unlike that of the Yanomami, described earlier in this chapter. Nevertheless, many of these peoples are showing a new resourcefulness in standing up to the forces of destruction arrayed against them. That these forces are formidable is illustrated in the following account by an anthropologist who lives in Brazil and has done fieldwork in the Amazon since 1976.

_____

[18]*Cultural Survival Quarterly, 15* (4), 38. (1991).

Violence on Indian Day in Brazil 1997[19]

▲▼▲

Sunday evening, April 20, 1997, the Brazilian television network Rede Globo on its weekly program Fantástico, carried the tragic story of a Pataxó Indian of Bahia who had been brutally murdered. The Pataxó are the same indigenous people whom Pedro Álvares Cabral encountered in his "discovery" of Brazil in 1500.

According to the news story, the 44 year old Pataxó leader, Gildino Jesus dos Santos, had gone to Brasilia with a number of his people to discuss their land claims with government officials, to participate in the demonstrations and festivities held in commemoration of Indian Day in Brazil, and to welcome thousands of landless poor, or Sem Terra, from all over Brazil—a historic moment in Brazilian struggles to institute agrarian reform. According to other Pataxós lodged in a FUNAI boarding house [FUNAI is the Brazilian Indian service], Gildino came back late from the festivities and was barred entrance to the boarding house by military police. He wandered around the area for awhile and decided to sleep on a bus stop bench. An eyewitness report declared that a car with five youths approached, poured flammable liquid over the body of the sleeping Indian and set fire to him. It was later determined that the youths thought the Pataxó was another of the numerous *mendingo* or street beggars that wander the streets in all the major cities of Brazil. Every month at least one mendingo is killed in this fashion just for the "fun" of seeing the beggar run in panic and attempt to extinguish the fire before it completely burns him.

In the case of Gildino dos Santos, 95% of his body was severely burned and he died the next day in the hospital where he had been taken by one of the few witnesses to the crime. Five youths between the ages of 16 and 19 years old were taken prisoner. All are from upper middle class families (one the son of a colonel, two others the sons of judges). The crime is punishable by a sentence of between 13 and 30 years of imprisonment. But will there be punishment? Certainly, the moment is propitious for an exemplary punishment since Brazilians are reeling from the recent shock of scenes of police brutality in Diadema, Saõ Paulo, and Cidade de Deus, Rio de Janeiro.

_____

[19]Wright, R. M. (1997). Violence on Indian Day in Brazil 1997: Symbol of the past and future. *Cultural Survival Quarterly, 21* (2), 47–49.

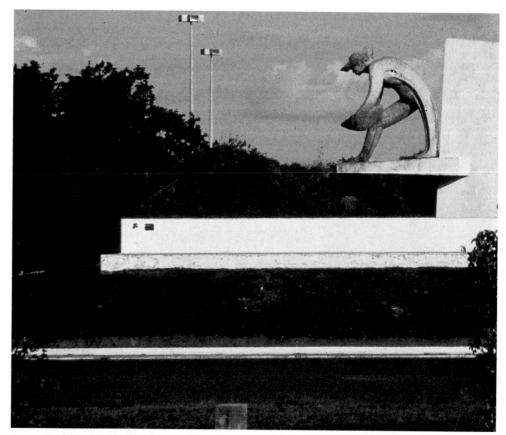

Statue "celebrating" gold miner in the main square of Boa Vista in Brazil. Gold miners and others who have invaded Indian lands have caused massive death and devastation. In 1993, when a group of Indians succeeded in evicting a rancher from their land, a man phoned one radio show, identified himself as a professional "hit man" and offered to kill the local Bishop (who supported the Indians), cut off his head, and display it in the miner's pan.

But, this threatens to be another horrible death statistic involving the Indians in Brazil.

When I was asked to prepare an article for this issue in commemoration of Cultural Survival's 25th anniversary—for me an honor considering Cultural Survival has focused on Brazil from its beginning—I initially intended to write about the political victories and "conquests" by the Indigenous movement in Brazil, as demonstrated in an exemplary fashion by the Federation of Indigenous Organizations of the Rio Negro (FOIRN) in the Northwest Amazon. Victories which mark significant advances for the approximately 20,000 Indians of various linguistic families in the region, with the demarcation of a large and continuous land reserve and the participation of indigenous leadership in key positions of municipal government. I intended to focus on this area because it is where I have conducted anthropological and historical research since 1976 and I have been in contact with the Federation over the past 12 years since I returned to live in Brazil. A remarkable situation has changed from complete subordination and dependence on external agents of contact (the missionaries and military, principally) 20 years ago, to an effervescence of local indigenous political associations (over 20), coordinated by a region-wide indigenous confederation. Cultural traditions long suppressed by the missionaries to the point where indigenous people were "embarrassed" with their identity, have evolved in the form of a brilliant leader, Baniwa Gersen Luciano Santos, whose intellectual contribution to the indigenous movement in Amazonia in general will surely have long-term consequences.

The Northwest Amazon has become a critical testing ground in Brazil for important questions revolving around sustainable development and how these models are to be translated into practice. Are such models viable alternatives in the Northwest Amazon context, or is there still an enormous distance between NGOs [nongovernmental organizations] and academic discourses about such models and the specific and immediate needs of native peoples? What are the effects of NGO involvement in local-level politics on Indian/white relations and the indigenous cultural revitalization movement in general in this area? The immediate problem, which the incident in Brasilia on Indian Day revealed in all its horror, is not the new models, but the old problems and the old wounds which have never had sufficient time to heal. Racism and impunity, the two principal villains, constantly tear away at the heart of victories. For those who have short memories and may have forgotten what these two villains have done in recent years, it may be well worth a quick review of other incidents and their outcomes.

Every year the Indigenous Missionary Council (CIMI, a branch of the Brazilian Catholic Church most directly involved in indigenous affairs) publishes a report on violence against the indigenous population in Brazil. The statistics show that not only is there an increase in violence year by year, but also in the kinds of aggression committed against indigenous peoples: murders of leaders, massacres, epidemic diseases caused by neglect of official health agencies, illegal detentions, and police brutality. One can only be shocked by the repeated acts of violence against Indians throughout the country. Yet how are these cases represented and reported in the national media and how are they dealt with by authorities? Are there patterns in the violence that characterize Indian/white relations?

Violence Against Indigenous People in Brazil

The most common pattern characterizing violence against indigenous people in Brazil is impunity. Violence against the indigenous people in Brazil is horrible and lamentable, but it is ultimately beyond control. In case after case, the same scenario is revealed in which violent acts against Indians are never brought to justice. Conflicts and tensions, particularly over land and resource rights, build up over the years, and coupled with the inertia of FUNAI, explode in traumatic massacres or murders. Investigations are immediately initiated and the accused are apprehended; in this initial phase, international pressure has played an important role. The second phase includes a long period of procrastination which takes the steam out of the initial urgency of the case. Next, the accused stall for time to manipulate the proceedings while the investigations drag on. When, or if the case is finally brought to the courts, there is never sufficient evidence to incriminate the accused who are then absolved or given light sentences. The consequence of this scenario is the reproduction of violence in interethnic relations.

For example, a well-known Guaraní leader, Marçal Tupã-y, was murdered in 1983 by the hired gunmen of a local rancher that disputed the lands of Marçal's people. An entire decade passed before the perpetrator of the crime —known to everyone in the region—was brought to trial in a local court. In the end, the rancher was absolved of the crime for "lack of evidence." Another example is the 1988 massacre of Ticuna Indians of the upper Solimões that left 14 dead, 23 wounded, and ten "disappeared." The massacre was perpetrated by 14 gunmen hired by a local lumber businessman in order to "settle" a land claim. This claim had dragged on for years because both federal authorities and local interests wished to suppress the movement. Despite the immediate national and international attention, today, nearly a decade later, news of the process has virtually disappeared from the press and the process of judicial procrastination has not gotten further than determining the jurisdiction for the trial—if there is to be one.

There is yet another scenario in which, through the manipulation of discourse about violence by the mass media, actual victims are transformed into perpetrators of violence against themselves or "blaming the victim," in which actual physical violence is compounded with symbolic violence against the victims. The case of the Yanomami in Brazil and Venezuela is certainly the most dramatic instance of this process.

In this case, structural amnesia and impunity have not been worse because the eyes of the world have focused on the Yanomami situation for so long. This has not immunized the Yanomami from physical violence (the 1993 massacre of 17 Yanomami of the village of Haxlmu), or from racist attacks such as those which characterized the articles published by Janer Cristaldo, an unknown journalist, in the Folha de São Paulo, two years ago. Cristaldo, in his initial article titled "Behind the Scenes of the Lano-Bluff," not only questioned the evidence of the massacre, but also systematically diverted the focus of the issue by claiming that numerous aggressions by indigenous peoples against the white man had never been brought to justice. Basing his characterization of the Yanomami on the "Fierce People" image popularized by Napoleon Chagnon, Cristaldo argued that Yanomami culture is itself "marked by violence" and that the international outrage over the Haxlmu massacre was nothing more than a conspiracy organized by anthropologists and indigenous defense organizations. He characterized the Yanomami as fodder for a supposed campaign to internationalize Amazonia "[e]ither the Armed Forces beware of this conspiracy by anthropologists," he warned, "or soon we will have the blue helmets [referring to UN intervention] in Amazonia." In this discourse, Brazilians are the victims while the Yanomami and their supporters are the aggressor.

"Sensationalizing" Violence

Numerous other cases could be analyzed to illustrate the kinds of structural violence that characterize Indian/white relations in Brazil today and the ways mass media has represented interethnic violence. In many cases, it is clear that media discourse serves the interests of local, regional and national power structures. It is also clear that the explanation of such violence is not sufficient to account for the incidents of brutality against individuals or whole groups of people. Indigenous peoples have shown that they are able to resist, adapt, and change, often in extraordinarily creative ways, to demands imposed on them from outside. Brazilian society, however, has repeatedly demonstrated that it is incapable of overcoming two of its deepest internal conflicts: racism and impunity. Governments continue to demonstrate their inability to implement viable political and economic models that could enable ethnic and social minorities to co-exist and live in dignity in a plural society.

As always, on Indian Day in Brazil, a kind of macabre ritual takes place. The mass media talk about the "inevitable extinction" of indigenous peoples as if they were a disappearing species. Ecologists and anthropologists reaffirm the vitality of socio-diversity and the necessity of indigenous peoples for the future survival of the planet. Brazilian consciousness, in relation to Indians and minorities in general, needs to change, not the Indians who have shown that they are not merely "survivors" or "remnants" of a once great past, but fully capable of forging viable models for their future.

At noon on Monday, April 21st, Tiradentes Day (Tiradentes is a Brazilian national hero), Brasilia declared three days of mourning for the Pataxó Indian who died. A requiem for the old models of Brazilian society as well?

MODERNIZATION AND THE "UNDERDEVELOPED" WORLD

In the examples we have just examined, we have seen how modernization has affected indigenous peoples in otherwise "modern" states. Elsewhere in the so-called underdeveloped world, whole countries are in the throes of modernization. Throughout Africa, Asia, and South and Central America we are witnessing the widespread removal of economic activities—or at least their control—from the family-community setting; the altered structure of the family in the face of the changing labor market; the increased reliance of young children on parents alone for affection, instead of on the extended family; the decline of general parental authority; schools replacing the family as the primary educational unit; the discovery of a generation gap; and many other changes. The difficulty is it all happens so fast traditional societies cannot adapt themselves to it gradually. Changes that took generations to accomplish in Europe and North America are attempted within the span of a single generation in developing countries. In the process they frequently face the erosion of a number of dearly held values they had no intention of giving up.

Commonly, the burden of modernization falls most heavily on women. For example, the commercialization of agriculture often involves land reforms that overlook or ignore women's traditional land rights. While this reduces their control of and access to resources, mechanization of food production and processing drastically reduces their opportunities for employment. As a consequence, they are confined more and more to traditional domestic tasks, which, as commercial production becomes peoples' dominant concern, are increasingly downgraded in value. To top it all off, the domestic workload tends to increase, because men are less available to help out, while tasks such as fuel gathering and water collection are made more difficult as common land and resources become privately owned and as woodlands are reserved for commercial exploitation. In short, with modernization, women frequently find themselves in an increasingly marginal position. While their workload increases, the value assigned the work they do declines, as does their relative and absolute health, nutritional, and educational status.

MODERNIZATION: MUST IT ALWAYS BE PAINFUL?

Although most anthropologists see the changes affecting traditional non-Western peoples caught up in the modern technological world as an ordeal, the more widespread opinion has been that it is a good process—that however disagreeable the "medicine" may be, it is worth it for the people to become just like "us" (i.e., the people of Europe and North America). This view of modernization, unfortunately, is based more on the hopes and expectations of Western culture than on reality. No doubt Western peoples would like to see the non-Western world attain the high levels of development seen in Europe and North America, as many Japanese, South Koreans, Taiwanese, and some other Asians, in fact, have done. Overlooked is the stark fact the standard of living in the Western world is based on a rate of consumption of nonrenewable resources whereby far less than 50% of the world's population uses a good deal more than 50% of these resources. By the early 1970s, for example, the people of the United States—less than 5% (approximately) of the world's population—were consuming more than 50% of all the world's resources. Figures such as this suggest it is not realistic to expect most peoples of the world to achieve a standard of living comparable to that

An urban slum near Juarez, Mexico. All over the world, people are fleeing to the cities for a "better life," only to experience disease and poverty in such slums.

of the Western world in the near future, if at all. At the very least, the countries of the Western world would have to cut drastically their consumption of resources. So far, they have shown no willingness to do this, and, if they did, their living standards would have to change.

Yet more non-Western people than ever, quite understandably, aspire to a standard of living Western countries now enjoy, even though the gap between the rich and poor people of the world is widening rather than narrowing. This has led to the development of what anthropologist Paul Magnarella has called a new "culture of discontent," a level of aspirations far exceeding the bounds of local opportunities. No longer satisfied with traditional values, people all over the world are fleeing to the cities to find a "better life," all too often to live out their days in poor, congested, and diseased slums in an attempt to achieve what is usually beyond their reach. Unfortunately, despite all sorts of rosy predictions about a better future, this basic reality remains.

CHAPTER SUMMARY

Although cultures may be remarkably stable, culture change is characteristic of all cultures to a greater or lesser degree. Change is often caused by accidents, including the unexpected outcome of existing events. Another cause is people's deliberate attempt to solve a perceived problem. Finally, change may be forced upon one group in the course of especially intense contact between two societies. Adaptation and progress are consequences rather than causes of change, although not all changes are necessarily adaptive. Progress is however a culture defines it.

The mechanisms involved in cultural change are innovation, diffusion, cultural loss, and acculturation. The ultimate source of change is innovation: a new practice, tool, or principle. Other individuals adopt the innovation, and it becomes socially shared. Primary innovations are chance discoveries of new principles—for example, the discovery that the firing of clay makes the material permanently hard. Secondary innovations are improvements made by applying known principles —for example, modeling the clay to be fired by known techniques into familiar objects. Primary innovations may prompt rapid cultural change and stimulate other inventions. An innovation's chance of acceptance depends partly, but not entirely, on its perceived superiority to the method or object it replaces. Its acceptance is also connected with the prestige of the innovator and recipient groups. Diffusion is the borrowing by one society of a cultural element from another. Cultural loss involves the abandonment of some trait or practice with or without replacement. Anthropologists have given considerable attention to acculturation. It stems from intensive firsthand contact of groups with different cultures and produces major changes in the cultural patterns of one or both groups. The actual or threatened use of force is always a factor in acculturation.

Applied anthropology arose as anthropologists sought to provide colonial administrators with a better understanding of native cultures so as to avoid serious disruption of the cultures or as anthropologists tried to help indigenous people cope with outside threats to their interests. A serious ethical issue for applied anthropologists is how far they should go in trying to change the ways of other peoples.

Reactions of indigenous peoples to changes forced upon them vary considerably. Some have retreated to inaccessible places in hopes of being left alone, while some others have lapsed into apathy. Some, such as the Trobriand Islanders, reassert their traditional culture's values by modifying foreign practices to conform to indigenous values, a phenomenon known as syncretism. If a culture's values get widely out of step with reality, revitalization movements may appear. Some revitalization movements try to speed up the acculturation process to get more of the benefits expected from the dominant culture. Others try to reconstitute a gone but not forgotten way of life. In some cases, a pariah group may try to introduce a new social order based on its ideology. Revolutionary movements try to reform the culture from within. Rebellion differs from revolution, in that the aim is merely to replace one set of officeholders with another.

Modernization refers to a global process of cultural and socioeconomic change whereby developing societies seek to acquire characteristics of industrially "advanced" societies. The process consists of four subprocesses: technological development, agricultural development, industrialization, and urbanization. Other changes follow in the areas of political organization, education, religion, and social organization. Two other accompaniments of modernization are structural differentiation and new forces of social integra-tion. An example of a modernizing society is the Skolt Lapps of Finland, whose traditional reindeer herding economy was all but destroyed when snowmobiles were adopted to make herding easier. In Ecuador, the Shuar Indians modernized to escape the destruction visited upon many other Amazonian peoples. So far they have been successful, and others are mobilizing their resources in attempts to achieve similar success. Nevertheless, formidable forces are still arrayed against such cultures, and, on a worldwide basis, it is probably fair to say modernization has led to a deterioration, rather than improvement, of peoples' quality of life.

POINTS FOR CONSIDERATION

1. Is tradition immutable? What is the role of tradition in conjunction with the concept of cultural change discussed in this chapter? Bearing in mind the Finnish and Brazilian examples, how important are tradition and change to a culture's health?

2. How might tradition and group identity encourage cultural change? Is this occurring, and, if so, is it restricted to nonindustrialized societies?

3. What areas within industrialized societies might benefit from anthropological investigation? Why?

4. How complete is the assimilation process that occurs with immigration into pluralistic states such as the United States, Great Britain, the former Soviet Union, and others? What has been the effect upon the dominant cultures?

SUGGESTED READINGS

Barnett, H. G. (1953). *Innovation: The basis of cultural change.* New York: McGraw-Hill.

This is the standard work on the subject, widely quoted by virtually everyone who writes about change.

Bodley, J. H. (1990). *Victims of progress* (3rd ed.). Mountain View, CA: Mayfield.

Few North Americans are aware of the devastation unleashed upon indigenous peoples in the name of "progress," nor are they aware this continues on an unprecedented scale today or of the extent their own society's institutions contribute to it. For most, this book will be a real eye-opener.

Gordon, R. J. (1992). *The Bushman myth: The making of a Namibian underclass.* Boulder, CO: Westview.

This is a remarkably enlightening study of how both Bushman culture and European myths about the Bushman have changed over the past 150 years. Not only does it demolish myths ranging from the "Bushmen as Vermin" stereotype of the colonial era to the childlike innocence of the film *The Gods Must Be Crazy,* but also it shows how these people have been part of the world system since before their first "discovery" by Europeans. To see how they have managed their interactions with outsiders and how outsiders have manipulated images of the Bushmen for their own economic, political, and social interests is enlightening.

Magnarella, P. J. (1974). *Tradition and change in a Turkish town.* New York: Wiley.

This book, one of the best anthropological community studies of the Middle East, is also an excellent introduction to the phenomenon known as modernization. It has none of the facile generalizations about modernization one so often finds, and the author's view of the phenomenon, which is well documented, is quite different from what was promoted in the optimistic days of the 1950s.

Stannard, D. E. (1992). *American holocaust*. Oxford: Oxford University Press.

Stannard deals with 500 years of cultural change in the Americas related to the contact of European and native cultures. In doing so, he focuses on genocide, relates it to "the holocaust" of World War II, and demonstrates how deeply rooted the phenomenon is in Western culture and Christianity.

Chapter 27
ANTHROPOLOGY AND THE FUTURE

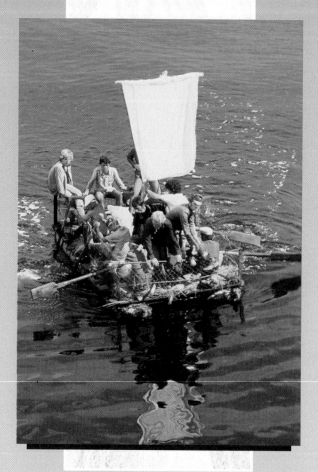

IF HUMANITY IS TO HAVE A FUTURE, IT WILL HAVE TO SOLVE THE POLITICAL AND ECONOMIC PROBLEMS THAT ARE RESPONSIBLE FOR A WORLDWIDE FLOOD OF REFUGEES. WHAT DRIVES THIS IS THE INCREASING ECONOMIC DISPARITY BETWEEN THE INDUSTRIALIZED COUNTRIES OF EUROPE AND NORTH AMERICA ON THE ONE HAND AND MOST OF THE OTHER COUNTRIES OF THE WORLD, AND THE POLITICAL TURMOIL CAUSED BY STATES CONTROLLED BY PEOPLE OF ONE NATIONALITY WHO TRY TO REPRESS ATTEMPTS BY PEOPLE OF OTHER NATIONALITIES TO RETAIN AND ASSERT THEIR OWN IDENTITIES AND TRADITIONS.

Chapter Preview

What Can Anthropologists Tell Us of the Future?

Anthropologists cannot any more accurately predict future cultural forms than biologists can predict future life forms or geologists future landforms. They can, though, identify certain trends we might otherwise be unaware of and can anticipate some of the consequences these might have if they continue. They also can shed light on problems nonanthropologists already have identified by showing how these relate to each other as well as to cultural practices and attitudes experts in other fields are often unaware of. This ability to place problems in their wider context is an anthropological specialty, and it is essential if these problems are ever to be solved.

What Are Some Present-Day Trends in Cultural Evolution?

One major trend in present-day cultural evolution is toward worldwide adoption of the products, technology, and practices of the industrialized world. This apparent gravitation toward a homogenized one-world culture is, however, opposed by another very strong trend of ethnic groups all over the world toward reasserting their distinctive identities. A third trend we are just becoming aware of is that the problems cultural practices create seem to be outstripping the capacity of cultures to find solutions to such problems.

What Problems Will Have to Be Solved if Humanity Is to Have a Future?

If humanity is to have a future, human cultures will have to find solutions to problems posed by slowed population growth in some areas and rapid growth in others, food and other resource shortages, pollution, and a growing culture of discontent. One difficulty is that, up to now, people tend to see these problems as if they were discrete and unrelated. Thus, attempts to deal with one problem, such as food shortages, are often at cross-purposes with other problems, such as an inequitable global system for the distribution of basic resources. Unless humanity has a more realistic understanding of the "global society" than presently exists, it cannot solve the problems whose solutions are crucial for its future.

Anthropology is often described by those who know little about it as a backward-looking discipline. The most common stereotype is that anthropologists devote all of their attention to the interpretation of the past and the description of present-day "tribal" remnants. Yet as we saw in Chapter 1, as well as in the Anthropology Applied boxes for Chapters 4 and 17, not even archaeologists, the anthropologists most prone to looking backward, limit their interests to the past, nor are ethnologists uninterested in their own cultures. Thus, throughout this book we constantly have made comparisons between "us" and "others." Moreover, anthropologists have a special concern with the future and the changes it may bring. Like many members of Western industrialized societies, they wonder what the "postindustrial" society now being predicted will hold. They also wonder what changes the coming years will bring to non-Western cultures. As we saw in the preceding chapter, when non-Western peoples are thrown into contact with Western industrialized peoples, their culture rapidly changes, often for the worse, becoming both less supportive and less adaptive. Since Western people show no inclination to leave non-Western people alone, we may ask, How can these threatened cultures adapt to the future?

THE CULTURAL FUTURE OF HUMANITY

Whatever the biological future of the human species, culture remains the mechanism by which people solve their problems of existence. Yet some anthropologists have noted with concern—and interpret as a trend—that the problems of human existence seem to be outstripping any culture's ability to find solutions. The main problem seems to be that while solving existing problems, cultures inevitably pose new ones. To paraphrase anthropologist Jules Henry, although cultures are "for" people, they are also "against" them.[1] As we shall

see, this dilemma is now posing serious new problems for human beings. What can anthropologists tell us about future cultures?

Anthropologists—like geologists and evolutionary biologists—are historical scientists; as such, they can identify and understand the processes that have shaped the past and will shape the future. They cannot, however, tell us precisely what these processes will produce in terms of future cultures, any more than biologists can predict future life forms or geologists future landforms. The cultural future of humanity, though, certainly will be affected in important ways by decisions we humans will be making in the immediate future. This being so, if those decisions are to be made intelligently, it behooves us to have a clear understanding of the world today. Here anthropologists have something vital to offer.

To comprehend anthropology's role in understanding and solving the future's problems, we must look at certain flaws frequently seen in the enormous body of future-oriented literature that has appeared over the past few decades, not to mention the efforts to plan for the future that have become commonplace at regional, national, and international levels. For one, rarely do futurist writers or planners look more than about 50 years ahead, and the trends they project, more often than not, are those of recent history. This predisposes people to think a trend that seems fine today will always be so and that it may be projected indefinitely into the future. The danger inherent in this is neatly captured in anthropologist George Cowgill's comment: "It is worth recalling the story of the person who leaped from a very tall building and on being asked how things were going as he passed the 20th floor replied 'Fine, so far.'"[2]

Another flaw is a tendency to treat subjects in isolation, without reference to pertinent trends outside an expert's field of competence. For example, agricultural planning is often predicated upon the assumption a certain amount of water is available for irrigation, whether or not urban planners or others have designs for that same water. Thus—as in the southwestern United States, where

---

[1]Henry, J. (1965). *Culture against man* (p. 12). New York: Vintage Books.

[2]Cowgill, G. L. (1980). Letter, *Science, 210*, 1305.

more of the Colorado River's water has been allocated than actually exists—people may be counting on resources in the future that will not, in fact, be available. One would suppose this would be a cause for concern, but as two well-known futurists put it, "If you find inconsistencies the model is better off without them."[3] These same two authorities, when editing a volume aimed at refuting the somewhat pessimistic projections of *Global 2000* (the first U.S. government attempt at a coordinated analysis of global resources), deliberately avoided discussing population growth and its implications, because they knew that to do so would lead their contributing authors to disagree with one another.[4] This brings us to yet another common flaw: A tendency to project the hopes and expectations of one's own culture into the future interferes with the scientific objectivity necessary to address the problem.

Against this background, anthropology's contribution to our view of the future is clear. With their holistic perspective, anthropologists are specialists at seeing how parts fit together into a larger whole. With their evolutionary perspective, they can see short-term trends in longer term perspective. With more than 100 years of cross-cultural research behind them, anthropologists can recognize culture-bound assertions when they encounter them; and, finally, they are familiar with alternative ways to deal with a wide variety of problems.

ONE-WORLD CULTURE

A popular belief since the end of World War II has been that the future world will see the development of a single homogeneous world culture. The idea such a "one-world culture" is emerging is based largely on the observation that developments in communication, transportation, and trade so closely link the peoples of the world that they are increasingly wearing the same kinds of clothes, eating the same kinds of food, reading the same kinds of newspapers, watching the same

kinds of television programs, communicating directly with one another via the Internet, and so on. The continuation of such trends, so this thinking goes, should lead North Americans who are traveling in the year 2100 to Tierra del Fuego, China, or New Guinea to find the inhabitants living in a manner identical or similar to theirs. But is this so?

Certainly striking is the extent such items as Western-style clothing, transistor radios, Coca-Cola, and McDonald's hamburgers have spread to virtually all parts of the world, and many countries—Japan, for example—have moved a long way toward becoming "Westernized." Moreover, looking back over the past 5,000 years of human history, one will see a clear-cut trend for political units to become larger and more all-encompassing while becoming fewer in number. A logical outcome of this trend's continuation into the future would be the reduction of all autonomous political units to one encompassing the entire world. In fact, by extrapolating this past trend into the future, some anthropologists even have predicted the world will become politically integrated, perhaps by the 23rd century but no later than 4850.[5]

One problem with such a prediction is that it ignores the one thing all large states, past and present, irrespective of other differences between them, share in common: a tendency to come apart. Not only have the great empires of the past, without exception, broken up into numbers of smaller independent states, but also countries in virtually all parts of the world today are showing a tendency to fragment. The most dramatic illustrations of this in recent years have been the breakup of the Soviet Union into several smaller independent states and the attempt of several Yugoslavian republics to regain their independence. It also can be seen in separatist movements such as that of French-speaking peoples in Canada; Basque and Catalonian nationalism in Europe; Scottish, Irish, and Welsh nationalism in Britain; Tibetan nationalism in China; Kurdish nationalism in Turkey,

---

[3]Holden, C. (1983). Simon and Kahn versus *Global 2000. Science, 221,* 342.

[4]Ibid., 343.

[5]Ember, C. R., & Ember, M. (1985). *Cultural anthropology* (4th ed., p. 230). Englewood Cliffs, NJ: Prentice-Hall.

The worldwide spread of such products as Pepsi is taken by some as a sign that a homogeneous world culture is developing.

Iran, and Iraq; Sikh separatism in India; Tamil separatism in Sri Lanka; Igbo separatism in Nigeria; Eritrean and Tigrean secession movements in Ethiopia; Namibian nationalism; and so on—this list is far from exhaustive. Nor is the United States immune, as can be seen from Puerto Rican nationalist movements and Native American attempts to secure greater political self-determination and autonomy.

These examples all involve peoples who consider themselves members of distinct nations by virtue of their birth and cultural and territorial heritage, over whom peoples of some other ethnic background have tried to assert control. An estimated 5,000 such national groups exist in the world today, as opposed to a mere 181 recognized states (up from fewer than 50 in the 1940s).[6] Although some of these national groups are quite

small in population and area—100 or so people living on a few acres—some are quite large. The Karen people of Burma (Figure 27.1), for example, number some 4.5 to 5 million, making them larger than 48% of the United Nations member states.

Reactions of these peoples to attempts at annexation and absorption by imposed state regimes other peoples control range all the way from Bangladesh's successful fight for independence from Pakistan (or the Igbos' unsuccessful fight for independence from Nigeria) to the nonviolence of Scottish and Welsh nationalism. Many struggles for independence have been going on for years, such as the Karen resistance to the Burmese invasion of their territory in 1948; the takeover of Kurdistan by Iraq, Iran, and Turkey in 1925; and the even earlier Russian takeover of Chechnya. Even in relatively nonviolent cases, the stresses and strains are obviously there. Similar stresses and strains even may develop in the absence of ethnic differences when regional interests within a large

---

[6]*Cultural Survival Quarterly, 15* (4), 38. (1991).

FIGURE 27.1
Ethnic nationalities of Burma.

stack emissions that cause acid rain, which is destroying resources and endangering the health of people in other states (not to mention other countries, Canada in particular).

Expansionist attempts by existing states to annex all or parts of other states also seem to be running into difficulty, as in the Iraqi attempt to take over Kuwait. It is just possible we are reaching a point where the old tendency for political units to increase in size while decreasing in number is being canceled out by the tendency for such units to fragment into a greater number of smaller ones.

THE RISE OF THE MULTINATIONAL CORPORATIONS

The world's resistance to political integration seems to be offset, at least partially, by the rise of multinational corporations. Because these cut across the boundaries between states, they are a force for global unity despite the political differences that divide people. Situations such as this are well known to anthropologists, as illustrated by this description of Zuni Indian integrative mechanisms:

> Four or five different planes of systemization crosscut each other and thus preserve for the whole society an integrity that would speedily be lost if the planes merged and thereby inclined to encourage

The 1997 confrontation between Republic of Texas separatists and law enforcement officials is symptomatic of the stresses and strains that exist in United States society.

country increasingly compete. Again, hints of this may be seen in the United States: for example, in arguments over access to Colorado River water, in attempts by oil- and gas-producing states to get the most out of their resources at the expense of other states ("Let the Bastards Freeze in the Dark" proclaimed bumper stickers in oil- and gas-producing states during the Arab oil embargo of the 1970s), and in the refusal by some states to curb smoke-segregation and fission. The clans, the fraternities, the priesthoods, the kivas, in a measure the gaming parties, are all dividing agencies. If they coincided, the rifts in the social structure would be deep; by countering each other they cause segmentations which produce an almost marvelous complexity, but can never break apart the national entity.[7]

Multinational corporations are not new in the world (the Dutch East India Company is a good example from the 17th century), but they were not common until the 1950s. Since then they have become a major force in the world. These modern-day giants are actually clusters of corporations of diverse nationality joined together by ties of common ownership and responsive to a common management strategy. Usually tightly controlled by a head office in one country, these multinationals organize and integrate production across the boundaries of different countries for interests formulated in corporate boardrooms, irrespective of whether or not these are consistent with the interests of people in the countries where they operate. In a sense they are products of the technological revolution, for without sophisticated data-processing equipment, the multinationals could not keep adequate track of their worldwide operations.

Though typically thought of as responding impersonally to outside market forces, large corporations are in fact controlled by powerful economic elites who benefit directly from their operations. For example, in 1994, just 10 individuals helped direct 37 North American companies whose combined assets of $2 *trillion* rival those of many governments, and this represented nearly 10% of all corporate assets in the United States "for profit" businesses. Yet, the world's largest individual stockholders and most powerful directors, unlike political leaders, are known to few people. For that matter, most people cannot even name the five largest multinational corporations.[8]

So great is the power of multinationals that they increasingly thwart the wishes of governments. Because the information these corporations process is kept from flowing in a meaningful way to the population at large, or even to lower levels within the organization, it is difficult for governments to get the information they need for informed policy decisions. Consider how it took decades for the United States Congress to extract the information it needed from tobacco companies to decide what to do about tobacco legislation. Nor is this an isolated case. Beyond this, though, the multinationals have shown they can overrule foreign-policy decisions, as when they got around a U.S. embargo on pipeline equipment for the Soviet Union in the 1980s. Although some might see this as a hopeful augury for the transcendence of national vices and rivalries, it raises the unsettling issue as to whether or not the global order should be determined by corporations interested only in financial profits.

If the ability of multinational corporations to ignore the wishes of sovereign governments is cause for concern, so is their ability to act in concert with such governments. Here, in fact, is where their worst excesses have occurred. In Brazil, for example, where the situation is hardly unique but is especially well documented, a partnership emerged, after the military coup of 1964, between a government anxious to proceed as rapidly as possible with development of the Amazon basin; a number of multinational corporations, such as ALCOA, Borden, Union Carbide, Swift-Armour, and Volkswagen, to mention only a very few; and several international lending institutions, such as the Export-Import Bank, the Inter-American Development Bank, and the World Bank.[9] To realize their goals, these allies introduced inappropriate technology and ecologically unsound practices into the region, converting vast tropical areas into semidesert.

Far more shocking, however, has been the practice of uprooting whole human societies because they are seen as obstacles to economic growth. Literally overnight, people are deprived of

---

[7]Kroeber, A. L. (1970). Quoted in Dozier, E., *The Pueblo Indians of North America* (p. 19). New York: Holt, Rinehart and Winston.

[8]Bodley, J. H. (1997). Comment. *Current Anthropology, 38*, 725.

[9]Davis, S. H. (1982). *Victims of the miracle.* Cambridge: Cambridge University Press.

Brazil's Grand Carajas iron ore mine is an example of the kind of project states favor in their drive to develop. Not only does this introduce ecologically unsound technologies, but it also commonly has devastating effects on the indigenous people whose land is seized.

the means to provide for their own needs and forcibly removed to places where they do not choose to live. Little distinction is made here between Indians and Brazilian smallholders who were brought into the region in the first place by a government anxious to alleviate acute land shortages in the northeast. Bad as this is for these Brazilian smallholders, the amount of disease, death, and human suffering unleashed upon the Indians can only be described as massive. In the process, whole peoples have been (and are still being) destroyed with a thoroughness not achieved even by Stalin during his "Great Terror" in the Soviet Union of the 1930s or the Nazis in World War II. Were it not so well documented, it would be beyond belief. This is "culture against people" with a vengeance.

The power of multinational corporations creates problems on the domestic as well as the international scene. Anthropologist Jules Henry, in his classic study of life in the United States, observed that working for any large corporation—multinational or not—tends to generate "hostility, instability, and fear of being obsolete and unprotected. For most people their job was what they had to do rather than what they wanted to do. . . . Taking a job, therefore, meant giving up part of their selves."[10]

The power of corporations extends far beyond governments and workers. Their control of television and other media, not to mention the advertising industry, gives them enormous power over the lives of millions of "ordinary" people in ways they little suspect. The following is a case in point.

---

[10]Henry, J. (1965). *Culture against man* (p. 127.). New York: Vintage Books.

Standard-izing the Body: The Question of Choice[11]

The question of choice is central to the story of how medicine and business generate controlling processes in the shaping of women's bodies. Michel Foucault [in *Madness and Civilization*] demonstrates how changes in the concept of madness led to changes in diagnosis and treatment of the insane and of social attitudes toward them. He describes how changing perceptions of madness in parts of Western Europe from the Middle Ages to the end of the 19th century led to the separation of "mad" persons from the rest of society, their classification as deviants, and finally their subjection to social control. He focuses on the cultural controls that led to the social controls; ideas about madness led to asylums for the mad. A similar incremental process is central to discussions of the commodification of a woman's body.

Images of the body appear natural within their specific cultural milieus. For example, feminist researchers have analyzed the practice of breast implantation in the United States from the vantage point of the cultural milieu, and in the Sudan, female circumcision and infibulation [the most extreme form of female genital mutilation] serve to accentuate a feminine appearance. Thus, Sudanese and other African women, North American women, and others experience body mutilation as part of engendering rites. However, many writers differentiate infibulation from breast implantation by arguing that North American women *choose* to have breast implants whereas in Africa women are presumably subject to indoctrination (and besides, young girls are too young to choose). One of the most heated debates arising from the public health concern over breast implants is whether the recipients are freely situated—that is, whether their decision is voluntary or whether control is disguised as free will.

An informed response to the free-choice argument requires knowing how the beauty-industrial complex works. It requires sensitive fieldwork in multiple sites and an understanding of emergent idea systems in incremental change. Linda Coco builds upon the insights revealed by Howard Zinn's *The Twentieth Century: A People's History*. Zinn cites a 1930s magazine article which begins with the statement, "The average American woman has sixteen square feet of skin." This is followed by an itemized list of the annual beauty needs of every woman. Sixty years later the beauty-industrial complex is a multibillion-dollar industry that segments the female body and manufactures commodities of and for the body.

As Coco shows, some women get caught in the official beauty ideology, and in the case of silicone-gel breast implants some hundreds of thousands of women have been ensnared. But who gets caught and when is important to an understanding of the ecology of power. The average age of a woman having breast implantation is 36 years, and she has an average of two children. She is the beauty industry's insecure consumer recast as a patient. She is somehow deviant; her social illness is deformity or hypertrophy (small breasts). Coco quotes a past president of the American Society of

---

[11]Adapted from Nader, L. (1997). Controlling processes: Tracing the dynamics of power. *Current Anthropology, 38,* 715–717.

Plastic and Reconstructive Surgery (ASPRS): "There is substantial and enlarging medical knowledge to the effect that these deformities [small breasts] are really a disease which result in the patient's feelings of inadequacies, lack of self-confidence, distortion of body image, and a total lack of well-being due to a lack of self-perceived femininity. . . . Enlargement . . . is therefore . . . necessary to ensure the quality of life for the [female] patient." In other words, cosmetic surgery is necessary to the patient's psychological health.

The plastic surgeon regards the construction of the official breast as art, the aim being to reform the female body according to the ideals of classic Western art. One surgeon pioneering procedures for correcting deformity took as his ideal female figure that of ancient Greek statues, which he carefully measured, noticing the exact size and shape of the breasts, their vertical location between the third and seventh ribs, the horizontal between the line of the sternal ["breastbone"] border and the anterior axillary line, and so forth. In Coco's analysis the exercise of the plastic surgeon's techno-art re-creates a particular static, official breast shape and applies this creation ostensibly to relieve women's mental suffering. The surgeon becomes a psychological healer as well as an artist.

Along with art and psychology, there is, of course, the business of organized plastic surgery, which responds to the demands and opportunities of market economics. By the late 1970s and early 1980s there was a glut of plastic surgeons. The ASPRS began to operate like a commercial enterprise instead of a medical society, saturating the media with ads and even providing low-cost financing. The discourse became a sales pitch. Women "seek" breast implants to keep their husbands or their jobs, to attract men, or to become socially acceptable. Coco calls this "patriarchal capitalism" and questions whether this is free choice or "mind colonization."

Understanding "choice" led Coco to an examination of the power both in the doctor-patient relationship and in the control of information. By various means certain women—the insecure consumers—are led to trust and believe in modern medical technology. What is most important in being "caught" is their internalization of the social message [cultural control]. Coco's conclusion that North American women are subtly indoctrinated to recognize and desire a certain kind of beauty presents an interesting possibility. Women "were told by the media, plastic surgeons, women's magazines, other women, and the business world that they could enhance their lives by enhancing their bust lines. . . . The social imperative for appearance was personalized, psychologized, and normalized." Social surveys indicate that, to the extent that women internalize the social imperative, they feel they are making the decision on their own.

Not surprisingly, women whose surgery resulted in medical complications often came to recognize the external processes of coercive persuasion that had led them to seek implants. In some ways, they resembled former cult members who had been deprogrammed: their disillusionment caused them to question the system that had encouraged them to make the decision in the first place. The result was a gradual building of protest against the industry, expressed in networks, newsletters, support groups, workshops, and seminars. As have some former cult members, women have brought suit, testified before lawmakers, and challenged in other ways some of the largest

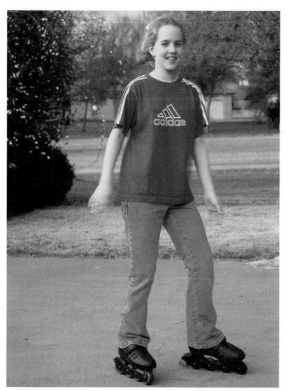

The power of corporations over individuals is illustrated by their ability to get consumers to pay, by purchasing goods such as this T-shirt, to advertise corporate products.

so than many even think it to be."[13] In the face of such seemingly mindless systems for making decisions in the corporate interest, employees become ever more fearful that if they ask too much of the corporation, it simply may shift its operations to another part of the globe where it can find cheaper, more submissive personnel, as has happened with some frequency to labor forces. Indeed, whole communities become fearful that if they do not acquiesce to corporate interests, local operations may be closed down.

In their never-ending search for cheap labor, multinational corporations more than ever have come to favor women for low-skilled assembly jobs. In so-called "underdeveloped" countries, as subsistence farming gives way to mechanical agriculture for production of crops for export, women are less able to contribute to their families' survival. Together with devaluation of the worth of domestic work, this places pressure on women to seek jobs outside the household to contribute to its support. Since most women in these countries do not have the time or resources to get an education or

---

[13]Wolfe, A. W. (1977). The supranational organization of production: An evolutionary perspective. *Current Anthropology, 18,* 619.

In so-called "underdeveloped" countries, women have become a source of cheap labor for large corporations, as subsistence farming has given way to mechanized agriculture. Unable to contribute to their families' well-being in any other way, they have no choice but to take on menial jobs for low wages.

to develop special job skills, only low-paying jobs are open to them. Corporate officials, for their part, assume female workers are strictly temporary, and high turnover means wages can be kept low. Unmarried women are especially favored for employment, for it is assumed they are free from family responsibilities until they marry, whereupon they will leave the labor force. Thus, the increasing importance of the multinationals in developing countries is contributing to the emergence of a prominent gender-segregated division of labor. On top of their housework, women hold low-paying jobs that require little skill; altogether, they may work as many as 15 hours a day. Higher paying jobs, or at least those that require special skills, are generally held by men, whose workday may be shorter since they do not have additional domestic tasks to perform. Men who lack special skills—and many do—are often doomed to lives of unemployment.

In sum, multinational corporations have become a major force in the world today, drawing people more firmly than ever into a truly global system of relationships. Although this brings with it potential benefits, it is also clear it poses serious new problems that now must be addressed.

ONE-WORLD CULTURE: A GOOD IDEA OR NOT?

In the abstract, the idea of a single culture for all the world's people has had a degree of popular appeal, in that it might offer fewer chances for the kinds of misunderstandings to develop that, so often in the past few hundred years, have led to wars. Many anthropologists question this, though, in the face of evidence that traditional ways of thinking about oneself and the rest of the world may persist, even with massive changes in other aspects of culture. Indeed, one might argue that the chances for misunderstandings actually increase; an example of this is the Original Study in Chapter 16.

Some have argued that perhaps a generalized world culture would be desirable in the future, because certain cultures of today may be too specialized to survive in a changed environment. Examples of this situation are sometimes said to abound in modern anthropology. When a traditional culture that is highly adapted to a specific environment—such as that of the Indians of

Brazil, who are well adapted to life in a tropical rain forest—meets a European-derived culture and the social environment changes suddenly and drastically, the traditional culture often collapses. The reason for this, it is argued, is that its traditions and political and social organizations are not at all adapted to "modern" ways. Here we have, once again, the ethnocentric notion (discussed in Chapter 26) that "old" cultures are destined to give way to the new. Since this is regarded as inevitable, actions are taken that by their very nature virtually guarantee the traditional cultures will not survive; it is a classic case of the self-fulfilling prophecy.

A problem with this argument is that, far from being unable to adapt, traditional societies in places such as Brazil's Amazon forest usually have not been given a chance to work out their own adaptations. It is *not* any laws of nature that cause the collapse of traditional cultures but, rather, the political choices of the powerful, their willingness to overpower traditional peoples, and their unwillingness to live and let live. That Amazonian Indians can adapt to the modern world if left alone to do so, without losing their distinctive ethnic and cultural identity, is demonstrated by the Shuar case, noted in the preceding chapter. In Brazil, however, the pressures to develop the Amazon are so great that whole groups of people are swept aside so that multinational corporations and agribusiness can pursue their particular interests. People do not have much chance to work out their own adaptations to the modern world if they are transported en masse from their homelands and deprived literally overnight of their means of survival to devote more acreage to the raising of beef cattle. Few Brazilians get to eat any of this meat, for the bulk of it is shipped to Europe; nor do many of the profits stay in Brazil, since the major ranches are owned and operated by corporations based elsewhere. The process continues apace, nonetheless.

An important issue is at stake in such situations, for what has happened is that some of the world's people with the power to do so have defined others—indeed, whole societies—as obsolete. This is surely a dangerous precedent, which, if allowed to stand, means any of the world's people may at some time in the future be declared obsolete by others who think they have, and might really have, the power to back it up.

ETHNIC RESURGENCE

Despite the worldwide adoption of such items as Coca-Cola and the "Big Mac" and despite pressure for traditional cultures to disappear, it is clear cultural differences are still very much with us in the world today. In fact, a tendency for peoples around the world to resist modernization, and in many cases retreat from it, is strengthening. Manifestations of this we have already alluded to are the worldwide separatist movements, the success so far of the Shuar in retaining their own ethnic and cultural identity, and the increasing political activism of Brazilian Indians—indeed, of native peoples throughout the world.

During the 1970s the world's indigenous peoples began to organize self-determination move-ments, culminating in the formation of the World Council of Indigenous Peoples in 1975. This now has official status as a nongovernmental organization of the United Nations, which allows it to present the cases of indigenous people before the world community. Leaders of this movement see their own societies as community based, egalitarian, and close to nature and are intent upon maintaining them that way. Further credibility to their cause came from the dedication of 1993 as the Year of Indigenous Peoples.

North Americans often have difficulty adjusting to the fact not everyone wants to be just like they are. As children, people in the United States are taught to believe "the American way of life" is one all other peoples aspire to (and how arrogant to appropriate the label "Americans" strictly to themselves!), but it isn't only people such as the Shuar who resist becoming "just like us." In the world today whole countries, having striven to emulate Western ways, have become disenchanted with these ways and suddenly backed off. The most striking recent case of such a retreat from modernity is Iran. With the overthrow of the shah, a policy of deliberate modernization was abandoned in favor of a radical attempt to return to an Islamic republic out of a past "golden age" (mythical though the latter is). A somewhat similar, though less radical, retreat from modernity seems to be under way in the United States, which, in the 1980s and again in 1994, elected governments dedicated to a return to certain "traditional values" from its past. To note just one other parallel between the two situations, in the United States the analogue to a fundamentalist religious leader controlling the Iranian government is the strong sympathy Republican Party members show toward fundamentalist religious views.[14]

Increasingly, indigenous peoples around the world are organizing to defend their own interests. Here, Kaiapo Indians in Brazil protest against planned hydroelectric dams.

---

[14]Marsella, J. (1982). Pulling it together: Discussion and comments. In S. Pastner & W. A. Haviland (Eds.), *Confronting the Creationists* (pp. 79–80). *Northeastern Anthropological Association, Occasional Proceedings*, No. 1.

Cultural pluralism. Social and political interaction of people with different ways of living and thinking within the same society.

Sometimes, resistance to modernization takes the form of a fundamentalist reaction, as it did in Iran and as is happening today in Algeria. This photo is of an FIS (Islamic Salvation Front) rally in Algiers.

CULTURAL PLURALISM

Since a homogeneous world culture is not necessarily the wave of the future, what is? Some see **cultural pluralism,** in which more than one culture exists in a given society, as the future condition of humanity. Cultural pluralism is the social and political interaction of people with different ways of living and thinking within the same society or multinational state. Ideally, it implies a rejection of bigotry, bias, and racism in favor of respect for the cultural traditions of other peoples. In reality, it has rarely worked out that way.

Elements of pluralism are found in the United States, despite its melting-pot ideology. For example, in New York City neighborhoods of Puerto Ricans, with their distinctive cultural traditions and values, exist side by side with other New Yorkers. Besides living in their own *barrio*, the Puerto Ricans have their own language, music, religion, and food. This particular pluralism, however, may be temporary, a stage in the process of integration into what is sometimes referred to as "standard American culture." Thus, the Puerto Ricans, in four or five generations, like many Italians, Irish, and eastern European Jews before them, also may become (North) Americanized to the point where

their lifestyle will be indistinguishable from others around them. Nevertheless, some Puerto Ricans, African and Asian Americans, American Indians, Hispanics, and others strongly have resisted abandoning their distinctive cultural identities. Whether this marks the beginning of a trend away from the melting-pot philosophy and toward real pluralism, however, remains to be seen.

Some familiar examples of cultural pluralism may be seen in Switzerland, where Italian, German, and French cultures exist side by side; in Belgium, where the French Walloons and the Flemish have somewhat different cultural heritages; and in Canada, where French- and English-speaking Canadians live in a pluralistic society (but where most native people are not accorded equal recognition). In none of these cases, though, are the cultural differences (save those of native people in Canada) of the magnitude seen in many a non-Western pluralistic society. As an example of one such society—and its attendant problems—we will look at the Central American country of Guatemala.

Guatemalan Cultural Pluralism

Guatemala, like many other pluralistic countries, came into being through conquest. In Guatemala's case the conquest was about as violent and brutal as it could be, given the technology of the time (the 1500s), as a rough gang of Spanish adventurers led by a man known even then for his cruelty and inhuman treatment of foes defeated a people whose civilization was far older than Spain's. The conquerors' aim was quite simply to extract as much wealth as they could, primarily for themselves but also for Spain, by seizing the riches of those they conquered and by putting the native population to work extracting the gold and silver they hoped to find. Although the treasures to be had did not live up to the conquerors' expectations (no rich deposits of ore were found), their main interest in their new possession continued to be whatever they could extract from it that could be turned into wealth for themselves. For the nearly 500 years since, their *Ladino* descendants have continued to be motivated by the same interests, even after independence from Spain.

Following its conquest, Guatemala never experienced substantial immigration from Spain or from anywhere else in Europe. The conquerors and their descendants, for their part, wished to restrict the spoils of victory as much as possible to themselves, even though those spoils did not live up to advance expectations. In fact, the country had little to attract outsiders. Thus, Indians have always outnumbered non-Indians in Guatemala and continue to do so today. Nonetheless, Indians never had been allowed to hold any important political power; the apparatus of state, with its instruments of force (the police and army) remained firmly in the hands of the *Ladino* (non-Indian) minority. This enabled them to continue exacting tribute and forced labor from Indian communities.

In the 19th century Guatemala's *Ladino* population saw the export of coffee and cotton as a new source of wealth for themselves. For this, they took over huge amounts of Indian lands to create their plantations while depriving Indians of sufficient land for their own needs. Consequently, the latter had no option but to work for the plantation owners on their enlarged holdings at wages cheap beyond belief. Any reluctance on the part of these native laborers was dealt with by brute force.

In the 1940s democratic reforms occurred in Guatemala. Although Indians played no role in originating them, they benefited from them; for the first time in more than 400 years native peo-

ples could at least hold municipal offices in their own communities. In the 1950s the Roman Catholic Church began to promote agricultural, consumer, and credit cooperatives in rural areas (which, in Guatemala, are predominantly Indian).

With the U.S.-engineered military coup of 1954, this brief interlude, when the government recognized Indians had social, economic, and cultural rights, came to an end. As before, the Indians stayed out of politics except within their own villages. And, for the most part, they remained aloof from the guerrilla activities that soon arose in reaction to a succession of military regimes. But because the guerrillas operated in the countryside and because of 400 years of *Ladino* distrust of Indians, these regimes came to regard all rural people, most of them Indian, with ever deeper suspicion. Inevitably, the latter were drawn into the conflict.

In 1966, the United States Advisory Mission introduced the use of terrorist tactics to maintain governmental control of the countryside.[15] By 1978, this escalated into a "reign of terror" known as *La Violencia:* Whole villages were razed, inhabitants killed, and bodies burnt and otherwise mutilated by either the army or by unofficial death squads the army turned a blind eye toward. Whether people were or were not guerrillas or guerrilla sympathizers was largely irrelevant as repression came to be seen as the most effective way to maintain order. At the height (between 1981 and 1983) of *La Violencia* an estimated 15,000 people were "disappeared," at least 90,000 were killed, half a million became refugees inside Guatemala, and 150,000 fled to Mexico, while another 200,000 found their way to other countries, including the United States. In the hardest hit areas, the population was reduced by almost half, and whole towns—some of which had existed for 1,000 years—were destroyed. The overwhelming majority of victims of this violence, which reached genocidal proportions, were Indians.

In the late 1980s, violence in the Guatemalan countryside lapsed from acute to merely chronic, although it began to escalate anew in the early

---

[15]Zur, J. (1994). The psychological impact of impunity. *Anthropology Today, 10* (3), 16.

In Guatemala, the military and other groups sanctioned by the government used violence to maintain the control of one nationality (*Ladino*) over another (Maya). As the illustration from a 1552 Spanish source shows, this has an eerie similarity to the way the Spanish treated the native Maya of Guatemala 450 years ago. Although the violence has now subsided, it has not ended completely.

1990s. Nevertheless, despite this and the fear Maya Indians still felt, political activism among them was on the rise. And forensic anthropologists, at considerable risk to themselves, were working with local communities to exhume victims' bodies to help bring the perpetrators to account (see the Anthropology Applied in Chapter 1). In 1992, the awarding of the Nobel Peace Prize to Rigoberta Menchú, the Maya woman who worked tirelessly for indigenous rights, focused international attention on Guatemala, and ultimately peace accords were signed in late December 1996. A parallel document,

Maya refugees in Mexico prepare to return home to Guatemala after 15 years of fleeing state-directed violence in their homelands.

"Accord on Identity and the Rights of Indigenous Peoples," would establish Guatemala officially as a multicultural, multilingual country where the cultural rights of all indigenous groups would be constitutionally protected.

How effectively these changes can be implemented remains to be seen. On the hopeful side, many refugees have begun to return, and Pan-Mayanists have begun various educational projects, as well as pressing for legal recognition of their customary norms, as called for in the accords. But not all Ladinos are happy with this outcome. Murders and intimidation have not stopped altogether. Meanwhile, in the neighboring Mexican state of Chiapas, an outbreak of violence by large landowners, condoned by local government officials, against native Maya supporters of the Zapatistas and their campaign for indigenous rights has been occurring. These events are reminiscent of the previous violence in Guatemala.

Also, in Guatemala, the *Ladino* elite are talking more about the need to forge a true national identity for their country, but will this be done in a manner consistent with the "Accord on Identity and the Rights of Indigenous Peoples"? We can, of course, remain hopeful, but we cannot escape that, historically, what has been called nation building, in all parts of the world, in most cases involves attempts to exterminate the cultures of peoples belonging to nations other than those who control the government.[16] Even in the 1980s, states were borrowing more money to fight peoples within their boundaries than for all other programs combined. Nearly all state debt in Africa and nearly half of all other debt in "underdeveloped" countries come from the weapons states purchase to fight people claimed to be citizens by those very same states.[17] So far, the situation in the 1990s is no better.

---

[16]Van Den Berghe, P. (1992). The modern state: Nation builder or nation killer? *International Journal of Group Tensions*, 22 (3), 194–198.

[17]*Cultural Survival Quarterly*, 15 (4), 38. (1991).

Although a peace agreement in Guatemala has greatly reduced violence against that country's Maya population, anti-Maya violence is on the increase in the neighboring Mexican state of Chiapas. Shown here are coffins with victims of the December 1997 massacre.

Of all the world's states, Switzerland is one of the very few where pluralism really has worked out to the satisfaction of all parties to the arrangement, perhaps because, despite linguistic differences, they are all heirs to a common European cultural tradition. In Northern Ireland, by contrast, groups being heirs to a common tradition has not prevented violence and bloodshed. It seems the more divergent cultural traditions are, the more difficult it is to make pluralism work.

Given this dismal situation, can anything be done about it? As anthropologists David Maybury-Lewis and Pierre Van Den Berghe point out, we tend to idealize the peace and social order the unitary state maintains and to exaggerate the danger to this vision the allowance of cultural distinctiveness and/or local autonomy to peoples of other nationalities presents.[18] The sooner we recognize this tendency, the better off we will be. After all, states as cultural constructs are products of human imagination, and nothing prevents us from imagining in ways more tolerant of pluralism. Obviously, this will take a good deal of work, but at least the recognition exists that such things as *group* rights exist.

Even though it often fails to act on it, the United Nations General Assembly in its Covenant of Human Rights, passed in 1966, states unequivocally that "In those states in which ethnic, religious or linguistic minorities exist, persons belonging to such minorities shall not be denied the rights, in community with the other members of their group, to enjoy their own culture, to profess and practice their own religion or to use their own language."[19] Besides education, one of the actions that can help make this acknowledged right a reality is the advocacy work on behalf of indigenous peoples substantial numbers of anthropologists engage in (see Anthropology Applied on the next page).

ETHNOCENTRISM

The major problem associated with cultural pluralism has to do with ethnocentrism, a concept introduced in Chapter 14. To function effectively, a culture must instill the idea its ways are "best," or at least preferable to those of all other cultures. This provides individuals with a sense of pride in and loyalty to their traditions, which they derive psychological support from and which binds them firmly to their group. In societies where one's self-

---

[18]Maybury-Lewis, D. (1993). A new world dilemma: The Indian question in the Americas. *Symbols*, 22. Van Den Berghe, P. (1992). The modern state: Nation builder or nation killer? *International Journal of Group Tensions*, 22 (3), 191–192.

[19]Quoted in Bodley, J. H. (1990). *Victims of progress* (3rd ed., p. 99). Mountain View, CA: Mayfield.

These pictures show a Chechen woman in front of her home that has been destroyed by a Russian rocket and federal marshals at Wounded Knee, South Dakota, where U.S. troops laid siege to the Sioux Indian town in 1973. Both exemplify the willingness of states one nationality controls to use their armies against people of other nationalities within their borders to promote the state's interests over those of the other nationality.

Advocacy for the Rights of Indigenous Peoples

Anthropologists are increasingly concerned about the rapid disappearance of the world's remaining indigenous peoples for a number of reasons, foremost among them the basic issue of human rights. The world today is rushing to develop parts of the planet Earth that have so far escaped industrialization, or the extraction of resources regarded as vital to the well-being of "developed" economies. These development efforts are planned, financed, and implemented both by governments and businesses (generally the huge multinational corporations), as well as by international lending institutions. Unfortunately, the rights of native peoples generally have not been incorporated into the programs and concerns of these organizations, even where laws exist that are supposed to protect the rights of such peoples.

For example, the typical pattern for development of Brazil's Amazon basin has been for the government to build roads, along which it settles impoverished people from other parts of the country. This brings them into conflict with Indians already living there, who begin to die off in large numbers from diseases contracted from the settlers. Before long, the settlers learn the soils are not suited for their kind of farming; meanwhile, outside logging, mining, and agribusiness interests exert pressure to get them off the land. Ultimately, the settlers wind up living in disease-ridden slums, while the Indians are decimated by the diseases and violence unleashed upon them by the outsiders. Those who survive are usually relocated to places where resources are inadequate to support them.

In an attempt to do what they can to help indigenous peoples gain title to their lands and avoid exploitation by outsiders, anthropologists in various countries have formed advocacy groups. The major one in the United States is Cultural Survival, Inc., based in Cambridge, Massachusetts. This organization's interest is not in preserving indigenous cultures in some sort of ro-

mantic, pristine condition so that they will be there to study or to serve as "living museum exhibits," as it were. Rather, it is to provide the information and support to help endangered groups assess their situation, maintain or even strengthen their sense of self, and adapt to the changing circumstances. It does not regard assimilation of these groups into the mainstream societies of states as necessarily desirable; rather, they should be allowed the freedom to make their own decisions about how they wish to live. Instead of designing projects and then imposing them on endangered societies, Cultural Survival prefers to respond to the requests and desires of groups that see a problem and the need to address it. Cultural Survival can suggest ways to help and can activate extensive networks of anthropologists, of other indigenous peoples who already have faced similar problems, and of government officials whose support can be critical to success.

Most projects Cultural Survival funds or assists have been focused on securing the land rights of indigenous peoples and organizing native federations. It also has identified and funded a number of locally designed experiments in sustainable development, such as the Turkmen Weaving Project, which helps Afghan refugees make profitable income from traditional rug weaving; the Ikwe Marketing Collective, through which Minnesota Indians market wild rice and crafts; and Cultural Survival Enterprises, which has developed and expanded markets for products such as the nuts used in the popular Rain Forest Crunch (itself a creation of Cultural Survival). Of major importance was the success of Cultural Survival in getting the World Bank, in 1982, to require a policy that the rights and autonomy of tribal peoples and minorities be *guaranteed* in any project the bank is involved in. Despite such successes, however, much remains to be done to secure the survival of indigenous peoples in all parts of the world.

identification derives from the group, ethnocentrism is essential to a sense of personal worth. The problem with ethnocentrism is that it all too easily can be taken as a charter for manipulating other cultures for the benefit of one's own, even though —as we saw in Chapter 23—this does not have to be the choice. When it is, however, unrest, hostility, and violence commonly result.

In a typical expression of ethnocentrism, President James Monroe, in 1817, said this of Native American rights:

> The hunter state can exist only in the vast uncultivated deserts. It yields to the . . . greater force of civilized population; and of right, it ought to yield, for the earth was given to mankind to support the greater number of which it is capable; and no tribe or people have a right to withhold from the wants of others, more than is necessary for their support and comfort.[20]

This attitude is, of course, alive and well in the world today, and governments frequently use the idea that no group has the right to stand in the way of "the greater good for the greater number" to justify the development of resources in regions subsistence farmers, pastoral nomads, and food foragers occupy—irrespective of the wishes of those peoples. But is it truly the greater good for the greater number? A look at the world as it exists today as a kind of global society, with all the world's peoples bound by interdependency, raises serious questions about such policies.

GLOBAL APARTHEID

Apartheid, which was until the mid-1990s the official governmental policy of South Africa, consists of programs or measures that aim to maintain racial segregation.[21] Structurally, it served to perpetuate the dominance of a White minority over a non-White majority through the social, economic, political, military, and cultural constitutions of society. Non-Whites were denied effective participation in political affairs, were restricted in where they could live and what they could do, and were denied the right to travel freely. Whites, by contrast, controlled the government, including, of course, the military and police. Although 4.7 non-Whites for every White live there, being White and belonging to the upper stratum of society have tended to go together. The richest 20% of South Africa took 58% of the country's income and enjoyed a high standard of living, while the poorest 40% of the population received but 6.2% of the national products. Even with the end of apartheid and White control of the government, the figures are not much different today.

What has South Africa to do with a global society? Structurally, the latter is very similar— almost a mirror image of South Africa's society, even though no conscious policy of global apartheid is practiced. In the world society, about two thirds of the population is non-White and one third is White. In the world as a whole, being White and belonging to the upper stratum tend to go together, even though some exceptions exist (Japan and Kuwait immediately spring to mind). Although this largely White upper stratum has not been a homogeneous group, divided until recently into communist and noncommunist peoples, neither was the upper stratum of South African society, where friction always has occurred between the English, who controlled business and industry, and the Afrikaners, who controlled the government and military. In the world today, the poorest 75% of the population make do with 30% of the world's energy, 25% of its metals, 15% of its wood, and 40% of its food. The greater percentage of these and other resources goes to the richest 25% of the population (Figure 27.2). Life expectancy, as in South Africa, is poorest among non-Whites. Most of the world's weapons of mass destruction are owned by Whites: The United States, Russia, France, and Britain. As in South Africa, death and suffering from war and violence are distributed unequally; in the world, the poorest 70% of the population suffer more than 90% of violent deaths in all categories.

One could go on, but enough has been said to make the point: The parallels between the current

---

[20]Quoted in Forbes, J. D. (1964). *The Indian in America's past* (p. 103). Englewood Cliffs, NJ: Prentice-Hall.

[21]Material on global apartheid is drawn from G. Kohler (1996), Global apartheid. Reprinted in W. A. Haviland & R. J. Gordon (Eds.), *Talking about people: Readings in contemporary cultural anthropology* (2nd ed., pp. 262–268). Mountain View, CA: Mayfield.

Structural violence in East Timor, where the Indonesian armed forces, trained and equipped with assistance from the United States, rely on force to maintain control over a population that has never consented to Indonesian rule.

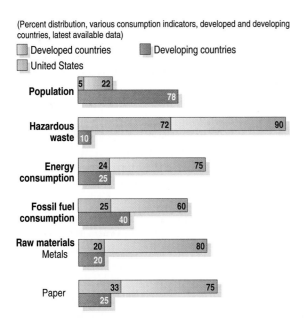

(Percent distribution, various consumption indicators, developed and developing countries, latest available data)

☐ Developed countries   ■ Developing countries
☐ United States

Population
5
22
78

Hazardous waste
72
90
10

Energy consumption
24
75
25

Fossil fuel consumption
25
60
40

Raw materials Metals
20
80
20

Paper
33
75
25

FIGURE 27.2
Though a minority of the world's population, people in the developed countries consume the most resources and generate the bulk of hazardous wastes.

world situation and that of apartheid South Africa are striking. To be sure, a number of non-White countries, such as South Korea, Taiwan, Malaysia, Thailand, and Indonesia, have shown dramatic economic growth in recent years. Unfortunately, the economic crash these countries experienced in 1997 has the potential to reduce much, if not all, of this progress. In any event, the price of obtaining help from the world's industrialized (mostly White) countries is to conform to requirements imposed by institutions they control, such as the International Monetary Fund. Moreover, it has become much easier for interests in the United States and other industrialized countries to buy up enterprises in countries in trouble, such as these east Asian countries. In previous financial bailouts in Latin America, the borrowers were hurt far more than the lenders of wealthy countries, and the current Asian bailouts seem headed in the same direction.[22]

[22]Avoiding the next crisis. (1998, January 12). *Washington Post National Weekly Edition*, p. 26.

We may sum up global apartheid as a de facto structure of world society that combines socioeconomic and racial antagonisms and that has these characteristics:

1. A minority of largely White people occupies the pole of affluence, while a majority composed mostly of other races occupies the pole of poverty.
2. Social integration of the two groups is made extremely difficult by barriers of complexion, economic position, political boundaries, and other factors.
3. Economic development of the two groups is interdependent.
4. The largely affluent White minority possesses a disproportionately large share of the world society's political, economic, and military power.

Global apartheid is thus a structure of extreme inequality in cultural, racial, social, political, economic, military, and legal terms, as was South African apartheid.

Around the world, condemnation of South African apartheid was close to universal, and even South Africa itself eventually abolished the system. Since global apartheid is even more severe than the South African version was, we ought to be much more concerned about it than we have been up to now.

PROBLEMS OF STRUCTURAL VIOLENCE

One of the consequences of a system of apartheid, whether official or unofficial and on the state or global level, is a great deal of **structural violence**: violence exerted by situations, institutions, and social, political, and economic structures. A classic instance of structural violence is the economic collapse of east Asian countries in 1997. To survive, these countries will have to make drastic cuts in social services, while industry downsizing and failures will cause untold numbers of people to lose their jobs. As far as the victims of this economic calamity are concerned, the effect is violent, even though the cause was not the hostile act of a specific individual. The source of the violence was an anonymous structure (the economy), and this is what structural violence is all about.

The remainder of this chapter leaves insufficient space to cover all aspects of structural violence, but we can look at some aspects of particular concern to anthropologists. Other specialists, too, are concerned, and anthropologists draw on the work of these specialists as well as their own, thereby fulfilling their traditional role as synthesizers (discussed in Chapter 1). Moreover, anthropologists are less apt than other specialists to see these aspects of structural violence as discrete and unrelated. Thus, they have a key contribution to make to our understanding of such modern-day problems as overpopulation, food shortages, pollution, and widespread discontent in the world.

WORLD HUNGER

As frequently dramatized by events in various parts of Africa, a major source of structural violence in the world today is our failure to provide food for all of its people. Not only is Africa losing the capacity to feed itself, but also 52 countries worldwide by 1980 were producing less food per capita than they were 10 years previously, and in 42 countries available food supplies were not adequate to provide the caloric requirements of their populations.[23] One factor contributing to this food crisis is a dramatic growth in the world's population.

Population growth is more than a simple addition of people. If it were just that, the addition of 20 people a year to a population of 1,000 would double that population in 50 years; but because the added people beget more people, the doubling

---

[23]Bodley, J. H. (1985). *Anthropology and contemporary human problems* (2nd ed., p. 114). Palo Alto, CA: Mayfield.

Structural violence.   Violence that situations, institutions, and social, political, and economic structures exert.

time is actually much less than 50 years. Hence, it took the whole of human history and prehistory for the world's population to reach 1 billion people, achieved in 1750. By 1950, world population had reached almost 2.5 billion, representing an annual growth rate of about 0.8%. By A.D. 2000, it will have increased to 6 billion (Figure 27.3).

The obvious question arising from the burgeoning world population is, can we produce enough food to feed all those people? The majority opinion among agriculturalists is that we can do so, but how far into the future we can is open to question. In the 1960s a major effort was launched to expand food production in the poor countries of the world by introducing new high-yield strains of grains. Yet despite some dramatic gains from this "green revolution"—India, for example, doubled its wheat crop in 6 years and was on the verge of grain self-sufficiency by 1970— and despite the impressive output of North American agriculture, millions of people on the face of the globe continue to face malnutrition and starvation. In the United States, meanwhile, *edible* food worth about $85 million is thrown out every day (far more food than sent out for famine relief), and farms are going out of business in record numbers.

The immediate cause of world hunger has less to do with food production than with food distribution. For example, millions of acres in Africa, Asia, and Latin America once devoted to subsistence farming have been given over to the raising of cash export crops to satisfy appetites in the world's "developed" countries for food such as coffee, tea, chocolate, bananas, and beef. Those who used to farm the land for their own food needs have been relocated either to urban areas, where all too often no employment exists for them, or to other areas ecologically unsuited for farming. In Africa such lands often are occupied by pastoral nomads; as farmers encroach upon these, insufficient pasturage is left for livestock. The resultant overgrazing, coupled with the clearing of the land for farming, leads to increased loss of both soil and water, with disastrous consequences to nomad and farmer alike. In Brazil, which is highly dependent on outside sources of fossil fuels for its energy needs, millions of acres in the northeast were taken over for sugar production for making alcohol to fuel the vehicles in Rio. The

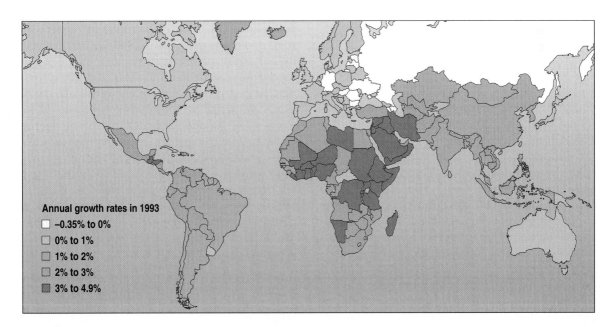

FIGURE 27.3
Population growth rates around the world.

Hunger stalks much of the world as a result of a world food system geared to satisfy an affluent minority in the world's developed nations.

people displaced by this were given small holdings in the Amazon, where they now are being uprooted to make way for huge ranches for raising export beef.

One strategy urged upon so-called developing countries, especially by U.S. government officials and development advisers, is to adopt the practices that have made North American agriculture so incredibly productive. On the face of it, this seems like a good idea, but it overlooks the fact it requires investment in expensive seeds and chemicals that neither small farmers nor poor countries can afford. Intensive agriculture by the U.S. model requires enormous inputs of chemical fertilizers, pesticides, and herbicides, not to mention the fossil fuels needed to run all the mechanized equipment. Even where high production lowers costs,

the price is often beyond the reach of impoverished farmers. It also has other problems: Farming U.S. style is energy inefficient. For every calorie produced, at least 8—some say as many as 20—calories go into its production and distribution.[24] By contrast, an Asian wet-rice farmer using traditional methods produces 300 calories for each 1 expended. North American agriculture is wasteful of other resources as well: About 30 pounds of fertile topsoil are ruined for every pound of food produced.[25] In the midwestern United States, about 50% of the topsoil has been lost over the past 100 years. Meanwhile, toxic substances from chemical nutrients and pesticides pile up in unexpected places, poisoning ground and surface waters; killing fish, birds, and other useful forms of life; upsetting natural ecological cycles; and causing major public-health problems. Despite its spectacular short-term success, serious questions arise about whether such a profligate food production system can be sustained over the long run, even in North America.

Pollution

It is ironic that a life-sustaining activity such as food production should constitute a health hazard, but that is precisely what it becomes when agricultural chemicals poison soils and waters and food additives (more than 2,500 are or have been in use) expose people to substances that all too often turn out to be harmful. This, though, is but a part of a larger problem of environmental pollution. Industrial activities are producing highly toxic waste at unprecedented rates, and factory emissions are poisoning the air. For example, smokestack gases are clearly implicated in acid rain, which is causing damage to lakes and forests all over northeastern North America. Air containing water vapor with a high acid content is, of course, harmful to the lungs, but the health hazard is greater than this. As surface water and groundwater become more acidic, the solubility of

---

[24]Ibid., 128.

[25]Chasin, B. H., & Franke, R. W. (1983). U.S. farming: A world model? *Global Reporter, 1* (2), 10.

In Guatemala, where these bananas are grown, agricultural development has caused increased malnutrition levels. As in many developing countries, modernization of agriculture has meant the conversion of land from subsistence farming to raising crops for export, making it increasingly difficult for people to satisfy their basic nutritional needs.

lead, cadmium, mercury, and aluminum increases sharply. The increase of dissolved aluminum, in particular, is becoming truly massive, and aluminum consumption has been associated with senile dementia as well as Alzheimer's and Parkinson's diseases. Today, these rank as major health problems in the United States.

Added to this is the global warming problem —the greenhouse effect—caused by the burning of fossil fuels. Although much is unknown about the extent of global warming, climatic scientists agree it is real and that its long-term effects will be harmful. Unfortunately, the response from energy interests has been similar to the campaign tobacco companies carried out for so long to convince the public smoking was not hazardous. The former have launched a massive public relations campaign to persuade the public global warming is not real; as a consequence, it becomes very difficult to do anything about it.

As with world hunger, the structural violence from pollution tends to be greatest in the poorest countries of the world, where chemicals banned in countries such as the United States are still widely used. Moreover, industrial countries have taken advantage of the lax environmental regulations of "underdeveloped" states to get rid of hazardous wastes. For instance, the president of Benin (in West Africa) not long ago signed a contract with a European waste company to dump toxic and low-grade radioactive waste on the lands of his political opposition.[26] In the United States, both government and industry have tried to persuade Indians on reservations experiencing severe economic depression that the solution to their problems lies in allowing disposal of nuclear and other hazardous waste on their lands.

Meanwhile, as manufacturing shifts from the developed to the developing countries of the world, a trend also encouraged by fewer safety and environmental regulations, lethal accidents such as the one in 1988 at Chernobyl, Ukraine, may be expected to increase. Here, a faulty reactor at a nuclear power plant released radiation, causing numerous deaths, relocation of 126,000 people, increased thyroid cancer and damaged immune systems even 10 years later, increased birth defects, and economic privation for people living as far

---

[26]*Cultural Survival Quarterly*, 15 (4), 5. (1991).

Environmental degradation is dramatically illustrated by the fires that burned out of control in southeast Asia in 1997, causing widespread health and visibility problems from massive amounts of smoke and particulate matter in the air.

away (the Arctic Circle) as the Saami, whose reindeer herds were contaminated by radioactive fallout. Indeed, development itself seems to be a health hazard; it is well known that indigenous peoples in Africa, the Pacific Islands, South America, and elsewhere are relatively free from diabetes, obesity, hypertension, and a variety of circulatory diseases until they adopt the ways of the developed countries. Then rates of these "diseases of development" escalate dramatically.

Modern humanity knows the causes of pollution and realizes it is a danger to future survival. Why, then, does not humanity control this evil by which it fouls its own nest? At least part of the answer lies in philosophical and theological traditions. As we saw in Chapter 23, Western industrialized societies accept the biblical assertion they have dominion over the earth with all that grows and lives on it, which it is their duty to subdue. These societies contribute most to global pollution. One North American, for example, consumes hundreds of times the resources of a single African,

with all that implies with respect to waste disposal and environmental degradation. Moreover, each person in North America adds, on average, 20 tons of carbon dioxide (a greenhouse gas) a year to the atmosphere. In "underdeveloped" countries, less than 3 tons per person are emitted.[27]

The exploitative worldview, characteristic of all civilizations, extends to all natural resources (Figure 27.4). Only when problems have reached crisis proportions, such as the destruction of the earth's protective ozone layer, have Western peoples protected or replaced what their greed and acquisitiveness have prompted them to take from the environment. In recent years, recognizing the seriousness of the environmental crisis people were creating for themselves, various bodies have passed laws against or restricting such activities as hunting whales out of existence, dumping toxic wastes

[27]Broecker, W. S. (1992, April). Global warming on trial. *Natural History*, 14.

Anthropology and the Future CHAPTER 27 817

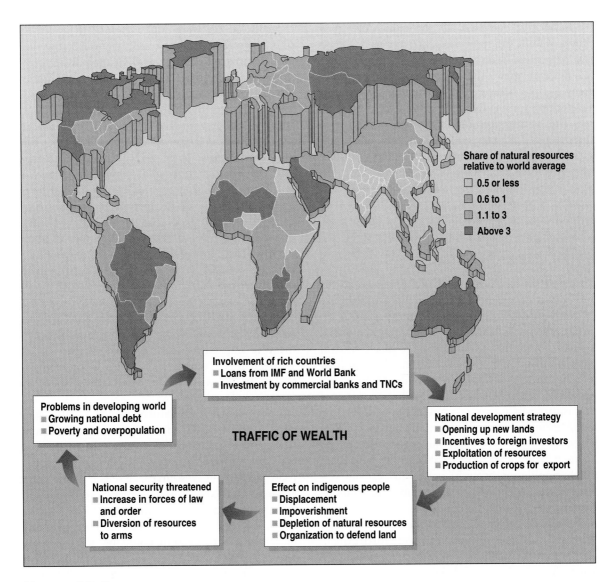

FIGURE 27.4

A high gross national product (tall blocks on map) is sustained in the world's industrial countries by a flow of mineral and land wealth from the lands of indigenous peoples.

into streams and rivers, and poisoning the air with harmful fumes. However, most such laws apply to the world's most affluent countries—the very ones where consumption levels drive the forces of exploitation responsible for environmental degradation in the world's poorer countries.

A large part of the problem in this and similar situations is a human reluctance to perceive as disadvantageous the practices that previously seemed to work well. Frequently, practices carried out on a particular scale or suited to a particular context become unsuitable when carried out on another scale or in another context. Because they are trained to view customs in their broader context, anthropologists would seem to have an important role to play in convincing people that solutions to many problems require changed behavior.

Indigenous peoples, in particular, also may play a significant role. They are apt to stand in awe of natural forces, bestowing on them a special place in their religious system. For example, many people believe rushing rapids, storms, the mountains, and the jungles possess awesome powers. This is also true of fire, which both warms and destroys. For farmers, the sun, rain, and thunder are important to their existence and are often considered divine. Such worldviews are not foolproof checks to the kind of environmental manipulation that causes severe pollution, but they certainly act as powerful restraining influences.

POPULATION CONTROL

Although the problems we have discussed so far may not be caused by population growth, they are certainly made worse by it. For one reason, it increases the scale of the problems; thus, the waste a small population generates is far easier to deal with than what a large one generates. For another, it often nullifies efforts people make to solve the problems, such as when increased food production is offset by increased numbers of people to be fed. Although solving the population growth problem does not by itself make the other problems go away, it is unlikely those problems can be solved unless population growth is arrested.

As our earlier look at population demonstrated, the world's population has grown enormously since the beginning of the industrial age. With the exception of European and North American populations, where birthrates are significantly lower than death rates (a balance between the two is required for **replacement reproduction**), the world saw no sign of a significant decline in birthrates prior to 1976. The reason impoverished people, in particular, tended to have so many children is simple: Children are their main resource. They provide a needed labor pool to work farms, and they are the only source of security for the elderly; hence, having many offspring makes sense (especially if infant mortality rates are high). His-

torically, people were apt to limit their family size only when they became wealthy enough that their money replaced children as their main resource; at that point, children actually *cost* them money. Given this, we can see why birthrates have for so long remained high in the world's poorest countries. To those who live in poverty, children are seen as the only hope.

Nevertheless, since 1976 some encouraging signs have occurred, such as China's steep decline in birthrates. China is one of 19 "underdeveloped" countries where birthrates actually have dropped *below* replacement levels (Chinese birthrates and death rates balance out at about 2.1 children per woman; the government's policy will be discussed later). In Africa, as well as much of south Asia and much of Central and South America (again, the world's poorest countries), birthrates also have declined, but far less dramatically. Examples include Bangladesh, where the rate has fallen from 6.2 to 3.4 (in just 10 years); Tunisia, where the rate has fallen from 7.2 to 2.9; and Mexico, which has moved 80% of the way to replacement level.[28]

Still, despite such improvements, fertility rates remain above replacement, so continual population growth makes it difficult for these countries even to maintain their present per capita share of food and other resources. Even if they could achieve immediate replacement reproduction, their populations would continue to grow for the next 50 years before the age distribution would flatten and zero growth could be achieved. The reason is that even though each woman has fewer children, more women are having them. This population momentum is exacerbated as life expectancy is improved. Current projections are that global population will peak around A.D. 2050 at about 8.5 billion people.

---

[28]Wattenberg, B. J. (1997, November 23). The population explosion is over. *New York Times Magazine*, 60.

Replacement reproduction. When birthrates and death rates are in equilibrium; people produce only enough offspring to replace themselves when they die.

The problem's severity becomes clear when it is realized the present world population of nearly 6 billion people can be sustained only by using up nonrenewable resources, which is like living off income-producing capital. It works for a time, but once the capital is gone, so is the possibility of even having an income to live on.

Desirable though it may be to halt population growth, programs to do so, and their consequences, pose many new problems. These are well illustrated by China's much publicized policy to promote one-child families. Although this has slowed the growth rate of China's population (birthrates are now below replacement level), it has given rise to some serious new problems. One difficulty stems from its basic contradiction to another policy, to raise agricultural productivity by granting more economic autonomy to rural households and the continued existence of families, which (as in old China) are strongly patriarchal. Within such families, men are responsible for farmwork, perpetuation of the male line of descent is considered essential to everyone's well being, and postmarital residence is strictly patrilocal. Under these circumstances, the birth of male children is considered essential; without them, the household will not have the workforce it needs and will suffer economically. Furthermore, the parents will have no one to support them once they are too old for physical labor. Daughters are of little use to them, since they will marry out of the household and can offer little aid to their parents. Since married couples are supposed to have only one child, the birth of a girl is greeted with dismay, for if the couple tries again for a boy, local state officials will exert tremendous pressures for the woman to have an abortion and for her or her husband to undergo sterilization.

Not surprisingly, in the face of all this, female infanticide is on the rise in China, and women who bear daughters are often physically and mentally abused by their husbands and mothers-in-law, sometimes to the point of committing suicide. (Although the state teaches that men determine a baby's sex, most rural Chinese believe the woman is still responsible for the outcome of a birth, perhaps through her diet and behavior.) Women pay in other ways with their bodies; when a second pregnancy occurs, the woman must have the abortion, and usually she is the one sterilized (surgical intervention for men in their prime is discouraged, owing to the importance of their agricultural labor). This leaves the man free to coerce his daughter-bearing wife into a divorce so that he can try again for a son

As birth rates fall around the world, there will be a rise in the percentage of the elderly, with an attendant rise in health care costs.

with a new wife, leaving the old one of no use to anyone and with no son to care for her in old age. One means of preventing a married woman's unauthorized pregnancy is by placing an intrauterine device (IUD) in her womb. This cannot be removed without official permission, which is hard to get even in the face of compelling medical reasons, since removal is contrary to official Chinese policy. Nor is an attached cord for removal provided, all of which have led to a proliferation of back-alley practitioners who remove IUDs with improvised hooks, often leading to infection and death.

If women in China's rural areas are seen to have little value, the same is not true where the manufacture of goods is an option. For this, female labor is in some demand, and, as a consequence, abduction of young women from rural communities has risen dramatically. Although firm figures are hard to get, an estimate for 1993 is that 100,000 women and children were kidnapped in that year.[29] Such women commonly are sold as brides to men in families who then control their labor, either sending them out to bring wages to the family or putting them to work without wages in family enterprises.

The problem of who will care for the elders in their old age is not just a problem for the Chinese but also will be a problem for any society whose birthrates are below replacement level. The inevitable consequence is the number of old people "explodes" relative to the number of productive people of younger age. Already the United States is beginning to worry about this. Care of the elderly is expensive, but fewer young have been born to assume the costs. Where will the money come from? As yet, nobody knows.

THE CULTURE OF DISCONTENT

Despite the difficulties, stabilization of the world's population appears to be a necessary step if the future's problems are ever to be solved. Without this, whatever else is done, the world's inability to provide enough food and distribute it equally seems inevitable. Up until about 1950, growth in

the world's food supply came almost entirely from expanding the amount of cultivated land. Since then, it has come increasingly from the high-energy inputs of chemical fertilizers that new high-yield varieties of crops depend on, of pesticides and herbicides, and of fuel to run tractors and other mechanical equipment, including irrigation pumps. The source of almost all this energy is oil, yet, although the demand for food is projected to rise until at least the middle of the 21st century, oil supplies are diminishing and will surely decline over this same period.

Insufficient food supplies are bound to result in increased structural violence in the form of higher death rates in the world's "underdeveloped" countries. This surely will have an impact on the "developed" countries, with their relatively stable populations and high living standards. It is hard to imagine how such countries could exist peacefully side by side with others experiencing high death rates and abysmally low living standards. Already, the combination of overpopulation and poverty is causing a rising tide of migration from the impoverished countries to the more affluent ones of Europe and North America, with a consequent rise of intolerance and antiforeign feeling and general social unrest.

Necessary though birth control may be for solving the future's problems, we have no reason to suppose it will be sufficient by itself. The result would be only to stabilize situations as they are. The problem is twofold. For the past several years, the world's poor countries have been sold on the idea they should enjoy a living standard comparable to that of the rich countries. Yet the resources necessary to maintain such a standard of living, even at moderate levels, are running out. As we saw in the last chapter, this situation has led to the creation of a culture of discontent, whereby people's aspirations far exceed their opportunities. The problem involves not just population growth outstripping food supplies, but it is also one of unequal access to decent jobs, housing, sanitation, health care, and adequate police and fire protection. And it is one of steady deterioration of the natural environment as a result of increasing industrialization and overuse of the land.

Some dramatic changes in cultural values and motivations, as well as in social institutions, are

[29]Gates, H. (1996). Buying brides in China—again. *Anthropology Today, 12* (4), 9.

required. The emphasis on individual self-interest, materialism, and conspicuous production, acquisition, and consumption, characteristic of the world's richest countries, needs to be abandoned in favor of a more human self-image and social ethic. These can be created from values still found in many of the world's non-Western cultures. Such values include a worldview that sees humanity as part of the natural world, rather than superior to it. Included, too,

is a sense of social responsibility that recognizes that no individual, people, or state has the right to expropriate resources at the expense of others. Finally, an awareness is needed of how important supportive ties are for individuals, such as seen in kinship or other associations in the world's traditional societies. Is humanity up to the challenge? Who knows, but it appears significant changes are bound to come, one way or another.

CHAPTER SUMMARY

Since future forms of culture will be shaped by decisions humans have yet to make, they cannot be predicted with any accuracy. Thus, instead of trying to foretell the future, a number of anthropologists are attempting to gain a better understanding of the existing world situation so that decisions may be made intelligently. Anthropologists are especially well suited for this, owing to their experience at seeing things in context, their long-term evolutionary perspective, their ability to recognize culture-bound biases, and their familiarity with cultural alternatives.

However humanity changes biologically, culture remains the chief means by which humans try to solve their problems of existence. Some anthropologists are concerned that there is a trend for the problems to outstrip any culture's ability to find solutions. Rapid developments in communication, transportation, and world trade, some believe, will link people together to the point that a single world culture will result. Their thinking is that such a homogenized superculture would offer fewer chances for conflict between peoples than in the past. Most anthropologists are skeptical of such an argument, in view of the recent tendency for ethnic groups to reassert their distinctive identities and in view of the persistence of traditional ways of thinking about oneself and others, even in the face of massive changes in other cultural aspects. Anthropologists also are concerned about people's tendency to treat many of the world's traditional societies as obsolete when they appear to stand in the way of "development."

Another alternative is for humanity to move in the direction of cultural pluralism, where more

than one culture exists in a society. To work, cultural pluralism must reject bigotry, bias, and racism. Some anthropologists maintain that pluralistic arrangements are the only feasible means of achieving global equilibrium and peace. A problem associated with cultural pluralism is ethnocentrism. All too often, in the name of "nation building," it has led one group to impose its control on others. Common consequences are prolonged violent and bloody political upheavals, including genocide.

Viewing the world today reveals a picture that is strikingly similar to South Africa's apartheid system. This world system serves to maintain the dominance of a largely White minority over a non-White majority through the social, economic, political, military, and cultural constitution of the current "global society."

One consequence of any apartheid system is a great deal of structural violence exerted by situations, institutions, and social, political, and economic structures. Such violence involves problems such as overpopulation and food shortages, which anthropologists are actively working to understand and help alleviate. One challenge the world over is to provide food resources to keep pace with the burgeoning population. The immediate problem, though, is not so much one of producing enough food as it is an existing food-distribution system geared to the satisfaction of appetites in the world's richest countries at the expense of those living in poorer countries.

Pollution has become a direct threat to humanity. Western peoples have protected their environments only when some crisis forces them to do so, and even at that their consumption rates continue to drive environmental degradation in other countries. Western societies have felt no long-term responsibilities toward the earth or its resources and could learn much from those non-Western peoples who see themselves as integral parts of the earth.

Meeting the problems of structural violence that beset the human species today probably can be done only if we continue to reduce the birthrate. Effective birth-control methods are now available. Whether or not these methods are used on a vast enough scale depends on their availability and acceptance. Many of the world's developing countries have policies aimed at controlling population growth, but these sometimes conflict with other policies, and in any case they give rise to new kinds of problems. Even if replacement reproduction were immediately achieved, populations would continue to grow for another 50 years.

Solving the problems of the global society depends also on lessening the gap between the living standards of impoverished and developed countries. This calls for dramatic changes in the values of Western societies, with their materialistic consumer orientation. All people need to see themselves as part of nature, rather than as superior to it. Also needed are a social responsibility that recognizes that no people has a right to expropriate important resources at the expense of others and an awareness of how important supportive ties are between individuals.

POINTS FOR CONSIDERATION

1. Of what practical value are the social sciences, particularly anthropology? What services can anthropologists provide beyond academics?

2. In your opinion, will continued modernization bring humanity, in the end, into a single homogenous world culture? Does modernization mean absolute assimilation? How might tradition play a part in this process?

3. Powerful states often feel they have a responsibility to intervene in foreign affairs to speed the development of other countries or to calm political and social distress. Is this necessarily a wise idea? Even when the intentions are good, is the outcome always positive? Explain your answer.

SUGGESTED READINGS

Bodley, J. H. (1985). *Anthropology and contemporary human problems* (2nd ed.). Palo Alto, CA: Mayfield.

Anthropologist Bodley examines some of the most serious problems in the world today: overconsumption, resource depletion, hunger and starvation, overpopulation, and violence and war.

Bodley, J. H. (1990). *Victims of progress* (3rd. ed.). Mountain View, CA: Mayfield.

This book explores the impact of industrial civilization on the world's indigenous peoples and how the latter are organizing to protect themselves.

Davis, S. H. (1982). *Victims of the miracle*. Cambridge: Cambridge University Press.

An anthropologist looks at Brazil's efforts to develop the Amazon region, the motivations behind those efforts, and their impact on indigenous peoples. Davis pays special attention to the role multinational corporations play, how they relate to the Brazilian government, and who benefits from it all.

Maybury-Lewis, D. (Ed.). (1984). *The Prospects for plural societies* (1982 Proceedings of the American Ethnological Society). American Ethnological Society.

In 1982, a group of anthropologists met to discuss one of the most crucial issues of our time, the prospects for multiethnic societies. What emerged as the "villain" of the conference was the state—not just particular countries but states as a kind of political structure and the hold they have over modern thought and political action. Maybury-Lewis confronts this issue in the concluding essay, which by itself makes this volume worth obtaining.

Miller, S. (Ed.). (1993). *State of the peoples: A global human rights report on societies in danger.* Boston: Beacon Press.

This important publication from *Cultural Survival Quarterly* systematically reports on the situation of indigenous people throughout the world, region by region. Also included are professional articles on critical issues affecting such diverse peoples as Bosnians and Bushmen, all sorts of useful maps and charts, and suggested solutions to many challenges indigenous peoples face. A "must read" for anyone who is in any way concerned with the "New World Disorder."

BIBLIOGRAPHY

Aberle, D. F., Bronfenbrenner, U., Hess, E. H., Miller, D. R., Schneider, D. H., & Spuhler, J. N. (1963). The incest taboo and the mating patterns of animals. *American Anthropologist, 65,* 253–265.

Abu-Lughod, L. (1986). *Veiled sentiments: Honor and poetry in a Bedouin society.* Berkeley, CA: University of California Press.

Adams, R. E. W. (1977). *Prehistoric Mesoamerica.* Boston: Little, Brown.

Adams, R. M. (1966). *The evolution of urban society.* Chicago: Aldine.

AIDS Monthly Surveillance Summary (through July 1997). (1997). San Francisco.

Al-Issa, I., & Dennis, W. (Eds.). (1970). *Cross-cultural studies of behavior.* New York: Holt, Rinehart & Winston.

Alland, A., Jr. (1970). *Adaptation in cultural evolution: An approach to medical anthropology.* New York: Columbia University Press.

Alland, A., Jr. (1971). *Human diversity.* New York: Columbia University Press.

Allen, S. L. (1984). Media anthropology: Building a public perspective. *Anthropology Newsletter, 25,* 6.

Allen, J. S., & Cheer, S. M. (1996). The non-thrifty genotype. *Current Anthropology, 37,* 831–842.

Amábile-Cuevas, C. F., & Chicurel, M. E. (1993). Horizontal gene transfer. *American Scientist, 81,* 332–341.

American Anthropological Association (1998). Statement on "race." Available at www.ameranthassn.org.

Amiran, R. (1965). The beginnings of pottery-making in the Near East. In F. R. Matson (Ed.), *Ceramics and man* (pp. 240–247). Viking Fund Publications in Anthropology, No. 41.

Anderson, C. M. (1989). Neanderthal pelvis and gestational length. *American Anthropologist, 91,* 327–340.

Andrews, L. B., & Nelkin, D. (1996). The bell curve: A statement. *Science, 271,* 13.

Ankel-Simons, F., Fleagle, J. G., & Chatrath, P. S. (1998). Femoral anatomy of *Aegyptopithecus zeuxis,* an early Oligocene anthropoid. *American Journal of Physical Anthropology, 106,* 413–424.

Appenzeller, T. (1998). Art: Evolution or revolution? *Science, 282,* 1451–1454.

Arensberg, C. M. (1961). The community as object and sample *American Anthropologist, 63,* 241–264.

Armstrong, D. F., Stokoe, W. C., & Wilcox, S. E. (1993). Signs of the origin of syntax. *Current Anthropology, 34,* 349–368.

Armstrong, S. (1991, February 2). Female circumcision: Fighting a cruel tradition. *New Scientist,* 42–47.

Ashmore, W. (Ed.). (1981). *Lowland Maya settlement patterns.* Albuquerque: University of New Mexico Press.

Avoiding the next crisis. (1998, January 12). *Washington Post National Weekly Edition,* p. 26.

Balandier, G. (1971). *Political Anthropology.* New York: Pantheon.

Balter, M. (1998). Why settle down? The mystery of communities. *Science, 282,* 1442–1444.

Banton, M. (1968). Voluntary association: anthropological aspects. In *International encyclopedia of the social sciences* (Vol. 16, pp. 357–362). New York: Macmillan.

Bar-Yosef, O. (1986). The Walls of Jericho: An Alternative Interpretation. *Current Anthropology, 27,* 157–162.

Bar-Yosef, O., Vandermeesch, B., Arensburg, B., Belfer-Cohen, A., Goldberg, P., Laville, H., Meignen, L., Rak, Y., Speth, J. D., Tchernov, E., Tillier, A-M., & Weiner, S. (1992). The Excavations in Kebara Cave, Mt. Carmel. *Current Anthropology, 33,* 497–550.

Barber, B. (1957). *Social stratification.* New York: Harcourt.

Barfield, T. J. (1984). Introduction. *Cultural Survival Quarterly, 8,* 2.

Barham, L. S. (1998). Possible early pigment use in South-Central Africa. *Current Anthropology, 39,* 703–710.

Barnett, H. (1953). *Innovation: The basis of cultural change.* New York: McGraw-Hill.

Barnouw, V. (1985). *Culture and personality* (4th ed.). Homewood, IL: Dorsey Press.

Barr, R. G. (1997, October). The crying game. *Natural History, 47.*

Barth, F. (1961). *Nomads of South Persia: The Basseri tribe of the Khamseh Confederacy.* Boston: Little, Brown (Series in Anthropology).

Barth, F. (1962). Nomadism in the mountain and plateau areas of South West Asia. *The Problems of the Arid Zone* (pp. 341–355). Paris: UNESCO.

Barton, R. F. (1919). Ifugao Law. Berkeley: *University of California Publications in American Archaeology and Ethnology,* Vol. XV.

Bascom, W. (1969). *The Yoruba of Southwestern Nigeria.* New York: Holt, Rinehart & Winston.

Bates, D. G., & Plog, F. (1991). *Human adaptive strategies.* New York: McGraw-Hill.

Beals, A. R. (1972). *Gopalpur: A South Indian village.* New York: Holt, Rinehart & Winston.

Beattie, J. (1964). *Other cultures: Aims, methods and achievements.* New York: Free Press.

Bednarik, R. G. (1995). Concept-mediated marking in the Lower Paleolithic. *Current Anthropology, 36,* 605–634.

Behrensmeyer, A. K., Todd, N. E., Potts, R., & McBrinn, G. E. (1997). Late Pliocene faunal turnover in the Turkana basin, Kenya and Ethiopia. *Science, 278,* 1589–1594.

Beidelman, T. O. (Ed.). (1971). *The transition of culture: Essays to E. E. Evans-Pritchard.* London: Tavistock.

Bell, D. (1997). Defining marriage and legitimacy. *Current Anthropology, 38,* 241.

Belshaw, C. S. (1958). The significance of modern cults in Melanesian development in W. Lessa & E. Z. Vogt (Eds.), *Reader in comparative religion: An anthropological approach.* New York: Harper & Row.

Benedict, R. (1959). *Patterns of culture.* New York: New American Library.

Bennett, J. W. (1964). Myth, theory and value in cultural Anthropology. In E. W. Caint & G. T. Bowles (Eds.), *Fact and theory in social science.* Syracuse, NY: Syracuse University Press.

Berdan, F. F. (1982). *The Aztecs of Central Mexico.* New York: Holt, Rinehart & Winston.

Bermúdez de Castro, J. M., Arsuaga, J. L., Cabonell, E., Rosas, A., Martinez, I., & Mosquera, M. (1997). A Hominid from the lower Pleistocene of Atapuerca, Spain: Possible ancestor to Neandertals and modern humans. *Science, 276,* 1392–1395.

Bernal, I. (1969). *The Olmec world.* Berkeley: University of California Press.

Bernard, H. R., & Sibley, W. E. (1975). *Anthropology and jobs.* Washington, DC: American Anthropological Association.

Bernardi, B. (1985) *Age class systems: Social institutions and policies based on age.* New York: Cambridge University Press.

Berra, T. M. (1990). *Evolution and the myth of creationism.* Stanford, CA: Stanford University Press.

Berreman, G. D. (1962). *Behind many masks: Ethnography and impression management in a Himalayan village.* Ithaca, NY: Society for Applied Anthropology (Monograph No. 4).

Berreman, G. D. (1968). Caste: The concept of caste. In *International Encyclopedia of the Social Sciences* (Vol. 2, pp. 333–338). New York: Macmillan.

Bicchieri, M. G. (Ed.). (1972). *Hunters and gatherers today: A socioeconomic study of eleven such cultures in the twentieth century.* New York: Holt, Rinehart & Winston.

Binford, L. R. (1972). *An archaeological perspective.* New York: Seminar Press.

Binford, L. R., & Chuan, K. H. (1985). Taphonomy at a distance: Zhoukoudian, the cave home of Beijing man? *Current Anthropology, 26,* 413–442.

Birdwhistell, R. (1970). *Kinesics and context: Essays in body motion communication.* Philadelphia: University of Pennsylvania Press.

Black, H. C. (1968). *Black's law dictionary.* St. Paul, MN: West.

Blumer, M. A. & Byrne, R. (1991). The ecological genetics and domestication and the origins of agriculture. *Current Anthropology, 32,* 23–54.

Boas, F. (1962). *Primitive art.* Gloucester, MA: Peter Smith.

Boas, F. (1966). *Race, language and culture.* New York: Free Press.

Bodley, J. H. (1985). *Anthropology and contemporary human problems* (2nd ed.). Palo Alto, CA: Mayfield.

Bodley, J. H. (1990). *Victims of progress* (3rd ed.). Mountain View, CA: Mayfield.

Bodley, J. H. (1997). Comment. *Current Anthropology, 38,* 725.

Bohannan, P. (Ed.). (1967). *Law and warfare: Studies in the anthropology of conflict.* Garden City, NY: Natural History Press.

Bohannan, P., & Dalton, G. (Eds.) (1962). *Markets in Africa.* Evanston, IL: Northwestern University Press.

Bohannan, P., & Middleton, J. (Eds.). (1968). *Kinship and social organization.* Garden City, NY: Natural History Press (American Museum Source Books in Anthropology).

Bohannan, P., & Middleton, J. (Eds.). (1968). *Marriage, family, and residence.* Garden

City, NY: Natural History Press (American Museum Source Books in Anthropology).

Bolinger, D. (1968). *Aspects of language.* New York: Harcourt.

Boone, E. S. (1987). Practicing sociomedicine: Redefining the problem of infant mortality in Washington, D.C. In R. M. Wulff & S. J. Fiske (Eds.), *Anthropological praxis: Translating knowledge into action* (p. 56). Boulder, CO: Westview Press.

Bordes, F. (1972). *A tale of two caves.* New York: Harper & Row.

Bornstein, M. H. 1975. The influence of visual perception on culture. *American Anthropologist, 77*(4), 774–798.

Brace, C. L. (1981). Tales of the phylogenetic woods: The evolution and significance of phylogenetic trees. *American Journal of Physical Anthropology, 56,* 411–429.

Brace, C. L. (1997). Cro-Magnons Я us? *Anthropology Newsletter, 38*(8), 1, 4.

Brace, C. L., Nelson, H., & Korn, N. (1979). *Atlas of human evolution* (2d ed.). New York: Holt, Rinehart & Winston.

Brace, C. L., Ryan, A. S., & Smith, B. (1981). Comment. *Current Anthropology, 22*(4), 426–430.

Bradfield, R. (1973). *A natural history of associations.* New York: International Universities Press.

Braidwood, R. J. (1960). The agricultural revolution. *Scientific American, 203,* 130–141.

Braidwood, R. J. (1975). *Prehistoric men* (8th ed.). Glenview, IL: Scott, Foresman.

Brain, C. K. (1968). Who killed the Swartkrans ape-Men? *South African Museums Association Bulletin, 9,* 127–139.

Brain, C. K. (1969). The contribution of Namib Desert Hottentots to an understanding of Australopithecine bone accumulations. *Scientific Papers of the Namib Desert Research Station, 13.*

Branda, R. F. & Eatoil, J. W. (1978). Skin color and photolysis: An evolutionary hypothesis. *Science, 201,* 625–626.

Brew, J. O. (1968). *One hundred years of anthropology.* Cambridge, MA: Harvard University Press.

Broecker, W. S. (1992, April). Global warming on trial. *Natural History, 14.*

Brothwell, D. R., & Higgs, E. (Eds.). (1969). *Science in archaeology* (Rev. ed.). London: Thames & Hudson.

Brown, B., Walker, A., Ward, C. V., & Leakey, R. E. (1993). New *Australopithecus boisei* calvaria from East Lake Turkana, Kenya. *American Journal of Physical Anthropology, 91,* 137–159.

Brown, D. E. (1991). *Human universals.* New York: McGraw-Hill.

Brues, A. M. (1977). *People and races.* New York: Macmillan.

Bull, J. J., & Wichman, H. A. (1998). A revolution in evolution. *Science, 281,* 1959.

Burling, R. (1969). Linguistics and ethnographic description. *American Anthropologist, 71,* 817–827.

Burling, R. (1970). *Man's many voices: Language in its cultural context.* New York: Holt, Rinehart & Winston.

Burling, R. (1993). Primate calls, human language, and nonverbal communication. *Current Anthropology, 34,* 25–53.

Butzer, K. (1971). *Environment and anthropology: An ecological approach to prehistory* (2d ed.). Chicago: Aldine.

Byers, D. S. (Ed.). (1967). *The prehistory of the Tehuacan Valley: Vol. 1. Environment and Subsistence.* Austin: University of Texas Press.

Cachel, S. (1997). Dietary shifts and the European Upper Paleolithic transition. *Current Anthropology, 38,* 590.

Calloway, C. (1997). Introduction: Surviving the Dark Ages. In C. G. Calloway (Ed.), *After King Philip's War: Presence and persistence in Indian New England* (pp. 1–28). Havover, NH: University Press of New England.

Campbell, B. G. & Loy, J. D. (1995). *Humankind emerging,* (7th ed.). New York: Harper Collins.

Carmack, R. (1983). Indians and the Guatemalan Revolution. *Cultural Survival Quarterly, 7*(3), 52–54.

Carneiro, R. L. (1970). A theory of the origin of the state. *Science, 169,* 733–738.

Caroulis, J. (1996). Food for thought. *Pennsylvania Gazette, 95*(3), 16.

Carpenter, E. (1973). *Eskimo realities.* New York: Holt, Rinehart & Winston.

Carroll, J. B. (Ed.). (1956). *Language, thought and reality: Selected writings of Benjamin Lee Whorf.* New York: Wiley.

Cartmill, M. (1998). The gift of gab. *Discover 19*(11), 64.

Cashdan, E. (1989). Hunters and gatherers: Economic behavior in bands. In S. Plattner (Ed.), *Economic Anthropology* (pp. 21–48). Stanford, CA: Stanford University Press.

Cavalli-Sforza, L. L. (1977). *Elements of human genetics.* Menlo Park, CA: W. A. Benjamin.

Cavallo, J. A. (1990, February). Cat in the human cradle. *Natural History,* 54–60.

Centers For Disease Control. (1997). *Centers For Disease Control Semi-Annual AIDS Report* (through June 1996). Atlanta, GA.

Chagnon, N. A. (1988). *Yanomamo: The fierce people* (3rd ed.) New York: Holt, Rinehart & Winston.

Chagnon, N. A., & Irons, W. (Eds.). (1979). *Evolutionary biology and human social behavior.* North Scituate, MA: Duxbury Press.

Chambers, R. (1983). *Rural development: Putting the last first.* New York: Longman.

Chang, K. C. (Ed.). (1968). *Settlement archaeology.* Palo Alto, CA: National Press.

Chapple, E. D. (1970). *Cultural and biological man: Explorations in behavioral anthropology.* New York: Holt, Rinehart & Winston.

Chasin, B. H., & Franke, R. W. (1983). U.S. farming: A world model? *Global Reporter, 1*(2), 10.

Childe, V. G. (1951, orig. 1936). *Man makes himself.* New York: New American Library.

Childe, V. G. (1954). *What happened in history.* Baltimore: Penguin.

Chodorow, N. (1971). Being and doing: A cross-cultural examination of the socialization of males and females. In V. Gornick & B. K. Moran (Eds.), *Woman in sexist society.* New York: Basic Books.

Ciochon, R. L., & Fleagle, J. G. (1987). Ramapithecus and human origins. In R. L. Ciochon and J. G. Fleagle (Eds.), *Primate evolution and human origins.* Hawthorne, NY: Aldine de Gruyter.

Ciochon, R. L., & Fleagle, J. G., (Eds.). (1987). *Primate evolution and human origins.* Hawthorne, NY: Aldine de Gruyter.

Ciochon, R. L., & Fleagle, J. G. (1993). *The human evolution source book.* Englewood Cliffs, NJ: Prentice Hall.

Clark, E. E. (1966). *Indian legends of the Pacific Northwest.* Berkley: University of California Press.

Clark, G. (1967). *The Stone Age hunters.* New York: McGraw-Hill.

Clark, G. (1972). *Starr Carr: A case study in bioarchaeology.* Reading, MA: Addison-Wesley.

Clark, G. A. (1997). Neandertal genetics. *Science, 277,* 1024.

Clark, J. G. D. (1962). *Prehistoric Europe: The economic basis.* Stanford, CA: Stanford University Press.

Clark, W. E. L. (1960). *The antecedents of man.* Chicago: Quadrangle Books.

Clark, W. E. L. (1966). *History of the primates* (5th ed.). Chicago: University of Chicago Press.

Clark, W. E. L. (1967). *Man-apes or ape-men? The story of discoveries in Africa.* New York: Holt, Rinehart & Winston.

Clarke, R. J., & Tobias, P. V. (1995). Sterkfontein member 2 foot bones of the oldest South African hominid. *Science, 269,* 521–524.

Clay, J. W. (1987). Genocide in the Age of Enlightenment. *Cultural Survival Quarterly 12*(3).

Clay, J. W. (1996). What's a nation? In W. A. Haviland & R. J. Gordon (Eds.), *Talking about people* (2nd ed., pp. 188–189). Mountain View, CA: Mayfield.

Clough, S. B., & Cole, C. W. (1952). *Economic history of Europe* (3d ed.). Lexington, MA: Heath.

Codere, H. (1950). *Fighting with property.* Seattle: University of Washington Press (American Ethnological Society, Monograph 18).

Coe, S. D. (1994). *America's first cuisines.* Austin, TX: University of Texas Press.

Coe, W. R. (1967). *Tikal: A handbook of the ancient maya ruins.* Philadelphia: University of Pennsylvania Museum.

Coe, W. R., & Haviland, W. A. (1982). *Introduction to the archaeology of Tikal.* Philadelphia: University Museum.

Cohen, J. (1997). Is an old virus up to new tricks? *Science, 277,* 312–313.

Cohen, M. N. (1977). *The food crisis in prehistory.* New Haven, CT: Yale University Press.

Cohen, M. N. (1995). Anthropology and race: The bell curve phenomenon. *General Anthropology, 2*(1), 1–4.

Cohen, M., & Armelagos, G. (Eds.). (1984). *Paleopathology at the origins of agriculture.* Orlando, FL: Academic Press.

Cohen, M. N. & Armelagos, G. J. (1984). Paleopathology at the origins of agriculture: Editors' summation. In M. N. Cohen & G. J. Armelagos (Eds.) *Paleopathology at the origins of agriculture.* Orlando, FL: Academic Press.

Cohen, M. L. (1967). Variations in complexity among Chinese family groups: The impact of modernization. *Transactions of the New York Academy of Sciences, 295,* 638–647.

Cohen, M. L. (1968). A case study of Chinese family economy and development. *Journal of Asian and African Studies, 3,* 161–180.

Cohen, R., & Middleton, J. (Eds.). (1967). *Comparative political systems.* Garden City, NY: Natural History Press.

Cohen, Y. (1968). *Man in adaptation: The cultural present.* Chicago: Aldine.

Colburn, T., Dumanoski, D. & Myers, J. P. (1996, March). Hormonal sabotage. *Natural History*, 45–46.

Cole, S. (1975). *Leakey's luck: The life of Louis Seymour Bazett Leakey. 1903–1972.* New York: Harcourt Brace Jovanovich.

Collier, J. F., & Yanagisako, S. J., (Eds.). (1987). *Gender and kinship: Essays toward a unified analysis.* (Stanford, CA: Stanford University Press).

Collier, J., Rosaldo, M. Z., & Yanagisako, S. (1982). Is there a family? New anthropological views. In B. Thorne & M. Yalom (Eds.), *Rethinking the family: Some feminist questions* (pp. 25–39). New York: Longman.

Connelly, J. C. (1979). Hopi social organization. In Ortiz, A. (Ed.), *Handbook of North American Indians, Vol. 9, Southwest* (pp. 539–553). Washington, DC: Smithsonian Institution.

Connor, M. (1996). The archaeology of contemporary mass graves. *SAA Bulletin, 14*(4), 6 & 31.

Conroy, G. C. (1997). *Reconstructing human origins: A Modern Synthesis.* New York: W. W. Norton.

Constable, G., & the Editors of Time-Life. (1973). *The Neanderthals.* New York: Time-Life.

Cook, S. F. (1972). *Prehistoric demography.* Reading, MA: Addison-Wesley.

Coon, C. S. (1957). *The seven caves.* New York: Knopf.

Coon, C. S. (1958). *Caravan: The story of the Middle East* (2nd ed.) New York: Holt, Rinehart & Winston.

Coon, C. S. (1971). *The hunting peoples.* Boston: Little, Brown.

Coon, C. S., Garn, S. N., & Birdsell, J. (1950). *Races: A study of the problems of race formation in man.* Springfield, IL: Charles C Thomas.

Cooper, A., Poinar, H. N., Pääbo, S., Radovci, C. J., Debénath, A., Caparros, M., Barroso-Ruiz, C., Bertranpetit, J., Nielsen-March, C., Hedges, R. E. M., & Sykes, B. (1997). Neanderthal genetics. *Science, 277,* 1021–1024.

Coppens, Y., Howell, F. C., Isaac, G. L., & Leakey, R. E. F. (Eds.). (1976). *Earliest man and environments in the Lake Rudolf Basin: Stratigraphy, paleoecology, and evolution.* Chicago: University of Chicago Press.

Cornwell, T. (1995, Nov. 10). Skeleton staff. *Times Higher Education,* p. 20.

Corruccini, R. S. (1992). Metrical reconsideration of the Skhul IV and IX and Border Cave I crania in the context of modern human origins. *American Journal of Physical Anthropology, 87,* 433–445.

Cottrell, F. (1965). *Energy and society: The relation between energy, social changes and economic development.* New York: McGraw-Hill.

Cottrell, L. (1963). *The lost pharaohs.* New York: Grosset & Dunlap.

Courlander, H. (1971). *The fourth world of the Hopis.* New York: Crown.

Cowgill, G. L. (1980). Letter. *Science, 210,* 1305.

Cowgill, G. L. (1997). State and society at Teotihuacan, Mexico. *Annual Review of Anthropology, 26,* 129–161.

Cox, O. C. (1959). *Caste, class and race: A study in dynamics.* New York: Monthly Review Press.

Crane, L. B., Yeager, E., & Whitman, R. L. (1981). *An introduction to linguistics.* Boston: Little, Brown.

Crocker, W. A., & Crocker, J. (1994). *The canela, bonding through kinship, ritual and sex.* Fort Worth, TX: Harcourt Brace.

Culbert, T. P., (Ed.). (1973). *The Classic Maya collapse.* Albuquerque: University of New Mexico Press.

Culotta, E. (1992). A new take on anthropoid origins, *Science, 256,* 1516–1517.

Culotta, E. (1995a). Asian hominids grow older. *Science, 270,* 1116–1117.

Culotta, E. (1995b). New finds rekindle debate over anthropoid origins. *Science, 268,* 1851.

Culotta, E. (1995c). New hominid crowds the field. *Science, 269,* 918.

Culotta, E., & Koshland, D. E., Jr. (1994). DNA repair works its way to the top. *Science 266,* 1926.

Cultural Survival Quarterly, 15(4), 5 (1991).

Cultural Survival Quarterly, 15(4), 38 (1991).

Dalton, G. (1971). *Traditional tribal and peasant economics: An introductory survey of economic anthropology.* Reading, MA: Addison-Wesley.

Dalton, G. (Ed.). (1967). *Tribal and peasant economics: Readings in economic anthropology.* Garden City, NY: Natural History Press.

Dalton, G. (1971). *Traditional tribal and peasant economics: An introductory survey of economic anthropology.* Reading, MA: Addison-Wesley.

Daniel, G. (1970). *The first civilizations: The archaeology of their origins.* New York: Apollo Editions.

Daniel, G. (1975). *A hundred and fifty years of archaeology.* (2d ed.) London: Duckworth.

Darwin, C. (1936; orig. 1871). *The descent of man and selection in relation to sex.* New York: Random House (Modern Library).

Darwin, C. (1967; orig. 1859). *On the origin of species.* New York: Atheneum.

Davenport, W. (1959). Linear descent and descent groups. *American Anthropologist, 61,* 557–573.

Davis, S. H. (1982). *Victims of the miracle.* Cambridge: Cambridge University Press.

Day, G. M. (1972). Quoted in Vogelman, T. C. (Director), and Department of Anthropology (Producer). *Prehistoric life in the Champlain Valley* [Film]. Burlington, VT: University of Vermont.

Death and disorder in Guatemala. (1983). *Cultural Survival Quarterly, 7*(1).

Dettinger, K. A. (1997, October). When to wean. *Natural History,* 49.

de Laguna, F. (1977). *Voyage to Greenland: A personal initiation into anthropology.* New York: Norton.

de Laguna, G. A. (1966). *On existence and the human world.* New Haven, CT: Yale University Press.

de Pelliam, A., & Burton, F. D. (1976). More on predatory behavior in nonhuman primates. *Current Anthropology, 17*(3).

de Waal, A. (1994). Genocide in Rwanda. *Anthropology Today, 10*(3), 1–2.

de Waal, F. (1996). *Good natured: The origins of right and wrong in humans and other animals.* Cambridge, MA: Harvard University Press.

de Waal, F., Kano, T., & Parish, A. R. (1998). Comments. *Current Anthropology 39,* 407–408, 410–411, 413–414.

Dean, M. C., Beynon, A. D., Thackeray, J. F., & Macho, G. A.. 1993. Histological reconstruction of dental development and age at death of a juvenile *Paranthropus robustus* specimen, SK 63, from Swartkrans, South Africa. *American Journal of Physical Anthropology, 91,* 401–419.

DeBeer, Sir G. R. (1964). *Atlas of evolution.* London: Nelson.

Deetz, J. (1967). *Invitation to archaeology.* New York: Doubleday.

Deevy, E. S., Jr. (1960). The human population. *Scientific American, 203,* 194–204.

Devereux, G. (1963). Institutionalized homosexuality of the Mohave Indians. In H. M. Ruitenbeck (Ed.), *The problem of homosexuality in modern society.* New York: Dutton.

DeVore, I. (Ed.). (1965). *Primate behavior: Field studies of monkeys and apes.* New York: Holt, Rinehart & Winston.

Diamond, J. (1994). How Africa became black. *Discover, 15*(2): 72–81.

Diamond, J. (1994). Race without color. *Discover, 15*(11), 83–89.

Diamond, J. (1996). Empire of uniformity. *Discover, 17*(3), 78–85.

Diamond, J. (1997). The curse of QWERTY. *Discover, 18*(4), 34–42.

Diamond, J. (1998). Ants, crops, and history. *Science, 281,* 1974–1975.

Dixon, J. E., Cann, J. R., & Renfrew, C. (1968). Obsidian and the origins of trade, *Scientific American, 218,* 38–46.

Dobyns, H. F., Doughty, P. L., & Lasswell, H. D., (Eds.). (1971). *Peasants, power, and applied social change.* London: Sage.

Dobzhansky, T. (1962). *Mankind evolving.* New Haven, CT: Yale University Press.

Doist, R. (1997). Molecular evolution and scientific inquiry, misperceived. *American Scientist 85,* 475.

Donnan, C. B., & Castillo, L. J. (1992). Finding the tomb of a Moche priestess. *Archaeology 45*(6), 38–42.

Douglas, M. (1958). Raffia cloth distribution in the Lele economy. *Africa, 28,* 109–122.

Dowson, T. A., & Lewis-Williams, J. D. (1993). Myths, museums, and southern African rock art. *South African Historical Journal, 29,* 44–60.

Dozier, E. (1970). *The Pueblo Indians of North America.* New York: Holt, Rinehart & Winston.

Draper, P. (1975). !Kung women: Contrasts in sexual egalitarianism in foraging and sedentary contexts. In R. Reiter (Ed.), *Toward an anthropology of women* (pp. 77–109). New York: Monthly Review Press.

Driver, H. (1964). *Indians of North America.* Chicago: University of Chicago Press.

Dubois, C. (1944). *The people of Alor.* Minneapolis: University of Minnesota Press.

Dubos, R. (1968). *So human an animal.* New York: Scribner.

Duncan, A. S., Kappelman, J., & Shapiro, L. J. (1994). Metatasophalangeal joint function and positional behavior in *Australopithecus afarensis. American Journal of Physical Anthropology, 93,* 67–81.

Dundes, A. (1980). *Interpreting folklore.* Bloomington, IN: Indiana University Press.

Durkheim, E. (1965). *The elementary forms of the religious life.* New York: Free Press.

Durkheim, E. (1964). *The division of labor in society.* New York: Free Press.

duToit, B. M. (1991). *Human sexuality: Cross cultural readings.* New York: McGraw-Hill.

Eastman, C. M. (1990). *Aspects of language and culture* (2nd ed.). Novato, CA: Chandler & Sharp.

Edey, M. A., & Johannson, D. (1989). *Blueprints: solving the mystery of evolution.* Boston: Little, Brown.

Edey, M., & the Editors of Time-Life. (1972). *The missing link*. New York: Time-Life.

Edmonson, M. S. (1971). *Lore: An introduction to the science of folklore*. New York: Holt, Rinehart & Winston.

Edwards, S. W. (1978). Nonutilitarian activities on the Lower Paleolithic: A look at the two kinds of evidence. *Current Anthropology, 19*(l), 135–137.

Eggan, F. (1954). Social anthropology and the method of controlled comparison. *American Anthropologist, 56*, 743–763.

Eiseley, L. (1958). *Darwin's century: Evolution and the men who discovered it*. New York: Doubleday.

Eisenstadt, S. N. (1956). *From generation to generation: Age groups and social structure*. New York: Free Press.

Elgin, S. H. (1994). I am not scowling fiercely as I write this. *Anthropology Newsletter, 35*(9), 44.

Elkin, A. P. (1964). *The Australian aborigines*. Garden City, NY: DoubleDay/Anchor Books.

Ellison, P. T. (1990). Human ovarian function and reproductive ecology: New hypotheses. *American Anthropologist, 92*, 933–952.

Ember, C. R., & Ember, M. (1985). *Cultural anthropology* (4th ed.). Englewood Cliffs, NJ: Prentice-Hall.

Ember, C. R., & Ember, M. (1996). What have we learned from cross-cultural research? *General Anthropology, 2*(2), 5.

Epstein, A. (1968). Sanctions. In *International Encyclopedia of the Social Sciences* (Vol. 14, p. 3). New York: Macmillan.

Erasmus, C. J., & Smith, W. (1967). Cultural anthropology in the United States since 1900. *Southwestern Journal of Anthropology, 23* 11–40.

Erasmus, C. J. (1950). Patolli, Pachisi, and the limitation of possibilities. *Southwestern Journal of Anthropology, 6*, 369–381.

Ervin-Tripp, S. (1973). *Language acquisition and communicative choice*. Stanford, CA: Stanford University Press.

Esber, G. S., Jr. (1987). Designing Apache houses with Apaches. In R. M. Wulff & S. J. Fiske (Eds.), *Anthropological praxis: Translating knowledge into action* (pp. 187–196). Boulder, CO: Westview Press.

Evans, W. (1968). *Communication in the animal world*. New York: Crowell.

Evans-Pritchard, E. E. (1937). *Witchcraft, oracles, and magic among the Azande*. London: Oxford University Press.

Evans-Pritchard, E. E. (1968). *The Nuer: A description of the modes of livelihood and political institutions of a Nilotic people*. London: Oxford University Press.

Fagan, B. M. (1995). The quest for the past. In L. L. Hasten (Ed.), *Annual Editions 95/96, Archaeology* (p. 10). Guilford, CT: Dushkin.

Fagan, B. M. (1998). *People of the earth* (9th ed.). New York: Longman.

Falk, D. (1975). Comparative anatomy of the larynx in man and the chimpanzee: Implications for language in Neanderthal. *American Journal of Physical Anthropology, 43*(1), 123–132.

Falk, D. (1989). Ape-like endocast of 'Ape Man Taung'. *American Journal of Physical Anthropology, 80*, 335–339. Falk, D. (1989). Ape-like endocast of 'Ape Man Taung'. *American Journal of Physical Anthropology, 80*, 335–339.

Falk, D. (1993). A good brain is hard to cool. *Natural History, 102*(8), 65.

Falk, D. (1993). Hominid paleoneurology. In R. L. Ciochon & J. G. Fleagle (Eds.) *The human evolution source book*, Englewood Cliffs, NJ: Prentice-Hall.

Farmer, P. (1992). *AIDS and accusation: Haiti and the geography of blame*. Berkeley: University of California Press.

Farsoun, S. K. (1970). Family structures and society in modern Lebanon. In L. E. Sweet (Ed.), *Peoples and cultures of the Middle East* (Vol. 2). Garden City, NY: Natural History Press.

Feder, K. L. (1999). *Frauds, myths, and mysteries* (3rd ed.). Mountain View, CA: Mayfield.

Federoff, N. E., & Nowak, R. M. (1997). Man and his dog. *Science, 278*, 305.

Fedigan, L. M. (1986).The changing role of women in models of human evolution. *Annual Review of Anthropology, 15*, 25–56.

Ferguson, T. J. (1996). Archaeology for and by Native Americans. Paper presented at the 95th Annual Meeting, American Anthropological Association.

Ferrie, H. (1997). An interview with C. Loring Brace. *Current Anthropology, 38*, 851–869.

Firth, R. (1952). *Elements of social organization*. London: Watts.

Firth, R. (1957). *Man and culture: An evaluation of Bronislaw Malinowski*. London: Routledge.

Firth, R. (1963). *We the Tikopia*. Boston: Beacon Press.

Firth, R (Ed.). (1967). *Themes in economic anthropology*. London: Tavistock.

Fishman, J. (1994). Putting a new spin on the human birth. *Science, 264*, 1082–1083.

Flannery, K. V. (1973). The origins of agriculture. In B. J. Siegel, A. R. Beals, & Stephen A. Tyler (Eds.), *Annual Review of Anthropology* (Vol. 2, pp. 271–310). Palo Alto, CA: Annual Reviews.

Flannery, K. V., (Ed.). (1976). *The Mesoamerican village*. New York: Seminar Press.

Fleagle, J. G. (1992, December). *Early anthropoid evolution*. Paper presented at the 91st Annual Meeting of the American Anthropological Association.

Folger, T. (1993). The naked and the bipedal. *Discover, 14*(11), 34–35.

Forbes, J. D. (1964). *The Indian in America's past*. Englewood Cliffs, NJ: Prentice-Hall.

Forde, C. D. (1955). The Nupe. In D. Forde (Ed.), *Peoples of the Niger-Benue confluence*. London: International African Institute (Ethnographic Survey of Africa. Western Africa, part 10).

Forde, C. D. (1953). *Habitat, economy, and society*. New York: Dutton.

Forde, C. D. (1968). Double descent among the Yako. In P. Bohannan & J. Middleton (Eds.), *Kinship and social organization* (pp. 179–191). Garden City, NY: Natural History Press.

Fortes, M. (1969). *Kinship and the social order: The legacy of Lewis Henry Morgan*. Chicago: Aldine.

Fortes, M., & Evans-Prichard, E. E. (Eds.). (1962; orig. 1940). *African political systems*. London: Oxford University Press.

Fortes, M. (1950). Kinship and marriage among the Ashanti. In A. R. Radcliffe-Brown & C. Daryll Forde (Eds.). *African systems of kinship and marriage*. London: Oxford University Press.

Fossey, D. (1983). *Gorillas in the mist*. Burlington, MA: Houghton Mifflin.

Foster, G. M. (1955). Peasant society and the image of the limited good. *American Anthropologist, 67*, 293–315.

Fox, R. (1967). *Kinship and marriage in an anthropological perspective*. Baltimore: Penguin.

Fox, R. (1968). *Encounter with anthropology*. New York: Dell.

Frake, C. O. (1992). Lessons of the Mayan Sky. In A. F. Aveni (Ed.), *The sky in Mayan literature* (pp. 274–291). New York: Oxford University Press.

France, D. L., & Horn, A. D. (1992). *Lab manual and workbook for physical anthropology* (2nd ed.), New York: West.

Frankfort, H. (1968). *The birth of civilization in the Near East*. New York: Barnes & Noble.

Fraser, D. (1962). *Primitive art*. New York: Doubleday.

Fraser, D. (Ed.). (1966). *The many faces of primitive art: A critical anthology*. Englewood Cliffs, NJ: Prentice-Hall.

Frayer, D. W. (1981). Body size, weapon use, and natural selection in the European Upper Paleolithic and Mesolithic. *American Anthropologist, 83*, 57–73.

Frazer, Sir J. G.. (1961 reissue). *The new golden bough*. New York: Doubleday, Anchor Books.

Freeman, J. D. (1960). The Iban of western Borneo. In G. P. Murdock (Ed.), *Social structure in Southeast Asia*. Chicago: Quadrangle Books.

Freeman, L. G. (1992). *Ambrona and Torralba: New evidence and interpretation* [paper]. 91st Annual Meeting of the American Anthropological Association. San Francisco.

Fried, M. (1972). *The study of anthropology*. New York: Crowell.

Fried, M. (1967). *The evolution of political society: An essay in political anthropology*. New York: Random House.

Fried, M., Harris, M., & Murphy, R. (1968). *War: The anthropology of armed conflict and aggression*. Garden City, NY: Natural History Press.

Fried, M. 1960. On the evolution of social stratification and the state. In S. Diamond (Ed.) *Culture in history: Essays in honor of Paul Radin*. New York: Columbia University Press.

Friedl, E. (1975). *Women and men: An anthropologist's view*. New York: Holt, Rinehart & Winston.

Fritz, G. J. (1994). Are the first American farmers getting younger? *Current Anthropology, 35*, 305–309.

Frye, M. (1983). Sexism. In *The politics of reality* (pp. 17–40). New York: The Crossing Press.

Furst, P. T. (1976). *Hallucinogens and culture* (p. 7). Novato, CA: Chandler and Sharp.

Gamble, C. (1986). *The Paleolithic settlement of Europe*. Cambridge: Cambridge University Press.

Gardner, R. A., Gardner, B. T., & Van Cantfort, T. E. (Eds.). (1989). *Teaching sign language to chimpanzees*. Albany, NY: State University of New York Press.

Gamst, F. C., & Norbeck, E. (1976). *Ideas of culture: Sources and uses*. New York: Holt, Rinehart & Winston.

Garn, S. M. (1970). *Human races* (3d ed.). Springfield, IL: Charles C Thomas.

Gates, H. (1996). Buying brides in China—again. *Anthropology Today, 12*(4), 10.

Gebo, D. L., MacLatchy, L., Kityo, R., Deino, A., Kingston, J., & Pilbeam, D. (1997). A hominoid genus from the early Miocene of Uganda. *Science, 276*, 401–404.

Geertz, C. (1963). *Agricultural involution: The process of ecological change in Indonesia.* Berkeley: University of California Press.

Geertz, C. (1984). Distinguished lecture: Anti-relativism. *American Anthropologist, 86,* 263–278.

Geertz, C. (1965). The impact of the concept of culture on the concept of man. In J. R. Platt (Ed.), *New views of man.* Chicago: University of Chicago Press.

Gelb, I. J. (1952). *A study of writing.* London: Routledge.

Gell, A. (1988). Technology and magic. *Anthropology Today, 4*(2), 6–9.

Gellner, E. (1969). *Saints of the atlas.* Chicago: University of Chicago Press (The Nature of Human Society Series).

Gennep, A. Van (1960). *The rites of passage.* Chicago: University of Chicago Press.

Gibbons, A. (1992). Mitochondrial Eve: Wounded, but not yet dead. *Science, 257,* 873–875.

Gibbons, A. (1996). Did Neandertals lose an evolutionary "arms" race? *Science, 272,* 1586–1587.

Gibbons, A. (1997). A new face for human ancestors. *Science, 276,* 1331–1333.

Gibbons, A. (1997). Ideas on human origins evolve at anthropology gathering. *Science, 276,* 535–536.

Gibbons, A. (1998). Ancient island tools suggest *Homo erectus* was a seafarer. *Science, 279,* 1635–1637.

Gibbons, A., & Culotta, E. (1997). Miocene primates go ape. *Science, 276,* 355–356.

Gibbs, J. L., Jr. (1965). The Kpelle of Liberia. In J. L. Gibbs (Ed.), *Peoples of Africa* (pp. 197–240). New York: Holt, Rinehart & Winston.

Glausiusz, J. (1995). Micro gets macro. *Discover 16*(11), 40.

Gleason, H. A., Jr. (1966). *An introduction to descriptive linguistics* (Rev. ed.). New York: Holt, Rinehart & Winston.

Glob, P. (1969). *The bog people.* London: Faber & Faber.

Gluckman, M. (1955). *The judicial process among the Barotse of Northern Rhodesia.* New York: Free Press.

Goddard, V. (1993). Child labor in Naples. In W. A. Haviland & R. J. Gordon (Eds.), *Talking about people* (pp. 105–109). Mountain View, CA: Mayfield.

Godlier, M. (1971). Salt currency and the circulation of commodities among the Baruya of New Guinea. In G. Dalton (Ed.), *Studies in economic anthropology.* Washington, DC: American Anthropological Association (Anthropological Studies No. 7).

Golden, M., Birns, B., Bridger, W., & Moss, A. (1971). Social-class differentiation in cognitive development among black pre-school children. *Child Development, 42,* 37–45.

Goodall, J. (1986). *The chimpanzees of Gombe: Patterns of behavior.* Cambridge, MA: Belknap Press.

Goodall, J. (1990). *Through a window: My thirty years with the chimpanzees of Gombe.* Boston: Houghton Mifflin.

Goode, W. (1963). *World revolution and family patterns.* New York: Free Press.

Goodenough, W. (1956). Residence rules. *Southwestern Journal of Anthropology, 12,* 22–37.

Goodenough, W. (1961). Comment on cultural evolution. *Daedalus, 90,* 521–528.

Goodenough, W. (Ed.). (1964). *Explorations in cultural anthropology: Essays in honor of George Murdock.* New York: McGraw-Hill.

Goodenough, W. (1965). Rethinking status. And Role: Toward a general model of the cultural organization of social relationships. In M. Benton (Ed.), *The relevance of models for social anthropology.* New York: Praeger (ASA Monographs l).

Goodenough, W. (1970). *Description and comparison in cultural anthropology.* Chicago: Aldine.

Goodenough, W. (1990). Evolution of the human capacity for beliefs. *American Anthropologist, 92,* 597–612.

Goodman, M., Bartez, W. J., Hayasaka, K., Stanhope, M. J., Slightom, J., & Czelusniak, J. (1994). Molecular evidence on primate phylogeny from DNA sequences. *American Journal of Physical Anthropology, 94,* 3–24.

Goodman, M. E. (1967). *The individual and culture.* Homewood, IL: Dorsey Press.

Goody, J. (Ed.). (1972). *Developmental cycle in domestic groups.* New York: Cambridge University Press (Papers in Social Anthropology, No. 1).

Goody, J. (1976). *Production and reproduction: A comparative study of the domestic domain.* Cambridge: Cambridge University Press.

Goody, J. (1983). *The development of the family and marriage in Europe.* Cambridge, MA: Cambridge University Press.

Goody, J. (1969). *Comparative studies in kinship.* Stanford, CA: Stanford University Press.

Gordon, R. (1981, December). [Interview for Coast Telecourses, Inc.]. Los Angeles.

Gordon, R. (1990). The field researcher as a deviant: A Namibian case study. In P. Hugo (Ed.), *Truth be in the field: Social science research in southern Africa.* Pretoria: University of South Africa.

Gordon, R. J. (1992). *The Bushman myth: The making of a Namibian underclass.* Boulder, CO: Westview.

Gordon, R. J., & Megitt, M. J. (1985). *Law and order in the New Guinea highlands.* Hanover, NH: University Press of New England.

Gorer, G. (1943). Themes in Japanese culture. *Transactions of the New York Academy of Sciences,* series 11, 5.

Gorman, E. M. (1989). The AIDS epidemic in San Francisco: Epidemiological and anthropological perspectives. In A. Podolefsky & P. J. Brown (Eds.), *Applying anthropology, An introductory reader.* Mountain View, CA: Mayfield.

Gornick, V. & Moran, B. K. (Eds.). (1971). *Woman in sexist society.* New York: Basic Books.

Gould, S. J. (1996). *The mismeasure of man* (Rev. ed.). New York: W. W. Norton.

Gould, S. J. (1983). *Hen's teeth and horses' toes.* New York: Norton.

Gould, S. J. (1985). *The flamingo's smile: Reflections in natural history.* New York: Norton.

Gould, S. J. (1986). Of kiwi eggs and the Liberty Bell. *Natural History, 95,* 20–29.

Gould, S. J. (1989). *Wonderful life.* New York: Norton.

Gould, S. J. (1991). *Bully for brontosaurus.* New York: W. W. Norton.

Gould, S. J. (1996). *Full house: The spread of excellence from Plato to Darwin.* New York: Harmony Books.

Gould, S. J. (1997). *Questioning the millennium.* New York: Crown.

Graburn, N. H. (1969). *Eskimos without igloos: Social and economic development in Sugluk.* Boston: Little Brown.

Graburn, N. H. (1971). *Readings in kinship and social structure.* New York: Harper & Row.

Graham, S. B. (1979). Biology and human social behavior: A response to van den Berghe and Barash. *American Anthropologist, 81*(2), 357–360.

Graves, P. (1991). New models and metaphors for the Neanderthal debate. *Current Anthropology 32*(5), 513–543.

Green, E. C. (1987). The planning of health education strategies in Swaziland. In R. M. Wulff & S. J. Fiske (Eds.), *Anthropological praxis: Translating knowledge into action* (pp. 15–25). Boulder, CO: Westview.

Greenberg, J. H. (1968). *Anthropological linguistics: An introduction.* New York: Random House.

Greenfield, L. O. (1980). A late divergence hypothesis. *American Journal of Physical Anthropology, 52,* 351–366.

Greenfield, L. O. (1979). On the adaptive pattern of *Ramapithecus. American Journal of Physical Anthropology, 50,* 527–547.

Griffin, B. (1994). CHAGS7. *Anthropology Newsletter, 35*(1), 12–14.

Grine, F. E. (1993). Australopithecine taxonomy and phylogeny: Historical background and recent interpretation. In R. L. Ciochon & J. G. Fleagle (Eds.), *The human evolution source book,* Englewood Cliffs, NJ: Prentice Hall.

Grün, R., & Thorne, A. (1997). Dating the Ngandong humans, *Science, 276,* 1575.

Gulliver, P. (1968). Age differentiation. In *International Encyclopedia of the Social Sciences* (Vol. 1, pp. 157–162). New York: Macmillan.

Gutin, J. A. (1995). Do Kenya tools root birth of modern thought in Africa? *Science, 270,* 1118–1119.

Haeri, N. (1997). The reproduction of symbolic capital: Language, state and class in Egypt. *Current Anthropology, 38,* 795–816.

Hafkin, N., & Bay, E. (Eds.). (1976). *Women in Africa.* Stanford, CA: Stanford University Press.

Hall, E. T., & Hall, M. R. (1986). The sounds of silence. In E. Angeloni (Ed.), *Anthropology 86/87* (pp. 65–70). Guilford, CT: Dushkin.

Hall, K. R. L., & DeVore, I. (1965). Baboon social behavior. In I. DeVore (Ed.), *Primate behavior.* New York: Holt, Rinehart & Winston.

Hallowell, A. I. (1955). *Culture and experience.* Philadelphia: University of Pennsylvania Press.

Halverson, J. (1989). Review of *Altimira revisited and other essays on early art American Antiquity, 54,* 883.

Hamblin, D. J., & the Editors of Time-Life. (1973). *The first cities.* New York: Time-Life.

Hamburg, D. A., & McGown, E. R. (Eds.). (1979). *The great apes.* Menlo Park, CA: Cummings.

Hammond, D. (1972). *Associations.* Reading, MA: Addison-Wesley.

Hannah, J. L. (1988). *Dance, sex and gender.* Chicago: University of Chicago Press.

Harlow, H. F. (1962). Social deprivation in monkeys. *Scientific American, 206,* 1–l0.

Harpending, J. H. & Harpending, H. C. (1995). Ancient differences in population can mimic a recent African origin of modern humans. *Current Anthropology, 36,* 667–674.

Harris, M. (1968). *The rise of anthropological theory: A history of theories of culture.* New York: Crowell.

Harris, M. (1965). The cultural ecology of India's sacred cattle. *Current Anthropology, 7,* 51–66.

Harrison, G. G. (1975). Primary adult lactase deficiency: A problem in anthropological genetics. *American Anthropologist, 77,* 812–835.

Hart, C. W., Pilling, A. R., & Goodale, J. (1988). *Tiwi of North Australia* (3rd ed.). New York: Holt, Rinehart & Winston.

Hartwig, W. C., & Doneski, K. (1998). Evolution of the Hominid hand and toolmaking behavior. *American Journal of Physical Anthropology, 106,* 401–402.

Hatch, E. (1983). *Culture and morality: The relativity of values in anthropology.* New York: Columbia University Press.

Hatcher, E. P. (1985). *Art as culture, an introduction to the anthropology of art.* New York: University Press of America.

Haviland, W. (1970). Tikal, Guatemala and Mesoamerican urbanism. *World Archaeology, 2,* 186–198.

Haviland, W. A. (1972). A new look at Classic Maya social organization at Tikal. *Ceramica de Cultura Maya, 8,* 1–16.

Haviland, W. A. (1974). Farming, seafaring and bilocal residence on the coast of Maine. *Man in the Northeast, 6,* 31–44.

Haviland, W. A. (1975). The ancient Maya and the evolution of urban society. *University of Northern Colorado Museum of Anthropology, Miscellaneous Series,* 37.

Haviland, W. A. (1983). *Human evolution and prehistory* (2d ed.). New York: Holt, Rinehart & Winston.

Haviland, W. A. (1991). Star wars at Tikal, or did Caracol do what the glyphs say they did? Paper presented at the 90th Annual Meeting of the American Anthropological Association.

Haviland, W. A. (1997). The rise and fall of sexual inequality: Death and gender at Tikal, Guatemala. *Ancient Mesoamerica, 8,* 1–12.

Haviland, W. A. (1997). Cleansing young minds, or what should we be doing in introductory anthropology? In C. P. Kottak, J. J. White, R. H. Furlow, & P. C. Rice (Eds.), *The teaching of anthropology: problems, issues and decisions* (p. 35). Mountain View, CA: Mayfield.

Haviland, W. A., et al. (1985). *Excavations in small residential groups of Tikal: Groups 4F-1 and 4F-2.* Philadelphia: University Museum.

Haviland, W. A., & Moholy-Nagy, H. (1992). Distinguishing the high and mighty from the hoi polloi at Tikal, Guatemala. In A. F. Chase & D. Z. Chase (Eds.), *Mesoamerican elites: An archaeological assessment.* Norman: Oklahoma University Press.

Haviland, W. A., & Power, M. W. (1994). *The original Vermonters: Native inhabitants, past and present* (Revised and expanded ed.). Hanover, NH: University Press of New England.

Hawkes, K., O'Connell, J. F., & Blurton-Jones, N. G. (1997). Hadza women's time allocation, offspring, provisioning, and the evolution of long postmenopausal life spans. *Current Anthropology, 38,* 551–577.

Hawkins, G. S. (1965). *Stonehenge decoded.* New York: Doubleday.

Hays, H. R. (1965). *From ape to angel: An informal history of social anthropology.* New York: Knopf.

Heichel, G. (1976). Agricultural production and energy resources. *American Scientist,* 64.

Heilbroner, R. L. (1972). *The making of economic society* (4th ed.). Englewood Cliffs, NJ: Prentice-Hall.

Heilbroner, R. L., & Thurow, L. C. (1981). *The economic problem* (6th ed.). Englewood Cliffs, NJ: Prentice-Hall.

Helm, J. (1962). The ecological approach in anthropology. *American Journal of Sociology, 67,* 630–649.

Henry, J. (1965). *Culture against man.* New York: Vintage Books.

Henry, J. (1966). The metaphysic of youth, beauty, and romantic love. In S. Farber & R. Wilson (Eds.), *The challenge of women.* New York: Basic Books.

Henry, J. (1974). A theory for an anthropological analysis of American culture. In J. G. Jorgensen & M. Truzzi (Eds.), *Anthropology and American life.* Englewood Cliffs, NJ: Prentice-Hall.

Herskovits, M. J. (1952). *Economic anthropology: A study in comparative economics* (2nd ed.). New York: Knopf.

Herskovits, M. J. 1964. *Cultural dynamics.* New York: Knopf.

Hewes, G. W. (1973). Primate communication and the gestural origin of language. *Current Anthropology, 14,* 5–24.

Hickerson, N. P. (1980). *Linguistic anthropology.* New York: Holt, Rinehart and Winston.

Hodgen, M. (1964). *Early anthropology in the sixteenth and seventeenth centuries.* Philadelphia: University of Pennsylvania Press.

Hoebel, E. A. (1960). *The Cheyennes: Indians of the Great Plains.* New York: Holt, Rinehart & Winston.

Hoebel, E. A. (1972). *Anthropology: The study of man* (4th ed.). New York: McGraw-Hill.

Hoebel, E. A. (1954). *The law of primitive man: A study in comparative legal dynamics.* Cambridge, MA: Harvard University Press.

Hogbin, I. (1964). *A Guadalcanal society.* New York: Holt, Rinehart & Winston.

Holden, C. (1983). Simon and Kahn versus Global 2000. *Science, 221,* 342.

Holden, C. (1996). Missing link for miocene apes. *Science, 271,* 151.

Holden, C. (1998). No last word on language origins. *Science, 282,* 1455–1458.

Hole, F. (1966). Investigating the origins of Mesopotamian civilization. *Science, 153,* 605–611.

Hole, F. & Heizer, R. F. (1969). *An introduction to prehistoric archeology.* New York: Holt, Rinehart & Winston.

Holloway, R. L. 1980. The O. H. 7 (Olduvai Gorge, Tanzania) hominid partial brain endocast revisited. *American Journal of Physical Anthropology, 53,* 267–274.

Holloway, R. L. (1981). The Indonesian *Homo erectus* brain endocast revisited. *American Journal of Physical Anthropology, 55,* 503–521.

Holloway, R. L. (1981). Volumetric and asymmetry determinations on recent hominid endocasts: Spy I and II, Djebel Jhroud 1, and the Salb *Homo erectus* specimens, with some notes on Neanderthal brain size. *American Journal of Physical Anthropology, 55,* 385–393.

Hostetler, J., & Huntington, G. (1971). *Children in Amish society.* New York: Holt, Rinehart & Winston.

Howell, F. C. (1970). *Early man.* New York: Time-Life.

Hsiaotung, F. (1939). *Peasant life in China.* London: Kegan, Paul, Trench, & Truber.

Hsu, F. L. (1961). *Psychological anthropology: Approaches to culture and personality.* Homewood, IL: Dorsey Press.

Hsu, F. L. K. (1977). Role, affect, and anthropology. *American Anthropologist, 79,* 805–808.

Hsu, F. L. K. (1979). The cultural problems of the cultural anthropologist. *American Anthropologist, 81,* 517–532.

Hsu, F. L. (1997). Role, affect, and anthropology. *American Anthropologist, 79,* 805–808.

Hubert, H., & Mauss, M. (1964). *Sacrifice.* Chicago: University of Chicago Press.

Hunt, R. C. (Ed.). (1967). *Personalities and cultures: Readings in psychological anthropology.* Garden City, NY: Natural History Press.

Hymes, D. (1964). *Language in culture and Society: A reader in linguistics and anthropology.* New York: Harper & Row.

Hymes, D. (Ed.). (1972). *Reinventing anthropology.* New York: Pantheon.

Ingmanson, E. J. (1998). Comment. *Current Anthropology, 39,* 409–410.

Inkeles, A., Hanfmann, E., & Beier, H. (1961). Modal personality and adjustment to the Soviet socio-political system. In B. Kaplan (Ed.), *Studying personality cross-culturally.* New York: Harper & Row.

Inkeles, Alex, & Levinson, D. J. (1954). National character: The study of modal personality and socio-cultural systems. In G. Lindzey (Ed.), *Handbook of social psychology.* Reading, MA: Addison-Wesley.

Ireland, E. (1991). Neither warriors nor victims, the wauja peacefully organize to defend their land. *Cultural Survival Quarterly, 15*(1), 54–59.

It's the law: Child labor protection. (1997, November/December). *Peace and Justice News,* 11.

Jacobs, S. E. (1994). Native American Two-spirits. *Anthropology Newsletter, 35*(8), 7.

Jacoby, R., & Glauberman, N. (Eds.). (1995). *The bell curve.* New York: Random House.

Jennings, J. D. (1974). *Prehistory of North America* (2d ed.). New York: McGraw-Hill.

Jennings, F. (1976). *The invasion of America.* New York: Norton.

Johanson, D. C., & Edey, M. (1981). *Lucy, the beginnings of humankind.* New York: Simon & Schuster.

Johanson, D., & Shreeve, J. (1989). *Lucy's child: the discovery of a human ancestor.* New York: Avon.

Johanson, D. C., & White, T. D. (1979). A systematic assessment of early African hominids. *Science, 203,* 321–330.

John, V. (1971). Whose is the failure? In C. L. Brace, G. R. Gamble, & J. T. Bond (Eds.), *Race and intelligence.* Washington, DC: American Anthropological Association (Anthropological Studies No. 8).

Johnson, A. (1989). Horticulturalists: Economic behavior in tribes. In S. Plattner (Ed.), *Economic anthropology* (pp. 49–77). Stanford, CA: Stanford University Press.

Johnson, A. W., & Earle, T. (1987). *The evolution of human societies, from foraging group to agrarian state*. Stanford, CA: Stanford University Press.

Johnson, D. (1996). Polygamists emerge from secrecy, seeking not just peace but respect. In W. A. Haviland & R. J. Gordon (Eds.), *Talking about people* (2nd ed., pp. 129–131). Mountain View, CA: Mayfield.

Jolly, A. (1985a). The evolution of primate behavior. *American Scientist 73*(3), 230–239.

Jolly, A. (1985b). *The evolution of primate behavior* (2nd ed.). New York: Macmillan.

Jolly, A. (1985). Thinking like a Vervet. *Science, 251,* 574.

Jolly, C. J. (1970). The seed eaters: A new model of hominid differentiation based on a baboon analogy. *Man, 5,* 5–26.

Jolly, C. J., & Plog, F. (1986). *Physical anthropology and archaeology* (4th ed.). New York: Knopf.

Jopling, C. F. (1971). *Art and aesthetics in primitive societies: A critical anthology*. New York: Dutton.

Jorgensen, J. (1972). *The sun dance religion*. Chicago: University of Chicago Press.

Joukowsky, M. A. (1980). *A complete field manual of archeology: Tools and techniques of field work for archaeologists*. Englewood Cliffs, NJ: Prentice-Hall.

Joyce, C. (1991). *Witnesses from the grave: The stories bones tell*. Boston: Little, Brown.

Kahn, H., & Wiener, A. J. (1967). *The year 2000*. New York: Macmillan.

Kaiser, J. (1994). A new theory of insect wing origins takes off. *Science, 266,* 363.

Kalwet, H. (1988). *Dreamtime and inner space: The world of the shaman*. New York: Random House.

Kaplan, D. (1972). *Culture theory*. Englewood Cliffs, NJ: Prentice-Hall (Foundations of Modern Anthropology).

Kardiner, A. (1939). *The individual and his society: The psycho-dynamics of primitive social organization*. New York: Columbia University Press.

Kardiner, A., & Preble, E. (1961). *They studied men*. New York: Mentor.

Kay, R. F., Ross, C., & Williams, B. A. (1997). Anthropoid origins. *Science, 275,* 797–804.

Kay, R. F., Theweissen, J. G. M., & Yoder, A. D. (1992). Cranial anatomy of *Ignacius graybullianus* and the affinities of the plesiadapiformes. *American Journal of Physical Anthropology, 89*(4), 477–498.

Kay, R. F. (1981). The nut-crackers—A new theory of the adaptations of the Ramapithecinae. *American Journal of Physical Anthropology, 55,* 141–151.

Kay, R. F., Fleagle, J. F., & Simons, E. L. (1981). A revision of the Oligocene apes of the Fayum Province, Egypt. *American Journal of Physical Anthropology, 55,* 293–322.

Keesing, R. M. (1975). *Kin groups and social structure*. New York: Holt, Rinehart & Winston.

Kendall, L. (1990, October). In the company of witches. *Natural History,* 92–95.

Kenyon, K. (1957). *Digging up Jericho*. London: Ben.

Kerri, J. N. (1976). Studying voluntary associations as adaptive mechanisms: A review of

anthropological perspectives. *Current Anthropology, 17*(1).

Kessler, E. (1975). *Women*. New York: Holt, Rinehart & Winston.

Kleinman, A. (1982). The failure of western medicine. In D. Hunter & P. Whitten (Eds.), *Anthropology: Contemporary perspectives*. Boston: Little, Brown.

Kluckhohn, C. (1994). Navajo witchcraft. *Papers of the Peabody Museum of American Archaeology and Ethnology, 22*(2).

Kluckhohn, C. (1970). *Mirror for Man*. Greenwich, CT: Fawcett.

Kluckhohn, C. (1994). Navajo witchcraft. *Papers of the Peabody Museum of American Archaeology and Ethnology, 22*(2).

Knauft, B. (1991). Violence and sociality in human evolution. *Current Anthropology, 32,* 391–409.

Koch, G. (1997). Songs, land rights and archives in Australia. *Cultural Survival Quarterly, 20*(4).

G. Kohler (1996), Global apartheid. Reprinted in W. A. Haviland & R. J. Gordon (Eds.), *Talking about people: Readings in contemporary cultural anthropology* (2nd ed., pp. 262–268). Mountain View, CA: Mayfield.

Koufos, G. (1993). Mandible of Ouranopithecus macedoniensis (hominidae: primates) from a new late Miocene locality in Macedonia (Greece). *American Journal of Physical Anthropology, 91,* 225–234.

Krader, L. (1968). *Formation of the state*. Englewood Cliffs, NJ: Prentice-Hall (Foundation of Modern Anthropology).

Kramer, P. A. (1998). The costs of human locomotion: maternal investment in child transport. *American Journal of Physical Anthropology, 107,* 71–85.

Kroeber, A. L. (1939). Cultural and natural areas of native North America. *American Archaeology and Ethnology* (Vol. 38). Berkeley, CA: University of California Press.

Kroeber, A. (1958). Totem and taboo: An ethnologic psycho-analysis. In W. Lessa & E. Z. Vogt (Eds.), *Reader in comparative religion: An anthropological approach*. New York: Harper & Row.

Kroeber, A. L. (1963). *Anthropology: Cultural processes and patterns*. New York: Harcourt.

Kroeber, A. L., & Kluckhohn, C. (1952). *Culture: A critical review of concepts and definitions*. Cambridge, MA: Harvard University Press (Papers of the Peabody Museum of American Archaeology and Ethnology, 47).

Kuhn, T. (1968). *The structure of scientific revolutions*. Chicago: University of Chicago Press (International Encyclopedia of Unified Science, 2[27].

Kummer, H. (1971). *Primate societies: Group techniques of ecological adaptation*. Chicago: Aldine.

Kuper, H. (1965). The Swazi of Swaziland. In J. L. Gibbs (Ed.), *Peoples of Africa* (pp. 479–511). New York: Holt, Rinehart & Winston.

Kurath, G. P. (1960). Panorama of dance ethnology. *Current Anthropology, 1,* 233–254.

Kushner, G. (1969). *Anthropology of complex societies*. Stanford, CA: Stanford University Press.

La Barre, W. (1945). Some observations of character structure in the Orient: The Japanese. *Psychiatry, 8.*

Lancaster, J. B. (1975). *Primate behavior and*

the emergence of human culture. New York: Holt, Rinehart & Winston.

Landes, R. (1982). Comment. *Current Anthropology, 23,* 401.

Lanning, E. P. (1967). *Peru before the Incas*. Englewood Cliffs, NJ: Prentice-Hall.

Lanternari, V. (1963). *The religions of the oppressed*. New York: Mentor.

Lasker, G. W., & Tyzzer, R. (1982). *Physical anthropology* (3d ed.) New York: Holt, Rinehart & Winston.

Laughlin, W. S., & Osborne, R. H. (Eds.). (1967). *Human variation and origins*. San Francisco: Freeman.

Laurel, K. (1990). In the company of witches" *Natural History,* 92.

Layton, R. (1991). *The anthropology of art* (2nd ed.). Cambridge: Cambridge University Press.

Leach, E. (1961). *Rethinking anthropology*. London: Athione Press.

Leach, E. (1962a). The determinants of differential cross-cousin marriage. *Man, 62,* 238.

Leach, E. (1962b). On certain unconsidered aspects of double descent systems. *Man, 214,* 13–34.

Leach, E. (1965). *Political systems of highland Burma*. Boston: Beacon Press.

Leach, E. (1982). *Social anthropology*. Glasgow: Fontana Paperbacks.

Leacock, E. (1981a). *Myths of male dominance: Collected articles on women cross culturally*. New York: Monthly Review Press.

Leacock, E. (1981b). Women's status in egalitarian society: Implications for social evolution. In *Myths of male dominance: Collected articles on women cross culturally*. New York: Monthly Review Press.

Leakey, L. S. B. (1965). *Olduvai Gorge, 1951–1961* (Vol. 1). London: Cambridge University Press.

Leakey, L. S. B. (1967). Development of aggression as a factor in early man and prehuman evolution. In C. Clements & D. Lundsley (Eds.), *Aggression and Defense*. Los Angeles: University of California Press.

Leakey, M. D. (1971). *Olduvai Gorge: Excavations in Beds I and II. 1960–1963*. London and New York: Cambridge University Press.

Leap, W. L. (1987). Tribally controlled culture change: The Northern Ute language revival project. In R. M. Wulff & S. J. Fiscke (Eds.), *Anthropological praxis: Translating knowledge into action* (pp. 197–211). Boulder, CO: Westview.

Leavitt, G. C. (1990). Sociobiological explanations of incest avoidance: A critical review of evidential claims. *American Anthropologist, 92,* 971–993.

Le Clair, E., & Schneider, H. K. (Eds.). (1968). *Economic anthropology: Readings in theory and analysis*. New York: Holt, Rinehart & Winston.

Lee, R. (1993). *The Dobe Ju/boansi*. Ft. Worth, TX: Harcourt Brace.

Lee, R. B., & DeVore, I. (Eds.). (1968). *Man the hunter*. Chicago: Aldine.

Leeds, A., & Vayda, A. P. (Eds.). (1965). *Man, culture and animals: The role of animals in human ecological adjustments*. Washington, DC: American Association for the Advancement of Science.

Lees, R. (1953). The basis of glottochronology. *Language, 29,* 113–127.

LeGros Clark, W. E. (1966). *History of the primates* (5th ed.). Chicago: University of Chicago Press.

Legros, D. (1997). Comment. *Current Anthropology, 38*, 617.

Lehmann, A. C., & Myers, J. E. (Eds.). (1993). *Magic, witchcraft and religion: An anthropological study of the supernatural* (3rd ed.). Mountain View, CA: Mayfield.

Lehmann, W. P. (1973). *Historical linguistics, An introduction* (2d ed.). New York: Holt, Rinehart & Winston.

Leigh, S. R., & Park, P. B. (1998). Evolution of human growth prolongation. *American Journal of Physical Anthropology, 107,* 331–350.

Leinhardt, G. (1964). *Social anthropology.* London: Oxford University Press.

Leinhardt, G. (1971). Religion. In H. Shapiro (Ed.), *Man, culture and society* (2nd ed.). London: Oxford University Press.

LeMay, M. (1975). The language capability of Neanderthal man. *American Journal of Physical Anthropology, 43*(1), 9–14.

Lenski, G. (1966). *Power and privilege: A theory of social stratification.* New York: McGraw-Hill.

Leonard, W. R., & Hegman, M. (1987). Evolution of P₃ morphology in *Australopithecus afarensis. American Journal of Physical Anthropology, 73,* 41–63.

Lerner, R. N. (1987). Preserving plants for Pomos. In R. M. Wulff & S. J. Fiske (Eds.), *Anthropological praxis: Translating knowledge into action* (pp. 212–222). Boulder, CO: Westview.

Leroi-Gourhan, A. (1968). The evolution of Paleolithic art. *Scientific American, 218,* 58ff.

Lett, J. (1987). *The human enterprise: A critical introduction to anthropological theory.* Boulder, CO: Westview.

Levanthes, L. E. (1987). The mysteries of the bog. *National Geographic, 171,* 397–420.

Levine, N. E., & Silk, J. B. (1997). Why polyandry fails. *Current Anthropology, 38,* 375–398.

Levine, R. (1973). *Culture, behavior and personality.* Chicago: Aldine.

Levine, R. P. (1968). *Genetics.* New York: Holt, Rinehart & Winston.

Lewin, R. (1983). Is the orangutan a living fossil? *Science, 222,* 1223.

Lewin, R. (1985). Tooth enamel tells a complex story. *Science, 228,* 707.

Lewin, R. (1986). New fossil upsets human family" *Science, 233,* 720–721.

Lewin, R. (1987a). Debate over emergence of human tooth pattern. *Science, 235,* 749.

Lewin, R. (1987b). The earliest "humans" were more like apes. *Science, 236,* 1062–1063.

Lewin, R. (1987c). Four legs bad, two legs good. *Science, 235,* 969.

Lewin, R. (1987d). Why is ape tool use so confusing? *Science, 236,* 776–777.

Lewin, R. (1988). Molecular clocks turn a quarter century. *Science, 235,* 969–971.

Lewin, R. (1993). Paleolithic paint job. *Discover, 14*(7), 64–70.

Lewis, I. M. (1976). *Social anthropology in perspective.* Harmondsworth, England: Penguin.

Lewis, I. M. (1965). Problems in the comparative study of unilineal descent. In M. Banton (Ed.), *The relevance of models for social organization* (A.S.A. Monograph No. 1). London: Tavistock.

Lewis-Williams, J. D. (1990). *Discovering southern African rock art.* Cape Town and Johannesburg: David Philip.

Lewis-Williams, J. D., & Dowson, T. A. (1988). Signs of all times: Entoptic phenomena in Upper Paleolithic art. *Current Anthropology, 29,* 201–245.

Lewis-Williams, J. D., & Dowson, T. A. (1993). On vision and power in the Neolithic: Evidence from the decorated monuments. *Current Anthropology, 34,* 55–65.

Lewis-Williams, J. D., Dowson, T. A., & Deacon, J. (1993). Rock art and changing perceptions of Southern Africa's past: Ezeljagdspoort reviewed. *Antiquity, 67,* 273–291.

Lewontin, R. C., Rose, S., & Kamin, L. J. (1984). *Not in our genes.* New York: Pantheon.

Linton, R. (1964). *The study of man: An introduction.* New York: Appleton. (Original work published 1936)

Little, K. (1964). The role of voluntary associations in West African urbanization. In P. van den Berghe (Ed.), *Africa: social problems of change and conflict.* San Francisco: Chandler.

Livingstone, F. B. (1973). The distribution of abnormal hemoglobin genes and their significance for human evolution. In C. Loring Brace & J. Metress (Eds.), *Man in evolutionary perspective.* New York: Wiley.

Louckey, J., & Carlsen, R. (1991). Massacre in Santiago Atitlán. *Cultural Survival Quarterly, 15*(3), 70.

Lorenzo, C., Carretero, J. M., Arsuaga, J. L., Gracia, A., & Martinez, I. (1998). Intrapopulational body size variation and cranial capacity variation in middle Pleistocene humans: The Sima de los Huesos sample (Sierra de Atapuerca, Spain). *American Journal of Physical Anthropology, 106,* 19–33.

Lounsbury, F. (1964). The structural analysis of kinship semantics. In H. G. Lunt (Ed.), *Proceedings of the Ninth International Congress of Linguists.* The Hague: Mouton.

Lovejoy, C. O. (1981). Origin of man. *Science, 211*(4480), 341–350.

Lowenstein, J. M. (1992, December). Genetic Surprises. *Discover 13,* 82–88.

Lowie, R. H. (1948). *Social organization.* New York: Holt, Rinehart & Winston.

Lowie, R. H. (1956). *Crow Indians.* New York: Holt, Rinehart & Winston. (Original work published 1935)

Lowie, R. H. (1966). *Culture and ethnology.* New York: Basic Books.

Lustig-Arecco, V. (1975). *Technology strategies for survival.* New York: Holt, Rinehart & Winston.

MacCormack, C. P. (1977). Biological events and cultural control. *Signs, 3,* 93–100.

MacNeish, R. S. (1992). *The origins of agriculture and settled life.* Norman, OK: University of Oklahoma Press.

MacNiel, R. (1982). *The right place at the right time.* Boston: Little, Brown.

Magnarella, P. J. (1974). *Tradition and change in a Turkish town.* New York: Wiley.

Mair, L. (1969). *Witchcraft.* New York: McGraw-Hill.

Mair, L. (1971). *Marriage.* Baltimore: Penguin.

Malefijt, A. de W. (1969). *Religion and culture: An introduction to anthropology of religion.* London: Macmillan.

Malefijt, A. de W. (1974). *Images of man.* New York: Knopf.

Malinowski, B. (1922). *Argonauts of the western Pacific.* New York: Dutton.

Malinowski, B. (1945). *The dynamics of culture change.* New Haven, CT: Yale University Press.

Malinowski, B. (1951). *Crime and custom in savage society.* London: Routledge.

Malinowski, B. (1954). *Magic, science and religion.* Garden City, NY: Doubleday/Anchor Books.

Marano, L. (1982). Windigo psychosis: The anatomy of an emic-etic confusion. *Current Anthropology, 23,* 385–412.

Marcus, J., & Flannery, K. V. (1996). *Zapotec civilization: How urban society evolved in Mexico's Oaxaca Valley.* New York: Thames & Hudson.

Marks, J. (1995). *Human biodiversity: Genes, race and history.* Hawthorne, NY: Aldine.

Marsella, J. (1982). Pulling it together: Discussion and comments. In S. Pastner & W. A. Haviland (Eds.), *Confronting the creationists.* Northeastern Anthropological Association, Occasional Proceedings, No. 1, 77–80.

Marshack, A. (1972). *The roots of civilization: A study in prehistoric cognition; The origins of art, symbol and notation.* New York: McGraw-Hill.

Marshack, A. (1976). Some implications of the paleolithic symbolic evidence for the origin of language. *Current Anthropology, 17*(2), 274–282.

Marshack, A. (1989). Evolution of the human capacity: The symbolic evidence. *Yearbook of physical anthropology* (Vol. 32, pp. 1–34). New York: Alan R. Liss.

Marshall, L. (1961). Sharing, talking and giving: Relief of social tensions among !Kung bushmen. *Africa, 31,* 231–249.

Marshall, M. (1990). Two tales from the Trukese taproom. In P. R. DeVita (Ed.), *The humbled anthropologist* (pp. 12–17). Belmont, CA: Wadsworth.

Martin, E. (1994). *Flexible bodies: Tracking immunity in American culture—from the days of polio to the age of AIDS.* Boston: Beacon Press.

Mason, J. A. (1957). *The ancient civilizations of Peru.* Baltimore: Penguin.

Matson, F. R. (Ed.). (1965). *Ceramics and man.* New York: Viking Fund Publications in Anthropology, No. 41.

Maybury-Lewis, D. (1960). Parallel descent and the Apinaye anomaly. *Southwestern Journal of Anthropology, 16,* 191–216.

Maybury-Lewis, D. (1984). The prospects for plural societies. 1982 Proceedings of the American Ethnological Society.

Maybury-Lewis, D. (1993, Fall). A new world dilemma: The Indian question in the Americas. *Symbols,* 17–23.

Maybury-Lewis, D. H. P. (1993). A special sort of pleading. In W. A. Haviland & R. J. Gordon (Eds.), *Talking about people* (pp. 16–24). Mountain View, CA: Mayfield.

McCorriston, J., & Hole, F. (1991). The ecology of seasonal stress and the origins of agriculture in the Near East. *American Anthropologist, 93,* 46–69.

McFee, M. (1972). *Modern Blackfeet: Montanans on a reservation.* New York: Holt, Rinehart & Winston.

McHale, J. (1969). *The future of the future.* New York: Braziller.

McHenry, H. (1975). Fossils and the mosaic nature of human evolution. *Science, 190,* 524–431.

McHenry, H. M. (1992). Body size and proportions in early hominids. *American Journal of Physical Anthropology, 87,* 407–431.

Mead, M. (1928). *Coming of age in Samoa.* New York: Morrow.

Mead, M. (1970). *Culture and commitment.* Garden City, NY. Natural History Press. Universe Books.

Mead, M. (1963). *Sex and temperament in three primitive societies* (3d ed). New York: Morrow.

Meadows, D. H., Meadows, D. L., Randers J., & Behrens III, W. W. (1974). *The limits to growth.* New York: Universe Books.

Melaart, J. (1967). *Catal Hüyük: A Neolithic town in Anatolia.* London: Thames & Hudson.

Mellars, P. (1989). Major issues in the emergence of modern humans. *Current Anthropology, 30,* 349–385.

Meltzer, D., Fowler, D., & Sabloff, J. (Eds.). (1986). *American archaeology: Past & future.* Washington, DC: Smithsonian Institution Press.

Merrell, D. J. (1962). *Evolution and genetics: The modern theory of genetics.* New York: Holt, Rinehart and Winston.

Merriam, A. P. (1964). *The anthropology of music.* Chicago: Northwestern University Press.

Mesghinua, H. M. (1966). Salt mining in Enderta. *Journal of Ethiopian Studies, 4*(2).

Michaels, J. W. (1973). *Dating methods in archaeology.* New York: Seminar Press.

Middleton, J. (Ed.). (1970). *From child to adult: Studies in the anthropology of education.* Garden City, NY: Natural History Press (American Museum Source Books in Anthropology).

Miles, H. L. W. (1993). Language and the orangutan: The old "person" of the forest. In P. Cavalieri & P. Singer (Eds.), *The great ape project* (pp. 42–57). New York: St. Martin's Press.

Millon, R. (1973). *Urbanization of Teotihuacán, Mexico: Vol. 1, Part 1. The Teotihuacán Map.* Austin: University of Texas Press.

Mintz, S. (1996). A taste of history. In W. A. Haviland & R. J. Gordon (Eds.), *Talking about people* (2nd ed., pp. 79–82). Mountain View, CA: Mayfield.

Minugh-Purvis, N. (1992). The inhabitants of Ice Age Europe. *Expedition, 34*(3), 23–36.

Mitchell, W. E. (1973, December). A new weapon stirs up old ghosts. *Natural History Magazine,* 77–84.

Mitchell, W. E. (1978). *Mishpokhe: A study of New York City Jewish family clubs.* The Hague: Mouton.

Molnar, S. (1992). *Human variation: Races, types and ethnic groups* (3rd ed.). Englewood Cliffs, NJ: Prentice Hall.

Montagu, A. (1964a). *The concept of race.* London: Macmillan.

Montagu, A. (1964b). *Man's most dangerous myth: The fallacy of race* (4th ed.) New York: World Publishing.

Montagu, A. (1975). *Race and IQ.* New York: Oxford University Press.

Moore, J. (1998). Comment. *Current Anthropology 39,* 412.

Morgan, L. H. (1877). *Ancient society.* New York: World Publishing.

Moscati, S. (1962). *The face of the ancient orient.* New York: Doubleday.

Mullings, L. (1989). Gender and the application of anthropological knowledge to public policy in the United States. In S. Morgan (Ed.), *Gender and anthropology* (pp. 360–381). Washington: American Anthropological Association.

Murdock, G. (1960). Cognatic forms of social organization. In G. P. Murdock (Ed.), *Social structure in Southeast Asia* (pp. 1–14). Chicago: Quadrangle Books.

Murdock, G. P. (1965). *Social structure.* New York: Free Press.

Murdock, G. P. (1971). How culture changes. In H. L. Shapiro (Ed.), *Man, culture and society* (2nd ed.) New York: Oxford University Press.

Murphy, R. (1971). *The dialectics of social life: Alarms and excursions in anthropological theory.* New York: Basic Books.

Murphy, Robert, & Kasdan, L. (1959). The structure of parallel cousin marriage. *American Anthropologist, 61,* 17–29.

Murray, G. F. (1989). The domestication of wood in Haiti: A case study in applied evolution. In A. Podolefsky & P. J. Brown (Eds.), *Applying anthropology, an introductory reader.* Mountain View, CA: Mayfield.

Myrdal, G. (1974). Challenge to affluence: The emergence of an "under-class. In J. G. Jorgensen & M. Truzzi (Eds.), *Anthropology and American life.* Englewood Cliffs, NJ: Prentice-Hall.

Nader, L. (Ed.). (1965). The ethnography of law. *American Anthropologist,* Part II, 67(6).

Nader, L. (Ed.). (1969). *Law in culture and society.* Chicago: Aldine.

Nader, L. (Ed.). (1980). *No access to law: Alternatives to the American judicial system.* New York: Academic Press.

Nader, L. (1981, December). [Interview for Coast Telecourses, Inc.]. Los Angeles.

Nader, L. (1997). Controlling processes: Tracing the dynamic components of power. *Current Anthropology, 38,* 714–715.

Nance, C. R. (1997). Review of Haviland's *Cultural anthropology* (p. 2). [Manuscript in author's possession].

Nanda, S. (1992). Arranging a marriage in India. In P. R. De Vita (Ed.), *The naked anthropologist* (pp. 139–143). Belmont, CA: Wadsworth.

Naroll, R. (1973). Holocultural theory tests. In R. Naroll & F. Naroll (Eds.), *Main currents in cultural anthropology.* New York: Appleton.

Nash, M. (1966). *Primitive and peasant economic systems.* San Francisco: Chandler.

Natadecha-Sponsal, P. (1993). The young, the rich and the famous: Individualism as an American cultural value. In P. R. DeVita & J. D. Armstrong (Eds.), *Distant Mirrors: America as a foreign culture* (pp. 46–53). Bellmont, CA: Wadsworth.

Needham, R., (Ed.). (1971). *Rethinking kinship and marriage.* London: Tavistock.

Needham, R. (1972). *Belief, language and experience.* Chicago: University of Chicago Press.

Neer, R. M. (1975). The evolutionary significance of Vitamin D, skin pigment and ultraviolet light. *American Journal of Physical Anthropology, 43,* 409–416.

Nesbitt, L. M. (1935). *Hell-hole of creation.* New York: Knopf.

Netting, R. M., Wilk, R. R., & Arnould, E. J. (Eds.). (1984). *Households: Comparative and historical studies of the domestic group.* Berkeley, CA: University of California Press.

Nettl, B. (1956). *Music in primitive culture.* Cambridge, MA: Harvard University Press.

Newman, P. L. (1965). *Knowing the Gururumba.* New York: Holt, Rinehart & Winston.

Nietschmann, B. (1987). The third world war. *Cultural Survival Quarterly, 11*(3), 1–16.

Norbeck, E. (1974). *Religion in human life: Anthropological views.* New York: Holt, Rinehart & Winston.

Norbeck, E., Price-Williams, D., & McCord, W. (Eds.). (1968). *The study of personality: An interdisciplinary appraisal.* New York: Holt, Rinehart & Winston.

Normile, D. (1998). Habitat seen as playing larger role in shaping behavior. *Science, 279,* 1454.

Nunney, L. (1998). Are we selfish, are we nice, or are we nice because we are selfish? *Science, 281,* 1619.

Nye, E. I., & Berardo, F. M. (1975). *The family: Its structure and interaction.* New York: Macmillan.

O'Barr, W. M. & Conley, J. M. (1993). When a juror watches a lawyer. In W. A. Haviland & R. J. Gordon (Eds.), *Talking about people* (2nd ed., pp. 44–47). Mountain View, CA: Mayfield.

O'Mahoney, K. (1970). The salt trade. *Journal of Ethiopian Studies, 8*(2).

Oakley, K. P. (1964). *Man the tool-maker.* Chicago: University of Chicago Press.

Oboler, R. S. (1980). Is the female husband a man? Woman/woman marriage among the Nandi of Kenya. *Ethnology, 19,* 69–88.

Offiong, D. (1985). Witchcraft among the Ibibio of Nigeria. In A. C. Lehmann & J. E. Myers (Eds.), *Magic, witchcraft and religion* (pp. 152–165). Palo Alto, CA: Mayfield.

Okonjo, K. (1976). The dual-sex political system in operation: Igbo women and community politics in midwestern Nigeria. In N. Hafkin & E. Bay (Eds.), *Women in Africa* (pp. 45–58). Stanford, CA: Stanford University Press.

Oliwenstein, L. (1995). New footsteps into walking debate. *Science, 269,* 476.

Olszewski, D. I. (1991). Comment. *Current Anthropology, 32,* 43.

Ortiz, A. (1969). *The Tewa world.* Chicago: The University of Chicago Press.

Oswalt, W. H. (1970). *Understanding our culture.* New York: Holt, Rinehart & Winston.

Oswalt, W. H. (1972). *Habitat and technology.* New York: Holt, Rinehart & Winston.

Oswalt, W. H. (1972). *Other peoples other customs: World ethnography and its history.* New York: Holt, Rinehart & Winston.

Otten, C. M. (1971). *Anthropology and art: Readings in cross-cultural aesthetics.* Garden City, NY: Natural History Press.

Ottenberg, P. (1965). The Afikpo Ibo of eastern Nigeria. In J. L. Gibbs (Ed.), *Peoples of Africa.* New York: Holt, Rinehart & Winston.

Otterbein, K. F. (1971). *The evolution of war.* New Haven, CT: HRAF Press.

Parades, J. A., & Purdum, E. J. (1990). Bye bye Ted.... *Anthropology Today, 6*(2), 9–11.

Parish, A. R. (1998). Comment. *Current Anthropology, 39,* 413–414.

Parker, R. G. (1991). *Bodies, pleasures, and passions: Sexual culture in contemporary Brazil*. Boston: Beacon Press.

Parker, S., & Parker, H. (1979). The myth of male superiority: Rise and demise. *American Anthropologist, 81*(2), 289–309.

Partridge, W. (Ed.). (1984). *Training manual in development anthropology*. Washington, DC: American Anthropological Association.

Pastner, S., and Haviland, W. A. (Eds.). (1982). Confronting the creationists. *Northeastern Anthropological Association Occasional Proceedings*, I.

Patterson, F., & Linden, E. (1981). *The education of Koko*. New York: Holt, Rinehart & Winston.

Patterson, T. C. (1981). *Archeology: The evolution of ancient societies*. Englewood Cliffs, NJ: Prentice-Hall.

Peacock, J. L. (1986). *The anthropological lens: Harsh light, soft focus*. New York: Cambridge University Press.

Pelliam, A. de, & Burton, F. D. (1976). More on predatory behavior in nonhuman primates. *Current Anthropology, 17*(3), 512–513.

Pelto, P. J. (1973). *The snowmobile revolution: Technology and social change in the Arctic*. Menlo Park, CA: Cummings.

Penniman, T. K. (1965). *A hundred years of anthropology*. London: Duckworth.

Peters, C. R. (1979). Toward an ecological model of African Plio-Pleistocene hominid adaptations. *American Anthropologist, 81*(2), 261–278.

Peterson, F. L. (1962). *Ancient Mexico, An introduction to the pre-Hispanic cultures*. New York: Capricorn Books.

Pfeiffer, J. E. (1977). *The emergence of society*. New York: McGraw-Hill.

Pfeiffer, J. E. (1978). *The emergence of man*. New York: Harper & Row.

Pfeiffer, J. E. (1985). *The creative explosion*. Ithaca, NY: Cornell University Press.

Piddocke, S. (1965). The potlatch system of the southern Kwakiutl: A new perspective. *Southwestern Journal of Anthropology, 21*, 244–264.

Piggott, S. (1965). Ancient Europe. Chicago: Aldine.

Pilbeam D. (1986). *Human origins*. David Skamp Distinguished Lecture in Anthropology, Indiana University.

Pilbeam, D. (1987). Rethinking human origins. In *Primate evolution and human origins*. Hawthorne, NY: Aldine de Gruytar.

Pilbeam, D., & Gould, S. J. (1974). Size and scaling in human evolution. *Science, 186*, 892–901.

Pimentel, D. (1991). Response. *Science, 252*: 358.

Pimentel, D., Hurd, L. E., Bellotti, A. C., Forster, M. J., Oka, I. N., Sholes, O. D., & Whitman, R. J. (1973). Food Production and the Energy Crisis. *Science, 182*.

Piperno, D. R., & Fritz, G. J. (1994). On the emergence of agriculture in the new world. *Current Anthropology, 35*, 637–643.

Pitt, D. (1977). Comment. *Current Anthropology, 18*, 628.

Plattner, S. (1989). Markets and market places. In S. Plattner (Ed.), *Economic anthropology*. Stanford, CA: Stanford University Press.

Podplefsky, A., & Brown, P. J. (Eds.). (1989). *Applying anthropology, an introductory reader*. Mountain View, CA: Mayfield.

Polanyi, K. (1968). The economy as instituted process. In E. E. LeClair, Jr. & H. K. Schnei-

der (Eds.), *Economic anthropology: readings in theory and analysis* (pp. 122–167). New York: Holt, Rinehart & Winston.

Pope, G. (1989, October). Bamboo and human evolution. *Natural History, 98*, 48–57.

Pope, G. G. (1992). Craniofacial evidence for the origin of modern humans in China. *Yearbook of Physical Anthropology, 35*, 243–298.

Pospisil, L. (1963). *The Kapauku Papuans of West New Guinea*. New York: Holt, Rinehart & Winston.

Pospisil, L. (1971). *Anthropology of law: A comparative theory*. New York: Harper & Row.

Powdermaker, H. (1966). *Stranger and friend: The way of an anthropologist*. New York: Norton.

Power, M. G. (1995). Gombe revisited: Are chimpanzees violent and hierarchical in the free state? *General Anthropology, 2*(1), 5–9.

Premack, A. J., & Premack, D. (1972). Teaching language to an ape. *Scientific American, 277*(4), 92–99.

Price, T. D., & Feinman, G. M. (Eds.). (1995). *Foundations of social inequality*. New York: Plenam.

Price-Williams, D. R. (Ed.). (1970). *Cross-cultural studies: Selected readings*. Baltimore, MD: Penguin (Penguin Modern Psychology Readings).

Prideaux, T., & the Editors of Time-Life. (1973). *Cro-Magnon man*. New York: Time-Life.

Pringle, H. (1997). Ice Age communities may be earliest known net hunters. *Science, 277*, 1203–1204.

Pringle, H. (1998). The slow birth of agriculture. *Science, 282*, 1446–1450.

Prins, A. H. (1953). *East African class systems*. Groningen, The Netherlands: J. B. Walters.

Prins, H. (1996). *The Mi'kmaq: Resistance, accommodation, and cultural survival*. Fort Worth, TX: Harcourt Brace.

Puleston, D. E. (1983). *The settlement survey of Tikal*. Philadelphia: University Museum.

Radcliffe-Brown, A. R. (1931). Social Organization of Australian tribes. *Oceania Monographs*, No. 1. Melbourne: Macmillan.

Radcliffe-Brown, A. (1952). *Structure and function in primitive society*. New York: Free Press.

Radcliffe-Brown, A. R., & Forde, C. D. (Eds.). (1950). *African systems of kinship and marriage*. London: Oxford University Press.

Rappaport, R. A. (1969). Ritual regulation of environmental relations among a New Guinea people. In A. P Vayda (Ed.), *Environment and Cultural behavior* (pp. 181–201). Garden City, NY Natural History Press.

Rappaport, R. (1984). *Pigs for the ancestors* (Enlarged ed.). New Haven, CT: Yale University Press.

Rappaport, R. A. (1994). Commentary. *Anthropology Newsletters, 35*(6), 76.

Rathje, W. L. (1974). The garbage project: A new way of looking at the problems of archaeology. *Archaeology, 27*, 236–241.

Rathje, W. L. (1993). Rubbish! In W. A. Haviland & R. J. Gordon (Eds.), *Talking about people: Readings in contemporary cultural anthropology*, Mountain View, CA: Mayfield.

Read-Martin, C. E., & Read, D. W. (1975). Australopithecine scavenging and human

evolution: An approach from faunal analysis. *Current Anthropology, 16*(3), 359–368.

Read, C. E. (1973). The role of faunal analysis in reconstructing human behavior: A Mousterian example. Paper presented at the meetings of the California Academy of Sciences, Long Beach.

Recer, P. (1998, Feb. 16). Apes shown to communicate in the wild. *Burlington Free Press*, p. 12A.

Redfield, R., Linton, R., & Herskovits, M. J. (1936). Memorandum of the study of acculturation. *American Anthropologist, 38*, 149–152.

Redman, C. L. (1978). *The rise of civilization: From early farmers to urban society in the ancient Near East*. San Francisco: Freeman.

Reid, J. J., Schiffer, M. B., & Rathje, W. L. (1975). Behavioral archaeology: Four strategies. *American Anthropologist, 77*, 864–869.

Reina, R. (1966). *The law of the saints*. Indianapolis, IN: Bobbs-Merrill.

Reiter, R. (Ed.). (1975). *Toward an anthropology of women*. New York: Monthly Review Press.

Relethford, J. H., & Harpending, H. C. (1994). Craniometric variation, genetic theory, and modern human origins. *American Journal of Physical Anthropology, 95*, 249–270.

Renfrew, C. (1973). *Before civilization: The radiocarbon revolution and prehistoric Europe*. London: Jonathan Cape.

Reynolds, V. (1994). Primates in the field, primates in the lab. *Anthropology Today, 10*(2), 3–5.

Rice, D. S. & Prudence, M. (1984). Lessons from the Maya. *Latin American Research Review, 19*(3), 7–34.

Richmond, B. G., Fleangle, J. K., & Swisher III, C. C. (1998). First Hominoid elbow from the miocene of Ethiopia and the evolution of the Catarrhine elbow. *American Journal of Physical Anthropology, 105*, 257–277.

Rightmire, G. P. (1990). *The evolution of Homo erectus: Comparative anatomical studies of an extinct human species*. Cambridge: Cambridge University Press.

Rightmire, G. P. (1998). Evidence from facial morphology for similarity of Asian and African representatives of *Homo erectus*. *American Journal of Physical Anthropology, 106*, 61–85.

Rindos, D. (1984). *The origins of agriculture: An evolutionary perspective*. Orlando, FL: Academic Press.

Rodman, H. (1968). Class culture. *International encyclopedia of the social sciences* (Vol. 15, pp. 332–337). New York: Macmillan.

Rogers, J. (1994). Levels of the genealogical hierarchy and the problem of hominoid phylogeny. *American Journal of Physical Anthropology, 94*, 81–88.

Romer, A. S. (1945). *Vertebrate paleontology*. Chicago: University of Chicago Press.

Roosevelt, A. C. (1984). Population, health, and the evolution of subsistence: Conclusions from the conference. In M. N. Cohen & G. J. Armelagos (Eds.), *Paleopathology at the origins of agriculture*. Orlando, FL: Academic Press.

Rosas, A., & Bermdez de Castro, J. M. (1998). On the taxonomic affinities of the Dmanisi mandible (Georgia). *American Journal of Physical Anthropology, 107,* 145–162.

Roscoe, P. B. (1995). The perils of "positivism" in cultural anthropology. *American Anthropologist, 97,* 497.

Rowe, T. (1988). New issues for phylogenetics. *Science, 239,* 1183–1184.

Ruhlen, M. (1994). *The origin of language: Tracing the evolution of the mother tongue.* New York: John Wiley & Sons.

Ruvdo, M. (1994). Molecular evolutionary processes and conflicting gene trees: The hominoid case. *American Journal of Physical Anthropology, 94,* 89–113.

Sabloff, J., & Lambert-Karlovsky, C. C. (1973). *Ancient civilization and trade.* Albuquerque: University of New Mexico Press.

Sabloff, J. A. (1989). *The cities of ancient Mexico.* New York: Thomas & Hudson.

Sabloff, J. A., & Lambert-Karlovsky, C. C. (Eds.). (1974). *The rise and fall of civilizations, modern archaeological approaches to ancient cultures.* Menlo Park, CA: Cummings.

Sahlins, M. (1968). *Tribesmen.* Englewood Cliffs, NJ: Prentice-Hall (Foundations of Modern Anthropology).

Sahlins, M. (1961). The segmentary lineage: An organization of predatory expansion. *American Anthropologist, 63,* 322–343.

Sahlins, M. (1972). *Stone age economics.* Chicago: Aldine.

Salthe, S. N. (1972). *Evolutionary biology.* New York: Holt, Rinehart & Winston.

Salzman, P. C. (1967). Political organization among nomadic peoples. *Proceedings of the American Philosophical Society, 3,* 115–131.

Sanday, P. R. (1975). On the causes of IQ differences between groups and implications for social policy. In A. Montagu (Ed.), *Race and IQ.* London: Oxford.

Sanday, P. R. (1981). *Female power and male dominance: On the origins of sexual inequality.* Cambridge: Cambridge University Press.

Sangree, W. H. (1965). The Bantu Tiriki of western Kenya. In J. L. Gibbs (Ed.), *Peoples of Africa.* New York: Holt, Rinehart & Winston.

Sapir, E. (1921). *Language.* New York: Harcourt.

Savage, J. M. (1969). *Evolution* (3d ed.). New York: Holt, Rinehart & Winston.

Scaglion, R. (1987). Contemporary law development in Papua New Guinea. In R. M. Wulff & S. J. Fiske (Eds.), *Anthropological praxis: translating knowledge into action.* Boulder, CO: Westview.

Scarr-Salapatek, S. (1971). Unknowns in the IQ equation. *Science, 174,* 1223–1228.

Schaller, G. B. (1971). *The year of the gorilla.* New York: Ballantine.

Scheflen, A. E. (1972). *Body language and the social order.* Englewood Cliffs, NJ: Prentice-Hall.

Schepartz, L.A. (1993). Language and human origins. *Yearbook of Physical Anthropology, 36,* 91–126.

Scheper-Hughes, N. (1979). *Saints, scholars and schizophrenics.* Berkeley: University of California Press.

Schlegel, A. (1977). Male and female in Hopi thought and action. In A. Schlegel (Ed.), *Sexual stratification* (pp. 245–269). New York: Columbia University Press.

Schrire, C. (Ed.). (1984). *Past and present in hunter-gatherer studies.* Orlando, FL: Academic Press.

Schurtz, H. (1902). *Alterklassen und Männerbünde.* Berlin: Reimer.

Schusky, E. L. (1975). *Variation in kinship.* New York: Holt, Rinehart & Winston.

Schusky, E. L. (1983). *Manual for kinship analysis* (2nd ed.). Lanham, MD: University Press of America.

Schwartz, J. H. (1984). Hominoid evolution: A review and a reassessment. *Current Anthropology, 25*(5), 655–672.

Sellen, D.W., & Mace, R. (1997). Fertility and mode of substance: A phylogenetic analysis. *Current Anthropology, 38,* 878–889.

Semenov, S. A. (1964). *Prehistoric technology.* New York: Barnes & Noble.

Sen, G., & Grown, C. (1987). *Development, crisis, and alternative visions: Third World women's perspectives.* New York: Monthly Review Press.

Seymour, D. Z. (1986). Black children, black speech. In P. Escholz, A. Rosa & V. Clark (Eds.), *Language Awareness* (4th ed.). New York: St. Martin's.

Shapiro, H. (Ed.) (1971). *Man, culture and society* (2nd. ed.). New York: Oxford University Press.

Sharer, R. J., & W. Ashmore. (1993). *Archaeology: Discovering our past* (2nd ed.). Palo Alto, CA: Mayfield.

Sharp, L. (1952). Steel axes for Stone Age Australians. In E. H. Spicer (Ed.), *Human problems in technological change.* New York: Russell Sage.

Shaw, D. G. (1984). A light at the end of the tunnel: Anthropological contributions toward global competence. *Anthropology Newsletter, 25,* 16.

Sheets, P. (1993). Dawn of a New Stone Age in eye surgery. In R. J. Sharer & W. Ashmore, *Archaeology: Discovering our past* (2nd ed.). Palo Alto, CA: Mayfield.

Shimkin, D. B., Tax, S., & Morrison, J. W. (Eds.). (1978). *Anthropology for the future.* Urbana, IL: Department of Anthropology, University of Illinois, Research Report No. 4.

Shinnie, M. (1970). *Ancient African kingdoms.* New York: New American Library.

Shipman, P. (1981). *Life history of a fossil: An introduction to taphonomy and paleoecology.* Cambridge, MA: Harvard University Press.

Shorto, R. (1997, December 7). Belief by the numbers. *New York Times Magazine,* p. 60.

Shostak, M. (1983). *Nisa: The life and worlds of a !Kung woman.* New York: Vintage.

Shreeve, J. (1994). "Lucy", crucial early human ancestor, finally gets a head. *Science, 264,* 34–35.

Shreeve, J. (1994). Terms of estrangement. *Discover, 15*(11), 56–63.

Shreeve, J. (1995). *The Neandertal enigma.* New York: Willliam Morrow.

Shuey, A. M. (1966). *The testing of Negro intelligence.* New York: Social Science Press.

Sillen, A. & Brain, C. K. (1990). Old flame. *Natural History, 4,* 6–10.

Simons, E. L. (1972). *Primate evolution.* New York: Macmillan.

Simons, E. L. (1989). Human origins. *Science, 245,* 1343–1350.

Simons, E. L. (1995). Skulls and anterior teeth of *Catopithecus* (primates: anthropoidea) from the Eocene and anthropoid origins. *Science, 268,* 1885–1888.

Simons, E. L., Rasmussen, D. T., & Gebo, D. L. (1987). A new species of Propliopithecus from the Fayum, Egypt. *American Journal of Physical Anthropology, 73,* 139–147.

Simpson, G. G. (1949). *The meaning of evolution.* New Haven, CT: Yale University Press.

Sjoberg, G. (1960). *The preindustrial city.* New York: Free Press.

Skelton, R. R., McHenry, H. M., & Drawhorn, G. M. (1986). Phylogenetic analysis of early hominids. *Current Anthropology, 27,* 21–43.

Slobin, D. I. (1971). *Psycholinguistics.* Glenview, IL: Scott, Foresman.

Small, M. F. (1997). Making connections. *American Scientist, 85,* 503.

Smith, A. H., & Fisher, J. L. (1970). *Anthropology.* Englewood Cliffs, NJ: Prentice-Hall.

Smith, B. H. (1994). Patterns of dental development in *Homo, Australopithecus, Pan,* and *gorilla. American Journal of Physical Anthropology, 94,* 307–325.

Smith, B. D. (1977). Archaeological inference and inductive confirmation. *American Anthropologist, 79*(3), 598–617.

Smith, F. H., & Raynard, G. C.. (1980). Evolution of the supraorbital region in Upper Pleistocene fossil hominids from South-Central Europe. *American Journal of Physical Anthropology, 53,* 589–610.

Smith, P. E. L. (1976). *Food production and its consequences* (2d ed.). Menlo Park, CA: Cummings.

Smith, R. (1970). Social stratification in the Caribbean. In L. Plotnicov & A. Tudin (Eds.), *Essays in comparative social stratification.* Pittsburgh: University of Pittsburgh Press.

Smuts, B. (1987). What are friends for? *Natural History.* 96(2), 36–44.

Snowden, C. T. (1990). Language capabilities of nonhuman animals. *Yearbook of Physical Anthropology, 33,* 215–243.

Speck, F. G. (1920). Penobscot shamanism. *Memoirs of the American Anthropological Association, 6,* 239–288.

Speck, F. G. (1935). Penobscot tales and religious beliefs. *Journal of American Folk-Lore, 48*(187), 1–107.

Speck, F. G. (1970). *Penobscot man: The life history of a forest tribe in Maine.* New York: Octagon Books.

Spencer, F., & Smith, F. H. (1981). The significance of Ales Hrdlicka's "Neanderthal phase of man": A historical and current assessment. *American Journal of Physical Anthropology, 56,* 435–459.

Spencer, H. (1896). *Principles of sociology.* New York: Appleton.

Spiro, M. E. (1966). Religion: problems of definition and explanation. In M. Banton (Ed.), *Anthropological approaches to the study of religion* (A.S.A. Monographs). London: Tavistock.

Spitz, R. A. (1949). Hospitalism. *The psychoanalytic study of the child* (Vol. 1). New York: International Universities Press.

Spradley, J. P. (1979). *The ethnographic interview.* New York: Holt, Rinehart & Winston.

Spradley, J. P. (1980). *Participant observation.* New York: Holt, Rinehart & Winston.

Spuhler, J. N. (1979). Continuities and discontinuities in anthropoid-hominid behavioral evolution: Bipedal locomotion and sexual reception. In N. A. Chagnon & W. Irons

(Eds.), *Evolutionary biology and human social behavior* (pp. 454–461). North Scituate, MA: Duxbury Press.

Squires, S. (1997). The market research and product industry discovers anthropology. *Anthropology Newsletter, 38*(4), 31.

Stacey, J. (1990). *Brave new families.* New York: Basic Books.

Stahl, A. B. (1984). Hominid dietary selection before fire. *Current Anthropology, 25,* 151–168.

Stanford, C. G. (1998). The social behavior of chimpanzees and bonobos: empirical evidence and shifting assumptions. *Current Anthropology, 39,* 399–420.

Stanley, S. M. (1979). *Macroevolution.* San Francisco: Freeman.

Stannard, D. E. (1992). *American holocaust.* Oxford: Oxford University Press.

Stanner, W. E. (1968). Radcliffe-Brown, A. R. *International Encyclopedia of the Social Sciences* (Vol. 13). New York: Macmillan.

Steward, J. H. (1972). *Theory of culture change: The methodology of multilinear evolution.* Urbana: University of Illinois Press.

Stewart, D. (1997). Expanding the pie before you divvy it up. *Smithsonian, 28,* 82.

Stiles, D. (1979). Early Acheulian and developed Oldowan. *Current Anthropology, 20*(l), 126–129.

Stiles, D. (1992). The hunter-gatherer "revisionist" debate. *Anthropology Today, 8*(2), 13–17.

Stirton, R. A. (1967). *Time, life, and man.* New York: Wiley.

Stocker, T. (1987, spring). A technological mystery resolved. *Invention and Technology,* p. 64.

Stocking, G. W., Jr. (1968). *Race, culture and evolution: Essays in the history of anthropology.* New York: Free Press.

Stoler, M. (1982). To tell the truth. *Vermont Visions, 82*(3), 3.

Stone, R. (1995). If the mercury soars, so may health hazards. *Science, 267,* 958.

Straughan, B. (1996). The secrets of ancient Tiwanaku are benefiting today's Bolivia. In W. A. Haviland & R. J. Gordon (Eds.), *Talking about people* (2nd ed., pp. 76–78). Mountain View, CA: Mayfield.

Straus, W. L., & Cave, A. J. E. (1957). Pathology and the posture of Neanderthal man. *Quarterly Review of Biology,* p. 32.

Stringer, C. B., & McKie, R. (1996). *African exodus: The origins of modern humanity.* London: Jonathan cape.

Suarez-Orozoco, M. M., Spindler, G., & Spindler, L. (1994). *The making of psychological anthropology, II.* Fort Worth, TX: Harcourt Brace.

Susman, R. L. (1988). Hand of *Paranthropus robustus* from Member 1, Swartkrans: Fossil evidence for tool behavior. *Science, 240,* 781–784.

Swadesh, M. (1959). Linguistics as an instrument of prehistory. *Southwestern Journal of Anthropology, 15,* 20–35.

Swartz, M. J., Turner, V. W., & Tuden, A. (1966). *Political Anthropology.* Chicago: Aldine.

Swisher III, C. C., Curtis, G. H., Jacob, T., Getty, A. G., Suprijo, A., & Widiasmoro. (1994). Age of the earliest known hominids in Java, Indonesia. *Science, 263,* 1118–1121.

Tague, R. G. (1992). Sexual dimorphism in the human bony pelvis, with a consideration of the Neanderthal pelvis from Kebara Cave, Israel. *American Journal of Physical Anthropology, 88,* 1–21.

Tannen, D. (1990). *You just don't understand: Women and men in conversation.* New York: William Morrow.

Tardieu, C. (1998). Short adolescence in early hominids: Infantile and adolescent growth of the human femur. *American Journal of Physical Anthropology, 107,* 163–178.

Tax, S. (1953). *Penny capitalism: A Guatemalan Indian economy.* Smithsonian Institution, Institute of Social Anthropology, Pub. No. 16. Washington, D.C.: GPO.

Tax, S. (Ed.). (1962). *Anthropology Today: Selections.* Chicago: University of Chicago Press.

Tax, S., Stanley, S., et al. (1975). In honor of Sol Tax. *Current Anthropology. 16,* 507–540.

Templeton, A. R. (1994). "Eve": Hypothesis compatability versus hypothesis testing. *American Anthropologist, 96,* 144–147.

The First Americans, ca. 20,000 B.C. (1998). *Discover, 19*(6), 24.

Thomas, D. H. (1974). *Predicting the past.* New York: Holt, Rinehart & Winston.

Thomas, D. H. (1998). *Archaeology* (3rd ed.). Fort Worth, TX: Harcourt Brace.

Thomas, E. M. (1994). *The tribe of the tiger.* New York: Simon & Schuster.

Thomas, W. L. (Ed.). (1956). *Man's role in changing the face of the earth.* Chicago: University of Chicago Press.

Thompson, S. (1960). *The folktale.* New York: Holt, Rinehart & Winston.

Thomson, K. S. (1997). Natural selection and evolution's smoking gun. *American Scientist, 85,* 516–518.

Thorne, A. G., & Wolpoff, M. D. H. (1981). Regional continuity in Australasian Pleistocene hominid evolution. *American Journal of Physical Anthropology, 55,* 337–349.

Thorne, B., & Yalom, M. (Eds.). (1982). *Rethinking the family: Some feminist questions.* New York: Longman.

Thornhill, N. (1993). Quoted in W. A. Haviland & R. J. Gordon (Eds.), *Talking about people* (p. 127). Mountain View, CA: Mayfield.

Tiffany, S. (Ed.). (1979). *Women in Africa.* St. Albans, VT: Eden Press.

Tobias, P. V. (1980). The natural history of the heliocoidal occlusal plane and its evolution in early Homo. *American Journal of Physical Anthropology, 53,* 173–187.

Tobias, P. V., & von Konigswald, G. H. R. (1964). A comparison between the Olduvai hominines and those of Java and some implications for hominid phylogeny. *Nature, 204,* 515–518.

Togue, R. G. (1992). Sexual dimorphism in the human bony pelvis, with a consideration of the Neanderthal pelvis from Kebara Cave, Israel. *American Journal of Physical Anthropology, 88,* 1–21.

Trager, G. L. (1964). Paralanguage: A first approximation. In D. Hymes (Ed.), *Language in culture and society.* New York: Harper & Row.

Trinkaus, E. (1986). The Neanderthals and modern human origins. *Annual Review of Anthropology, 15,* 197.

Trinkaus, E., & Shipman, P. (1992). *The Neandertals: Changing the image of mankind.* New York: Alfred A. Knopf.

Tuden, A. (1970). Slavery and stratification among the Ila of central Africa. In A. Tuden

& L. Plotnicov (Eds.), *Social stratification in Africa.* New York: Free Press.

Tumin, M. M. (1967). *Social stratification: The forms and functions of inequality.* Englewood Cliffs, NJ: Prentice-Hall (Foundations of Modern Sociology).

Turnbull, C. M. (1961). *The forest people.* New York: Simon & Schuster.

Turnbull, C. M. (1983). *The human cycle.* New York: Simon & Schuster.

Turnbull, C. (1983). *Mbuti Pygmies: Change and adaptation.* New York: Holt, Rinehart & Winston.

Turner, T. (1991). Major shift in Brazilian Yanomami policy. *Anthropology Newsletter, 32*(5), 1 & 46.

Turner, V. W. (1957). *Schism and continuity in an African society.* Manchester, England: University Press.

Turner, V. W. (1969). *The ritual process.* Chicago: Aldine.

Tylor, E. B. (1871). *Primitive culture: Researches into the development of mythology, philosophy, religion, language, art and customs.* London: Murray.

Tylor, Sir E. B. (1931). Animism. In V. F. Calverton (Ed.), *The making of man: An outline of anthropology.* New York: Modern Library.

Ucko, P. J., & Rosenfeld, A. (1967). *Paleolithic cave art.* New York: McGraw-Hill.

Ucko, P. J., Tringham, R., & Dimbleby, G. W. (Eds.). (1972). *Man, Settlement and urbanism.* London: Duckworth.

Valentine, C. A. (1968). *Culture and poverty.* Chicago: University of Chicago Press.

Van Allen, J. (1979). Sitting on a man: Colonialism and the lost political institutions of Igbo women. In S. Tiffany (Ed.), *Women in society* (pp. 163–187). St. Albans, VT: Eden Press.

Van Den Berghe, P. (1992). The modern state: Nation builder or nation killer? *International Journal of Group Tensions, 22*(3), 191–207.

Van Gennep, A. (1960). *The rites of passage.* Chicago: University of Chicago Press.

Van Willigen, J. (1986). *Applied anthropology.* South Hadley, MA: Bergin & Garvey.

Vansina, J. (1965). *Oral tradition: A study in historical methodology* (H. M. Wright, Trans.). Chicago: Aldine.

Vayda, A. P. (1961). Expansion and warfare among swidden agriculturalists. *American Anthropologist, 63,* 346–358.

Vayda, A. (Ed.). (1969). *Environment and cultural behavior: Ecological studies in cultural anthropology.* Garden City: Natural History Press.

Vincent, J. (1979). On the special division of labor, population, and the origins of agriculture. *Current Anthropology, 20*(2), 422–425.

Vogelman, T. C., et al. (1972). *Prehistoric life in the Champlain Valley* (Film). Burlington, VT: Department of Anthropology, University of Vermont.

Voget, F. W. (1960). Man and culture: An essay in changing anthropological interpretation. *American Anthropologist, 62,* 943–965.

Voget, F. W. (1975). *A history of ethnology.* New York, Holt, Rinehart & Winston.

Vogt, E. Z. (1990). *The Zinacantecos of Mexico, a modern way of life* (2nd ed.). New York: Holt, Rinehart & Winston.

Wagner, P. L. (1960). *A history of ethnology.* New York: Holt, Rinehart & Winston.

Wallace, A. F. C. (1956). Revitalization movements. *American Anthropologist, 58,* 264–281.

Wallace, A. F. C. (1965). The problem of the psychological validity of componential analysis. *American Anthropologist, Special Publication* (Part 2), 67(5), 229–248.

Wallace, A. F. C. (1966). *Religion: An anthropological view.* New York: Random House.

Wallace, A. F. C. (1970). *Culture and personality* (2nd ed.). New York: Random House.

Wallace, E., & Hoebel, E. A. (1952). *The Comanches.* Norman, OK: University of Oklahoma Press.

Ward, C. V., Walker, A., Teaford, M. F., & Odhiambo, I. (1993). Partial skeleton of *Proconsul nyanzae* from Mfangano Island, Kenya. *American Journal of Physical Anthropology, 90,* 77–111.

Wardhaugh, R. (1972). *Introduction to linguistics.* New York: McGraw-Hill.

Wattenberg, B. J. (1997, November 23). The population explosion is over. *New York Times Magazine,* p. 60.

Washburn, S. L., & Moore, R. (1980). *Ape into human: A study of human evolution* (2d ed.). Boston: Little, Brown.

Weatherford, J. (1988). *Indian givers: How the Indians of the Americas transformed the world.* New York: Fawcett Columbine.

Weaver, M. P. (1972). *The Aztecs, Maya and their predecessors.* New York: Seminar Press.

Weiner, A. B. (1977). Review of Trobriand cricket: An ingenious response to colonialism. *American Anthropologist, 79,* 506.

Weiner, A. B. (1988). The Trobrianders of Papua New Guinea. New York: Holt, Rinehart & Winston.

Weiner, J. S. (1955). *The Piltdown forgery.* Oxford: Oxford University Press.

Weiner, M. (1966). *Modernization: The dynamics of growth.* New York: Basic Books.

Weiss, M. L., & Mann, A. E. (1990). *Human biology and behavior* (5th ed.). Boston: Little, Brown.

Weitzman, L. J. (1985). *The divorce revolution: The unexpected social and economic consequences for women and children in America.* New York: The Free Press.

Werner, D. (1990). *Amazon journey.* Englewood Cliffs, NJ: Prentice-Hall.

Wernick, R., & the Editors of Time-Life. (1973). *The Monument Builders.* New York: Time-Life.

Westermarck, E. A. (1926). *A short history of marriage.* New York: Macmillan.

Wheeler, P. (1993). Human ancestors walked tall, stayed cool. *Natural History, 102*(8), 65–66.

Whelehan, P. (1985). Review of Incest, A Biosocial View. *American Anthropologist, 87,* 677–678.

White, D. R. (1988). Rethinking polygyny: Co-wives, codes and cultural systems. *Current Anthropology, 29,* 529–572.

White, E., Brown, D., & the Editors of Time-Life. (1973). *The first men.* New York: Time-Life.

White, L. (1949). *The science of culture: A study of man and civilization.* New York: Farrar, Strauss.

White, L. (1959). *The evolution of culture: The development of civilization to the fall of Rome.* New York: McGraw-Hill.

White, Peter. (1976). *The past is human* (2d ed.). New York: Maplinger.

White, R. (1992). The earliest images: Ice Age "art" in Europe. *Expedition, 34*(3), 37–51.

White, T. D. (1979). Evolutionary implications of Pliocene hominid footprints. *Science, 208,* 175–176.

Whitehead, N., & Ferguson, R. B. (Eds.). (1992). *War in the tribal zone.* Santa Fe, NM: School of American Research Press.

Whitehead, N. L., & Ferguson, R. B. (1993, November 10). Deceptive stereotypes about tribal warfare. *Chronicle of Higher Education,* p. A48.

Whiting, B. B. (Ed.). (1963). *Six cultures: Studies of child rearing.* New York: Wiley.

Whiting, J. W. M., & Child, I. L. (1953). *Child training and personality: A cross-cultural study.* New Haven, CT: Yale University Press.

Whiting, J. W. M., Sodergem, J. A., & Stigler, S. M. (1982). Winter temperature as a constraint to the migration of preindustrial peoples. *American Anthropologist, 84,* 289.

Willey, G. R. (1966). *An introduction to American archaeology: Vol. 1. North America.* Englewood Cliffs, NJ: Prentice-Hall.

Willey, G. R. (1971). *An introduction to American archaeology, Vol. 2: South America.* Englewood Cliffs, NJ: Prentice-Hall.

Williams, A. M. (1996). *Sex, drugs and HIV: A sociocultural analysis of two groups of gay and bisexual male substance users who practice unprotected sex.* Unpublished manuscript.

Williamson, R. K. (1995). The blessed curse: Spirituality and sexual difference as viewed by Euro-American and Native American cultures. *The College News, 17*(4).

Willigan, J. V. (1986). *Applied anthropology* (pp. 128–129, 133–139). South Hadley, MA: Bergin & Garvey.

Wills, C. (1994). The skin we're in. *Discover, 15*(11), 77–81.

Wilson, A. K., & Sarich, V. M. (1969). A molecular time scale for human evolution. *Proceedings of the National Academy of Science, 63,* 1089–1093.

Wingert, P. (1965). *Primitive art: Its tradition and styles.* New York: World. 1965.

Wirsing, R. L. (1985). The health of traditional societies and the effects of acculturation. *Current Anthropology 26*(3), 303–322.

Wittfogel, K. A. (1957). *Oriental despotism, a comparative Study of total power.* New Haven, CT: Yale University Press.

Wolf, E. (1959). *Sons of the shaking earth.* Chicago: University of Chicago Press.

Wolf, E. (1966). *Peasants.* Englewood Cliffs, NJ: Prentice-Hall.

Wolf, E. (1982). *Europe and the people without history.* Berkeley: University of California Press.

Wolf, M. (1972). *Women and the family in rural Taiwan.* Stanford, CA: Stanford University Press.

Wolf, M. (1985). *Revolution postponed: Women in contemporary China.* Stanford, CA: Stanford University Press.

Wolfe, A. W. (1977). The supranational organization of production: An evolutionary perspective. *Current Anthropology, 18,* 165–635.

Wolpoff, M. H. (1971). Interstitial wear. *American Journal of Physical Anthropology, 34,* 205–227.

Wolpoff, M. H. (1977). Review of earliest man in the Lake Rudolf Basin. *American Anthropologist, 79,* 708–711.

Wolpoff, M. H. (1982). *Ramapithecus* and hominid origins. *Current Anthropology, 23,* 501–522.

Wolpoff, M.H. (1993). Evolution in *Homo erectus*: The question of stasis. In R. L. Ciochon & J. G. Fleagle (Eds.), *The human evolution source book.* Englewood Cliffs, NJ: Prentice-Hall.

Wolpoff, M. H. (1993). Multiregional evolution: The fossil alternative to Eden. In R. L. Ciochon & J. G. Fleagle (Eds.), *The human evolution source book.* Englewood Cliffs, NJ: Prentice-Hall.

Wolpoff, M. (1996). *Australopithecus*: A new look at an old ancestor. *General Anthropology, 3*(1), 2.

Wolpoff, M. & Caspari, R. (1997). *Race and human evolution.* New York: Simon and Schuster.

Womack, M. (1994). Program 5: Psychological anthropology. *Faces of culture.* Fountain Valley, CA: Coast Telecourses, Inc.

Wong, K. (1998, January). Ancestral quandary: Neanderthals not our ancestors? Not so fast. *Scientific American,* pp. 30–32.

Wood, B., & Aiello, L. C. (1998). Taxonomic and functional implications of mandibular scaling in early Hominines. *American Journal of Physical Anthropology, 105,* 523–538.

Wood, B., Wood, C., and Konigsberg, L. (1994). *Paranthropus boisei*: An example of evolutionary stasis? *American Journal of Physical Anthropology, 95,* 117–136.

Woodward, V. (1992). *Human heredity and society.* St. Paul, MN: West.

Woolfson, P. (1972). Language, thought, and culture. In V. P. Clark, P. A. Escholz, & A. F. Rosa (Eds.), *Language.* New York: St. Martin's.

World Bank (1982). *Tribal peoples and economic development.* Washington, DC: World Bank.

Wright, R. (1984). Towards a new Indian policy in Brazil. *Cultural Survival Quarterly 8*(1).

Wright, R. M. (1997). Violence on Indian day in Brazil 1997: Symbol of the past and future. *Cultural Survival Quarterly, 21*(2), 47–49.

Wulff, R. M., & Fiske, S. J. (1987). *Anthropological praxis: Translating knowledge into action.* Boulder, CO: Westview.

Zohary, D., & Hopf, M. (1993). *Domestication of plants in the Old World* (2nd ed.). Oxford: Clarendon Press.

Zur, J. (1994). The psychological impact of impunity. *Anthropology Today, 10*(3), 12–17.

INDEX

Abell, Paul, 159
Abenaki people, 472, 681–682. *See also*
  Western Abenakis
  music of, 739
  patrilocal residence and, 29–30
Abkhasian people, 507
Abnormal behavior, 388
Abnormal personality, normal personality
  and, 458–464
Aborigines. *See also* Australian Aborigines
  in Tasmania, 766
Abortions, in China, 819–820
Absolute (chronometric) dates, 55, 56–59
Abu Hureyra, Syria, 289
Abu-Lughod, Lila, 588n, 671n, 735
Abuse
  domestic violence and, 593
  within family, 571
"Accord on Identity and the Rights of Indige-
  nous Peoples" (Guatemala), 807
Acculturation, 764–766
  extinction and, 764–766
Acheulean tool tradition, 209–215
Acquired immune deficiency syndrome. *See*
  AIDS
Action theory of civilization, 338–339
Adapids, 134, 138
Adaptation, 74, 77–85, 379
  of Bakhtiari people, 490–493
  change and, 758
  climatic, 357–358
  culture and, 396–398
  defined, 396
  evolutionary, 471–473
  to food production, 484–490
  as interaction between organism and envi-
    ronment, 469–470
  material technology, and, 482–483
  Paleolithic and Mesolithic, 275
  ramamorph, 144–147
  skin color and, 359–363
  subsistence patterns and, 468–476
  unit of, 470–471
Adaptive radiation, 130, 133
Advertising, 800
Adzes. *See* Axes
Aegyptopithecus, 139, 140
Aesthetics. *See* Art(s)
Afar people, craft specialization of, 511
Afar region, Ethiopia, 154
Affinal kin, 544
Africa. *See also* Bushmen; East Africa;
  "Eve" hypothesis (study); South Africa;
  West Africa; specific groups and regions
  age grouping in, 629, 630–631
  bride-price in, 561
  civilizations of, 495 (map)
  farming in, 299
  gender and political power in, 666–667
  H. erectus from, 204–206
  pigment uses in, 228
African American English (AAE), 426
African Americans
  body shapes of, 359
  infant mortality among, 589–590
  race, intelligence, and, 364, 365
  sickle-cell anemia and, 79
  social dialects and, 424–425
Afrikaners, porphyria among, 369
Age
  care of elderly and, 820
  culture and, 384
  division of labor by, 509–510
  grouping and, 628–631
Age grade, 629–630
  political organization by, 660–661

Age sets, 629–630
  Tiriki people and, 630–631
Aggression, dependence training and, 451
Agnatic descent, 600
Agricultural development, modernization and,
  777
Agriculture. *See also* Farmers and farming;
  Food production; Horticulture; World
  hunger
  adaptation and, 397
  in Aztec cities, 495–498
  in Bolivian Altiplano region, 494
  food-producing societies and, 484–490
  health and, 305
  intensive, and nonindustrial cities, 493–
    498
  irrigation, 475
  land control and, 511–512
  Natufian culture and, 273–274
  Neolithic progress and, 308–309
  in New World, 304
  in Tikal, 320
  urban innovations in, 321
AIDS, 540–542, 759
Alaska, fossils in, 38–43
Aleut, use of term, 357
Alleles, 66. *See also* Race
  dominant and recessive, 68–69, 70
  farming and, 299
  physical variability and, 346, 347
  sickle-cell anemia and, 78–79
  skin color and, 362
Alliance, marriage as, 554
Allies, polymorphic species and, 346
Alphabet, phonetic, 410
Alpha males. *See* Primates
Altered fossils, 42–43
Altered states, 459–461
Altimira Cave, Spain, 264
Altiplano region, 494
Alva, Walter, 332
Amazon region. *See also* Brazil; Yanomami
  people; specific groups and countries
  advocacy for indigenous peoples of, 809
Ambilineal descent, 607–609
Ambilocal residence, 584
Ambrona, Spain, 217
American Indians. *See* Native Americans; spe-
  cific groups
American Sign Language, 406, 407
  chimpanzees and, 429–430
  orangutan study and, 118–122
Americas. *See also* New World; specific
  regions
  archaeology in, 296
  Archaic cultures in, 274
  Maritime archaic culture in, 274
  Neolithic culture in, 304
  Paleoindians in, 268
  plant domestication in, 295
  tales in, 734
  Upper Paleolithic peoples in, 267
Amino acid racemization dating, 57–58
Amino acids, protein consumption and, 192–
  194
Amiran, R., 758n
Amish people, as subculture, 384–385, 386
Amok disorder, 462
Analogies, 94
Anatomically modern peoples
  Cro-Magnons as, 250–251
  transition to, 268–271
Ancestral spirits, 697–698
Ancestry, descent groups and, 598–609
Andaman Islands, 356
Andes Mountains, Tiwanaku in, 494

Andrews, L. B., 366n
Anemia
  adaptation and, 469–470
  sickle-cell, 69, 78–80
Angiosperm plants, 131
Animal life
  faunal regions and, 346–347
  human diseases and, 307
  transhumant nature of, 292–293
Animals. *See also* Cave painting; Domestication; Hunting; Meat eaters
  adaptation of, 77–78
  anthropomorphism and, 64
  disease transfer to humans, 373
  domestication of, 285–286, 292–294, 296,
    484, 485 (map)
  geographic variation in, 352
Animatism, 700–701
Animism, 698, 699
  language use and, 121
Ankel-Simons, F., 139n
Anorexia nervosa, 462
Anthropoid origins (study), 135–137
Anthropologists
  advocacy for rights of indigenous peoples
    and, 809
  agricultural development and, 494
  applied anthropology and, 768–771
  in business, 530
  dispute settlement and, 678
  infant mortality and, 589–590
  mental health and, 460
  protecting cultural heritages, 727–728
  social-impact assessment and, 635–636
Anthropology, 6. *See also* Archaeology; specific branches of anthropology
  contemporary life and, 31–33
  development of, 7–8
  discipline of, 9–22
  economic, 504–506
  ethics and, 31
  future of, 790, 792–822
  humanities and, 30–31
  overview of, 6–7
  sciences and, 8–9
  scientific approach and, 22–30
Anthropomorphism, 64
Antibiotics, innovation and, 758–759
Apache Indians, housing for, 384–385
Apartheid, global, 810–812
Apes. *See also* Primates
  bipedalism and infants of, 171
  culture and, 389
  families of, 576
  human evolution and, 147–148
  learning in orangutans (study), 118–122
  locomotion of, 160
  from Miocene epoch, 139–141
  in Oligocene epoch, 138–139
  small and great, 107–109
  speech of, 428–430
Appalachia, revitalization in, 773
Appearance. *See also* Race; Skin color
  of *Homo sapiens,* 226–232
Appenzeller, T., 258n
Applied anthropology, 768–771. *See also*
  Anthropologists
Arapesh people, 447
  war and, 680
Arboreal animals, 98, 99–100, 103–104,
  107, 133
Archaeological and Historical Preservation
  Act (1974), 46
Archaeological fieldwork, 28
Archaeology, 12–14
  Alaska discoveries and, 38–43

data recovery and, 36–43
evidence from, 52–59
forensic, 234
fossil sites, localities, and, 43–52
paleoanthropology and, 36
Archaic cultures, in Americas, 274
Archaic *H. sapiens. See Homo sapiens*
Arctic peoples, shamans of, 704
Ardipithecus ramidus, 152, 164
Arensburg, B., 240n
Aristocracy. *See* Social stratification
Armelagos, George, 305n, 308, 321n
Armstrong, D. F., 406n, 430n
Armstrong, J. D., 457n
Armstrong, S., 706n
Arnhem Land studies, 28
Aroostook Band of Micmacs (ABM), 611–612
Aroostook Indians, 611–612
Arranged marriage, in India (study), 554–559
Arsuaga, J. L., 226n
Art(s), 412. *See also* specific arts
of anatomically modern *H. sapiens*, 248
anthropological study of, 726–728
cultural role of, 724–726
functional nature of, 725
music as, 736–741
pictorial, 741–750
pottery and, 302–303
rock art, 219, 221, 742–750
rock art and political power (study), 747–749
social role of, 651
Upper Paleolithic, 248, 258–265
verbal, 728–736
Artifacts, 36
symbolic, 218–219
Asbestos, 374
Ashmore, W., 251n
Asia. *See also* China; Southeast Asia; Southwest Asia; specific regions
civilizations of, 495 (map)
H. erectus and bamboo use in (study), 211–213
Asian, use of term, 357
Asian Americans, 364, 365
Association of Aroostook Indians (AA), 611
Association patterns
political organization by, 661
social class and, 639
Astronomy, 325
Mayan, 319
Aurignacian tradition, 237–240
Australia, 266
rock art in, 259, 262
Australian Aborigines, 28
divorce among, 563–564
land control and, 512
male initiation rites of, 705
music of, 740–741
reciprocity among, 515
Australopithecus, 142, 144, 150, 152–172
afarensis, 153, 154–159, 178, 182, 183
africanus, 152–153, 154–159, 163, 182, 183
anamensis, 153, 164–165
boisei, 153, 159–164, 178, 182, 183
cranial capacity of, 194
environment, diet, and origins of, 165–166
homo habilis and, 181–183
locomotion of, 160
robustus, 153, 159–164, 182
Authority. *See* Control; Political systems
Avunculocal residence, 585–586
Awlad 'Ali Bedouins, "little songs" of, 734–735
Axes, 209–210, 213, 271, 272
Aymara Indians, 494
Azande people, 673–674
Aztec empire
agriculture and city life of, 495–498

legends of, 732
marketplaces of, 526–527
metals and, 323, 325
money in, 527
religion and, 696
sacrifice and, 400, 709

Baboons, 103, 107
families of, 576
infant transporting by, 147
relocation of, 110
Baby boom, family and, 574–575
Bach, Johann Sebastian, 725–726
Baffier, D., 239n
Bakhtiari people
as pastoralists, 490–493
polygamy among, 587
Balanced opposition, 660
Balanced reciprocity, 516–517
Bali, cremation ritual in, 690
Balter, M., 315n, 373n
Bamboo
H. erectus and (study), 211–213
species of, 213
Band, 654–656
Bantu people, food-foraging societies and, 477
Barfield, T. J., 490n
Barham, L. S., 228n, 259n
Baringo fossil, 182
Barley, 292
Barnett, Steve, 529
Barr, R. G., 12n
Barrio, 804
Barrow, Alaska, 38–43
Barter, trade and, 517–518
Barth, F., 491n
Bar-Yosef, O., 240n, 301n
Basket making, of Pomo Indians, 738
Basque language, 299
Baton method, 214
Bay, E., 666n
Beans, 297
Beard, K. Christopher, 136, 137
Beauty, standardization of (study), 798–800
Beck, Benjamin, 118
Bednarik, R. G., 219n, 239n, 269n
Bedouin people, limits on power among (study), 670, 671–673
Behavior. *See also* Personality
abnormal, 388
problem-solving and, 379
race and, 363–364
self and, 436–446
Behavioral environment, self and, 436–446
Behrensmeyer, A. K., 192n
Belfer-Cohen, A., 240n
Belgium, cultural pluralism in, 804
Bell, D., 544n
Bella Coola people, 607
Bell Curve, The (Herrenstein and Murray), 365
Benedict, Ruth, 455, 456
Berdache (two-spirit), 458n
Berdan, F. F., 495n
Bermdez de Castro, J. M., 206n
Bible, 7
social control and, 716
Big business. *See* Multinational corporations
Big Man (New Guinea), 522, 523–524
political organization and, 657, 658
Bilateral descent, 613–615
Bilzingsleben, Germany, 217, 218
Biological avoidance theory, incest taboo and, 545–546
Biology
evolution and, 64
gender and, 383
human evolution and, 368–374
mating and, 548–549
Neolithic period and, 305–308

race and, 349–362
sexual division of labor and, 507
Biotechnology, 694
Bipedalism, 147
of apes, 158–159, 160
of *Australopithecus*, 152, 153, 158–159, 160, 161
forest region and, 212
heat stress and (study), 168–171
of *Homo sapiens*, 158–159, 160
of humans, 166–172
scavenging and, 192
Birds, classification of, 351–352
Birdsell, Joseph, 348, 358
Birth control
in China, 819–820
sexual activity and, 544
Birthrate, population control and, 818, 819
Bison, cave paintings of, 264
Black, Davidson, 202–203, 238
Black, H. C., 677n
"Black" ancestry, of all humans, 361
Black Elk, 701
Black English, 21, 424–425. *See also* African American English (AAE); Ebonics
Black Muslims, 773
"Black pride" movement, 362
Blacks
social dialects and, 424
in South Africa, 637, 643–644
"Black Skull," 161, 163
Black's Law Dictionary, 677
Blades
from Kenya, 242
Upper Paleolithic, 253
Blade technique, 253
Blood types, 68. *See also* Alleles
distribution of, 346, 347
race and, 348
Blumenschine, Robert J., 190
Blumer, M. A., 291n
Blurton Jones, N. G., 478n, 509n
Boas, Franz, 26, 770
Boats, trade and, 324
Bodies, ornamentation of, 264–265
Bodley, J. H., 22n, 400n, 529n, 780n, 796n, 808n, 812n
Body decoration, 724
Body differences, race and, 348, 357–359
Body language. *See* Kinesics
Body temperature, of mammals, 132
Bohannan, P., 607n
Bolivian Altiplano, 494
Bones
from Sima de los Huesos, 226
Weidenreich and, 238
Bonobos, 109, 111. *See also* Primates
hunting by, 124
individual interaction among, 112, 113
sexual behavior among, 113–114
sharing among, 195
tools and, 123, 166
Boone, E. S., 589n
Boone, Margaret, 589–590
Border Cave, 241
Borrowing. *See* Diffusion
Bosnia
as pluralistic society, 387
Serbs in, 652
Bound morpheme, 410
Bow and arrow, 258, 272
Boxgrove, England, fossils from, 206, 207
Boys, puberty rites and, 705–706
Brace, C. Loring, 230, 250n, 299n
Brachiate, 102
Brachiation, 148
Brahmans (India), 637, 640–641
Braidwood, Robert, 287
Brain. *See also* Cranial capacity
of *A. afarensis* and *A. africanus*, 157–158, 159

of *A. robustus* and *A. boisei,* 159, 161
of archaic *H. sapiens,* 230, 231
bipedalism and, 168–171
of Chinese *H. erectus,* 204
cooling of, 170
of Cro-Magnons, 250, 251
of *H. erectus,* 207
of *Homo habilis,* 178–180, 181–182
meat eating and, 194
of primates, 99–100
primate skeleton and, 101–102
size of, 170
spoken language and, 237
tools, meat, and, 185–194
Brain, C. K., 189–190, 216
Branch Davidians, 717, 719
Branda, R. F., 360n
Brazil. *See also* Yanomami people
extinction in, 764–766
forcible change and, 771
multinationals in, 796, 797
one-world culture and, 802
Breast feeding, 438
Breeding. *See also* Sex and sexuality
of animals, 293
of plants, 292
Bride-price, 560–561
Brides. *See also* Arranged marriage; Marriage;
Spouse
Chinese purchases of, 820
Bride service, 562
Broecker, W. S., 816n
Bronze Age, 322–323
sites from, 44
Broom, Robert, 159
Brown, P. J., 769
Buka, Solomon Islands, 716–717
Bull, J. J., 85n
Bunn, Henry, 188
Burial mounds, 44–45
Burials, 41
African ritual activity and, 228
in Australia, 266
of Moche priestess (Peru) (study), 330–334
Neandertal, 235
Neolithic, 304
social stratification and, 329–330, 334–
336
Burins (tools), 254
Burling, R., 406n
Burns, Karen, 234
Bushmen, 447, 447 (map). *See also* Ju/'hoansi
Bushmen
acculturation and, 765
nursing and ovulation among, 480
rock art and, 742–750
subsistence patterns and, 466, 477
war and, 680
Business
culture, economics, and, 529–531
multinational corporations and, 795–796
Butcher, J. N., 463n
Butchering practices, 217
Byrne, R., 291n

Cacaxtla, Mexico, 319
Calendar, Maya, 319, 325
Calloway, C., 732n
Camels, Southeast Asia fossils of, 211–212
Camp, in food-foraging society, 482
Canaanites, 696
Canada. *See also* North America
cultural pluralism in, 804
nuclear family in, 579
Canary Islands, cultural loss and, 763–764
Cancer
lung, 374
skin, 371
thyroid, 371
Cannibalism, ritual, 707–708
Carbohydrates, protein and, 233

Carbon dioxide gas, 816
Cargo cults, 514, 773
Caribbean region. *See also* specific locations
and peoples
female-headed households in, 592
Carneiro, Robert, 337
Carnivores, scavenging by (study), 188–191
Caroulis, J., 389n
Carretero, J. M., 226n
Carrying capacity, 479
Carrying devices, 192
Carson, R. C., 463n
Cartmill, M., 220n, 237n
Carver, George Washington, 365
Carvings, 258–259
Cashdan, E., 477n
Caspari, R., 237n, 250, 251n
Castaneda, Carlos, 701
Caste. *See also* Social class
defined, 636
in India, 636–637
in South Africa, 637
Castillo, I. J., 330n
Çatalhöyük, Turkey, 315
Catarrhines, 97, 104, 105, 106, 128, 140. *See
also* Primates
evolution of, 145
origins of (study), 135–137
sharing and sexual activity among, 195–
196
Catholic Church. *See also* Nuns
marriage, family life, and, 570–571
Catopithecus, 134–135, 138
origins of (study), 135–137
Caucasoid, 348
Cavalieri, P., 118n, 430n
Cavallo, J. A., 188n
Cave art, 218
in Europe, 259–264
recreation of (study), 261–264
"Cave bear cult," 235
"Caveman" image, of Neandertals, 229
Cave sites, 45. *See also* specific sites
Cell division, 66–69
Celtic cultures, music and, 740
Central America. *See also* Americas
Teotihuacan and, 315–316
Tikal and, 317–321
Central government, 326–329
Centralized political systems, 661–665
chiefdoms as, 662–663
state systems as, 663–665
Cereal grasses, 284–286
Ceremonies
Hopi, 606
religious, 705–708
Chagnon, N. A., 196n
Chambers, Robert, 27–28
Chance
in evolution and cultural innovation, 289
genetic drift and, 72–73
Change. *See* Change mechanisms; Cultural
change
Change (genetic), factors for, 70–72
Change mechanisms, 757–764
cultural loss and, 763–764
diffusion as, 761–763
innovation as, 757–761
Channel Islands, 233
Chantek (orangutan). *See* Project Chantek
Characteristics, shift from Neandertal to
anatomically modern, 239
Chase, A. F. and D. Z., 642n
Chasin, B. H., 814n
Chatrath, P. S., 139n
Chechen people, 808
Chemicals
hormone-disrupting, 371–374
poisoning by, 371
Chemical separation, of archaeological evi-
dence, 53

Chenchu people, divorce among, 563
Chernobyl accident, 815–816
Cheyenne people, 471, 473, 474–475, 478,
661
Chiapas, Mexico, 490, 681
violence in, 807
Chicago Commodities Exchange, 526
Chiefdoms, 662–663
Child, Irving L., 449, 452, 453n
Childbirth, of Neandertals, 235
Child care. *See* Child rearing; Day-care centers
Childe, V. Gordon, 287, 288, 289
Child labor, 509–510, 818
Child rearing, 434, 436–465
dependence training and, 448–451, 452
family and, 568, 576–577
group personality and, 452–458
independence training and, 451–452
personality and, 446–452
Children. *See also* Child rearing; Family and
family life
age grouping and, 628, 630
cosleeping and, 11–12
in family, 576
female-headed households and, 591–593
food production and, 298
in Ju/'hoansi society, 448
raising of, 434–465
in single-parent households, 553
Chimpanzees, 104, 109
child-rearing of, 437
compared with *A. afarensis,* 156
Goodall's work with, 111, 112
group behavior and, 111
home ranges of, 117
hunting by, 124
individual interaction among, 112, 113
infanticide among, 113
protein sources of, 193
sexual behavior among, 113–114
speech and, 428–430
tool use by, 123
China. *See also* Tsu (family unit); specific
locations
ancestors in, 698
archaic *H. sapiens* from, 232
birth control in, 819–820
birthrate in, 818, 819
civilization of, 315, 495 (map)
core values and national character in, 456–
457
cultural role of food in, 380
extended family in, 588
female infanticide in, 819
fossils in, 43, 229
Great Wall in, 326
H. erectus from, 202–204
patrilineal society in, 600–601
revolutionary goals in, 775–776
Chinampas, 495, 496, 497
Chlorofluorocarbons, 371
Chodorow, Nancy, 459
Choice, women's bodies and (study), 798–
800
Choking, in humans, 237
Choppers. *See also* Acheulean tool tradition;
Oldowan tool tradition; Tools
regional distribution of, 212–213
in Zhoukoudian, China, 212
Christianity. *See also* Catholic church;
Evangelism
masculine-authoritarian concept of god in,
697
symbolic ritual cannibalism in, 708
in United States, 693
Christian Zionists, 759
Chromosomes, 66. *See also* Cell division
DNA and movement of, 245
Y, 270
Chronometric dating, 55, 56–59

Church. *See* Catholic Church
Churinga, 236, 237, 259
Ciochon, R. L., 143n, 178n, 216n
Cities. *See also* Civilization; Urban society
  agricultural innovation in, 321
  of Aztecs, 495–498
  central government in, 326–329
  civilization and, 314
  cultural change and, 321–336
  diversification of labor in, 322–325
  intensive agriculture in nonindustrial, 493–498
  Neolithic, 314
  preindustrial, 498–499
  slums in, 786
  social stratification in, 329–336
  Teotihuacan, Mexico, 312
Civilization
  in Çatalhöyük, Turkey, 315
  definition of, 314–317
  environmental and social circumscription theory of, 337
  locations of major early, 495 (map)
  Neolithic origins of, 314, 315 (map)
  religion theory of, 337–339
  stress and, 339–340
  in Teotihuacan, Mexico, 315–316
  theories on emergence of, 336–339
  in Tikal, 317–321
  trade networks theory of, 337
  warfare and, 340
Clan of the Cave Bear, 229, 250
Clans
  as descent groups, 610–613
  of Five Nations, 616
  in Hopi society, 605–606
  in Scotland, 596
  totemism among, 612–613
Clark, Ella, 6
Clark, W. E. LeGros, 100
Class. *See* Social class
Classic Maya civilization. *See* Maya people
Classification, racial, 348, 350–354
Classification system, 94–95
  for humans, 96
Clavicle, 102
Clay, J. W., 664n
Clay cooking, 758
Cleavers, 209–210
Climate
  adaptation to, 357–358
  archaeological evidence and, 52
  cold Mousterian, 233–234
  primate changes and, 138
  in Tikal, 320
Climatic determinism, 287
Clinton, Hillary Rodham, body language and, 413
Clinton, James, 617
Closed-class societies, 641
Clothing, 217
  Neolithic, 303
  Upper Paleolithic, 265, 266
Coco, Linda, 798–800
Code, Navajo language as, 431
Code of ethics, of American Anthropological Association, 31
Code of Hammurabi, 329
Code switching, 428
Codrington, R. H., 700
Coe, W. R., 318n
Coercion, law and, 676
Cognatic descent, 607
Cognitive capacity. *See also* Learning
  of archaic and modern *H. sapiens,* 242
  cultural adaptation and, 279
  Paleolithic and Mesolithic trends in, 274
  of Upper Paleolithic peoples, 269–270
Cohen, J., 373n
Cohen, Mark N., 305n, 308, 321n, 365n
Cohen, Yehudi, 547

Colburn, T., 372n
Coleman, J. C., 463n
Collier, J., 564, 571n, 581n
Colonization, Upper Paleolithic, 266
Colonizers, plants as, 291
Coloring. *See also* Skin color
  in African ritual activity, 228
  of artifacts and bodies, 219, 235
  in Aurignacian tradition, 239
  for decorating, 259
Comanche people, 471, 472
Comhaltas Ceoltoiri Eireann, 740
Coming of Age in Samoa:.... (Mead), 449
Common-interest associations, 631–634
  men's and women's, 632–634
Communes, extended family life and, 582
Communication, 404. *See also* Language;
  Project Chantek; Vocalization
  among animals, 406
  group membership and, 418
  among primates, 115–117
Complementary opposition, 660
Compliance, child rearing and, 452
Conception, perception and, 438–439
Conflict. *See also* Wars and warfare
  cultural, 462
  dispute settlement and, 677–679
Conflict resolution, 651
Conjugal bond, 544
Conjugal families, 549, 579
Connelly, J. C., 605n
Connor, M., 234n
Conroy, G. C., 144n, 171n, 180n, 235n, 238n
Consanguineal ("blood") relationship, 545, 549, 570, 577
Conservation, of primates, 110
Conspicuous consumption, 521
Construal, 745
Consumption patterns, 529
Contagious magic, 710
Continents
  Paleolithic spread over, 275
  separation of, 132–133
Contrastive pairs, of Lévi-Strauss, 548
Control. *See also* Cultural control; Order
  of crime, 677–679
  externalized, 669–674
  internalized, 668–669
  through law, 674–679
  religion and, 716
  witchcraft for, 673–674
Convergent evolution, 81, 473
Cooking, 216
  innovation in, 758
Coon, Carleton, 211, 358, 764n
Cooperation, 651
  economic, in family, 576–578
  groups and, 535
  among hominids, 195–196
Cooperative work groups, 510
Core-fringe-legume pattern (CFLP), 297
Core values, 456
Core vocabulary, 417
Corn. *See* Maize (corn)
Cornplanter (Seneca chief), 666
Cornwell, T., 234n
Corporations. *See* Multinational corporations
Correspondence, social stratification and, 334–335
Corruccini, R. S., 240n, 241n
Cortex, 100, 131
Cosleeping, 11–12
Courts, dispute settlement and, 678–679
Cousin marriage, 559–560
Cousins club, among Jewish people, 609, 628
Covert, Herbert, 135, 136
Covert Causation: Linguistic Traces of Effective Organizational Control (Wasson), 530
Cowgill, George, 317n, 792
Crabtree, Don, 251

Crafts
  growth of civilization and, 322, 338
  pottery as, 301–303
Craft specialization, 511
Cranial capacity
  in *H. erectus,* 205, 207
  of KNM ER 1470, 207
  of Neandertals, 228–229
Cranium, 102
Creation myths, 6, 77
Cremation burials, in Australia, 266
Cretaceous period, 132
Crick, Francis, 64
Cricket, in Trobriand Islands, 771–772
Crime, 677–679
  culture and, 401
Croatia, skull from, 269
Crocker, J., 399n
Crocker, W. A., 399n
Cro-Magnons, 250–251
  gene flow and skulls of, 270
  skeletons of, 24
Crop failures, 297
Crops. *See also* Agriculture; Domestication;
  Farmers and farming; Food production;
  Horticulture
  complexes of, 489–490
  in Mexico, 295–296
  Native American, 297
  vegeculture and, 295
Cross-cultural perspective, 11, 22, 28–29
  Murdock and, 23
Cross-cultural studies
  of child rearing, 448–452
  kinesics and, 413–414
Crow people, 471, 481, 516–517, 701–702
  women among, 633–634
Crow system, of kinship terminology, 619–621
Crusades, 682
Culotta, E., 71n, 135n
Cultivation. *See* Agriculture; Farmers and farming
Cults. *See* Revitalization movements
Cultural adaptation, 279
  Cro-Magnon and, 251
  Paleolithic and Mesolithic, 275, 279
Cultural anthropology, 9–12
  scientific approach and, 22–30
Cultural borrowing. *See* Diffusion
Cultural change, 754, 756
  adaptation and, 397–398, 758
  forcible, 764–774
  Haiti deforestation and, 769
  linguistic, 416–420
  modernization and, 777–787
  processes of, 753
  rebellion, revolution, and, 774–776
  stability and, 473
Cultural control, 668
Cultural deprivation theory, 21
Cultural ecology, 475
Cultural identity, protecting, 727–728
Cultural loss, 763–764
Cultural pluralism, 803, 804–808
  in Guatemala, 804–808
Cultural relativism, defined, 400
Cultural resource management, 46
Cultural Survival, Inc., 809
Cultural Survival Enterprises, 809
Culture. *See also* Art(s); Civilization; Domestication; specific topics
  abnormal behavior and, 388
  adaptation and, 79, 396–398, 482–483
  Apache houses and, 384–385
  archaeology and, 13
  Archaic, in Americas, 274
  change and, 398
  characteristics of, 382–392
  Chinese, 456–457

cities and changes in, 321–336
concept of, 382
defined, 382, 699
economics, business, and, 529–531
environment and, 439–440
ethnicity and, 803
ethnocentrism and, 808–810
evaluation of, 399–402
evolution of, 288
field studies of, 392–396
food in, 380
function of, 397–398
genetics, 368–369
global apartheid and, 810–812
of *H. erectus,* 209–221
human survival and, 379
integrated nature of, 390–392
Japanese, 456
language and, 389
as language setting, 420–428
learned nature of, 388–389
Maritime archaic, 274
marriage and, 548–549
Mesolithic, 273–274
Neandertal, 235
needs in, 393
Neolithic, 299–304
one-world, 793–795, 802
personality and, 446–452
protecting heritages, 727–728
race and, 356
racism and, 363–374
religion and change in, 716–719
reproduction and, 369
society, individual, and, 399
society and, 382–388
structural violence and, 812–821
symbols and, 389
tools and, 194–195
Upper Paleolithic, 258–266, 269
Culture areas, 473–475, 474 (map)
Culture-bound theories, 11
cross-cultural research and, 25–30
man as hunter and, 193
Culture core, 475–476
Culture of discontent, 787
Culture type, 474
Culturological approach, 390
Cushing, Frank Hamilton, 8
Cuzco, 329
Czech republic, skulls from, 269

Dade County, mental health program in, 460
Dahomey
    dual sex orientation of, 508
    women in, 507
Dali, China, skull from, 227
Darrington, Wilshire, 45
Dart, Raymond, 152
Darwin, Charles R., 24, 64, 76. *See also* Evolution; Heredity
Darwin, Erasmus, 76
Dating of past, 55–59
Datum point, 47
Davis, S. H., 796n
Dawson, Charles, 24
Day, G. M., 733n
Day-care centers, 437–438
Deacon, J., 447n
Death penalty, 709
Deception, language use and, 121
Deforestation, in Haiti, 769
Delinquency, culture and, 401
Demands, supply of goods and services and, 504
Dendrochronology, 56–57
Deniker, J., 348
Density of social relations, 479
Dentition. *See* Teeth
Dependence training, 448–451, 587
    defined, 449–450

D'Errico, F., 239n
DES, 371–372
Descent groups, 598–609
    ambilineal descent, 607–609
    bilateral descent, kindred, and, 613–615
    clans as, 610–613
    defined, 599
    double descent and, 607
    evolution of, 615–616
    forms and functions of, 609–616
    kinship and, 596, 616–621
    lineage and, 610
    matrilineal descent and, 604–607
    patrilineal descent and, 600–604
    phratries, moieties, and, 613
    unilineal descent and, 599–600
Descent of Man, The (Darwin), 24
Descriptive linguistics, 416
Descriptive system, of kinship terminology, 621
Desiccation theory. *See* Oasis theory
Dettinger, K. A., 438n
Developed countries. *See* Industrialized societies; West
Developing countries. *See also* Nonindustrial societies; Underdeveloped countries
    world hunger and, 814
Developmental stages, primate births at, 104
Deviance. *See* Abnormal personality; Core values; Personality
DeVita, P. R., 457n
DeVore, Irven, 251
De Waal, A., 644
De Waal, F., 111n, 114n
Diabetes, thrifty genotype and, 371
Dialects, social, 424–428
Diamond, J., 283n, 350n, 356n, 761n
Diet. *See also* Food; Food production; Hunting; Teeth
    animal fats and, 233
    Australopithecus and, 165–166
    of Eosimias, 138
    lactose intolerance and, 369–371
    meat in, 185–194
    tools and, 184
Diffusion, 761–763
Digestion, cooking and, 216
Dinosaurs, 86
Directed change, 768–771
Directional selection, 75
Discontent, culture of, 820–821
Discrimination, race and, 357
Disease. *See also* Health
    emergence of new, 373
    genetic, 72
    in Neolithic, 307
Displacement, 430
    symbolic language and, 120
Dispute settlement, 677–679
Distribution
    exchange and, 514–529
    of wealth, 521–525
Divergent evolution, 81
Diversification of labor, 322–325
Diversity, of modern humans, 344, 346
Divination, 714
Division of labor, Neolithic, 304
Divorce, 548, 553
    in non-Western societies, 563–564
    in North America, 574
Dixon, Roland B., 348
Dmanisi, Georgia, fossils from, 206, 207
DNA (deoxyribonucleic acid), 64–65
    gene flow and, 270–271
    mitochondrial, 241, 243–245
    mutation and, 70–72
Dobuan people, 455, 458
Doist, R., 80n
Dole, Robert, body language and, 413
Domestication, 283–287
    animal, 285–286, 292–294, 296

beginnings of, 286–287
    centers of, 294–297
    food production and, 484, 485 (map)
    plant, 284–285, 289, 290–292, 294–295
    productivity, instability, and, 298
    in Southeast Asia, 294–295
Domestic violence, 593
Dominance, sexual dimorphism and, 274
Dominant traits, 68–69, 70
Donnan, C. B., 330n
Double descent, 607
Dowry, 562
Dowson, T. A., 447n, 461n, 747n
Dozier, E., 796n
Dragon Bone Hill site, 203
Dragon teeth, 204
Draper, P., 447n
Drunkard's walk (study), 82–83
Dryomorph fossils, 142, 162
Dual sex configuration, 508
Dubois, Eugene, 202
Dumanoski, D., 372n
Dundes, Alan, 458
Dvorak keyboard, 760–761
Dwellings, social stratification and size of, 334
Dyes. *See* Coloring

Early Pleistocene Djetis beds, 202
Earoil, J. W., 360n
East Africa
    cooperative work in, 510
    pastoralists in, 492
East Asia
    "Eve" ("Out of Africa") hypothesis and, 242–243
    skulls from, 227
Ebonics, 21, 424
    study of, 425–427
Ecological niches, 132
Ecological zones, 292
Ecology, cultural, 475
Economic anthropology, 504–506
Economic development, tropical forests and, 323
Economics
    Aztec institutions, 496–497
    cooperation and family life, 576–578
    culture, business, and, 529–531
Economic systems
    distribution and exchange in, 514–529
    industrial, 505
    markets and, 502
    of nonliterate peoples, 504
    in Trobriand Islands, 504–506
Economy
    descent system and, 599
    in industrialized and nonindustrialized societies, 810–811
    informal, 528–529
    multinationals and, 796–797
Ecosystem, 471
Ecuador. *See* Shuar (Jivaro) people
Education
    Native Americans and, 445
    religion and, 716
    social class and, 640
Efe people, 348
Egalitarian societies
    food-foraging societies as, 483–484
    groupings in, 635
    leveling mechanism and, 514
    Neolithic, 304
Eggs, chromosomes and, 68
Egypt. *See also* Fayum Depression
    brother-sister marriages in, 546, 547–548
    centralized authority in, 327
    cities in, 314
    irrigation theory of civilization and, 336–337
    social class in, 638–639

Einstein, Albert, 365
Elderly. *See also* Age
  among Neandertal, 235
Electra complex, 545
Electron spin resonance, 58
Elizabeth II (England), ceremonies and, 708
Elkin, A. P., 705
Elk Soldier Society, 676
Ember, C. J., 400n
Ember, C. R., 793n
Ember, M., 400n, 793n
Empires. *See* specific empires
Enamel hypoplasias, 305, 306
Enculturation, 388–389
  defined, 436
  personality and, 446
Endogamy, 547–548
Enga patrilineage group, 522–523
England, archaeological sites in, 44, 45, 227
English language, 411
  family of, 418
  nonstandard English and, 426
  Standard English and Ebonics in, 424
Engraving, Bushman rock art and, 742–750
Entoptic phenomena, 259, 265, 745–747
Environment(s). *See also* Adaptation; Agriculture; Ecology; Pollution
  adaptation and, 469–470
  Australopithecus and, 165–166
  behavioral, 439–441
  bipedalism and, 171–172
  change and, 398
  ecosystem and, 471
  expansion into, 346–347
  fire and, 216–217
  human adaptations and, 469
  intelligence and, 366
  plant domestication and, 289–290
  tool use and, 211–213, 214
Environmental and social circumscription, 337
Eocene primates, 134–138
Eosimias, 136–137, 138
Epicanthic eye fold, 359, 360
Epics, 732
Epiglottis, 407
Epipaleolithic period, 283
Esber, George, Jr., 385
Eskimo. *See also* Inuit peoples
  kinship terminology system of, 617–618
  use of term, 357
Essay Concerning Human Understanding, The (Locke), 436
Essock, Susan, 118
Estrus, 102. *See also* Sex and sexuality
Ethics issues, 31
Ethiopia, skull from, 227
Ethnic groups
  in Burma, 795 (map)
  linguistic nationalism and, 419–420
  resurgence of, 803
  in Russian Federation, 387 (map)
Ethnic psychoses, 462–464
Ethnocentrism, 808–810
  business and, 529–531
  defined, 400
  in economic studies, 504
  in United States, 401
Ethnographic Atlas (Murdock), 23
Ethnographic fieldwork, 28
Ethnography, 15
  business and, 530
Ethnohistory, 29–30
Ethnolinguistics, defined, 421
Ethnology and ethnologists, 15
Ethnomusicology, 736–741
Ethnoscientists, 476
Europe. *See also* specific locations
  Cro-Magnons from, 250
  family life in, 570–571
  gender grouping and, 627–628

H. erectus from, 206–207
  lactose intolerance and, 369–370
  Neandertals from, 228–231
  nuns and, 564
  rock art in, 259–264
  warfare and, 682
Evangelism, 693, 702
Evans-Pritchard, E. E., 674n
"Eve" hypothesis (study), 240, 241, 243–245
Evolution, 64. *See also* Genes
  apes and human, 147–148
  of catarrhine primates, 145
  convergent, 81, 473
  Darwin and, 24, 76
  defined, 70
  divergent, 81
  of female sexuality, 539–540
  of genus *Homo,* 270
  human biological, 368–374
  nondirectedness of, 84–85
  paleoanthropology and, 36
  parallel, 473
  of populations, 80–81
  practical importance of, 85–87
  primate behavior and, 104–105, 125
  variation and, 346–348
Evolutionary adaptation, 471–473
Evolution of Culture, The (White), 390
Excavation. *See also* Archaeology
  archaeological, 47–50
  records and dating of, 52–59
  of Tikal, 319–321
Exchange
  distribution and, 514–529
  market, 525–529
Existence, 692
Exogamy, 547–548
  lineage, 610
  residence patterns and, 582
  Trobriand Islanders and, 392, 394–396
Expansion, environmental, 346–347
Expressions, 413–414
Extended family, 581–582, 587–588
Extermination programs, race and, 357
Externalized controls, 669–674
Extinction, 764–766
  of primate species, 110
Eyes
  epicanthic fold and, 359, 360
  of primates, 98

"Face" in extended families, 587–588
Fact, 23
Fagan, B. M., 52n
Falk, D., 158n, 178n, 181n
Family and family life. *See also* Child rearing; Descent groups; Divorce; Enculturation; Infant mortality; Marriage; Sex and sexuality
  abuse within, 571
  child rearing and, 568
  children and, 576
  conjugal family, 549, 579
  consanguine family, 549
  defined, 577
  descent groups and, 598–609
  domestic violence and, 593
  extended family, 581–582, 587–588
  female-headed household and, 591–593
  of food foragers, 484
  functions of, 575–578
  income and, 591–592
  kinship terms and, 423–424
  marriage and, 549
  in North America (study), 572–575
  nuclear family, 549, 579–581, 588–593
  organization of, 586–589
  patterns of, 535
  polygamy in, 586–587
  residence patterns and, 582–586
Family circles, among Jewish people, 608–609

Family life, in North America, 570–571
Farmers and farming, 280, 282. *See also* Agriculture; Food production; Horticulture; Plants
  in Africa, 531
  diversification of labor and, 322
  food foraging and, 287
  food-producing lifestyle and, 484–490
  geographical spread of, 297–299
  innovation in, 321
  irrigation theory and, 336–337
  in Jericho, 300–301
  land control and, 511–512
  in New World, 304
  settlements and, 299–300
  swidden farming and, 486
Faunal region, 346–347
Fayum depression, fossils from, 128, 134–135, 138
Feelings, chimpanzee vocalization and, 116
Female infanticide, 819
Female Power and Male Dominance (Sanday), 23
Females. *See also* Gender; Primates; Reproduction; Sexual dimorphism; Women
  A. afarensis, 154
  bipedalism and, 167
  households headed by, 591–593
  Paleolithic and Mesolithic trends and, 274
  reproduction and care of young in primates, 102–104
  sexual behavior in primates, 113–114
  sexuality of, 539–540
Feminine identity, of Native American men, 442–446
Femininity, child rearing and, 459
Ferguson, R. B., 656n, 681n
Ferguson, T. J., 296
Ferrie, H., 230n, 362n
Fertile Crescent, food domestication in, 287–288
Fertility
  food production and, 298
  humans and, 539
  in Neolithic villages, 307–308
Fieldwork, 15. *See also* specific studies
  archaeological evidence and, 53
  ethnographic, 16–20, 21, 28
  questionnaire surveys and, 27–28
Fingerprint patterns, human classification and, 354
Finland, Skolt Lapps and, 779–780
Fire, *H. erectus* and, 215–217
Fischman, J., 235n
Fishing, 283. *See also* Food-foraging societies
Fiske, S. J., 420n, 589n, 713n
Fission, in descent group, 610
Five Nations, 616
  gender grouping in, 626–627
  political power in, 666
  warfare and, 682
Flakes, of Klasies River people, 241
Flake tools, 210, 212
  Levalloisian, 227–228
  Mousterian, 232–233
Flannery, K. V., 338n
Fleagle, J. G., 139n, 143n, 178n, 216n
Flea markets, 528–529
Fleming, Alexander, 758–759
Flexible/integrated labor pattern, 507–508
Flores, Indonesia, 218
Flotation, 47
Fluorine test, 55
"Flying lemurs," 134
Folger, T., 168n
Folk healers, 460
Folklore, 728
  tales and, 733–734
Folkloristics, 728
Folk singers, 740
Folktales. *See* Folklore; Tales

Food. *See also* Diet; Farmers and farming;
  World hunger
  bipedalism and, 171–172
  cooking of, 251
  cultivation of, 280, 282
  culture and, 380
  diffusion and, 761–762
  fire and, 216
  and Neolithic health, 305–306
Food distribution, generalized reciprocity and,
  515–516
Food-foraging societies, 28, 29, 185, 279
  characteristics of, 479–480
  cultivation and, 282
  egalitarianism of, 483–484
  farming and, 299
  food production and, 287
  food sharing in, 482
  human fertility and, 298
  impact on human society, 480–484
  music among, 737
  subsistence patterns in, 476–484
  tools of, 512–513
  women in, 509
Food-producing societies, subsistence patterns
  in, 484–498
Food production, 279, 286–294. *See also*
  Agriculture
  in Americas, 295–297
  cultural diversification and, 308
  reasons for, 287–294
  spread of, 297–299
  in Tropics, 323
Food transporting, by ramamorphs, 146
Foramen magnum, 102
Forbes, J. D., 810n
Forcible change, 764–771
  acculturation and, 764–766
  directed change, 768–771
  genocide and, 766–767
  reactions to, 771–774
Forde, C. D., 582n, 607n
Foreign policy, multinationals and, 796
Forensic anthropology, 10–11, 234
Forensic archaeology, 234
Forests
  deforestation in Haiti and, 769
  economic development and, 323
  environment and, 212–213
  fire and, 216–217
Formal sanctions, 670
Form classes, 411
Fossey, Dian, 112, 162
Fossils, 37–43. *See also Australopithecus;*
  Skulls; specific types
  altered, 42–43
  of archaic *H. sapiens,* 228–231
  "Eve" ("Out of Africa") hypothesis and,
    241
  excavation of, 50
  of *H. erectus,* 200, 202–209
  of *H. habilis,* 178
  preservation of, 51–52
  primate, 128, 130–148
  sites and localities of, 43–52
Fossil studies, of human development, 24–25
Foucault, Michel, 798
Four-corners region, archaeological sites at,
  44
Fovea centralis, 98
Fox, Robin, 30, 401n, 579n
Fragile X Syndrome, 72
Frake, C. O., 325n
Frame substitution, 410
France. *See also* specific sites
  cave paintings in, 260
  jaw from, 227
  Mousterian sites in, 233, 235
Franke, R. W., 814n
Frayer, D. W., 255n
Frazer, George, 709

Freeman, L. G., 217n
Free morphemes, 410
Freud, Sigmund, 545
Frye, Marilyn, 412–413
Fundamentalism, 693
  in Iran and Algeria, 804
Funerals. *See also* Burials
  ritual, 707
Furlow, R. H., 32n
Furst, P. T., 461n

Galdikas, Birute, 112, 162
Gamble, C., 216n
Garbage Project (University of Arizona), 13–
  14, 393
Gardner, Allen and Beatrice, 429
Garn, Stanley, 348, 358
Gates, H., 776n, 820n
Gathering, by females, 192
Gays. *See* Homosexuality
Geertz, C., 12n
Gell, A., 726n
Gender. *See also* Females; Males; Sex and
  sexuality
  animal breeding and, 293
  bipedalism and, 167
  child rearing and, 459
  in Chinese society, 775–776
  common-interest associations and, 632–
    634
  defined, 383
  division of labor and, 506–508
  egalitarianism in, 627
  family life and, 575
  family roles and, 577–578
  female-headed households and, 591–592
  grouping by, 626–628
  initiation rites and, 705–706
  in Jewish, Christian, and Islamic traditions,
    716
  in Ju/'hoansi society, 448
  kinesics and, 412–413
  language and, 424
  marriage and, 544
  Paleolithic and Mesolithic trends and, 274
  personality and, 446–447
  political leadership and, 666–668
  roles and, 383–384
  scavenging and, 192, 193
  social stratification by, 641–642
  subsistence patterns and, 480–482
Gene flow, 73–74
  in genus *Homo,* 270–271
  in human development, 238
  race and, 355–356
Gene pools, 70
  culture and, 368–374
  "Eve" hypothesis and, 243–245
  farming and, 299
  human-chimpanzee comparisons and, 105
  ozone depletion and, 369–371
  plant domestication and, 291
  population, 69–77
  racial types and, 356
  radiation and, 371
  skin color and, 362
  variation and, 346, 357–359
Genera (genus), 94
Generalized reciprocity, 515–516
Genes, 64, 65–66
  polygenetic inheritance and, 69
  sickle-cell, 352
Genesis myths. *See* Creation myths
Genetic drift, 72–73
Genetic engineering, 374
Genetics. *See also* Gene flow; Gene pools;
  Genes
  incest taboo and, 545
Genital mutilation, 706–707
Genocide, 766–767
  in Rwanda (study), 644–646

Genotypes, 68, 346
  thrifty, 370
Genus *Homo,* 157
Geographic variation, in animals, 352
Geography. *See* Culture areas
Germanic subgroup, of Indo-European lan-
  guage family, 418
Germany
  Neandertal in, 228
  skull from, 227
Gesture-call system, 197, 411–416, 430–431
Gestures. *See also* Gesture-call system
  primates, humans, and, 429
Ghana, tale from, 733
Ghost Dance, 717, 773
Gibbons, A., 218n, 245n, 270n, 373n
Gibbons (apes), 108
Gibbs, J. L., Jr., 630n, 662n
Gingerich, Philip, 136, 137
Girls. *See* Femininity; Women
Girl Scouts, 624
Glaciers, 233
  food production and, 287
  migration and, 267
Glauberman, N., 366n
Glausiusz, J., 72
Global 2000, 793
Global warming, 815
Glottochronology, 417
Gluckman, Max, 775
Gluskabe (quasi-human being), 700
Goddard, V., 509n
Gods and goddesses, 696–697. *See also*
  Supernatural
Goldberg, A., 240n
Golden Bough, The (Frazer), 709–710
Gold miners, in Brazil, 782
Goldschmidt, Walter, 400
Gombe. *See* Goodall, Jane
Gonzales, Antonio, 633
Goodall, Jane, 111, 112, 117, 162, 166n,
  194n
Goodenough, W. H., 217n, 543, 549n
Goods and services, in cities, 314
Goody, J., 571n
Gordon, Robert J., 15, 297n, 400n, 447n,
  494n, 509n, 551n, 664n, 680n, 768, 810n
Gorer, Geoffrey, 456
Gorilla, 109. *See also* Apes; Primates
  group behavior of, 111
  home ranges of, 117
  Homo habilis compared with, 179
  individual interaction among, 112–113
  male dominance among, 543
  sexual behavior among, 114
  sign language and, 429
  tools and, 123, 166
Gornick, V., 459n
Gould, Stephen Jay, 6n, 25, 80, 80n, 83n,
  86–87, 238n, 285n, 718n, 763
Government
  central, 326–329
  as characteristic of civilization, 326–329
  earliest, 328–329
  of Hammurabi, 329
  of Inca, 329
  political organization and, 654
  in Tikal, 319
  in West, 665
Graburn, N. H. H., 581n
Gracia, A., 26n
Grains, domestication of, 284–285
Grammar, 411
Grasses, 284–286
Great Basin region, Native Americans of, 474
Great Plains region. *See also* Plains Indians;
  specific peoples
  Indians of, 458, 471, 472, 473–475
Great Pyramid, centralized authority and,
  327
Great Wall of China, 326

Green, Edward C., 713n
Greenhouse effect, 815
Grid system, 47, 48
Groom. *See* Arranged marriage; Marriage;
  Spouse
Grooming, among primates, 112, 114
Gross national product, wealth traffic and,
  817 (map)
Gros Ventre people, 481
Group(s), 535. *See also* Descent groups; Fam-
  ily and family life
  by age, 628–631
  common-interest associations as, 631–634
  by gender, 626–628
  Girl Scouts as, 624
  linguistic change and, 418
  primate, 111
  social stratification of, 634–647
Group marriage, 552
Group membership, descent groups and,
  599–600
Group personality, 452–458
  modal personality and, 453–455
  national character and, 455–458
Guaraní people. *See* Yanomami people
Guatemala, 387
  cultural pluralism in, 804–808
  genocide and, 766
  violence in, 805–807
Guatemala City, Tikal and, 317–321
Gusii people, divorce among, 563

Habitat disturbance, disease transfers and,
  373
Hadar tools, 183
Hadza people, 509
Haeri, N., 639n
Hafting, 228, 233
  Cro-Magnons and, 251
  in South Africa, 242
Hair, race and, 348
Haiti
  deforestation in, 769
  U.S. soldiers in, 683
Half-life, 56
Hall, Edward and Mildred, 531
Hallowell, A. I., 461–462
Hallucinogens, 460–461
Halverson, J., 264n
Hammurabi (Babylon), 329
Handedness, speech and, 197, 207–208
Hands (primate), 102, 103. *See also* Arboreal
  animals
Haplorhines, 97, 104, 106–109
Hardenbergh, Firmon, 252
Hardy-Weinberg Principle, 70
Harpending, Henry, 244, 271n
Harris lines, 305, 306
Harrison, G. G., 369n
Haviland, W. A., 32n, 297n, 318n, 319n,
  337n, 400n, 473n, 494n, 509n, 551n,
  582n, 642n, 664n, 729n, 803n, 810n
Hawaiian system, of kinship terminology, 617
Hawkes, K., 478n, 509n
Hazda people, 478
Heads. *See also* Brain; Fossils; Skulls
  childbirth and, 235
Healers. *See also* Shamans
  in Swaziland (study), 713
Health
  in Neolithic, 305–307
  pollution and, 814–818
Heat exchange, in *Homo habilis,* 181–182
Heat stress, bipedalism and (study), 168–171
Heaven's Gate cult, 717, 718
Hebrew people, 696
Hegman, M., 155n, 192n
Heilbroner, R. L., 504n
Heizer, Robert F., 47
Hemoglobin, 68–69
  abnormal, 307
Henry, Jules, 521n, 553, 792, 797

Herds and herding. *See also* Domestication;
  Pastoralists and pastoralism
  mechanized, 779–780
Heredity, 64–69. *See also* Evolution; Genes
  adaptation and, 77–85
  of blood types, 68–69
  intelligence and, 366
  population genetics and, 69–77
Herodotus, 7
  on Great Pyramid, 327
Herrenstein, Richard, 365
Herskovits, M., 510n
Heterozygous pair, 68
Hieroglyphics, of Maya, 328
Highland bagpipe, 739–740
"Hilly flanks" theory, 287
Hinton, Leanne, 425
Historical linguistics, 416
Historic Preservation Act (1966), 46
History
  archaeology and, 13
  cultural change and, 756
  ethnohistory and, 29–30
  legends and, 731–732
Hitler, Adolf. *See* Nazi Germany
HIV, 541–542. *See also* AIDS
  global distribution of, 540 (map)
  transmission of, 85
Hocquenghem, Anne Marie, 332
Hoebel, E. A., 472n, 661n, 675n, 775n
Holden, C., 793n
Hole, Frank, 47, 290n
Holistic perspective, 15
Holloway, R. L., 208n
Holocaust, genocide and, 766
Holy wars, 682, 685
Home ranges, of primates, 117
Hominid, 143
Hominidae family, 105
Hominines, 144, 148. *See also Australopithe-
  cus;* Gesture-call system; Language
  earliest, 150
  Homo sapiens and, 226
  Oldowan tools and, 184–185
  posture of, 166–172
  scavenging by (study), 188–191
  transitional culture of, 227–228
Hominoids, 104, 140–141
  cooperating and sharing among, 195–196
  similarities among, 105
Homo (genus), 175. *See also* specific types
  ancestors of, 133
  early, 178–183
  spread of, 200
Homo erectus, 25, 46, 157, 184
  Acheulean tradition and, 209–215
  from Africa, 204–206
  bamboo use and (study), 211–213
  from China, 202–204
  cranial capacity of, 194
  culture of, 209–221
  early *H. Sapiens* and, 226–227
  from Europe, 206–207
  fire use by, 215–217
  fossils of, 43, 200, 202–209
  and *H. habilis,* 208–209
  from Java, 202
  physical characteristics of, 207–208
  relationship with *H. habilis,* 208–209
  transitional skull of, 226
  variation and, 347–348
Homogeneous world culture, 793–795
Homo habilis, 178–180
  and *Australopithecus,* 181–183
  cooperation and sharing by, 195–196
  cranial capacity of, 194
  gorilla compared with, 179
  H. erectus and, 208–209
  language and, 197
  stone tools of, 186
  tools and, 183–184, 185
Homologies, 94, 95

Homo sapiens, 6. *See also* Upper Paleolithic
  appearance of, 226–232
  archaic (Neandertals), 224, 228–231
  cognitive capacity and, 269–270
  late *H. erectus* and, 226–227
  locomotion of, 160
  modern human origins and, 237–240
  transitional skull of, 226
  transition from archaic to anatomically
    modern, 268–269
  Upper Paleolithic people, 250–271
  variations in, 279
Homosexuality. *See also* AIDS
  gay or lesbian couples and, 544
  Native American intersexuality and, 442–
    446, 458, 481–482
Homozygous pair, 68
Hooton, Earnest, 348
Hopi Indians, 470, 489, 613
  divorce among, 563, 564
  extended families of, 582
  innovation and, 757
  matrilineal society of, 605–607
  matrilocal extended family among, 584
  residence patterns and food production,
    585
  stratification among, 642
  syncretism and, 772
  totemism among, 612–613
  war and, 680
Hormone-disrupting chemicals, 371–374
Horses, Southeast Asia fossils of, 211–212
Horticulture, 308, 468
  slash-and-burn, 469
Horticulturists
  land control and, 511–512
  tools of, 513
Hostetler, Jr., 384n
Household, 551
  defined, 578–579
  female-headed, 591–593
  organizational types, 586–589
  production by, 508
Housing, 551. *See also* Shelter
  for Apaches, 384–385
  Neolithic, 303
HRAF. *See* Human Relations Area File
  (HRAF)
Hsu, Francis, 441, 456
Human diversity, 344
Humanities, 30–31
Human Relations Area File (HRAF), 23, 29
Human rights. *See* Cultural pluralism; United
  Nations
Humans. *See also* Adaptation; Cro-Magnons;
  Human diversity; Neandertals
  apes and evolution of, 147–148
  bipedalism of, 166–172
  classification of, 96
  continuing biological evolution of, 368–374
  disease transfer from animals, 373
  "Eve" ("Out of Africa") hypothesis of,
    240–245
  as food producers, 287–294
  fossil preservation of, 38–43
  genetic variation among, 357–359
  multiregional hypothesis of, 237, 238
  origins of modern, 237–240
  physical variation of, 346–348
  primate evolution and, 104–105
  ramamorphs and origins of, 143–144
  separate ancestral populations of, 244
  simultaneous evolution of, 237
  theories of evolution of, 238
  Upper Paleolithic, 250–271
Human sacrifice, in Aztec empire, 400, 709
Hunger. *See* World hunger
Hunter-gatherers, 478. *See also* Food-foraging
  societies; Subsistence patterns
Hunting, 282. *See also* Domestication; Food
  foraging
  animal domestication and, 293

in food-foraging society, 482
gender and, 193
by *H. erectus*, 217–218
by Mousterian peoples, 233–234
Paleoindian, 268
Paleolithic and Mesolithic trends in, 274–275
by primates, 124
Upper Paleolithic, 254–258
Huntington, G., 384n
Huntington's Disease, 72
Husband. *See also* Arranged marriage; Marriage; Spouse
female, 562–563
Hussein, Saddam. *See* Kurdish people
Hutu people, 645, 646
Hybrids, 270
Hydraulic theory of civilization, 336
Hypoglossal canal, 220, 237
Hypotheses, 24
cross-cultural research and, 28–29

"I" ("me"), development of, 439
Ibibio people, witchcraft and, 710, 711–712
Ibn Khaldun, 7
Ice Age. *See also* Glaciers
cave paintings from, 261–264
Iconic images, 745
Ideograms, 327–328
Igbo people, 666–667, 794
Ikwe Marketing Collective, 808
Imagination, 22
Imitative magic, 710
Immigrants, intelligence testing of, 366
Implants, and standardization of women's bodies (study), 799–800
Inbreeding, incest taboo and, 546–547
Inca empire
government of, 329
redistribution in, 519–521
Incest taboo, 545–547
endogamy, exogamy, and, 547–548
Income, in single-parent household, 591–592
Incorporation, 706
in rites of passage, 705
Independence training, 451–452
defined, 451
India
arranged marriage in (study), 554–559
caste system in, 636–637
Indian. *See also* Native Americans
use of term, 356
Indigenous peoples. *See also* specific groups
advocacy for rights of, 809
in Guatemala, 807
pollution and, 818
wealth traffic and, 817 (map)
World Council of Indigenous Peoples, 803
Individual, culture, society, and, 399
Individual interaction, among primates, 112–113
Indo-European language family, 417, 417 (map), 418
Indonesia, structural violence in, 811
Indus River region, civilization of, 495 (map)
Industrial economies, 505
Industrialization, modernization and, 777
Industrial societies. *See also* Underdeveloped countries; West
conspicuous consumption in, 521
labor specialization in, 511
resource uses and waste generation by, 811
Indus Valley, cities in, 314
Infancy, in primates, 104
Infanticide, female, 819
Infant mortality, 589–590
stress and, 339
Infants. *See also* Child rearing; Children
food transport, bipedalism, and, 172
transporting of, 147
Informal economy, 528–529
Informal sanctions, 670

Informants, 15
Ingmanson, E. J., 124n
Inheritance. *See also* Genes; Heredity
of intelligence, 366–367
of skin color, 362
Initiation rites, 705–706
and cave paintings, 264
Inkblot test, 454
Innovation
acceptance of, 759–761
as change mechanism, 757–761
cultural dynamics and, 759
Integration
of culture, 390–392
defined, 390
Integrative mechanisms, 778
of Zuni, 795–796
Intelligence
brain size and, 158
defined, 366–368
environment and, 366
frequency distribution and, 367 (map)
heredity and, 366
of orangutans (study), 118–122
of primates, 117
race and, 364–366
Intensification rites, 707–708
Intensive agriculture, 308
of Aztecs, 495–498
and nonindustrial cities, 493–498
Interdependence of goods and services, in cities, 314
Interests. *See* Common-interest associations
Internalized controls, 668–669
International Indian Treaty Council, 633
International Monetary Fund, 811
Intersexuality, 458
among Native Americans, 442–446, 481–482
Inuit people, 357, 358, 552. *See also* Eskimo system
arts and, 727
family of, 579–581
Inupiat people. *See* Alaska
IQ. *See also* Cognitive capacity; Intelligence
race and, 364, 365–368
twin studies and, 366
Iran. *See* Bakhtiari people; Zagros Mountains, Iran
Iraq, 235. *See also* Kurdish people
Irish potato famine, 298
Irons, W., 196n
Iroquoian people, 616, 682
gender grouping of, 626
kinship terminology and, 618–619
stratification among, 642
Irrigation, 489
Irrigation agriculture, 475
Irrigation theory of civilization, 336–337
Islam, masculine-authoritarian concept of god in, 697
Isolating mechanisms, 83
Israel, 235
excavations in, 34
kibbutz relationships and, 546, 577
Ituri forest, people in, 439
IUDs, in China, 820

Jacobs, Sue Ellen, 458n, 635–636
Jacoby, R., 366n
Jain, R. K., 544n
James, Gideon, 633
Japanese, national character of, 456
Java
H. erectus from, 202
H. sapiens from, 231
Jaws. *See* Teeth
Jenkins, Carol, 373
Jensen, Anne, 38
Jericho, 293
farming in, 300–301
Jewish people. *See also* Hebrew people; Israel

age grouping and, 628
ambilineal descent in New York, 607–609
Nazis and genocide policy, 766
religion and, 693
Jivaro people. *See* Shuar (Jivaro) people
Johanson, Donald, 42, 154
Johnson, A., 522n
Johnson, D., 551n
Jolly, Allison, 406
Jolly, C. J., 147n
Jorgensen, J. G., 521n
Joyce, C., 11n
Juarez, Mexico, slum near, 786
Judgments, cultural relativism and, 400
Ju/'hoansi Bushmen, 437, 447, 477, 479, 481, 484. *See also* Bushmen
age division of labor among, 509
band organization of, 655
directed change and, 768
family life and, 578
generalized reciprocity among, 515
genocide and, 766
land control and, 512
music of, 739
shamans of (study), 703–704
tools of, 513
trances and, 461
Julien, M., 239n
Jungers, William L., 188

Kaiapo people, 803
Kaiser, J., 80n
Kalahari Desert, 447. *See also* Ju/'hoansi Bushmen
lion behavior in, 389
Kambili epic, 732
Kangaroo rat, 77
Kanin, Leon, 366
Kanjera, Kenya, 162
Kano, T., 111n
Kanzi (chimpanzee), 429
Kao Poh Nam, Thailand, 215
Kapauku Papuans, 390–391, 658, 684
law and, 676
marriage and, 550, 551
Karen people, 794
Kay, Richard, 137, 138n, 144n
Kayapó Indians, 765
Keller, Albert, 23
Kendall, Lauren, 709
Kenya. *See also* Lake Turkana region, Kenya; Leakey, Louis S. B.; Leakey, Mary
blades from, 242
Kenyapithecus, 143, 146
Kenyatta, Jomo, 510
Kephart, Ron, 425n, 427
Khufu, Great Pyramid of, 327
Kibbutz
child rearing on, 577
marriage and, 546
Kidnapping, of women and children, 820
Kin
affinal, 544
consanguineal, 545
isolation from, 588–590
Kindred, 614–615
Kinesics, 412–414
defined, 412
King, Martin Luther, Jr., 428
King Philip's War, legend about, 732
Kinship, 535
Crow system of terminology, 619–621
descent and, 596, 598–599
Eskimo system of terminology, 617–618
groups of, 617–621
Hawaiian system of terminology, 618
Iroquois system of terminology, 618–619
marriage and, 547
among Native Americans (study), 611–612
Omaha system of terminology, 621
as political organization, 659–660

Sudanese (descriptive) system of terminology, 621
terminology of, 616–617
Kinship terms, 423–424
Kitsunetsuki disorder, 463
Kiwi birds, adaptation of, 80
Klasies River people (South Africa), 241–242
Kluckhohn, Clyde, 382, 517n, 714
Knauft, B. M., 663n, 680n
KNM ER 1470, 178, 182
cranial capacity of, 207
Knuckle-walking, 107, 109
Koch, G., 741n
Kohler, G., 810n
Kolata, Alan, 494
Koloddday, A., 627n
Konigsberg, L., 165n
Königswald, G. H. R., 202
Koobi Fora, skulls from, 181
Koro disorder, 463
Koshland, D. E., Jr., 71n
Kota people, 517
Kottack, C. P., 32n
Koufos, G., 143n
Kpelle people, 662–663, 679
Kroeber, A. L., 382, 796n
Kroll, Ellen, 188
Kromdraai, South Africa, 159
Kula ring, 518–519
Kuper, H., 665n
Kurdish people, genocide and, 766
Kwakiutl people, 455, 607

LaBarre, Weston, 456
Labor
child, 509–510, 818
craft specialization and, 511
diversification of, 322–325
Labor patterns, 506–511
age division of labor and, 509–510
cooperation and, 510
craft specialization and, 511
sexual division of labor and, 506–508
La Chapelle-Aux-Saints, France, 229, 235
Lactase, 369
Lactose, 369
Lactose intolerance, thrifty genotype and, 370–371
Ladakh people, 552
Ladinos, 356
in Guatemala, 805, 806, 807
in Mexico, 774
Laetoli, Tanzania, 154, 159, 161, 162
La Ferrassie, France, 224
Lagash, Mesopotamia, 322, 340
Laguna, Frederica de, 736
Lake Champlain area, 46
Lake Titicaca, 494
Lake Turkana region, Kenya, 152, 161, 204
Lake Victoria region, 162
Lake Zurich, Switzerland, 45
Lana (chimpanzee), 429
Land, control of, 511–512
Land bridge, between Siberia and Alaska, 267
Language, 404. See also Linguistic anthropology
culture and, 389, 420–428
defined, 406
farming and, 299
gender and, 424
gesture-call system of, 411–416
grammar and, 410
of H. erectus, 207–208, 220
of H. habilis, 180, 197
kinesics and, 412–414
kinship terms in, 423–424
linguistic change and, 416–420
morphology and, 410
nature of, 407–411
of Neandertals, 236–237

among Northern Ute, 419–420
origins of, 428–431
phonology and, 409–410
social class and, 638–639
sound and shape of, 408–411
spread into Americas, 267
syntax and, 410
vocalizations and, 416
word usage in, 416–417
Language family, 418
defined, 417
Lapps. See Skolt Lapps
La Quina, France, 233
Larynx, 407
Last Supper, The (Leonardo da Vinci), 744, 745
Latah disorder, 462
Laville, H., 240n
La Violencia (Guatemala), 805
Law
defined, 670, 674–675
functions of, 675–676
Hammurabi and, 329
social control through, 674–679
Law of competitive exclusion, 164
Law of Primitive Man, The (Hoebel), 675
Leach, Edmund, 21
Leakey, Louis S. B., 112, 161, 162, 178
Leakey, Mary, 154, 161, 162, 178
Leakey, Richard, 148
Leap, William L., 420–421
Learned behavior, 388–389
Learning. See also Cognitive capacity
by primates, 117, 118–122
Leavitt, G. C., 546n
LeClair, E. E., Jr., 514n
Lee, Richard, 479
Legends, 731–733
Legitimacy, of political systems, 683–685
Legros, D., 476n
Lehmann, C., 710n
Leigh, S. R., 216n
Leinhardt, G., 700n
Lemuriformes, 97
Lemurlike primates, 134
Leonard, W. R., 155n, 192n
Leonardo da Vinci, 744, 745
Leopards, hominine scavenging and (study), 188–191
Lerner, Richard N., 728
Lesbians. See Homosexuality
Levalloisian technique, of tool manufacturing, 227–228
Leveling mechanism, 513–514
Levine, N. E., 552n, 587n
Levirate, 552
Lévi-Strauss, Claude, 547, 548
Lewin, Roger, 143n, 167n, 178n, 260, 261n
Lewis, I. M., 15
Lewis-Williams, J. D., 447n, 461n, 744n, 747n
Lewontin, Richard, 366
Lie detector, 679
Lifestyle
of Americans, 803
food-foraging and, 476–484
social class and, 639–640
Light, fire and, 217
Lineage, 610. See also Segmentary lineage system
in Hopi society, 606
Lineal system, of kinship terminology, 617–618
Lingua franca, English as, 411
Linguistic anthropology, 14–15
Linguistic change, 416–420
Linguistic divergence, 417
Linguistic nationalism, 419, 421
Linguistics. See also Language; Verbal arts
defined, 408
Linnaeus, 95

Linton, Ralph, 761
Linton, Sally, 193
Literature. See also Art(s); specific types
Native American influences on, 762
"Little songs," of Awlad 'Ali Bedouins, 734–735
Locke, John, 436
Locomotion. See also Bipedalism
of A. anamensis and Ardipithecus, 164
of Homo sapiens, Australopithecus, and apes, 160
Lorblanchet, Michel, 260, 261–264
Lorenzo, C., 226n
Lovejoy, C. O., 167n
Lovers. See Marriage; Sex and sexuality
Lowenstein, Jerold, 66
Lower Paleolithic, tools from, 183–197
Lowie, Robert, 516, 761
"Lucy," 154, 158, 188
Lung cancer, asbestos and, 372–374
Lyon, Patricia, 332

Mabal skull, 232
MacCormack, C. P., 706n
Mace, R., 298n
MacNeil, R., 682n
MacPhee, Ross, 137
Madness and Civilization (Foucault), 798
Magic, 708–710
Magnarella, Paul, 787
Mair, L., 712n
Maize (corn), 286, 297
domestication of, 284
Makapansgat, 154
Makhubu, Lydia, 713
Malaria, 352–353, 369. See also Sickle-cell gene
adaptation and, 469
Male descent. See Patrilineal descent
Male dominance, in Kapauku culture, 391
Males. See also Gender; Primates; Reproduction; Sexual dimorphism
dominance of, 543
Paleolithic and Mesolithic trends and, 274
sexual behavior in primates, 113–114
status in society, 193
Malinowski, Bronislaw, 392–393, 674, 707
on needs, 393
Trobriand Islanders study and, 392, 394–396
Maliseet people, 611
Mammals, 95–98. See also Primates
development of, 130–132
Southeast Asia fossils of, 211–212
Mammary glands, adaptation and, 80
Mandela, Nelson, 536
Mande people, 732
Man Makes Himself (Childe), 288
Mao Tse-tung, 457
Marcus, Joyce, 338n
Maritime archaic culture, 274
Market exchange, 502, 525–529
marketplace and, 525–526
Marketplace
market exchange and, 525–526
structure and function of, 528
Markets, flea markets as, 528–529
Marquesan Islanders, 552
Marriage, 535. See also Polygyny; Sex and sexuality
as alliance, 554
bride-price and, 560–561
bride service and, 562
choice of spouse and, 553–559
between cousins, 559–560
cultural nature of, 536
defined, 543
dowry and, 562
family and, 549
forms of, 550–563

group, 552
levirate, 552
in lineage exogamy, 610
mating and, 548–549
monogamy and, 550
within and outside the group, 547–548
polyandry and, 551–552
polygyny and, 550–551
same-sex, 544, 562–563
serial monogamy and, 552–553
sororate, 552
Marriage exchanges, 560–562
Marsella, J., 803n
Marshack, Alexander, 219, 236
Marshall, M., 16n
Martin, Emily, 541
Martin, Robert D., 136
Martinez, I., 226n
Mason, J. A., 519n
Massacres, genocide and, 766
Mathematics, 325
Mating, marriage and, 548–549
Matriarchy, myth of, 730–731
Matrilateral cross-cousin marriage, 559–560
Matrilineal descent, 599, 604–607
divorce and, 564
Matrilocal residence, 584
Matson, F. R., 758n
Mauer, Germany, fossils from, 206, 207
Mau Mau, 717
May, Elaine, 574
Maya people, 25–27, 45, 681. See also Tikal
agriculture of, 321, 322
calendar of, 325
children's work and, 509
cooperative work among, 510
descent groups of, 598
development of stratification among, 642–643
diffusion and, 761
extended family of, 582, 583
gender stratification of, 641–642
Guatemala violence and, 806–807
metals and, 323
patrilocal residence patterns of, 582–584
religion and, 337–338
Venus tables of, 718
writing of, 328
Maybury-Lewis, David, 400, 808
Mbuti people, 439, 477–478, 483
ambilocal residence of, 584
family life and, 578
McBrinn, G. E., 192n
McCarthy, Joseph, 740
McCorriston, J., 290n
McFarlane, Len, 251
McHenry, H. M., 155n
McVeigh, Timothy, 676
Mead, Margaret, 456
cross-cultural studies of, 448
personality and, 446
work of, 449
Meat eaters
Mousterian peoples as, 233
protein consumption and, 192–194
scavengers and, 185
tools, brains, and, 185–194
tools for butchering, 184
Mechanized herding, 779–780
Mediation, dispute settlement and, 678
Medicine. See also Surgery
selection and, 369
standardization of women's bodies and (study), 798–800
Western vs. folk healers, 460
Mediterranean region, plant domestication in, 289
Meignen, L., 240n
Meiosis, 67–68
Mekranoti Kayapo Indians (study), swidden farming among, 486–489

Melanesia
cargo cults in, 773
ritual cannibalism in, 707
Melanin, 359
Melemchi people, 459–461
Mellars, P., 233n
Melody, 737
Melting pot ideology, 764
Men. See also Gender; Group(s); Patrilineal descent; Sex and sexuality
abnormal personality and, 458
body language and, 412–413
common-interest associations among, 632–634
division of labor and, 506–508
in food-gathering societies, 481–482
Native American feminine identities and, 442–446
in Trobriand Island culture, 394–396
Menchú, Rigoberta, 806
Mendel, Gregor, 64, 65, 68, 70
Mende people, female initiation rites of, 706
Mental ability. See also Intelligence
of orangutan, 121
Mental health. See also Personality
anthropology and, 460, 462
Mesghinua, H. M., 511n
Mesoamerica
civilization in, 315
Neolithic culture in, 304
writing in, 328
Mesolithic era, 58, 271–274. See also Pale-olithic period
cultural diversity in, 273–274
farming, pastoralism, and, 283
food foraging in, 292
tools and weapons in, 271–273
trends in, 274–275
Mesopotamia
cities and, 314
irrigation theory of civilization and, 336–337
stress of civilization and, 340
writing in, 328
Mestizo, 356
Metals
in Americas, 323
trade in, 324
Mexico. See also Aztec empire; Zapatista movement (Mexico)
armed conflict in, 681
food production in, 323
plant domestication in, 295–296
Teotihuacan in, 312
Mexico City, 317
Miami Community Mental Health Program, 460
Microlith, 271–272, 274
Middle East
Bakhtiari pastoralists in, 490–493
farming settlements in, 301
fossil sites in, 46, 228
plant domestication in, 290–294
religious persecution in, 715
Middle Paleolithic traditions, 232
Middle Stone Age. See Mesolithic era
Middleton, J., 607n
Migraine sufferers, entoptic phenomena and, 745, 746
Migration
to Americas, 267
gene flow and, 73–74
population growth and, 233
temperature and, 217
during Upper Paleolithic, 266–268
Mi'kmaq people, 611–612
Millennium, Revitalization movements and, 718
Miles, H. L. W., 118n, 188, 197n, 430n
Milk, lactose intolerance and, 369–370
Miller, Henry, 455

Minangkabau people, matrilineal society of, 609
Mintz, Sidney, 297, 297n
Miocene epoch, 139–141. See also Ramamorphs
Mire, Soraya, 707
"Missing link," 24, 202
Missionaries
as change agents, 768
technological, 772
Trobriand Islanders and, 771–772
Yanomami and (study), 783
Mitchell, W. E., 608n, 668n
Mitochondrial DNA, human evolution and, 241, 243–245
"Mitochondrial Eve." See "Eve" hypothesis (study)
Mitosis, 66
Mobility
scavenging and, 192
social, 640–641
Moche priestess (Peru), burial of (study), 330–334
Moctezuma, 498
Modal personality, 453–455
Modernization, 777–787
defined, 777
among Shuar people, 780–781
Skolt Lapps, snowmobiles, and, 778–780
and "underdeveloped" world, 785–786
unpleasant aspects of, 786–787
Mohawk Indians, 613, 616
Moholy-Nagy, H., 642n
Moiety, 613
Monaghan, Leila, 425
Money, 527
Mongaloid, 348
"Mongaloid face," 358–359
Monkeys. See also Primates
in Oligocene epoch, 138–139
Monogamy, 548–549, 550
among primates, 114
serial, 548, 552–553
Monroe, James, 810
Montagnais people, 483
Montagu, M. F. A., 364n
Monuments, in Tikal, 319
Moore, J., 111n, 196n
Moran, B. K., 459n
Morgan, Lewis Henry, 619
Morgen, S., 592n
Mormons and Mormonism, 717, 719, 773
Morocco, skull from, 227
Morotopithecus, 140, 141
Morphemes, 410
Morphology, 410
Mortality
infant, 589–590
in Neolithic, 305–307 (study)
stress and, 339
Moseati, S., 335n
Moths, adaptation by, 78
Motif, 733
Mousterianlike tradition, 232
Mousterian tradition, 232–235
symbolic plaque from, 236
Movement. See Migration
Movius, Hallam, 211
Movius line, 211
Mullings, L., 592n
Multinational corporations, 795–802
Multiregional hypothesis, 237, 238
"Eve" ("Out of Africa") hypothesis and, 240, 241
gene flow and, 271
Mundugamor people, 447
Mundurucu people, 627
family life and, 578
household among, 579
Murdock, George Peter, 23, 607
Murray, Charles, 365

Murray, Gerald F., 769
Music, 736–741
  functions of, 739–741
  as identifier, 739
  manual labor and, 740
  systems of, 737–738
  Upper Paleolithic, 258
Mutagenic agents, 371
Mutation, 70–72
  DNA analysis and, 245
  isolating mechanisms and, 84
  plant domestication and, 291–292
  sickle-cell gene as, 352
Mwindo epic, 732
Myanga people, 732
Myers, J. E., 710n
Myers, J. P., 372n
Myth(s), 700–701
  creation, 6, 77
  verbal arts and, 729–731
Mythology, 700
  legends and, 732

Nader, Laura, 31, 647, 800
Nafkin, N., 666n
Nakedness, of human skin, 170
Namibia, 643
  Ju/'hoansi people of, 447–448, 447 (map)
  rock art in, 260
Nanda, S., 554n
Nandi people, same-sex marriage among, 562–563
Naples, Italy, children's economic role in, 509
Nash, Philleo, 20–21
Naskapi people, 483
Natadecha-Sponsal, P., 457n
Nation. See also State
  defined, 664
  state compared with, 664–665
National character, 455–458
  Japanese and, 456
  objections to studies of, 456–458
National Endowment for the Arts, 724
National Environmental Policy Act (1969), 46
National Historic Preservation Act, 296
Nationalism, linguistic, 419
Nationalist movements, 793–794
Native Americans. See also specific groups
  animatism of, 700
  archaeology and, 54, 296
  bison hunts and, 471
  blood types of, 347
  culture areas and, 473–475
  dual sex orientation of, 508
  education of, 445
  European American borrowing from, 761–762
  food production by, 286–287, 295–297
  gender roles in, 388
  genocide and, 766
  government policy and, 450
  of Great Basin region, 474
  of Great Plains, 458
  intersexuality among, 442–446, 458
  kinship organization of (study), 611–612
  North of Mexico, 297
  patrilocal residence and land claims of, 30
  Penobscot and, 440–441, 442–446
  religion and, 445
  social stratification among, 642
  spirits and, 699
  tribes of, 656
  warfare and, 681–682
  Windigo psychosis among, 463–464
Natufian culture, 273
  plant domestication and, 289, 290–294
Naturalistic worldview, 694–695. See also Worldview

Natural selection, 74–77
  evolution of populations and, 80–81
  geographically variable human traits and, 352
  race and, 353
  single births and, 104
Nature/nurture. See Intelligence
Navajo Indians
  code talkers of, 431
  culture and environment of, 470
  witchcraft and, 712–714
Navajo Tribal council, 657
Nayar people
  consanguine families of, 549
  family of, 579
  households among, 578
  sexuality among, 543–544
Nazi Germany
  genocide in, 766, 767
  racial worldview of, 357
Neandertals, 24, 52, 224, 228–231. See also Mousterian tradition
  archaic moderns and, 269
  Aurignacian tradition and, 237–238
  childbirth among, 235
  coexistence with modern humans, 237–240
  society of, 235
  spoken language and, 236–237
  symbolic life of, 235–236
Needs
  cultural meeting of, 401
  Malinowski on, 393
Neer, R. M., 359n
Negative reciprocity, 517
Negative sanctions, 669, 670
Negroid, 348
Nelkin, D., 366n
Neolithic period, 282
  civilization and, 314, 315 (map)
  clothing in, 303
  culture of, 299–304
  domestication in, 283–287
  housing in, 303
  human biology and, 305–308
  and idea of progress, 308–309
  irrigation theory of civilization and, 336–337
  pottery in, 301–303
  social structure in, 303–304
  technology in, 301–303
  transition to urban life during, 321–336
Neolocal residence, 585
Nepal, Melemchi of, 459–460
Nepeña Valley. See Moche priestess (Peru)
Nesbit, L. M., 511n
Net hunting, 251, 255–256
Neurotic individual, 462
"New Age" revitalization movement, 717
Newburyport, Massachusetts. See "Yankee City" study (Warner)
New Guinea, 266
  divorce in, 563
  people of, 447
  warfare in, 680
Newly-emerged countries
  cultural change in, 774–775
  mental health in, 460
New Stone Age. See Neolithic period
New World. See also Americas
  civilization in, 315
  writing in, 328
New World monkeys. See Platyrrhines
New York City, Jewish ambilineal descent groups in, 607–609
Nez Perce people, 6
Ngandong, Java, 231
Nichols, Johanna, 267
Nietschmann, B., 775n

Nile River region, civilization of, 495 (map)
Nobel Prize, 669
  Menchú, Rigoberta, and, 806
Nomads and nomadism. See also Pastoralists and pastoralism
  environment and, 398
  pastoral, 491
  pottery and, 302
Noninindustrial modern cities, subsistence patterns in, 484–498
Noninindustrial societies
  children's work in, 509
  common-interest associations in, 632
  conspicuous consumption in, 522–525
  craft specialization in, 511
  economies of, 504
  household production in, 508
Nonstandard English. See Black English; English language
Nonunilineal descent, 607
Non-Western societies. See also Divorce; Marriage
  future and, 792
  marketplaces in, 525–528
Non-whites, apartheid and, 810–812
Normal personality, abnormal personality and, 458–464
Normative orientation, 440
Normile, D., 109n, 111n
North America. See also Canada; United States
  age grouping in, 628
  civilizations of, 495 (map)
  core values in, 457–458
  extended family in, 588
  family life in, 570–571, 572–575 (study)
  female-headed households in, 591–593
  genocide in, 766
  independence training in, 451, 452
  individual in, 399
  nuclear family in, 588–590
  religion in, 693
  witchcraft in, 711
Northern Ireland, cultural pluralism in, 808
Northwest Coast Indians, pictorial arts of, 742
Notochord, 96
Nuclear accidents, 815–816
Nuclear family, 549, 570, 579–581, 588–593
  in North America, 572–575
  relationships in, 570–571
Nuer people
  kinship organization of, 659–660, 661
  language and, 423
Nulliak, Labrador, 273
Nunney, L., 77n
Nuns, in Europe, 564
Nursing, food production and, 298

Oakland Schools, Ebonics in, 425–427, 428
Oasis theory, 287
Oaxaca, Mexico, 317
Obi, 666–667
Object orientation, 440
Obler, R. S., 562n
Obsidian
  Aztec use of, 325
  surgical use of, 251–252
  trade in, 324
Occupations, in Tikal, 320
O'Connell, J. F., 478n, 509n
Octave, 737, 738
Oedipus complex, 545
Offiong, D., 710n
Oglala Sioux, 701
Ojibwa people, totemism and, 612
Okonjo, K., 666n
Old age. See Age
Oldowan tool tradition, 184–185
  Acheulean and, 209

Old Stone Age. *See* Paleolithic period
Olduvai Gorge, Tanzania, 47, 161, 162, 178
    Oldowan tool tradition and, 184–185
    scavenging study and, 188, 191
    tools from, 183–184
Old World, civilization and, 315
Old World monkeys. *See* Catarrhines
Oligocene epoch, 138–139
Oliwenstein, L., 158n
Olszewski, D. I., 291n
Omaha system, of kinship terminology, 621
O'Mahoney, K., 511n
Omomyids, 134, 138
Omu, 667
One-world culture, 793–795
On the Origin of Species (Darwin), 76
Open-class societies, 641
Orangutans, 106, 108–109, 144. *See also*
    Apes
    intelligence of (study), 118–122
    sign language and, 429
Order
    political organization and, 652, 668–674
    state and, 665
Orientation, behavioral environment and, 440
Ortiz, Alfonso, 605n, 692
Ouranopithecus, 143
"Out of Africa" hypothesis. *See* "Eve" hy-
    pothesis (study)
Overtones, 737
Ozone depletion, gene pools and, 371

Painting. *See also* Art(s); Cave art
    Bushman rock art and, 742–750
    on pottery, 303
    from rock shelters, 259
    in Tikal, 319
Paiute people, 474
Paleoanthropology, 36. *See also* Archaeology
Paleocene Epoch, 134
Paleoindians, 268
Paleolithic period, 58, 175, 209. *See also*
    Mesolithic era
    food sources in, 282
    forensic archaeology and, 234
    Lower, 183–198
    Middle, 232
    population increase and movement in,
        233–234
    sites from, 45
    trends in, 274–275
    Upper, 237–240, 250–271
Palynology, 56
Pan (genus), and humans, 105
Pañamarca. *See* Moche priestess (Peru)
Papago people, 489
Papua New Guinea (study), conspicuous con-
    sumption and, 522–525
Parades, Anthony, 400
Paralanguage, 415
Parallel evolution, 473
Parapithecids, 138–139
Parish, A. R., 111n, 117n
Park, P. B., 216n
Parker, Richard, 541
Participant observation, 15
Pastner, S., 803n
Pastoralists and pastoralism, 283, 292, 308.
    See also Domestication; Food-foraging so-
    cieties
    Bakhtiari people as, 490–493
    defined, 490–493
Pataxó Indians, 781
Patriarchal religion, 697
Patrilateral parallel-cousin marriage, 559
Patrilineal descent, 599, 600–604
    in Taiwan (study), 602–604
Patrilocal residence, 29–30, 582–583
Patterns of affect, 441

Patterns of Culture (Benedict), 455
Pech Merle cave paintings, 261–262, 263
Pelegrin, J., 239n
Pelto, P. J., 778n
Penicillin, 758–759
Penobscot Indians, 440–441, 697
    study of, 442–446
Pentadactyly, 102
Pentatonic music system, 737, 738
Pequot Indians, 766
    genocide and, 767
Perception, child rearing and, 438–439
Percussion method, 184
Permian period, 130
Permissive child rearing, 452
Persecution, religion and, 715
Personality, 446–452
    child rearing and, 434, 436–465, 448–452
    defined, 446
    group, 452–458
    modal, 453–455
    normal and abnormal, 458–464
Peru
    civilization in, 315
    Inca government in, 329
Pesticides, 371
Phenotype, 68, 346
Phenotypic traits, 356
Phonetic alphabet, 410
Phonology, 409–410
    group differences and, 418–419
Phratries (superclan units), 613
    in Hopi society, 605
Phylogenies, 85
Physical anthropology, 9
    archaeology and, 36
    scientific methodology and, 24
Physical appearance. *See* Appearance
Physical characteristics, of *H. erectus,* 207–
    208
Physical variable
    human, 346–348
    racial, 357–359
Physiological stress, in Neolithic (study),
    305–307
Phytoliths, 285
Pibloktoq disorders, 463
Pictographs, 327
Pictorial art, 741–750
Pig domestication, 294, 301
Piggot, Stuart, 36
Pigments, 228, 259. *See also* Coloring; Skin
    color
    in cremation burials, 266–267
Pilbeam, David, 141–142, 146n
Piltdown discoveries, 24–25
Pima Indians, 370
Pimentel, D., 371n
Pithecanthropus erectus, 202
Pitt, D., 800n
Plains Indians, 458, 471, 472–473, 473–475
    gender roles among, 481–482
Planets, Maya and, 325
Plant foods, 283. *See also* Farmers and farm-
    ing; Food foraging
    Natufian culture and, 273–274
Plants
    angiosperms, 131
    domestication of, 284–285, 289, 290–292,
        294–295, 484, 485 (map)
    protein from, 192–193
Plastic surgery, 799
Plattner, S., 477n, 526n
Platyrrhines, 97, 106, 107
    origins of (study), 135–137
Play, among primates, 115
Plesiadapiformes, 134
Plog, F., 147n
Plows, 301

Pluralism, cultural, 386, 803, 804–808
    Russian Federation and, 387, 387 (map)
Podolefsky, A., 769n
Poetry, songs and, 735–736
Point Franklin Project, 38
Pokotylo, David, 251
Polanyi, K., 514n
Political organization
    order and, 652, 668–674
    religion and, 684, 685
    social role of, 651
    war and, 680–683
Political organization, Bushman rock art and
    (study), 747–749
Political systems, 654–668
    centralized, 661–665
    leadership and gender in, 666–668
    legitimacy and, 683–685
    multinationals and, 796–800
    uncentralized, 654–661
Politics, music and, 740
Pollution, 814–818
Polyandry, 549, 551–552, 587
Polycentric theory of human evolution, 238
Polygamy, families and, 586–587
Polygenetic inheritance, 69
Polygraph, 679
Polygyny, 549, 550–551. *See also* Polygamy
    in Kapauku culture, 391
    among Nandi people, 562–563
    sororal, 587
    wealth-generating, 551
Polymorphic species, 346–347
    polytypic species and, 374
Polytheism, 696
Polytypic genetic variants, 347, 355
Polytypic species, 374
Pomo people, basket making of, 728
Pongidae family, 105
Pope, G. C., 211n, 215n, 243n, 270n
Population(s), 70
    in ancient Mexico, 317
    control of, 818–820
    evolution of, 80–81
    expanding (study), 243–244
    food production and, 484
    genetic drift and, 72–73
    global, 818
    natural selection and, 74–77
    organisms in, 470
    within species, 83
    Tikal Mayan, 320–321
    world hunger and, 812–814
    worldwide growth rates, 813 (map)
Population density, among food-foragers,
    479–480, 480
Population genetics, 69–77
Population growth
    farming and, 298
    food production and, 288–289
Porphyria, 369
Positive sanctions, 669
Pospisil, Leopold, 390, 550n, 658–659, 676n
Postindustrial society, 792
Posture. *See also* Bipedalism
    of humans, 166–172
Potassium-argon analysis, 57, 58
Potato famine, 298
Potlatches, 522, 524
Pottery
    Neolithic, 301–303
    from New World, 304
Potts, R., 192n
Poverty
    in female-headed households, 591
    among women, 592
Powell, John Wesley, 26
Power. *See* Political organization
Power, M. G., 117n

Power, M. W., 337n, 473n, 729n
Predmost, Czechoslovakia, 258
Prehensile, 102
Prehistoric Indian sites, 45
Preindustrial cities, 498–499
Premarital sexual activity, 539
Preservation of fossils, 51–52
Pressure flaking, 253–254
Priests and priestesses, 701
    burial of Peruvian (study), 330–334
    Tikal Mayan priesthood and, 320
Primary innovation, 757, 758
Primates
    anthropoid origins and (study), 135–137
    characteristics of, 98–105
    conservation of, 110
    cultural behavior among, 389
    fossils of, 128, 130–148
    modern, 105–109
    monogamy among, 549
    as order, 64, 95–98
    rise of, 132–147
    sexuality and, 539–540
    social behavior of, 110–125
    Temple monkeys as, 92
Pringle, H., 255n, 289n, 294n
Prins, Harald, 611–612
Problem solving, 379
Proconsul, 139–141
Production, household, 508
Products, worldwide, 794
Progress. *See also* Evolutionary adaptation
    concept of, 753, 754
    Neolithic and, 308–309
Progressive income tax, 520
Project Chantek, 118–122
Property
    Catholic Church and, 564, 570–571
    dowry and, 562
    leveling mechanism and, 514
Propliopithecidae, 138
Protein, sources of, 192–193
Psychological disorders, ethnic psychoses and, 462
Psychological tests, modal personality and, 454
Psychology, 12
Psychotic individuals, 462–464
Puberty
    genetic changes and, 372
    rites of Australian Aborigines, 705–706
Public works, centralized authority and, 326–327
Pueblo. *See* Hopi Indians
Puerto Ricans, 804
Puleston, D. E., 319n
Punishment, 670
Purdum, Elizabeth D., 400
Putnam, Fredric Ward, 26
PVCs, 372
Pyramids, Aztec, 498

Qafzeh, Israel, 58, 239–240, 241
Queens, as political leaders, 666
Quercy paintings, 262
Questionnaire surveys, 27–28
QWERTY keyboard, 759–761

Race, 83, 348–362. *See also* Racism
    American Anthropological Association statement on, 357n
    as biological concept, 349–355
    Census Bureau categories of, 356–357
    classification of (study), 350–354
    concept of, 355–357
    culture and, 356
    intelligence and, 364–366
    IQ testing and, 364, 365–368
    physical variables and, 357–359
    skin color, adaptation, and, 359–362
    traits and, 348–349

Racemization. *See* Amino acid racemization dating
Races (Coon, Garn, and Birdsell), 348–349
Racial barriers, 84
Racism, 363–374. *See also* Apartheid; Race
Radcliffe-Brown, A. R., 391, 612, 669
Radiation, 371
    adaptive, 130
Radioactivity, mutation and, 71
Radiocarbon analysis, 56, 58
Rain Forest Crunch, 809
Raised-field technology, 494
Rak, Y., 240n
Ramamorphs, 141–143
    adaptations of, 144–147
    and human origins, 143–144
Ramphele, Mamphela, 7
Rappaport, R. A., 468n
Rappaport, Roy A., 30
Rathje, William, 14
Rationalism, religion and, 692–694
Raw materials, of early civilizations, 324
Reagan, Ronald, legends and, 731
Reality, language and, 422
Rebellion, cultural change and, 774–776
Recer, P., 117n
Recessive traits, 68–69, 70
Reciprocity, 514–515
    balanced, 516–517
    generalized, 515–516
    negative, 517
Records, writing as, 327–328
Redistribution, 519–521
Red ochre. *See* Coloring; Pigments
Regionalism, Paleolithic and Mesolithic trends in, 275
Reina, R. E., 761n
Reindeer, snowmobiles and, 779–780
Reischauer, Edwin, 32–33
Reiter, R., 447n
Relationships, family households and, 571
Relative dating, 55–56
Relatives. *See* Kindred
Relethford, John, 244, 271n
Religion. *See also* Missionaries
    anthropological approach to, 694–695
    civilization and, 337–339
    cultural change and, 716–719
    defined, 694
    functions of, 692, 714–716
    gods, goddesses, and, 696–697
    magic and, 708–714
    Native Americans and, 445
    persecution and, 715
    politics and, 684, 685
    practice of, 695–708
    rituals, ceremonies, and, 705–708
    social role of, 651
    specialists in, 701–705
    supernatural and, 690–701
    among Tewa people, 692
    of Tikal Maya, 320, 337–338
Replacement
    cultural loss and, 763
    cultural loss without, 763–764
Replacement reproduction, 818
Reproduction
    and care of young, 102–104
    culture and, 369
    hormone-disrupting chemicals and, 372–374
    isolating mechanisms and, 83
    population control and, 818–820
Reptiles, 130
Republic of Congo, diseases in, 373
Residence patterns
    ambilocal, 584
    avunculocal, 585–586
    of families, 582–586
    matrilocal, 584
    neolocal, 585

patrilocal, 582–583
Resources. *See also* Population(s)
    land control and, 511–512
    leveling mechanisms and, 513–514
    patterns of labor and, 506–511
    pollution and, 816
    technology and, 512–513
Retirement, 628–629
Retroviruses, 73–74
Revitalization movements
    cultural change and, 772–774
    religion and, 716–719
Revolts, revolution and, 775
Revolution
    cultural change and, 774–776
    defined, 774
Reynolds, V., 389n
Rhythm, 738
Rice, D. S., 323
Rice, P. C., 32n
Rice, P. M., 323
Rice cultivation, 280, 294–295
Rickets, 360
Rightmire, G. P., 205n
Rindos, D., 282n, 284n
Rites. *See also* Ritual(s)
    of intensification, 705, 707–708
    of passage, 705–707
Ritual(s). *See also* Rites
    in Africa, 228
    in Australia, 266–267
    collective, 695
    magic and, 708–710
    religious, 690, 705–708
Ritual cannibalism, 707–708
Ritual cleaning, by primates, 112
Robertson, Pat, 773
Robinson, George Augustus, 766
Robinson, John, 159
Rock art, 259–264
    Australian, 259, 262, 266
    of Bushmen, 742–750
    study of, 747–749
Rock carvings, 219, 221
Rogers, J., 105n
Roles. *See also* Gender
    age and, 384
    gender and, 383–384, 459, 480–482
Roman Catholic Church. *See* Catholic Church
Roman Egypt (Roman). *See* Egypt
Romer, Alfred S., 99
Roosevelt, A. C., 305, 321n
Root crops, 295, 296
Rorschach test, 454
Rosaldo, M. Z., 564, 571n, 581n
Rosas, A., 206n
Roscoe, Paul, 28
Roscoe, Will, 444–445
Rose, Steven, 366
Ross, C., 138n
Rumbaugh, Duane, 118
Rural Development (Chambers), 27
Rusinga Island, 162
Russian Federation, ethnic groups in, 387 (map)
Rwanda, genocide in (study), 644–646

Saami people. *See* Skolt Lapps
Sacrifice Ceremony, in Peru, 332–334
Sacrifices, Aztec, 400, 709
Sahlins, M., 517n, 659n
Saint Césaire, France, 239, 269
Salem, Massachusetts, witchcraft in, 710
Salzman, P. C., 491n
Same-sex marriage, 544, 562–563
Samoan people, 607
Sanctions, control and, 669–670
Sanday, Peggy R., 23, 364n, 507n, 609, 731n
Sand paintings, 725
Sangree, W. H., 630n

Sanitation, cities, towns, and, 339
San José de Moro. *See* Moche priestess (Peru)
Sapir, Edward, 410
Sapir-Whorf hypothesis, defined, 421–422
Sarah (chimpanzee), 429
Savanna
    bipedalism and, 168–171
    forest environment and, 212–213
    protein sources of, 192–194
Scalpels, stone, 251–252
Scapula, 102
Scavenging
    bipedalism and, 167–168
    gender roles and, 193
    by *H. habilis*, 185–188
    hunting and, 217, 218
    study of carnivores, 188–191
Schepartz, L. A., 235n, 237n
Schizophrenia, 462–463
Schlegel, A., 607n
Schliemann, Heinrich, 45
Schneider, H. K., 514n
Schoningen, Germany, 46
Schools, age grading in, 628
Schurtz, Heinrich, 632–633
Science
    of Maya, 325
    religion and, 692–693, 693
Scientific approach, 22–30
Scotland, clan affiliation and, 596
Scottish pipers, 739–740
Sea, resources from, 241
Seasonal uplands, 489–490
Secondary innovation, 757
Sedentary community. *See* Settlement(s)
Sedentary lifestyle, food production and, 484–490
Seeds
    crops from, 287
    in Natufian subsistence, 290–291
    plant domestication and, 284–285, 291
Seeger, Pete, 740, 741
Segmentary lineage system, 659
Selassie, Tekle Haile, 771
Selection. *See also* Natural selection
    Cro-Magnons and, 251
    mitochondrial DNA and, 245
    reproduction, culture, and, 369
    unconscious, 284–285
Self
    and behavioral environment, 436–446
    Native Americans and, 450
    Penobscot view of, 440–441, 442–446
Self-awareness, 436–437
Self-determination, 803
Self-identification
    music and, 739
    racial categories and, 357
Seligman, C. G., 15
Sellen, D. W., 298n
Semenov, S. A., 53
Semitonal music system, 737–738
Seneca people, 666
Sense organs, of primates, 98–99
Separation, in rites of passage, 705
Separatist movements, 793–794, 795
Serbs, in Bosnia, 652
Serial monogamy, 548, 552–553
Serpent Mount (Ontario, Canada), 53
Settlement(s). *See also* Cities; Civilization
    of farmers, 484–490
    farming and, 282
    food production and, 287–288
    at Jericho, 301
    Neolithic, 299–304
    pottery and, 302
Sex and sexuality. *See also* Gender
    biological nature of, 383
    cave art and, 264
    control of sexual relations, 539–549
    dependence training and, 451

Native American intersexuality and, 442–446
    primate reproduction and, 102–104
    among primates, 113–115
    racial traits and, 353–354
    rules of sexual access, 542–545
    sharing, cooperation, and, 195–196
    in society, 399
    among Trobriand Islanders, 538–539
Sex roles. *See* Gender; Roles
Sexual dimorphism, 114–115, 155, 157
    bipedalism and, 167
    of *Homo habilis*, 178
    Neandertal pelvis and, 231n
    Paleolithic and Mesolithic trends in, 274
Sexual division of labor, 506–508
Sexual segregation, 508
Shamans, 701–705
    pictorial arts and, 747
Shanidar Cave, Iraq, 235, 239, 240
Shapiro, H., 700n
Sharer, R. J., 251n
Sharing
    of food, 482
    among hominoids, 195–196
Shaw, Dennis, 32
Shea, John, 251
Sheehan, Glenn, 38
Sheep, domestication of, 292, 293
Sheets, Payson, 251, 252
Shelter. *See also* Housing
    of *H. erectus*, 217
    Mesolithic, 273
    Mousterian, 234
    Upper Paleolithic, 265–266
Sherente people, 642
Shorto, R., 693
Shoshone Indians, 474
Shostak, M., 793n
Shreeve, Jane, 230n, 237n, 245n, 251n, 355
Shuar (Jivaro) people, modernization and, 780–781
Siamangs, 108
Siberia, colonization of, 266
Sickle-cell gene, 69, 78–79, 307, 352–353, 369
    adaptation and, 469–470
Sight. *See* Vision
Signal, defined, 406
Sign language, 406, 407
    chimpanzees and, 429–430
Silent trade, 517–518
Silk, J. B., 552n, 587n
Sillen, Andrew, 216
Sima de los Huesos (Spain), 226, 228
Simons, Elwyn, 135, 136, 270n
Simpson, O.J. and Nicole, 593
Simpson, S., 38n
Sinanthropus pekinensis, 203
Singer, P., 118n, 197n, 430n
Single mothers, 591–593
Single-parent households, 553, 579
Sioux Indians, 471
    Wounded Knee and, 808
Sipán. *See* Moche priestess (Peru)
Sites (fossil), 43–52. *See also* specific sites
    of *H. erectus*, 203
    Mousterian, 233–234
    of Neandertal burials, 235
Sivapithecus, 141, 143
Sjoberg, G., 329n
Skara Brae, Orkney Islands, 45
Skeletons. *See also* Fossils; Skulls
    of archaic *H. sapiens*, 230–231
    of Cro-Magnons, 24, 251
    domestication and, 285–286
    of *H. erectus*, 207–208
    primate, 96, 101–102
Skepticism, 22–23
Skilled labor, growth of civilization and, 322
Skin, naked, 170

Skin cancer, ozone depletion and, 371
Skin color
    adaptation and, 359–363
    culture and, 388
    depigmentation and, 361–362
    distribution of pigmentation, 362 (map)
    inheritance of, 69
    melanin and, 359
    race and, 348, 350–354
Skolt Lapps, snowmobiles and, 778–780
Skuhl, Israel, 240
Skulls. *See also* Fossils; Skeletons; Teeth
    of archaic *H. sapiens,* 228–230, 231, 232
    from Dali, China, 227
    from Ethiopia, 227
    "Eve"" ("Out of Africa") hypothesis and, 241
    transition from *H. erectus* to *H. sapiens,* 226
    Upper Paleolithic, 269, 270
Slash-and-burn farming, 469
    Maya and, 26–27
Slavery, of women, 820
Small, M. F., 480n
Snaketown, Arizona, 51
Snow, Clyde C., 10–11
Snowmobiles, Skolt Lapps and, 778–780
Social behavior, of primates, 110–125
Social class, 535
    Aztec, 497
    caste and, 636–638
    defined, 636
    family life and, 575
    Rwanda genocide and (study), 644–647
    social stratification and, 329–336
Social control. *See* Control
Social dialects, 424–428
    Ebonics study and, 425–427
Social factors, race, racism, and, 356–357, 363–374
Social-impact assessment, 635–636
Social isolating mechanisms, 84
Social rank, 535
Social sciences, cultural anthropology and, 11
Social stratification
    burial of Peruvian Moche priestess and, 330–334
    in cities, 329–336
    of groups, 634–647
    indicators, 334–336
Social structure
    of Aztecs, 497
    defined, 382
Social Structure (Murdock), 23
Société de Linguistique de Paris, 428
Society. *See also* Cultural anthropology; Culture; Family and family life; Food-foraging societies
    action theory and, 338–339
    Aztec, 497
    civilization and, 314
    culture, individual, and, 399
    culture and, 382–388
    defined, 382
    egalitarianism of food-foraging, 483–484
    food-producing, 484–498
    ills of, 401
    impact of food foraging on, 480–484
    multinationals and, 796–797
    Neandertal, 235
    Neolithic, 303–304
    in nonindustrial agricultural cities, 493–498
    nuclear family in, 570–571
    pluralistic, 386
    sexually segregated, 508
    status of men in, 193
Sociolinguistics, 424–428
Sociology, 12
    anthropology and, 27–28
    cultural anthropology and, 11

I-16 INDEX

Sodergem, J. A., 217n
Soil marks, 44
Solutré, France, 258
Solutrean laurel leaf blades, 254
Somalia intervention, 32
Sorcery, 712–714
    in Swaziland (study), 713
Sororal polygyny, 551, 587
Sororate, 552
South Africa. *See also Australopithecus,*
    afarensis and *africanus*
    apartheid in, 810–812
    fossils from, 241–242
    rock art in, 260, 742–750
    social stratification in, 643
South America. *See also* Americas; Central
    America
    civilizations of, 495 (map)
    Upper Paleolithic peoples in, 267
Southeast Asia. *See also* China
    Andaman Islanders of, 356
    domestication in, 294–295
    forest adaptation and, 213
    H. erectus and, 218
    H. erectus bamboo tools in (study), 211–
    213
    tools from, 210
Southwest Asia
    coexistence of Neandertal and modern hu-
    mans, 239
    domestication in, 289, 290–294
    "Eve" ("Out of Africa") hypothesis and, 241
Soviet Union, ethnic groups in former, 387
    (map)
Spain, 228
    cave paintings in, 260
    hominine fossils from, 226
Spatial orientation, 440
Spear hunting, Upper Paleolithic, 254–255,
    258
Specialization
    among Aztecs, 496
    diversification of labor and, 322
Speciation, 81–83
Species, 81
    evolution of, 86
    polymorphic, 346–347
    populations within, 83
Speck, F. G., 440n
Speech, 220. *See also* Language; Vocalization
    human biology and, 407
    voice qualities and, 415–416
Sperm
    chromosomes and, 68
    decline in counts, 372, 374
Speth, J. D., 240n
Spirits
    ancestral, 697–698
    Native Americans and, 700
    Penobscot view of, 443–444, 697
Spoken language
    and gestural language, 430–431
    of Neandertals, 236–237
    written records and, 327
Spouse, choice of, 553–559
Spuhler, J. N., 196n
Squires, Susan, 530
Stabilizing selection, 75–76
Stacey, J., 552n, 571n, 591n
Stahl, A. B., 193n
Standard English, 424
Standardization, of women's bodies (study),
    798–800
Standard of living, modernization and, 786–
    787
Stannard, D. E., 756n
Starvation. *See* World hunger
State
    defined, 663
    nation compared with, 664–665
    order and, 665

political organization and, 654
    as political system, 663–665
    war and, 680
Status. *See also* Caste; Social class
    in food-foraging societies, 483–484
    skin color and, 362
Status symbols, 639–640
Stereoscopic vision, 98
Stereotypes, racial, 357
Sterkfontein, South Africa, 154
Stern, Jack T., 188
Stevenson, Matilda Coxe, 8
Steward, D., 678n
Steward, Julian H., 474, 474n, 475
Stigler, S. M., 217n
Stiles, D., 478n
Stoker, W. C., 406n, 430n
Stoler, M., 731n
Stone, R., 369n
Stone Age. *See also* Neolithic period; Pale-
    olithic period
    language in, 431
Stonehenge, 303
Stone tools, 251–252
Stories. *See* Verbal arts
Strapping Youth fossil, 204
Stratified site, 47–48
Stratified society, 635
    class, caste, and, 636–640
    gender and, 641–642
    Rwanda genocide and (study), 644–646
Stratigraphy, 55
Straughan, B., 494n
Strepsirhines, 97, 104, 105–106
Stress
    civilization and, 339–340
    in Neolithic, 306–307
Structural differentiation, 777, 778
Structural-functionalist school of thought, 391
Structuralism, Lévi-Strauss and, 548
Structural violence
    in Brazil, 781–785
    culture of discontent and, 820–821
    defined, 812
    in Indonesia, 811
    pollution and, 814–818
    population control and, 818–820
    world hunger and, 812–814
Strum, Shirley, 110
Subculture
    defined, 384
    use of term, 386
Subgroup, in pluralistic society, 387–388
Sub-Saharan Africa, farming in, 299
Subsistence patterns, 466. *See also* Food pro-
    duction
    adaptation and, 468–476
    food-foraging lifestyle and, 476–484
    food-producing society and, 484–498
    gender and, 480–482
    and nonindustrial cities in modern world,
    498–499
    scavenging and, 190
Subspecies, races as, 83
Sudan, religious persecution in, 715
Sudanese (descriptive) system, of kinship ter-
    minology, 621
Sumer
    civilization of, 314–315
    farming in, 321
Supernatural
    ancestral spirits and, 697–698
    animatism and, 700–701
    animism and, 698
    religion and, 690, 696–701
Surgery, stone tools for, 251–252
Surveys, questionnaire, 27–28
Survival of the fittest, 75
Susman, Randall L., 188
Swanscombe, Kent (England), 46, 227
Swartkrans, South Africa, 159, 216

Swaziland, medicine and sorcery in (study),
    713
Swazi people, state of, 665
Sweat glands, 361
Swidden farming, 486
    in Chiapas, Mexico, 490
Switzerland, cultural pluralism in, 804, 808
Symbolic indicators, 639–640
Symbolic language, primate use of, 120
Symbolic life
    of *H. erectus,* 218–219
    of Neandertals, 235–236
    spoken language and, 237
Symbols
    cultural role of, 389
    defined, 406
Syncretism, 771–772
Syntax, 410–411
    defined, 410
Systemic nature of society, environment and,
    338–339
Systems of Consanguinity and Affinity of the
    Human Family (Morgan), 619

Taboos
    incest, 545–547
    sexual access and, 542–543
Taghan people, divorce among, 563
Taiwan, patrilineal society in (study), 602–
    604
Tales, 733–734
Talking. *See* Language; Spoken language
Tanner, Nancy, 193
Tanzania, fossils from, 154, 227
Tardieu, C., 159n
Tarsierlike primates, 134
Tarsiers, 97, 106
Tasmanians, genocide and, 766
TAT. *See* Thematic Apperception (TAT) test
Tata, Hungary, 236
Taung (ape man), 158n
Taurus Mountains, animal domestication and,
    289
Taxonomy, 95
Tchernov, E., 240n
Techno-economic aspect of culture, 390
Technology. *See also* Tools
    in Americas, 268
    archaeological evidence and, 53–59
    cultural adaptations and, 482–483
    fire and, 215–217
    of Klasies River people, 241–242
    labor and, 512–513
    Mesolithic tools and weapons, 271–273
    metals and, 325
    modernization and, 777
    Neolithic, 301–303
    raised-field, 494
    of Tikal, 319
    tools and, 213, 214
Teeth. *See also* Primates
    of *A. boisei* and *A. robustus,* 161–162
    of *Ardipithecus,* 164
    of *Australopithecus,* 155–156, 165, 182
    cooking and, 216
    of Cro-Magnons, 251
    enamel hypoplasias and, 305, 306
    of *Homo habilis,* 182
    meat eating and, 185
    primate, 96–97, 100–101, 130
    sexual dimorphism and, 155, 157
Tegrean people, craft specialization and, 511
Tells (archaeological sites), 46
Temple monkeys (Thailand), 92
Tenochtitlán, 495, 497–498
Teocallis, 498
Teosinte, 285, 286
Teotihuacan, Mexico, 312, 315–316
    bureaucracy in, 329
    centralized authority in, 326–327
    infant and child mortality in, 339

Terra Nullius, 740
Territory, food forager concept of, 484
Terrorism, in Guatemala, 805
Tewa people, 692
Text. See also Writing
    Mayan, 328
Textiles, from New World, 304
Thailand, family group in, 568
Thematic Apperception (TAT) test, 454
Theology, of Western society, 697
Theory, 24
Thinking. See also Intelligence
    language and, 422
Third World. See Newly emerged countries;
    specific locations
Thomas, Elizabeth Marshall, 389, 389n
Thomas, Peter A., 46
Thomson, K. S., 76n
Thorne, B., 564n, 581n
Thornhill, Nancy, 546–547
Threat gestures, among primates, 147
Thrifty genotype, 370
Thurow, L. C., 504n
Thyroid cancer, 371
Tibetan people, 552
Tiffany, S., 667n
Tiger, Jerome, 450
Tikal, 27, 45, 48, 49, 52, 317–321. See also
    Maya people
    agriculture at, 321
    centralized authority in, 326
    excavation evidence, 319–321
    religion and, 338
    social class and, 335n
Tillier, A. M., 240n
Tiriki people, age grading by, 629, 630–631,
    661
Tiv people, money of, 527–528
Tiwanaku, 494
Tlatelolco, 496
Tlingit people, 736
Tobacco, diffusion of, 762 (map)
Tobias, P. V., 202n
Todd, N. E., 192n
Togue, R. G., 231n
Tolland Man, 37
Tombs
    of Moche priestess (study), 331
    as public works, 327
Tonality, 737
Tonowi, as Kapauku headman, 658–659
Tools. See also Technology
    A. boisei and, 178
    Acheulean tradition and, 209–215
    of Australopithecus, 165–166
    butchering and, 217
    culture and, 194–195
    diversification of, 210
    of early civilizations, 324
    Levalloisian technique and, 227
    from Lower Paleolithic, 183–197
    of Maritime archaic culture, 274
    meat, brains, and, 185–194
    modern stone, 251–252
    Mousterian tradition and, 232–235
    Neolithic, 301, 302
    objects as, 123
    Oldowan tradition and, 184–185
    of Paleoindians, 268
    Paleolithic and Mesolithic trends in, 274
    for plant domestication, 291
    pre-hominine use of, 167
    technology and, 512–513
    of Upper Paleolithic peoples, 253–258
Torralba, Spain, 217
Tory Islanders, family of, 579
Totemism, 612–613
Touch, of primates, 98–99
Toulouse-Lautrec, Henri, 72
Towns. See Cities
Toxic wastes, 815

Trade
    barter and, 517–518
    of Jericho, 301
    in Mesoamerica, 324
    networks of, 337
    silent, 517–518
    technology and, 325
    in Tikal, 319
    Upper Paleolithic, 266, 275
Tradition, modernization and, 778
Training. See Dependence training; Independence training
Traits, 68. See also Heredity
    adaptation and, 469–470
    racial classifications and, 348–349, 352–
        354
    sexual, 542
Trances, 459–461, 702
    entoptic phenomena and, 744–747
    rock art and, 259, 260, 744
Transhumance, 292, 492
Transition, in rites of passage, 705–706
Transportation, cultural loss and, 763
Transporting
    of food, 146, 171–172
    of infants, 147
Triassic period, 131
Tribe
    among Native Americans, 611–612, 656
    as political organization, 656–659
Trobriand Islanders
    avunculocal residence and, 586
    Kula ring of, 518–519
    marriage and, 547, 560–561
    sexuality among, 538–539
    study of, 392, 394–396
    syncretism among, 771–772
    yam production among, 504–506
Tropical regions
    economic development and, 323
    H. erectus in, 217
    hominine development and, 360
    wetlands in, 489, 490
Troy, 45
Trukese study, 16–20
Truzzi, M., 521n
Tsembaga people, 476
Tsu (family unit)
    in China, 601–602
    fission in, 610
Turkana people, marriage and, 550
Turkey, 292, 293
    civilization in, 315
    pig domestication in, 294, 301
Turkmen Weaving Project, 809
Turnbull, Colin, 451, 712n
Turner, T., 765
Tutchone people, 476
Tutsi people, 349, 645–646
Twa people, 645, 646
Twentieth Century, The: A People's History
    (Zinn), 798
Twin studies, intelligence and, 366
Two-spirit, 458n
Tylor, Edward B., 547, 699
Typewriters, innovation and, 759–760
Tyrolean Alps, Neolithic man in, 45
Tyrosinase (enzyme), 360

UFOlogy, 718
Uganda Kob (antelope), 75
Ugandan people, 642
Ukkuqsi excavation (study), 38–43
Ukraine, 265
Ultraviolet radiation. See Vitamin D
Unaltered fossils, 38
Unarias Academy of Science, 717
Uncentralized political systems, 654–661
    age-grade organization as, 660–661
    association organization as, 661
    band organization as, 654–656

kinship organization as, 659–660
    tribal organization as, 656–659
Uncle Remus stories, as tales, 734
Unconscious selection, 284–285
Underdeveloped countries, 529, 531
    modernization and, 785–786
    women as labor in, 801–802
Under Mount St. Elias (De Laguna), 736
Unification Church, 717
Unilateral descent. See Unilineal descent
Unilineal descent, 599
    ancestral spirits and, 698
United Nations. See also specific
        organizations
    Covenant of Human Rights and, 808
    cultural understanding and, 32
United States. See also North America; Nuclear family
    age grouping in, 628–629
    child rearing in, 451
    Christianity in, 693
    cultural role of food in, 380
    extended family in, 581, 582
    family life in, 570
    flea markets in, 528–529
    government of, 665
    homosexuality and, 458
    linguistic nationalism in, 421
    nuclear family in, 579, 581
    redistribution of wealth in, 520
    religion and politics in, 685
    social stratification in, 640
    warfare and, 683
United States Advisory Mission, 805
United States Agency for International Development (AID), 769
United States government, cultural resource management by, 46
Untouchables, 637
Uplands. See Seasonal uplands
Upper Paleolithic, 237–240
    anatomically modern people from, 248,
        250–271
    arts in, 248, 258–265
    origins of peoples, 268–271
    Paleoindians and, 268
    spread of peoples during, 266–268
    tools of, 253–258
Urbanization, modernization and, 777
Urban society. See also Cities; Civilization
    transition from Neolithic period, 321–336
Urukaginal, 340
Ute people (study), language renewal among,
    419–420

Values. See also Religion; Revitalization
        movements
    core, 456
Van Allen, Judith, 667
Van Den Berghe, Pierre, 656n, 665n, 766n,
    775, 807n, 808
Vandermeersch, B., 240n
Van Willigen, J., 636n
Variation. See also Race
    in animals, 352
    in Homo sapiens, 279
    human physical, 346–348, 357–359
    in intelligence, 364–368
Vayda, A. P., 468n
Veblen, Thorstein, 521
Vegeculture, 295
Venezuela, Yanomami and, 453
Venus figures, 259–260, 264
Verbal arts, 728–736
    legend and, 731–732
    little songs of Awlad 'Ali Bedouins, 734–
        735
    myth and, 729–731
    poetry and, 734
    tales and, 733–734
Verbal evaluation, 638–639

Vernacular English, 424–425
Vikings, 507
Villages
  cities and, 314
  Neolithic, 304
Vindija fossil, 238, 239
Violence, 651. *See also* Structural violence
  domestic, 593
  in Guatemala, 805–806
  against Yanomami people (study), 781–785
Viruses, 73–74, 75, 373
Vision, stereoscopic, 98
Vitamin D
  ozone depletion and, 371
  skin pigmentation and, 360, 361
Vocabulary, core, 417
Vocalization, 416. *See also* Language
  by chimpanzees, 115–116
  by chimpanzees and gorillas, 428–430
  gesture-call system, 197
Vocal qualifiers, 416
Vocal segregates, 416
Vogelman, Thomas C., 733n
Vogt, E. Z., 509n, 582n
Voice qualities, 415
Voluntary association, 632
Vrindaban, 693

Walker, Alan, 140
Wallace, Anthony F. C., 694, 718
Wallace, E., 472n
Wants, supply of goods and services and, 504
Wape people, 668, 697
Warm Springs Dam-Lake Sonoma Project, 728
Warner, W. Lloyd, 20, 22
Wars and warfare
  in early civilizations, 340
  political organization and, 680–683
Washington, D.C., infant mortality in, 589–590
Washoe (chimpanzee), 429
Wasson, Christina, 530
Wastes, pollution and, 815
Watercraft, 266
Watson, James, 64
Wattenberg, B. J., 818
Wealth
  distribution of, 521–525
  gross national product and, 817 (map)
  polygynous households and, 551
  redistribution of, 519–521
Weaning, 438
Weapons. *See also* Tools
  of *H. erectus*, 218
  Mesolithic, 271–273
Weatherford, J., 295n, 762n
Weaving, in New World, 304
Weidenreich, Franz, 203–204, 238–239
Weights and measures, cultural diffusion and, 762–763
Weiner, Annette, 394n, 504n, 505, 539
Weiner, J. S., 25
Weiner, S., 240n
Weitzman, L. J., 553n
Werner, D., 486n
West. *See also* Underdeveloped countries
  abnormal personality in, 458
  art in, 744
  future and, 792
  law in, 674, 675
  theology of, 697

West Africa. *See also* specific kingdoms
  land control in, 512
Western Abenakis, 472. *See also* Abenaki people
  legend of, 732–733
  verbal arts of, 729–730
Westernization, 793
West Indies, serial monogamy in, 552–553
Wetlands. *See* Tropical regions
We'wha (Zuni), 444
What Happened in History (Childe), 288
Wheat, 291
Wheeler, Pete, 147n, 168
Whelehan, P., 545n
White, J. J., 32n
White, Leslie A., 390
Whitehead, N. L., 656n, 681n
White House Conference on Families, 570
White Man's Bad Medicine, The (Tiger), 450
Whites
  apartheid and, 810–812
  social dialects and, 424
"Whites." *See* Skin color
Whiting, Beatrice, 449
Whiting, J. W. M., 217n, 449, 452, 453n
Wicca, 711
Wichman, H. A., 85n
Wife. *See also* Arranged marriage; Marriage; Spouse
  in same-sex marriage, 562–563
Wilcox, S. E., 406n, 430n
Williams, B. A., 138n
Williams, Jody, 669
Williams, M., 540
Williamson, Rhonda Kay, 441, 442–446
Willigan, J. V., 460
Wills, C., 360n
Windigo psychosis, 463–464
Witchcraft, 673–674, 710–714
  functions of, 712–714
  magic and, 709
  and medicine in Swaziland (study), 713
Wittfogel, Karl, 336
Wolf, M., 588n, 602n
Wolfe, Alvin, 800–801
Wolf Lies Down, 676
Wolpoff, M. H., 216n, 220n, 237n, 241n, 250, 251n
Womack, M., 459n
Women. *See also* Family life; Females; Gender; Group(s); Marriage; Matrilineal descent; Patrilineal descent; Sex and sexuality
  abnormal personality and, 458
  and African farming, 531
  as anthropologists, 8
  body language and, 412–413
  burial of Peruvian Moche priestess, 330–334
  child rearing and, 576–577
  in China, 775–776
  common-interest associations among, 632–634
  division of labor and, 506–508
  in food-gathering societies, 480–482
  gender roles of, 384
  gender stratification and, 641–642
  in Guatemala, 806
  in Kapauku culture, 391
  labor of, 801–802
  modernization and, 785–786
  myth of matriarchy and, 730–731
  as political leaders, 666–668
  in single-parent households, 553

standardizing bodies of (study), 798–800
in Taiwanese patrilineal society (study), 602–604
in Trobriand Island culture, 394–396
Wong, K., 245n
Wood, B., 165n
Wood, C., 165n
Woodward, Louise, 590
Woolfson, Peter, 422
Words, language families and, 417
Work. *See* Labor; Labor patterns
Work songs, 740
World Bank, indigenous peoples and, 809
World Council of Indigenous Peoples, 803
World Ethnographic Sample (Murdock), 23
World Health Organization (WHO), 460, 540
World hunger, 812–814
Worldview, 681
  religion and, 694
Wounded Knee
  genocide and, 766
  violence at, 808
Wright, 118
Wright, R. M., 781n
Writing. *See also* Text
  as evidence of centralized authority, 327–328
Written documents, social stratification and, 334–335
Wulff, R. M., 420n, 589n, 713n

Xochimilco, 496

Yakö people, double descent among, 607
Yale University, Cross Cultural Survey at, 23
Yalom, M., 564n, 581n
Yam production, among Trobriand Islanders, 504–506
Yanagisako, S., 564, 571n, 581n
"Yankee City" study (Warner), 20
Yanomami people, 453, 454
  in Brazil, 453 (map)
  Brazilian Independence Day violence and (study), 781–785
  extinction and, 764–766
  state, nation, and, 664–665
Yoruba people, family life of, 578
Young, care of, in primates, 104
Yugoslavia (former), religious persecution in, 715

Zagros Mountains, Iran, 292, 293. *See also* Bakhtiari people
  animal domestication and, 289
Zapatista movement (Mexico), 681, 774, 807
Zapotec people, 31
Zawi Chemi Shanidar, Iraq, 286
Zhoukoudian, China, 206
  fossils from, 203, 204, 238
  tools from, 210
Zihlman, Adrienne, 193
Zilhão, J., 239n
Zimmerman, Michael, 41
Zinjanthropus boisei, 161
Zinn, Howard, 798
Zuni Indians, 455
  integrative mechanisms of, 795–796
  We'wha of, 444
Zuni Man-Woman, The (Roscoe), 444–445
Zur, J., 805n

PHOTO PERMISSIONS

Page	Credit
Page 2	John Cancalosi/DRK Photo
Page 4	Michel Zabe/Art Resource, NY
Page 7	Courtesy of Vice-Chancellor Mamphela Ramphele. © Shawn Benjamin
Page 8 left	The Granger Collection, New York
Page 8 right	Smithsonian Institution Photo No. 56196
Page 10	Susan Meiselas/Magnum Photos
Page 12 left	Michael Newman/PhotoEdit
Page 12 right	Charles Gupton/Tony Stone Images
Page 13	Photographs furnished by the U.S. General Services Administration
Page 14	William Rathje by Louie Psihoyos
Page 16	1996 Richard Lord
Page 21	Courtesy of Dr. Miriam Lee Kaprow, New York
Page 23	UPI/Corbis-Bettmann
Page 24	Galen Rowell 1985/Peter Arnold, Inc.
Page 26 left	Corbis-Bettmann
Page 26 middle	The Granger Collection, New York
Page 26 right	Culver Pictures
Page 29	Don Smetzer/Tony Stone Images
Page 32	Corbis-Bettmann
Page 34	Kenneth Garrett/NGS Image Collection
Page 37	Jan Friis & Torben Petersen/Bonniers/Silkeborg Museum 1997. Reprinted with permission of Discover Magazine
Page 39	Courtesy of Glenn Sheehan and Anne Jensen
Page 42	1985 David L. Brill
Page 43	John Veltri/Photo Researchers, Inc.
Page 44	Mike Andrews/Ancient Art & Architecture Collection
Page 45	G. Gorgoni/Leo de Wys, Inc.
Page 49	William A. Haviland
Page 50	William A. Haviland
Page 51	James B. Petersen, Dept. of Anthropology, University of Vermont
Page 52	Tikal, A Handbook of the Ancient Maya Ruins by William R. Coe. University of Pennsylvania Museum, Philadelphia 1967.
Page 55	University of Pennsylvania Museum, neg. #T4-398
Page 58	James B. Petersen, Dept. of Anthropology, University of Vermont
Page 62	Martin Harvey/The Wildlife Collection
Page 65	Photo Researchers, Inc.
Page 66	SuperStock
Page 69	Meckes/Ottawa/Photo Researchers, Inc.
Page 71	1999 Don Couch Photography
Page 72	Archive Photos
Page 73	AP/Wide World Photos
Page 74 top left	Obremski/The Image Bank
Page 74 top right	Steve Elmore
Page 74 middle left	Lawrence Manning/Woodfin Camp and Associates
Page 74 middle right	Ronald L. Kienhuls
Page 76	Corbis-Bettmann
Page 77 left	E. R. Degginger/Color-Pic, Inc.
Page 77 right	E. R. Degginger/Color-Pic, Inc.
Page 78 left	E. R. Degginger/Color-Pic, Inc.
Page 78 right	E. R. Degginger/Color-Pic, Inc.
Page 80	Otorohanga Zoological Society
Page 84	1999 Don Couch Photography
Page 86	O. Louis Mazzatenta/NGS Image Collection
Page 90	Gerard Sioen/Rapho
Page 92	Jodi Cobb/NGS Image Collection
Page 95 top left	Anthro-Photo
Page 95 top right	Stephen Dalton, Oxford Scientific Films/Animals, Animals
Page 95 bottom left	Cleo Freelana Photos/PhotoEdit
Page 95 bottom right	Colin Milkins, Oxford Scientific Films/Animals, Animals
Page 99	James Moore/Anthro-Photo
Page 103 left	Irven DeVore/Anthro-Photo
Page 103 right	Grant Heidrich/Anthro-Photo
Page 106 left	N. R. Christiansen/Taurus Photos
Page 106 right	David Agee/Anthro-Photo
Page 107	Michael Dick/Animals, Animals
Page 108 top	E. R. Degginger/Color-Pic, Inc.
Page 108 bottom	Peter Drowne/Color-Pic, Inc.
Page 109 left	Miriam Agron/Animals, Animals
Page 109 right	David Watts/Anthro-Photo
Page 112	Irven DeVore/Anthro-Photo
Page 113	AP/Wide World Photos
Page 114 left	Anita de Laguna Haviland
Page 114 right	Anita de Laguna Haviland
Page 115	Amy Parish/Anthro-Photo
Page 123	Gerry Ellis/ENP Images
Page 124	David Bygott/Anthro-Photo
Page 128	E. L. Simons/Duke Primate Center
Page 131	Anita de Laguna Haviland
Page 132	Martin Harvey/The Wildlife Collection
Page 137	Nancy J. Perkins
Page 139	Ollie Ellison/Duke University
Page 140	1985 David L. Brill
Page 143	1985 David L. Brill; artifact credit, Peabody Museum, Harvard University
Page 144	David Agee/Anthro-Photo
Page 146 left	National Museums of Kenya
Page 146 right	Irven DeVore/Anthro-Photo
Page 147	Anita de Laguna Haviland
Page 150	Dr. R. J. Clarke, University of the Witwatersrand
Page 152	AP/Wide World Photos
Page 154	1985 David L. Brill by permission of Owen Lovejoy
Page 155	1985 David L. Brill; artifact credit, Transvaal Museum, Pretoria
Page 158	William H. Kimbel, Ph.D., Institute of Human Origins
Page 160	Institute of Human Origins
Page 161	Tim White, Department of Anthropology, University of California at Berkeley
Page 162	Melville Bell Grosvenor/National Geographic Society
Page 163 top	National Museums of Kenya
Page 163 bottom	1985 David L. Brill; artifact credits, (left) A. africanus, Transvaal Museum, Pretoria, (right) A. boisei, National Museum of Tanzania, Dar es Salaam
Page 164	1994 Tim O. White/David L. Brill, Atlanta
Page 166	Photo by Dr. Rose Sevcik. Courtesy of The Language Research Center, Georgia State University
Page 167	John Giustina/The Wildlife Collection
Page 171	Michael Nichols/NGS Image Collection
Page 174	E. R. Degginger/Photo Researchers, Inc.
Page 176	National Museums of Kenya
Page 182	National Museums of Kenya
Page 186 top	David L. Brill, copyright The National Geographic Society
Page 186 bottom left	David L. Brill, copyright The National Geographic Society
Page 186 bottom right	David L. Brill, copyright The National Geographic Society
Page 186 middle left	David L. Brill, copyright The National Geographic Society
Page 186 middle right	David L. Brill, copyright The National Geographic Society
Page 187 top	William A. Haviland
Page 187 bottom	J & B Photo/Animals, Animals
Page 189	E. R. Degginger/Color-Pic, Inc.
Page 193	Andy Freeberg 1991 Discover Magazine
Page 194	Sue-Savage-Rumbaugh/Language Research Center
Page 195	Anita de Laguna Haviland
Page 196 left	1993 Mary Ann Fittipaldi
Page 196 right	1993 Mary Ann Fittipaldi
Page 200	Javier Trueba/Madrid Scientific Films
Page 202	Negative No. 319781. Courtesy Department of Library Sciences, American Museum of Natural History
Page 203	Courtesy of Dr. Phillip V. Tobias, South Africa
Page 204 top	John Reader/Photo Science Library/Photo Researchers, Inc.
Page 204 bottom	National Museums of Kenya
Page 206 left	Transparency No. 626. Courtesy Department of Library Sciences, American Museum of Natural History
Page 206 right	1985 David L. Brill; artifact credit, National Museum of Kenya, Niarobi
Page 207	Kenneth Garrett/NGS Image Collection
Page 208	Kenneth Garrett/NGS Image Collection
Page 209	National Museum of Kenya
Page 214	1985 David L. Brill
Page 215	Geoffrey G. Pope, Anthropology Department, The William Paterson College of New Jersey
Page 218	1985 David L. Brill
Page 219 left	Kenneth Garrett/National Geographic Image Collection
Page 219 right	Kenneth Garrett/NGS Image Collection
Page 221	Alexander Marshack
Page 224	David L. Brill 1985
Page 226	Javier Trueba/Madrid Scientific Films
Page 227 left	1985 David L. Brill; artifact credit, National Museum of Ethiopia, Addis Ababa
Page 227 right	Zhou Guoxing, Beijing Natural History Museum
Page 229	Kenneth Garrett/National Geographic Society Image Collection
Page 229	McBrearty/Anthro-Photo
Page 230	1995 David L. Brill\Atlanta, original housed in the British Museum
Page 231	Mimi Brace
Page 232	Professor Wu Xinzhi, Bejing, China
Page 233	Photo Researchers
Page 236 left	Alexander Marshack, New York University
Page 236 right	Alexander Marshack, New York University
Page 238	Negative No. 335658. Courtesy Department of Library Sciences, American Museum of Natural History
Page 241	Courtesy of Dr. B. Vandermeersch. Item from Israel Antiquities Authority
Page 242 top	L. W. T. Lawrence, The South African Museum
Page 242 bottom	Sally McBrearty
Page 248	Slide n. 10, Panel with horses. This fesco covers more than 6 square metres big and is part of a larger composition reaching about 6 m. height. Courtesy of French Ministry of Culture and Communication, Regional Direction for Cultural Affairs-Rhone-Alpes region-Regional Department of Archaeology.

Page 250	1985 David L. Brill; artifact credit, Musee De L'Homme, Paris
Page 252	William A. Haviland/UVM Photo Service
Page 252	William A. Haviland/UVM Photo Service
Page 259	Alexander Marshack, 1997
Page 260 left	Anita de Laguna Haviland
Page 260 right	Anita de Laguna Haviland
Page 261 top left	Negative No. K15806. Courtesy Department of Library Services, American Museum of Natural History
Page 261 bottom left	Negative No. K15823. Courtesy Department of Library Services, American Museum of Natural History
Page 261 right	Negative No. K15872. Courtesy Department of Library Services, American Museum of Natural History
Page 263	Jean Vertut
Page 265 top	Randall White
Page 265 bottom	Stanley H. Ambrose
Page 266	Göran Burenhult
Page 268 top	Peabody Museum
Page 268 bottom	Joe Ben Wheat Photo, University of Colorado Museum, Boulder
Page 269	Courtesy of Anthropos Institute, Brno
Page 270 left	Professor Wu Xinzhi, Bejing, China
Page 270 right	Drawing from *Up From The Ape* by Earnest A. Hooton, Copyright © 1931, 1946 by The MacMillan Company, New York.
Page 273	W. Fitzhugh
Page 278	Louis Goldman/Photo Researchers, Inc.
Page 280	Courtesy of Zhijun Zhao
Page 282	Paul Conklin/PhotoEdit
Page 284	William A. Haviland
Page 285 top left	Dr. W. van Zeist, Biologisch-Archaeologisch Institut, Rijksuniversiteit Gronigen
Page 285 top right	Dr. W. van Zeist, Biologisch-Archaeologisch Institut, Rijksuniversiteit Gronigen
Page 285 bottom	Dr. Dolores Piperno/Smithsonian Tropical Research Institute
Page 286	New York Botanical Garden, Bronx, drawing by Dr. Waltin Galinat
Page 288	AP/Wide World Photos
Page 290	Mark Richards/PhotoEdit
Page 291	Courtesy of the Oriental Institute of the University of Chicago
Page 292	Pierre Boulat/Woodfin Camp & Associates
Page 297	Courtesy of Michael Coe
Page 299	Harvey Finkle/Impact Visuals
Page 300 left	British School of Archaeology in Jerusalem
Page 300 right	British School of Archaeology in Jerusalem
Page 301	Ankara Archaeological Museum/Ara Guler, Istanbul
Page 303	John Kegan/Tony Stone Images
Page 304	Peabody Museum, Harvard University. Photography by Hillel Burger.
Page 306 top	Alan H. Goodman, Hampshire College
Page 306 bottom	Alan H. Goodman, Hampshire College
Page 307	Richard Hutchings/PhotoEdit
Page 312	Richard Reed/Anthro-Photo
Page 316	Arlette Mellaart
Page 318	Anita de Laguna Haviland
Page 319	Enrico Ferorelli
Page 320	Anita de Laguna Haviland
Page 321	The University Museum, University of Pennsylvania (neg. #T4-398)
Page 322	Dr. Peter D. Harrison
Page 324 top	Ban Chiang Project, University of Pennsylvania Museum
Page 324 bottom left	Ronald Sheridan/Ancient Art & Architecture Collection
Page 324 bottom right	Ronald Sheridan/Ancient Art & Architecture Collection
Page 325 top	Negative No. 330878. Courtesy Department of Library Sciences, American Museum of Natural History
Page 325 bottom	Heather Angel/Biofotos
Page 326	Tony Stone Images
Page 331 left	Dr. Christopher B. Donnan
Page 331 right	Dr. Christopher B. Donnan
Page 333 top left	Dr. Christopher B. Donnan
Page 333 top right	Dr. Christopher B. Donnan
Page 333 middle	Dr. Christopher B. Donnan. Drawing by Donna McClelland.
Page 333 bottom left	Dr. Christopher B. Donnan
Page 333 bottom right	Gonzalo de Reparaz, Painting by Felix Caycho.
Page 334	Anita de Laguna Haviland
Page 335	William A. Haviland
Page 338	Victor R. Boswell/National Geographic Society
Page 339	Mohenjo/Anthro-Photo
Page 340	Cultural Relics Bureau, Beijing, and the Metropolitan Museum of Art, New York
Page 344	A. Ramey/PhotoEdit
Page 349 left	Lauré Communications/Eliot Elisofon/National Museum of African Art
Page 349 right	Jean-Pierre Hallet/The Pygmy Fund
Page 354 middle	Laurence Dutton/Tony Stone Images
Page 355	Lawrence Migdale/Tony Stone
Page 356 left	Dinodia Picture Agency
Page 356 right	A. Ramey/PhotoEdit
Page 358	AP/Wide World Photos
Page 359	AP/Wide World Photos
Page 360	AP/Wide World Photos
Page 361 top	Beryl Goldberg
Page 361 bottom left	Farrell Grehan/Photo Researchers, Inc.
Page 361 bottom middle	Richard Wood
Page 361 bottom right	E. R. Degginger/Color-Pic, Inc.
Page 363	Royal Anthropological Institute Photographic Collection
Page 364 left	Dr. Cloyce G. Coffman/Texas A & M University
Page 364 right	Dr. Cloyce G. Coffman/Texas A & M University
Page 365 left	AP/Wide World Photos
Page 365 right	AP/Wide World Photos
Page 368	Bill Clark/The Daily Progress
Page 370	Arizona State Museum, University of Arizona, Helga Teiwes, Photographer
Page 372	1999 Don Couch
Page 374	AP/Wide World Photos
Page 378	Charles Henneghien/Bruce Coleman, Inc.
Page 380	Christian Vioujard/Gamma
Page 383 left	Laura Dwight/PhotoEdit
Page 383 right	Tony Freeman/PhotoEdit
Page 386	Dennis MacDonald/PhotoEdit
Page 387	AP/Wide World Photos
Page 388	Bettina Cirone/Photo Researchers, Inc.
Page 390	Photo by Napoleon A. Chagnon
Page 391	UPI/Corbis-Bettmann
Page 392	David Tejada/Tony Stone Images
Page 393	Phoebe A. Hearst Museum of Anthropology, University of California at Berkeley
Page 395	Annette Weiner
Page 397	Alec Duncan
Page 398	1991 Sean Sprague/Impact Visuals
Page 399	Mark Richards/PhotoEdit
Page 401 top	Tom McCarthy/PhotoEdit
Page 401 bottom	Wasyl Szkodzingsky/Photo Researchers, Inc.
Page 404	Tom McCarthy/PhotoEdit
Page 406	1994 Norbert Rosing/Mauritius
Page 408	Megan Biesele/Anthro-Photo
Page 412 left	Comstock Inc./Russ Kinne
Page 412 right	AP/Wide World Photos
Page 413	AP/Wide World Photos
Page 414 top left	1995 Richard Lord
Page 414 bottom	1996 Richard Lord
Page 414 top	Jeff Greenberg/PhotoEdit
Page 415	Tony Freeman/PhotoEdit
Page 421	Paul Conklin/PhotoEdit
Page 422	Chip Hires/Gamma Liaison
Page 423	Klaus Francke/Peter Arnold, Inc.
Page 426	AP/Wide World Photos
Page 428	AP/Wide World Photos
Page 429	John Chellmann/Animals, Animals
Page 431	UPI/Corbis-Bettmann
Page 434	Anne Day/Contact Press Images
Page 437	Martin Bell/Mary Ellen Mark Library
Page 438 top	1991 Richard Lord
Page 438 bottom	David Young-Wolff/PhotoEdit
Page 439 left	Mark Jenike/Anthro-Photo
Page 439 right	Irven DeVore/Anthro-Photo
Page 444	Smithsonian Institution Photo No. 85-8666
Page 448	Anthony Bannister/ABPL
Page 449	UPI Corbis-Bettmann
Page 450	The Native American Painting Reference Library
Page 452	Tony Freeman/PhotoEdit
Page 454	N. Chagnon/Anthro-Photo
Page 455	The Granger Collection, New York
Page 457 top	Jeff Greenberg/PhotoEdit
Page 457 bottom	AP/Wide World Photos
Page 458	PhotoEdit
Page 461	Anthony Bannister/ABPL
Page 466	Shostak/Anthro-Photo
Page 469	Mark Richards/PhotoEdit
Page 470 left	Neidhardt Collection /Underwood Archives, SF
Page 470 right	1993 Kirk Condyles/Impact Visuals
Page 471	ARCHIV/Photo Researchers, Inc.
Page 472	Anita de Laguna Haviland
Page 475	Courtesy of the University of Illinois at Urbana-Champaign
Page 477	Anthony Bannister/ABPL
Page 478 top left	Anita de Laguna Haviland
Page 478 bottom	Vanessa Vick/Photo Researchers, Inc.
Page 478 top right	Robert Brenner/PhotoEdit
Page 480	Anthony Bannister/ABPL
Page 481 left	Anthony Bannister/ABPL
Page 481 right	Anthony Bannister/ABPL
Page 485	Paul Conklin/PhotoEdit
Page 489	Underwood Photo Archives, SF
Page 490	1980 James D. Nations/DDB Stock
Page 491	Teas/Anthro-Photo
Page 492	Adrian Arbib/Anthro-Photo
Page 496	D. Donne Bryant/DDB Stock
Page 497	Courtesy of the Department of Library Services, The American Museum of Natural History
Page 498	Jeff Greenberg/PhotoEdit
Page 502	1993 Rick Browne/Photo Researchers, Inc.
Page 506	Annette Weiner
Page 507 left	David H. Wells/The Image Works
Page 507 right	Guy Gillette/Photo Researchers, Inc.
Page 508 left	D. Donne Bryant/DDB Stock
Page 508 right	Eric Kroll
Page 510	PhotoEdit
Page 511	Kenneth Murray/Photo Researchers, Inc.
Page 513	Anthony Bannister/ABPL
Page 515	Stan Washburn/Anthro-Photo, Inc.
Page 516	AP/Wide World Photos
Page 519 left	Annette Weiner

LITERARY PERMISSIONS